32.35

SELECTED WRITINGS OF *T. C. SCHNEIRLA*

Dr. T. C. Schneirla ready for a field expedition on Barro
Colorado Island, Panama Canal Zone, March 1966.
(Photo by Ralph Buchsbaum.)

SELECTED WRITINGS

of

T. C. Schneirla

EDITED BY

LESTER R. ARONSON   ETHEL TOBACH

Department of Animal Behavior
The American Museum of Natural History, New York

JAY S. ROSENBLATT   DANIEL S. LEHRMAN

Institute of Animal Behavior
Rutgers University, Newark

W. H. FREEMAN AND COMPANY

San Francisco

© Copyright 1972 by W. H. Freeman and Company.

No part of this book may be reproduced
by any mechanical, photographic, or electronic process,
or in the form of a phonographic recording,
nor may it be stored in a retrieval system, transmitted,
or otherwise copied for public or private use
without the written permission of the publisher.

Library of Congress Catalog Card Number: 71–135632
International Standard Book Number: 0–7167–0930–9
Printed in the United States of America

1 2 3 4 5 6 7 8 9

Contents

Preface

The papers by T. C. Schneirla that constitute this book have been selected to provide insight into his theories, methods, and observations, and to show how they developed from his experiments in comparative psychology and animal behavior. In a companion volume, *Development and Evolution of Behavior,* a collection of essays written as a memorial to Dr. Schneirla by his colleagues and associates, the influence of Dr. Schneirla's thinking is clearly evident. Together, the book of essays and this volume of selected papers exemplify his most significant contributions to the behavioral sciences, as viewed from the present historical perspective.

Dr. Theodore C. Schneirla was born on July 23, 1902 into a farming family in modest economic circumstances in Michigan. He completed his early academic training in Michigan and matriculated in the University of Michigan to earn a Doctor of Science degree in the Psychology Department. At age 23, he began his experiments on maze learning in ants at the University of Michigan under the direction of Dr. John F. Shepard, with whom he had studied comparative psychology. In the fall of 1927, Schneirla left Ann Arbor to teach at New York University, where he finished writing his Ph.D. thesis, "Learning and orientation in ants." In 1930, after three years of his teaching at New York University, Schneirla, and his wife, neé Leone Warner, went to Chicago, where he spent a year in Karl Lashley's laboratory as a National Research Council Fellow. While in Chicago, the Schneirlas met and made lifelong friends with another young couple, Norman and Ayesha Maier. From this friendship came the classic book, *Principles of Animal Psychology,* which was published in 1935 and was reissued in a paperback edition in 1964 with additional material. Dr. Schneirla returned to New York University in 1931 and he remained on the faculty of this institution until his death in 1968.

In 1932, Dr. Schneirla made his first field trip to the Canal Zone Biological Area on Barro Colorado Island in Gatun Lake, Panama. Before this trip was over, he had developed the hypothesis that the migratory and nonmigratory episodes of the army ant colonies were related to the condition of the brood. He concluded that the high degree of stimulation by the active larval brood arouses the workers to large raids, ending in emigrations. When the larvae become enclosed as pupae, and the rest of the brood consists of nonmotile eggs, stimulation of the workers is reduced, the raids are smaller and do not end in emigrations. With this hypothesis, he demonstrated that the changes in behavior of these ants are intimately related to changes in morphology and in physiological processes. This radical hypothesis stood in sharp contrast to the then prevalent and static explanations of the migratory phenomenon, which either relegated the phenomenon to the category of innate behavior controlled by the genes (and hence requiring no further investigation) or related it to a decline in the abundance of food in the raiding areas.

In 1943, Dr. Frank Beach, Chairman of the Department of Animal Behavior of The American Museum of Natural History, invited Schneirla to become an Associate Curator there in recognition of his fine field work and ability as an experimentalist and theoretician. Schneirla remained as an Adjunct Professor at New York University where he continued to give courses until 1962 in Comparative Psychology, Thinking and Development of Behavior. Through the years he directed the research of doctoral candidates not only from New York University, but from several other universities in the New York metropolitan area.

In September 1944, Dr. Schneirla was awarded a John Simon Guggenheim Fellowship, which enabled him to spend six months in the Tehuantepec region of Mexico where he studied the social behavior of army ants under dry season conditions. In 1955, having recovered from a viral infection of the spinal cord that had almost completely paralyzed his body and legs, Dr. Schneirla returned once again to Barro Colorado Island for his strenuous field work.

The progress of Schneirla's theoretical position during these productive years is not only a reflection of his personal experience, but is part of the growth of behavioral science. Fundamental to his position was the emphasis on the use of the inductive method in the attainment and organization of knowledge. He was guided by the law of parismony, by Morgan's canon, and, above all, by the need to avoid the fallacies of anthropomorphism and zoomorphism.[1] His work reflects the meaningful application of a truly comparative approach to behavior, one that stresses the differences as well as the similarities of various species.

He viewed the concept of integrative levels as a fundamental tenet in all

---

[1] Zoomorphism, as used here, denotes giving animal-like qualities to human beings. This meaning is derived from the classical definition "the representation of God, or gods in the form, or with the attributes of the lower animals."

comparative and ontogenic studies as well as in the analysis of every aspect of the physiology and behavior of the individual organism. For example, he maintained that there is little scientific value in viewing the feeding behavior of all animals from protozoa to man as equivalent just because it results in the intake of food. There are major qualitative differences in form, function, nervous system, and behavior at various phyletic levels and all these must be considered in the analysis of feeding.

Dr. Schneirla contributed creatively to the understanding of three basic behavioral processes: motivation, social organization, and development. At first, he conceptualized the biphasic processes of approach and withdrawal as related to the state of the organism and the intensity of the effective stimuli and as critical in the initiation and maintenance of activity. This concept of the biphasic approach-withdrawal process was expanded later by considering it to be a fundamental feature both in the behavior of simple animals such as protozoa and in the early stages of behavioral development of the more complex forms.

Another of Schneirla's early contributions was a significant broadening of Wheeler's original concept of trophallaxis by formulating the new concept of reciprocal stimulation, that is, the exchange of all forms of stimulation between organisms. He explained socialization phenomena by integrating the process of reciprocal stimulation with the concepts of phyletic and organismic levels of organization. By doing so, he clarified the basis for the varieties of social behavior in the animal world and for the changes in such behavior during the history of the individual.

Development was thought of as a fusion of growth, experience, and maturation. Experience was redefined as the total history of all stimulation to which the organism is exposed during all stages of development. This formulation resolved the apparent dilemma of heredity versus environment, of nature versus nurture, and of instinct versus learning. Long before he published his first paper on behavioral development, Schneirla had been concerned with the unscientific concept of "instinct" and its wide acceptance by behavioral scientists who came from diverse fields, such as anthropology, sociology, psychology, psychiatry, biology, and animal breeding. He was especially opposed to such ethological terms as "innate releasing mechanism," "vacuum and displacement reactions," "fixed action potential" and "action specific energy," which he considered to be reifications deduced from the basic assumption of the existence of instincts. Even when the terms "vacuum and displacement reactions" are used in a strictly descriptive fashion, they are applied to behavior in widely disparate groups of animals in which the structural and functional bases of behavior are very different.

Although Dr. Schneirla appreciated the observations and data gathered through the field and experimental observations of the classical ethologists, he questioned the premises and assumptions underlying their research and the interpretations of the results of their investigations. In the earliest stages of his critical analysis of "natively determined behavior," he pointed out the need to understand and to take into consideration the developmental history of the individual, as was done in the discussions of pecking behavior in his and Maier's book, *Principles of Animal Psychology* (1935). His emphasis on behavioral development led also to a revitalization of the concept of levels of organization by the inclusion of development and change as important processes inherent in the concept. This new integration of a levels and a developmental approach provides, thereby, the alternative to theories of behavior that are based on concepts of instinct. In essence, at a given phyletic level and at a given stage of ontogeny, the total behavior of the individual is seen as a derivative of the continuous synthesis and fusion of experience, growth, and maturation with the genome. At higher phyletic levels and in later stages of ontogeny, specific learning processes are involved in the maturational processes. Moreover, learning, itself, is not unitary, but occurs in various levels of complexity. Only at the highest phyletic level—man, behaviorally speaking, and even then, at a late stage of child development—does the individual begin to use the most complex mental processes. This view of the development and evolution of behavior is a far cry from the traditional and still popular, but ideologically weak, dichotomy between "the innate and the acquired."

Dr. Schneirla not only saw the fallacies of the concept of instinct in the confines of behavioral research and theory, but in its application to man's behavior. Among his latest writings was a sharp denunciation of such theorizing under the rubric of "aggression" and the application of ethological theory to the complex human social behavioral patterns such as international politics, war, social conflict within a nation, and interindividual hostility. He pointed out that the uncritical extrapolation of incompletely supported conclusions from research with infrahuman species to specious solutions of the problems of humanity was the result of anthropomorphism, zoomorphism, and a disregard of the law of parsimony and of Morgan's canon. The pessimistic implications of such fallacious thinking for human society were countered by Schneirla's reliance on the highly evolved plasticity of human behavior for solutions to the problems of human aggression and violence.

The interest in animal behavior and its relevance to human societal problems has focused attention on the various scientific approaches to the subject and the differences among these approaches. Such inquiry has had many effects, one of which has been the crystallization of what some people call "Schneirla's Theory." Dr. Schneirla, of course, never referred to his work in this way. Rather, he was concerned with the formulation of concepts that would make it possible by laboratory experimentation and field observation to explain behavioral phenomena in evolutionary and developmental terms, without recourse to vitalistic or static assumptions. He formulated his concepts inductively, as in the example of his unique analysis of the behavior of army ants and their social organization. The inductive procedures that he used, together with the complexity of the problems to which he addressed himself, resulted in his developing a style of writing that does not conform with the usual presentations found in the biological and psychological literature. As often happens in such cases, his publications have been overlooked by some and misunderstood by others.

Although the articles selected deal with various behavioral phenomena, the integrity of Schneirla's approach to behavior is evident throughout. This integrated conceptualization is repeated in many of the papers because he considered this to be essential in developing his analysis of each problem in behavior that he studied. Such a *modus operandi* created some difficulty for us in the presentation of his work. Dr. Schneirla's bibliography contains over 120 items. The task of selection was therefore a considerable one. We originally planned to reprint a large number of papers and to eliminate from these portions of specialized or minor interest. We soon discovered that this procedure led to a loss in continuity, as all the parts of his papers tend to be highly interrelated. We, therefore, reduced the number of articles and, with few exceptions, they are reprinted in their entirety. Deletions are indicated by ellipses.

Dr. Schneirla kept a set of bound volumes of his reprints. On these he had penned a number of corrections—a word here and there that improved the clarity of a sentence, or a brief factual change based on later evidence. We decided that it would benefit the readers to include these changes in the reprinted papers. Such changes, as well as editorial corrections, are enclosed by brackets [ ].

In those papers that were originally printed in foreign journals, punctuation and spelling were changed to conform to American usage.

Line drawings have been recopied to make for stylistic consistency, but half-tones have been reprinted from the originals with the exception of one color plate, from a *Natural History Magazine* article, which is reproduced in black and white (Figure 111). Figures have been renumbered to run consecutively throughout the book. Tables have been renumbered, when necessary, to run consecutively from the number 1 within a paper. Reference lists and bibliographies have been reprinted, with only those changes necessary to achieve a consistent style.

We have also omitted from this volume the very detailed reports of his field observations and experiments on the behavior and reproductive cycles of army ants. Before his death, Dr. Schneirla had almost completed the manuscript of a definitive book on this subject which effectively summarizes all of this research. Dr. Howard R. Topoff has edited this manuscript, and it has been published by W. H. Freeman and Company as a related volume.

Although Schneirla's interests ranged widely in the field of behavioral science, we were able to organize the papers under particular rubrics. The integration of his thinking was such, however, that there are repeated references to particular ideas, and our system of arrangement is just one of several possibilities. We hope that it is a felicitous one, but we are sure that many of Schneirla's associates who have read his papers, listened to his lectures, or collaborated with him in research could offer excellent alternative ways of presenting his work. We are also sure that new perspectives of Schneirla's scientific contributions will emerge in later years as others begin to apply and deal with the concepts that he developed. In the introductions to the sections that follow, we present briefly some of our thoughts concerning the interrelatedness of the papers and our reasons for including some and omitting others.

March 1971

Lester R. Aronson
Ethel Tobach

SELECTED WRITINGS OF *T. C. SCHNEIRLA*

I

ON THEORY AND METHODS OF COMPARATIVE PSYCHOLOGY

The articles in this section present Schneirla's overall views of the contemporary status of comparative psychology and animal behavior. The first paper, *The Relationship between Observation and Experimentation in the Field Study of Behavior* (No. **50**),* is a discussion of basic techniques and goals of field research in behavior. Schneirla shows that observation, experimentation, and control are attributes of both field and laboratory investigation and that in favorable situations these two procedures complement each other. This article adds to today's discussions of the differences between American and European approaches to field and laboratory studies of animal behavior. At a time when laboratory studies dominate

* This and subsequent numbers in this introduction refer to the items in the complete bibliography of Schneirla's works, p. 1017. Bold face numbers denote articles that are included in this volume.

this area of science, the article is still most timely although it was written twenty years ago.

The *Encyclopaedia Britannica* article, *Psychology, Comparative* (No. 42), was first written in 1948 and was revised in 1959 and 1962 to include new developments in the field. Although planned for the layman, this clearly stated review has proven to be highly useful to students and investigators in other fields who wish to obtain a basic understanding of comparative psychology. In the *Preface* to the 1964 Dover edition of *Principles of Animal Psychology* (No. 12), Maier and Schneirla discuss their then current views of comparative psychology, particularly those related to the processes of learning. Other articles on the state of the science of comparative psychology not printed here include *Some Comparative Psychology* (No. 6), *Contemporary American Psychology in Perspective* (No. 37), and the two earlier editions of the *Encyclopaedia Britannica* article. The article *A Consideration of Some Conceptual Trends in Comparative Psychology* (No. 57) is placed in Part VIII (On Aspects of Mammalian Behavior) becaus of its theoretical relevance to that section.

The American Museum of Natural History was the first natural history museum to expand beyond the traditional role of taxonomy and systematics and to include animal behavior as an integral part of its biological research and exhibition programs. In the *Curator* article (No. 86), written in 1958 and 1959, Dr. Schneirla reviews the historical development of the study of animal behavior, the then current activities of the Department of Animal Behavior and their relevance to the scientific and educational endeavors of the Museum; included also is a discussion of his views of the relationship between science and the layman. Although the research in the Animal Behavior Department has changed in the intervening years, the arguments and historical perspectives of this article are still pertinent.

Dr. Schneirla was always concerned about strong anthropomorphic tendencies in students of animal behavior, tendencies which were, until recently, a major block to progress in the field and are still prevalent among nonspecialists and laymen. He dealt with this problem in many papers. Two little gems, which are not included in this collection, *"Cruel" ants—and Occam's razor* (No. 26) and *Postscript to "Cruel" ants* (No. 29) are recommended to readers interested in this problem.

Lester R. Aronson
Ethel Tobach

T. C. SCHNEIRLA

The Relationship between Observation and Experimentation in the Field Study of Behavior

Bibliography No. 50

THE OBSERVER AS INVESTIGATOR

Man goes to nature to learn what nature is, but, in so doing, he introduces possibilities of distortion through his own presence. These risks Bacon had in mind when he stressed the importance of scientific investigation as a means of supplementing and correcting our sense impressions, which are likely to be "infirm and erring."

After a tendency of long standing, observation is frequently viewed as the one necessary field method, and the laboratory is considered the place for experimentation. This view seems justified in part by the fact that field investigation is more obviously dependent, as a rule, upon the worker's immediate perception than is laboratory research. Yet this involves an oversimplification, not only in the sense that the resources of observation as a technique are minimized but also in that the relation of field investigation to the laboratory is misrepresented.

The laboratory holds its place traditionally as the investigative situation in which the scientific study of given phenomena may proceed without the intervention of unknowns of any large magnitude. Unfortunately, this justified emphasis upon laboratory techniques of control has led to the mistaken impression that control may be obtained only under laboratory conditions. This sectarian conception of the "sanctity of the laboratory" has encouraged a narrow view of experimental science, at the expense of the social sciences, in which field procedures are of paramount importance (10). The difference is not that abrupt. As Warden, Jenkins, and Warner (56) have said, "Obviously, no sharp line can be drawn between careful field observation and simple experimental procedure. In a very

Annals of The New York Academy of Sciences, vol. 51, art. 6 (November 7, 1950). Copyright © 1950 The New York Academy of Sciences. Reprinted with permission.

proper sense, the laboratory may be considered as a limited and controllable field in which isolation and quantitative measurement of selected aspects of behavior can be made." Properly speaking, in terms of the logic of science, there is really no experimental method as distinct from observation (59), and the field study of behavior is no exception. A consideration of the advancing scope of experimentation from the physical to the biological to the psychological and social sciences in the present century inevitably broadens our concept of research beyond the scope of the laboratory proper.

Actually, in numerous ways, observation and experimentation are as closely related in field study as they are in other areas of scientific investigation. The role of experimentation in the social sciences, as in science generally, is the refinement of observational techniques (18). In all scientific research, in field or laboratory, the function of the investigator as an observer of natural phenomena is involved in a variety of ways, which require appropriate control. "Control," in this larger sense, concerns all measures taken to increase the reliability and validity of methods and procedures in a scientific investigation.

In comprehensive studies of individual and social behavior under natural conditions, an effort should be made to advance progressively from a preliminary stage, in which mainly perceptual procedures (such as viewing the animals from a blind) are depended upon, to a stage in which specialized and appropriate manipulative procedures are introduced. The systematic investigator aims at an effective control of conditions throughout, but he learns that this end is achieved in different ways at different stages. From the beginning, any steps taken to facilitate the observer's technique of approach, his mobility and the adequacy of his perception, constitute a regulation of conditions in the phenomenon directed toward promoting reliability and validity of results. Hence all are control measures. From a comparable standpoint, Poincairé (35) appraised the methods of physics, to clarify the observer's influence on the phenomenon he studies through his very intrusion into the situation and his selection of the objects to be studied (37).

The care taken with preliminary details, from articles of clothing to notebooks and instruments (13), is designed to introduce the investigator quietly and inconspicuously into contact with the phenomenon, so that he may establish the characteristic nature of the given behavior pattern and its range of variations with dependability. This emphasis upon a maximal intimacy of access to the phenomenon under study brings out a valuable feature of field investigation, in that, first of all, it opens to study and appraisal the entire pattern of the animal's adjustment to its environmental niche-situation. The fundamental precautions directed toward adequacy of preliminary observations thus provide a basis for a later introduction of systematic changes designed to explore what may be termed the inner nature of the phenomenon. The paper of Dr. Emlen will involve a consideration, from this viewpoint, of techniques for the investigation of social behavior in birds.

If scientific methods are means of extending our perception, fundamentally, these means are recognizable in many forms in field work. The assiduous study of terrain, the binoculars and the blinds, living on the study area, and aiming for the fullest expertness of orientation and mobility within it, are such means. Measures of this type are controls in that they reduce the disruptive effect of variables which might be introduced through the intrusion of the observer into the lives of the animals. Such procedures contribute on the one hand to a maximal perception of situation and animals and hence facilitate learning how variations in the phenomenon can be introduced and explored to advantage. On the other hand, they serve to control the "intrusion" factor effectively, provided they are based upon an adequate knowledge of the animal's biological and psychological makeup. For example, the elusive and retiring nature of gibbons in their forest environment was overcome by Carpenter (8) through approach methods and scheduling of operations based upon the typical activities and response tendencies of the animal. Comparably, Nissen (31) designed his approach to chimpanzee groups on such knowledge as the fact that they are chiefly disturbed not so much by human noises and activity in their vicinity as by sudden movements and by "actions which might be effective as directed toward them."

Field work may be thought of as furnishing opportunities for investigation not initially available under laboratory conditions, to be gained through access to the complete natural phenomenon. The two are best considered overlapping and mutually complementary areas of investigation. They are basically similar in method, in that both include perceptual observation in some form as an essential procedure, and the fundamental criteria of reliability and validity of evidence are similarly involved, as are techniques of control through an established basis of understanding and a systematic variation of conditions with reference to this basis. Comparable mental operations are present in both, especially the use of hypothesis, analysis, and synthesis and theorizing in gathering and interpreting results. A common body of problems is studied, although in somewhat different ways.

The field investigator must never be considered simply a "watcher," even when the results of his observations are gathered and reported in a most naïve and uncontrolled form. He is always a perceiver, who is, as Woodworth (60) notes, "not an unbiased registering instrument." As a perceiver, he makes some attempt to interpret what he views, and often his degree of assurance has no relation to whether his acuity and understanding are quite inadequate or are close to the scientific ideal of reliability and validity in these respects. These matters differ, of course, with his sensitivity, intelligence, and personal make-up, his general and special training, his interest in problem and animal, and his bias or expectation of a particular outcome.

About intelligence, we may be hopeful. The other characteristics require further consideration. In the first place, the effective perception and report of meaningful situations is a technique which benefits from systematic training. It is not surprising that in a test by Raymond Pearl (33), fifteen professional men and scientists, all very interested in genetics, disagreed widely in their results from the sorting of 532 grains of stock and hybrid corn in two characters only, color and form. Obviously, personal differences in acuity, perception, training, and judgment contributed to the outcome. From this, the inference should not be drawn that, in studying behavior under natural conditions, we must resort to a mechanical collection of data which will exclude all personality factors. For one thing, investigators must plan any such procedures in view of their approach to the problem and understanding of it. Then, also, whatevc. sampling procedures are used cannot be random but must be selective, because behavior phenomena in the wild are not indiscriminate and random but are characteristically systematic and ordered in time and space, with characteristic types of variability (19). However excellent the mechanical facilities may be, their use must be planned and applied by the intervention of perceiving and thinking individuals.

With reasonably good qualifications at the start as concerns sensitivity, intelligence, and motivation in particular, the observer's technique as a skilled perceiver, reasoner, and manipulator of his subject matter may be advanced through experience to a high degree of scientific reliability and control. The point is emphasized by W. H. Hudson (22) in his comparison of gambler and naturalist: the former able to distinguish readily the most minute differences on the engraved backs of playing cards but quite unable to discern differences in the appearance and behavior of species of common birds, differences readily apparent to the naturalist, who on his part finds the cards all alike on their reverse sides. Some ways in which an improvement in field perception may come about are suggested in Darling's (13) discussion of observational techniques, based on his classical study of group behavior in the red deer of Scotland:

> It takes time for the eye to become accustomed to recognize differences, and, once that has occurred, the nature of the differences has to be defined in the mind by careful self-interrogation if the matter is to be set down on paper. . . . The fact remains that an observer has to go through a period of conditioning of a most subtle kind. . . . [He] must

empty his mind and be receptive only to the deer and the signs of the country. . . . This is quite severe discipline, calling for time and practice. . . . It is necessary intellectually to soak in the environmental complex of the animal to be studied until we have a facility with it which keeps us, as it were, one move ahead. We must become intimate with the animal. . . . In this state the Observer learns more than he realizes.

A cardinal point is that the observer must consider the single observation only a small part of his task, to be repeated, enlarged upon, and varied as a matter of necessary control. As Carpenter (8) puts it: "The reliability and completeness of the first observation of any given activity can always be increased by repeated checking." That this is a question of the validity of sampling procedures, and not simply one of piling up data, is emphasized by Fisher's (15) statement: "The salutary habit of repeating important experiments, or of carrying out original observations in replicate, shows a tacit approach to the fact that the object of our study is not the individual result, but the population of possibilities of which we do our best to make the experiments representative."

To facilitate the development of observational skills, the observer checks his perception of groupings of animals and of details in their relations to given situations, repeating his work systematically at frequent intervals, to promote his discernment of similarities and of differences according to time and place. He sets out to predict variations in the phenomenon according to known or suspected conditions, noting his predictions so that they may be checked against what actually occurs. Beyond increasing the reliability and validity of perceptual data, such procedures should lead into a progressive experimentalistic approach to the phenomenon.

OBSERVATIONAL CONTROL THROUGH RECORD-TAKING [1]

Adequate techniques in taking records establish a firm basis for minimizing perceptual and mnemonic errors. One must record as he watches events, keeping his eyes and ears on the animals and setting down notes with tactual control as far as possible, in order not to lose "visual touch" with occurrences. Much practice at writing in the dark helps improve the mechanics of this process, and also anticipates inevitable needs in nighttime observation. The habit of taking records at all times, regardless of inconveniences such as rain, eliminates lapses of time between perception and statement and stimulates watchful attention to events and their relationships in time. Through such procedures, the investigator becomes a

---

[1] Experts who find any of this material somewhat tediously familiar are advised to skip as may seem desirable, provided they do not skip the main point.

dynamic perceiver of his phenomenon, a "participant" rather than merely a "spectator," in Heidbreder's sense (20). Qualitative accuracy in note-taking is thereby promoted, rather than mere quantity.

Because the processes of organization and interpretation begin with the initial perception and notation of occurrences, good notes inevitably assist methodology at all stages from observation to explanation. The first aim is an adequately complete and accurate report made at the time of oc-currence, containing all essentials from routine information (such as date, time, weather, special and general nature of situation) to unusual or specialized matters.[2] Adequate field notes are stated in a connected and organized manner, following a standard form when appropriate. Usual patterns of events should be noted, not taken for granted and omitted, or variations and exceptions, and opportunities for special tests, will be passed over. An appropriate system of symbols should be devised for representing important aspects of the phenomenon, to promote organiza-tion, scope, and depth in the survey.[3]

For many types of work, a full use of shorthand or speed-writing is almost mandatory. On-the-spot illustrations, such as an outline sketch of a behavioral situation, or some appropriate form of graph which indicates the essential nature of change in a situation, become useful assets when developed systematically. Opportunities for new ways of quantifying rec-ords should be sought, from measurements of spatial dimensions to the calibration of important behavioral characteristics. Frequent practice in the estimation of distances is desirable, as in other matters, such as count-ing animals in groups, judging their spatial arrangement, and so on. Emphasis upon improving and polishing such techniques not only saves valuable time but also stimulates the development of an investigative at-titude. Speculative or interpretive comments should be marked distinc-tively in the notes.

Notes should not be permitted to "rest" once they are in the record books. Each day's notes should be summarized and critically reviewed before one retires for the night. At intervals of a few days, more inclusive surveys of notes should be made, directed not only toward general analytical study, but also toward catching discrepancies, omissions, and latent meanings and otherwise checking the adequacy of the record. Any changes, additions, or deletions which are made in the original notes, at

---

[2] In Shelford's (49) basic work on ecological methodology the importance of a thorough-going ecological and behavioral coverage in notes is explored.

[3] For example, in his field study of chimpanzee behavior, Nissen (31) devised convenient symbols for discernibly different sounds he was able to identify according to situation of arousal. Thus "FP" designated "fear or pain situation," and "TT" a situation of general excitement. In part, this system aided the investigator to differentiate the organic and ex-ternal conditions under which different sounds occurred.

any time after the original observation, should be marked distinctively. These and comparable procedures aid accuracy in perception and record, as well as insight in the planning of further work.

It is assumed that the notes will be supplemented instrumentally whenever appropriate or feasible, through the use of still and motion-picture photography, sound recorders, activity recorders, and the like, with the precaution that such measures shall not displace essential perceptual observations. It is clear that photographic records, opportunely made, have value for subsequent study of the phenomenon in various ways, such as inspecting the scene for overlooked details, quantifying various aspects of behavior, and so on. Sound-recording procedures have possibilities not only for later analysis of the records, but also for experimental use in playing them back to the animals under selected conditions in the field. In fundamental and original studies, however, such records should be considered as secondary and supplementary to the written and graphic notes from observation.

In each field project, an adequate account of the typical daily march of events is essential, as a basis for studies on variations, and to assist the planning of specialized surveys and tests. Such accounts of the daily routine are comparable to laboratory protocols. It is well to bear in mind that even original notes on field events are not to be regarded as mere catalogues of occurrences, but as perceptual accounts which invariably include some interpretation as well. If this fact is taken into account, it can be controlled appropriately. The well-schooled field investigator sets down his hypotheses as clearly as possible in advance, then records his perceived events with an attempt to distinguish what is focal and what peripheral under the conditions, significant variations and their conditions, and discernible relationships. Frequently, the records will include on-the-spot comparisons with other situations, and features worth following up comparatively will be noted. An emphasis upon newly revealed features and relationships makes for a progression and development from one situation to another, and assists the investigator to enlarge his understanding as well as his data concerning the phenomenon.

Specifically, these practices may be regarded as elementary controls guarding against the types of errors made under the conditions of so-called "observational memory" reports, in which results are reported or set down after an interval of time has elapsed. (From studies such as those of Bartlett (3) on this type of report, we may expect the perceiving, thinking, and remembering of observers who attempt to recall their material with inadequate records or without notes to be sprinkled liberally with subtle or gross errors, such as the inclusion of outside material, omissions, and alterations generally dependent upon personal motivation and attitude.) Emphasis upon notetaking techniques also increases adequacy of initial perception. Because observational memory is notoriously low in reliability and in validity, training in the technique of perceiving and emphasis upon adequate record-taking are imperative for control in field observation.

"PERSONAL EQUATION" IN FIELD INVESTIGATION

Because natural phenomena are not random aggregates but are found to be organized, in some respect, in all cases, systematic and controlled methods of selecting cases and collecting data must be found. The field study of social behavior in animals is not unlike that in opinion-poll and survey investigations on the human level, in that the methods cannot be directly transferred from the laboratory but must be developed through study of conditions in the respective field situations. Selected questions considered important must be investigated in (i.e., put to) groups considered representative of their populations. How the operations of selection are carried out is crucial for the adequacy of the study.

These considerations make the psychology of the investigator a matter of importance. The fact that different observers often obtain very different results from what is objectively the same phenomenon emphasizes the existence of individual differences in the psychological factors underlying perception and report, a condition known since 1795 as "personal equation" (5). Toward the control of such matters, we may bring an adequate training in the techniques of approach, of perceptual observation, of record-taking, and of logical processes. Such techniques are, to some extent, general but, in specific detail, must be developed appropriately on an empirical basis for each type of problem.

Obviously, the use of methods supplementing general observation is dependent upon the observer's psychology, in view of the fact that he must select the times and places at which to use particular instruments, according to his conception of the phenomenon and the relative importance of events in it. With sufficient cameras and sound pick-ups, he might conceivably get a fairly complete record of visual and auditory aspects. However, the general worth of the record would depend upon the skill and insight with which the recorders were placed, and finally the task of editing and interpretation would remain to tax his perceptual processes and judgment. Thus, whether or not the use of supplementary mechanical devices aids over-all control is a matter dependent upon the observer, and in particular upon his attitudes toward the subject matter.[4]

---

[4] In the light of recent critiques of the subject (e.g., Sherif and Cantril, 50), we may define attitude as an established and relatively enduring readiness to think and react in given selective ways with respect to objects or situations, under the influence of varying affective

It is evident that in studies of social behavior, our attitudes toward the nature, origin, and relationship of competition, cooperation, and natural-selection processes exert subtle influences not readily controlled in the planning and prosecution of investigations. For example, if our investigations are initiated on the hypothesis that a peck-order conception of social organization is adequate, some inertia is to be expected in our attention to other possible factors in social organization.[5] The nature of the effective "whole" that is investigated in a given problem depends upon factors of attitude. Whether in field or laboratory, the experimenter's responsibility for control involves the regulation of such matters, and not only the manipulation of objective factors in the phenomenon under study.

OBSERVATION-SELECTIVE AND DIRECT-MANIPULATIVE CONTROLS

Field study involves a variety of ways of regulating factors in the phenomenon under study. These may be differentiated roughly as *observation-selective controls* (including procedures of regulating approach, selective techniques in observation, and selection of variations for study) and *direct-manipulative controls* (which are more or less similar qualitatively to regular laboratory controls). All observational investigation involves the first type of control. The relative prominence of the second type depends upon the nature of problem and subject. We have been discussing observation-selective types of control, principally. Now we may turn to a discussion of a class of field problem in which the second type of control holds a prominent place.

Investigations on the problem of ant orientation, used here to illustrate use of direct-manipulative controls in field work, have the longest history of any systematic experimentation upon a behavior problem. They began in 1745, when Bonnet extended his observations on ant columns by the simple "finger test."[6] Merely rubbing a finger across the route disrupted travel in the column, suggesting the presence of a chemical trail. From that time, research on the way-finding of ants has developed through a long series of investigations, to which Huber, Lubbock, Forel, and Brun (6) have been notable contributors. Since Lubbock, much of the work, particularly that of Brun, has been performed in field and laboratory in a

---

and motivational aspects of personality, which owes its characteristic pattern to current situations interactive with the influence of learning and social experience.

[5] The available evidence suggests that cooperation and competition may have different biological bases in social behavior, and may differ in the degree and nature of their relationship according to phyletic level and environmental conditions (1, 45).

[6] For references on the general subject of orientation in ants, see Brun (6) and Schneirla (41).

coordinated way. For example, following preliminary observations and tests, the factor of light-compass orientation (i.e., a reaction to direction of light) was postulated, and Santschi developed his "mirror test" to investigate it in the field. Working with an established column of ants, direct sunlight was first shut off by setting up a board beside the trail; then a mirror was placed to reflect sunlight oppositely to the original direction. A typical result in ants such as *Lasius niger* was a clear reversal of traffic, indicating virtual orientation to light direction. Under certain conditions, however, the experiment is not effective with the same species.

Investigating this matter in the laboratory, Brun used Lubbock's procedure of reversing or interchanging cardboard floor sections of an established *Lasius* trail between nest and food-place. He found that when the trail was chemo-polarized (by interchanging floor-sections), a dominant reliance upon the chemical gradient made the ants less dependent upon direction of light than was the case with more homogeneous chemical trails.

In other ant species, such as *Formica*, field experiments demonstrated that, under given conditions, the chemical factor may dominate orientation at given times (e.g., when the path is narrow and canalized), whereas, under other conditions, the visual factor of light direction may dominate (dependent upon compound-eye processes), and, under still other conditions, a visual light-and-shadow factor (dependent upon the ocelli) may dominate. In demonstrating the last point, Brun first established, through observational records of individual foraging trips by *Formica* ants, that a polygonal course might be taken, with a succession of definite changes in direction, before the ant headed rather directly for the nest. The use of appropriate tests indicated that chemical and light-direction factors were not responsible. Finally, Brun established a reaction to large objects (e.g., trees) as basic here, through his finding that disorientation occurred when object-masking changed the situation in given ways. Appropriate observation-selective controls also were employed.

Through the combined field and laboratory methods developed in this area (7), characteristic species differences in the pattern of orientation have been demonstrated, as well as variations in the relative importance of sensory factors under different environmental conditions. As a further step, the maze method may be used in the laboratory, offering a controlled situation essentially equivalent to the situation of foraging in the field, to study the manner in which the way-finding pattern develops through learning (41, 43).

The tendency to be selectively preoccupied with certain results in particular sometimes distracts attention from essentials. For example, Cornetz was led by results of the polygonal-course type described above to minimize visual factors and resort to an "unknown direction sense." The matter was clarified by Brun through further tests and a comparison of results for numerous species under varied environmental conditions. At one stage, it was necessary to demonstrate, contrary to an assertion of Cornetz's, that the foliage of a eucalyptus wood did not exclude directed light and thereby obviate light-compass orientation. A comparable tendency is frequently seen, in the literature on bird migration and homing, to minimize or exclude the role of certain factors (e.g., visual, thermal, food) in favor of some other one in focus at the time. According to a critique by Odum (32), this error has been made in a recent purported demonstration of magnetic-field orientation in pigeons, in which no adequate controls were introduced on the function of topographical gradients and other environmental aspects favoring visual cues in particular.

An interesting illustration of the way in which direct-manipulative controls advance in field investigation is furnished by some experiments on bird homing. In the well-known experiments of Watson and Lashley (57) with terns, groups of birds were transported over considerable distances, in some cases over hundreds of miles, in different directions from their home on Bird Key in the Tortugas off Florida, and approximately half of them returned successfully. The explanation of their homing over long distances through presumably strange territory is a matter of conjecture, due to the fact that the birds could not be followed. Recently, Griffin and Hock (17) have performed similar experiments with the gannet, transporting the birds to a point more than 100 miles inland from their nesting area on the coast of New Brunswick. A new feature of experimentation was, that upon release, the course of individual birds (in half the cases) was followed by means of an airplane. The plane following above did not affect the behavior of the released bird in its flight, as was indicated by the fact that the frequency of return was the same in the experimental birds and in a control group not followed in the return. There was no indication of a direct flight in the followed birds, through long distances after their release, but all exhibited clear indications of spiralling. The results suggest that some of the birds may have become oriented when they chanced within visual range of landmarks in the coastal area. With this new technique, the orientation process in transport-and-release tests may now be studied effectively with wider controls than before.

Because of the basic reliance of most field investigation upon the observation-selective type of control, for effective analysis and synthesis it is very desirable to survey the results broadly after each test in which a segment is focused upon. The investigator aims at a systematic exploration of the phenomenon. For example, my studies on the army-ant behavior pattern involved, in essence, an examination of the following parts of the system in succession: first, the development and organization of raids;

then, the relationship between raiding and emigration; next, the nature of rhythmic processes in colony behavior; and so on (42). After studying each subproblem, a renewed concentration upon the pattern as a whole became more advantageous.

At first in this program, with the exception of secondary manipulative controls in studying chemical-trail orientation, only observation-selective procedures were followed. The object was to discover essential events and relationships by significant comparisons through observation. As an outcome of this procedure on a small scale, a major comparison study became possible. A condition was established in which a given colony staged large daily raids and emigrated each night. Through the time, a great brood of developing larvae was present. The hypothesis that a superadded excitatory effect from this brood served to keep the colony maximally active was supported by events when the larval brood came to maturity. Precisely on the day when the brood of grown larvae was enclosed in cocoons and its excitatory effect (presumably) reduced to a minimum, the colony began to stage very small raids, and emigrations ceased. In effect, maturation and enclosure of the brood constituted a control (observationally selected) on the factor of brood stimulation, for no other significant changes were discovered at the time. As a further check, the given colony remained sessile until this brood matured pupally and callow workers emerged, then broke abruptly into its maximal behavior condition of large raids and nightly emigrations. As a direct-manipulative test, the larval brood of a colony (then definitely nomadic) was removed, whereupon the level of raiding decreased sharply and nomadism ceased. Appropriate manipulative tests in the laboratory, and various detailed laboratory observations, confirmed the existence of a strong direct excitatory effect exerted by larvae upon adult workers, in contrast to a relatively weak effect of enclosed pupating broods. The results supported the postulation of a "drive" factor underlying colony behavior changes, exerted at periodic intervals by developing broods. This relationship proved to be the focal process in the highly organized behavior pattern of these social insects.

The essential procedure in such an investigation involves the comparison of major changes in the phenomenon with other conditions, which are focused upon successively, to probe their suspected relationship. As the selective observational studies advance, direct-manipulative tests become possible. Leading alternative hypotheses are checked similarly. For instance, the leading alternative to the above explanation of migration in army ants was the Vosseler concept of food depletion in the nesting area. Among the comparisons which ruled this out, there was the fact that on several occasions, after a given nomadic colony had evacuated its site of the day, another colony settled down in the area for an extended stay.

The variations in colony behavior occurred very regularly, but always in relation to identifiable brood changes, and not food supply.

It should be noted that, in field research, we are not merely observing events as concomitant or nonconcomitant, as one might pull markers of like or unlike color from a container by chance. Rather, we study concurrent series of events with the object of demonstrating the presence or absence of system inductively, and plan to explore selectively all crucial aspects of the phenomenon and their variations so that the nature of underlying relationships may be revealed. The research is qualitative in the sense that we are examining all relationships indicated as important among the events and processes of a system or pattern. In such instances, the existence and the nature of a pattern cannot be demonstrated readily by quantitative procedures, which are, however, useful when a specialized stage of analysis and synthesis is reached.

THE ARTIFACT METHOD: A COMBINATION OF PROCEDURES

An example of a specialized use of direct-manipulative controls in observational investigation is the "artifact method," in which given stimulus-episodes are introduced artificially, to find what aspects of the animal's environment figure critically in its ordinary behavior. Thus, in Audubon's studies of the role of smell in food-location by vultures, objects such as a painting of a sheep's body and a stuffed deer skin were placed on the ground in the open. From the fact that vultures came down to the artifacts but not to covered food, Audubon was drawn to the conclusion that smell could play no great part in the vulture's carrion responses, in contrast to vision (51). Results were later obtained by Chapman (9) indicating that both turkey buzzards and vultures reacted to hidden carrion on the basis of smell, although a visual guidance to food occurred when it was in the open.

The artifact method has found its most systematic use in the investigations of Tinbergen (53), with insects, birds, and fishes. A representative study was that of Tinbergen and Kuenen (54) on the appearance of the gaping response in young nestling thrushes. Tactual and visual stimuli of various kinds (e.g., tapping of bill or of nest edge, movement of a stick end or of black discs of different sizes and forms) were presented to the nestlings from an early time. The gaping reaction was first elicited by mechanical stimuli alone. Then visual stimuli began to elicit the response, the most effective artifacts being objects larger than 3 mm in diameter, such as black discs, moved at or above head level. Shortly after the first visual stimuli produced gaping, it was observed that, when a small convexity protruded from the upper margin of the disc, the gaping of the young bird was distinctively directed toward this part of the stimulus field.

This method is related to the psychophysical "method of limits" (55) in the sense that it involves presenting stimuli in a more or less graded series (i.e., in size, pattern) to find the threshold below which a given activity is not elicited. It is a departure in the sense that aspects of the stimulus (e.g., its size, its figural aspects) are varied, with the object of finding which of them are essential to response under given conditions. The artifact method is similar to the "method of equivalence" as used by Klüver (25), Lashley (26), and Maier (29), in their laboratory studies of mammalian visual discrimination, in that both methods are aimed at finding which of varied types of stimuli effectively produce the same response.[7]

In such experiments, the investigator's attitude and theory are especially crucial for the selection of stimuli and their manipulative use. One of Tinbergen's remarks (53) about the method is very interesting in this connection: "Experimentation with releasers . . . seems a very simple business indeed. However, this is true only in appearance. The technique is simple enough, but as a method of thinking and planning it has some treacherous pitfalls. It is easy to meddle with animals, to experiment in a vague and random way, but it requires some knowledge of ethology as a whole and some insight into the nature of a given problem to plan really convincing experiments that are relevant to the problem." In other words, the essence of the method is the selection, on the basis of preliminary studies of the animal in its environment, of stimulus patterns or part-patterns judged relevant to the elicitation of a given response, with the object of studying the conditions of appearance of this response and aspects of the pattern essential for its elicitation under given conditions.

The method has been effective for studying behavior such as the early reactions of young birds, and for analysis of stimulus patterns involved in the interaction of members of sexual pairs in different animals. However, the Tinbergen and Kuenen conclusions, for instance, advance beyond such matters to the conclusion that the order of responsiveness to mechanical and to visual stimuli has an entirely innate basis and also that the gaping response proper and the directional character of this response are innately differentiated. It should be considered that the theoretical attitude of the experimenters may have caused them to overlook quite inadvertently the desirability of controls on the influence of experience in these develop-

---

[7] The investigation with nestling thrushes was first carried out under laboratory conditions, then was repeated in the field (with adult birds absent in both cases) with entirely comparable results.

ments. In their study, adequate controls are not apparent on the possibility that extrinsic factors and experience are influential in the sequence of various changes in the gaping of nestlings. For instance, some results obtained by D. Lehrman (unpublished) indicate that there is a critical period during which gaping is first elicited by mechanical stimuli, when the eyes open secondarily during each reaction, thereby introducing incidentally a concomitance of gaping activity and visual effect which may have some importance for the later occurrence of gaping specifically to visual stimulation. To be comprehensive, investigations of this kind, with behavior appearing during early stages of development, must involve distinctive controls on the possible involvement of conditioning or learning factors in the phenomenon.

CROSS-SECTIONAL AND LONGITUDINAL INVESTIGATIONS COMBINED

The observation-selection methods may be described as the scheduling of cross-sectional studies of behavior in time so that strategic comparisons may be made within the underlying system. Studies which involve the comparison of a few cross-sectional episodes of behavior must be regarded as tentative and incomplete. When a consecutive series of cross-sectional surveys is made, with investigations timed at intervals during a period in which the pattern is suspected to be undergoing significant developments, a more adequate synthesis can be made. An example of this type of study is the investigation of eel migration carried out by Schmidt (40), in which the eel population of the North Atlantic ocean was sampled frequently in a spatially systematic way. From the fact that, through one interval of time, young eels increased in size and age as Europe was approached, whereas, through another distinct period, adults in the samples increased in age and sexual maturity westward from Europe, the conclusion was drawn that adult eels migrate westward from Europe to reach a given spawning ground in the ocean, and that young eels (of European species) migrate eastward from this area toward Europe. This kind of investigation approaches the longitudinal type of study, in which behavior trends are followed consecutively through considerable periods of time. For a thoroughgoing coverage of behavior patterns and their effective conditions of origin and change, such a method is imperative, whether we are studying problems in group or individual behavior.

The longitudinal plan, combined with intensive cross-sectional studies, has brought significant results in the investigation of both individual and group phenomena. As concerns individual patterns, a representative example is furnished by study of the pecking response in the chick (29). The group behavior functions and organization of birds and mammals have been explored advantageously from this point of view, as other authors in this monograph demonstrate. As an example from another level of organization, the writer's experiments on the army ant behavior pattern were designed so that all cross-sectional records of different colonies at critical stages could be compared with (presumably) equivalent stages in given colonies studied over long periods of time. Although shorter studies on different individuals or groups are contributive, beyond doubt the greatest degree of control and depth of comparative study is gained in a programmatic combination of short-term comparisons with long-term surveys. This is particularly true in the study of phenomena which are complexly organized and subject to change in time, as are the cases of individual development and of social organization.[8]

We should not omit mentioning the fact that in many instances, excellent field research has fallen short of its deserved gains through a concentration upon mature stages of given phenomena to the exclusion of developmental studies. For instance, although the field study of ant wayfinding is of long standing and reaches a point of effective theoretical clarity in the work of Rudolf Brun (6), we are still limited to hypothesis so far as the development of phenomena of field orientation is concerned, or to inferences from laboratory investigation (41). The paper of Dr. Riess will deal specifically with the important topic of studying developmental phenomena.

CONTROL IN LOGICAL PROCESSES OF INVESTIGATION

The concept of observation-selective control may be extended into a consideration of the conditions of reliability and validity in any specialized logical processes of investigation. In the behavior literature, controls of this sort may be found not only in the positive but also in the negative sense.

Because perceiving, thinking, and action are related in subtle and complex ways, the mental processes of hypothesis and theory are inevitably involved at all stages of scientific investigation. The desirability of controlling personal factors (such as attitude) in the framing and execution of a project is behind the frequent emphasis upon distinguishing between fact and hypothesis. Such a distinction, although difficult, is desirable, for it should increase our alertness to recognize the marks of our hypothesizing and theorizing, and thereby lead to a more effective use of such processes in reporting the nature of natural phenomena.

From a consideration of psychological processes underlying the ob-

---

[8] Of course, there are technical problems to be solved, such as the necessity of marking permanently all individual animals in the study group, if such programs are to be carried out advantageously.

servation-selective functions of an observer, even as brief a one as ours has been, it is apparent that the standards of validity in scientific reporting must reach considerably beyond the implications of Karl Pearson's statement (34) that the laws of nature are only descriptions of the order of our perceptions. To point the matter, we may consider Cohen and Nagel's (12) recognition of four different senses in which the word "fact" is frequently used in the literature of science. As illustration, we may consider a hypothetical case in which four statements of "fact" are made by the same observer at four different times. These are, let us say:

1. "The animal was heard to utter two sounds."
2. "The animal uttered a low grunting sound and a high whining sound."
3. "The animal uttered two sounds, a high-pitched 'whining' sound as an expression of hunger, and a low-pitched grunting sound in reaction to a female."
4. "The high-pitched whining sound, a response to hunger, was broken off when the male sighted a female; whereupon the low-pitched grunting sound was made in order to attract her."

All four types of statement will be found in scientific protocols as statements of "fact," in the *"Results"* section of publications as well as in the *"Discussion of Results"* section, although the careful scientist as a rule endeavors to limit his use of the term to statements on a par with the first two. All are "factual" in the sense that all four statements contain evidence bearing on some problem. On the other hand, each contains a degree of interpretive implication and statement of relationship, and it will be noticed that from the first statement to the fourth this aspect increases in prominence and in complexity. As a fifth possibility, a generalization is sometimes offered as a statement of "fact," for example, that

5. "Animals of this species usually leave off their concern with food, and hunger squealing is displaced by grunting, when a female passes, in order to attract the female."

It is clear from these considerations that the term "fact" is frequently used by scientists in very different constructions, which differ in the extent to which "evidence" and "interpretation" are combined in different cases. The "bare datum of evidence" ordinarily regarded as the essence of fact must be recognized as a hypothetical construct; and our problem is to approximate it as validly as we can. But it should be apparent that "fact" in the sense of the hypothetical "bare datum" will not be dealt with validly in behavior reporting as distinct from interpretation, until the role played by initial concepts and "direction" (27) is taken into account.

When initial concepts are strong and vivid, and metaphorically very appealing, they may be carried through an entire study without ever being examined effectively from the standpoint of validity. Stated plainly, this type of study is likely to be deductive rather than mainly inductive, as would appear desirable. The possibility should be recognized that an initial proposition may be sufficiently broad to enfold almost any datum of evidence in the given field in a cloak of indelible deductive coloration. A clear example is the initial statement of Hingston (21), in his book "Instinct and Intelligence," that "Everybody knows what instinct is." A more subtle one is the assertion of Russell (38) that ". . . inborn impulse to carry out a specific mode of action is the fundamental thing in instinctive behavior. . . ."

The manner in which presumptive concepts may be brought under effective control through a constant checking of earlier processes retroactively is suggested by William James's (23) caution that "The most useful investigator, because the most sensitive observer, is always he whose eager interest in one side of the question is balanced by an equally keen nervousness lest he become deceived."

A good example of an investigator's earnest efforts toward control in gathering and reporting evidence is offered in Jennings's (24) classical studies on protozoan behavior, which have all of the essential aspects of field investigation. The book is an important exercise in the technique of bringing out an inductively established behavior principle, namely the relevance of variability in behavior to the accomplishment of environmental adaptations on the given level. It must be said that, on the whole, Jennings succeeded (47).

The observer's attitude toward what constitutes an adequate sample of data to represent the phenomenon is dependent to a great extent upon his attitude and initial hypothesis. One extreme is represented by the "anecdotal tendency" (56), popularized by the Plinys and still in evidence in the public prints. Typically, a single outstanding case, considered representative and strikingly convincing in itself, is recounted to "prove the point." The storyteller is not out to *test* the adequacy of his view. Rather, he undertakes to convince the skeptics that his interpretation is the only one. Quite often, validity and reliability are implied by virtue of good social reputation or a "long experience close to nature." [9] Often, the account is very eloquently and sincerely presented, as in an article in which a "veteran guide" (39) recounts several instances in which animal sagacity is proved, as, for instance, a case in which a "smart little wolf" used a bull elk to dig out mice for him, and another in which beavers rebuilt a destroyed dam by ingenious devices involving reasoning. In each instance,

---

[9] Long experience close to nature may make an anecdotalist into an artist in that practice, or may make him a valid reporter of events, depending for one thing, upon his developing an interest in scientific validity.

there is a single observation, reported sincerely but with a heavy load of assumption and emotionally toned words. In his answer to the article from the standpoint of the scientific student of animal behavior, Beach (4) emphasized in particular the incompleteness of such reports, as well as the tendency to overlook alternative interpretations involving fewer assumptions. Scientific field investigators will sympathize with the attitude of the anecdotalist who is fond of animals and is struck by their apparent brilliance on occasion. Yet they also know that a single observation, especially when incomplete and reported from "observational memory," can have no valid bearing on the solution of a problem.

The question of validity in field notes obviously involves the fact that our language is loaded with preexperimental terms, which govern the use of specific imagery in our metaphors, and often dictate thought patterns which canalize our perception and our thinking. Validity is promoted in field records when metaphorical terms and "as if" devices are put in quotes, a practice which encourages later reexamination of the account for soundness of expression. It often happens that conceptual terms, first used as convenient symbols for partially understood things and relationships, slip through automatic transitions into a permanent form. No important term should be kept in use without frequent careful examination, for the unchallenged crystallization of a key concept in a much used verbal expression may prevent the observer from ever noticing exceptions to its chief implications.

An adequate observation-selective procedure calls for a carefully planned and consecutive study. As an example, let us take a hypothetical investigation of "fighting" between males of a given species of mammal, in its possible relation to mating. Evidence is needed which will permit testing available hypotheses logically. To broaden our receptivity, we focus, to begin with, on how fighting comes about, then on possible relations of fighting to other activities in the species. First, we must obtain as adequate an account of all cases of combat and their conditions as possible, both in and out of rutting season. We collect data on the relative frequency of variations in the initiation and conduct of combat. To test the hypothesis of a direct sexual-selective function of fighting, we would take note of the conduct of participants and other members of the group after each fight. If the "loser" then mates as frequently as the "winner," perhaps fighting does not play a direct part in sexual selection but has some other role, such as facilitating reproduction in a generalized manner. This hypothesis would then be examined appropriately, and so on.

In our study of the representative phenomenon and its variations, reliability and validity are promoted by repeating studies, to check on what is relevant to the phenomenon, the order of importance of relevant aspects, and other points. Once the principal pattern of factors and relationships is outlined, in further studies our leading hypothesis may be checked back into the phenomenon under selected variations in conditions. Such a review of occurrences, with a new approach to the phenomenon, may afford a needed control by reducing the canalizing effect of a previously dominant attitude which emphasizes certain items and excludes others.

The need to reexamine our initial premises at intervals, in the light of current findings, may be illustrated in terms of a frequent cause of ambiguity, a confusion of the factual existence of adaptive behavior systems with the hypothesis of purposive causation. The fact of adaptivity concerns the extent to which given activities adjust the animal to, or fit it for, its life zone. This aspect of behavior has no necessary relation to complex psychological functions such as anticipation and purpose, although McDougall (30) and some others have treated them as virtually synonymous. The property of adaptive function is common in the behavior patterns of animals from amoeba to man, but without the demonstrated involvement of anticipation or purpose except in the higher vertebrates (29). The danger of generalized expressions for adaptive adjustments in behavior, such as Russell's use of "perception" and "objective purpose" on all levels, is that they obscure important differences which appear to exist in the nature of psychological processes underlying adaptive adjustment at different phyletic levels.

The fact-gathering and interpretive aspects of science are closely related. We start out in laboratory and in field, in observation and experiment alike, by noting resemblances. But *degrees* of similarity are often important and sometimes crucial, and, by watching out for them and using special techniques to identify them, as by quantifying the main aspects of behavior, we may uncover important relationships of difference in our phenomena. Our investigation thereby constitutes an analysis of the phenomenon, which centers around the comparison of events and relationships in situations (e.g., social groups) which are similar in some respect considered important. When a number of different types of phenomena are assigned to a common category (e.g., Alverdes's (2), "open society"), the grouping must be considered tentative in dependence upon the extent to which the essential basis of similarity has been demonstrated. The process of synthesis, in which a theory is constructed to interpret the nature of a given behavior pattern or the interrelationship of a series of such patterns, often hinges upon the extent to which biological processes underlying the various behavioral events have been examined.

THE COMPARATIVE METHOD IN FIELD AND LABORATORY INVESTIGATION

The advantages of the comparative method to the processes of analysis and synthesis in animal study are clear. A difference in the homologous behavior patterns of two closely related species frequently is critically useful in uncovering important problems or basic principles. For example, by a comparison of group functions in the red deer and the roe deer of Scotland, Darling (13) found a significant difference meriting further examination, that, in the matriarchal groups of red deer, a close social organization prevailed, whereas organization was considerably looser in the roe groups with buck leadership. The advantages of species comparisons are demonstrated in this monograph, for example, in the papers of J. P. Scott on social behavior of dogs and wolves and of J. W. Scott on species of grouse.

As an example from another level, it was helpful in studying the basis of migration in army ants to note, first of all, that daily emigrations occurred in two closely related species despite wide differences in their patterns of raiding (42, 44, 48). A comparison of the relationship between raiding and the daily emigration process in colonies of the two species clarified the part played by similar factors, such as the process of afternoon rearousal of raiding in particular. Thereby the essentials of nomadic behavior in the general group became more apparent.

The ideal program for the future study of animal behavior would involve a coordination of field and laboratory investigation. Each has its characteristic advantages. Field investigation offers an opportunity to work with the animal's full pattern of activities from various approaches, with a broad perspective, with the relevance and, to a great extent, the validity of laboratory findings in view. In the laboratory, one may focus on specialized problems such as sensory discrimination, motivation, learning, and higher processes, pursuing them in detail and under conditions involving refined controls. Such studies require a further unification which may be gained in field applications and extensions. Programmatic studies along these lines may be anticipated.

If we know the typical behavior pattern of a given animal under natural conditions, and its usual variations, as well as the range of natural conditions to which the animal is capable of adjusting, the manner in which it may be investigated to advantage in the laboratory becomes clarified. Then the nature of crucial aspects of natural adjustment may be explored, as in gradient tests, discrimination and sensitivity tests, tests of adjustment through learning, and others as appropriate. Such a coordination of efforts will ward off errors in the planning of laboratory problem environments. Such difficulties have been apparent in the past, in that too little attention has been paid to the influence of the laboratory environment, the cage, on the functioning of laboratory animals in problem situations. It is only recently that serious study has been turned to such matters for animals in laboratory (36) and zoo environments (19). Hediger's comparison of the effects of confinement on caged animals, in relation to their behavior patterns in the wild, is certainly of interest from the standpoint of work with cage-confined laboratory animals also.

To represent one aspect of this important type of problem which has been much neglected, we may consider the fact that, in the case of confined animals, there is certain to be a considerable variation in activity, according to organic condition and related factors. Despite the fact that degrees of difference in the tendency to vary activity appear to be important for animal responsiveness under differing organic conditions, our chief tests have involved offering an opportunity for *homogeneous* activity, as in the exercise wheel. Measures such as Dashiell's (14) "exploratory maze" and Whitaker's (58) light-dark cage represent a partial escape from the idea that measuring "general activity" brings responsiveness adequately under measurement. These matters call for a reappraisal of methods and procedures from the standpoint of field-laboratory environmental conditions and their effects upon animal personality, considered comparatively.

We may agree in part with the European criticism (52) that in some respects American investigators have become overspecialized on certain laboratory problems and that a preoccupation has developed to some extent with specialized methods for their own sakes. In part, such tendencies may be due to ethnocentric attitudes which have influenced the planning of laboratory projects (46). It is to be expected that the artificialities often seen on this basis will be reduced in laboratory study which is planned more adequately in relation to the animal's situation under natural conditions.

It is probable that projects calling for the correlated investigation of given problems in laboratory and field will be undertaken more frequently and extensively when more field stations are available at which behavior studies may be carried out to advantage in typical ecological settings. Situations are desirable where a certain amount of laboratory investigation can be done in connection with a field program, to test possibilities for more extensively controlled work in regular laboratories. From the laboratory side, in addition to devising new experimental methods which will fit the special conditions and needs of the field, some of our most transportable and conformable methods may be used in the field. It is evident, for example, that more should be known of how far an animal's adaptations in the natural situation of the species are influenced by its capacities for learning and plastic behavior in general. Environmental emergencies of appropriate types may be devised to study how various obstructions are met, and comparable methods may be developed for investigating the establishment of behavior routines under natural conditions. For example, Gordon (16) used a variety of standard laboratory tests, including jumping situation to test discrimination, simple mazes, problem boxes, and string problems, to test the capacities of the western chipmunk in its native habitat. It should be possible to carry many of our laboratory methods into a direct-manipulative use in the field, with appropriate modifications. The possibilities are promising, and open the way for the comparative use of a great body of laboratory evidence.

An important question awaiting investigation concerns the extent to which animals under natural conditions are led to use their potentialities for plastic adjustments through learning and higher processes. Nissen (31) was led to the conclusion that the chimpanzees he observed in French Guinea were not very much extended to employ such capacities in this habitat: "It is hardly surprising that when wants can be satisfied by what we may call primitive behavior, complicated and therefore difficult behavior mechanisms will not be brought into play, even if potentially present." He thought the emotional aspects of life in these chimpanzees were much more developed, relatively, than the intelligence capacities, as compared with known laboratory conditions of behavior. What differences may be found on this point within the same species under differing environmental conditions, and from species to species under the respectively characteristic environmental conditions, remain to be investigated.

Not only do field and laboratory supplement each other in these respects, they also may be used to correct each other in appraising the relative prominence of different capacities in the two general settings. Carpenter (8) concluded that laboratory investigations of an animal such as the gibbon help to disclose possible misjudgments in the relative prominence of characteristics in the field, such as the minimizing of how far sensory capacities are used and the emphasizing of motor capacities. At the same time, he notes that there are problems, such as group organization, intergroup relations, and communicative behavior, which may be first and most validly studied in free-ranging animals under natural conditions. Further control will be obtained in planning investigations and in the interpretation of results when laboratory findings are referred to the field and field results to the laboratory as a matter of course.

RESUMÉ

To sum up, our purpose has been to show that, in each type of problem in animal psychology, there exist opportunities for correlated field and laboratory research. These problems may be pursued most adequately in the field when we think of field and laboratory research as basically similar. We have considered several means whereby control, in the sense of greater adequacy, may be obtained through emphasis upon training, upon the technique of the observer's approach to the problem and situation, through his strategy in selecting variations for study in contrast, and through adequate techniques in logical operations.

Working with animal behavior under natural conditions, the problems of reliability and validity in the collection and interpretation of data begin with the observer's perception. The influence of his attitudes and pattern of thinking begins with his selection of a problem and his preliminary survey of the field. By recognizing the essential function of hypothesis and other logical processes, such as analysis, synthesis, and comparison, from early to late stages in the gathering and interpretive use of evidence, methods may be worked out to bring their influences under control and improve their dependability.

Observation-selective controls involve the basic techniques of field method, from the perceiving of a phenomenon, and its regulated variation, to measures promoting exactness in taking records and rechecking them at suitable intervals. The concept of control subsumes our attitude toward the problem and its characteristics, which governs whether important relationships involved and factors underlying the phenomenon will be explored in adequate ways. From these considerations, programs become most comprehensive when investigation of the phenomenon is varied systematically in both a cross-sectional and a longitudinal sense. As an investigation proceeds, ways in which the direct-manipulative type of control may be applied will become apparent, according to the nature of the phenomenon studied. The study of natural phenomena from the standpoint of their developmental stages is a necessary feature of method in field investigation.

Errors attributable to the psychology of the investigator will not be eliminated through using supplementary instrumental methods, because these will be used according to his observation-selective techniques. The nature of these techniques will dominate his procedures in quantifying the records, in selecting instruments and determining their use in time and space, and in selecting and introducing direct-manipulative procedures of any character. These and other modes of extending the scope of field observation are subject to systematic controls similar to those needed for "bare observation." Supplementary methods are especially valuable when they sharpen attention to the basic phenomenon and promote a thoroughgoing exploration of its aspects through systematic variations.

Thus, control is gained in the field, not simply by mechanizing or quantifying our work or by multiplying cases, but by repeating given aspects of the investigation under methodically varied conditions. The object is to derive an adequate interpretation of the phenomenon through the logical processes of comparison, analysis, and synthesis. In the sense of psychological control (over attention, perception, and reasoning in the problem situation), the object is gained by means of systematically shifting our direction of approach to the problem, as concerns aspects of environment and animal, and relationships disclosed as important. Such procedures, if applied adequately to research from the preliminary stage of general observation to the specialized stages, should lead to planning more intensive investigation along new or expanded lines. In these respects, a close coordination of field and laboratory work is to be encouraged. The experimental attitude should play a leading role at all stages in field investigation.

REFERENCES

1. Allee, W. C. 1945. Social biology of subhuman groups. *Sociometry* 8: 21–29.
2. Alverdes, F. 1927. *Social life in the animal world*. New York: Harcourt, Brace.
3. Bartlett, F. C. 1932. *Remembering: A study in experimental and social psychology*. Cambridge: University Press.
4. Beach, F. A. 1947. Of course animals can think. *Nat. Hist.* 51: 116–118, 144.
5. Boring, E. G. 1929. *A history of experimental psychology*. New York: Appleton-Century.
6. Brun, R. 1914. *Das Raumorientierung der Ameisen und das Orientierungsproblem im Allgemeinen*. Jena: Gustav Fischer.
7. Brun, R. 1926. Psychologische Forschungen an Ameisen. *Abderhalden's Handbuch der biologischen Arbeitsmethoden*. Abt. VI, Teil D, *Methoden der Vergleichenden Tierpsychologie*. Pp. 179–230.
8. Carpenter, C. R. 1940. A field study in Siam of the behavior and social relations of the gibbon (*Hylobates lar*). *Comp. Psych. Monogr.* 16(5): 212.
9. Chapman, F. 1938. *Life in an air castle*. New York: Appleton-Century.
10. Churchman, C. W. 1948. *Theory of experimental inference*. New York: Macmillan Co.
11. Cohen, M. R. 1931. *Reason and nature*. New York: Harcourt, Brace.
12. Cohen, M., and E. Nagel. 1934. *An introduction to logic and scientific method*. New York: Harcourt, Brace.
13. Darling, F. F. 1937. *A heard of red deer*. London: Oxford.
14. Dashiell, J. F. 1925. A quantitative demonstration of animal drive. *J. Comp. Psych.* 5: 205–209.
15. Fisher, R. A. 1935. *The design of experiments*. London: Oliver and Boyd.
16. Gordon, K. 1943. The natural history and behavior of the western chipmunk and the mantled ground squirrel. *Oregon St. Mon., Zool.*, no. 5, pp. 104.
17. Griffin, Donald R., and Raymond J. Hock. 1948. Experiments on bird navigation. *Science* 107: 347–349.
18. Haring, D. G., and Mary E. Johnson. 1940. *Order and possibility in social life*. New York: Smith.
19. Hediger, H. 1942. *Wildtiere in Gefangenschaft*. Basel: Benno Schwabe & Co.
20. Heidbreder, Edna. 1924. An experimental study of thinking. *Arch. Psychol.* no. 73.

21. Hingston, R. W. G. 1928. *Problems of instinct and intelligence.* New York: Macmillan.
22. Hudson, W. H. 1893. *Idle days in patagonia.* New York: Appleton.
23. James, W. 1896. *Will to believe, and other essays in popular philosophy.* New York: Longmans, Green.
24. Jennings, H. S. 1906. *Behavior of the lower organisms.* New York: Columbia.
25. Klüver, H. 1933. *Behavior mechanisms in monkeys.* Chicago: Univ. Chicago Press.
26. Lashley, K. S. 1938. The mechanism of vision: XV. Preliminary studies of the rat's capacity for detail vision. *J. Gen. Psychol.* 18: 123–193.
27. Maier, N. R. F. 1930. Reasoning in humans. I. On direction. *J. Comp. Psych.* 10: 115–144.
28. Maier, N. R. F. 1939. Qualitative differences in the learning of rats in a discrimination situation. *J. Comp. Psych.* 27: 289–327.
29. Maier, N. R. F., and T. C. Schneirla. 1935. *Principles of animal psychology.* New York: McGraw-Hill.
30. McDougall, W. T. 1924. *Outline of psychology.* New York: Charles Scribner's Sons.
31. Nissen, H. W. 1931. A field study of the chimpanzee. *Comp. Psych. Monogr.* 8: 122.
32. Odum, H. T. 1948. The bird navigation controversy. *Auk* 65: 584–597.
33. Pearl, R. 1911. The personal equation in breeding experiments involving certain characters of maize. *Biol. Bull.* 21: 339–366.
34. Pearson, K. 1900. *The grammar of science.* London: Black.
35. Poincairé, H. 1912. *La valeur de la science.* Paris: Flammarion.
36. Riess, B. F. 1945. "Freezing" behavior in rats and its social causation. *J. Soc. Psychol.* 24: 249–257.
37. Rosenthal-Schneider, Ilse. 1945. The scientist's interference with the things he studies. *Australian J. Sci.* 7: 166–169.
38. Russell, E. S. 1944. The stereotypy of instinctive behavior (with an appendix on valence as "meaning for action"). *Proc. Linn. Soc. London,* 155th Session, Pt. 2: 186–208.
39. Russell, G. A. 1946. Can animals think? *Nat. Hist.* 55: 478–480; 490–492.
40. Schmidt, E. J. 1922. The breeding places of the eel. *Phil. Trans. Roy. Soc. London,* Ser. B, 211: 179–208.
41. Schneirla, T. C. 1929. Learning and orientation in ants. *Comp. Psychol. Monogr.* 6: 1–143.
42. Schneirla, T. C. 1938. A theory of army-ant behavior based upon the analysis of activities in a representative species. *J. Comp. Psychol.* 25: 51–90.
43. Schneirla, T. C. 1942. The nature of ant learning. II. *J. Comp. Psychol.* 35: 149–176.
44. Schneirla, T. C. 1945. The army-ant behavior pattern: nomad-statary relations in the swarmers and the problem of migration. *Biol. Bull.* 88: 166–193.

45. Schneirla, T. C. 1946a. Problems in the biopsychology of social organization. *J. Abnormal & Soc. Psychol.* 41: 385–402.
46. Schneirla, T. C. 1946b. Contemporary American animal psychology in perspective. *Twentieth century psychology*. New York: Philosophical Library. Pp. 306–316.
47. Schneirla, T. C. 1947. Herbert Spencer Jennings: 1868–1947. *Am. J. Psychol.* 60: 447–450.
48. Schneirla, T. C. 1949. Army-ant life and behavior under dry-season conditions. III. The course of reproduction and colony behavior. *Bull. Am. Mus. Nat. Hist.* 95.
49. Shelford, V. E. 1929. *Laboratory and field ecology*. Baltimore: Williams & Wilkins.
50. Sherif, M., and H. Cantril. 1945. The psychology of "attitudes." *Psychol. Rev.* 52: 295–319; 53: 1–24.
51. Strong, R. M. 1911. On the olfactory organs and the sense of smell in birds. *J. Morph.* 22: 619–662.
52. Tinbergen, N. 1942. An objectivistic study of the innate behaviour of animals. *Bibliotheca Biotheoretica*, Ser. D, 1(2): 39–98.
53. Tinbergen, N. 1948. Social releasers and the experimental method required for their study. *Wilson Bull.* 60: 6–51.
54. Tinbergen, N., and D. J. Kuenen. 1939. Über die auslösenden und die richtunggebenden Reizsituationen der Sperrbewegung von jungen Drosseln. (Turdus merula L. und T. e. ericetorum Turton). *Z. Tierpsychol.* 3: 37–60.
55. Titchener, E. B. 1915. *Experimental psychology*. Vol. II. *Quantitative experiments*. Part II. Instructor's Manual. New York: Macmillan.
56. Warden, C. J., T. N. Jenkins, and L. H. Warner. 1940. *Comparative psychology; A comprehensive treatise*. Vol. I. *Principles and methods*. New York: Ronald Press.
57. Watson, J. B., and K. S. Lashley. 1915. Homing and related activities of birds. *Carn. Inst. Wash.*, Publ. no. 211, pp. 9–60.
58. Whitaker, W. L. 1937. A method for studying environmental choices of laboratory animals. *Science* 86: 314.
59. Wolf, A. 1929. Scientific method. *Encyclopedia Brit.*, 14th Edition, 20: 127–133.
60. Woodworth, R. S. 1937. Situation-and-goal set. *Am. J. Psychol.* 50: 130–140.

T. C. SCHNEIRLA

Psychology, Comparative

Bibliography No. 42

Psychology, comparative, concerns the study of similarities and differences in capacities for environmental adjustment and for behavioral organization among the important types of living beings, from plants and unicellular organisms to the primates including man. A view of the subject held earlier by W. Wundt and others included human comparisons now generally studied under the titles of genetic or child psychology, abnormal psychology and ethnology or folk psychology. The present article is concerned with an examination of the psychological nature and capacities of lower animals and man in comparison with one another.

Comparative psychology is studied because the behavior of animals is in itself interesting, because of important applications in fields such as medicine and animal training, and also because of significant bearings on human psychology. With the rise of an experimental comparative psychology in the latter half of the 19th century and its rapid growth during the 20th century, the scientific study of lower animals has cast increasing light on questions in human psychology, such as the development of individual behavior, motivation, the nature and methods of learning and many others. Psychologists often employ lower animals as subjects in their experiments because these are easier to obtain in numbers and can be much better known as to background and better controlled under experimental conditions than human subjects, and because of relationships in behavior. Much can be learned about man by studying lower animals; moreover, the discovery of differences illuminates the similarities.

In primitive times man had to learn about animals because of his constant struggle with them for existence. Animals became familiar members of human households, and many cultures used animals as totems or worshiped them as magical beings. The common-sense tendency to endow lower animals with human capacities always has been strong. People often talk to animals, appealing for action or for sympathy as though dealing with human beings. An extreme development of this tendency is the doctrine of metempsychosis, or transmigration of souls, which holds that after

Psychology, Comparative, by T. C. Schneirla, is reproduced with permission from the *Encyclopaedia Britannica*, 1962.

death the human soul may reside either in another person or in a lower animal.

In recorded history two different views have developed concerning man's relation to the lower animals. One, termed for convenience the man-brute view, stresses differences often to the point of denying similarities altogether; the other, the evolutionary view, stresses both similarities and differences. Aristotle formalized the man-brute view, attributing a rational faculty to man alone, lesser faculties to the animals. On the other hand, from the 19th century Darwinism led scientists to look for relationships between man, considered a highly evolved animal, and the other animals. This has come to be the modern view in science. Scientific evidence indicates that continuity in the evolution of organisms provides a basis for essential psychological similarities which exist, together with differences, between lower and higher animals.

I. METHODS

1. GATHERING EVIDENCE

The evolutionary position, which has been substantiated in its main contentions concerning mental relationships among animals, has its basis in experimental evidence. Fact gathering, whether by observation or by experiment, requires, beyond a keen interest in animals, special training in the scientific methods of investigation for which personal feelings are no substitute. An animal story, even when reported by a person of repute and veracity, carries no automatic guarantee of its soundness. All reports, whether from laboratory experiments or from studies of animals in their natural habitats, must be evaluated for reliability according to what investigative conditions prevailed and what precautions were taken against error in gathering the facts.

In comparative psychology, as in science generally, the soundest method of study at hand is used. An observer of nesting behavior in birds constructs a hide-out or blind to minimize disturbances resulting from his presence. Binoculars, a camera and special mechanical means for recording the bird's reactions may further increase the reliability of his investigation.

Experiments in the laboratory are designed to obtain the maximal control over conditions. There it is possible to regulate general factors such as age and physiological condition of the subjects, to exclude disturbances, to change environmental conditions or keep them constant, according to the experimental plan, and to introduce apparatus designed to ensure accuracy both in the test itself and in recording results. Thus animal psychology has employed the maze method as one means of testing learning, special problem boxes to test intelligent behavior and a variety of other techniques planned to increase the significance of the evidence obtained.

2. INTERPRETING EVIDENCE

No theory can be sounder than the validity of its evidence or the logic of its construction. To illustrate the necessity of checking evidence at the source and logically examining theory, a famous case in which humanlike abilities were claimed for a performing animal may be cited. Late in the 19th century, several horses owned by a Herr von Osten of Berlin, particularly one named Hans, became renowned for purported mathematical capacities. When a problem was written on a blackboard before him, Hans, by tapping first with right forefoot and then with left, indicated the answer in digits and tens respectively, with such success as seemingly to support the owner's claim for mental calculations by the horse. Although skepticism was expressed by many, and some alleged trickery, others asserted that the owner must be honest and his claims therefore valid. Scientific surveys of the case, particularly by the psychologist O. Pfungst, supported the following analysis. The horse performed well whether the owner was present or not, apparently ruling out trickery due to the owner's presence. But Hans failed unless the trainer or someone else was present who knew the answers; hence success depended somehow on human influence. The fact that the horse failed when blindfolded excluded telepathy while indicating some other effect from persons present. Observing the audience carefully, the psychologists found that when a problem was written down, someone who knew the answer would bend forward very slowly, whereupon the horse would begin tapping. After the correct number of taps, the person would relax, usually with a little movement, as of the head, and the horse would stop. Slight movements of this kind were known to psychologists as inadvertent activities accompanying acts of close attention. From these facts, Pfungst concluded that, without the owner's knowing it, the horse had learned to start and stop his taps according to appropriate sensory cues. This interpretation was favored by still other facts. The horse was equally successful whether the problem was in simple arithmetic or in calculus; also, his responses to easy and to difficult problems alike often were incorrect by only one or two digits, suggesting a direct control of the tapping that could operate now early, now late, rather than mental operations. Supporting this conclusion was the fact that Hans typically began tapping mechanically when all was ready, without even looking at the figures.

This case brings out some important principles of interpretation in comparative psychology. The investigator selects a likely hypothesis, but considers it tentative until it is supported by experiments in which all factors of possible importance are controlled. (In the Clever Hans case, the roles of sensitivity and habit in the horse, the factors of audience knowledge and of subtle motor aspects of attention, and still others were tested.) After his experiments, the scientist sifts and organizes the available evidence logically, using mathematical techniques when possible, to find what theory best fits the facts. These safeguards are elementary, whatever the nature of the behavior problem.

3. ANTHROPOMORPHISM

There is an irresistible human tendency to ascribe human attributes, emotions and capacities to other beings. Thus it is said that moths and other insects fly to the light out of curiosity; the rattlesnake sounds its rattle in order to warn intruders; pets and domestic animals are noble or sly and deceitful according to conditions; and so on. The practice of interpreting behavior on the basis of selected stories is called anecdotalism. Thus Plutarch in ancient Rome, La Fontaine in 17th-century France and countless other writers have busied themselves in narrating stories about mental feats in lower animals.

Although valuable literary works may be created by authors attributing human traits to animals, anthropomorphic literature risks two fundamental flaws which make it an undependable source of evidence. First, it typically involves the implicit assumption that any person is well acquainted with his own behavior and thoughts and even understands their causes. About this belief modern psychology is seriously doubtful, advising caution to writers about behavior and particularly those unskilled in observation or interpretation. Another difficulty is that a scientifically untrained person, however well intentioned, may rest content with a single outstanding occurrence in the life of an animal as a basis for his interpretation, especially one with dramatic features making its telling and retelling a gratifying act. But a single observation has low reliability, as have any number, when perception is influenced by prejudices and preconceived notions. Furthermore, with each narration, new features are usually introduced and old ones changed so that the report becomes increasingly unreliable.

4. ADAPTIVE BEHAVIOR OR PURPOSE

Unnecessary complexities often arise in interpretation because of the interpreter's point of view. Under natural conditions, for example, animal behavior generally conforms to what a human observer might call "appropriate" or "best" in the given situation. Thus the Venus's-flytrap closes its hinged leaf when a fly alights upon it, but not when stirred by a breeze; the scallop closes the valves of its shell as its common enemy, the starfish, approaches; the octopus frequently remains secluded until its common prey, the crab, is nearby; the chimpanzee, attracted by food out of reach, may attain it by piling boxes. Acts that seem well adapted to the given animal's welfare under particular conditions are often described as purposive. For those interested in obtaining valid explanations, this generalization of purposiveness in behavior raises difficulties.

The above cases are typical—what can be said about them? First, these acts occur as described: the reports are reliable. Also, the acts have in common one characteristic: each of them furthers the life processes of the animal and fits it to its surroundings. In this respect they are all adaptive, and indeed, animal behavior tends to be adaptive. Although many theorists mean only this when they use the term purposive to describe behavior, a distinction seems desirable between what is adaptive and what is purposive in behavior.

The names of H. Driesch and W. McDougall are associated with a view in the nature of teleology, through which all animal behavior of the type termed above adaptive is endowed with directive forces comparable with human volition. When a man behaves purposively, with the assistance of thought processes he strives for an end which he anticipates or expects. If all animals actually performed their adaptive behavior on the basis of such a process, the theoretical problems of comparative psychology would be relatively simple, for the same type of solution would apply to all cases. But the danger exists that the teleological type of explanation may arise from the theorist's preconceived notions rather than from reliable supporting evidence.

5. MORGAN'S CANON

A useful rule in scientific interpretation is the principle of parsimony, which may be stated as follows: of alternative explanations for a given phenomenon, choose the simplest, that requiring the fewest assumptions, provided it meets the facts adequately. This principle was stated for comparative psychology by C. L. Morgan (*An Introduction to Comparative Psychology*, 1894) as follows: "In no case may we interpret an action as the outcome of the exercise of a higher psychical faculty, if it can be interpreted as the outcome of the exercise of one which stands lower in the psychological scale."

The purposive type of explanation for the above examples would be that the Venus's-flytrap needs food, hence closes when touched by insects but not by inedible objects; the scallop recognizes the starfish as an enemy and closes its valves to avoid destruction; the octopus hides so that its enemies cannot see it and its prey may come close; the chimpanzee stacks boxes in order to obtain suspended food. Although at first sight these purported explanations all may appear simple, actually they are all complex and no one of them should be adopted until alternatives have been considered in the light of Morgan's canon. Each hypothesis assumes that the animal anticipates the consequences of one action or its alternative (e.g., the scallop anticipates death if it does not close) and can weigh the possibilities somewhat as a reasoning man might. Humanlike capacities, such as understanding meanings, anticipating results and choosing between alternatives, are thereby implied by these purposive explanations. The evidence, however, favours a purposive explanation in only one of the described instances, the case of the box-stacking chimpanzee. W. Köhler and others have shown that this animal can anticipate success when jumping from the ground to suspended food, can understand the significance of a box as a means of reaching food and can solve problems by reasoning. Conversely, to account for the flytrap's reaction, only a simple reflexlike reaction to stimulation need be assumed, for the leaf closes when its delicate filaments are touched by a foreign object. As for the scallop, experiments show that it closes in response to any sufficient chemical effect, as to starfish broth released in the water nearby, but not to a starfish presented behind glass (visual control). In the case of the octopus, an intent to hide is excluded by J. A. Bierens de Haan's finding that the animal slips between plates of glass, where it remains in full sight, as readily as between pieces of slate. The simpler explanation consistent with the facts is that the octopus comes to rest when its body touches between surfaces, not because it understands hiding.

These cases illustrate the value of investigation in comparative psychology to test assumptions and reach an adequate explanation. Too frequently a purposive account merely names the gains of an activity (e.g., protection, food) without clarifying the process involved. But a name alone is no explanation, and may in fact suggest an incorrect interpretation. Adaptive acts must be explained through evidence from investigation rather than by analogies between lower animals and man, for activities which lead to similar adaptive results (e.g., both the leaf closing of the flytrap and the box stacking of the chimpanzee are "food-getting behavior") may be very different psychologically.

6. OBJECTIVE ATTITUDE

Early in the 20th century the view gained ground that careful experimentation on behavior under controlled conditions should produce evidence improving psychological theories of animal capacities. A chief contribution of this movement to comparative psychology was its emphasis on objective techniques as against subjective procedures for evaluating and comparing the psychological resources of different animals. To appraise any animal activity, the psychologist must consider its nature and adaptive value, the situation and what factors in the species' organic make-up and in individual experience may have contributed to it.

The first task in comparative study is to discover the characteristic capacities and resources of behavior in each animal type; the next is evaluation. It is not sufficient to assign positions in a series, classifying some animals as inferior and others as superior; the presumed inferiority or superiority must be clarified through comparisons. Neither the stability nor the adaptive efficiency of behavior are as indicative of superior psychological status as are modifications of behavior to fit new conditions. The principal weakness of a topical study is the implication that capacities such as "memory" are much the same wherever found. But any given capacity, such as learning, overlaps others and may also differ greatly according to the animal type involved. Higher animals do not necessarily repeat the make-up of lower animals with the addition of certain new abilities. Rather than a recapitulation of the characteristics of lower animals in the higher, research discloses similar properties and others which assume new psychological significance. These matters may be illustrated by passing in review some outstanding differences observed among various types of animals.

II. PSYCHOLOGICAL STANDING

1. PSYCHOLOGICAL LEVELS

The earliest formal statement of psychological levels was the scheme of Aristotle, endowing plants with a nutritive faculty alone, the lowest animals with sensory faculties also, higher animals with an appetitive faculty also and man alone with a rational faculty. Descartes's ideas embodied a simpler scheme: a lower level of animals, viewed as automata, and man as the sole rational being, on a higher level. In 1905, R. M. Yerkes differentiated levels on the basis of functional criteria and experimental evidence: (1) discrimination, a general form of reaction, shown by lower invertebrates; (2) docility, or modifiable reactions, shown by rodents; and (3) initiative, or variability in reaction, shown by primates.

One objection to such systems is that they are speculative and may restrict the experimenter's viewpoint. Another is that they tend to oversimplify animal nature, even in the lowest animal forms, and encourage categorical interpretations of animal capacities. Distinctions of psychological levels are rejected by those who believe that capacities such as perception and learning exist in all animals. Experience, however, favors the concept of psychological levels to usefully represent transitions from lower to higher psychological stages and validly summarize knowledge of animal relationships, so long as complete discontinuities from level to level are not assumed.

2. CONSCIOUSNESS

Attributing consciousness to any lower animal and speculating as to how it must feel to be that animal is a popular tendency which has its formal counterparts in speculative philosophy. When we see another individual behaving more or less as we do under comparable conditions, that being, whether man or lower animal, is assumed to have an experience similar to our own. Thus Montaigne, from occurrences such as the starting and barking of dogs in their sleep, thought that brutes must possess the power of imagination. Late in the 19th century when experimental comparative psychology began to develop, the prominence of introspective methods in general psychology encouraged a strong tendency to analogize consciousness. This tendency weakened in time, mainly through objective tendencies succeeding the failure of attempts to use consciousness as a criterion of animal mentality. The chief objections were, first, that introspection, a method considered low in validity for human psychology, could not be valid for studying lower animals, which lack speech; and, second, that if inferences concerning the subjective aspects of even the simplest mental states in man are held doubtful, little justification exists for applying the method of anthropomorphic analogy to lower animals. In the words of M. F. Washburn (from *The Animal Mind,* 3rd ed., 1926, Macmillan Co.) :

> We speak, for example, of an "angry" wasp. Anger, in our own experience, is largely composed of sensations of quickened heart beat, of altered breathing, of muscular tension, of increased blood pressure in the head and face. The circulation of a wasp is fundamentally different from that of any vertebrate. The wasp does not breathe through lungs, it wears its skeleton on the outside, and it has the muscles attached to the inside of the skeleton. What is anger like in the wasp's consciousness? We can form no adequate idea of it.

Comparative psychologists have thus come to favor objective procedures for understanding lower animals, and to mistrust analogies from human states when these stand alone.

A. Critical Points of Change in the Animal Series

1. PROTOZOANS AND THE CONCEPT OF "SIMPLICITY"

Protozoans frequently are termed the simplest animals. This cannot mean that their activities are few, for H. S. Jennings and F. Alverdes found that the reactions of the ciliate *Paramecium,* for one, are many and varied.

This organism is propelled forward, rotating about its long axis, by the beating of minute, hairlike cilia covering its ovoid body. When stimulated, it pauses momentarily, rotating narrowly or widely before continuing in a new direction, or backs away at an angle varying from acute to obtuse. Specific properties of the stimulus, particularly its intensity, may be critical; for example, weak contact typically elicits slight interruptions of forward movement, strong contact a pronounced backing reaction, and physicochemical properties of stimulation directly influence the extent and the duration of modifications in forward swimming. Although the protoplasmic changes underlying the many variations of ciliary stroke in these different reactions doubtless are biochemically complex, this behavior is simple in the sense that it can be understood in terms of psychologically simple concepts, for a dictation of response by the physical properties of stimulation is the lowest order of psychological process.

Protozoan behavior, nevertheless, is adaptive. When Jennings dropped a stream of carmine particles upon the disc of the attached trumpet-shaped ciliate *Stentor*, there occurred a series of reactions from a slight contraction of the oral disc to increasing general contractions which at length broke the animal free from the substratum. Jennings characterized these variable reactions to conditions of repeated stimulation as a series of "trials." More objectively considered, such behavior is the product of protoplasmic changes forced by repetitive stimulation. At first only the funnel end reacts; then as internal excitation spreads, the stalk contracts progressively toward its attached base. Behavior thus changes successively through a progression of physiological summations producing new results as they reach more remote localities. Although the notion of "trials" emphasizes the adaptive aspects of these processes, it misrepresents the acts, which are forced by stimulation rather than arising as attempts to attain expected results.

This case illustrates how, in the simple psychological system of the protozoan, variable reactions widen an animal's adaptation to surrounding conditions. Jennings demonstrated that paramecia collect around a drop of acid in their medium not through direct approaches to the acid but because they first swim readily into the area, then recoil from the acid-deficient border zone on each encounter. Since, in the ciliates, stimulus changes typically interrupt forward swimming differently according to their intensity and other physicochemical properties, the organisms thereby can avoid injurious and approach beneficial agents in their environment. The adaptability of such reactions in unicellular organisms, through the gaining of optimal conditions thereby, stems from the persistence of variable swimming until conditions favor normal locomotion.

The status of behavior changes in protozoans has been much discussed. As examples, amoebae, repeatedly exposed to bright light, put forth fewer pseudopodia before each further reversal of direction; *Paramecium,* introduced successively into a capillary tube from which it can escape only by doubling around, reverses with increasing promptness. Some writers consider such changes equivalent to the "learning" of higher organisms, pointing to graphic records of reduced time or movement in these cases. Others, conversely, stress the limited duration of such changes in protozoans, also that many of them have been duplicated (as by chemical treatment) without putting the organism through "trials." Thus, although F. Bramstedt reported that repeatedly combining light (generally ineffective) with heat (generally avoided) caused *Paramecium* to avoid light in tests, J. B. Best found that light avoidance came about in *Paramecium* through experimental exposures to high temperature alone. Best therefore interpreted Bramstedt's results not as "conditioned responses" but as hysteresis, or a general sensitizing of the protoplasm to the action of one physical agent through the effect of another. Perhaps the most relevant point favoring the latter, simpler interpretation is that the described changes soon disappear without evidencing any lasting alteration of the species behavior pattern.

2. PSYCHOLOGICAL LIMITATIONS OF LOWER INVERTEBRATES

Significant for determining the psychological level of an animal is its behavioral organization. Perhaps least endowed in these respects are low multicellular animals such as adult sponges. The sponge is a bottom-attached organism of the colonial type that feeds by filtering organic substances from water drawn through chambers in the body wall. The reactions of sponges are simple, local and sluggish. As G. H. Parker (*The Elementary Nervous System*, 1919) found, sponges lack integration among their parts except that resulting from structural unity and a crude transmission of mechanical impulses through certain primitive cells around the opening to the body cavity, combining sensory and motor properties. Such limitations may have characterized the early ancestors of multicellular animals prior to the appearance of neural tissue.

In the coelenterates, behavioral organization has improved so that a measure of integration exists in activities such as feeding, locomotion and withdrawal from intense stimulation. These gains were found by G. J. Romanes and by Parker to be attributable to a generalized conduction system, with a nerve net, a continuous conduction network permeating the body wall and transmitting impulses from specialized sensory cells to specialized muscle tissue. Activities here, although far better integrated than in sponges, are still relatively sluggish and considerably below the level of cephalopods, for example. One limitation is in the low-grade centralization of the conduction system, which distinctly handicaps behavioral organization.

Activities are better integrated in echinoderms such as starfish and sea urchins. In normal behavior, local activities are so effectively combined that J. von Uexküll, who investigated the neurophysiology, was led to characterize the echinoderm in action as a "community of reflexes." In a reflex, stimulated sensory cells transmit impulses to association cells in the neural system, which arouse muscular contractions. Thus, the tube feet, small fingerlike muscular structures capable of adhering to the substratum by their terminal sucking discs, when stimulated lightly, bend toward the affected side through one muscular action; when stimulated intensely, they bend away through another action. An appreciable local autonomy is indicated by the fact that the characteristic echinoderm structures, tube feet, pedecillariae (nippers) and spines, when cut from the animal and appropriately mounted, react to stimulation much as before. To be sure, throughout the animal series, reflexlike actions enter into the normal functioning of internal organs (e.g., the vertebrate heartbeat), controlled reflexly in a more or less automatic manner. Even in mammals, reflexes may intervene in general behavior, as in scratching or sneezing, but with a very different significance than in lower invertebrates. For the latter, the community-of-reflexes concept has some validity for a behavior in which somewhat autonomous local activities are combined differently according to the conditions of arousal.

Yet the behavior of lower invertebrates such as coelenterates and echinoderms is more than a chain-reflex combination of functions, as sense organs and motor structures are linked functionally together by the nerve net. Thus, soon after pedecillariae have caught prey, the tube feet extend, attach and "walk" the object toward the centrally located mouth, which meanwhile everts and folds around the victim. The simplest nerve nets (as in the coelenterate *Hydra*) have a minimal polarization related to the growth gradient, and conduct according to the strength and localization of external stimulation without strict directionality. Such nerve nets exemplify the function of primitive conduction systems, joining local operations without specifying the behavior pattern. Although in mammals nerve-net functions are visceral and local (as in coordinating intestinal activities in digestion), in the lower invertebrates nerve-net correlation is the main agency unifying behavior.

Echinoderms advance materially in behavioral organization as compared with coelenterates. A more versatile integration of local function exists in the righting response, aroused when the animal is turned on its back. In the inverted starfish, with previous stimulation and handling equalized, two or three rays twist about, and when the ventral surfaces of these rays touch the ground, tube feet progressively closer to the central disc attach. These rays thereby swing the body of the starfish, overbalance and right it. For this reaction to occur, it is necessary that the rays of one side become dominant.

A. R. Moore demonstrated that this organization normally depends on impulses through the nerve ring interconnecting the radial nerves of the five arms. When this nerve ring is sectioned, all rays attach, behavior is uncoordinated and righting occurs slowly and abnormally. Through nervous impulses, therefore, the normal unitary behavior of echinoderms involves the temporary subordination of certain local activities to others dominating general action. The studies of J. E. Smith on the starfish nervous system reveal new complexities, including ganglion-cell mechanisms involved with the nerve net, advancing behavioral organization beyond that of the coelenterates.

An improved organization of behavior thus enters with the subordination of local, reflexlike functions to wider patterns, as when scratching is inhibited as a dog sees food. The local activities themselves are then not only more elaborate and diversified, as in the reflex-cleaning activities of insects, but also better related to other behavior. Echinoderm behavior is more than a community of reflexes; sponge behavior is far less.

Although echinoderm adaptive activities are impressive, they are sluggishly performed and their level of organization should not be overestimated. Jennings endowed the starfish with the capacity to learn, on the basis of tests in which individuals shortened the time required to right themselves. One pair of rays was prevented from attaching by a glass rod used to disengage the tube feet from the substratum, and after 180 trials these arms attached less readily than before the trials. Although Jennings interpreted this as "habit formation," Moore produced similar results merely by rubbing the tube-foot surfaces of particular rays with a glass rod or treating them with weak acid. He therefore attributed Jennings's results not to "learning," or changes in central organization through experience, but to injury of restrained arms through continuous friction with the rod which altered sensory and motor function in further trials. These results are therefore equivalent to the impairment of action through motor fatigue, or its reduction through sensory adaptation or injury, not ordinarily classed as learning in higher animals.

B. Cephalization and Centralized Control

1. FUNCTIONS OF A SIMPLE BRAIN

Improvements in both organization and capacities of behavior appear in worms, mollusks and particularly insects. Basic advances are illustrated in a simple form in the earthworm. Whereas echinoderms are radially structured, and any of the body sections can lead in locomotion or other activities according to circumstances, worms have an anterior specialized end, which is not only the most sensitive and mobile of all body sections but also the dominant one by virtue of a superior ganglionic centre or brain. Cephalization, or head dominance, improves organization basically, widens the range of environment and action, and carries behavioral organization beyond the conditions prevailing in protozoans, coelenterates and echinoderms. The significance of specialized head receptors and a brain for efficient behavior in a marine worm is indicated, after the brain has been destroyed, by irregular crawling about, by turning much more clumsily on contact and burrowing less readily than a normal worm. The animal after operation cannot extend from its burrow (on chemical stimulation) and seize prey as does the normal individual. Removal of the worm's brain, although not preventing normal reactions altogether, materially reduces their directness and precision. This is therefore a primitive type of brain, a collector and a transmitter of impulses from the most sensitive parts of the organism, presumably also an amplifier, but not a major organizing centre. The brain of insects, in contrast, is an indispensable organizing centre. Although a bee or ant with its brain destroyed may stagger about for a time before dying, with a degree of locomotor coordination, only scattered reflex acts such as stinging occur and the complex normal repertory (e.g., foraging, building) is gone.

2. ADVANCES IN ORIENTATION

Regulation of locomotion and way finding under changing external stimulation improves in worms, mollusks and arthropods over its status in lower invertebrates. J. Loeb emphasized that the evolution of a specialized anterior and bilateral symmetry opens the way for new patterns of orientation in space. These improvements admit more appropriate changes in adjustment to external stimulation, as when an octopus turns toward the side on which a crab is seen but does not pursue if the object moves too swiftly. At this stage the crude energic properties of stimulation are dominant, as when a worm or snail approaches the source of a weak chemical but withdraws from the source of an intense stimulus, with variable behavior at intermediate concentrations. The directive effect of stimuli of different intensity acting on receptors of the opposite sides of the body is shown by experiments in which a fly with its right eye covered turns toward the right under strong light but toward the left under weak light.

Progress in the organization and variability of orientation is indicated from the worms to insects, depending on the complexity and specialization not only of receptors but also of the central nervous system. The octopus, for example, has eyes much better fitted than those of marine worms for general vision, with accommodation to distance, and can inhibit its dash at a crab until within range. Social insects such as ants and bees have compound eyes, admitting versatile reactions to visual movements as well as movement with reference to changing visual stimuli. Although the evolution of orientation in space involves receptor specializations, advances in this capacity are especially correlated with the nervous system. Operative longitudinal sectioning of the brain introduces progressive impairments in the orientation of animals from worms to insects. Z. Y. Young demonstrated that the octopus, through experience, can master conditioned responses to a crab, or to visual forms experienced with food. In such func-

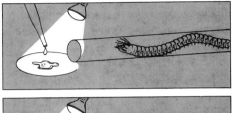
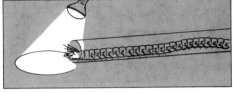

FIGURE 1
Copeland's study of conditioning in the
marine worm *Nereis*. At first, light is ineffective, but after having been combined several
times with meat juice, light alone brings
the worm from the tube.

tions the octopus, far superior to worms, loses correspondingly much more
through brain operations. Although in the lower invertebrates quantitative
aspects of stimulation such as intensity, size and rate of change basically
control the timing and precision of orientation, in the cephalopods and insects, as compared with the worms, the patterns not only become more
complex but also more changeable according to experience.

3. SIMPLE LEARNED MODIFICATIONS

Clear evidence for learning appears first in the worms, in which conditioned responses have been demonstrated. H. B. Hovey found that, although light ordinarily keeps the marine flatworm *Leptoplana* active, presenting a light together with head contact (which stops movement) trained
the worm within 20 five-minute periods to stop moving in light. Comparably, M. Copeland conditioned the marine worm *Nereis* to emerge from a
tube in response to light or to dark, whichever condition had been paired
with meat juice in training. A more complex habit was acquired by earthworms in Yerkes's experiment, in which turning to the left at a T junction
led to electric shock, to the right into a dark box. Within 160 trials some
of the worms regularly turned right on reaching the junction. This habit
does not depend on specific sensory or muscular changes; when L. Heck
reversed the electrodes and dark box after the habit was learned, worms
which required more than 120 trials to acquire the right turn now reversed
it within 75 trials. Such modifications indicate a basis in central nervous

organization rather than in peripheral function. No learning comparable to this adjustment in worms has been demonstrated in coelenterates or echinoderms.

The organization of behavior is greatly enhanced by a capacity for learning. Worms, through simple learned changes, can alter their normal activities, though not as much as higher invertebrates. In learning, illustrated by the conditioned response, through experience a specific reaction is given to a stimulus previously incapable of eliciting such behavior. In Copeland's experiment, light (the conditioned stimulus) initially did not bring the worm from its tube. Meat juice (the unconditioned stimulus) was effective, however, and pairing these two stimuli brought for light a new control over reactions. In the worm's T-maze behavior, through comparable changes, stimuli near the junction control the right-turning reaction, rendering contact with the electrodes unnecessary. An adequate basis for such changes is afforded by a central nervous system with ganglionic centres and interconnections admitting appropriate new sensory-motor organizations. The mere presence of ganglion cells is not enough, for the starfish despite such equipment seems incapable of true learning. In arthropods, neural evolution admits further advances in the learning capacity.

III. EVOLUTION OF BEHAVIOR

1. BEHAVIOR AND THE PROCESSES OF EVOLUTION

Modern science interprets behavioral differences in animals, from protozoans to man, as the outcome of long and complex evolutionary processes. The role of behavior in evolution is by no means obvious, however, as inferences from fossils must be validated by evidence on the relationships of structure and behavior in existing organisms and these, rather than forming a linear series, represent different branches of a complex related system of which many sections have vanished. Also, the relations of structure and behavior not only resist unraveling, but seem to have very different properties in the principal types of existing animals. Despite these and other obstacles, behavior has clearly evolved.

There is little question that behavior has played a critical and major role in organic evolution. Efficiency in widely different activities, from foraging to defense and shelter getting, has much bearing on the success of reproductive processes and hence on species survival. In many ways, behavior must have influenced intimately the selective processes underlying evolution.

The initiatory mechanism for evolutionary change, biologists conclude, involved mutations in the chromosomes, effected through the action of radiation on the organism through chemical, mechanical or other extrinsic agencies. Mutations may have involved any aspect of structure in the organism, thereby altering behavior in diverse ways from the specific to the general. Widespread effects of structural mutations on behavior probably were commoner in higher animals such as mammals, with more complex interrelationships between structures and functional systems, than in phyletically primitive organisms such as echinoderms. As further mutations affected existing structures, modifying function from its previous basis, behavior may have changed in different directions from the patterns of the principal ancestral types.

According to conditions, success in behavior affecting reproduction must depend on what responses are made both in everyday existence and in critical or marginal situations. Because behavior results from the interactions of functional systems (sensory, neural, secretory, motor and others), a mutation affecting structure locally can often influence functions in the organism as a whole. For example, a more sensitive eyespot may improve directed responses to light so that orientation and foraging become more efficient, and adding a lens to the system widens the range and efficiency of adaptation still more.

Structural changes through mutations therefore admit behavioral specializations giving surviving species distinctive habitats or "niches." Within any period, the relative success of behavior affecting reproduction determines which strains and species can adapt to appropriate niches and survive and which types perish through mutations leading to detrimental or inefficient behavior. As accumulating mutations favor diversity, successful animal types tend to expand into lineages differing increasingly in their adaptive patterns. The survival of a species then depends on its possessing a set of genes contributing under appropriate conditions to the development of a behavior pattern adequate to maintain the reproducing population in its species niche.

2. EVOLUTION, STRUCTURE AND BEHAVIOR

Structure, physiology and behavior are intimately related in all animals, and the principles of evolution therefore apply to all three. The course of evolution does not reinstate earlier conditions, but transforms and adds to them in new phyletic settings. The fate of species and species relationships in evolution depends primarily on the relative efficacy of structures rather than on purposive considerations, which involve a basic misconception of species-typical acts and their dependence on structures. Thus a dragonfly which ordinarily lays her eggs on water may lay them on a freshly tarred roof, not by mistake, but because she responds to the sensory characteristics of any shimmering surface.

At early stages in evolution, structure bears rather directly on behavior, favoring stereotyped patterns. Invertebrate activities thus are dominated by the functional characteristics of specific sensory, motor or other equipment or of particular physiological conditions. These relationships can be misunderstood, particularly when they are complex. Thus J. H. Fabre believed in an "inflexibility of instincts" in insects, attributed to inherited nervous patterns, arguing from cases in which performance presumably could occur only once, as he reported the callow mason bee able to escape only once from the paper cell of pupation. But L. Verlaine found that in this case the critical matter was strength of the jaws, for when the cell wall was not too tough, the bee could escape more than once even on the first day. Dependence of behavior on particular organic conditions is illustrated by the fact that spiders can repair their torn webs or not according to the supply of secretion in their different silk glands. As we shall see, structure is much less directly related to behavior in mammals.

Throughout evolution, and particularly at times of crisis and other turning points, there evidently was a premium on mutations increasing the complexity and functional relationships of structures favoring wider and more versatile environmental adjustments. Significant sequences thus are indicated, as when local specialization of the skin of early vertebrates added a lens to the primitive eye, increasing the efficiency of space perception, which increased still further when specializations in retina, eye muscles and brain admitted binocular vision and an augmented depth effect.

New adaptive levels were achieved in evolution not just through added complexity of existing structures affecting function but through qualitative changes as well. In a succession of adaptive radiations from the acellular to the multicellular, and from the primitive vertebrate ancestor to the reptilelike mammalian ancestor, basic changes occurred in the conduction system with important consequences for behavioral organization and for new behavior. The result presumably was not so much that mechanisms of lower levels were repeated on higher levels as that they were modified in relation to the new context. Accordingly, it is probable that in vertebrate evolution from fish to man the "old brain" was not merely retained in a more complex form, but was progressively repatterned correlatively with increasing cortex. In mammals, as compared with invertebrates, not only are structural mechanisms much more versatile in their functional relationships but limitations of action by specific structures relax increasingly, widening the breadth and plasticity of behavior in its bearing on species adaptation.

3. ANCESTRY AND BEHAVIORAL RESEMBLANCE

In the animal series, behavior patterns tend to exhibit similarities in proportion to the degree of phylogenetic relationship and dissimilarities in inverse proportion. All animals are similar in the general sense that behavior is adaptive and that each type, in characteristic ways, behaves so as generally to attain beneficial and avoid injurious conditions. This similarity depends on the fact that all species have mechanisms favoring approach to stimuli of weak intensity, withdrawal from stimuli of strong intensity. In phyla from bacteria to man, however, these reactions differ in their structural bases and in their ontogeny.

In principle, existing animals represent parts not so much of a linear series as of a multibranched system, hence discontinuities as well as continuities prevail among them. Body form exerts a basic influence on general type of behavior, as in the head-first progression and bilaterality in orientation of all bilaterally symmetrical animals. Superimposed on such general patterns are disparities among groups from phyla to species, roughly proportional to ancestral affinities.

Striking differences among the specific adaptive patterns of surviving phyla show that the principle of continuity in evolution must be qualified in view of different branch lines in ancestry. For example, arguments, on grounds of evolutionary continuity, that a learning capacity exists in protozoans analogous to that of mammals oppose the fact that since unicellular and multicellular animals diverged in remote geologic times they have differed progressively, and the advent of mechanisms basic to the learning capacities of multicellular organisms may well have postdated the common ancestry.

Because structure may influence function very differently on different animal levels, both in the relative directness and in the nature of its effect, the principle of structural homology (i.e., basis in common ancestry) cannot be generalized directly to behavior. A different reservation concerns resemblances through convergence, or adaptations evolving independently, whereby similar niches are occupied or similar activities arise. Owls and bats, for example, have analogous adaptations for flight and the nocturnal capture of prey; termites and ants have similar patterns in nesting and other social activities.

O. Heinroth, particularly, and later K. Lorenz stressed behavioral characteristics as an additional clue to evolutionary relationships. Thus similar activities in closely related species often exhibit gradations evidently corresponding to the relative recency of the species. For example, in the mating patterns of empid flies prior to coupling, in one species the male presents to the female a freshly killed insect, in another species he presents the booty within a cocoon he has spun and in still another he presents only an empty cocoon. The last pattern is presumably the most recent.

Striking similarities, not convergences, are often found between related species living in widely separated habitats, as, for example, both English and South American thrushes line their nests with mud. Comparisons are complicated, however, in the similar patterns of related species which are sympatric (i.e., live in the same habitat) by the rise of specialized differences through competitive processes influencing natural selection. Thus two closely related species of army ants in the genus *Eciton,* sharing the same tropical forest habitat, differ strikingly in the patterns of their predatory raids, with colonies of one species pillaging in large swarms, colonies of the other in complex systems of columns. These species also differ in the booty they capture, with the first taking mainly hard-bodied arthropods, the second soft-bodied brood of various insects, and significant differences are also found in the properties of their cyclic nomadic activities.

4. PHYLOGENY, ONTOGENY AND "INSTINCT"

The traditional view that ontogeny recapitulates phylogeny, questioned for structure by G. R. de Beer and others, is even more doubtful for behavior. What individuals in each species inherit are their chromosomes, influencing ontogeny in species-characteristic ways provided development occurs under species-typical conditions. Under other extrinsic conditions, different phenotypes (developmental forms) appear, diverging from the species-typical pattern not only structurally but often also behaviorally. Species-characteristic behavior patterns, considered in relation to species genetics, constitute the problem of "instinctive behavior."

A useful way of stating this problem is to say that although heredity influences all behavior in all animals, its influence is more direct in some animals (evidently the more primitive) than in others and may be very different on different phyletic levels. This interpretation contradicts the traditional view that the "instinctive" and the "learned" may be clearly distinguished in animal behavior, with the latter increasingly prominent in higher animals. It is more likely that behavior evolves through new and increasingly complex reorientations, with the old rebuilt and extended in terms of the new, than through the replacement of the "innate" by the "learned."

On each phyletic level, striking differences appear in the relationships between genes, species-typical structures and physiology, situational conditions at successive developmental stages, and the predominance of species-typical behavior as against genotypical patterns. In the sense that the activities of invertebrate animals are more directly dominated by structure than are those of mammals, invertebrate behavior is more instinctive. Accordingly, agencies mediating among genes, organic mechanisms and behavior are fewer, with less numerous and less involved interrelationships, in protozoans and sponges than in insects, with insects in turn below rodents and rodents below mammals. In this succession, the role of heredity in behavioral development is not decreased, but rather becomes increasingly indirect and plastic as further and more diverse intervening variables are added. Consequently, contrasting behavior patterns arise which are not only increasingly complex but also qualitatively progressive. For understanding these differences, the classical nature-nurture dichotomy is not only too simple but also misleading. Psychological superiority must have emerged in higher animals not through less nature and more nurture but through increasingly complex and qualitatively new properties of nature and nurture, inextricably interrelated in development in ways characteristic of the level.

As an example, function varies strikingly with age both in invertebrates and in mammals. In honeybees, G. Rösch attributed such differences to growth-conditioned organic changes. Young workers emerging from pupation tend to specialize in feeding larvae, but when the salivary glands atrophy at about the 15th day the main function becomes comb construction. The wax glands seem influential in the latter work, as building drops off sharply when these glands end their active phase at about the 25th day. Foraging outside the hive then typically begins. In mammals, however, ontogenetic changes in function usually cannot be correlated readily with specific structural changes.

It is therefore probable that the relationship of behavior to survival, always important in evolution, is very different on various phyletic levels. As it is realized that assumptions of innateness in apposition to the acquired can explain no activity, increasing emphasis is placed upon the need for analytical investigation.

Although geneticists often state that the genes impose species-characteristic limitations on development, even after the mid-20th century this generalization lacked proof for behavior. Actually, the influences of the genes are not direct or exclusive in determining behavior in any animal but are exerted through diverse interrelationships between organism and developmental medium. The gaps between genes and somatic characters are great; those between genes and behavior, which are far greater, can be bridged only through investigations directed at disclosing the intervening variables and their interrelationships.

In all phyla, the functioning of organic factors underlying the rise of instinctive activities requires a developmental situation typical of the species. Frequently, certain conditions of stimulation (i.e., experiences) can be detected as critical for the development of the species-typical pattern. Thus J. E. Harker found that the normal day-night activity rhythm of the adult May fly does not appear when developing individuals have been subjected to continuous light or darkness, but only when eggs or larvae have been exposed to at least one daily light-dark cycle. Comparably, species patterns such as the spinning of characteristic cocoons by caterpillars result from a close relationship between structural growth and features of the developmental situation. G. van der Kloot and C. Williams found that if a *Cecropia* larva cannot attain an upright posture against a support such as a twig, no cocoon is spun. Instead, the thread is arranged, as, for example, a cone around a peg or a sheet lining a balloon, according to prevalent physical conditions. In the parasitic ichneumon fly *Nemeritis,* responses to the host upon which eggs are laid are influenced by larval experience, as such responses can be modified by changing the type of insect on which the individual feeds as a larva. Indicating the possibility that conditioning influences insect development, although in a secondary and obscure role, is evidence that the act of following odor trails arises in many ants on the basis of individual habituation to nest chemicals beginning as early as the period of larval feeding.

In lower vertebrates, species-typical behavior such as mating and nesting have the characteristic of stereotypy, as in insects, but with a different aspect relevant to the level. The claim of Lorenz and others that certain critical acts called "instinctive movements" arise through innate neural patterns determined isomorphically by the genes lacks effective support. Rather, Z. Y. Kuo, from his significant studies on pecking in chicks, concluded that intimate relationships exist between factors in growth and in the extrinsic situation. Comparably, D. Lehrman found that adult ringdoves experimentally injected with the hormone prolactin did not feed their young. Instead they underwent organic changes such as the production of "pigeon's milk" by the crop and an increased thoracic sensitivity, contributive to action although not specific action. The characteristic pattern of feeding the young did not occur unless the adult had experienced a sequence of reciprocal stimulative exchanges with nestlings. Therefore, although such patterns are species typical and involve genetic influences, they are not predetermined neurally, but result from a development in which organic processes interact intimately with situational factors. In vertebrates, the development of behavior involves more diverse and plastic relationships between organic and extrinsic factors than in any of the invertebrates.

5. ONTOGENY OF VERTEBRATE BEHAVIOR

Vertebrate behavior patterns characteristically exhibit essential differences from those of invertebrates, evidently due not only to organic differences basic to perception and motivation but also to the potentialities of a nervous system with a fundamentally different central pattern. Although certain functions, such as locomotion and equilibrium, are well developed even in fishes, in mammals these too may vary according to the conditions of individual development.

6. "MATURATION"

The concept of maturation, emphasizing the role in behavioral development of organic changes through growth and differentiation, has been focused by many upon the nervous system. In the study of G. E. Coghill on the salamander *Ambystoma,* successive stages in action were observed with correlated histological changes in the nervous system. In this tailed amphibian, an early nonmotile stage was identified when, with sensory surfaces still unconnected nervously with muscles, the only action was an anterior bending to the side of direct muscular stimulation. At about 30 hours of age, the head bent away from the stimulated side, paralleling the appearance of crossed nerve connections from the skin of the head to muscles on the opposite side. Then S movements of the body and, later, rapid swimming movements were correlated with further growth changes in the nerve tube. Coghill concluded that in the development of swimming in this vertebrate, the status of neural growth is critical. This conclusion found support in the research of L. Carmichael, who immobilized salamander embryos with Chloretone during the period in which swimming normally appears, yet found that when later released from the drug, these animals apparently swam as well as undrugged normal specimens. The conclusion that organic neural growth alone is sufficient for development of normal swimming in this amphibian is tentative, however, in view of evidence obtained by A. Fromme. His results indicate that opportunities for action and stimulation at certain stages in development also contribute to the swimming pattern, since embryos immobilized then, when later released from the drug, swam less well than normals.

Maturation, as defined, seems basic to the behavioral development of lower vertebrates from fishes to birds. The concept needs revision, however, in view of evidence cited below, bearing on the interaction of processes within the developing organism and between organism and external situation, characteristic of growth stage but extending beyond the specific bounds of growth and differentiation.

Although the development of behavior patterns is often held to depend on an innate central neural control, this question is still controversial. Certainly, neural growth limits behavior at any stage (e.g., the salamander cannot bend its head until crossed neural connections have grown). Other factors also are involved. The characteristic head lunge of lower vertebrates probably requires sensory maturation as well as neural maturation. Several such mechanisms evidently contribute to the adult lunging response, which, as in many fishes, amphibians and birds, occurs on weak stimulation. Thus the characteristic lunge is elicited by objects below a certain size if these are in motion at not too rapid a rate. Presumably, in lower vertebrates, tissue growth promotes adult patterns such as feeding and mating in discrete ways as through sensory-threshold factors in visual-movement responses. To understand the ontogeny of behavior, however, the study must be broadened. Although, for example, gonadal hormones are basic to the appearance of mating behavior in all vertebrates, evidence suggests that they may function in diverse ways beyond their possible neural effects, as by increasing local sensitivity.

7. FACTORS IN ORGANIZATION

Against the traditional predeterministic view that instinctive behavior is organized neurally on a native basis, the alternative epigenetic view holds that such behavior develops through coordinations of many organic resources in the organism interacting with the developmental medium. Experience, definable as the effect of stimulation on the organism, participates in all development, and in diverse forms, including learning.

From the same genotype, variations in the conditions of development may result in phenotypes differing behaviorally as well as organically. Under different temperature conditions in development, M. H. Harnly obtained fruit flies which were flightless, limited and eccentric, or species typical in flight; and K. Moore in a comparable experiment obtained rats differing in both body form and learning ability.

For the organization of instinctive behavior, evidence for invertebrates and for vertebrates shows that species-typical factors both of maturation and of experience in the standard developmental situation are essential. Certain poecilid fishes, raised apart from species mates in neutral surroundings in which, for example, they never saw their own reflections from the water film or other surfaces, scored much lower than normals in mating tests at maturity. That the role of experience may involve learning in amphibian larvae is suggested by the fact that N. L. Munn found the early swimming stages of certain amphibians capable both of being conditioned and of learning a simple T-maze habit.

Although the roles of maturation and of experience are fused in all behavioral development and resist experimental separation, certain generalizations are possible. Thus organic factors seem relatively more determinative of behavioral development in lower vertebrates than in mammals. In the former, accordingly, naive responses to stimulation are less readily modified through experience than in the latter. The lizard *Lacerta,* studied by H. Ehrenhardt, gave its forward (feeding) lunge most readily to the movement of figures such as circles with even outlines, least readily to figures such as crosses with irregular outlines. When a circle was presented with a quinine-treated meal worm, a cross with an untreated meal worm, initial responses were virtually unmodified within 850 trials. In comparison, mammals such as rats normally change their initial responses readily according to the conditions of training. In lower vertebrates, discrete properties of the stimulus such as movement, size and brightness characteristically dominate behavior, evidently as a result particularly of correlated factors in sense organs and nervous system. N. Tinbergen and others use the term "releasers" for stimuli which typically elicit certain types of response; however, this concept has been criticized as too simple and as obscuring ontogenetic processes. For example, the gaping (mouth-opening) response of nestlings in passerine species such as thrushes is first aroused by mechanical stimulation, as by vibrations of the nest, later by the movement of any object (e.g., a black disk) of sufficient size presented above the nest edge. The facts suggest that, through conditioning, naive responses (e.g., to nest vibration) become attached to specific features of the external situation, such as first the parent bird's bulk at the nest edge, then the parent's head. The organization of such responses in birds is a complex matter in which experience may figure in various ways.

In this sense, birds have a far more extensive and complex repertory of instinctive, organically determined activities than have mammals. In the organization of activities such as migration, the role of maturation seems predominant, that of experience secondary. The investigations of W. Rowan and others show that the northward spring migration of birds such as juncos is set off through the excitatory effect of internal changes (e.g., pituitary and gonadal secretions) caused by a progressive increase in daily illumination. How these factors relate to those influencing the direction and the course of migration (e.g., temperature gradient; angle of the sun) requires further investigation.

For activities such as homing, in contrast, the influence of organic factors, although undoubted, is difficult to discern; the role of experience, clearer. Whereas the studies of E. Schüz and others show that some species on release in strange territory may be oriented as in migration, homing in birds such as the pigeon is known to be strongly dependent on experience with landmarks and topography.

The organization of species-typical activities such as pecking in fowl is known to have a complex individual history, starting in the egg. Kuo showed that, with maturation in sensory, nervous and muscular tissue, the embryo's head lunge to touch modifies under the influence of self-stimulation through its own actions. Crude conditioning processes are evident before hatching. Shortly after hatching, the significant activities of the head lunge, bill opening and closing and swallowing are crude and essentially separate. Head lunging occurs, however, on the appearance of small, moving objects and (limited by maturational properties such as muscular strength) within a few days an organized and discriminative pecking at edible objects comes about. Thus it appears that whereas maturation dominates the development of individual components of pecking such as the head lunge, experience factors are required even for the early appearance of these components and are heavily involved in organizing the eventual efficient act. The influence of maturation is emphasized by the fact that, when chicks are kept in the dark and hand-fed for varying times after hatching, the process of improvement leads sooner to efficient pecking than in normal chicks; i.e., experience is more advantageous when strength and other organic factors have advanced. The influence of experience is emphasized by the fact that chicks fed artificially for longer than two weeks after hatching learn only with great difficulty to peck at food, since they have learned to feed otherwise than through pecking. The greater predominance of stereotypy in lower vertebrates than in birds seems attributable to the greater influence of experience in the behavioral development of the latter.

8. NERVOUS SYSTEMS AND BEHAVIOR

An important approach to understanding psychological differences between lower animals and mammals is through the role of the nervous system. Although in worms the appearance of a dominant brain permits definite advances over the radial pattern of the starfish, this center is of a low order, mainly a transmitter rather than an organizer. Insects, much advanced in organization, still reflect a strong influence of sensory and other local components in behavior.

As comparative neurologists have shown, the anterior nervous system of lower vertebrates is not only more sparsely supplied with interconnections than is that of mammals, but the brain exerts only a rudimentary control over lower centers and is not equipped to influence general behavior in terms of numerous changing sensory factors in a situation. The olfactory system, dominating the forebrain, and the visual system, in the midbrain, are best equipped for integrations within the status of reflexes. Such characteristics go far toward accounting for the characteristic stereotypy of behavior in these animals and for their shortcomings in modifying naive responses based on specific stimulus aspects such as intensity.

With the appearance of cerebral cortex, correlation among the principal centres of the vertebrate brain improves greatly. Cortex, although restricted in reptiles to a small area in the upper forebrain and obscure in birds, covers the entire forebrain in mammals. Cortex interconnects the principal centers of the nervous system both directly and indirectly, admitting new types of organization which override specific sensory effects and local activities according to the animal's experience. The evolution of cortex, particularly, admits for mammals their psychological superiority.

IV. PSYCHOLOGICAL SUPERIORITY OF MAMMALS

In mammals, from marsupials to man, the psychological limitations of lower animals are overcome progressively. Through more versatile capacities and better organization of behavior, the world of the individual increases in content and in variety. The general superiority of mammals shows itself particularly in their resources for developing new behavior. For example, reptiles, although they can be tamed so that they become docile, do not form attachments or take the initiative in play with the person who satisfies their needs, as do mammals.

A. Development of Behavior in Mammals

1. MATURATION

Correlated with the longer developmental period typical in mammals, their resources admit a greater weight for experience and a greater variety of behavior appropriate to changing circumstances than in inframammalian animals. In general, higher mammals require a longer time than lower to develop. Accordingly, whole-body adaptive behavior appears earlier in lower mammals, which often fend for themselves sooner after birth than the young of higher mammals. For example, the young opossum, just 12–15 days after development begins, crawls from the mother's cloaca over her abdomen to the pouch, moving along by a reflex hair-clutching and forelimb progression. At 60 days it leaves its nipple in the pouch on occasional excursions to the outside, where it runs and climbs about. The young of ungulates, such as the goat, are capable of upright progression shortly after birth; the human infant, in contrast, is incapable of self-progression until it crawls at about eight months of age.

Most mammals are relatively more immature at birth than the young of lower vertebrates, and hence cope less effectively with their environments. Young marine turtles, on emerging from the egg, crawl toward the moonlit sea (in response to reflected light). Newborn kittens and puppies, however, accomplish only a highly variable, nonvisual locomotion to the mother, and in specific activities have little more than crude sucking and righting responses. These mammals improve very slowly from birth in orientation and locomotion. At one week (before vision enters) the kitten returns slowly and inefficiently to the nest when set down nearby, mainly requiring tactual guidance. Although in the appearance of crawling in kittens and walking in human infants maturation is basic, limiting the rate of development somewhat as in lower vertebrates, in mammals the factors of experience have increasing weight.

Man's adult behavior pattern appears later than that of any other animal and is the least specifically influenced by maturation. When a chimpanzee and a human infant were raised from birth in the same household, with similar treatment, the advantages of more rapid maturation were at first all in the chimpanzee's favor. At five months it exceeded the average one-year performance level of human infants in climbing, manipulating objects and responding to companions. Although the chimpanzee's motor superiority continued, soon the human infant excelled in other respects. At one year, in acquiring word sounds, object meanings and social meanings, the human infant far surpassed the chimpanzee. Man's psychological superiority over other animals rests on his greater capacity for profiting from experience and not simply on his longer infancy and childhood.

2. GENETICS OF BEHAVIOR

Although genetic factors underlie all animal activities, heredity seems to influence behavior more directly in the lower mammals than in the higher. Sexual patterns, for example, are less stereotyped in chimpanzees than in rats, as a result of evolutionary advances in the primate cortex which admit new relationships between structure and behavior and make experience and learning more influential.

The study of correlations between genetics and behavior, in psychogenetics, offers techniques for comparison. For example, the trait "wildness" appears to be dominant in the offspring when the gray Norway rat is crossed with the docile albino rat, and the behavior of future generations as well as that of backcrosses of the hybrids indicates the opposed influence of different gene combinations. With this knowledge the organic basis of such behavioral differences can be studied in different strains. The increasing difficulty, as maturity approaches, of taming the young of genetically "wild" strains of rats, much greater than in domesticated strains, indicates that glandular secretions contribute to strain differences of this type. Supporting evidence is found in the fact that the adrenal glands of wild strains are larger than those of domesticated strains.

3. INFLUENCE OF EXPERIENCE

Traditionally, species-typical activities appearing soon after birth, in isolated animals, have been considered inborn. But experience is not excluded thereby, as conditioned-response learning is demonstrated prior to hatching in certain birds and before birth in certain mammals, including man. Furthermore, under equivalent developmental conditions, experience may influence different individuals similarly and its role therefore may be overlooked. For example, Kuo found that the appearance of mouse-hunting behavior in kittens depends upon a situation in which organic equipment is utilized. The kitten's first pounce is not "hunting," but darting toward a moving object. This response resembles the forward lunge of certain lower vertebrates, except that in the kitten the new stimuli that enter and the patterns that eventuate are largely matters of experience. In the typical feline environment, pouncing soon leads to tasting blood, since the kitten inherits sharp claws capable of piercing the mouse's skin; tasting blood stimulates biting, and with experience the kitten becomes a mouser. Kuo obtained different results by varying developmental conditions. By always

shocking kittens with mice present, he displaced pouncing with a fear reaction; by raising kittens with mice, pouncing was inhibited and social
companionship developed. Thus, although certain species-typical equipment favors pouncing, drawing blood and other events essential for mous-
ing, mouse killing as a pattern requires certain interactions of organism and
developmental field most likely to occur in the normal species environment.

4. DRIVE AND MOTIVATION

Certain classes of behavior once called instincts are related by modern
psychology to drives. Drive is a term for physiological processes energizing individual behavior. Examples are the thirst, sex and hunger drives.
Each of these patterns has its basis in physiological processes; for example,
the sex drive emanates from complex conditions centering around glandular
secretions, the hunger drive from both gastric processes and changes in
blood chemistry. The influencing of changes in general behavior by internal drive fluctuations has been established experimentally for many
different animals. A classical example is G. H. Wang's demonstration of
relationship between the ovarian (egg-maturation) cycle and periodic
fluctuations of general activity in the female rat. Organic examinations
showed that oestrous or heat periods recurred at four- to five-day intervals, and at corresponding times striking increases occurred in the daily
amount of activity. Wang concluded that the activity rhythm depended on
glandular changes incident to oestrus, as it disappeared in mature females
after spaying and during pregnancy and was absent in immature females.

Some broad differences exist in the responses of different types of animals to drives. On maturing sexually, invertebrates and lower vertebrates
tend to behave in more stereotyped ways than do higher vertebrates. A
female solitary wasp of certain species, fertilized and with mature eggs,
stirs about and excitedly stings a spider or other characteristic prey when
it is encountered; an egg-laden jewel fish is particularly attracted by objects having certain general properties of movement, coloration and size.
The effective stimuli are species typical. In contrast, the incentives or
stimuli governing the drive-impelled responses of mammals, increasingly
broadened and individually more variable than in lower vertebrates, seem
related to superior capacities for learning through experience.

A related difference exists between lower and higher mammals in the
ability to satisfy or change a drive tension through conditions related only
indirectly to the original incentive. Thus a pat on the head stimulates a
properly trained dog to intensive efforts but affects a rat much less. Chimpanzees can learn to work for poker chips which are then inserted into a
food-delivery slot, whereby an inedible object acquires a measure of drive
satisfaction for the animal. A comparable mammalian superiority in moti-

vated behavior is seen in the individual's ability to initiate the secondary stimulus, as when a dog "ready for a walk" brings out his leash. Such behavior has not been established reliably in reptiles or other lower vertebrates.

5. SENSITIVITY AND PERCEPTION

Von Uexküll and others have undertaken to describe the world of lower animals in terms of what is known about sensitivity. Thus one might speculate that for the honeybee in flight a flower patch is a flickering mosaic of colour with a glimmer of ultraviolet here and there; for the bird skimming low the patch has a distinct color geometry without ultraviolet effects; for the house cat the scene has a washed out, colorless appearance. Such descriptions, from subjective inferences, are in the class of rudimentary speculation.

Only the first step toward understanding an animal's effective environment is accomplished by exploring its sensitivity. The chief problems are: what types of physical effects the animal is equipped to sense, what upper and lower limits (thresholds) hold for the various aspects (e.g., intensity) in vision and other modalities, and what the acuity is in each field. In the sensory properties of animals, striking differences are found. Among the insects, the housefly, honeybee and others, although blind to the long wave lengths of light seen by man as red, are visually sensitive to very short rays (the ultraviolet band) not seen by most vertebrates including man. Carnivores such as dogs, cats and rats are insensitive to wave-length differences in light which man sees as colors; whereas bees, many fishes and most diurnal birds and primates have a distinct wave-length sensitivity. Although these animals may not see hues as does man, they have color vision, since under experimental conditions they can discriminate between wave lengths and between wave lengths and grays of corresponding brightness.

Important differences also are found in the ranges of corresponding types of sensitivity. Most fishes can discriminate among intensities and pitches of sound; many crickets and other insects possess receptors known as chordotonal organs, sensitive to high frequencies of sound; many lower animals react to auditory frequencies above the human limits. The hunter's dog responds to the tone of a whistle near 30,000 cycles per second, soundless to the hunter, whose upper threshold lies below 18,000 cycles.

Striking sensory adaptations, important for orientation, are common. In bats, insect-feeding species and certain others have remarkable aptitudes for flying in the dark, long attributed to tactual sensitivity but found to depend on a keen perception of the bat's own ultrasonic utterances reflected from objects. When D. R. Griffin released bats in a dark room they flew skillfully among wires strung close together, but when hearing was eliminated by plugging the ears, or when the sounds were stopped by fastening shut the mouth, the skill disappeared. The work of K. von Frisch shows that honeybees and other arthropods can orient with reference to the plane of polarization of light, a visual capacity still undemonstrated for any vertebrate animal. In primitive vertebrates, such as sharks, olfaction tends to be a highly developed and dominant sensory field; in higher vertebrates, and especially in primates, the dominant field is vision. In most birds, taste is acute but smell is poor; in honeybees and many other insects, olfaction through antennal reception is exquisitely acute but taste seems poorer than in man.

An animal's sensory equipment fundamentally influences its way of life. Bats and oilbirds can live in dark caves because of their delicate ultrasonic auditory sensitivity; mammals with keen olfaction can track prey by scent and tend to become night foragers, particularly (as in the cats) when dark adaptation processes favor dim-light vision. In contrast, animals with superior bright-light vision and inferior smell, as the diurnal monkeys, settle into a routine of daytime activity and nighttime sleep. Interesting relationships are often found between the fields of sensitivity and differences in habitat. There are species such as cave fishes living in complete darkness that have poor vision or are blind, with tactual and chemical sensitivity highly developed. Comparable inverse relationships between vision and olfaction prevail in many insects. Most diurnal birds have excellent vision but are low in olfaction. Sensory equipment basically defines the limits and the nature of an animal's world.

6. SENSING VS. PERCEIVING

Sensory data, although indispensable for behavior, are not the best indicators of an animal's psychological standing. Many birds, for example, approximate man and are far superior to most lower mammals in visual acuity. Yet, in the critical matter of using sensitivity to master object meanings and their relationships, in which sensory factors are secondary, birds are inferior.

An animal's capacity for perception, definable as sensing in terms of meanings, is best judged according to how it deals with objects under varying conditions. The relatively stereotyped responses governing food-getting activities in cold-blooded vertebrates seem best interpreted in terms of "taxis" types of relatively direct stimulus-response relationships. For these vertebrates, object-organism relationships evidently depend mainly on specific characteristics, such as intensity and rate of movement, and not object meanings, and feeding depends essentially on what stimuli are adequate in their physical properties to elicit a reflexlike combination of forward lunge and mouth opening. These animals seem to behave far more in terms of seeing than of perceiving.

7. SIMPLEST PERCEPTUAL RELATIONSHIPS

The organic basis of capacities for response to sensory change and for perceiving is evidenced in the lowest vertebrates. Minnows trained by P. Schiller to snap at the movement of a small bar of light presented with food then reacted to the light when it was presented twice within $\frac{1}{20}$ sec in closely adjacent positions. The fish evidently perceived a movement, somewhat as would a human subject under comparable conditions. Experiencing "apparent movement" thus may be present throughout the vertebrate series. Many psychologists, and especially Gestaltists, consider this class of phenomenon an index of capacity for relationships, basic to perception.

It is probable that such capacities are essential to a meaningful sensing of objects. G. Révész presented chickens with successive pairs of circles, triangles and arcs differing in size, the smaller one of each pair bearing food, thereby training the bird to peck only at the smaller figure in grain-free test pairs. Then two identical arcs were presented, one directly above the other, both with grain. The trained chickens pecked mainly at the upper figure, apparently seeing it as smaller than the lower arc, thus evidencing an illusion of size similar to that of human subjects under comparable conditions. Correspondingly, chickens trained by Köhler to peck at the brighter member of a training pair pecked mainly at the brighter card in new test pairs of different brightnesses. Similar results were obtained in equivalent tests of a chimpanzee and a human child, except that the training was more quickly accomplished.

Thus widely different vertebrates have a capacity for reacting to successive visual situations as unities in which the members are bound together reciprocally. An organization of this type may be termed a relationship, although in the simplest cases the unity seems due to processes on a physiological level rather than to qualitatively superior functions involving intelligence.

8. CONTRASTS IN PERCEPTUAL CAPACITY

Social insects normally accept members of their own colony but attack nestmates bearing the odor of another colony. That the perceptual capacities of lower vertebrates are comparably low is indicated in tests with species mates. Male Siamese fighting fish, for example, respond similarly to females and to artificial objects such as clay plugs, unless size is too great or movement too rapid, whereupon the artifact is attacked as are other males. Hence the male's responses to species mates evidently depend on physical characteristics but not meanings such as "mate" or "enemy." In pigeons, kittiwakes and numerous other birds, a parent which feeds young regularly on the nest will neglect them when they are off the nest even if close by. Evidently the young have a very simple meaning for the mother bird, rigidly dependent on the nest locus (at least in the early stages of incubation) and much below the level of maternal perception in monkeys, in which mothers feed and protect their young under a variety of conditions.

Sensory discrimination. Critical for evaluating perceptual levels is the extent to which experience brings more versatile adjustments to objects under changing conditions. The first step is sensory discrimination, a learning to distinguish sensory differences and respond appropriately. As far as sensitivity permits, stimulative discriminations in every sensory field can be learned with appropriate responses by insects and other higher invertebrates, and by vertebrates from fish to man. The learning is relatively simple for a mammal, which characteristically requires fewer trials than lower vertebrates; the critical matter is whether the animal is sensitive and reactive to stimulative differences under the conditions. Thus dogs discriminate tones more readily than do rats because of better reception as well as superior sound localization and learning capacities. A hunting dog must first discriminate among types of animal scents (e.g., raccoons and rabbits), then he must learn to set himself for the one aspect of scent emphasized by his master.

Complex discriminations. The next degree is mastering complex discriminations, forming schemata in which successful response under experimental conditions depends on two or more characteristics of the positive pattern (e.g., brightness *and* size), two or more characteristics of the negative pattern, or on relationships *between* the positive and negative patterns. Correspondingly, the tracking dog at this stage distinguishes the "correct" scent from similar "false" scents depending on different combinations of characteristics.

Conditional discrimination. A qualitative advancement is that of conditional discrimination, which demands intelligence well beyond that required for simple discriminations and schemata. This step is not indicated for reptiles and birds, and may exceed the capacities of rodents. Problems requiring conditional discrimination arise when similar schemata are encountered in many situations with important differences in their relevance. For example, not all pet dogs can learn that unless the master also wears his hat he does not necessarily intend to go walking when he holds the leash. When an animal can give the critical response to the essentials of related schemata without mistakes due to conflicting details, he has mastered a set of contingent relationships termed an abstraction. For example, white rats after long training can jump to a triangle, however it stands, rather than to a circle; whereas chickens, having learned to differentiate these two figures in set positions, are lost if the triangle is tilted.

For success in conditional discrimination, aspects such as complexity in the combination of critical details from experience to experience are crucial. Discerning patterns in varying circumstances, in which confusing differences may obscure key details, is an accomplishment in the discrimination of relationships excluded to all but higher mammals. In contrast to the rat, whose limits for abstraction are soon reached, chimpanzees progress well in matching-from-sample tests, as N. Kohts found, and can single out a schema such as a triangle even when it is presented with others matching it in details such as color and size. Monkeys, although less apt pupils than chimpanzees, as H. Harlow has shown can advance from simple discriminations of objects to very complex discriminations involving a number of characteristics.

Very different attitudes have been taken in animal psychology toward the subject of perception. Some would use this term for any reaction to sensory effects, others would reserve it (as above) for grasping meaningful patterns through sensitivity. The former practice seems to have its basis in implicit analogies between any animal sensitivity and human "consciousness of environment." On this view, the simplest sensory processes indicate perception. Such analogies, however, are vague. Modern experimenters prefer objective methods in which judgments of perceptual capacities depend on data from systematic object-discrimination tests under controlled conditions. The critical matter is not sensitivity alone, but how the animal organizes sensory data in adapting to new conditions. For this, resources for learning are critical.

B. Learning Capacity

The rich endowment of lower animals in species-typical adaptations related to structural specializations is well balanced in mammals by superior capacities for modifying behavior. Writers such as E. Hering believe, however, that all organisms have "memory," in that the action of a stimulus on protoplasm always leaves traces which influence further responses. In this very general sense, the term learning would be extended to the simplest types of behavior changes through stimulation, as in plants and protozoans. An alternative view is that such changes should be classed as equivalent to the general kinds of trace effect termed hysteresis in physical systems rather than to learning as in higher organisms. For comparative psychology, the primary fact is not just the production of some trace effect through stimulation, but what class of trace is involved and what its relevance to the organization of behavior may be.

1. VARIETIES OF LEARNING

Adaptation and fatigue phenomena. The simplest types of trace phenomena are based on processes akin to sensory adaptation or muscular fatigue. A dog or a man kept in the dark for even a few minutes undergoes chemical changes in the retinas of the eyes increasing the sensitivity of the rod cells so that dark vision is good, but on release to bright light, vision is poor and orientation inefficient. A worm, after circling counterclockwise inside a dish, is likely to turn left when transferred into a T maze; a dog after running all day scratches himself weakly, because chemical products of action and associated phenomena (fatigue) have temporarily changed muscular contraction. Similar instances based on changes in receptors or muscles are common throughout the animal series. They are not classed with learning because they centre around peripheral changes and not directly around central-nervous traces altering individual behavior in persistent ways.

Sensory integration; habituation. Certain classes of experience may arouse neural trace effects influencing behavior without altering it specifically. For example, the larvae of many ants and other social insects, through feeding on substances characteristic of the species (chemical stimulus I) in the nest situation of the colony (chemical stimulus II), may accomplish a sensory integration with neural traces influencing adult behavior in varied ways as in trail following and in foraging. In a comparable phenomenon in mammals, termed "sensory preadaptation," after different stimuli such as a light and a buzzer are experienced together repeatedly without any specific action being involved, a response then conditioned to one of these stimuli also is elicited by the other without further training. In a similar phenomenon, generally termed habituation, commonly experienced disturbing stimuli lose their initial effect, and may even facilitate ongoing behavior. Thus snails in an aquarium, bumped and otherwise disturbed for weeks by fish, then carry out their activities without the initial stoppages; a clerk becomes able to work in a noisy office. In such cases, through common experiences, nervous traces are set up which influence behavior in general ways. These phenomena seem related to conditioning because new integrations are formed; they are, however, distinguishable from other types of learning in that specific behavioral changes are not primarily essential.

Conditioned responses. In conditioned-response learning, the gain is a new stimulus-response connection, the nature of which depends on what specific stimuli are experienced together. To take an example from the lowest animal in which learning has been demonstrated, a flatworm moves about in response to stimulus A (light), but halts at stimulus B (head contact); stopping occurs to A, however, after the stimuli have been combined many times. Conditioning, therefore, depends on what stimuli are combined under appropriate conditions, through everyday experience or the plans of an experimenter or animal trainer. With each repetition, an "unconditioned stimulus" (B) which arouses the critical response (B_R)

at the outset is experienced by the animal together with a conditioned stimulus (A) which initially does not arouse this response. Through experiencing the combination, the animal forms both an A-B integration and neural traces permitting A to control the critical response B_R. In the pioneering experiment of I. Pavlov with dogs, A was a bell sound; B, meat powder in the mouth, was a stimulus arousing B_R, a reflex salivation. Through repeated combinations of bell and meat powder, at length A-B_R was accomplished and the bell controlled salivation.

In vertebrates, and in the invertebrates including worms, probably most reflexes and other local reactions may be conditioned if stimuli are appropriately paired. Although at first young dogs scratch only in response to local skin irritation (e.g., flea bites), appropriately pairing this unconditioned stimulus with the smell of flea powder, hearing "scratch!" or seeing his collar normally conditions the dog to form the corresponding A-B_R pattern. The potentialities of the conditioning principle for practical animal training depend mainly on ingenuity and patience, as is illustrated by a popular Russian film of the 1950s portraying an animal enterprise in which dogs run trains, rabbits behave excitedly on missing them, cats punch tickets and theatrical doings are also represented convincingly, although evidently without understanding, by the actors.

In the mammals, particularly, aspects of the situation other than the focal stimuli can control behavior through conditioning, thus serving as secondary conditioned stimuli. In Pavlov's work, stimuli incidentally seen and heard in the test room (e.g., hearing experimenter's movements) at length elicited the critical response in the absence of the experimental stimuli. This enlargement of the habit was indicated also by a reduced responsiveness when the animal was tested in another room or without his harness. In such ways, in laboratory experiments or with pets at home, stimuli considered incidental or even overlooked come to control a habit, as in the Clever Hans case.

Conditioning is not the same in all animals capable of it but varies considerably in its internal pattern and relations to other behavior. For this fact, differences in neural resources are critical. In invertebrates capable of it, and in lower vertebrates, conditioning is largely restricted to combining simple stimuli with reflex or stereotyped responses, and naive responses to potent stimuli are reversed only with difficulty if at all. Examples are the difficulty of conditioning an inhibition of the snail's foot retraction to intense contact or the lizard's snapping at figures of complex but not smooth outlines. Mammals can form systems of conditioned responses in which a wider range of responses may be controlled by the same stimuli, the responses themselves varying more than in lower animals. The traditional milkman's horse, starting and stopping skillfully according to combinations of footstep-and-bottle sounds, is an everyday example. The significance of such learning is illustrated by the great variety and flexibility of combinations possible through systematic training in almost any mammal, compared with the limitations of turtles, toads and fish, increasing in that order.

From the lowest to the highest mammals the ability expands to modify conditioned responses according to prevailing conditions. It is difficult to condition a fish to move one fin alone to a light combined with shock, but with a dog, in time a light paired with shock to one leg controls not only the flection of that leg, without the shock, but other changes also. Reduced forms of the conditioned stimulus and subtle secondary stimulus effects enter, and the response is curtailed and modified until at length the paw alone moves just enough to avoid the shock. Cases of learning in this class, in which both stimulus and response undergo precise modifications according to motivation and the consequences of action (e.g., obtaining food or evading shock), evidently represent the merging of the conditioning type with the selective type of learning (see below). The inferiority of lower vertebrates to mammals in such learning doubtless corresponds to differences in neural equipment. Thus, although normal dogs can be conditioned to withdraw a specific paw skillfully on signal, dogs deprived surgically of cerebral cortex advance little beyond the stage of general excitement and variable responses to the conditioned stimulus. The limitations of dogs without cortex remind the experimenter somewhat of lower vertebrates with their inferior neural equipment.

Operant learning. Variations of conditioning are possible depending on the animal and technique used. A method known as operant learning approximates conditioning by routinizing stimuli and other conditions, but differs from it in that initiating the response depends specifically on the animal. In the classical experiment of B. F. Skinner, a rat learns to approach and press a bar for a food reward. If the reward is given only in the presence of a signal, say a light, the rat will tend to press the bar during presentation of the light and not in the dark. If his hunger is reduced, he stops pressing, and so on. This method is very useful for research on the properties of sensory discrimination, reaction and drive; however, it may not be suited to the comparative study of learning. In the operant method, the experimenter plans the situation for the animal so that the successful response is sure to occur, thereby greatly reducing the time and variable behavior for solution (if indeed the "solution" otherwise could be learned at all). Despite the specific utilities of this method, the fact remains that by selecting what action is to be "correct," and by maneuvering the animal's behavior so that this action occurs, the experimenter substitutes his own role for unexamined selective processes otherwise dependent upon the animal. By this method, therefore, similarities are obtained for pigeons, rats and men which may be very misleading as

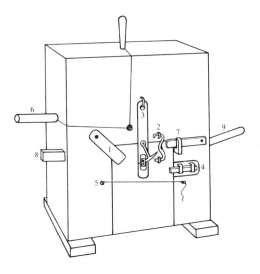

FIGURE 2
Combination problem box used in testing
monkeys. To enter the box and obtain food,
the animal must deal with the items in the
sequence indicated by the numbers. (From
Kinnaman, *Am. J. Psych.* 13:112.)

to how far the basic processes of learning may actually be similar or different through the animal series.

Trial-and-error or selective learning. This complex form of learning, not clear below arthropods, reaches its peak in the mammals. It is illustrated by the behavior of a hungry dog outside a food box that can be opened only by pulling a cord. The first responses of dogs to such problems are highly varied, and include nearly all activities possible under the conditions, from pawing and sniffing at the box and at the floor nearby to running about at intervals and also, finally, sitting and howling. At length the dog, in the course of biting and pawing at objects, happens to pull the cord and enters the door to food. The first trial, particularly, is likely to be very long, but, as E. L. Thorndike found in his pioneering work with cats, random activities decrease and the cord is pulled more and more promptly in further trials. From these characteristics, such learning is called trial and error. Because the animal improves by working more frequently in the correct locus and adapts more efficiently through organizing appropriate responses from initial variable behavior, the process may be termed selective learning. When D. K. Adams prehabituated animals to the general situation, thereby reducing initial disturbance and emotional excitement, random behavior decreased and the correct solution was more promptly and efficiently acquired than in naive animals.

Many kinds of problem situations have been used in studying selective learning, including types in which escaping shock or getting food depends on pressing a pedal or pulling a string, combinations of these and other devices. Higher mammals such as the chimpanzee can solve problems involving latch combinations which are difficult for the monkey and insoluble for rats and lower mammals, not merely because the chimpanzee excels in manipulative ability but because of his superior capacity for organization in learning. Birds, in contrast to mammals, are limited to easier problems, which they learn more slowly. Sparrows are slow, pigeons much slower, in learning to press a string admitting them to a food box, then do not relate the string response to the act of entering the door. The bird's inferior organization of the habit is shown by the fact that, with the habit learned, if the string is moved he tends to work in the habitual place instead of directing his efforts at the shifted string, as most dogs would. The inferiority of lower vertebrates to mammals in problem solving, as W. Fischel has shown, lies especially in their shortcomings for interrelating the critical act (e.g., string pulling), the object acted upon (e.g., the string) and the goal (food).

A method much employed in studying selective learning involves the maze, in which establishing a correct route despite blind alleys makes possible investigating both the elimination of errors and the organization of a complex orientation habit. Animals from earthworm and crab to chimpanzee and man have been tested, and striking differences are found. To learn a T maze with only one blind alley the crab *Cambarus* needed more than 60 trials, chimpanzees only a few. In about half the trials needed by the crab for its simple learning, *Formica* ants master mazes containing six blind alleys. Rats, on the other hand, given this pattern used for the ant in an appropriate scale, need only 12 runs or less.

As T. C. Schneirla found, submammalian animals require more trials to learn comparable problems, commit far more errors than mammals and accomplish an inferior habit in a different and more limited way. The ant, to learn the six-blind maze mentioned, first became habituated, next mastered local difficulties, finally a general organization of the habit, all very gradually. The rat, in contrast, exhibited no distinct stages but mastered local difficulties and organized the general route simultaneously. The superiority of the rat's habit is shown by its facile modification when maze changes shift the correct route through a former blind alley. The rat reverses maze habits readily when required to start at the former exit, whereas for the ant this is a very difficult problem. The ability to reorganize behavior in new situations is a particular mark of the mammal's superior capacity for selective learning.

Tests requiring modifications in learned habits reveal even more clearly than do studies of initial learning how strikingly different the capacities of ants and rats are for organizing solutions of comparable tasks. To com-

68

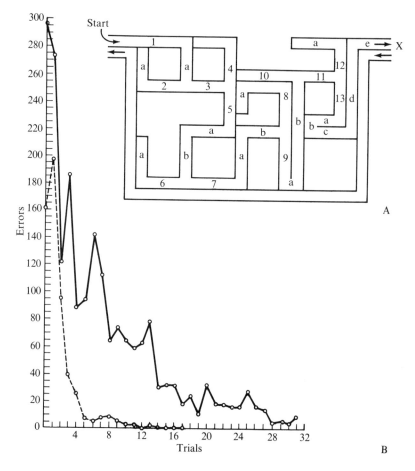

FIGURE 3
A. Six-blind maze problem used for testing both ants and rats. B. Solid line
indicates total error scores of eight ants. Broken line, the total error scores of
eight rats. (From Roeder, ed., *Insect Physiology*. New York: Wiley, 1953.)

pare fish and rat in this respect, M. E. Bitterman and J. Wodinsky used a
technique requiring successive reversals to the stimuli of a discrimination
habit. Although in these experiments the rats improved steadily from
day to day in shifting between two similar alternative habits, the fish
usually failed to improve except within given days, and in successive
reversals their habits seemed to interfere with each other. Differences
thus are indicated between ant and rat and between fish and rat, with the
rat excelling not only in its method of acquiring habits but also in changing
mastered habits.

When learning is reviewed comparatively (as in the foregoing discussion) the possibility arises that the chief difference between invertebrates and lower vertebrates, on the one hand, and mammals on the other may not so much involve the formation of neural traces, emphasized by S-R learning theory, as in capacities for organizing traces, emphasized by other theories. Thus, using food or shock in training techniques may be important in inframammalian forms mainly for the rate of forming the neural traces themselves, although in mammals its influence on the course and organization of selective learning can be much greater.

For good results in training mammals, although conditioned-response procedures may be held basic, the use of punishment or reward to control what is learned must be tempered by a broader conception of the role of incentives and motivation than would be necessary for lower animals. Accordingly, for mammals, punishment is advisedly used only in mild forms (as intense stimuli emphasize avoidance reactions to trainer and situation) and reward, similarly, to encourage desirable responses and their efficient organization.

2. EXPERIENCE AND CAPACITIES IN LEARNING

Mammals surpass invertebrates and lower vertebrates not only in learning new problems but also in reorganizing habits adaptively. Adapting to this comparison the neurophysiological theory of D. O. Hebb for the ontogeny of perception, one would say that rodents and higher mammals, with further related experiences, advance much more readily than lower forms from trace effects to linkages to complex neural patterns. Mammalian learning is typically more efficient in familiar situations, not only because the animal is less excited and behaves less erratically than under strange conditions, but also because mammals can extend habits progressively to better effect than can lower animals.

Virtually any type of problem is mastered more readily by mammals, not only because of their superior organic equipment for original learning, but because experience is brought more effectively to bear on further problems. Harlow investigated these matters at length with monkeys given long series of discrimination tests with problems of increasingly difficult natures. Results showed that monkeys master more complex discrimination problems of the same general type with progressive facility. Harlow applied the term "learning sets" to the successive stages of the monkey's progress in "learning to learn." He was inclined to emphasize the similarity of learning at successive stages and to doubt that qualitatively new processes enter at the advanced stages. But, as N. R. F. Maier and Schneirla suggested, the discrimination method may not be adequate to reveal qualitative differences in learning. This problem seems to require other methods more appropriate for the investigation of similarities and differences in learning and intelligence at different animal levels.

C. Intelligent Behavior

1. CRITERIA

Intelligence is definable as the capacity to utilize experience in adapting to new situations. Intelligence is not efficiency in adaptive behavior, a quality shared by all surviving animals. Furthermore, although intelligence depends to some extent on the organism's aptitude for conditioning, and more so on its capacities for selective learning, the crucial matter is how readily the gains of past experience are adapted to new problems.

It is difficult to diagnose any solution correctly without adequate knowledge of the animal's background. Morgan described a case in which, after he had observed a dog in repeated erratic attempts to pull a crooked stick through a paling fence, the animal finally yanked the stick through when the crooked part accidentally broke off. A passer-by, who saw only the last and successful part of the series, remarked, "Clever dog that, sir, he knows where the hitch do lie." Whether success results through accident, a gradual process of selective learning or an efficient reorganization of experiences appropriate to the problem may depend on (1) species capacities, (2) the capacities and experience of the individual and (3) the conditions under which the difficulty is encountered.

2. INSIGHT

Commonly accepted as an index of intelligent behavior are short-cut solutions known as insight, in which the animal appears suddenly to "see the point." Calling such solutions insightful does not of course explain them but may only analogize success with a hypothetical process of seeing into something. The mere rate of accomplishment does not indicate insightful solution, for insects in certain problems occasionally achieve rapid but noninsightful improvements. Insight involves a kind of organizing ability not demonstrated in insects or lower vertebrates, superior to both conditioning and selective learning for overcoming new difficulties.

Pioneer studies by M. Haggerty and others shortly after 1900 revealed that problem solutions by monkeys are often better than would be expected through trial-and-error processes alone. For example, a monkey, after having watched another, in four successive trials, climb the side of a cage and reach into a chute to obtain fruit, when given the problem himself soon solved it by working directly around the chute until he reached the fruit. Later, in the research of Köhler and Yerkes particularly, similar abilities were demonstrated for chimpanzees, superior to those of monkeys.

In these experiments, chimpanzees were presented with problems such as food overhead or behind a fence, unobtainable by direct responses such as reaching or jumping but obtainable only by indirect procedures. Although there were failures and some animals never did well, some of the chimpanzees reached distant food by means such as stacking boxes or raking it in with a stick. One of Köhler's chimpanzees, which had previously used only single sticks as rakes, was shown food beyond reach, requiring a stick longer than any available. First there were actions such as merely reaching out with the arm, or using one bamboo piece alone or to push out another, for getting at the incentive. Even though inappropriately, the animal in such behavior was using foreign objects as a means to an end—in other words, as crude tools. After an hour, the goal was unattained and the animal sat facing away from the food, idly handling two bamboo sticks. Then a change appeared, as follows:

> Sultan . . . picks up the two sticks, sits down again on the box, and plays carelessly with them. While doing this, it happens that he finds himself holding one rod in either hand in such a way that they lie in a straight line; he pushes the thinner one a little way into the opening of the thicker, jumps up and is already on the run toward the railings, to which he has up to now half turned his back, and begins to draw a banana towards him with the double stick. (W. Köhler, *The Mentality of Apes,* Eng. trans., 1925, Harcourt Brace.)

That the sticks were perceived as a useful tool and not combined by accident was indicated by the fact that when the pieces happened to separate, the animal straightway recombined them in a manner impossible without some understanding of their function together.

3. RELATIVE CAPACITY FOR INDIRECT SOLUTION

Solutions of such types resemble the pattern recognizable in mammals as "perception of relations." Much evidence indicates that lower mammals are inferior to primates in this respect. Cats and dogs can learn to manipulate levers, but neither can assemble a tool or use it as chimpanzees can in solving problems.

Köhler emphasized the superiority of primates over lower vertebrates in correcting their initial direct responses to the incentive, when necessary, with indirect ones. A hen separated from food by a wire fence persists in zigzag running against the fence, opposite the food, whereas dogs in time abandon direct responses for a detour to the food, and monkeys do so sooner than dogs. Fischel demonstrated that although dogs can respond to one of two incentives with the direct or indirect action that is appropriate, thus solving a task failed by turtles and by birds, they master the critical relationships less effectively than primates do. Chimpanzees clearly surpass monkeys at solving the type of problem requiring the subject to push food away from him around a barrier before raking it in, indicating a superior mastery of the relationship of the subject's position, the barrier and the goal.

4. REASONING AS REORGANIZED LEARNING

Indirect or insightful solutions are frequently differentiated from patterns acquired directly through selective learning in that the former type of solution often appears suddenly, after a period of apparently fruitless trial and error. Sudden improvements in progress toward or in attaining a new type of solution are notable in the problem-solving behavior of higher primates such as chimpanzees, less prominent in monkeys, still less in dogs, cats and rats in that order. This fact does not mean that insightful solutions occur independently of previous learning.

Insightful solutions have not been clearly demonstrated in any inframammalian animal, and various anecdotal claims for such processes, as in insects, seem attributable rather to uncontrolled possibilities for direct responses. What is unique about insightful solutions is that they are attained by reorganizing two or more patterns of response available from experience in similar situations, although previously independent of each other. Thus, perceptual adjustments such as jumping to food and handling a box may exist separately in the animal's repertory until he combines them in solving a new problem. In one of the experiments of Maier, who studied simpler forms of this type of solution in the rat, the subject was first habituated to the elevated pathway shown in Figure 4, passing between each two tables frequently, without receiving food. In the test, the rat was first given food on one of the tables, e.g., no. 3, then was transferred to no. 1, for example. On the basis of his specific habits, the rat in this case would have turned with equal readiness to tables no. 2 and no. 3; the results, however, showed that adult rats were able to return with better than 80% success to the one food table correct in the particular test. Achieving correct solutions when a direct recall of learned responses would have led to chance scores indicates a capacity for combining learned items which had been separate in previous experience.

Maier emphasizes the qualitative similarity of such solutions to reasoning in man. As an example of a solution by reasoning, not demonstrated in mammals below primates, the joining of short sticks when a longer one is needed has been mentioned. As H. Birch found, however, chimpanzees cannot solve this stick-combination problem by reasoning unless they have previously handled sticks as in play and appropriate unitary perceptual

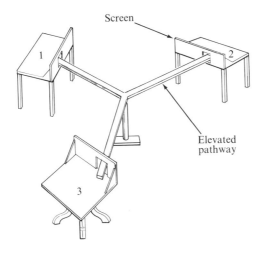

FIGURE 4
Maier three-way apparatus for testing
reasoning in the rat. (Adapted from Maier and
Schneirla, *Principles of Animal Psychology.*
New York: McGraw-Hill, 1935.)

adjustments are thereby made available. The feat then is to combine
these elements insightfully in an intelligent adaptation to new difficulties.

5. RELATIVE INDEPENDENCE OF STEREOTYPY

Nonsoluble tests. Mammals differ greatly in their freedom from stereotyped behavior in problem situations, as G. V. Hamilton found. In his
nonsoluble test, the subject was presented with four doors, one door
unlatched on each trial, but never that unlatched on the preceding trial.
This fact was discovered by the human subjects, but not by any lower
animal. Next in complexity of response were monkeys, the other primate
tested, which often tried all four doors successively and distributed their
efforts without trying any one door repeatedly on any one trial. Stereotypy
of response, or repeating particular reactions frequently, occurred often
in dogs and cats and very often in horses. Significantly, the tendency for
stereotypy and persistent repetition of errors is marked in the maze learning of rats in which 20% or more of the cerebral cortex has been destroyed. Maier found partially decerebrate rats very inferior to normal
subjects on reasoning problems, much as lower mammals are distinctly
inferior to primates on such problems. Superior cortical endowment thus
inhibits stereotypy in mammals so that new adaptations become possible.

Multiple-choice test. The Hamilton situation was adapted by Yerkes
in further studies of plastic behavior in his multiple-choice test. Here the

subject faced nine doors in an arc, with a sequence of five doors unlatched on each trial, but (to eliminate simple position habits) always a different set. Food was to be found behind just one door each time, and the problem was to discover how the correct door was systematically related to the others. Sample problems were: (1) always first at the right; (2) always second from the left; (3) always the middle door. The aim here was to compare the levels of intelligence in different animals. In the above problems (1), presumably the simplest, was solved both by the crow and the rat, which both failed (2). Problem (3) was solved by the monkey but not by the pig. Chimpanzees solved problems more difficult than (3), in which success may have depended on capacity to abstract a significant pattern from among complex settings, or on what Yerkes called "ideational processes." To the claim that the multiple-choice method is valid for testing animal intelligence comparatively, critics object that the method affords no basis for clearly appraising such processes; also that this situation handicaps some animals unduly by admitting irrelevant features such as emotional reactions, which may have caused gorillas to fail problems solved by chimpanzees.

6. REPRESENTATION AS A SECONDARY FACTOR IN REASONING

Attaining solutions by combining previously independent experiences, demonstrated in lower mammals including rodents, represents the reasoning process in simpler outline than in man. Animal psychologists have studied "mental processes" in lower mammals, in comparison with man, to find what other factors are contributive. One interesting method is that of delayed response, an outcome of earlier attempts to test capacities for "ideas." In the form developed by W. S. Hunter, this method involved first training the animal to go through the one of three doors marked by a light; then, in tests, the lamp over one of the doors was first lit briefly and after a given delay the animal had to respond without the light. In modifications of this test by others, the animal was first shown food under one of several cups or saw food buried, and after a delay had to locate it.

The general result of such experiments, although specific results differ according to procedure and situation, is that lower mammals require more preparatory training for success and in general rely more on specific bodily orientation during certain types of tests than primates do. In food-concealment tests, monkeys and chimpanzees can delay successfully over intervals of 24 hours or longer. The general interpretation is that success depends on a capacity to represent the absent object or the appropriate adjustment to this object as a cue for recalling its location after the delay. Ability to delay the correct act over an interval is often interpreted as centering around an abbreviated form of the actual adjustment; lifting a box, for example, might be represented by a slight tensing of the arm muscles as in raising the box. In comparison with man's great advantage of symbolizing experiences verbally, lower mammals are handicapped by having to represent their adjustments in much less versatile ways.

A related capacity indicated in lower primates and certain other mammals is the anticipation of particular absent objects. In one delayed-response experiment with monkeys, in which banana was used in some of the trials and lettuce (less preferred) in others, the subject became disturbed and refused a piece of lettuce surreptitiously substituted for the banana he had seen concealed before the delay. Evidently the animal then specifically anticipated banana, for lettuce was accepted readily in delayed trials preceded by the showing of lettuce.

The ability to represent absent objects and situations may be considered a contributory factor in reasoning. This type of process is suggested by trials in which a chimpanzee, after having worked at suspended food for some time without success, suddenly rushes around the corner for a box previously seen there, then promptly uses this box in a solution. The ability to represent absent objects, although it aids solutions by reasoning, cannot alone account for such solutions, for merely representing an experience without change or recombination would constitute a direct recall rather than a new solution. In the primates, the newness of solutions achieved through reasoning is far more striking than in other mammals.

V. MAN COMPARED WITH THE LOWER ANIMALS

Although man is not structurally the most highly evolved animal, he is psychologically the highest. His superiority is not absolute, however, for most of his advantages are also possessed, though to lesser extents, by mammalian relatives.

1. TIME, REASONING AND FORESIGHT

Although reasoning is found in mammals down to rodents, in the lower orders it is simpler and evidently plays a far smaller part in adaptive behavior than it does in man.

One of man's psychological advantages is foresight, or reasoning with reference to problems in the more distant future. Time, for lower primates, is largely restricted to the present and is much less extensive and meaningful for the past than it is for man, who lives in the future as well as in the past and present. The anticipations of lower animals can be conditioned within limits to coming phases of recurrent events, through internal or external stimuli characteristic of given times of day. In rodents, discrimination of short intervals of time in terms of action has been demonstrated; however, their anticipations are held to shorter times and simpler processes than they are in primates. Even in apes, anticipation is far shorter than it is in man, and largely involves more familiar occurrences. The capacity to think far forward in time requires a wider reorganization of the traces of experience than is found in any lower animal.

Man's intelligence is capable of systematic sequential reasoning, or planning, organizing into systems the traces of very different experiences with reference to future goals. Foresight in the chimpanzee is typified by his food expectancies, anticipative of specific episodes only a day or two off. If lower primates are capable of utilizing reasoning to obtain goals or forestall hazards expected in the more distant future, these abilities remain undemonstrated.

Planning for future needs requires not only foresight but also reflective thought or reasoning about one's own conditions in relation to the past, present or future. Differentiating and identifying the self in thinking, marked typically by the first significant use of personal pronouns such as "me" around two years of age, is a major event in human mental development. This symbolic accomplishment is far superior to reacting emotionally about one's own behavior or appearance, as might a monkey observing himself in a mirror or a growling dog preparing to fight.

Foresight involves taking note of one's own status or condition, in reference to that of other individuals, objects and situations, to achieve appropriate measures. This type of self-reactive reasoning expresses man's superiority over the lower primates better perhaps than any other aspect of development. The comparison is weakened neither by subnormal human intelligence nor by the fact that any man at times uses his mental capacities poorly. The best human foresight infinitely surpasses the best in subhuman primates.

2. VERBAL LANGUAGES AND COMMUNICATION

Although language and communication are often confused, the former constitutes a special case of the latter. In communication the behavior (or related processes; e.g., odors) of one animal influences the behavior of others; in language, a special system of symbolic processes is used with the expectation of influencing others in given ways. Odors produced reflexly from an excited bee's scent gland or vibrations produced in a termite colony through the head rapping of excited individuals on gallery walls are communicative events but not language. Processes such as the flashing of fireflies, the chirping of crickets and the color changes, movements and sounds of mating animals are by-products of excited behavior rather than language symbols initiated in view of expected effects on other individuals.

Communication approaches closer to language when social responses advance through conditioning, as in groups of birds or mammals when the excited cries of one individual throw others into flight. Another advance is made when a general activity is modified through experience into a special device used to influence the behavior of others, as when barking and biting in a dog change into baring fangs and growling as means of intimidation. When merely beginning the act often causes flight, the abbreviated form is learned as a special social device. Instances of simple, discrete communicative processes of this sort are not uncommon in the everyday life of mammals, as in the "begging" of hungry dogs and the mewing of cats before closed doors. When used with even a limited anticipation of their social effects, such acts approach the stage of language.

Infrahuman primates seem not to develop systems of symbols in the class of language. Yerkes, however, from his extensive experience, indicated in the chimpanzee a variety of sounds and movements which influence other individuals, keeping them in touch with and informed about the presence and attitude of one another as well as about significant features of their environment. To be sure, these sounds and movements of lower primates more often appear as incidental features of the first animal's excitement (e.g., the "hunger cry") than as intentional means of informing others of something. Although proof is lacking that chimpanzees use sounds symbolically, S. Crawford and H. Nissen demonstrated experimentally that these animals can use gestures as language symbols, as in tapping the shoulder of a lagging companion when food can be obtained only with his cooperation.

Man alone has the capacity for systematic codes of language symbols. Nonmimetic, conventional types of symbols, particularly, qualitatively distinct from the acts or objects they represent, account for the great efficiency of human language. In contrast, the communicative activities of lower mammals are essentially mimetic in that the sign or signal is a specific part of a series of experiences which represent the whole. Even the chimpanzee, which has a facility for vocal utterances and an intelligence that makes it perhaps the best candidate for language next to man, falls short of achieving verbal language symbols. Attempts to teach chimpanzees true words attain only the stage of stereotyped responses given under set stimulus conditions. Parrots can learn to repeat frequently heard sound patterns, which, however, constitute skilled acts largely devoid of any meaningful association with the objects or situations eliciting them and are not manipulated with anticipation of the results; hence, not language.

3. CONCEPTUALIZATION AND INTELLIGENCE

The psychological deficiencies of chimpanzee as compared with man, and of monkey as compared with chimpanzee, relate significantly to the elaboration of cerebral cortex. In the mammalian series rat-dog-monkey-chimpanzee-man, there is not only a progressive increase in the proportion of cerebral cortex to body weight but also an increase in the number of cortical cells and the complexity of their interconnections. Such increases parallel improvements in capacities for complex functions centering around learning and its reorganization in perceptual, conceptual and language processes. This is validated by findings such as K. Lashley's of a high positive correlation in rats between amount of intact cerebral cortex and performance in learning problems, and Maier's that losses exceeding 20% of cortex abruptly reduce to a minimum the scores of rats in reasoning tests. Limitation of symbolic behavior by the amount and pattern of cerebral cortex is emphasized for man by the deficiencies of imbeciles and by the degeneration of symbolic functions in step with progressive cortical loss as in tumors. In the final stages of such disorders, the patient may see once familiar objects without being able to name them or recall their meanings.

Mastery of verbal language symbols evidently require a foundation in object meanings beyond the resources of subhuman intelligence. To be sure, a chimpanzee can be taught human activities such as using utensils, yet the circumstances of training and of use indicate a limited perceptual and conceptual command over the adjustments and a performance more rigidly bound to specific sensory properties and motor routines than in man. The chimpanzee thus can learn to ride vehicles without forming the abstraction "ride" and using it verbally to initiate the act as does the human child through mastering the common properties of vehicles. Although human infants in their first symbols are bound to particular situations and concrete uses, later they progress steadily with verbal symbols whereas chimpanzees remain in the nonverbal stage.

Chimpanzees are not sufficiently intelligent to attain the level of perceptual development essential for human conceptual processes. Their concepts do not reach the stage of conventional symbols such as words, and are too simple and rigid to be combined in symbol sentences. Correspondingly, their adult problem-solutions are simple and discrete and, like their tool concepts, cannot be interrelated into systems to form progressive principles. From the lower primate's episodes of reasoning, discontinuous as compared with man's, the gains therefore are not consolidated as communicable knowledge or social heritage.

4. EMOTION

In higher and lower animals alike, a relationship may hold between outer causes and the individual's initial excited, emotionalized responses. Although in the higher mammals these processes progressively involve perceptual states of variable stability and psychological complexity characterized as pleasant or unpleasant, they are grounded in visceral conditions. Primitively, strong stimuli elicit withdrawal and an interruptive visceral condition, weak stimuli approach and a vegetative visceral condition. What may be called the strong emotions, characterized by interruptive visceral changes such as hampered digestion, quickened heartbeat, secretion of adrenin and impulsive responses such as flight or fighting, are aroused by intense stimulation. W. Cannon identified equivalent interruptive physiological reactions of these types as accompaniments of strong emotional excitement in both lower mammals and man, "putting the organism on a war footing." Conversely, weak stimulation promotes vegetative changes such as facilitated digestion, and the related overt response is an approach toward the stimulus source, naïvely in mammals a general relaxation and reflex extension of limbs. The interruptive condition seems inherently episodic, the vegetative condition relatively continuous and potentially basic to social life. In mammals, however, with their capacities for psychological plasticity, which of these becomes dominant in personality and society seems increasingly dependent on the prevalent development conditions. Lower mammals and very young children readily tend to perceive objects and situations in terms of their general emotional associations, as conditioned-response learning prevails first. Under severe environmental conditions, with punishment and strong stimulation frequent, interruptive emotional tendencies may become dominant, as in the trembling, cringing, whining behavior of a frequently punished dog when the whip, his master or a stranger is encountered. In contrast, an emphasis on approach tendencies and selective learning in development brings intelligence to the fore and contributes to social rather than asocial behavior.

In man, visceral processes play a far more indirect and delicate role in emotional reactions which are much more influenced by the perceptual significance of the situation than they are in lower mammals. Because man's emotional development is dominated by his perceptual and conceptual processes, according to circumstances, it is unsafe to infer experiences of "fear" in the human sense in the excited flight of insect or fish from a suddenly moved object or "maternal love" in the queen ant licking her first brood. That the difference depends particularly on the intimate involvement of cerebral function in man's emotional development is indicated by lapses in emotional specialization and social restraint with cortex-inhibiting agents such as alcohol or more lasting deficits when brain tumors or injuries reduce cortical function. Comparably, in cats and other lower mammals, when the cortex and brain stem are disconnected surgically there are marked increases in activities such as snarling, biting, panting and other signs of interruptive visceral disturbances normally episodic and associated with high emotional excitement. Man's cortical equipment admits an emotional specialization comparable with his intelligence and involved with it in an intimacy well beyond the range of lower mammals in general.

The temperamental resemblance of lower primates to man appears much closer than their intellectual resemblance to him. Although well-domesticated dogs are frequently very sensitive to subtle differences in human behavior, acting almost as members of the family, domesticated chimpanzees seem far more delicately and complexly attuned both to man and to chimpanzee companions. Hebb, by simulating the approach of a "timid man" and of a "bold man" in successive tests, obtained significant chimpanzee responses, with one animal friendly in the former situation but aggressive in the latter, two others interested but aggressive and unafraid in both. The first animal may have been hoodwinked by the act, the other two not, as the experimenter was known to them.

Experienced observers report patterns meriting terms such as confidence and discouragement, bluff, suspicion and others, appearing under comparable conditions in the ape and the human child. These responses involve rough similarities in external signs of emotionality, including facial expressions and general tensional changes, reliably interpreted as indicating emotional attitudes. A common difference is that, in excited emotional responses, overt processes tend to emerge more readily in adult lower primates, with the whole body involved as in stamping and shrieking when rejecting something, and in this sense they are much more "dominated emotionally" than adult man.

5. AESTHETIC PERCEIVING

The capacity for perceiving objects or situations in emotional terms such as distress or reassurance appears first in mammals. Although in lower vertebrates and some invertebrates stimuli such as body colors or characteristic sounds may be excitatory or calming, repellent or attractive, evidence suggests that specific effects such as intensity (controlling physiological changes), and not their perceptual significance, dominate such responses. Neither simple conditioned responses nor naive responses to stimuli are truly aesthetic, in that emotional effects accompanying attraction or repulsion reach the level of appreciating object significance, object qualities and emotional effects as related.

Simple aesthetic perceiving, so defined, is indicated in the subhuman primates. Köhler observed chimpanzees hanging material such as plants or fruit skins about their necks or shoulders or applying clay or other substances to their bodies or to surrounding objects. Other behavior was seen which Köhler considered rudimentary dancing, as when animals pranced around a circular path in single file or stood in pairs, one stamping the feet alternately as the other rotated with outstretched arms. Such actions are accepted as primitive types of aesthetic perceiving both because individuals evidently derive an emotional gratification from manipulating object qualities with reference to themselves and because these actions exert an emotional effect on others. D. Morris, from studies of finger painting by chimpanzees in the London zoo, suggested that free-choice and project methods often reveal indications of aesthetic appreciation in selecting and combining colors, somewhat comparable to the tendencies of human infants. B. Rensch thought that the preferences of *Cebus* monkeys for certain combinations of colors and grays, and certain geometrical patterns, express processes resembling some of the simpler aesthetic tendencies in man.

The capacities of lower primates for aesthetic perceiving are slight in comparison with the potentialities of man, who alone seems able to create systematically visual patterns such as thematic paintings, auditory patterns such as symphonies or dances worthy of choreography with the expectation of exciting appreciative emotional responses in himself and others. Not only are the chimpanzee patterns vague and lacking in subtlety, but their significance apparently involves only a momentary emotional appreciation, as capacities are lacking for the intellectual synthesis of emotional effects and patterning of material essential for a wider orientation in time. The human artist, with an appreciation of his own relationship to the theme and resources for planning his work to play upon the emotional susceptibilities of others, can treasure and recreate aesthetic experiences. Through his foresight, experiences remote in time and space and with disparate meanings are continued creatively to enrich the environment for himself and others.

6. PERSONALITY AND ABNORMAL BEHAVIOR

Normal behavior is definable as the developmental pattern characteristic of the given animal group. The major animal forms have been compared here in terms of their normal or typical patterns. Although this is justified, it is also true that every species presents individual differences in all characteristics of behavior. Individual differences in organic characteristics and in adaptive behavior constitute an important fact in evolution. Generally such variations are predictable, in that correspondingly fewer individuals deviate from the species norm in more radical ways. Some ants or bees are superior and others inferior to most of their colony mates in orientation, foraging and nest activities; chimpanzees differ widely in capacities from reaction time to reasoning, and so on for every psychological property of every animal species.

Individual differences that are matters of degree in sensory acuity or in the efficiency of learning may be considered regular or ordinary. Radical psychological deviations from typical species behavior are uncommon in the lower animals, although special departures may result from extraordinary conditions as in development. Pathological and disease conditions affecting the nervous system can produce behavioral eccentricities. Thus the signs of rabies in dogs and other mammals are extreme emotional excitability with indiscriminate running and biting; brain tumors produce sleepiness, reduced sensitivity, irritability or depression and other extraordinary signs according to their locus and extent. In these disorders, however, psychological disturbances are secondary results rather than causes. Man seems to be the one animal frequently plagued by psychological complications arising through disrupted organization of personality and behavior rather than primarily through organic defects.

Under special stress, lower vertebrates may exhibit emotional disorders resembling those of man. Gun-shy dogs tend to be extremely fearful in specific situations, and perhaps generally, because of emotional conditioning. Disturbances resembling neuroses have been produced in mammals and also birds with Pavlovian conflict technique, in which an animal, trained, for example, to respond to a circle but inhibit response to an ellipse, is then forced to respond to a figure intermediate between these two. As the animal cannot both respond and inhibit response simultaneously, a conflict condition results, with tension, excitement and even violent movements, and usually great difficulty in repeating either habit. Under marked frustration in problem situations, with strong hunger but with no response adequate to get food, chimpanzees and other mammals become emotionally disturbed, negativistic and neurotic. Frequent experiences of this sort cause lower primates and human children alike to exhibit symptoms such as temper tantrums or chronic sulkiness with evasion of or dependence on others rather than attempts at direct solutions. By frustrating chimpanzees from infancy, with frequent stress and blocking of strong motivation (as many human parents treat their children), one may obtain abnormal personality trends resembling human neuroses.

One important reason why types of personality disorganization common in man are less prominent in his animal relatives centers around their deficiencies for redirected motivation, perception and reasoning and their consequent freedom from morbid anxieties about unobtainable goals. When a chimpanzee is away from the scene of its frustrations, its limited capacities for symbolism hold down related emotional stress in other situations. The effects of frustration are thereby reduced for the animal and it is freer to recuperate than is a man, who can recreate the situation with its tensions and even enlarge on these.

Lower animals are protected from mental illnesses in still other ways, also related to their psychological inferiorities. Not so dominated as man by remote goals or dangers or by attitudes of personal prestige, they can leave the frustrating situation outright when this is possible, or hit on some irrelevant response as an escape. Even so, similar personality defects frequently arise, with some resemblance to human reactions in frustrating work situations, as in caged mammals persistently circling their enclosures. Stereotyped habits arising under these conditions tend to reduce emotional tensions from conflicts between escape motivation and the necessity to remain. Although such behavioral fixations, as a rule, neither satisfy the dominant motivation nor resolve persistent emotional difficulties, they help the animal to survive frustration without excessive emotional tensions; hence they are adaptive. Similarly, in man, characteristic delusions and other fixations in behavior and thinking may save the individual from more serious personality disorganization and thus permit survival in society.

7. CONTRASTING SOCIAL PATTERNS

Aggregations are fairly common among all animals. Cells of sponges and other colonial organisms are unified organically, members of general associations remain together temporarily through common responses to the same extraneous stimuli. Social groups as in insects, birds and men are unified and organized on the basis of interdependence among the individual members and their responses one to another.

Natural selection has placed a premium on mechanisms making for interattraction and grouping of species members. As W. C. Allee demonstrated, even the biochemical products of death facilitate survival of others in various invertebrate associations. In insects and mammals, secretions and other processes have evolved which attract members of the species one to another, facilitating unity in local groups while repelling strangers. In various animals, and particularly birds, specialized visual and auditory mechanisms have a comparable function. Variously, the conditions of development favor the effectiveness of such processes and in many ways grouping contributes to species survival.

Striking similarities in social patterning, as between insects and man, encourage analogies as in A. E. Emerson's stress on the social group as supraorganism and his argument that natural selection affects different animal groups in the same ways. Such views can usefully attract attention to comparable organic factors ensuring social life in very different animals, but they also may obscure major differences. In social insects, cuticular secretions, tactual and other factors promote reciprocal stimulation among workers, queen and brood, unifying the colony; in mammals, including man, the organic products of parturition assure the female's attention to and licking of young; suckling and approach to the female by neonates strongly promote the development of a parent-young bond basic to individual socialization. Yet Schneirla has emphasized the significance of differences in the socialization process itself on different animal levels, terming the insect patterns biosocial, the mammalian patterns psychosocial.

Analysis shows that, on different levels, comparable biological factors promoting specialization can differ greatly in their developmental consequences, according to phyletic psychological differences such as those discussed in this article. The abiding characteristic of the biosocial level, as exemplified differently by insects and birds, is that organic processes exert their effects rather directly on group behavior; that of the psychosocial level is plasticity and diversity of outcome according to conditions in development and in the social situation. Whereas the many types of insect social pattern over the world had reached substantially their present forms by Tertiary times, more than 60,000,000 years ago, man has passed from the Stone Age to the space age, producing complex cultural systems, civilizations, science and recorded knowledge, within the past 50,000 years. Insect social evolution was achieved through organic evolution, whereas man has developed socially within a period when his organic make-up, particularly his cerebral cortex, seems not to have changed in any important respect. Insects have fixed communication patterns, men have plastic symbolic languages; insects have structurally canalized caste functions, men only those fixed circumstantially, through social heritage or through differences in intelligence; insects have organically stereotyped forms of cooperation but men are capable of intentional forms of concerted goal striving or of competition, according to upbringing and prevalent conditions.

It is valid to speak of a "worm nature," an "ant nature" or even a "bird nature" but not of a "human nature," for man can have whatever nature the conditions of his rearing and social situation permit. He may be tolerant or intolerant, with narrow prejudices and violent hatreds or broad interests and congenial attitudes dominant, depending on developmental, social and cultural background. The resources of his maturation may be directed either to avariciousness and cruelty or to charity and kindness, but none of these patterns is inherent in him. If one tendency seems more convenient for man than another, it is to discover or create a habitat in which interruptive, excited emotional disturbances are minimized most of the time. He shares this tendency with most of the other animals, but as a psychosocial being he has his own conventional, sophisticated ways of achieving it. Man stands on the psychological pinnacle not only intellectually but also emotionally, and the struggle for social conditions of peace and quiet has predominated in his history despite frequent disturbed, noisy exceptions.

It is not only through his intellectual but also through his emotional capacities that man has succeeded in merging small groups into widespread integrated societies as against the local groups to which all lower animals are held. He has achieved not only vast unitary social organizations, but true *internationales* in art, literature, music and science. Perhaps the most important task of comparative psychology is to show in what respects these achievements are unique and in what respects they are equivalent to the various ways in which lower animals adapt to their worlds.

REFERENCES

Colloque internationale sur L'instinct animale (1956).
J. Dembowski, *Tierpsychologie* (1955).
W. Fischel, *Die Seele des Hundes* (1950).
D. O. Hebb, *The organization of behavior* (1949).
H. Hediger, *Wild animals in captivity* (1950).
F. Hempelmann, *Tierpsychologie* (1926).
H. S. Jennings, *Behavior of the lower organisms* (1906).
N. R. F. Maier and T. C. Schneirla, *Principles of animal psychology* (1935).
C. L. Morgan, *An introduction to comparative psychology* (1894).
A. Roe and G. G. Simpson (eds.), *Behaviour and evolution* (1958).
S. S. Stevens (ed.), *Handbook of experimental psychology* (1951).
C. P. Stone (ed.), *Comparative psychology,* 3rd ed. (1951).
C. J. Warden, T. N. Jenkins, and L. Warner, *Comparative psychology,* 3 vol. (1935–40).
J. B. Watson, *Behavior: an introduction to comparative psychology* (1914).
H. Werner, *Comparative psychology of mental development* (1940).
See also the journals: *Animal Behaviour; Behaviour; Journal of Comparative and Physiological Psychology; Journal of Genetic Psychology; Zeitschrift für Tierpsychologie.*

NORMAN R. F. MAIER

T. C. SCHNEIRLA

Preface to
Principles of Animal Psychology
(Dover edition)

Bibliography No. 12

Since the early 1930s, interest in problems in the psychology and behavior of animals has increased and broadened greatly. The continued demand for this book warrants reissuing it in a form adapted to a wider group of readers. The chapters in the Supplement are added for a contemporary discussion and for current references on problems raised in the book itself.

Organization of the book along phyletic lines emphasizes the importance of an evolutionary approach to the psychological and behavioral study of animals. No linear arrangement of behavior types was advanced; rather, discussions of the evidence led to the recognition of qualitative as well as quantitative differences in the organization and underlying abilities of major adaptive patterns. The doctrine of psychological levels represents a concept basic to comparative psychology, often neglected by those who would apply a single general formula to the adaptive behavior of animals. We need to carry out comparisons of phyletic types as well as of more closely related groups. Also, thoroughgoing comparisons are needed of the abilities and organization underlying behavior, based upon analyses of the interrelationships among these properties, as against the mere listing of data and behavioral descriptions that often passes as comparative psychology.

We favor theory as a tool and not as an immutable end in itself. The classical distinction between the innate and the acquired, the unlearned and the learned, has become more questionable than ever in the face of mounting evidence on behavioral development. In Articles I and II of the

From *Principles of Animal Psychology* by N. R. F. Maier and T. C. Schneirla. New York: Dover Publications, Inc., 1964. Reprinted with permission of the publisher.

Supplement, therefore, the concepts of "maturation" and "experience" are extended into new applications for the ontogeny of behavior. Ethological terms such as "imprinting," IRM, and "releasers," however convenient they often seem to be, are still essentially hypothetical, do not emphasize developmental comparisons among the major animal types, and are phenomenalistic rather than calling attention to the quantitative aspects and range of early behavioral ontogeny. The last point is the aim of the concepts of "approach-fixation" and "withdrawal-fixation" advanced by us in Article I of the Supplement.

A survey of our 1935 Subject Index brings out important qualitative contrasts as suggested by terms such as "sensory integration," "perception," "variability," and "plasticity." These ways of emphasizing qualitative differences among the psychological resources of different animal types we find supported by subsequent developments, as regards learning theory, for example. With respect to learning, our 1935 terms "contiguity" and "selection," extended in our 1942 article (Article III in the Supplement) and elsewhere, find strong present-day support. The fact that items such as food and shock can have dual roles in learning, serving according to conditions either as reinforcing or as selective agents, deserves increased emphasis. We would extend our differentiation of *ability* and of *motivational factors* in behavior study, to distinguish between what is learned and what motivationally selected, against the questionable practice of merging motivational factors into learning as presumed stimulus-excitatory agents.

Our emphasis upon the need for analytically studying situational differences is borne out, for example, by a contrast of *contiguity,* or "classical" conditioning methods in which a specific unconditioned stimulus is used to control the critical response, with methods employing the maze or problem box in which no such means is used to control response. Or, as another example, the methods of Köhler and of Adams permit the influence of insight whereas the methods of Guthrie and Harlow exclude opportunities for insight. In Articles III and V of the Supplement we distinguish the importance of such differences both for results and for theory in the study of learning. In these articles we also suggest a resolution of the problem of S-S vs. S-R bonds, which from Hull's notions of conditioning and Tolman's cognitive views might be considered an issue in pure conditioning.

Unnecessary conflicts in learning theory are propagated when one specific type of test situation is emphasized to the exclusion of others. Properly to stress differences that arise in learning according to the prevalent test situation, we suggest functional terms such as "contiguity" and "selectivity" rather than the conventional terms "classical" and "instrumental" conditioning, as the former is historical only and the latter carries insufficient emphasis on functional differentiation. Emphasis upon operations, although convenient for reporting results, often obscures what effects the particular test situation has upon the animal. Thus the tendency of Skinner operationists to overlook the effects of their planful controls over the subject's behavior during an elicited sequence of responses in lever-pressing or teaching-machine situations turns attention from processes of selectivity and of organization in learning in favor of an emphasis upon automatization.

Biologists find existing animals to be an incomplete series of numerous ramifications in which transitional ancestral types have been widely eliminated through natural selection. The psychologist, who must therefore study animal types as he finds them and must rank them from his evidence, must also expect to find differing complexities and patterns of variables intervening between structure and behavior on each level. From experience, we know what difficulties may be anticipated in relating behavioral organization and capacities to morphological turning points, for at progressively higher psychological levels the relationship of structure to behavior becomes increasingly devious, especially through the intervention of new variables.

The comparative approach to behavior study in man and lower animals can become more useful and significant through specific techniques such as those employing drugs and biochemical agents. As another example, the use of implanted electrodes to apply intraneural stimulative effects at different levels has widening potentialities for the investigation of developmental and social phenomena. It is to be hoped that such potentialities can be realized through adequate emphasis upon training the researchers in the principles and disciplines of comparative psychology. Through use of the comparative methodology, psychological differences as well as similarities between man and lower animals may become known.

From the stage of behavior modification through simple tissue adaptation in the lowest animals, great advances are found in modifying behavior, first through contiguity and then also through selective learning. Our qualitative distinction between learning and reasoning, the latter a capacity to solve problems by combining previously disparate experiences, now finds additional support through research on animal problem reactions and on creativity in man. In man, this last capacity advances beyond the plasticity evidenced by certain other mammals in their selective learning and perhaps also in their reasoning to a stage of increasing novelty of solution gained through an ability to accomplish the *fragmentation* of entire learned patterns and thereby to reorganize and recombine the results of experience in a creative manner.

Comparative investigation and study of behavioral development and capacities on different animal levels have increasingly stimulated investigations on human capacities and personality. One important reason for encouraging such a discipline is to understand each animal in its own psychological terms; another is to know what similarities and what differences exist among animals including man. As a further ideal, the effective use of the comparative method in basic studies of animal, child, and social psychology is certain to advance the conceptual development of all these fields and thus benefit zoology, psychology, and science generally.

T. C. SCHNEIRLA

The Study of Animal Behavior: Its History and Relation to the Museum

Bibliography No. 86

PART I

Human records show abundantly that anyone who directs his attention seriously towards animals for any reason is likely to become interested in their behavior. Notwithstanding this fact, which has held since prehistoric times, only within the past half-century has society developed methods for representing animals in its museums, not just as effigies or as specimens in formal, didactic series, but as living and functional creatures referred to natural settings. Although an intention to represent animals in action is apparent in many of the surviving traces of man's early artistry, to understand the relatively recent advent into museums of the habitat group and of live exhibits is a problem for the philosopher of museums as well as for the historian of museum exhibition. The development of organized research under museum auspices, focused on problems in the behavior of animals, which is very recent, seems to be a closely related part of this interesting problem.

This subject, still considered tentative and debatable by many, has roots in the history of man and his science so deep as to fall well beyond the limits of the present article. Consequently, our attention is here directed mainly to the phenomenon of departmentalized investigation of animal behavior problems in museums, considered against its historical background.

Human interest in what animals do always involves some recognizable orientation to the practical needs of the times, on the one hand, and to current beliefs and prejudices on the other. From the beginning man's progress in domesticating animals undoubtedly required him to learn about their conduct, and his improving knowledge about what might be expected of neighboring animals undoubtedly guided his defenses against their real

---

Part I is taken from *Curator* 1: 17–35 (1958). Reprinted with permission.

or fancied threats to his welfare and existence. Techniques of hunting, based on such knowledge, were necessary both to man's existence and to his social mores long before they became matters of recreation. When in such vital activities man pitted himself against the beasts, or sought their tolerance or their companionship, the relationships activated not only his tensions and superstitions, but also, in time, other and more cultural concerns. It is interesting to imagine what speculative advances beyond the practical motives of defense and of food may have stimulated the artisans of our primitive cave paintings (Fig. 5). These paintings suggest, beyond a considerable curiosity derived from knowledge about animals in action, thoughts concerning the meaning of all this for man.

Seemingly, there have always been deeper interests in man's attention to animal conduct, related to his outlook on life and habits of interpreting his world. Abundant illustrations are found in the history of totem, tabu, and folklore, of witchcraft and of metaphysics. Aristotle's *Historia Animalium, De Anima,* and other works involving or touching on what may be called "natural history" reflected long study of records of the past concerning animal function, as well as the enthusiasm of a direct student of animal being and animal ways—the work of a naturalist disposed to combine gleanings from folklore with the results of his own wide observations. Earnest investigator of nature by land and by sea, inquiring into all things as to their growth or "becoming," he developed a pervasive concept of life as progressing from the lower to the higher. For him, the highest faculty was *reason,* which distinguishes man from the mere animal, the creature of impulse. The animal, however, can actualize its inner potentiality, or "entelechy," in appropriate behavior, as an end forecast in its inner being. For this principle Aristotle, as vitalist and teleologist, found much evidence in his information and anecdotes about animal ways. This great philosopher, although limited by his times to mere scraps of information, maintained an attitude of insistent inquiry into the active nature of things and towards the comparison of beings in terms of function.

In the early centuries of the Christian era, the spirit of direct investigation of nature declined, as, with Pliny and others after him, man's sophisticated interpretations prompted indirect approaches to nature in the accumulation of anecdotes about animals and their behavior. This practice, strongly influenced by superstition and folklore, tended to increase the gap between man and nature and at the same time to encourage interpretations of nature that were far more subjective than objective. In the thirteenth century a new era began in biological history, when Thomas Aquinas and others brought again to the fore the naturalistic works of Aristotle, or at least certain aspects of these writings. In an atmosphere of dogma, however, it was Aristotle's body of "facts," rather than his spirit of inquiry, that became the center of attention. The old statements were now revived

FIGURE 5

A representation of animal behavior by prehistoric man: From among the oldest traces of human art yet discovered, a section of printed mural from the cave in Lascaux, southeastern France, found only recently, in 1940. This work, assigned an age of roughly 20,000 years, is attributed to artists among ancestors of *Homo sapiens* overlapping Cro-Magnon man. Throughout this branching cave, the walls bear pictures of a cavalcade of animals, beautifully done in color. In this section, a cow-like animal leaps over the frieze of little horses at the right, considered the work of a different artist, as is the bovine head sketched at the upper right. (From *Lascaux: Prehistoric Painting*. New York: Skira, Inc.)

with the intention of proving (in the sense of demonstrating but not of putting to the test) the thesis that animals are controlled in their behavior by a divinely endowed, nonrational instinct, rather than by the faculty of reason assigned to soul-possessing man alone. Not until the sixteenth century did the questioning attitude towards nature again become vigorous in the studies of naturalists such as Gesner and Belon. The tendency, then revitalized, to investigate nature directly, rather than by speculation and citation of authority, continued to Darwin and to the present time.

The practice of studying animals directly as whole, active beings did

FIGURE 6
A modern habitat group photographed in the Hall of North American Mammals of The American Museum of Natural History. This diorama represents a behavioral situation, typical of moose indigenous to subarctic America, as their autumn mating season advances. Normally forest dwellers, the moose at that time frequently cross territorial lines in the tundra areas and muskeg. When the bulls meet, fierce battles may occur, with alternate cautious approaches and charges, which often result in serious injury or death. These encounters have a complex relationship to mating.

not, however, spring up at once. Although in the few centuries preceding Darwin, explorers and early field naturalists accumulated a considerable body of general facts on the remarkable activities of animals in the wild, such information was treated by and large as relatively incidental, or was overlooked altogether by the principal biologists of the times—the early morphologists, embryologists, and physiologists. In their laboratories and studies they were working on the organism from the ground up, or (better) from within out, and had plenty to occupy them in their young specialties. After Linnaeus launched the science of taxonomy in the mid-eighteenth century with his *Systema Naturae,* the conventional criteria for the differentiating and cataloging of species were morphological, the general method was one of categorical description, and it might be said that biologists in general then adhered more to Plato's emphasis on the animal's "form" or "being" than to Aristotle's concept of the "becoming."

Yet at about the same time Réaumur was carrying out his pioneering observations on insect behavior, including tests of trail-forming in ants, and meticulously recording the results for others to study and improve upon. Also, as an indication of the rise of an interest in function among specialists of the times, who were mainly devoted to studying structure, early eighteenth-century botanists began to investigate not only the physiology but the reactions (tropisms) of plants. Such work, however, was relatively desultory, and, while the question of the animal psyche remained largely in the provinces of philosophers and popular writers, scientists on the whole devoted their principal efforts and attention to subjects other than function and behavior.

It was Darwin who brought the question of the animal mind and related adaptive functions solidly into natural science. Considerations about mental evolution and the meaning of the adaptive activities of animals figured prominently in his *On the Origin of Species,* and in other books a comparative approach was made to the study of structure in its bearing on behavior. A reliance on behavioral evidence for biological theory, as related to anatomical and other evidence, was indicated, for example, in his *The Expression of the Emotions in Man and Animals,* in the comparisons he made of muscular structures underlying similar "expressions" and postures in different vertebrates. For example:

> The Anubis baboon (*Cynocephalus anubis*) was first insulted and put into a furious rage, as was easily done, by his keeper, who then made friends with him and shook hands. As the reconciliation was effected the baboon rapidly moved up and down his jaws and lips, and looked pleased. When we laugh heartily, a similar movement, or quiver, may be observed more or less distinctly, in our jaws; but with man the muscles of the chest are more particularly acted on, whilst with this baboon, and with some other monkeys, it is the muscles of the jaws and lips which are spasmodically affected. (Darwin, 1872, p. 133.)

Such methods characterized Darwin's rather new approach to nature. But as much as the Darwinian evolutionary movement stimulated a distinct renascence of interest in the activities and functions of animals, the strong controversial atmosphere of the times turned discussion into debate and stimulated the practice of anecdotalism—simple story-telling—directed at demonstrating the psychological continuity of animals and man. The anecdotalists were motivated dominantly to prove a point rather than to investigate the unknown, so for evidence they were content to rely on fragmentary reports of usually vague origin, and for reliability on appeals to the social standing of the narrator, rather than to checks and balances in the subject matter. They were anthropomorphists by and large, given to interpreting the doings of animals in terms of their predilections concerning man's mental make-up and motivation, who saw fit to support their claims with vague analogies and specious reasoning from general similarities. But, as experiments on human perceptual learning have since shown, limited observation and personal report are notoriously inaccurate (especially when biased) unless subjected to careful controls and reënforced by sound training in the essential techniques.

Neither the practice of anecdotalism nor the scientific reaction to it was new. In the early eighteenth century Réaumur, brilliant mathematician and physicist, also turned his talents to behavioral investigation, and in his treatise on ants interjected a comment on the practice of investigating behavior through anecdotes, as follows:

> Not only Pliny but all the ancient naturalists laud the ants because they honour their dead in the same manner as we honour our own. They assure us that each formicary has its cemetery. It is believed, furthermore, that the dead ant is not carried thither till after it has been placed in a coffin; but that the living do not have to trouble to make one, because empty husks or follicles of certain seeds furnish coffins all but ready-made, among which they know how to choose the most suitable. Ælian tells us what decided Cleanthes to ascribe reason to animals, although he had always obstinately refused to do so. He was an eye-witness of what happened while the corpse of an ant—apparently not one of the common herd—was being borne away. Those carrying the body passed too near the entrance of another formicary, an act which is apparently contrary to the regulations among ants. The corpse was therefore seized by the members of the alien formicary. After several speeches, which the spectator failed to hear but the sense of which he could clearly divine, the corpse was released, but not till after the ants that were conducting the funeral had ransomed the corpse from those that had seized it by the payment of a piece of earthworm. If I report such stories it is surely not with the intention of either rendering them credible or of refuting them, but because they show us the progress of the human mind. What the erudite of former times seriously proclaimed to other savants would today scarcely be recounted by credulous nurses to their nurselings. . . .
>
> In a word, the attempt has been made to convert the ants into little men, more perfect than the large ones to whom they have been proposed as models worthy of imitation. It is certainly permissible to regard the ants as small animals of even greater accomplishments if one have need of them in the composition of a pretty and instructive fable; but . . . it seems to me that it is not permitted to naturalists to represent them otherwise than Nature has made them or rather such as we can observe them. . . . (Wheeler, 1926, pp. 132–133, 134.)

These are not matters of only incidental concern for the historian of museums, as man's public accounts of the functional properties of objects must always have been strongly influenced by the dominant ideas and prejudices of the times. In the "temples of the Muses" in ancient Greece, the natural objects and artifacts displayed for veneration and study doubtless were offered with a generous amount of folklore and anecdote. Even more probable, natural objects in the cabinet collections of medieval times were likely to have been described in terms of antique beliefs projected through heritages such as the silly and far-fetched anecdotes of Pliny (and that astounding compendium of animal folklore, the "Physiologus") rather than as an expression of the best scientific thought of the age. (Unfortunately for the latter, in no age can the object be depended upon to tell its own story.) Even in modern times, although progress may have reduced the degrees of freedom of anecdotalism in the scientific study of behavior, crude analogy and story-telling as approaches to nature continue as favorite public pastimes and from time to time raise their heads in our newspapers and public institutions, even including museums.

Analogy solely by similarity is always the pillar of anthropomorphism in the interpretation of animal ways, and the degree of license permitted this tendency usually plays a strong role in popular attitudes towards the scientific study of animal activities. It was not mainly Darwin's fault that a popular resurgence of anecdotalism and an outburst of anthropomorphism in scientific as well as in public circles were among the immediate outcomes of his work. To be sure, Darwin's own writings, against the background of the times, contained their share of anecdote and anthropomorphism, yet the development of an objective attitude in studying animal life was another and far better representation of his contributions. This theme, however, developed its scientific repercussions more slowly than did the other.

The objectivistic reform, distinctly a reaction to the early post-Darwinian anthropomorphic excesses, arose only late in the nineteenth century, with its roots both in the naturalism of Darwin and in general scientific history. Earlier traces of this movement, really the direct forerunners of modern behavior study, were not confined altogether to science. Notably, the great sixteenth-century battle in France over the animal soul involved as principal figures two philosophers, Descartes and Gassendi, who directed their polemic and dialectic *con* and *pro,* respectively. This controversy, which mirrored rather well the political and social tensions of the times, as Rosenfeld's (1941) excellent analysis has shown, also involved men of several other professions, including writers, clerics, a gamekeeper to the king, and a writer of fables. Yet it might be called a draw, in view of the indefiniteness of the rules and the paucity of valid evidence available. One of the most valuable contributions was made by the essayist Montaigne, who carefully evaluated all the evidence at hand and decided, in effect, that the difference was a relative one. In his judgment, man must also be considered a member of the animal kingdom, and not the only in-

AFTER THE BATH.

FIGURE 7

Alfred Russel Wallace, co-discoverer with Charles Darwin of the theory of
natural selection, in a scene representing his characteristic interest in the lives and
behavior of animals. Having adopted an orphaned orangutan, found in the Malayan
forest, Wallace functioned as foster father by giving it rice-water, spliced with
sugar and coconut milk, from a bottle with a quill in the cork. In a few trials it
learned to suck very well. He "fitted up a little box for a cradle, with a soft mat for
it to lie upon, which was washed every day, and the little one as well." Soon
"it enjoyed the wiping and rubbing dry amazingly, and when I brushed its hair
seemed to be perfectly happy, lying quite still . . ." (However, "at other times,"
Wallace said, "I had to be careful to keep my beard out of its way.")

The illustration (from Morgan, 1891) shows in the box at the left a young
macaque monkey, which Wallace "gave the little fellow as a companion."
(Wallace, 1872.)

telligent member at that—certainly not the highest in "moral sensibility,"
as witness his wars, and not the only one with imaginative powers, as witness evidence for dreaming in horses and dogs. As a comparative psychologist, examining the case in depth in terms of evidence for differences as
well as for similarities, the essayist was ahead of his time and may be ex-

cused the contemporary device of citing cases of devotionally contemplative elephants and tunnies with mathematical insight. In all seriousness, and well ahead of Swift, Montaigne cast man in the role of "Yahoo" rather than of the one rational being, and must have helped at least a few of his readers towards a more critical, objective study of the general problem.

Such influences, unfortunately, did not ward off the wave of anthropomorphism immediately following Darwin's impact. In any case, Darwin's position that "the mental faculties of man and the lower animals do not differ in kind, although immensely in degree" opposed the traditionally strong brute versus man dichotomy on a scientific basis, and paved the way for comparative studies which might disclose differences in kind as well as in degree. Towards the development of an objective investigation of "animal mind," the advance of biological research from Renaissance times also contributed strongly. As Lewinsohn (1954, p. 199) says,

> Under the microscope the differences between man and animal seemed to vanish completely. . . . For all its multiplicity, nature was one. The theory that the mind, or soul, was something higher than the body ran hard up against the facts of modern anatomy and physiology.

But diversified answers were offered from science. One was the "mental evolution" doctrine of the physiologist Romanes, who was quite an anecdotalist away from his laboratory and at his desk, postulating for human ontogeny successively higher stages of mentality from that of birth, approximating lower invertebrates, to that of about fifteen months, approximating the mental level of the dog. This doctrine of metempsychoses in series in one generation, so to speak, was a literal application of the mental-continuity principle that made interesting popular reading and was taken seriously by many contemporary scientists.

As an anecdotalist, Romanes was enthusiastic, if not too critical of content. For example, of the cat, he said (1883, p. 425):

> . . . as one other instance of high reasoning power in this animal, Mr. W. Brown, writing from Greenock to *Nature* (vol. xxi, p. 397) gives a remarkable story . . . , the facts in which do not seem to have admitted of mal-observation. While a paraffine lamp was being trimmed, some of the oil fell upon the back of the cat, and was afterwards ignited by a cinder falling upon it from the fire. The cat with her back "in a blaze, in an instant made for the door (which happened to be open) and sped up the street about 100 yards," where she plunged into the village watering-trough, and extinguished the flame. "The trough had eight or nine inches of water, and puss was in the habit of seeing the fire put out with water every night." The latter point is important, as it shows the data of observation on which the animal reasoned.

Whatever the possibility for mal-observation in this case, the likelihood of mal-interpretation would seem to have been high. For, although careful experimentation has shown that adult domestic cats are capable under appropriate conditions of effecting simple solutions by reasoning, the probability is much stronger that the highly excited feline of Greenock reacted on another and simpler psychological basis.

It was to promote safeguards of reliability in fact-gathering, as well as logic and comprehensiveness in the interpretation of behavioral evidence, that C. Lloyd Morgan (an eminent psychologist and contemporary of Romanes) brought forward his "Canon," a reasonable rule of parsimony which stated that:

> In no case may we interpret an action as the outcome of the exercise of a higher psychical faculty, if it can be interpreted as the outcome of the exercise of one which stands lower in the psychological scale. (Morgan, 1894, p. 53.)

Morgan, usually more careful than Romanes to know the facts about reported behavioral feats and to assess them systematically, offered numerous examples from his own wide experience to mark out the pitfalls. In one case, he had been trying without any success to train a fox terrier in the best way to pull a crooked stick through a paling fence, but after many trials the dog indicated no particular progress in his behavior.

> Nothing could apparently be simpler than to push the stick up, free the crook, and pull the whole thing through; but the dog continued to pull. I repeated the experiment many times, and tried to show the dog how the difficulty could be overcome. But each time the crook caught, he pulled with all his strength, seizing the stick now at the end, now in the middle, now near the crook. At length he seized the crook itself, and with a wrench broke it off. A man who was passing, and who had paused for a couple of minutes to watch the proceedings, said, "Clever dog that, sir; he knows where the hitch do lie." The remark was the characteristic outcome of two minutes' chance observation. During the half-hour or more that I watched the dog he had tried nearly every possible way of holding and tugging at the stick. (Morgan, 1894, pp. 257–258.)

It would be interesting to know in what form the passerby transmitted to others his knowledge about the Professor's remarkable dog.

Morgan himself, although favorable to the doctrine of mental continuity, was somewhat reserved on the subject. But to many other scientists, mental continuity spelled "anthropomorphism," and the anecdotal sequel of Darwinism was sure to receive its appropriate reaction: a severe lashing of objectivistic criticism based on research. Towards this movement in the nineteenth century the relatively new experimental psychology contributed, beginning with psychophysics (finding the quantitative relation between stimulus strength and degree of sensation) around mid-century and accelerating with Wundt's psychological laboratory at Leipzig (the first in the world) and with Ebbinghaus' pioneering research on human learning and memory. These events strikingly outlined the possibility of experimenting not only with phenomena of sensitivity and reaction and of learning and recall, but also with other mental processes. Contrary to traditional dogma, the "mind" was now being accepted as a legitimate object of research. To test the psychological problems raised by evolution theory, why not investigate lower animals in these respects, as well as man? These problems of mental evolution never could be settled well by citing anecdotes or by writing non-experimental polemics to prove a favored point.

Within two decades before the turn of the century, scores of investigators in biology and psychology were busy studying the behavioral resources of animals from Protozoa to man. In England in 1882, Lubbock reported the results of experiments and critical observations on insect sensitivity and behavior, and Morgan reported on the behavior, "instincts," and mental processes of birds and mammals. Both of these men, with others such as the protozoologist Verworn in Germany, strongly opposed anthropomorphism as a practice and condemned any reliance on anecdotes in the study of behavior. These investigators, and others, such as the German physiologist Bethe, even more vigorously emphasized the indispensability of experimental methods and of an objective viewpoint in studying the problems of behavior. "Objective" in this context meant a reliance on experimental method and scientific controls in obtaining the facts, and a vigilance against subjective preconceptions and prejudices in interpreting the evidence, so as to overlook or distort none of the relevant facts in the theoretical treatment.

Even before 1900 the naturalistic approach to behavior study had been taken up vigorously in the United States by psychologists such as W. S. Small, who originated the maze method of studying animal learning, and soon notably by E. L. Thorndike, who studied learning with chicks, rats, and cats as subjects, and whose concept of "trial and error" in learning (after C. L. Morgan) eventually influenced international education perhaps fully as much as did the later Pavlovian concept of conditioned reactions. A major criticism was leveled against Thorndike's methods by Small, W. Mills, and others for the unnaturalness of testing animals in situations so restricted as the problem cages that were used. This matter, with related criticisms bearing on technique, received the attention of an increasing number of investigators as advances were made in adapting laboratory conditions and methods to research on the behavior and psychological capacities of lower animals. The anthropomorphic indulgences of the immediate post-Darwinian period had found their antidote in experimental investigation and theoretical skepticism, although the way to truth still promised to be long and hard.

This movement acquired a strong impetus, particularly in the United States. With the founding of the *Journal of Animal Behavior* in 1911, it became clear that man, in whose attention to animals practical motives and prejudicial ideas had always dominated, at last seriously accepted their behavior as an object of study in its own right. This journal, combining behavioral and psychological studies on a variety of invertebrate and vertebrate animals, carried forward for eight years a vigorous naturalistic advance to which both biologists and psychologists contributed. Then, rather abruptly, the series ended in 1918, and new, complicating developments changed the orientation and content of succeeding journals in the post-war years.

The range and depth of the post-Darwinian development of behavior study are best appreciated in terms of the objectivistic, experimentalist movement expressed in the work of such men as Jennings and Parker in biology and Thorndike and Yerkes in psychology. Although, after the First World War, Jennings turned from behavior to more specific biological areas of study, such as genetics, Parker, to secretory functions and other specialized problems, and Thorndike, to human psychology, Yerkes returned from leadership of the U.S. Army's intelligence-testing program to comparative psychology proper. Yerkes is our best example of the continuity, for, in his active career spanning the first half of this century, he made contributions clearly marking out the Darwinian sequelae in scientific behavior study. By following some of his representative publications chronologically, we see that in his life program he literally mounted the phyletic and psychological ladders, as follows: 1901, reactions of Daphnia, learning in the turtle; 1902, habit formation in the green crab; 1903, habits and reactions in the frog; 1904, behavior and reactions of medusa, and space perception in tortoises; 1905, hearing in frogs, and facilitation and inhibition in the reactions of frogs; 1906, behavior of coelenterates; 1907, behavior and psychology of the dancing mouse; 1909, behavior modifiability in the dancing mouse; 1911, methods of studying vision in vertebrates; 1912, learning in the earthworm; 1915, comparative studies of intelligence in birds and mammals (multiple-choice method); 1916, mental capacities of lower primates; 1917–1921, army intelligence-testing program; 1921 and thereafter, primate psychology (Yerkes and Yerkes, 1929). From these years until his death in 1956, Yerkes was active in promoting the investigation of primate psychological and biological functions. Clearly, he was foremost among those whose studies served to give evolutionary theory a sound basis in psychological research. It was he especially who demonstrated that, in their behavioral and psychological capacities, animals throughout the phyletic series may be compared validly in terms of both similarities and differences. From such work it is clear that, as between lower primates and man, the predominant note is one of relationship and continuity, notwithstanding man's wide leadership in psychological capacities essential to language, conceptualization, and, particularly, social heritage.

Zoological museums had been developing as scientific institutions with the rise of biology and reflect in various ways and to varying degrees the stages of growth in scientific biology. These changes seemed indicated significantly in the field representation of museums. Bates, Belt, and Hudson, who were collectors for museums, and many others carried into the field around the world an objective approach to nature that exemplified the scientific advances of their times. These men were interested in the natural situation and activities of animals as well as in their structures and classification when collected. In contrast to their predecessors of the "cabinet" period, they showed in their writings an endeavor to observe, investigate, and carefully report nature as they found it. They, as well as the curators at home, lived more or less under the influence of developments in science that centered increasingly around function as a key problem in the study of nature. Although the rise of taxonomy seemed to emphasize structural bases for classification to the exclusion of nearly everything else, this discipline inevitably felt the influence of morphology, which was developing as a science increasingly aware of the need to study animal structure in its relation to function.

Other scientific changes also played their part, including especially the revival after 1890 of the organismic theory through the work of biologists such as C. O. Whitman. Another was the advancing subject of embryology: the closer relationship of anatomy and physiology inevitably increased interest in the development of individual structures and functions as interrelated. Emphasis on the function of the organism as a whole in physiology and other branches of biology promoted a new discipline, ecology, devoted to the investigation of the environmental relationships of the organism. In the literature of this period, many important instances are found of an increasing emphasis on the integrated study of animal structure and function. As one example, W. M. Wheeler's classic *Ants, their Structure, Development, and Behavior,* published in 1910, symbolized the work of a man who, after having received a doctorate on an embryological problem, had entered upon a versatile scientific career centering around taxonomy and museum curatorship (including a period in The American Museum of Natural History), but extending readily into studies of function and behavior.

Modifications appeared meanwhile in the museums themselves, meriting specialized historical study in relation to the times. To be sure, the influence on museums of scientific advances seems on the whole to have involved an appreciable latency; to what extent, and on what basis, only historical study will reveal. Most intriguing of the changes, perhaps, as reflecting a growing tendency for a representation of the functional relationships of the organism, is the habitat group or diorama. This striking exhibitive device reified the animal and its behavior for the museum audience by the mounting of the individual animal or group in postures that suggested a typical action situation in nature, by the introduction of third-dimensional techniques to heighten the impression of living beings existing in space and time, and by the merger of the foreground into a painted background for a broader suggestion of the natural relationships and biotic zone of the animal. The idea of the habitat group seems to have developed slowly, in part as a heritage from the earlier period of nature-pioneering in America. In essence, these characteristics are reported to have been used in a museum of nature privately set up by the American artist Charles Willson Peale, shortly after 1800. By 1900, exhibits of this general type appeared in various museums on both sides of the Atlantic. In The American Museum of Natural History the full technique of the habitat group was utilized in a series of bird displays, the first of which, the "Bird Rock Group," was presented in 1900. This series of exhibits represented birds, indigenous to very different parts of the world, in their life and behavioral situations. Emphasis on function had grown apace. In these new exhibits, and in comparable ones concerning other animals, soon to follow, man's progressing insight into nature became translated into vivid representations of animals functioning in their species niches.

In the new era, this Museum's representatives in the field went out not only as collectors, but also as investigators of animal life. In the *Bulletin* of 1892, the change was signaled by an article by F. M. Chapman, then in his fourth year as Assistant Curator of Birds and Mammals, which reported a study of these vertebrates found in the locality of Trinidad, Cuba. Careful notes were added to the taxonomic descriptions, on the flight, nesting, and song of the birds, and the habitats and activities of the mammals. The attitude was clear: a collector's report could not be considered complete without some substantial information concerning behavior.

From the early days, this Museum has had a strong tradition of function-and-behavior study in the zoological departments as well as in anthropology. W. M. Wheeler, Curator of Invertebrates from 1903 to 1908, never collected ants in the field without close attention to the details of behavior. Chapman's work on the bird dioramas revealed the fascination behavior held for him, an absorbing interest which developed into specific field studies. In several books (e.g., Chapman, 1929) and in articles in *Natural History,* he reported the results of field studies directed at the resources of behavior in both birds and mammals. He carried out both systematic observational projects such as his survey of the tropical social bird, the Oropendola, and actual field tests of behavior, such as his work on booty-finding in the vulture. Comparably motivated was F. E. Lutz, Curator of Insects, who went into the field both as collector and as experimentalist, to make pioneering investigations on problems ranging from insect sensitivity and responses to ultra-violet and other types of stimuli to a variety of problems concerning general behavior. These included questions such as how certain insects and birds are awakened to their daily routine, and the relationship between body structure and burden carried by the polymorphic workers of a leaf-cutter ant. Lutz's experimentation also extended to indoor work, both in his basement at home and in his laboratory at the Museum, where he made controlled experiments on such problems as the basis of day-night activity rhythms in crickets and other insects. There, too, he maintained a variety of living insects, from Orthoptera to ants, in artificial nests in order to study their development and their behavioral repertoires.

A staff member of similar interests was G. Kingsley Noble, who in 1920 became assistant curator, administering the Department of Herpetology. As were Chapman and Lutz, Noble was a taxonomist who was also interested in studying the whole animal, alive and functioning, as well as in the form of a specimen. Not disposed to confine his life studies to taxonomy and collecting, Noble began by maintaining rare tropical frogs and salamanders in the laboratory, where he induced them to breed and was able to study their life histories and activities. As his department grew, its work extended from taxonomy to investigations of structural and functional relationships, and to animal ecology. For him, descriptions of structure and behavior were only the beginning of the biologist's task, and he pressed on to investigate problems considered fundamental: mating and other aspects of sex behavior, the functions of hormones in structural development and behavior, and aspects of social behavior.

Noble's interests in structure led him from the anatomy of a species into its histology; his interests in function led him from studying the role of mechanisms, such as the adhesive toe-discs of tree frogs, to problems in the evolution of adaptive structures in general, as means of working out principles underlying the relations of animals to their environments. As with Chapman and Lutz, but much more intensively and extensively, his investigation of nature moved from descriptive methods to the working out of analytical techniques designed for wider inductive attacks on the problems (Noble, 1941). In exhibition, similarly, he soon advanced beyond the descriptive stage, for he believed that:

> The curator's task only begins with the habitat group. He must in supplementary exhibits dissect and analyze nature in such a way that the public will understand the principles controlling the life of the creatures

FIGURE 8
Rat learning a maze to the advantage of public interest and information, in the Hall of Animal Behavior set up in the first floor of the African Wing of The American Museum of Natural History during the late 1930s. This hall, planned by Drs. Noble and Beach, contained a variety of three-dimensional exhibits showing phenomena and principles of the adaptive behavior of animals.

portrayed—the fundamental biological principles controlling life in general. (Beach, 1944.)

So Noble's exhibits on animal behavior covered a wide range of problems, from the role of the sense organs in the behavior of fishes, birds, and mammals to tests of mammalian learning involving animals running mazes in full view of the visitor (Figure 8).

A museum that sponsors such research activities and organizes exhibitive procedures so advanced pedagogically certainly has come a long way from the cabinet and curio collections of earlier times. Of course, as the twentieth century advanced, museums, as conceived by many persons over the world, continued solely as repositories of natural objects, their program confined essentially to the display and classification of these objects. In many of these institutions, however, the business of the curators had expanded from the care, description, and classification of specimens to include the study and explication of their function. Previously, behavior had been inserted incidentally, if at all, in the collecting and taxonomic reports, in the form of fragmentary, scattered references to "habits" or "instincts," by which was meant, simply, "activities typical of the animal." In the early days, such information usually was the result of very casual observations and was reported rather incidentally. But function and behavior, in the hands of the curators we have discussed, became important as goals in the study of the organism. These men perhaps characterized the period in which Theodore Roosevelt had lambasted exploiters and those who misrepresented nature as "nature fakers." In their own contributions they exemplified the basic necessity for reliability and validity in the study and explanation of natural events. Accuracy in the description of structure and the determination of taxonomic status is but one step, moreover, towards the goal of understanding nature, and, if the principle is well mastered, it will be extended (although not easily) to function and behavior as well.

Our own period has faced the need for specialization as one of its trials in science, as well as in other professions. At the same time the crossing of professional lines is urged upon us by a deepening study of relationships among different fields. In the museum, as naturalistic evidence and theory on each type of animal enlarge in scope, and the tasks of collation and study increase, the corresponding departments of specialization must focus still more on problems specific to their respective animal groups. But also, as science grows, the several departments must widen their horizons to consider problems of functional relationships extending beyond their own animal specialties. The task is a very demanding one, and even in museums with the best of resources, not all members of every specialized department can go very far in applying themselves to broad problems along interphyletic lines. In the earlier days only a few, such as Chapman and Noble, had much time for intensive study of common problems in adaptive function and evolution. The growing need, expressed by these curators, was to find better research tools and appropriate animal subjects in order to realize the unique potentialities of museums in the effective investigation of such problems.

The history of one department illustrates the growth of this aspect of the Museum's work in the investigation of phenomena accepted as fundamental in natural history: adaptive function, speciation, and the evolution of behavior. With its increasing scope of experimentation in focusing on such problems, Noble's department in 1928 had "and Experimental Biology" added to its name. In 1934 it became two separate departments. The range and depth of research had advanced well beyond the earlier departmental lines, held as they were to taxonomic and other problems specific to two lower vertebrate classes. So the new department had to be fitted with laboratories equipped for the investigation of broad problems of biological function and behavior by modern techniques, with animals from fish to mammals as subjects. In the words of Frank Beach (1944), under whose chairmanship after Noble's death this division became the Department of Animal Behavior,

> Objective and quantitative analysis of complex behavior patterns cannot be accomplished merely by assiduous and painstaking observation (as) . . . observational and descriptive methods are no longer sufficient in any branch of science. The determination of the basic causes of behavior rests upon a genuinely analytical approach (necessarily involving) not only the general fields of zoology and biology but also . . . psychology, physiology, neurology, endocrinology, etc.

This department, devoted to the investigation of broad phyletic principles underlying behavior patterns and their evolution, is in no small part a contribution of those curators in the specialized departments of this Museum, who, from the early days of the institution, had shown a devoted interest in the observation and description, and also to an appreciable extent the testing, of animal activities.

One point in particular is clear from the experience of these men and others who began their museum work essentially as taxonomists. Curators in the special fields, in their research, must make inferences from structure concerning behavior, often of remote or historically extinct animals. But the inferential, theoretical path from structure to function and behavior is seldom, if ever, as direct as it may seem at first sight, and in any case the inferences from structure must be tested away from the desk. What is more important, the inferences and the hypotheses must be tested by sound techniques—with adequate experimental set-ups, instrumentation, and controls—and the results must be evaluated in terms of comprehensive theory. Not all these necessary instruments may be readily accessible to the specialist in taxonomy or to the biologist whose research has been devoted to certain specialized aspects of one group of animals. In our time, behavior has become a major category of natural history for scientific study, and its problems can be attacked adequately only through the cooperation of numerous disciplines and the use of many tools in science.

PART II

Research in a modern museum of natural history is distinguished by its evolutionary approach to nature, covering the entire range of adjustments to natural situations. Here the study of behavior can play an important role, not only in scientific evidence and theory, but also as one means of

---

Part II is taken from *Curator* 2: 27–48 (1959). Reprinted with permission.

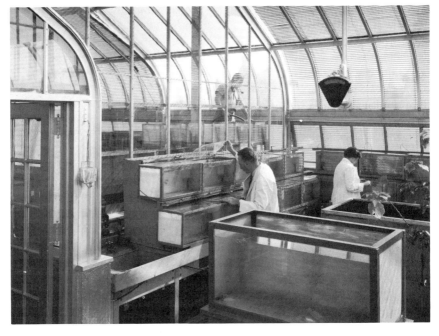

FIGURE 9
Routine procedures in maintaining fish for laboratory experimentation. The commodious greenhouse on the seventh floor of the African Wing of the Museum houses the large tanks and furnishes the ecological conditions necessary for behavior studies of fish such as the West African mouthbreeder. In nature, this fish lives in shallow coastal lagoons, river deltas, and other situations where long daily periods of exposure to tropical sunlight prevail.

linking the research aspect of the museum program with exhibition and education.

A department devoted to the investigation of problems in animal behavior can be helpful in other ways as an integrative agency in the museum's program. Such a department facilitates the correlation of research and theory about animal functions, through its emphasis on the organism as a unitary, organized system coping with its world. For in the course of life the animal may often need its entire resources—whatever the species limits of structural, physiological, and psychological capacities—to meet the emergencies of its habitat.

The activities of each distinctive type of existing animal are mainly, by hypothesis, adaptive, adjusting the species to the conditions of its particular environmental niche. Accordingly, the program of a museum department of behavior is directed first of all at the study of adaptive behavior and its biological basis in the important types of animals. To be sure, in this day in natural science, particularly in America, emphasis often falls on the study of adaptive functions in particular animals as specialized subjects; thus, geneticists have used the fruit fly, physiologists the dog, and psychologists the white rat, as a common lower-animal subject. Even in behavior research itself, at the present time, the evolutionary approach is often passed over for the study of the activities of different animals in terms such as shelter-getting, food-getting, social, imitative, reproductive, and other general classes of adjustments. In the museum, however, such procedures should be carried out by a comparison of the major types of animals with respect to these adaptations.

In a natural history museum, behavior study is inherently phyletic and comparative in its major emphasis. In research on the principal types of behavior, methods for studying common properties can be planned so as to work out general principles that hold for all phyla, and, at the same time, to assay important differences among animals. Thus, although the aspect of stereotypy among individuals is prominent in the food-getting and other behavior of lower invertebrates such as the starfish, and appears strikingly in the behavior of insects, it now takes on different and far more complex forms, as is also the case, but still differently, in birds. In the mammals, in contrast, plasticity and change characterize normal species behavior, and stereotypy becomes an exceptional, eccentric feature. Probably adaptive behavior can be understood best in terms of how it is very differently achieved in contrasting animal types. The postulation of qualitatively different levels in various animal phyla and in the classes of vertebrates seems a sound guide for the study of behavior.

The direct investigation of behavior, of course, involves living animals. Even when these are accessible to investigation in museum laboratories and not only in the field, studying their behavior and its biological basis demands evidence from many scientific sources. Thus, a combination of research on the anatomy, physiology, ecology, and behavior of living echinoderms in comparison with those of living insects sheds light not only on modern conditions but also on the circumstances of ancient times and ancestral forms and on the evolution of adaptive functions in general. Projects thus organized in a museum program may thereby serve as means for comparing the relative efficiency and durability of behavior patterns in existing animals with those of ancestral forms. One can imagine a ghostly clinic of the extinct, in which representatives of trilobites, mastodons, and sabre-tooth tigers discuss the question: "Was it something we grew, ate, or did wrong?" For enlightenment on such problems we may look to comparative psychology as well as to anatomy, physiology, and ecology. In the museum, therefore, behavior can be studied to advantage in terms of both its different phyletic settings and its underlying biological and psychological processes.

Linkage of present and past is through heredity in all organisms, often also with mechanisms resembling the "traditions" of higher organisms, via the developmental medium. Students of systematics and animal classification, orienting their theories progressively in terms of a coalescence of structure and function, now give behavior more weight than ever before. Emphasis on behavior in systematics has brought with it a strong tendency to view species-typical systems as strictly inherited, and, in view of correlations observed between species structure and characteristic responses, the conclusion is often drawn that behavior patterns may be considered homologous, much as structures of common ancestry are considered homologous. This answer, however, to what for museum scientists is a key question, is not necessarily correct. For, although heredity may be considered basic to all behavior in all animals, genetic mechanisms may underlie behavior very differently in different types of animals, according to how the nongenetic factors intervene and what these may be in the various cases. That is to say, no direct, closed relationship can be presumed to link genes, structures, and behavior in any species, and structures may mediate very differently between genes and the activity systems of Protozoa, pigeons, and primates (11).[1]

Consequently, the problem of "instinctive behavior," that is, of species-typical behavior considered in the light of underlying hereditary mechanisms, is a focal one for study in a natural history museum. On the thesis that the term "instinct" merely raises the general problem of behavior ancestry in animals but offers no clear, valid solution, the program of our own department centers around the question of how behavior patterns characteristic of species develop in different phyla and classes. Under museum auspices, two important avenues of research are open for such a program.

The union of laboratory and field research traditionally is best achieved through the facilities of a natural history museum. In the program for behavior, the emphasis ideally is on a close relationship between studies of species under controlled conditions in the laboratory and of the same or related species in their natural situations. But, as the history of animal psychology shows, coordinated field and laboratory investigations of behavior are difficult to carry through, except on a limited, sporadic basis, because of inevitable handicaps in techniques, personnel, time, and funds. The handicaps are not mainly in obtaining the funds, for progress seems to depend first of all on advances in techniques and methods and on improvements in planning related to the sharpening of goals as theoretical insights are clarified.

---

[1] The numbers in parentheses throughout this part of the article refer to items numerically listed in the bibliography at the end of this article.

One important aspect of planning concerns what animal is to be studied. The selection, presumably, should be guided first of all by considerations of theory and method and by an interest in comparative research. These are severe criteria, it seems, for they oppose the common preference for domesticated species for psychological and other research. Domesticated animals, such as the pigeon and the white rat, are in wide use, no doubt more because they are relatively cheap to obtain and to maintain in numbers and adapt well to a variety of laboratory situations, than because they are the best animals for the study of many problems. That the transferral of a species sample to the laboratory from nature is hardly ever a simple matter and the maintenance of sufficient numbers for research often may be very difficult are no excuse for our letting the course of science be dominated by conditions of mere convenience in subject matter. To free themselves from such stereotypy, scientists must pursue energetically the answers to problems, from health and breeding techniques to laboratory habituation and research use, that now oppose systematic scientific study of species from the wild. As the need for coordinated field and laboratory research is more widely recognized, solutions to these problems should be found for an increasing variety of animal forms.

Comparative investigation of the behavior and psychology of animals should advance best in well-organized programs of field and laboratory investigation of common problems. With good planning, field and laboratory approaches may be combined advantageously (e.g., 7). Progress should accelerate and broaden as the realization spreads that these approaches to animal study actually are closely related (10). Experience has shown that field study is not just a matter of "watching the animal" and jotting down notes, for if systematically pursued it must solve problems of method and attack problems of theory closely allied with those of laboratory research. Even a general observation, uncomplicated by gadgets or special procedures, represents an intrusion into the animal's world and a distortion of the phenomenon under study. To control such factors, and to develop adequate methods of analysis, techniques for entering the situation and for mastering the details of perception and record-taking at successive stages must be worked out and procedures for analyzing results must be developed that are appropriate to the animal, situation of the study, and the problem. For, in principle, there is a close equivalence between laboratory and field research on behavior, as concerns the logic of controls, adequate design, a sufficient number of cases, and systematic organization of results. With increasing experience, field investigations increase in reliability and resemble experiments more, and laboratory research becomes more naturalistic and better adapted to the animal under study, than when field and laboratory are regarded as largely disconnected or just mutually supplementary.

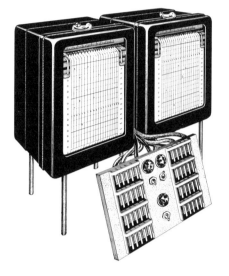

FIGURE 10
Electro-mechanical recording system used in the laboratory of the Department of Animal Behavior. The observer operates the keys on the board "by touch," without taking his eyes off the animal. Each key stands for a different item of behavior, and pressing the respective keys controls electrically the movement of corresponding pens tracing lines on the moving paper roll of the recorder. In this manner, a graphic record of the animal's behavior is obtained. Figure 11 illustrates the use of this sytem.

In this type of approach to problems, facilitated in the museum situation, the behavioral investigation of any species can advance by regular stages. The first stage aims at obtaining information both about the behavior pattern and about the animal's typical adjustment to laboratory conditions, viewed in relation to behavior under natural conditions. This may be an introductory probing of the problem, or a "pilot phase," in which the behavior repertoire of the species is charted and the nature and circumstances of occurrence of the chief items in this repertoire are explored.

The pilot stage can guide the planning of an intensive, better-controlled investigation. In our laboratory, from the empirical evidence obtained in the first stage, tentative lists are made up of behavior items according to their evident importance, for use in more systematic studies. A mechanical means has been devised by which frequencies, durations, and combinations of the acts can be recorded by a trained observer who "keeps his eyes glued to the animal" (Figures 10 and 11). By such means we have worked out methods for the analytical investigation of behavior in several vertebrate species.

Methods of this kind can involve operations of synthesis as well as of analysis, in that the experienced observer may concentrate in one series on particular aspects of the behavior and in the next on a perceptual survey of the pattern as a whole. When carried out successively, these operations facilitate each other—giving evidence about both the woods and the trees, so to speak. In field investigation, method should result in ideas

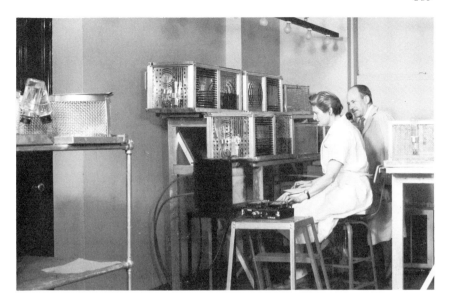

FIGURE 11
Routine observations preliminary to an investigation of environmental factors
affecting behavioral development in mammals. Female rodents with litters live in
cages of a design under study for possible experimental use. Daily records of their
behavior are taken with the apparatus shown in Figure 10, with a dictaphone
for qualitative notes.

for special tests as supplemental to observation; in laboratory research, it
should produce hypotheses to be tested in specific experiments.

In the program of our department, the first goal is to gain evidence
both on the development and the adult pattern of behavior in each of
several important animal types, to assay the species-typical behavior system of each. The next step is to devise methods for discerning the similarities and differences of species patterns in comparison with those of closely
and of distantly related animal types. As the following perspective will
show, in terms of some representative studies, we have concentrated on
the first stage and, up to the present time, have entered the second only in
an exploratory way.

Investigating a species behavior pattern as an adaptive system calls for
studies of its repertoire of items, its psychology, its biological basis, and
its environmental relationships. Much of our research has been directed
at species reproductive behavior, as critical for species survival and therefore as a strategic means of our understanding the inclusive behavior
of the animal. Studies of reproductive behavior in species of the West
African mouthbreeding fish *Tilapia* began with observations of adults

114

FIGURE 12
Temporary exhibit of projects carried out with the African mouthbreeding fish, *Tilapia macrocephala,* illustrating techniques for investigating and collecting these fish in the field, and for maintaining and studying them in the laboratory.

engaged in nest-building, mating, and incubation. Specialized studies followed. On the biological side, certain important differences were found between these fish and mammals with respect to the role of ovarian hormones. Evidence was also found on the function of social stimulation in spawning and on the influence of early experience in the ontogeny of mating behavior (2, 3). In another series of studies, the reproductive behavior of the marine goby fish was analyzed (15). Depending on the combinations, certain visual, chemical, and other stimuli could elicit combat, courtship, or territorial defense from the male. A female ovarian secretion was found, excitatory to the male. Sounds were also involved, and it was discovered, for example, that a peculiar "grunting" noise emitted by the male could be distinctly excitatory to females (16).

In our research, emphasis is placed first on analyzing the behavior and discovering underlying factors, then on studying interrelationships of processes involved in the species system. Research on species of army ants in field and laboratory has revealed a complex pattern of cyclic behavior in which phases of vigorous predation and nomadism alternate with relatively quiescent phases in the colonies (12). The key relationship proves to be an increased "social stimulation" of the worker population at specific intervals by the active stages of successive immense broods, which accounts for the regular intervention of "nomadic" phases between successive "statary" phases. Also critical to this system are changes in the stimulative action of the larval brood on the colony at specific (histologically identifiable) stages, so altering adult behavior as to set off through various channels a critical change in the queen's reproductive processes. In the army-ant behavior pattern and its species variants, many different agencies are involved, some deriving from the properties of each different type of individual in the colony (i.e., from queen, broods, and workers), others from specific environmental influences such as the day and night cycle.

Studies of reproductive patterns in mammals have been focused in detail on the role of hormones in behavior organization. An important class difference is indicated here. In mammals low in the scale, such as rats, castration results in an early disappearance of the male pattern; in certain higher mammals (including man), however, the male sex responses often persist for a long time after castration. Experiments both on hamsters and domestic cats ruled out a replacement hormone from the adrenal gland as cause, although replacement tests revealed hormone relationships. Male cats, however, given appropriate experience prior to castration, continued sexually responsive for several months after the operation, whereas males without such experience lost function quickly (8). The results tend to support Beach's thesis that the role of experience in the sexual sphere is significantly greater in the higher mammals than in rodents.

Widely indispensable to reproduction in the vertebrates are parental relations with young, which are typical of the species. Such behavior is often attributed to specific hormones presumed to arouse it by priming an innate neural control. Results from the mouthbreeding fish, mentioned above, indicate that this hypothesis may be too simple or even misleading, as do also findings concerning the ring-neck dove (6). In this bird, both parents normally feed the young by regurgitating "pigeon's milk" from the crop. The act seems automatic and explicable on the above basis. Experiments showed, however, that whereas injections of the pituitary hormone, prolactin, caused the crop substance to be produced, parent doves did not deliver this to the young unless they had experienced certain stimulus-response relations with the young in the early nesting stage. Prolactin does not arouse feeding of young directly; its effect rather involves both a suppression of mating responses and arousal of organic changes underlying production of the crop substance and crop engorgement, and hence contributes partially and indirectly to the act. From such changes, however, two among several essential events, the opening of the parent's bill and regurgitation from the crop, can occur in turn as the sensitive parental thorax is stimulated incidentally by hungry nestlings in stirring about. Beyond the organic factors, therefore, the parental-young exchanges of stimuli and response on the nest seem essential to the rise and integration of the feeding pattern.

Our studies with domestic cats, which involve both analyses of normal behavior and experiments in which kittens are isolated for subsequent tests, support the following account of the normal feeding relationship (9). After the litter has been delivered, the female initiates nursing by approaching and licking the neonate kittens, then lying down and enclosing them in an arc. Each new-born kitten, thus aroused to activity in its turn, moves towards the female's abdomen, as into a commodious enclosure, slowly and with infinite obtuseness from the observer's view, but in effect guided, over all, by gradients in thermal and tactual stimuli from the female—"the closer, the warmer," as it were. On touching the warm, hairy surface, the kitten gives the crude, variable response of nuzzling, so that through many different occurrences its sensitive nose finally meets, fumbles about, and at last secures, a nipple. We find that from the first hour the kittens improve in their ability to reach the mother and to attach after separation. What is more, they also improve in reaching and suckling at individually specific nipples—one fore, another aft, and so on. To all of these matters the female's presence and movements contribute, as factors in a progressive, reciprocal process.

In these very different cases of species-typical behavior in invertebrates, the patterns seem to develop as complexes in which the roles of organic structures and functions, with those of stimulation from the situation of development, are interrelated very intimately. In the parental-young system of the cat, however, individual developmental plasticity and the role of learning seem to assume a much greater weight, and to figure very differently, than in the insects and lower vertebrates studied.

In the museum research environment, stress is both on the problem of origins and on that of animal nature, consistent with the relevance of behavior to systematics, evolution, and environmental adaptations. As regards the question of how species heredity influences the development of species-typical behavior, emphasis on developmental processes avoids both the barren issue of "nature vs. nurture" and other blind alleys, such as the sharp cleavage of "instinct" from "intelligence." Prospects are that both these distinctions will come to be held as relative; at any rate, at present neither behavior development nor learning in any of its forms is sufficiently known to support them. Rather, our thesis is that in various phyla and classes of animals structure and function may interact and influence ontogeny in many different ways and may enter into very different relations with the developmental situation (11).

The bearing of the life situation on development demands a close investigation in all animals, for *experience,* defined objectively as "the effect of stimulation on the organism," always plays a part in species development. In the agencies of developmental experience at various animal levels, general similarities are indicated as well as differences. In the cyclic functional system of army ants, interactions with the prevalent situation evidently condition the emergence of individual social function in a manner characteristic of the insect (11, 12). Because, for example, the feeding of individuals as larvae and later as newly emerged adults occurs in an odor field typical of the colony as well as of the species, these specific interactions of the developing worker with its situation seem to contribute in essential ways to the rise of normal adult responses such as trail following. Observations and tests show that young workers, after emerging from their cocoons, exhibit the normal behavior of adults only after a preliminary phase lasting a few days, in which time their crude initial responses evidently are modified into reactions such as the efficient laying down and following of chemical trails, discrimination of strangers from nest mates, and other adult responses integral to the colony behavior system. Callow workers released artificially from their cocoons and raised in the laboratory apart from nest mates are slow and defective in their responses after a few days, as compared with normal young. The conclusion, supported by other evidence in the army ant and certain other social insects, is that species behavior in these cases does not appear as a purely "inborn" pattern.

Because reproductive behavior is critical for species survival, museum research and theory require that its development in individuals be appraised accurately. Laboratory findings (14), referred to below, indicate that even in the lower vertebrates patterns such as mating are not organized independently of the situation of development. Experiments on parental behavior in birds (6), also, as described, reveal that intricate relationships often exist within a cluster of organic and experiential factors essential to the normal development of such behavior. The point here is definitely not that such behavior in any species is due to "learning" rather than to "instinct," for these are false alternatives. "Experience," as we define the term, is not always equivalent to learning, although, depending on species capacities, it may involve one or another form of learning. This point is supported by evidence on parental behavior in cats, already mentioned, in still other ways.

Investigations of delivery in the cat indicate that this act is not natively organized in that the female automatically "knows what to do" (18). Rather, she possesses certain organic processes which promote a successful birth, provided that indispensable interactions of factors in organism, behavior, and situation become possible. Experiments with rats indicate that such processes begin early in life and include experience of the female with her own body and the genital areas particularly. Organic factors involved in the birth episode are uterine contractions, birth fluids, afterbirth and expelled membranes, and the neonate itself. Each of these in its turn exerts potent, incidentally directive stimulative effects on the female's behavior. Quantitative and qualitative studies of many parturitions show, for example, that the processes of licking the attractive fluids exert an over-all integrative influence by shifting the female's attention from one aspect to another in the changing situation, as from her own body first to the substratum and then to the neonate. Events are consequently so channeled that a reciprocal stimulative relationship between female and neonate starts and progresses into a suckling-nursing pattern, and thus a social bond can develop along psychological lines in the litter situation. The female's pattern of behavior in parturition thus is not preformed but is literally assembled in the delivery situation itself.

The idea still is widely held that activities appearing in an organism raised away from species mates (i.e., in "isolation") must *ipso facto* be "inborn" or "innate." Isolation of young from the species is a useful method for studying behavior, and we have employed it, but not with its traditional interpretation. Our policy is rather to examine the relation of structure and function to the changing developmental situation in successive stages of development. As one example, platyfish reared from birth to sexual maturity away from species mates, not experiencing even their own reflections from the water film or other surfaces, scored low in mating tests at maturity (14). In contrast, mating scores were much higher in fish given earlier experience with species mates, but scores were intermediate in subjects which, although deprived of experience with species mates, had seen their own reflections and a heterogeneous environment during early life. Even in this lower vertebrate, therefore, the ontogeny of the mating pattern seems to require both a maturation of organic mechanisms such as hormone factors and a developmental environment in which typical species experiences, including self experiences, promote an important socializing process.

To investigate the development of behavior in the domestic cat, the isolation method in a more involved form was used (9). First, the normal development of reciprocal mother-young relations as in suckling and nursing was quantified for a control group. In the experimental groups, the variable factor was experience in the litter situation, with kittens isolated for scheduled intervals, starting at birth or later, under separate maintenance in incubators serving as "artificial mothers." After their isolation periods, the respective kittens were returned to mother and litter for a detailed study of their initial and later reactions. It was found that kittens isolated from birth to two weeks or longer only very slowly establish a suckling relationship with the female and social relations with litter mates. The readjustments vary individually and never quite reach normal standards. Kittens isolated during later times in the litter period show marked asocial tendencies on return, as in sleeping apart, and there are other signs of their avoiding litter mates. Although, in such cases, responses to other kittens improve appreciably within a few days, relations with the mother improve more slowly and never become altogether normal. It is the deprived kitten who is responsible for the strained, abnormal relations that arise, not the mother, who as a rule accepts the returned isolate readily. Even limited species experience, however, may benefit ontogeny, as is indicated by the fact that kittens, when paired in the incubator, were much more relaxed and versatile there and also in their readjustment to the litter situation on return than were isolates. The greatest deficit was shown by kittens isolated from species experiences (except for sounds and odors) from birth to sexual maturity. These animals, facing species mates for the first time, never reacted "normally," but varied in their responses from "indifference" to intense disturbance, and the males seemed incapable of mating except through experience in many successive tests.

Although species behavior patterns undeniably depend on characteristic organic factors, as a rule these influences cannot be readily identified or traced out in development. One promising line of research from this standpoint concerns species orientation, or adjustment to the conditions of space and time, as in establishing a territory and mastering a route. A problem of this type was studied in the trail-following responses of newly emerged army ants. Another, also investigated in the field, concerned the orientative adaptation of goby fish in the Caribbean area to a seashore habitat despite emergencies arising daily through tidal changes (4). When these fish get cut off in isolated pools during the ebb, they are able to escape by jumping from pool to pool or to open water below and can thus evade disturbances as from predators. Observations and tests show that the fish learns the general topography of the shore habitat at high tide by swimming over the borders of the "pool" areas and roundabout in the vicinity; then, as an outcome of this experience, it can jump accurately as emergencies arise at low tide.

Migration is a type of orientative behavior that is vital to the environmental adaptations of many animals and especially of many birds. As a first step in our study of the basis of this behavior, the properties of adult vision are under investigation comparatively in birds of species that are regularly, partially, or not at all migratory (1). By training the birds to discriminate visual stimuli by using their conditioned responses appropriately, the capacities of visual acuity are studied under both daylight and twilight conditions in the starling (in which one race is migratory) and the robin (a fairly regular migrant). This research paves the way for studies on the wider use of visual sensitivity in migratory birds.

Although new-born mammals are often described as helpless, sessile creatures, their orientative adventures actually begin soon after birth. Developmental research with cats involved studies of how the neonate improves in its ability to adjust to the home base and to navigate at a distance from it (9). With kittens at successive ages, observations and tests were carried out both in the home cage and in a facsimile area. Improvements in control over emotional disturbance were indicated by significant decreases in the loudness and pitch of the kitten's soundmaking and also in its readiness to cry in the tests of successive days. These changes, as well as locomotor signs of an improving environmental adjustment, appeared first in the home corner within a few hours after birth, within a few days had expanded to the border of the home base, in the second week extended to the adjacent corners, and in the third week reached the corner diagonally opposite the home base. In studies at corresponding times, in an experimental area with the same type of floor and the same dimensions as the home cage, comparable improvements in behavior appeared, but always much more slowly than in the living cage itself. The results indicate a process of emotional and psychological adjustment to the home area and its vicinity, dependent both on local sensory cues and presumably also on individual factors related to experience.

Tests were carried out on the changing role of sensory factors in the kitten's orientation, paralleling behavior improvement, in a program of interchanges or renewals of the usual floor or wall units, or of their replacement by units differing in some one aspect such as odor. The results show that chemical cues become dominant in the described adjustments from within an hour or two after birth. Even at that early time, the neonate has begun a general adaptation to the home corner, the locality that is first scented strongly by the mother during the period of pregnancy and once more during parturition. The kitten's navigation about the cage improves slowly, mainly on a chemical basis but also through use of tactual cues. The eyes open after about one week, and a few days later the kitten has begun to orient more widely afield and with a new efficiency, on a dominantly visual basis, now reaching the home corner on the diagonal across an open space rather than near the walls as before. Towards weaning time the kitten can range freely about the cage. These tests disclose the interplay of sensory, organic, and motor processes in the development of way finding in the cat. Involvement of learning in the orientative process is shown by the fact that kittens tested regularly on each day from birth are clearly superior in their orientation to kittens first tested at a later age.

These results seem relevant to species living under natural conditions. Littering females of many carnivores, in leaving their nests to forage, scatter their suckling young nearby, as these happen to disengage from the nipples. Such occurrences, as our findings suggest, may introduce for the kittens both emergencies requiring adjustment and opportunities for practice in orientation, at first near the home base and later (as attachment strengthens with age) farther afield. Independent exploratory excursions

FIGURE 13
Temporary exhibit of a colony of *Eciton hamatum,* set up in the Museum after a field investigation in Panama. From the wire transportation cage (left), the ants make their way through plastic tubes into the glass-walled enclosure (above), in which a typical nesting cluster of workers is formed, with queen and brood in the center. Through other tubes, the ants reach the feeding chambers and return to the nest with booty.

outside the nest would be facilitated thereby. As success in the independent returns would depend on factors such as strength, sensitivity, and learning capacity, these occurrences may well have an appreciable selective importance.

Museum biologists are concerned about the relative weight of similarities and differences in the adaptive characteristics of closely related and of distantly related species of animals. This question, bearing on species backgrounds in natural selection, enlists the behavior specialist, and several projects of the kind have been carried out in our program. In these comparisons, the ecological and population characteristics of the species have been studied in relation to their behavior and general biology.

A long-term investigation of two closely related species of army ants in the genus *Eciton* has shown that, although their behavior patterns have equivalent biological bases, differences in nesting, predation, and nomadic functions are sufficiently great to enable these species to live in the same forest habitat throughout the American tropics (12). One of these two species raids in large swarms and captures hard-bodied arthropods as its principal prey; the other raids in branching columns and takes mainly soft-bodied booty. Variations in the colony populations and functional cycles of the first species on Trinidad, perhaps related to a distinct release from competition there, may be due less to the absence from that island of the second species than to the absence of a species in the genus *Labidus*. On the mainland, the latter overlaps the two *Eciton* species in habitat, but, like the first of these, is a swarmraider, hence is more competitive with it than is the second *Eciton* species.

Comparisons of closely related genera also have been undertaken in our program. In the field, the adaptive patterns of two different genera of army ants have been compared, one represented by species indigenous to the tropics, the other by a species of the North Temperate zone (13). Fundamental similarities exist between the two in their functional cycles, and in the organic processes underlying them, but with significant differences seemingly referable to secondary biological mechanisms arising through evolution of seasonal adaptations in the latter. In the mammals, comparisons of strains of domestic mice and rats have been made, particularly with respect to the tensional and "emotional" properties of their behavior. Inclusion in this comparison of members of a related genus brought in from their natural habitat is contemplated.

Our research necessarily involves a vigilance for the role of heredity in species-typical behavior. Such a consideration, in view of the traditional museum interest in the processes of evolution, is consistent with an increasing awareness in modern systematics of the merging of behavioral, ecological, and structural evidence in the study of selective processes. In the defining of a species, for example, a criterion now generally stressed is a reproductive isolation or failure to cross with related groups living in the same or adjoining natural areas. Factors underlying such reproductive insulation, the so-called "isolating mechanisms," are incompletely known. One of our projects (5) concerned what reproductive barriers might exist between two closely related species of poeciliid fishes, the platyfish and the swordtail, found living in close proximity in their native rivers in Mexico, without their crossing, or at least without their producing viable hybrids. Under appropriate conditions, however, these species were made to cross in the laboratory. Behavior analysis and appropriate tests disclosed the influence of numerous isolating mechanisms, and not, as is often suggested for such processes, just one or two. These factors varied in nature and in their combinations, including items in behavior (e.g., differences in movement), physiology (e.g., differences in sperm viability), and morphology (e.g., male gonopod structure). Studies such as this, in which specialists in genetics, ecology, and behavior join forces, exemplify a type of research that progresses well in the museum situation.

Our general emphasis is on the normal range of behavior within a population living in the species niche or typical environment. Yet in science

FIGURE 14
Putting "Tiger's" sound effects on record. Illustrating one of numerous projects involved in study of the everyday behavior of animals. (Photograph by Don Rice, courtesy of W. C. C. Publishing Co.)

much can be learned about the normal or usual from the abnormal, and attention has been turning therefore to studies on how organisms meet abnormal or extreme conditions. A notable example is Selye's research on physiologically taxing conditions or "stressors," such as extremes of temperature. But the role of other types of extreme conditions, including the psychological, has not been explored very systematically. If we are to understand adaptive behavior well, it is necessary to go beyond the physiological to examine the effects of emotional crises and problem situations that tax species resources. One study in our laboratory measured the relationship between the mild stress of a variable environment early in life and degree of susceptibility to tuberculosis infection in several strains of rats and mice (17). It was found that animals that reacted to stressful conditions with greater locomotor and emotional disturbance were more susceptible to the disease than were those less affected by the stresses. Also, the various genetic strains ranked in the same order in their susceptibilities to the environmental stresses as in their proneness to the disease, and a high correlation was found between these two characteristics among individuals in each of the groups.

A striking result of these experiments was the extent to which individuals in the same group might differ one from another in their reactions to a common stressful test. Examining the basis of individual differences within a species population subjected to taxing conditions is one object of an experiment with mammals now in its pilot stage in our laboratory. The principal aim of this research is to examine how controlled instabilities in different aspects of environment affecting individuals during the early stages of life may influence their capacities to meet stresses of various kinds introduced later under test conditions.

Research of this kind should help to clarify variations in the adaptive efficiency of behavior under natural conditions, particularly as concerns emergencies beyond the normal limits of species tolerance. The study of adjustments to sensory, physiological, and problem stresses under experimental conditions may cast some light on what factors influence the normal properties of a species for tolerating such conditions, and what types of maladjustments may arise in a population when the intensity of stresses presented by predators, scarcities, over-population, and other hazards exceeds its resources for readjustment. This line of research should be increasingly valuable when it is carried into the area of species comparisons.

Although scientific departments specializing in the investigation of animal behavior and psychology are still exceedingly rare among the natural history museums of the world, advances in science have prepared the way for them. In such programs, museums, which are best fitted to integrate field and laboratory methods and to utilize the comparative approach, have an important opportunity for scientific pioneering. The natural history museum, because of its time-strengthened goals, appropriate facilities, and experienced staff, offers an optimal environment for doing such work well. Let us hope that this opportunity will be accepted.

In keeping with their responsibilities in modern times, natural history museums have a real need for comprehensive programs in the comparative study of behavior. Nature faking is as much out of place in animal psychology as it is recognized to be in other fields of natural history. Yet loose analogy and anecdote still frequently govern public interpretations of animal activities and capacities, even occasionally in science. If museum scientists are not prepared to offer sound interpretations of behavior, they have small reason to complain when hearsay and uncritical inference hold sway in books, the press, and even in classrooms. Increasingly, in these times, conclusions vital to man's welfare are drawn from inferences about lower animals in areas from education to the mental clinic. To avoid harmful misconceptions in this field, as in other areas of science, evidence must meet good standards of reliability, and theory good standards of validity, before either can be taken seriously into account.

Only with the first real scientific investigations of animal behavior after Darwin did man become impelled to study his own origin and his own nature through systematic comparisons with lower animals as well as through studying himself. He has learned that his superiority in the phyletic scale is indicated not so much by specific organic details, which (except for cerebral cortex, grasping hand, facial musculature, and a few other details) in fact often reverse it, as by his mental capacities from perception to reasoning. To be sure, man's verbal, conceptual language and broader reasoning capacity, based on advances in cerebral cortex, so vastly extend his control over space, time, and social processes as to give the impression of absolute differences from lower animals. Through experience, however, scientists who study animal psychology have become cautious about any sweeping use of the terms "absolute" and "relative" in such respects. Solutions by reasoning, for example, have been demonstrated in mammals down to the rodents; also a gestural language has been demonstrated in chimpanzees; and beyond doubt the intellectual attainments of primitive, small-brained men were limited indeed. From such considerations, scientists realize the defects of dogmatic answers, such as were prevalent in preexperimental times, about the mental capacities of animals as compared with those of man and are wary of their modern counterparts.

Not only in research, in which the comparative study of animal psychology encounters many unanswered problems, but also in interpretation, there must be an adequate rapprochement of biology and psychology if the needs of the future are to be met adequately. Only an effective comparative study in science of the psychology of the lower animals in relation to that of man can meet the atavistic dogma that evolutionary principles do not apply to man in the psychological sense. Clearly, much remains to be done, for only during the past few decades has man seriously directed his scientific resources to the end of investigating such questions systematically.

The general responsibility of museum research on behavior is to integrate studies of specific problems and of representative animal types with the derivation of general principles concerning adaptive behavior. In recent decades, the results of psychological research on lower animals often have been applied formally to the human level, in the study of general problems such as learning, with some freedom, although not always with due regard to scientific support for the extrapolation. Science, of course, has found that man can learn much about himself through studying lower animals, also about lower animals through studying man, and psychological problems are included. The conclusions, however, do not follow at once from general similarities alone; rather, they must be worked out through procedures in method and theory adequate to the task of evaluating both the similarities and the differences. The functions of the zoological museum to investigate nature and to teach about nature inevitably involve considerations such as these, when questions are raised about what animals do and why they do it.

A department devoted to investigating broad problems in the behavior and psychology of animals, although a new feature in the natural history museum, should become a commonplace as museums better realize their potentialities, responsibilities, and goals in keeping with the advances of science and the increasing problems of man in modern times.

REFERENCES

PART I

Beach, Frank A. 1944. Reports by the chairmen of the scientific departments of The American Museum of Natural History. (Unpublished)
Chapman, Frank M. 1929. *My tropical air castle*. New York: Appleton and Co.
Darwin, Charles. 1872. *The expression of the emotions in man and animals*. New York: Appleton and Co.
Lewinsohn, R. (tr. German). 1954. *Animals, men and myths*. New York: Harper and Brothers.
Maier, Norman R. F., and T. C. Schneirla. 1935. *Principles of animal psychology*. New York: McGraw-Hill Book Co.
Montaigne, Michel de. 1580. *Essais*. (tr. E. J. Trechmann, 1927).
Morgan, C. Lloyd. 1891. *Animal sketches*. London: Arnold.—1896. *Habit and Instinct*. London.
Noble, G. Kingsley. 1941. The museum and science. *Nat. Hist.*, 47: 5.
Romanes, G. J. 1883. *Animal intelligence*. London: Kegan Paul.
Rosenfeld, Leonora C. 1941. *From beast-machine to man-machine*. New York: Oxford Univ. Press.
Wallace, Alfred R. 1872. *Malay archipelago*. London: Macmillan.
Walden, Carl J., Thomas N. Jenkins, and Lucien H. Warner. 1935. *Comparative psychology*, vol. I. *Principles and methods*. New York: Ronald Press.
Wheeler, William Morton (tr). 1926. *The natural history of ants from an unpublished manuscript in the Archives of the Academy of Sciences of Paris, by René Antoine Ferchault de Réaumur*. New York: A. A. Knopf.
Yerkes, Robert M., and Ada W. Yerkes. 1929. *The great apes*. New Haven: Yale Univ. Press.

PART II

1. Adler, H. E., and J. I. Dalland. Spectral sensitivity in the starling (*Sternus vulgaris*). *J. Comp. Physiol. Psychol.* (In press.)
2. Aronson, L. R. 1948. Problems in the behavior and physiology of a species of African mouthbreeding fish. *Trans. New York Acad. Sci.*, ser. 2, 2: 33–42.

3. Aronson, L. R. 1949. An analysis of the reproductive behavior of the mouthbreeding cichlid fish, *Tilapia macrocephala* (Bleeker). *Zoologica* 34: 133–158.
4. Aronson, L. R. 1951. Orientation and jumping behavior in the gobiid fish *Bathygobius soporator*. *Am. Mus. Novitates*, no. 1486, pp. 1–22.
5. Clark, E., L. R. Aronson, and M. Gordon. 1954. Mating behavior patterns in two sympatric species of xiphophorin fishes: their inheritance and significance in sexual isolation. *Bull. Am. Mus. Nat. Hist.* 103: 141–225.
6. Lehrman, D. L. 1955. The physiological basis of parental behavior in the ringdove. *Behaviour* 7: 241–286.
7. Noble, G. K., M. Wurm, and A. Schmidt. 1938. Social behavior of the black-crowned night heron. *Auk* 55: 7–40.
8. Rosenblatt, J. S., and L. R. Aronson. 1958. The decline of sexual behavior in male cats after castration with special reference to the role of prior sexual experience. *Behaviour* 12: 285–338.
9. Rosenblatt, J. S., G. Turkewitz, R. Cohn, and T. C. Schneirla. Studies of early socialization and adjustment to the litter situation in the domestic cat. (In MS.)
10. Schneirla, T. C. 1950. The relationship between observation and experimentation in the field study of behavior. *Ann. New York Acad. Sci.* 51: 1022–1044.
11. Schneirla, T. C. 1956. Interrelationships of the "innate" and the "acquired" in instinctive behavior. In P.-P. Grassé, ed., *L'instinct dans le comportement des animaux et de l'homme*. Paris: Masson. Pp. 387–452.
12. Schneirla, T. C. 1957. A comparison of species and genera in the ant subfamily Dorylinae with respect to functional pattern. *Insectes Sociaux* 4: 259–298.
13. Schneirla, T. C. 1958. The behavior and biology of certain Nearctic army ants. *Insectes Sociaux* 5: 215–255.
14. Shaw, E. 1957. Sexual behavior of male platyfish reared in altered environments. *Anat. Rec.* 128: 621. (MS in preparation.)
15. Tavolga, W. N. 1954. Reproductive behavior in the gobiid fish *Bathygobius soporator*. *Bull. Am. Mus. Nat. Hist.* 104: 431–459.
16. Tavolga, W. N. 1956. Visual, chemical and sound stimuli as cues in the sex discriminatory behavior of the gobiid fish *Bathygobius soporator*. *Zoologica* 41: 49–64.
17. Tobach, E. 1955. A study of the relationship between behavior and susceptibility to tuberculosis in rats and mice. *Adv. Tuberc. Res.* 6: 62–89.
18. Tobach, E., M. L. Failla, R. Cohn, and T. C. Schneirla. 1955. Analytical studies of maternal behavior and litter relations in the domestic cat. I. Parturition. *Anat. Rec.* 122: 423–424. (MS in preparation.)

II

ON INSTINCTIVE BEHAVIOR

Dr. Schneirla objected strenuously to nativistic concepts of behavior such as instincts, innate, inborn, and, more recently, "encoded in the genes." His concern was based on the conviction that such concepts tend to minimize or discourage a more valid approach to the basic problems in behavior, namely, the development of behavior in the individual as a function of the continuous interaction and fusion of changing genic (biochemical) and experiential factors. The arguments in favor of a nonnativistic view appear in many of his papers and his search for alternative ways of understanding and explaining behavior (see Parts IV and VIII) occupied much of his scientific life. The three papers selected for this section are directed specifically to the problem of nativism and represent his more recent thinking. The article, *Interrelationships of the "Innate" and "Acquired" in Instinctive Behavior* (No. **77**),* was pre-

---

* This and subsequent numbers in this introduction refer to the items in the complete bibliography of Schneirla's works, p. 1017. Bold face numbers denote articles that are included in this volume.

sented at a colloquium in Paris on the question of instincts and is his most extensive and well-rounded discussion of the subject. Interesting comments by Schneirla on the presentations of the other participants are scattered throughout the proceedings of the conference.

The second article, *Instinctive Behavior* (No. **90**), is a greatly condensed version of the argument with a somewhat different emphasis. The third article, *Instinct and Aggression* (No. **115**), a book review, is a critical evaluation of two books by Konrad Lorenz who is the chief protagonist of traditional instinct theory.

Lester R. Aronson
Ethel Tobach

T. C. SCHNEIRLA

Interrelationships of the "Innate" and the "Acquired" in Instinctive Behavior

Bibliography No. 77

The title assigned to me by Dr. Grassé offers an opportunity to question the concepts of innate and acquired as the mental tools with which to investigate instinctive behavior. For too long these concepts have been accepted a priori, on the questionable assumption that they represent separable entities in behavior determination. This dichotomy is a heritage from our preexperimental past, incorporated with too little question in the basic statement of the "instinct problem." But instinct theory, like all other theories, must have concepts substantiated through reliable evidence.

In this colloquium we have for convenient reference an influential contemporary theory of the nativistic, preformistic type, in which the above concepts and their basic distinction form a prominent part of the groundwork. Lorenz (1950) has indicated his point of view in these words: "We shall call instinctive only a sequence of motions that occurs with an inborn coordination of all its components, independent of training or understanding."

Not only the basic activities, but much of their inner organization, are considered inborn as effected through specific integral neural mechanisms. Such claims require careful examination.

To explain what we mean by challenging these concepts and also what we *do not* mean, the case of the so-called "Anti-instinctivists" may be mentioned. In the 1920s certain scientists, American psychologists (e.g., Kuo, 1924) in particular, raised objections to nativism and in favor of a more objective attitude. For Watson, a chief figure, this was not merely a reaction to the practices of others. He himself had attempted a classification of animal "instincts" (1914) and in his drive against Mentalism he

From Grassé, *L'Instinct dans le comportement des animaux et de l'homme,* Masson et Cie, 1956, édit., publications de le Fondation Singer-Polignac, 43 avenue George Mandel, Paris.

later (1919) defined "instinct" as "an hereditary pattern reaction, the separate elements of which are movements, principally of the striped muscles."

Here we find a suggestion of hereditarily-determined organization and of "the instinctive movement," not unrelated to Lorenz's (1935, 1950) ideas. But the resemblance soon stops, for Watson did not encapsulate the inherited determiners in the nervous system, and mistrusted the Freudian influences to which Lorenz may have been susceptible (Kennedy, 1954). Watson had a conception of hereditary influence that although rather positively held was not too consistent, for he (1925) denied "it" on the human level.

The anti-instinctivist movement, although criticized as having gone "too far" (Hunter, 1947), made two contributions of value, first an emphasis on objectivity and an insistence on experimentation. In a preceding period of naturalistic investigation, essentially descriptive methods had been followed by Whitman (1899), Mills (1898) and others, and indeed Mills, zealous investigator of behavior and founder of a club at McGill so dedicated, seemed convinced that the "animal mind" was closed to experimentation. Watson in contrast favored experimental study of behavior both in laboratory and field (e.g., Watson and Lashley, 1915), but disengaged it strongly from mentalism. The second contribution of the anti-instinctivists was a stress upon diagnostic, analytical research. This is exemplified in the work of Kuo, who asked not only "What happens?" but also "How?" His investigations (Kuo, 1930, 1932) raised serious difficulties for dogmatic distinctions of innate and acquired. In fact Kuo disowned both "instinct" and "learning" as obscure, emphasizing ontogenetic processes in the development of behavior.

The fresh methodological improvements built upon the earlier naturalistic approaches, with their further emphasis on qualitative methods, we can accept, and these might be used to better advantage in behavior study today. Through this movement particularly, a healthy skepticism developed to balance overconfident statements such as Hingston's (1928) that "Everybody knows what instinct is." The challenge was directed mainly at the traditional criteria for distinguishing the innate from the acquired, which were: *universality* of given activities through a species, *early appearance* in the individual, *absence of learning,* and *appearance in isolation.* As we shall see, present evidence supports this challenge strongly.

That these objections have survived is indicated by the frequency of calls (e.g., Leuba, 1940; Howells, 1945; Anastasi and Foley, 1948) for a reconsideration of the "nature-nurture" dichotomy. But the situation is not as unequivocal as might be implied by Beach's (1947) remark in a recent symposium on instinct that the "artificiality of the implied dichotomy" (i.e., heredity-environment) "is apparent to everyone." Much uneasiness exists about discarding the distinction, witnessed by the chairman's statement ending the same symposium, that all five contributors had "emphasized the role of heredity in the determination of behavior" (Hunter, 1947).

The need for a contemporary stock-taking is accented by Hebb as follows (1953, p. 46 f):

> I would not suggest for a moment that the problems in this area are unreal; I do suggest that they have been poorly stated, inasmuch as we cannot dichotomize behavior into learned and unlearned, environmentally determined and hereditarily determined. I urge that there are not two kinds of control of behavior, and that the term, "instinct," implying a mechanism or neural process independent of environmental factors, and distinct from the neural processes into which learning enters, is a completely misleading term and should be abandoned.

As Anastasi and Foley (1948) have said, the term heredity is often defined "indirectly, vaguely or inconsistently, especially when it comes to the domain of behavior phenomena." To replace the unsatisfactory dichotomy, these authors suggest a reconsideration of behavior etiology in terms of structural and functional factors. But progress in biology has emphasized increasingly how intimately functional properties are bound into the principles of morphology, and neither the idea of isolated morphological factors nor that of isolated *function* fits the needs of a dynamic behavior theory. As Cobb (1944) has said, ". . . no function is possible without an organ that is functioning and therefore no function takes place without structural change."

Consistently we may say that all problems of development are inherently both functional and structural.

Doubtless the traditional criteria have inherent weaknesses. Confidence about excluding learning from any given activity is inversely related to appreciation of the scope of learning and how incompletely this phenomenon is known; early appearance becomes unreliable with demonstrations of conditioning at early stages in insects, birds and mammals; and, as will be shown later, appearance in isolation, however sound at first sight, rests too heavily upon an incomplete understanding of equivalence between environments. Even universality is questionable, first of all because of acts that normally are likely to be learned widely throughout a species (Smith and Guthrie, 1921). Actually there seem to be no hard and fast rules for distinguishing hypothetically innate behavior from other kinds.

Undeniably, the influence of genetic constitution is expressed somehow in the functions and behavior of every animal. Raccoons, for instance, could not readily be brought to peck at their food as do chicks. The "instinct problem" therefore centers around the occurence of behavior that may be termed species-stereotyped or species-specific, species-characteristic or species-typical. A species, defined dynamically, concerns groups capable of interbreeding under natural conditions, but reproductively isolated from other such groups (Mayr, 1942). Investigations of the mechanisms underlying such isolation in insects (Spieth, 1952) and in fishes (Clark, Aronson and Gordon, 1954) indicate that behavior factors are involved as well as physiological, structural and environmental ones. But what is the causal nexus?

The simplest answer might seem to be that species-typical behavior is inherited, as nativistic theories suggest; yet the unreliability of the criteria for innateness reminds us that the genes do not directly translate themselves into behavior by any means. Between the fertilized ovum and properties of the mature organism lie the complex processes of development. The following preliminary considerations of these matters encourage a broad perspective on the problem of the individual rise of species-typical behavior.

1) Preformism is misleading. "That which is directly inherited . . . is the set of genes, with the accompanying cytoplasm" (Jennings, 1930). This is the initiating cause of development, designated by Johannsen the *genotype* as distinguished from the *phenotype,* i.e., from the organism and its functions produced through development. Now, as David and Snyder have said (1951, p. 54):

> Limitations in the early concept of genes as individual "determiners" of Mendelian characteristics, and of a one-to-one correspondence between gene and characteristic, were exposed by the discovery of genic interactions and of environmentally contingent gene effects. The newer concept of *genic balance* implies that genetic variability is a function of the genotype as a whole and that isolation of individual gene effects involves an artificial disjunction of gene and total genotype.

Clearly, it is the phenotype that can be studied more or less directly, but from the beginning of development the effects of the genotype can be examined only indirectly through evidence gained thereby. Haldane (1946) thus points out that a given genotype promoting ontogeny can lead in one environment to adaptive results, in a different environment to neutral or maladaptive results. And, as Dobzhansky (1950) has put it:

> The so-called "nature-nurture" (genotype-environment) problem is not to distinguish which traits are genotypic and which are environmental, for all traits are genotypic and environmental.
>   . . . The outcome of development at any stage is a function of both

the heredity of the developing individual and the environment in which the process has taken place. The development is apparently epigenetic, not preformistic. . . .

The concept of a direct determination by the genes, a one-to-one relationship with developmental processes, might be considered at least for the molecular plane of development. But modern investigators have their reservations even here. As Weiss states (1954, pp. 193–194):

> The genome of the zygote endows all descendant cells with a finite repertoire of modes of reaction. What is commonly called "differentiation potency" may be interpreted as a finite assortment of chemical entities. These entities, of course, must not be viewed as direct precursors of any final results, but as a reactive system, the constant interaction of which with systems of the extragenic space will only gradually yield the later specific characteristics of the various cell strains.
>
> . . . Since the extragenic space, i.e., the genic environment, is thus undergoing progressive transformation, it is evident that every new reaction must be viewed in terms of the cellular system in its actual condition at that particular stage, molded by the whole antecedent history of transformations and modifications, rather than solely in terms of the unaltered genes at the core. Incidentally, keeping this in mind ought to stop the confusing practice of labelling all intrinsic properties of a cell at an advanced stage as "genetic," but those brought out by still later interactions with neighboring cells or diffusable agents as "environmentally" or "hormonally" introduced, forgetting that no cell develops independently, but that all of them have gone through a long chain of similar "environmental" interactions with neighboring cells and the products of distant ones.
>
> Theories concerning how behavior and behavior patterns arise through this mass of finite events must do more than bridge initial and terminal stages with hypothetical shielded intraorganismic determiners.

2) *Genic effects are indirect and mediated.* As Stern (1954) says, we have barely touched the surface of the problem concerning how genic factors actually influence organic development, and to investigators like Dobzhansky (1954) it seems improbable that these factors have anything like a complete determinism at any stage. Systems of intervening variables, which always include the influence of developmental conditions, both intrinsic and extrinsic to cell, tissue, organ, system or organism, mediate the initial genic effects at each successive stage. There is evidence that these variables may range from biochemical (e.g., enzymatic) conditions to the repercussions of action and specific extrinsic effects. Moreover, their effects on development appear to be self-reactive and cumulative. Thus at any stage further development and new organizational gains oc-

cur through interrelationships that are only partially the products of genic influence.

3) Distinctions of the "native" and "acquired" ambiguous. These considerations suggest the unwisdom of attempts to distinguish what is "innate" from what is "acquired," or to estimate the proportionate effects of these or to judge what kinds of effects they might produce separately. There exist no separate entities of this sort, for conditions at any stage are the complex product of trace effects from previous stages entering into interactions with prevalent extrinsic-intrinsic conditions, themselves composite acquisitions. Learning, the most complex form of acquisition, may have very different forms (Maier and Schneirla, 1935, 1942), and as Hebb (1953) reminds us, is known so incompletely that its effects may be far from obvious. But indirectly, all learning is somehow influenced by the genes (Howells and Vine, 1945).

4) The "instinct" problem is one of development, different for each phyletic level. In each type of organism, the genotype varies characteristically in its range and complexity of effects as evidenced by different types and degrees of sensitivity to surrounding conditions as well as complexity and plasticity of neural and reactive functions. The problem of "instinct" therefore demands careful attention to phyletic differences in those configurations characterized as "levels" (Needham, 1929; Redfield, 1942; Schneirla, 1946, 1949). "Instinct" is not a real and demonstrated agency in the causation of behavior, but a word for the problem of species-typical behavior at all phyletic levels.

Consequently, "instinct" study must examine the ontogeny of behavior in each type of organism, so as not to miss any aspect of the expanding field of relationships in development. Each organism must be studied in its own terms, since when new capacities enter the developmental situation, new configurations must be expected in adaptive behavior as well as variations in patterns more similar to the "phyletically old." Consequently, valuable evidence, both as to the ontogenetic causation and the evolutionary history of behavior patterns, lies in the comparison both of closely related and of distantly related organisms.

THE RELATION OF DEVELOPMENT TO BEHAVIOR AT DIFFERENT PHYLETIC LEVELS

Behavior patterns often reach similar ends in different phyla, as a result of parallel evolutionary processes. To the teleologist, an equivalence of ends signifies equivalence in the organizations attaining these ends. But actually the accomplishment of adaptively comparable results, as through feeding, tells us nothing of the antecedent processes. These may involve complex anticipations, as in a socialized human being, or may be reflex-like and automatic, as in a lower invertebrate. Calling two such acts in different phyletic contexts "instinctive" mainly conveys the information that they are both species-typical and nutritively beneficial, but leaves doubt as to what else they may have in common. The implication is of course that both somehow depend upon mechanisms resulting through evolution; however, these may be either homologous or analogous, or both, and if convergent may function to similar ends although very different in internal makeup. Thus great doubt exists that a common formula can be found for "instinctive behavior" at all phyletic levels.

Feeding in a coelenterate and in a cat would both be called instinctive, since both acts are species-typical products of ontogeny in the normal species habitat. Both are adaptive. Yet the patterns may arise through very different developmental processes with different underlying organizations resulting.

In the typical feeding pattern of the medusoid coelenterate the stimulus, typically a chemotactic effect, if too weak produces only a brief local response of tentacles, if too strong brings a vigorous contraction of the bell which turns the animal away. But adequate stimulation elicits first a contraction of the local marginal tentacles which curl about the object, then a local contraction of the bell margin which, spreading centrally, pulls object and tentacles toward the mouth tube. Meanwhile this tube, the manubrium, has bent toward the stimulated sector and by expanding its opening now engulfs the object.

This response pattern can be obtained normally from an animal of given structure acted upon by stimulation within a given range of intensity. Its respective components depend first of all upon the functional properties of the tentacles, bell and manubrium. In the mature organism, the integration of these into well-timed series depends particularly upon the conductile functions of the nerve net (Bullock, 1943) which tie them into a predictable functional sequence. Their functional patterns are strongly influenced first of all by the morphology of the parts, in locations fixed through development. In one important aspect of control in the act, perhaps the most critical, Bozler's (1926) findings support the hypothesis of Loeb that the diffuse nerve-net impulses first reach and adequately activate the basal part of the mouthtube on the side nearest the highly aroused marginal sector. Hence typically the manubrium bends directly, "purposively" through functional conditions imposed by its structure and its location in the animal (Maier and Schneirla, 1935).

Pantin's (1943, 1950) studies on hydroid coelenterates show in detail how a patterned action of parts can result from a nerve-net system connecting the components in a given spatial way. Thresholds of receptors and of muscles, together with nerve-net conductile properties of irradiation and summation, are critical for this behavior system. The system is capable of considerable variation according to the conditions of arousal and the current state of the organism. One such variation, a temporary failure of the tentacle responses to food, obviously depends upon intraorganic changes thought by Jennings (1905) to be a "loss of hunger," perhaps grounded in widespread neural changes. But Parker (1919) was able to narrow the cause experimentally to a peripheral adaptation effect which temporarily raised the excitation threshold of the tentacular receptor cells.

Such patterns in lower invertebrates are stereotyped in that they are produced directly through arousal of the functional properties of the species-characteristics tissues. The intervening variables therefore are those of a specific developmental process, and the activity pattern is in this sense "directly determined" without the intervention of special variables such as learning. Yet even these simple organic systems do not arise in a vacuum, for if the individual is to develop in the characteristic form with the typical species activity repertoire, there must be a representative succession of developmental stages, each involving interactions between the respective organic conditions and standard extrinsic conditions.

A marked variability is seen in the activities of these lower invertebrates, but only that possible in a simple organic system of radial symmetry—a variation of multitudinous changes about a fixed center as it were and within set organic limits. Although from time to time behavior can change in somewhat more persistent ways, these seem limited to alterations in sensory adaptation or muscle tonus, peripheral changes which are ephemeral in the sense that the organization of behavior is held to the species norm—the typical individual behavior system that is approximated through life. Despite temporary variations behavior thus is essentially stereotyped, and lacks the plasticity found in higher phyla. In phyletic behavior comparisons, many types of variability and many types of plasticity are to be expected.

Feeding in the domestic cat also is a species-typical pattern which results through development in the standard habitat. But the rise of the chief properties and the organization of feeding in this mammal hardly follows a course duplicating that in coelenterates. For one of the prominent typical patterns of food-acquisition, rodent killing, a study of Kuo's (1930) has revealed that the developmental factors, both intraorganic and extrinsic, are complexly and variably interrelated at all stages. The contributions of bodily growth are essential, but so is a learning process through which the components are integrated into a pattern. These components depend on features of bodily makeup which adapt the cat to being excited by small moving objects, to making swift movements, and to capturing and devouring small animals.

But the normal outcome is by no means inevitable. By appropriately regulating the situations in which kittens encountered rodents, Kuo was able to produce adult cats which attacked and ate rodents, and others which obtained their food in other ways, either fearing and avoiding rodents or living peaceably with them according to experience. It is also possible, for example, to train young kittens to eat solid food without using their paws, which are frequently used normally. Still other variations are possible in dependence upon the kind of situation in which the animal develops.

In both coelenterates and birds, the typical feeding pattern emerges in the normal habitat through an organic development basically initiated by the genic constitution. But these ontogenetic processes in the different phyla involve strikingly different intervening variables, particularly in neural resources determining plasticity. In both organisms, intraorganic relationships introduced through growth influence further stages and the outcome. But in the coelenterate these are held within narrow limits, whereas in the mammal, through wider and more complex intrinsic and extrinsic interrelationships, they become major factors in behavioral development. The eventual mammalian pattern owes its specific organization particularly to the superior capacities of the nervous system for change. In the cat, the function of components such as use of the paws may be eliminated or changed through training; in the coelenterate, comparable changes (e.g., in tentacle responses) are relatively fluctuant and dependent upon peripheral modifications. The developmental system of the mammal therefore may be termed *plastic* in the sense that under appropriate conditions one or more patterns differing from the species norm may be produced and retained. But in the coelenterate pattern, variability occurs about a fixed axis, at is were, and is not to be confused with plasticity.

INTERRELATIONSHIPS IN COMPLEX STEREOTYPED BEHAVIOR PATTERNS

The insects are often cited for their "instinctive" behavior. The insect nervous system appears to be first of all a transmitter and summator of impulses from afferent systems. The arrangement of tracts and centers seems particularly to favor direct discharge under the predominant afferent effect, rather than plasticity of organization as in the very different mammalian system (Schneirla, 1953b). Consequently, and with the added important fact of rapid conduction over short arcs, we should expect patterns of activities rigidly governed by organic mechanisms and, in the mature individual, readily dominated by abrupt external sensory change. In relation to these conditions, highly sensitive receptors have evolved such as the compound eye, permitting delicate reflex adjustments as to slight movements in the visual field (Autrum, 1952), illustrated by the attack-reaction of the praying mantis.

In a system of this kind, specific organic factors readily translate themselves into behavior. By means of the successive operative removal of head, thorax, legs and various abdominal segments in the mature silkworm moth, McCracken (1907) demonstrated in the egg-laying pattern of this insect an olfactory control as link to the external situation, a reciprocal neuromotor function in the postural execution, and an abdominal process serving as nucleus of the whole pattern. Although the functional systems are typically complex with an organization resisting analysis, Spieth (1952) found the mating patterns of closely related species of Drosophila so well differentiated as to be taxonomically reliable. And Adriaanse (1947), in a population of *Ammophila campestris,* a solitary wasp previously considered a single species, found two distinctive behavior patterns which with previously overlooked morphological differences indicated the existence of two distinct species.

Insect behavior cannot be adequately studied in terms of one functional stage alone, since any stage emerges through relationships effective earlier in development. Critical factors may even be extrinsically introduced by other individuals, as when an ovipositing female incidentally fixes the early environment of her young by laying her eggs in a particular place (e.g., on the species food-plant in a phytophagous insect). Through this act the newly emerged insect is given not merely food and a feeding station (Kennedy, 1953) but also a shelter with predators, diseases and other properties (Dethier, 1954)—a ready-made environmental complex. In this case the main determinative factor through which the next generation is so weightily influenced may be some organic factor affecting adult sensitivity (e.g., in a metabolic influence upon olfaction—Dethier, 1947). Or in certain species, it is even an olfactory habituation established in larval feeding which may persist to the adult stage (Thorpe and Jones, 1937).

To discover the nature of the organization in each type of behavioral pattern and its prerequisite developmental relationships, analytical investigation is essential. Although evidence from this source is not plentiful, some of the salient points may be brought out in the consideration of one such study of a solitary insect and one of a social insect behavior pattern.

The spinning behavior of the *Cecropia* silkworm was studied by Van der Kloot and Williams (1953). Normally, after a period of wandering, the mature caterpillar settles down at a twig-crotch and spins a double cocoon with a thinner upper end through which the adult eventually escapes. Cessation of feeding is attributable to glandular changes of the period, as is the wandering, which is absent in caterpillars deprived of silk glands. This extirpation also eliminates two movements, the "stretch-bend" and the "swing-swing," basic in normal spinning, which thus depend at least in part upon sensory input from the spinning apparatus itself. The genesis and temporal order of these movements are attributed largely to stimulation from the changing internal environment, but their execution depends predominantly upon tactual and gravitational cues from without. For example, for the termination of either basic movement, contact of the spinnerets is essential at full flexion or full extension. The pattern of the normal cocoon thus may be considered a compound expressed through a spatial relationship of the body to the external world. (So, in a highly uniform environment such as the interior of a balloon, the larva spins a flat layer of silk.) This behavior pattern therefore comes about through a complex progressive relationship between changing organic conditions and the sensory input from these states, interacting with that from sets of external circumstances which are altered according to how the act progresses.

In a sense, insect social patterns have evolved as permutations of individual characteristics, since each has arisen in a dynamic environment defined chiefly by complexly interrelated individual properties (Schneirla, 1941, 1946, 1952b). Some of the functional principles involved in one highly specialized pattern of this type may be examined in terms of a case which I have studied (1938, 1944, 1953a) in some detail—the nomadic, predatory system of the terrestrial army ants.

One central feature of army-ant life is the formation and regulation of the temporary nest or bivouac, a complex outcome of worker behavior critical for the functional pattern of the colony. The bivouac is a mass of living workers which not only affords a temporary base of operations and a population reservoir for the colony, but also is an excellent incubator for the great broods that energize the colony (Schneirla and Brown, 1954). Indirectly, as a result of colony behavior, each new bivouac site is opportunely sheltered in the general environment; and may be readjusted to disturbing variations in surrounding atmospheric conditions. A stable microclimate is so regularly established for the successive broods that the periodicity of the developmental stages is highly predictable in brood after brood. Thereby the bivouac, and the worker behavior accounting for its properties, serve as fundamental regulators of colony "drive."

These bivouac properties facilitate the occurrence of a regular cycle of behavior changes in the colony, each successive one caused by a further massive excitation of the adult population by the brood. The shelter properties of the bivouac are greatly enhanced by a diurnal behavior routine in the worker population which, although related only indirectly to environmental atmospheric changes, buffers the brood securely against potentially harmful exposure. Reciprocally, through indirectly contributing to the existence of a rhythmic colony behavior, a normally developing brood makes the bivouacs possible. Through complex interactive organic and behavioral events, adult behavior, brood processes and environmental conditions are interrelated in the functioning of this complex behavior pattern.

An indispensable component in the nomadism and predation of the army ants is their foraging pattern which centers around the making and following of chemical-trail systems. These raiding systems are typical of the species. For example, *Eciton burchelli* may be called a swarm-raider in that it conducts its forays in large masses or swarms connected by columns with the bivouac; *E. hamatum* is in contrast a column-raider in that it operates in systems of branching columns terminating in small raiding groups. Certain characteristics of the adult workers of these species, identifiable in simple tests, seem implicated, no doubt with others less readily identified. Chief among these are differences in olfactory threshold, glandular secretions and their intensity, level and range of excitability. In all of these respects, *E. burchelli* is the more generalized, *E. hamatum* the more specialized. Thus *E. hamatum* can advance in relatively small numbers and follow its trails readily, with more precise trail-division responses than *burchelli,* which requires greater numbers. *E. hamatum* is more specialized in its booty, taking soft-bodied prey evidently found mainly through odor; *E. burchelli* takes a wide variety of booty primarily through response to motion.

Certain basic organic factors thus may be postulated as centrally involved in the species pattern. Another, and a critical one, centers around the fact that the newly emerged worker does not enter at once into an adult function. Instead a few days are required, first within the bivouac, then after a day or two in gradually extending the scope and efficiency of operations on raiding trails. An experience factor is suggested by the fact that callows artificially removed from their cocoons typically are accepted in other colonies of their species and are undisturbed on being introduced, whereas older callows are attacked and are noticeably disturbed on introduction. To account for such results, we may assume a simple habituation to the specific colony odor, perhaps begun in larval feeding, progressing after emergence when the callow feeds voraciously in the presence of this odor (Schneirla, 1941). The young worker therein has the basis for a following reaction to the colony odor trails when she first ventures outside the bivouac. The improvement shown within a few days from the initial clumsy and hesitant condition may be partially due to further maturation, but this cannot be the entire answer. There is also one specialized trail reaction, turning toward the bivouac at trail junctions when booty-laden, which may have its basis in early feeding on the typical booty.

These assumptions find support. Conditioning is a well known phenomenon in social insects (Schneirla, 1953b), and Thorpe and Jones (1937) appreciably shifted the adult oviposition response of a solitary insect, the ichneumon *Nemeritis,* to an abnormal host upon which experimental subjects had fed as larvae. A conditioning process for the ants is not considered the sole factor, rather as implementing and extending the function of organic factors (e.g., mouth reflexes). That developmental factors place a distinct limit upon such processes would follow from the difficulty of artificially hatching callow workers of *Eciton burchelli* into *hamatum* colonies, and vice versa. Comparable results have been obtained for the highly socialized camponotine species (Schneirla, 1952b).

It is suggested that discrete morphological and physiological properties of the individual insect can enter into patterned interrelationships through types of facilitation effective in the group environment. In ants such as *Formica,* it is possible that early discrete mouth-part reflexes may be extended from simple passive feeding, through colony interactions, into active feeding of others and finally into individual foraging (Maier and Schneirla, 1935; Schneirla, 1941, 1952b, 1953b). The conditioning process assumed is doubtless a rudimentary one, with limitations typical for insects, but nonetheless indispensable to the species functional pattern.

In insect colonies, other individuals are prominent environmental agents facilitating such integrations, thereby being somewhat equivalent to the role which the general environment may serve in solitary insects. In social insects, relationships of this kind are indispensable for the functional patterns of individual and group. General colony function in the army ants depends upon adult responsiveness to the brood, which through its physiology and activity furnishes attractive and excitatory tactual and chemical stimulation. The regular rhythmicity which is essential to the species behavior pattern as well as to colony unity depends upon such relationships (Schneirla, 1938, 1952b). When active larvae are present, intensively exciting the worker population, large raids and regular nomadism are the rule; when the brood is quiescent and social stimulation low, raids are small and emigration absent. These findings offer strong support for extending the Wheeler (1928) concept of trophallaxis to all classes of stimulative relationship among individuals in the social group, rather than merely to "exchange of food" (Schneirla, 1946, 1952b).

In the insect social system, each type of individual enters into group relationships more or less indispensable to the species pattern. In the army ants, for example, the prodigious ovulation processes of the queen come into action for short periods of a few days at regular intervals somewhat more than one month apart. This is of great importance for the Eciton functional cycle, since it determines the timing of broods which in turn governs timing of the cycle through predictable brood excitatory effects.

At first sight, time relations in the functional pattern might be attributed to an endogenous control in the queen, who becomes physogastric and delivers a new brood approximately midway in each statary phase. But recent findings show that the queen is brought into this condition by a critical extrinsic effect (Schneirla, 1953a). The specific cause arises anew near the end of each active or nomadic phase, when the larval brood then present is nearing maturity. A few days before this phase ends, the larvae begin to undergo a glandular change which underlies the cessation of feeding and the approach of cocoon spinning (Lappano, unpubl.). At this point, although feeding less and less, the brood is constantly more active and capable of stimulating the adult population increasingly. The queen soon begins to feed voraciously, but this is probably not an automatic reaction to the mere presence of abundant food. More likely, she is started and maintained in the process by an intensified trophallactic stimulation from the excited workers, and augmented social stimulation should increase her capacity to consume food. A recrudescence of the fat bodies soon begins and with a maturation of eggs in the ovarioles causes her gaster to swell. These processes accelerate and reach their peak toward the middle of the statary phase, when the actual egg-laying episode occurs.

This theory finds a natural test. A second physogastric episode begins near the end of each statary phase, when reflex activities of the nearly mature pupal brood stimulate the workers to larger raids, thereby indirectly causing a food surplus (although the brood is still enclosed and not feeding). But soon after the new brood of workers has emerged from cocoons and a new nomadic phase has begun, physogastry in the queen is cut short. Evidently a large-scale feeding by callows, reducing the food, and a diversion of workers to trophallactic relations with callows, account for the abrupt return of the queen to the nonreproductive condition. This condition persists until the current nomadic phase nears its end, when a new episode of egg-production begins and advances to completion.

It seems clear that the normal reproductive episode of the queen is initiated extrinsically and can complete itself only when the essential extrinsic conditions persist. The necessary cause evidently lies in a complex relationship arising periodically between brood and worker population, an interaction indirectly introduced through the queen's own function at an earlier point in the cycle (i.e., when the preceding egg-batch was laid). The cyclic pattern thus is self-rearoused, so to speak, in a feedback fashion. This rearousal is timed with relative precision and is therefore the product of a reciprocal relationship between queen and colony function, not of a timing mechanism endogenous to the queen. Essential to

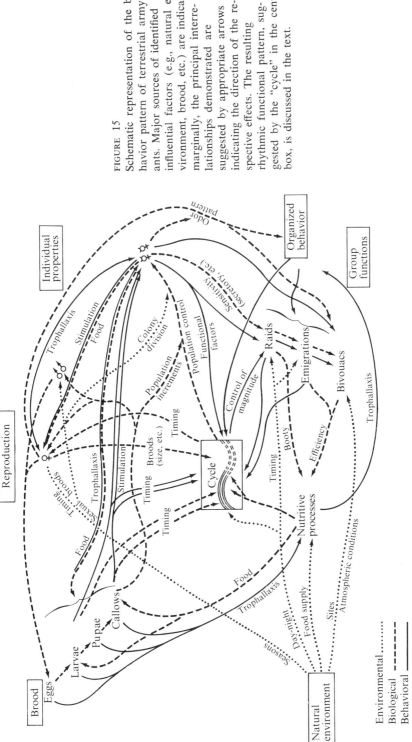

FIGURE 15

Schematic representation of the behavior pattern of terrestrial army ants. Major sources of identified influential factors (e.g., natural environment, brood, etc.) are indicated marginally, the principal interrelationships demonstrated are suggested by appropriate arrows indicating the direction of the respective effects. The resulting rhythmic functional pattern, suggested by the "cycle" in the center box, is discussed in the text.

the timing of intervals is the duration of developmental stages in the brood, which owes its regularity particularly to the bivouac as "brood incubator."

The schema of the Eciton functional cycle, in Figure 15 indicates that the interrelationships of the principal contributive factors and their current effects upon the system are numerous and varied. Relationships with the physical conditions of the general environment, under which the pattern has evolved, are crucial. As one example, heterogeneity in the operating terrain is indispensable for execution of the typical raiding-emigration sequence (Schneirla, 1944). There is also the diurnal cycle to which the timing of daily raids and nightly emigrations is geared in the terrestrial species. Light sensitivity, although unimportant for orientation, thus is a key factor in the cyclic pattern of these species. Emigration in the terrestrial species normally occurs in the evening, at the one time of day when atmospheric conditions are most nearly homogeneous throughout the forest and sufficiently near the brood optimum to permit exposing this delicate part of the population during the change of colony base (Schneirla and Brown, 1954).

The complex Eciton cyclic pattern therefore arises through the diverse interrelationships of its component processes—the morphological, physiological, behavioral and environmental factors which interact under given conditions. The organization does not preexist in the heredity of any one type of individual—workers, brood or queen—nor is it additive from these alone. The organic factors basic to the species pattern have evolved in close relationship to the general environment, which therefore supplies key factors essential for their contemporary integration into a functional system.

"MATURATION" AND "EXPERIENCE" IN BASIC VERTEBRATE ONTOGENY

The concept "maturation" in modern morphogenetic theory includes, with growth as such, the excitatory and stimulative effects that arise through growth processes and influence further stages of development. Development is much more than growth therefore. This definition suggests a need to broaden the traditional view of "maturation" as the direct or specific effect of growth processes on development. Their indirect effects, and their interaction with surrounding conditions, can become cumulative. A broader causal pattern is suggested by Holt's (1931) view of self-stimulative relationships in the development of coordinated movements.

The actual breadth of the pattern of relationships governing early behavioral development on different vertebrate levels is not well known. Locomotion is frequently taken as a critical case, and Coghill's (1929) classical experiment with larval salamanders is accepted as demonstrating an innate intraneural determination of coordination. Yet this experiment was not an analysis of function; it was a histological and descriptive study which disclosed a parallel course in the appearance of successive new types of neural connectives and the respective phases of a series of locomotor changes. The functional aspects of the correlation remain unclarified.

The experiment of Carmichael (1926) with drugged salamanders has been widely accepted as eliminating peripheral factors in favor of a neural determination of functional development. When embryos were drugged with chloretone to prevent movement during development, the experimenter reported that within 30 minutes for recovery from the drug, adult specimens swam in a manner "indistinguishable" from that of control animals. But Fromme (1941), repeating and extending this experiment with tadpoles, did not altogether confirm this conclusion. In his investigation the recovered experimental subjects differed from normals not only in a slower swimming speed but also in details suggesting deficiencies in coordination, when time-conditioned drug effects were controlled. Particular deficiencies were noted in an experimental group chloretonized only during the advanced stage of "partial movements." Fromme concluded that "without opportunities for the practice of rudimentary movements, the earliest swimming does not compare favorably with that of a control group." It should be noted also that in such experiments, the role of other possible factors such as subtle afferent effects has not been excluded.

Coghill's view that an initial generalized pattern is primary, with partial patterns individuating secondarily from it, is a broad generalization which seems to require secondary qualification. The concept of a preset total neurogenic pattern, subsumed under such generalizations, only roughly fits available evidence. Early generalized activities are variable and not too well patterned. On the other hand, discrete activities may appear very early, as Kuo (1932, 1939) found in embryonic chicks, and Carmichael and Smith (1939) in early guinea pig embryos from which they readily elicited local responses with low intensities of tactual stimulation. So many conditions determine the extent or inclusiveness of movements at different stages (Werner, 1940; Carmichael, 1951) that variability and flux deserve equal emphasis with broad patterning in early action. Windle (1940, 1950), in fact, holds that the earliest responses to stimulation are local reflexes, which provide a basis for the integrated patterns of later stages.

The alternatives for the causation of patterning in ontogeny are not simply *growth vs. learning.* Doubtless, mechanisms like some of the vestibulo-ocular reactions "are not patterned by training but are laid down directly in growth," *somehow,* as Sperry (1946) concludes from his study of compensatory eye movements appearing in tadpoles without optic nerves. But the "laying down" would (even here) seem to be a matter of *development,* of intraorganic interrelationships involving other tissues, organs and even systems, rather than just an accretion of tissues, or *growth* specifically. As a matter of principle, the possibility of even wider relationships cannot be excluded.

Apparent support of a predetermination of behavior by a neural control from specific centers is found in the investigations of Hess (1949), in which, for example, during electrostimulation of different localities in the cat's hypothalamus, movements suggesting activities such as feeding and sleeping appeared, although unrelated to the present external situation. As Lehrman (1953) points out, Hess himself does not conclude from this that a strict localization of functional control exists in the hypothalamus, and variations in afferent input may account at least in part for the discovered temporal variations in responses to localized electrostimulation. Moreover, as Masserman (1941) found, such "pseudo-affective" reactions obtained by electrostimulation of the hypothalamus differ strikingly from the normal in a number of respects. It should be emphasized that these experiments involved the adult stage only. The role of peripheral loopline processes in normal central coordination may have been underestimated. Thus in the adult cat, Gellhorn, Loella and Ballin (1954) found the responsiveness of cortical auditory and projection areas in lightly anesthetized subjects appreciably increased through peripheral application of nociceptive ("pain") stimuli together with the respective exteroceptive stimuli. Strychnine tests indicated that this is a result of interactions of cortical projection processes with impulses set up in the hypothalamus through nociceptive stimulation.

Adherents of the Lorenz theory often attach considerable weight to certain results from studies on locomotion in fish and amphibians as evidence for an innate central nervous determination of behavior in vertebrates. One such study is that of Weiss (1941), who obtained motor activity in a transplanted salamander limb which had motor connections only with a deplanted section of spinal cord. In the absence of afferent connections, the movements may be attributed to spontaneous neural impulses from the displaced section of cord. But the actual relationship to normal behavior of these effects and of spontaneous discharges such as those recorded by Prosser (1936) from isolated arthropod ganglia has not been established. There also are numerous technical details opposing an unequivocal interpretation of such results (Gray, 1950).

The findings of von Holst (1935, 1950) with the teleost *Tinca vulgaris* and other fishes are often taken to support an innate neural determination of coordinated locomotion. But Lissman (1946), in experiments with dogfish in which *all* afferent inlets to the central nervous system had been removed, could not obtain such automatic central control. Rather, carrying deafferentation beyond a certain point abolished the rhythm completely. Although positive conclusions await further evidence, it is indicated that the central control in this case depends upon some intact peripheral connections. Since previous experiments have concentrated on mature animals, there is an unfortunate lack of evidence concerning how neural coordination may be established through earlier development in such activities.

Of course nothing is to be gained by minimizing neural capacities for organization appearing through development (Lashley, 1947; Hebb, 1949). To throw needed light on the condition of such functions through ontogeny, let us hope that further studies will involve comparisons of neural control in immature and in adult stages. With respect to hypothalamic functions, it is conceivable, for example, that in the adult, central control may have usurped the role of peripheral functions indispensable in early development. Hence the James-Lange and Cannon theories of emotion may both be valid but for different stages. In regard to the coordination of locomotion, however, Lissman (1950) concludes that ". . . the proprioceptors may well determine the disposition and the state of activity of the central nervous system more permanently than is often assumed."

And this, after all, is only one of the peripheral systems to be considered as influencing central coordination. The complexity of such relationships would appear to underlie findings such as those of Aronson and Noble (1948), who in a systematic operative exploration could not resolve an amphibian behavior pattern, that of mating, into a control of its components within respective neural centers.

There has been a considerable number of observational studies on vertebrate ontogeny, summarized by Carmichael (1946, 1951). These studies, although impressively detailed, exhibit a chiefly descriptive character and a general shortage of systematic analytical procedures which may stem from concepts of an ontogeny dominated by the maturation of predetermined "growth" processes. A concept of maturation thus circumscribed does not seem valid for any stage of development including the earliest and for any vertebrate including the lowest classes. It would seem useful to define the concept more broadly to cover interactions within the developing organism, cumulative from stage to stage, without assuming any sharp cleavage of these processes from changes introduced by extrinsic conditions.

For a discussion of this point at an elementary level, we may refer to some findings of Tracy (1926) in his studies of toadfish ontogeny. The early larva of this fish lies quiescent on the bottom for successive intervals, but intermittently exhibits quick jerking movements, called "spontaneous" because they have no apparent extrinsic cause. According to Tracy's analysis, these movements occur through the presence in the blood of metabolic products, accumulating as growth processes reduce available oxygen during each quiescent period. At a critical point in the buildup, an intrinsic excitation somehow occurs. The existing biochemical condition may either cause the direct firing of motor neurones, or may alter thresholds so that sensory impulses from other sources excite motor discharge to muscles. The rhythmicity of the process may be due to the fact that each movement phase alters the embryo's condition so that a further resting phase may ensue, in which metabolites accumulate to the point of setting off another movement, and so on.

These early movements are endogenous in the sense that their basis is mainly within the organism. But for their occurrence, not only must there be interactions of metabolic processes within the embryo, but also interactions of these processes with extrinsic conditions. The point may be stressed by taking up an interesting conclusion of Tracy's, to the effect that if external conditions could be kept constant, the organism's activities would be determined by its own life processes. Such statements can be misleading. What this *cannot* mean is that extrinsic conditions ever are passive or neutral, much less dispensable, for the developing organism is in constant and progressively changing interaction with its medium. This principle becomes increasingly significant for development as it advances to organizations of processes which include as subordinate the biochemical and other basic functions.

From the initial stages of development, extrinsic conditions are thus implicated in developmental processes. They are not to be included within "maturation" as defined, yet they influence development and activities constantly and vitally. These effects constitute instances of "experience," defined as *the effects of extrinsic stimulation upon development and behavior*. This concept may be only roughly apposed to "maturation" in its significance for development. It denotes a wide range of phenomena, from the influence of biochemical changes and growth-induced activities to an afferent input variously aroused, with possible trace effects not usually classed as "learning" (e.g., cases of sensory adaptation). It is only at later stages that learning, a higher order of process resulting from "experience," contributes to behavioral development.

No absolute or sharp distinction is intended between these concepts of maturation and experience at their border-line, which may be considered a common zone of overlapping functions. As McGraw (1940) pointed out with respect to attempts to distinguish "maturation" from "learning" through a separation of stimulation from extra- and intraorganismic environments, respectively, ". . . the definition is confusing and calls for a clarification of the terms *organism* and *internal and external environments*. . . . To what are these environments internal or external?"

Stimuli at first effective externally may, at a later stage, function through their organic traces, as admitted by and in interaction with new orders of function which have entered meanwhile.

Undue stress upon one of these concepts to the exclusion of the other must give a misleading picture of behavioral development. For example, Grohmann (1939) reared young pigeons in narrow tubes intended to prevent incipient flight movements, yet in free tests at the age of normal flight these birds were judged equal in their flying to previously unrestrained controls. This case has been cited (e.g., by Tinbergen, 1951) as evidence for an innate control and against experience. But developments contributing to actual flight may still include wing-muscle contractions despite enclosure within a tube, as well as wing movements known to occur in embryonic stages (Kuo, 1932). Also, developmental functions preliminary to flight may be very different in various species of birds. Thus, young turkey vultures kept by Dennis (1941) in restricted quarters until the normal flight time showed poor balance and could not fly on release, without further experience in the open. Was this a case of muscular weakness, or was it lack of experience?—What is experience? Tinbergen (1951, p. 132) mentions observations of butterflies and dragonflies which, when disturbed after emergence, made long flights without benefit of incipient flight movements. But previous developmental relationships may actually be relevant in cases of this kind. Also, after such insects emerge, there is a process of wing spreading attended by local actions as the wings dry, which obviously involves a facilitation of respiration to the point necessary for flight. It is not clear how peripheral loop-line relationships and their build-up can be excluded from the development of nervous control in such mechanisms.

The principles of behavioral organization are not to be satisfied by a priori postulations of innate organizing centers, but must be worked out in investigations appropriate to each type of behavior. For this purpose, Kuo (1932) directed his attention to the embryonic history of pecking in the domestic fowl. He recorded a time table of events as viewed through a window made in the shell, and in this way could also work out interactions. He traced the development, from indistinct beginnings, of three general kinds of activity significant for the adult pecking pattern. These were, the head lunge, bill-opening and -closing, and swallowing. The head movement first occurs passively as the head, bent down and resting on the thorax, is pushed upward and falls back rhythmically with the heart beat. On the fourth embryonic day a more vigorous nodding movement is observed, interpreted as an active response of the head to touch or to neural irradiation. After the sixth day, flexion of a leg may brush the toes against the head, eliciting a head movement. Such movements are reflex-like in the sense that they are local and automatic, but at the same time they are at first highly variable in form, a feature only partially reduced at hatching. In the course of time, limited integrations appear between the activities of head, bill and throat. At about the eighth day head-nodding may be followed closely by opening and closing of the bill, very possibly through the effect of nervous impulses irradiating from the head action. This movement in time gains increased frequency and amplitude, so that after the ninth day bill-clapping admits fluid into the mouth. Swallowing may then occur, probably as a reflex response to the sensory effect of amniotic fluid drawn into the mouth. A few days before hatching, when the head lifts and thrusts forward, beak-first, opening and clapping of the bill may follow, often with swallowing. All of these movements now are somewhat less stereotyped than before, and would seem to have come predominantly under neural control.

At hatching, the interconnection of these activities is at a relatively low point, with each "component" still variable and remote from its condition in the adult pecking pattern. Then a critical new feature enters:

Visual arousal of the lunge on visual stimulation. As suggested by Maier and Schneirla (1935), this response may be aroused de novo by visual effects through a diffusion of impulses from the optic lobe into adjacent midbrain centers, thereby setting off neural mechanisms previously established in terms of a tactual control of the head lunge.

These results seem best accounted for not in terms of an initial central nervous organization, but by an inclusive organization which emerges from the processes and interrelationships of maturation and experience as we have defined them. The eventual components are only vaguely suggested in the unformed, variable and unorganized events of earlier stages. Each component has its own developmental history into which many causes, both directly and indirectly related to organic growth, may enter. Thus tactual effects which at first accompany head movement incidentally, may acquire a direct neural control over this response through the formation of a functional neural pattern—an elementary conditioned response. In each stage, maturation gives rise to effects which influence other activities occurring at the same time and also, through contiguous neural traces, form new integrations influencing further stages. Experience here means the relationship of the organism with its own activities in self-stimulative processes, as well as with its extraorganic situation, at each stage. Typical "experience" in the egg, arising through and related to growth processes, thus seems essential for the normal development of head lunge and other components of the eventual pecking pattern. For the advance of the entire sequence of events, the involvement of feedback processes and their trace effects upon later stages is indispensable.

An efficient pecking response appears after hatching through a discrimination-motor learning in close relation to and in dependence upon further maturation. Studies of this learning process, with due attention to the role of maturation, have been carried out by Shepard and Breed, Bird, Cruze and Padilla (see Maier and Schneirla, 1935). The eventual neural correlation pattern of food-pecking evidently arises as the composite product of an interplay of forces variously introduced into the typical growth situation. Although the contributions of physical growth are of course indispensable, their role alone is insufficient for the rise of the normal pattern or any other. Also indispensable are the wider reactions into which the growth factors enter as partial contributors. When these wider relationships are changed, the outcome is not the species-typical one. Thus in the experiment of Padilla (1935), a critical change in the post-hatching situation of the chick facilitated the establishment of a pattern significantly different from the typical one.

It would seem to be the prevalence of an intimate, dynamic relationship between the factors of maturation and experience that renders analytical study of behavioral ontogenesis so difficult. Methods must be devised appropriate to the complexity and subtlety of these processes and their trace effects influencing later stages. In such work, little may be expected from attempts to estimate the specific or the proportionate contributions of the innate versus the acquired in ontogeny (Howells, 1945; Anastasi and Foley, 1948). It is another matter to attempt an appraisal of maturational effects as limiting capacity to change through experience (McGraw, 1940, 1946). An example is Shirley's (1931) reference to a cephalo-caudad maturational gradient underlying a described ontogenetic sequence of motor changes in the human infant. This is essentially an introductory procedure for appraising how far development has progressed at given stages, and is not the same as attempting to estimate the overall weight of "maturation" as against "learning" in the particular animal. The latter practice can become a dangerous limiting influence in research and theory, especially when one member of the pair is favored unduly. It is thus probable that Gesell (1945, 1950) carried the idea of "maturation" conceived as an innate "growth plan" much too far in his theory of behavioral development in the human infant. For a true picture, "experience" factors must not be held from consideration until advanced ontogenetic stages are reached.

"Experience," as the term is used by Beach and Jaynes (1954), concerns only cases that involve learning and habit acquisition more or less specifically. But the meaning and relevance of the "experience" concept as used here subsumes *all* types of relationships dependent on extrinsic conditions, including gains through "learning" as one type. Learning concerns only a part of the range of relevant experiences—a chronologically later and more specialized part. For example, indications of conditioning have been reliably identified by Munn (1940) and by Moore and Welch (1940) in the swimming stage of larval amphibia, but we have suggested intrinsic-extrinsic interactions for stages much earlier than this, the organic trace effects of which must be considered as factors in later development. Not the earliest, but an important concurrence of this type, is suggested by the coincidence of a proprioceptive or other organic-arousal process with an exteroceptive effect, as illustrated in Kuo's results. Carmichael (1936) suggested that through such combinations of events, transition to an exteroceptive control might begin and advance, with the stimulus-response pattern thereby assuming a more specific form. Such processes in early stages cannot be expected to fit traditional notions of conditioning.

Prenatal conditioning thus far has been demonstrated only on the bird and human levels. Gos (1935) obtained a specific conditioning of general movement to vibration after the 16th day in the chick embryo; Hunt (1949) after 15 days. The human embryo has been conditioned by Ray (1932) and by Spelt (1948) after 6½ months. The criteria of conditioning appeared broadly satisfied by the results, although the Wickens (1939) rightly questioned whether the ordinary type of conditioning is closely duplicated in the embryonic stage. Significantly, at 10 days in the chick embryo, before a specific conditioning was demonstrable, Gos began to notice signs of habituation to experimental stimulation. Very possibly, with adequate techniques, changes of a simple order may be demonstrated at still earlier stages. Thus far, conditioning in utero seems to be characteristically rather generalized, variable, and unstable in its trace properties. It is likely that, whatever their degree of specialization, processes involving the consolidation of the trace effects of experience must be reckoned with as implementing maturational processes and as indispensably interrelated with them at all stages.

THE "NATIVE" AND THE "ACQUIRED" IN STIMULATION AND PERCEPTION

Objectivity in attempts to appraise an animal's relation to its environment always is influenced by our own perception, which inevitably colors our notions of the adjustment (Schneirla, 1950). From this standpoint Lehrman (1953) has criticized Lorenz's view of the external stimulative effect, conceived as "releaser," triggering off an innately organized neural center and thereby eliciting the appropriate instinctive act.

The stimulative effect in "instinctive" behavior tends to resist analysis as to its nature, and unfortunately we are too much limited to general impressions which are likely to be unreliable. But the difficulty is only increased by referring to situational adjustments as "perception" in widely different animal types from psychologically lowest to highest (Schneirla, 1948, 1949). The risk is distorting the actual relationship of situation and animal. As an example, Hertz (1931, 1933) found that untrained bees in their initial visual tests approached most readily the stimulus cards of greatest contour richness and inner detail (e.g., paddlewheel figures as against crosses). This spontaneous response opposed training, although von Frisch (1923) and others had conditioned bees to brightness, color, and odor differences. Some writers are inclined to interpret the Hertz finding in terms of a fairly complex configurational process comparable to mammalian pattern perception. However, Wolf (1933) found that bees were attracted more readily to rapidly flickering stimulus areas than to slowly flickering areas. He concluded from these and other facts, and in consideration of the poor analyzing power of the bee's eye, that flowers are visually effective for the bee in flight according to the gross effects of intermittent visual change rather than to their unitary figural patterns as such.

The specialized response of the bee is selectively determined first of all by the properties of the receptor and afferent-neural system and not a hypothetical neural releasing center. The afferent mechanism, a product of development, puts the organism directly into relationship with the kinds of external situation under which these mechanisms have evolved. Many other spontaneous responses of insects may depend comparably on receptor properties, for example as responses to air vibrations first depend upon the properties of chordotonal organs or related receptors in insects. The corresponding processes seem to be more adequately characterized as "sensing" than perceiving.

A promising contemporary theory of perception, that of Hebb (1949), describes a process through which cumulative neural organizations arise through further experience in external situations. Perception, the capacity for appropriately organized adjustments to the sensed situations according to their properties, is viewed as additive, starting virtually from zero and progressing to further specializations in dependence upon opportunities for experience and capacity for change through experience. Thus, rats raised in darkness need about six times as many trials as normally reared animals to master a discrimination of vertically from horizontally striped fields (Hebb, 1949). Comparable evidence for other vertebrates will be taken up presently. In the perceptual task itself, the configurational effect evidently is gained essentially through learning, aided in still unidentified ways by early experience.

One difficulty with terms such as *releaser* is their ambiguity. Even if this term could be limited to the elicitation of spontaneous reactions not dependent upon specific experience with the object involved, the concept of triggering off an innate neural coordination remains unsupported. Nor does "releaser" seem applicable to conditioned stimuli, which must be qualitatively different from those arousing spontaneous responses in their corresponding organic mechanisms, and not merely in the number of items as Baerends (1950) concludes. This view finds support in results to be considered.

Stimuli eliciting "spontaneous" reactions (thus termed for convenience) seem to be simple and generalized, not configurational. The ant guest, for example, does not appear to be initially attracted to the ants as stimulus constellations, but to effects such as odor. The conditions under which impulses through different sensory channels can be equivalent in evoking a common response, as described under the Seitz concept of heterogeneous summation (e.g., Tinbergen, 1951), are not clear. The best examples of this phenomenon seem to exist in the class of postural and locomotory control (e.g., Friedrich, 1932). More specialized types of adjustments often are dominated by specific afferent mechanisms, as in the plant responses of phytophagous insects, frequently odor-specific evidently by virtue of a biochemical aspect of the receptive process (Dethier, 1947).

The influence of afferent equipment in early behavior in higher vertebrates usually depends upon wider properties of the organism. In birds and mammals, the initial "naive" receptor-influenced responses in many cases soon become specialized in species-typical ways. For example, chicks and ducks show differences in their initial encounters with water, due in part, Schooland (1942) thinks, to differences in temperature sensitivity of the feet. Influenced by this afferent property, and also by visually-dependent pecking tendencies, a characteristic water-reaction soon becomes established in the first encounters. In the rise of incubation and nesting in birds (Tucker, 1943; Davis, 1945), a hormonally produced condition of seasonally increased tactual and temperature sensitivity in specialized ventral areas known as "brood patches" is considered basic. But a considerable amount of variable, random activity is required in the organically disturbed bird before the typical locality adjustments of nesting and incubation can be worked out (Craig, 1948; Lehrman, 1953). Comparably, a hormonally increased temperature sensitivity may be allotted a major role in the "working out" of nest-building activities in parturient rodents (Kinder, 1927).

Doubtless the relation of afferently determined susceptibilities to spontaneous reactions must be established for each type of organism, in terms of prevalent extrinsic conditions. Often the key effect is relatively simple. For example, the nestling herring gull typically pecks at the parent's bill in the feeding situation, and through tests with models Tinbergen and Perdeck (1950) found the critical factor to be a red patch on the adult bill. By varying the position of this spot on the models, these investigators found that the young bird would peck most readily when it was placed near the tip of the bill. The simplest interpretation would seem to be that the spot is effective according to its degree of prominence as a moving object, i.e., on the head it is moving axially and more slowly, near the bill tip circumferentially and faster.

In lower vertebrates, the controlling effect in spontaneous reactions seems more understandable in quantitative than in qualitative terms. Thus the visually-determined "lunge" responses common in fishes, amphibians and reptiles are elicited most effectively by moving stimuli of small area. Toads snap in dependence upon such properties and not the nature of the object (Honigmann, 1945; Freisling, 1948). Critical for the response seems to be energy of the delivered stimulus effect; thus toads snap at small moving objects with the tongue alone, at larger ones with the jaws assisted by the forelegs, but still larger ones bring withdrawal (Eibl-Eibesfeldt, 1952). Specific details may acquire a limited effectiveness as modifiers of the spontaneous response through conditioning (Schaeffer, 1911; Cott, 1936; Eibl-Eibesfeldt, 1952).

Facts such as the above suggest that the mechanism of a spontaneous reaction may depend upon some general organic relationship, such as a critical ratio between afferent, neural and effector thresholds. Deficiency in central nervous correlation capacity seems to be a prime condition, since stereotyped, spontaneous response tendencies are strongest in animals with the lowest supply of internuncial neurones. It may be the resultant dominance of specific peripheral conditions over simplified neural channels that makes spontaneous responses so resistant to reversal through conditioning. Ehrenhardt (1937) found that in its initial visual response, the lizard *Lacerta agilis* snapped most readily at figures with smooth outlines, least readily at those with more varied outlines (e.g., at squares as against circles). In conditioning tests, with stimuli close together in preference, although limited changes were possible, reactions to extremes such as circle versus cross could not be changed in as many as 850 trials. The neural changes of conditioning may thus be effectively resisted by the wider base of stereotyped response in the organism, fixed through organic development.

When the area of a stimulus model is varied experimentally, and the smallest sizes produce "feeding" responses, intermediate sizes "courting," and still larger sizes "fright" or "attack" (as is typical in fishes and many other lower vertebrates), the underlying response mechanisms would seem to have evolved in relation to the usual energy effects of the respectively different external situations. Thus there tends to be a correspondence in

different animals between body size and the magnitude of stimulus thresholds critical for the respective reactions.

The actual effect of a stimulus situation may elude identification through
the observer's tendency to offer a diagnosis dependent upon apparent
adaptive significance. There is a well-known experiment (Tinbergen,
1948, 1951) in which an airplane-shaped model of a "bird of prey"
elicited alarm and escape reactions from young nestling birds when
moved over them with the "short-neck" end first, but not when moved
"tail-first." This appears sensible since it is the way a man first recognizes
a hawk. But the initial effect on young birds may be simple and perceptually nonqualitative, perhaps a shock reaction produced by a sufficiently
abrupt stimulus change rather than anything more specific to a "bird of
prey flying overhead"—a hypothesis of mine discussed by Ginsberg
(1952). This idea finds support in a study by McNiven (1954) with
nestling young of various birds, which showed disturbance when an airplane-shaped model was moved rapidly overhead, but not when it moved
slowly, *whichever end was in advance.* The artifact method requires careful control against subjective impressions of what common external object
or situation the test model may represent to the animal. "Short-necked-
ness" in the above situation is a cue to the human observer, a perceptual
"sign" indicating an innate escape reaction to him but not necessarily to
the bird. The animal's actual relation to the situation and its developmental basis may be very different from what the "sign" interpretation
suggests.

The "isolation" technique is often considered a critical means of appraising the contributions of the normal environment to the species behavior pattern; and even as the one crucial way of separating "innate"
from "acquired" in behavior (e.g., Tinbergen, 1951). But actually, isolation may involve only a relative change from the situation typical for the
species (Riess, 1950). The effect of the "normal environment" is not
readily diagnosed, and the possibility must be considered that altered
situations (e.g., "isolation") may contain extrinsic effects more or less
equivalent to those, regarded as species-typical. Isolation merely shows
what responses may be obtained in divergent situations. For example,
Craig (1914) found that young male doves raised in isolation from species
mates, upon sexual maturity would give their mating responses to a
miscellany of objects, including the human hand or foot. Such results tell
us only that the "abnormal" stimuli are somehow equivalent to the normal
one, the species mate. The isolation technique, then, is essentially an
introductory means of finding what behavior can appear under different
conditions. But what the situation of isolation may have contributed to
the observed behavior may not be altogether different from what associations with species mates may contribute normally. In simple logic, the

"isolated" animal is not shut off from itself; it is obviously no less a member of its own species, and thus may present *to itself,* through the processes of its own development and self-stimulative associations, at least some of the influences which normally affect later species associations, as in mating. This must be determined experimentally.

Pattie (1936) reported an "innate gregarious tendency" in chicks raised in isolation; Howells and Vine (1940) described a limited differential association with species-mates in chicks raised with mice; and Schooland (1942) found a similar gregarious tendency in chicks raised with ducklings, interpreted not ". . . in terms of the differentiated environment," but ". . . as rooted in innate constitution." Does "constitution" as used here exclude environmental relationships after hatching? The possibility should be tested that the isolated chick, peeping in situations of organic relief as when fed or warmed, may "develop" a tendency to approach the source of such species-typical stimuli, hence species-mates in the tests. The "tendency" demonstrated in these studies is partial, relative, and quantitative. Such conceivable relationships are based on still earlier stages of development. An isolated chick even when satiated will resume pecking when pecking sounds are heard. By the criterion of isolation this response becomes "innate," but what is its actual basis?

Parr (1937) excludes the possibility of self-stimulative gains in an isolated fish, which, without appendages, cannot touch himself and thus become acquainted with his own body. Even occasional natural miror effects are excluded. The argument is that the psychological capacities of these lower vertebrates would not permit sufficient gain from occasional self-stimulative experiences to affect later associations with the animal's own kind. This seems reasonable with respect to total, integrated impressions, but should not be taken to exclude limited experiences through repetitive partial effects as with a self-produced chemical exuded under given conditions, or occasional direct glimpses of a specific part of the body or of the whole as an area. Although psychologically incapable of learning an organized self-reference perception, these lower vertebrates may be prepared through such partial experiences to react to species mates as more than "foreign objects." The value of such relationships through experience presumably is greater for most birds and more contributive still in mammals.

The psychological inferiority of lower vertebrates as compared with man in this respect, although difficult to appraise, is probably not absolute even when judged in terms of the adult stage. But it is great, since man, as Hallowell (1954) concludes, ". . . through language and reflective thought is able to integrate perceptions of his own body and his personal experience with a meaningful concept of self that is the common property of other groups of his society."

The difference no doubt is least marked when man is in the prelinguistic stage of his individual perceptual development, before a well-integrated self-perception of the "body-image" type has been established. Then his gains, more like those of his closer mammalian relatives, come through self-stimulative, environmentally linked contiguities experienced in connection with basic adaptive adjustments such as locomotion and feeding.

Developmental relationships are often judged too narrowly as concerns the distinction of maturational and experiential contributions. For instance, conceptions of the ontogeny of bird song have changed since the finding (Scott, 1902, 1904; Conradi, 1905) that singing in many species is influenced by early auditory experience. But other species have been viewed as independent of this factor, as in the roller canaries which Metfessel (1940) found singing recognizable parts of the species song after isolation from hatching. To say that the first type learns its song, the second type has the pattern innately, would be superficial. In Metfessel's isolated birds, organic factors in the development of singing are suggested by the "fatigue curve" trend of individual tours when graphed. The influence of self-hearing experience is suggested by the fact that the order of elements varied and was different from the normal; also, the song tended to be higher in pitch, the song elements were modified when tones were experimentally introduced, and later group experience changed all songs toward the median. The higher pitch may have been due to the fact that isolated birds, more excited and tense than socially-raised birds, produce and hear higher tones than do the latter.

We have postulated one common characteristic among all cases of development:

Namely, they come about through continuous interactions between intraorganic developmental processes (maturation) and the effects of extrinsic conditions (experience). Hypothetically, gains from experience may represent very different types of process, contrasting orders of organization, from direct physiological effects of limited scope to the most advanced patterns of learning. The lowest orders of interaction predominate at early developmental stages; qualitatively more advanced orders (including learning) enter later, based on the accomplishments of preceding stages. The phyla, and the vertebrate classes, differ in their respective capacities for reaching higher orders in maturation, in experience, and in the interrelationships of these (Schneirla, 1949). Therefore, learning cannot be viewed as superimposed upon the effects of maturation and sharply separable from them; rather, these processes occur together in close interaction. But since learning subsumes earlier developmental processes and often therefore represents larger changes, its effects tend to be more discernible than those of simpler orders of experience.

How shall we differentiate gains through learning from other gains through experience as defined above? Attempts to distinguish learning from other processes in development presuppose a more exact knowledge of learning and its organic basis than we now have (Hebb, 1953). Cases of learning, simple or complex, seem all to involve the experiencing of sensory contiguities which modify individual behavior by effecting neural changes. But neither S-R theories with their rigid formula, nor cognition theories with their looser one, have been validated for phyletic comparisons or for individual ontogeny on any phyletic level (Schneirla, 1952a). A theory postulating more than one qualitative process of learning is required. Thus Maier and Schneirla (1935) distinguished conditioned-response patterns from selective (trial-and-error) learning, in that the animal's response in the latter case is fixated in dependence upon changes in the motivational situation. Then, on further evidence, they (1942) distinguished an afferent-afferent type of conditioning from the better known afferent-motor (classical, Pavlovian) pattern, the latter being more wholistic in that a specific change is effected in response control.

In the lowest animal phyla, experience, as we have defined it, is limited to simple, directly effective maturational relationships with learning never involved as a factor. In higher phyla, improved capacities for neural correlation admit learning to varying and increasingly broader roles in behavior development. But attempts to distinguish a stage in ontogeny at which "learning begins," and to separate learning from maturation, are based upon classical notions of learning tailored from the study of adult stages. Simpler forms of change through experience may prevail early in ontogeny, basic to conventionally recognizable signs of learning in later stages. Kuo's pioneer findings indicate how earlier stages may lead into later stages. The earliest changes (as through proprioceptive-tactual contiguities), although variable, imprecise and very slowly cumulative, may nevertheless promote improvements in neural organization essential to the normal succession of stages. Present techniques, although useful to demonstrate what animals can be conditioned in later stages of ontogeny, are insufficient for more than vague glimpses of the form and scope of the process, and admit no view of its antecedent conditions.

Hatching or birth means appearance into a new and complex environment, the occasion for novel behavioral acquisitions arising through a new set of relationships between maturation, growth attainments, and experience. The new environment is a variable, heterogeneous one, only partially equivalent to the former relatively monotonous embryonic setting, and presents new contiguities which promote some striking changes. In many of the changes in birds and mammals, further accessions follow a predictable course in which learning is an essential component. A striking example is the phenomenon which Lorenz (1935) described as "imprinting," after his observation that young goslings, exposed only to the experimenter in the period just after hatching and kept away from species mates, would thereafter follow him but not adult geese. Cushing and Ramsay (1949) were able to form heterospecific groups by placing young birds with a foster mother (e.g., bob-white quail with a Bantam hen) directly after hatching from an incubator. Fabricius (1951), studying imprinting in ducklings of various species, found that the initially effective visual stimulus was not specific, but concerned movement of the attractive object and its parts, and particularly movement-away. A generalized initial effect is indicated by the fact that the size of the "foster parent" could vary within wide limits and that sound (soft, rhythmic effects) was needed in many cases. The imprinted following-reaction to the experimenter was often interfered with by a tendency to retreat. This effect was found to increase steadily after hatching, which may account for the fact that the period of effective imprinting is relatively short and typically limited to the first few hours after hatching. In some species such interference operates from the start, as Lorenz found with the incubator hatched young of wading birds such as curlews. Turning-to reactions thus may be considered products of prehatching stages which at hatching are elicited by "unconditioned" stimuli of a very generalized nature but with the common property of relatively low intensity. In contrast, stimuli of higher intensity (e.g., "disturbances" such as sudden movements), elicit escape reactions (Schneirla, 1939, 1949). The specific stimuli which may acquire a conditioned control over such reactions through early contiguities may produce fixations for inanimate as well as for living objects (Thorpe, 1944; Fabricius, 1951). As Whitman (1919) and Craig (1914) reported for pigeons, in some species later affiliations (e.g., in mating preferences) depend almost entirely upon the early environment and contiguities it may introduce. This seems to be a relative matter (Cushing and Ramsay, 1941), since in many others barriers exist which Cushing (1941) attributed to "genetically controlled factors." These are developmentally-furnished effects, presumably related first of all to species size and other gross morphological characteristics, to which correspond through evolution the thresholds for arousal of "unconditioned" turning-to or withdrawal reactions, respectively.

Evidence on the effects of early experience in later behavior of birds and mammals is summarized by Beach and Jaynes (1954). It is probable that such lists will be enlarged and their meaning clarified when our conceptions improve as to how still earlier experience antedates and prepares for learning, and how these processes are related to maturation in vertebrate ontogeny. As an example, Tinbergen and Kuenen (1939) concluded that the initial visual arousal of the gaping reaction in nestling thrushes is due to excitation of an innate releasing mechanism, independent of experience. But Lehrman (1953) questions this interpretation from his studies in our laboratory with nestling red-winged blackbirds. In these birds, as in the thrush, the eyes open for an interval during the latter phase of gaping at the stage when this reaction is still *initiated* only by mechanical stimuli. Visual movement then would augment the response, as would any other stimulus to which the young bird was sensitive. This may be a nonspecific neural irradiative effect. But through this summative effect, an object (e.g., the parent) regularly present and visible at such times may, in its specific visual properties, come to initiate and control the response in later stages. This would seem to explain why, when the "visual releaser" stage is reached, the stimuli which Tinbergen and Kuenen consider "innate" have pattern features like those of an adult outlined above the nest edge. For this process, which actually seems to be a case of conditioning, it is important that from the start feeding accompanies each repetition of the critical stimulus combination (Craig, 1913).

Gains through early experience are likely to be elusive and only indirectly identifiable. In Siegel's (1953) study carried out in our laboratory with ring doves, the heads of young doves were encased in translucent hoods from 3 days of age, starting before the eyes opened, and the birds were fed by hand. Opportunity for visual form definition was thereby excluded to the time of testing as young adults, although there was normal stimulation by light. Then, in learning to discriminate a circle and triangle by jumping from a perch (a response previously conditioned to contact), the experimental doves were inferior to normal subjects, both in the original learning and in further transfer tests. (Condition of the eye and visual acuity seemed normal in the hood-reared birds, which behaved equivalently to normal birds in optomotor tests). Thus in ring doves, experience somehow provides a perceptual basis essential for form perception and discrimination in the adult.

Nissen, Chow and Semmes (1951) deprived a young chimpanzee of opportunities for tactual and manipulative experience, first by binding the arms, then from the fifth week by encasing all four extremities in tubes. When the impediments were removed at 31 months, the animal although not noticeably deficient in general visual discrimination was very inferior to normal subjects in various tests of tactual-motor coordination and in discriminating touched points on the body. In the following four months these reactions improved, but some deficiences persisted. Grooming behavior and the sounds normally accompanying it were absent throughout. The chimpanzee's normal tactual adjustments to its own body evidently are established through action in experience, as Werner (1940) finds for the human infant. The absence of grooming would suggest an impaired capacity for social adjustment, based on deficient self-stimulative experience in early life.

Hebb (1949) theorized that early experience benefits later learning in the widest sense, and that the benefit is inversely proportional to age. This idea finds support in numerous studies (Bingham and Griffiths, 1952; Forgays and Forgays, 1952; and Fuller, 1953). Thompson and Heron (1954) raised Scottish terriers under home conditions and later compared them with litter mates moderately or severely restricted in their upbringing, in performance on barrier, delayed-reaction, and other tests. Scores were higher in relation to degree of freedom from restriction in early life. Although the deficit was not specifically defined, the restricted animals seemed handicapped by deficiencies in early perceptual experience rather than by a specific motor impairment. Birch (1945) has shown that chimpanzees lacking the specific earlier experience of "extending" the arm with perceived foreign objects are seriously backward in their ability to use sticks insightfully in later reasoning tests.

The environment does not merely elicit preorganized mechanisms of behavioral adjustment, but is itself implicated in the development of such mechanisms. Isolation experiments do not tell us what is native in the normal patterns, for *if the animal survives,* the atypical situation also must have contributed to the development of some adaptive pattern. For each organism, a range of environmental situations exists, variously deviant from the normal or typical, in which may arise functional patterns sufficiently adaptive for survival. Techniques of the "isolation" type thus concern relative-abnormality-of-setting rather than isolation in the full sense, and help tell us how far extrinsic conditions may be changed at a particular developmental stage without preventing or altering further development based on the gains of preceding stages.

The "innate differential" of Howells and Vine (1940) we may paraphrase something like this:

Under given extrinsic conditions, admitting given types of experiences to interact with maturational attainments at any stage, some behavior patterns develop more readily than others in each type of organism. The relative case or difficulty in obtaining any result is a function both of the species genic constitution and of conditions under which a development may be completed. Since, within limits characteristic of the species, different configurations can develop according to the prevailing extrinsic context, the latter factor must be throughout an indispensable contributor to the rise of a functionally organized system.

Postulation of an original isomorphism, or a functional correspondence of stimulus and reaction, presupposes a preformed organization. But the behavior organization eventually obtained is, from the considerations raised, a developmental product and not one that exists initially as a potential or miniature schema. The eventual relations of stimulation or perception to adaptive behavior can arise only through the conjunction of a whole set of conditions requiring interactions of the endogenous and exogenous at all stages. Instead of expanding from a miniature anlage, a behavior pattern must become synthesized through progressive sets of relationships, and real functional isomorphism is an end product. It is not forecast, but requires the cumulative interactions of many factors in the developmental processes of which the species is capable in the given milieu.

If the developmental capacities of the species permit, one or another neurophysiological organization may arise according to the extrinsic context. Thereby, part-processes such as local reflex-like functions, introduced through development, may be incorporated in wider patterns as nuclear or as peripheral components (Kuo, 1939; Windle, 1940, 1950). The role of implicated factors may vary greatly according to species. Often an afferent factor is crucial, as in spontaneous reactions to visual movement. In the cat, as Kuo (1930) has shown, this factor is nuclear for the rise of the typical reaction to rodents: pouncing and killing. But it is only one component, and the pattern does not arise in its typical form unless circumstances in early infancy admit other factors (as the pounce; claws, jaws and teeth—drawing blood, tasting, biting and eating) for which the kitten is also structurally fitted through normal development. In the typical environs, these combinations are almost certain to rise through experience, permitting the quick formation of an integrated pattern. But, as we have seen, by modifying early experience Kuo was able to produce the patterns of attacking rodents, avoiding them, or living peaceably with them. Are these alternative patterns all to be considered innate for cats? (Crafts et al., 1938).

PLASTIC DEVELOPMENTAL RELATIONSHIPS IN MAMMALS

On the mammalian level, where successive stages in ontogeny involve the most diversified relationships of maturation and experience in the animal series, variability and plasticity take on new meanings for behavior. Here we find the greatest involvement of *feedback* processes—a convenient term for relationships in which the functions and activities (i.e., the output) of an organism affect the further course of events in the system that produced them.

There are great differences both in nature and in degree in the capacities of various mammals for such relationships at different ontogenetic stages. Carnivores for instance are doubtless much more limited shortly after birth than ungulates; when the former are still low in sensory, neural correlation, and other capacities, the latter relatively mature with prompt use of visual sensitivity and quadrupedal locomotion (Cruikshank, 1946). Early adjustments in newborn puppies center predominantly around reactions to a "tactile deficit" (James, 1952); kittens improve within the first few hours in finding the mother and their individual feeding stations, utilizing sensory effects gained actively through the individual's own movements (Rosenblatt et al., unpubl.). As these processes vary, we should expect to find important differences in behavior development at later stages (e.g., mating). For cats, as scattered reports indicate for other mammals, an early life apart from species mates accounts for later inhibition of mating reactions, in part through disturbed reactions to "strangeness." Kagan and Beach (1953) found that later sexual responsiveness was significantly limited in male rats held to brief bisexual encounters with species mates in early life, evidently through the disrupting effect of "playful responses."

In mammals, previous experience is closely associated with other age-conditioned variables in affecting developments at later stages (Beach and Jaynes, 1954). There is little doubt that Holt's (1931) conception of self-stimulative relationships in such trace effects will find ample confirmation (Schneirla, 1946, 1949). Many experiences related to this class, influential in later behavioral development, doubtless are gained through the animal's activities in relation to objects and situations apart from its own body. Riess (1950) reports that female rats deprived of early experience with movable objects are deficient maternally, building no definite nests, retrieving young and artifacts seemingly alike, and losing their young through deficient suckling. Carrying of young by the parent, a widespread pattern of behavior in mammals (Causey and Waters, 1936), may depend to an appreciable extent upon previous individual stimulative relationships.

To test the influence of self-stimulative experience in the development of an adaptive pattern normally appearing in maturity, Birch (unpubl.) reared young female rats provided with wide rubber collars worn continually until their first parturition. The rats adapted well to their collars and gained weight normally, although these accessories prevented touching or licking the posterior body including the genitalia, which were licked frequently in the controls. In 13 of 14 observed parturitions with experimental rats, all of the young were lost through cannibalism or neglect. Chewing at unconsumed bodies was common. In the remaining case, 9 of 11 young (rather fortuitously) survived parturition, but most of these were killed by the mother before the 14th day, when the last two died of inanition. These young were at a disadvantage for nursing through being gathered forward under the mother's body instead of being pushed posteriorly in the normal way.

The collars may have deprived these rats of self-stimulative relationships essential for normal parturitive behavior. (Control rats with collars just as heavy but narrower, permitting stimulative access to the posterior body, behaved normally in parturition.) One distorted factor in the experimental rats might be physiological, a deficiency in salt metabolism; another psychological, concerning a self-perception normally gained through adjustments established to the animal's own body in youth. It is possible that normally, a sufficient stimulative equivalence of the newborn pups to the genitalia, which the female has learned earlier to lick but not bite, would prevent cannibalism; but that without this perceptual adjustment the experimental mothers readily chewed and ate their young. An interesting item is the normal huddling which facilitates nursing. Ordinarily, tactual stimulation from the young causes the mother to maintain and to increase their pressure against her. This reaction is impelled not only through the female's augmented ventral sensitivity, an effect of hormonal processes in pregnancy and parturition, but also through a perceptual adjustment learned in previous grooming and licking of the posterior body and the genital area in particular.

Although no preestablished neural organizer is indicated for parturitive behavior, on the basis of hormonally-induced organic changes and through the intervention of learned perceptual adjustments an adaptive pattern may be integrated. The experience factor here is not the specific practice of a preexisting pattern, since it involves not the young themselves but perceptual effects having an appreciable stimulative equivalence to the young. Uyldert (1946) found that specific experience with young is also beneficial. Virgin females made pseudopregnant with high estrogen were given opportunities to lick, nurse, and tactually encounter young rats. When later tested in their primiparous behavior in comparison with animals lacking previous experience with young, the experimental animals brought through all of their young in 88% of the cases, whereas only 11% of the control animals did so.

Our studies on normal parturitive behavior in rats and domestic cats (Tobach et al., unpubl.) are relevant to this discussion. We are led to characterize the event, for cats, as an interplay or even competition between the stimulative effects of endogenous events (e.g., uterine contractions, emergence of fetus) and the external results of such events (e.g., fluids, neonate). These stimulative by-products of organic processes tend to intrude themselves upon the female's attention in a somewhat variable order, timing and duration. Each one, as it arises, demands a specific perceptual and behavioral adjustment on her part. The parturitive phenomenon here is not a regular, patterned flow of events, but a series of rather sporadic organic and behavioral episodes, together with variable activities not specifically parturitive in themselves. Thus the female exhibits, in a not very predictable order, the predictable items of self-licking, licking newborn or floor, eating after-birth, general movement and sitting or lying. Intervals of intense activity indicating a high level of excitement, *a condition facilitating delivery operations,* are interspersed with intervals of exhaustion and rest, *facilitating initiation of nursing and other stimulative relations of mother and newborn.*

In these mammals parturitive behavior is indicated as a loose assemblage of functions centering around the stimulative consequences of organic events. A sequence of hormonally-induced endogenous changes sets a loose temporal order for behavioral adjustment, dependent in sequence and timing upon the female's variable attention to competing organic and environmental stimuli. Persistently in evidence is an orientation to the posterior body and particularly the vaginal area, a perceptual set which enormously aids normal parturitive operations. This factor, presumably based upon self-stimulative experience in youth, is very possibly indispensable for an adaptive outcome and survival of the young.[1]

Reciprocal stimulative relationships between parent and young may provide the unifying basis for a progressive organization of behavioral adjustments in the litter situation. Such relationships initiated in parturition may be sustained both by the physiological condition of the lactating mother and the organically enforced sensory susceptibilities of the young. Within a few days the mother evidences an appreciable discriminative specialization in stimulative interchanges with the young, pointing up her strong attachment to them. And on their side the kittens, as our studies (Rosenblatt et al., unpubl.) indicate, acquire individualized adjustments to the mother (tending, for example, to nurse at specific nipples) which begin within a few hours after delivery. There is much to be said for the theory that maternal reactions in mammals develop and become motivated on the basis of stimulative relationships ("trophallaxis"—Schneirla, 1946, 1949) between parent and young.

Doubtless, afferent susceptibilities initiating and promoting "trophallactic" behavior, together with organic tensions underlying and maintaining the pattern, may be traced back to hormonal processes. But the relationships are more than unidirectional. The existence of feedback relationships in the pattern is indicated by evidence that the endocrine conditions themselves are facilitated and reinforced by stimulation received in routine litter operations, as in nursing (Selye, Collip and Thompson, 1934; Selye and McKeown, 1934; Leblond and Nelson, 1937; Uyldert, 1946; Beach, 1948).

---

[1] Labriola (1953) confirmed the finding of Wiesner and Sheard that female rats display maternal behavior after their young have been delivered by caesarean operation. Nest-building and retrieving can occur, he finds, without the actual process of parturition and associated events such as cleaning young, consuming after-birth, and lactating normally. Since further care of young is not reported, the full effect of the omitted events in the normal process cannot be gauged. Nor has this experiment eliminated the experiential factors indicated by Birch's results as crucial for an adaptive pattern. Labriola's conclusion that the "hormonal changes associated with pregnancy and its termination" can directly and solely in themselves produce maternal behavior, seems premature. Rather, these factors would seem to act as partial contributants to a more inclusive and complex process.

Processes accounting for the usual cessation of maternal behavior at weaning are not well understood. It is possible that age-conditioned behavioral changes in the young so reduce the mother's afferent input from trophallactic processes as to cause a sharp fall in the endocrine secretions maintaining her litter reactions. This change in turn may reduce the female's afferent susceptibilities sufficiently to admit other hormonal processes favoring different behavior (e.g., high estrone promoting heat). Such changes presumably interfere with organic tensions in the mother which evidence (Wiesner and Sheard, 1933; Uyldert, 1946) indicates are normally conditioned to stimulation from the young.

An interesting instance of how the mother's organic processes and behavior may relate to the young is offered by Martins (1949). Some female dogs, in the last stages of lactation and for a few days after weaning, following a meal at a distance from the nest, disgorge regularly in the presence of the pups on returning to the nest. An adaptive relation to weaning is evident, since the pups eat the regurgitated material. Martins suggests an endocrine control for the act; but it is also clear that perception of the young, related to litter experience, also plays a critical part. Regurgitation occurs on the female's return to the nest, but may be inhibited for as long as an hour if the pups are not there, with the mother disgorging promptly when they appear.

Peripheral processes not only contribute to the rise of the components but may also facilitate integration in the "instinctive behavior" of mammals. In sexual behavior, for example, cutaneous stimulation has an important function in promoting activities just before and during coitus (Beach, 1951). In rodents, stroking the rump produces lordosis in hormonally aroused females, and genital stimulation contributes heavily to effective mating behavior in both sexes (Bard, 1939; Beach, 1951). It has been maintained (Lashley, 1938) that the behavior pattern is produced through the priming action of hormones on a surrogate neural mechanism, with peripheral (nonnervous) components playing incidental roles. But the possibility exists that the afferent system is intimately involved in the systemic organization. This is suggested by findings like that of Dusser de Barenne and Koskoff (1934) that male cats with cords sectioned just above the lumbar region responded to stimulation of the penis with gross movements resembling intercourse. Since these movements are not only aroused but maintained for a time, an appreciable measure of interplay is indicated between efferent components, nervous centers (e.g., the sacral autonomic system) and local afferent mechanisms as agents in the production of organized behavior.

The investigations of Kruchinsky (1947) indicate a critical peripheral factor in the pelvic-thrust response of the rabbit's copulatory pattern, involving afferent connections of penis and urethra. In pretested male rats castrated and then given regular injections of testosterone in different amounts, Beach and Holz-Tucker (1949) obtained a sex-responsiveness score directly corresponding to the amount of hormone received. The experiment was extended by Beach and Levinson (1950), who found a positive correlation between hormone dosage and the number of receptor papillae in the skin of the penis in experimental subjects. These findings may be taken to suggest hormone effects both in central nervous processes and in peripheral mechanisms relevant to sex behavior.

Although reproductive behavior is grounded on the effects of strong hormonal and related organic processes in development, cortical resources admitting learning as a component increase steadily through the mammals (Beach, 1947, 1951). Even in rodents and lower mammals, this function is indicated. Rosenblatt (1953) found that early experience increases hormonal effects promoting mating in castrated male cats; Warren (1954) reported comparable results with hamsters. Appearance of the mating pattern in previously isolated rodents (Beach, 1942) does not rule out experience as a contributor to the normal pattern, on grounds already mentioned. Partial or complete failure of mating in cats visually and tactually isolated from their kind during early life may signify a larger role of learning than in rodents, perhaps magnified by perceptual emotional components. Here also, the learning factor, as distinguished from the influence of developed organic functions, resists disentangling in its specific contributions.

Results reported by Kent and Liberman (1949) seem to offer direct support for a "neural priming" hypothesis. Doses of progesterone too small to produce "psychic estrus" when given subcutaneously to spayed estrogen-primed female hamsters, brought typical mating responses when injected directly into the lateral ventricle of the brain. On this basis the investigators suggest that ". . . progesterone may act directly upon one or more neural nuclei, facilitating, in an unknown manner, the manifestation of reflex mating activity in the female hamster, thus effecting the physiological state known as psychic estrus."

But in our laboratory Warren and Rosenblatt (unpubl.), to test the possibility that the Kent-Liberman results may have resulted at least in part from a peripheral or non-nervous differential, injected groups of spayed female hamsters equivalently in the lateral ventricle of the brain, the jugular vein, and subcutaneous tissues. From the results, the factor of differential absorption of hormone into the blood stream (depending on injection site) must be taken into account before results such as those of Kent and Liberman can be interpreted with respect to a hypothetical priming effect on nerve centers.

Available evidence recommends considering the mating pattern as resulting from the interactions of several organic systems. Factors in the excitation and function of specific components and in the organization of the inclusive pattern are not necessarily identical. With respect to the latter, extirpative experiments significantly indicate that in rats the cortex is not directly involved in the integration of mating behavior, but rather facilitates lower centers essential to the responses, in the male although not strongly in the female (Beach, 1952). The possibility is not excluded that cortical facilitation may influence both central and peripheral mechanisms as well as their integration in this behavior.

Another interesting case is the micturition pattern of the dog. This response appears as a squatting posture in young animals and adult females but as elevation of one rear leg in adult males (Berg, 1944). The adult male response is displaced in castrated males by the female-young squatting posture, but testosterone restores it (Martins and Valle, 1948); at discontinuance of injection, however, the squat returns (Berg, 1944). A direct hormonal action on a surrogate neural mechanism might seem indicated; but Clark (1945), in a consideration of the neurological evidence, found conflicting results and appealed for behavioral analysis. Freud and Uyldert (1948) investigated the fact that leg elevation follows object-sniffing, and on the side toward which sniffing occurs. (The urine of females in heat is especially potent for eliciting this response—Beach and Gilmore, 1949). Since leg elevation can occur with or without release of urine, the afferent effect seems important. Osmoanesthesia abolished leg elevation and produced the squatting pattern in four-fifths of the trials, with the male posture returning on recovery from the anesthetic. From their evidence, the authors regard the micturition pattern as a conditioned response involving both the connections of olfactory receptors and the bladder proprioceptors. Without these afferent limbs the adult male pattern cannot function, and in their absence during ontogeny it is possible that this distinctive pattern could never arise. The action of hormones, in addition to possibly arousing or priming nervous centers involved, thus may extend more widely in the organism to afferent mechanisms essential for such behavior.

Problems of behavioral organization such as these converge in the study of motivation. Simply definable as the impulsion of behavior, motivation in different animals is not soluble in simple, one-process terms. Although the ontogeny of motivation in mammals is still incompletely glimpsed, many of the difficulties doubtless stem from a concentration on adult stages, for at different ages organic tensions may be related very differently to external conditions. Motivational processes certainly are no exception to the rule that plasticity in using organic mechanisms varies with learning capacity. Hebb (1949) postulates proportionately greater gains from early experience than later, but for adequate comparison more evidence is needed. The first step is to analyze the ontogenetic background. For example, food deprivation in youth increases food-hoarding in adult rats (Hunt, 1941), but the nature of the trace effect is still obscure. Perhaps related is the fact that, after regular experiences of thirst and hunger during infancy, rats as adults learn the location of food and water more readily than do normal subjects (Christie, 1952). Related to physiological aspects of the problem, such findings suggest a subtle perceptual factor in the development of motivation, perhaps similar to that already suggested in the case of maternal behavior.

Visceral processes are undoubtedly basic to motivated behavior, yet the relationship has been incompletely explored (Bard, 1939). Emphasis upon the complexity of motivational processes in any mammal suggests a close attention to ontogenetic advances under the influence of contrasting experiences. No visceral mechanism seems immune to a conditioned extrinsic control (Crafts et al., 1938, Chap. 18), although such processes are not as readily modified through conditioning as are so-called voluntary reactions. Trace effects may influence motivation on very different levels of qualitative organization and complexity.

Although visceral processes are considered subsequent energizers of organized motivated behavior, other than in respiration and circulation they are arhythmic at birth, as Carlson and Ginsburg (1916) demonstrated for stomach contractions in the dog. Later, however, visceral rhythms develop in relation to new functions such as feeding, or come under external control (Seward and Seward, 1937). In the neonate as in the embryonic mammal, visceral activities are considered a chief source of the characteristic generalized, diffuse activity then prodominant (Carmichael, 1951). A radical distinction may be necessary in the external relevance of these tensions according to stage. Initially, visceral tensions evidently serve as indiscriminate excitants, *deficiency conditions* or *lacks* produced by a shortage of some metabolic ingredient. Only later, when specific relationships of incentive-bound types develop between them and external conditions, may the respectively different visceral deficiency-processes be referred to as "needs." It is probable that a *need,* or motivating-tension with incentive relevance, cannot exist prior to learning through experience.

The term "striving," which implies an object- or goal-relevance in energized behavior, seems applicable therefore only to motivated behavior at later stages of ontogeny. The basic condition is an internal disruption which, while it is in operation, keeps the animal active. In the naive animal the aroused behavior tends to be strikingly variable and persistent, and these characteristics, together with the typical adaptiveness of the outcome, account for the insistence of many authors that all motivated behavior is "purposive." But later behavior can be very different according to how the exciting tensions have been removed or changed on previous occasions and in dependence upon limiting factors peculiar to the ontogenetic stage.

The relation of the neonate mammal to its situation is facilitated in the direction of an adaptive outcome by the proximity and behavior of the mother—whether she bites instead of licking, pushes the newborn forward or backward with respect to her body, and the like. As our studies on the cat indicate, a variety of circumstances in the initial relationship of neonate and mother facilitate the first occurrence of sucking. The newborn is brought into abdominal contact partly through maternal complicity, as in licking, partly by its own crude orienting responses to parentally-furnished tactual and thermal stimulus gradients. A process is thereby initiated whereby the kitten's essentially reflex sucking response becomes the focus around which a more inclusive adaptive pattern can arise. Similar roles often played by specific reflex mechanisms cannot be overlooked (Maier and Schneirla, 1935, Chaps. 6, 11 and 12; Kennedy, 1954). For integration of stimuli and responses into a pattern the crucial occurrence is reduction of the disturbing organic tensions through sucking. The feeding adjustment of the neonate to the mother, initially random and lacking in organization, thus may become specialized as a process of food motivation.

In the neonate, the responses which resolve the drive episode soon become organized thereby into an elementary striving, a crude perceptual adjustment to extrinsic conditions which acquire incentive valence. Repeated combinations of organic tensions and given activities alleviating them increase the directive potency of stimuli recurring at such times. For the kittens, the mother's characteristics, and for the mother, those of the kittens, become strong incentives. In the kitten, an initially random behavior when "hungry" is replaced by efficient responses to incentives leading to resumption of a habituated postural relationship to the mother and consummation at an individually preempted nipple. Thus a randomly disturbing organic "lack" acquires an externalized perceptual relevancy and becomes a motivating "need."

Different principles seen to be involved in behavior changes at later ontogenetic stages. Although the parturient female rodent or cat is not initially capable of patterned adjustments, her behavior is predictably influenced in direction by organic changes, by external circumstances, and by the effects of previous experience. As the Birch "collar" experiment indicates, a preexisting perceptual factor can influence a trend toward an adaptive combination of these various initially disconnected elements. There are also organic factors which, in their external effects, facilitate the integration of a pattern. One is the licking reaction, which after delivery readily transfers from self-trophallactic reactions to genitalia to amniotic fluids, sac and then to newborn. The equivalence seems purely chemotropic, yet, to an appreciable extent because they bear the fluids, the newborn can become specifically attractive objects, incentives which increase in motivational potency the more they accompany afferent satisfactions and tension-relief.

In the rat's nest-making, as in parturition, a hormonally produced set of organic tensions dominates the animal's activity, and under typical conditions, also can enter into externalized relationships such that an adaptive adjustment to the situation must work itself out. The induced physiological condition and increased sensitivity of ventral surfaces accounts for a temperature reactivity critical for the termination of operations in a situation called a "nest" (Kinder, 1927). In variable activities aroused through heat-loss disturbance, materials are carried and pushed about until an organism-situation relationship exists in which the animal is quieted through sufficient reduction of the disturbing afferent condition (Lashley, 1949). The behavior is not altogether random; for one thing because, as Riess' results indicate, in the absence of earlier object-experience the materials might be handled differently with maladaptive results. Dependence of environmental susceptibilities upon organic condition is emphasized by Richter's (1942) experiment in which the critical afferent condition was introduced hormonally through removing the thyroid or pituitary gland, thereby bringing about nest-building in rats of either sex.

Presumably each type of motivation may be considered a pattern that develops through progressive interrelationships between organism and environment. Hunger is an example of one complex system. Although initially and basically it depends upon gastric contractions (Wada, 1922; Patterson, 1933), food-striving may later exist independently of stomach contractions (Bash, 1939; Morgan and Stellar, 1950). For some time it has been known that, as in the dog (Carlson and Ginsburg, 1916), hunger contractions of the empty stomach decrease with age. This change with age may parallel increases in the process Anderson (1941) terms "drive externalization," in which incentives can arouse the drive independently of internal facilitation. The relationship of organic tensions to activities and their various stimulative agents must normally become specialized in mammals according to individual experience with responses changing or removing tensions under specific stimulus conditions. Thus Harris et al. (1933) found that rats deficient in vitamin B1 could learn a preference for food rich in this vitamin, provided that such food was distinctively flavored in discrimination-learning. The cocoa flavor used then became a controlling property of the incentive.

The complexity of motivation is seen when the act occurs in a situation that seems biologically inappropriate for it, as in "displacement activity," (Armstrong, 1950) when feeding activity occurs in a presumed "mating" situation, or the reverse. This reminds us that presumably different "consummatory" reactions may be closely related basically. Similar autonomic functions may underlie differently motivated acts, as for example stroking a satiated cat may initiate cranio-sacral activity capable of supporting either a rearousal of feeding or a rubbing against the hand. Thus under appropriate conditions the special stimuli for different responses based upon a given autonomic function may exhibit an appreciable equivalence. The explanation, it would seem, lies in the ontogeny of motivational patterns.

The pattern of motivation characteristic of a species must develop through progressive functional relationships between organism and environment. The adult patterns are most complex and plastic in mammals, yet even here, although experience is a factor of importance, the function of learning is not readily separable. Most accessible to description are specific conditioning episodes, in which a new or conditioned stimulus can be discerned in temporal contiguity with an unconditioned stimulus. In such cases, the latter is called "unlearned" in the sense that it produces the critical response (e.g., feeding) somehow as an outcome of earlier development. Even less distinguishable are the old and the new in trial-and-error or selective learning, and particularly at early ages, as in the shifting of appetites at weaning. The solution seems to lie in closer study of ontogeny, with less arbitrary separation of "innate" from "acquired" influences.

The traditional instinct problem has much in common with that of motivation, in that both require a theory which can account wholistically for behavioral organization through development. The former emphasizes genetic constitution, but this is also central to motivation study, in which the role of organic factors is apparent at all stages. Although Hebb (1949) mistrusts configurational theories because they have neglected the experience factor, this is by no means an essential gap in them, but one that can be repaired by a systematic attention to ontogeny (Werner, 1940; Birch, 1945).

The analysis of behavior patterns in relation to hereditary background, or "psychogenetics," although potentially valuable, is "as yet more a promise than an actuality" (Hall, 1951). Useful beginnings have been made in the description of correspondences between phenotypic behavioral traits and genes (e.g., Keèler and King, 1942; Fuller, 1953). But such facts emphasize the need for analytical studies of ontogeny to avoid an over-simplification of both genetic mechanisms and developmental processes through which these exert their effects. The gaps between genes and somatic characters are great; those between genes and behavior, which are greater still, can be bridged only by studies directed at understanding the intervening variables and their interrelationships. Earlier notions of a one-to-one relationship between these agencies and their effects have fallen away before advances in physiological genetics.

As an example, the general characteristic "wildness" broadly differentiates many animal species. Each species has its characteristic "flight distance" (Hediger, 1950), only relatively reducible through taming. Strain differences may be demonstrated in rats, with "wild" dominant over "tame" (Yerkes, 1913; Dawson, 1932; Keeler, 1942). Other studies (Donaldson, 1928; Yeakel and Rhoades, 1941; Richter, 1952) point to the adrenal gland as foremost among somatic factors basic to this behavior character. This discovery improves upon the statement that the behavior trait is hereditary, yet merely points up the need for analysis of the developmental processes producing the gland in the milieu of early ontogeny, on the one hand, and of its functional relationships in behavior on the other. To this system there are contributants of many kinds, including even learning, as indicated by the fact that experience in being reared with a mother or other species mates which are relatively "wild" promotes wildness in young rats (Rasmussen, 1939).

Genetic influences in the development of behavior characters can be exerted only indirectly, as we have seen for various phyletic levels, through the mediation of organismic processes requiring the interaction of given intrinsic and extrinsic conditions. The traditional dichotomy of heredity and environment promotes a fundamental misstatement of these matters. Rather, the picture is one of a typical species ontogeny in which a flux of relationships exists between the developing organism and the species environment, differing with the conditions of each developmental stage. Aspects of behavior may be termed "genetic" only in the sense that they come about through the ontogenetic processes of the different species or strains under their respective typical developmental conditions.

Two points will bear final emphasis. First, the tendency to oversimplify statements of genetic-behavioral correspondences on the strength of their heuristic value, as for taxonomy, may lead to serious misrepresentation. Thus with respect to one conception of reproductive isolation, Clark, Aronson and Gordon (1954) point out that this condition is not a simple lock-and-key mechanism controlled by a few genes, merely because a striking character of structure or behavior may often seem to be *the* critical factor isolating two species. Actually, there are complex patterns composed of many small characteristic differences. Many inherited characters, most of which are probably overlooked, are undoubtedly involved. Genotypically, these accumulations of small differences, which probably underlie determinations such as behavioral isolating mechanisms (Muller, 1940), despite their multiple and complex nature may be easier to build up than a single-factor basis (Mayr, 1948). And on the phenotypic side, only confusion is added and problems obscured when a single alleged crucial intervening variable is postulated, such as a preorganized neural mechanism, a function not sufficiently known to have theoretical validity.

The second point concerns the validity of interphyletic extrapolations of common mechanisms based upon broad adaptive similarities in behavior. It is probable, for example, that major qualitative differences exist between the "motivation" of animals which operate on a physiological or biosocial level in their interindividual behavior, and those animals which operate on an involved psychosocial level (Schneirla, 1946; David and Snyder, 1951).

The complexity of intelligent behavior in mammals and its resistance to psychogenetic analysis may be illustrated by studies of rats in the Tryon "bright" and "dull" strains, progeny of selective breeding for highest and lowest performance, respectively, in a multiple-T maze. One important difference is sensory, since Krechevsky (1933) found the brights more responsive tactually, the dulls more visual in discrimination situations. Still other factors are indicated in Searles' (1949) finding that the brights are higher in food-getting and lower in water-avoidance motivation, also more timid in open spaces although less disturbed by mechanical maze sounds than the dulls. On a lower phyletic level, as in insects, the development of comparable adaptive behavior might well involve lesser capacities, differently organized than in mammals (Schneirla, 1949).

"Instinct" is thus a problem concerning not only the lower animal phyla with their more stereotyped behavior, but developmental relationships producing species-typical behavior throughout the animal series. To the extent that it has gradually revealed this fact, and thereby has stimulated the rise of appropriate methods of comparative behavior study, the traditional instinct controversy may have made its best contribution to science.

CONCLUSIONS

1) In the development of any animal, systems of intervening variables mediate between genic influences and processes in ontogeny through which adaptive behavior appears. The range of these variables, from biochemical and physical conditions to the effects of experience, depends basically upon limitations imposed by the genic constitution of the species.

2) On all phyletic levels, behavioral organization arises in development through the interrelationships of intrinsic and extrinsic factors influencing growth and differentiation. Only in a misleading sense can the genic constitution be said to determine the organization of behavior patterns, even in phyla characterized by the most rigid lines of development.

3) In a strict theoretical sense the terms "innate" and "acquired" cannot therefore be applied validly to behavior or to the organization of behavior. Accordingly, it is suggested that the term "instinct" be retired from scientific usage, except to designate a developmental process resulting in species-typical behavior.

4) "Maturation," as conceptualized for behavioral development, subsumes not only growth of the morphological basis but also the excitatory and stimulative effects arising through growth processes in their influence upon further stages of development. "Experience" is defined as the effects of extrinsic stimulation upon development and behavior. The effects of maturation and experience tend to overlap and become integrated through

their interactions and organic trace effects. These concepts involve fewer trammeling theoretical assumptions than do "innate" and "acquired," and should replace the latter in theoretical usage.

5) The role of experience may have narrow or wide limits in behavioral development and may range into simple or complex learning functions according to phyletic properties.

6) Intervening variables in the development of behavior differ characteristically on each phyletic level as to their relative weight and patterns of relationships. It is therefore extremely doubtful that a single formula of "instinctive" behavior can be devised for the animal series in general.

7) There are characteristic phyletic differences in the degree of relationship between stages in behavior development, later stages being based upon earlier ones and modifiable under conditions of maturation and experience admitted according to phyletic capacities.

8) In the more advanced invertebrates and the vertebrates, functions of a disparate, local character appearing in early ontogenetic stages frequently serve as foci or nuclei in the later integration of more complex patterns.

9) In behavior development on various phyletic levels, "feedback" relationships involving interactions between the progressing system, its component processes and its "output," frequently play an essential role in the rise of integration and in advances from stage to stage.

REFERENCES

Adriaanse, M. S. 1947. *Ammophila campestris* Latr. und *Ammophila adriaansei* Wilcke. Ein Beitrag zur vergleichenden Verhaltensforschung. *Behaviour* 1: 1–34.
Anastasi, A. and J. P. Foley. 1948. A proposed reorientation in the heredity environment controversy. *Psychol. Rev.* 55: 239–249.
Anderson, E. C. 1941. The externalization of drive. I. Theoretical considerations. *Psychol. Rev.* 48: 204–224.
Armstrong, E. A. 1950. The nature and function of displacement activities. In *Sympos. Soc. Exper. Biol.*, IV. New York: Academic Press. Pp. 361–384.
Aronson, L. R., and G. K. Noble. 1948. The sexual behavior of Anura. 2. Neural mechanisms controlling mating in the male leopard frog, *Rana pipiens. Bull. Am. Mus. Nat. Hist.* 86: 87–139.
Autrum, H. 1952. Über zeitliches Auflösungsvermögen und Primarvorgänge im Insektenauge. *Naturwiss.,* 39 Jg., 13: 290–297.
Baerends, G. P. 1950. Specializations in organs and movements with a releasing function. In *Sympos. Soc. Exper. Biol.*, IV. New York: Academic Press. Pp. 337–360.

Bard, P. 1939. *The hypothalamus and central levels of autonomic function.* Baltimore: Williams and Wilkins.

Bash, K. W. 1939. An investigation into the possible organic basis for the hunger drive. *J. Comp. Psychol.* 28: 109–135.

Bastock, M., D. Morris, and M. Moynihan. 1953. Some comments on conflict and thwarting in animals. *Behaviour* 6: 66–84.

Beach, F. A. 1940. Effects of cortical lesions upon the copulatory behavior of male rats. *J. Comp. Psychol.* 29: 193–239.—1942. Analysis of the stimuli adequate to elicit mating behavior in the sexually-inexperienced male rat. *J. Comp. Psychol.* 33: 163–207.—1947. Evolutionary changes in the physiological control of mating behavior in mammals. *Psychol. Rev.* 54: 297–315.—1948. *Hormones and behavior.* New York: Hoeber.—1951. Instinctive behavior: reproductive activities. In S. S. Stevens, ed., *Handbook of experimental psychology.* New York: Wiley. Chap. 12.

Beach, F. A., and R. Gilmore., 1949. Response of male dogs to urine from females in heat. *J. Mammol.* 30: 391–392.

Beach, F. A., and A. M. Holz-Tucker. 1949. Mating behavior in male rats castrated at various ages and injected with androgen. *J. Comp. Physiol. Psychol.* 42: 433–453.

Beach, F. A., and J. Jaynes. 1954. Effects of early experience upon the behavior of animals. *Psychol. Bull.* 51: 240–263.

Beach, F. A., and G. Levinson. 1950. Effects of androgen on the glans penis and mating behavior of castrated male rats. *J. Exper. Zool.* 114: 159–171.

Berg, I. 1944. Development of behavior: the micturition pattern in the dog. *J. Exper. Psychol.* 34: 343–367.

Bingham, W. E., and W. J. Griffiths, Jr. 1952. The effect of different environments during infancy on adult behavior in the rat. *J. Comp. Physiol. Psychol.* 45: 307–312.

Birch, H. G. 1945. The relation of previous experience to insightful problem-solving. *J. Comp. Psychol.* 38: 367–383.—The relation of factors involved in early experience to maternal behavior in the rat. (*Unpubl.*)

Bozler, E. 1926. Sinnes-und Nervenphysiologische Untersuchungen an Scyphomedusen. *Z. Vergl. Physiol.* 4: 37–80; 797–817.

Bullock, T. H. 1943. Neuromuscular facilitation in Scyphomedusae. *J. Cell. Comp. Physiol.* 22: 251–272.

Carlson, A. J., and H. Ginsburg. 1916. Contributions to the physiology of the stomach. XXX. *Am. J. Physiol.* 39: 310–312.

Carmichael, L. 1926–1927–1928. The development of behavior in vertebrates experimentally removed from the influence of external stimulation. *Psychol. Rev.* 33: 51–58.—34: 34–47.—35: 253–260.—1936. A re-evaluation of the concepts of maturation and learning as applied to the early development of behavior. *Psychol. Rev.* 43: 450–470.—1946. The onset and early development of behavior. In *Manual of child psychology.* New York: Wiley. Pp. 43–166.—1951. Ontogenetic behavior. In S. S. Stevens, ed., *Handbook of experimental psychology.* New York: Wiley. Chap. 8.

Carmichael, L., and M. R. Smith. 1939. Quantified pressure stimulation and the specificity and generality of response in fetal life. *J. Genet. Psychol.* 54: 425–434.

Causey, D. C., and R. H. Waters. 1936. Parental care in mammals. *J. Comp. Psychol.* 22: 241–254.

Christie, R. 1952. The effect of some early experiences in the latent learning of rats. *J. Exper. Psychol.* 43: 281–288.

Clark, E., L. R. Aronson, and M. Gordon. 1954. Mating behavior patterns in two sympatric species of Xiphophorin fishes: their inheritance and significance in sexual isolation, *Bull. Am. Mus. Nat. Hist.* 103: 139–335.

Clark, G. 1945. The central control of micturition. *Urol. Cutan. Rev.* 49: 612–617.

Cobb, S. 1944. *Borderlands of psychiatry.* Cambridge: Harvard Univ. Press.

Coghill, G. E. 1929. *Anatomy and the problem of behavior.* New York: Macmillan.

Conradi, E. 1905. Songs and call notes of English sparrows when reared by canaries. *Am. J. Psychol.* 16: 190–198.

Cott, H. B. 1936. The effectiveness of protective adaptations in the hive bee, illustrated by experiments on the feeding reactions, habit formations, and memory of the common toad (*Bufo bufo bufo*). *Proc. Zool. Soc. Lond.* 1: 111–133.

Crafts, L. S., T. C. Schneirla, E. N. Robinson, and R. W. Gilbert. 1938. *Recent experiments in psychology.* New York: McGraw-Hill. (Rev. Ed., 1950).

Craig, W. 1914. Male doves reared in isolation. *J. Anim. Behav.* 4: 121–133.—1918. Appetites and aversions as constituents of instinct. *Biol. Bull.* 34: 91–107.

Cruikshank, R. M. 1946. Animal infancy. In L. Carmichael, ed., *Manual of child psychology.* New York: Wiley. Chap. 3.

Cruze, W. W. 1938. Maturation and learning in chicks. *J. Comp. Psychol.* 19: 371–409.

Cushing, J. E. 1941. Non-genetic mating preference as a factor in evolution. *Condor* 43: 233–236.

Cushing, J. E., and A. O. Ramsey, 1949. The non-heritable aspects of family unity in birds. *Condor* 51: 82–87.

David, P. R., and L. H. Snyder, 1951. Genetic variability and human behavior. In J. H. Rohrer and M. Sherif, eds., *Social psychology at the crossroads.* New York:Harper. Chap. 3.

Davis, D. E. 1945. The occurrence of the incubation patch in some Brazilian birds. *Wils. Bull.* 57: 188–190.

Dawson, W. M. 1932. Inheritance of wildness and tameness in mice. *Genetics* 17: 296–326.

Dennis, W. 1941. Spalding's experiment on the flight of birds repeated with another species. *J. Comp. Psychol.* 31: 337–348.

Dethier, V. G. 1947. *Chemical insect attractants and repellents.* Phila.: Blakiston.—1954. Evolution of feeding preferences in phytophagous insects. *Evolution* 8: 33–54.

Dobzhansky, T. 1950. Heredity, environment, and evolution. *Science* 111: 161–166.

Donaldson, J. 1928. Adrenal gland in wild gray and albino rat: corticomedullary relations. *Proc. Soc. Exper. Biol. Med.* 25: 300–301.

Dusser de Barenne, J. G. 1934. Further observations on the flexor rigidity in the hind legs of the spinal cat. *Am. J. Physiol.* 107: 441–446.

Ehrenhardt, H. 1937. Formensehen und Sehscharfebesrimmungen bei Eidechsen. *Z. Vergl. Physiol.* 24: 258–304.

Eibl-Eibesfeldt, I. 1952. Nahrungserwerb und Beuteschema der Erdkröte. (*Bufo bufo* L.). *Behaviour* 4: 1–35.

Fabricius, E. 1951. Zur Ethologie junger Anatiden. *Acta Zool. Fenn.* 68: 1–175.

Forgays, D. G., and J. W. Forgays. 1952. The nature of the effect of free-environmental experience in the rat. *J. Comp. Physiol. Psychol.* 45: 322–328.

Freisling, J. 1948. Studien zur Biologie und Psychologie der Wechselkröte (*Bufo viridis* Laur). *Östl. Zool. Zsch.* 1: 383–440.

Freud, J., and I. E. Uyldert. 1948. Micturition and copulation behavior patterns in dogs. *Acta Brev. Neerl.* 16: 49–53.

Friedrich, H. 1932. Studien über die Gleichgewichtserhaltung und Bewegungsphysiologie bei Pterotrachea. *Z. Vergl. Physiol.* 16: 345–361.

Frisch, K. V. 1923. Über die Sprache der Bienen. *Zool. Jahrb., Zool. Physiol.,* 20: 1–186.

Fromme, A. 1941. An experimental study of the factors of maturation and practice in the behavioral development of the embryo of the frog, *Rana pipiens. Genet. Psychol. Monogr.* 24: 219–256.

Fuller, J. L. 1953. Cross-sectional and longitudinal studies of adjustive behavior in dogs. *Ann. N.Y. Acad. Sci.* 56: 214–224.

Fuller, J. L., and J. P. Scott. 1954. Genetic factors affecting intelligence. *Eugen. Quart.* 1: 28–43.

Gellhorn, E., W. Koella, and H. M. Ballin. 1954. Interaction on cerebral cortex of acoustic or optic with nociceptive impulses: the problem of consciousness. *J. Neurophysiol.* 17: 14–21.

Gesell, A. 1954. *The embryology of behavior: The beginnings of the human mind.* New York: Harper.—1950. Human infancy and the ontogenesis of behavior. *Am. Sci.* 37: 529–553.

Ginsberg, A. 1952. A reconstructive analysis of the concept "Instinct" *J. Psychol.* 33: 235–277.

Gos, M. 1935. Les réflexes conditionnels chez l'embryon d'Oiseau. *Bull. Soc. Sci. Liége* 4–5: 194–199; 6–7: 246–250.

Gray, J. 1950. The role of peripheral sense organs during locomotion in the vertebrates. *Sympos. Soc. Exper. Biol.* 4: 112–126.

Grohmann, J. 1939. Modifikation oder Funktionsreifung? *Z. Tierpsychol.* 2: 132–144.

Haldane, J. B. S. 1946. The interaction of nature and nurture. *Ann. Eugen.* 13: 197–205.

Hall, C. S. 1951. The genetics of behavior. In S. S. Stevens, ed., *Handbook of experimental psychology*. New York: Wiley. Chap. 9.

Hallowell, A. I. 1954. The self and its behavioural environment. In E. S. Carpenter, ed., *Explorations Two*. Toronto: Univ. of Toronto.

Harris, L. J., J. Clay, J. Hargreaves, and A. Ward. 1933. Appetite and choice of diet. The ability of the vitamin-B deficient rat to discriminate between diets containing and lacking the vitamin. *Proc. Roy. Soc., Ser. B*, 113: 161–190.

Hebb, D. O. 1949. *The organization of behavior*. New York: Wiley.—1953. Heredity and environment in mammalian behavior. *Brit. J. Anim. Behav.* 1: 43–47.

Hediger, H. 1950. *Wild animals in captivity*. London: Butterworths.

Hertz, M. 1931. Die Organisation des optischen Feldes bei der Biene. *Z. Vergl. Physiol.* 14: 629–674.—1933. Ueber figurale Intensitäten und Qualitäten in der optischen Wahrnehmung der Biene. *Biol. Zbl.* 53: 10–40.

Hess, W. R. 1949. *Das Zwischenhirn—Syndrome, Lokalisationen, Funktionen*. Basel: Schwabe.

Hingston, R. W. 1929. *Problems of instinct and intelligence*. New York: Macmillan.

Holst, E. von. 1935. Erregungsbildung und Erregungsleitung im Fischrückenmark *Pflüg. Arch.* 235: 345–359.—1935. Über den Prozess der zentralnervosen Koordination. *Pflüg. Arch.* 236: 149–158.—1950. Quantitative Messung von Stimmungen im Verhalten der Fisch. *Sympos. Soc. Exper. Biol., IV. New York:* Academic Press. Pp. 143–174.

Holt, E. B. 1931. *Animal drive and the learning process*. London: Norgate.

Honigmann, H. 1945. The visual perception of movement by toads. *Proc. Roy. Zool. Soc., Ser. B*, 132: 291–307.

Howells, T. H. 1945. The obsolete dogmas of heredity. *Psychol. Rev.* 52: 23–34.

Howells, T. A., and D. O. Vine. 1940. The innate differential in social learning. *J. Abnorm. Soc. Psychol.* 35: 537–548.

Hunt, E. L. 1949. Establishment of conditioned responses in chick embryos. *J. Comp. Physiol. Psychol.* 42: 107–117.

Hunt, J. McV. 1941. The effects of infant feeding-frustration upon adult hoarding in the albino rat. *J. Abnor. Soc. Psychol.* 36: 338–360.

Hunter, W. S. 1947. Summary comments on the heredity-environment symposium. *Psychol. Rev.* 54: 348–352.

James, W. T. 1941. Morphological form and its relation to behavior. In *The genetic and endocrinic basis for differences in form and behavior*. Am. Anat. Mem., vol. 19, Sect. VI, p. 525–643.—1952. Observations on the behavior of newborn puppies. I. Method of measurement and types of behavior involved. *J. Genet. Psychol.* 80: 65–73.—1952. Observations on the behavior of newborn puppies. II. Summary of movements involved in group orientation. *J. Comp. Psychol.* 45: 329–335.

Jennings, H. S. 1911. 1905. Modifiability in behavior. I. Behavior of sea anemones. *J. Exper. Zool.* 2: 447–472.

Jennings, H. S. 1930. *The biological basis of human nature.* New York: Norton.

Kagan, J., and F. A. Beach. 1953. Effects of early experience on mating behavior in male rats. *J. Comp. Physiol. Psychol.* 46: 204–208.

Keeler, C. E. 1942. The association of the black (non-agouti) gene with behavior in the Norway rat. *J. Hered.* 33: 371–384.

Keeler, C. E., and H. D. King. 1942. Multiple effects of coat color genes in the Norway rat, with special reference to temperament and domestication. *J. Comp. Psychol.* 34: 241–250.

Kennedy, J. S. 1953. Host plant selection in Aphididae. *Tr. IXth Int. Cong. Entom., Amsterdam,* pp. 106–113.—1954. Is modern ethology objective? *Brit. J. Anim. Behav.* 2: 12–19.

Kent, G. C., Jr., and M. J. Liberman. 1949. Induction of psychic estrus in the hamster with progesterone administered via the lateral brain ventricle. *Endocrinology* 45: 29–32.

Kinder, E. F. 1927. A study of the nest-building activity of the albino rat. *J. Exper. Zool.* 47: 117–161.

Krechevsky, I. 1933. Hereditary nature of "Hypotheses." *J. Comp Psychol.* 16: 99–116.

Kruchinsky, L. 1947. The role played by peripheral impulses in the sexual form of behaviour of males. C. Rend. (Doklady) *Ac. Sci. U. S. S. R.* 55: 461–463.

Kuo, Z. Y. 1921. A psychology without heredity. *Psychol. Rev.* 31: 427–448. —1930. The genesis of the cat's response to the rat. *J. Comp. Psychol.* 11: 1–30.—1932. Ontogeny of embryonic behavior in Aves. I. The chronology and general nature of the behavior of the chick embryo. *J. Exper. Zool.* 61: 395–430.—1932b. Ontogeny of embryonic behavior in Aves. II. The mechanical factors in the various stages leading to hatching. *Ibid.,* 62: 453–489.—1932c. Ontogeny of embryonic behavior in Aves. III. The structure and environmental factors in embryonic behavior. *J. Comp. Psychol.* 13: 245–272.—1932d. Ontogeny of embryonic behavior in Aves. IV. The influence of embryonic movements upon the behavior after hatching. *Ibid.,* 14: 109–122.—1939. Total pattern or local reflexes? *Psychol. Rev.* 46: 93–122.

Labriola, J. 1953. Effects of caesarean delivery upon maternal behavior in rats. *Proc. Soc. Exper. Biol. Med.* 83: 556–557.

Lashley, K. S. 1938. Experimental analysis of instinctive behavior. *Psychol. Rev.* 45: 445–471.—1947. Structural variation in the nervous system in relation to behavior. *Ibid.,* 54:325–334.—1949. Persistent problems in the evolution of mind. *Quart. Rev. Biol.* 24: 28–42.

Leblond, C. P., and W. P. Nelson. 1937. Maternal behavior in hypophysectomized male and female mice. *Am. J. Physiol.* 120: 167–172.

Lehrman, D. S. 1953. A critique of Lorenz's "objectivistic" theory of animal behavior. *Q. Rev. Biol.* 28: 337–363.

Leuba, C. 1940. The need for a systematic study of innate nature. *Psychol. Rev.* 47: 486–490.

Lissman, H. W. 1946. The neurological basis of the locomotory rhythm in the spinal dogfish (*Scyllium canicula, Acanthias vulgaris*). II. The effect of de-afferentation. *J. Exper. Biol.* 23: 162–176.—1950. Proprioceptors. In *Sympos. Soc. Exper. Biol.,* IV. New York: Academic Press. Pp. 34–59.

Lorenz, K. 1935. Der Kumpan in der Umwelt des Vogels. *J. Ornithol.* 83: 137–213, 289–413.—1950. The comparative method in studying innate behaviour patterns. In *Sympos. Soc. Exper. Biol.,* IV. New York: Academic Press. Pp. 221–268.

Maier, N. R. F., and T. C. Schneirla. 1935. *Principles of animal behavior.* New York: McGraw-Hill.—1942. Mechanisms in conditioning. *Psychol. Rev.* 49: 117–134.

Martins, T. 1949. Disgorging of food to the puppies by the lactating dog. *Physiol. Zool.* 22: 169–172.

Martins, T., and J. R. Valle. 1948. Hormonal regulation of the micturition behavior of the dog. *J. Comp. Physiol. Psychol.* 41: 301–311.

Masserman, J. 1941. Is the hypothalamus a center of emotion? *P. Med.* 3: 3–25.

Mayr, E. 1942. *Systematics and the Origin of Species.* New York: Columbia Univ. Press.—1948. The bearing of the new systematics on genetical problems. In M. Demerec, ed., *Advances in genetics.* New York: Academic Press. Vol. 2, pp. 205–237.

McCracken, I. 1907. The egg-laying apparatus in the silkworm (*Bombyx mori*) as a reflex apparatus. *J. Comp. Neurol. Psychol.* 17: 262–285.

McGraw, M. 1940. Basic concepts and procedures in a study of behavior development. *Psychol. Rev.* 47: 79–89.—1946. Maturation of behavior. In *L. Carmichael, ed., Manual of child psychology.* New York: Wiley. Chap. 7, pp. 332–369.

Mcniven, M. A. Responses of the chicken, duck and pheasant to a hawk and goose silhouette—A controlled replication of Tinbergen's study. (*Unpubl.*)

Metfessel, M. 1940. Relationships of heredity and environment in behavior. *J. Psychol.* 10: 177–198.

Mills, W. 1898. *The nature and development of animal intelligence.* London: Unwin.

Moore, A. R., and J. C. Welch. 1940. Associative hysteresis in larval Amblystoma. *J. Comp. Psychol.* 29: 283–292.

Morgan, C. T., and E. Stellar. 1950. *Physiological psychology,* 2nd ed. New York: McGraw-Hill.

Muller, H. J. 1940. Bearings of the "Drosophila" work on systematics. In J. Huxley, ed., *The new systematics.* Oxford: Clarendon.

Munn, N. L. 1940. Learning experiments with larval frogs. *J. Comp. Psychol.* 29: 97–108.

Needham, J. 1929. *The skeptical biologist.* London: Chatto.

Nissen, H., K. L. Chow, and J. Semmes. 1951. Effects of restricted opportunity for tactual, kinesthetic, and manipulative experience on the behavior of a chimpanzee. *Am. J. Psychol.* 64: 485–507.

Padilla, S. G. 1935. Further studies on the delayed pecking of chicks. *J. Comp. Psychol.* 20: 413–443.

Pantin, C. F. A., and A. M. P. Pantin. 1943. The stimulus to feeding in *Anemonia sulcata. J. Exper. Biol.* 20: 6–13.—1950. Behaviour patterns in lower invertebrates. In *Sympos. Soc. Exper. Biol.,* IV. New York: Academic Press. Pp. 175–195.

Parker, G. H. 1919. *The elementary nervous system.* Philadelphia: Lippincott.

Parr, A. E. 1937. On self-recognition and social reaction in relation to biomechanics, with a note on terminology. *Ecol.* 18: 321–323.

Patterson, T. L. 1933. Comparative physiology of the gastric hunger mechanism. *Ann. N.Y. Acad. Sci.* 34: 55–272.

Pattie, F. A., Jr. 1936. The gregarious behavior of normal chicks and chicks hatched in isolation. *J. Comp. Psychol.* 21: 161–178.

Prosser, C. L. 1936. Rhythmic activity in isolated nerve centers. *Cold Spr. Harb. Sympos. Quant. Biol.* 4: 339–346.

Rasmussen, E. W. 1939. Wildness in rats. *Acta Psychol.* (Hague) 4: 295–304.

Ray, W. S. 1932. A preliminary study of fetal conditioning. *Ch. Devel.* 3: 173–177.

Redfield, R., ed. 1942. *Levels of integration in biological and social systems.* Lancaster: Cattell Press.

Richter, C. P. 1942–1943. Total self-regulatory functions in animals and human beings. *Harvey Lect.* 38: 63–103.—1952. The effect of domestication on the steroids of animals and man. In *Ciba Found. Colloq. Endocrin.,* III. London: Churchill.

Riess, B. F. 1950. The isolation of factors of learning and native behavior in field and laboratory studies. *Ann. N.Y. Ac. Sci.* 51: 1093–1102.

Rosenblatt, J. 1953. Mating behavior of the male cat. The role of sexual experience and social adjustments. Ph. D. thesis: Library, New York Univ.

Rosenblatt, J., J. Wodinsky, M. L. Failla, R. Cohn, and A. Frank. 1953. Analytical studies on maternal behavior and litter relations in the domestic cat. II. From birth to weaning. (Unpubl.)

Schaeffer, A. A. 1911. Habit formation in frogs. *J. Anim. Behav.* 1: 309–335.

Schneirla, T. C. 1938. A theory of army-ant behavior based upon the analysis of activities in a representative species. *J. Comp. Psychol.* 25: 51–90.—1939. A theoretical consideration of the basis for approach-withdrawal adjustments in behavior. *Psychol. Bull.* 37: 501–502.—1941. Social organization in insects, as related to individual function. *Psychol. Rev.* 48: 465–486.—1944. A unique case of circular milling in ants, considered in relation to trail following and the general problem of orientation. *Am. Mus. Nov.,* no. 1253, pp. 1–26.—1946. Problems in the biopsychology of social organization. *J. Abnorm. Soc. Psychol.* 41: 385–402.—1948. Psychology, comparative. In *Encyclop. Brit.,* vol. 18, pp. 690–760.—1949. Levels in the psychological capacities of animals. In R. W. Sellars et al., eds., *Philosophy for the future.* New York: Macmillan. Pp. 243–286.—1950. The relationship between observation and experimentation in the field study of behavior. *Ann. N.Y. Acad. Sci.* 51: 1022–1044.—1952a.

A consideration of some conceptual trends in comparative psychology. *Psychol. Bull.* 49: 559–597.—1952b. Basic correlations and coordinations in insect societies with special reference to ants. *Coll. Int. Cent. Nat. Rech. Sci.* 34: 247–269.—1953a. The army-ant queen: keystone in a social system. *Eull. Un. Int. Etude Ins. Soc.* 1: 29–41.—1953b, In K. Roeder, ed., *Insect physiology.* New York: Wiley. Basic problems in the nature of insect behavior. Chap. 25.—Insect behavior in relation to its setting. *Ibid.,* Chap. 26.—Modifiability in insect behavior. *Ibid.,* Chap. 27. —Collective activities and social patterns among insects. *Ibid.,* Chap. 28.

Schneirla, T. C., R. Z. Brown, and F. Brown. 1954. The bivouac or temporary nest as an adaptive factor in certain terrestrial species of army ants. *Ecol. Monogr.* 24: 269–296.

Schooland, J. B. 1942. Are there any innate behavior tendencies? *Genet. Psychol. Monogr.* 25: 219–287.

Scott, W. E. D. 1902. Data on songbirds. *Science* 15: 178–181.—1904. The inheritance of song. *Science* 19: 957–959.

Searle, L. V. 1949. The organization of hereditary maze-brightness and maze-dullness. *Genet. Psychol. Monogr.* 39: 279–325.

Selye, H., J. B. Collip, and D. L. Thompson. 1934. Nervous and hormonal factors in lactation. *Endocrinology* 18: 237–248.

Selye, H., and T. McKeown. 1934. Further studies on the influence of suckling. *Anat. Rec.* 60: 323–332.

Seward, G. H., and J. P. Seward. 1937. Internal and external determinants of drives. *Psychol. Rev.* 44: 349–363.

Shepard, J. F., and F. S. Breed. 1913. Maturation and use in the development of an instinct. *J. Anim. Behav.* 3: 274–285.

Shirley, M. 1931. The sequential method for the study of maturing behavior patterns. *Psychol. Rev.* 38: 507–528.

Siegel, A. I. 1953. Deprivation of visual form definition in the ring dove. I. Discriminatory learning. *J. Comp. Physiol. Psychol.* 46: 115–119.— 1953. Deprivation of visual form definition in the ring dove. II. Perceptual-motor transfer. *Ibid.,* 46: 249–252.

Smith, S., and E. R. Guthrie. 1921. *General psychology in terms of behavior.* New York: Appleton.

Snyder, L. H. 1950. *The principles of heredity* (4th Ed.). Boston: Heath.

Spelt, D. K. 1948. The conditioning of the human fetus in utero. *J. Exper. Psychol.* 37: 338–346.

Sperry, R. W. 1946. Ontogenetic development and maintenance of compensatory eye movements in complete absence of the optic nerve. *J. Comp. Psychol.* 39: 321–330.

Spieth, H. T. 1952. Mating behavior within the genus *Drosophila* (Diptera). *Bull. Am. Mus. Nat. Hist.* 99: 401–474.

Stern, C. 1954. Two or three bristles? *Am. Sci.* 42: 212–247.

Thompson, W. R., and W. Heron. 1954. The effects of restricting early experience on the problem-solving capacity of dogs. *Canad. J. Psychol.* 8: 17–31.

Thorpe, W. H., and F. G. W. Jones. 1937. Olfactory conditioning in a parasitic insect and its relation to the problem of host selection. *Proc. Roy. Soc. Lond., Ser. B,* 124: 56–81.

Tinbergen, N. 1948. Social releasers and the experimental method required for their study. *Wilson Bull.* 60: 6–52.—1951. *The Study of Instinct.* New York: Oxford Univ. Press.

Tinbergen, N., and D. J. Kuenen. 1939. Über die auslösenden und die richtunggebenden Reizsituationen der Sperrbewegung von jungen Drosseln (*Turdus m. merula* L. und *T. e. ericetorum* Turton). *Z. Tierpsychol.* 3: 37–60.

Tinbergen, N., and A. C. Perdeck. 1950. On the stimulus situation releasing the begging response in the newly hatched herring gull chick (*Larus argentatus argentatus* Pont). *Behaviour* 3:1–39.

Tobach, E., M. L. Failla, and T. C. Schneirla. Analytical studies on maternal behavior and litter relations in the domestic cat. I. Parturition. (*Unpubl.*)

Tracy, H. C. 1926. The development of motility and behavior reactions in the toadfish (*Opsanus tau*). *J. Comp. Neurol.* 40: 253–369.

Tucker, B. W. 1943. Brood-patches and the physiology of incubation. *Brit. Birds* 37: 22–28.

Uyldert, I. E. 1946. A conditioned reflex as a factor influencing the lactation of rats. *Acta Brev. Neerl.* 14: 86–89.

Van der Kloot, W. G., and C. M. Williams. 1953a. Cocoon construction by the Cecropia silkworm. I. The role of the external environment. *Behaviour* 5: 141–156.—1953b. Cocoon construction by the Cecropia silkworm. II. The role of the internal environment. *Ibid.,* 5: 157–174.

Wada, T. 1922. An experimental study of hunger in its relation to activity. *Arch. Psychol.* 57: 1–65.

Warren, R. P. 1954. The sexual behavior before and after castration of the adrenalectomized male golden hamster treated with DCA. Ph. D. thesis: Library, New York Univ.

Warren, R. P., and J. Rosenblatt. Does progesterone induce estrus behavior by action on the hypothalamus? (*Unpubl.*)

Watson, J. B. 1914. *Behavior: An introduction to comparative psychology.* New York: Holt.—1919. *Psychology from the standpoint of a behaviorist.* Philadelphia: Lippincott.—1925. *Behaviorism.* New York: Norton.

Watson, J. B., and K. S. Lashley. 1915. Homing and related activities in birds. (Papers Dept. Mar. Biol., 7). *Carn. Inst. Wash. Publ.,* no. 211, pp. 9–60.

Weiss, P. 1941. Autonomous versus reflexogenous activity of the central nervous system. *Proc. Am. Phil. Soc.* 84: 53–64.—1954. Some introductory remarks on the cellular basis of differentiation. *J. Embryol. Exper. Morphol.* 1: 181–211.

Werner, H. 1940. *Comparative psychology of mental development.* New York: Harpers.

Wheeler, W. M. 1928. *The social insects.* New York: Harcourt, Brace.

Whitman, C. O. 1899. Animal behavior. Biological lectures, 1898, *Marine Biol. Lab., Wood's Hole, Mass.,* pp. 285–338.—1919. *Behavior of pigeons.* (v. 3, post. works; H. A. Carr, Ed.), Carn. Inst. Publ., no. 257, pp. 1–161.

Wickens, D. D., and C. Wickens. 1939. A study of conditioning in the neonate. *Psychol. Bull.* 36: 599.

Wiesner, B. P., and N. M. Sheard. 1933. *Maternal behavior in the rat.* Edinburgh: Oliver and Boyd.

Windle, W. F. 1940. *Physiology of the fetus: Origin and extent of function in prenatal life.* Philadelphia: Saunders.—1950. Reflexes of mammalian embryos and fetuses. In P. Weiss, ed., *Genetic neurology.* Chicago: Univ. Chicago Press.

Wolf, E. 1933. Das verhalten der Bienen gegenüber flimmernden Feldern und bewegten Objekten. *Z. Vergl. Physiol.* 20: 151–161.

Yeakel, E. H., and R. P. Rhoades. 1911. A comparison of the body and endocrine gland (adrenal, thyroid and pituitary) weights of emotional and non-emotional rats. *Endocrinol.* 28: 337–340.

Yerkes, R. M. 1913. The heredity of savageness and wildness in rats. *J. Anim. Behav.* 3: 286–296.

T. C. SCHNEIRLA

Instinctive Behavior

Bibliography No. 90

Instinctive behavior—any species-typical pattern of responses not clearly habitual or acquired through experience. This wording is preferred to the traditional term instinct, which denotes an innate impulse, blindly impelling action appropriate to attaining certain ends. The adjective instinctive is used by some, the Freudians for example, to signify certain complex, motivated behavior, and thus leans toward the classical meaning, that of an innate drive or predisposition to given acts.

THE PROBLEM

In every animal species, certain characteristic patterns or systems of adaptive action appear under certain conditions. Thus, many spiders spin webs typical of their species, most birds make species-typical nests, and beavers build dams and lodges. These activities, instinctive in the above sense, pose important questions concerning their evolutionary basis and genetics, their ontogeny and psychology, and their adaptive significance.

CRITERIA

Earlier theorists seeking objective approaches to this problem devised certain criteria of the instinctive in behavior, particularly appearance shortly after birth or hatching, no essential dependence upon learning, and appearance in the individual raised in isolation. With further research, however, these criteria all met with objections. For example, the first is contradicted by evidence that species-typical behavior may appear at stages other than birth; the second, by evidence that experience and learning often exert their effects in ways resisting clear identification, for example, embryonic stimulation or prenatal conditioning; and the third by the fact that isolation may not exclude extrinsic influences, that is, stimulative properties

From *Encyclopedia of Science and Technology*. New York: McGraw-Hill, 1960. Pp. 146–147. Reprinted with permission.

of the individual itself, which are characteristic of the species. But the last two of these criteria still influence many students of comparative animal behavior who synonymize with "instinctive" such concepts as innate, native, and endogenous.

FOCAL POINTS IN RESEARCH AND THEORY

Objective study demands that the behavior patterns of representative animals be studied analytically, and that basic assumptions be tested. Research must cover environmental conditions and stimuli, the range of behavioral variation, and organic conditions underlying the development and appearance of the behavior. Both longitudinal and cross-sectional studies of behavioral ontogeny are needed, obtained by methods appropriate to the species, and with genetic controls.

In theorizing, all conceptual terms must be evaluated. Thus skepticism about the instinct concept centers around traditional dogma which differentiates psychologically between man, conceived as the sole possessor of reason, and lower animals ruled by instinct. This idea is contradicted by much evidence in comparative psychology. The related assumption that animals possess an original, innate nature modified only secondarily (if at all) by experience is opposed by evidence on behavior development. The related idea of sharply distinguishing instinctive from intelligent behavior is in contrast to evidence that instinctive behavior is often plastic in relation to the situation. Differences in the nature of such behavior, and in its developmental basis, doubtless exist on different phyletic levels.

Other unsettled, controversial points in research and theory concern the role in such behavior of (1) neural organization, (2) nonnervous organic factors such as hormones, and (3) sensitivity and perception, together with the relation of these in ontogeny (development). Some authorities postulate the existence of innate central neural coordinations to account for the rise and control of instinctive behavior; others emphasize the role of peripheral mechanisms, interwoven with neural processes, in behavioral ontogeny. Classical distinctions between reflex and instinct are questioned on the ground that such functions may differ in degree rather than in kind. Theories distinguishing sharply between instinct and learning meet the objections that neither of these is sufficiently well understood, and that both may vary greatly in their forms and in their relationships to development on different phyletic levels.

Although all behavior is related to heredity, the influence of the genes upon behavior is a complex question, still unanswered. Genes in the chromosomes must exert basic influences on structural growth, and, through structure, on behavior. Examples of behavior determined or influenced by structure are readily found, as in limb structure and characteristic gait, cellular equipment in the retina of the eye and proneness for day or night activity, size of certain glands, such as the adrenal, and degree of docility or of wildness. However, it is another matter to trace out such correspondences from the fertilized egg through the complexities of ontogeny.

The genetics of some of the species-predictable behavioral characteristics of animals have been worked out, and are impressive. Thus, through selective breeding of parental generations, it has been possible to produce hybrids and backcrosses of certain insects, fishes, birds, and mammals differing predictably from the parents in behavioral characteristics such as level of excitement, parental behavior, and reproductive behavior.

The facts do not yet indicate how directly or in what manner the genes may influence development of behavior in any animal. Preformists postulate a direct relationship between genes and behavior; epigeneticists postulate an indirect relationship through many interlacing factors in organism and developmental situation. The traditional nature-nurture controversy has waned; instead, the emphasis is on the study of the rise of typical and atypical ranges of species behavior in evolution and in ontogeny.

REFERENCES

D. O. Hebb, *The organization of behavior,* 1949.
N. R. F. Maier and T. C. Schneirla, *Principles of animal psychology,* 1935.

T. C. SCHNEIRLA

Instinct and Aggression

Bibliography No. 115

A review of two books by Konrad Lorenz, *Evolution and Modification of Behavior* (The University of Chicago Press) and *On Aggression* (Harcourt, Brace & World).

Dr. Lorenz, Director of the Max Planck Institute for Physiology of Behavior, Germany, and the author of works on animal behavior, has written two new books on important subjects. In *Evolution and Modification of Behavior* he discusses his theory of animal behavior; in *On Aggression* he applies this theory to a problem in social behavior. Both books stem from dubious assumptions.

Aggression is defined as "The fighting instinct in beast and man which is directed against members of the same species." The thesis for man and beast alike is: Aggressive instincts dominate behavior unless curbed. The importance of this point for man is stressed: Someone from another planet, "looking upon man as he is today, in his hand the atom bomb, the product of his intelligence, in his heart the aggression drive, inherited from his anthropoid ancestors, which this same intelligence cannot control, would not predict long life for the species."

Instinctual aggression is, of course, not a new concept. Its dominance in natural selection is an idea Lorenz shares with Herbert Spencer (first to speak of "survival of the fittest") and Freud. Lorenz considers aggression and fighting common and thinks they must have been potent in the evolution of all animals.

On Aggression opens with vividly described observations of strikingly colored coral reef fishes in tanks and in the sea. In each case a territory holder, excited by an invader of his own species, drives off the trespasser. Territorial defense fighting, common in lower vertebrates, birds, and mammals, is found crucial as a basis for food getting, mating, rearing young, and other behavior promoting species survival. In lower animals, instinctive aggression is viewed as working well; in man, however, it seems to be getting out of hand.

Mechanisms that inhibit fighting, Lorenz holds, are essential to survival

From *Natural History*, 75 (10): 16 (1966). Reprinted with permission.

in lower animals and man alike. Chief among these are ritualistic displays in which aggressors are warded off with little or no combat. In man, however, the inhibitory controls imposed on aggression both through natural selection and through cultural processes may fail in the split-second emergencies created by modern weaponry and accessory bellicose patterns. Man is "the only being capable of dedicating himself to the highest moral and ethical values" but one "whose animal properties bring with them the danger that he will kill his brother, convinced that he is doing so in the interests of these very same high values. *Ecce homo!*" Behold man, that is, as Lorenz sees him.

Lorenz shares this somber view with Freud, who also saw conflict and war as inevitable, violent expressions of irresponsible, aggressive instincts. Lorenz, like Freud, considers the social bond and related influences inadequate to inhibit man's aggressive biological nature in the modern world.

In his chapter "Avowal of Optimism," Lorenz suggests that, under the described threat, we must find methods for ritualizing and channelizing instinctive aggressions, must encourage people of differing ideologies and races to get acquainted, must direct "the militant enthusiasm" of youth toward "genuine causes that are worth serving in the modern world," and must improve our understanding of behavioral mechanisms fundamental to aggression, the better to control them. We must use all our resources of humor and of knowledge to these ends. These suggestions, although helpful, seem to reveal an aspect of Freudian sublimation—making the best of a bad deal.

A different picture of man, however, based on current scientific methodology and theory, is at odds with Lorenz's out-dated negative view. Results of research on human group behavior emphasize man's great social potentials arising from his developmental plasticity and his versatility for constructive behavior. At the same time, evidence on the origins of asocial behavior suggests that those hypotheses in which instinctual aggression explains the rise of wars are tangential and naive.

The question is, not whether results concerning behavior in lower animals are applicable to man, but whether the application is as simple a matter as Lorenz's procedures imply. Responsible scientists must carry out their behavioral research within the broadest perspective and evaluate evidence in terms of the most valid theory possible. Evidence on individual differences, on the conditions of development, and on the state of the population must be featured, for these surely were all crucial in the natural selective background of every animal. The results of research must be presented in comprehensive reports open to searching analysis, not in descriptive, subjective terms as Lorenz has done.

The significance Lorenz gives his results is too great to justify his non-experimental, anecdotal treatment of the subject. An appropriately broad systematic presentation of the behavioral facts would have aided readers to understand, for example, how differently individual fish responded according to the conditions (as stressful crowding in aquariums), and how results from observations of animals in confinement actually compared with the behavior of species mates under natural conditions.

Studying social phenomena and other behavior under natural conditions is extremely important, and the ethological approach inspired by Lorenz and Tinbergen has aided such work, which ideally goes hand in hand with laboratory research. The field of behaviorial development is highly controversial, however, in ways that do not emerge clearly in *Behavior*. Lorenz's critics dispute neither his emphasis on "the great fact of adaptiveness in behavior" as he implies, nor on the correlations between genotypes (empirically described species genetics) and phenotypes (individual patterns developed). Rather, they reject much of his evidence as partial and unreliable, and question the assumptions he applies dogmatically to these problems.

It is not clear from *Behavior* whether or not science will be aided by Lorenz's terms, "phyletic information" and "individually acquired information," which he consistently confuses with reality. These concepts, notwithstanding the impressive cybernetic aura he gives them and the polemical deftness with which he uses them, seem not to differ much from their traditional synonyms, "nature" and "nurture," respectively.

Space precludes discussing the obfuscations raised in *Behavior* for readers attempting to judge the theoretical issues involved in the book. Lorenz admits that the terms "innate" and "learned," used (by "earlier ethologists") to denote mutually exclusive agencies, are fallacious. But at the same time, in speaking of "information" that is either "phyletically acquired" or "individually acquired," he revives the fallacious dichotomy by using the word *information* in two different senses. He repeats his old assertion that others (whose evidence and ideas he evades) offered "learning in the egg and in utero" to explain ontogenesis, although he should know by now that this is both an untrue statement and a misrepresentation of important evidence.

Two related devices stand out in the book. One is the term "innate schoolmarm" for hypothetical genetic agencies governing what the animal is to learn as it develops. Another is the "deprivation experiment," formerly the "isolation experiment," offered here as *the* method for determining what is innate. The author directs these ideas at the separation of innate and learned elements in behavior with a faith in their soundness hardly justified by evidence or comprehensive theory. The implication that the genes rigidly "program" the animal's learning is opposed by the results of many experiments, as well as by evidence from animal training. Under appropriate developmental conditions, animals do many things they never would do ordinarily. The deprivation experiment, widely used to study behavioral differences in young animals raised under conditions other than those presumed to be natural for them, is better termed change-of-environment test. Believing that "it can only tell us directly what is not learned," the author must assume that he knows beforehand the developmental significances of these "natural" conditions. This, however, is a major aspect of the problem under study. Actually, this method is only one of those now widely used in developmental research far wider in scope than is considered in *Behavior*.

Lorenz's entire argument rests on the single assumption that patterns such as aggression are seated specifically in the genes. It is a long way from the genes to behavior, however, and the books under review do not light the path. This key assumption is not only unsupported, it is denied by a sizable weight of evidence. As is well known, the frequency and nature of aggression varies among members of both interspecies and intraspecies groups raised under conditions favorable to one or another pattern of behavioral development.

Lorenz seems interested neither in the study of individual differences nor in phyletic comparisons in behavioral development, yet these problems are vital to understanding how aggression, for example, arises and varies in different animals. The question of why, when two fish react to invasions of their territory, one flees whereas the other attacks, or why some people generally are peaceable whereas others are quarrelsome, is not easy. Neither is it the same question for fish and for people. All methods (including deprivation tests) must be used for studying such differences in function and in behavior throughout development.

The more scientists study behavioral development and its properties through the animal series, the less likely are they to follow Lorenz's oversimplified formula which he applies to all levels. As an example, in certain animals on what I have called the "biosocial level," chemical secretions, according to concentrations, attract or repel species mates, thereby dominating behavior. Ants, bees, and wasps offer good examples of biological processes controlling behavior directly. On the "psychosocial level," in contrast, structural and physiological factors contribute indirectly to behavior and differently according to the conditions of individual development. In man, adrenalin—a neurosecretory, excitatory substance—arouses fighting, loving, poetizing, singing, or fleeing according to the individual's background and his current situation. The assumptions underlying the theory expounded in these books are open to question for lower animals; their extrapolation to man is doubtful.

It is as heavy a responsibility to inform man about aggressive tendencies assumed to be present on an inborn basis as it is to inform him about "original sin," which Lorenz admits in effect. A corollary risk is advising societies to base their programs of social training on attempts to inhibit hypothetical innate aggressions, instead of continuing positive measures for constructive behavior. Major aggressions of history, including Hitler's, may be attributed superficially to instincts or studied systematically with evidence known to historians and scientists.

III

ON THE CONCEPT OF INTEGRATIVE LEVELS IN THE STUDY OF BEHAVIOR

Dr. Schneirla developed the concept of integrative levels as the most important theoretical formulation for considering the evolution of behavior in its broadest sense, i.e., from the most primitive to the most complex and specialized animal species. When comparing behavior in disparate species (say, a worm, a fish, a lower mammal, and man), one must always take into consideration major differences in morphology and physiology, which at higher levels are more differentiated and specialized, thereby providing the basis for more complex and qualitatively different behavioral processes. This was one reason that he found so much difficulty with well-known ethological constructs, such as "releasers," "displacement reactions," "specific action potential," etc., that are applied equivalently at many phyletic levels without regard to major qualitative differences in neural and other relevant physiological processes.

The levels concept is introduced in the paper, *Levels in the Psycho-*

logical Capacities of Animals (No. **46**),* the first in this section, and the application of the concept to the evolution of social organization is considered in the second paper, *The Concept of Levels in the Study of Social Phenomena* (No. **65**). Two other papers dealing particularly with the question of levels in social behavior, *The "Levels" Concept in the Study of Social Organization in Animals* (No. **52**) and *The Biopsychology of Social Behavior of Animals* (No. **119**), are included in Part V, On Social Organization. An early paper on the subject, *Problems in the Biopsychology of Social Organizations* (No. 38) has been omitted.

The levels concept permeates every aspect of Schneirla's thinking, research, and writing. His papers on behavioral development and approach-withdrawal behavior (Part IV) and on social organization (Part V) are examples of his theoretical application of this concept to the analysis of different behavioral phenomena. Similarly, his research on the behavior of army ants (in Part VII) and on the comparison of learning in insects and mammals (in Part VI) are examples of his experimental application of the concept.

Lester R. Aronson
Ethel Tobach

---

* This and subsequent numbers in this introduction refer to the items in the complete bibliography of Schneirla's works, 'p. 1017. Bold face numbers denote articles that are included in this volume.

T. C. SCHNEIRLA

Levels in the Psychological Capacities of Animals

Bibliography No. 46

The concept of psychological levels in its modern form is due especially to the investigative attack of experimental science upon evolutionary processes. To a large extent these lines of research have been materialistic in the sense that their principal method drives for explanations of events in terms of properties discovered through systematically broadened and controlled investigative experience. Such empirically grounded methods have been introduced broadly into investigation and theory as well, challenging in both of these departments the predominantly deductive and subjective procedures which have infiltrated science from preexperimental philosophy through mystical and animistic conceptions of nature. An inevitable characteristic of the materialistic approach to problems is the drive for naturalistic explanations.

The term "levels" is a convenient conceptual device for developing a systematic theory of different patterns of adaptation to the given conditions of existence in different organisms. Our methods of investigating, describing, and explaining the similarities and differences which prevail among different animal types must adjust themselves as precisely as possible to the real state of affairs prevalent in each case. Both Mechanists and Vitalists seem to have missed this course by divergently emphasizing different phenomena; the former by endeavoring to fit all adaptive capacities directly under physicochemical rubrics, the latter by setting out to bring all cases under a universal supernatural causal principle. Both seem to have erred in generalizing too widely an incomplete characterization of a different portion of the animal series. In effect, both have slipped into what Sloane (105) aptly terms the error of "reductionism"—they have tended to reduce organisms to a single level by distracting attention from the nature of differences among levels. To offer seriously a theory of human thinking couched throughout in terms of brain biochemistry is vague in

Reprinted with permission of The Macmillan Company from *Philosophy for the Future: The Quest of Modern Materialism,* edited by Roy Wood Sellars, V. J. McGill, and Marvin Farber. Copyright © 1949 by The Macmillan Company.

that the nature of the general capacity is lost in a welter of unorganized details. To offer an explanation of food-taking in a protozoan organism as "purposive striving" is assuredly vague in a somewhat different sense, in that a humanized label is applied which has barely more than a literary suitability in the given situation.

It is necessary to ask what questions are properly subject to investigation by animal psychologists—that is, what constitutes a psychological problem in animal behavior? A classical answer has been rephrased by Bierens de Haan (10), who considers Psychology as a science of "psychic realities" which man can first know in himself through introspection, and then study in lower animals through "sympathetic intuition." The difficulty is not merely that such an approach to the subject is ethnocentric and limits procedures mainly to anthropomorphically colored analogies, but—even more serious—that human introspection as the proposed source of concepts offers a most unsound point of departure. Modern experimental psychologists studying human capacities employ introspection only with numerous reservations as a secondary adjunct to method, admitting such data as evidence only after adequate checks and balances have been imposed. Many difficulties await one who operates through analogy on a phenomenalistic basis such as the above.

The general problem of the animal psychologist is the nature of behavioral capacities on all levels of accomplishment. He must contrive to understand how each animal type functions as a whole in meeting its surrounding conditions; what its capacities are like and how they are organized in admitting given functions of individual-unit or of group. The principle of levels has come into current usage through a recognition of important differences in the complexity, the degree of development, and the interdependent organization of behavior functions through the animal series. The evidently superior properties that appear on a new level of organization are not to be explained as due to a new kind of energy (85) or new vital properties (83), but as functional properties arising from a new system of organization which differs in given ways from "lower" and "higher" systems. Thus local autonomy in food-taking is less in the snail than in the jellyfish, the learning of social insects is subject to limitations evidently not typical of mammals, internal condition can have a more or less restricted significance in the general behavior of different animals, and so on (75).

The terms "part" and "whole" must be regarded as convenient abstractions which have a different relationship to each other on different animal levels. For example, in the sponge behavior of the individual aggregate is little more than a summated action of individual parts or chimneys, whereas in a food-snatching kitten the details of local muscle contraction are subsumed under superior functional organizations describable in part as learned habits. The problems of animal psychologists, then, involve discerning the similarities and differences in capacities and whole-functioning on different levels.

A reminder is essential at this point. A comparative study of capacity for organization does not presuppose a reduction of psychology to biological terms. We are cautioned by Novikoff (85) that the error of reducing all properties of the organism to the physicochemical is not to be corrected by ignoring biochemistry. Psychological properties must be regarded as derivatives of biological processes—hence the construction of appropriate new concepts must be undertaken when required by evidence at progressively higher levels. Put in another way, experience in behavior investigation reminds us not to expect the "wholes" of lower levels to be encountered as specific constituent parts on higher levels. If the lower-level wholes appear to be represented as subsystems in the higher organism, these are likely to be differentiated qualitatively by the nature of the given more inclusive system in which they occur. For instance, it is superficial and really misleading to say that "instinctive man" is like a given lower animal, since this implies that by removing the top layers we encounter substratal units which duplicate lower-animal behavior. A social group, as another example, is involved very differently as a unit in a population than an individual as a unit in a social group. The student of levels in capacities must be alert for qualitative differences as well as for similarities.

Theoretical validity is endangered in fundamental ways when concepts such as those offered by Vitalism are generalized a priori to all animal levels. Along with Vitalism have been inherited from preexperimental times the practices of a predominant deductivism, of widely generalizing certain unquestioned and uninvestigated concepts regarded as basic, thus imposing a strait-jacket upon whatever investigation may be attempted.

ANECDOTALISM

An inevitable outcome is the practice of anecdotalism, in which there is a selection and mustering of instances which fit given preconceived explanations at the expense of a broad study of relevant events. Anecdotalism is chronically subjective and not experimental in tendency. Here we are confronted with a curious explanatory procedure in which a final interpretation exists in advance of any appreciable amount of evidence. This practice is by nature restrictive and nonstatistical, promoting the selection of given events for description without much consideration of the wide population of events in the classes to which these belong. It can lead irresponsibly to an emphasis upon instances or of characteristics which may well be exceptional in nature and unrepresentative of their classes. One who sets out to demonstrate that protozoan organisms or any others have the mental characteristics of man may convince himself at least, provided he singles out opportunely the brief episodes which seem describable as instances of perception of danger, of reasoning, or what not. By the same method, the absence of reasoning in man can be proved with ease.

Another difficulty with anecdotalism lies in its dependence upon the false assumption that an uncontrolled perceptual observation must possess some intrinsic validity of its own. The shortcomings of observational memory and its corollary procedure of unchecked verbal report have been emphasized repeatedly by general psychologists, from Stern to Bartlett (6). The best intentioned subjects typically report their observations with alterations, additions, and various types of motivated rearrangement in the material. Such defects emphasize the basic importance of a dependable technique and method for studying animal capacities. Actually, observation involves techniques subject to improvement through practice, just as do more formal methods of experimentation.

It is a safe rule that rigid distinctions, particularly those offered with pretensions to fundamental significance, should be held as highly tentative in scientific procedure and not accorded fundamental explanatory roles in advance of adequate evidence. Yet the separate existence of "mental" and "physical" realities still enters almost without question into the theorizing of many scientists and philosophers about animal nature. When we admit the dichotomy mind versus body without challenging its applicability to scientific investigation, anecdotal practices are a foregone conclusion as ingrown features of method. For the concept "mind" offers a convenient ground against which seemingly representative instances can be selected perceptually to the exclusion of others. And the blanket concept of the animal's "psyche" offers a convenient device for relegating the biological actualities underlying adaptive existence to limbo in favor of hypothetical agencies such as "purpose," "vital principle," or "mental faculties."

It is possible to introduce anecdotalism without seeming to do so, by selecting evidence which emphasizes apparent similarities among animal levels. To say that a particular instance of behavior is a case of "learning" does not explain it and assuredly does not demonstrate that it is necessarily related very closely to other instances in which the same term has been used. The similarity may be so partial and superficial that use of the common term actually misrepresents the various phenomena considered by minimizing the existence of wide areas of difference among them. Has an amoeba "learned" in any important sense when in the course of repeated head-on exposures to a beam of light it extends progressively fewer pseudopodia? (77) The phenomenon appears to resemble light adaptation more closely than it does learning in a higher animal, especially since it evidently involves a progressive reduction in the biochemical action of light which has a distinctive and relatively short time limit. It is doubtful whether Jennings (59), merely by using the term "learning," suggested an adequate explanation for his discovery that individual starfish can be induced to use much less frequently two of their five radial arms originally used predominantly in moving from a set of restraining pins, especially after another investigator has shown that the results can be duplicated by persistently rubbing the given arms or by applying acid to them. It is questionable whether Bramstedt (14) by using the term "conditioned response" has found the most suitable conceptual device to indicate what has occurred in given paramecia which remain predominantly in darkened water, out of a lighted area, without then requiring a temperature difference initially present in the two areas. At first sight these cases appear to have the essential aspects of "conditioned response" and "learning." Yet there are reasons to believe that this generalization has been very premature. Grabowski (42) found that paramecia would react as did Bramstedt's subjects even though they were kept from the experimental areas until the final "tests" and the water alone was subjected to the light-temperature combinations used in the training procedure of Bramstedt. The term "learning" seems to be very misleading for phenomena in lower invertebrate behavior which resemble instances of sensory adaptation and muscle fatigue more closely than they do a representative learning through experience. The breadth of the difference is suggested by the fact that no persistent and progressive changes of the species behavior system have been demonstrated in the lower invertebrates, at all comparable to what "learning" may involve in higher animals. On the strength of such evidence as Bramstedt's, Chauvin (19) believes that the psychological similarity of lowest and highest organisms has been underestimated. It is more likely that an uncritical generalized use of the higher-level concept has tended to distract attention from the vast area of difference separating these phenomena.

When terms such as "learning" are used in sweeping fashion on widely separate levels they encourage thinking conclusively of homogeneous agencies presumably understood in the various cases, rather than processes of very different nature still requiring explanation. Such practices have the characteristic of mysticism inherent in Vitalism, as well as its effect of distracting attention from the need for further analysis and comparison.

ANALOGY

A serious charge to which vitalistic theories are vulnerable is that their premature generalization of concepts such as "mind" and "purpose" tends to vitiate the close comparison of animal levels which evolutionary doctrine encourages. If vitalistic precepts were generally followed, scientific procedure in studying animal capacities would be reduced to a mere general description of events under the label presumed to apply (cf. 49). For a dynamic theoretical process based upon inductive method would be substituted a system of concepts derived from initial "intuition" and enforced by authority, or prestige, or by the sheer inertia of wide acceptance. Matters have not been improved when concepts are imposed upon lower levels anthropocentrically, as the term "learning" has been generalized widely by some writers and "perception" by others (e.g., Russell, 92). Inevitably, an insistent generalization of mentalistic terms throughout the animal series, whether or not it is designedly vitalistic, has much in common with vitalistic thought-ways.

These procedures both involve centrally a dominant deductivism, which elevates the use of analogy at the expense of analysis. The term "mind" suggests close qualitative similarity wherever it is used, evading explanation but at the same time implying it with such propagandistic success that the issue seems fairly settled. The word then effectively infers a causal agency sui generis, in a procedure which lacks little to become animistic (52). A very similar strategy is accomplished through the generalization of terms such as "instinct" to several animal levels. Actually the practice is atavistic in the sense that the discussion of phenomena is transferred to preexperimental conditions under which it becomes easy to overlook or ignore evidence that does not agree with the given position.

A sound generalization deriving from the comparison of a wide variety of levels in animal capacity is that a given behavioral adjustment (e.g., food-taking) may be based in different instances upon very different patterns of cause-effect relationship. When an author asserts that an amoeba extending a pseudopod and a man asking for a sandwich are both acting "purposively," readers may be justified in taking the statement to allege that a similar "intention" underlies both acts. Whether the author really means this, or merely wishes to call attention to a similarity in the adaptive adequacy of behavior in the two cases, the effect of the common term is to imply that a closely related organization of underlying processes exists in both instances. A common feature of Vitalism, Animism, Mentalism, and other procedures featuring the use of analogy is that the organization of processes underlying behavioral systems is not subjected to very close study. Seldom do these doctrines encourage a critical comparison of presumably similar phenomena in different animal forms. Actually the analogies are preliminary and descriptive; the common terms, nothing more than tentative lables. Yet the customary emphasis upon a central theme tends to crystallize the terms and to obscure the unsoundness of applying them in purported explanatory roles to very different orders of events.

IDOLS OF THE THEATER

Many of the difficulties we have been discussing rest upon a failure to recognize that concepts are ways of representing and thinking about things and their relationships; explanatory symbols which should change and develop with advances in our evidence about things and relationships. For example, in the premating behavior of birds there are special activities which have been called "display" because, after Darwin, they have been regarded as special appeals designed to win over a desired individual of the opposite sex. For Pycraft (88) and some later writers such as Armstrong (4), the strutting and posturing of a male bird which serves to expose brilliant and striking plumage (not seen ordinarily) can have no other explanation. However, on further investigation, difficulties have arisen with this view. New factors of different nature have been discovered, which have led recent investigators such as Marshall (76) and Lack (64) to abandon the purposivistic concept of "display" for the notion that plumage is exposed incidentally in the course of behavior not designed to expose it as an appeal for mating, but appearing rather as a product of a generalized emotional excitement. Marshall came to the conclusion that the concept of a conscious sexual selection, as proposed by Darwin, must be replaced for birds by the view that such behavior is emotionally and not deliberately aroused. The other bird may be attracted through the behavior, but not because of a deliberate enticement, and in many cases the only identifiable adaptive role is that of promoting glandular processes. The behavior remains; our conception of it has been greatly improved.

Many instances may be found in which traditional concepts through long usage have come to represent presumable real forces underlying animal capacity. Frequently, after the example of Aristotle, students of animal ways have concluded that, because highly appropriate activities often seem to be without benefit of special experience, the impulse toward such activities must logically be inborn, or "instinctive." Modern animal psychology has had to struggle against the tremendous weight of authority always found behind this concept, and its seeming reasonableness. However, a growing body of experimental fact and theory now favors the view that "instinct" denotes a wide variety of behavior processes all influenced in one or another way by hereditary factors, rather than inborn urges to carry out a given process. In different animals, it now appears, the hereditary factors may be of very different nature, and may influence the appearance of given behavior patterns in different ways and to different degrees (75). The word "instinct" is reductionistic and fallacious in the sense that it tends to level over these important group differences, and to obscure the real nature of their influence.

As Warren (114) has shown very succinctly, conceptual devices such as "instinct" and "mind" are products of a major nominalistic error, in that they involve substituting a mere name for a problem requiring solution. For a long time after Aristotle, while it was confidently proffered and widely accepted as standing for an explanation, the word "instinct" served to distract attention from the need for serious study of the subject matter. Increasingly in recent decades scientists with good reason have balked at following the instinct dogma. Distinctive processes have been found in the rise of individual behavior in different species as well as in the broadest groups, the animal phyla; very different processes which are not adequately represented by the word "instinct." Coghill's (21) investigations, for instance, have shown that aquatic locomotion of salamanders arises mainly through the maturation of given neural centers and connectors, whereas the research of Kuo (63), Shepard and Breed (101), and other investigators has revealed that pecking in domestic fowl is dependent upon the maturation of given part-process activities (e.g., head lunging at bright objects, and swallowing reflex) and a learning to use them together (75). In the chick's typical environment one type of learning becomes possible and the typical pecking pattern appears; under changed extrinsic conditions other learning occurs and the resulting pattern is quite different. Neither pattern is "instinctive" in the sense of resulting from an inborn urge to perform it as a system. This holds even more forcibly for the development of behavior in mammals, which in the higher orders involves learning to relatively greater extents, and eventuates in patterns which differ very plastically in relation to the special external conditions of development. Thus, although the word "instinct" loosely represents a type of problem, it no longer meets the requirement; namely, to express the relationships between hereditary factors and behavior patterns on different animal levels.

Animal psychologists can point to some five decades of real progress in the materialistic and empirical study of animal capacities (75, 81, 82, 113). However, some of their own concepts, which lead into lines opposing comparative practice, have developed into reductionistic procedures operating almost as special disciplines within science itself. An example is the concept of "dominance" in social study.

The idea of dominance relationships in an animal group arose most specifically through the work of Schjelderup-Ebbe (93), who was first to demonstrate a "peck order" in his investigation of domestic fowl. Since then "dominance hierarchies" have been revealed in the group relationships of many other species of birds and other animals from fish to (and, of course, including) primates (1).

Typically the concept implies an aggressive type of relationship, in which one member of the group forces another to submit by actually attacking it or by threatening attack (25). It affords a convenient way of quantifying the behavior of individuals in a group, and for this reason alone its popularity is understandable. However, it is doubtful that the "dominance" concept is qualified to serve as a chief theoretical device for understanding group organization. Aggression dominance is not necessarily coupled with other important characteristics of group behavior such as ascendance, prestige, and (especially in higher types of social organization) social approval. However prominent a characteristic of group behavior it may be in many instances, dominance after all emphasizes part-processes, the discrete aspects of individuals and of specific individual interchanges, and serves to distract attention from the broad problem of accounting for group unity on the various social levels. It is doubtful whether "dominance theory" alone, as dictating a method of study, would ever lead to an investigation of factors which are involved in the formation of groups and in the socialization of individuals under varying conditions.

Here is an example of a way of thinking which tends to restrict the comparative aspect of animal psychology. On different animal levels there are pronounced differences in the quality and complexity of group unity, and capacities for plastic change in such unity, which dominance theory does not prepare us to understand (95). The essence of social organization consists in the approach-relationships of individuals, yet dominance thinking emphasizes withdrawals. Summated, withdrawals describe one prominent aspect of many groups; however, this aspect clearly is secondary to the factors which brought the parts together in the first place and keep them together long enough for dominance relationships to develop and pass through various changes (2). Actually, dominance relationships as such are absent in many effective types of social organization from primates (18) down through insects.

Although it has arisen from an effort to introduce quantitative method into the study of animal societies, the "dominance" procedure thus tends to lead away from the central question of group organization, and tends to discourage a thoroughgoing comparative study of groups. The trouble is that a partial and really descriptive procedure has become confused, in "dominance" emphasis, with the broad problem of investigating and explaining group unity. "Dominance" theory is reductionistic in this sense, as well as in the sense that it stresses partial similarities among groups on different levels, at the expense of studying other similarities and differences which may be much more significant for the nature of social organization.

But these are similar to the difficulties which we find in animistic conceptions of group organization, such as Maeterlinck's "spirit of the hive" on the insect level and McDougall's "crowd mind" on the human level. Such concepts implying a social psychic agency either are used frankly as literary conceits, or are fraudulent devices substituted gratuitously for any real effort to study the factors underlying a given level of group performance (22). They are simply descriptive, and circular—as for example, to the "spirit of the hive" may be attributed any properties which are noted in the collective performance of bees, whatever these may be. This type of concept is misleading, not merely because it tends to crystallize descriptive and observational errors in literary metaphors, but also because the metaphors furnish a veneer for ignorance. Thus "group mind" offers a spurious explanation for human social phenomena, in that it implies the existence of a close similarity between group function and individual mental function, with no more than anecdotal suggestions to support the analogy. This concept, far more than "dominance" doctrine, evades the issue of accounting for the origin and nature of social organization (16, 84).

We have considered some ways in which animal psychology has deviated from comparative method at the expense of scientific validity. One, the reifying of concepts into presumed forces, is often paralleled in its results by practices which have no apparent relation to Animism. When a single aspect of behavior, such as dominance, is studied on different levels without adequate attention to its origin and its background in the whole phenomenon, significant differences in addition to the most essential similarities may be obscured. Fallacies of metaphor are involved when terms are applied to different orders of capacities so loosely that the essential similarities are blurred and the important differences among capacity levels confused or ignored. Thus, nervous conduction in an individual may be assumed analogous to communication in a social group; but the similarity actually seems to have only an introductory or descriptive significance, and to lack any particular utility for explaining the nature of individual and social group comparatively. The procedure is "reductionistic" (105) in the sense that it isolates part-functions or single characteristics from their respective whole settings without adequate consideration of their relations to and dependence upon the wholes to which they belong. The chief shortcoming of "organism-superorganism" theory (37) lies in the fact that it is based upon this same kind of procedure (95).

We may consider two further examples of concepts which are often generalized in misleading ways. The term "stimulus" has been variously applied to causes of behavior ranging from specific energy effects to complex systems in motivation and perception. In the first sense it is frequently used in a positivistic manner by an experimenter who assumes that, because he has made no deliberate change in the external situation, no extrinsic difference can exist from a preceding observation. With his impression that the "same stimulus" is effective externally, he may refer prematurely to unknown internal processes to explain the difference in behavior. Through forgetting that the term "stimulus" actually is a convenient conceptual device which may or may not denote delimited and invariable causal factors, an inadequate control of extrinsic factors often is introduced which vitiates a realistic theory. The same type of positivistic and artificialized delimitation often is involved in speaking of *"the* environment" of a given organism, or of *"an* environment" which is optimal for different organisms. The development of ecological investigation and of methods for studying animal sensitivity and adaptiveness has shown that the term "environment" must be used in a statistical sense, keeping in mind what range of conditions is optimal for a given animal and what consequences ensue when conditions vary beyond this range. Through scientific investigations of animal adjustment it is becoming truistic to say that "the environment" of a given animal form is relative to the nature of its biological properties (e.g., temperature sensitivity and tolerance) and psychological capacities (e.g., learning capacity). Yet it is often forgotten that the "same environment" beneath a particular tree is very different for sitting rabbit and crawling slug on the "same" patch of grass. In a similar sense, when an animal psychologist refers to "the problem" which he has presented to animal subjects, the very expression may stem from a positivistic leveling effect in perception which scarcely prepares him to be alert for possible important differences in "the problem" for various individuals.

PURPOSES OF "PURPOSE"

No conceptual term has tended to obscure differences in capacity level more than generalized "purpose." Recently Bahm (5) has discussed concisely some of the chief logical weaknesses of the concept "purpose" as it is involved in teleological writings on natural history subjects. Closest to our present discussion is his reminder that the teleological purposivistic argument is always post hoc, since it ignores the fact that "survival of purpose does not imply survival for a purpose." This fact seldom dissuades purposivists from resorting to Animism on one or another basis.[1] A com-

---

[1] How effectively this ancient practice becomes accepted in a particular social setting through institutional propagation of concepts encouraging nonlogical and nonempirical thought processes, is clearly apparent, for example, in Rosenfield's (91) valuable treatise on the Cartesian controversy.

mon ground for such practices is a presumption of proof through elimination. A traditional proponent of purposivistic theory in biology and psychology, William McDougall (70) held steadfast to the argument that, since materialistic procedures in science cannot account for the phenomena of (a) growth and (b) adaptivity in behavior, only Animism remains adequate as a basis for metaphysical theory. McDougall (71) held persistently to the weight of point a although through the next two decades the sweeping conclusions of Driesch (34) from experimental embryology, on which it was based, were progressively carried toward negation by the researches of Spemann, Child (20), and other investigators. The second argument bears more directly upon animal psychology, where its considerable contemporary influence is evident in the writings of Tolman (111), Lorenz (68), and Russell (92) in particular.

Undeniably, behavior generally is describable as adaptive. From bacteria to man, living organisms universally tend to behave in ways beneficial to survival. Dating mainly from Darwin's work, this fact has been accepted as a widely prevalent characteristic of animal activities. However, the purposivists customarily underplay a corollary fact that even among contemporary species the adaptive aspect of behavior is a relative and not an absolute value throughout the population. In animal species maladaptive behavior commonly accounts for a death curve of individuals ranging from early to advanced ages. The biological factors underlying adaptive behavior, on one level or all levels, are by no means covered by the term "purpose." Mounting evidence favors the view that more or less complex processes of mutation in germ plasm compounded with the intricacies of propagative process and of environmentally enforced selection (32, 78) underlie the appearance of new or changed biological processes and animal types. The relative significance for adaptation of given biological factors is in the long run critical for survival, with mechanisms which promote maladaptive behavior constituting potential causes for elimination in the processes of so-called natural selection. To take an extreme example, a species of protozoa which through mutational innovations possessed organic mechanisms favoring consistent movement toward the source of intense stimulation and away from weak stimulation, assuredly would be wiped out in the course of time. Survival is favored, on the other hand, when factors arise which favor the reverse of these types of response. Adaptive behavior, directly or indirectly dependent upon biological factors on whatever level it occurs, is basically attributable to the processes of organic evolution which condition the phyletic development of such factors. It is strange to find these processes slighted or even ignored by writers who set out to account for the basic nature of adaptive behavior.

Adaptivity is an inevitable characteristic of all levels of adjustment. But is "purpose"? A basic mistake inherent in all Vitalistic and Animistic thinking is to confuse a fact, the great predominance of adaptive or life-promoting behavior throughout the animal series, with generalized "purpose." The latter term thus used is ambiguous, from the standpoint of science. Experimental psychologists find that "purpose" can be identified on the human level as "anticipation of a goal." "Purpose" in this scientifically acceptable sense of acting persistently and appropriately with reference to anticipated results, is a difficult technique which is present in the human child not automatically but only by dint of much gradually accomplished learning through experience. Hard come by in development, it is a capacity not to be taken lightly.

To what extent are such capacities, not readily acquired even by man, possessed by lower animals? From evidence on mature adjustments in the mammals, purposive behavior when it arises may be considered as the product of ontogenetic development. The adaptivity of purposive acts is devious and is relative to the given situation, as discussions of ethical and moral standards in different human cultures illustrate. In contrast, the behavior of animals on respective lower levels is more and more directly conditioned by organic factors, and hence its predominantly adaptive trend is attributable more and more specifically to the processes of evolution and heredity (75, Chapters 7 and 12). The kind of teleological doctrine which asserts that "purpose" is present wherever adaptive behavior exists either has theological implications which are hardly relevant to scientific theory, or rests upon a gratuitous a priori endowment of all living animals with higher-level psychological functions.

A great variety of biological processes underlies adaptive behavior functions on different animal levels, as is abundantly demonstrated in descriptive summaries of food-getting and other behavior such as those offered by Warden, Jenkins, and Warner (113). It is well to distinguish constantly between description and analysis, remembering the rule that similar adaptive consequences may result from very different causal processes. To refer to classes of behavior such as "protective behavior," "courtship," and "food-getting" behavior throughout all animal levels is entirely permissible on a descriptive basis which emphasizes the kind of adaptive result obtained; however, such a scheme has no essential validity at all for explaining the ontogenetic causal processes involved in producing given behavior in one or another animal type. For example, "protective behavior" may depend upon a shock-elicited tonic immobility of a given physiologically determined duration, as studied by Hoagland (50) in the lizard, or it may involve anticipated evasion of the source of disturbance, as is possible in a socialized chimpanzee or human child. The manner in which effective food-taking occurs in the starfish is explicable as a "community of reflexes" (112), a pattern of local reflex functions systematically unified through the generalized conductile properties of a nerve-net system

(45); but in contrast, chimpanzees are able to bring in food out of reach by constructing simple tools, and the "table manners" of a human child are essentially the product of socialized learning. We have used very wide contrasts here only to emphasize that broadly similar adaptive results may depend upon lower-level or higher-level processes. Certainly we are not implying the fallacious distinction that in lower animal groups behavior is "instinctive" and in higher animal groups behavior is learned. Differences in developmental patterns are not that crude and simple.

LEVELS IN ADAPTIVE BEHAVIOR

Perhaps the most basic problem in adaptive behavior concerns the manner in which animals on all levels avoid some types of stimulation, generally injurious, and approach other types which are generally adaptive or beneficial in effect. In the lower invertebrates such responses as "approach" tend to involve the whole body, and they are characteristic of the species without evident benefit of learning (75). The nature of the responsible hereditary mechanisms is suggested by some of the relevant evidence. A significant fact is that approaches toward the source of stimulation, as in food-taking, typically occur in response to effectively weak energies of stimulation, whereas withdrawals occur in response to effectively intense energies of stimulation. The earliest clear demonstration of opposed response types dependent upon quantitative aspects of stimulation was offered by Jennings (58) from his studies on protozoa and other invertebrates. In the invertebrate groups which have specialized receptors, the differentiation of response occurs in dependence upon strength of stimulation in various fields, such as light-, chemical-, and contact-sensitivity. The shift in "sign" of adjustment is not an "all-or-none" process, but occurs much as in the light responses of earthworms in Hess's (48) experiment, in which there was a gradual decrease from a maximum of approach reactions and an increase to a maximum frequency of withdrawal when a source of light was changed from low to high intensity.

The critical matter underlying such differences must be the amount of energy delivered to reactive tissues, since Hess found that adaptation to light causes earthworms to turn toward light of abnormally high intensities and to turn from the source only when intensities at the upper end of the scale were much higher than in worms unadapted to light. In contrast, dark adaptation (by effecting an increased sensitivity to light) lowered the entire scale of relationships. The nature of other important biological mechanisms basically involved in adaptive approach and withdrawal in these organisms is not altogether obscure (75). In the earthworm the principal effector systems are also differentiated in thresholds of responsiveness, with the circular muscles (extending the body forward by thinning it) first and predominantly aroused when stimulation is weak, the longitudinal muscle system (drawing back the body by thickening it) predominating when stimulation is strong. When stimulation is very intense the threshold of the most rapid conductor lines in the nervous system, the "giant fibers," is exceeded, and the invariable response is a highly adaptive backward jerking of the entire animal. This we may term the *principle of differential organic thresholds* underlying the adaptive orientation of behavior.

We are reminded here that in the lowest animals adaptive orienting responses can involve movements of the entire organism with respect to the stimulus source. The basis evidently lies in the evolution of generalized organic processes differing appropriately in threshold of arousal. Moreover, these responses appear directly upon the maturation and functioning of heritable structures. The literature on tropism and orientation offers abundant evidence for the broad applicability of this theory among invertebrate animals (38, 75).

The principle of adaptive-threshold systems seems applicable in the case of vertebrate animals, as well, although there evidently exist wide group differences in the nature of heritable mechanisms involved and in the relative directness of their influence upon the eventual behavior pattern. Complicating factors, rather incompletely known at present, are involved on all levels, with learning variously influencing the outcome especially in mammals (98). On the whole, there is no doubt that the unlearned components are more directly effective in the submammalian group than in the mammals. And among the submammalian classes, birds appear to rank above the others in this respect. For instance, the typical lower-vertebrate forward lunge, highly important in feeding, is regularly given to small moving objects in a mainly stereotyped way; whereas we have seen that the pecking response of some birds to edible objects evidently arises through the initial presence of a similar part-process but one eventually combined with others into a pattern through an early learning process.

In the mammals, and especially in man, adaptive organic thresholds seem to be most complexly and deviously influential in behavior development. With a very few doubtful exceptions, whole-body patterns are no longer attributable directly to maturation. The evidence suggests that certain local mechanisms of the reflexive type are present, first clearly demonstrated in Sherrington's (104) finding that the extensor-thrust response of the spinal mammal has a distinctly lower threshold of arousal than the limb-flexion reflex. Combine these facts with the further fact that weak stimulation has a typically localized effect, whereas intense stimulation of the neonate mammal produces a widespread mass action as Carmichael and Smith (17) reported, and it becomes apparent that these differential effects of stimulative energy furnish a broad basis for the establishment of specialized adaptive adjustments through learning (98).

Evidence for such underlying mechanisms may at first sight seem to be lacking in the case of man; yet there are scattered suggestions of their presence, as in the case of the plantar response (41, 87) and of an unlearned arm withdrawal to intense local stimulation (103). The latter fact seems very important, yet limb extension to weak stimulation remains to be demonstrated clearly in early neonate behavior. Careful studies made with graded intensities of stimulation are essential. A general hint of what may exist may be gathered from Watson's (116) trio of "love," "fear," and "rage" responses in the very young infant, in that he elicited "love" (simply a pacified effect, with relaxation and some limb extension) by mild stimulation such as patting, and the "fear-rage"—better, "excited" —responses (high excitement, crying, generalized contraction, and limb flexion) by definitely intense stimulation. Significantly, there is a suggestion here of an unlearned basis for a differentiation of the emotional component, in that craniosacral autonomic signs predominate with weak stimulation, and sympatheticoautonomic signs with strong stimulation. To be sure, Sherman's (102) critique of Watson's emotional trio demonstrated that "fear" and "rage" were not differentiable in early neonates as Watson claimed, but neglected to examine comparatively the more excited ("fear-rage") and milder responses ("love") reported by Watson. Bridges's (15) description of an originally undifferentiated basis for emotion in the human infant after the scheme of Stratton (106) has no substantiation, because she did not work with infants below the age of three months, when some differentiation was found. Although the evidence is at present rather meager, the possibility is worth examining experimentally, that organic mechanisms such as those mentioned above provide an initial basis not only for the overt adaptive adjustments of man to his world, but also for their differentiated emotional backgrounds (98).

How these indistinctly glimpsed organic processes provide an initiating basis for purposive adaptive behavior in man can only be suggested here. Purposive reaching is centrally important, but arises only gradually as an outcome of a lengthy developmental process. In Halverson's (44) study of grasping it seems significant that six-weeks-old infants responded at first to a small cube of sugar (i.e., weak visual stimulus) by a somewhat variable extension and abduction of arm, together with a rolling of eyes toward the object (visual "regard"). These first arm movements in the situation seem to constitute incidental products of the mild stimulative change, and to be not at all purposive in the sense of representing "attempts" to reach or get the object. The initial dependence of such movements upon organic maturation is indicated by the fact that after the age of three months the record steadily worsens for a number of weeks, in that the infant's arm is extended variably sideward and farther from the object than in earlier tests. The reason seems to be a more rapid maturation of the abductor muscles than of arm-extensor muscles at this stage (44). The act has all the aspects of an incidental "getting the arm out" upon excitation, rather than a directed reaching in anticipation of obtaining something. Circumstances indicate that the latter condition develops slowly through learning, as Holt (51) suggested. During early months the hand virtually never reaches to and touches the seen object. Then a reasonably efficient pattern of reaching out directly, grasping, and pulling in ordinarily appears, at seven or eight months of age, only after several months of variable activity. It is a reasonable hypothesis that this eventual directed, anticipatory pattern is a perceptual system which develops through organic maturation and learning-in-use from the initial physiological process of incidental arm extension to weak stimulative effects.

LEVELS: COMMON FACTORS AND HETEROGENEITIES

It would appear that the initial physiological mechanisms underlying approach and withdrawal responses are broadly similar on several animal levels. Wide differences appear, however, in their relation to the eventual behavior pattern. On the mammalian and especially the primate level the process is most indirect and involved of all, and the appearance of the eventual purposive pattern is most influenced by special learning. Here ontogeny plays the foremost role, with individual variation and capacity for plastic modification as outstanding features. This plasticity is effective also in the influence of visceral components upon the development of perceptual and emotional processes.

The fact that systems of approach and withdrawal behavior are widely adaptive on all animal levels often causes them to be treated as though they were effectively similar throughout the animal series. Our evidence is sufficient to show wide stages of difference. On the lowest animal levels their function is present through maturation alone; the physical properties of stimulation are effective in a similar stereotyped fashion in an animal's life from beginning to end. It is thus a serious error to apply the word "perception," as does Russell (92), to the "food-getting" and other adaptive responses of invertebrate and lower vertebrate animals, as if these animals could sense a meaningful environmental pattern by virtue of *anticipating* further stages of the process and the eventual significance of the object to them. The disordered and confused epistemology involved in such errors can be corrected only through comparative study of the underlying processes. A survey is not comparative if it deals with the acts in cross-sectional manner as mere episodes of accomplishment, taking adaptive significance as adequate proof of a similar process of underlying "purposeful perception" in all cases. To be adequate, the survey must be carried out in a consistent longitudinal way, with cross-sectional investigations at suspected turning points.

There is ample evidence from developmental experiments with human infants that "perception" of the nature of objects, and "purposeful striving" to deal with them in given ways, result from a complicated ontogeny involving much learning and social-selective influence (cf. 90). Such evidence is lacking for inframammalian forms in particular. Unless we rest content with the gratuitous assumption that "innate knowledge" is possessed by lower organisms such as starfish and spiderling which give *initially* appropriate reactions, detailed comparisons will be made which show that the latter must be regarded as qualitatively different from mammalian "perceptual" adjustments.

Impressed by apparent signs of qualitative equivalence, writers often prematurely generalize particular concepts so that significant functional differences are placed subordinately or are even overlooked. Thus the term "perceptual pattern" has been used to imply a meaningful visual organization equivalent to that of man, whereas in fact the nature of visual organization may be significantly different from that of man. For example, the work of Mathilde Hertz (47) on visual discrimination in bees was impressive, especially in demonstrating what a variety of "patterns" of intricate design could be discriminated. Taken as a matter of Gestalt differentiation, the process appeared to lie qualitatively close to the human level. However, Wolf's (119) results suggest that the process in the bee involves a differentiation of gross flicker effects rather than the appreciation of inclusive figural patterns involved in mammalian perception. Thus although "pattern" has been a convenient term in studying behavior systems on various levels, the time has come to use it with greater care so that qualitative heterogeneity is not obscured.

The fact is that organic maturation makes very different contributions on different animal levels. Adjustment patterns so called appear on widely different bases in ontogeny. The feeding pattern of the jellyfish is largely present through maturation alone, whereas systems such as food-pecking in birds are complexes resulting from a close and progressive interaction between maturation and learning. This learning is much more generalized and qualitatively simpler than learning generally is in human ontogeny. It would seem advisable to avoid dogmatism concerning the sense in which adjustive patterns as such may be inherited, even on lower levels such as social insects in which complex behavior systems seem to arise without benefit of learning. (As a matter of fact, insect social patterns *do* involve some learning.) For no animal inherits its environment except in an indirect sense, and behavior patterns must always be considered as the products of an intimate interaction between organism and environment. For example, the behavior pattern of an army ant colony, with its intricate system of daily raids and nightly migratory movements, constitutes an impressively complex and highly stereotyped system (96, 99). The pattern is the outcome of a cumulative interaction of processes contributed by colony queen, developing brood, and worker individuals in the characteristic environmental setting. Broadly considered, it is the outcome of genetic properties, yet in no sense is it inherited as a pattern even by the colony queen who functions as "pacemaker." The significance of this statement is indicated by the fact that learning functions at certain strategic points; and, although simple and rudimentary in nature, the learning component is essential for the rise and maintenance of the pattern (97).

LEVELS IN SUBSOCIAL AND SOCIAL ADJUSTMENT

Actually, phenomena such as the above represent complex systems of interrelated individual and subgroup adjustment patterns. They constitute one level in the scale of social phenomena—"social" because the integrity of the group depends upon the interdependence of individuals and upon their mutual responsiveness. The nature of such interdependence and the complexity of intragroup relationships differs widely among animals exhibiting social behavior. Group systems may be termed "subsocial" (118) when interdependence is incidental to the presence of other individuals and their role may be replaced by given environmental effects such as temperature. Allee (2) has demonstrated the broad adaptive significance of grouping in numerous lower phyla, in which an incidental kind of "cooperation" occurs. Or on the other hand, the interdependence may hinge qualitatively upon the nature of the composite effect of other members of the group as individuals with given properties. The great popular and even scientific prominence which the struggle and destruction aspects of evolution have received has tended to obscure the significance which "mutual aid" assumes in phylogeny on a wide variety of levels (62). "Cooperation" may be systematically present on the basis of a simple stereotyped system or on qualitatively specialized grounds. Other individuals of the species, or other animals, always must be considered as members of the effective environment of each individual, variously influencing the trend of its adjustments both pro and con on one or another qualitative level.

How similar and how different are social levels? A common factor evidently involved in the origin and maintenance of any social aggregation is based upon the biologically prepotent effect of weak stimulation in eliciting turning-toward reactions (95). The process seems to underlie interindividual responsiveness on all levels of complexity and qualitative elaboration in social behavior. This factor, which after Wheeler (118) may be termed "trophallaxis," is basic to the development of both stereotyped social patterns (as in insects) and more plastic social patterns (as in mammals). Its elaboration in lower-level societies involves learning only in a simple and secondary form delimited by hereditary mechanisms; in mammals its potentialities for plastic modification and elaboration are relatively greater. It is basic to and accounts for the gregariousness of individuals, however that gregariousness may be expressed and modified in a variety of ways through social heritage and special learning. The fundamental role of trophallactic processes in socialization derives from the fact that, from the first moment, interchanges which canalize and mold the early learning processes occur between the newborn mammal and its surroundings. Factors of relative dominance, ascendancy, or tendencies toward seclusiveness and the like, must be considered as of secondary and modifying significance, influencing the form of relationships in the social organization without being themselves basic to the *fact* that a social organization of some kind occurs.

Although the initiating factor in social aggregation evidently is broadly similar on levels from insects to man, differences of the widest magnitude appear in its expression in various social patterns. Such patterns are all adaptive in some important sense. In natural selection those organisms would appear to be favored which develop one or another mechanism of interindividual facilitation (2, 62). But it must also be recognized that the adaptive significance of a capacity for mutual assistance and its general role in selection may differ considerably according to the psychological level of its process. While mutual assistance on the insect level, developing on the basis of direct trophallactic interchanges, is limited to a relatively simple interindividual facilitation (95, 97) the chimpanzee can anticipate the result of joint effort in relation to a group goal (27). The possibilities on the human level are vastly greater, and moreover are psychologically cumulative. While any environmental changes effected through the "interindividual facilitation" to which insects are functionally restricted are typically standard for the species through innumerable generations for eons, important changes may occur in human society within a matter of years.

Of all the factors conditioning the potentialities of individual development and socialization on different levels, the most crucial is the extent to which the central nervous system has evolved. Although it appears that some capacity for learning plays an essential part in socialization on all levels, differences in the learning potential undoubtedly are of first importance in setting limits upon socialization, as upon the relative plasticity of adaptive functions in general.

Learning capacity, definable as susceptibility for effective individual changes through experience in the organization of the characteristic behavior pattern, has been demonstrated experimentally even in lower invertebrates such as flatworms (53, 75). Though learning can occur in the absence of cerebral cortex (65), experiments with lower animals show convincingly that it is qualitatively much reduced (29). The maximal accomplishments possible in inframammalian animals such as insects, although impressively complex in some respects, nevertheless show qualitative limitations such as a proneness for stereotypy and a sluggish development of habit organization. For example, the learning capacities of ants, evidently at their best in the *Formica* species, are relatively situation-bound and rotelike, resembling the showing of lower mammals (e.g., rats) deprived of much of their cortex (94). The behavior changes which have been reported for invertebrates such as protozoa and echinoderms appear to belong on a distinctive sublearning level, especially since they represent transient effects which do not alter the characteristic behavior pattern in any effective way.

Unfortunately psychologists have paid insufficient attention to the analysis of differences in learning capacity through the animal series. An influential contemporary learning theorist, Hull (56), endeavors to account for learning in general by applying the conditioned-response concept deductively. Various limitations of this approach have been pointed out by critics (66). A serious shortcoming of the Hull doctrine is its basic implication that differences in learning are secondary to the homogeneity which all cases are held to possess. It is characteristic of conditioned-response learning, however, that emphasis is upon the situation as set for the animal (e.g., by the experimenter). The role of the animal is relatively passive, with the pattern of its acquisition canalized by the prescribed stimulus-combination. Simpler instances, like the varieties of "habituation" or "negative adaptation," are similar in this respect. On the other hand, the "selective learning" or "trial and error learning" which is accomplished when an animal is free to act in terms of its own behavior resources, appears to be qualitatively distinct from and superior to "conditioning" in important respects. One critical aspect distinguishing "selective" learning, as Culler (28) and Maier and Schneirla (74) have pointed out, is that here the response of the animal changes the effective situation so that new types of adjustment may occur permitting a learning to anticipate the terminating condition, which can become a "goal." Through conditioning a child may be taught to pull a string until an object is encountered, then to pick it up and play—whereupon disconnecting string from object in a test will not inhibit pulling. When, however, through selective learning the child masters a more highly organized response in which string is pulled in relation to toy, then he both anticipates future play while pulling and notices a disconnected string before pulling. The qualitative inferiority of a conditioned-response learning often is not perceptible until the subject is required to use it in a changed situation (60).

It would appear very significant that in the lowest levels on which learning has been clearly demonstrated, the flatworms (53) and the annelids (26, 46, 121), conditioned-response patterns are possible but there is no clear evidence for selective learning. When *Formica* ants and rats are tested in an objectively identical maze pattern, the ants begin their specific learning with locally restricted unitary processes of a conditioned-response character, and selective learning enters gradually, whereas the rats evidence selective learning and intersegmental relationships at an early point (94). Such results suggest that, in addition to a qualitative difference between conditioning and selective learning, there exist different levels of qualitative accomplishment in selective learning itself.

In mammals, and particularly in the psychologically highest orders of mammals, maturation alone provides few specialized adaptive behavior mechanisms, whereas large repertoires of relatively stereotyped behavior are found in the lower groups. Among mammals as a rule the general adaptive pattern is initially unformed or very loosely formed. Their deficiency of organically stereotyped activities is coupled with an initial period of slow maturation in the atmospheric environment, typically under parental protection. Participation of the parents in the selective learning of young, a process first seen in birds, broadens the social environment according to degree of learning capacity. Organic factors such as those underlying nursing and brooding facilitate a prolonging of early trophallactic relations into a period of family life and perhaps higher-level socialization as well. Thus in various ways the mammal's superior learning capacity greatly broadens its environment and introduces more degrees of freedom under changing environmental conditions. Yet along with this progressively increasing adaptive plasticity, through a linkage of intervening stages, new possibilities for maladaptive behavior are also introduced (40). Thus among mammals according to group psychological capacities, "adaptive" and "maladaptive" become more relative to special value systems than they are in lower animals.

When "learning" is used as a generalized term, it is necessary to remember that a longer ontogenetic preparation usually combined with superior cortical equipment in the "higher" mammals introduces not only greater complexity in attainments but also a greater qualitative variation in the organic traces of experience. The inevitable outcome is a greater qualitative heterogeneity in the eventual adult pattern in dependence upon special conditions. Only man has the time, capacity, and special social assistance adequate for the guidance of learning by reasoning and long-term anticipation or special planning. Yet often through hampering conditions or conflicting special factors his individual and group attainments are arrested on lower stages.

One of the most important contributions of the kinds of selective learning admitted by the progressive evolution of cerebral cortex is that a more effective interrelationship becomes possible among the animal's organic processes and behavioral capacities. Thus visceral processes underlying emotion and motivation can enter into wider relations with capacities of the whole individual such as perception and anticipation in environmental adjustment. Lower mammals to some extent and man to an extent great in potential may thus learn to inhibit or divert hampering emotional and motivational processes.

A most important criterion of higher status in the psychological scale would appear to be group capacity for variable and plastic adjustments. The young individual in inframammalian and lower mammalian orders receives a rather standard preparation for social participation; hence the outcome is more or less typical for the standard environment. There is good reason to believe that organic differences (e.g., brood patches) exist among bird species which account for the young of one species taking more readily to a solitary life than a social one, or the reverse. In man the influence of surrounding individuals upon selective learning is vastly greater from the start and is potentially more variable—witness the striking differences which eventuate in children according to the nature of the "social heritage" dominating their upbringing (7). There is no evidence for the "instinctive" prepotency of individualistic or egocentric attitudes in man (31, 54, 79). The relative predominance of patterns such as competition or cooperation depends upon what system of cultural influences canalizes and guides the socialization process, not upon any known racial or national differences in germ plasm (79). When an educational program is unscientific in that it emphasizes a mass acquisition of predigested categorical results and discourages questioning and search for better answers to old questions, the conditioned-response pattern of learning obviously is in the ascendance and the intelligence potential of the given society is broadly wasted (39).

DRIVES, MOTIVATION, AND GOALS

One necessity is to understand the relation of goals to the basic organic energizing conditions which are conveniently denoted as "drives." We owe to Jennings (58) the first adequate emphasis upon an important basic fact about adaptive behavior patterns, that a given organic disturbance or deficiency leads inevitably to an increased variability in behavior, through which readjustment may occur by chance. An organic change which merely disturbs the subject in a generalized way may be termed a "lack." In organisms capable of learning through experience to the essential extent, "lacks" can become effective as "needs," since through conditioned-response or selective learning a special direct adjustment may be added to the behavior repertoire. Thus chicks learn to peck at grains when hungry. The effective need then becomes the focus of a "drive" or energizing tissue condition leading to given readjustments, and the special stimulus pattern promoting a given readjustment process may be termed an "incentive." Special incentive patterns the properties of which are not directly apparent but are anticipated in terms of their expected outcomes may be termed "goals." Here activities are more or less efficiently organized into a unitary system controlled by special "stimulus cues" and really projected into future time. Token-reward solutions as demonstrated for certain carnivores and primates illustrate "goal-wards" adjustments (120).

In situations of deficiency or "lack," the lowest organisms respond on a direct organic basis governed by the immediate biochemical stimulation, according to its intensity. Much the same is true of higher organisms at early stages before ontogenetic specialization has begun. On this level potentially harmful objects may elicit approach reactions much as Jennings's (58) observations disclosed—provided the effective stimulus is weak. Thus, at first the human infant does not "reach," but *gets the arm out* on appropriate stimulation. The difference is that, through experience, animals on successively higher levels can become "conditioned" or can learn selectively to respond according to the special properties of objects, i.e., what *kind* of object is involved. Frequently, as in orthodox Freudian doctrine and in typical "purposive" psychology, a given set of goals and perceptual processes is viewed as innate. Such practices are possible when the significance of ontogenetic psychological development in a given social setting is not really taken into account. Ontogenetic study of mammals discloses no innate "perception"; rather, "appreciating the nature of the object" in simple or involved ways depends upon the given animal's capacity to learn and its opportunity to learn through experience. The stages of perceptual learning are most numerous and complex in man, whose knowledge of objects and effective environment can expand progressively through reaching, crawling and walking toward the finally "calling"—that is, through codifying socially the anticipation of a desired object or situation. It is only through a developmental study of the socialization process, in which the interrelationship of successive stages is adequately considered, that the dependence of advanced stages of perceptual anticipation of "goals" upon initial nonperceptual processes of organic "lack" may be appreciated.

As Dashiell (30) puts it, "A man's interests and desires may become ever so elaborate, refined, socialized, sublimated, idealistic; but the raw basis from which they are developed is found in the phenomena of living matter." To say that fundamentally all behavior derives from and is motivated by the organic processes of the individual is not, however, tantamount to claiming that everything from impulse to attitude and purpose is traceable *directly* to a specific "drive" or energizing tissue condition. Those who insist upon such a narrow interpretation of the materialistic viewpoint underestimate the levels of complexity involved in mammalian, and especially human, psychological development. Yet progressive research in child psychology shows with increasing clarity that the relationship of motivated conduct to organic processes is at first insistently direct in the infant, and later steadily more indirect and devious. The sequence of interlocking stages involved in the education of motivational processes may be suggested by the progress of individuals in attaining their effective incentives and goals, as described by Shaffer (100) and other students of human adjustive behavior. Earliest to become recognizable are sustenance motives clearly related to tissue conditions; then are evident the more specialized "security" motives, and in different relative strengths "dominance," "social approval," "special sex motives," and so on.

Socialized human motivation functions on widely different qualitative levels, according to the complexity of the satisfactions afforded, and to the closeness of the relationship between basic organic factors and accepted goals. Only a failure to consider evidence from the ontogenetic processes of socialization can explain the neglect of the function of organic factors at all stages. Shaffer (100) has pointed out how each of the principal types of motivation, from sustenance to social approval, arises through the involvement of given initially reflexively functional tissue conditions in stimulative interchanges between infant and environment. The earliest situations inevitably combine more or less uniformly the various physiological states of interruptive (disturbance) or vegetative (relief) character with given environmental changes which through conditioned-response learning come to serve as special cues (e.g., the infant's response to special sounds much as to feeding). Then selective learning enters the picture and the infant becomes able to respond differentially to cues (e.g., turning toward one sound, "mother's voice," rather than another). The mother's voice soothes him as did feeding or patting originally, and thus functions as an early "substitute satisfaction." The selective process in time leads to a versatile anticipation of given social results and an initiation of his own cues as a means of manipulating and controlling these events. For example, the statement "Bub hungry" may become a special device if it has served to set the feeding process into action or hurry it along. Thus language symbols become involved in an infinite variety of ways both as especially efficient cues (e.g., "Love me?") and as anticipated ends in themselves (e.g., working hard, anticipating "We're proud of you!"). Here we realize that any attempt to write a social psychology based on individual motivation must fall short, since, highly individualistic or not, whatever system of effective incentives and accepted goals may prevail is a product of training in some kind of social environment.

The weakness in Lewin's (67) valence-vector conception of human motivation is that it presumes the existence of given adult systems of effective incentives and goals, without examining variations dependent upon the determining role of an ontogenetic socialization process effective according to selective conditions in the given social heritage and culture. In mammals such as rodents and carnivores, social heritage is limited to secondary and relatively disparate influences like structure of the burrow or parental activities in dealing with prey, so that nature of incentives and goals and the entire picture of motivation remains closely related to the basic integral organic processes themselves. In man, culture and intellectual heritage as selective agencies have so thoroughgoing an influence that even sustenance and security adjustments may become rather completely controlled and modified by factors of prestige, dominance, social approval, and the like. If one neglects ontogenetic development and does not endeavor to trace the influence of organic factors (i.e., the basic drives) up through the various stages of socialization, it is easy to forget that these organic factors are always involved directly or indirectly in adult behavior. Hence mystics and occasional idealistic philosophers may gain adherents for the view that sophisticated, well sublimated purposes and goals never have any relation to man's vulgar organic processes, but are present intuitively or instinctively. These last words denote procedures of evasion.

The elusiveness of the connection between the initial organic states, including processes such as trophallaxis on the one hand and the stages of psychological elaboration in socialization on the other, has permitted sophisticated men to forget that the organic factors are implicated as facilitators and reenforcing agents on all levels of development. The connection is readily overlooked or denied mainly because organic processes seldom appear in relief on higher psychological levels, but are modified and merged in qualitatively new adjustment patterns. Thus socialized man even under stress of extreme organic need or persistent frustration does not regress to the "brute level." Rather, he shifts to some eccentric and distorted variation of his ordinary personality, which varies from his prevalent socialized make-up according to the degree of integrity and organization attained by that adjustment system. The view that man's "higher psychological processes" constitute a single agency or unity which is capable of being sloughed off under hypothetically extreme provocation is a naive outcome of the mind-body conception of man's nature which stands in need of correction.

MIND, ADAPTIVE BEHAVIOR, AND REASONING

"Mind," ostensibly a term for a generalized functional entity, a very impressive term, actually is only an introductory expression for all of man's intellectual capacities and attainments considered as a system. It is only in a relative and not at all an absolute sense that the processes denoted by terms such as reasoning, thinking, imagining, knowing, perceiving, anticipating, learning, and attitudinizing constitute a unitary and integral system. Attempts to conceive these functions as constituting a single noncorporeal agency, distinct at all times from "body," have failed dismally as a basis for prediction in science. Notable examples may be found: from the Kantian prediction of complete failure for an experimental psychology since "mind" was held to be nonorganic and hence not subject to measurement, to the endeavors of the "formal discipline" school to train "memory" as though it were a unitary and discrete thing rather than a term for a set of deviously related characteristics of learning and recall.

The various forms of mentalism in psychology tend to give spurious answers to the problems of reality and of knowledge. They confuse the evasive *phenomenon* of "awareness" with a postulated general causal agency, a functional or structured "consciousness" to which are imputed various descriptively familiar properties such as "knowing" and "choosing." As Holt (52) has put it, for an explanation of these functions is substituted a "little man inside," endowed a priori with all the properties to be explained. Unfortunately this preexperimental and nonscientific procedure is insistently maintained by a social pressure grounded in social heritage and propagated in our everyday vocabulary and dictionary as in our mores. The reductio ad absurdum is reached when the capacities of lower animals are attributed to "animal mind," when animals are spoken of as "instinctively knowing," and when anthropocentric ideas dominate comparative psychology to the detriment of a really comparative investigation.

In endeavoring to understand the nature of higher psychological processes, it is dangerous to accept one characteristic as if it were critically representative of the whole system, or central to it. Early American experimenters in animal psychology (23, 24, 43, 107) thus endeavored to test for the presence or absence of "ideas" or "imagery" in lower mammals, as somehow critically indicative of thought processes. The results were not at all conclusive (75, 115). Even in man, where imagery may be studied with far greater directness than in lower mammals, various experimenters (13, 86) have found its role generally of secondary importance in reasoning, if not actually detrimental to best results. Theories such as Binet's (11) and Titchener's (110) which account for reasoning in terms of the association of memory images are at best very incomplete.

The concept of imagery denotes only the sensory aspect of representation, which is but one phase of the capacity for dealing perceptually with objects or situations in their absence. Its relation to an action basis, or lack of such basis, is highly significant, as Werner (117) has shown ontogenetically. Significantly, the principal contribution of delayed-response method has been made in the demonstration that to relatively different extents rodents, carnivores, and other mammals below primates possess capacities for the representation of absent situations. Differences are found, with anthropoids superior to lower mammals, both in the time limit and in the qualitative complexity of the represented situation. This capacity both widens the boundaries of the immediate spatial environment and extends the effective temporal limits of integrated environmental adaptation.

The term "anticipation" signifies the more dynamic type of representation, in which the organism projects itself into an organized sequence of specialized adjustments of representational character dominated by the expected development of a given outcome—a "goal." Although orthodox teleologists generously endow all animals with this capacity, its presence has been demonstrated adequately only in the mammals. Comparisons are helpful here. The excitatory function in insect "communication" is performed in a stereotyped way without any evidence of expecting given results; whereas the shoulder-tapping gesture of a chimpanzee in a joint rope-pulling problem clearly involves an expectation of producing given changes in the partner, with a readiness to join in the projected future activity (27). The nature and elaboration of symbolic cues in anticipatory behavior appears to depend upon the relative development of cerebral cortex as a basis for advance in perceptual learning. Thus the chimpanzee's inability to advance beyond gestural cues in his anticipatory adjustments, to the mastery and employment of verbal language cues, does not seem to lie mainly in an incapacity to make the sounds, but rather in his restricted ability to organize meaningful relationships in anticipation. In view of the fact that the perceptual anticipation we have been discussing is an instance of thinking, the lower primates may be considered as chronically inferior to man in the qualitative nature of these processes.

Qualitative differences in thinking often are somewhat confused through the use of the term "insight." Thus Thorpe (108) has considerably exceeded the scope of his evidence by generalizing the insight concept to some insect accomplishments which superficially appear to involve "insightful" processes. If "insight" is taken rather vaguely to mean "seeing through to the solution of a difficulty," such an analogical extension of the term may seem justifiable, for insects often do overcome difficulties in ways which might appear similar to primate solutions. Thus, numerous observers have reported Ammophila wasps tamping down earth with a pebble in closing their burrows. However adaptive, such behavior seems more susceptible to explanation as an act arising spontaneously in the course of stereotyped activities than as problem-thinking (8). Neither is the complexity of insect behavior in learning problems, or the relatively sudden improvement in efficiency which sometimes occurs, any necessary indication of "insight" processes, for analytical study of such accomplishments reveals that they have a much simpler character within the limits of rather stereotyped selective learning (94).

It seems necessary to study instances of suspected "insight" not only in terms of the given problem situation, but also in the ontogenetic background of preparation for the event. Thus, in working toward a fuller understanding of the stick solutions reported for chimpanzees by Köhler (61), Birch (12) found that previous use of sticks in play, although not in food-getting, provided a generalized background of preparation for the accomplishment of "insightful" food-attainment solutions with sticks. From our theory of the ontogeny of purposive action, it may be suggested that the basis for solution was provided by the previous perception of stick-in-hand-lengthening-arm, which now can lead to an anticipation of stick-in-hand when the food is seen beyond arm-reaching distance. A relationship of this kind was in fact suggested by Köhler (61) himself.

On the human level, comparable differences in action experience seem to condition the occurrence of "insight" in surrogate ways. In Durkin's (35) experiment with human subjects assembling a complex patchwork puzzle, insightful or sudden-integration solutions were accomplished most frequently by subjects who had previously worked with the component sections of the complex problem as subpuzzles, but scarcely at all by those subjects who had no previous experience with any part of the puzzle. It is significant that the latter subjects were the ones who worked most persistently with their hands, by "overt trial and error," whereas the "insight" subjects spent more time thinking—that is, in anticipating or dynamically representing the prospective results of their working processes. The trial-and-error subjects merely perceived the pieces as belonging to a puzzle to be solved, the "insight" subjects more readily perceived them in terms of an anticipated use in-relation-to-something-else in a possible type of solution. An intermediate "gradual analysis" solution type combined features of these two.

Human thinking has many types, from simple representation and anticipation through more complex daydreaming and free imagination, from simple rationalization to rather elaborate autistic patterns, and from creative imagination to more or less systematic reasoning. All these types involve two characteristics in particular—various meaning-systems are dealt with in terms of representative processes, and these processes (or "concepts") function in a highly reduced (i.e., schematized) form which under the most efficient conditions obviates recourse to overt behavior. The ontogeny of human thinking is a long process, proceeding from an early basis of direct perceptual adjustments, to the development of a capacity to represent and anticipate absent situations, and next the imaginative interrelating of represented meaning-systems. Infrahuman primates fall far behind the human infant in the basic perceptual and object-meaning acquisitions (57), quite evidently through deficiency in the organic prerequisites for complex learning (i.e., cortical equipment). This deficiency may well account for their inability to master the use of sounds as symbols, an accomplishment which is well under way in the human infant, as a rule, shortly after one year of age. The chimpanzee reaches his limit at the level of representative (conceptual) cues which grew out of the meaning-system itself and remain qualitatively similar to it —as do simple gestures.

Findings in comparative psychology lead to the conclusion that lower primates, and even many psychologically lower mammals such as dog and rat, are capable of solving problems through identifiable processes of thinking. Maier's work (73) suggests that processes which serve as cues for overt adjustments may be reorganized implicitly even in rodents; the studies of Köhler (61) and of Yerkes (122) demonstrate this for lower primates. The above conception of animal reasoning has been arrived at inductively, through experimental investigation; it might well be used as a simple definition of the basic and essential process in human reasoning. In this sense, on experimental grounds, we are able to recognize that a capacity to reason is present in lower mammals.

The qualitative superiority and immensely greater versatility of human reasoning is of course undeniable. However, the difference although great is a relative one. T. V. Moore (80) has endeavored to make it absolute, through the following dialectic argument:

> Do animals reason? Reasoning in human beings has a specific meaning: the deduction of conclusions from general principles. This is the sense in which the term is used in most works on logic. To depart from this meaning is likely to give rise to various ambiguities and any such clouding of expression must by all means be avoided.

If we recognize that the nature of reasoning must be worked out in scientific investigation and cannot be limited a priori through categorical speculative procedures, this argument loses its basis. The "specific meaning" favored by Moore would in fact lead to the categorical elimination of vast areas of human reasoning, from the rambling generative processes of "creative imagination" to the inductive processes which underlie and permeate scientific theorizing.

The evidence from lower mammals indicates that their reasoning is characteristically a matter of synthetic processes in which relatively simple recombinations and reorganizations of learned representational systems permit overcoming difficulties in ways not covered by unmodified recall of experience (75). Man at his best is of course vastly superior in such accomplishments; however, for an adequate comparative study of human capacity it is necessary to study him also in his varying degrees of efficiency and of preparation, and to examine his progress through the ontogenetic stages underlying various types of adult thought patterns. In the lower levels of intelligence and of education, and in early childhood, we find that human reasoning is not at all conveniently divisible into deductive and inductive patterns, any more than it is in lower mammals (31, 54, 69). On the other hand, in the unsophisticated struggles of young children (3, 90) or of poorly prepared adults with new problems requiring reasoning (35, 61) we note significant features basically similar to the reasoning of lower primates as described by Yerkes and Köhler.

MAN AND LOWER ANIMALS

There are two extreme views concerning man's relationship to lower animals: one, the nonscientific position that man possesses an immortal soul which sets him sharply and forever apart from the "brute"; the other, the scientifically developed evolutionary conception of man as a higher animal who has emerged gradually by a process of continual evolution from ancestral forms similar to what he now calls "animals." The latter approach, experimentally grounded, has opened the way for a recognition of basic similarities to lower animals on essentially biological levels, and of important potentialities for superior development on psychological and social levels (33). Such a comparative procedure has guided the foregoing discussion.

The comparative study of man in the various sciences, from biology to psychology and anthropology, assuredly does not mark human beings off as different from lower animals in absolute ways. The differences are of course striking and outstanding, when one considers the impressive continuity and development of man's languages, his literary and artistic creativity, his social and political institutions, his long-term propagation and improvement of knowledge in history and in science. There is one capacity in particular, man's facility in the technique of articulate language, which seems to be prerequisite to his superior attainments (9, 89). Yet his qualitative distinction is not an absolute or complete one in this respect, since the most essential psychological characteristic of language, the formulation and delivery of symbols in directive, purposive ways, has been demonstrated in the lower primates (27). Furthermore, man is not absolutely different from lower animals in his capacity for thinking and reasoning, because levels of difference have been demonstrated among lower mammals both in the capacity for implicit representation and self-signaling essential to thinking and in the extemporaneous reorganization of different meaning-systems central to problem-solving thought or reasoning.

Neither is man absolutely different in social respects from lower animals. Fundamentally similar biological factors are traceable in the processes underlying gregarious behavior on very different social levels from insect to human society. The outcome of their influence, and the nature of behavior patterns producible through their elaboration, naturally differ according to the nature of psychological capacities and other special factors (e.g., sexual rhythms, social heritage) involved on the different levels. Lower-level societies exhibit social heritage in different but always limited respects, from the presence of particular nest constructions and prevalent chemical patterns as in insects to the parental and family influences upon selective learning in the ontogeny of various mammals. Culture in the ethnopsychological sense is not absent from lower primates, as witness Köhler's (61) report of observing self-decoration and crude quasi-ritualistic group dancing in chimpanzees, and Tinklepaugh's (109) note that monkeys (like chimpanzees) often pluck fur with evident anticipation of an adornment effect. These last similarities, particularly, are outgrowths of the trophallactic basis of social unity.

It is of course truistic to say that man's ways of life are far more complex and plastic than those of lower animals, in relation to infinitely more variable ontogenetic contributions in his case. Lower animals always exhibit marked stereotypy although to different extents in their constructions and dwellings, strongly in contrast to man's versatility in artistic forms and in architecture. Potentially, man's degrees of freedom are far greater through his superior learning and thinking capacities, his incentive and goals far more extensive and elaborately specialized beyond the bounds of initially effective and physiologically dominated sustenance motivation, than those of lower mammals. Man is capable of goals and purposive behavior on many different levels. Unfortunately, this superiority is often misused to the point of maladaptiveness. It is a prevalent hazard of the human level of psychological versatility that superior logical attainments may be used ingeniously to favor the propagation of illogical and unscientific practices in society, and that superior social groups may beat each other down. The systematic institutional propagation of mysticism and narrow stereotyped patterns in human society is responsible to no small extent for the fact that, contemporaneously, human science is far ahead of social capacities to utilize its advances.

Scientists and philosophers, who are bound to be intimately concerned professionally with the principles of validity in reasoning, must consequently become interested in the verifiability and validity of the ethical and moral precepts which are influential in their society. Such attitudes represent a full appreciation of the fact that man's supremacy in cortical equipment permits his attainment educationally of a superior capacity level on which episodes of reasoning may extend into organized sequences of plans and programs. However, when this superior capacity of ontogenetic versatility leads into the cultivation of barrier-building techniques and fetishistic intergroup conflicts, the potentialities of reasoning are blunted inevitably in individual and group, and there occur widespread lapses to lower-level types of adjustment among the human possibilities.

CONCLUSION

The foregoing discussion has emphasized the fallacious nature of a generalized teleology which argues for a purposive agency in all organisms, and thereby obscures the fact that somewhat similar effectiveness in adaptive behavior may exist on rather different biological and psychological levels of organization. Indicating some of the pitfalls which are introduced through a reliance upon analogy, we have tried to suggest the manner in which comparative study reveals the actual nature of similarities and differences among the many adaptive levels. The levels considered lowest are those on which specific biological processes account directly for the character of adaptive behavior, without further hierarchies of complexity in the organization; the progressively higher levels are marked by the presence of progressive linked stages of organization typified by increased qualitative complexity in perception and learning; the highest levels are those of plastic adaptive adjustments arising through widened learning capacities and the entrance of thinking. Reasoning arises as a specialized problem-solution type of thinking. Biological processes are involved indispensably at all levels, yet their discrete functions and simpler interrelationships do not account directly for the superior capacities of the higher organisms as mechanistic theorists have claimed. On the other hand, the inadequacy of Mechanism at higher levels does not warrant resorting to Vitalism. The far sounder alternative is the practice of continuing to study all levels comparatively, discarding concepts and dichotomies which are outgrown, and constructing theories which better represent the nature of similarities and differences in animal capacity throughout the series.

REFERENCES

1. Allee, W. C. 1942. Social dominance and subordination among verte-brates. *Biol. Symposia* 8: 139–162.
2. Allee, W. C. 1938. *The social life of animals.* New York: Norton.
3. Alpert, A. 1928. *The solving of problem-situations by Preschool children: An analysis* (Contributions to Education, No. 323). New York: Teachers College, Columbia Univ.
4. Armstrong, E. A. 1942. *Bird display.* London: Cambridge Univ. Press.
5. Bahm, A. J. 1944. Teleological arguments. *Sci. Mon.* 58: 377–382.
6. Bartlett, F. C. 1932. *Remembering: A study in experimental and social psychology.* New York: Macmillan.
7. Benedict, R. 1934. *Patterns of culture.* Boston: Houghton.
8. Berland, L. 1935. Quelques traits du comportement des Hyménoptères Sphégiens. *Ann. Sci. Nat.,* 10th Series, 18: 53–66.
9. Bierens de Haan, J. A. 1930. Animal language in its relation to that of man. *Biol. Rev.* 4: 249–268.
10. Bierens de Haan, J. A. 1947. Animal psychology and the science of ani-mal behaviour. *Behaviour* 1: 71–80.
11. Binet, A. 1899. *The psychology of reasoning.* Chicago: Open Court.
12. Birch, H. B. 1945. The relation of previous experience to insightful problem-solving. *J. Comp. Psychol.* 38: 367–383.
13. Bowers, H. 1935. The role of visual imagery in reasoning. *Brit. J. Psychol.* 25: 436–446.
14. Bramstedt, F. 1939. Ueber die Dressur-Fähigkeiten der Ciliaten. *Zool. Anz.* 12: 111–127.
15. Bridges, Katherine M. 1931. *The social and emotional development of the pre-school child.* London: Kegan Paul.
16. Brown, J. F. 1936. *Psychology and the social order.* New York: McGraw-Hill.
17. Carmichael, L., and M. F. Smith. 1939. Quantified pressure stimulation and the specificity and generality of response in fetal life. *J. Genetic Psychol.* 54: 425–434.
18. Carpenter, C. R. 1934. A field study of the behavior and social relations of howling monkeys (Alouatta palliata). *Comp. Psychol. Monogr.* 10: 1–168.
19. Chauvin, R. 1947. Les Progrès de la psychologie animale moderne et leur intérêt en psychologie humaine. *Rev. Quest. Sci.* 20: 188–204.
20. Child, C. M. 1924. *Physiological foundations of behavior.* New York: Holt.
21. Coghill, G. E. 1929. *Anatomy and the problem of behavior.* London: Cambridge Univ. Press.
22. Cohen, M. R. 1931. *Reason and nature.* New York: Harcourt.
23. Cole, L. W. 1915. The Chicago experiments with raccoons. *J. Anim. Behav.* 5: 158–173.

24. Cole, L. W. 1907. Concerning the intelligence of raccoons. *J. Comp. Neurol. Psychol.* 17: 211–261.
25. Collias, N. E. 1944. Aggressive behavior among vertebrate animals. *Physiol. Zool.* 17: 83–123.
26. Copeland, M. 1930. An apparent conditioned response in *Nereis virens*. *J. Comp. Psychol.* 10: 339–354.
27. Crawford, M. P. 1937. The cooperative solving of problems by young chimpanzees. *Comp. Psychol. Monogr.* 14: 1–88.
28. Culler, E. A. 1938. Recent advances in some concepts of conditioning. *Psychol. Rev.* 45: 134–153.
29. Culler, E. A., and E. Mettler. 1934. Conditioned behavior in a decorticate dog. *J. Comp. Psychol.* 18: 291–303.
30. Dashiell, J. F. 1937. *Fundamentals of general psychology.* Boston: Houghton.
31. Deutsche, J. M. 1937. *The development of children's concepts of causal relations.* Child Welfare Monograph Series, No. 13. Minneapolis: Univ. of Minnesota Press.
32. Dobzhansky, T. 1941. *Genetics and the origin of species,* 2nd ed. (rev.) I. New York: Columbia Univ. Press.
33. Dobzhansky, T., and M. F. Ashley Montagu. 1947. Natural selection and the mental capacities of mankind. *Science* 105: 587–606.
34. Driesch, H. 1908. *The science and philosophy of the organism.* 2 vol. London: Black.
35. Durkin, H. E. 1937. Trial and error, gradual analysis, and sudden reorganization. *Arch. Psychol.,* No. 210, pp. 1–85.
36. Emerson, A. E. 1942. Basic comparisons of human and insect societies. *Biol. Symp.* 8: 163–176.
37. Emerson, A. E. 1939. Social coordination and the superorganism. *Am. Midland Nat.* 21: 182–209.
38. Fraenkel, G., and D. D. Gunn. 1940. *The orientation of animals.* Oxford: Clarendon Press.
39. Freeman, E. 1940. *Conquering the man in the street.* New York: Vanguard Press.
40. Galt, W. 1940. The principle of cooperation in behavior. *Quart. Rev. Biol.* 15: 401–410.
41. Goldstein, K. 1939. *The organism.* New York: American Book Co.
42. Grabowski, U. 1939. Experimentelle Untersuchungen über das angebliche Lernvermögen von Paramaecium. *Z. Tierpsychol.* 2: 265–282.
43. Gregg, F. M., and C. A. McPheeters. 1913. Behavior of raccoons to a temporal series of stimuli. *J. Anim. Behav.* 3: 241–259.
44. Halverson, H. M. 1933. Acquisition of skill in infancy. *J. Genet. Psychol.* 43: 3–48.
45. Hamilton, W. F. 1922. Coordination in the starfish: II, Locomotion. *J. Comp. Psychol.* 2: 61–76.
46. Heck, L. 1920. Ueber die Bildung einer Assoziation beim Regenwurm auf Grund von Dressurversuchen. *Lotos Naturwiss. Z.* 68: 168–189.

47. Hertz, M. 1931. Die Organisation des optischen Feldes bei der Biene. *Z. vergl. Physiol.* 14: 629–674.
48. Hess, W. 1924. Reactions to light in the earthworm, *Lumbricus terrestris* L. *J. Morphol. Physiol.* 39: 515–542.
49. Hingston, R. W. G. 1929. *Instinct and intelligence.* New York: Macmillan.
50. Hoagland, H. 1928. On the mechanism of tonic immobility in vertebrates. *J. Gen. Physiol.* 11: 715–742.
51. Holt, E. B. 1931. *Animal drive and the learning process.* New York: Holt.
52. Holt, E. B. 1937. Materialism and the criterion of the psychic. *Psychol. Rev.* 44: 33–53.
53. Hovey, H. B. 1929. Associative hysteresis in flatworms. *Physiol. Zool.* 2: 322–333.
54. Huang, I. 1930. Children's explanations of strange phenomena. *Psychol. Forschung.* 14: 63–182.
55. Huang, I., H. Yang, and F. Y. Yao. 1945. Principles of selection in children's "phenomenistic" explanations. *J. Genet. Psychol.* 66: 63–68.
56. Hull, C. L. 1944. *Principles of behavior.* New York: Appleton-Century.
57. Jacobsen, C. F., M. M. Jacobsen, and J. G. Yoshioka. 1932. Development of an infant chimpanzee during her first year. *Comp. Psychol. Monogr.* 9.
58. Jennings, H. S. 1906. *The behavior of lower organisms.* New York: Columbia Univ. Press.
59. Jennings, H. S. 1907. Behavior of the starfish, *Asterias forreri de Loriol. Univ. Calif. Publ. Zool.* 4: 53–185.
60. Katona, G. 1940. *Organizing and memorizing.* New York: Columbia Univ. Press.
61. Köhler, W. 1926. *The mentality of apes.* New York: Harcourt.
62. Kropotkin, P. M. 1917. *Mutual aid: A factor of evolution.* New York: Knopf.
63. Kuo, Z. Y. 1932. Ontogeny of embryonic behavior in Aves: IV, The influence of embryonic movements upon the behavior after hatching. *J. Comp. Psychol.* 14: 109–122.
64. Lack, D. 1940. Pair-formation in birds. *Condor* 42: 269–286.
65. Lashley, K. S. 1932. Integrative functions of the cerebral cortex. *Physiol. Rev.* 13: 1–42.
66. Leeper, R. 1944. Dr. Hull's principles of behavior. *J. Genet. Psychol.* 65: 3–52.
67. Lewin, K. 1935. *A dynamic theory of personality.* New York: McGraw-Hill.
68. Lorenz, K. 1937. The companion in the bird's world. *Auk* 54: 245–273.
69. Lorimer, F. 1929. *The growth of reason.* New York: Harcourt.
70. McDougall, W. 1911. *Body and mind.* New York: Macmillan.
71. McDougall, W. 1929. *Modern materialism and emergent evolution.* New York: Van Nostrand.
72. McGill, V. J. 1945. The mind-body problem in the light of recent psychology. *Sci. and Soc.* 9: 335–361.

73. Maier, N. R. F. 1929. Reasoning in white rats. *Comp. Psychol. Monogr.* 6.
74. Maier, N. R. F., and T. C. Schneirla. 1942. Mechanisms in conditioning. *Psychol. Rev.* 49: 117–134.
75. Maier, N. R. F. and T. C. Schneirla. 1935. *Principles of animal psychology.* New York: McGraw-Hill.
76. Marshall, A. J. 1944. Display and bower-building in bower-birds. *Nature* 153: 685.
77. Mast, S. O., and L. Pusch, 1924. Modification of response in amoeba. *Biol. Bull.* 46: 55–59.
78. Mayr, E. 1942. *Systematics and the origin of species.* New York: Columbia Univ. Press.
79. Mead, M., ed. 1937. *Cooperation and competition among primitive peoples.* New York: McGraw-Hill.
80. Moore, T. V. 1941. Human and animal intelligence. In *Scientific aspects of the race problem.* New York: Longmans. Chap. III.
81. Moss, F. A., ed. 1942. *Comparative psychology.* New York: Prentice-Hall.
82. Munn, N. L. 1933. *An introduction to animal psychology: The behavior of the rat.* Boston: Houghton.
83. Needham, J. 1929. *The sceptical biologist.* London: Chatto.
84. Newcomb, T., ed. 1947. *Readings in social psychology.* New York: Holt.
85. Novikoff, A. 1945. The concept of integrative levels and biology. *Science* 101: 209–215.
86. Pear, T. H. 1937. The place of imagery in mental processes. *Bull. John Rylands Libr.* 21: 3–24.
87. Pratt, K. C. 1934. Generalization and specificity of the plantar response in newborn infants: The reflexogenous zone: I. *J. Genet. Psychol.* 44: 265–300; II. *Ibid.,* 45: 22–38.
88. Pycraft, W. P. 1914. *The courtship of animals.* London: Hutchinson.
89. Révész, G. 1944. The language of animals. *J. Gen. Psychol.* 30: 117–147.
90. Richardson, H. M. 1932. The growth of adaptive behavior in infants: An experimental study at seven age levels. *Genet. Psychol. Monogr.* 12: 195–359.
91. Rosenfield, L. D. 1941. *From beast-machine to man-machine: Animal soul in French letters from Descartes to La Mettrie.* New York: Oxford Univ. Press.
92. Russell, E. S. 1938. *The behaviour of animals.* London: Edward Arnold.
93. Schjelderup-Ebbe, T. 1922. Beiträge zur Sozialpsychologie des Haushuhns. *Ztschr. Psychol.* 88: 225–252.
94. Schneirla, T. C. 1945. Ant learning as a problem in comparative psychology. In P. L. Harriman, ed., *Twentieth Century Psychology.* New York: Philosophical Library. Pp. 266–305.
95. Schneirla, T. C. 1946. Problems in the biopsychology of social organization. *J. Abnorm. Soc. Psychol.* 41: 385–402.
96. Schneirla, T. C. 1944. The reproductive functions of the army-ant queen

as pace-maker of the group behavior pattern. *J. N. Y. Entom. Soc.* 52: 153–192.

97. Schneirla, T. C. 1941. Social organization in insects, as related to individual function. *Psychol. Rev.* 48: 465–486.

98. Schneirla, T. C. 1939. A theoretical consideration of the basis for approach-withdrawal adjustments in behavior. *Psychol. Bull.* 37: 501–502.

99. Schneirla, T. C. 1938. A theory of army-ant behavior based upon the analysis of activities in a representative species. *J. Comp. Psychol.* 25: 51–90.

100. Shaffer, L. F. 1936. *The psychology of adjustment: An objective approach to mental hygiene.* Boston: Houghton.

101. Shepard, J. F., and F. S. Breed. 1913. Maturation and use in the development of an instinct. *J. Anim. Behav.* 3: 274–285.

102. Sherman, M. 1927. The differentiation of emotional responses in infants: (I) Judgments of emotional responses from motion picture views and from actual observation. *J. Comp. Psychol.* 7: 265–284.

103. Sherman, M. and I. C. Sherman. 1925. Sensorimotor responses in infants. *J. Comp. Psychol.* 5: 53–68.

104. Sherrington, C. S. 1906. *The integrative action of the nervous system.* New Haven: Yale Univ. Press.

105. Sloane, E. H. 1945. Reductionism. *Psychol. Rev.* 52: 214–223.

106. Stratton, G. M. 1928. Excitement as an undifferentiated emotion. In C. Murchison and M. L. Reymert, eds., *Feelings and emotion.* Worcester, Mass.: Clark Univ. Press. Chap. 17.

107. Thorndike, E. L. 1911. *Animal intelligence.* New York: Macmillan.

108. Thorpe, W. H. 1943. Types of learning in insects and other arthropods. *Brit. J. Psychol.* (Gen.) 33: 220–234; 34: 20–31, 66–76.

109. Tinklepaugh, O. 1931. Fur-picking in monkeys as an act of adornment. *J. Mammal.* 12: 430–431.

110. Titchener, E. B. 1909. *Lectures on the experimental psychology of the thought processes.* New York: Macmillan.

111. Tolman, E. C. 1932. *Purposive behavior in animals and men.* New York: Appleton-Century.

112. Uexküll, J. v. 1900. Die Physiologie des Seeigelstachels. *Ztschr. Biol.* 39: 73–112.

113. Warden, C. J., T. N. Jenkins, and L. H. Warner. 1935. *Comparative Psychology: A comprehensive treatise* (3 vols.). New York: Ronald Press.

114. Warren, H. C. 1930. The organic world and the causal principle. *Science,* 71: 204–208.

115. Washburn, M. F. 1926. *The animal mind,* 3rd ed. New York: Macmillan.

116. Watson, J. B. 1919. *Psychology from the standpoint of a behaviorist.* Philadelphia: Lippincott.

117. Werner, H. 1940. *Comparative psychology of mental development.* New York: Harper.

118. Wheeler, W. M. 1928. *The social insects.* New York: Harcourt.

119. Wolf, E. 1933. Das Verhalten der Bienen gegenüber flimmernden Feldern und bewegten Objekten. *Z. vergl. Physiol.* 20: 151–161.

120. Wolfe, J. B. 1936. Effectiveness of token-rewards for chimpanzees. *Comp. Psychol. Monogr.* 13: 1–72.
121. Yerkes, R. M. 1912. The intelligence of earthworms. *J. Anim. Behav.* 2: 332–352.
122. Yerkes, R. M., and A. W. Yerkes. 1929. *The great apes.* New Haven: Yale Univ. Press.

T. C. SCHNEIRLA

The Concept of Levels in the
Study of Social Phenomena

Bibliography No. 65

There are many types of animal aggregations typically formed under natural conditions, from groups of the protozoan organism, Paramecium, to human organizations (15). How are we to understand them? Despite their apparent diversity, all such groups have in common a "togetherness" of individuals. In every such aggregation, unity is evident to some extent, suggesting properties more or less different from those of the separate, unassembled individuals. The nature of the properties of group unity is by no means immediately apparent in any case. More than one writer has conceived it mystically, as an intangible agency and even a kind of collective mentality, exemplified in Maeterlinck's concept "spirit of the hive" for an insect colony (12), and Le Bon's "crowd mind" for human groups (10). However appealing they may be, such ideas serve only to emphasize the existence of a unified group, and make no substantial contribution toward explaining the question of its nature. More recently, a realistic method has developed which promises to correct such difficulties.

Modern scientific investigations have sharpened the realization that there are numerous types of aggregations typically formed by different animals, similar to one another in certain respects and different in other respects. Understanding what holds various types of groups together and what principles underlie their organizations derives from insight not only into their common features but also into their differences.

The concept of "levels" has developed as a means of organizing our evidence concerning the types of collective behavior exhibited in the animal series. In this approach, various kinds of aggregation are ranked "higher" or "lower" in a scale, according to our evaluation of these groups in terms of criteria of tested validity. Of course it is not a simple matter to determine what clues in the evidence are most valid as indicators of relative superiority or inferiority in group function. In the scientific study of varied types of aggregations, however, it is understood first of all that the

From *Groups in Harmony and Tension,* by Muzafer Sherif and Carolyn Sherif. New York: Harper and Brothers, 1953. Reprinted with permission.

principles whereby higher groups are considered superior to lower-level types can be worked out dependably only through actual investigations of groups to learn their real characteristics. In this chapter the point will be discussed principally in terms of some comparisons of human and insect aggregations.

The primary purpose of the *levels concept* is to understand the relationships of varied natural phenomena in general, and not social phenomena alone. Although all types of animals are basically regarded as having had a common ancestry, animals now living may be considered the representatives of different stages attained through evolution. The levels concept represents the different types of individual organisms as differing in stage of organization, from the viruses, considered at a lower level than the Protozoa, to various multicellular organisms, considered respectively higher. With justification we may consider the viruses a simpler type of organism than a multicellular animal, but differences in organization other than relative complexity must be taken into account as well, in the study of organismic levels. In what respects, finally, is a bird considered an organism on a higher level than a starfish, a monkey on a higher level than a bird? Further and more elaborate difficulties arise when we pass beyond the comparison of types of individual organisms to compare *groups* of organisms in regard to their respective levels.

First of all, social levels are not to be distinguished in terms of how successful various types of groups have been in meeting (i.e., how well they are adapted to) the conditions of their environments (1), because environmental conditions are not the same for various types of organisms, but differ greatly according to the different capacities of their members— their sensory equipment, for example. A large group of "tent caterpillars," reassembled each night within its enclosure of silken threads spun on a tree, may be as relatively successful at surviving in its environment as human inhabitants of a nearby settlement are in theirs, notwithstanding the far greater total and greater variety of sensory impressions received by members of the human group from their surroundings. For the rise of all animal species has occurred through natural-selection processes in the course of which poorly adjusted animal types are "weeded out." These varied events in evolution have led to the survival of animals which acquire (through mutation and related biological processes) adequate adaptive resources and to the elimination of those acquiring inadequate adaptive resources. Thus a species so constituted that its members were always attracted to intense stimulus changes would risk extinction through an unusual frequency of serious injury to member individuals. Surviving species, animals now existing, may be ranked high or low with respect to social characteristics but do not have *corresponding* ranks with respect to adaptive success. Colonies of the swimming protozoan, Paramecium, colonies of a social insect, and communities of mankind are not clearly different in this respect. For present purposes we may assume that all meet their respective environmental conditions reasonably well, although these conditions are very different in complexity and other respects more important for the psychologist. The differences crucial for social levels depend upon the *ways* in which various types of animal groups adjust to their typical surroundings.

In other words, differences in "levels" depend upon *what kinds of processes and capacities are available* to an animal and its species mates in adapting to their environments. Because of their sensorimotor capacities in particular, social insects such as ants and bees in their colony settings may be ranked higher in the group-level array than the sponge, a colonial organism very deficient in such capacities. Furthermore, a higher status in this respect depends more upon advantages in the *kind* of capacities available in the group than upon complexity. Thus the pattern of community life in social insects evidently is influenced only in limited ways through learning—ways which may be considered meager in group potentialities compared with the relatively vast functions of learning in the socialized life of man. This is the case despite the fact that the social life of insects tends to be very complex. This point bears further study.

It seems also true that animal aggregations of the most different types (and levels) exhibit certain basic similarities (1, 19). A point that soon impresses even casual observers is that very different aggregations often attain recognizably similar end results. Thus, for example, man builds huts or grand skyscrapers, termites simple ball-nests of mud or impressive rock-hard spire nests; human cities are complexly organized, but insect communities also show an amazing complexity in their daily affairs. However, in the internal and basic processes whereby these assemblages function, maintain their organization, and attain their characteristic results, the social phenomena are very different.

We must discard both the notion that sheer complexity is the most dependable guide to the level of a social phenomenon and the corollary idea that the kind of result achieved through group action is a necessary guide to the level of a society. On the contrary, the problem is not that simple, for as suggested above, the key of social levels must be sought in underlying processes. Let us consider one of many possible examples in which great functional complexity exists in a group which, qualitatively considered, is relatively low in level.

In certain species of army ants living in tropical forests, mass or swarm raids are organized anew each day by the colonies (16). These forays are amazingly complex as to both numbers of participants and the variety and organization of their behavior. They are also highly successful (i.e., very adaptive) in their tangible outcome, which is great quantities of living prey delivered as booty to the temporary nest of the colony. The swarms of one common species often grow larger than fifteen yards in width each forenoon and then may contain more than 30,000 individuals. The intricacy of internal organization is suggested by the fact that, although such a body becomes very large, it continues to sweep along as a growing unified group moving roughly in a single direction away from the temporary nest. The movement of the body is not strictly linear but is complicated by alternate wheeling or "flanking" movements, first right and then left in rhythmic fashion, whereby more ground is covered and more booty captured. The size of a swarm and the complexity of its internal organization develop from the first beginnings after dawn, until near midday a maximum is reached in size and complexity, whereupon the sections of the main body interfere with one another and unity decreases. Here a process of swarm division occurs, through which two or more subswarms arise. These influence one another through indirect connections with the nest far in the rear. Actually, the study of swarm-division processes throws valuable light upon the nature of organization in the unitary swarm which first develops.

Such highly complex and adaptive collective maneuvers might well encourage exaggerated notions of both individual capacities and group processes involved. To a casual observer the effective strategy seems to depend upon a central officership of some kind, carried out "as if by word of command," as one writer puts it. However, a systematic investigation of this seemingly very intelligent social strategy shows that it rests not upon humanlike processes of leadership and group communication but on the complex interaction of very simple behavioral processes (17).

By studying how these complex raids develop through the day, and how oversize swarms divide, one basis for understanding their organization and function is provided. Another is provided by studying the behavior of groups comparatively, in laboratory and field. The individual army ant, psychologically considered, is very simple—indeed, much simpler than many other ants. No worker ant in the swarm ever adds more than a very limited and uncomplicated contribution to proceedings. The swarm advance involves a "relay" process carried out through simple responses of successive myriads of individuals when they encounter new (chemically unsaturated) ground ahead of the swarm. Organization within the mass is attained through an interplay of columns and masses among the sections of the whole, based upon individual reactions to chemical and tactual stimulation. Observations and appropriate tests of individual workers in these species reveal a small repertoire of reaction capacities which may lead to results which are complex and variable or simple and stereotyped according to the complexity of the prevalent environment. In the heterogeneous forest environment, a swarm raid builds up after dawn each day; but under the simplified conditions of a large enclosed space in the laboratory the ants will run for days in an endless circular column, unladen or carrying their brood (18). In the forest environment, where the complex phenomenon of the raid can build up, stage upon stage, only humanized (i.e., anthropomorphic) terms might seem adequate for the group action. But such terms are not adequate for the student of animal societies, comparing group patterns.

Insect and mammalian societies are a well-known source of analogies. For example, the terms "king" and "queen" are commonly used for the male and fertile female of the termite colony, or "royal pair" for them both. The terms certainly are descriptive in a literary sense, but their use is not always free of the implication that a mysterious overlordship beyond biological functions may be exerted by reproductive individuals over the colony. To discuss the queen seriously as "ruler" over her colony is plain nonsense. More seriously, analogies are frequently drawn between conditions such as a government or social pattern in man and a type of colony organization in insects, or between communication in man and social coördination in insects. Let no one dismiss such analogies on the plea that they are generally intended figuratively or for literary purposes, and not seriously and meaningfully. They are used too frequently and relied upon too heavily by writers and speakers to be lightly cast aside.

Analogies between human and insect behavior are frequently encountered in serious discussions with often impressive but usually not very sound reasons given. The patterns of insect society seem to resemble some of those in human society—why should we not use the same terms and apply conclusions from the insect situation directly to man?

A book by Friedrich Christian Lesser (*Insecto-Theologia*, 1738) served as one of the principal sources for the many English writers in the following century who used insects as examples for worthy human moral conduct. One such writer, the Reverend W. Farren White (*Ants and Their Ways*, 1884) endeavored to make clear how many important lessons could be derived from ants, with

> . . . their industry, their well-regulated government, the *devotion of the queen for the commonwealth, loyalty of her subjects,* their affection for their youthful charges . . . *their public works and national enterprises, planned and executed with the most surprising promptitude, uncontrolled by parliamentary committees, orders in council, and circumlocuous offices* . . . their social institutions, their provident clubs, and savings banks . . . their habits of early rising, of cleanliness, of moderation, of economy, of temperance, their love of fresh air . . . their skill in industry in many trades . . . their language, which though more difficult to acquire than Chinese, yet is to them so intelligible that there are no misunderstandings, all speaking it fluently . . .

In a sentence from which these few portions are taken, the Reverend Mr. White draws many lessons for mankind from the ants, not the least of which is the one (indicated by our italics) which implies that human monarchial systems might do well to follow those of ants in dispensing with trammeling parliamentary procedures.

Social groups of insects commonly share food among all members of the colony, without regard to labor or other social contributions—is this not equivalent to socialism or communism in human society? Do not both insect societies and human societies have their "social parasites"? Have not many insects "worked out" a form of warmaking state which resembles a human pattern such as fascism rather closely in many respects? If striking similarities such as these appear, why should we not use illustrations from insect societies in a *direct* application to man?

Such writers seem not to have been sufficiently industrious or careful to have read the writings of scientific students of ant life such as R. Réaumur, *Mémoires pour Servire à l'Histoire des Insectes,* T. VI, 1742, who expressed himself as follows: ". . . But writers have not been content to admire what the ants permit us to see. They have sought to interpret to their advantage all their actions, even those whose motives are most obscure. . . . A government has been said to exist among them which ours might take as a model; they have been made to appear as civilized as ourselves. . . . They have endeavored 'to convert the ants into little men.'" (From R. Réaumur, *The Natural History of Ants,* tr. W. M. Wheeler, 1926.)

Because general analogies of this type usually depend upon superficial similarities rather than evidence for significant common processes, they cannot be tested readily; hence they may be turned whichever way may suit the purposes of the user. A particular value judgment is determinative, rather than the validity of a comparison. Such arguments therefore are likely to be not only specious but hazardous to truth when the analogy is used to force home an important point. For example, in social insects there are many forms of social parasitism and dependency, of predation and pillaging, of food-sharing and mutual relationships, but their adaptive importance in the respective insect social patterns has no direct or necessary bearing upon the advantages or disadvantages of roughly similar patterns in man. For insect social patterns have developed through the processes of biological evolution, and have persisted with minimal and slow change through more than sixty million years. In man, however, we may look to tradition and institutional factors for the elaboration and continuance of existing social patterns. Any human pattern must be evaluated as desirable or undesirable in terms of its psychological bases, its meaning, and its consequences for human society, and no argument from the biological processes underlying an insect pattern can have an immediate and decisive bearing upon the human issue. The point here is that conclusions taken from apparent similarities alone are questionable, *not* that a comparative study of animal societies can fail to increase our insight into *all levels* of social behavior.

The analogy between human and insect communication is a subtle one, likely to depend upon the application of similar names rather than how insects on the one hand and men on the other hand actually influence one another in social situations. Insect communication frequently is complex and difficult to understand—witness in particular the dances of the returning honey bee forager on the comb, as von Frisch has described them (7, 8). This investigator has reported that hive mates are somehow influenced by the finder's dance, so that they are able to locate the food place sooner than by chance, not only in its direction but also in its distance. *How* this particular effect occurs is still unclear although its occurrence is factual. Those who are inclined to regard it as symbolic, in the human sense, should consider the really nonsymbolic nature of other social interactions which are well known in bees. From other research of von Frisch we know that a returning finder bee, through the stimulative effect of a perfume carried back on her body from the flower she has visited, may arouse other bees somehow to a specific "set" for the odor of this type of flower. This effect is produced even when the experimental perfume is a different one from that of her own nectar source, dusted incidentally upon her body as she feeds.

Types of insect communication are known in which the community is aroused through the rapid propagation of excitement from individual to individual, often by antennal contact with or without an accompanying odor effect. In other cases, an effect is transmitted through the air from specialized vibratory (stridulatory) organs set into action when the insect becomes excited, affecting specialized receptors (chordotonal organs) in other individuals within range. These types are well known in many species of ants and other social insects. A cruder form is effective when vibrations are transmitted through the ground or nest structure, as when the "sender" is an excited ant or termite striking its head or abdomen repeatedly against the wooden walls of the nest galleries. Although perhaps tempting, it is very unsafe to conclude that these interchanges are qualitatively like human symbolic forms in which one man calls a command or an appeal to others, or beats a drum to them in code.

The known insect interchanges appear to have in common an important limitation, that if the behavior of the finder insect not only arouses others but also guides them to some extent the latter effect is an incidental product of the finder's behavior and not the cause of it (13). Experiments by Eidmann and others show this fact clearly for various species of ants. For example, in a standard laboratory test with certain ant species, one ant finds food while wandering about, then returns across an area to the place where her nestmates are confined. Her behavior on entering arouses them, many of them soon leave by the now open door, and some of these soon find the food place. They find the food sooner than by chance, but is this because the finder has directed them to it? She has, but incidentally and *not by code*. If, after the finder has returned, the paper floor across which she ran is replaced with a fresh one, the newcomers (aroused by her) wander about and find the food place only by accident. The excited finder during her feeding and return has released a glandular secretion which the others can follow so long as its traces remain on the floor. However, she does this by virtue of reflex responses, and not intentionally any more than a man sweats under certain atmospheric conditions *in order to* furnish a social cue to others that he is uncomfortably warm.

Only in its general adaptive function as social transmission does insect "communication" resemble human language. When men speak to one another, the following criteria are satisfied: (1) The words are used more or less intentionally, with respect to anticipated social consequences; (2) the words are typically symbolic, in that they have learned, meaningful connections with objects and situations; (3) the words are directive, in that they influence others as well as the speaker in characteristic ways; and (4) the words may be patterned and rearranged according to the motivation of the speaker and his perception of situation and listeners. Human language is a symbolic discourse, mastered through long experience. There is no evidence that the social transmission of insects in the typical pattern of the species is learned, or that it is symbolic in the sense that human words are symbolic. Rather, the insect forms are derived through biological processes characteristic of the species and are fixed in nature rather than culturally changeable and socially versatile, as are those of man. Since the insect colony can exhibit only rigid forms of social transmission produced through the predominant influence of species heredity, they stand in sharp contrast with those of a human culture, which are psychologically very different in their origin, character, and social potentialities.

Symbolic transmission in social groups is not, however, confined to the human level alone. For example, in experiments at the Yerkes Laboratories of Primate Biology, chimpanzees were able to learn a gestural form of communication and use it symbolically. When a food box was made too heavy for one chimpanzee alone to pull it within reach, chimpanzees which had previously pulled alone learned to pull together. Then, with further experience, they became able to summon one another by means of self-initiated gestures such as gentle taps on the shoulder (6). These were truly symbolic, and not merely signals to action. The chimpanzee who tapped was presenting, in anticipation of its social effect, a special cue which had come to symbolize, that is, to stand for meaningfully, the expected social result. The symbolic, anticipative, and directive nature of this gestural cue was indicated by the fact that when shoulder taps were insufficient, or slow in producing cooperation, the active animal would turn to pulling alone, or might act forcibly and directly to get the second animal involved in pulling. Although it is not known how far and in what ways such gestural devices may be involved in chimpanzee group communication under natural conditions, their use is probably very limited.

In lower primates, it is probable that there is virtually no symbolic communication outside of gestural procedures. Although the sounds produced by chimpanzees have an excitatory function in various settings, they are evidently uttered interjectionally as parts of excited behavior, to which the responses of other animals become conditioned according to the social situation in which the different types of sounds are usually heard. In lower primates, it is doubtful that vocal communication can attain the status of a symbolic language, much less a conventionalized language, as in human society. Here is an important difference in levels, resulting from the limited capacities of lower primates for the processes of learning, perception, and reasoning—inferiorities which account for their meager social training as well as their low social heritage and institutionalized behavior, as compared with man.

How are we to recognize a true "social" group in a lower animal, since these groups appear to differ widely in their organizations? First of all, let us recognize that not all groups are necessarily social; unless the aggregation is grounded upon the interdependence of individual members, upon their responsiveness to one another, it is not a social group. There are invertebrate assemblages in which such intragroup relationships are lacking; these are termed "associations" rather than social groups. Thus in many species of flies, individuals gather together because all of them approach the same environmental stimulus and remain within the area of its effect. At twilight or dawn, large clouds of male mosquitoes may form on a basis of common response to environmental features such as light and temperature. In contrast, the members of a clan of monkeys remain in a group by virtue of an interindividual attraction within the group and not merely because there happens to be an independent individual attraction to the same area. What is common to all "social" groups is this responsiveness to other individuals as having definite attractive properties of their own apart from those of the physical environment.

Nothing is gained except obscurity when we say that some animals are social because they are "gregarious." This term means simply that they tend to come together; it merely describes what we already know but does not suggest an explanation for it. Progress is made in these problems only when students become impatient with impressive but really hollow terms such as "gregarious instinct" and look behind them for the real meanings.

A promising approach has been made through the study of "trophallaxis" processes in a social group, that is, processes based upon the interchange of mutually attractive stimuli in the group. As Wheeler (20) developed the term for social insects, it signified food exchange; however, we may extend it to mean all stimuli which are equivalent to food in their organic effects, and all which come to elicit approach to other individuals. Thus a newborn sheep is licked by its mother, then nurses and is soothed by cuddling with her; soon it is following her about, and later follows other sheep. On the basis of reflex processes which are at first limited and rather random in their influence upon general behavior, organized group responses appear through learning and the young lamb becomes socialized. After such early socialization it is disturbed and restless when it is away from the group for very long. By virtue of the initial crude reflex processes (e.g., nursing upon finding the nipple) the young individual experiences tension relief in the presence of another individual (its mother), thus learns to approach the other and finally the group. Bottle-raised lambs kept apart from the flock do not approach the group or mix with it on later tests, except after special training. Thus gregarious behavior does not appear automatically but requires an initial ontogenetic process, characteristic of the species, for its development.

The attraction of a young mammal to the mother develops as a part of a mutual bond, for the mother also obtains tension relief in various ways from the young, relief from mammary-gland tension, for example. The group-adjustment process of course differs considerably in its form according to the condition of the young at birth, their sensitivity, and other developmental features characteristic of the species. In insects, the bond seems assured by the presence of physiological equipment such as body-surface secretions of the larvae which attract adults, arouse licking, and thereby open the way for feeding of larvae by adults. The process of a conditioned approach to the colony chemical and to individuals bearing it may really begin with larval feeding. Unity in the colony thus depends upon trophallactic effects which insure that each individual is attracted by and is attractive to all others.

Although we may postulate a fundamentally similar biological basis for the trophallactic processes through which gregariousness develops on different social levels, there are of course marked differences in the final social patterns. These depend especially upon how far adjustments to other individuals may develop psychologically, and what other individuals come to mean to the responder, that is, upon processes limited by the psychological capacities of the species. Thus, the limitations of social interactions in insects are suggested by the predominance of *present* chemotactual stimulative effects from *present* individuals. Even crudely daubing an ant of species A with the body fluids of species B may lead to her acceptance for a time in a colony of species B, although normally A is attacked by B. The partially stimulated B-colony odor is her badge, so to speak, and she is accepted more or less as a nestmate until the chemical has dissipated; then she becomes a "stranger." This social process must not be likened to human recognition of a fellow group member and friend; for we have no evidence that social interactions in insects involve the meaningful properties of human social perception. To be sure, somewhat similar results are achieved in the group affiliations of ant and man, but through processes which may differ very radically in their psychological nature. Not only does a *present* social stimulus such as his mother's "frown" come to have an increased perceptual meaning for an infant, but its meanings become more subtle and indirect in time, as when he perceives the frown according to his anticipation of what an *absent* individual (his father) may do when he enters the situation.

Even in insects, a responsiveness to species mates, however simple and apparently automatic it may appear to be, depends to an appreciable extent upon the conditions of early experience. Thus mixed colonies of ants may be created by putting individuals of different species together from the time they are removed from their cocoons. This type of evidence suggests that normally a conditioned responsiveness to the prevalent nest-colony chemical arises in ontogeny. After an infant chimpanzee had been raised to the age of nine months in a human household but away from chimpanzees (other than itself), when placed with an infant chimpanzee of similar age it was first disturbed and noticeably aggressive. These two young chimpanzees require a few weeks of experience together for relationships of acceptance and companionship to develop (9). Their behavior reminds us of the characteristics of "unsociability" and "shyness" which may appear in an only child deprived of early experience with other children. Whether on a lower or a higher social level, interpersonal relationships do not develop automatically or "instinctively" into a pattern; rather, they arise through a socialization process of progressive interrelationships between an organism and surrounding conditions.

The contributions of the social environment and of group history to the socialization process are very different according to the species, as we have said. In insects they are narrow and rigid; in man they are both wide and plastic. Although insects are capable of learning, so far as our evidence goes this capacity seems to be secondary in the early adjustments of new individuals to the social group. Its function may be largely held to a generalized conditioned approach to the colony chemical, established through early adjustments of new individuals to the social group. Its function may be largely held to a generalized conditioned approach to the colony chemical, established through early feeding. Such processes are dominated by hereditary properties of the species, for example, by the relatively automatic character of certain insect feeding reflexes. On the other hand, the wide and predominant role of learning in the socialization of a human individual cannot be disputed. Some specific organic processes such as the sucking reflex are prominent, of course; however, their social function and their significance change greatly in the course of time. The predominance of biological factors in the insect social pattern may be emphasized by terming such a pattern *biosocial;* that of psychological factors in the human pattern by terming it *psychosocial.*

These differences may be illustrated in another way by asking what influences may be exerted by the past upon animals at different social levels. In insects, through genetic factors underlying growth, the evolutionary past of the species is rather directly dominant over the development of social behavior and thus accounts for the persistence of such behavior in an insect group. Hence, as we have mentioned, the principal social insects have had their characteristic group patterns for many millions of years. Furthermore, because these patterns are dominated by organic, hereditary factors developed through evolution, as behavior systems they are typically very stable. In contrast, human social patterns are changeable, plastic, and often unstable. Man has a cultural pattern characteristic of the social climate in which he lives, since he acquires it through learning under the conditions of that social setting. In his individual acquisition of language, ways of dressing, attitudes toward books, and judgments of the beautiful, the process is profoundly influenced by group circumstances and by the conditions of individual social experience from start to finish. Continuity in this process is maintained through a cultural heritage, transmitted from generation to generation through psychological functions such as learning, understanding, and symbolic communication. In this sense, insects have only a very negligible culture: their social heritage is limited to the general influence of a spatial odor-pattern and various physical properties of a nest built up by earlier generations. In a comparable sense, chimpanzees in the wild have their established group territories, their regular feeding and nesting places, to which the young learn to conform as an inevitable part of their socialization. Their gesture language doubtlessly is involved in aiding the transmission of such effects to further generations. Wide psychological differences are represented here. The insect level is very stereotyped and limited in comparison with the primates', yet that of chimpanzees like other lower primates is vastly below the representative social level of man (21).

We have considered some of the concepts derived through analogy which tend to obscure differences among social levels in the animal series. A further one, originally developed in studies of group behavior in domestic fowl, is that of "dominance hierarchy" (5). As illustrated with a flock of chickens in the barnyard, the dominance hierarchy constitutes a so-called peck order, or a series of different aggression-submission relationships in the group. In the simplest case, approximated in small groups of chickens placed together experimentally, a linear dominance ranking develops in which superior members dominate all those lower in the group but are dominated by all those of higher dominance rank. With chickens these relationships at first involve actual aggression by pecking, with A pecking B and all others, but not being pecked by them; B pecking C and all others except A; C pecking D and all others except A and B; and so on. Through learned discriminations depending upon the consequences of initial encounters in the group situation, the amount of overt pecking of others steadily decreases, especially in the most dominant members, and a mere beginning of such behavior or the mere approach of a socially dominant member becomes sufficient to obtain withdrawal or other submissive behavior. Of course, social situations may be described in which rats, dogs, chimpanzees, and people seem to behave in a way closely approximating the peck-order situation of the henyard. However, it would be a serious fallacy to assume that all of these group situations are adequately covered by the peck-order outlines described for hens in the yard.

This type of behavior situation is readily recognized in many animal groups; however, the idea can easily be carried too far. Even in birds, with their characteristically stereotyped group relationships, prominence of the peck-order feature of group behavior differs greatly according to the limitations of space, food, and other basic conditions. Moreover, its prominence differs greatly among species, and its form varies considerably in groups under natural conditions. For example, the dominance-hierarchy aspect is not easy to recognize among the score or more of individuals in a clan of Central American howler monkeys (4); on the other hand, rather sharp differences in dominance with frequent overt aggressive interchanges characterize the group behavior of Old World monkeys such as the rhesus. Leadership in the former group is mainly a matter of ascendance and other nonconflict relationships, but in the latter it is more clearly a result of aggression and conflict interactions. It is also to be noted, with respect to the rhesus as example, that the dominance pattern of primate groups seems much more complex in its origin and variations than that characteristic of birds.

Social patterns such as aggression-dominance relationships, as would be expected, are most involved and most variable in form and degree in human groups. Here the relative prominence of such aspects of social life varies most widely according to differences in the conditions of early socialization. Investigations in the United States have shown that hostile and aggressive social attitudes and behavior are prominent or are minimal in the group adjustments of children according to earlier experiences in groups (11) and the extent of unfriendly or aggressive relationships with adults (3). It is an elementary principle of social psychology that human group patterns may differ widely in their nature according to the background of the groups and their members. To say that this statement holds relatively less for social patterns in lower animals obviously does not mean that early family adjustments and socialization can be ignored in their case.

Social organization on any level must be studied first of all in terms of factors responsible for group unity. A condition such as dominance is really a secondary part of this question, since instead it opposes group unity. More properly, trophallactic relationships in the early life of individuals in the social group may be postulated as furnishing group-approach tendencies opposing aggression and withdrawal tendencies underlying dominance relationships. Aggression-dominance adjustments arise through conflict and friction among group members, as in sharp competition over limited food or space; hence they have to do with "social distance" rather than with group unity directly. In the more solitary lower vertebrates such as many birds, male dominance and aggressiveness in the breeding season tend to ward off all species members save one, keeping neighboring mated pairs at their distance (2). When aggression-dominance and intragroup conflict reach a high point, a weakening or even a disappearance of group unity may be expected. Group organization depends first of all upon the strength of social-approach tendencies. Modifications and limitations in group organization then may be understood in terms of the function of such basic factors in relation to the strength of aggression-dominance and other modifying influences.

On the whole, social levels are relatively, but not absolutely, different. We have noticed indications of a basic similarity in the biological factors underlying trophallactic relationships and determining group unity in a variety of animal societies. Yet the social patterns which can develop on this general basis in different species must be referred in their specific nature to the psychological capacities (and particularly learning capacities) of the different animal types. Differences in psychological endowment account for qualitative social differences which are very striking in widely separated groups. Thus, while insects, chimpanzees, and man all communicate after their fashions, in insects this function is stereotyped and non-symbolic, and in chimpanzees although symbolic it is tremendously limited in its social scope in comparison with the symbolic systems of man. Thus, change is possible in insect social patterns only as it is enforced to limited extents through environmental alterations or through exceedingly slow processes of biological evolution. In man, on the other hand, social patterns change through psychological processes which are not at all directly dependent upon evolution since their relationship to a biological basis (e.g., function of cerebral cortex) does not determine or limit their pattern in any direct way. This means that, in an animal capable of greatly extended learning and mastery of symbolic processes, important qualitative differences in social pattern may arise and develop rapidly in a short succession of generations.

Unfortunately, the processes of psychosocial evolution, like those of biosocial evolution, have their negative as well as their positive aspects. An insect species, by and large, can rid itself of maladaptive social behavior only through appropriate changes in the organic characteristics promoting such behavior, by virtue of natural selection in evolution. Man, on the other hand, has far more efficient ways of correcting maladaptive behavior through use of his psychological facilities. However, to say that human social patterns occupy a "higher" level than those of lower animals does not mean that man's social procedures are always better adapted to his needs than are those of lower animals to theirs. When man attempts to settle his social difficulties by resorting to physical combat, no analogy with lower animals can adequately explain his failure to use the maximal psychological facilities at his disposal. For man's patterns of social misconduct are as characteristic of him under the conditions, and as different from any to be found in lower animals, as are his more desirable social processes. Sufficient emphasis on the human conditions which characteristically produce human social disasters may finally teach man how to improve his group procedures.

REFERENCES

1. Allee, W. C. 1938. *The social life of animals.* New York: Norton.
2. Allee, W. C. 1942. Social dominance and subordination among vertebrates. In R. Redfield, ed., *Biological Symposia.* 8: 139–162.
3. Anderson, H. H. 1946. Domination and social integration in the behavior of kindergarten children and teachers. *Genet. Psychol. Monogr.* 21: 287–385.
4. Carpenter, C. R. 1934. A field study of the behavior and social relations of howling monkeys. *Comp. Psychol. Monogr.* 10: 1–168.
5. Collias, N. 1944. Aggressive behavior among vertebrate animals. *Physiol. Zool.* 17: 83–123.
6. Crawford, M. P. 1937. The cooperative solving of problems by young chimpanzees. *Comp. Psychol. Monogr.* 14: 1–88.
7. Frisch, K. von. 1947. The dances of the honey bee. *Bull. Animal Behavior,* No. 5, pp. 1–32.
8. Frisch, K. von. 1950. *Bees, their vision, chemical senses, and language.* Ithaca: Cornell Univ. Press.
9. Jacobsen, C. F., M. M. Jacobsen, and J. G. Yoshioka. 1932. The development of an infant chimpanzee during her first year. *Comp. Psychol. Monogr.* 9: 1–94.
10. Le Bon, G. 1920. *The crowd: A study of the popular mind.* London: Fisher Unwin.

11. Lewin, K., R. Lippitt, and R. K. White. 1939. Patterns of aggressive behavior in experimentally graded "social climates." *J. Soc. Psychol.* 10: 271–299.
12. Maeterlinck, M. 1903. *The life of the bee.* New York: Dodd, Mead.
13. Maier, N. R. F., and T. C. Schneirla. 1935. *Principles of animal psychology.* New York: McGraw-Hill. Chap. 6.
14. Pear, T. H. 1950. Peace, war, and culture patterns. In T. H. Pear, ed., *Psychological factors of peace and war.* New York: Philosophical Library. Chap. 2.
15. Redfield, R., ed. 1942. *Biological Symposia,* Vol. 8, Lancaster: Cattell Press. Especially articles by Jennings, Allee, and Carpenter.
16. Schneirla, T. C. 1940. Further studies in the army-ant behavior pattern— Mass organization in the swarm raiders. *J. Comp. Psychol.* 29: 401–460.
17. Schneirla, T. C. 1941. Social organization in insects, as related to individual function. *Psychol. Rev.* 48: 465–486.
18. Schneirla, T. C. 1944. A unique case of circular milling in ants. *Am. Mus. Novitiates,* No. 1253, pp. 1–26.
19. Schneirla, T. C. 1946. Problems in the biopsychology of social organization. *J. Abn. Soc. Psychol.* 41: 385–402.
20. Wheeler, W. M. 1928. *The Social Insects.* New York: Harcourt, Brace.
21. Yerkes, R. M., and A. W. Yerkes. 1935. Social behavior in infrahuman primates. In C. Murchison, ed., *Handbook of social psychology.* Worcester: Clark Univ. Press.

IV

ON THE DEVELOPMENT OF BEHAVIOR AND THE CONCEPT OF APPROACH-WITHDRAWAL

In criticizing the instinct-learning dichotomy, Schneirla recognized the need to formulate an adequate alternative. This he did by the application of a holistic developmental theory to behavior study in which maturation and experience are redefined. Maturation, he stated, is the "contribution to development of growth and tissue differentiation, together with their organic and functional trace effects surviving from earlier development." Experience is "the contribution to development of the effects of stimulation from all available sources (external and internal) including their functional trace effects surviving from earlier development." Moreover, the developmental contributions of the two complexes, maturation and experience, must be viewed as a long series of intervening variables, that are *fused* (i.e., inseparably coalesced) at all stages in the ontogenesis of any organism (see No. 112).* Thus, *maturation,* in contrast to concepts

---

* This and subsequent numbers in this introduction refer to the items in the complete bibliography of Schneirla's works, p. 1017. Bold face numbers denote articles that are included in this volume.

of "innate" behavior or behavior that is "programmed in the genes," is a developmental process, and *experience* is much more inclusive than learning, which is only one facet of experience. Of major importance is Schneirla's insistence that these two factors (which he calls "conceptual conveniences") are inseparable at all times and that attempts to assign behavior to one or the other are futile—just as in the older writings he vigorously questioned the validity of describing some behavior as innate and other behavior as learned.

The reformulation of maturation and experience is just a small portion of a broad theory of behavioral development presented in the first paper in this section, *The Concept of Development in Comparative Psychology* (No. **80**). In this paper, Schneirla pays particular attention to fundamental differences in the development of behavior at different phyletic levels. The article *"Critical Periods" in the Development of Behavior* (No. **105**) exemplifies the complexities that Schneirla emphasized in analyzing the development of social behavior. The application of Schneirla's theory of development to the ontogeny of sucking behavior and home orientation in kittens is illustrated in article No. **121** in Part VI and article No. **99**.

The subject of development is treated in several other articles (Nos. 89, 112, 113) not included in the collection.

Even with the more heuristic concept of maturation and experience, Schneirla recognized that the study of behavioral development was extremely difficult, and he was constantly looking for conceptual tools to further such studies. This led him to elaborate the concept of approach-withdrawal and its application to behavioral development. He first mentions approach-withdrawal in the abstract of a paper that he presented at the meeting of the American Psychological Association in 1939—*A Theoretical Consideration of the Basis for Approach-Withdrawal Adjustments in Behavior* (No. **18**), the second paper in this section. In this paper, he suggested that approach to the source of mild stimulation and withdrawal from the source of intense stimulation of the same modality is a basic physiological process in early development and could provide the ontogenetic basis for several psychological theories based upon negative-positive differentiation in behavior. However, his first definitive paper on the subject, *An Evolutionary and Developmental Theory of Biphasic Processes Underlying Approach and Withdrawal* (No. **87**) (reprinted in this section), was not written until 20 years later, and his major theoretical presentation of the subject, *Aspects of Stimulation and Organization in Approach-Withdrawal Processes Underlying Vertebrate Behavioral Development* (No. **108**) (reprinted in this section), did not appear until 1965. The subject is also considered briefly in articles **80** (in this section), 89, 112, and 113 on behavioral development and in *Levels in the Psychological Capacities of Animals* (No. **46**) in Part III.

Of all Schneirla's theoretical propositions, the approach-withdrawal theory seems to have engendered the most opposition. It is also the least understood. A common source of misunderstanding is the failure to recognize that approach-withdrawal is both a phylogenetic and ontogenetic concept and that this threshold phenomenon might be altered, obliterated, or even reversed in adult stages. On the other hand, one can cite a great many examples of this phenomenon in adults of various species especially at lower phyletic levels. Although there are many current criticisms of this concept, this unique postulation of biphasic processes underlying approach and withdrawal as a fundamental developmental process may in the long run prove to be his most important contribution to behavioral science.

Lester R. Aronson
Ethel Tobach

T. C. SCHNEIRLA

The Concept of Development in Comparative Psychology

Bibliography No. 80

PERSPECTIVE

The concept of *development,* connoting a pattern of changes occurring in a system through time, is fundamental to the psychological study of animals. This is a cardinal precept of animal psychology, stimulated by the evolutionary movement in biology and emphasized in modern times by an increasing interest in comparing man with the lower animals and the animals with one another. But a comparative psychology as scientific discipline does not arise merely through the general recognition that relationships exist on some basis between the phenomena of phylogenetic and of ontogenetic change (94). Nor can it be expected to arise automatically, merely through the behavioral study of different animal forms.

It should be clear that a comparative psychology is not to be established by the same methods as a comparative anatomy or a comparative embryology. Although, as investigation progresses, the molecular basis of behavior and of psychological capacities is revealed with increasing clarity in organic processes, it is becoming evident that the principles holding for the molecular and molar levels of organic reality cannot be the same (79,93). Although the principles for *the molecular* are basic to the molar level, *the molar* requires operations in investigation and theory beyond the specific terms of the molecular. No matter how thoroughgoing the studies of the embryologist and his colleagues in cognate biological fields may be, in themselves they cannot be expected to give an inclusive, comprehensive basis for dealing adequately with questions concerning the behavior and psychology of animals (79, 111). The same is true of morphology and of physiology, although each discipline in its appropriate ways is indispensable to comparative psychology for evidence as well as for theory.

The phyletic and ontogenetic aspects of behavior study are generally considered related. But the type of relationship presupposed, or tested for,

From *The Concept of Development,* edited by D. B. Harris. Minneapolis: University of Minnesota Press. Copyright © 1957 University of Minnesota. Reprinted with permission.

has differed widely according to personal or scientific predilections. However, even an anthropocentrist on the one hand and an anthropophobe on the other, if scientifically orientated, must investigate the organization and capacities of behavior in a wide variety of phyletic types, for better understanding of man's status or that of any lower animal. And from a broad scientific outlook it is necessary to go further, to study the ontogenetic or individual development of each principal animal type, to the end of comparing the respectively different adaptive patterns attained by these animals for better understanding of the animal series inclusively.

It may not be altogether clear why a science of behavioral development should be responsible for deriving its own theories and validating its own principles, rather than accepting them fully formed from other fields in Biology. But the probability exists that in all types of organisms, in ways depending on the characteristics of each respective phyletic level, behavior has differing degrees of indirectness in its relation to structure (95). The issue is often complicated by a confusion of abstractions, or preliminary working attempts to represent phenomena, with a positivistic or finalistic view of "reality" itself. To emphasize these considerations, a conceptual distinction which is both empirically grounded and heuristically recommended is suggested here, to differentiate what is connoted by the terms *growth, differentiation,* and *development.* With "growth," the emphasis is on change by tissue accretion, and with "differentiation," on variation, in the changing of structural aspects with age in an organism. With "development" the emphasis is on progressive changes in the organization of an individual considered as a functional adaptive system, throughout its life history. Growth processes, as well as those of tissue differentiation, are subsumed by the term development, which further stresses the occurrence of progressive changes in the inclusive, organized function of the individual.

This distinction has great theoretical importance for the study of behavioral and psychological capacities in the animal series. For it stresses the fact—increasingly apparent with the advance of morphology on the one hand and of psychology on the other—that although tissue and organ, local movement and inclusive behavior are closely and inseparably related in functions, for represented phenomena are not fully describable in the same terms. The problems of behavioral development are approached very differently according to what attitude is taken in this regard. For example, the term *maturation* is often used to denote a casual agency representing the role of genetic constitution in behavioral development (31). The next step, equally unsound, is acceptance of the traditional nature-nurture dichotomy, with the position that "nurture" is equivalent to "learning" and that there must be some specific turning point in development at which this agency enters the picture. This practice unduly limits our perspective in developmental psychology. The term *maturation* seems useful for developmental study and theory, but demands a broader connotation.

The Problem of Behavioral Development

For an adequate perspective in the methodology of research and theory, we cannot accept an a priori definition of behavioral development either as an unfolding of the innate, with gains through learning presumably superimposed in superior phyla, or as a continuum expanding mainly through the pressure of environmental forces, with the genes merely contributing an initial push to the process. Rather, a defensible generalization is that species' genetic constitution contributes in some manner to the development of *all* behavior in *all* organisms, as does milieu, developmental context, or environment. The "instinct" question, then, is regarded as merely a traditionally favored way of posing the question of behavioral development in a general, preliminary way, with emphasis upon the role of genetic constitution (95).

The question of behavioral development is posed from the above standpoint not to be ecletic, but first of all to encourage behavioral analysis, an emphasis badly needed in all developmental psychology. In the history of this subject, an insufficient stress upon analytical methodology has resulted from specific biases and theoretical inhibitions at least partially accountable for the fact that our studies of psychological development have been too predominantly descriptive, too discontinuous as to stages investigated, and too preoccupied with certain stages (as the adult, in particular) to promote the rise and use of adequate analytical methods.

The critical problem of behavioral development should be stated as follows:

1) To study the organization of behavior in terms of its properties at each stage, from the time of egg formation and fertilization through individual life history; and
2) to work out the changing relationships of organic mechanisms underlying behavior;
3) always in terms of the contributions of earlier stages in the developmental sequence,
4) and in consideration of the properties of the prevailing developmental context at each stage.

In attacking this problem, an adequate programmatic combination of cross-sectional and longitudinal studies must be carried out through an analytical methodology suited to the phyletic level under study, with the results then synthesized to the end of valid phyletic comparisons. This is a large assignment.

DEVELOPMENT CONSIDERED PHYLETICALLY

Behavioral Relationships in the Animal Series

The phyletic study of development naturally presupposes some kind of series or order among contemporary animals as to their respective evolutionary backgrounds. However, no clear and supportable series, except in the broadest terms, has been established with respect to the behavioral properties of the respective animal phyla (46, 74). We know at least that existing animals, considered in terms of organizations and capacities underlying behavior, form not a linear series but a discontinuous one. The phyletic tree has numerous long branches, with large sections now extinct, and present-day animals fall into a very irregular pattern on it. Although the order of evolutionary antiquity and recency is usually paralleled by degree of specialization in the sense of behavioral plasticity, exceptions are numerous. For instance, the horse, which as a specific form of organism has had about the same evolutionary time as man to reach its present adap- tive status, compared favorably with man only in specializations other than psychological.

Our comparative behavioral study therefore must include all principal existing animal forms, and not just those that form some type of series (91, 94). In the comparison, undue concentration on any one animal form at the expense of others must be avoided. The recent history of this subject has taught us impressively how a preoccupation with one animal such as the rat can lead into scientific blind alleys (91, 94). Both types of theory most prevalent at the present time in American psychology, the behavioristic (S-R or operant) and the cognitive, exhibit a focalization such that neither of them has made any appreciable headway along naturalistic or developmental lines. After decades of concentration on the rat as favorite subject, we still do not know just how far this rodent may be considered equivalent to man as an experimental subject, and how far different. Many adopt the rat for research as an adequate psychological equivalent to man, without accepting the theoretical obligation of comparison.

To repeat, animal psychology in its developmental aspect cannot rely chiefly on any other biological field such as morphology, although it is sometimes argued that a comparative psychology can be founded directly on comparative anatomy (70). This may presuppose or favor a preformistic answer to the instinct problem (67). But the concept of *homology*, connoting a significant evolutionary relationship between comparable species mechanisms, has not been validated as yet for behavior and its organization. To the extent that this may be possible in the future, what homologies may exist in the behavioral properties of different animals must be worked out essentially by psychological and behavioral methods; always, of course, in view of evidence from comparative anatomy and other biological sciences. For the chief difficulty, as we shall see, is that behavior seems to have very different relations to structure in different types of animals. Reliable methods must be devised to investigate how far different animals from protozoa to primates have species-characteristic behavior in which similar capacities are similarly organized, or different capacities differently organized.

Psychological Levels

For this task of phyletic comparisons, a theory of psychological levels promises to be useful, in which the capacities and organizations in behavior are compared as *high* or *low* in respect to psychological status (79, 93). For example, insects, with their behavior pattern characteristically dominated by specific sensory mechanisms and stereotyped reactions, may be judged lower in the psychological scale than cats, which have a more plastic behavioral organization and can adapt to a much wider and more complex environment. If one knew only the reactive repertoire of the sea anemone's tentacle, the insect's antenna and the cat's forepaw in their normal situations of use by the respective organisms, he would conclude without much doubt that among these three, the tentacle indicates by far the lowest psychological status in total behavior, the paw the highest. What we know about the respective owner organisms would not change this judgment.

Psychological level cannot depend upon *adaptive success,* for by hypothesis, all existing animal forms must be ranked more or less on a par in this respect. The principle of *homeostasis,* which concerns physiological readjustment of an organism to biologically nonoptimal conditions, applies well to all animals considered against their respective environments. As Pick (85) has emphasized, the degree of efficiency of homeostatic mechanisms is substantially the same for animals low and high in the phyletic series. But at the same time, the mechanisms underlying homeostasis, along with other capacities crucial for behavioral organization, show progressive changes in their internal organization and in their relationships to other individual functions, from psychologically low-status to high-status animals.

Complexity is often advanced as a criterion for distinguishing psychological standing. This, however, is a doubtful procedure until we know *what* it is that is complex. For instance, the compound eye is very complex in many insects, but in action it lacks associated perceptual capacities present in a mammal through experience. Insect visual discriminations through the compound eye are based on flicker vision rather than on pattern perception in the mammalian sense (93). *Formica* ants can learn rather complex mazes, although needing more than twice as many trials as rats need to master the same pattern; also, the ant's habit once acquired is not readily reversed in spatial terms, and is otherwise far less plastic than that of the rat (91). The significant feature of behavior for psychological appraisal is not specifically dependent upon a multiplicity of molecular units (e.g., many sensory endings and the like); it is rather a difference in *kind,* depending upon the qualitative aspects of behavioral organization and capacities. To be sure lower organisms, considered as integrated wholes, are simpler than the higher, although in the composition of their specific mechanisms of sensitivity and of reaction they often excel so-called higher organisms. But a rat may often utilize a relatively poor visual capacity with greater adroitness in novel situations than might an insect in adjusting to comparable conditions.

From what might be termed the additive point of view, *capacity for most lasting neural trace effects* gained through experience (that is, for modifying behavior in quantitative terms) often is regarded as crucial for the psychological appraisal of an animal. But it is probable that higher mammals do not necessarily retain behavioral modifications better than do many birds, or even insects, for example; it is in the versatile use of the traces under new conditions of emergency that mammals typically excel (91). Also, on higher levels, the nature of variability in behavior becomes much more than the capacity for some kind of change. Unless *variability* is defined with care as to what kind of behavioral organization is varied, it becomes a capricious term indeed. For example, the word "trial," as in "trial and error," ranges in the literature from the category of an incidental, forced behavior change, as Jennings (57) used the term for protozoan behavior, to an anticipation or expectation of the consequences of an act, as in much behavior of higher mammals (74, 93). To say that higher levels are characterized by plasticity means that capacities and organizations appear which admit the possibility of systematic variations appropriate to new environmental conditions. Adjustments to changing conditions are no longer made merely through the random shifting of items in a fixed repertoire, but through the appearance of opportune new patterns.

The developmental process characterized as behavioral evolution therefore cannot be viewed as a process of accretion, by addition of further mechanisms similar to the old. If this were true, phyletic comparison would be easier than it seems to be. Rather, development evidently has taken place in evolution through the progressive transformation of "old" mechanisms (e.g., homeostasis—85,) as well as though the appearance of new mechanisms (e.g., neural patterns underlying reasoning). In the vertebrate series, gill-arch structures through evolution have contributed to auditory ossicles (107), forebrain to a diversified complex dominated by

cortex (47, 60); both of these changes facilitating greater plasticity in behavioral organization, although in very different ways and with different
degrees of directness. Through organic evolution, higher functional levels
appear which, as individual adaptive systems and as behaving wholes, may
be considered qualitatively new.

ONTOGENY AND PHYLETIC COMPARISONS

Phyletic Differences in Behavioral Attainments

Accordingly, on each further psychological level, the contribution of individual ontogeny is a characteristically different total behavior pattern
arising in a different total context. This fact cannot be appreciated unless
the comparison of different animal types is made in terms of their entire
ontogenetic ranges, and not just certain stages such as the adult. This is a
principle to which Orton (82) recently has called attention from the
standpoint of biological procedures in systematics. After all, a stage is just
one developmental cross-section, or limited interval between turning points
in ontogeny, and without an adequate longitudinal perspective an investigator is prone to basic misconceptions when he undertakes to compare
phyletic types on this basis alone. A tunnel vision for natural events is the
risk thereby, whether the properties of immature stages alone or those of
adult stages alone are used for the comparison. The "waggle dance" as
described for the honey bee by von Frisch (28) is an efficient communicative device and an impressive event, but when considered in the light of
its stereotyped ontogenetic basis must be viewed—contrary to a frequent
conclusion from general similarity—as fundamentally inferior in its qualitative organization to symbolic processes in higher mammals and language
in man. The appearance of behavioral stereotypy through ontogeny, if
found characteristic of a species, indicates a lower psychological level,
whereas a systematic plasticity in the organization of behavioral cues made
broadly representative through experience indicates a high level. Similar
behavioral adjustments may be grounded very differently in ontogeny, and
that through a more versatile course of individual development, analagous
or homologous mechanisms may vastly extend and vary their functional
range in behavior (93). Consider, for example, how differently the vertebrate forelimb is involved in the feeding operations of a toad, an adult
monkey, and a five-year-old human child.

Homologous mechanisms are transformed functionally in a new setting
on each higher level, as through ontogeny a characteristically different total
behavior pattern arises in a different total context. The same principle may
hold roughly for analagous adaptive mechanisms in very different phyletic

settings. For instance, the group unity and organization of an insect colony is held (92), as an extension of Wheeler's (116) concept of "trophallaxis," to derive from reciprocal stimulative processes reinforced by a variety of sensitive zone and special secretory effects. In different but comparable ways, parallel intragroup processes of this type may be held basic to social behavior on *all* levels from invertebrates to man. The fundamental mechanisms are similar, in that specialized sensitivity and responses affecting the formation of individual affiliations and reactivities in the group situation are always involved; however, the various resulting patterns of collective behavior are distinctively different. I have characterized that of social insects as *biosocial,* in that it is evidently dominated by specific mechanisms of sensitivity, physiological processes and responses; that of mammals as *psychosocial,* in that, although trophallactic mechanisms are still basic and indispensable to them, group behavior is now characterized by plastic processes arising through learning, anticipation and the like (92, 93). The principle is: that similar biological processes can lead to very different behavior patterns through ontogeny, depending upon what species developmental capacities and limitations are effective in the prevailing context.

Animals at different points in the phyletic scale tend to be adapted very differently to their respective niches, with ontogeny producing strikingly different adjustive repertoires according to species capacities. Protozoan and mammal, evaluated psychologically, represent widely different levels of adjustment. The predominant or leading properties of any level, considered particularly with respect to the plasticity aspect of behavior, must decide its status in comparison with other levels. Within each level there is a range of behavioral capacities differing in underlying organization— as in carnivores, from random emotionalized escape to a roundabout food-getting response. The different patterns in the behavioral repertoire of any level may be termed *functional orders,* and ranked high or low in organizational status. In a chimpanzee, for example, incidentally flicking away a fly represents a pattern of low functional order, gesturing to another chimpanzee a pattern of high functional order, although the actual movements are similar. The highest functional orders characterizing any psychological level are those utilizing its maximal possible gains through ontogeny. Thus higher mammals, in a longer ontogeny, attain functional orders ranging from reflexes through learning to reasoning; fishes, in a relatively short ontogeny, do not advance beyond learning, in which their capacities seem much more limited than are those of mammals. Each species, then, masters successively higher functional orders to the extent that, in its ontogeny, intervening variables in behavioral organization can prepare it for individual adjustment to increasingly shifting environmental conditions.

With respect to behavior and its organization, the ontogeny of any level is not so much a retracing through the stages and functional orders of successive ancestral forms as a new composite leading to a new total pattern characteristic of the level. For example, the types of variable, generalized behavior typical of the early stages in mammalian ontogeny (11) are not clearly equivalent in recapitulâtive terms to any type of variable behavior at lower phyletic levels. Vandel (108) sees in evolution a phenomenon of the same nature as in the ontogeny which gives rise to individuals, basing this conclusion on analogous principles (e.g., phyletic morphology cf. species allometry at different stages) postulated for the two cases. However, the appearance of morphological homologies in the ontogeny of a phyletic type, out of sequence with presumed phyletic antiquity or recency, was among the evidence bringing de Beer to the conclusion that: "Phylogeny plays no causal part in determining ontogeny, except in so far as past external factors have been responsible for exerting selection and preserving those internal factors which are operative in the ontogeny of the descendants" (19, p. 139). Functional orders characteristically attained through ontogeny on any phyletic level are not replicas of those appearing through ontogeny at other levels, either with respect to their order of appearance, their individual makeup, or their properties of organization as part-processes in the inclusive behavior pattern.

Genes and Behavior

It would be misleading to say that the behavioral patterns of lower psychological levels are inherited or innate, those of higher levels learned. The traditional heredity—environment dilemma stands out more and more clearly as a pseudo-problem as further evidence indicates that in all animals, intrinsic and extrinsic factors are closely related throughout ontogeny (95). As a guide to investigation, it is no wiser to regard development as a natively determined unfolding of characters and integrations than as the result of the molding effect of extrinsic forces. We may therefore hold that genetic constitution contributes to *all* behavioral development at *all* phyletic levels, just as modern geneticists hold that without a participating environmental context at all stages there could be no development in any animal (101, 111). The question is *how* development occurs in the particular animal under prevailing conditions, not *what* heredity specifically contributes or environment specifically contributes, or how much either contributes proportionally, to the process. Genes are complex biochemical systems, integrated from the beginning of ontogeny into processes of increasing complexity and scope, the ensuing progressive processes always intimately influenced by forces acting from the developmental context (111, 114).

In each species, genetic factors contribute indirectly to advances in stabilizing organismic functions with species-characteristic limits, at which they tend to resist change. But as Dobzhansky (20) has emphasized, it is undesirable to confuse this natural state of affairs with the impression of heredity *directly* determining development. Nor does a correspondence of the theoretical genotype with strain-specific behavioral characteristics appearing in any animal in the standard environment demonstrate a *more direct* relationship of genetic constitution and behavior in highly selected than in relatively unselected strains (38, 95). The more predictable phenotypic outcome in the former case does not automatically demonstrate that the genes have operated directly in ontogeny to produce certain behavior. In fact, it does not convey to us *any* evidence as to *what* type of causal nexus may intervene between the fertilized ovum and any stage of development. It is reasonable to assume that in the cases of both inbred and outbred strains the causal nexus has involved equivalently complex formulae of intervening variables characteristic of the species. At the same time, experiments with inbred strains under standard conditions represent a promising method for inductive study of genotypic contributions to development (38, 95).

The fact that in all phyletic types, modified or even radically different phenotypic alternatives may arise through ontogeny according to variations in the context of development militates against a doctrine of genic anlagen directly determining the rise of behavior. A concept of behavioral development as a direct unfolding of patterns through growth seems attributable to the kind of incomplete or inadequate analysis of organismal processes often characteristic of preliminary or descriptive studies. Gesell's (31) conception of a human ontogeny in which early behavior expands through "the innate processes of growth called maturation" seems more adequate for insects, although not really suitable in their case (95). Harnly (42) found, in experiments with the fruit fly *Drosophila melanogaster,* that the same gene may influence the development of different wing size and structure according to what temperature prevails during development of the phenotype. The types produced from the same genotypic strain were capable of full normal flight, erratic flight, or no flight, depending upon conditions of development. Not only wing size but also wing articulation and neuromuscular control were believed differently affected according to what temperature prevailed during specific early stages of ontogeny. It is impossible to account adequately for such facts in terms of a preformistic theory of behavioral development.

Intervening Variables in Development

The nervous system is often represented as the carrier of an innate determination for behavior patterns presumed to arise solely through its passive development. For this type of conclusion, Coghill's (16) investigation of larval salamanders is often cited as evidence. However, it cannot be presumed that the full significance of this research is understood as yet, even for *amphibian* development (29). On any phyletic level, the nervous system develops as *one* part of the organism, closely interrelated with other mechanisms throughout, and like them, indirectly influenced by the genes (67, 95). Nativistic views of behavioral development (53) may often seem to furnish the sole available theoretical resolution of a problem in the appearance of individual behavior, but only when the developmental system is so incompletely understood that the burden can be placed upon neural growth alone. Investigations on the ontogenetic causation of species behavior patterns, to carry weight, must involve a throughgoing analysis of behavioral development as related to other processes at successive stages. Conclusions not based on such analyses are premature.

The problem of ontogeny is not one of instinctive patterns directly determined by the genes, but one of understanding what changing integrations of development underlie successive functional stages characteristic of the species. Two concepts may be used to represent the factorial complexes essential to the entire flow of events in development. The first is *maturation,* which connotes growth and differentiation together with all of their influences upon development. *Maturation* is neither the direct, specific representative of genic determination in development, nor is it synonymous with structural growth. Much as an environmental context is now recognized as indispensable to any development (20, 101, 111, 114), students of behavioral development (62, 76) emphasize the roles of structure and function as inseparable in development. The second of these two fundamental concepts is *experience,* which connotes *all* stimulative influences upon the organism through its life history, ranging from physical and biochemical effects exerted from the start to stimulative combinations underlying learning and other higher functional orders possible for the species at later stages in ontogeny.

As an abstract operation, for heuristic purposes, these factorial complexes may be conceptualized disjunctively in their effects upon development, and there are indications that this logical procedure may be carried further as experimental methodology advances. But realistically, the two concepts must be considered as standing for complex systems of intervening variables closely integrated at all stages of development. On the one hand, the processes of maturation are certainly integral to all behavioral ontogeny. The chick, for example, after hatching, could not improve in its discriminative pecking at food without the factor of increasing muscular strength promoting the head lunge and supporting postural activities (18, 74, 98). But even this factor makes its contribution intimately in relationship with exercise in the lunging activity itself, a function closely allied to advances in perceptual discrimination through learning. For development, the factors of maturation and experience are as inseparably related as are physiological processes, stimulation and action.

Circular Functions and Self-stimulation in Ontogeny

An indispensable feature of development is that of circular relationships of self-stimulation in the organism (95). The individual seems to be interactive with itself throughout development, as the processes of each given stage open the way for further stimulus-reaction relationships depending on the scope of intrinsic and extrinsic conditions then prevalent. At early embryonic stages, circular biochemical effects of expanding range, thus in a sense *spiral,* may be invoked in these terms; somewhat later, proprioceptive processes capable of integrating neurally with the early cutaneous stimulative effects (10, 65). From the time of fertilization, development is continuous and progressive (33, 117), its processes and stages closely interrelated in their intrinsic and extrinsic aspects (95).

The potentialities of redundant stimulative processes for development have been incompletely investigated. For instance, Fromme (29) found, in replicating Carmichael's (9) test with early amphibian embryos immobilized by chloretone, that specimens held inactive during stages 17 and 20, in particular, in later tests swam more slowly and with dificient coordination as compared with normal specimens. The need for further work along the lines of the Carmichael experiment is indicated, as to its bearing on the interpretation of Coghill's (16) findings. The effects, particularly in the earliest stages, may not be those of obvious action or readily recorded impulses, so much as electromotive changes and action twitches of minute magnitude, slight afferent pulses, or other subtle energy releases capable of contributing in some way to the changing of patterns in development. For the early neurogenic stage, Carmichael (10) suggested the significance of the concomitance of circular proprioceptive and tactual effects for widening the scope of control of the latter. Kuo (64, 65, 66) demonstrated for the chick embryo ways in which stimulative effects from early functions such as heartbeat and rhythmical pulsations of the amnion membrane could influence the development of a head-lunge response. Early self-stimulative relationships, influencing the rise of a basic generalized response, contribute (with the entrance of extrinsic, differentiated conditions) to the specialization of this act into pre-hatching responses such as egg-chipping or to post-hatching patterns such as preening, drinking, and food-pecking (66).

Self-stimulation may contribute to development in a variety of ways in different phyla. Insect larvae radically change their environment by spinning cocoons, and later, again modify their stimulative setting by opening the cocoon or incidentally stimulating adults to do so (95). Mature bird embryos chip their way from the shell; early marsupial embryos shift from the mother's uterus to an external environment, still in a close although very different nutritive association with the mother. But although hatching and birth are to be considered turning points in development, partially self-induced through the embryo's own processes and movements, the change produced by these events in the developmental context is a relative and not absolute one. The embryo is still the embodiment of cumulative gains from preceding stages, and continues to participate in its own development in comparable ways; however the different environmental setting may modify the expression of this complex. Hatching or birth represents only one of the stages at which the young individual influences a notable change in its own environment made possible by stimulative gains through its own prior development. Although opening the way for a wider scope of action in a more heterogeneous environment, neither involves an absolute change for the stimulus-response progressions of development.

At all stages, the individual possesses the maturational properties of its species, which inevitably exert species-typical feedback effects upon its development. That the relationship of such effects to the rise of behavior at later stages may be elusive is suggested by Nissen's (81) statement that: "Among animals at all levels in the phyletic scale there can be observed highly motivated, almost compulsive forms of behavior which have no relation to homeostasis in the usual sense of the term, . . ." He cites the nest-building and brooding behavior of birds as examples of activities which ". . . have no obvious effect on maintaining the physiological equilibrium of the individual engaging in these activities." But, actually, in many birds maturational processes affecting temperature change and irritability of the skin at the hypersensitive brood patches lead to active, variable readjustments, and appear to be key functions in the appearance of nesting and incubation. The outcome may be physiological adaptations of the homeostatic type. For mammals, Kinder's (61) research indicated that temperature conditions at the skin must somehow provide a basis for nest-building in rats. But such factors are likely to influence behavioral development only as part-processes in a complex of interrelated organic events. Lehrman (68) found that feeding of the young by the parent ring dove did not occur except through the development of a behavior-influencing integration of: (1) hormonal factors; (2) afferent effects (and in particular, processes centering around the delicately sensitive brood patches); (3) neural factors (including certain processes bearing on a generalized "drive" excitation); also (4) closely related circular processes in individual behavior and (5) parent-young reciprocal stimulative processes occurring in a complex sequence. Without the latter—an involved succession of stimulative exchanges between the two participants—there could be no feeding response by the parent to the perceived squab. Such findings suggest that the developmental pattern underlying behavior is a global one, including a range of circular stimulative and reactive processes based upon the gains of earlier stages.

Early self-stimulative relationships may provide a significant basis for later adjustments to new conditions involving members of the same species. For example, Birch (5) found that female rats, provided from early youth with wide collars which prevented stimulative access to the posterior body and genital zones, in a later test at primiparous parturition lost their young through neglect or cannibalism. Controls indicated that it was not the weight or general disturbing effect of the collar, but the effect of the wide flange in preventing stimulative relations with the posterior body, that accounted for the abnormal outcome in experimental animals. Thus self-stimulative experiences normally inevitable in every day behavior during youth seem essential for efficient delivery and care of young in this animal. One normal gain denied to the experimental rats may have been a general perceptual orientation to the posterior bodily areas as familiar objects; another, the capacity of responding to the genital zones—and to objects such as neonate young, bearing equivalent olfactory properties—by licking and not biting.

For such stimulative relationships in the developmental system, maturation and experience are intimately cooperative in ways characteristic of the species. Van der Kloot and Williams (109, 110) investigated analytically the cocoon-spinning of the Cecropia silkworm, as an event centering around larval maturity. Maturation of the spin-glands introduces a complex of organismic and stimulative events, including an essential negative geotropic reaction (prerequisite for an upright position on a twig in the natural situation), two critical movements (the "swing-swing" and the "stretch-bend") which introduce the mouth contacts necessary for spinning, and still other factors. It is evident that this complex arises through transitional processes from earlier stages, and that, throughout, the extrinsic context is intimately interrelated with endogenous factors. Thus the pattern of spinning depends first of all upon the availability of the silkgland secretion, upon impulses from these glands arousing the two principal types of movement critical for spinning, upon mouth contact with a surface essential to stimulate release of the fluid, and finally upon the topography of the external situation in which the caterpillar finds itself when capable of spinning. In a situation in which the animal cannot arrive in an upright posture against a support such as a twig, no cocoon can be spun, but a different pattern arises depending upon the prevalent physical surroundings, as for example, either a cone around a peg or a sheet of silk lining a balloon.

This point of view, of the maturation and experience complexes always intimately related in behavioral development, may be adapted to advantage in the study of turning points and intervening stages in mammalian development. The fact that the term *stage* has been extrapolated from embryology to the study of behavioral ontogeny and reminds us that to deal with the latter, we must accept embryological evidence as integral, but we must advance beyond this to higher functional orders in development to which organic maturation is *one* contributor. To be sure, the accomplishment of given maturational events often seems to influence behavioral changes rather promptly, particularly at lower phyletic levels, as when an active sponge larva transforms and settles into the sessile adult condition (37), or an amphibian larva metamorphoses into an adult with rather different properties of sensitivity and response. Higher in the psychological scale, the relationship of one stage with following stages seems to be more involved. But the principle is much the same for all. Investigations of domestic cats in our laboratory (88) indicate how behavioral advances centering around birth, eye-opening and weaning occur through complex intrinsic-extrinsic integrations. For a time after eye-opening, the kitten's approach to the mother evidently proceeds much as before, on a proximal sensory basis. Within a few days, changes appear which seem attributable both to new gains through maturation (e.g., an increasing visual acuity, 113) and to an integration of previously established nonvisual perceptual processes with new visual cues, controlling a somewhat different adjustment to the mother. Transfer to solid food involves nutritive and behavioral adjustments which are accomplished by degrees, and through the participation of various factors. Stages in behavioral development at higher psychological levels, thus may be regarded as overlapping. Their turning points occur in a more gradual manner, than may be true of the events in maturation which contribute to them.

Ontogenetic Progress and the Role of Experience

Under normal conditions, *experience,* the effect of stimulation on the organism—including especially stimulative effects characteristic of the species ontogenetic milieu—is indispensable to development at all stages. How far this factor contributes to advances beyond the primary limits of the physical and biochemical into modifications through conditioning and learning depends upon species capacities. The growing organism takes more from its environment than the energy essential for nutrition; it is affected from the first by energy changes in its environs, and responds in a manner depending on its developmental stage. *Trace effects,* or organismic changes influential in the course of further development result.

Experience may contribute to ontogeny in subtle ways. From insects to man, not only the general developmental progression, but also events critical for the pattern changes of later stages, may involve factors of experience. We may expect to find that many physiological and behavioral rhythms, now often considered purely endogenous and "innate," may result from an interrelationship of intrinsic and *essential* extrinsic factors. For insects, Harker (40) has found that the normal day-night activity rhythm of the adult mayfly does not appear unless the egg has been subjected to at least one 24-hour light-dark cycle. The regular daily activity variations typical under natural conditions do not appear in adults raised from eggs grown experimentally in continuous light or in continuous darkness. In some manner, the organic effect of a specific physical condition acting for a limited time at a very early stage becomes deeply ingrained and influences complex daily behavioral variations in the adult stage. Comparable results were obtained by Brett (8) for the rhythm of pupal emergence in *Drosophila*.

In all animals, not only factors influencing the current developmental progression, but also trace effects critical for the pattern changes of later stages, may be introduced through experience. In birds and mammals, organic periodicities basic to the development of adult drives may be stimulatively influenced at their ontogenetic basis by periodic experiences, as through changes in the behavior of the incubating mother. Comparably, tidal, diurnal, and other rhythms in the physical environment, as well as nonrhythmic changes, may effect the developing stages of animals from lower invertebrates to mammals, influencing the basis for both periodic and aperiodic processes underlying adult behavior. A striking case in which lower vertebrate behavior is influenced in the adult stage by a subtle habituation effect accomplished during early stages of development has been demonstrated by Hasler and Wisby (43) in Pacific salmon. Their findings indicate the probability that when adult salmon leave the ocean and ascend a river system to spawn, turns at stream branches are made toward the tributary carrying the chemical essence of the headwaters in which the individual developed from the egg before descending to the ocean.

There is evidence that the effects of early experience may be diffuse, and that they may influence the later stages of development in a nonparticulate manner. Moore (78) found that neonate rats raised in an environment of 95° F temperature had longer, more slender bodies and tails, and performed less well in maze-learning tests as adults than did others kept at an environmental temperature of 55° F. It is not surprising that such extrinsic-intrinsic relationships are often overlooked or their effects misinterpreted in behavior studies.

It is a classical rule that incompleteness of maturation tends to restrict the scope of developmental susceptibility to extrinsic effects. In relation to species properties, the nature of gains through experience is both canalized and limited by the relative maturity of species-typical afferent, neural, and efferent mechanisms, in dependence upon the developmental stage attained. A definite conditioned response could not be demonstrated in the chick embryo to a combination of contact and shock stimuli before about 16 days (34), in the neonate dog before about 20 days (30). According to phyletic capacities, the influence of experiential effects upon later behavior often seems to depend critically upon the stage at which they act. Thus in ungulates the mother is a prominent feature of the environment for the neonate who, susceptible to specific exteroecptive effects such as odors, and with the eyes open, soon established a strong bond with the parent (6). In the phenomenon first described for birds by Lorenz (69) as "imprinting," primacy of some available and conspicuous attractive object which happens to be initially conspicuous and ubiquitous after hatching seems crucial for the normal bond with the parent first of all, and secondly with species mates. A specific initial susceptibility is indicated by the fact that newly hatched goslings or other birds first exposed to stimulation from a person are later unresponsive to stimuli from species mates as against the prepotent human object. In normal hatching, parent and species mates of course have the advantage of primacy (23). The initially prepotent stimulus for eliciting the approach seems to be highly generalized and definable in quantitative terms such as size and rate of movement. Through a process apparently related to conditioning, stimuli specific to the initially adequate object soon become prepotent, and canalize later response tendencies rather fundamentally. It is not surprising that such early adjustments are often found to be virtually irreversible.

The trace effects of early experience seem to be characteristically generalized, diffuse and variable, their influence at later stages nonparticulate and difficult to identify. Even so, they must be reckoned with as important influences in the later behavior pattern. In tests of conditioning in chick embryos, Gos (34) found that specific conditioned responses to a touch-shock pairing could not be accomplished before approximately 16 days. But subjects stimulated repeatedly after about the 10-day stage changed in their general responsiveness to the extrinsic stimuli used, indicating some trace effect. Hypothetically, we might expect that the extent to which a vertebrate embryo is mechanically disturbed in egg or uterus, and perhaps also the conditions under which such disturbance occurs, could affect the later level of individual emotional excitability. Experiences common to the usual species environment, such as knocking about of the eggs as they are turned by the incubating parent, or as the parent leaves the nest and returns to it, might have trace effects influencing similarly the development of all normally-raised young. Therefore, from early biochemical effects to later experiences promoting learning, the characteristic properties of the species-standard environment are never to be taken for granted or minimized, but always admitted to the field of possible indispensable factors in normal development.

Relative maturity at birth differs widely among the mammals, and is to be considered a cardinal factor in development, particularly as to what selective effects in organism-environmental relationships may depend thereon. In ungulates such as goats, from shortly after birth the social bond seems to advance with acceleration to the stage of visual perception, greatly facilitated by a precocious quadrupedal motility as well as by specific olfactory, auditory and tactual effects (6). In contrast, the advance of the neonate in carnivores such as cats and dogs seems to be much slower, against stricter early postnatal limitations along afferent, neural and motor lines. Reciprocal stimulative relationships of the neonate with species mates seem based upon strong organic gratification from such stimulative processes, and must be considered fundamental to the wider social integration of the individual (92). Differences during and subsequent to the establishment of the primary bond with the mother, as well as in other group experiences bearing upon the litter period, may contribute basically to certain striking contrasts in group behavior tendencies characteristic of the various lower vertebrate orders. In carnivores, the typical disruption of such associations at the time of weaning would seem to be significantly related to organic and behavioral changes in the participants (e.g., maternal hormone effects) not common in ungulates, in which group associations typically persist with only secondary changes in the pattern of intragroup relationships. Receptivity of the sexually mature mammal to a species mate may represent the rearousal of a perceptual responsiveness established earlier in life, as during the litter period. The appearance of this typical susceptibility, even in relatively nonsocial animals, would seem also to involve the lowering (through a hormonal priming of certain organic mechanisms) of afferent and other functional thresholds which serve as key items underlying the mating reaction. But the adjustments are perceptual, and for them, early experience may well be critical. Thus individual carnivores raised apart from species mates are likely to display disturbance reactions upon encountering them for the first time in adult tests, and mate only after long delays and much disturbance, if at all.

In each species, the specificity and the nature of the effects of early experience upon later behavioral development seem to differ more or less characteristically according to developmental stage. Such trace effects may be major factors in ontogeny, but thus far have been difficult to identify as originating in the embryonic and early neonate stage of carnivores and other mammals with a protracted period of early development. One striking contrast is opened by the experiment of Fuller et al. (30), who found that puppies, presented with a combination of electric shock with a visual, auditory or other exteroceptive stimulus, exhibited no specific signs of conditioning before the 20th postnatal day. This result was confirmed by James and Cannon (56). It seems probable, however, that a less specific type of conditioning may occur at earlier postnatal stages in young carnivores, and perhaps others as well, evidently mainly on a somesthetic and chemoceptive basis, and in terms of lower functional orders of neural integrations. Studies in our laboratory (118) on the behavior of neonate kittens show that specialized feeding adjustments to the mother begin soon after birth and have taken on an individually characteristic pattern within the first day or two. The adaptations concern both a direct approach to the mother and the attachment of a given kitten to a particular nipple with increasing frequency, i.e., posted at the front, center or rear in the nipple series. These adjustments, which usually are individually stabilized within the first four days after birth, clearly involve learning, and form a basis for wider social adaptations in the litter situation.

The impression has steadily gained ground among American psychologists that species behavior patterns depend not only on characteristic maturation but also upon experiences normal to the species (62, 74, 100). On this basis Kuo (63) manipulated the early experiential context of kittens to control their later reactions to rodents; and Patrick and Laughlin (83), by raising young rats in open areas as on table tops, obtained adults inclined to range more and to follow walls less than is usual for the species. Through tests with an isolated rhesus monkey, Foley (25) emphasized early associations with species mates as a factor in normal grooming reactions. Such results prepare us for Hebb's (44, 45) proposition that through early experience basic perceptual organizations are built up, and that the gains from experience are likely to be greater at opportune early phases in ontogeny than at later stages. This generalization has received further support from a variety of experiments. With rats (26, 27) and with dogs (104), early environments of greater scope and heterogeneity provide a more adequate basis for perceptual adjustment to new situations than do more restricted, simpler environments, and a more adequate basis for performance in maze and problem-solving tests at later stages (3, 54). In mammals (1, 14), a wide variety of conditions in early postnatal experiences, from trauma (39) and deprivation (49, 52) to litter conditions (97) and maternal behavior (59) can influence behavioral development to differing extents and in very different ways. Although the research still falls short of what would be desirable in longitudinal and analytical scope, it seems clear that age normally brings a variety of accretions, substitutions and changes, attributable to progressive conditions in the organism and in its experience. For example, Seitz (96) found that young foxes, although they had been well tamed from an early age, from the age of about 36 days began to defend themselves against handling. Taming evidently serves to raise the excitation threshold for certain familiar perceptual patterns, but its inhibitive potency suffers at sexual maturity. Species properties as learning capacity, excitation threshold, tension adjustment and a host of other characteristics must be considered among potential determinants of what experience may contribute at any stage.

Early generalized training often is basic to later more specialized adjustments. In Maier's (72) tests of reasoning in rodents, which required the combination of previously separate perceptual experiences, chance scores were made by rats younger than six months, scores of 80% or more by adults. Young chimpanzees given early experience in handling of sticks in play later proved superior to chimpanzees lacking such experiences, when given reasoning tests requiring the combination of sticks into tools for reaching food (4).

The range and nature of developmental gains through early experience naturally depend first of all upon species capacities for learning. In insects and lower vertebrates, gains through experience are less pervasive in later life than is typical for mammals (91). But for any species capable of learning, what is acquired must depend in part upon the conditions of exposure. Whether or not a mammal's response to an attractive or disturbing situation serves to change its motivational adjustment to that situation may determine whether a simple conditioned reaction or a selective-learning pattern is acquired (74, 75). Also, the tension level of the animal at the time of an experimentally-introduced experience may determine the functional order of what is learned.

Finally, any generalization about stereotypy or variability in behavior through development must depend upon the phyletic level as well as on the conditions of individual experience and individual background. For instance, shock or punishment, as one well-studied condition, may promote variability (102) or stereotypy (73) in habit formation, according to the intensity of the shock and also in dependence upon how it is administered. Many other conditions may determine whether experience in a mammalian species contributes to the individual repertoire a stereotyped habit of restricted scope or a more versatile pattern useful in new situations (74, 80).

"Original Nature" and Development

It is often held that in all animals, the adult behavior pattern results from the modification of an initial instinctive core (e.g., 80). Notwithstanding its traditional potency, this view seems to be at odds with the trend of ontogeny in a variety of animals. Either, as in lower vertebrates, behavior patterns, once stereotyped in the course of a relatively short ontogeny, are not very widely changed later on; or, as is increasingly the case up to the mammalian scale, they have a generalized beginning, and are built up to the adult pattern in a longer and more complex development. Rather than assuming an "original nature," more or less modifiable secondarily, it seems preferable to regard behavior patterns on all levels as results of a developmental process representative of the species.

In this process, genetic constitution is regarded as indirectly influential in the rise of structural-functional mechanisms through progressive intrinsic-extrinsic relationships characteristic of the level. In higher animals, developmental processes are progressively more labile in relation to capacities for profiting by experience and for behavioral plasticity. In the higher mammals, early behavior, although not formless, is most generalized of all, and the individual is most radically influenced by experience in the course of later development. But in no case can experience be considered a late-comer in development, limited to learning at later stages, for its earliest influences seem indispensable in the ontogeny of all animals. This is the case despite the fact that the trace effects of embryonic experiences seem qualitatively inferior and limited in comparison with higher functional orders of learning entering later on. For any animal, whether high or low in the scale, development is not correctly represented by the view of a primary innate pattern, broken and recast to different extents by virtue of learning at later stages. The "original nature" view is a product of traditional instinct doctrine, and is not just an oversimplification, but seems to be false.

The concept of an "original nature" has found its main support in the widely used *isolation method,* purported to separate innate behavior from the acquired (e.g., 105). Typically, in an animal separated at birth and raised apart from species mates, the principal responses appearing are considered innate or inborn (e.g., 89, 96, 120). The argument is that, because these responses have appeared in the artificial environment, (i.e., away from species mate) without benefit of any experience in the environment considered natural and normal for the species, their normal counterparts cannot have been influenced to any important extent by experiences in the "natural" environment. The logic is doubtful (87). As a rule, this assumption places far too much weight on the experimenter's knowledge of the typical developmental setting and its effect in ontogeny (87). Actually, isolation tests unaccompanied by an appropriate analytical methodology show only what behavior can or cannot develop in either of the two situations—usual and unusual—through causes not demonstrated. For one thing, the contexts may be equivalent in certain important but unidentified respects, as, for example, that the individual through its *own* organic and behavioral properties has introduced a sequence of stimulative effects normal to the species (95).

Although the isolation method is not necessarily decisive either for the intrinsic or for the extrinsic factors in ontogeny, it is suggestive, and potentially very helpful to analytical studies of ontogeny. It is the concept of the "innate" that is misleading for behavior (119) and that should be replaced by concepts better suited to the actualities of development at different phyletic levels.

LEVELS OF ATTAINMENT THROUGH ONTOGENY

Perception

Adaptive behavior may be achieved at different phyletic levels through capacities low or high in functional order, in relation to the species niche. Through ontogeny, irritability or sensitivity arises in all animals, in very different forms and basic to a variety of adaptive patterns. This fact does not justify generalizing the capacity *perception* through all phyletic levels, as is often done (e.g., 80), reducing it to any stimulative reaction whatever. This practice may be convenient for some purposes, but its broad effect is to distract attention from critical phyletic differences in capacities for organizing sensory data (74). It is imperative to investigate whether a given species really can progress, through development, beyond the lowest functional order (mere reaction to stimulation) to the mastery of organization, qualitative relationships, and the meaning differential dependent upon qualitative differences in objects and situations. Actually, critical phyletic differences in capacities for organizing sensory data seem evident, not as differences in degree but as differences in kind (44, 93). Stimulative irritability, in its simpler forms, need entail no more than simple sensory effects far inferior to and qualitatively very different from the specialized perceptual processes of which higher mammals are capable.

Experimental psychologists have been unable to analyze out the raw-sensory-effect element, as it might be called, from other components in a perceptual adjustment (36), possibly because adequate investigations along these lines have yet to be made at early ontogenetic stages and with different phyla. The matter seems different with the fully developed stage in lower phyletic levels. Protozoa assuredly possess stimulative irritability, but it remains to be demonstrated that they perceive, i.e., *sense with meaning*. Recognizable perceptual adjustments of a low organizational order appear in lower vertebrates, in a form which resists later ontogenetic modification. Ehrenhardt (21) could train lizards only to a limited extent to snap at the member of a stimulus pair with the more irregular outline, in opposition to the characteristic naïve response of this animal, i.e., the response most easily established early in ontogeny. In mammals, specialized and more plastic perceptual adjustments are mastered more slowly in ontogeny, but are modifiable to far greater extent as a rule than is possible in lower vertebrates.

Perceptual habits seem very different on lower and higher vertebrate levels. Within a few trials after hatching, the chick begins to discriminate grains from small bright inedible objects, improving on the nonparticulate stimuli which initially evoked the embryonic head lunge (74). In contrast, young carnivores require more time to integrate visual cues with non-visual perceptual adjustments established to mother and litter-mates earlier in the neonate period (88). Methods must be devised adequate to the task of tracing ontogenetic progress from sensory naivete to perceptual adequacy in animals at different phyletic levels.

Claims for "innate perceptual schemata" have not been validated in adequate experimental investigations. Presumed innate "sign stimuli" (105, 106) seem to resolve themselves, not into initially meaningful patterns, but into very generalized stimulus effects (32, 93). For example, the "hawk reaction" of nestling birds in certain species, which has been attributed to an innate meaning content, seems due rather to a diffuse stimulative shock effect than to an inborn pattern significance (32, 77). For perceptual meaning and organization, experience seems necessary, although its gains are much more restricted in lower vertebrates than in mammals. Through experiments in which, by means of translucent hoods, ring doves were deprived of early experience in visual definition, Siegel (99) found that even in this psychologically inferior bird, such experience normally must contribute an essential perceptual basis for learning pattern discriminations in adulthood. In a similar study of the chimpanzee, Chow and Nissen (13) found that experience is very essential for adult interocular equivalence in pattern discrimination. Experiments with the rat led Teas and Bitterman (103) to conclude that initial visual adjustments are "loosely organized wholes out of which the perception of objects and relations is subsequently differentiated."

Although investigations are still preliminary, it is safe to say that, in the vertebrates from fish through mammals, perception increases greatly in the scope and depth of the developmental process which makes possible the recognition of objects patterns and their relationships. The sensing of the new and strange is increasingly striking in ontogeny, from rodents to primates (44), and invites further study as indicating the integration of a wider scope of environmental cues. Correspondingly, from the fact that the chimpanzee's curiosity seems dominantly destructive in its motor outlets, men's on the whole constructive, Nissen (81) refers to the greater command of object and situation relationships in the latter. In a comparative study of early development in the chimpanzee and human infant, Jacobsen et al. (55) found the chimpanzee well ahead in all aspects of sensitivity and reactivity during the first nine months. However, as the human infant began to accelerate in perceptual accomplishments and in early concept formation, as indicated by the mastery of his first words, his superiority in psychological development became increasingly apparent.

Motivation

The manner in which differentiated drives appear through ontogeny is still unclear for any animal. Comparative investigations are needed as to the ontogeny of motivation, and I wish here to offer some theoretical considerations with respect to this problem.

It is probable that *homeostasis* affords a comparable basis for adaptive behavior in all vertebrates: a generalized excitation set up by some marked deviation from the theoretical "steady state" forces a readjustment to the pattern of metabolic processes normal to the species. But, as Pick (85) has pointed out, homeostatic mechanisms elaborate and change from fishes to man. It is not only in the organic mechanisms of homeostasis themselves that the evolutionary elaboration occurs, but also in their potentialities for widened behavioral relationships through ontogeny. Progressively higher in the mammals, these processes, through higher orders of capacity attained in ontogeny, become increasingly capable of entering into wider behavioral relationships. The result is a marked increase in the specialization of drive-impelled anticipations of incentive conditions satisfying *needs,* and in a corresponding elaboration of consummatory reactions in motivation. A primary question is: How do these reactions become differentiated appropriately as adjustments of approach or of withdrawal?

Theoretically, in all organisms, evolution has involved the selection of mechanisms favoring approach to *mild* stimulative effects, avoidance of *intense* stimulative effects (90, 93). This set of relationships between individual and environment may be proposed as a primary condition in the ontogeny of all animals, accounting for basic tendencies of the types traditionally contrasted as "appetite" and "aversion" (17, 50). It is also considered a primary condition in the ontogeny of higher levels, however extensively the initial conditions are steadily more extensively and elaborately modified and even reversed in specific detail through the higher functional orders influencing individual development. However this may be, species violating this condition as basic in ontogeny would risk extinction. It is evidenced, in one way or other and to an important extent, in the basic ontogenetic processes of all animals. Other things equal, the pseudopod of an Amoeba shrinks with intense local stimulation, extends with weak stimulation; correspondingly, the forelimb of a neonate mammal flexes or adducts, extends or abducts, according to the energy of local stimulation (11, 12).

.

The selective process postulated as operative in these terms throughout the phyletic series presumably has included all types of functional thresholds, from afferent and neural to those of visceral and motor systems. Fundamentally, before ontogeny advances very far, these mechanisms are specifically dominated by the intensity of stimulative energy presented in any given experience. The response here depends critically upon the intensity of the neurophysiological energy discharge produced, and not upon what *kind* of object or situation produced it, nor upon its potentialities for eventually benefit or harm to the organism. Evidence available for certain well-studied invertebrates such as the earthworm (48, 74) admits a clear illustration of the principle in its case. In the earthworm (48, 74) the response is typically a whole-body approach or withdrawal, stereotyped and appearing early in ontogeny, a forced type of reaction not much changed throughout life in its typical relationship to the intensity range of stimulation (other things—e.g., temporary sensory adaptations—being equal). Once ontogenetically established, as with the typical lunge reaction of lower vertebrates to small moving objects, withdrawal from larger moving objects (22, 51), the stereotyped patterns resist modification (21).

The described stimulus-response relationships, then, are regarded as fundamental processes operating in ontogeny at all levels, the particular nature of the mechanisms differing according to the species. Degree of elaboration, change or reversal through ontogeny on any given phyletic level would depend upon the extent to which higher functional orders are attainable there in individual behavior. On higher levels, motivation must be thought of as having an increasingly complex ontogeny, through which individual perceptual discriminations of objects and situations relevant to the aroused organic conditions influence incentives and goals—conditions to be approached or avoided. In superior animals, new rules are possible in these respects through ontogeny. The primary naive relationship of response with objective stimulus intensity may then be modified and, indeed, reversed, according to species capacities and the external circumstances encountered in individual experience.

In mammals, a more generalized condition of drive is postulated in early ontogeny, although still paralleling the described diphasic basis for response according to stimulus energy effect, viewed as a central feature of development in all animals. Theoretically, the ontogeny of mammalian *withdrawal* adjustments is primarily centered around high-threshold mechanisms in afferent, neural, flexor-adductor muscles, and in sympathetic autonomic and related visceral systems; of *approach* adjustments around low-threshold afferent, neural, extensor-abductor muscles, and parasympathetic and related visceral systems. It is presumed that the neural changes underlying learning are maximally effected through conditions activated either one of these systems in a synergic manner; as when intense stimulation is reduced or the source evaded through withdrawal, weak stimulation held or the source gained through approach. The ontogenetic basis of individual learning is thus viewed as essentially biphase in these terms, although of course, the relationships must be viewed as subject to alternation through experience, depending upon species capacities.

The development on this basis of overt reactive adjustments appropriate to conditions to be approached or avoided depends upon capacities for attaining superior functional orders in modifying behavior, according to what consequences typically occur as sequelae to approach or withdrawal under given conditions. In contrast to the stereotypy characteristic of lower levels, higher mammals attain increasingly plastic and individually specialized drive, incentive, and consummatory relationships. "Searching for . . . ," as a term applied to lower animals, is a loose generalization usually indicating random behavior under drive impulsion; but through ontogeny in a mammal with advanced capacities for learning the expression can mean the specific, drive-impelled anticipation of an incentive. Infant rats, subjected to regular experiences of food and water deprivation, as adults learn to locate these objects with greater facility than do normal subjects (15). Such results would not be expected in reptiles; but in chimpanzees, capable of more involved differentiations in motivation, assemblage of appropriate symbolic tokens could occur under comparable conditions. Mammalian motivation is a superior attainment through higher functional orders in behavioral development than are possible in lower phyla.

Conditions Widening Ontogenetic Attainment

The potentialities of ontogeny depend most significantly upon the extent to which the central nervous system has developed a basis for processes underlying learning. Notwithstanding arguments for "learning" in the radially symmetrical invertebrates below flatworms (112), a general distinction of qualitative differences seems necessary here (74). The trace effects of experience in organisms such as Protozoa and coelenterates seem to be diffuse or peripheral and not a basis for more lasting changes in the individual behavior pattern. For example, in paramecia subject to the combined effect of light and temperature, temporary behavior changes may be produced which suggest conditioned responses (7, 112). However, these changes depend upon some evanescent condition in metabolism, due solely to thermal effects (2, 35) altering sensitivity to light for a limited time. In contrast, invertebrates such as worms and insects are capable of neural trace effects through experience (74), as a basis for more lasting changes in the individual behavior pattern.

In addition to neural trace effects, or *fixation,* there is the capacity of advanced neural systems for *correlation,* or the organization of trace effects. Phyletic differences in capacity of the nervous system for correlating the effects of experience must account for the fact that although many insects are capable of forming rather complex habits, these patterns seem much more limited in plasticity (i.e., in properties for change and transfer) and far more situation-bound than is typically the case with mammals (74, 81).

Qualitative differences in learning at different phyletic levels have been insufficiently investigated, as have differences in the functional orders of behavioral modification possible in ontogeny at various levels. For example, simple conditioned responses established when the animal's reaction alters the situation in some critically adaptive way have different properties than have the simpler conditioned-reflex types of change learned by more passive subjects; the former pattern is more similar to selective learning in its properties (74, 75). The conditioned response of the flatworm, in its general make-up, vaguely resembles that typical of decerebrate carnivores (e.g., as generalized), but seems far inferior to the gains possible through learning in normal mammals. The cerebral cortex, evolving as a special modification of the vertebrate forebrain (47, 58, 60), introduces new properties and higher functional orders of attainment in species ontogeny, freeing the individual from the domination of specific afferent or motor mechanisms.

With the rapid acceleration of this correlative asset to predominance in the mammals, there appear striking advances in species attainments related to experience in ontogeny. Penfield (84) attributes man's superior intellectual attainments to the frontal and parietal lobes of the cerebral cortex, increasing through the mammals to man but without a specific counterpart in lower vertebrates. In man alone, vast strides in behavioral development are possible, depending on the availability of a superior cultural heritage in ontogeny (86). This superiority is also, although less obviously, due to evolutionary advances in the lower-center neural mechanisms (85) which specifically favor the individual acquisition of more extensive organizations of central and peripheral processes (as in motivation—95). Improved neural correlation promotes the attainment of a wider, more intricate set of environmental adjustments and of new behavioral patterns as individual accomplishments, provided that such acquisitions are favored by the circumstances of ontogeny.

From these considerations, one would anticipate significant improvements in animal intelligence tests through measuring plasticity in modifying learned habits, rather than through measuring acquisition or retention. This seems to be the case. After equivalent experience, rodents are on the whole less gifted in the roundabout type of adjustment than are dogs, but carnivores fall short of the primates in this respect. Accordingly, in a test requiring the selection of the alternative learned response appropriate to which of two experienced incentives is presented, Fischel (24) found that although turtles and birds failed and dogs succeeded, the latter were distinctly inferior to human subjects in the psychological organization of their adjustment in the problem. In higher animals, responses to young, food, and other goal objects are not necessarily more intense in energy output, but are richer in meaning content and more versatile in their appropriateness to changing environmental situations than in lower forms. With increasing cortical correlation capacity influencing ontogeny, species attainments in behavior are marked increasingly by the characteristics of appropriate variation and newness.

The existence of qualitative differences in species capacities for behavioral organization cannot be doubted, and more extensive comparative studies are overdue (91, 94). Learning clearly furnishes the ontogenetic basis for higher attainments such as reasoning; but reasoning does not therefore reduce to learning, any more than these capacities may be considered fully distinct from each other. Harlow (41) has shown for the monkey how cumulative experience in "learning to learn" object discriminations may progress to a high degree of complexity and skill. However, visual-discrimination methods may not be well suited for the analysis of higher mental functions based on learning (74). If systematic tests adequate for this purpose can be devised for a variety of animal forms, phyletic differences in potentialities for psychological development may prove more striking than has been suspected.

The advantages of the comparative method have been scarcely explored in the study of behavioral development (91, 115). A child's attainment of sentences marks a new advance from the stage of unitary verbal symbols, and contrasts sharply with a monkey's inability to master symbolic relationships beyond the simplest abstractions. In a far wider sense, man's capacity for repatterning verbal symbols serially, or for attaining such symbols at all, is qualitatively far above the functional order represented by the gestural symbolic processes to which the chimpanzee seems developmentally limited, although not altogether dissimilar in its ontogenetic basis.

SUMMARY AND CONCLUSIONS

As recapitulation doctrine has not been validated for behavior, the concept of *psychological levels* is advanced to express the phyletic range of behavioral organization and psychological capacities, and the concept of *functional orders* is advanced to express the ontogenetic range on any one level.

The term *development* with respect to individual behavior stresses progressive changes in organized adaptive function through ontogeny. Behavioral development on any phyletic level is not so much a retracing through the stages and levels of successive ancestral forms as a new composite leading to a new pattern distinctive of the level.

Genetic constitution and developmental setting influence *all* behavioral development in *all* organisms, operating jointly through a complex formula of intervening maturation-experience variables in a causal nexus typical of the level. *Maturation* connotes processes contributed through growth and differentiation, and *experience* connotes the effects of stimulation of the organism.

In any species, maturational and experiential effects operate at each stage as closely interrelated systems of selective factors influencing the scope of attainments at that and further stages.

The nature and specificity of the developmental effects of early experience depend upon species capacities, developmental stage, and setting. The trace effects of early experience, although mainly generalized and diffuse in comparison with those of later stages at which specific conditioning and learning enter, may be fundamental to behavioral development. At higher levels, simple conditioning must be considered a possible developmental factor even in prenatal stages.

Within the usual developmental setting of the species, typical patterns of successive self-stimulative effects, as well as of other feedback effects and of inevitable experiences, offer key factors for the progression of stages characteristic of species ontogeny. In many species, ontogeny may also entail characteristic reciprocal stimulative ("trophallactic") processes between individuals, essential to the rise of group behavioral affiliations as well as of mating.

In lower phyla, behavior patterns are stereotyped within a relatively short ontogeny in terms of lesser functional orders, and thereafter resist change; in higher phyla, after generalized early stages, through a longer ontogeny they involve functional orders of increasing scope and plasticity. But for no species is ontogeny based upon an initial innate pattern ("original nature") modified to different extents at later stages.

Generalizations about stereotypy or variability in behavioral ontogeny must depend upon species-characteristic maturational resources as well as upon individual experience. *Plasticity,* a superior functional order in variable behavior, depends both upon species capacities for the fixation and correlation of neural trace effects and upon the range and character of individual experience.

From a simple sensory irritability prevalent in the lowest phyla, animals in higher phyla advance through ontogeny to higher orders of relationships and meaningful organization in perception. In mammals, early naive sensory responses are basic in ontogeny to progressively higher perceptual orders attained according to species capacities and opportunity through experience.

A wide parallelism exists among phyla in the mechanisms underlying adaptive behavior, susceptible to specializations of approach and withdrawal adjustments according to ontogenetic capacities and opportunities on the respective levels. On this basis, increasingly elaborate drive processes underlie the attainment of successively higher orders of anticipative motivational adjustments.

Superior behavioral attainments at higher psychological levels depend not only upon capacities for neural correlation and systematic organization, but also upon advances in phyletically "old" mechanisms (e.g., those of homeostasis). Species attainments in behavioral plasticity broaden correspondingly, with greater situation-appropriate variation and newness when extrinsic conditions are favorable in ontogeny.

REFERENCES

1. Beach, F., and J. Jaynes. 1954. Effects of early experience upon the behavior of animals. *Psychol. Bull.* 51: 240–263.
2. Best, J. B. 1954. The photosensitization of *Paramecium aurelia* by temperature shock. *J. Exper. Zool.* 126: 87–99.
3. Bingham, W. E., and W. J. Griffiths, Jr. 1952. The effect of different environments during infancy on adult behavior in the rat. *J. Comp. Physiol. Psychol.* 45: 307–312.
4. Birch, H. B. 1945. The relation of previous experience to insightful problem-solving. *J. Comp. Psychol.* 38: 367–383.
5. Birch, H. Unpubl. Ontogenetic sources for order in the maternal behavior of the rat.
6. Blauvelt, H. 1955. Dynamics of the mother-newborn relationship in goats. In *Group processes,* 1st conference, 1954. New York: Josiah Macy, Jr., Foundation. Pp. 221–258.
7. Bramstedt, F. 1935. Dressurversuche mit *Paramecium caudatum* und *Stylonychia mytilus. Z. Vergl. Physiol.* 22: 490–516.
8. Brett, W. J. 1955. Persistent diurnal rhythmicity in Drosophila. *Ann. Ent. Soc. Am.* 48: 119–131.
9. Carmichael, L. 1926. The development of behavior in vertebrates experimentally removed from the influence of external stimulation. *Psychol. Rev.* 33: 51–58.—1927. A further study of the development of behavior in vertebrates experimentally removed from the influence of external

stimulation. *Psychol. Rev.* 34: 34–47.—1928. A further experimental study of the development of behavior. *Psychol. Rev.* 35: 253–260.

10. Carmichael, L. 1936. A re-evaluation of the concepts of maturation and learning as applied to the early development of behavior. *Psychol. Rev.* 43: 540–470.

11. Carmichael, L. 1946. The onset and early development of behavior. In L. Carmichael, ed., *Manual of child psychology.* New York: Wiley. Pp. 43–166.

12. Carmichael, L., and M. F. Smith. 1939. Quantified pressure stimulation and the specificity and generality of response in fetal life. *J. Genet. Psychol.* 54: 425–434.

13. Chow, K. L., and H. W. Nissen. 1955. Interocular transfer of learning in visually naïve and experienced infant chimpanzees. *J. Comp. Physiol. Psychol.* 48: 229–232.

14. Christie, R. 1951. Experimental naiveté and experiential naiveté. *Psychol. Bull.* 48: 327–339.

15. Christie, R. 1952. The effect of some early experiences in the latent learning of rats. *J. Exper. Psychol.* 43: 281–288.

16. Coghill, G. E. 1929. *Anatomy and the problem of behavior.* New York: Macmillan.

17. Craig, W. 1911. Appetites and aversions as constituents of instinct. *Biol. Bull.* 34: 91–107.

18. Cruze, W. W. 1935. Maturation and learning in chicks. *J. Comp. Psychol.* 19: 371–409.

19. de Beer, G. R. 1951. *Embryos and ancestors.* London: Oxford.

20. Dobzhansky, Th. 1950. Heredity, environment, and evolution. *Science* 3 (2877): 161–166.

21. Ehrenhardt, H. 1937. Formensehen und Sehscharfebestimmungen bei Eidechsen. *Z. Vergl. Physiol.* 24: 258–304.

22. Eibl-Eibesfeldt, I. 1952. Nahrungserwerb und Beuteschema der Erdkröte (*Bufo bufo* L.). *Behaviour* 4: 1–35.

23. Fabricus, E. 1951. Zur Ethologie junger Anatiden. *Acta Zool. Fennica* 68: 1–177.

24. Fischel, G. 1950. *Die Seele des Hundes.* Berlin: Paul Parey.

25. Foley, J. P. 1934. First year development of a rhesus monkey (*Macaca mulatta*) reared in isolation. *J. Genet. Psychol.* 44: 390–413.

26. Forgays, D. G., and J. W. Forgays. 1952. The nature of the effect of free-environmental experience in the rat. *J. Comp. Physiol. Psychol.* 45: 322–328.

27. Forgus, R. H. 1954. The effect of early perceptual learning on the behavioral organization of adult rats. *J. Comp. Physiol. Psychol.* 47: 331–336.

28. Frisch, K. von. 1950. *Bees: Their vision, chemical senses, and language.* Ithaca: Cornell Univ. Press.

29. Fromme, A. 1941. An experimental study of the factors of maturation and practice in the behavioral development of the embryo of the frog, *Rana pipiens. Genet. Psychol. Monogr.* 24: 219–256.

30. Fuller, J., C. A. Easler, and E. M. Banks, 1950. Formation of conditioned avoidance responses in young puppies. *Am. J. Physiol.* 160: 462–466.
31. Gesell, A. 1945. *The embryology of behavior: The beginnings of the human mind.* New York: Harper.
32. Ginsberg, A. 1952. A reconstructive analysis of the concept "instinct." *J. Psychol.* 33: 235–277.
33. Gluecksohn-Waelsch, S. 1954. Some genetic aspects of development. In the mammalian fetus. Physiological aspects of development. *Cold Spr. Harb. Sympos. Quant. Biol.* XIX.
34. Gos, M. 1935. Les reflexes conditionels chez l'embryon d'oiseau. *Bull. Soc. Sci. Liège,* 4me Année (4–5), 194–199: (6–7), 246–250.
35. Grabowski, U. 1939. Experimentelle Untersuchungen über das angebliche Lernvermögen von Paramaecium. *Z. Tierpsychol.* 2: 265–281.
36. Graham, C. H. 1950. Behavior, perception and the psychophysical methods. *Psychol. Rev.* 57: 108–120.
37. Gregory, W. K. 1946. The roles of motile larvae and fixed adults in the origin of the vertebrates. *Quart. Rev. Biol.* 21: 348–364.
38. Hall, C. S. 1951. The genetics of behavior. In S. S. Stevens, ed., *Handbook of experimental psychology.* New York: Wiley. Pp. 304–329.
39. Hall, C. S., and P. H. Whiteman. 1951. The effects of infantile stimulation upon later emotional stability in the mouse. *J. Comp. Physiol. Psychol.* 44: 61–66.
40. Harker, J. E. 1953. The diurnal rhythm of activity of mayfly nymphs. *J. Exper. Biol.* 30: 525–533.
41. Harlow, H. 1949. The formation of learning sets. *Psychol. Rev.* 56: 51–65.
42. Harnly, M. H. 1941. Flight capacity in relation to phenotypic and genotypic variations in the wings of *Drosophila melanogaster. J. Exper. Zool.* 88: 263–274.
43. Hasler, A. D., and W. J. Wisby. 1951. Discrimination of stream odors by fishes and its relation to parent stream behavior. *Am. Nat.* 85: 223–238.
44. Hebb, D. O. 1949. *The organization of behavior.* New York: Wiley.
45. Hebb, D. O. 1953. Heredity and environment in mammalian behaviour. *Brit. J. Anim. Behav.* I: 43–47.
46. Hempelmann, F. 1926. *Tierpsychologie vom Standpunkte des Biologen.* Leipzig: Akad. Verlagsges.
47. Herrick, C. J. 1924. *Neurological foundations of animal behavior.* New York: Holt.
48. Hess, W. 1924. Reactions to light in the earthworm, *Lumbricus terrestris* L. *J. Morphol. Physiol.* 39: 515–542.
49. Holland, J. G. 1954. The influence of previous experience and residual effects of deprivation on hoarding in the rat. *J. Comp. Physiol. Psychol.* 47: 244–247.
50. Holt, E. B. 1931. *Animal drive and the learning process.* London: Williams and Norgate.

51. Honigmann, H. 1945. The visual perception of movement by toads. *Proc. Roy. Zool. Soc.,* Ser. B, 132: 291–307.

52. Hunt, J. McV. 1941. The effects of infant feeding-frustration upon adult hoarding in the albino rat. *J. Abnorm. Soc. Psychol.* 36: 338–360.

53. Hunter, W. S. 1947. Summary comments on the heredity-environment symposium. *Psychol. Rev.* 54: 348–352.

54. Hymovitch, B. 1952. The effects of experimental variations on problem solving in the rat. *J. Comp. Physiol. Psychol.* 45: 313–320.

55. Jacobsen, C. F., M. M. Jacobsen, and J. G. Yoshioka. 1932. Development of an infant chimpanzee during her first year. *Comp. Psychol. Monogr.* 9 (41): 1–94.

56. James, W. T., and D. J. Cannon. 1952. Conditioned avoiding responses in puppies. *Am. J. Physiol.* 168: 251–253.

57. Jennings, H. S. 1906. *Behavior of the lower organisms.* New York: Columbia Univ. Press.

58. Jerison, H. J. 1955. Brain to body ratios and the evolution of intelligence. *Science* 121 (3144): 447–449.

59. Kahn, M. W. 1954. Infantile experience and mature aggressive behavior of mice: some maternal influences. *J. Genet. Psychol.* 84: 65–75.

60. Kappers, C. U. A., G. C. Huber, and E. C. Crosby. 1936. *The comparative anatomy of the nervous system of vertebrates, including man.* New York: Macmillan Company.

61. Kinder, E. F. 1927. A study of the nest-building activity of the albino rat. *J. Exper. Zool.* 47: 117–161.

62. Kuo, Z. Y. 1924. A psychology without heredity. *Psychol. Rev.* 31: 427–448.

63. Kuo, Z. Y. 1930. The genesis of the cat's response to the rat. *J. Comp. Psychol.* 11: 1–30.

64. Kuo, Z. Y. 1932. Ontogeny of embryonic behavior in Aves. II. The mechanical factors in the various stages leading to hatching. *J. Exper. Zool.* 61: 395–430.

65. Kuo, Z. Y. 1932. Ontogeny of embryonic behavior in Aves. III. The structure and environmental factors in embryonic behavior. *J. Comp. Psychol.* 13: 245–272.

66. Kuo, Z. Y. 1932. Ontogeny of embryonic behavior in Aves. IV. The influence of embryonic movements upon the behavior after hatching. *J. Comp. Psychol.* 14: 109–122.

67. Lehrman, D. S. 1953. A critique of Lorenz's "objectivistic" theory of animal behavior. *Quart. Rev. Biol.* 28: 337–363.

68. Lehrman, D. S. 1955. The physiological basis of parental feeding behavior in the ring dove (*Streptopelia risoria*). *Behaviour* 7: 241–286.

69. Lorenz, K. 1935. Der Kumpan in der Umwelt des Vogels. *J. Ornith., Leipzig,* 83: 137–213, 289–413.

70. Lorenz, K. 1950. The comparative method in studying innate behaviour patterns. In *Physiological mechanisms in animal behaviour.* New York: Academic Press. Pp. 221–268.

71. Luchins, A. S., and R. H. Forgus. 1955. The effect of differential post-weaning environment on the rigidity of an animal's behavior. *J. Genet. Psychol.* 86: 51–58.
72. Maier, N. R. F. 1932. Age and intelligence in rats. *J. Comp. Psychol.* 13: 1–6.
73. Maier, N. R. F., and J. B. Klee. 1943. Studies of abnormal behavior in the rat. XII. The pattern of punishment and its relation to abnormal fixations. *J. Exper. Psychol.* 32: 377–398.
74. Maier, N. R. F., and T. C. Schneirla. 1935. *Principles of animal psychology.* New York: McGraw-Hill.
75. Maier, N. R. F., and T. C. Schneirla. 1942. Mechanisms in conditioning. *Psychol. Rev.* 49: 117–134.
76. McGraw, M. 1946. Maturation of behavior. In L. Carmichael, ed., *Manual of child psychology.* New York: Wiley.
77. McNiven, M. A. 1954. Responses of the chicken, duck and pheasant to a hawk and goose silhouette—A controlled replication of Tinbergen's study. Thesis: Pennsylvania State Univ. Libr.
78. Moore, K. 1944. The effect of controlled temperature changes on the behavior of the white rat. *J. Exper. Psychol.* 34: 70–79.
79. Needham, J. 1929. *The sceptical biologist.* London: Chatto and Windus.
80. Nissen, H. W. 1951. Phylogenetic comparison. In S. S. Stevens, ed., *Handbook of experimental psychology.* New York: Wiley. Pp. 347–386.
81. Nissen, H. W. 1954. The nature of the drive as innate determinant of behavioral organization. In *Nebraska symposium on motivation, II.* Lincoln: Univ. Nebraska Press.
82. Orton, G. 1955. The role of ontogeny in systematics and evolution. *Evolution* 9: 75–83.
83. Patrick, J. R., and R. M. Laughlin. 1934. Is the wall-seeking tendency in the white rat an instinct? *J. Genet. Psychol.* 44: 378–389.
84. Penfield, W. 1954. Some observations on the functional organization of the human brain. *Proc. Am. Phil. Soc.* 98: 293–297.
85. Pick, J. 1954. The evolution of homeostasis. *Proc. Am. Phil. Soc.* 98: 298–303.
86. Piéron, H. 1953. De l'animale à l'homme: les origines du psychisme. In H. Beer, ed., *À la recherche de la mentalité préhistorique.* Paris: Albin Michel. Pp. 37–73.
87. Riess, B. 1950. The isolation of factors of learning and native behavior in field and laboratory studies. *Ann. N.Y. Acad. Sci.* 51: 1093–1102.
88. Rosenblatt, J., J. Wodinsky, A. Frank, and T. C. Schneirla. Unpubl. Analytical studies on maternal behavior and litter relations in the domestic cat. II. From birth to weaning.
89. Schneider, K. M. 1950. Aus der Jugendentwicklung einer künstlich aufgezogenen Schimpansin. III. Vom Verhalten. *Z. Tierpsychol.* 7: 485–558.
90. Schneirla, T. C. 1939. A theoretical consideration of the basis for approach-withdrawal adjustments in behavior. *Psychol. Bull.* 37: 501–502.
91. Schneirla, T. C. 1945. Ant learning as a problem in comparative psy-

chology. In P. Harriman, ed., *Twentieth century psychology*. New York: Philosophical Library. Pp. 276–305.

92. Schneirla, T. C. 1946. Problems in the biopsychology of social organization. *J. Abnorm. Soc. Psychol.* 41: 385–402.

93. Schneirla, T. C. 1949. Levels in the psychological capacities of animals. In R. W. Sellars et al., ed., *Philosophy for the future*. New York: Macmillan. Pp. 243–286.

94. Schneirla, T. C. 1952. A consideration of some conceptual trends in comparative psychology. *Psychol. Bull.* 49: 559–597.

95. Schneirla, T. C. 1956. Interrelationships of the "innate" and the "acquired" in instinctive behavior. In *Colloque Int. sur l'Instinct Animale, 1954*. Paris: Fond. Singer-Polignac. Pp. 387–432.

96. Seitz, A. 1950. Untersuchungen über Varhaltensweisen bei Caniden. *Z. Tierpsychol.* 7: 1–46.

97. Seitz, P. F. D. 1954. The effects of infantile experience upon adult behavior in animal subjects: I. Effects of litter size during infancy upon adult behavior in the rat. *Am. J. Psychiat.* 110: 916–927.

98. Shepard, J. F., and F. S. Breed. 1913. Maturation and use in the development of an instinct. *J. Anim. Behav.* 3: 274–285.

99. Siegel, A. I. 1953. Deprivation of visual form definition in the ring dove. I. Discriminatory learning. *J. Comp. Physiol. Psychol.* 46: 115–119. II. Perceptual-motor transfer. *J. Comp. Physiol. Psychol.* 46: 250–252.

100. Smith, S., and E. R. Guthrie. 1921. *General psychology in terms of behavior*. New York: Appleton.

101. Snyder, L. H. 1950. *The principles of heredity*. Boston: Heath.

102. Stone, G. R. 1946. The effect of negative incentive on serial learning. I. The spread of variability under electric shock. *J. Exper. Psychol.* 36: 137–142.

103. Teas, D. C., and M. E. Bitterman. 1952. Perceptual organization in the rat. *Psychol. Rev.* 59: 130–140.

104. Thompson, W. R. 1954. The effects of restricting early experience on the problem-solving capacity of dogs. *Canad. J. Psychol.* 8: 17–31.

105. Tinbergen, N. 1951. *The study of instinct*. New York: Oxford Univ. Press.

106. Tinbergen, N., and D. J. Kuenen. 1939. Uber die auslösenden und die richtunggebenden Reizsituationen der Sperrbewegung von jungen Drosseln (*Turdus m. mercula* L. und *T. e. ericetorum* Turton) *Z. Tierpsychol.* 3: 37–60.

107. Tumarkin, A. 1955. On the evolution of the auditory conducting apparatus: A new theory based on functional considerations. *Evolution* 9: 221–243.

108. Vandel, A. 1955. L'évolution considerée comme phénomène de développement. *Bull. Soc. Zool. Fr.* 79: 341–356.

109. Van der Kloot, G., and C. M. Williams. 1953. Cocoon construction by the cecropia silkworm. I. The role of the external environment. *Behaviour* 5: 141–156.

110. Van der Kloot, G., and C. M. Williams. 1953. II. The role of the internal environment. *Behaviour* 5: 157–174.

111. Waddington, C. H. 1940. *Organizers and genes.* Cambridge: Cambridge Univ. Press.

112. Warden, C. J., T. N. Jenkins, and L. Warner. 1940. *Comparative Psychology.* Vol. II. *Plants and invertebrates.* New York: Ronald.

113. Warkentin, J., and K. U. Smith. 1937. The development of visual acuity in the cat. *J. Genet. Psychol.* 50: 371–399.

114. Weiss, P. 1954. Some introductory remarks on the cellular basis of differentiation. *J. Embryol. Exper. Morphol.* 1: 181–211.

115. Werner, H. 1940. *Comparative psychology of mental development.* New York: Harper.

116. Wheeler, W. M. 1928. *The social insects.* New York: Harcourt, Brace.

117. Willier, B. H. 1954. Phases in embryonic development. *J. Cell. Comp. Physiol.* 43: 307–317.

118. Wodinsky, J., J. S. Rosenblatt, and T. C. Schneirla. Unpubl. The establishment of stable individual nursing adjustments by neonate kittens.

119. Woodger, J. H. 1953. What we mean by "inborn." *Brit. J. Phil. Sci.* 3: 319–326.

120. Zippelius, H. M., and F. Goethe. 1951. Ethologische Beobachtungen an Haselmäusen (*Muscardinus a. avellanarius* L.) *Z. Tierpsychol.* 8: 348–367.

T. C. SCHNEIRLA

A Theoretical Consideration of the Basis for Approach-Withdrawal Adjustments in Behavior

Bibliography No. 18

Various theoretical systems in psychology have been built upon a priori acceptance of a negative-positive differentiation in behavior. However, the conditions which are responsible for the ontogenetic appearance of such a differentiation appear to be unclearly glimpsed.

A consideration of the evidence for inframammalian animals shows a more or less distinctly inherent basis for a "sign" differentiation of behavior. This rests upon the properties of stimulation at different intensities in accounting not only for quantitative differences, but especially for qualitative differences in adjustment to the environment. An analysis of adaptive behavior in one well-investigated animal shows that stimuli at high intensities typically elicit a general reaction in which the predominance of a differentiated excitation-reaction system virtually insures withdrawal from the source. Conversely, weak stimuli predominantly arouse the antagonistic system and typically produce an approach to the source of stimulation.

This conception envisages negative-positive responses as fundamentally attributable to the differential arousal of excitation-reaction systems which function as though they possessed distinctively different activation thresholds. Through natural selection, we may hypothecate the evolution of such mechanisms along adaptive lines.

This view has utility as a hypothetical basis for understanding approach-withdrawal behavior in man. The problem has been dealt with previously in a rather fragmentary way, evidently because of complexity and the initial absence of directionalized general reactions in neonate behavior.

From *Psychological Bulletin* 37: 501–502 (1939). Courtesy of the American Psychological Association.

Evidence from general studies of early behavior, of emotional development, and of certain crucial adjustments such as the reaching reaction, may be profitably organized on this basis. The bearing of this "reaction-system-threshold" theory upon concepts such as "appetite-aversion," "vectors," "sign-gestalt" and the like, will be considered.

An Evolutionary and Developmental Theory of Biphasic Process Underlying Approach and Withdrawal

Bibliography No. 87

I

The aspect of *towardness* or *awayness* is common in animal behavior. Our problem is to consider, from the phylogenetic and the ontogenetic approaches, the question of how animals generally manage to reach beneficial conditions and stay away from the harmful, that is, how *survivors* do this. Although this valuable series of conferences has by now covered nearly all phases of the motivation problem, the evolutionary and developmental aspects are perhaps the ones touched on lightly in evidence and theory. My purpose is to discuss some promising theoretical ideas and evidence bearing on these questions.

Motivation, broadly considered, concerns the causation and impulsion of behavior. The question here is what impels the approach and withdrawal reactions of very different animals from protozoans to man and how each level develops its characteristic pattern. Have these levels anything in common, or does each have a basis very different from the others?

Reprinted from *Nebraska Symposium on Motivation,* vol. 7, edited by Marshall R. Jones, by permission of University of Nebraska Press.

The theory presented in this article was first developed in a book on comparative psychology (75); its application to behavioral phylogeny and ontogeny was sketched a few years later (99) and discussed in subsequent publications (101, 102, 103). The concept of biphasic adaptive mechanisms has been developed from the writings of Ch. Darwin, H. S. Jennings, W. Cannon, C. S. Sherrington, J. B. Watson, and F. H. Allport, in particular, all of whom have used it implicitly or in specific ways. The concept of antagonistic functional mechanisms has been discussed teleologically by Kurt Goldstein (44) with reference to adaptive behavior, and recently W. Kempf (68) has developed a theory of conflict and neurosis based on a wholistic study of biphasic mechanisms in man. All of these sources may be consulted for detailed references on this ramifying subject.

In studying this broad problem of behavior, an objective methodology is indispensable. To be specific, I submit that *approach* and *withdrawal* are the *only* empirical, objective terms applicable to *all* motivated behavior in *all* animals. Psychologically superior types of adjustment are found, but only on higher psychological levels and after appropriate individual development.

As elementary definitions, an animal may be said to *approach* a stimulus source when it responds by coming nearer to that source, to *withdraw* when it increases its distance from the source. This point is not sufficiently elementary, however, to escape confusion. Confusion is indicated when the term "approach" is combined with "avoid," as if these were opposite concepts for motivation. This practice, common in the literature, is indulged in even by psychological dictionaries. But however conventional, it is psychologically wrong, for *withdrawal* is the conceptual opposite of *approach,* and the opposite of avoidance is seeking, which means "to look or search for" something. Seeking and avoidance are of a higher evolutionary and developmental order than approach and withdrawal, and these terms should not be mismated.

To put it differently, whereas all behavior in all animals tends to be adaptive, only some behavior in some animals is purposive. Behavior is *adaptive* when it contributes to individual or to species survival, especially the latter. To take a contrast, when an amoeba is stimulated by directed weak light, typically there occurs a local flow of protoplasm toward the source, perhaps followed by a general movement in that direction: an approach. This is a forced protoplasmic reaction, very different at basis from behavior observed in a rat (75, frontispiece). Uneasy about coming into the open, this animal does so however when food is placed there. But instead of eating in the open, it manipulates the dish across to and over the barrier, and ends by feeding in its retreat. On inductive grounds, both amoeba and rat act adaptively, but only the rat accomplishes goal-directed responses to an incentive, and therefore behaves *purposively*. The response of the amoeba is energized directly by protoplasmic processes set off by the stimulus—that of the rat involves specialized, higher-level processes not indicated in the protozoan.

The real issue concerns what assumptions we made about teleology or the problem of final causes. Vitalists such as Driesch and McDougall settle the problem of behavior causation by assuming a priori that all adaptive behavior is "aimed at" resolving a difficulty, and that all animals, at whatever level, can "see" the beneficial and "avoid" the injurious. Warburton (118), however, believes that telic usage of the term "goal," a frequent indulgence in biology, implies only that the phenomenon is held selectively advantageous to the reacting organism. If this is really so, confusion can be avoided by using the term "adaptive," unless psychological "purposing" is adequately demonstrated.[1] It is becoming more and more evident that adaptive behavior, which has attained many specialized forms through natural selection, is basically natural and organic in all animals, from those of lowest psychological status to those capable of reaching solutions by specialized anticipative processes.

How, then, does behavior in surviving animals, even the lowliest, come to have the character of adaptiveness, centering around efficient approach and withdrawal responses? The main reason seems to be that behavior, from its beginning in the primitive scintilla many ages ago, has been a decisive factor in natural selection. For the haunts and the typical niche of any organism must depend on what conditions it approaches and what it moves away from—these types of reaction thereby determine what future stimuli can affect the individual, its life span, and the fate of its species.

The principle may be stated roughly as follows: *Intensity of stimulation basically determines the direction of reaction with respect to the source, and thereby exerts a selective effect on what conditions generally affect the organism.* This statement derived from the generalization that, for all organisms in early ontogenetic stage, *low intensities of stimulation tend to evoke approach reactions, high intensities withdrawal reactions with reference to the source* (99). Doubtless the highroad of evolution has been littered with the remains of species that diverged too far from these rules of effective adaptive relationship between environmental conditions and response.

The chief difficulty of the vitalists seems to arise from an unwillingness to accept the possibility that mechanisms correlated with physical reality could start very simply as forced-reaction types and then permute through long evolution to provide a basis for psychologically advanced types such as seeking or avoiding. Although terms such as "appetite-aversion" imply that all animals know what to look for and what to avoid, this is not so in all cases. Jennings's (67) discovery that protozoans such as Paramecium approach the source of potentially lethal chemicals and withdraw from potentially beneficial or innocuous chemicals obviously does not prove that the animal has made a mistake, but only that the experimenter has been ingenious enough to find stimulative situations reversing the normal formula that low-energy stimulation leads to food or other benefits, including no harm, and high-energy stimulation leads to harm or death.

---

[1] A positivistic generalization of "purpose" was used by Bertocci (3) in arguing against Gordon Allport the problem of causal factors in motivation. The present writer finds himself in agreement with Allport (2) that if these problems are to be investigated scientifically, a really objective set of concepts is needed, not contaminated by unexamined a priori assumptions. The latter form of obfuscation frequently is accompanied by disarming protests such as that of the biologist McKinley (80), who, while holding that purposive striving underlies the adaptive behavior of all organisms through evolution, denies that his assumption is teleological (i.e., that it is purpositivistic!).

Although at first glance all animals seem to act as though they could seek or avoid things in view of benefits or dangers, it is the methods of objective science that must be directed at this question, and not the forensic arts.

Much evidence shows that in *all* animals the species-typical pattern of behavior is based upon biphasic, functionally opposed mechanisms insuring approach or withdrawal reactions according to whether stimuli of low or of high intensity, respectively, are in effect. This is an oversimplified statement; however, in general, what we shall term the A-type of mechanism, underlying approach, favors adjustments such as food-getting, shelter-getting, and mating; the W-type, underlying withdrawal, favors adjustments such as defense, huddling, flight, and other protective reactions. Also, through evolution, higher psychological levels have arisen in which through ontogeny such mechanisms can produce new and qualitatively advanced types of adjustment to environmental conditions. Insects are superior to protozoans, and mammals to insects, in that ontogeny progressively frees processes of individual motivation from the basic formula of prepotent stimulative-intensity relationships.

Mistakes in the psychological level of adaptive processes are common risks (101). What this means is illustrated by a controversy over the status of sea-anemone motivation (75, p. 45). Jennings found that after he had dripped meat juice for a time over one side (A) of an individual's crown of tentacles, neither the tentacles of side A nor those of the unstimulated side B would respond by extending and waving. The results suggested to Jennings a general motivational change in the animal, which he characterized as a "loss of hunger." Parker repeated this test, but with an additional control, that of injecting a current of meat juice into the body cavity through the body wall. Here also the entire disc presently became quiescent, leading Parker to conclude that the meat juice had adapted all tentacles alike by entering the hollow interiors and diffusing through the walls to the recepter cells. On this low level, peripheral (i.e., molecular) types of change seem dominant rather than central (i.e., molar) types produced through organized neural conditions as in mammals. In contrast, a satiated rat can become unresponsive to food through an avoidance process involving perceptual rejection, and not just local or restricted physiological changes in some property such as sensitivity. The difficulty with terms such as *sensitization* and *satiation* for animal drive is that they are vague and may run a wide range of qualitatively different processes in different animals.

Thus, although acceptance and rejection, beneception and nociception, love and hate, and other motivational dichotomies are based on perhaps similar organic properties arising through evolution, they involve widened potentialities for behavior organization and superior capacities such as anticipation demonstrable only in higher mammals.

I recall a psychologist expressing surprise that a worker bee participates in comb-building although, as he supposed, it is "not hungry at the time." This type of case must remain enigmatic for those who assume without question that the insect is motivated by an anticipation of the over-all result to which its act contributes. But I believe the relationships of food and actions leading to it are rather different for insects than for mammals (75, 100, 104). The insect builds its maze habit slowly and by stages: first a general habituation to the situation develops, then a process of very gradually mastering the local choice-points, and in a final stage an over-all integration of the habit comes about only through stereotyped interactions between segmentally anchored habits. The rat masters the "same" maze pattern very differently, starting its local learning and over-all integration together even on the first run. Unlike the ant, he can soon anticipate distant parts of the maze, and this may get him into trouble at times. The ant's habit is built up in sections, without any indications that the subject is capable at any time of specifically anticipating the end-point from a distance. Her drive processes are evidently rather different from those of the rat, which can anticipate either by stages as a habit builds up or by leaps to the end-point, depending on the circumstances.

Our theory of animal motivation is likely to be influenced strongly by the views we hold as to whether learning can differ qualitatively at different phyletic levels. Even the sparse existing evidence indicates that differences of a fundamental nature exist, not to be understood in terms of "complexity." Basic differences in the nature of learning seem involved in the fact that ants do not reverse a learned maze readily, although rats do, as also in the fact that the two animals initially acquire the habit very differently. Accordingly, it is significant that repeatedly reversing alternative responses differing greatly in difficulty can result in neurotic behavior in rats (124) but not in ants (100, 104). The results indicate that *drive* in the ant's habit is much more strictly bound to specific effects from extrinsic stimulation (e.g., from food carried) and from internal condition than in the rat's. The finding of Bitterman et al. (5) that fish progress very differently than rats in a reversal problem, with slight indications of day-to-day progress in only a few of the fish and strong evidence for such progress in all of the rats, indicates basic differences in how lower vertebrates and mammals learn the "same" problem. Concerning the extent to which reasoning may differ qualitatively from learning, much evidence points to the existence of a fundamental distinction, which discrimination-generalization methods for example may not be valid to test (75, Chap. 20).

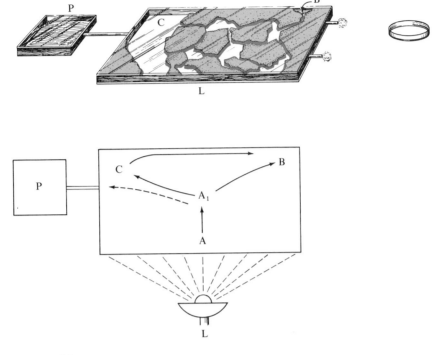

FIGURE 16
Nest setup for comparison of reactions of *Formica* ants and inquiline beetles
to intense stimulative conditions. Top: Ant nest water-dish removed; L, lamp; P,
food-box; bottom: A,A₁, B, C (see text).

I believe that a strong case can be made for differentiating the following
levels in capacity to modify behavior (101):

1) fluctuant changes, through peripheral effects (e.g., protozoans);

2) sensory integration, habituation, based on central trace effects (e.g.,
flatworms);

3) contiguity-type conditioned responses (worms);

4) selective learning (different in insects; mammals);

5) insight, reasoning (higher mammals).

On different phyletic levels, therefore, the relation of the fundamental
biphasic mechanisms to drive may differ significantly according to the
scope and nature of capacities for modifying behavior through ontogeny.

Such differences may be crucial for survival in emergency situations.
As an example, one of my nests of *Formica* ants had been overfed and
developed a large population of tiny parasitic beetles. To get rid of the
beetles, I put a lamp on side A (Figure 16). At first both ants and beetles
gave strong taxis reactions to the light and heat, all withdrawing towards

side B-C. But soon certain of the ants began running to the chamber P, taking a previously learned foraging route, then returned to the nest and carried their more sluggish species-mates into the box and safety. Meanwhile, the beetles collected increasingly in corner B, the last part of the nest to dry out in the heat. At length all of the beetles were at B and were dead or dying; all of the ants were in the box P and alive. The predominant initial drive process of both animals was of the *taxis* type, governed by intense extrinsic stimulation, with varying A- and W-type adjustments as the nest situation changed. This pattern led to the extinction of the beetles, whereas a qualitatively different adjustment process admitted by ontogenetic specialization saved the ants.

II

Through biphasic adjustive mechanisms, stimulative energy fundamentally dominates the approach and withdrawal responses of all animals. A simple, inclusive pattern is that involved in the gel-sol cycle of the protozoan amoeba. In this animal, stimulus energy, whether in the form of light, chemical, or tactual effects, if weak, sets up solation in the locality, perhaps with pseudopod formation and extension toward the source following; if strong, it sets up gelation or contraction on the stimulated side or perhaps widely, then solation may occur on the opposite side with movement away from the source. Mast (77) demonstrated that with different intensities of light the protoplasmic effects graduate from solation and prompt forward locomotion to delays in movement based on different degrees of reversal in the protoplasmic flow and, finally, a movement from the source. Such differences may be seen clearly under the microscope. The intervening variables are here exposed as different degrees of change ranging to a complete reversal of the gel-sol cycle; the drive is generalized in protoplasmic activity.

Biphasic mechanisms facilitating approach-withdrawal adjustments are present in all functional systems, from sensory to motor, in multicellular animals. One important type of biphasic afferent process enters with what Hecht (55) called the "duality of the sensory process." In the clam *Mya* he demonstrated two opposed photochemical processes, one (A-type) aroused in weak light, the other (W-type) in strong light, the A-process eliciting siphon extension and feeding, the W-type siphon retraction and valve closure. Hecht generalized this dual-process formula for the photoreceptors of widely different animals, including man.

The biphasic properties of receptor mechanisms are sometimes not apparent until their relations to general function are analyzed. Earthworms, for example, lack specialized eyes but have light-sensitive cells

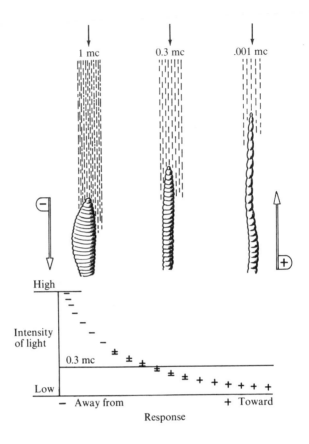

FIGURE 17
Reactions of dark-adapted earthworms to light
(W. Hess. 59). Top: at the high intensity, prompt anterior shortening, movement from source predominate;
at the middle intensity, less prompt shortening, increasing movement towards source; at the low intensity,
thinning and movement towards the source predominate. Bottom: Graph of intensity and response
relationships.

distributed in the skin. In W. Hess's (59) experiment, dark-adapted
earthworms turned from a light source of 0.3 mc in 99% of 144 trials but
turned from a source of 0.001 mc in just 43% of the trials (Figure 17).
As earthworms lack specialized eyes, this difference is due to the differential arousal of light-sensitive cells in the skin. The weak light evidently
stimulated relatively few of these generalized receptors, those of lowest
threshold, producing a low-energy neural discharge with approach the

dominant response, whereas the stronger light aroused also many of the cells with higher thresholds, resulting in a stronger neural discharge forcing W-type reactions.

Specialized eyes of many types exist in the animal series, their properties bearing on action in diversified ways. In many invertebrates, the sectors of the compound eye are known to differ significantly in the sensitivity and relation to action of their afferent elements (75, Chap. 6). In Clark's studies on water beetles, as an example, specimens with left eyes covered turned to the left when light reached anterior sections of the open compound eye, but to the right when sections farther back were stimulated by light of the same intensity. The reason, effective for many animals from flatworms to arthropods, is that sensillae of lower threshold in certain zones of the eye discharge neural patterns of higher energy, inducing the animal to react as to a more intense stimulus than when sensillae of higher thresholds in other zones are aroused. That a forced difference in action results is indicated for example by the finding that varnishing over the lower part of both eyes in certain flies causes extension of the anterior legs and raising of the body, whereas covering the upper parts causes flexion of anterior legs and lowering of the body (Fraenkel and Gunn, 38). Research such as that of Mittelstaedt (83) with insects shows that such relationships are often complexly involved in the control of action.

According to the type of eye possessed by an animal, basic differences may arise in the relative potency of stimuli to excite neural discharges affecting action mechanisms. As we shall see, certain lower vertebrates, with lens eyes, are directly opposite to the bee, with compound eyes, in their tendency to approach figures of simpler rather than more complex outlines. Hertz reported that the honeybee's approach to visual figures varied in proportion to the heterogeneity of outlines and internal articulation, e.g., a star was approached more frequently than a square, and both of these more frequently than a circle (57a). Wolf (125), analyzing such behavior, found that bees approached visual areas in frequencies directly related to the rate of flicker. From such results he concluded that responses to flickering fields and to articulated figures had a common basis, namely, the number of pulses per unit time produced in the sensillae of the eye as the bee flies across the stimulus fields. Lower vertebrates, which instead, as we shall find, approach circles more readily than figures of more complex outlines, evidently have afferent properties opposite to those of the compound eye as concerns action.

Thus, in vision and other modalities, types of mechanism have evolved which, by regulating the potency of neural discharge in specialized ways, serve to canalize the stimulative conditions under which animals approach or withdraw. The vertebrate ear, considered a specialization of the cutaneous system, significantly extends reactivity to vibratory stimuli.

This has occurred through the evolution of afferent specializations, as of a cochlea from the lagena of lower vertebrates, and of changes in the anatomy of the auditory ossicles affecting both the range and the acuity of hearing (Tumarkin, 115). In chemoception, also, many end-organ specializations have arisen which admit species-typical thresholds and other differences in sensitivity. Striking cases may be found in the responses of insects to chemicals (Dethier, 25), from approaches to odor of food plants or of animal hosts to withdrawals from other plant or insect odors. In many cases, as with affinities for colony odors in social insects, species secretory functions as well as earlier feeding experience also influence reactivity; in others, as when a former food odor becomes repellent, changes in susceptibility clearly occur in dependence upon organic condition or age. Many types of secretory and other organic specializations have evolved, variously significant for such reactions. One interesting type of adaptive effect was discovered by von Frisch (41), who extracted an essence from the skin of the minnow which proved strongly repellent to species mates. This phenomenon is evidently widespread, as Heintz (57) found it in worms and insects also.

A great diversity of mechanisms affecting attraction or repulsion along species-typical lines is evidenced in the natural behavior of animals.

Correlated with biphasic afferent functions are neural mechanisms with distinctive arousal thresholds or other functional properties dependent on stimulus intensity. One interesting type of specialization is known for the earthworm and certain other invertebrates, in which intense stimulation of the head elicits a sudden jerk of the entire animal backward. In this response, the function of regular short-relay conductors underlying smooth locomotion is interrupted by the arousal of W-type effectors through the "giant fibers" (Stough, 112; Bullock, 11), a specialized high-threshold conductor especially responsive to intense stimulation.

Whatever their equipment of specialized neurones may be, the nervous systems of multicellular animals are all capable of discharging differentially according to afferent intensity. The general formula supported by much neurophysiological research on both invertebrates (e.g., 51) and vertebrates is that, with increasing stimulus intensity in any modality, successive increases are evoked not only in the volley rate of discharge into the central nervous system but also in the number of neurones conducting (Brink, 10). Consequently, instead of type-A actions, predominant at lower stimulus intensities, type-W actions of higher threshold can be aroused increasingly.

Primary to all such phenomena is a dependence of the neural discharge on the quantitative aspects of stimulation. For particular types of discharge, Sherrington (109) remarked that "The accuracy of grading within a certain range of intensities is so remarkable that the ratio between stimulus intensities and response-intensity has by some observers been assigned mathematical precision." From Sherrington's pioneer work on the differential arousal of flexion and extension reflexes through the spinal cord, with his associates (Creed et al., 17) he derived the principle of "half centers," which may be characterized as *reciprocally functioning ganglionic sub-centers*. This principle outlines the functional differentiation of partially overlapping neurone groups adjacent to each other in the same neural center, differing in their arousal thresholds and capable of working reciprocally in the excitation of antagonistic effector systems. The view that such reciprocally related neurone groups normally operate to oppose the strong arousal of A-type and W-type effectors simultaneously, but favor the predominance of one or the other type in a smoothly working pattern, is well supported (Eccles, 31). This principle, first demonstrated for antagonistic neurone groups in the cord, may have a considerably wider application to neural correlation in the control of biphasic effector systems.

A finding of significance for mammalian ontogeny is that of Adrian (1), that impulses from deep or protopathic and impulses from epicritic or superficial cutaneous receptors, selectively aroused according to stimulus intensity, may take different paths and have typical discharge-pattern differences, as in the lesser opportunities for summation in epicritically aroused than in protopathically aroused patterns. The quantitative aspects of stimulation and of conduction therefore would tend to favor a routing of impulses in the first case predominantly through that neurone group in the spinal level discharging to A-type effectors, and in the second case through its antagonist discharging to W-type effectors. This may be considered the paradigm for neural discharge to common centers in early ontogeny, dependent on stimulus energy delivered to any modality.

Although most of the research on the functions of the autonomic nervous system has been done with *adult* mammals, and the evidence is understandably complex, the generalization seems justified that, according to stimulus magnitudes acting upon the central nervous system, the two principal sections of the autonomic system are selectively aroused to characteristically different functions. Through the cranial and sacral regions of the central system, the *parasympathetic* outflow tends to arouse visceral and skeletal functions of an A-type of vegetative character; through the thoracic and lumbar regions the *sympathetic* outflow arouses functions of a W-type of interruptive nature. The antagonism of these systems may be illustrated by Kuntz's (70) description of the selective arousal by weak stimuli of impulses over a dorsal cord depressor path of long fibers and low resistance, associated with the parasympathetic system and arousing vasodilitation, and by strong stimuli of impulses over a ventral cord pressor relay of short fibers and high resistance, associated with the *sympathetic* system and eliciting vasoconstriction.

Significantly, although the autonomic nervous system is old in vertebrates, in its full biphasic function in higher mammals it is highly specialized. Recently, Pick (88) has concluded that whereas primitively in vertebrates the dorsal-outflow (*parasympathetic*) system is the predominant system of visceral arousal from the cord, the ventral outflow, although at first negligible, from amphibians to man increases steadily in potency and specialization as the *sympathetic* system, and becomes progressively more effective as the antagonist of the parasympathetic.

Evidence concerning metabolic processes effected largely through smooth muscles and the autonomic nervous system widely supports the Cannon-Langley theory of antagonistic functioning dependent on opposition of the *parasympathetic* and *sympathetic* autonomic divisions. As Darling and Darrow (20) demonstrated, the biphasic character of human visceral function shows through even in the *adult* in blood pressure and other physiological aspects of emotional reactivity, notwithstanding certain exceptions (e.g., galvanic skin response) in which the divisions of the autonomic tend to reinforce each other. Starting with Cannon's research, the patterning of opposed function has been revealed in all types of visceral actions, including smooth muscle and the neurohumoral. Neurophysiological research gives a familiar picture of *vegetative* (A-type) changes (homeostatic, smooth-running processes occurring within a range characteristic of species and developmental stage), aroused characteristically by low-intensity stimulation through the parasympathetic system, and of *interruptive* (W-type) changes supported by secretion of adrenin and aroused characteristically by high-intensity stimulation through the *sympathetic* system. With experience, the functional relationships of these systems become more complex and varied, perhaps often to the point of cancelling or reversing aspects of their basic antagonistic, reciprocal relationship.

The effectors, also, seem to function biphasically in all animals. In the earthworm, under weak stimulation the circular muscles are dominantly aroused, thinning and extending the body and facilitating movement toward the source; under strong stimulation the longitudinal muscles are dominant, thickening the body and facilitating withdrawal from the source. A striking interruption of normal smooth reciprocal function of the two systems occurs when high-intensity stimulation causes the body to contract suddenly backward through a rapid maximal innervation of the W-system via giant fiber conduction. In other invertebrates, through corresponding mechanisms in tentacles and other local structures, the mobile part typically swings toward the side of weak stimulation, away from that of strong stimulation, and through comparable synergic action the entire organism may react equivalently.

For vertebrates, the principle of differential and antagonistic systems in skeletal muscle function was established by Sherrington (109), who demonstrated it in the action of sets of muscles working against each other at the same joint or on different joints of the same limb. Between extensor dominance with weak stimulation and flexor dominance with strong stimulation, a gradation of functional combinations was demonstrated both by myographic recordings and by direct palpation of muscles to intact limbs. In the developing organism, relationships of threshold may be stated conveniently in terms of the Lapique concept of chronaxie, as a measure of arousal threshold. Bourguignon (6) found that adult mammalian extensors tend to have a low chronaxie and flexors a high chronaxie, particularly in the limbs. These two muscular systems commonly act concurrently in the general behavior of animals (Levine and Kabat, 74); however, summaries of the evidence (e.g., Fulton, 42; Hinsey, 60) leave no question that their antagonistic function in synergic patterns is a primary fact in mobility and action, and that their reciprocal arousal is essential to the development of coordinated patterns of behavior (Hudgins, 65). For research on vertebrates generally, flexion of a limb to strong stimulation is a response taken for granted as available for conditioning from early stages. Although Sherrington described extension as postural and flexion as a "reflex to noxious stimulation," their biphasic function, as we shall see, constitutes a mechanism of expanding relationships basic to ontogeny.

In sum, diverse biphasic mechanisms of the receptors, central and auxiliary nervous systems, and effectors are fundamental to ontogeny in all animals. They have in common, generally, the property of A-type arousal by weak stimuli, facilitating local or general approach to the source, and W-type arousal by strong stimuli, facilitating local or general withdrawal. Recently Kempf (68) has reviewed the evidence for such antagonistic functional systems in man, in relation to problems of conflict and neurosis. The thesis here is that relationships between stimulus magnitude and the degree and direction of response, although different on the various psychological levels as to their form and the extent to which their function may be modified, are always critical for the determination in ontogeny of what conditions may attract and what may repel members of a given species. These matters must not be oversimplified, of course, as many conditions besides experience, including adaptation, fatigue, and health, may affect the potency and directness of the biphasic processes.

The property of differential thresholds in biphasic systems may take a more specific origin in early ontogeny when the probing termini of developing neuroblasts react selectively to the biochemical properties of tissue fields nearby, and may influence their environs in turn. Threshold differences evidently progress throughout the organism along biphasic lines. Many types are as yet little understood, as for example that involved in Eccles's (31) distinction between "fast" and "slow" muscles in the cat. Such differences, paralleling biphasic differences in afferent, visceral, and neural systems, underlie the rise of specialized patterns of approach and withdrawal, the detailed character of which is a matter of phyletic level and ontogenetic attainments.

III

It should be emphasized that whether the described biphasic processes influence behavior in rudimentary or in specialized ways depends particularly upon species capacities for their modification through ontogeny into correlations and organized adaptive systems.

In early ontogeny in all animals, the quantitative aspects of stimulation evidently dominate both the direction and vigor of action. To illustrate the effectiveness of this relationship on the invertebrate level, let us consider a phenomenon known as the "reversal of taxis." Here the animal is reported as reversing its normal responses to stimulus intensity, or in conventional terms it becomes "positive" to bright light rather than "negative" as usual. In W. Hess's (59) experiments, light-adapted earthworms approached a source of 0.3 mc in 55% of the trials, in contrast to only 1% for dark-adapted worms to the same intensity (cf. Figure 17). It seems likely, however, that no reversal of response polarity has occurred, as the light-adapted worm does not withdraw from weak light. Instead, the intensity threshold has been raised so that physically strong light exerts an effect equivalent to that normal for weak light. Significantly, removal of the earthworm's brain comparably brought a greater readiness to approach bright light. As any means taken to raise the animal's threshold to anterior stimulation has this effect, the so-called reversal of taxis to extrinsic stimulation involves instead a temporary decrease in sensitivity.

It is well known that the "sign" of the taxis responses of many insects and other animals varies according to age or excitability, developmental stage, and external conditions (e.g., Dolley and Golden, 27; Dolley and White, 28; Fraenkel and Gunn, 38). These phenomena appear to have in common an effect on metabolism, decreasing or increasing functional thresholds according to their direction. There are many physiological means of changing an animal's readiness to respond, which may acquire more or less involved relationships in the motivational pattern according to species and ontogeny. Consider two rather different example, both more specialized with respect to motivation than taxis-change cases of the type mentioned. Evans and Dethier (35) analyzed the rise through feeding of the blowfly's tarsal thresholds to four sugars, all of which had been found tasteless for the fly and two of them completely nonnutritious.

By eliminating factors such as blood chemistry, the experimenters narrowed the locus of the inhibitory effect to some part of the gut other than the crop. In contrast, Harris et al. (50) trained vitamin-B-deficient rats to take a stock food containing this vitamin, as against the same food without the vitamin, by adding a trace of cocoa to the former. With this subtle cue, the B-deprived rats discriminated between foods critically different for their organic deficiency, although normal rats ate these foods equally. In these instances, worm, blowfly, and rat are clearly motivated at very different psychological levels, at which the term "sensitization" would have very different meanings. There are many ways of increasing or decreasing the responsiveness and drive of any organism, which, particularly at higher levels, may have very different relationships to the directionality and plasticity of response.

Lower vertebrates present many striking species-typical approach and withdrawal tendencies. Many reptiles respond differently to long and short rays of the spectrum, a tendency attributed to aspects of their retinal chemistry. The nocturnal approach of newly hatched loggerhead turtles to the sea, which Daniel and Smith (18) attribute to the reflection of moonlight from the surf, may thus be analogous to the proneness of *Lacerta* lizards to approach green as against other spectral stimuli. These are strong tendencies, since Wagner (117) found lizards persisting through several hundred trials in snapping at a green disc bearing a quinine-soaked mealworm as against one of another hue bearing an untreated mealworm. Ehrenhardt (32) investigated with similar results another of Lacerta's persistent responses, its approach to figures such as discs with smooth outlines as against figures such as squares with broken outlines. The possibility that such tendencies relate to characteristic properties of the receptor and afferent system, governing neural discharge to viscera and effectors, is suggested by the fact that the honeybee approaches figures of *broken* outlines as against those with smooth outlines, due, as Wolf (125) demonstrated, to compound-eye properties making visual-flicker effects attractive. Without doubt they bear a significant relationship to phenomena of approach described for birds (36, 58) as "imprinting" and "following."

The general disposition of lower vertebrates to approach the source of low-energy stimulation is clear. The fish *Coris,* studied by von Holst (61), reacts to weak contact or light by bending towards the source and by spreading dorsal and anal fins, to strong stimuli by bending away and *folding* these fins. In many fishes, changes in skin coloration also occur, differentiated as to stimulus intensity, indicating disparate visceral components in the excitation processes. Many fishes, amphibians, and reptiles respond rather consistently to moving stimuli of small area by lunging forward. The snapping responses of toads depend upon quantitative

312

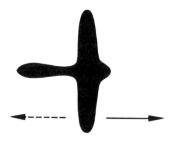

FIGURE 18
From Eibl-Eibesfeld and Kramer (34): "Model
of bird of prey releases escape reactions
(flight) among young gallinaceous birds, ducks
and geese when moved to the right. Moved
to the left (broken arrow) it has no releasing
function. In this case, shape in relation to the
direction of movement provides the active
sign stimulus. (After Tinbergen, 1948)."
    This caption presents the ethologists' hypothe-
sis of "innate schemata." For a different interpretation, see text.

properties of the stimulus such as rate of movement rather than its
qualitative nature, as Honigmann (63) and also Freisling (40) demonstrated in tests controlling size, intensity, and rate of movement. These
stimulus characteristics seem to be effective as quantitative values, hence
essentially equivalent to one another in their control over neural discharge
in the visually naive animal. With any one of these as independent variable, the lunge characteristically occurs to stimulus intensities below a given
magnitude, above which turning and withdrawal increase in frequency.
Although toads flick the tongue alone at very small moving objects, they
lunge at somewhat larger ones and use the jaws, but still larger stimuli
bring retreat (33).

    Such response tendencies, dominated by stimulus magnitude, may be
basic to the differentiation of patterns such as feeding, mating, and flight
in the lower vertebrates. In these animals the naive responses to quantitative sensor effects have a compulsive character and, as we have seen,
tend to resist change through experience. At best they can be changed
only within strict limits, as Schneider (98) found in the extensive training
required by the toad to inhibit snapping at edible objects presented behind glass, a training much less effective in young animals than in adults.
Deficiencies in central nervous correlation evidently restrict the extent to
which such processes can be changed through ontogeny. Results of this
general type, signifying resistance to the modification of stimulus-intensity-
dominated reactions, are obtained characteristically with cold-blooded
vertebrates having a low supply of internuncial neurones.

    From these considerations, it is more likely that, for lower vertebrates
predominantly and for mammals at earlier stages, approach or withdrawal
depends on generalized effects governed by stimulus energy, rather than on
what ethologists have called an "inborn schema." Lorenz's and Tinbergen's
interpretation (Figure 18) of the effect of their hawk-goose figure (cf.
34), which reportedly caused goslings to crouch in disturbance when it
was pulled blunt end first above them, but to show no disturbance or

extend when it was pulled across narrow end first, has been attributed to innate figural effects. I have suggested (101, 102) that instead the results may have been due to a sudden retinal change in the first case versus a gradual one in the second, and not to innate figural effects as such. The corresponding opposite behavioral effects should then be produced by triangles drawn across the visual field base or apex first, sounds breaking suddenly or gradually, and the like. Thus an "enemy" may exert an initial flight-provoking effect because of its size and brusque movements rather than in specific, qualitative appearance. In vertebrates such as birds, however, the qualitative appearance of objects may soon become effective according to adjustive circumstances in which they appear. Lehrman (72) suggests that the gaping responses of young perching birds are given to artificial stimuli resembling the general shape of the parent sitting at the nest edge, not because these approximate a native releaser pattern, as some ethologists maintain, but because they have been glimpsed briefly through opening of the eyes during earlier gaping responses to weak mechanical stimuli. Significantly, the "flight distance," or minimal space within which animals in the wild tolerate a strange object without retreating (56), generally corresponds roughly to body size, to which through natural selection the threshold properties of the species may have become adjusted.

Light is generally the most potent extrinsic stimulus influencing movements of animals in space, and has therefore been featured in this discussion. Consequently it is important to distinguish from typical orienting responses, in which directionality of response tends to correspond to the intensity of the neural effect, a type which Verheijen (116) has called the "trapping effect." This arises through the animal's encountering an isolated powerful light in a dark field, when the stimulus disorients the animal and literally forces a tonic fixation to the source. In this way, intense lights on dark nights cause injury and death to countless insects and birds. Had such effects been common as natural hazards during evolution, the course of natural selection in flying animals might have been somewhat different. No species could survive long with processes facilitating a compulsive approach to the source of potentially destructive stimuli, were such conditions common in its environment.

An elementary type of orientation is that in which an animal approaches a low-energy stimulus source, as a neonate kitten nears the abdomen of its mother through crudely directionalized responses to thermal and tactual stimuli from her. In more specialized cases, if the source moves off, *following reactions* occur. In the simple type of following reaction illustrated in Figures 19 and 20, an army ant trails one of another species in the column, evidently adjusting her locomotory movements to a stimulative field in which weak olfactory and tactual effects predominate.

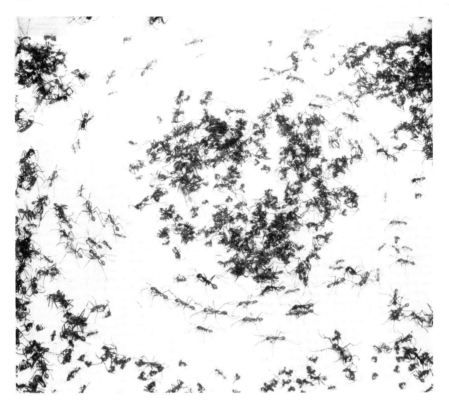

FIGURE 19
Circular column in army ants of the species *Eciton burchelli* and *E. hamatum,*
35 minutes after these ants (previously separated by gauze for mutual olfactory
habituation) were released together into a common area. While the excited ants
circle, "following" reactions predominate, based on common tactual and olfactory
stimuli. When circling stops, disturbed reactions to species odor differences appear.

Comparably, the neonates of many birds and precocial young of many
mammals approach an object centered in their visual field, evidently
through responses to low-intensity stimulation from it, and subsequently
may follow if the object moves away. The initially generalized character of
the stimulus is suggested by the finding of Fabricius (36) and E. Hess
(58) investigating "imprinting," that auditory and other stimuli also influence the reaction.

An important instance from natural behavior is the activity of a blind
altricial neonate mammal readjusting to a changed stimulus gradient
created when its mother disengages from the litter but remains nearby.
The weakly directionalized stimulus pattern still promotes A-responses but
is suboptimal for the A-type organic set, and thereby energizes effectively

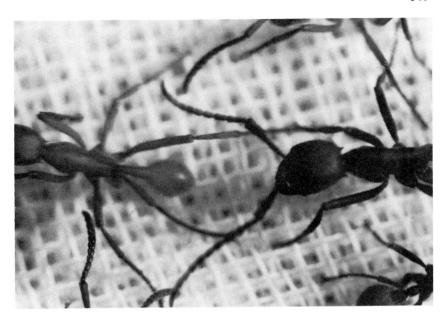

FIGURE 20
Close-up of a worker of *Eciton burchelli* following one of *hamatum* in the circular column. (See text.)

(i.e., facilitates) reactions maintaining or increasing this set. The function of the stimulus at this stage is suggested by the fact that, if it drops suddenly to zero, the rapid change acts as a disturbance which is likely to inervate interruptive visceral processes, mass action, and loud vocalization.

It would appear that following may be considered an extension of approaching in which locomotion is adjusted in such a way that a given range of stimulus magnitude prevails. The basis may be postulated as the arousal of low-energy stimulation of both A-type extension or approach reactions and A-type (vegetative) organic processes. Through this concurrence of events, there becomes established (according to species capacities) an organic set in terms of which the animal can readjust its position so that the external stimulus is maintained within an intensity range optimal for this set. The attractive stimulus then not only arouses approach movements, but also the A-type set capable of facilitating recovery movements when the stimulus changes away from the optimum. The status of the extrinsic stimulus then governs whether approach continues into following, and whether following accelerates, changes direction, or stops. Disparities between the organic set and the stimulus magnitude can thereby be readjusted reciprocally, and following reactions are balanced off against this pattern according to the direction of its variations. Ontogenetic changes in these relations vary in nature and extent according to species capacities. Leuba's (73) "optimal-stimulation" theory for mammalian learning represents one potentially useful way of studying such phenomena.

In the altricial young of certain mammals, the species-typical pattern of relationships between stimulus magnitude, organic set, and action is established much more slowly than in the precocial young of other mammals, and on a higher level than in lower vertebrates. Investigations in our laboratory (95) show that neonate kittens improve from the first hour in reaching the mother after separations and soon begin to establish individually differentiated suckling positions: fore, aft, or between. In the same period orientation in the nest vicinity, first established on the basis of proximal stimulation, decreases somewhat in efficiency after the eyes open at about one week, then rises steadily to a new pattern of organization based on visual perception. Regular progress of the kitten after about the tenth day in close approaches leading into suckling as well as in following the mother when she disengages indicates a growing capacity to hold or augment cues from a meaningful object. Then, after about the eighteenth day when the mother no longer "presents" regularly to the young and initiates feeding less and less, the kittens become steadily more proficient in a process of mutual approach (Figure 21). At length, after about the thirtieth day, the kittens themselves not only initiate feeding increasingly, but can follow the mother more efficiently and persistently as she decreases in responsiveness to them. A complex and changing set of seeking-avoidance relationships is indicated, doubtless basic and important to weaning. For the kittens, these studies reveal a behavioral development in which perceptual learning undergoes a succession of qualitative adjustments to objects which are first approached as naively attractive, then sought out as meaningful patterns in relation to organic condition.

In early stages, then, the approaching and following reactions are generalized; when and how far they specialize to environmental and species cues depends on properties of the species, the individual, and the changing developmental situation. It is often claimed that the mating patterns of lower vertebrates are natively given and little influenced by experience. But Shaw (106), working in our laboratory, has found that platyfishes raised from birth apart from species mates and surrounded by plates of ground glass scored minimally in mating tests at maturity. In contrast, individuals raised similarly in isolation during the first month but thereafter with species mates made much higher scores, though still inferior to those made by individuals normally raised with species mates. In this species, therefore, the elicitation of approach and other reactions in the complex repertoire of mating depends to a major extent on processes of perceptual development requiring earlier social experience as one factor.

Group adjustments such as those of schooling in fishes and flock-flying

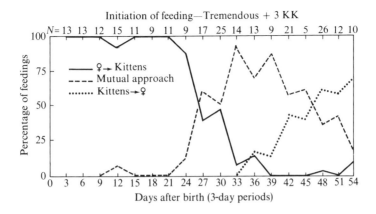

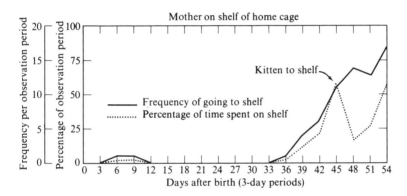

FIGURE 21

Top: Graphic summary of the frequency of different patterns of initiating feeding in a representative litter of domestic cats consisting of the mother ("Tremendous") and her three kittens (95). Legend: Initiations by the female alone, solid line; by mutual approach, broken line; and by kittens alone, dotted line.

Bottom: Graph of results for female's reactions to a wall shelf in the living cage. Note the sharp drop in the female's "time on shelf" when the kittens begin to reach the shelf at about 45 days of age.

in birds are specialized following reactions of obvious adaptive significance. To their development, early behavioral relationships with species mates may contribute, judging by preliminary findings in our research. In the schools of fishes such as mackerel, and in the circling mills these species may form, Parr (86) finds evidence that each participant fixes others unilaterally, and in the circular movement accelerates, slows, or turns in such a manner as to hold the size of a retinal image relatively constant. Such adjustments, in which nonvisual factors also play a part, doubtless have a specialized ontogeny appropriate to species mechanisms, capacities, and typical experiences.

As it is likely that the ontogeny of such adjustments is characteristic of the phyletic level, the claim that species behavior patterns represent an "original nature," later changed more or less through learning, is misleading. In what particular developmental stage is "original nature" to be identified? For vertebrates, evidence from the work of Carmichael (13) and others suggests the possibility that in early embryonic stages integrations may form between postural and visceral stimulation, characteristically diffuse, and cutaneous stimulation, localized in its effects when at low intensities. On such a basis in the embryo, a local response such as raising and pushing forward the head might gradually come under the control of local tactual stimulation when linked with vegetative visceral states. The careful research of Kuo (see 75) on the chick embryo indicates that such integrations in the embryo, although still unstable, may set up trace effects furnishing a basis for later reactions such as the head lunge, a response critical for feeding, and numerous other postnatal reactions in vertebrates.

There may be a significant clue here to the understanding of initial visual reactions in vertebrates. Carmichael and Smith (14) established for the early guinea pig embryo that lightly touching a limb typically arouses local responses, often with limb extension. Comparably, with appreciable frequency in the embryos of this and other mammals, weak stimulation of one cheek elicits a turning of the head toward the touched side. Strong local stimulation, in contrast, arouses generalized and variable activity. Not only may the integration of postural impulses with cutaneous stimuli provide a basis for progressive specialization of such actions, but an important part of the complex may be the role of organic processes of low threshold. Maier and Schneirla (75) suggested that at hatching or birth, such local action patterns, then tactually controlled, might be directly accessible to control by low-energy visual stimulation. The idea is that, when the animal is first visually stimulated, a diffusion of neural impulses from optic centers could arouse adjacent centers in midbrain through which might be activated one or another tactuo-motor pattern already partially integrated. The first visual stimuli might then, through their partial equivalence to weak anterior contact, elicit local or even general approach responses. This phenomenon may be a crude early form of the effect well known for mammals in later stages and termed "sensory preconditioning" (76); also, it bears a distant resemblance to the spontaneous integrative effects demonstrated for fishes and other vertebrates and termed "intersensory transposition" by von Schiller (97). On such a basis, local or even general approach responses to visual stimulation could occur in visually naive vertebrates, or local extension movements in neonates incapable of general progression at birth.

IV

These considerations suggest that ontogenetic attainments in motivational and perceptual adjustment arise through biphasic processes dominated in early stages by stimulus magnitude, progressing later as species capacities may permit. Lower invertebrates seem to maintain a species status quo close to minimal deviation from this pattern; insects vary more from it, although their motivation is dominated by specific extrinsic and organic conditions; it is higher mammals that deviate most from the biphasic pattern through ontogeny. Psychologists who emphasize disproportions, reversals, and exceptions between stimulus magnitude and response properties are therefore talking of adult stages at higher psychological levels.

Our review has stressed the existence of interrelationships between biphasic afferent, organic, and response processes at all phyletic levels. Because such organizations underlie ontogeny in all animals, the concept of stimuli as having a "drive" status seems inadequate for any animal at any stage. Neither is it adequate to stress endogenous processes without recognizing their changing role in ontogeny, as do the ethologists, who with their "releaser" concept minify changing stimulus relevances in development.

From the phyletic and ontogenetic perspectives, the changing relationships of stimulation, organic processes, and reaction in animal motivation, although grounded in biphasic conditions in all phyla, are seen as different kinds of processes at each level. For the blowfly, Dethier and Bodenstein (26) discovered that although sucking is aroused and controlled in rate by afferent input from tarsal chemoreceptors, continuation and termination of the act comes about through impulses relayed to the brain from the foregut, hence "hunger can be equated [in this insect] with the absence of stimulating fluids in the foregut. . . ." To illustrate the complex relationships of afferent to organic factors in a higher vetebrate, consider pigeon behavior. Light at dawn arouses mature pigeons to strut and coo, both actions known to stimulate endogenous functions such as crop manufacture of "pigeon's milk." Sight of the strutting male also facilitates ovulation in the female, with related organic changes promoting activities such as nest-making (72). At various stages in this behavior, extrinsic stimuli play the role of arousers, general organic excitants, specific excitants, or perceptual cues. Extrinsic stimuli, endogenous processes, and action can play such versatile roles in these patterns, with action differences so dependent on what conditions may affect each and what stage the sequence of events has reached, as to make the classical distinction between stimulus, drive, and mechanism an oversimplified and misleading thought pattern.

The role of early experience in motivational development is still inadequately understood; however, our evidence indicates that the part played by stimulative gains in development enlarges and specializes qualitatively from insects to mammals. Although in early stages, reactivity is dominated in all by stimulus intensity, mammals progress most in changing the relationships between biphasic processes and extrinsic conditions. The concept of "original nature" is vitiated by the fact that, on all levels, ontogeny constitutes a series of adjustive processes elaborating and changing under the conditions of each stage and not a process beginning suddenly at some one stage; moreover, attempts to distinguish sharply between the unlearned and the learned in development are unrealistic (102, 103).

Through early experience, particularly in mammals, A-type processes become cued to special stimuli such as odors accompanying food, W-type processes to the special stimuli of predators, and the like. But the relevance of stimulation to motivation is not episodic; rather, as sensory-deprivation research shows clearly (54), one prerequisite is a continuous afferent input maintaining a metabolic pattern essential to all activities from nesting to problem-solving. From our research with cats (95), it is evident that from birth the regular presence of a complex of chemical and tactual stimuli from the nest environment and maternal and litter associations is needed for normal perceptual development. Through certain types of focal experience, in which mild stimuli are contiguous with optimal metabolic or trophic processes, A-type patterns become environmentally conditioned, and certain intense, disturbing stimuli contiguous with interruptive processes become environmental controllers of W-type patterns. Focal stimuli in the litter situation thereby facilitate mating reactions at maturity, focal predator odors help put the animal on guard wherever encountered. The pattern of contiguity or S-R learning evidently is elementary for the early stimulus-cueing of organic sets of A-types and W-types.

For later developments, however, selective-learning processes must be postulated. Specifically, Maier and Schneirla (75, 76) suggested that whereas the contiguity formula could account for conditioning withdrawal or escape reactions to intense stimuli, a selective-learning formula is needed when changing relationships of action to stimuli and to endogenous conditions affect further adjustments. Accordingly, Roberts (94) discovered that although cats learned to avoid "an apparently strong noxious motivational set elicited by hypothalamic stimulation," with the strongest or "flight" intensity, there were no signs of *avoidance* training within as many as 270 trials. The strong shock, by forcing an immediate withdrawal, may have admitted only contiguity learning, whereas the two lesser intensities by producing milder disturbances admitted selective learning. Furthermore, concepts of "tension reduction" are much too general to deal adequately with ontogenetic progress. From the results of Thompson (114) and others, it appears that from early infancy mammals establish approach and withdrawal habits differently. Accordingly, the theory of "optimal stimulation" recently advanced by Leuba (73) admits processes of selective cue adjustments made in relation to organic optima of different types.

The practice of combining the terms "approach" and "avoidance," although rather prevalent, is misleading. Whereas in its earliest stages a mammal evidently approaches or withdraws according to sheer stimulus intensity, operations of seeking or avoidance under particular conditions can be accomplished only later, depending on capacity and opportunity to learn perceptual adjustments to qualitatively specific conditions. For reasons stated, the term "tension reduction" is deemed unsuitable for endogenous processes in learning, as processes of A-types and of W-types differ significantly in their relevance both to contiguity and to selective-learning. In fact, ontogenetic considerations suggest that specialized seeking patterns typically are mastered by young mammals *before* withdrawal reactions have well begun to differentiate into avoidances. The literature accordingly suggests that the human infant specializes perceptually in reaching and smiling before he avoids and sulks discriminatively.

Processes of behavioral organization and motivation cannot be dated from any one stage, including birth, as each stage of ontogeny constitutes the animal's "nature" at that juncture and is essential for the changing and expanding accomplishments of succeeding stages. Such improvements arise through an intimate interrelationship of "maturation" and "experience," representing all conditions introduced in any stage through tissue growth and through stimulative effects, respectively (103). Thus we have suggested that early integrations between postural, tactual, and organic conditions may be basic to later adaptive specializations as in feeding. Also, the concept "organic set" has been used to represent the gains of early stages underlying an endogenously facilitated readiness to adjust to something (e.g., to approach) without demonstrable perception of object qualities as such. I believe that ants do not advance appreciably beyond this level in their ontogeny, whereas mammals clearly do. Mammalian ontogeny leads into further stages in which "attitudes" become effective, involving readinesses to organize adjustments relevantly to discriminated situational meanings. In mammalian ontogeny, it is likely that motivated learning of the anticipative type enters soon after distance (i.e., more comprehensive) cues effective through progressive visual perception really begin to modify and dominate the more restricted proximal processes of orientation and adaptation carried over from earlier stages.

V

The view has been followed here that processes of perception, motivation, and emotion progress in an intimate relationship in animal ontogeny. Modification of early biphasic excitatory states inevitably overlaps the processes of perceptual development and anticipative motivated adjustments. Consider the frequency with which terms such as "pain" or "pleasure" are used to designate excitatory effects of stimuli through brainstem-implanted electrodes in mammals. It appears from such studies that disturbed responses termed "pain" or "fear" can be elicited through stimulating specific areas, "pleasure" or "reward" effects from other areas (82, 23). In the Olds and Milner (85) experiment, rats stimulated through the septal area acted as though rewarded, repeatedly operating a level turning on the shock, as though in "strong pursuit of a positive [i.e., A-type] stimulus," whereas through areas nearby the stimuli seemed to have a "neural or punishing effect" instead (cf. 43). These tests may have "cut in" on A- or W-type patterns, tapping critical way-stations in circuits of distinctively different arousal thresholds. But also, Bower and Miller (8) made implantations in the middle to anterior forebrain bundle of the rat through which a reward effect was obtained at the onset of stimulation and aversive effects with continued stimulation. Evidently A-type patterns were first aroused here, but were displaced by W-type patterns when the effective intensity reached their threshold through summation. It is important to emphasize the fact that *adult* animals were used in this research.

Although in recent years the term "anxiety" has been much used in psychology to denote a so-called "secondary drive" reinforcing learning, the ontogenetic background of this type of process is really no better understood than that of "hope" or "faith" drives. Actually, the nature of such processes may vary from organic set to anticipation, with corresponding differences in relevance to learning, according to ontogenetic stage and situation. "Fear" also raises many problems. Hebb's (52) conclusion from tests of captivity-raised chimpanzees that many primate fears are "spontaneous" may involve both (1) and stimulus equivalences, in seemingly very different object characteristics and types of movement, referable to stimulus intensity-effects, and (2) effects of the "strange" on partially socialized animals, with unidentified relationships to earlier experience. Other problems which may be investigated to advantage through considering interrelated perceptual, motivational, and emotional processes in development concern the nature of "uncertainty" and "danger," and the ontogeny of "psychological distance under threat" (81, 122).

The interrelationships of these processes of perceptual, motivational, and emotional ontogeny are suggested if we define "emotion" broadly as: (1) episodes or sequences of overt and incipient somatic adjustment, (2) often loosely patterned and variable, (3) usually with concurrent exciting sensory effects, perhaps also perceptual attitudes characterizable as desirable or undesirable, pleasant or unpleasant, (4) related to the intensity effects or perceptual meaning of a stimulus, (5) synergic with organic changes of A- or W-types.

The cautious but significant acknowledgment by W. A. Hunt (66), after Woodworth, of the relevance of attitudes of acceptance or rejection to "feelings of pleasantness or unpleasantness with respectively different organic backgrounds," suggests a synthesis of the concepts of motivation, emotion, and perception in human ontogeny significant for comparisons with lower animals. One crucial property of these processes is that from fishes to man, as Pick has emphasized, the *sympathetic* nervous system increases in prepotency as an energy-expending system, antagonistic to the *parasympathetic* as energy-conserving system.

This view agrees with Leeper's (71) point that a motivational theory of emotion is needed, and that Hebb's concept of emotion as disorganized response is misleading. In A-type adjustments as ontogeny progresses, it is not so much disorganization as a *re*organization of organic processes that occurs, depending on advances in motivated perception. Studies such as Rowland's (96) revealing a low correlation between "intensity" and type of organic changes in emotion are from adult subjects, for whom object-meaning tends to overweigh stimulus magnitude. With ontogenetic progress in higher vertebrates, perceptual meanings often modify, occlude, or reverse the earlier effects of stimulus intensity.

I therefore conclude that although the James-Lange type of theory provides a useful basis for studying the early ontogeny of mammals, in which A-type or W-type patterns dominate behavior according to stimulus magnitude, a Cannon-type theory of higher-center control is *indispensable* for later stages of perceptual and motivational development. If ontogeny progresses well, specialized patterns of A- and W-types, or their combinations, perceptually controlled, often short-circuit or modify the early viscerally dominated versions. Proposals like that of Harlow and Stagner (49) that thalamic centers are functionally differentiated as to processes of pleasure versus pain, and the like, seem applicable as ontogeny progresses, suggesting for later stages *brainstem* patterns such as implanted-electrode results indicate. Comparisons with results from needed studies on earlier stages will be most interesting. But, from this approach, recent proposals, e.g., Golightly (46), that the James-Lange theory be abandoned as outmoded must be held premature until the ontogeny of emotion is better understood.

Doubtless, as Bousfield and Orbison (7) state, the infant mammal is "essentially precorticate at birth." Also, as a perceptually naive animal, his emotional-motivational processes seem diffuse and dominated by stimulus magnitude swaying autonomic-visceral susceptibilities. But, contrary to impressions that seem general in the child-psychology literature, there is significant evidence that at birth the infant mammal already has a crudely dichotomized organic basis for his perceptual-motivational-emotional ontogeny. In this context, however, the question, "Are there any innate emotions?" should be dismissed as posing the false alternatives of *finding* or *not finding* adultlike patterns in psychologically barren early stages.

This interpretation differs sharply from that of Bridges (9), that an "undifferentiated excitement" prevails for the human neonate (Figure 22), differentiated only later into conditions of "delight" and "distress." Textbook writers who adopt this conclusion seem to have overlooked the fact that Bridges's research on infant emotionality did not involve intensive research on neonates. Many psychologists seem also to have been influenced in their views by a conventional rejection of Watson's (119) theory of infant emotions. Watson, as many will recall, concluded from studies with neonate infants that their emotions may be differentiated as "love," "fear," and "rage," arousable by stimuli such as stroking and patting, loud noises, and restraint, respectively. Sherman (107), however, found competent judges unable to distinguish the fear and rage patterns without knowing the stimuli, and Taylor (113) reported that Watson's conditions did not initiate "constant pattern responses" in infants he tested. Watson would have been well advised to call his emotional reactions X, Y, and Z (as he himself once suggested), differentiating them by effective stimulus intensities rather than arousal patterns, for then the differentiation can be made of X as relatively unexcited responses of A-type from XY as excited responses of W-type, to weak and strong stimuli, respectively (Figure 23). With gentle tactual stimulation of neonates Pratt et al. (90) obtained pacifying reactions and relaxation of limbs; with stroking Watson obtained extension of limbs and quiescence as a rule; with intense light Canestrini (12) observed typically an intake of breath and sudden contraction of the abdominal wall, rising fenestral and breathing curves, and external signs of "fear"; with strong contact Peiper (87) noted a withdrawal of the part affected, general action, and crying; with sudden intense auditory stimuli the Shermans (108) noted arm flexion, crying, and signs of visceral disturbance or "colic"; with intense stimuli a "startle pattern" is obtained involving strong general limb flexion and signs of visceral disturbance (79). In the general evidence, the biphasic aspects of neonate reactions, and their general correlation with stimulus intensity, seem clearly indicated.

The conclusion seems warranted that in neonate mammals generally these early biphasic processes of a physiological order, aroused according to stimulus magnitude, furnish a basis for individual perceptual, motiva-

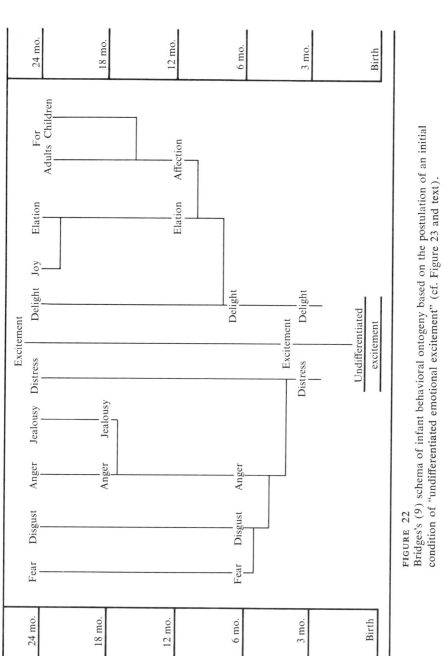

FIGURE 22

Bridges's (9) schema of infant behavioral ontogeny based on the postulation of an initial condition of "undifferentiated emotional excitement" (cf. Figure 23 and text).

Schema: ontogeny of approach-withdrawal and emotional stimulation in man

	Reaction	Adequate stimuli	
		High intensities	*Low intensities*
Initial stages: incidental "approach-withdrawal"	Somatic component	Vigorous mass action: flexion, adduction, crying, tension	Pacified, local action: extension, abduction, turning-to, "smile"
	Visceral component	"Interruptive" effects, sympathetic-autonomic predominant	"Vegetative" effects, parasympathetic-autonomic predominant
		Focal to disturbing situations	*Focal to "gratifying" situations*
Social adaptation: purposive approach-withdrawal	Perceptual adjustment	Specialized withdrawal: pulling, walking off; Indirect modes of escape, negation, aggression; "Sulk" gestures, sounds symbolizing NO	Specialized approach: reaching, walking to; Indirect modes of approval, acquisition; Social smile, gestures, sounds symbolizing YES
	Visceral background	Conditioned interruptive patterns; sympathetic-autonomic facilitation	Conditioned vegetative patterns; parasympathetic-autonomic facilitation

FIGURE 23
Schema of theory outlining biphasic functional conditions basic to the ontogeny of early approach or withdrawal and of related subsequent perceptual and emotional differentiation in man (cf. Figure 22).

tional, and emotional development. The theory is schematized in Figures 23 and 24. The foregoing discussion, in this sense, supports Leeper's (71) position that the processes of emotion and motivation are fundamentally related. The socialization of early physiologically given biphasic excitatory states and the specialization of motivation and emotion seem to advance hand in hand in the education of the infant mammal in perceptual processes and action. To suggest the relevance for human psychological development of the theory of biphasic processes sketched in this article, I shall outline evidence bearing on the ontogenetic course of two adjustive processes unquestionably crucial in man's perceptual and motivational adjustment to his world: *smiling* and *reaching*.

After Darwin, the general recognition advanced the primate evolution must have involved concurrent organic changes admitting an upright posture, an increase in visual range, a freeing of the limbs for specialized prehension and the face for social expression, and a specialization of the brain

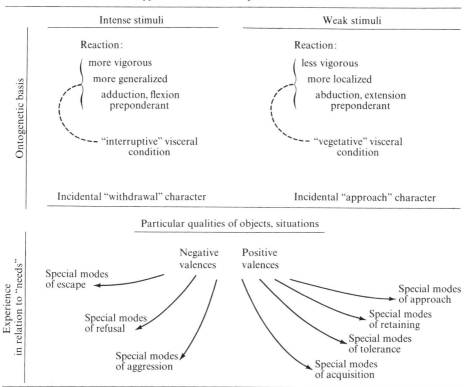

Approach-Withdrawal Adjustments in Man

FIGURE 24
Schema of theory basing approach and withdrawal reactions on biphasic processes dependent in early stages (top) on effective stimulative intensity, subsequently (bottom) on developmental processes related particularly to experience (cf. Figures 22 and 23).

admitting conceptual plasticity. These superior human assets for perceptual-motivational development may be considered marks of a stage in natural selection far advanced beyond that at which lower vertebrates with far less advanced properties for cephalic dominance are limited to the simple lunge as an approach. Significant also in this impressive evolutionary progression are changes such as Pick (88) has described, underlying a steady specialization of the *parasympathetic* autonomic division, an energy-conserving system, correlated with an even more rapid advance of its antagonist, the sympathetic system, an energy-expending system in adjustive behavior. In the organismic setting available on the human level, emphasizing adaptive plasticity, the potential ontogenetic relevance of the

328

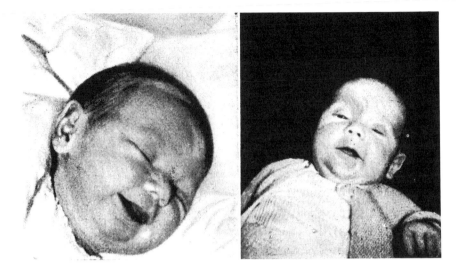

FIGURE 25
Photographs of facial reactions in a neonate infant, from O. Koehler (69), who describes this reaction as an "innate smile." Unilateral "smile" on the fourth postnatal day (left) and on the seventh postnatal day (right).

autonomic divisions, as with that of other biphasic processes, reaches far beyond an elementary status of simple antagonism.

Consistent with Darwin's (21) concept of *antithesis* in mammalian emotional expression, anatomists find evidence for the rise of two antagonistic systems of facial muscles in mammals, one elevating the lip corners, the other pulling them down, in close correlation with progressive elaboration of the trigeminal or facial-cutaneous sensory system (64). Significantly, physiological and behavioral evidence indicates that the *levator* system has a lower arousal threshold than the *depressor* system. With low-intensity shocks to cheek or mastoid regions of adult human subjects, Dumas (29, 30) noted a mechanical "smile" resembling that of hemiplegics; with higher intensities, a different grimace involving facial musculature more widely.

Now O. Koehler (69) represents the view of many who consider smiling innate as a social pattern in man, pointing out that a semblance of this reaction can occur in premature and neonate infants (Figure 25). Strictly considered, however, this early response is a *grimace,* a physiologically forced response to low-intensity stimulation, and the "smile" is a specialized social adjustment appearing only after much perceptual-motivational development. Although light facial contact, particularly near the lip corners, is generally most effective in producing the neonate grimace, Dennis

(24) obtained it with other weak stimuli such as light patting of the chest and asafetida released at the nostrils. In the early neonate this action is infrequent and has a fleeting character, occurring "incidentally with other facial activities in an overflow reaction," according to Spitz and Wolf (111). A concurrence with vegetative visceral conditions is indicated by its appearance when the infant is calming down, relieved from disturbance, or recently satiated.

Neither Dennis nor Spitz and Wolf, however, reported any "unconditioned" stimulus for this reaction. The difficulty seems to have been that they looked for a *specific* unconditioned stimulus. For there is evidence, including their own, that although a variety of stimuli can arouse this reaction, *all* have in common the property of *low intensity*. Even interoceptive changes after feeding may be effective, as suggested by the traditional "gas smile," which seems more often a response to a gentle stomach pressure (as during "burping") than to "belly-ache" as Spitz and Wolf maintain. The conclusion seems in order that this action first specializes through a gradual conditioning process, in which the unconditioned stimulus is a facial-nerve arousal by low-intensity stimulation.[2] Such a process, elicited most frequently by factual stimuli when the neonate is in a vegetative organic condition, would later be available for control by visual stimuli of low intensity, when visual centering of stimuli has improved sufficiently.

A diffuse, generalized conditioning process is indicated initially. Although within the first two months Spitz and Wolf obtained few grimace reactions to visual stimuli, these came increasingly after the third month, when Dennis noted also a growing reactivity by grimacing to a face presented over the crib. The face *as such* cannot be credited for this effect, as Spitz and Wolf obtained the response with a variety of stimuli, including sounds and horror masks. The visual effect evidently is initially very general and diffuse, but in time becomes more specific. A crude contiguity-conditioning process is indicated, through the concurrence of certain visual effects with satiation or relief from disturbance. By six months, as a rule, Spitz and Wolf observed definite advances in the specificity of stimulus control, "in the direction of increased discrimination," with the response not only elicited selectively by faces rather than masks, but also changed in pattern from the "fleeting grimace" of the first three months, "not well differentiated from general facial action," to a "more definite expression."

Next indicated is a discriminative "social smile," to familiar as against

---

[2] Spitz and Wolf conclude from the fact that they found the nursing bottle ineffective as a stimulus for this response during the first six months, that "this disposes of the hypothesis that smiling is a conditioned reflex established in response to gratification of being satiated with food." This does not follow, however, as the nursing bottle usually is seen only briefly before feeding, as a rule, and thereafter is touched rather than seen. An experiment on this point seems in order.

unfamiliar faces. That the "smile" comes about through a progressive perceptual-motivational learning process dependent on the developmental situation to an important extent is indicated by Spitz's and Wolf's finding that this response developed precociously in infants who had the "best relations with attentive mothers," but was delayed, infrequent, and unspecialized in infants who had experienced poor relations with indifferent mothers. From its initial status as a crude reaction forced through low-intensity arousal, under optimal conditions this response appears to specialize simultaneously in its afferent, organic, and motor aspects, first with a general set to associated stimuli, then with a rudimentary perceptual anticipation of more specifically "desirable" stimuli. It is difficult to fit these results within the framework of contiguity conditioning alone; rather, from the circumstances of development, it is probable that a process of selective learning underlies the metamorphosis of this and related aspects of the infant's expanding repertoire of "seeking" adjustments.

The *reach,* another significant approach response, seems to develop concurrently in the infant with the "smile," as a related adjustment. These early stages, as Frank (39) has pointed out, involve a progressive self-contact process of individual adjustment, which, as Nissen, Chow, and Semmes (84) demonstrated for chimpanzees, progresses badly without adequate opportunities for tactual experience through limb mobility. The matrix of this process in earlier stages evidently consists in the characteristically variable and diffuse reactions of relaxation and local limb extension to gentle limb contact, when a vegetative organic condition prevails. These types of reaction occur characteristically with low-intensity stimulation of many kinds, usually tactual but also at times auditory or olfactory. The local reactions typically elicited by such stimuli stand in definite contrast to the mass-action type obtained with strong stimulation. To stimulation of the foot with a needle, termed "pain," the Shermans (108) usually obtained a "pulling away of the leg or the face, associated with movements of the arms and crying." Although neonate behavior seems chaotic and often unpredictable, limb flexion is typically obtained with strong stimulation, and this was the unconditioned response used both by Wenger (120) and by the Wickens (123), who conditioned it to previously ineffective stimuli within the first ten postnatal days. Watson, who noted limb flexion as a typical response to loud sounds or dropping, conversely identified arm extension as a frequent response to gentle stroking of the neonate's arm or cheek.

The infant's approach or A-type reactions normally seem to change from soon after birth in a more regular manner than do the more episodic, excited W-type reactions. At first the face takes the lead, with close functional relationships between sucking, lip-contact, and hand movements. As Davis (22) concluded, the initial afferent control seems to be tactuopostural, with vision entering gradually into a steadily more dominant role. A progressive self-communication through tactuo-motor channels, emphasized by E. B. Holt (62) as basic to motivation and learning, underlies gradually developing integrations between proximal sensory control and visual control in early space perception.

Initially the infant gets his arm out incidentally, as part of a forced overt A-type response to *low*-energy stimulation. One significant aspect of the tactuo-visual integration that gradually assumes control of this reaction is the concurrence of head-turning to the side of gentle stimulation with progressive efficiency in centering the eyes on the focal area. McGinnis (78) reported for the first six weeks an increased frequency of head turning towards small objects seen in motion. Centering objects in the visual field, as it improves, elaborates into an eye-following of both the infant's head and objects.

Advancing the anterior body or its parts extends the infant's "space," as Werner (121) puts it, and in its early posturo-tactual basic may relate to reactive trends begun in utero. Progress through tactuo-visual integration represents complex psychological developments in which maturation *and* experience factors are doubtless interrelated inextricably (103). A dependence of progress in learning and motivation on the trophic aspects of reciprocal stimulative exchanges with self and environs is emphasized by Spitz's and Wolf's finding that smiling is likely to be retarded when infants have an inferior maternal adjustment, and without much doubt this is also true of the closely related response of reaching.

Halverson's (48) studies on grasping and reaching began with the infant at about 12 weeks, supported in a chair with a small cube of white sugar on the table before him. At this stage the infants tended to "regard" this stimulus or center it variably in the visual field, with frequent head-bending forward. Responses were quantified in terms of the nearest approach of the hand to the cube in each trial. Early deviations were large, as the infant's arms moved in various directions from his vertical axis but not particularly towards the exciting stimulus. From the data, these responses may be interpreted as crude arm extensions forced by low-intensity stimulation, a getting-out-the-arm reaction rather than a reaching for something. Significantly, in infants from 12 to 24 weeks there was an actual increase in the average digression from the stimulus, evidently due mainly to an accelerated maturation of shoulder muscles, so that the arm struck out laterally rather than forward in the trials.

It is significant that during this period the infant continued to respond to the stimulus by extending and abducting his arms, although he seldom touched or grasped the object and hardly ever got it into his mouth. But, as Castner (15) noted, in these months the duration of visual "regard" increases steadily, along with the frequency of arm extensions to visually centered stimuli. Daily life of course offers many experiences to the infant, in which he handles just-seen objects in A-type situations, as when the waving hand is seen, then gets into his mouth and stays there after feeding. It is a question of equivalent processes facilitating one another in the learning of related adjustments, and Halverson's results show steady progress after about 24 weeks in arm extension through elbow straightening, paralleled by increasing efficiency in getting the hand to the pellet. In the test situation the infant progressed steadily in directing his arm *to* a seen object, rather than just extending the limb as at first. Around six months, therefore, as the infant starts his reach, we may infer the presence of a simple anticipation of having the object in hand, *then* a different anticipation of mouthing it.

The significant point is that forelimb extension, the local adjustment central to the infant's perceptual-motivational development in the first year, begins as an incidental response to low-energy stimulation but, through progressive integrations of vision with pre-existing tactuo-proximal adjustments, becomes first a specific approach response, then a perceptually directed seeking response (Figure 24).

Motivation and learning theory meet difficulties here, of course, partly through insufficient evidence and partly through logical shortcomings. It is plain that research on infant perception and motivation has taken us beyond the stage of Watson's kinaesthetic-motor theory and Holt's reflex-circle theory. But for reasons advanced before, S-R or connectionistic theories seem limited to early stages, when events are dominated by what contiguities of stimuli and A-type processes are sufficiently experienced. Such occurrences might explain attainment of a simple visually directed arm approach based on earlier tactuo-proximal adjustments. But to understand progress into the stage of perceptually directed reaching, we must postulate qualitatively new processes of selective learning developing through the situation-altering effect of action (76). Related aspects concern relevance of stimulus properties to the optimal organic condition (73), changing relationships between action and its organic consequences (76, 105), and qualitative differences between nonperceptual and perceptual learning (92).

Reaching may well be the most significant indicator of early approach-responsiveness in man. Fundamental to processes changing incidental limb extension to perceptual seeking is an intimate relationship to A-type organic processes, first as concomitant events, then in versatile roles influencing the plastically utilized relationships of selective learning (Figures 23 and 24).

In these ways, the human infant normally acquires in his first half year an anticipative way of dealing with objects at a distance. Anticipative reaching, in *its* turn, is basic first to approach and *then* to seeking by crawling and walking respectively. These developments themselves provide a perceptual-motivational basis for approaches and seeking of the *conceptual* type. What earlier stages may contribute to the more vicarious forms of reaching is suggested by the difficulties experienced in completing approach reactions in the period when "the infant must touch everything." Richardson's (93) study of infant learning showed that infants must pass through many months of progressive toil before they can perceive a string and lure as related, with the former a means of getting the latter. From Fishel's (37) tests it appears that dogs never deal with such relationships as well as do young children.

Early progress in motivated reaching, providing a basis for perceiving and using the arm as an *extension* of the body towards incentives, thereby leads in some primates to the use of objects as means to increase still more the scope of approaching and seeking responses. Such attainments are limited in monkeys, but accelerate from chimpanzee to man. This view of motivated problem-solving is supported by Birch's (4) evidence that chimpanzees achieve few insight solutions in the Köhler stick-combination test unless sticks have been handled previously in play. After the animal has perceived a stick in an arm-extending pattern, a reasoned combining of sticks evidently can arise through anticipating further extensions of a single held stick. Dependence of this indirect *seeking* response on the animal's motivated condition was demonstrated when Birch made the subject hunger excessive before tests, whereupon chimpanzees capable of insight solutions limited themselves to reaching *directly* for the distant food with the arm alone.

By means of comprehensive rules of conduct, inhibitive procedures and the like, man is capable of extending his motivated approach adjustments under conditions of stress beyond the limitations of direct response. But even man, schooled as he can be in ways of seeking what may lie in hyperspace, at times follows the wrong rules or for other reasons reaches short through petty motivation.

REFERENCES

1. Adrian, E. D. 1935. *The mechanism of nervous action.* Philadelphia: Univ. Pennsylvania Press.
2. Allport, F. H. 1924. *Social psychology.* New York: Houghton-Mifflin.
3. Bertocci, P. A. 1940. A critique of G. W. Allport's theory of motivation. *Psychol. Rev.* 47: 501–532. (Cf. Allport's reply, *ibid.,* pp. 533–553.)
4. Birch, H. 1945. The relation of previous experience to insightful problem-solving. *J. Comp. Psychol.* 38: 367–383.
5. Bitterman, M. E., J. Wodinsky, and D. K. Candland. 1958. Some comparative psychology. *Am. J. Psychol.* 71: 94–110.

6. Bourguignon, G. 1929. Classification fonctionnelle des muscles par la chronaxie. *Traité Physiol. Norm. Path.* 8: 157–238.

7. Bousfield, W. A., and W. D. Orbison. 1952. Ontogenesis of emotional behavior. *Psychol. Rev.* 59: 1–7.

8. Bower, G., and N. E. Miller. 1958. Rewarding and punishing effects from stimulating the same place in the rat's brain. *J. Comp. Physiol. Psychol.* 51: 669–674.

9. Bridges, K. M. B. 1931. *The social and emotional development of the preschool child.* London: Kegan Paul.

10. Brink, F., Jr. 1951. Excitation and conduction in the neuron. Chap. 2, pp. 50–93.—Synaptic mechanisms. Chap. 3, pp. 94–120. In S. S. Stevens, ed., *Handbook of experimental psychology,* New York: Wiley.

11. Bullock, T. H. 1948. Physiological mapping of giant fiber systems in polychaete annelids. *Physiol. Comp. Oecol.* 1: 1–14.

12. Canestrini, S. 1913. Über das sinnesleben des Neugeborenen. *Monogr. Neurol. Psychiatr.,* No. 5. Berlin: Springer.

13. Carmichael, L. 1936. A re-evaluation of the concepts of maturation and learning as applied to the early development of behavior. *Psychol. Rev.* 43: 440–470.

14. Carmichael, L., and M. F. Smith. 1939. Quantified pressure stimulation and the specificity and generality of response in fetal life. *J. Genet. Psychol.* 54: 425–434.

15. Castner, B. M. 1932. The development of fine prehension in infancy. *Genet. Psychol. Monogr.* 12: 105–193.

16. Craig, W. 1918. Appetites and aversions as constituents of instincts. *Biol. Bull.* 34: 91–108.

17. Creed, R. S., D. Denny-Brown, J. C. Eccles, E. G. T. Liddell, and C. S. Sherrington. 1932. *Reflex activity of the spinal cord.* London: Oxford Univ. Press.

18. Daniel, R. S., and K. U. Smith. 1947. The migration of newly hatched loggerhead turtles toward the sea. *Science* 106: 398–399.

19. Darrow, C. W. 1937. Neural mechanisms controlling the palmar galvanic skin reflex and palmar sweating. *Arch. Neurol. Psychiatr.* 37: 641–663.

20. Darling, R., and C. W. Darrow. 1938. Determining activity of the autonomic nervous system from measurements of autonomic change. *J. Psychol.* 5: 85–89.

21. Darwin, Charles. 1873. *Expression of the emotions in man and animals.* New York: Appleton.

22. Davis, R. C. 1943. The genetic development of patterns of voluntary activity. *J. Exper. Psychol.* 33: 471–486.

23. Deigado, J. M. R., W. W. Roberts, and N. E. Miller. 1954. Learning motivated by electrical stimulation of the brain. *Am. J. Physiol.* 179: 587–593.

24. Dennis, W. 1935. Experimental test of two theories of social smiling in infants. *J. Soc. Psychol.* 6: 214–223.

25. Detheir, V. G. 1947. *Chemical insect attractants and repellents.* Philadelphia: Blakiston.

26. Detheir, V. G., and D. Bodenstein. 1958. Hunger in the blowfly. *Z. Tierpsychol.* 15: 129–140.
27. Dolley, W. L., Jr., and L. H. Golden. 1947. The effect of sex and age on the temperature at which reversal in reaction to light in *Eristalis tenax* occurs. *Biol. Bull.* 92: 178–186.
28. Dolley, W. L., Jr., and J. D. White. 1951. The effect of illuminance on the reversal temperature in the drone fly *Eristalis tenax*. *Biol. Bull.* 100: 84–89.
29. Dumas, G. 1922. L'expression des émotions. *Revue Philosophique* 47: 32–72, 235–258.
30. Dumas, G. 1948. *Le sourire, psychologie et physiologie.* (3me Ed.) Paris: Presses niver.
31. Eccles, J. C. 1953. *The neurophysiological basis of mind.* Oxford: Clarendon.
32. Ehrenhardt, H. 1937. Formensehen und Sehscharfebestimmungen bie Eidechsen. *Z. Vergl. Physiol.* 24: 258–304.
33. Eibl-Eibesfeldt, I. 1951. Nahrungserwerb und Beuteschema der Erdkröte (*Bufo bufo* L.). *Behaviour* 4: 1–35.
34. Eibl-Eibesfeldt, I., and S. Kramer. 1958. Ethology, the comparative study of animal behavior. *Quart. Rev. Biol.* 33: 181–221.
35. Evans, D. R., and V. G. Dethier. 1956. The regulation of taste thresholds for sugars in the blowfly. *J. Ins. Physiol.* 1: 3–17.
36. Fabricius, E. 1951. Some experiments on imprinting phenomena in ducks. *Proc. Xth Internatl. Ornith. Cong., Uppsala,* pp. 375–379.
37. Fischel, G. 1950. *Die Seele des Hundes.* Berlin: Parey.
38. Fraenkel, G. S., and D. L. Gunn. 1940. *The orientation of animals.—Kineses, taxes and compass reactions.* New York: Oxford Univer. Press.
39. Frank, L. 1957. Tactile communication. *Genet. Psychol. Monogr.* 56: 209–255.
40. Freisling, J. 1948. Studien zur Biologie und Psychologie der Wechselkröte (*Bufo viridis* Laur.). *Öst. Zool. Zeitschr.* 1: 383–440.
41. Frisch, K. v. 1941. Über einen Schreckstoff der Fischhaut und seine biologische Bedeutung. *Z. Vergl. Physiol.* 29: 46–145.
42. Fulton, J. F. 1926. *Muscular contraction and the reflex control of movement.* Baltimore: Williams and Wilkins.
43. Glickman, S. E. 1958. Deficits in avoidance learning produced by stimulation of the ascending reticular formation. *Canad. J. Psychol.* 12: 97–102.
44. Goldstein, K. 1939. *The organism.* New York: American Book Co.
45. Goldstein, K. 1950. On emotions: considerations from the organismic point of view. *J. Psychol.* 31: 37–49.
46. Golightly, C. L. 1953. The James-Lange theory: a logical port-mortem. *Phil. Sci.* 20: 286–299.
47. Greenfield, A. 1955. Alteration of a conditioned avoidance tendency by a procedure of adaptation to the unconditioned stimulus. *Ann. N. Y. Acad. Sci.* 62: 277–294.
48. Halverson, H. M. 1937. Studies of the grasping response of early infancy. *J. Genet. Psychol.* 51: I, 371–392; II, 393–424; III, 425–449.

49. Harlow, H., and R. Stagner. 1932. Psychology of feelings and emotions: I. Theory of feelings. *Psychol. Rev.* 39: 570–589.

50. Harris, L. J., J. Clay, J. Hargreaves, and A. Ward. 1933. Appetite and choice of diet. The ability of the vitamin-B deficient rat to discriminate between diets containing and lacking the vitamin. *Proc. Roy. Soc., B,* 113: 161–190.

51. Hartline, H. K. 1935. The discharge of nerve impulses from the single visual sense cell. *C. Spr. Harb. Symp. Quant. Biol.* 3: 245–250.

52. Hebb, D. O. 1946. On the nature of fear. *Psychol. Rev.* 53: 259–276.

53. Hebb, D. O. 1949. *The organization of behavior.* New York: Wiley.

54. Hebb, D. O. 1958. The motivating effects of exteroceptive stimulation. *Am. Psychol.* 13: 109–113.

55. Hecht, S. 1929. Vision: II. The nature of the photoreceptor process. In C. Murchison, ed., *Foundations of experimental psychology.* Clark Univ. Press. Chap 4.

56. Hediger, H. 1950. *Wild animals in captivity.* London: Butterworths.

57. Heintz, E. 1955. Actions attractives et répulsives spécifiques de broyats et de substances extraites de broyats chez *Apis mellifica* et *Tubifex tubifex. C. R. Soc. Biol.* 149: 2224–2227.

57a. Hertz, M. 1933. Die Organisation des optischen Feldes bei der Biene. *Z. Vergl. Physiol.* 14: 629–674.

58. Hess, H. 1958. "Imprinting" in animals. *Sci. Am.* 198: 81–90.

59. Hess, W. 1924. Reactions to light in the earthworm, *Lumbricus terrestris* L. *J. Morph. Physiol.* 39: 515–542.

60. Hinsey, J. C. 1934. The innervation of skeletal muscle. *Physiol. Rev.* 14: 514–585.

61. Holst, E. v. 1937. Bausteine zu einer vergleichenden Physiologie der lokomotorischen Reflexe bei Fischen. II. Mitteilung. *Z. Vergl. Physiol.* 24: 532–562.

62. Holt, E. B. 1931. *Animal drive and the learning process.* New York: Holt.

63. Honigmann, H. 1945. The visual perception of movement by toads. *Proc. Roy. Zool. Soc., B,* 132: 291–307.

64. Huber, E. 1930. Evolution of facial musculature and cutaneous field of trigeminus. *Quart. Rev. Biol.* 5: 133–188, 389–437.

65. Hudgins, C. V. 1939. The incidence of muscular contraction in reciprocal movements under conditions of changing loads. *J. Gen. Psychol.* 20: 327–338.

66. Hunt, W. A. 1939. A critical review of current approaches to affectivity. *Psychol. Bull.* 36: 807–828.

67. Jennings, H. S. 1906. *The behavior of lower organisms.* New York: Columbia Univ. Press.

68. Kempf, E. J. 1953. Neurosis as conditioned, conflicting, holistic, attitudinal, acquisitive-avoidant reactions. *Ann. N. Y. Acad. Sci.* 56: 307–329.

69. Koehler, O. 1954. Das Lächeln als angeborene Ausdrucksbewegung. *Z. Menschl. Vererb.-u. Konstitutionslehre* 32: 390–398.

70. Kuntz, A. 1929. *The autonomic nervous system.* Philadelphia: Lea and Febiger.
71. Leeper, R. W. 1948. A motivational theory of emotion to replace 'emotion as disorganized response.' *Psychol. Rev.* 55: 5–21.
72. Lehrman, D. 1953. A critique of Lorenz's "objectivistic" theory of animal behavior. *Quart. Rev. Biol.* 28: 337–363.
73. Leuba, C. 1955. Toward some integration of learning theories: the concept of optimal stimulation. *Psychol. Reports* 1: 27–33.
74. Levine, M. G., and H. Kabat. 1952. Cocontraction and reciprocal innervation in voluntary movement in man. *Science* 116: 115–118.
75. Maier, N. R. F., and T. C. Schneirla. 1935. *Principles of animal psychology.* New York: McGraw-Hill.
76. Maier, N. R. F., and T. C. Schneirla. 1942. Mechanisms in conditioning. *Psychol Rev.* 49: 117–134.
77. Mast, S. O. 1931. The nature of response to light in *Amoeba proteus* (Leidy). *Z. Vergl. Physiol.* 15: 139–147.
78. McGinnis, J. M. 1930. Eye-movements and optic nystagmus in early infancy. *Genet. Psychol. Monogr.* 8: 321–430.
79. McGraw, M. 1937. The Moro reflex. *Am. J. Dis. Children* 54: 240–251.
80. McKinley, G. M. 1956. *Evolution: the ages and tomorrow.* New York: Ronald.
81. Meyer-Holzapfel, M. 1955. Unsicherheit und Gefahr im Leben höherer Tiere. *Schweiz. Z. Psychol. Anwend.* 14: 171–194.
82. Miller, N. E. 1958. Central stimulation and other new approaches to motivation and reward. *Am. Psychol.* 13: 100–108.
83. Mittelstaedt, H. 1957. Prey capture in mantids. *Rec. Adv. Invert. Physiol.,* Univ. Oregon Publ. Pp. 51–71.
84. Nissen, H., K. L. Chow, and J. Semmes. 1951. Effects of restricted opportunity for tactual, kinesthetic, and manipulative experience on the behavior of a chimpanzee. *Am. J. Psychol.* 64:485–507.
85. Olds, J., and P. Milner. 1954. Positive reinforcement produced by electrical stimulation of septal area and other regions of rat brain. *J. Comp. Physiol. Psychol.* 47: 419–427.
86. Parr, A. E. 1927. A contribution to the theoretical analysis of the schooling behavior of fishes. *Occas. Papers Bingham Oceanogr. Coll.,* no. 1, pp. 1–32.
87. Peiper, A. 1926. Untersuchungen über die Reaktionzeit im Säuglingsalter: II. Reaktionzeit auf Schmerzreiz. *Monatschr. Kinderheilk.* 32: 136–143.
88. Pick, J. 1954. The evolution of homeostasis. *Proc. Am. Phil. Soc.* 98: 298–303.
89. Pratt, K. C. 1946. The neonate. In L. Carmichael, ed., *Manual of child psychology.* New York: Wiley. Chap. 4.
90. Pratt, K. C., A. K. Nelson, and K. H. Sun. 1930. The behavior of the newborn infant. *Ohio State Univ. Stud., Contr. Psychol.* no. 10.
91. Prosser, C. L. 1934. Effect of the central nervous system on responses to light in *Eisenia foetida* Sav., *J. Comp. Neurol.* 59: 61–91.

92. Razran, G. 1955. Conditioning and perception. *Psychol. Rev.* 62: 83–95.
93. Richardson, H. M. 1932. The growth of adaptive behavior in infants: An experimental study of seven age levels. *Genet. Psychol. Monogr.* 12: 195–359.
94. Roberts, W. W. 1958. Rapid escape learning without avoidance learning motivated by hypothalamic stimulation in cats. *J. Comp. Physiol. Psychol.* 51: 391–399.
95. Rosenblatt, J. S., J. Wodinsky, G. Turkewitz, and T. C. Schneirla. Analytical studies on maternal behavior in relation to litter adjustment and socialization in the domestic cat. II. Maternal-young relations from birth to weaning. III. Development of orientation. (In ms.)
96. Rowland, L. W. 1936. The somatic effects of stimuli graded in respect to their exciting character. *J. Exper. Psychol.* 19: 547–560.
97. Schiller, P. v. 1933. Intersensorielle Transposition bei Fischen. *Z. Vergl. Physiol.* 19: 304–309.
98. Schneider, D. 1954. Beitrag zu einer Analyse des Beute und Fluchverhaltens einheimischer Anuren. *Biol. Zentralbl.* 73: 225–282.
99. Schneirla, T. C. 1939. A theoretical consideration of the basis for approach-withdrawal adjustments in behavior. *Psychol. Bull.* 37: 501–502.
100. Schneirla, T. C. 1946. Ant learning as a problem in comparative psychology. In P. Harriman, ed., *Twentieth century psychology*. New York: Philos. Library. Pp. 276–305.
101. Schneirla, T. C. 1949. Levels in the psychological capacities of animals. In R. W. Sellers *et al.*, eds., *Philosophy for the future*. New York: Macmillan.
102. Schneirla, T. C. 1956. Interrelationships of the "innate" and the "acquired" in instinctive behavior. In *L'Instinct dans le comportement des animaux et de l'homme*. Paris: Masson. Pp. 387–452.
103. Schneirla, T. C. 1957. The concept of development in comparative psychology. In D. B. Harris, ed., *The concept of development*. Minneapolis: Univ. Minnesota Press. Pp. 78–108.
104. Schneirla, T. C. L'apprentissage et la question du conflit chez la fourmi. Comparaison avec le rat. *J. de Psychol.* (In press)
105. Seward, J. P. 1952. Introduction to a theory of motivation in learning. *Psychol. Rev.* 59: 405–413.
106. Shaw, E. Studies on sexual behavior in platyfish reared under altered or reduced environmental conditions. (In ms.)
107. Sherman, M. 1927. The differentiation of emotional responses in infants. I. Judgments of emotional responses from motion picture views and from actual observation. *J. Comp. Psychol.* 7: 265–284.
108. Sherman, M., and I. C. Sherman. 1925. Sensory-motor responses in infants. *J. Comp. Psychol.* 5: 53–68.
109. Sherrington, C. S. 1906. *The integrative action of the nervous system.* (1923 Ed.) New Haven: Yale Univ. Press.
110. Spitz, R. A. 1957. *No and yes—on the genesis of human communication.* New York: International Univ. Press.

111. Spitz, R., and K. M. Wolf. 1946. The smiling response: a contribution to the ontogenesis of social relations. *Genet. Psychol. Monogr.* 34: 57–125.
112. Stough, H. B. 1936. Giant nerve fibers of the earthworm. *J. Comp. Neurol.* 40: 409–464.
113. Taylor, J. H. 1934. Innate emotional responses in infants. *Ohio State Univ. Stud., Contrib. Psychol.,* no. 12, pp. 69–81.
114. Thompson, R. 1954. Approach versus avoidance in an ambiguous-cue discrimination problem in chimpanzees. *J. Comp. Physiol. Psychol.* 47: 133–135.
115. Tumarkin, A. 1955. On the evolution of the auditory conducting apparatus: A new theory based on functional considerations. 9: 221–243.
116. Verheijen, F. J. 1958. The mechanisms of the trapping effect of artificial light sources upon animals. *Arch. Néerl. Zool.* 13: 1–107.
117. Wagner, H. 1932. Über den· Farbensinn der Eidechsen. *Z. Vergl. Physiol.* 18: 378–392.
118. Warburton, F. E. 1955. Feedback in development and its evolutionary significance. *Am. Nat.* 89: 129–140.
119. Watson, J. B. 1919. *Psychology from the standpoint of a behaviorist.* Philadelphia: Lippincott.
120. Wenger, M. A. 1936. An investigation of conditioned responses in human infants. *Univ. Iowa Stud. Child Welfare* 12: 8–90.
121. Werner, H. 1940. *Comparative psychology of mental development.* New York: Harper.
122. Werner, H., and S. Wapner. 1955. Changes in psychological distance under conditions of danger. *J. Pers.* 24: 153–167.
123. Wickens, D. D., and C. Wickens. 1939. A study of conditioning in the neonate. *Psychol. Bull.* 36: 599.
124. Witkin, H. A. 1942. Restriction as a factor in adjustment to conflict situations. *J. Comp. Psychol.* 33: 41–74.
125. Wolf, E. 1933. Das Verhalten der Bienen gegenüber flimmernden Feldern und bewegten Objekten. *Z. Vergl. Physiol.* 3: 209–224.

T. C. SCHNEIRLA

JAY S. ROSENBLATT

"Critical Periods" in the Development of Behavior

Bibliography No. 105

Scott's interesting article (1) on "critical periods" in behavioral development merits a thoroughgoing critical review bearing on the validity of his general conceptions of behavioral ontogeny basic to the idea which he has extrapolated from embryology to the study of behavior. Here, however, we comment specifically on certain inferences that might be drawn from his allusion to our recent article on behavioral development in cats (2).

In discussing his concept of critical periods, Scott reports us as having "suggested that there are critical stages of learning—that what has been learned at a particular time in development may be critical for whatever follows."

Although we are not disposed to dispute this broad statement, it is not ours. In our view, any such sentence should have a more comprehensive context, to the effect that what the young animal may attain in behavior at any phase of ontogeny depends upon the outcome of earlier development in its every aspect. The point we wish to emphasize here, however, is that our position might be seriously misunderstood in at least two important respects from Scott's allusion to our article. (i) Although, as our study of social behavior in newborn kittens (2, 3) indicated strongly, learning is involved at all phases in behavior development, our findings have broader and very different implications for social ontogeny than might be gathered from Scott's mention of the work. (ii) The context indicates that Scott has misunderstood the criticisms we have offered (2, 3) of his "critical periods" concept.

The gist of our objection is not that we favor describing three critical periods of social development, corresponding to the three main stages in the ontogeny of social-feeding behavior in kittens for which we found evidence, or whatever number of critical periods might be advanced as an alternative. We were interpreting our results from a viewpoint definitely at odds with Scott's notion of "critical periods" when we wrote (2):

> These considerations favor a very different view of the concept of "critical periods" from the one now held by many writers. In the social development of the cat, we are led to the idea that striking changes in the essential progression are grounded not only in the growth-dependent processes of maturation but also, at the same time, in opportunities for experience and learning arising in the standard female-litter situation. This conception of social ontogeny encourages stressing not just one or a few chronologically marked changes in the behavior pattern, but rather indicates that normally each age period is crucial for the development of particular aspects in a complex progressive pattern of adjustment.

We consider the implications of this theoretical viewpoint for developmental research very different from those of Scott's concept.

Evidence supporting our view demonstrated that in kittens, at all age periods, social approaches preliminary to feeding behavior undergo a course of development in the litter situation significantly different from the behavior of kittens reared under conditions of isolation and fed from an "artificial mother" (2, 3). No evidence was found for any time interval in which the different conditions of rearing failed to produce a pattern of feeding approaches and suckling in kittens reared in isolation that was significantly different from that in normally reared kittens of corresponding ages. This result has been predicted from the theory of social ontogeny (4) which guided our work.

Those who examine this theory (4, 5) and related considerations (2, 6, 7) will find an emphasis upon the fusion of maturation (growth-contributed) and experience (stimulation-contributed) processes at different stages in behavioral ontogeny, together with the contention that the contributions both of maturation and of experience (the latter including, but not confined to, conditioning and learning), as well as the interrelations of these contributions, may differ greatly according to stage in any animal. This theory thus differs sharply from Scott's, with its emphasis (see 8) upon factors of maturation presumably specific for "critical periods" and its apparent assumption that "learning" is a distinct and probably a delayed contributor.

From our theory of behavioral development (4–6), we conclude that factors of maturation may differ significantly in their influence upon ontogeny, both in the nature and in the timing of their effects, according to what relations to the effects of experience are possible under the existing conditions. We found, in support of this view, that gains in suckling made by kittens reared in isolation differed greatly from gains made by litter mates reared by the mother, and that the kittens reared in isolation were, at best, only partially adapted to the demands of social feeding and suckling of the mother at the time of their return to the litter. The differences between the experimental animals and the control litter mates were striking. In no single phase of development during the first 2 months of life did these two very different conditions of rearing—with mother and litter or isolated, with an "artificial mother"—fail to have very different effects on the development of suckling responses, despite the presumable equivalence of potential factors of maturation for kittens in the two groups. The results indicate that the actual effects of maturation differed considerably in the two cases. We do not find such evidence compatible with the meaning of maturation that would seem to follow from the critical-period hypothesis.

What is social behavior? Scott states (1) that in puppies the period of socialization begins at approximately 3 weeks of age. We submit, however, that much of the evidence he cites bears only tangentially on the question of when socialization really begins. Although his article is mainly concerned with social behavior, it does not deal primarily with intraspecies behavioral relationships but deals, instead, with the responses of puppies to human handlers, of young birds to artifacts, and the like. Under the heading, "Process of primary socialization" we find, for example, citations of tests in which machine-fed and hand-fed puppies "became equally attached to people . . . ," hand-fed puppies "yelped more when they saw the experimenter . . . ," "hungry puppies became more rapidly attached to the handlers . . . ," and "separating young puppies overnight from their mother and litter mates . . . speeded up the process of socialization to human handlers."

The degree of equivalence between such results and the ontogeny of interactions among species mates may prove to be appreciable, but it has not been determined. We suggest that Scott, in basing his principal treatment of social development upon experimental interventions featuring responses to conditions other than association with species mates has been led astray.

In our studies of the social-feeding behavior of kittens we were able to distinguish early forms of intraspecies social responses not evident in reactions to human handlers or to artifacts such as the "artificial mother." A dependence upon the latter two sources of evidence might have led us to neglect aspects of intraspecies behavior which we found crucial for the understanding of social ontogeny.

With due emphasis upon intraspecies behavioral relations, we maintain that processes of socialization and formation of the social bond begin at birth, if not earlier (2–6). Kittens make consistent progress from an hour or two after birth in becoming oriented to their environment and to species mates, in becoming adjusted to the litter situation and the "home area," and in making individual, distinctive responses to particular nipples. Such aspects of behavior concern reciprocal relations of dependency with the mother and with litter mates, hence are social.

Because Scott was concerned with giving an account of the critical-period concept and illustrating it, evidence centered on the ontogeny of intraspecies responses may not have seemed relevant to him. Yet, because his reference to our article might imply that it supports his own concepts of behavioral development, we assert that there is an important difference between his view and our own.

REFERENCES

1. Scott, J. P. 1962. *Science* 138: 949.
2. Schneirla, T. C., and J. S. Rosenblatt. 1960. *Am. J. Orthopsychiat.* 31: 223.
3. Rosenblatt, J. S., G. Turkewitz, and T. C. Schneirla. 1961. In B. M. Foss, ed., *Determinants of infant behaviour.* London: Methuen. Pp. 51–74.
4. Schneirla, T. C. 1956. In P.-P. Grasse, ed., *L'Instinct dans le comportement des animaux et de l'homme.* Paris: Masson. Pp. 387–452.
5. Schneirla, T. C. 1946. *J. Abnormal Soc. Psychol.* 41: 385.
6. Schneirla, T. C. 1951. In M. J. Senn, ed., *Problems of infancy and child-hood.* New York: Josiah Macy, Jr. Foundation. Pp. 81–124.
7. Thomas, A., H. G. Birch, S. Chess, M. E. Hertzig. 1962. In *Proc. World Congr. Psychiat.* 3rd, Montreal, 1962. Pp. 722–726.
8. Scott, J. P. 1958. *Psychosomat. Med.* 20: 42.

T. C. SCHNEIRLA

Aspects of Stimulation and Organization in Approach-Withdrawal Processes Underlying Vertebrate Behavioral Development[1]

Bibliography No. 108

I. DEVELOPMENTAL IMPLICATIONS OF THE BIPHASIC APPROACH-WITHDRAWAL THEORY

In the evolution of behavior, operations which appropriately increase or decrease distance between organisms and stimulus sources must have been crucial for the survival of all animal types. The success of a species in reaching food, in mating, in evading noxious situations, and thus in surviving, presumably depended first of all upon the efficiency of its members in dealing with differences in the stimulative intensities naturally characterizing such situations.

For an understanding of such matters especially in their relationships to behavioral ontogenesis, the writer has developed a theory of biphasic approach-withdrawal (A-W) processes (Schneirla, 1939, 1959). This theory derives support from many sources—from the findings of Darwin, Jennings, Cannon, Sherrington, the Pavlovian school, and others whose work has borne on relevant problems. The concept of biphasic functional mechanisms, on which this theory centers, has been applied to adaptive behavior by Holt (1931) and by Goldstein (1939), and Kempf (1953) has derived a theory of human conflict and neurosis from evidence on biphasic mechanisms in man.

From *Advances in the Study of Behavior,* vol. 1, edited by D. S. Lehrman, R. Hinde, and E. Shaw. New York: Academic Press, 1965. Reprinted with permission.

[1] I am grateful to Drs. Lester R. Aronson, James Atz, Jay S. Rosenblatt, William Tavolga, and Ethel Tobach of the American Museum of Natural History, and to Dr. Gilbert Gottlieb of the Dorothea Dix Hospital, Raleigh, North Carolina, for their help in critically reading the manuscript of this chapter.

A. *Résumé of the Principal Concepts and Some Definitions*

The A-W theory, begun in a general treatise on comparative psychology (Maier and Schneirla, 1935), has been carried further along comparative lines and as a basis for studying behavioral development. The main postulate for phylogenesis in this theory is that, according to the behavioral resources of each species, approach responses and their perceptual sequelae arise through the agency of A-processes, withdrawal responses and their perceptual sequelae through the agency of W-processes. The key postulate for ontogenesis is that, in early developmental stages, low or decreasing stimulative effects can selectively arouse organic processes of the A-system (i.e., vegetative) and, conversely, that high or increasing stimulative effects can selectively arouse organic processes of the W-system (i.e., interruptive).

In all animals (Schneirla, 1959, pp. 1–42, 78–81) low stimulative intensities tend to elicit and maintain A-processes, the energy-conserving metabolic processes normal for the species and basic to approach responses, whereas high stimulative intensities tend to arouse W-processes, energy-expending metabolic changes underlying disturbed responses and withdrawal. Evidence for the existence of two functionally opposed systems has been summarized by Kuntz (1929), Gellhorn (1943), Kempf (1953), and Schneirla (1959). Familiar examples of A-processes in mammals are the regular heartbeat, smooth-running respiration and digestion, and other processes maintained or increased predominantly through activation by the parasympathetic division of the autonomic nervous system; examples of W-processes are the irregular heartbeat, inhibited digestion, adrenin-related excitement, and other changes aroused mainly through sympathetic activation. In general, it is evident that A-processes and W-processes involve much the same organs but in functionally very different ways.

To clarify the use of special terms relevant to this theory and to facilitate an objective use of the concepts, the following definitions are offered:

Approach—A response to extrinsic stimulation through which the animal orients to and may also reduce the distance between itself and the stimulus source.

Withdrawal—A response to extrinsic stimulation through which the animal orients from and may also increase the distance between itself and the stimulus source.

Seeking; searching—Specialized approaches, whereby the animal responds to stimuli in ways appropriate to finding the object.

Avoidance—Specialized withdrawals, whereby the animal responds to stimuli in ways appropriate to breaking off or forestalling behavioral relations with the object.

A-stimulus—A low-intensity energy change (Section I, B) which can elicit neural input patterns of the regular, low magnitudes and limited quantitative variations adequate for A-system arousal.

W-stimulus—An energy change objectively definable as high-intensity, which can elicit neural input patterns of the irregular, high magnitudes adequate for W-system arousal.

A-processes—Low-threshold mechanisms which in their tonic aspects are energy-conserving and basic to species-typical development and to regular behavior, and in their phasic aspects underlie and facilitate actions of approach or seeking.

W-processes—Visceral and other mechanisms with a high component of sympathetic-autonomic control, related to disruptive or tensional conditions basic to withdrawal or avoidance reactions.

Approach-fixation; withdrawal-fixation (Schneirla, 1959, pp. 78 ff.)—The establishment of neural trace effects through which (1) behavior is directed toward or away from a given stimulus, respectively, (2) the behavioral functions become specialized and stimulus-discriminative through the repetition of contiguities reinforced by A-processes or by W-processes.

Tonic—Continuous processes such as those of the A-system basic to species-typical development and to regular behavior.

Phasic—Processes arising by degrees or stages through the repetition of temporary, short-lived increases in A-processes or in W-processes which are at first typically episodic (cf. Section IV, B).

Maturation; experience—(See Section I, D).

B. Biphasic Approach-Withdrawal Theory Focuses on the Developmental Effects of Stimulation

The A-W theory seems applicable to behavior in all animals, although the extent to which basic A-responses and W-responses may change from early stages is naturally dependent upon species resources for plasticity through experience (Section V, A). Species differences in the basic properties, such as stimulus filtering (Section IV, A), and in functional plasticity, concern how far specializations have evolved in afferent, neural, and other mechanisms central to behavioral development. The emergence of such properties must have rested, above all, on conditions in natural selection favoring the survival of animals equipped for consistent approaches to low-intensity sources and withdrawals from high-intensity sources of stimulation. Whatever mutations were key items in determining thresholds of sensitivity and functions such as those of conduction and response, meeting this formula for adaptive behavior, must have had a heavy weighting for survival. Such mechanisms, as Orton (1955) has recognized, may function at any stage of ontogenesis as critical agents for survival.

Certain interpretations will bear emphasis here. First, "stimulus intensity" in A-W theory is interpreted as *effective stimulus input* affecting neural input under the given conditions. It was in these terms that Maier and Schneirla (1935, Chapters 1–11; Table 21) concluded that *low* stimulative intensities favor approach, high intensities withdrawal, in all animals. As a rule, stimulus values for approach lie nearer the lower stimulus threshold than the median of the species range, with threshold functions changing within limits according to conditions. Thus, for taxis responses, the threshold for any sensory field may increase under conditions such as adaptation, excitement, or age, so that the animal now approaches stimulus sources of higher intensities, which normally produce variable responses or withdrawal (e.g., Dolley and White, 1951; Perttunen, 1958). The conditions of activity depend, however, not only upon species-specific properties of the receptors, but also upon other conditions of the organism, its experience, and the developmental circumstances governing the primary quantitative effects of stimuli on individual behavior.

A species norm of stimulus intensity is first of all a function of receptor stimulus-filtering properties governing what energy changes can affect action in development (Sections III, A; IV). Under species-normal developmental conditions, vertebrates with rod-dominated retinas tend to be nocturnal, those with cone-dominated retinas diurnal (Walls, 1942). Evidently through different properties in light thresholds and retinal photochemistry, particularly, these animals normally function most effectively at very different extrinsic intensity levels.

Such elementary conditions provide a species-typical matrix determining the direction of extrinsic change optimal for arousal and continued activity. Migratory locusts (*Locusta migratoria*), which often carry out mass flights at night, starting at dusk, respond in laboratory tests to a decrease in intensity of dim light with a steady firing of optic fibers which continues in the dark (Hoyle, 1955). In comparable tests, Roffey (1963) obtained similar results with desert locusts (*Schistocerca gregaria*), although these insects when highly excited commonly start their mass flights at dawn (i.e., when a shift from darkness to light starts optic firing). Among the doryline ants, certain surface-adapted species start their daily predatory raids at dawn and end them at dusk (Schneirla, 1940), whereas more subterranean species begin their raids at dusk and end them before dawn (Schneirla, 1958). Changes in light intensity activate both types, but in diurnal species, typically, an increase from a low intensity is excitatory whereas in nocturnal species it is a decrease that is excitatory.

Most animals are capable of opposite types of reaction to low and to high stimulus intensities, depending upon input magnitudes and individual condition. This, the A-W principle, was clearly demonstrated in Hecht's (1929) study of the clam (*Mya* sp.), in which weak light set up one type of input process arousing siphon extension and feeding, strong light an opposed process arousing siphon retraction and closure. Thus, a low-intensity range is optimal for the species' A-system, a high intensity range for its W-system.

Experience and aging, especially in the higher vertebrates, normally bring significant, sweeping changes in the relationships of extrinsic intensities to responses typical of the species in early stages (Schneirla, 1959, p. 26). For example, Crozier and Pincus (1927) reported for neonate rats at 1 week a "negative phototaxis" to relatively low intensities of light. But D'Amato and Jagoda (1962), by raising young rats under fairly intense light, increased frequencies of turning to the bright side of a Y-maze significantly over those of controls in postlitter-period tests. No reliable differences appeared, however, in group responses to bright light in an open-field test, in which all subjects were presumably much more excited than in the Y-maze test. The developmental change in the typical species photic response level was evidently a relative one, therefore. To what are such changes normally relative?

Inevitably, in both evolution and ontogenesis, these functional conditions are related to the fact that low-intensity stimulative changes are likely to be followed by beneficial results, high-intensity stimulative changes by noxious results. My biphasic A-W theory is grounded on the universality of this state of affairs in the relationship of every species to its characteristic habitat. (Selection pressure would favor a corresponding approach-withdrawal dichotomy, and would promote its stabilization in the genotype through genetic assimilation.) This fundamental fact has affected the evolution of all mechanisms underlying adaptive behavior.

But certain critics of the A-W theory have somehow been led to view it in a much narrower perspective. P. T. Young (1961), for one, in criticizing this theory as one of mere "stimulus intensities," evidently did not look beyond superficialities. On the contrary, I have stated repeatedly that the A-W theory is based on the utilization, through development, of the animal's *inclusive* resources for adaptive behavior (Schneirla, 1939, 1956, 1959). This is a wholistic theory designed for studying *all* adaptive patterns of behavior attainable in a species under the conditions of individual development.

Through evolution, then, biphasic mechanisms underlying directionally opposed orientative responses, governed first of all by quantitative properties of stimulation, are present in all animals from protozoans to primates. But, through natural selection, specializations have appeared in all of the mechanisms underlying adaptive behavior. They have emerged in a variety of types which have brought sensory-neural input effects increasingly under the influence of species properties bearing on behavioral plasticity through experience. In discussing relevant problems, therefore, due weight must be given both to peripheral and to central resources for behavioral development typical of the species.

C. *Relevance of the Approach-Withdrawal Theory*
   to Proximal and to Distance Sensitivity

Although animal perception has often been studied as though visual functions arose independently of other modalities, there is every reason to believe that proximal sensory functions were generally antecedent to those of the distance modalities in evolution, as they generally are in ontogenesis. Vertebrate behavior will be viewed in this chapter from the standpoint that somatic-afferent functions are (with those of related proximal fields) basic to behavioral development both in precocial and in altricial animals, although in somewhat different ways (Section V).

A principal thesis in this chapter will be that the early organization of functions in the proximal afferent fields of somaesthesis (i.e., cutaneous, proprioceptive, and visceral sensitivity) and chemoception furnish the necessary basis for later functioning of the species-typical distance modalities (Sections III and IV). This order of functioning, effective as a basis for the orientative behavior of diverse organisms (Fraenkel and Gunn, 1940), seems to hold widely in vertebrate perceptual development.

Despite the probability that the basic mechanisms of approach and of withdrawal in animals have evolved through the effects of natural selection upon factors of proximal sensitivity, the scientific literature on animal orientation and on perception has stressed visual functions with the auditory next in order. The principal reason seems to have been the priority of these fields in research on the adult behavior patterns of higher animals generally.

In accordance with the weight of evidence, my first extensive discussion of the A-W theory was stated mainly in terms of distance sensitivity, with occasional references to proximal modalities (Schneirla, 1959, pp. 28 ff.). As this chapter is concerned with specific problems in vertebrate behavioral development, its major premise is that early patterns derived through proximal sensitivity provide the major basis in most species for the subsequent stages of specialization in approach and in withdrawal.

Because of the evident ontogenetic primacy of proximal sensory mechanisms, it is essential to examine the relevance of A-W theory to proximal modalities such as chemoception, in terms of which certain criticisms have recently been directed against this theory.

Without regard to organism or developmental stage, Pfaffmann (1961) has stated that ". . . the general applicability of the A-W formulation to all stimuli must be qualified by certain qualitative differences among stimuli and their receptor systems." His criticism applies specifically to gustation, on the grounds that although certain taste stimuli are accepted in weak concentrations but at stronger ones drop to rejection, others are rejected in weak concentrations and increasingly so in higher concentrations, with the sugars in particular activating what might be called a high-threshold system which is "positive" throughout its range.

It is worth noting that the evidence given to support this criticism is derived from research with adult subjects, whereas I have referred A-W theory to higher vertebrates specifically in the context of early developmental stages. Evidently some of the critics of this theory have not noticed statements to this effect, as for example (Schneirla, 1959, p. 26) that its application to later stages in higher animals must take into account modifications, occlusions, and reversals that arise inevitably through perceptual and social development.

All of this considered, the A-W theory seems to apply appreciably to gustation *even* in adult stages. Apparent exceptions such as the sugars are understandable, for as Dethier (1947) has suggested the absence of appreciable preference reversal with these substances may be attributed to the impossibility of holding them in solution at sufficiently high concentrations to arouse rejection. With saccharin, a perceptually similar substance that is soluble through a wide range of concentrations, Beebe-Center et al. (1948), in tests with adult rats, found that whereas the subjects took more test fluid than water at concentrations not far above threshold, as concentration rose their preferences first varied and then at high values turned to the water as against the saccharin.

The frequent statement that specific gustatory stimuli owe their primary "positive" or "negative" values to innate consumatory tendencies seems vague. Adult rats tested by Weiner and Stellar (1951), when offered saline solutions as against water, took the saline at values just above threshold but switched to the water as the concentration of saline continued to rise. Another test case of importance is presented by the bitter-tasting alkaloids of certain plants, as shunning these must be of appreciable adaptive value to most terrestrial animals. Investigating this problem, Warren (1963) tested the effect of the alkaloid, sucrose octaacetate (bitter-tasting to man) on fluid-deprived mice. In choices against water, preference concentrations were established for eight of ten subjects, indicating a trend toward acceptance of low concentrations and rejection of high concentrations.

As these results suggest, the quantitative aspects of gustatory reactivity, even in adult subjects, generally indicate a determination of acceptance or of rejection consistent with A-W theory, namely, that a low quantitative input selectively excites A-processes underlying acceptance, a high input

W-processes underlying rejection. For gustation, as with other modalities, the relationship between stimulus intensity and input potency holds, for as Pfaffmann himself concluded from electrode records of input along the chorda tympani nerve: "A behavioral inversion occurs at a concentration where the intensity of the neural input is still increasing. We have been as yet unable to find any change in the sensory neural activity, *beyond that of magnitude,* that might correspond to this point of inversion" (Pfaffmann et al., 1961, p. 468—italics mine). Zotterman (1961) reached a similar conclusion.

Processes of sensory integration are fundamental to early individual behavioral development as they are also to a considerable extent to subsequent processes (Maier and Schneirla, 1935, 1942). It is therefore essential to recall a previous discussion of the ontogenesis of approach and withdrawal, which stressed the primacy for individual overt function of embryonic integrations such as those between cutaneous and proprioceptive sensitivity (Schneirla, 1959, pp. 22 ff.) The priority of proximal sensitivity both for early stages of functional development and for differential reinforcements underlying the perceptual and behavioral specializations of later stages will be discussed in the following sections.

D. Relationship of the Concepts "Maturation" and "Experience" in Developmental Theory

The question of *what* aspects of the surrounding medium affect the developing organism and *how* they affect it demands investigations centered on quantitative techniques not dominated by qualitative preconceptions. The classical concept of innate responses "made prior to experience in the natural situation" is a subjective alternative, dependent upon assumption rather than upon evidence as to when experiences relevant to behavioral development begin, what their nature is, and how they are effective.

In the absence of concerted research on this problem, the embryonic antecedents of species behavior patterns are very incompletely known. The doctrine of reflexes and the Coghill concept of "specific actions individuating from the generalized" are still very influential, although insufficiently validated for developmental research, and at best neither of them seems to be more than a part of the story (Kuo, 1963). One difficulty is that both of these notions embody the unproved doctrine of an innate intraneural patterning of behavior directly from genic sources, as does the IRM (innate releasing mechanism) concept of Lorenz (1935, 1957, 1961).

As an alternative to instinctivist views, A-W theory envisages behavioral development as a program of progressive, changing relationships between organism and environment in which the contributions of growth are always inseparably interrelated with those of the effects of energy changes in the environs (Schneirla, 1949, 1956). This formulation corresponds to a fundamental concept of modern embryology (e.g., Balinsky, 1960), according to which organism and developmental medium are inseparably related.

Although ethologists (e.g., Lorenz, 1961; Tinbergen, 1951) have viewed the "unlearned" and the "learned" as separable in behavioral development, this distinction seems unsupported and unrealistic.[2] Instead, the concept of "maturation," redefined as the contributions of tissue growth and differentiation and their functional trace effects at all stages, and "experience," defined as the contributions of stimulation from the developmental medium and of related trace effects, seem preferable (Schneirla, 1957). These terms are not to be taken as representing a mutually exclusive separation, but as convenient abstractions.

The logical alternative to nativism is neither to minimize the weight of genomic influences underlying development, nor is it compatible with shifting the emphasis to "experience" by interpreting this term incorrectly as synonymous with conditioning and learning. Nativists typically underestimate the subtlety, indirectness, and variety of relationships prevalent in development between the complexes denoted by the terms "maturation" and "experience," which are not simply interrelated but constitute a *fused* system in each stage (Schneirla, 1956, 1957). This theory, then, is much more than "interactionistic."

In examining the ontogenesis of approach and withdrawal reactions, we are of course studying the individual basis of perceptual abilities. The manner in which qualitative effects such as shape may arise for the neonate demands careful investigation as a developmental problem in each vertebrate type.

II. STIMULATIVE EQUIVALENCE AND GENERALIZATION IN BEHAVIORAL DEVELOPMENT

A. Equivalence; the Qualitative and the Quantitative in Development

The *quantitative* is widely understood to be that which is measurable or statable in degrees or amounts, the *qualitative* that which is different in kind. But actually, in studying ontogenesis, the meanings of these terms seem often to be confused, often because of inadequate techniques or a paucity of data, often because of a bias for the qualitative in this type of research. Research on the approach-withdrawal responses of neonatal vertebrates is a complex field in which experimenters often seem to follow a qualitative imagery that introduces an unknown number of independent variables in a single test.

---

[2] The fact should be emphasized, however, that in recent years Tinbergen (1963) has rather drastically changed his position on this entire question.

An asset to the study of stimulative effects in behavioral development is the Klüver (1962) principle of *equivalence,* to the effect that when physically different stimuli elicit the same response, the first assumption is that a common psychological effect is involved rather than different effects, such as of perceptual meanings. The parsimonious hypothesis, that under these conditions the animal cannot discriminate among the stimuli (e.g., Lashley and Wade, 1946), represents the type 1 condition of generalization which prevails in neonate vertebrate animals (Section V, A; Point 4). This type can be distinguished by means of appropriate tests from those [type 2] in which different responses indicate an ability to discriminate among the stimuli, and [those, type 3, in which] the same response is given to stimuli (otherwise different for the animal) on the basis of a learned property they have in common. For types 2 and 3 of this series, postnatal experience is a necessary factor (Section V, A; Points 6 and 7).

Difficulties arise in the interpretation of results from tests of neonate animals with stimuli presumably new to their experience. Even with subjects that are defined as visually "naive" in these terms, only the first test may be considered a strict measure of naiveté, for with each repetition the stimulus can acquire a further degree of familiarity (Sections III, B; V, B).

Later on, I shall give evidence for the hypothesis that the *initial* postnatal responses of any vertebrate are elicited comparably by "new" stimuli through a quantitative equivalence these stimuli bear to somaesthetic stimuli effective for A-responses in embryonic stages. This consideration offers a new perspective for interpreting the phenomenon of "imprinting," a major topic in this chapter.

The working principle thus arises that, in studying behavioral development, the hypothesis of equivalent *quantitative* stimulus effects has priority over that of *qualitative* effects (i.e., those centered on the *kind* of object involved). Premature conclusions as to the ontogenetic basis of qualitative perceptual abilities have been derived from partial evidence such as the following: (1) quantitative differences in afferent output unaccompanied by evidence on concurrent physiological or behavioral effects; (2) different afferent outputs elicited by stimuli in *adult* stages; and (3) variations in afferent output elicited by different stimuli in a *lower* vertebrate. These points apply to the significance for perceptual development of evidence on afferent electrophysiological effects, such as that obtained by Hartline (1938), Kuffler (1953), and Maturana et al. (1960) with frogs and other lower vertebrates. Evidence of this kind has been used (as by Sackett, 1963) to support conclusions for "innate" perceptual patterning in higher vertebrates, although its meaning for the sensory physiology of the animals and the stages from which it derives is still unclear

(Rushton, 1962; Horn, 1962). Quantitative evidence on specific functions at any stage has no necessary significance for behavior until its application to the development of organization in behavior has been clarified.

B. The Question of Innate Figural Schemata

In investigations of early behavior, both the nature of the tests and the
interpretation of findings often have been strongly influenced by the observer's impressions that the neonate's initial reactions to stimuli disclose
aspects related to the *kind* of object involved. This is the hypothesis of
innate schemata, for which an alternative will be offered in Section II, D.
The difficulty of these questions may be illustrated in terms of three familiar instances from the literature on vertebrate behavior.

1. BILL PECKING IN NEONATE GULLS

Neonate gulls of many species peck at the parent's bill within a few
hours after hatching, thereby soon obtaining food. In a study by Tinbergen and Perdeck (1950) on the Herring Gull (*Larus argentatus*), in
which the adult has a red spot at the tip of a yellow bill, neonates presented with a variety of models pecked more often at the spot in its normal position at the bill tip than on the head or near the base of the bill.
The "releasers" of the response thus seemed to be effects such as a "certain shape," nearby and moving, with a red patch at the tip. This qualitative view of the essential stimuli was to be expected for, after the hypothesis of an innate schema, the models had been designed to look more or
less like the head-and-bill patterns of adult gulls.

But the ability of neonate gull chicks to behave appropriately in this
situation may have a simpler, quantitative basis (Schneirla, 1955; Lehrman, 1955b). As the models were made with handles, the experimenter
might inadvertently have presented this object much as the adult head
nears the chick in nature, i.e., with the bill tip closest to the chick's head,
prominent and moving as though at the end of a rotating arm (Figure 26).
Thus, by virtue of his subjective construction of the situation, the tester
would inevitably cause the spot to be effective through ". . . its degree
of prominence as a moving object, on the head . . . moving axially and
more slowly, near the bill tip circumferentially and faster" (Schneirla,
1956, p. 411).

Collias and Collias (1957) studied this problem in the Franklin's Gull
(*Larus pipixcan*), in which the adults have red bills. Hatchlings of this
gull were placed before two adult head-models facing each other with
downward-converging bills, one bill red and the other green, both bills
flashing at 75 pulses per minute. Because the chicks pecked 5 times more

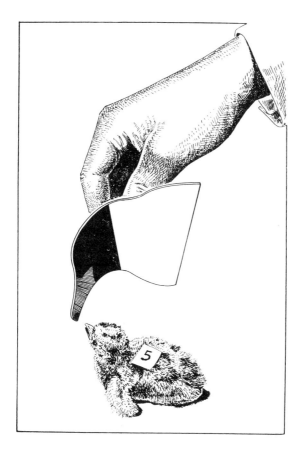

FIGURE 26
Situation of testing black-headed gull chick with
artifact. (From Tinbergen and Perdeek, 1950.)

often at the red bill than at the green one, despite wide variations in intensity in some of the tests, the experimenters concluded, "At least in
part the red bill is an adaptation to stimulate and direct the initial feeding
responses of the young." Although the conditions of this test were complex, the results indicate the role of disparate, quantitative factors initially
favoring a retinal centering of the spot, rather than pre-organized, qualitative factors.

Weidmann and Weidmann (1958), in a similar experiment with the
Black-headed Gull (*Larus ridibundus*), in which adults also have red
bills, obtained results emphasizing specific factors such as background
contrast and motion of a small, prominent object below the chick's eye
level. Hailman (1962) carried out field tests on hatchlings of the Laugh-

ing Gull (*L. atricilla*) with series of models, also laboratory tests (Hailman, 1964) with stimuli such as moving rods and flickering panels. His results also point to simple, disparate visual factors such as flicker and a moving spot as equivalent for these early responses, rather than complex effects or evidence of an innate pattern (cf. Section III, A).

2. THE "HAWK EFFECT"

Another much discussed case has derived from tests in which Lorenz (1939) and Tinbergen (1948) passed artifacts over the nest of young goslings (*Anser anser*). The models marked with arrows (Figure 27, *1*), when passed overhead broadside forward, were reported to have released "escape responses" by virtue of one aspect of their shape, the "short neck," but independently of other features (Tinbergen, 1951). Hence this artifact has been referred to as the "hawk figure." Passed in the other (i.e., the "goose") direction, the artifacts are reported to have produced negligible effects. This test, the results of which are often interpreted as evidence for an innate ("hawk") schema, dependent on the specific effect short neck as a "sign stimulus," has been repeated by others with somewhat different results [3] (e.g., Hirsch et al., 1955). One major source of difficulty has been the prevalence of artifacts dominated by complex, qualitative aspects (Figure 27), evidently suggested by the innate schema hypothesis. Under these conditions, experimental control becomes very difficult.

But the "hawk figure" somehow does disturb the hatchlings of many species, as Melzack et al. (1959) reported excitement, escape, and fear reactions in laboratory-hatched Mallard ducklings (*Anas platyrhynchos*) when a replica of this figure was passed overhead in tests. For ducklings inexperienced with such figures, at first the "hawk" model was considerably more fear-provoking than the "goose," but for other ducklings given early experience with the figure pulled over them in either direction, the disturbance was negligible. In another test, although the ducklings seemed unaffected by a stuffed eagle simply moved overhead, most of them "showed fear" when it was suddenly swooped down upon them. Similar responses were given to the sudden swoops of a stuffed teal and a tea tray directed upon the hatchlings by the investigators.

McNiven (1960) investigated the problem in a manner more specifically directed at object movement as a factor. His subjects were presented in tests with the hawk-goose artifact (Figure 27, *4*) moved over them in two different ways. This model, in black and brown, was pulled along a thin wire over 2-day-old domestic chicks and over 4-day-old

---

[3] Although Hirsch et al. (1955) investigated a different species than had Tinbergen, their results are consistent with those of other recent investigators on a variety of species.

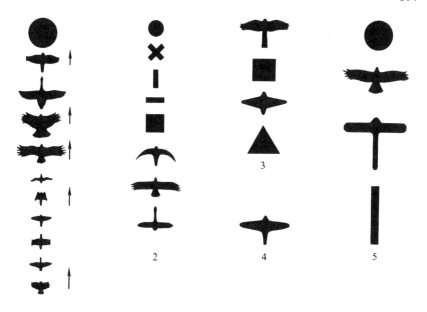

FIGURE 27

Artifacts used by investigators testing the reactions of young precocial birds to figures moved past them overhead. 1. Lorenz and Tinbergen (Tinbergen, 1948). A "hawk effect" was reported for the figures and direction indicated by arrows. 2. Kràtzig (1940). 3. Goethe (1940). 4. McNiven (1960). 5. Schleidt (1961).

ducklings and pheasants, either (1) as *sailing* (i.e., straight overhead and parallel to the ground) or (2) as *swooping* (i.e., on a sharp angle directly toward the bird). Escape reactions, recorded when the subject under test crouched or ran off, were obtained in 59.0% of the tests with swooping but in only 5.3% of the tests with sailing.

These investigations, with that of Schleidt (1961), confirm the hypothesis (Schneirla, 1949, 1956) that the necessary factor for the hawk effect is a *sudden, massive increase in retinal stimulation*. The condition of swooping ensures, much better than does sailing, that the subject will receive quickly an intensive increase in the visual input adequate to elicit W-processes (Sections I, A; IV). The quantitative aspects of this phenomenon are emphasized by Schleidt's (1961) comparison of results in terms of a standardization of conditions such as size, height, and speed of motion of the model.

The hawk effect, although obtained with naive hatchlings, is not a figural effect in the sense the innate schema hypothesis would predict. Rather, the adequate stimulus may be defined, as above, in terms of its high quantitative potency for the forced arousal of W-processes. For eliciting such processes in inexperienced hatchling gallinaceous birds, objects as different as stuffed birds and a tea tray (Melzack et al., 1959), a black rectangle (Schaller and Emlen, 1963), a green box (Moltz, 1961), and either the "hawk figure" or a large black disk (Schleidt, 1961) all have been found effective. Although these investigators differ in the detailed conditions of their tests, significant factors are visual naiveté in the subjects (Melzack et al., 1959) and the increase of retinal stimulation as by swooping the object down (McNiven, 1960) or moving it toward the subject on the level (Moltz, 1961; Schaller and Emlen, 1963).

3. THE "VISUAL CLIFF"

In the visual cliff[4] phenomenon, described by Walk and Gibson (1961), both neonate precocial and young altricial vertebrates turn from a centerboard toward the "shallow" side of a situation in which a checkerboard pattern is located close below glass, but away from the "deep" side on which the same pattern is located 50 cm or more below the glass. As examples of results obtained with a series of both precocial and altricial vertebrates, both 1–4-day-old chicks and 1-month-old kittens in their first tests turned to the shallow side in more than three fourths of the cases, but always backed up and displayed other signs of disturbance when placed on the glass over the deep side.

Although visual experience can modify this response (Carr and Mc-Guigan, 1964), it appears in dark-raised animals and the findings of Walk and Gibson justify their conclusion that *motion parallax* is the main factor differentiating these responses, without specific visual experience as a necessary factor. This means that, as the visually naive animal moves between the test surfaces, the near one is seen as relatively unchanged whereas the deep one is seen as more in flux the greater its distance.

This of course emphasizes the chief visual effect but leaves other necessary factors unrevealed. How it happens that strong motion parallax can be disturbing may be understood in terms of A-W theory, by which the visual sector of least motion parallax is considered equivalent to a low-intensity stimulus adequate for A-arousal, the sector of rapid motion parallax as equivalent to a high-intensity stimulus adequate for W-arousal and disturbance (Table 1).

From this interpretation, the visual cliff phenomenon would be expected to have its parallels in the previsual behavior of altricial vertebrates. As an example, in studying the development of orientation in

---

[4] See the chapter by Walk in [*Advances in Study of Behavior*, vol. 1, edited by D. S. Lehrman et al. New York: Academic Press, 1965].

neonate kittens we (Rosenblatt et al., 1962) found that 1-day-old subjects readily moved back into the nest corner in tests, provided the regular floor section was in place there. But with this replaced by a new floor sector, the neonate under test would stop short on reaching the border and recoil, indicating its disturbance by nose tapping at the floor, by vocalizing and not moving forward.

This last example, although involving nonvisual experience as a principal factor, bears a significant resemblance to both the "visual cliff" and the "hawk effect" reactions. In each of these cases, without specific experience of the event, a sudden quantitative change from attractive stimulation adequately arouses W-processes and disturbance in the animal.

C. Equivalence and Quantitative Stimulative Effects in Lower Vertebrates

The idea is well supported that different types of visual and other stimuli can force approach or withdrawal in lower vertebrates on a quantitative basis and equivalently according to stimulus intensity (Schneirla, 1956, 1959). Thus small moving objects of various types generally arouse (from fish, amphibians, reptiles, and birds) a rapid head-advancing response, interpreted as a generalized vertebrate head-lunge reaction (Maier and Schneirla, 1935). Honigmann (1945) demonstrated that object movement, also background movement (with the object stationary), are equivalent for this response in lizards (*Lacerta viridis*), and von Schiller (1933), testing minnows (*Phoxinus* sp.) with a conditioning procedure, made the disappearance and reappearance of a lighted bar within $\frac{1}{20}$ sec equivalent to the actual movement of this object.

In an experiment with lizards of *Lacerta* spp., Ehrenhardt (1937) presented on two-pronged stimulus forks various paired combinations of items from a series of visual stimuli ranging from a disk to a cross. Finding that in free tests the disk was snapped at most, the square less, and the cross least frequently, he then attempted to train the animals against this preference order. Although the disk now was always presented with a quinine-treated mealworm and the cross with an edible one, no subject substantially reduced the proportion of its lunges at the disk in hundreds of trials. For this animal, therefore, the disk is a potent stimulus for eliciting the lunge, its effect resisting adverse training. With a similar method, Wagner (1932) had demonstrated a comparably strong tendency in these lizards to lunge at green disks as against disks of other spectral values.

Local and general approach movements often occur in the same episode as well as separately in lower vertebrates in response to repeated low-intensity stimuli. Von Holst (1937) reported that the labrid fish

Labrichthys psittacula reacted to weak contact or to weak light by bending its anterior end toward the stimulated side with a spreading of dorsal and anal fins, and to intense stimuli in either of these fields by bending contralaterally and folding its fins. In Breder and Halpern's (1946) studies on the cyprinid *Brachydanio rerio,* the fish approached moving stimuli such as a black rectangle up to a certain size, but above that value began to retreat. In more than 100 trials, the response to movement of cards larger than 32 sq in was withdrawal, whereas smaller sizes increasingly elicited approach responses culminating in a consistent approach at 4 sq in.

To the continued movement of small stimuli, numerous fishes, amphibians, and reptiles respond by first turning the eyes and head and then the body—holding the stimulus centered retinally—then by lunging forward and snapping at the object. Other things equal, tongue flicking occurs with the smallest moving objects, the body lunge with summation or with increased stimulus size up to values that begin to elicit withdrawal (Eibl-Eibesfeldt, 1951). There is a distinct quantitative aspect in these relationships, in which extrinsic variables such as intensity, size, duration, and rate of movement are equivalent one to another in arousing head-advancing and related species-typical actions (Seitz, 1940). Evidence on the equivalence of stimulus factors such as these for the lunging-snapping responses of toads (*Bufo* sp.) has been reported by Honigmann (1945) and Freisling (1948).

Modifications demonstrated for such responses in the adults of these lower vertebrates include some discrimination of edible objects from others that force rejection through their tactual or gustatory effects, as well as inhibitory or facilitative changes according to attainability or individual condition. Endogenous facilitation is greatest when the individual is hungriest; then the extrinsic quantitative values can be the least that ever elicit the responses. In fishes, which as juveniles snap readily at small objects but seem generally to require many trials to inhibit snapping at inedible objects or at movement behind glass, hunger tends strongly to oppose the effects of training. Much the same conditions seem to hold for frogs.

The developmental basis of such patterns in these lower vertebrates and the manner in which changing relationships of extrinsic and endogenous factors may be involved are not well known. Although the larvae of both urodele (Moore and Welch, 1940) and anuran (Munn, 1940) amphibians have been conditioned to simple visual stimulus changes, to my knowledge no transfer across metamorphosis has yet been demonstrated. Some progress of considerable theoretical interest has been made with birds, however, as we shall see.

D. *Nonvisual Embryonic Antecedents of Approach-Withdrawal Processes in Birds*

Even the traditional force of the concept of innate patterns cannot hide the fact that all behavior develops. Oviparous birds and oviparous reptiles offer promising material, as results obtained with them seem to reveal a perspective of developing embryonic functions. In the chick embryo, an early stage of a progressive relationship between endogenous and somatic processes is indicated by Waddington's (1937) finding that, near the end of the second day of incubation, early heart action affects circulation so that the embryo's anterior axis twists leftward. This postural change normally causes the left side of the head to touch the yolk sac as the right side is raised. It is from about this time, as Kuo's (1932a–e) findings indicate, that a progression of events ensues through the effects of heart function upon the embryo. Kuo concluded that, as a consequence of early postural changes, the head comes to rest against the thorax; it is consequently first passively lifted and dropped with the heartbeats, but within a few days has begun an active nodding motion, suggested by Kuo as a conditioned response to gentle pressure from the thorax each time it is raised. After the sixth day, an increased responsiveness of the head is marked by a concurrence of head movements with periodic yolk-sac pressure, also with the contact of toes against the head during occasional flexions of a leg (Kuo, 1932b, c).

A wider responsiveness of the chick to stimulation, with signs of a progressive neural organization, is next indicated by an alternate opening and closing of the beak as the head nods. After the ninth day, fluid enters the mouth as bill clapping occurs with the head action, and the swallowing of this fluid may well reinforce the action. On the 17th day when the head, now more mobile and with more room to move, occasionally lifts and thrusts forward, this action is clearly followed by opening and clapping of the bill. The entire set of acts then would appear excitable by somatic and endogenous stimulation, perhaps independently as well as jointly. The possibility is worth noting that, as the retina is first electrically excitable late on the 17th day (Peters et al., 1958), diffuse light penetrating the egg may then also begin to exert some effect upon action.

The developmental course of stimulation and action may begin earlier in the vertebrate embryo and may be much more complex than has been realized. A postulation from the evidence (Kuo, 1932a–e; Orr and Windle, 1934) is that, as a consequence of the series of events described, the actions of advancing, turning, or raising the head to gentle contact assume a role as facilitators of endogenous A-processes which may be a weighty factor in development. The evidence suggests that reactivity of the head increases significantly to low-intensity contact with soft, yielding tissues in the environs. In the described stages, through steady or repeated contact with these tissues, the embryo's anterior may increase in its effectiveness as an overt agency maintaining or at times increasing postural and visceral A-processes. Head reactivity to low-intensity contact may thus be not only the potentially dominant overt component of the A-system, but also a major factor underlying a central neural control of the A-system and its arousal (see Bykov, 1957). The A-system, as its functions are outlined for birds, may be the prototype of that in mammals (Section V, B and C).

III. ROLE OF EXTRINSIC SIMULATION IN EARLY APPROACH-WITHDRAWAL RESPONSES

A. Local Approach Responses in Birds: Gaping and Pecking

Neonate altricial birds are normally fed by the parents through a nestling period in which the bill-gaping response predominates (Lehrman, 1955a). The gaping response is at first given to a wide variety of low-intensity mechanical stimuli, such as contact with bill or head, shaking of the nest, sounds, and air currents, as Holzapfel (1939) reported for the Starling (*Sturnus vulgaris*), Schaller and Emlen (1961) for the Common Grackle (*Quiscalus quiscula*), Impekoven (1962) for the Reed Warbler (*Acrocephalus scirpaceus*), and Tinbergen and Kuenen (1939) for thrushes. In time, however, during the initial nonvisual stage the range of adequate stimuli narrows considerably, until the slightest nest shaking or bill contact produces the response.

After a little more than a week, visual stimuli begin to be effective for gaping reactions, starting with moving stimuli such as a finger or a stick within a general range of sizes and rates. Tinbergen and Kuenen (1939), from their study on hatchling thrushes (*Turdus merula* and *T. ericetorum*), distinguished between visual stimuli with a "releasing" effect (e.g., a moving stick) and stimuli with a "directing" effect (e.g., a small black disk atop a larger black disk). The difference, however, may be one between stages of increasing differentiation. Lehrman (1953), in fact, from tests with nestling Red-winged Blackbirds (*Agelaius phoeniceus*), suggested that the parent's form may become effective through being seen regularly during feedings in the late nonvisual stage, when the eyes begin to open briefly during gaping responses to bill contact. In this situation, a conditioning to specific visual stimuli is a strong possibility. In their study on nestling grackles, Schaller and Emlen (1961) found that although at first a wide range of visual artifacts elicited gaping, after about

200 hours these failed increasingly although gaping to the parent continued. In these cases, a learning reinforced by A-processes as well as by feeding is indicated.

The pecking of neonate precocial birds, as is well known, may be elicited soon after hatching by small, moving visual stimuli (Shepard and Breed, 1913; Cruze, 1938). Investigations to be cited show that such stimuli are effective on a naive visual basis, prior to feeding.

The pecking of dark-raised, unfed White Rock chicks was tested by Rheingold and Hess (1957) with an array of six visual stimuli in an arc, each below a circular opening of about 2.5-cm diameter. In 67 responses by 3-day-old chicks before drinking had occurred, the frequency of pecking was: mercury, 26; plastic, 19; blue water, 12; water, 8; metal, 8; and red water, 0. To show the potency of this reaction, these same chicks, after 4 days of drinking experience and a final 12 hours without water, pecked at the stimuli in much the same order. Brightness of reflecting surface, considered by the investigators the principal attractive property, was even more effective when combined with movement.

Still other factors may elicit pecking in naive chicks. Engelmann's (1941) results with mash-raised Bantam pullets suggested a tendency to peck at rounded grains in preference to other shapes. But Altevogt (1953), Curtius (1954), and Rettler (1960), although confirming his results for size preferences, obtained negative evidence for shape. As concerned size, Curtius obtained preference norms for diameters of 5 mm in turkeys and 2.5 mm in chicks. Comparisons of results for "shape" are rendered difficult by differences in method and in conditions, such as age and experience of the subjects, with feeding prior to testing or in the tests a frequently uncertain variable.

An initial "shape" factor may be involved, however. In a test by Fantz (1957), groups of White Rock chicks, tested in pairs on their second day and before any feeding, were presented with combinations of two or more flat and solid objects differing in shape. Excluding trials in which chicks pecked at the stimuli equally or did not respond, most of the pairs pecked more frequently at the rounded figure in both flat and solid forms than at the angular one. Accentuation of the rounded aspect was a factor, since group differences were as striking for the disk and triangle as raised figures as they were with these as flat figures in the test that followed.

These results indicate that precocial birds (as with lizards in Ehrenhardt's study) give their head-lunge response more readily to rounded than to angular objects. In another of Fantz's experiments, an introductory period of feeding on rounded grains strengthened the tendency to peck at rounded figures in tests, whereas introductory feeding on angular grains weakened this tendency. It should be noted, however, that the main factor in modifying the visual responses may have been the influence of throat contact and gustatory effects favoring rounded grains as against angular grains in the training period.

With respect to initial differences in pecking at colored stimuli, Altevogt (1953), among others, reached a negative conclusion, and Curtius (1954) attributed indications of distinctions among wavelength stimuli to background contrast. But Schaefer and Hess (1959b), who considered color an effective variable under their conditions, found yellow by far the most attractive hue for the early pecking responses of Vantress broilers. The order of preference for pecking, however, was the reverse of that obtained by them with the same hues presented in larger disks in distance tests (Figure 28).

B. Stimulative Basis of Early Locomotor Approach Responses in Birds

As we have seen, reptiles and other lower vertebrates lunge at stimuli of given general properties; young birds respond to comparable stimuli with gaping or pecking. Related actions are those of approaching and following attractive stimuli, observed by Spalding (1873) and Heinroth (1910) and described by Lorenz (1935) in connection with the phenomenon called "imprinting." The initial approach response, distinguished theoretically from other actions in the sequence (Section V, A), will be discussed here.

In studies reviewed recently by Fabricius (1962), Hinde (1962), and Salzen (1962), investigators have found rather different visual stimuli effective for eliciting the early locomotor approaches of many precocial birds. Any characteristic tendencies in such responses are of course relevant to the hypothesis of innate schemata, if it can be shown that specific experience is not a factor. Lorenz (1935, 1957), from his observations, described two different species tendencies: (1) a "correlative type," exemplified by the Greylag Goose (*Anser anser*), in which a wide range of objects including a walking man could elicit approach and following, and (2) a "mosaic type," exemplified by the Curlew (*Numenius arquata*) and the Godwit, in both of which naive young are reported as following their parents but fleeing from a man in motion. It seemed to Lorenz that the latter type, in contrast to the first, must possess highly differentiated "innate perceptual patterns."

But Fabricius (1962) has emphasized the finding of Seitz (1949) that a naive young Curlew will approach and follow a man provided that *only* the man's head is first seen, whereas the bird flees if the man is first seen at full length. The aspects of stimulation for the initial approach thus seem not to be qualitatively distinctive for either species, although the range of object size is evidently smaller for the curlew than for the Greylag Goose for this response. The stimulus size range for Mallard Ducks also seems to be wide, as with the Greylag Goose, since the ducklings will approach and follow a variety of moving objects of sizes from those of a walking man down to a box 4 cm in diameter, with still smaller objects pecked at or not responded to (Fabricius and Boyd, 1954). Hence Lorenz's distinction seems to need a reinterpretation.

Within general limits of size and rate of motion, naive precocial birds seem to approach a great variety of objects. Fabricius (1951) reported the neonates of Mallards and diving ducks approaching objects as different as a man and models of their own or of other species and small boxes, especially if these test objects were in motion. In comparable tests by Ramsay (1951), young Muscovy ducklings approached and followed very different stimuli including a green box and a football. Fabricius and Boyd (1954) reported that ducklings on their first day approached and followed white and brown boxes and a balloon of 14-cm diameter. Ramsay and Hess (1954), Jaynes (1956), Moltz and Rosenblum (1958), and others have reported approach responses by neonate ducklings and chicks to moving objects ranging from boxes and cylinders of various colors, shapes, and sizes to adult models of their own and other species.

These results indicate that the range of visual stimuli effective for eliciting approach in presumably naive precocial birds is fairly wide, and that the aspects of stimulation adequate for eliciting approach in most if not all precocial birds may be not specific (i.e., dependent upon the *kind* of object involved) but, rather, generalized. It would seem that the initial approach responses of these birds do not involve qualitative aspects, but that ranges of size, intensity, and rate of movement are effective as quantitative variables.

In the course of time, investigators increased their precautions to ensure that the neonates were visually naive (i.e., uninfluenced by previous *visual* experience) by keeping them in dark containers from the time of hatching to their first tests. With this preparation, Schaefer and Hess (1959a) tested the approach responses of Vantress broilers with pairs from the series of objects represented in Figure 28, in trials lasting 17 minutes each. The plain ball proved most attractive and the other objects significantly less attractive, as gauged in terms of the distance each was followed in any one of the three colors under test. In other tests, a stuffed Brown Leghorn rooster proved less attractive than any of these stimuli. A comparable preference for a plain disk as against one with projections is indicated by one of Gray's (1961) findings with White Rock chicks. Barred Rock × Rhode Island Red chicks tested by Abercrombie and James (1961) in postnatal days 1 and 2 were attracted to a stationary turquoise ball presented alone; this ball, however, was still more attractive to another group of chicks given the same stimulus against a flickering light. Thus, for general approach, as for pecking, *round* objects seem to be specifically attractive to neonate precocial birds. The effective size for pecking is about 2.5-cm diameter or less, whereas for general approach the stimulus can be 15 cm or larger according to the distance and other conditions.

Results have differed concerning the attraction of spectral hues. Jaynes (1956) reported a green cube to be somewhat more attractive than a red cylinder for 1–4-day-old New Hampshire Red chicks, but Smith and Hoyes (1961) obtained negative results in tests of 18–30-hour-old Light Sussex × Brown Leghorn chicks with equal-intensity flickering disks of red, green, and white. In neither of these studies, however, was a range of spectral values tested. Schaefer and Hess (1959b) exposed naive chicks during their first day to successive 17-minute tests, in each of which one of a series of hues and brightnesses was presented on a ball of 7-inch diameter. In these distance tests, blue and red were followed the most, with yellow last (Figure 28), reversing the order of attractiveness for these stimuli in pecking tests. Because equal brightnesses were used in this study, the results support the hypothesis of a naive differential attraction in chicks to wavelengths.[5] Gray (1961), who tested neonate White Rock chicks with painted disks, found no differences until the second day, when red and yellow were attractive; green, blue, and white were not significantly attractive. This is a complex matter, of course, dependent upon subjects and procedure as well as upon the physical conditions of stimulation used by different experimenters.

Evidence that flicker attracts insects, and that the pecten introduces this factor in many birds (Menner, 1938; Pumphrey, 1948), suggests also that this variable may be attractive to naive vertebrates (Schneirla, 1956). James (1959) supported this hypothesis with his finding that Barred Plymouth Rock chicks, from their second day, responded increasingly with approach to a flickering light as against a steady light. A different breed tested by Smith (1960) was similarly responsive from about the 16th postnatal hour. Flicker rate is a factor, as James (1959) found disks flickering in pulses of 1 sec each more attractive than disks flickering in ¼-sec or in 5-sec pulses.

The influence of size of the flickering area is shown by the fact (Smith, 1960; Smith and Hoyes, 1961) that, in distance tests, disks flickering at intensities of 0.6–1.0 foot candle (in ½-sec pulses) were more attractive at diameters of 15–28 cm than at smaller sizes. The intensity of flicker is significant also, since Smith and Hoyes (1961) found that when the total light is the same—e.g., with a 15-cm disk of 0.03 foot candle and one of 5 cm at 0.24 foot candle—the frequencies of approach are much the

---

[5] It is still possible that the psychological effects may have been to sensory *intensity* differences and not to wavelength differences as such, since these experimenters did not control for the equivalence of brightness in their stimuli.

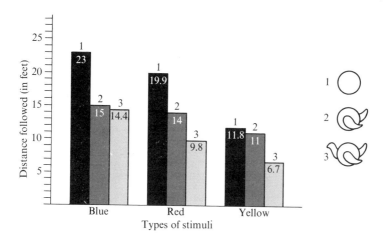

FIGURE 28
Models used by Schaefer and Hess (1959a) in testing the reactions of young chicks in 17-minute periods 1 day after imprinting sessions. Numbers above bars indicate the model used in each type of test; numbers within bars indicate the distance each type of stimulus was followed in the tests.

same. But Smith (1960) found a flickering disk of 0.36 foot candle more attractive to naive chicks than one of 0.002 foot candle.

The range of flicker intensity has yet to be tested for approach vis-à-vis withdrawal, as for chicks which are evidently somewhat light-adapted these stimuli seem relatively low in the scale. Another significant need is for studies of *irregular* as compared with regular flicker at the same intensities (see Table 1).

Although the role of audition in vertebrate development generally may be secondary to that of vision, it is important and, at times, may be crucial. Fabricius (1951) noted that whereas in man-imprinted Tufted Ducks (*Aythya fuligula*) no specific visual cues could be discerned at early ages, the ducklings reacted to the keeper's voice by hurrying in his direction although not to other voices. In precocial birds also (Fabricius and Boyd, 1954), early approaches to a seen object are facilitated by low, repetitive sounds.

Detailed studies were carried out by Collias (1952) on sound production and sound reactions in neonate chicks. The hatchlings were soon attracted by (1) short, repetitive tones at low frequencies; (2) recordings of light, repeated and regular pencil tapping; (3) clucking, records of clucking, or human imitations of this sound; and, finally, (4) the so-called "pleasure notes" typical of young chicks in equable situations. From a few minutes after hatching, the chicks typically responded to all of these sounds by producing the last type themselves and often by moving toward the source.

The chick's pleasure notes are a series of short, predominantly low-pitched tones of regular timing, all at the same low intensity at an even output of 4–5 per second. These sounds were given regularly to low-intensity stimuli such as the slow movement of a finger, more often when the motion and the tapping sound were combined (Collias and Joos, 1953). Artificially presented tones of the same even, low intensity and regularity were similarly effective, as were organ tones of this description at low frequencies. But increasing the duration, the intensity, or the predominant pitch too far could abruptly reduce the attractive effect and soon reverse the nature and direction of the response.

From his studies on ducklings of various species, Klopfer (1959) reported the neonates as attracted to a number of different sounds but to no one particular sound initially, concluding that ". . . no unlearned preferences for any particular auditory signal seemed to exist." But, as Collias's results indicate, this conclusion cannot be correct (at least for the Franklin's Gull) as concerns the neonatal effects of low-intensity, repetitive sounds against others.

In studies of neonate Peking ducklings by Gottlieb and Klopfer (1962), responsiveness to visual and to auditory stimuli was found different according to the conditions of developmental age (i.e., days from the initiation of incubation) or of experience (i.e., group rearing vs. isolation). In an initial exposure of 20 minutes to a moving decoy from which a repetitive sound issued, more of the isolated than group-reared ducklings were attracted, and responded more strongly. In tests within 10–14 hours after the training, the isolated subjects showed a difference not indicated in the group-reared subjects, in that those trained at the early developmental age of 26.5–27.5 days were more responsive to the auditory stimulus, those trained at the later age of 27.5–28.5 days were more responsive to the visual stimulus. Thus, auditory and visual stimuli both influence the approach responses of ground-nesting ducklings, although their relative potencies depend upon factors both of developmental age and of rearing (cf. Klopfer and Gottlieb, 1962).

In hole-nesting ducks, auditory stimuli play a critical role in early behavior. Gottlieb (1963) studied the exodus of young Wood Ducks (*Aix sponsa*), in which the nestlings first crawl upward in the dark to the nest hole and then leap down to the ground or water where they soon trail after the calling parent. The nest cavity is dark, hence crawling upward to the patch of light presented by the nest hole is specifically aroused by the parent's repetitive sound from outside. The ducklings evidently are attracted to the nest hole when first aroused by the sound and, once there, by the orienting effect of the parent's sound and moving figure together.

In Table 1 are listed a number of stimulative characteristics which, as evidence cited in this section indicates, are largely equivalent for arousing neonatal A-reactions. Presumably, the first overt response aroused is that of head advancing, accompanied by a phasic increase of endogenous A-processes as indicated by pleasure notes and nestling on head contact

TABLE 1

Stimuli equivalent for neural-input effects adequate to arouse approach or withdrawal in neonate vetebrates.

Types of effective stimuli	Corresponding neural-input effects	
	Equivalent for arousal of A-processes	Equivalent for arousal of W-processes
Proximal	Tactuo-proprioceptive, chemoceptive patterns of low magnitude, regular timing	Tactuo-proprioceptive, chemoceptive patterns of high magnitude, irregular timing
Distance		
Visual		
Succession	Gradual changes, regular intervals (e.g., *regular* visual flicker), low motion-parallax	Abrupt changes, irregular intervals (e.g., *irregular* visual flicker), high motion-parallax
Intensity	Low to low-medium, or decreasing	Medium-high to high, sharply or irregularly increasing
Contour	Rounded (e.g., a disk)	Angular, abrupt corners
Movement	Regular; low to medium rate; *away* from subject	Irregular; high rate; *toward* subject
Size	Small to medium-small	Large
Auditory		
Succession	Regular	Irregular
Intensity	Low to low-medium	High
Frequency	Medium-low to low; regular	Medium to high; irregular
Pattern	Simple	Complex; irregular ("noisy")

(Collias, 1952; Salzen, 1962). The processes whereby these embryonic reactions become aroused by visual and auditory stimulation, and the general trend of their extension and further specialization, will be discussed in Sections III, D, IV, and V.

C. Stimulative Basis of Early Withdrawal Responses

The idea has often been expressed that the disturbance and escape reactions of birds to certain stimuli are aroused on the basis of an "innate recognition" of natural enemies and strange objects (e.g., Nice and ter

Pelkwyk, 1941). A very different hypothesis, however, is favored by the evidence reviewed here.

Collias and Joos (1953), in systematic observations on neonate chicks from the time of hatching, noted that they were disturbed from the first by "harsh" sounds, with the frequency and scope of response increasing in time (cf. Salzen, 1962). The adequate auditory stimuli for such responses were abrupt, loud, extended in duration, irregular ("unsegmented"), and rich in high frequencies, as were the recorded sounds of sneezing, chair scraping, and horn blaring. To such sounds, neonate chicks showed signs of disturbance such as cessation of pleasure notes, frequent "distress calling," and, later, escape reactions.

Collias (1952) and Collias and Joos (1953) recorded from newly hatched chicks a typical "distress call," a loud, protracted peeping repeated only 2–3 times per second at descending frequencies, a sign of disturbance which they significantly attributed to ". . . loss of contact with the egg shell and . . . cooling of the moist down." These excited calls, evidently attributable to disturbances incident to hatching, are frequent during the first hour but then decrease as the neonate settles. This type of call, which as Collias notes is given to conditions—such as isolation, cold, pain, restraint, or hunger—that inhibit pleasure calls, thus seems to indicate the episodic arousal of W-processes. Even during the first day, chicks give this call persistently after having been changed to a new pen (Hess, 1959) or when influenced by temperatures well above or below the body norm (Kaufman and Hinde, 1961).

Although naturally hatched birds are likely to be protected by darkness, artificially hatched ones are frequently disturbed by exposure to bright light or to sudden movement. Such disturbances may intrude even under laboratory test conditions (Moltz, 1961). These matters soon change, however, as an experiment by Salzen (1962) with day-old chicks indicates. In a group of 41 chicks tested at 24–36 hours with a 3-minute exposure to an intermittently moving box, responses of the pleasure type (e.g., contentment calls, nestling, approach) were given by 26 of the subjects at the beginning of the test and by 30 at the end, in contrast to responses of the fear type (e.g., distress calls, crouching, flight) in 15 of the subjects at the beginning and 11 at the end.

The proneness of subjects to such behavior depends upon posthatching experience to an appreciable extent. In this same experiment of Salzen's, another set of neonates, that had spent their first 24 hours grouped with other chicks, mainly gave W-type responses as contrasted with the predominance of A-type responses in isolated chicks. The fact that chicks grouped for the first 6 hours only and then isolated were not very different in these respects from the 24-hour isolates seems to indicate a lesser responsiveness at first, but increasing after the first few hours, to experiences affecting reactions to moving stimuli.

An experiment by Schaller and Emlen (1963) recalls the "hawk test" (Section II, D). In tests on hatchlings of five species of gallinaceous birds and three species of waterfowl, the stimulus object (most often a black rectangle of 12×22 cm) was advanced toward and close to the subject from the end of the nest box (a maximal distance of 1 meter) at a rate of 25 cm per second. Eight grades of response were noted, from "no response," "watching object," and "stepping back" to "dashing away" and "frantic running or jumping." From the first signs of disturbance, which were generally detectable as distress calls around 5 hours, overt W-type responses increased to a highly excited, variable "avoidance" as the common response after 2–35 days. Although the authors emphasize "strangeness" as the feature accounting for their results, the hypothesis of "sudden retinal impact," offered in Section II, B as adequate for W-process arousal in the "hawk effect," seems more applicable. Under their conditions, variations in specific aspects such as shape and size of the stimulus had no apparent effect upon the response, which therefore seemed to be maximally aroused even by the relatively low values of these aspects in the stimulus field.

D. Transition from Prenatal to Neonatal Approach-Withdrawal Reactions

At this juncture, a set of mechanisms considered essential for the transition from fetal A-W functions to neonatal behavior may be postulated.

The species-typical vertebrate reaction of advancing or turning the head toward low-intensity stimulation rests not upon neural maturation alone, but upon progressive structural-functional processes to which growth is one contributor (Sections I, A, B; II, D). Through a series of stages, this overt action and its afferent feedback come to be the focal components of the A-system, with which accessory actions such as bill clapping, swallowing, and a complex of A-processes become associated. The normal A-type components are those optimal for species development and these, through stimulus integrations, come to be smoothly and regularly facilitated by low-intensity feedback patterns of the A-system including its mechanosensory and proprioceptive components. The organization and integrity of the A-system in this regular development-sustaining function—its *tonic* function—afford a basis for the continued organization and differentiation of its component parts.

An extension of great importance is the facilitation of anterior-body turning-to reactions by A-processes under episodic arousal by surges of low-intensity stimulation (Table 1). In earlier sections, as a basis for this point, discussion has centered on the manner in which head-advancing reactions in birds and lower vertebrates come to be elicited by stimuli which are quantitatively equivalent for A-arousal. With repetition, such a low-intensity stimulus effect may become *phasic* (cf. Section I, A) as a specific excitant of A-processes. Gottlieb's (1963b) studies of wood ducks under natural conditions suggest two ways in which auditory stimuli may thus become effective. The duck, sitting on her nearly full-term eggs, utters her call continuously from the early stages of egg pipping. As analyses of recordings show, the repetitive sound is first very low, but accelerates in rate and intensity to the time of exodus about 20–30 hours later. Further investigations indicate that the *necessary* factor in the neonate's later responsiveness to the adult call, however, may be a repetitive vocalization by the embryo itself for some time before hatching. Gottlieb (1963a) has obtained evidence that a self-stimulative process may thereby function which is essential for the neonate's approach to and following of the parental call in the exodus.

The formation of a basis for phasic A-processes in the embryo may be emphasized by a brief review. From the myogenic stage, the embryo may acquire phasic A-responses through early integrations by which both current postures and visceral processes can be sustained or increased under the control of low-intensity mechanical stimulation and of afferent feedback effects (Schneirla, 1956, 1957). Expanding relationships of action and function are indicated for A-processes by Kuo's (1932a–e) observation that bill opening and the consequent swallowing of amniotic fluid, first occurring incidental to head movement, seem to gradually form a pattern. Through such occurrences, the gustatory and other afferent effects of these actions can function as agents reinforcing a progressive neural control of the head and bill actions by extrinsic stimuli.

The arousal of somatic-visceral A-processes as phasic responses to repeated low-intensity stimulative episodes in the embryo is suggested by evidence such as Collias's (1952) observation that contentment notes may be heard from the unopened chick egg when it is gently turned or warmed, and that occasional distress notes from within a (cooling) pipped egg are stopped when clucking sounds are played. From what has been suggested, extrinsic stimuli such as clucking may owe their potency not only to their quantitative effects as such (Table 1) but also to conditioning through self-stimulation and through parental stimuli prior to hatching. As I have suggested (Schneirla, 1956), processes of mechanical and auditory self-stimulation may provide one basis for the attraction of naive isolated hatchlings to species mates as in Pattie's (1936) and Ohba's (1962) tests. The role of embryonic self-stimulative processes seems clearly indicated by Gottlieb's findings, mentioned above.

The A-system, with its somatic and visceral components appreciably organized, thus seems normally available for adequate extrinsic arousal (Table 1) after hatching or birth. The occurrence of pleasure notes in late embryo chicks indicates that A-processes may increase at times of reduced tension, as when a chilled egg is warmed or a postural change occurs as the egg is turned. Significantly, disturbances in neonate chicks such as those reported by Brückner (1933) to loud noises or loss of equilibrium may be quieted by applying a gentle, firm pressure against the top of the head—a low-intensity stimulus which presumably has often stabilized A-processes in the embryo. Several authors (e.g., Hess, 1959; Moltz, 1961) have noted that the act of *nestling,* an active pressing of the head against an object, quiets neonate subjects that have been disturbed. Under natural conditions, this is the dominant neonatal response to parental incubation.

The functions discussed here for the A-system are presumably antecedent to those which at later stages constitute the basis of the animal's approach-following responses (Section V). We now turn to the neural aspects of this transition.

IV. HYPOTHESES OF NEURAL FUNCTIONS BASIC TO EARLY APPROACH-WITHDRAWAL RESPONSES

A. Factors of Neural Input Adequate for Neonatal Approach-Withdrawal Arousal

To the primitive vertebrate nervous system, characterized by small, slow-conducting fibers, more highly evolved systems have added mechanisms which although admitting great modifications have not displaced the old types entirely (Herrick, 1924; Bishop, 1959). The new organizations, dominated by larger, faster-conducting units, although gaining vastly in fine discrimination and in correlation, also possess mechanisms such as the reticular and limbic formations and some cutaneous and nociceptive elements which may be basic in embryonic function. These, although "primitive" in the sense that they resemble corresponding structures in lower vertebrates, nevertheless have changed appreciably in their form in relation to later-evolved structures such as cortex. Davis (1961) has suggested that cutaneous and vibratory sensitivity may bear the same relationship to audition, for example, that Head's protopathic tactual sense bears to the specialized, epicritic sense of touch. In vertebrate functional development, early stages evidently are dominated by the first type of conductile mechanism, with the superior discriminations and correlations of the second type appearing to increasing extents in phyletically advanced animals, although arising more slowly in ontogenesis than the first.

These considerations are relevant to the idea that a tactuo-proprioceptive integration opens the way for the organization of somatic actions such as head advancing both with tonic and with phasic A-processes. As a consequence *new* stimuli, equivalent in essential respects (Table 1) to those earlier controlling these somatic actions, can elicit A-system functions after hatching or birth.

In the preceding discussion a basis was formed for the postulation, suggested by findings such as those of Coghill and Kuo, that in neonatal vertebrates a diffusion of impulses from aroused optic centers reaches and activates somatic afferent centers, exciting functions controlled by the latter in embryonic states (Schneirla, 1959). The low-intensity visual and other stimuli involved owe their adequacy to afferent output effects quantitatively equivalent to those of general-sensory stimuli which assume control of A-processes in the embryo. Through this link, patterns of head advancing and A-processes facilitating them are now susceptible to activation by equivalent exteroceptive stimuli, such as those listed in Table 1.

Evidence on the conditions of stimulative equivalence effective in the neonate's initial responses to visual stimuli particularly, with the behavioral evidence, constitutes a basis for characterizing initial environmental effects as *quantitative* rather than qualitative. Grundfest (1959) has generalized for all modalities that the input or receptive elements of excitable cells respond to specific stimuli with an electrogenesis proportional to the strength of the stimulus and equalling the stimulus in duration. (The next stage, conduction of the effect, is an all-or-none phenomenon.) Simple relationships between stimulus intensity and other receptor functions to output and to central effects cannot be assumed for active organisms at any stage. But the evidence (Eccles, 1953; Granit, 1955; Rosenblith, 1961) supports the assumption that low-intensity stimuli owe their potency for eliciting A-processes to the setting up of afferent output patterns of low fiber-number and volley-rate values adequate to meet the low thresholds of these processes (Maier and Schneirla, 1935, pp. 314 ff.; Schneirla, 1959). The essentials are typified by data such as those of Kuffler (1953) on the relationship between stimulus intensity and frequency of the peripheral optic discharge and of Katsuki et al. (1958) on the comparable increases in peripheral auditory discharge with increasing stimulative intensities. Doubtless the distortions of centripetal discharge patterns by the effects of concurrent afferent or endogenous events, inevitable in research on adult stages (Horn, 1962; Rosenblith, 1961), are potent in the neonate also. The behavior evidence for early postnatal stages, however, seems to support the general terms of A-W theory well.

Results on vertebrate behavior in neonatal stages indicate an appreciable degree of equivalence among sensory modalities in their neural discharge properties meeting the arousal thresholds of A- and W-processes. These relationships may be somewhat comparable to those described by Davis (1961) as an "overlapping of fields" in adult stages. The initially adequate stimuli for A-system arousal seem to be generalized (i.e., non-specific, nonqualitative—Section III, B), the consequences for action depending upon quantitative afferent-discharge effects rather than upon the nature of the object. So long as the afferent output is low in magnitude, regular, and only gradually increased or decreased, head advancing can occur in an episodic A-system arousal which on repetition becomes phasic and expands into locomotor approach. In Table 1 are listed some of the chief aspects of afferent discharge adequate for A-arousal, basic to the attraction for neonates of stimuli as different as flicker, low motion-parallax, and a disk for vision, and low, repetitive sounds for audition.

But suddenly increasing the effective intensity of any stimulus, as by presenting a noise or by moving the visual stimulus *toward* the neonate, raises the mass of the neural input to the W-system threshold. Various stimuli of this type are listed in Table 1, all of them sharing potential input properties, such as *high magnitude, irregularity,* or *abrupt change,* adequate for eliciting high-threshold W-processes.

Some problems in early behavior may be considered in their relationship to afferent discharge effects. As vision soon becomes dominant in most precocial vertebrates, a tendency is noticeable for other responses to follow head turning toward the stimulus, centering the visual image on the fovea. This behavior, which takes place in response to low-intensity stimuli, has been insufficiently investigated. Two mechanisms may be postulated for its occurrence: (1) the arousal by neural diffusion of head-advancing reactions and other phasic A-processes already under tactuo-proprioceptive control, and (2) the reinforcement by A-processes of those body, head, and eye movements whose stimuli occur contiguously with the retinal centering of the stimulus.

Evidence has been cited in Section III, A that small, rounded objects as well as gleaming or moving spots attract the lunge responses of lower vertebrates and the pecking responses of neonatal chicks. These reactions, which seem to have similar A-system bases, are forced by the afferent discharge effects of the aforementioned stimuli, into which the research of Hartline (1938), Kuffler (1953), and Granit (1955) on retinal functions has given insight. Barlow (1953) found that the receptive fields of single ganglion cells in the retina of the frog are concentric and of a size fitted well by the image of a fly at 5 cm. Small, bright objects nearby seem to exert a comparable effect on the chick retina. The better the image fits the elementary receptive field, the higher the attraction, as the superiority of rounded over angular objects for the head-advancing responses of lizards, frogs, and chicks would indicate. The simplest reason for this seems to be that individual ganglion-cell fields are concentric, with the center of each generally negative to its periphery (Kuffler, 1953), so that although small rounded objects can elicit regular firing, angular or larger objects—by jutting into adjacent fields—set up irregular firing patterns which may result in nonresponse or in disturbance.

As the intensity, size, and frequency of small spots of light used as stimuli are made to vary, corresponding electrical changes may be detected in the retina, optic nerve, and optic centers of adult vertebrates (Adrian and Matthews, 1928; Granit, 1955). In a recent study on the frog, Maturana et al. (1960) found evidence for four classes of ganglion cells responding in distinctive ways to the movement of small contrast contours across the retina. These cells differed in their responses to rates of motion as well as to contour differences and to the "on," "off," and "on-off" properties reported by Hartline (1938). Grüsser-Cornehls et al. (1963) confirmed these results with a technique showing that the ganglion cells actually respond to successive stimulation of the same unitary field or of neighboring fields. Units in the periphery of the frog retina have higher latencies of response and also higher thresholds to the movement, the contrast, and the size properties of small dark or white spots than do central units. It is significant (Lettvin et al., 1961) that these ganglion cells differ anatomically from simple to complex both in breadth on the same level and in number of levels on which they make dendritic connections.

Although the detailed significance of these aspects of retinal function is not clear as yet (Rushton, 1962; Horn, 1962), particularly for behavioral development, it is probable that peripheral factors such as these play a much more specific role in the stereotyped behavior of lower vertebrates than in birds and mammals. Although Hubel and Weisel (1961, 1962) reported comparable concentric unitary receptive fields for both the retina and the geniculate body of the cat, their results indicate that the cat has much less differentiation and specificity in its retinal function than has the frog, but much more in its geniculate body than the frog has in its superior colliculus. In the cat, ". . . the specification of cells for complex functions is postponed to a higher level," and as a consequence there is a greater scope for changes in development. On circumstantial grounds, it is probable that birds are intermediate in developmental plasticity, closer to mammals than to lower vertebrates in this respect. This inference is supported by the relative facility with which precocial birds modify their initial forced visual responses (Section V, B), in comparison with the fixity of lower vertebrates in this respect.

The fact is that although small bright nearby objects attract the head-approach (pecking) responses of chicks, larger objects at a distance are attractive at lower intensities. This difference, together with the reversal of effective wavelength stimuli in nearby and in distance visual tests (Schaefer and Hess, 1959a, b), seems attributable to the fact that the retinal input effects of small areas at higher intensities are equivalent to those of larger areas at lower intensities (Granit, 1955).

For larger stimuli at a distance, I have noted the greater attractiveness of disks than of angular objects for neonate chicks. This comparison in terms of shape involves multiple ganglion-cell functions, hence raises new questions. In general terms, the best hypothesis would seem to be that a *disk* excites neural input effects which are simpler and more regular than those of an angular object and thus fits low A-system thresholds better. A disk, when retinally centered, would stimulate a concentric zone, whether its image fell within the *fovea,* within the *area,* or within a larger zone of the retina. Fovea, area, and retina are all concentric, and from the general facts of vertebrate retinal structure (Walls, 1942; Polyak, 1957) the working generalization may be derived that units equidistant from the center have similar functional properties, those at unequal distances different properties in proportion to differences in their locations with respect to the center. The hypothesis is sketched in Figure 29. With a retinally centered plain disk or sphere, for which background contrast would be the major factor of retinal difference, retinal elements (all) of the hypothetical type 'O' around the outer border of the stimulated zone should make uniform output contributions, and elements of type 'I' around the inner border contributions of a different kind from those of 'O' elements but all alike. So long as the object remains centered, the combined effect of all 'O' and all 'I' impulses would then form a retinal-output pattern of marked regularity. The disk, when centered, thus is attractive through exciting a neural input adequate to arouse and maintain A-processes.

Contour angularity, on the other hand, to the extent that it excited retinal elements of diversified types at more scattered contrasting borders than with the disk (Figure 29), would set up retinal output patterns of such irregularity as to adequately excite W-processes, with disturbing effects in behavior.

Visual flicker, also an attractant to neonate precocial birds, has the essential character of low intensity and of regular periodicity adequate for A-system arousal (Schneirla, 1959). Its equivalence to object movement for this effect seems based upon the efficiency of successions of stimuli or of smooth image movement over the retina to excite the same types of output. Comparably, an object movement, on the one hand, and a background movement behind the object, on the other, can equivalently elicit the amphibian lunge (Honigmann, 1945) and the pecking response in neonate birds (Collias and Collias, 1957). The fact that flicker has a special potency for many birds over object movement as such has been clarified by Pumphrey's (1948) proposal, extending the findings of Menner (1938) and of Crozier and Wolf (1943), that an intermittency effect

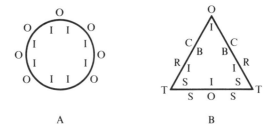

FIGURE 29

Hypothesis to account for the greater attraction of a disk than of an angular figure for neonate precocial vertebrates (cf. Fig. 28 and Table 1). A: O, I—Principal types of retinal elements firing from the outer and inner contrasting borders (respectively) of the disk. B: O, C, I, B, etc.—Principal types of retinal elements firing from the outer and inner contrasting borders of the triangle.

is accentuated each time one of a series of borders passing over the retina coincides with a shadow cast by the pecten. A contrast of this mechanism in birds with that involved in the excitation of well-spaced peripheral cells in the kitten's retina emphasizes the divergent ways in which stimulus-intermittency effects can become attractive in vertebrates.

The fact deserves emphasis, however, that if intermittent stimuli such as a flickering light are to be adequate for A-system arousal and approach, they must be relatively low in intensity (or increase gradually) and must be *regular*—or a different result may occur. Although evidence on *irregular* flicker is sparse, its potencies as a disturbance may be predicted. In vertebrates, as in certain insects (Hassenstein, 1961), increasingly irregular flicker may arouse retinal-output patterns reaching the point of a sudden "white noise" effect (Reichardt, 1961), beyond which the stimulus is adequate for a strong W-arousal.

A convenient way to emphasize the canalizing effect of afferent-output properties is through the analogy of afferent filtering mechanisms, in terms of which Marler (1961) has reviewed the evidence for sensory variables and behavior. This concept is useful for pointing out end-organ properties such as the frequency-differentiating auditory mechanisms of lower vertebrates (Davis, 1961) or retinal mechanisms responding differently to spectral stimuli (Granit, 1955). The nature of the oil droplets in vertebrate retinas may be relevant to the behavioral effects of wavelengths (Walls, 1942) and of corresponding differences in retinal electrophysiology (e.g., Muntz, 1963).

But the receptor-filtering analogy has limitations for phyletic comparisons in which, as mentioned, species differences in afferent-output properties must be appraised in terms of relative developmental plasticity. An example is offered by the study of Peters et al. (1958) on early visual functions in chicks. Although fibers of the optic nerve are myelinated 6 days before hatching (Schifferli, 1948), photic stimuli bring no electrical responses from the retina until weak spikes appear late on the 17th day. Recorded impulses are stronger on the 18th and 19th days, however, so that the retina may respond before hatching both to diffuse light reaching it through the shell and to endogenous arousal. Evidence for the facilitation of embryonic retinal responses through repeated stimulation suggests ". . . that the use of an organ, even in the embryo, is a factor in bringing it to an actual functional state, and that continued use along certain patterns may enhance a definite type of response" (Peters et al., 1958). Such effects may facilitate the transition from the embryonic condition to neonate function on this level.

B. Neural Functions Basic to the Development of Approach-Withdrawal Processes

In the embryo and early neonate, two functions of the A-system develop, evidently prior to the rise of W-processes. The first of these functions may be described as that of *tonic* or continuous involvement, on which development centers (Section I, A). From early stages, A-processes seem predominant in the embryo, which is generally exposed only to energy changes of weak or mild intensity. In contrast to the continuity of the tonic A-processes, interruptive effects then may occur rarely, as when a change is introduced by an interaction of systems developing at different rates. Thus, reactions of the vascular system to the rise of the muscular system, or of both of these to the growth of the nervous system, may introduce disruptions of W-types requiring readjustments in A-functions. An example of such a readjustment may be the development of tactual and postural integrations in the neural stage.

The second A-function may begin with brief, episodic increases in A-arousal in connection with a new developmental integration (Section II, D). *Phasic* arousals of A-processes can thus arise at hatching or birth or in the neonate, facilitating adjustments to new conditions, as in the extension of turning-to reactions into locomotor approach in a manner typical of the species.

From the embryonic to neonatal stages, both the tonic and the phasic A-functions are evidently facilitated by somesthetic feedback patterns in progressively effective ways. The characteristic of regularity in afferent output which marks somesthetic patterns in the adult (Pringle, 1962) presumably is available increasingly as a steadying influence both of developmental functions and of the postural and overt actions typical of each stage.

The phasic role of A-processes, that of facilitating overt actions such as embryonic postural adjustments and neonate nestling, is a changing one. This function, as suggested, may progress from an episodic to a phasic, more regularly patterned character. It is with the support of phasic A-processes that overt actions such as head advancing may develop into approach specializations through neonatal experience.

The diagram presented in Figure 30 emphasizes the basic roles played by both the tonic and the phasic A-functions in the normal life and readjustments of embryo and neonate. Together, these functions may form a progressively more efficient A-*system* underlying species-normal behavioral development. Deviations of these functions from the species norm of A-system dominance presumably would depend upon what exceptional conditions might force individual tensional patterns toward extremes, such as those discussed by Selye (1956).

The everyday progress of embryonic and neonatal functions appears to rest substantially upon tonic A-processes, with deviations readjusted first through episodic and then through phasic A-arousal (Figure 30). Normally, W-processes evidently arise episodically at first, becoming phasic only gradually and with an appreciable latency in the neonate (Section V, A). In the early neonate chick, a decrease in A-processes as through chilling may arouse W-processes episodically and, on repetition, in a phasic form, with effects such as quickening of circulation and increased general activity which can be adaptive. That such changes may bring about phasic A-arousal is suggested by Collias's (1952) observation that a chilling of the neonate chick elicits distress calling (i.e., W-arousal), which changes to contentment calling (i.e., A-arousal) soon after the hatchling comes into head contact with a surface or hears clucking. Here, the adaptive change may be facilitated by the concurrent action of A-stimuli and of W-arousal.

Basically the A-system and W-processes, with low and high excitation thresholds, respectively, are antagonistic and reciprocal. Salzen (1962) has discussed the occurrence of pleasure and of fear responses in neonatal chicks, which as instances of A-arousal and W-arousal, respectively, conform well to the functional terms of my A-W theory. But the suggestion after Collias (1952) that "antithetical nervous systems" are major agents at that early time assumes a degree of perceptual-central organization appropriate to a later stage. Evidence on neonatal function and behavior indicates that initially the visceral and somatic components of A-W processes are dominant, with interaction of the autonomic divisions developing slowly. As Figures 30 and 31 suggests, neonatal stages dominated by

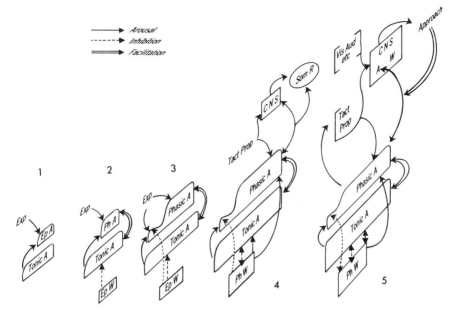

FIGURE 30
Theoretical schema for the embryonic development of vertebrate A-W processes
as a basis for neonatal approach and following (cf. Section III, D, IV, B, V, A, and
V, B). 1–4: the *embryonic* progression (Section VI, stage 1). 5: the *neonatal*
status of precocial vertebrates (Section VI, stage 2). *CNS*, central neural function;
Ep, episodically aroused processes; *Exp*, effects of stimulation from developmental
medium; *Ph*, phasic processes; *Som R*, somatic actions (e.g., head lifting); *Tact
Prop* (tactuo-proprioceptive integrations); *Vis Aud*, "new" stimuli equivalent to
Vis Aud. For definition of A-W terms, see Section I, A.
   1. Progressive *Tonic A* processes, low-threshold mechanisms central to development. At their peak, these involve occasional or sporadic increases (*Ep A*) in
certain components. Low-intensity stimuli from the developmental medium (*Exp*),
through contiguity with such increases, begin to Control *Ep A*.
   2. Repetition of contiguities of *Tonic A, Exp,* and *Ep A* increases the latter
by stages into a pattern (*Ph A*), now effectively aroused by *Exp* (e.g., tactual, proprioceptive stimuli). *Ph A* enters a relationship of reciprocal facilitation with
Tonic A. Tensional changes in development now arouse episodic *W* processes (*Ep
W*) which can partially inhibit *Tonic A* processes.
   3. Arousal and facilitative relationships between *Tonic* and *Phasic A* processes
now occur in a more smoothly patterned system in which *Exp* both arouses *Ph A* and
opposes inhibition of *Ph A* by *Ep W*. *Ep W*, although still not phasic, can now
inhibit *Ph A* directly.
   4. W processes now are phasic (*Ph W*) and capable of facilitating *Ph A* and
Tonic A processes or inhibiting them according to conditions. Somesthetic integrations (*Tact Prop*), as low-energy input effects, now can arouse *Phasic A* processes
both through autonomic and through central (*CNS*) neural channels. Neural patterns are established through which *Tact Prop* stimuli directly arouse somatic responses (*Som R*) such as head lifting or head turning.
   5. In the neonate, relations of arousal, facilitation, and inhibition between
A processes and W processes have become complicated and advanced. An outstanding neonatal event (Sections IV, B and V, A) is that "new" extrinsic stimuli
(*Vis Aud etc.*) can arouse somatic A response by eliciting *CNS* patterns previously
controlled by nonvisual (*Tact Prop*) stimuli. An extension of the embryonic
somatic responses into perceptual patterns of locomotory approach arises both
through direct neural feedback from A responses and indirect feedback from A
system facilitation (Section V).

382

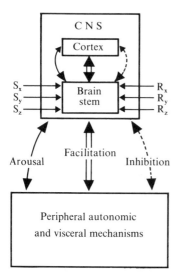

FIGURE 31
Schema of neural control in the orientative and perceptual adjustments of advanced neonate, juvenile, and adult birds and mammals (cf. Section IV, B). CNS, central nervous system; $S_{x,y,z}$ discriminated stimuli; $R_{x,y,z}$ perceptually differentiated responses. Arrows as in Figure 30. Functional advances from embryonic and neonatal conditions (Figure 30) are indicated by evidence for higher-level neural patterns, now capable of dominating and short-circuiting peripheral mechanisms in perceptual adjustments of approach or withdrawal.

peripheral and autonomic mechanisms may be essential to reach the degree of central control disclosed by the results of implanted electrode research (e.g., Olds and Olds, 1962). The functional and behavioral sequence through which central control may progress to adult conditions is suggested in the next section and has been outlined in a hypothesis relating the A-W theory to emotional development (Schneirla, 1959, p. 28 ff.). The idea is sketched for the development of perception in Figure 31.

It is in the context of behavioral ontogenesis that the rise of correlative functional patterns linking the central nervous system and the autonomic nervous systems in progressive behavioral control may be explored to best advantage. Recent advances indicate that the functions of both the limbic (MacLean, 1959) and the reticular formations (Brodal, 1957) may play significant roles in the changing ontogenetic relationships, as Lindsley (1958) has suggested for the latter in regard to perceptual development. The ontogenetic path of such functions is not at all clear at present, however.

For example, Sokolov (1960), with emphasis on the reticular system, has outlined a theory as to how the "mechanisms of the orienting reflex" may function in conditioning and extinction, by activating the animal and facilitating its afferent discriminations. But the W-processes discussed in this chapter, which seem relevant to the "orienting reflex" and "defensive reflex" functions of the Pavlovians, evidently arise only gradually and segmentally in the neonate, through stages in which they are generally subordinate to the A-processes. As is indicated in a review by Antonova (1961) this complex, perhaps best termed the "orientational response," begins in neonate mammals as a set of variable reactions of disturbance to stimuli of intermediate (or higher) strengths. Studied in their relationship to vegetative reactions such as sucking, which is typically one of interruption, the orientational reactions were at first unstable in both their occurrence and extinction but gradually increased in individual and group frequency. The increase was more rapid in the precocial rabbit than in altricial mammals such as dogs and cats. The developmental study of such relationships represents a problem of the first importance.

The reasonable hypothesis, represented in Figure 30, is that neonatal functions underlying behavior rest on a basis of A-system dominance. Evidence bearing on the limitations of neural function early in ontogenesis (Bishop, 1959) suggests that the neonate begins life in its new environment on an essentially embryonic level with its A-processes dominated by a "drowsy" vegetative condition, then progresses in discriminating stimuli and differentiating its behavior mainly through sequences of A-arousal. The involvement of episodic W-arousal in these developments may be secondary as a rule, and variable according to individual conditions (Section V, D).

Significantly, in adult subjects, processes of discrimination and reinforcement which are selective and precise in the waking state are imprecise and generalized under sleepy or drowsy conditions (Sokolov, 1960; Hernández-Peón, 1961). The latter approximates the immature condition of embryo and neonate. Evidence that the reticular system includes both activating mechanisms and components which oppose these (Cordeau, 1962) suggests that this system—with other midbrain mechanisms—may contribute to the neonate's progress in approach-following discriminations and in related reactions to disturbance. For the latter, two principal W-functions are postulated (Sections III and IV), the first of these inhibitory or interruptive in function, the second one an arousal mechanism through which the restoration of A-processes may be facilitated. The latter is discussed by Sokolov (1960) in its state of relatively mature function.

In the following section, the stages postulated for the development of phasic A-system functions in neonatal vertebrates will be outlined, with a suggestion of the manners in which W-processes may be involved in behavioral development.

V. APPLICATION OF APPROACH-WITHDRAWAL THEORY TO CONTRASTING DEVELOPMENTAL PATTERNS IN VERTEBRATES

A. Postulates Applicable to Both Precocial and Altricial Types

The key postulates for behavioral ontogenesis discussed in this chapter center on the primary role of A-processes in adaptive behavior. These are the mechanisms normal to ontogenesis which, especially in their phasic roles, are basic to the stages of change in approach and withdrawal. The A-processes are potentially reinforcing to the rise of approach-following responses (i.e., imprinting). Aroused by low-intensity stimuli or by stimuli changing toward the optimum, phasic A-processes, underlying approach, have the advantage of a facilitation from tonic processes of the A-system with their normal feedback (Figure 30). The W-processes, basic to withdrawal, are adequately aroused by high-intensity stimuli. Lacking a tonic support, in the usual course of behavior their involvement is either interruptive or one of indirectly facilitating A-arousal —with the possibility of a continuity in individuals of abnormally high tension.

In this section, the principal sequences of events in approach-withdrawal development will be outlined in a manner applicable to most vertebrates. The vertebrates, and particularly birds and mammals, may be classified into *precocial, altricial,* and *transitional* types (Nice, 1962) according to their relative state of development at birth, with the altricial the least advanced of the three.

As a framework for the comparison of these types in the following sections, conclusions from previous sections of this chapter broadly applicable to all will be stated below, summarizing the A-W theory of behavioral development. The special terms have been refined in Section I, A.

1. Input effects adequate for A-processes. The stimuli adequate for eliciting A-processes are those exciting neural input effects which are quantitatively low, regular, and limited in their ranges of magnitude. Stimuli adequate for eliciting W-processes are those exciting neural input effects which are quantitatively high, irregular, and of variable, extensive ranges.

The neural basis of this statement is given in Section IV; relevant species-specific receptor-filtering mechanisms have been discussed by Granit (1955), Schneirla (1956), Marler (1961), Horn (1962), and various authors in Rosenblith (1961).

2. Embryonic development of A-processes; stimulative control. Embryonic A-processes, through associated mechanisms in maturation and in stimulus integration (Section I), come by stages under the control of low-intensity mechanical (tactual; proprioceptive) and visceral feedback impulses.

Consequently, both A-processes and overt actions (e.g., head advancing) coupled with them can be aroused or facilitated either mechanically —as by gentle head contact—or endogenously.

3. Arousability of A-processes in the neonate. Upon hatching or birth, the stage to which the A-system has developed in the mature embryo

opens it to excitation by low-intensity visual stimulation or to other extrinsic stimuli equivalent to the previous somesthetic control. The equivalent effect arises through a diffusion of neural impulses from optic or other newly excited centers into general-sensory and other areas through which A-processes have been aroused in the embryo (Section IV, A).

W-processes, normally excitable by high-intensity stimuli, are episodic and low in organization in embryo and neonate (Sections III, C and D).

4. Range of A-stimuli in the neonate. Depending upon their equivalence in quantitative neural-input effects, a broad range of extrinsic stimuli may elicit head-advancing or turning-to actions shortly after birth or hatching, their efficacy in further stages depending upon relative potencies and upon which object appears initially and frequently.

Through feedback from A-processes aroused to episodic action, mechanisms of overt response are sustained under given stimulus conditions so that, with repetition, plastic A-patterns develop. Thus reinforced, head-advancing or turning-to reactions become extended into locomotor approaches.

5. The fixation of approach-following patterns through A-reinforcement. A stage of contiguity learning then ensues through reinforcement by A-processes of approach and related responses to the primary, frequent, and prominent stimuli.

The reinforcement of neural changes underlying this learning process is available through repeated A-system arousals by the adequate stimulus. As a contiguity is repeated with such reinforcement, the approach-fixation soon extends into one of following objects equivalent in their stimulative effect. The neonate can thereby maintain—through phasic A-system readjustments—actions of forward locomotion to the object, turning or hurrying so that it stays visually centered (or auditorially prominent) and near the optimal input magnitude.

6. Selective learning and specialization. As experiences continue with the fixated object and related ones, a stage of stimulus differentiation and of response specialization ensues, through a selective learning dependent upon the outcome of the subject's response as related to consequences such as feeding and nestling (Maier and Schneirla, 1935, 1942).

Selective learning can arise through competitions of alternative contiguity patterns continuing according to how the consequences of actions reinforce them differently through A-system arousal. In time, this process advances to a stage of *seeking* the object in its absence.

7. Stages of disturbance, "fear" and "avoidance." W-processes first appear in the neonate as diffuse disturbances, then as segmental reactions leading to withdrawal or flight. Through contiguity learning based on their frequency or prominence, objects presenting adequate stimuli for W-arousal may first reach the status of being feared, then (through selective learning) that of being avoided.

A consistent arousal of W-processes may set up first a contiguity conditioning to the object's general properties, then a selective learning by which the object is avoided on partial or specialized cues. According to conditions, such processes may at times be inhibitory to action, at times may facilitate A-arousal, and at times may facilitate W-arousal and flight.

8. Social responses through the fixation of approach-following responses. In both precocial and altricial vertebrates, the processes described under Points 1–7 commonly underlie the formation of discriminative social bonds, of participation in social groups, and of courtship and mating. But, under given conditions, they may become subordinate to cues from other objects favored by contiguity or by selective learning.

The eight groups of statements listed above, concerning the development of approach-withdrawal reactions, derived from discussion in earlier sections centered particularly on precocial birds, will now be discussed in their relevance to both precocial and altricial birds and mammals.

B. Approach-Fixation and Withdrawal-Fixation in Precocial Vertebrates

1. PRECOCIAL BIRDS

Although pecking is considered here a local approach response, its behavioral properties and diversified roles are significantly different from those of general approach. Through further experience—as in fighting (Tobach and Schneirla, 1964)—these responses may come to vary considerably in their relevance to behavior in different individuals.

The biphasic A-W theory seems to adapt well to developmental events such as imprinting, justifying the term *approach-fixation* for that phenomenon (Schneirla, 1959, p. 78). This term denotes (1) active responses by the animal to initially attractive stimuli (Table 1) (2) eliciting A-processes which enhance their effectiveness and reinforce contiguity learning (3) centered on *trace effects* accounting for progressively discriminative approaches to and following of these stimuli, and moreover (4) the fact that stimuli of high intensity may conversely elicit the reinforcing basis for a *withdrawal-fixation*.

The relevance of this theory to the development of approach-following reactions has been discussed by Moltz (1960, 1961)—with whose version, considered later in this section, I do not agree—and by Salzen (1962). These authors, Fabricius (1962), and Hinde (1962) have reviewed the evidence on imprinting.

The embryonic basic for approach-fixation in the neonates of precocial birds is afforded by self-stimulative processes (Section V, A, Points 1 and 3). Under natural conditions the neonatal course of this process is influenced strongly by self-derived stimuli, as well as by stimuli from the parent which contribute toward structuring the situation. Under early post-hatching conditions, visual and auditory stimuli generally act together, with their roles differing according to species equipment and developmental situation. In the wood duck, structuring of the dark nest situation with the tree hole visible above makes the female's call from outside an effective directionalizer of the exodus but, once in the open, the young are visually as well as aurally responsive to the parent (Section III, B).

The process whereby anterior tactual stimuli acquire a control over head advancing in the embryo is considered basic (Section II, D). The potency of head contact for visual approach-fixations is indicated by the proneness of hatchlings to stop or to move along with their heads touching the object, giving pleasure notes meanwhile (Salzen, 1962). Furthermore, this tendency is stronger in neonates than at later stages (Hess, 1959). Ohba (1962) noted that approaches, although predominant in the responses of naive chicks to other chicks on their first posthatching day, rarely extended into following until after physical contact had occurred on one or more trials (Section V, B; Points 2 and 3). A reinforcement of approach by A-processes is indicated thereby.

Under favorable conditions, the acts of head advancing and turning, with visual centering of the object, are soon succeeded by the first locomotion toward adequate stimuli (Section V, B; Point 4), often early on the first day. The primary condition may be described as one of a locomotion toward low-intensity stimuli, positively reinforced by A-processes. Recurrences of situations presenting adequate visual-input effects soon lead to a contiguity conditioning to the object and, as Hinde (1962) says, "Rapid learning occurs." The parent normally structures the situation by her presence at the scene, by moving slowly at intervals, and usually also by producing a low, repetitive sound (Section III, B) so that, with repetitions, head advancing leads rapidly into movement toward the object and into following as it moves away. Repetitions involve cumulative reinforcement and enhance afferent differentiations. Moltz (1961) stresses the fact that following is commonly stimulated by the object moving *away from* but not towards the neonate. Incidental occurrences of the latter situation stimulate W-processes that may interfere with the approach-fixation.

Numerous generalized visual and auditory stimuli are equivalently adequate for approach (Section III, B; Table 1), so long as they fall within the species quantitative range for A-processes. After hatching, as conditions permit, A-system reinforcement applies to these dominant stimuli much as it did to the mechanical stimuli previously effective. Under natural conditions the species-typical qualitative effects of appearance and behavior are prominent from the first, facilitating the transfer from quantitative to qualitative control (Section V, B; Points 1–5) so smoothly that the parent's crucial role in canalizing the approach-fixation is often underestimated.

In tests, correspondingly, object prominence is an important factor (Fabricius, 1951), as are the conditions of primacy and frequency (Jaynes, 1956, 1958a; Hess, 1959). Of 150 first-day chicks given ten trials daily with a moving green box, only 57% responded with approaches, but of another 150 given 50 such experiences daily, 80% so responded (Salzen and Sluckin, 1959).

Two mechanisms may be prerequisite to these events in the neonate, the one a neural diffusion through which extrinsic stimuli are *added* to the embryonic mechanical control of head advancing and A-processes, the other a mechanism of approach-fixation to the adequate stimulus. Both of these agencies are reinforced by A-processes (Section V, B; Points 3–5). The first one is indicated by the behavior protocols of Jaynes (1956), Schaefer and Hess (1959a), and others, who report contentment chirps as common in approaches to the object, with nestling and pecking frequent in its vicinity. Normally, with further trials (Jaynes, 1956; Salzen and Sluckin, 1959), active approaches to the moving object increase in frequency and vigor, indicating that the process of contiguity learning is well begun.

But individual differences are usually notable in these events (Hinde, 1962), since in tests of naive chicks with a flickering disk, for example, some subjects soon were approaching consistently while others continued to vary and others to turn away (Smith and Hoyes, 1961). Conditions of "physiological maturation" (Jaynes, 1956) doubtless contribute subtly to these differences, as by influencing individual levels of excitability. In the neonate, however, much as in the embryo, the roles of maturation and of experience seem inseparable (Sections I, A, II, D, and IV, A). As suggested in Section IV, B, all individuals may pass from a relatively lethargic embryonic neural condition into a postnatal stage of increasing responsiveness. Differences appear to exist among the neonates of any group in the extent to which phasic A-processes may become effective as facilitators of approach reactions (Sections III, B and C).

The optimal or so-called "critical" period for the fixation of approach-following responses in precocial birds varies with developmental circumstances and species resources. Under Hess's (1959) conditions, its peak was 18 hours and its termination around 30 hours for chicks and ducklings. But the shape and duration of the curve for this interval, rather than depending solely (or directly!) upon factors of physiological maturation such as the presumably age-conditioned fear postulated by Hess

(1959), seem complex and strongly dependent upon the extrinsic conditions of development. Under research conditions in which an attractive
object is presented consistently, the potency of A-processes elicited by
the object stimulus *alone* is likely to wane in time, so that in a sense the
process of imprinting is self-terminating (Hinde, 1962; Salzen, 1962).
But with controlled differences in the vectors of stimulation (Smith and
Bird, 1963), in intervening reinforcements (Baron and Kish, 1960), in
the degree and timing of social experiences (Guiton, 1959; Salzen, 1962),
and in other conditions of rearing and experience (Gottlieb and Klopfer,
1962; Waller and Waller, 1963) such as the deterrent effects of low
temperature (Hinde et al., 1956; Salzen and Tomlin, 1963), it is not a
question of an all-or-none critical period but of differences "in the probability that imprinting will occur" (Kaufman and Hinde, 1961), i.e., of
differences in its strength, pattern, and duration.

Although many (e.g., Jaynes, 1956; Moltz, 1960; Hinde, 1962) now
regard imprinting as a case of learning, it is perhaps better termed a
process of *approach-fixation* which is like adult learning to the extent that
trace effects modifying behavior are evidently established according to
experience. It differs from conventional learning, however, not only in its
aspect of primacy, but also in what appears to be the inextricable involvement of developmental processes peculiar to the stage.

The early neonatal stages of approach-fixation evidently involve a
rudimentary contiguity learning reinforced by A-processes, hence they
progress best when experience with the object is consistent (Jaynes, 1957;
1958a,b) and involves a minimum of disturbance (Salzen, 1962). As
Weidman (1956) concluded for ducklings, when the condition of repeated, regular experiences with the object (i.e., the A-stimulus) is fulfilled, increases in readiness to follow, to discriminate the object from
others, and to search for it in its absence readily ensue.

The reinforcing effects of A-processes are a *necessary* basis for extending the initial naive approach into the stage in which a fixation of approach-following for a specific object-pattern can occur. In laboratory
tests, an adequate stimulus presented *alone* continues for a considerable
time to be "its own reward," and reinforcement through A-processes
invoked through its quantitative effect is indicated by the subject's vocali-
zations and other behavior in approaching it. Occasional intrusions of
W-processes, in contrast, are indicated by distress notes and flight tendencies (Salzen, 1962) which delay or may block the approach-fixation.

In early stages of approach-following, contiguity learning progresses
best when experience with the object is most regular, as reinforcement by
A-processes can be interrupted if disturbances are frequent. The frequent
statement that "reward-type reinforcement" is unnecessary for this stage
appears to have distracted attention from the fact that, under natural

conditions, the maternal object not only has the property of directly eliciting A-processes in embryo and neonate, but does so in varied and progressive ways as through gentle contact, warmth, clucking, and food. Thus the mother, as species agent, induces and maintains the initial forced approaches to A-stimuli, the stage of A-reinforced contiguity learning which overlaps it, and the stage of selective learning. The rate at which these processes can be effected is suggested by occurrences in community-nesting birds such as the Adelie Penguin (*Pygoscelis adeliae*), in which neonates within a few hours show a striking accuracy in approaching their own parents as against other adults in a group (Sladen, 1955).

In the group situation, other neonates in their visual appearance alone can elicit approaches (Pattie, 1936; Ohba, 1962), and as this response strengthens through contiguity it can interfere with the attractive effect of new stimuli (Guiton, 1961). Normally, changes in the social situation through varied individual encounters must soon introduce competing contiguities and then selective learning (Section V, A; Points 5–8). The siblings as they develop compete increasingly with the parent as attractive objects (Jaynes, 1956). These relations no doubt are also complicated by variations in incidental food cues, food competition, and other relationships. One factor of importance is the changing behavioral relationship of the young to the hen (Maier, 1963), which may bear interesting similarities to litter-period relationships in certain mammals (cf. Section V, C).

Evidence on approach-following reveals two rather different stages of stimulus-generalization, the first interpreted (Section III, B) as an indiscriminate initial approach to stimuli which are A-process-reinforced and quantitatively equivalent for arousal, the second as a transferral of the discriminated aspects of an initially dominant object to others. Transfer effects to different objects often depend upon how consistently the original object was followed (Hinde et al., 1956), although contradictory results have been reported on this point (Jaynes, 1956; Moltz, 1960), perhaps related to different conditions of rearing and testing.

The approach-following sequence of the biphasic functional systems is marked by the frequent occurrence of an "ambivalence" towards the attractive object (Fabricius, 1951; Hinde, 1961). Within the first hour the distress notes of the posthatching interval have subsided. But the increase of similar vocalizing later on the first day, when a test object is presented (Hess, 1959), seems based upon disturbances from the new situation (as from jerky object motion). This is especially the case with oversensitive subjects that withdraw from stimuli approached readily by others (Fabricius, 1951; Salzen, 1962). As an example, an object that is being approached is retinally centered and, let us assume, is then magnified appreciably by the deep avian fovea (Walls, 1942; Pumphrey, 1948). But then, through a chance movement, the centered object is lost—an occurrence which enforces a *sudden* drop in the A-stimulative input with the effect of a sharp disturbance. With repetition, however, the W-processes thereby aroused may be reduced (i.e., adapted) sufficiently to activate variable movements and recovery of the object (i.e., rather than increased tension, as at first). Thus in experienced subjects, the retinal "jump" that may occur as a retinally centered object is lost can become a specific cue for recovering and recentering the image without reducing the main adjustment to the object itself.

Such readjustments in the neonate must, however, remain for some time on a rudimentary neural level. The postulation of qualitative stages in the approach-withdrawal development of higher vertebrates, for which a neural basis is suggested in Section IV, can accommodate the concept of a "neuronal model" (cf. Sokolov, 1960; Salzen, 1962) only for advanced stages. In neonatal stages, rudimentary as they seem to be, it is likely that the autonomic-visceral-somatic components of A-W processes lose their embryonic dominance only by degrees, as suggested in Section IV, B.

The hypothesis has been offered here that the necessary reinforcement for the initial approach-fixation consists in phasic A-processes aroused by the low-intensity stimulus itself (Section V, A; Points 1–3). That is to say, the fixation of approach-following responses to a specific object is a *positive* type of process for which W-processes are not basically necessary. Although Hinde et al. (1956) suggested that imprinting might have its basis in the removal of fear, the idea has no necessary relevance to early stages.

But the fear type of concept was applied to the entire process *including* early stages by Moltz (1961) in his hypothesis that the perceived stimulus acquires "anxiety-reducing" properties which themselves account for the following of the object, for pursuing it when it is seen anew, and for seeking it later in anxiety-producing situations. As a test of this hypothesis, Moltz and Rosenblum (1958) gave to ducklings that had been following an experimental object well, on their fourth posthatching day, a pretest interval in the test situation *minus* the object. There was a decline in their subsequent following-scores as compared with those of controls detained in a situation other than that of testing. But anxiety reduction was not shown to be the factor *necessary* for these results, nor have further experiments (Moltz et al., 1959) shown it to be essential for the fixation of either object approach or following.

The preferable view is that the fixation of approach-following responses normally involves processes of A-system reinforcement as *necessary* from the first and basic—with W-processes secondary, minor, or dispensable, depending upon the individual and conditions. Hinde (1962), Salzen (1962), and others have noted that many of their subjects approached the object from the beginning and made their following responses to it without any signs of fear (Section V, B). It is significant also that W-processes have an appreciable latency, since Jaynes (1957) found New Hampshire Red chicks that increased their approaches to the test object from the first trial with signs of W-responses appearing only at 30 hours as "weak flight" and at 60 hours as "strong flight." In the isolated chicks tested by Salzen (1962) at 24 hours of age, A-type responses to a moving object predominated greatly over the W-type, as also with isolated chicks tested at 7 days of age.

The occurrence and fixation of approach-following responses depend upon both developmental status and experience. Gottlieb and Klopfer (1962), with a technique grouping Peking ducklings according to "developmental age" (cf. Section III, B), found that of 21 ducklings imprinted before 27.5 days (i.e., postincubative), in the tests 13 were dominantly auditory and 8 visual, whereas of 21 imprinted after that age these proportions were virtually reversed. Illustrating the role of training, 42 of 60 visually isolated subjects were approach-following-fixated, but only 28 of 60 group-raised subjects were so fixated.

The role of W-processes may differ considerably according to the conditions (i.e., of development, experience, and test situation) affecting the subject. Socially reared chicks, for example, make lower scores in following a test object than do previously isolated chicks of the same age (Guiton, 1959; Abercrombie and James, 1961), indicating that prior approach-fixations may interfere with the following of new stimuli. Salzen (1962) found that the effects of periods of group experience ranging from 1 and 3 to 7 days were sufficient to make a moving test object (a box) far more disturbing to these subjects than to isolated chicks. These results, with comparable disturbance effects produced by a static test object in subjects used to one in motion, indicated that the aspect of *sudden change* was common to the situations in which W-type responses predominated. But Moltz et al. (1960), by rearing chicks in diffuse light in a plain cage, increased their scores in object following over those of chicks raised normally, evidently because the *lack* of specific object-fixations made these chicks more responsive to the new stimuli than were controls.

Earlier in this section, the idea was advanced that W-processes may have one of two different roles vis-à-vis A-processes in object-fixation: that of inhibiting or excluding them or that of facilitating them according to conditions. The first of these roles is illustrated in the "hawk test" and in the comparable test of Schaller and Emlen (1963), in which a black rectangle repeatedly moved *toward* ducklings or chicks elicited an increasing disturbance to the point of strong W-fixations of frantic flight and specific avoidance. The second role of W-processes, that of facilitating A-processes, would appear to be frequently involved in precocial birds raised and tested under relatively stable conditions. Normally, in the second stage of stimulus generalization, when even familiar objects may be disturbing in new circumstances, a selective learning occurs in which a facilitation by W-processes may sharpen the discrimination of approach-fixated objects from objects increasingly W-fixated.

Presumably, the relationships of A-processes to W-processes attain varying patterns of central control through development, depending upon species abilities, individual tensional level, and other conditions. The limitations of generalizing in these matters are shown not only by comparisons of vertebrate classes and of precocial and altricial types within classes, but also of individuals within a species, in their patterns of A-W development.

2. PRECOCIAL MAMMALS

In mammals such as goats and sheep, signs of approach-fixation normally appear soon after birth and evidently the process continues into a discriminative following of the mother and of species mates. Hediger (1950) and Collias (1956) mention the occurrence of imprinting in mammals as different as guinea pigs, sheep, and buffaloes.

Generalized stimuli seem initially effective for approach, as the young of ungulates and other mammals raised apart do not later flock or mate with others of the species. Neonate kids and lambs squirm about and bleat feebly, thereby facilitating both visually and aurally their being licked by the parent. The licking, which usually starts at the head end (Herscher et al., 1963), elicits turning-to responses and is one factor orienting the neonate toward the parent. The relationship, which is bilateral and complex, forms rapidly. The mother's first attraction to the newborn is often stimulated by its bleating, to which she responds with approach and a series of low sounds (Herscher et al., 1963). Licking aids the process of drying and also stimulates the neonate; furthermore it furnishes a quick and effective olfactory basis for maternal fixation to the neonate (Collias, 1956; Blauvelt, 1955). The first rising of the elk calf (*Cervus canadensis*) to its feet is stimulated by maternal licking (Altmann, 1963). Newborn kids and lambs, which usually can stand and move about within an hour or two, tend to approach large objects and especially moving objects, a visual factor canalizing motion toward the parent (Hersher et al., 1963). In proportion to their own body size, however, these neonates approach objects of much the same quantitative range as do precocial birds.

Responses of turning toward the parent are thus oriented by maternal licking, responses of general approach by the visual effect of the parent as a moving object. Further licking, as it progresses posteriorly, tends to shift the neonate toward the udder. Hediger (1950) calls attention to the fact that, in suckling, neonate ungulates stand in toward the udder from in front. This response may be influenced by more than one factor, as by maternal licking of anogenital areas and by a local visual effect. This effect, described by Hediger (1950) as the "abdominal-leg angle," may be first exerted through the visual stimulative agency of leg movement specifically. Neonate chamois, bison (*Bison bison*), and wild boars follow the mother soon after birth (Altmann, 1956). In the "heeling" responses of young moose (*Alces americana*) and elk calves, which are clearly visual as they function better on land than in water, the calf follows the mother and as her pace quickens moves closer to her (Altmann, 1963). Altmann notes that this response is reversible, also more flexible and less limited in respect to its "sensitive period" than would be prescribed by Lorenz's (1955) definition of imprinting, a judgment now viewed as also true for birds (Sections III, B; V, B).

The significance of the parental figure as a visual controller is suggested also by Collias's (1956) observation that neonate kids do not move about much when the mother is absent—I have noted this also with young fawns in the forest; within a few weeks, kids and lambs tend to graze closely beside the mother, wandering farther in time but running back when frightened.

It is probable that the rooting and nuzzling responses significant for early orientation to the mother in mammals (Spitz, 1957; Fraser, 1963) have an embryonic basis analogous to that described for the head-advancing reaction in birds (Section II, D). From the evidence, A-W theory seems to apply comparably to neonatal approach and following responses in both precocial birds and mammals (Section III, D).

C. Approach-Fixation and Withdrawal-Fixation in Altricial Vertebrates

1. ALTRICIAL BIRDS

Evidence on the gaping responses of altricial birds, considered a local approach-response comparable to pecking (Section III, A), suggests as basic for visual responses a mechanically controlled embryonic head-advancing mechanism comparable to that indicated in precocial vertebrates (Sections II, D; III, D). Although the neonate enters the nonvisual stage with a generalized responsiveness to mechanical stimuli, discrimination sharpens in this respect and auditory cues become effective, so that a substantial perceptual-motor basis is available for the visual stage. A pattern of conditioning, which facilitates the transition to the visual stage, has been suggested (Section III, A). From a detailed study of gaping and related behavior in the Reed Warbler, Impekoven (1962) has described the manner in which gaping begins to appear with forward locomotion in the visually elicited food-begging reactions of postnestling young around the 12th day.

In Ring Doves, as in altricial birds generally, the parents' attachment to the nest transfers to the eggs and young, admitting a series of parental-young interactions basic to the feeding process. In these events, head-pushing actions of the young stimulate the parent to the point of regurgitating crop material ("pigeon's milk") which is taken by the nestling through actions of bill clapping in the parent's throat (Lehrman, 1955a). The last response is clearly a specialization of the head-advancing movement. These relationships of nestling and parent, arising through a typical developmental sequence, provide a sufficient basis, Lehrman concluded, for the parent's feeding the young squab on its first locomotor approaches. The initial approach of the squab to the parent may be aroused by generalized visual characteristics with auditory facilitation, much as in precocial birds. There follows a stage in which the parent's specific visual and auditory properties are effectively discriminated from those of other members of the species.

The influence of these early approach adjustments on adult behavior is indicated by the results of Warriner et al. (1963), in which the systematic presentation to young pigeons of a series of adult colors including black and white reliably influenced later mating responses of the males although not of the females. This result, as the authors suggest, would be expected from the high degree of male dominance in the selective functions of courtship and mating in pigeons.

2. ALTRICIAL MAMMALS

The developmental formula outlined in Section V, A seems generally valid for altricial mammals also. The potency of low-intensity somatic afferent effects for eliciting the head-advancing and turning-to responses has been emphasized (Schneirla, 1959). In Lincoln's (1933) study of rat fetuses delivered by Caesarian section and tested with localized anterior tactual stimuli, head extension appeared alone in 17% of the animals on day 16.5 but had increased to 82% on day 17. Although on day 17 head movement toward the stimulus was accompanied by mouth opening and tongue movements in less than half of the animals, on day 17.5 and thereafter these actions were combined in nearly all of the cases.

These actions are of course central to feeding in the neonate, in which the snout and anterior head are centers of stimulative liaison with the environment. Neonate puppies can be led about by touching the head appropriately (James, 1952), responses of advancing or turning the head to light contact being especially predictable under conditions of nonoptimal temperature and hunger (Welker, 1959).

In neonate kittens we (Schneirla and Rosenblatt, 1961) studied the initial period of nonvisual orientative development as a basis for visual perception. In this research, Turkewitz (1962) found that 1-day-old kittens readily advanced their heads in response to light head-contact with the soft undersurface of a canopy, particularly when it was warm. The concept of an embryonic head-advancing response given by the neonate to low-intensity anterior stimuli may thus underlie in these mammals a behavioral transition to postnatal approach responses resembling that set forth in Section V, A, Points 1–3. The process seems to be facilitated in cats by maternal situation-structuring through licking and the "functional U" posture in nursing (Rosenblatt et al., 1962).

How this progression of responses may be facilitated by A-processes in the transition from embryo to neonate is indicated by Salk's (1960, 1963) study in which a regular heartbeat sound was played continuously at low intensity to human infants in their first 4 neonatal days, but not to control subjects otherwise treated similarly. Around two thirds of the experimental infants, but only one third of the controls, gained weight on the same food intake during this period. The experimental subjects also cried less, were less restless, and had deeper and more regular breathing and fewer gastro-intestinal upsets than the controls. Salk attributed this evidence of increased well-being and "better coordination of the autonomic nervous system" in his experimental infants to an imprinting of the maternal heartbeat in the embryo. This and other effects may arise in lower vertebrates also, with the embryo's own heartbeat as another possible source of tonic A-system facilitation.

Our results (Rosenblatt et al., 1962) shows that in neonate kittens local adjustments to the female such as "nipple preference" improve from the first hour or two after birth. The first approach responses seem generalized to mild tactual, thermal, and olfactory stimulation, with the nest and female largely equivalent in their attractive potencies. In our large experimental cage, within 3–4 days the kittens had become able to return to the nest corner from the adjacent corner 75 cm distant. Control tests showed that the basic attraction lay in olfactory cues from the nest (cf. Section II, B, 3), with the processes soon extending spatially, first through wall following and then through cues admitting a course parallel to the wall with occasional contacts. By 7–10 days, most of the kittens were able to reach the home corner from the corner diagonally opposite, paralleling the two walls successively as distinct stages. Although the median time for eye opening was 7–10 days in our kittens, only after the 12th day could they replace the wall-following pattern with a visually controlled course directly across the diagonal to the nest corner (Figure 32). The nonvisual perception of the living cage thus provides a basis for perceiving it visually, but is effective only through a transitional process which requires time and action after the eyes have opened.

Although neonate kittens enter the stage of efficient visual perception

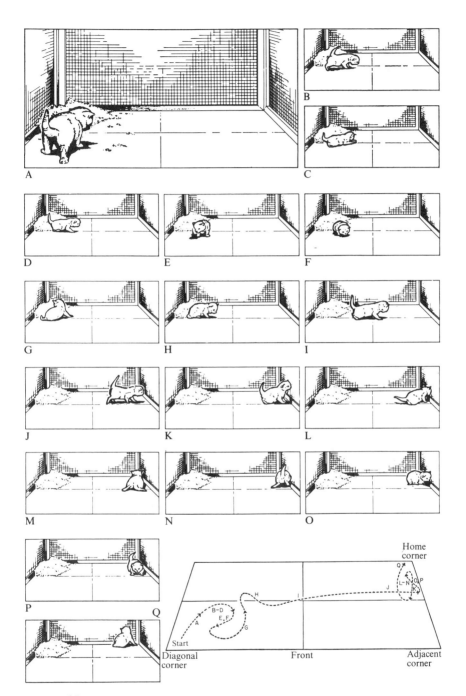

FIGURE 32
Successive actions in an orientation test of a 20-day-old kitten in reaching the home corner of its living cage from the corner diagonally across the field. The drawings show positions at 5-second intervals; the diagram at the lower right indicates the general path. (From Schneirla and Rosenblatt, 1961.)

within 2 weeks, nursing sessions are initiated by the female until around the 20th day (Rosenblatt et al., 1962). Then the kittens begin to initiate the process, first in short approaches to the female and then in longer ones in more varied situations. Behavioral interchanges in this stage seem to involve increasingly subtle visual, auditory, and other sensory cues. Soon after the kittens have begun this progress, they transfer their perceptual affinity from the nest to their mother, who is followed more and more. Then, after about 5 weeks, their following changes to pursuit or to searching as the female first withdraws and then begins to avoid them. The more she slips away, however, the more expertly they can search her out. Comparable stages from local feeding adjustments through active approaches and harrying the female have been observed in the rat (Rosenblatt and Lehrman, 1963). As the female's avoidance of them increases, young altricial mammals transfer gradually to new sources of food and then, under natural conditions, the litter group dissolves.

The relation of the described changes in the mother's behavior to increasing disturbances through approach actions by the young is shown by comparisons of multikitten and single-kitten litters, with the maternal-kitten bond enduring for months in the latter. Conversely, the extent to which the female's changing behavior influences changes in approach reactions by the young is indicated by the difficulties of isolated kittens in readjusting to the female on their return. For example, kittens isolated from the 23rd to 44th day—the interval in which the female changes from withdrawal to progressive avoidance of her young (Schneirla et al., 1963) —on their return soon exhibit rising tension and excitement when near the female. Their disturbance is clearly indicated by hissing and other W-responses, which mount as they change from mere withdrawals to consistently avoiding her.

It is plain that in the normal situation, the sequence of changes in the mutual approach-withdrawal relationships of parent and young cannot be mainly the result of critical periods synchronized to inevitable processes of physiological maturation. Instead, these behavioral changes must represent a progression of stimulative-response relationships in which maturational influences must be complexly related to influences of experience and of mutual behavioral effects (Schneirla and Rosenblatt, 1963). In the rat (Rosenblatt and Lehrman, 1963) the succession of approach-withdrawal patterns in the normal litter period similarly involves changing stimulative effects upon the female, which are major factors underlying the stages of her maternal behavior cycle. Through such reciprocal behavioral relations, the young normally pass through a stage of local approaches to one of active locomotor approaches, then enter a preadult stage of distinctive seeking or avoidance of the female.

VI. RÉSUMÉ AND CONCLUDING REMARKS

The biphasic A-W theory was designed to account for the development of approach-withdrawal patterns in animals. The derivation of this theory for vertebrates is continued in Sections I–IV of this chapter. In Sections V, B and C the theory is applied to postnatal behavioral development in precocial and altricial vertebrates, with a summary statement in Section V, A and a glossary in Section I, A.

Writers such as Werner (1940) and Hebb (1949), notably, who have presented important theories of perceptual development, have admitted on principle the priority of proximal sensory factors for visual perception in particular, but have not clarified the developmental processes necessary for this basis, nor has Taylor (1962) for the "unlearned reactions" from which his Hullian theory of perception takes its departure.

The A-W theory, in contrast, makes use of significant findings such as those of Kuo and Coghill to discern how functional conditions and active responses of the organism become related in early development. This theory lays the basis for approach behavior in vertebrates in progressive relationships between low-intensity somaesthetic stimuli and the energy-conserving A-processes in development. Three early stages are differentiated, in which the developmental rôles of the factors of "experience" and of "maturation" are viewed as intimately related in a changing progression. These factors, with their trace effects, contribute to (1) an embryonic stage in which sensory integrations and feedback effects give rise to crude directional vectors (Section II, D); (2) a stage in the maturing embryo and the neonate in which these processes elaborate, come under the control of new, extrinsic stimuli, and influence the formation of early contiguity-type conditioning (Sections III, B and D); and (3) a further postnatal stage in which behavioral development is marked by progressive contiguity conditioning and the entrance of selective learning.

The key postulate of A-W theory is that progress through early developmental stages is based upon the adequacy of low-intensity stimuli for eliciting A-processes which reinforce the functional mechanisms described above. Low-intensity stimuli, together with progressive maturational factors, are considered the primary agencies in functional development, as they arouse neural-input effects of the magnitudes adequate for the thresholds of A-processes.

The embryonic basis for approach behavior in vertebrates, according to this theory, lies in episodic increases of the tonic, continuous A-processes normal to development, which may begin in the preneural and early neural stages. Then, under repeated arousal by incidental A-stimuli, progressive increases can occur in A-processes which bring them by degrees to the condition of specialized patterns of phasic types. Next, through the rise of tactuo-proprioceptive integrations and related feedback mechanisms, the phasic A-processes come to include such overt actions as head-advancing and turning-to responses. These somatic components of the A-system, necessary for the specialization of postnatal locomotor approach responses, give the organism a basis for two of its principal orientative directions— i.e., head-first and to the sides. Through their postnatal extensions, these functions under proximal sensory control in the embryo also furnish the principal anchorages for perceptual development in the new environment.

The phasic A-processes of stage 1, above, are thus considered necessary for the postnatal orientative developments of approach-fixation (i.e., imprinting), following and seeking. The third main vector, withdrawal, seems to arise with greater latency than that of head advancing, with fewer episodic arousals in the embryo than A-processes because the higher quantitative input effects eliciting W-processes arise less frequently than do A-stimuli. This theory thus finds the essential basis for the postnatal processes of approach-fixation and following-fixation in the progress of A-processes and their somatic components from embryo to neonate. In the embryonic and early neonatal stages, the role of W-processes (e.g., as invoked by hypotheses of anxiety reduction) seems to be secondary and subject to individual conditions.

Because this theory views behavioral development as a progression of patterned changes resulting from the roles of the "maturation" and "experience" variables functioning intimately together in fused complexes, both structural and behavioral phenotypes would be expected to arise according to circumstances (Schneirla, 1956, 1957). Depending upon individual conditions, such phenotypes might diverge toward the dominance of either A-processes or of W-processes over behavior. An interesting example of such variations in the same species has been reported by Emlen (1963) from studies on the "visual cliff" responses of neonate gulls.

As an alternative to the hypothesis of "innate schemata," A-W theory conceptualizes early quantitative differentiations grounded on the development of the A-system and its overt components as basic to orientation and perception, with qualitative differentiations (i.e., of kinds of objects) subsequently derived on this basis. Thus, the visual effects of a disk or of regular flicker, or the hearing of repetitive sounds, if not too intense, are quantitatively equivalent for arousing A-processes antecedent to neonatal approach. Conversely, abrupt visual changes or harsh noises are equivalent for arousing W-processes, as in the hawk effect and visual cliff phenomena.

In stage 2, several developmental properties aid the transition from embryonic to neonatal conditions. The basis of tonic A-processes is facilitated by self-stimulative processes centered on the heartbeat. Comparably, the availability of phasic A-processes to species-typical stimuli such as quacking in ducks seems to be enhanced by self-stimulative effects in the embryo. Two important functional properties seem essential for the transition. First, there occurs a diffusion of neural impulses from newly aroused afferent centers (e.g., in precocial vertebrates, the optic centers) into the general-sensory channels which controlled phasic A-processes in the embryo. Through this agency (cf. Figure 30), the somatic afferent components of phasic A-processes in the embryo can be activated by "new" but quantitatively equivalent stimuli (cf. Table 1)—incidental situation-structuring by species mates, as an outcome of natural selection, presents such stimuli (Section III, B). Second, the physical nature of stimuli adequate for A-arousal may be canalized by the characteristics of receptor and other structural-functional specializations. The range of physical effects equivalent for visually attracting neonate precocial vertebrates thus includes rounded objects and regular flicker, that for audition low, repetitive sounds. These individual situation-canalizing factors also are of course results of natural selection.

Thus, neonatal vertebrate behavior has a nonvisual functional basis which through low-intensity stimuli develops the approach vectors, or through high-intensity stimuli develops the disturbance-withdrawal vectors of orientation and perception. Neonates of precocial and altricial vertebrates are influenced comparably by such processes in their perceptual development (cf. Section V, A), although with differences in both the rate and the patterning of the nonvisual and the distance-orientative stages (cf. Sections V, B and C). These important functions, which cannot be considered innate in the traditional sense, are the product of a complex progression of changes in embryonic and postnatal development which, with the species-normal genotype under species-standard ontogenetic conditions, seems inevitable.

Evidence on embryonic and neonatal functions indicates that developmental processes centered on peripheral and autonomic mechanisms are fundamental to vertebrate orientative and perceptual development (Figure 30). The conclusion therefore is that stages 1, 2, and 3 of behavioral development, as described above, are prerequisite for attaining the degree of higher-level central neural control indicated for adult vertebrates by evidence from implanted electrode research and by concepts such as the Pavlovian neuronal model (cf. Section IV, B; Figure 31).

The human neonatal responses of head advancing, arm extension, and grimacing have been discussed as reactions to generalized low-intensity stimulation under A-system facilitation (Schneirla, 1959). These can develop into the individual's major devices for entering into relations with his environment. The results of Dennis (1935) and Spitz (1957) indicate that the grimace, for example, is at first a diffuse response to a variety of low-intensity tactual, auditory, and visual stimuli, including *disk-like* masks. The idea, developed in this chapter, that the necessary reinforcement for the fixation of approach-type responses to such stimuli rests in the A-processes they elicit seems applicable comparably to the grimace and arm-extension responses of human neonates and to the locomotor approaches of lower vertebrates. The further idea that such reinforcement is available on new bases for the discriminative and reactive specialization of approach mechanisms through contiguity and selective learning (Section V, A) also seems applicable on both of these levels.

REFERENCES

Abercrombie, B., and H. James. 1961. The stability of the domestic chick's response to visual flicker. *Anim. Behav.* 9: 205–213.
Adrian, E. D., and R. Matthews. 1928. The action of light on the eye. Part III. The interaction of retinal neurones. *J. Physiol.* 65: 273–298.
Altevogt, R. 1953. Untersuchungen über das optische Differenzierungsvermögen der Amsel, *Turdus merula* L. *J. Orn., Lpz.* 94: 220–251.
Altmann, M. 1956. Patterns of social behavior in big game. *Trans. 21st N. Am. Wildl. Conf.,* pp. 538–545.
Altmann, M. 1963. Naturalistic studies of maternal care in moose and elk. In H. D. Rheingold, ed., *Maternal behavior in mammals.* New York: Wiley. Pp. 233–253.
Antonova, T. G. 1961. A comparative evaluation of the activity of analyzers in newborn animals. Transl. from *Materialy po evolyutsionnoy fiziologii,* vol. 4, pp. 77–81. U.S. Joint Publ. Res. Serv., Washington, D.C.
Balinsky, B. I. 1960. *An introduction to embryology.* Philadelphia: Saunders.
Barlow, H. B. 1953. Summation and inhibition in the frog's retina. *J. Physiol.* 119: 69–88.
Baron, A., and G. B. Kish. 1960. Early social isolation as a determinant of aggregative behavior in the domestic chicken. *J. Comp. Physiol. Psychol.* 53: 459–463.
Beebe-Center, J. E., P. Black, A. C. Hoffman, and M. Wade. 1948. Relative per diem consumption as a measure of preference in the rat. *J. Comp. Physiol. Psychol.* 41: 239–251.
Bishop, G. H. 1959. The relation between nerve fiber size and sensory modality: Phylogenetic implications of the afferent innervation of cortex. *J. Nerv. Ment. Dis.* 128: 89–114.
Blauvelt, H. 1955. Dynamics of the mother-newborn relationship in goats. In B. Schaffner, ed., *Group processes: Transactions 1st conference.* New York: Josiah Macy, Jr., Foundation. Pp. 221–258.
Breder, C. M., and F. Halpern. 1946. Innate and acquired behavior affecting the aggregation of fishes. *Physiol. Zoöl.* 19: 154–190.

Brodal, A. 1957. *The reticular formation of the brain stem. Anatomical and functional correlations.* Edinburgh: Oliver & Boyd.

Brückner, G. H. 1933. Untersuchungen zur Tierpsychologie insbesondere zur Auflösung der Familie. *Z. Psychol.* 128: 1–110.

Bykov, K. M. 1957. *The cerebral cortex and the internal organs.* New York: Chemical Publ.

Carr, W. J., and D. I. McGuigan. 1964. The stimulus basis and modification of visual cliff performance in the rat. *Animal behaviour* (in press).

Collias, E. C., and N. E. Collias. 1957. The response of chicks of the Franklin's gull to parental bill-color. *Auk* 74: 371–375.

Collias, N. 1952. The development of social behavior in birds. *Auk* 69: 127–159.

Collias, N., and N. Joos. 1953. The spectrographic analysis of sound signals of the domestic fowl. *Behaviour* 5: 175–188.

Collias, N. E. 1956. The analysis of socialization in sheep and goats. *Ecology* 37: 228–239.

Cordeau, J. P. 1962. Functional organization of the brain stem reticular formation to sleep and wakefulness. *Rev. Canad. Biol.* 21: 113–125.

Crozier, W. J., and G. Pincus. 1927. Phototropism in young rats. *J. Gen. Physiol.* 10: 519–524.

Crozier, W. J., and E. Wolf. 1943. Flicker response contours for the sparrow, and the theory of the avian pecten. *J. Gen. Physiol.* 27: 315–324.

Cruze, W. W. 1938. Maturation and learning in chicks. *J. Comp. Psychol.* 19: 371–409.

Curtius, A. 1954. Über angeborene Verhaltenswiesen bei Vögeln, insbesondere bei Hühnerkücken. *Z. Tierpsychol.* 11: 94–109.

D'Amato, M. R., and H. Jagoda. 1962. Effect of early exposure to photic stimulation on brightness discrimination and exploratory behavior. *J. Genet. Psychol.* 101: 267–271.

Davis, H. 1961. Some principles of sensory receptor action. *Physiol. Rev.* 41: 391–416.

Dennis, W. 1935. Experimental test of two theories of social smiling in infants. *J. Soc. Psychol.* 6: 214–223.

Dethier, V. 1947. *Chemical insect attractants and repellents.* New York: McGraw-Hill (Blakiston).

Dolley, L., Jr., and J. D. White. 1951. The effect of illuminance on the reversal temperature in the drone fly, *Eristalis tenax. Biol. Bull., Wood's Hole* 100: 84–89.

Eccles, J. C. 1953. *The neurophysiological basis of mind.* London and New York: Univ. Press, Oxford (Clarendon).

Ehrenhardt, H. 1937. Formensehen und Sehscharfebestimmungen bei Eidechsen. *Z. Vergl. Physiol.* 24: 258–304.

Eibl-Eibesfeldt, I. 1951. Fahrungserwerb und Beuteschema der Erdkröte (*Bufo bufo* L.). *Behaviour* 4: 1–35.

Emlen, J. T. 1963. Determinants of cliff edge and escape responses in herring gull chicks in nature. *Behaviour* 22: 1–15.

Engelmann, C. 1941. Versuche über den Geschmacksinn des Huhnes. VI. Über angeborenen Formvorlieben bei Hühnern. *Z. Tierpsychol.* 5: 42–59.

Fabricius, E. 1951. Zur Ethologie junger Anatiden. *Acta Zool. Fenn.* 68: 1–177.

Fabricius, E. 1962. Some aspects of imprinting in birds. *Symp. Zool. Soc. Lond.* 8: 139–148.

Fabricius, E., and H. Boyd. 1954. Experiments on the following-reaction of ducklings. *Rep. Wildfowl Trust* 6: 84–89.

Fantz, L. 1957. Form preferences in newly hatched chicks. *J. Comp. Physiol. Psychol.* 50: 422–430.

Fraenkel, G., and D. L. Gunn. 1940. *The orientation of animals—Kineses, taxes and compass reactions.* London and New York: Oxford Univ. Press. (Reissue, 1962: Dover, New York).

Fraser, A. F. 1963. The significance of the "pushing" syndrome. *Anim. Behav.* 11: 51–52.

Freisling, J. 1948. Studien zur Biologie und Psychologie der Wechselkröte (*Bufo viridis* Laur.) *Öst. Zool. Z.* 1: 383–440.

Gellhorn, E. 1943. *Autonomic regulations—their significance for psychology and neuropsychiatry.* New York: Wiley (Interscience).

Goethe, F. 1940. Beobachtungen und Versuche über angeborene Schreckreaktionen junger Auerhühner (*Tetrao u. urogallus* L.). *Z. Tierpsychol.* 4: 165–167.

Goldstein, K. 1939. *The Organism.* New York: American Book.

Gottlieb, G. 1963a. The facilitatory effect of the parental exodus call on the following response of ducklings: one test of the self-stimulation hypothesis. *Am. Zool.* 3: 518; and personal communication.

Gottlieb, G. 1963b. A naturalistic study of imprinting in wood ducklings (*Aix sponsa*). *J. Comp. Physiol. Psychol.* 56: 86–91.

Gottlieb, G., and P. H. Klopfer. 1962. The relation of developmental age to auditory and visual imprinting. *J. Comp. Physiol. Psychol.* 55: 821–826.

Granit, R. 1955. *Receptors and sensory reception.* New Haven: Yale Univ. Press.

Gray, P. H. 1961. The releasers of imprinting: differential reactions to color as a function of maturation. *J. Comp. Physiol. Psychol.* 54: 597–601.

Grüsser-Cornehls, U., O. Grüsser, and T. H. Bullock. 1963. Unit responses in the frog's tectum to moving and nonmoving visual stimuli. *Science* 141: 820–822.

Grundfest, H. 1959. Evolution of conduction in the nervous system. In A. D. Bass, ed., *Evolution of nervous control.* Washington, D.C.: Am. Assoc. Advanc. Sci. Pp. 43–86.

Guiton, P. 1959. Socialization and imprinting in brown leghorn chicks. *Anim. Behav.* 7: 26–34.

Guiton, P. 1961. The influence of imprinting on the agonistic and courtship responses of the Brown Leghorn cock. *Anim. Behav.* 9: 167–177.

Hailman, J. P. 1962. Pecking of Laughing Gull chicks at models of the parental head. *Auk* 79: 89–98.

Hailman, J. P. 1964. Ontogeny of pecking in Laughing Gull chicks. Unpublished Ph.D. thesis, Duke Univ., Durham, North Carolina.

Hartline, H. K. 1938. The response of single optic nerve fibers of the vertebrate eye to illumination of the retina. *Am. J. Physiol.* 121: 400–415.

Hassenstein, B. 1961. Ommatidienraster und afferente Bewegungsintegration. *Z. Vergl. Physiol.* 33: 301–362.

Hebb, D. O. 1949. *The organization of behavior.* New York: Wiley.

Hecht, S. 1929. Vision: II. The nature of the photoreceptor process. In C. Murchison, ed., *Foundations of experimental psychology.* Worcester, Mass. Clark Univ. Press. Pp. 169–272.

Hediger, H. 1950. *Wild animals in captivity.* London: Butterworths.

Heinroth, O. 1910. Beitrage zur Biologie, namentlich Ethologie und Physiologie der Anatiden. *Verhandl. 5th Int. Orn. Kongr., Berlin, 1910,* pp. 589–702.

Hernández-Peón, R. 1961. Reticular mechanisms of sensory control. In W. A. Rosenblith, ed., *Sensory communication.* New York: Wiley. Pp. 497–520.

Herrick, C. J. 1924. *Neurological foundations of animal behavior.* New York: Holt.

Hersher, L., J. B. Richmond, and A. U. Moore. 1963. Maternal behavior in sheep and goats. In H. L. Rheingold, ed., *Maternal behavior in mammals.* New York: Wiley. Pp. 203–232.

Hess, E. H. 1959. The relationship between imprinting and motivation. In M. R. Jones, ed., *Current theory and research on motivation.* vol. 7. Lincoln: Univ. Nebraska Press. Pp. 44–77.

Hinde, R. A. 1961. The establishment of the parent-offspring relation in birds, with some mammalian analogies. In W. H. Thorpe and O. Zangwill, eds., *Current problems in animal behaviour.* London and New York: Cambridge Univ. Press. Pp. 175–193.

Hinde, R. A. 1962. Some aspects of the imprinting problem. *Symp. Zool. Soc. Lond.* 8: 129–138.

Hinde, R. A., W. P. Thorpe, and M. A. Vince. 1956. The following response of young coots and moorhens. *Behaviour* 9: 214–242.

Hirsch, J., R. H. Lindley, and E. C. Tolman. 1955. An experimental test of an alleged innate sign stimulus. *J. Comp. Physiol. Psychol.* 48: 278–280.

Holt, E. B. 1931. *Animal drive and the learning process.* New York: Holt.

Holzapfel, M. 1939. Analyze des Sperrens und Pickens in der Entwicklung des Stars. *J. Orn., Lpz.* 87: 525–553.

Honigmann, H. 1945. The visual perception of movement by toads. *Proc. Roy. Soc.* B132: 291–307.

Horn, G. 1962. Some neural correlates of perception. In J. D. Carthy and C. L. Duddington, eds., *Viewpoints in biology.* London: Butterworths. Pp. 242–285.

Hoyle, G. 1955. Functioning of the insect ocellar nerve. *J. Exp. Biol.* 32: 397–407.

Hubel, D. H., and T. N. Weisel. 1961. Integrative action in the cat's lateral geniculate body. *J. Physiol.* 155: 385–398.

Hubel, D. H., and T. N. Weisel. 1962. Receptive fields, binocular interaction and functional architecture in the cat's visual cortex. *J. Physiol.* 160: 108–164.

Impekoven, M. 1962. Die Jugendentwicklung des Teichrohrsängers. (*Acrocephalus scirpaceus*). *Rev. Suisse Zool.* 69: 77–191.

James, H. 1959. Flicker: an unconditioned stimulus for imprinting. *Canad. J. Psychol.* 13: 56–67.

James, W. T. 1952. Observations on the behavior of new-born puppies: II. Summary of movements involved in group orientation. *J. Comp. Physiol. Psychol.* 45: 329–335.

Jaynes, J. 1956. Imprinting: The interaction of learned and innate behavior: I. Development and generalization. *J. Comp. Physiol. Psychol.* 49: 201–206.

Jaynes, J. 1957. Imprinting: the interaction of learned and innate behavior. II. The critical period. *J. Comp. Physiol. Psychol.* 50: 6–10.

Jaynes, J. 1958a. Imprinting: the interaction of learned and innate behavior. III. Practice effects on performance, retention and fear. *J. Comp. Physiol. Psychol.* 51: 234–237.

Jaynes, J. 1958b. Imprinting: the interaction of learned and innate behavior. IV. Generalization and emergent discrimination. *J. Comp. Physiol. Psychol.* 51: 238–242.

Katsuki, Y., T. Sumi, H. Uchiyama, and T. Watanabe. 1958. Electric responses of auditory neurons in cat to sound stimulation. *J. Neurophysiol.* 21: 569–588.

Kaufman, I. C., and R. A. Hinde. 1961. Factors influencing distress calling in chicks, with special reference to temperature changes and social isolation. *Anim. Behav.* 9: 197–204.

Kempf, E. J. 1953. Neurosis as conditioned, conflicting, holistic, attitudinal, acquisitive-avoidant reactions. *Ann. N.Y. Acad. Sci.* 56: 307–329.

Klopfer, P. H. 1959. An analysis of learning in young Anatidae. *Ecology* 40: 90–102.

Klopfer, P. H., and G. Gottlieb. 1962. Imprinting and behavioral polymorphism: auditory and visual imprinting in domestic ducks (*Anas platyrhynchos*) and the involvement of the critical period. *J. Comp. Physiol. Psychol.* 55: 126–130.

Klüver, H. 1962. Psychological specificity—does it exist? In F. O. Schmitt, ed., *Macromolecular specificity and biological memory*. Cambridge: M.I.T. Press. Pp. 94–98.

Krätzig, K. 1940. Untersuchungen zur Lebensweise des Moorschneehuhns, *Lagopus l. lagopus,* während der Jugendentwicklung. *J. Orn., Lpz.* 88: 139–166.

Kuffler, S. W. 1953. Discharge patterns and functional organization of mammalian retina. *J. Neurophysiol.* 16: 37–68.

Kuntz, A. 1929. *The autonomic nervous system.* Philadelphia: Lea & Febiger.

Kuo, Z. Y. 1932a. Ontogeny of embryonic behavior in Aves. I. The chronology and general nature of the behavior of the chick embryo. *J. Exp. Zool.* 61: 395–430.

Kuo, Z. Y. 1932b. Ontogeny of embryonic behavior in Aves. II. The mechanical factors in the various stages leading to hatching. *J. Exp. Zool.* 62: 453–489.

Kuo, Z. Y. 1932c. Ontogeny of embryonic behavior in Aves. III. The structure and environmental factors in embryonic behavior. *J. Comp. Psychol.* 13: 245–272.

Kuo, Z. Y. 1932d. Ontogeny of embryonic behavior in Aves. IV. The influence of embryonic movements upon the behavior after hatching. *J. Comp. Psychol.* 14: 109–122.

Kuo, Z. Y. 1932e. Ontogeny of embryonic behavior in Aves. V. The reflex concept in the light of embryonic behavior in birds. *Psychol. Rev.* 39: 499–515.

Kuo, Z. Y. 1963. Total patterns, local reflexes, or gradients of response? *Proc. 16th int. Congr. Zool., Washington, D.C.* 1963. Vol. 4, pp. 371–374.

Lashley, K. S., and M. Wade. 1946. The Pavlovian theory of generalization. *Psychol. Rev.* 53: 72–87.

Lehrman, D. S. 1953. A critique of Lorenz's "objectivistic" theory of animal behavior. *Quart. Rev. Biol.* 28: 337–363.

Lehrman, D. S. 1955a. The physiological basis of parental feeding responses in the ring dove (*Streptopelia risoria*). *Behaviour* 7: 241–286.

Lehrman, D. S. 1955b. The perception of animal behavior. In B. Schaffner, ed., *Group processes: Transactions 1st conference.* New York: Josiah Macy, Jr., Foundation. Pp. 97 ff., 259–267.

Lettvin, J., H. R. Maturana, W. H. Pitts, and W. S. McCulloch. 1961. Two remarks on the visual system of the frog. In W. A. Rosenblith, ed., *Sensory communication.* New York: Wiley. Pp. 757–776.

Lincoln, A. W. 1933. The early development of the feeding reaction in the albino rat. Unpublished M.A. thesis, Brown University, Providence, Rhode Island.

Lindsley, D. E. 1958. The reticular system and perceptual discrimination. In H. H. Jasper, L. D. Proctor, R. S. Knighton, W. C. Noshay, and R. T. Castello, eds., *Recticular formation of the brain.* Boston: Little, Brown. Pp. 513–534.

Lorenz, K. 1935. Der Kumpan in der Umwelt des Vogels. *J. Orn., Lpz.* 80: 50–98.

Lorenz, K. 1939. Vergleichende Verhaltensforschung. *Zool. Anz.* Suppl. to vol. 12: 69–102.

Lorenz, K. 1957. Companionship in bird life. In C. H. Schiller, ed., *Instinctive behavior: The development of a modern concept.* New York: International Univ. Press. Pp. 239–263.

Lorenz, K. 1961. Phylogenetische Anpassung und adaptive Modifikation des Verhaltens. *Z. Tierpsychol.* 18: 139–187.

MacLean, P. D. 1959. The limbic system with respect to two basic life principles. In M. A. B. Brazier, ed., *The central nervous system and behavior: Transactions 2nd conference.* New York: Josiah Macy, Jr., Foundation. Pp. 31–118.

McNiven, M. A. 1960. "Social-releaser-mechanisms" in birds—A controlled replication of Tinbergen's study. *Psychol. Rec.* 10: 259–265.

Maier, N. R. F., and T. C. Schneirla. 1935. *Principles of animal psychology.* New York: McGraw-Hill. (Reissue, 1964. Dover, New York).

Maier, N. R. F., and T. C. Schneirla. 1942. Mechanisms in conditioning. *Psychol. Rev.* 49: 117–134.

Maier, R. A. 1963. Physical contact between mother and young. *Science* 139: 673–674.

Marler, P. 1961. The filtering of external stimuli during instinctive behaviour. In W. H. Thorpe and O. Zangwill, eds., *Current problems in animal behaviour.* London and New York: Cambridge Univ. Press. Pp. 150–166.

Maturana, H. R., J. Y. Lettvin, W. H. Pitts, and W. S. McCulloch. 1960. Physiology and anatomy of vision in the frog. *J. Gen. Physiol.* 43: Suppl. 129–175.

Melzack, R., E. Penick, and A. Beckett. 1959. The problem of "innate fear" of the hawk shape: an experimental study with mallard ducks. *J. Comp. Physiol. Psychol.* 52: 694–698.

Menner, E. 1938. Die Bedeutung des Pecten im Auge des Vogels für die Wahrnehmung von Bewegungen, nebst Bemerkungen über seine Ontogenie und Histologie. *Zool. Jb., Abt. Allg. Zool. Physiol. Tiere* 58: 481–538.

Moltz, H. 1960. Imprinting: empirical basis and theoretical significance. *Psychol. Bull.* 57: 292–314.

Moltz, H. 1961. An experimental analysis of the critical period for imprinting. *Trans. N.Y. Acad. Sci.* 23: 452–463.

Moltz, H., and L. A. Rosenblum. 1958. The relation between habituation and the stability of the following response. *J. Comp. Physiol. Psychol.* 51: 658–661.

Moltz, H., L. A. Rosenblum, and N. Halikas. 1959. Imprinting and level of anxiety. *J. Comp. Physiol. Psychol.* 52: 240–244.

Moltz, H., L. Rosenblum, and L. J. Stettner. 1960. Some parameters of imprinting effectiveness. *J. Comp. Physiol. Psychol.* 53: 297–301.

Moore, A. R., and J. C. Welch. 1940. Associative hysteresis in larval *Amblystoma. J. Comp. Psychol.* 29: 283–292.

Munn, N. L. 1940. Learning experiments with larval frogs. *J. Comp. Psychol.* 29: 97–103.

Muntz, W. R. A. 1963. The Development of phototaxis in the frog. (*Rana temporaria*). *J. Exp. Biol.* 40: 371–379.

Nice, M. M. 1962. Development of behavior in precocial birds. *Trans. Linn. Soc. N.Y.* 8: 1–211.

Nice, M. M., and J. J. ter Pelkwyk. 1941. Enemy recognition by the song sparrow. *Auk* 58: 195–214.

Ohba, K. 1962. Studies in socialization of white leghorn chicks. (I) Behavior of day old chicks at their first paired meeting. *Ann. Animal Psychol.* (*Tokyo*) 12: 113–114.

Olds, M. E., and J. Olds. 1962. Approach-escape interactions in rat brain. *Am. J. Physiol.* 203: 803–810.

Orr, D. W., and W. F. Windle. 1934. The development of behavior in chick embryos: the appearance of somatic movements. *J. Comp. Neurol.* 60: 271–285.

Orton, G. 1955. The role of ontogeny in systematics and evolution. *Evolution* 9: 75–83.

Pattie, F. A., Jr. 1936. The gregarious behavior of normal chicks and chicks hatched in isolation. *J. Comp. Psychol.* 21: 161–178.

Perttunen, V. 1958. The reversal of positive phototaxis by low temperatures in *Blastophagus piniperda* L. (Col., Scolytidae). *Ann. Ent. Fenn.* 24: 12–18.

Peters, J. J., A. R. Vonderahe, and T. H. Powers. 1958. Electrical studies of functional development of the eye and optic lobes in the chick embryo. *J. Exp. Zool.* 139: 459–468.

Pfaffman, C. 1961. The sensory and motivating properties of the sense of taste. In M. R. Jones, ed., *Current theory and research on motivation,* vol. 9. Lincoln: Univ. Nebraska Press. Pp. 71–110.

Pfaffman, C., R. P. Erickson, G. P. Frommer, and B. P. Halpern. 1961. Gustatory discharges in the rat medulla and thalamus. In W. A. Rosenblith, ed., *Sensory communications.* New York: Wiley. Pp. 455–474.

Polyak, S. 1957. *The vertebrate visual system.* Chicago: Univ. Chicago Press.

Pringle, J. W. S. 1962. Prologue: The input element. *Symp. Soc. Exp. Biol.* 16: 1–11.

Pumphrey, R. J. 1948. The sense organs of birds. *Ibis* 90: 173–199.

Ramsay, A. O. 1951. Familial recognition in domestic birds. *Auk* 68: 1–16.

Ramsay, A. O., and E. H. Hess. 1954. A laboratory approach to the study of imprinting. *Wilson Bull.* 66: 196–206.

Reichardt, W. 1961. Autocorrelation, a principle for the evaluation of sensory information by the central nervous system. In W. A. Rosenblith, ed., *Sensory communication.* New York: Wiley. Pp. 303–317.

Rettler, M. 1960. Untersuchungen zur Ontogenese des Lernvermögens beim Haushuhn. *Zool. Jb.* 69: 193–222.

Rheingold, H. L., and E. Hess. 1957. The chick's "preference" for some visual properties of water. *J. Comp. Physiol. Psychol.* 50: 417–421.

Roffey, J. 1963. Observations on night flight in the desert locust (*Schistocerca gregaria* Forskal). *Anti-Locust Bull.,* no. 39, pp. 1–32.

Rosenblatt, J. S., and D. S. Lehrman. 1963. Maternal behavior of the laboratory rat. In H. L. Rheingold, ed., *Maternal behavior in mammals.* New York: Wiley. Pp. 8–58.

Rosenblatt, J. S., G. Turkewitz, and T. C. Schneirla. 1962. Development of suckling and related behavior in neonate kittens. In E. L. Bliss, ed., *Roots of behavior.* New York: Harper. Pp. 187–197.

Rosenblith, W. A., (ed.). 1961. *Sensory communication.* New York: Wiley.

Rushton, W. A. H. 1962. The retinal organization of vision in vertebrates. *Symp. Soc. Exp. Biol.* 16: 12–31.

Sackett, G. P. 1963. A neural mechanism underlying unlearned, critical period and developmental aspects of visually controlled behavior. *Psychol. Rev.* 70: 40–50.

Salk, L. 1960. The effects of the normal heartbeat sound on the behavior of the newborn infant: implications for mental health. *World Ment. Hlth.* 12: 168–174.

Salk, L. 1963. The importance of the heartbeat rhythm to human nature; theoretical, clinical, and experimental observations. *Proc. World Congr. Psychiat. 1963,* 3(3): 740–746. Univ. of Toronto Press. Toronto.

Salzen, E. A. 1962. Imprinting and fear. *Symp. Zool. Soc. Lond.* 8: 199–217.

Salzen, E. A., and W. Sluckin. 1959. The incidence of the following response and the duration of responsiveness in domestic fowl. *Anim. Behav.* 7: 172–179.

Salzen, E. A., and F. J. Tomlin. 1963. The effect of cold on the following response of domestic fowl. *Anim. Behav.* 11: 62–65.

Schaefer, H. H., and E. H. Hess. 1959a. Innate behavior patterns as indicators of the "critical period." *Z. Tierpsychol.* 16: 155–160.

Schaefer, H. H., and E. H. Hess. 1959b. Color preferences in imprinting objects. *Z. Tierpsychol.* 16: 161–172.

Schaller, G. B., and J. T. Emlen, Jr. 1961. The development of visual discrimination patterns in the crouching reactions of nestling grackles. *Auk* 78: 125–137.

Schaller, G. B., and J. T. Emlen, Jr. 1963. The ontogeny of avoidance behaviour in some precocial birds. *Anim. Behav.* 10: 370–381.

Schifferli, A. 1948. Über Markscheidenbildung im Gehirn von Huhn und Star. *Rev. Suisse Zool.* 55: 117–212.

Schleidt, W. M. 1961. Reaktionen von Truthühnern auf fliegende Raubvögel und Versuche zur Analyse ihrer AAM's. *Z. Tierpsychol.* 18: 534–560.

Schneirla, T. C. 1939. A theoretical consideration of the basis for approach-withdrawal adjustments in behavior. *Psychol. Bull.* 37: 501–502.

Schneirla, T. C. 1940. Further studies on the army-ant behavior pattern. Mass organization in the swarm-raiders. *J. Comp. Psychol.* 29: 401–460.

Schneirla, T. C. 1949. Levels in the psychological capacities of animals. In R. W. Sellars, V. J. McGill, and M. Farber, eds., *Philosophy for the future.* New York: Macmillan. Pp. 243–286.

Schneirla, T. C. 1955. Comments. In B. Schaffner, ed., *Group processes: Transactions 1st conference.* New York: Josiah Macy, Jr., Foundation. P. 95 ff.

Schneirla, T. C. 1956. Interrelationships of the "innate" and the "acquired" in instinctive behavior. In P.-P. Grasse, ed., *L'Instinct dans le comportement des animaux et de l'homme.* Paris: Masson. Pp. 387–452.

Schneirla, T. C. 1957. The concept of development in comparative psychology. In D. B. Harris, ed., *The concept of development.* Minneapolis: Univ. Minnesota Press. Pp. 78–108.

Schneirla, T. C. 1958. The behavior and biology of certain Nearctic army ants. Last part of the functional season, Southeastern Arizona. *Ins. Soc.* 5: 215–255.

Schneirla, T. C. 1959. An evolutionary and developmental theory of biphasic processes underlying approach and withdrawal. In M. R. Jones, ed., *Current theory and research on motivation,* vol. 7. Lincoln: Univ. Nebraska Press. Pp. 1–42.

Schneirla, T. C., and J. S. Rosenblatt. 1961. Behavioral organization and genesis of the social bond in insects and mammals. *Am. J. Orthopsychiat.* 31: 223–253.

Schneirla, T. C., and J. S. Rosenblatt. 1963. "Critical periods" in the development of behavior. *Science* 139: 1110–1115.

Schneirla, T. C., J. S. Rosenblatt, and E. Tobach. 1963. Maternal behavior in the cat. In H. L. Rheingold, ed., *Maternal behavior in mammals.* New York: Wiley. Pp. 122–168.

Seitz, A. 1940. Die Paarbildung bei einigen Cichliden. *Z. Tierpsychol.* 4: 40–84.

Seitz, A. 1949. Über das Verhalten zweier isoliert aufgezogener Brachvögel (*Numenius arquata* L.). *Orn. Ber.* 11: 32–39.

Selye, H. 1956. *The stress of life.* New York: McGraw-Hill.

Shepard, J. F., and F. S. Breed. 1913. Maturation and use in the development of an instinct. *J. Anim. Behav.* 3: 274–285.

Sladen, W. J. L. 1955. Social structure among Adelie penguins. In *Group processes: Transactions 2nd conference.* New York: Josiah Macy, Jr., Foundation. Pp. 28–93.

Smith, F. V. 1960. Towards definition of the stimulus situation for the approach response in the domestic chick. *Anim. Behav.* 8: 197–200.

Smith, F. V., and M. W. Bird. 1963. The relative attraction for the domestic chick of combinations of stimuli in different sensory modalities. *Anim. Behav.* 11: 300–305.

Smith, F. V., and P. A. Hoyes. 1961. Properties of the visual stimuli for the approach response in the domestic chick. *Anim. Behav.* 9: 159–166.

Sokolov, E. N. 1960. Neuronal models and the orienting reflex. In M. A. B. Brazier, ed., *The central nervous system and behavior: Transactions 3rd conference.* New York: Josiah Macy, Jr., Foundation. Pp. 187–276.

Spalding, D. 1873. Instinct, with original observations on young animals. *MacMillan's Mag.* (reprinted 1954: *Brit. J. Anim. Behav.* 2: 2–11).

Spitz, R. A. 1957. *No and Yes—on the genesis of human communication.* New York: International Univ. Press.

Taylor, J. G. 1962. *The behavioral basis of perception.* New Haven: Yale Univ. Press.

Tinbergen, N. 1948. Physiologische Instinktoforschung. *Experientia* 4: 121.

Tinbergen, N. 1951. *The study of instinct.* London and New York: Oxford Univ. Press.

Tinbergen, N. 1963. On aims and methods of Ethology. *Z. Tierpsychol.* 20: 410–433.

Tinbergen, N., and D. J. Kuenen. 1939. Über die auslösenden und richtunggebenden Reizsituationen der Sperrbewegung von jungen Drosseln (*Turdus m. merula* L. und *T. e. ericetorum* Turton). *Z. Tierpsychol.* 3: 37–60.

Tinbergen, N., and A. C. Perdeck. 1950. On the stimulus situation releasing the begging response in the newly-hatched Herring Gull chick (*Larus a. argentatus*). *Behaviour* 3: 1–38.

Tobach, E., and T. C. Schneirla. 1964. The biopsychology of social behavior in animals. In R. E. Cooke, ed., *Biological basis of pediatric practice.* New York: McGraw-Hill. In press.

Turkewitz, G. 1962. Personal communication.

von Holst, E. 1937. Bausteine zu einer vargleichenden Physiologie der loko-motorischen Reflexe bei Fischen. II. Mitteilung. *Z. Vergl. Physiol.* 24: 532–562.

von Schiller, P. 1933. Intersensorielle Transposition bei Fischen. *Z. Vergl. Physiol.* 19: 304–309.

Waddington, C. H. 1937. The dependence of head curvature on the development of the heart in the chick embryo. *J. Exp. Biol.* 14: 229–231.

Wagner, H. 1932. Über den Farbensinn der Eidechsen. *Z. Vergl. Physiol.* 18: 378–392.

Walk, R. D., and E. Gibson. 1961. A comparative and analytical study of visual depth perception. *Psychol. Monogr.* 75(17): 1–44.

Waller, P. F., and M. B. Waller. 1963. Early experience and later social behavior in ducklings. *Behaviour* 20: 343–363.

Walls, G. 1942. *The vertebrate eye and its adaptive radiations.* Bloomfield Hills, Michigan: Cranbrook Inst. Sci.

Warren, R. P. 1963. Preference aversion in mice to bitter substance. *Science* 140: 808–809.

Warriner, C. C., W. B. Lemmon, and T. S. Ray. 1963. Early experience as a variable in natural selection. *Anim. Behav.* 11: 221–224.

Weidmann, R., and U. Weidmann. 1958. An analysis of the stimulus-situation releasing food-begging in the black-headed gull. *Anim. Behav.* 6: 114.

Weidmann, U. 1956. Some experiments on the following and the flocking reaction of mallard ducklings. *Brit. J. Anim. Behav.* 4: 78–79.

Weiner, I. H., and E. Stellar. 1951. Salt preference of the rat determined by a single-stimulus method. *J. Comp. Physiol Psychol.* 44: 394–401.

Welker, W. I. 1959. Factors influencing aggregation of neonatal puppies. *J. Comp. Physiol. Psychol.* 52: 376–380.

Werner, H. 1940. *Comparative psychology of mental development.* New York: Harper.

Young, P. T. 1961. *Motivation and emotion.* New York: Wiley.

Zotterman, Y. 1961. Studies in the neural mechanism of taste. *In Sensory communication.* W. A. Rosenblith, ed., New York: Wiley. Pp. 205–216.

V

ON SOCIAL ORGANIZATION

Dr. Schneirla's views on social organization are based to a considerable extent on his concepts and formulations that have been presented in the previous sections of this book. These views serve as examples of the kinds of dynamic conclusions concerning important human social problems that derive from his theoretical orientation (see in this section *The "Levels" Concept in the Study of Social Organization in Animals*, No. **52**).* His emphasis on changing developmental processes, levels of integration, and his concept of "reciprocal stimulation" forms the core of these papers, while his position on instinct, maturation, experience, and approach-withdrawal forms the framework. Wheeler had used the concept of trophallaxis to denote the mutual exchange of nutriment chemicals, and

---

* This and subsequent numbers in this introduction refer to the items in the complete bibliography of Schneirla's works, p. 1017. Bold face numbers denote articles that are included in this volume.

stimulation related to such exchanges, between adult insects and their larval young as a basis for insect social organization. Schneirla modified this concept to include a wide range of mutual activities which he termed "reciprocal stimulation." He considered this process essential to the formation and maintenance of group organization in all animals. At the same time he emphasized that reciprocal stimulation differs materially at different phyletic levels (see in this section *The Biopsychology of Social Behavior of Animals,* No. **119**).

Based on his extensive research on army ants, and his work with collaborators on parturition and maternal relationships in domestic cats, Schneirla compared the basis for social organization in insects and mammals (in the article *Behavioral Organization and Genesis of the Social Bond in Insects and Mammals,* No. **94**). In contrast to the popular belief that social processes are basically similar in both groups (see *The Concept of Levels in the Study of Social Phenomena,* No. **65**, in Part III). Schneirla showed how they differ in fundamental ways. In insect groups the cohesive effect of reciprocal stimulation is based rather directly on physiological functions and their by-products, such as pheromones. Schneirla named the direct response to this type of stimulation *biotaxis.* Social organization depending essentially on this level of reciprocal stimulation he named *biosocial,* and insects, he maintained, characteristically form such groups. Early stages of the socialization process in mammals are also *biosocial,* as for example, in the organic events associated with parturition. As development proceeds, however, reciprocal stimulation based on more complex psychological processes, such as conditioning, learning, and concept formation, lead to *psychosocial* groups, as are found in mammalian social organization. Thus, although some of the features of insect and mammalian societies may seem similar, the processes leading to the formation and maintenance of social organization are basically different. Therefore, in comparing representatives of these two societies, one must take cognizance of the differences as well as the similarities and must recognize that factors attributed to one level do not necessarily apply at the other level.

The first paper in this section on social organization, *Problems in the Biopsychology of Social Organization* (No. **38**), appeared in 1946, and the subject was developed more fully in several later papers. This article was included, not only because of its historical interest, but also, because Schneirla treated two items, namely the superorganism concept and "dominance" concepts more fully here than in his later articles. These concepts have attracted less attention in recent years, and when writing later papers, Schneirla apparently felt that they no longer warranted extensive discussion.

Other papers relevant to Schneirla's views on social organization are

Development of Home Orientation in Newly Born Kittens (No. **121**) in Part VI; *The Army Ant* (No. **44**), *Collective Activities and Social Patterns among Insects* (No. **64**), and *Theoretical Consideration of Cyclic Processes in Doryline Ants* (No. **81**) in Part VII; and *A Consideration of Some Conceptual Trends in Comparative Psychology* (No. **57**), *Psychological Problems in the Orientation of Mammals* (No. **72**), and *Maternal Behavior in the Cat* (No. **104**) in Part VIII.

Additional papers on social organization not included in this volume are *A Consideration of Some Problems in the Ontogeny of Family Life and Social Adjustments in Various Infrahuman Animals* (No. 53), *Early Socialization in the Domestic Cat as Based on Feeding and Other Relationships, Between Female and Young* (No. 95), and *Development of Sucking and Related Behavior in Neonate Kittens* (No. 99).

Lester R. Aronson
Ethel Tobach

T. C. SCHNEIRLA

Problems in the Biopsychology
of Social Organization

Bibliography No. 38

There is an ancient and understandable tendency to draw moral conclusions from apparent similarities between man and lower animals, for
which the social insects have served as convenient material. Solomon's ad-
vice to the sluggard, "Go to the ant . . . ," comes readily to mind as an
outstanding instance of seemingly infallible repute. Unfortunately, in the
light of present knowledge about individual differences among insects in
social participation (Combes, 24; Chen, 21), this moral cuts two ways,
for the sluggard might well find all his time taken up in contemplating the
leisurely ways of those relatively sessile and less productive members
which any ant-hill is almost certain to contain. On the other hand, we who
are not sluggards may learn much from a more careful comparison of social activities in lower animals and in man, very possibly to the great advantage of better insight into man's social capacities and potentialities.

Scientists exhibit a growing tendency to study comparatively the makeup
of what are considered different levels of organization in the inorganic and
organic worlds (Redfield, 61). Simple and complex levels are recognized
among inorganic phenomena, and in an evolutionary sense certain of the
inorganic levels are recognized as prerequisite to the occurrence of organic
wholes such as viruses which are regarded as primary. Among biologists
and students of behavior there is an increasing alertness for what can be
learned from the investigation of one level or type of organization that will
assist in the improved understanding of others. An interest in comparative
study leads to a closer examination of the various instances of organization
describable as levels, for example the individual organism, the animal aggregation, social group and society (Allee, 2). We shall want to inquire
how far such studies have advanced beyond the stage of description and
naming, exemplified by Alverdes's (5) general survey, and are searching
out the essential qualities of different animal organizations. And since
there is implicit in the contemporary study of both individual organisms

From *The Journal of Abnormal and Social Psychology* 41(4): 385–402 (1946). Reprinted
with permission.

and social groups a conviction that such phenomena must be regarded as unitary wholes in some important sense, we should be concerned about the meaning and validity of this doctrine in the study of different social organizations. In what sense is an individual ant a unitary whole, or an ant colony, a species, a human city, nation, or a "United Nations"?

SUPERORGANISM CONCEPT AND ANALOGY

The first stage of comparative study generally involves a focusing upon similarities between observed phenomena. It is thus convenient to open our consideration of social-group comparisons with the concept of "superorganism" as it has been developed by certain students of insect behavior (Wheeler, 81, 84; Emerson, 31). This concept derives from an old notion entertained by Plato and Aquinas, that a society exhibits the principal attributes of an individual and may be considered a superior type of individual. In the writings of Wheeler and Emerson we find the idea developed to a high degree of elaborateness and in great detail as a technique for analogical study of organic systems. How interesting the study of insect social attributes becomes when approached from this point of view, may be represented by a brief sketch of Emerson's description of the insect "superorganism." His scheme of the insect colony as "superorganism" in relation to organisms and other "superorganisms" on different levels rests upon the premise that scientific methodology is fundamentally the same whether it applies to the mechanisms of the individual organism, the insect society, or human society. A careful comparison and correlation of these levels of organization leads, he believes, to the formulation of important principles; thus a detailed examination of the insect society leads to the discovery of many parallels to the properties of organisms. Some of these parallels we may outline as follows, condensed from his detailed survey (31):

1. Division of labor. Social insects commonly have castes, such as the differentiation of fertile individuals from infertile workers, analogized to the differentiation of gametes and somatic cells in the individual organisms; or the special function of infertile workers may be analogized to the function of cells in the individual's gastrovascular tract.

2. Intersectional communication. Insect communities are aroused by an interindividual transmission of impulses (e.g., excited termite soldiers rap their heads against wooden gallery walls, thereby exciting others; ants transmit excitation to nestmates by touching antennae), and such effects are compared with the intraorganismic transmission of nervous impulses, or to a chemical transmission among tissues through the blood stream.

3. Rhythmic periodicities. Social insects characteristically produce their

sexual forms seasonally, a process compared with the rhythmic production of gametes in an individual organism.

4. Life cycles. Birth, growth, and senescence in the individual organism are paralleled by colony foundation, expansion, and degeneration in social insects.

5. Organismic and superorganismic phylogeny. Emerson believes that the above similarities and others are not accidental, but that in the two cases natural selection operates in comparable ways, eliminating given mechanisms (i.e., of individual structure or those underlying group functions) according to their relative adaptive value.

Thus it is Emerson's conviction that the method of analogies is a valid way of studying organization on different levels, for in his view essentially the same biological processes have accounted for the evolution of organism and superorganism alike. He points to the comparable operation of selection as a factor in the evolution of individual and group at various integrative levels as a working assumption used by many biologists (e.g., Maidl, 49; Sturtevant, 73), and by Fisher (35) as a biometrician. However, the manner in which natural selection operates at different levels is very incompletely known at present. Simpson (71), for instance, has insisted that the superorganismic-organismic analogical procedure cannot be justified beyond the field of observation, for individual and social group are entities in very different senses of the word, differently subject to selection in evolution. It is questionable whether the deductive leaps of the analogy method provide a legitimate means of studying either the past history of animal societies or the nature of their present integrations.

CRITICAL DIFFERENCES BETWEEN LEVELS

Although it may be granted that the superorganism concept is a serviceable device for teaching the observed characteristics of organism and of group levels, beyond the unsettled question of whether similar evolutionary processes actually have been involved there is the further question, upon which we wish to concentrate in this discussion, whether the organization of different levels as they exist really involves similar factors (biological and psychological) of equivalent significance in the respective cases. In a recent critique of the superorganismic concept, Novikoff (58, 59) has concluded that it is inadequate both for discovering the actual nature of qualitative differences among levels of organization and for revealing the nature of the part-whole relationship in each given level. Although many students believe, as does Collias (23), that "integrated systems at one level may themselves be units in a more inclusive grouping," we may ask whether lower-level processes *as such* are really incorporated into higher levels of organization. To what extent are lower-level principles adequate for the understanding of higher levels? In what sense is the insect colony a *lower*-level phenomenon and human society a *higher*-level phenomenon, and to what extent does a study of the former contribute to understanding the latter?

While it is true as Gerard and Emerson (39) maintain that the method of analogy has an important place in scientific theory, its usefulness must be considered introductory to a comparative study in which differences may well be discovered which require a reinterpretation of the similarities first noted. As Emerson (32) has admitted, striking differences are found between insect and human society which may be too great to make the analogy significant. Perhaps the most significant differences come to light in a closer examination of the analogies described above. Outstanding contrasts are found especially in the nature of communication, in the occurrence of castes, and in "tradition."

The essential characteristics of communication in human society are (1) its symbolic and conventionalized character, (2) its directive function (i.e., using symbols to influence others), (3) its intentional use in social situations, and (4) its capacity for arrangement or rearrangement according to the requirements of meaning (cf. Bierens de Haan, 9). These characteristics are mastered in the socialization of the child, and are apparent both in linguistic and written communications, and in necessary modifications such as the finger codes of speechless individuals. In the social insects not one of these characteristics has been demonstrated in careful studies such as those of von Frisch (37) on bees, Eidmann (29) on ants, and Emerson (30) on termites. Instead, there is a direct transmission of excitement from individual to individual through antennal (and sometimes also front-leg) stroking as in most ants, special air-transmitted stridulatory vibrations in ants such as the tropical American *Paraponera clavata,* and through body vibrations transmitted via the substratum as in termites. These effects are not codified in any real sense, do not convey "information," and lack any directive effect in themselves. If the recipient is influenced in any describable way beyond being aroused to some activity, it is because of incidental stimuli such as the chemical effects described by von Frisch among flower gatherers, the existence of a chemical trail as Eidmann demonstrated, or because of previous individual learning (Maier and Schneirla, 50). Although the acquisition of the transmissive function by an individual appears to require a simple initial process of learning, which may occur through a modification of the first feeding reactions as Heyde (42) found in ants (Maier and Schneirla, 50), it cannot be regarded as psychologically comparable to human language acquisition (Révész, 62).

The occurrence of castes is a common characteristic of insect societies (Wheeler, 84). In addition to the sexual dichotomy of male and fertile females, there may be structurally different subtypes in the caste or castes of completely infertile or only partially fertile individuals. In many ants there occur polymorphic differences among the workers, sometimes in a continuous series from workers major on one extreme to workers minor on the other as in the leaf-cutter ant *Atta cephalotes,* sometimes in a discontinuous series with major and minor workers only. Because of their structural differences the various polymorphic castes differ in function: males and fertile females (queens) in sexual function, the workers serving as colony defenders in the case of the majors, as brood-tenders within the nest in the case of the minors, and the intermediates typically as foragers in the surrounding area. In the ants the basis of castes is typically biologically established, as follows—queens appearing from overfed fertilized eggs and males from unfertilized eggs, the various polymorphic worker castes from fertilized eggs which have been underfed to different extents. The differences in feeding which determine whether a queen or a worker type will develop from a fertilized egg are effective during the larval stage, and when the individual emerges as a young adult, fully grown at birth so to speak, its functional capacities may be predicted on the basis of its organic makeup. Thus through very long series of generations in a given species, the caste functions of individuals are stereotyped, and essentially changeless unless new developments occur through genetic evolution.

On the human level, in contrast to insects, castes in the sense of social or functional classes of different social ranks exist essentially on a psychological basis. The one clear biological foundation for a human functional "caste" differentiation is a sexual dichotomy, in which the organic differentiation of sexes imposes a qualitative differentiation of general reproductive function. It does not, however, impose any inevitable behavioral or psychological differentiation of social function; these are matters which anthropologists find attributable to social heritage and cultural pattern.[1] The social emancipation of women in relatively recent times, and their successful entrance into a variety of social and professional functions formerly considered the nature-given right of man alone, offer countless examples of the relatively limited extent to which human sex biology *in itself* channelizes social function. In insects, biological factors alone determine the channelizing (Schneirla, 66). Male ants or drone bees lack any organic basis for brood-tending or foraging, which are set functions of the hereditarily and trophically differentiated workers; whereas human males under appropriate conditions may even excel females in baby-tending, in cook-

---

[1] That is to say, genetico-physiological differences such as muscular strength existing between the sexes would facilitate certain differences in social function, but such differences are quantitative or relative rather than absolute, and are subject to alteration under appropriate social conditions.

ery, and in almost the entire range of domestic functions except giving birth.

In man, castes are not biologically differentiated in fixed ways as in insects, but exist essentially on an ideological and traditional basis. The fact that, whereas in the social insects germination has become highly centralized in a few individuals, in man it is a general property of individuals, Crowell (27) believes, is a biological characteristic contributing in man to a generalization of individual function in the family and hence in the social sphere. Thus the generalization of human reproductive functions throughout the population, other things being equal, would militate against a generation-to-generation stereotypy in human social function, facilitating the influence of the major biological factor basic to plastic adjustments—cerebral cortex.

It is often asserted that, while evidence is lacking for an anatomical specialization of human castes comparable to that of insects, an equivalent differentiating factor exists in the organic basis of intelligent behavior. For instance, R. B. Cattell (20) has reported intelligence-test results which differ according to the social level of the subjects, with the implications that biological factors necessarily play a maximal role and social factors a minimal role in accounting for the differences. Without adequate control (e.g., special tests) of the factors pertaining to social and economic background which are known to influence intelligence-test performance, such conclusions are widely open to question. As long as a satisfactory technique for such controls is lacking, scores on intelligence tests can have no clear meaning as to what native differences may exist among cultural, professional, or class groups (Neff, 55; Loevinger, 48; Mann, 53). In contrast to the stereotyped organic basis of insect social castes, the differentiation of human social castes appears to be dominantly influenced by essentially nongenetic factors.[2] However, by introducing vaguely hypothecated native factors, theories of "social instincts" such as that offered by McDougall tend to obscure the *relatively* homogeneous biology of the human population, and its great psychological plasticity as evidenced by the shifting of individuals across class lines. Such theories, as Brown (13) makes clear, stem from the ideology of a particular caste rather than from a scientific study of social organization. It is definitely not established that native (i.e., biological) factors play any major role in restricting human societal differentiations as found in the castes of India and the class hierarchies of Western countries.

---

[2] This statement is of course consistent with the view that genetically based individual differences in intelligence also play a selective role, according to the relative strength of other factors. The role of the diversified procedures which have been in social practise from ancient times to the present to limit or block upward shifting across the traditional class lines of a given society has been discussed by Veblen (78) and numerous other writers.

A third principal difference between insect and human societies arises through man's extensive human capacity for learning and reasoning based especially upon the elaboration of cerebral cortex in evolution. Dependent upon the use of these capacities through many generations but within a relatively short space of time as compared with insect social evolution, mankind has worked out many highly diversified societies, with very different forms of organization, institutions, and traditions (Benedict, 8). In each cultural setting man exhibits somewhat differently his capacity for transmitting the conceptualized traditions of previous generations to his descendants; yet all are alike in possessing some form of "social heritage."

Moreover, the members of each generation may increase, change, or even displace given aspects of the social heritage, rather than merely transmit the given system passively. Men are capable of a degree of plastic learning and reasoning which inevitably dynamizes and revises this process for better or worse. Furthermore, on the human level, not only do changes occur in the heritage of a given society on an internal basis, but also through interactions among societies (Malinowski, 51). Insect societies, on the other hand, appear to be limited essentially to passing on given social patterns on a biological basis, with changes appearing only through genetic evolution. Thus Wheeler (84) suggests the probability that the principal patterns of insect social behavior now extant were in substantially their present condition in remote Tertiary times. This is because insect social transmission is gametic transmission, and changes can be effected only through that process. A learning capacity is present, but ineffective in such matters. In certain genera of ants such as *Formica* the workers are capable of mastering fairly complex maze patterns (Schneirla, 64), and similarly they learn individually different routes in foraging outside the nest under natural conditions. Yet the learning process is stereotyped and rote in character, and as a process is limited to the individual and to the given situation (Schneirla, 68). Consequently new advances by the individual in learning a route contribute substantially nothing to the colony except additional increments of food, and the special learning of each individual dies with it. The activity of an insect colony, beyond furnishing food which maintains the population, offers little to further generations except an existing nest structure and the effect of certain simple interindividual behavior patterns, contributions of minimal plasticity rather directly depending upon the germ-plasm pattern of the social species. To know the contribution of a given ant colony to its brood, one need only know the taxonomic group and the given environment, and not the century in time beyond the Tertiary period; to know the contribution of given human parents, it is necessary to know very specifically not only the year and locality of residence, but also innumerable data concerning the given family, cultural influences, social affiliations, and the experience background of various individuals involved.

These differences are far-reaching ones, and in view of them we may say that, whereas social insects are biosocial, man is psycho-social. The differences appear to be far more significant than the similarities for understanding the characteristic nature of the respective phenomena, and the procedure of analogizing involved in applying the concept of superorganism consequently appears to be misleading for analytical study. The difference in interpretation, it should be remarked, is not one of mere emphasis but of logical procedure in studying the evidence. But fortunately, Wheeler (83) and Emerson as serious students of insect society have not employed the superorganism concept rigidly. Although Emerson (33) finds "a remarkable similarity between insects and human social systems," he also remarks: "In spite of many common analogous attributes, human society shows fundamental differences from insect social organization and these also must be analyzed for a proper perspective." He recognizes important differences in intelligence, leadership, the human use of symbolization, and in the fact that "the human species is the only organism which has developed an additional mechanism supplementing such biological heredity" (i.e., genic transmission). Yet, having noted these differences he returns to emphasize the analogues, as follows (33, pp. 168–169):

> The development of human social heredity through learned symbols is of such importance that this human attribute would seem to indicate the valid division line between the social and biological sciences. . . . However, even though techniques may differ and phenomena are diverse in numerous instances, I personally believe that scientific method is fundamentally the same whether applied to human social mechanisms or insect social mechanisms or whether applied to the social supraorganism or to the individual organism. In spite of the real differences between the societal types, careful comparison and correlation leads us to the formulation of important principles.

But instead of relying upon a method of analogy in studying social levels, stressing apparent but unclear similarities, it is preferable to compare phenomena by looking for the basis of both similarities and differences and endeavoring to emphasize these according to their respective importances. If biological analogues are "similarities in the function or use to the organism" (Boyden, 12), it seems necessary to find how far-reaching or how limited these similarities may be before they can be used in explaining social phenomena. For example, "communication" on the insect and human levels appears to be sufficiently different, both in its mechanisms and in the qualitative consequences of its function in social organization, as to require different conceptual terms in the two instances. In view of the very basic psychological differences which exist between the two processes, it seems preferable to use a term such as "social transmission" for interindividual arousal in insects, reserving the term "communication" for higher levels on which a conceptual process of social transmission is demonstrable. The similarity between these processes appears to have only a minimal and an illustrative, descriptive importance for theory.

A FUNDAMENTAL BIOLOGICAL FACTOR PROMOTING GROUP ORGANIZATION

Thus far our discussion has tended to be particularistic or "reductionistic" (Sloane, 72), in that describing characteristics of similarity or difference serves to emphasize part-processes and not unity of the social group, so far as the group is organized as a unit. Now we must look into the nature of organization process. Wheeler (84) offered an important contribution toward understanding insect social organization in his concept "trophallaxis," which signifies the reciprocal exchange of food or of equivalent tactual and chemical stimulation among individuals in a colony. An approach or "turning-toward" response is established to such stimuli, because of their adequacy to elicit (i.e., to *force* organically) the appropriate reflexes in dependence upon the conditions of presentation. Thus the queen feeds her first young larvae not because of a "maternal-care instinct," but because of larval secretions which effectively attract her to the larvae and which she licks up readily. The workers, while tending queen eggs, and brood, lick from the integument of these other individuals fatty exudates and salivary secretions, or regurgitate food as a reflex reaction to the antennal strokings of a nestmate. Wheeler (82) also presented abundant evidence for the existence of trophallactic relations between the ants and other insects (e.g., various staphylinid beetles) as "guests" in the colony, the latter eliciting a regurgitation of food through tactual stimulation as would nestmates, and attracting the ants through special glandular secretions or exudates. Thus the relation between ant hosts and "symphiles" is insured by much the same factors which are responsible for the existence of basic colony organization.

The process of trophallaxis is based upon the presence of inherited biological factors which insure simple stimulus-response relationships among individuals. In ants the behavior is not inherited in the sense that it is present as an adult pattern when the callow worker appears in the nest. It is probable that a rudimentary conditioning process is involved in the social adaptation of the individual as larva or as callow to the given species-colony chemical which is prevalent in the environment during feeding and equivalent activities. A simple learned basis is thereby provided for more versatile approaches to nestmates, following of colony chemical-trails, and returns to the nest as a foraging adult. This postulation (Schneirla, 66) is based especially upon observations by Heyde (42) of early behavior in young ants, and upon the investigations of Thorpe (75), which demonstrate olfactory conditioning in larval insects as an influence upon adult behavior. As a consequence of the inheritance by its individuals of the stable biological factors underlying trophallaxis, the insect colony acquires a unity which persists throughout the life of the group (Bodenheimer, 11), with disunity occurring only under exceptional conditions involving incidental changes in the trophallactic factors themselves.

It will be recognized that the trophallaxis process depends upon general biological factors somewhat comparable to those involved in the formation of simple and temporary aggregations, the incidental or subsocial groupings ("associations"—Alverdes, 5; Allee, 1) established through the independent approach responses of numerous related individuals to a common external stimulus (e.g., temperature). It is the hereditary specialization and diversification of such responses, as dependent upon particular types of stimuli from other individuals, and their generalization from early reflex-like reactions through simple habituation-learning, which accounts fundamentally for the integrity and persistence of the complex insect social organization. Throughout, the dominance of specific biological factors is apparent; thus the pattern of colony organization retains an essential insect-like constancy almost indefinitely in biological time, unless biological evolution intervenes.

TROPHALLAXIS AS INVOLVED IN HUMAN SOCIALIZATION

A somewhat comparable process of trophallaxis is basically involved in the socialization of the human infant. From the infant the mother receives agreeable stimulation, especially tactual stimulation (Allport, 4), as well as physiological relief exemplified by the effect of suckling, which affords not only agreeable and even erotic sensory effects but also relief from painful tension of the mammary glands and thus is sought by the mother (Ford, 36). Carpenter's (18) discussion of mother-infant relationships in the chimpanzee is enlightening in this connection. In the lower primates and other mammals the mother also receives a chemo-stimulative and physiological gratification through consuming the afterbirth, and licking and handling the young (Tinklepaugh and Hartman, 76, 77; Yerkes and Tomilin, 87). In the primates such intense gratification derives from holding and cuddling the young that in captivity it is sometimes impossible to constrain the mother to release a baby dead for hours or even for days (Lashley and Watson, 46). These and other physiological factors of direct stimulation and sensory gratification to the mother insure maternal orientation toward and psychological attachment to the young in most of the mammals, in which the duration and quality of parent-young association appears to be an important factor contributing to the degree of social organization (Darling, 28; Scott, 69). On the human level of course such developments usually advance to a high degree of elaboration, facilitated by an anticipation of the offspring and a psychological preparation for its arrival.

Because of the human mother's perceptual schema of the process of childbearing and care—typically influenced as it is by a great variety of effects from tradition and social experience—from the beginning the trophallactic relationship has a psychological setting of great importance. This means that by no means can the process of trophallaxis be termed with accuracy "the same process" on the ant and human levels. There is little doubt, however, that in mammals generally the entire maternal process is based upon and energized by the physiological and trophallactic processes, especially since the mother's responsiveness to young generally is intensive even in the primiparous females of lower mammals incapable of psychological preparation for the event and its significance (Wiesner and Sheard, 85; Beach, 7; Cooper, 25).

On the side of the infant human individual the trophallactic processes provide a necessary and effective basis for the development of a psychological affiliation with the mother and, through her, with society. "The child is part of his mother before he becomes an individual for himself and is part of a definite group for a long time before he can enter and join any group actively" (Bühler, 15). We cannot hope to do more here than to sketch the general outlines of the early socialization process deriving from this physiological foundation. Initially the infantile behavior is essentially unpatterned and on a reflexive basis (Pratt, Nelson, and Sun, 60), and those crude differences which may be identified in the infant's overt responses are attributable to the direct physiological *energy* effects of stimulation rather than to the nature of the given situation as adults know it. Under strongly stimulating conditions, as when extreme visceral tension exists or abrupt or intense extrinsic changes come about, vigorous mass action and usually crying result. Two incidental but important characteristics of such reflexive behavior should be emphasized. First, it serves to force the infant and his needs upon the mother and society, at first quite unintentionally of course, later more systematically through learning, thus coming to have a crude "signal-function" in the trophallactic process. Secondly, the mass-action response, although highly variable, also is characterized by a doubling up or flexion of the limbs. Predominance of the flexion response when the limb itself is intensely stimulated locally (Sherman and Sherman, 70) shows the forced reflexive character of the response, and also emphasizes its adaptive character, a getting-away-from the stimulus source (Goldstein, 41). Although at first this is a purely physiological factor, through it in the course of time specialized withdrawal reactions develop to particular objects and situations in which intense stimulation has been encountered (Schneirla, 65). Thus what is initially a purely *biological* part-process provides the basis for learned avoidances and later for negative attitudes in the social situation—a psychological process.[3]

More important for the early trophallaxis process is the fact that weak stimulation, such as the stroking of skin or relieving organic tensions, exerts a soothing effect and relaxes the infant.[4] Not only that, but the reflexive physiological effects under these conditions appear to involve an extension or abduction (i.e., a "getting-out") of the limbs as frequent component. At first reflexive, this response through conditioning becomes transformed into a specialized *reaching toward* or holding to objects or situations which have had soothing or tension-relieving effects. Thus holding out the arms toward the mother indicates (*to her*) that the infant needs her, and is an important objective sign of a growing specialized attachment to the mother and what she represents. *This is the nucleus of the infant's training to approach things, situations and people—first by reaching out, then by crawling and walking toward, and finally by positive attitude and conceptual expression indicating approval of given aspects of society* (Schneirla, 65). In the early stages of this social-training process the initial reflexive biological part-process becomes socially specialized and rather completely transformed into an externalized, psychologically organized system. The nature of this system, soon greatly expanded through selective learning rather than simple conditioning as at first, reaches conceptual status and comes to vary according to the relative emphasis of the given social and cultural environment upon things-and-people-and-ideas-to-be-approved.

DIFFERENT ROLES OF TROPHALLAXIS IN ANTS AND MEN

In comparison with this highly specialized psychological outcome of early trophallaxis on the human level, the stereotyped social repertoire

---

[3] In thus differentiating biological and psychological processes, it is not intended to suggest that psychological processes are nonorganic in the last analysis; rather, that psychological functions represent the elaboration and reorganization of the biological on a qualitatively new and higher level.

[4] Such effects were observed in the early studies at Johns Hopkins and were labeled "love" by Watson (80), although not at all "love" in the adult sense of an emotional attitude.

appearing in the young ant is rudimentary and limited, dominated throughout as it is by native factors. The social outcome of insect trophallaxis is largely set by hereditary factors; the social outcome of human trophallaxis is highly variable and plastic, in dependence upon the given cultural setting. On the human level the close trophallactic bond first established with the mother, family and immediate social environment expands into diversified and widened social relationships in very different ways according to what social agencies canalize and redirect the organization process. The trophallaxis process, a biological factor which is initially somewhat similar in the insects and in man (more on the human infant's side, and far less on the mother's) has a very different significance in the two cases for the eventual social pattern. In both cases it is a central factor in permitting the rise of a group organization and in molding the individual into the existing group organization, but in highly different ways as to how far the strictly biological processes are modified.

We are led to the conclusion that although important biological processes such as trophallaxis are represented both on lower and higher levels of social organization, their significance may vary greatly according to capacity for learning and in dependence upon factors influencing learning in the social situation. If space permitted, a similar conclusion might be reached from an analysis of individual "drives" or tissue needs in relation to social participation. Their role in insect social behavior is relatively stereotyped; on the human level it is plastic and highly modifiable. In man to be sure they are also fundamental, since tissue needs exist and compel adjustments, but the kinds of adjustments made depend widely upon the particular socialized selective-learning process involved. The socially acceptable satisfaction under given cultural conditions may be very different in nature from those tolerated and approved under other conditions. In all human societies most of the socially acceptable incentives appear to vary more or less widely from objects and processes which directly relieve drive tensions. In the socialization of the individual, his drive-reactions are greatly modified and elaborated through taboo and custom. Thus the relative importance of the principal types of incentives (sustenance, security, acquisitiveness, dominance, and social approval) may vary greatly among human societies and among different sections of the same society (Kornhauser, 44). Maller (52) found American school children from poorer neighborhoods somewhat less acquisitive and more cooperative in classroom situations than were children from well-to-do neighborhoods; and anthropologists (Goldman, 40) find some human societies (e.g., the Zuni) predominantly cooperative in their internal organization, others (e.g., Kwakiutl) predominantly competitive. Essentially similar biological part-processes are involved in these different human instances, but are metamorphosed very differently into psychological relationships according to the predominant pattern. The role of trophallaxis is so different in the socialization of insects and men that, in the final analysis, it cannot be considered the *same* process by any means. On the higher level it has a qualitatively distinct significance as compared with the insect level.

"DOMINANCE" CONCEPTS INADEQUATE FOR STUDYING ORGANIZATION

The role of trophallaxis has not been explored in the general study of vertebrate social organization. Instead, both investigation and theory have featured "dominance" relationships as presumably the most essential factor. As described by Schjelderup-Ebbe (63) in his classical studies with newly assembled groups of barnyard fowl, a social rank or dominance hierarchy is established in time by dint of reciprocal pecking among individuals. After an initial period of fighting and social instability, a ranking is established in which (in the simplest case of a linear peck-order) hen No. 1 pecks all of the others but is not pecked in turn, No. 2 pecks all but No. 1 and is pecked only by No. 1, and so on to the most subordinate member which is pecked by all and may never peck any of the superior members. Dominance orders have been described for a considerable number of bird species and for various other vertebrates including some primates (Allee, 2). Typically, dominance order is considered dependent upon aggressive behavior (Collias, 23); for example, Maslow (54) defines the dominant animal as "one whose behavior patterns are carried out without deference to the behavior of his associates."

However, the term does not always have this meaning and in general is not used very consistently. For instance, Noble, Wurm, and Schmidt (57) used the relative height of bill-holding between the members of a heron pair as an indication of dominance, on the assumption that this indirectly resulted from superiority in food-snatching as nestlings. And Maslow, who lays much stress upon dominance in studying primate social relationships, as the above definition suggests, appears to lapse both from consistency and from clarity when he states that "dominance in the chimpanzee is mostly of a friendly kind. . . . The dominant chimpanzee (at least in young animals) is a friend and a protector of the subordinate chimpanzee. . . . They form a close contact group and are dependent on each other. . . ." "Dominance in the macaque is usually brutal in nature, and . . . dominance in the cebus is in the first place tenuous and in the second place relatively non-contactual" (54, pp. 314–315). What these diversified relationships have in common would seem better characterized as "ascendancy," a behavior trait not necessarily dependent upon aggressiveness.

It is highly important to note that describable dominance hierarchies appear under rather special conditions, particularly when groups of birds or primates are confined within a small space, when incentives (i.e., food or drink) are restricted in quantity or in accessibility, or when sexual responsiveness is high. Moreover dominance relationships do not always stand out in grouping lower vertebrates, even in groups of fowl and especially when the groups are large, when social organization displays different characteristics (Fischel, 34). In certain animals studied carefully under field conditions, as for instance the howler monkeys studied by Carpenter (16), an efficient group organization exists without signs of intragroup dominance or aggressive relationships, whereas in others (e.g., baboons) aggression-dominance is prominent (Carpenter, 17, 19).

We must seriously entertain the possibility that dominance theory is an inadequate basis for the study of vertebrate social behavior. "Dominance" appears to be just one characteristic of social behavior, sometimes outstanding in group behavior and sometimes not, according to circumstances. Since the true "dominance" relationship is one of real or abbreviated aggression and withdrawal (Collias, 23), dominance must be considered a factor promoting the isolation and greater psychological "distance" of individuals, and thus more or less counteractive to factors which hold the group together. Perhaps a dominance situation may be viewed as one in which positive unifying factors are relatively weak but are somewhat artificially reinforced by special conditions, such as food scarcity or sexual receptivity (which serve to heighten reactivity to specific stimuli from other individuals), or by physical confinement of the group.

Factors related to social facilitation (Allee, 2, 3), and probably based upon original trophallactic relationships of one kind or another, may well furnish the major unifying basis in groups of lower vertebrates (e.g., schooling fishes), as seems to be the case in the social insects and in mammals. As an alternative to emphasizing dominance in adult groups, it would be well to examine carefully the nature and persistency of early contacts with one or both parents during the period of incubation in relation to "gregarious tendency" in later life. In the domestic fowl, as Brückner's (14) study shows, an intimate trophallactic relationship first exists between hen and chicks, only to be displaced after a few weeks by a condition in which the hen drives off the young. Comparably in mammals, the age of young when weaning occurs, if this change abruptly enforces separation from family conditions, presumably has an influence upon subsequent readiness to group and upon group behavior (e.g., the prominence of interindividual aggressiveness).

In a real sense, aggressive or dominance reactions are an indication of weak social responsiveness either because of individualistic reactions (e.g., sexual reactions) or an incompletely established group organization. Actually, interindividual adjustments in the formation of a new vertebrate group often pass from a stage of overt aggression to one in which tolerance reactions and social facilitation exist (Taylor, 74; Collias, 23). In different animals, the readiness with which early aggressive reactions change into qualitatively different relationships permitting a closer group unity may be opposed to different extents by the individualizing influence of factors such as sexual responsiveness, but otherwise may depend upon species capacity for modifying behavior. Bard (6) and Collias (23) have remarked that as cerebral cortex increases in the animal series, aggressive dominance relationships appear to drop back as prominent characteristics of social behavior. The importance of interindividual grooming, clearly a trophallactic unifying factor of compelling force in primate groups, has been emphasized by Yerkes (86). An infant chimpanzee first raised in isolation from others of its kind (Jacobsen, Jacobsen, and Yoshioka, 43), was at first aggressive when placed with a strange young chimpanzee, but within a few weeks there developed a pacific relationship of mutual dependence between the two.

Concepts such as dominance hierarchy tend toward a particularistic, static type of thinking about social organization, actually distracting attention from the essential problem of group unity. In studying social organization on any level, a theoretical procedure is desirable which centers around the conception of a dynamic integrative process rather than given characteristics such as dominance which may be sometimes absent. We believe that a more thoroughgoing ontogenetic survey of social behavior in the vertebrates will reveal the prerequisite importance of trophallactic processes for group unity wherever it occurs and whatever its strength.

CONTRASTS IN "COOPERATION" ON DIFFERENT GROUP LEVELS

The probability that trophallactic relationships intimately underlie intragroup approach reactions on all social levels suggests the importance of the principle of cooperativeness, elucidated by Kropotkin (45) as a factor in evolution. But of course the outcome in the group behavior pattern is very different according to the general level on which this factor operates. Some comparisons may be suggested.

Trophallaxis may be represented on its lowest or purely biological level by the common benefiting of individuals in an assemblage of lower invertebrates through the biochemical products of their own activity. Allee (1) cites many examples of such incidental byproducts of subsocial associations. It is clear that the result is an *incidental physiological facilitation of individual* metabolism, without any consequent elaboration of interindividual adjustments through learning. Such an elaboration occurs to a limited extent in the social insects, not only on the basis of hereditary specializations promoting such behavior, but also by virtue of a limited extension of interindividual responsiveness through social conditioning. Group function as a dynamic process thereby acquires a greater persistence and is extended into important functions such as reciprocal feeding and foraging; however, the psychological poverty of the process has been suggested above in our discussion of insect "communication." It is probably more accurate to term the capacity for mutual assistance in social insects *biosocial facilitation,* rather than "cooperation," because of these psychological limitations.

In contrast, *psychosocial cooperativeness* as it is found on the primate level involves an ability to anticipate the social consequences of one's own actions and to modify them in relation to attaining a group goal. The capacity for such behavior does not appear automatically, merely through the possession of cerebral cortex. The basis for some form of "cooperative" behavior in all probability is laid in early trophallactic relationships in family or intimate groups, as suggested above. The social consequences of this foundation may vary according to a variety of circumstances. In the social insects, the predominance of genetic factors in the socialization process assures the appearance of a highly stable "cooperative" pattern of very low psychological calibre. But in the vertebrates, such a pattern is by no means inevitable. The individualization of sexual responsiveness and other genetically contributed or learned factors may reduce its prominence greatly, as shown in dominance patterns.[5] The evolution of cerebral cortex through the mammalian series admits plastic learning as an increasingly important influence, and makes possible greater versatility in social patterning according to ontogenetic circumstances. Thus Crawford (26) has demonstrated the development through learning of cooperative relationships in the problem-solving and food-sharing of chimpanzees, a process very different in its psychological nature from the relatively stereotyped interindividual facilitation process of social insects, and qualitatively superior to the insect system. But even where cortex is most highly evolved, in man, it must be recognized that the predominance of a trend toward higher-type cooperation patterns is by no means inevitable. It is because man's group behavior depends mainly upon elaborated psychosocial pat-

---

[5] The appearance of dominance behavior in social activities is related by Collias (23) to the function of male sex hormone in particular. However, in a recent study of dominance behavior in chimpanzees, Birch and Clark (10) have been led to a different view on the basis of their finding that not only male hormone but female hormone as well (when in the necessary replacement amounts) (Clark and Birch, 22) can account for the appearance of dominance behavior.

terns of motives, attitudes and purposes and plans, and is not determined in its *patterning* by biological factors, that his societies are qualitatively distinct from those of insects.

It is frequently stated that, as Novikoff (58, 59) puts it, ". . . higher level phenomena always include phenomena at lower levels. . . ." This statement holds only if it is recognized that phenomena appearing in direct relation to biological processes on lower levels are not represented in the same fashion on higher levels, but there may influence group patterns very differently as they are modified, transformed and elaborated in new and diversified ways. They are not really analogues in a logical sense, for as we have found they do not have the *same* functions on different group levels except in a teleological and descriptive sense.

CONCLUDING REMARKS

To sum up, although similar biological factors underlie group unity on various levels of organization, these factors are not identical even in their basic or initial form, and their eventual significance for social patterning varies greatly from level to level. Analogical procedures such as those involved in using the "superorganism" concept are not adequate for studying social levels comparatively, because such procedures become preoccupied with general similarities rather than working toward an understanding of group unity through an evaluation of social similarities and differences.

Underlying the appearance of group unity on all levels are biological factors contributing to the facilitation of primary interindividual stimulative relationships, which, after Wheeler (83), we have termed *trophallaxis*. On different levels these factors are roughly similar in their general significance for grouping. Yet when we compare the insect social level with the simple-aggregation level on the one hand and with the human social level on the other, critically important differences are found in the basic form of trophallaxis and in its functional potentialities for group behavior. In view of qualitatively different consequences evident in the group activities of different animals, the "cooperation" factor as generalized by Kropotkin and Allee is subject to revision. It is necessary to differentiate interindividual relationships as "physiological facilitation" and as "biosocial facilitation" on the levels of simple aggregation and insect colony, respectively, and as "cooperation" on the psychosocial level typified by human society. In the light of this necessary conceptual differentiation, we are prepared to recognize the existence of a qualitatively different process of individual socialization on the human level, influenced very differently by psychological factors according to cultural pattern and social heritage, rather than in dependence upon the direct function of hereditary organic agencies as on the insect level.

The psychological plasticity contributed by human cortex admits the possibility that the role of the basic physiological factors (trophallaxis and drives) may be very different according to circumstances. We have endeavored to sketch a theoretical explanation of the manner in which individual socialization involves a different transformation and elaboration of the physiological factors into psychosocial patterns under different social conditions. As an analytical statement and not simply a value judgment, it may be said that from the standpoint of breadth of social organization and multiplicity of interindividual relationships a cooperative pattern (rather than a "dominance-hierarchy" pattern) represents the fuller attainment of human psychological resources. Dominance factors which emphasize individualistic motivation represent only a partial realization of group resources, on a lower psychological level, on which the clash of different subgroup motivations increases intragroup conflict and promotes tensions which make for social disorganization (Galt, 38). In criticizing "dominance" theory as applied to the vertebrates, we called attention to its reductionistic emphasis upon just those special characteristics which are not essential to group unity but in fact tend to operate against and reduce the psychological level of group integrity. For this reason in particular, "dominance" theory cannot be regarded as adequate for a comparative psychology of social organization.

Although insect-human analogies may offer an interesting way to introduce social comparisons, as investigation advances we must pass from them to a study of qualitative contrasts, if types of organization are to be understood and their relationships adequately evaluated. Superorganism theory and dominance theory have a common weakness, in that both emphasize particular group characteristics without directing attention toward the nature of group unity and toward conditions which favor or oppose it. Studies with chimpanzees (Crawford, 26; Nissen and Crawford, 56) show that infrahuman primates plastically acquire cooperative relationships under appropriate conditions, working purposively together toward common goals. Under other conditions, as we have seen, "dominance" aspects may be emphasized in interindividual behavior.

Similarly, the studies of Lippitt (47) with boy groups show convincingly that human behavior patterns and attitudes toward cooperative participation differ greatly according to whether the prevailing social climate has encouraged and facilitated the formation of a democratic or an autocratic group organization. Under the former conditions, individual psychological participation is considerably wider in its group references. Such studies assist social scientists to discern and emphasize the procedures which best realize the qualitative superiority of the human social level over subhuman levels. For although an insect society is limited to the biosocial level of organization, its genetically canalized social pattern considered as an adaptive device is obviously superior to a human social climate in which group members are taught not group participation for group goals but subgroup motivation and schismatic attitudes.

REFERENCES

1. Allee, W. C. 1931. *Animal aggregations.* Chicago: Univ. Chicago Press.
2. Allee, W. C. 1938. *The social life of animals.* New York: Norton.
3. Allee, W. C. 1945. Social biology of subhuman groups. *Sociometry* 8: 21–29.
4. Allport, F. H. 1924. *Social psychology.* New York: Houghton Mifflin.
5. Alverdes, F. 1927. *Social life in the animal world.* New York: Harcourt, Brace.
6. Bard, P. 1942. Neural mechanisms in emotional and sexual behavior. *Psychosomatic Med.* 4: 171–172.
7. Beach, F. A. 1937. The neural basis of innate behavior. I. Effects of cortical lesions upon the maternal behavior pattern in the rat. *J. Comp. Psychol.* 24: 393–439.
8. Benedict, R. 1934. *Patterns of culture.* New York: Houghton Mifflin.
9. Bierens de Haan, J. A. 1930. Animal language in its relation to that of man. *Biol. Rev.* 4: 249–268.
10. Birch, H., and G. Clark. Hormonal modifications of social behavior: II. *Psychosomatic Med.* (in press).
11. Bodenheimer, F. 1937. Population problems of social insects. *Biol. Rev.* 12: 393–430.
12. Boyden, A. 1943. Homology and analogy. *Quart. Rev. Biol.* 18: 228–241.
13. Brown, J. F. 1936. *Psychology and the social order.* New York: McGraw-Hill.
14. Brückner, G. H. 1933. Untersuchungen zur Tiersoziologie, insbesondere zur Auflösung der Familie. *Z. Psychol.* 128: 1–110.
15. Bühler, C. 1931. The social behavior of children. In C. Murchison, ed., *Handbook of child psychology.* Worcester: Clark Univ. Press. Pp. 374–416.
16. Carpenter, C. R. 1934. A field study of the behavior and social relations of howling monkeys. *Comp. Psychol. Monogr.* 10: 1–168.
17. Carpenter, C. R. 1940. A field study in Siam of the behavior and social relations of the gibbon (Hylobates lar.). *Comp. Psychol. Monogr.* 16: 1–202.
18. Carpenter, C. R. 1942. Societies of monkeys and apes. *Biol. Symposia* 8: 177–204.
19. Carpenter, C. R. 1945. Concepts and problems of primate sociometry. *Sociometry* 8: 56–61.
20. Cattell, R. B. 1937. *The fight for our national intelligence.* London: King.

21. Chen, S. C. 1937. The leaders and followers among the ants in nest-building. *Physiol. Zool.* 10: 437–455.
22. Clark, G., and H. Birch. 1945. Hormonal modifications of social behavior. I. The effect of sex-hormone administration on the social status of a male-castrate chimpanzee. *Psychosomatic Med.* 7: 321–329.
23. Collias, N. E. 1944. Aggressive behavior among vertebrate animals. *Physiol. Zool.* 17: 83–123.
24. Combes, M. 1937. Existence probable d'une elite non differenciée d'aspect, constituant les veritables ouvrieres chez les Formica. *C. R. Acad. Sci.* (*Paris*), 204: 1674–1675.
25. Cooper, J. 1944. A description of parturition in the domestic cat. *J. Comp. Psychol.* 37: 71–79.
26. Crawford, M. P. 1937. The cooperative solving of problems by young chimpanzees. *Comp. Psychol. Monogr.* 14: 1–88.
27. Crowell, M. F. 1929. A discussion of human and insect societies. *Psyche* 36: 182–189.
28. Darling, F. F. 1937. *A herd of red deer.* London: Oxford Univ. Press.
29. Eidman, H. 1925. Das Mitteilungsvermögen der Ameisen. *Die Naturwiss., Berlin,* 13: 126–128.
30. Emerson, A. E. 1928. Communication among termites. *IV Int. Cong. Entom.,* II, 1928.
31. Emerson, A. E. 1939. Social coordination and the superorganism. *Am. Midl. Nat.* 21: 182–209.
32. Emerson, A. E. 1941. Biological sociology. *Den. Univ. Bull.* 36: 146–155.
33. Emerson, A. E. 1942. Basic comparisons of human and insect societies. *Biol. Symposia* 8: 163–176.
34. Fischel, W. 1927. Beiträge zur Soziologie des Haushuhns. *Biol. Zent.* 47: 678–695.
35. Fisher, R. A. 1930. *The genetical theory of natural selection.* Oxford: Oxford Univ. Press.
36. Ford, C. S. 1945. *A comparative study of human reproduction.* New Haven: Yale Univ. Press, Publ. Anthrop.
37. Frisch, K. v. 1923. Über die Sprache der Bienen. *Zool. Jahrb., Zool. Physiol.* 20: 1–186.
38. Galt, W. 1940. The principle of cooperation in behavior. *Quart. Rev. Biol.* 15: 401–410.
39. Gerard, R., and A. E. Emerson. 1945. Extrapolation from the biological to the social. *Science* 101: 582–585.
40. Goldman, I. 1937. The Kwakiutl Indians of Vancouver Island (Chap. 6), and The Zuni of New Mexico (Chap. 10). In M. Mead, ed., *Cooperation and competition among primitive peoples.* New York: McGraw-Hill.
41. Goldstein, K. 1939. *The organism.* New York: American Book Co.
42. Heyde, K. 1924. Die Entwicklung der psychischen Fähigkeiten bei Ameisen und ihr Verhalten bei abgeänderten biologischen Bedingungen. *Biol. Zent.* 44: 624–654.
43. Jacobsen, C., M. Jacobsen, and J. G. Yoshioka. 1932. Development of an

infant chimpanzee during her first year. *Comp. Psychol. Monogr.* 9: 1–94.

44. Kornhauser, A. W. 1939. Analysis of "class" structure of contemporary American society—psychological bases of class divisions. In G. Hartmann and T. Newcomb, eds., *Psychology of industrial conflict.* New York: Dryden Press. Chap. II.

45. Kropotkin, P. M. 1917. *Mutual aid: A factor of evolution.* New York: Knopf.

46. Lashley, K. S., and J. B. Watson. 1913. Notes on the development of a young monkey. *J. Anim. Behav.* 3: 114–139.

47. Lippitt, R. 1940. An experimental study of the effect of democratic and authoritarian atmospheres. *Univ. Iowa Stud.* 16, no. 3.

48. Loevinger, J. 1940. Intelligence as related to socio-economic factors. *39th Yearbook, Nat. Soc. Stud. Educ.,* vol. I.

49. Maidl, F. 1933–1934. *Die Lebensgewohnheiten und Instinkte der staatenbildenden Insekten.* Wien.

50. Maier, N. R. F., and T. C. Schneirla. *Principles of animal psychology.* New York: McGraw-Hill.

51. Malinowski, B. 1945. *The dynamics of cultural change.* New Haven: Yale Univ. Press.

52. Maller, J. B. 1929. Cooperation and competition, an experimental study of motivation. *Tch. Coll. Cont. Educ.* no. 384.

53. Mann, C. W. 1941. Mental measurements in primitive communities. *Psychol. Bull.* 37: 366–395.

54. Maslow, A. H. 1940. Dominance-quality and social behavior in infrahuman primates. *J. Soc. Psychol.* 11: 313–324.

55. Neff, W. A. 1938. Socioeconomic status and intelligence: a critical survey. *Psychol. Bull.* 35: 727–757.

56. Nissen, H. W., and M. P. Crawford. 1936. A preliminary study of food-sharing behavior in young chimpanzees. *J. Comp. Psychol.* 22: 383–419.

57. Noble, G. K., M. Wurm, and A. Schmidt. 1938. Social behavior of the black-crowned night heron. *Auk* 55: 7–40.

58. Novikoff, A. 1945. The concept of integrative levels and biology. *Science* 101: 209–215.

59. Novikoff, A. 1945. Continuity and discontinuity in evolution. *Science* 102: 405–406.

60. Pratt, K. C., A. K. Nelson and K. H. Sun. 1930. The behavior of the newborn infant. *Ohio St. Univ. Stud., Contrib. Psychol.,* no. 10.

61. Redfield, R., ed. 1942. Levels of integration in biological and social sciences. *Biol. Symposia* 8: 1–26.

62. Révész, G. 1944. The language of animals. *J. Gen. Psychol.* 30: 117–147.

63. Schjelderup-Ebbe, T. C. 1922. Beiträge zur Sozialpsychologie des Haushuhns. *Z. Psychol.* 88: 225–252.

64. Schneirla, T. C. 1929. Learning and orientation in ants. *Comp. Psychol. Monogr.* 6: 1–143.

65. Schneirla, T. C. 1939. A theoretical consideration of the basis for approach-withdrawal adjustments in behavior. *Psychol. Bull.* 37: 501–502.

66. Schneirla, T. C. 1941. Social organization in insects, as related to individual function. *Psychol. Rev.* 48: 465–486.
67. Schneirla, T. C. 1944. A unique case of circular milling in ants, considered in relation to trail following and the general problem of orientation. *Am. Mus. Novitates,* no. 1253, pp. 1–26.
68. Schneirla, T. C. 1945. Ant learning as a problem in comparative psychology. In *Twentieth century psychology.* New York: Philosophical Library. Pp. 276–305.
69. Scott, J. P. 1945. Group formation determined by social behavior; a comparative study of two mammalian societies. *Sociometry* 8: 42–52.
70. Sherman, M., and I. C. Sherman. 1925. Sensorimotor responses in infants. *J. Comp. Psychol.* 5: 53–68.
71. Simpson, G. 1941. The role of the individual in evolution. *J. Wash. Acad. Sci.* 31: 1–20.
72. Sloane, E. H. 1945. Reductionism. *Psychol. Rev.* 52: 214–223.
73. Sturtevant, A. 1938. Essays on evolution. II. On the effects of selection on social insects. *Quart. Rev. Biol.* 13: 74–76.
74. Taylor, W. S. 1932. The gregariousness of pigeons. *J. Comp. Psychol.* 13: 127–131.
75. Thorpe, W. H. 1939. Further studies on preimaginal olfactory conditioning. *Proc. Roy. Soc. London* 127-B: 424–432.
76. Tinklepaugh, O. L., and C. G. Hartman. 1930. Behavioral aspects of parturition in the monkey (*M. rhesus*). *J. Comp. Psychol.* 11: 63–98.
77. Tinklepaugh, O. L., and C. G. Hartman. 1932. Behavior and maternal care of the new-born monkey (*M. rhesus*). *J. Genet. Psychol.* 40: 257.
78. Veblen, T. 1931. *The theory of the leisure class.* New York: Viking Press.
79. Warden, F. J., and W. Galt. 1943. A study of cooperation, dominance, grooming, and other social factors in monkeys. *J. Genet. Psychol.* 63: 213–233.
80. Watson, J. B. 1919. *Psychology from the standpoint of a behaviorist.* Philadelphia: Lippincott.
81. Wheeler, W. M. 1911. The ant colony as an organism. *J. Morph.* 22:307–325.
82. Wheeler, W. M. 1923. *Social life among the insects.* New York: Harcourt, Brace.
83. Wheeler, W. M. 1928. *Emergent evolution and the development of societies.* New York: Norton.
84. Wheeler, W. M. 1928. *The social insects.* New York: Harcourt, Brace.
85. Wiesner, B. P., and N. M. Sheard. 1933. *Maternal behavior in the rat.* Edinburgh: Oliver & Boyd.
86. Yerkes, R. M. 1933. Genetic aspects of grooming, a socially important primate behavior pattern. *J. Soc. Psychol.* 4: 3–25.
87. Yerkes, R. M., and M. Tomilin. 1935. Mother-infant relations in chimpanzees. *J. Comp. Psychol.* 20: 321–359.

T. C. SCHNEIRLA

The "Levels" Concept in the Study of Social Organization in Animals

Bibliography No. 52

NATURE OF THE "LEVELS" CONCEPT

Individuals and groups in the animal world may be thought of as being more or less advanced with respect to one or more series of different but related stages. Such a concept, which concerns the theory of "levels," may afford a useful and effective way in which to evaluate both the biological and psychological properties of individuals and the psychological properties of individuals and groups (Needham, 1929; Woodger, 1929; Redfield, 1942).

Organisms of different types exist under similar or widely different conditions. Even the "same" conditions may be met in terms of very different adjustment patterns in different groups. For the student of social phenomena it is important to know what similarities and what differences may underlie the adaptations of both solitary and collective organisms of different types in their respective settings. Widely different scientific opinions are encountered on this question. Some are inclined to believe that the similarities of the "lowest" and "highest" organisms have been underestimated (e.g., Chauvin, 1947), others take the view that vast and inescapably significant differences exist (e.g., Maier and Schneirla, 1935).

Metaphysical Devices in Characterizing Functional Levels

Although the writer has discussed the more philosophical aspects of this problem elsewhere (Schneirla, 1949), one question will bear consideration here. One of the most trammeling habits in traditional studies

---

From *Social Psychology at the Crossroads,* edited by M. Sherif and E. Rohrer. New York: Harper, 1951. Reprinted with permission.

of individual and society is the tendency to characterize complex phenomena in the simple terms of some metaphorical expression. Thus organized community functions are conceptualized on the insect level by Maeterlink as "spirit of the hive" and on the human level by McDougall as "group mind." A fallacy of metaphor is inherent in such naming. The conceptual term is so reified that functional characteristics of the phenomenon, which represent problems demanding investigation, are viewed as aspects of some vaguely generalized entity and are thereby held as already explained. Procedure in studying the phenomenon thereby becomes descriptive, and analytical, comparative investigation becomes superfluous.

The tendency to analogize individual and society is strong, and opens the way for irresponsible ethnocentric and subjective projections on the part of the individual who chooses the analogies. Thus, once Strecker (1940) has found the "mass mind" paranoic, it follows for him that world society must be saved by small elite groups of superior intellects, presumably participants in a nonparanoic mind. Analogies may be useful, of course, for introductory, pedagogical purposes, to emphasize and stress the characteristics of the phenomena under study. Certainly, for example, a most dramatic point is made when nervous conduction in an individual is analogized with communication in a social group. Events are no less dramatic when someone like Goebbels takes the analogy seriously, and sets himself up as the social neocortex sending out impulses to the spinal subgroups of society. Concern about the scientific adequacy of theoretical procedures is excluded when analogical devices are relied upon uncritically in studying adaptive processes.

It would seem necessary to develop the central conceptual terms in our study of individual and society in accordance with scientific standards of reliability and validity, recognizing that analogy is only introductory and illustrative and possesses no inherent dependability as a means of understanding the nature of individual and of group. Since the time H. Spencer seriously analogized human society as an organism, wide advances have been made both in biology and psychology which reveal the misleading character of this metaphor (Schneirla, 1946, 1949). Perhaps the most important risk inherent in this analogy is that it distracts attention from the extent to which a social group, composed of individuals, develops properties of its own that are not realizable within an organism considered as unit.

Views such as "supraorganism" (Emerson, 1939, 1942) are reductionistic from their inherent implication that the physiological integration and interaction of the cells, tissues, and organs in an organism are somehow qualitatively equivalent to the interactions of individuals and of subgroups in a society. In contrast, on the principle of levels, we recognize the necessity for constructing an appropriate new set of concepts when qualitatively distinctive functions are encountered. Thus, the alternative postulation to the supraorganismic interpretation is that the biology of the organism and the biology and psychology of individual and of group represent phenomenal levels which may be similar and even related to some extent but which possess important qualitative differences.

"Levels" as Differentiated Adaptive Systems

The levels concept postulates the existence of intraorganic and organic systems of phenomena which are comparable in their evolution and ontogenetic function but which also exhibit significant qualitative differences and in some important sense may be described as related but distinctive stages. Considered as surviving adaptive systems, the viruses, independent unicellular organisms, colonial organisms, metazoan organisms, and subsocial and social groups of different kinds, may be studied as members of a hierarchy of related functional systems in which basic relationships are present in very different settings of special functional properties and functional patterns (Woodger, 1929; Redfield, 1942; Novikoff, 1945). The expansion and development of each system represents not only a different condition of internal complexity, but, more important, a very different stage of qualitative integrity, marked by a capacity of the higher systems to function adaptively under more inclusive and more heterogeneous and variable surrounding conditions. A group or society, for example, has the advantage over an individual in adaptive resourcefulness in that it more freely plays multiple roles in space and in time. Hence groups and societies on the whole represent qualitatively superior systems in adaptive function.

In abstract terms, perhaps the most important qualitative similarity among surviving functional levels is that they are all more or less adaptive, presumably in basically related ways in some respects, in basically unrelated ways in others. What conditions may make for the survival or extinction of a system is obviously an important consideration for our entire discussion. Their most important differences evidently arise in their degrees of plasticity under conditions of environmental emergency and their properties for admitting opportune and well-integrated changes in the characteristic patterns. In order to evaluate the adaptive adequacy of a whole system, however, it is necessary to proceed from the objective fact of relatively successful environmental adjustment to an examination of the internal make-up or organization which is evidently responsible for the functional characters in question.

CHARACTERISTICS OF LEVELS
AND THEIR INTERRELATIONSHIPS

Internal Organization and Resemblances of Levels

Implicit in the concept of levels is the assumption that, in adaptive systems representing qualitatively inferior or superior stages, the part-processes exhibit important differences in their mutual interrelationships and in their various relationships with the inclusive aggregate. First of all, this brings up a fundamental question in the interrelationship of different levels; the question whether, as Collias (1944) states, "integrated systems at one level of organization may themselves be units of a more inclusive grouping. . . ." This might be the simplest basis for a relationship among levels, except that the objective world does not appear to function in the way implied.

Actually, when a part-process of a higher level resembles a "whole" of some lower level, it is likely at the same time to have a qualitative uniqueness by virtue of the setting in which it is incorporated (rather, has *become* incorporated *through elaboration in development and growth*) in the superior system. In other words, to say that evolutionary doctrine implies that higher integrative levels are derivatives of lower levels does not mean that "lower wholes" are repeated as such, as units, in the higher systems.

Two very different examples are: (1) the "cell" that has grown into relationship with an organismic matrix is not the same kind of functioning system as the independent, unicellular (rather, *acellular*) organism which may be *loosely* designated a "cell"; (2) there exists no such entity as "instinctive man" or "emotional man" considered as "animal nature" with a "cortical component" overlaid. A component functioning as a closely meshed unit in an organismic whole, or an individual organism functioning in a group, is qualitatively very different from the same component or individual when alone. The point here is that the concepts "whole" and "unit" as concepts actually are only abstract conveniences to be considered as preliminary devices in the study of adaptive systems. It is unfortunate that they can be very misleading.

Part and Whole as Relative in the Study or Organization

We may think of adaptive systems as physical, biological, biopsychological, psychological, subsocial and social. In a sense, these may be regarded as overlapping and interrelated adaptive stages. In evaluating and comparing their respective conditions of organization, it is often necessary to study parts or part-processes intensively as though they existed separately from the whole. This procedure is methodologically and theoretically sound only if it is combined appropriately with an investigation of the pattern as a whole. It is necessary to bear in mind that the "part" is only an abstraction and that the concept of parts as isolated units is paradoxical and unreal. As Sloane (1945) has suggested, our preoccupation with the part or unit as isolated may be considered a derivative of our folkways and socialized thought-patterns which conceptualize the individual as an independent object making social contacts.

From the failure of "atomistic" theories in biology and social psychology we learn, on the contrary, that the part functions or units may be adequately conceptualized only in view of their relations to and their dependence upon the wholes to which they belong. Actually, an atomistic conception of adaptive systems seems most adequate on the lowest organic levels, in which the "whole" (e.g., a sponge) may be described with a measure of validity as not only a morphological but also a functional sum of its parts. Even here, however, the view becomes false and misleading if carried very far in a functional study of the whole. It is inevitably less and less applicable to the understanding of progressively higher levels.

Preliminary Comparison of Individual, Association, and Social Group

The metazoan ancestral forms which were presumably first differentiated from protozoan organisms are conceivable as hollow masses of flagellated cells among which functional differences appeared, opening the way for specialized properties of the whole in nutrition and in locomotion (Hyman, 1931). In the course of evolution, further versatility of the whole appeared with additional differentiations among component parts, and at the same time with greater dependence and interconnection among the parts. With such changes, the organic unity imposed upon the mass through growth and division was supplemented by an increasingly complex and qualitatively superior functional unity. Living sponges, which are essentially colonies of growth-aggregated individuals having only a limited neuroid-mechanical transmission system, are decidedly more limited in the scope, variety, and orientation of their activities than is a jellyfish, in which diversified parts are unified functionally through a simple nerve-net system. Behavior of the sponge as an aggregate is little more than a summated action of individual parts or chimneys, with a virtual absence of diversified patterns of function, whereas in the insect one observes a variety of behavior patterns smoothly performed in a well-coordinated fashion by a well-integrated individual. The advances in whole-function were gained through greater intraindividual specialization coupled with a wider range of interrelationship among individual units, and the correlative reduction of autonomy and of functional independence in the components.

A contrast of colonial organism and metazoan organism is not to be taken a priori as a direct parallel of a contrast between social group and individual. The first pair represents different kinds of organic aggregates, all appearing through growth from a basic form, possessing in the metazoan organism a closer physiological interrelationship of the components. Subsocial aggregates (e.g., "associations") did not appear through the internal specialization of an ancestral unit-type, but through the assembling of individuals which in the most generalized associations became incidental parts of one another's environments by virtue of generalized properties. In contrast, in the more specialized social groups, individuals began to be environmental necessities of one another. Even wider and more important differences are found between organism and social group in the relation of the part to the aggregate. Study of individual variations through the animal series is in a sense preparatory for the study of social organization, but not in the sense that intraorganic relationships are directly parallel to those of animal groups.

PREREQUISITES FOR ADVANCED ORGANIZATION IN INDIVIDUAL AND GROUP

Discarding the analogy of individual and group on theoretical grounds does not mean that we turn away from the study of individuals in their group settings. Rather, we gain thereby a healthy skepticism concerning attempts to find common principles which will hold for part-to-whole relations in both individual and group situations. It seems clear that in the scientific study of individual and social group the problem of organization must be approached by different although not entirely independent methods. We may expect to find that advances in integration have different prerequisites in individuals, considered as a series of adaptive types, than in groups.

Individual Properties Underlie Group Functional Pattern

An intriguing picture is presented by studies of progressive organization in individuals through the animal series. The morphological basis may be sketched somewhat as follows: in the lower metazoan invertebrates (e.g., jellyfish), there first appear various patterns of radial symmetry in structure, with interchanging dominance-subordination relationships among the parts in physiological function and behavior. There next appear (e.g., in flatworms) patterns of bilateral symmetry and cephalization (antero-posterior polarity), a condition which admits stable patterns of physiological function and behavior. The radially symmetrical types have generalized nervous centers of limited properties; a "brain" or clearly dominant center first develops with bilateral symmetry, as an efficient transmitter from sensitive anterior regions (e.g., in earthworms). In the arthropods and especially in the insects it has also become a coordinator, while the coordinating efficiency of the nervous system as a whole is on the increase. With the appearance of cerebral cortex, in the higher vertebrates, the controlling function of the brain reaches its highest point, the coordination of parts and the unity of the organism are at their maximum in the animal series. These characteristics roughly set the limits of individual attainment and the pattern and qualitative level of intraindividual organization, hence are correlated with differences in the psychological level of the individual organism (Maier and Schneirla, 1935).

Those properties of individual organisms which set limits for the level of individual behavioral capacity also are among the factors involved in setting the qualifications of individuals, as wholes, for participation in group situations—considered as wholes of qualitatively different types. We are concerned here with what individual properties influence the *kind* of group pattern which emerges. Perhaps the most significant organic factor conditioning the qualitative level of the social pattern is the extent to which the central nervous system has developed. In the lower invertebrate organisms, capable only of temporary behavior changes largely involving peripheral sensory and motor processes (e.g., coelenterates), the persistence of more than the simplest type of group through active individual responses is hardly to be expected. The capacity for conditioning and stereotyped learning evidently contributes to the persistent integrity of groups in insects, but on the other hand, it is subordinate to the stereotyped mechanisms insuring interindividual responsiveness which predominate in the insects (Schneirla, 1946). It is difficult with our present knowledge to discern precisely what organic and functional characteristics contribute to the presence of social life on different animal levels and what characters influence variations in its form. The fact seems to be that organic maturation makes somewhat similar but also very different contributions on different levels, in both of these respects. Differences in the potential capacity to learn must be involved in very different ways, both setting limits upon the elaboration of organization and upon its relative plasticity in different animals.

In a preliminary way, the speculation may be advanced that a social pattern which is dominated by specific and reflexively stereotyped organic mechanisms must have definite qualitative limitations. Insect social patterns are an example. On the other hand, when individual capacities for perceptual development and learning through experience are greater (e.g., in primates), the social pattern may not only gain in complexity and in stages of organization within a species, but also become more versatile and more variable according to conditions. The relative plasticity of the social pattern in relation to new emergencies presented by the environment would appear to depend particularly upon the extent to which a capacity for conditioning and learning can modify the influence of specific organic factors underlying social behavior. Group comparisons on this basis afford an advantageous approach to the understanding of levels in social patterning.

Individual Properties Limiting the Level of Group Function

It is apparent that the characteristic organic and psychological qualifications of the component individuals must basically condition the nature of the social structure attainable by the species. In the lower animals the individual functional contributions are more or less uniform for the species, hence the species social pattern is highly predictable under the species-typical environmental conditions. Although in such cases individual capacities limit group function more rigidly than in higher forms, for reasons suggested above, group function even then is not to be considered a simple aggregate or sum of individual components. However limited the individuals may be, biologically and psychologically, every group pattern must be regarded as the product of components functioning in a system. To understand the level of organization, it is evident that its dynamic properties must be examined under conditions which are sufficiently varied to reveal representative properties of the pattern.

The *complexity* of group function and its *adaptive adequacy* are not necessarily dependent upon superior individual capacities in the psychological sense. To take what may be a somewhat extreme example, the behavior of certain army-ant species in their mass raids under forest conditions is amazingly complex, and the observer might well be led by the sight of highly adaptive collective maneuvers to an exaggerated estimation of the level of behavioral capacities of individuals functioning in the raid. Analysis of the complex function, however, shows that the workers themselves are capable of only very simple reactions, which within the progressively more complex group situations of daily raids carried out in a heterogeneous forest environment, can result in a seemingly very intelligent social strategy. In a homogeneous action setting, however, with the possibility of progressive developmental stages excluded through smaller numbers of participants, the group either is virtually unorganized or is limited to a simple milling phenomenon (Schneirla, 1944).

SIMILARITIES AND DIFFERENCES
AMONG ANIMAL SOCIAL PATTERNS

Outstanding Similarities Between Insect and Mammalian Societies

One of the most common sources of analogies in animal societies is that between insect and mammalian societies. In the hands of Emerson (1938, 1942) this procedure has advanced to a serious and specialized stage at which analogies are offered as a means of scientifically studying the respective social phenomena, and the process is extended to include individual organisms. Some of the outstanding analogies are as follows:

1. Communication within the whole. Within the individual organism, nervous impulses from one locality arouse other localities to a simultaneous action, or hormones transmitted through the blood stream coordinate the action of separate organs or systems. The insect community is aroused through the propagation of excitement from individual to individual; for example, excited termite soldiers rap their heads repeatedly against wooden gallery walls, transmitting a vibratory effect which arouses other individuals close by or at a distance. An ant excites her nest mates through antennal vibrations; a man sends a message by telegraph, arousing certain distant individuals to action.

2. Division of labor. The differentiation of gametes and somatic cells in individual organisms is analogized to the presence of fertile individuals and infertile workers in insect societies; the transmission of food by infertile insect workers may be analogized to the function of cells in an individual's gastrovascular tract. The worker and soldier castes of insect colonies may be compared with the various strata or castes in human society.

3. Rhythms, life cycles. The individuals of many animal forms produce their gametes at fairly regular intervals in a recognizable rhythm; social insects characteristically produce their sexual forms seasonally. The life cycle of birth, development, and senescence in an individual organism is paralleled in social insects by colony foundation, expansion, and degeneration.

4. Phylogeny in organism and superorganism. Many biologists besides Emerson believe that similarities such as those outlined above afford a valuable basis for studying the nature of organisms and social groups. From their point of view, essentially the same biological processes have been involved in the evolution of individual organism and of social group considered as supraorganism. Natural selection is regarded as having been involved in closely comparable ways in the evolution of individual and

of group; that is to say, individuals or groups have been eliminated in an equivalent fashion whenever the internal processes of the system have been maladaptive to a sufficient extent.

To be sure, the assumption that selection has worked comparably in the evolution of individual and of group at different phyletic levels has been utilized as a theoretical tool by numerous biologists (e.g., Fisher, 1930). On the other hand, this preliminary, trial conception of evolutionary processes at different levels is now opposed by evidence indicating that natural selection frequently has different properties for the individual organism than for the social group (Simpson, 1949). The bold deductive leaps of analogy certainly afford a stimulating set of devices for general and preliminary comparisons, but do not call attention to important differences among organism and group levels.

Individual Properties Which Promote Group Formation

The analogical procedure really is teleological in that individuals and social groups are compared in terms of the end results of their functions, without emphasizing underlying processes which may be very different. Hence, analogy has serious shortcomings as a means of understanding the nature of different types of functional systems in the animal world. If we are seriously comparing individual organism and social group, we must attempt to find what characteristics of individual organisms permit them to aggregate on different levels of group function. This is the problem raised, but not really answered in any sense, by traditional concepts such as "symphilic instincts" or "gregarious instinct" (Schneirla, 1949).

Jennings (1942) has described in some detail the groupings which appear in *Paramecium,* the ciliate protozoan. The appearance of such groups contrasts with the fact that solitary activity is common among paramecia. Paramecia frequently alter their direction of swimming, and frequently come by chance close to the borders of zones containing weak acids. Thereupon they typically move toward and enter such zones (Jennings, 1906). Since faintly acid products are given off by these ciliates themselves, groups of the paramecia are likely to form where a few have concentrated. Groups of genetically related paramecia (clones) form most readily, since the free daughter individuals produced by the division of a single parent are alike organically, and react more similarly to outer conditions than do the progeny of different parents. Because one of the adequate conditions for eliciting the reaction may be brought about through *Paramecium* activity, groups frequently form among these organisms. Because the reactions are not given to other individuals as such but to specific biochemical conditions which elicit the approach reaction, the grouping thus depends directly upon physiological conditions.

In simple association or in subsocial aggregations, groups commonly form through the approach reactions of different individuals to environmental conditions influencing all of them separately (Allee, 1938). Thus swarms of dance flies form through similar individual responses to local conditions such as light, humidity, and temperature. The example of *Paramecium* represents a somewhat more advanced case, in which the products of individual metabolism may exert a stimulative effect equivalent to that of an attractive environmental stimulation. Aggregations on the latter basis are common among otherwise solitary Arthropods such as the sowbug, *Oniscus* sp., groups of which may be found under stones and in similar places, where they assemble through common environmental effects but remain together for a time by virtue of added individual stimulative effects commonly available as chemical products of metabolism. In such aggregations the unity of the group is incidental to the presence of the individuals as such, and the role of individuals may be replaced by essentially equivalent environmental influences.

What differentiates a social group of any complexity from the above situation is that in social aggregations the unity rests upon an interdependence of individuals, a condition deriving from the effects exerted by group members as individuals with given qualities. In persistent social groups, the attractive effect of group members for one another has become more fixed and specialized, and typically produces in some characteristic manner a fixation of individuals for the group situation as well. The assemblage is thus held together particularly by the approach-responses of members based upon the individual properties of members. These reactions may be simple and primitively physiological, as when based upon characteristic "colony odor" effects in the case of social insects, or more elaborate and dependent upon a recognition of cues through learning as in higher mammals. Hence important psychological differences must be recognized in the "knowing of kind" in various types of social groups.

Adaptive Adequacy not a Criterion of Levels

The influences of individuals upon one another vary greatly among subsocial groups as well as among the social types. Incidental aggregations under similarly effective environmental conditions, and even accidental collections of individuals, introduce a variety of possible adaptive benefits, as Allee (1938) in particular has pointed out. For example, in swarms of various small flies, the meeting of sexual forms often is thereby assured, an advantage even more specific to stable social groups. Another kind of adaptive outcome, demonstrated in the associations of various lower invertebrates, is the modification of the microclimate or effective local environment through the products of individual metabolism, or, in some instances, even of organic degeneration. Both overcrowding and (frequently) undercrowding may result in results harmful to many or to all of the animals concerned. The involvement of what Allee has called "unconscious mutualism" in incidental assemblages and in environmental-response associations must be considered a potentially important factor in the survival or extinction of population segments or entire species, also in the rise of new factors influencing aggregation-responsiveness. Even under the simplest conditions of grouping, other individuals of the species may function as parts of the effective environment of each component individual, and thereby constitute factors in its potentialities for reproductive function and for survival.

The significance of grouping for individual and species survival is potentially great in representative social types, in which the interdependence of individuals is more specialized and group integrity is more systematic and persistent. In a pattern which is at the same time more stable and persistent and more varied and complex in its characteristics, the aggregation of individuals and its potentialities for mutuality may have a considerably greater adaptive significance than in the case of presocial groupings. The meeting of the sexual forms is assured through their proximity and also through the rise of facilitative behavioral (epigamic) situations in the social group. Furthermore, in the social setting, increasingly complex and systematic controls may function which introduce characteristic selective processes in the operations of pairing and mating. The behavior patterns of vertebrate groups frequently involve interindividual relationships describable as dominance hierarchies, involving differential individual adjustments based upon relationships of aggression, ascendancy, or some other form of priority which is demonstrably important for pairing and mating in many species. Thus in the prairie grouse a well-marked dominance hierarchy is present in which the apical male individual or "master cock" carries out most of the mating operations (J. W. Scott, 1941). In clans of howler monkeys, on the other hand, which have low dominance gradients within the group, priority in mating is virtually absent except in the case of "marginal males" excluded from the group proper but loosely affiliated with it (Carpenter, 1934).

There are many and varied additional consequences of the social condition on various levels, which have recognizable survival values for the functional groups, their individual members, and for the species. Defensive functions are promoted, not only through various kinds of individual specialization (as in insect castes) but also through the establishment of a more or less regular territory (as in various vertebrates) which is more defensible by virtue of group behavioral properties. Through the construction of nests or shelters, an increased environmental control is attained which promotes the longevity of individuals and also supports group survival through facilitating propagation and the raising of young. Obtaining a regular food supply is promoted through the rise of routine foraging operations, and on the side of group health, a social stimulative effect upon feeding (very probably accompanied by a facilitation of digestive processes) through the presence of other individuals has been demonstrated (Allee, 1938) in various bird and mammal groups.

It is doubtful whether adaptive adequacy is a criterion of diagnostic value in the evaluation of "levels," since groupings of all types, both presocial and social, are more or less effectively adaptive in relation to their respectively different settings. There is little point, for example, in comparing insect and mammalian social groups in terms of adaptive success, for very different environmental conditions have been met successfully by each in its characteristic way. The properties influencing behavior on different levels, according to how they restrict the potentialities for group function, open environments which are narrow or broad, and simple or complex, to which the respective aggregations adjust according to their behavioral and biological capacities.

It is not the relative adequacy of environmental adaptation, then, but the potentialities for qualitative elaboration and for plastic modification of group organization under emergencies which may be present in different patterns of animal aggregation, which are most relevant to the question of "levels."

FACTORS UNDERLYING GROUP UNITY ON DIFFERENT SOCIAL LEVELS

Differential Organic Thresholds—A Process Basic to All Aggregations

Preparatory to a consideration of group organization on different levels, it is desirable to look more closely at the question of group affiliations and group unity. The primary consideration, as already mentioned, is the problem of the gregarious tendency itself. It is probable that in most types of groups, from incidental associations to specialized social patterns, the coming together and remaining together of individuals is based in some essential way upon fundamentally similar biological factors. An important basis for such factors may be found in threshold differences in sensitivity, and in motor function (and probably also neural function), which directly or indirectly promote orientation toward the source of weak stimulation (Schneirla, 1946, 1949). This type of factor also is identifiable in characteristically solitary animal types, varying in nature according to organic condition (e.g., in normal feeding, cf. pairing and mating reactions), and in their case often promoting the temporary survival of incidental aggregations.

Although this condition, which may be termed the factor of "differential organic thresholds," appears to be a basic physiological contribution promoting gregariousness on all levels, there seem to be important differences in its relative organic specialization in different animal types. For example, on the level of associations, the groups are relatively unstable and internally uncomplicated and become formed in response to environmental stimulus effects rather than specifically to stimulation from other individuals. In various subsocial groups such as the ear-wigs, the young of which remain with the mother for some time after their appearance, a specific individual-attractiveness factor enters as a specialization with greater potentialities for group cohesion. The effectiveness of this factor, as concerns biological mechanisms underlying both individual attractiveness and responsiveness to others of the species, is greatest in the animals capable of social organization. As a common biological basis for all types of animal aggregation, we are thus postulating organic (threshold) properties as a basis for individual processes of approach to stimuli of low intensities and individual capacities to contribute attractive effects in the group situation. Theoretically, these two types of mechanisms must have evolved in relation to each other.

Although the fundamental basis of the grouping tendency apparently is broadly similar throughout the animal series, the manner and the relative directness of its expression (i.e., the variables intervening between organic basis and behavioral outcome) are widely different in various social patterns. On the lowest aggregational levels (e.g., *Paramecium*) the "threshold" factor is evidently simplest and most directly expressed in the sense that it is least subject to ontogenetic modification. In the complex social forms of some insects, some ontogenetic modification is identifiable, although stereotypy dominates the patterns; on the higher mammalian levels stereotypy is least and implementation through learning is greatest. The organic process underlying the origin and maintenance of aggregation on different levels evidently lies in the biologically prepotent effect of weak stimulation in eliciting a form of approach reaction peculiar to the given level. Comparisons of food-taking and other approach responses in the animal series show that through this process essentially similar functional results may be achieved in very different ways on different animal levels (Maier and Schneirla, 1935). How different the expression of this "approach" process may be on different levels is revealed in a contrast of insect and mammalian aggregations.

The "Trophallaxis" Factor in Social Insects and Mammals

In both social insects and social vertebrates, hereditary factors centering around the "differential organic-threshold factor" have become elaborated to an extent which permits the maintenance of a more or less involved form of group behavior pattern. In addition to factors of sensory threshold in social insects, Wheeler (1928) outlines in some detail the availability and function of larval exudates and other nutritive and sensory sources of effects insuring approach responses in the social group. Organic mechanisms of this type are identifiable in the various types of social insects in the brood, reproductive individuals, and developed workers, providing a basis for establishing and continuing adult relations to the brood and to other adults. Wheeler's term for the resultant social condition is "trophallaxis," which may be taken to signify a more or less widespread process of mutual stimulation and responsiveness among all members of the colony, underlying both colony unity and colony organization. In the foundation of the insect colony, the social process begins when the queen licks and handles her eggs, responding to attractive fluids upon them, and on a similar basis licks and feeds the larvae as they develop. A comparable process is involved in the attraction of adult workers to the brood, the queen, and to other workers, in various mutual relationships involving licking of body surfaces, stroking with antennae, and feeding with liquid food regurgitated by adequately stimulated individuals.

The nature of the trophallaxis process as a basis for colony function was first described by Wheeler (1928) and has been discussed in relation to colony behavior by Schneirla (1941). It is significant that in the ants, which exhibit social organization universally in all species, some form of trophallactic process is recognizable in all cases. Moreover, corresponding to the relative development of trophallactic properties in the species, the elaboration of the social pattern may be limited or expanded. For example, colony unity and organization are near their peak in the Formica species in which interindividual stimulation processes are most extensive, and near their low point in certain Ponerine species in which interindividual stimulation is limited in type and in scope, and feeding by regurgitation is absent.

There is much evidence that the "trophallaxis" factor is also basic to the appearance of social behavior in mammals. In insects, the function of the organic basis (i.e., differential thresholds, glandular attractants) is expressed in a relatively stereotyped way which depends upon learning and ontogeny to a relatively low although evidently essential extent. Here factors pertaining to the germ plasm and arising through organic growth more directly canalize the elaboration of individual behavior in the characteristic environment than in the case in mammals. On the other hand, in mammals the role of factors promoting plasticity and learning is wide, and the potentialities for modification and elaboration through experience are much greater than in insects. The influence of trophallactic factors begins to be exerted in the earliest relations between mother and newborn infant, which progressively become specialized and elaborated in the social situation according to its make-up. The hereditary basis for trophal-laxis in mammals includes not only properties of differential thresholds in exteroceptive sensitivity and in the principal antagonistic muscle systems, but also in the autonomic nervous system and viscera (Schneirla, 1949). On mammalian levels, however, and especially in primates, these factors are not themselves finally determininative of the nature of social pattern, except that through learning they insure the presence of one or another type of socialized adjustment.

Contrasting Social Levels: Insect and Human Societies

Although the organic basis for group formation by animals appears to be broadly similar on all levels, the genetic factors also differ both in complexity and in degree of specialization from the presocial to the so-cial, and from one social level to another. Even more striking differences are attributable to the involvement of ontogenetic processes centering around learning on different social levels.

Differences of this type may be illustrated in a further comparison of insect and mammalian societies. As Emerson (1942) has pointed out, some of the most prominent similarities between these societies are in the involvement of communication and the presence of division of labor (i.e., functional specialization).

"Communication" in the social insects may be understood as a direct transmission of excitement from individual to individual through tactual encounters (e.g., of antennae) or through substratal vibrations or even air-transmitted vibrations in some species. In ants and other social insects, a finder individual returning to the nest from a food-place is able to arouse her nestmates, which thereby are often enabled to find the food source sooner than by chance. If the secondary individuals are not merely aroused by the finder but also are oriented to some extent, the latter effect is at-tributable to incidental stimuli which differ in character according to the species. For example, certain ants are able to find a new food source through following chemical traces incidentally deposited on the substratum by the excited finder during her wandering return to the nest. The situa-tion in honeybees is not altogether clear at the present time. Although it has been demonstrated that finder bees may present directive olfactory stimuli to secondary bees in an incidental manner during their stay in the hive after foraging flights, von Frisch (1948) has recently reported that presumably nonolfactory directive effects may be received by secondary bees through the finder's "dance" on the comb. Until the actual nature of the effect transmitted from the finder to secondary bees becomes known, it seems preferable to consider this type of communication qualitatively similar to the types which are already known for insects. Only in its general adaptive function as social transmission does insect "communication" resemble human language.

In the language processes of human society, the following distinctive characteristics are identifiable: (1) the words are typically symbolic, in that they have meaningful and representational identifications with objects and situations, and as abstractions are frequently conventionalized; (2) the items are directive, in that they are used to influence the behavior of other individuals as well as to influence oneself; (3) they are used in social situations in relation to anticipated effects, i.e., intentionally, with the expectation of producing given desired or expected results; (4) the symbolic items or words are patterned and rearranged according to the effective motivation of the user or the nature of the anticipated outcome (Bierens de Haan, 1930). As parts of the process of their individual socialization, children normally master the meanings and composition of language so that the symbols can be expressed in spoken and also in a written form if appropriate education is available. The capacity to learn and to elaborate symbolic cues in anticipatory ways apparently depends upon the relative development of cerebral cortex as a basis for advances in perceptual and conceptual learning. The chimpanzee's inability to use vocal sounds as language cues thus seems attributable to his failure to reach the essential level in organizing meaningful perceptual and conceptual relationships, a level which the human infant normally attains before the end of his first year.

The essential characteristics of language as it appears on the human level are not apparent in social insect communication, which evidently is not conceptualized or abstract but is limited to a generalized excitation effect performed in a stereotyped way without anticipation of given social results. In contrast, Crawford (1937) found mature chimpanzees able to use gestures such as shoulder tapping in social signalling or perhaps even symbolic ways, with evidence of anticipating a given effect in the signalled individual and a readiness to participate in the joint activities (e.g., rope pulling for food).

To a certain extent, insect and human societies are alike in having caste-like patterns, or a division of labor. Morphological types are characteristic in insect societies, correlated with differences in individual function (Wheeler, 1928). Beyond the sexual dichotomy of male and female, many species have structurally differentiated subtypes in one or both sexes. In many ant species there are polymorphic worker types, sometimes in a clearly dimorphic distribution, sometimes in a continuous series from the smallest or minor type of worker to the largest or major type. Correlated with organic differences, the various polymorphic castes exhibit functional differences: the males and fertile females are more or less completely specialized in reproductive function, with workers major predominant in defensive activities, workers minor as brood-tenders within the nest, and intermediate workers most frequently as foragers. The genetic basis of caste differentiations is typified in most ant species by conditions in which males appear from unfertilized eggs and females from fertilized eggs, the queen-type female from overfed larvae and the worker-type female from underfed larvae raised from eggs of equivalent germ plasm make-up. These differences in feeding are effective during the larval stage, and after the worker individual emerges from the pupal condition as a young adult (incapable of further growth) the characteristic functional capacities of its caste appear within a few days, in a predictable correlation with its organic make-up. The caste functions are stereotyped on the basis of the predominant role of germ plasm factors, and lasting changes can appear only through further organic evolution in the species.

Castes on the human level, in contrast to those of insects, exist in the form of social or functional classes differentiated essentially according to processes of learning in a given social context. The psychological plasticity of human society is evidenced by the frequency with which individuals shift across class lines in a democratic situation, as well as by the possibility of recognizing the cultural and traditional fixation of such barriers when they are impermeable (Newcomb and Hartley, 1947). The one social feature in which there is a distant biological basis for the caste differences of many human societies is a sexual dichotomy, with its differentiation of reproductive functions. Few behavioral differences follow in a fixed manner from this dichotomy, as in the case of insects; rather, in many ways organic differences express themselves indirectly in behavior, and psychological differences in attitudes and values in their characteristic nature are products of social heritage and cultural pattern. Human experience, and in particular the widely different practices of distinctive cultural groups, indicate that in man biological differences between the sexes, in themselves, can have a very indirect influence upon social function, or a very different influence according to individual socialization.

The case is different in insect societies, in which biological factors dominantly channelize social function. Drone bees, like the males of most other social insects, lack any organic basis for brood tending, foraging, or feeding other individuals—these are functions peculiar to the genetically and trophically differentiated workers. The human male on the other hand is capable of performing most of the functions popularly termed "female," other than the specific female reproductive functions.

Although social functions are in many cases generalized among the worker individuals of many insect species, they are often highly differentiated to an extent dependent upon polymorphic differences, and reproductive function in most cases is limited to a relatively small number of individuals. In the higher primates and particularly in man, on the other hand, reproductive function for the most part is a general property of adult individuals throughout the population, and no restrictive biological properties are involved. Crowell (1929) has suggested that this generalization of germinal properties throughout the population has tended away from biologically-based functional specializations and has facilitated a generalization of individual function in the family and social sphere. Highly stereotyped human social forms quite often are characterized by one or another type of arbitrary sexual delimitation (e.g., celibate castes); these however are maintained culturally rather than through the germ plasm as in insects.

It is unnecessary to elaborate upon the vast differences between social insects and man in the matter of how social patterns develop and change. Insect social patterns, arising ontogenetically through the predominant role of hereditary factors, require chromosomal and evolutionary processes as a basis for lasting changes. The individual learning capacity of insects, stereotyped and situation-limited as it is (Schneirla, 1949) plays a subordinate (facilitative) role in individual socialization and shows its greatest elaboration in the foraging act (i.e., outside the nest). The various individuals make reproductive or nutritive contributions to colony welfare, and no individual learning that occurs can change the standard pattern of the species in lasting ways. The society is biosocial in the sense that it is a composite resultant of individual biological characteristics dominating group behavior.

In contrast, human societies may be termed psychosocial in that cultural processes dominate which are the cumulative and nongenetically transmitted resultants of experience and learning, under the influence of human needs and desires interacting variably with the procedures of labor or conflict, reasoning or routine. That is to say, although the trophallactic basis of human society is similar in a very general way to that of insects, it is very different in specific ways in its biological basis, and quite different in the predominant importance of individual learning and group experience for its realization in social intercourse.

ONTOGENETIC FACTORS INFLUENCING GROUP ORGANIZATION

Factors Introduced Through Individual Socialization

On all social levels, the formation of the group depends in some manner upon the initial reciprocal stimulative relationship between adults and young. In all cases this association evidently centers around some type of trophallactic process, which establishes a basis for a bond between the individual and the social group. For the young individual, the social group is thereby first represented by the attending parent or parents. The qualitative differences in the nature of this bond may be readily seen through carrying further our comparison of insect and mammalian societies.

In the social insects, the period of development during which the young individual typically is cared for by adults may involve a limited behavioral socialization through the trophallaxis process. In connection with feeding, the individual, as a callow and perhaps earlier as a larva, may be habituated and conditioned to the characteristic colony odor. After emergence, in many social insects there is a short period of a few days in which the callow attains to the adult behavior pattern, including particularly trophallactic relations, i.e., interindividual stimulation and a capacity for mutual feeding.

It has been suggested (Maier and Schneirla, 1935; Schneirla, 1941) that this pattern may be elaborated from a basis of early reflex-like responses, and that the early transition of trophallactic processes within the nest may be a factor in the later appearance of individual foraging outside the nest. The involvement of hereditary organic characteristics as factors in the process is indicated in the honey bee, in which the early socialization of the worker passes through three principal stages ending with adult foraging, each of these stages correlated with a demonstrable change in secretory function. It is our suggestion that this process, whereby the individual is incorporated into the colony, involves a simple learning factor which may be essential to the process although not prominent in it. The fact appears significant that in certain Ponerine ants in which no definite initial socialization process can be identified in the worker, trophallaxis is greatly reduced in the colony, and members of the population are very loosely integrated.

The term "biosocial" seems adequate for the insect social level, with its predominance of specific organic factors accounting for a representatively stereotyped pattern with (at best) only a secondary learning factor. However, it is not adequate in any real sense for the mammalian level.

The development of infant primates entails a far longer and more complex process of acquiring reciprocal relationships with the mother, then with the wide social environment, than in any other animal. The process evidently is one of a developing trophallactic integration of mother and young, involving reciprocal cutaneous stimulation, relief of mammary-gland tension in the mother by the young, and conversely, a relief of food-lack in the young and a presentation of optimal cutaneous stimulation by the mother (Schneirla, 1939, 1946). Apparently a process of conditioned learning in the young, involving an increased responsiveness first to the stimuli accompanying the feeding act, then to secondary accompanying stimuli, sets the stage for a process of selective learning. In the latter type of learning, the individual acquires the capacity to change a situation through particular reactions rather than others, according to the degree or kind of organic "satisfaction" received under different stimulative conditions. In the lower mammals the process of weaning typically initiates a considerable change or even a break in this relationship, and the family association of the young often does not continue into a protracted group affiliation. However, the young have acquired a motivated responsiveness to the exteroceptive cues (e.g., visual, auditory) of the species, which may function later in the initiation of pairing and in its sequel events, and in the formation of loose social groups (e.g., rat colonies) or of temporary groups.

In primates, including man, a similar process is based upon and is energized by certain physiological factors and the trophallactic interchanges to which they lead. The infrahuman primate mother, like that of many lower mammals, typically consumes the fetal membranes, licks the embryo and her own sexual zones, and consumes the afterbirth. For the infant the major initial effects are optimal cutaneous stimulation and relief of physiological tensions in feeding, for the mother, comparable cutaneous effects and organic relief through a reduction of tensions. However, the resulting process of learned attachment between mother and young is manifestly more complex and highly organized than in lower mammals (Yerkes and Tomilin, 1935). The primate parent-young attachment typically leads beyond the weaning stage and constitutes a basis of great importance for the subsequent wider affiliation of the young animal with the social group.

On the human level the initial organic processes have substantially the same role in principle, and their effect as a basis for some kind of trophallactic reciprocal relationship between mother and young is also the same in principle. Yet it is manifest that the socialization process may be very different in its outcome, depending upon the social context in which the early family relationships develop. Whereas the human mother typically anticipates the infant as such, it is doubtful that the lower primate mother's growing attentiveness to her changing sexual zones during pregnancy has a forward reference of definite perceptual expectancy, even in multiparous females. The chimpanzee mother is much quicker to become attached emotionally and perceptually to the infant as a social object than are the mothers in lower mammals, yet the relative complexity of her perceptual schema and understanding of this object has its limitations far below the psychological level attainable by the human mother.

It is possible that we shall begin to find the solution to the difference in the patterning of social behavior in different mammals in the characteristics of the early socialization situation. In all cases the basic aggregation-responsiveness of the young apparently arises through the initial trophallactic situation of the young. Approaches to the mother afford a basis for approaches to others of her kind, and expand inevitably into the social group. Dependence upon the mother generally shifts after weaning into a dependence upon the social group in primates, but not as closely or as continuously in lower mammals. The lower mammals and particularly the rodents generally have more than one young born at a time, which inevitably introduces a competitive factor into their demands upon the mother. Such experiences, together with other factors such as the abruptness of weaning, may exert important influences upon the later sociability of the young and hence perhaps the entire species social pattern.

It is possible that the character of the early social environment of the young mammal may have a considerable influence upon its capacity for subsequent group behavior. Preliminary evidence suggests that the amount of time spent by young rats with their mother and the opportunity for free trophallactic relationships with her and for associations with litter mates have bearing upon the later "sociability" of the individual. Early deprivation of this sort seems to result in an abnormally great tendency for aggressiveness toward species mates or independence from them. A female lamb which J. P. Scott (1945) raised on the bottle from birth, and kept apart from other sheep until nine days of age, never became an integrated member of the flock. She showed almost no tendency to play with other lambs, and as a rule behaved independently of the other sheep. She did not approach the flock to any extent until her first heat period, and only briefly then. When Jacobsen, Jacobsen, and Yoshioka (1932) raised a young chimpanzee apart from others of its kind from the time of birth, and at nine months of age this animal was placed with another chimpanzee infant, he was at first disturbed and aggressive, and required a few weeks of companionship before relations became acceptant and dependent between them.

Priority Factors and Dominance Hierarchies

As an approach to the study of vertebrate groups, the "dominance hierarchy" concept has occupied a foremost position since the first studies of Schjelderup-Ebbe (1922) with barnyard fowl brought the "peck-right" type of social pattern to contemporary attention. This type of hierarchy is the most readily identified in birds as well as in numerous other vertebrates, and lends itself easily to quantification. Within less than two decades a relatively voluminous literature has developed concerning this type of group structure in all of the principal vertebrate groups from fishes to primates (see summaries by Allee, 1938, 1948, and Collias, 1944).

The "dominance-hierarchy" concept usually implies a series of aggression-subordination relationships in the group, in which one member forces the submission of another by attacking fully or partially, or "threatening" an attack. A dominance hierarchy centering around aggression-submission relationships is an outstanding characteristic of group behavior in many vertebrate animals. As Allee (1948) has pointed out, however, the best known cases of dominance hierarchy are from studies of captive animals. In the forefront of attention are the results of studies with domestic fowl artificially confined in enclosures which hold all animals in the situation. The results of such studies do not necessarily suggest what kind of group pattern if any might arise if the group had been formed on another basis, or if the subjects had been free to group in dependence upon their initial responsiveness to one another.

It would seem that the ecological, psychological, and sociological conditions which lead to clear-cut dominance-subordination relationships must become better known before the real significance of this characteristic in social study may be appraised. In mammalian groups in their natural situation, the appearance of dominance patterns in a species may depend first of all upon the characteristic early parental and family relationships of the young, and its prominence in the group situation may also depend upon the manner of feeding and other typical environmental conditions. It is an interesting fact that whereas dominance relationships are minimal and cooperative relationships outstanding in the organization of the bisexual clans of Central American howler monkeys (Carpenter, 1934), male despotism and relative differences in dominance are prominent in groups of rhesus monkeys (Carpenter, 1942). One important difference in the origin of these patterns may concern the fact that young rhesus males separate from their groups in early adolescence and live in distinct groups with other young males until early adulthood, when they join a bisexual group and compete for social rank. Not only the trophallactic situation in the family and in early group life, but also factors influencing sexual behavior apart from these, must be considered as a basis for understanding typical group patterns in a species.

The problem is of course much more complex on the human level. Investigations with human groups in the United States have shown that the extent to which hostile aggressive behavior is involved in the group relations of children depends for one thing upon the individual's experience of aggression in previous group contacts according to how they involve dominance relations or group integrative patterns (Lewin, Lippitt, and White, 1939), and in experiences of aggression contacts with adults (Anderson, 1939).

It seems desirable to subject the dominance concept to a thoroughgoing appraisal, in order to identify more validly its relationship to other factors and characteristics in group organization. If trophallaxis factors may be postulated as the source of individual behavioral properties leading to aggregation and group unity, it seems necessary also to recognize the intervention of factors which lead to intragroup conflict according to their "strength." The administration of testosterone propionate to vertebrate subjects results in behavior changes through which group status of the injected individuals is likely to rise. Exclusive possession of females by certain males is outstanding in groups of prairie grouse (J. W. Scott, 1941) and rhesus monkeys (Carpenter, 1942) in which the dominance hierarchy is strongly developed, whereas generalized intercourse between the sexes is more prevalent in groups of howler monkeys (Carpenter, 1934) in which dominance differences are low.

If dominance status is a matter of aggressive tendencies for the most part, and has its main basis in factors such as adult sexual drive and individualistic food-taking, it is a process which concerns interindividual "distance" in social patterns and not group unity. As a distance-governing pattern in the more solitary vertebrates it is involved in the warding off of other males from territory held by a male in breeding season, in more social vertebrates it is a source of pair conflicts which may hold the group to a low degree of cohesion (Collias, 1944; Allee, 1948). In the Scottish roe deer, as Darling (1937) has reported, the group is male-led and is held to a small size by intragroup aggressive relationships. On the other hand, the female-led groups of red deer, with far lower aggression-dominance, become much larger and retain the young animals in the herd for a longer time than do the roe deer. It is probable that when aggression-dominance as a source of intragroup conflicts exceeds a given intensity and persistence, an effective social group with cohesion and stability may become impossible.

If it is true as Zuckerman (1932) states that "an adequate primate sociology is impossible without reference to the principle of dominance," it is even truer that if this principle is not viewed in its proper relation to other social factors, an adequate animal sociology is still less attainable. A reductionistic motif is not lacking in dominance doctrine, for when intergroup relationships are stated as matters of aggression or withdrawal; social patterns are most readily compared in terms of the relative prominence of dominance-hierarchy characters, and phyletic differences receive less attention. As Anderson (1946) has put the matter for social-adjustment studies on the human level, we are aware of domination but are not sufficiently aware of socially integrative behavior.

As a matter of fact, the dominance concept itself cannot validly be used as though it referred to a qualitatively equivalent process on all vertebrate levels. In the social behavior of lower vertebrate animals the dominance characteristic seems to be outstandingly of the peck-order type, although there are known to be many exceptions. In mammals the status of dominance relationships is much more complex and variable. In primates such as howler monkeys and chimpanzees, an ascendance factor must be recognized independently of a conflict-based dominance. In herds of red deer the leader usually is an experienced female, who does not gain her position through fighting (Darling, 1937). Scott (1945), reported no significant correlation between dominance and leadership order in a flock of sheep, and Stewart and Scott (1947) found a similar absence of any indication of relationships between these characteristics in a flock of goats. The "Spitzentier" animals (Fischel, 1927) which act for short times as pioneers in groups of fishes or birds, although they require facilitation from the group to maintain their role and typically hold it only in a temporary and limited sense, nevertheless represent a function of ascendancy which must be considered as important for group organization. The point holds even in the simpler situation of insect group function, in which some of the workers in a colony are "leaders" in the sense that they exert a greater facilitative effect through their work-rate in the group than do others (Chen, 1937) or as in the mass activities of army ants, the "leadership" is generalized and held briefly by any members of the group in dependence upon their happening to reach the front border of the swarm (Schneirla, 1940).

Although Maslow (1936) has defined a dominant animal as "one whose behavior patterns (sexual, feeding, aggressive, social) are carried out without deference to the behavior patterns of his associates," it is doubtful that this statement would be valid for the whole pattern of any functioning social group, even for those of very sharply defined dominance character. In monkeys and chimpanzees, even the most dominant male changes in behavior and attitude toward his sexual partner when she is sexually receptive (Yerkes, 1939). Grooming, or mutual preening, is one reciprocal activity in which the dominant animal is responsive to and dependent upon the subordinate, or the reverse (Yerkes, 1933). Chapple (1940) concluded from his study of human group relations that, basically, hierarchies as developed in human society tend to rest upon the ability of one individual to evoke responses from others at a given time.

Individual Motivation and Group Pattern

The primary factor underlying social aggregations on all levels appears to be the capacity of the mother or both parents to stay with the young, which opens the way for relations of mutual stimulation, response, and dependence to be set up as the young are reared. On all levels the evolution of organic factors underlying this capacity has involved the appearance of special mechanisms insuring mutual stimulation of parent and young. Larval secretions and adult regurgitation in social insects have a function basically similar in this sense to that of mammary glands in mammals. It is evident that the complexity of superimposed factors is greatest in the mammals, which are far less stereotyped in their social patterns than are most insects. The contrast is greatest with the primates, in which a prolonged association of the young with parents opens the opportunity for an extensive learning in group functions (Yerkes and Yerkes, 1935). Presumably the organic factors which facilitate the lengthy associations of parents and young, and those accounting for a slow and complex maturation process, have evolved in relation to those underlying a superior capacity for behavior modification through learning.

The socialized modification of the insect worker individual is relatively simple and is dominated by stereotyped processes arising through the involvement of the individual in group-feeding situations. That of mammals is infinitely more complex and variable, also very different in complexity and in elaboration on different levels, as new factors become involved. In higher mammals, learning contributes increasingly to individual socialization, which therefore is subject to wider differences in dependence upon group and environmental conditions of development than is the case in lower forms. This also means that maladaptive social behavior may appear more readily than in the stereotyped patterns of lower levels.

We have suggested that the limits of individual psychological capacities, particularly as they affect the socialization process, constitute an important factor imposing boundaries on the kind of group organization possible under given conditions. For example, when the parents are able to participate actively in the selective learning of the young, as some birds evidently can do to an extent and many mammals to a greater extent, the social environment of the young individual is inevitably limited or expanded in dependence upon the social and psychological capacities of the parents. The human ability to develop an abstraction of "one's kind" is a vastly less space-limited and more versatile process for group unity than is the dependence of lower mammals upon direct sensory cues and that of insects upon odor.

The ontogeny of the individual approach to the group underlies his group motivation. The human infant first reaches for his mother incidentally and on a physiologically-forced basis (Schneirla, 1946, 1949), then through a learned act of skill in manipulating his arm in a simple "purposive" manner, later through the use of a learned perceptual symbol, first in language, then in thought. Thus reaching toward social objects is fundamentally a matter of an action-based perception, then may also become symbolic and represent the consequences of an approach far more effectively. Throughout the process, there function social taboos and encouragements which influence learning selectively and serve to control the conditions under which the individual participates in the group. The socialization of young animals in lower primates is far simpler especially because no ability to initiate vocal "reaching" symbolically in the group situation is present.

The socialization process in man may be viewed as a matter of progressive interrelated stages, each arising upon the basis of previous ones, in which through the development of socialized motives and "goals" the individual is assimilated into the culture. In another connection the writer has discussed the relationship between the basic physiological processes and the socialized outcome, on different levels (Schneirla, 1949). In man, the process seems to depend upon the occurrence together of certain interruptive (disturbance) or vegetative (relief) processes in the organism with respectively different environmental situations which arouse them. This type of coincidence provides the basis for simple conditioning processes which open the way for a more complex selective learning of incentives, adjustments, and goals, in which the parents assist. In lower mammals the nature of incentives and goals and the whole pattern of motivation is always rather directly related to the underlying organic conditions ("drives") and the related environmental situations themselves. In man even adjustments to sustenance and security incentives (and of course, to those of sex) become highly modified according to cultural factors concerning prestige, dominance, social approval, and the like. Because the young of lower mammals receive a more standardized and stereotyped preparation for social participation, the result in their case is typical of the species.

SUMMARY CONSIDERATION: ORGANIZATION IN INDIVIDUALS AND IN GROUPS

How well a "whole" is organized depends upon the extent to which its parts function together as a system. The degree to which a system is organized may be evaluated in terms of the complexity and qualitative elaborations in the interaction of its parts and in the formation of interactive subsystems among them. In an important sense these remarks may be applied both to individual organisms and to aggregations of organisms, so far as these may both be considered as types of whole systems.

The levels of individual organisms and the levels of aggregated organisms presumably are interrelated, if the view is correct that aggregations must have arisen and developed selectively in evolution when the daughter products of fission or of sexual reproduction remained together or associated in some sense other than one of common growth. Despite this consideration, individuals and groups cannot be considered parts of a single continuous series of levels, and the parts of an organism do not necessarily function together in the same way that individuals function together in a social group. Some of the similarities are striking; the differences are also significant and essential to a diagnostic, analytical study.

Our real problem in this paper has been to consider the principal forms of animal aggregation in terms of their comparable characteristics. The first question in understanding group organization concerns the basis on which the component individuals happen to be together, the second their behavior (i.e., group pattern) in remaining together. The *gregarious factor* as it may be called appears to have basic similarities on all levels, although its relation to the eventual group pattern is very different in dependence upon superimposed factors. Incidental associations, insect groups, and the various forms of vertebrate aggregation all possess widely similar reaction tendencies to stimulative effects which may be encountered by individuals. In the simplest forms, the associations, the reactions are to localized environmental effects; in the higher types of aggregations they emanate from the individuals themselves. The attraction of individuals to one another forms and holds the group together, in the simplest cases through similar responses throughout the group, then on the basis of more specialized types of adjustment which become progressively more modifiable in the course of ontogeny on the respective higher levels.

The similar genetic basis underlying the gregarious factor in different organic settings we have characterized as a physiological process accounting for a turning toward weak stimulation. The incidental facilitation described by Allee for the association level typically involves physiological effects of the products of metabolism,—the biosocial cooperation typical in insect groups is qualitatively superior in that through a certain development in ontogeny a "trophallaxis" or specialized stimulus-exchange relationship of individuals can develop. This process is traceable through all higher levels, although it appears in different organic forms and in very different psychological and social contexts. Pattern differences among the levels may be understood in terms of (1) the different psychological capacities of individuals which limit potentialities for individual function and for plastic ontogenetic socialization, and (2) the ecological, environmental, and social conditions under which the early stages of group development have occurred.

The second type of influence (i.e., the "social setting") is more or less standard for lower levels; however, its variability becomes increasingly important in progressively higher levels. Social-aggregation tendencies are initially elaborated in many forms through behavioral relationships arising in the early association of parents and young. In the higher levels, this situation contributes important new formative potentialities for the assimilation of the individual into the social group. In insect groups and higher types, more or less specialized responses are established to group members as distinct from strangers, as an outcome of the trophallactic process and initial individual socialization.

Numerous other processes may be termed *social distance* factors in the sense that they tend to modify, reduce, or to vitiate the influence of the aggregational factor. That is, while the gregarious factor promotes the formation of some type of group which may be close and maximally facilitative or loose and diffuse according to the strength of this factor, the "social distance" factors tend to modify the pattern by complicating the conditions of interindividual approach and by introducing tendencies for withdrawal from other individuals or from the group situation. Individualistic sexual factors, in the males particularly, frequently serve this function, leading to the formation of group patterns or "dominance hierarchies" the nature of which depends upon intragroup aggressive relationships. The formation of groups of this pattern apparently requires the fixation of social position through individual discriminative learning of differences among others in the group, hence such groups are size-limited in subhuman animals. In some animal forms the establishment of dominance hierarchies apparently depends to a great extent upon access to reproductive relationships within the group, and may thereby play a selective role. Whether the aggression-dominance process accounts for a distinctively organized group, is minimal in the group pattern, or prevents any group formation except sexual pairing, seems to depend in particular upon the nature of the reproductive biology of the species. Dominance patterns are also facilitated through the overpopulation of small areas or through the availability of limited incentives (e.g., food) when the organic needs of associated individuals are high.

By definition, the highest social levels are those in which qualitative elaboration and plasticity in new emergency situations are greatest. The effective environments of primate social organizations are much more complex and variable than are those of social groups in lower organisms. Under different environmental conditions the capacities for modifiability in individuals and group are expressed differently and to varying extents. Under laboratory conditions when problems arise demanding collective effort, chimpanzees become able to cooperate on an adjustment level which is not apparent in the field (Nissen, 1931), utilizing gestural abstractions as means of influencing the behavior of others (Crawford, 1937) and hence as an effective group coordinating device. In human social situations, the amount of individual conformity required under given conditions differs from one culture to another, and within any one culture may vary temporally in dependence upon current social conditions. In the socialization of Hopi Indian infants, there is a noticeable lack of avoidance training, a characteristic which stems from an absence of social emphasis upon individual possession of objects (Dennis, 1940). American college students solve syllogistic problems very differently according to whether the problems are presented in terms of emotionally-loaded political and social symbols or in less preceptually coercive terms (Lefford, 1946); in the first case their solutions are dominated by the social-conformity (J-curve) factor (Allport, 1934), but in the second there are indications that individual reasoning abilities have been involved much more effectively. The vitiation of reasoning and higher psychological capacities in complex mammalian societies does not mean that what emerges will be equivalent to the nonreasoned stereotyped patterns of lower levels. The conditions are very different, and the result is very likely to be maladaptive with respect to group welfare.

On the social levels which are potentially highest in the above sense, factors may intervene which favor the retention of a stereotyped culture, or in other cases a plastic and progressive culture. The outcome is especially dependent upon whether a demand for maximal individual emotion-supported adherence to traditional forms excludes from the social situation the species potentials in new contributions from individuals and from subgroups. On lower levels, the characteristic species social patterns arise through an effective domination of the underlying biological processes over the interindividual relationships involved in socialization and in environmental adjustment. For example, studies of group function in lower mammals indicate that the characteristic pattern of group leadership depends to a considerable extent upon species reproductive processes. On the human level, a wide range of processes may be involved, producing leadership relations which are contracted or wide in their intellectual, economic, and social representation of subprocesses throughout the group, or on the other hand represent few or none of the subprocesses.

In order to dispense with sharp distinctions between individual and group which are actually paradoxical in studying social patterns, the tendencies expressed in individual socialization must be studied on different levels in terms of the growth and elaboration of group dependence and group relationships. Even in social patterns showing a maximal individual articulation, a socialized individual always lives with reference to a group in some sense in the processes of group integration, and coordination. Also according to the nature of social pattern, there exist various transitional stages between individual and group, individual and subgroups. Group organization needs to be studied in terms of interindividual dependence and subgroup interrelationship in their bearing upon group patterns on different levels. Further evidence is needed concerning what types of factors dominate individual and subgroup contributions to group organization on the respective levels.

In the last analysis, the utility of postulating different social levels depends upon our discerning the relative roles of biological factors underlying aggregation and those modifying or opposing it. Particularly important is the relationship of these processes in various animal types to psychological capacities which can facilitate or oppose aggregation and well-integrated group organization according to the special conditions of culture and social situation. It seems clear that any progressive modification of social patterns on the lowest levels is rigidly dependent upon the slow processes of natural selection and biological evolution. This long-time process occurs, as we have seen, in a variety of ways as concerns the entrance of qualitative specialization and behavioral versatility in group function. The importance of discernible differences in this process in different animals makes analogizing by similarity from level to level a procedure of doubtful validity, unless the analogies lead to thoroughgoing comparison.

Man, due to his potentially great freedom from the restrictions of biological processes, or to the opportune utilization of socially beneficial biological factors in the evolution of social patterns, can attain a far higher standard than in lower levels, depending upon how his psychological capacities are permitted to influence social progress. As Simpson (1949) puts the matter, "Under our ethics, the possibility of man's influencing the direction of his own evolution also involves his responsibility for doing so and for making that direction the best one." The problem of what is "best" for man's social welfare is properly a preeminent concern of the scientist in his investigation and theory.

REFERENCES

Allee, W. C. 1938. *The social life of animals.* New York: Norton.
Allee, W. C. 1948. Animal sociology, *Encyclop. Brit.*, 1948 ed.
Allport, F. W. 1934. The J-curve hypothesis of conforming behavior, *J. Soc. Psychol.* 5: 141–183.
Anderson, H. H. 1946. Domination and social integration in the behavior of kindergarten children and teachers. *Genet. Psychol. Monogr.* 21: 287–385.
Bierens de Haan, J. A. 1930. Animal language in its relation to that of man. *Biol. Rev.* 4: 249–268.
Carpenter, C. R. 1934. A field study of the behavior and social relations of howling monkeys (*Alouatta palliata*). *Comp. Psychol. Monogr.* 10.
Carpenter, C. R. 1942. Societies of monkeys and apes. *Biol. Sympos.* 8: 177–204 (Redfield, R., ed.).
Chapple, E. D. 1940. Measuring human relations: an introduction to the study of the interaction of individuals. *Genet. Psychol. Monogr.* 22:1–147.

Chauvin, R. 1947. Le progrès de la psychologie animale moderne et leur intérêt en psychologie. *Rev. Quest. Sci.* 20: 188–204.

Chen, S. 1937. The leaders and followers among the ants in nest-building. *Physiol. Zool.* 10: 437–455.

Collias, N. E. 1944. Aggressive behavior among vertebrate animals. *Physiol. Zool.* 17: 83–123.

Crawford, M. P. 1937. The cooperative solving of problems by young chimpanzees. *Comp. Psychol. Monogr.* 14: 1–88.

Crowell, M. F. 1929. A discussion of human and insect societies, *Psyche* 36: 182–189.

Darling, F. F. 1937. *A herd of red deer*. London: Oxford Univ. Press.

Dennis, W. 1947. Does culture appreciably affect patterns of infant behavior? In T. Newcomb and E. L. Hartley, eds., *Readings in social psychology*. Ch. 6, Sect. I.

Emerson, A. E. 1939. Social coordination and the superorganism. *Am. Midl. Nat.* 21: 182–209.

Emerson, A. E. 1942. Basic comparisons of human and insect societies. *Biol. Sympos.* 8: 163–176 (Redfield, R., ed.).

Fishel, W. 1927. Beiträge zur Sociologie des Haushuhns. *Biol. Zent.* 47: 678–695.

Fisher, R. A. 1930. *The genetic theory of natural selection*. Oxford: Oxford Univ. Press.

Frisch, K. von. *Aus dem Leben der Bienen*, 4th ed. Wien: Springer.

Galt, W. 1940. The principle of cooperation in behavior. *Quart. Rev. Biol.* 15: 401–410.

Hyman, L. H. The transition from the unicellular to the multicellular individual. *Biol. Sympos.* 8: 27–42.

Jacobsen, C. F. and M. M., and J. G. Yoshioka. 1932. Development of an infant chimpanzee during her first year. *Comp. Psychol. Monogr.* 9: 1–94.

Jennings, H. S. 1906. *Behavior of the lower organisms*. New York: Columbia Univ. Press.

Jennings, H. S. 1942. The transition from the individual to the social level. *Biol. Sympos.* 8: 105–119.

Lefford, A. 1946. The influence of emotional subject matter on logical reasoning. *J. Gen. Psychol.* 34: 127–151.

Lewin, K., R. Lippitt, and R. K. White. 1939. Patterns of aggressive behavior in experimentally graded "social climates." *J. Soc. Psychol.* 10: 271–299.

Maier, N. R. F., and T. C. Schneirla. 1935. *Principles of animal psychology*. New York: McGraw-Hill.

Maslow, A. H. 1936. Dominance-quality and social behavior in infra-human primates. *J. Soc. Psychol.* 11: 313–324.

Needham, J. 1929. *The skeptical biologist*. London: Chatto.

Newcomb, T., and E. L. Hartley, eds. 1947. *Readings in social psychology*. New York: Holt.

Nissen, H. W. 1931. A field study of the chimpanzee. *Comp. Psychol. Monogr.* 8: 1–105.

Novikoff, A. 1945. The concept of integrative levels in biology. *Science* 101: 209–215.

Redfield, R., ed. 1942. *Levels of integration in biological and social systems, Biol. Sympos.* 8. Lancaster: J. Cattell, Pr.

Révész, G. 1944. The language of animals. *J. Gen. Psychol.* 30: 117–147.

Schjelderup-Ebbe, T. 1922. Beiträge zur Sozialpsychologie des Haushuhns. *Z. Psychol.* 88: 225–252.

Schneirla, T. C. 1939. A theoretical consideration of the basis for approach-withdrawal adjustments in behavior. *Psychol. Bull.* 37:501–502.

Schneirla, T. C. 1940. Further studies on the army-ant behavior pattern.—Mass organization in the swarm-raiders. *J. Comp. Psychol.* 29: 401–460.

Schneirla, T. C. 1941. Social organization in insects, as related to individual function. *Psychol. Rev.* 48: 465–486.

Schneirla, T. C. 1944. A unique case of circular milling in ants, *Am. Mus. Nov.* no. 1253, 1–26.

Schneirla, T. C. 1946. Problems in the biopsychology of social organization. *J. Abnorm. Soc. Psychol.* 41: 385–402.

Schneirla, T. C. 1949. Levels in the psychological capacities of animals. In R. W. Sellars et al., eds., *Philosophy for the future.* New York: Macmillan. Pp. 243–286.

Scott, J. P. 1945. Social behavior, organization, and leadership in a small flock of domestic sheep. *Comp. Psychol. Monogr.* 18: 1–29.

Scott, J. W. 1941. Behavior of the sage grouse during mating cycle. *Bul. Ecol. Soc. Am.* 22: 38.

Shaffer, L. F. 1936. *The psychology of adjustment.* Boston: Houghton Mifflin.

Simpson, G. G. 1949. *The meaning of evolution.* New Haven: Yale Univ. Press.

Sloane, E. H. 1945. Reductionism. *Psychol. Rev.* 52: 214–223.

Stewart, J. C., and J. P. Scott. 1947. Lack of correlation between leadership and dominance relationships in a herd of goats. *J. Comp. Physiol. Psychol.* 40: 255–264.

Strecker, A. E. 1940. *Beyond the clinical frontiers.*

Wheeler, W. M. 1928. *The social insects.* New York: Harcourt, Brace.

Woodger, J. H. 1929. *Biological principles—A critical study.* New York: Harcourt, Brace.

Yerkes, R. M. 1933. Genetic aspects of grooming, a socially important primate behavior pattern. *J. Soc. Psychol.* 4: 3–25.

Yerkes, R. M. 1939. Social dominance and sexual status in the chimpanzee. *Quart. Rev. Biol.* 14: 115–136.

Yerkes, R. M., and M. I. Tomilin. 1935. Mother-infant relations in chimpanzee. *J. Comp. Psychol.* 20: 321–458.

Yerkes, R. M., and A. W. Yerkes. 1929. *The great apes.* New Haven: Yale Univ. Press.

Zuckerman, S. 1932. *The social life of monkeys and apes.* London: Kegan Paul.

T. C. SCHNEIRLA

JAY S. ROSENBLATT

Behavioral Organization and Genesis of the Social Bond in Insects and Mammals

Bibliography No. 94

Our discussion centers on the topic of instinctive behavior, which may be defined operationally as species-typical behavior studied from the standpoint of development. Insects and mammals both commonly exhibit group and parental behavior distinctive of the species and typical of their developmental patterns. Certain basic similarities are discernible in the different group-behavior phenomena of insects and mammals, and yet striking differences appear, in that the former may be characterized as *biosocial,* the latter as *psychosocial* (Schneirla, 10). Two such patterns, that of the army ants and that of domestic cats, may be compared on the basis of evidence from our departmental research program.

PROPERTIES OF THE ARMY-ANT FUNCTIONAL SYSTEM

Evidence bearing on the incorporation of the individual insect into its colony and on the maintenance of a species-standard pattern of relationships between individual and group is organized most effectively in terms of a doctrine of reciprocal-stimulative processes (Schneirla, 7, 9).

The tropical American army ants of *Eciton* species, as investigated both in field and laboratory (Schneirla, 7, 13), are characterized by frequent predatory raids and by a nomadic life involving frequent emigrations. Their daily raids involve immense numbers and are well organized, constituting in fact the most intricate unitary social operation carried out regularly away from the home site by any animal except man. Their periodic emigrations, also highly organized in typical ways, are found

From the *American Journal of Orthopsychiatry* 31: 223–253. Copyright © the American Orthopsychiatric Association, Inc. Reproduced with permission.

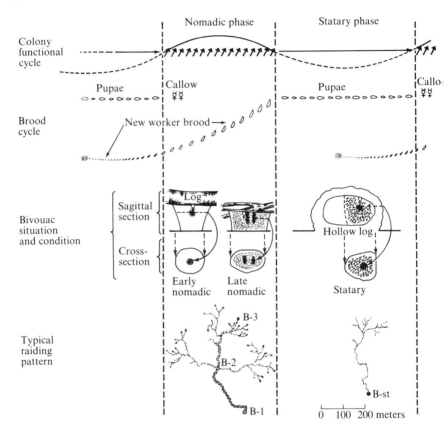

FIGURE 33

Schema of the functional cycle of the army-ant species *Eciton hamatum*. From the top: (1) the two phases in the cycle indicated by a sine curve; arrows indicate large daily raids and nightly emigrations in the nomadic phase; (2) typical correspondence between phases in the colony cycle and developmental stages of successive broods; (3) types of bivouac in each of the two activity phases, indicating placement of brood in each; (4) type of raiding system prevalent in each of the principal activity phases (B-1, 2, 3, successive bivouac sites; B-st, statary bivouac site). (From Schneirla, reference 13.)

closely related to the predatory expeditions from which they arise. Investigation discloses regular fluctuations in the occurrence and intensity of these activities which, studied analytically, throw significant light on the nature of the group functional pattern and of group unity.

The functional pattern of one army-ant species, *Eciton hamatum*, schematized in Figure 33, is typified by nomadic phases and statary phases of predictable duration which alternate in regular cycles throughout the year. Functional conditions in the two phases are very different, as the figure indicates. Throughout each nomadic phase, the daily raids are large, and emigration occurs nightly; throughout each statary phase daily raids are small or absent and no emigrations occur.

Brood-Stimulation Processes Basic to Colony Unity

The figure also represents the striking and prevalent fact that the phase of the functional cycle existing at any time in a colony corresponds directly to the developmental stage of the brood. Regularly, as indicated, in the statary phase a brood in the pupal condition is present and a new brood in the egg stage is produced, whereas in the nomadic phase a brood developing through the larval stage is present. This correspondence of conditions, as much evidence shows, is based upon the fact that colony function in these ants is grounded in an intimate adult responsiveness to the brood. Through its metabolic condition and activities, the brood furnishes to the workers a variety of attractive and excitatory tactual and chemical stimulation. The all-worker broods appear in regular succession at intervals of about 36 days in *Eciton,* are very large (about 80,000 in *hamatum* and 200,000 in *burchelli*) and exert a major stimulative effect on the colony population. In the nomadic phase, when active, feeding larvae are present, great daily raids and nightly emigrations occur; but when these larvae reach maturity and spin their cocoons the general level of excitation falls to a low ebb and a statary phase is entered. That statary phase ends when this pupal brood matures and, emerging as excitable callow workers, stimulates the worker population once again to a high level at which a new nomadic phase is entered by the colony.

This evidence supports a brood-excitation theory (7) by which the brood is held the decisive agency in the *Eciton* cycle, entering into diverse relationships of reciprocal stimulation with the worker population which at a high level maintain nomadism, at a low level maintain the statary condition. This view of a reciprocal relationship involving diverse types of stimuli goes considerably beyond Wheeler's concept (17) of "trophallaxis" (or "food exchange") to contend that stimuli from many organic sources, summating through a regular behavioral interplay among the members of a colony, are basic to the unity and the functional conditions of that colony. In other words, the communicative relationships—i.e., behavior and the products of behavior influencing function in other individuals—determine not only the functional pattern of the colony and its excitatory level, but also the very existence of the colony.

This fact is shown clearly by a test in which most of the young brood (eggs; microlarvae) is removed from a colony near the end of a statary phase. Emergence of the pupal brood from cocoons excites the colony greatly and initiates a nomadic phase in the typical way; but within a few days, when the stimulative effect from the callows has waned, daily raids lessen and emigration begins to fail through the absence of the major stimulative factor normally maintaining nomadic function. Comparably, when a colony loses its queen through death or removal, it maintains a fairly normal cyclic function only so long as the broods she has produced are still in development; thereafter the colony enters a statary condition in which it will eventually perish unless fusion occurs with another colony of that species.

Factors in the Species Raiding Pattern

Analytical investigations show that the characteristic organization of the colony behavior pattern in these ants is not determined by any one type of individual but, as evidence schematized in Figure 34 suggests, is a composite result of factors contributed by all types of individuals—queen, brood, workers and males—interacting in the colony situation. Let us consider the species raiding pattern. In *Eciton hamatum,* as Figure 33 indicates, this pattern is one of branching columns; in the closely related species *Eciton burchelli,* on the other hand, the raid is headed by a large unitary swarm, with branching columns a secondary feature. Field and laboratory results point to certain characteristics of the adult workers as basic to these species differences. Identifiable among these are properties of glandular equipment (accounting for a heavier, more diffuse trail-chemical in *burchelli* than in *hamatum*), of olfactory threshold (accounting for a less precise discrimination and, with secretory factors, for a much more facile massing of individuals in *burchelli* than in *hamatum*) and of individual excitability (which can rise to a significantly higher level in *burchelli* than in *hamatum*).

Eciton workers make and follow their raiding trails in highly stereotyped ways, essentially dependent upon tactual and olfactory sensitivity, as their minute eyes and degenerate visual equipment normally play little part in their orientation. For this, however, hypotheses of "blind instinct" or of innate patterns offer little and are misleading, for the functioning of individuals in colony adjustments has many variable aspects dependent upon the developmental situation. Species-specific organic factors such as olfactory thresholds and glandular properties are clearly basic in this complex. We must, however, also consider the fact that the worker, on emerging from her cocoon, does not attain adult function directly, but instead requires a few days in which she first circulates within the temporary nest of the colony, then gradually extends the scope and efficiency of operations outside the nest on the raiding trails. Callow workers artificially removed from their cocoons and held apart from the colony for several days cannot follow the trails efficiently as young workers of corresponding

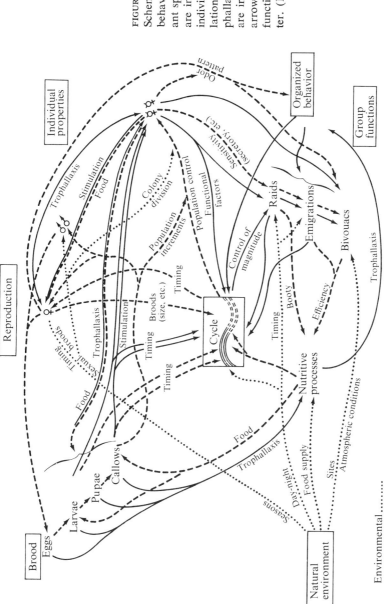

FIGURE 34
Schema of factors underlying the behavior pattern of terrestrial army-ant species. Major sources of factors are indicated marginally (e.g., individual properties); principal relationships demonstrated (e.g., trophallaxis = reciprocal stimulation) are indicated by appropriate arrows; arrows also indicate relevance to functional cycle, represented in center. (From Schneirla, reference 13.)

Individual properties

Reproduction

Brood

Natural environment

Organized behavior

Group functions

Trophallaxis
Stimulation
Food
Odor pattern
Colony division
Population increments
Population control
Functional factors
Sensitivity (secretory, etc.)
Broods (size, etc.)
Timing
Timing
Control of magnitude
Raids
Emigrations
Bivouacs
Cycle
Nutritive processes
Timing
Booty
Efficiency
Trophallaxis
Timing
Stimulation
Trophallaxis
Food
Timing
Sexual broods
Timing broods
Larvae
Pupae
Callows
Food
Trophallaxis
Day-night
Food supply
Sites
Atmospheric conditions
Seasons
Eggs

Environmental..........
Biological -----
Behavioral ———

ages normally do, but instead blunder about ineptly. Although organic maturation may account partially for the improvement shown in trail-following within the first few days, we must also postulate a factor of simple habituation learning, through which disturbance reactions are inhibited and general responses of approach and turning-to become conditioned by experience with a pervasive stimulus aspect. Despite evidence that this indicated gain from experience represents an exceedingly low-level type of learning, it is doubtful that the army-ant adaptive pattern could be maintained without it.

The problem of distinctive colony reactions or "nest-mate recognition" in ants is not simple but has numerous variable aspects. One of these is suggested by the fact that although the workers of *Eciton burchelli* and *hamatum* normally attack each other when brought together, a certain modification may be effected by the procedure of juxtaposing representative groups of workers of these two species for a few days, separating them only by a cheesecloth partition through which air circulates. Each thereby evidently acquires some of the other species' odor, as is shown by what happens when they are then introduced through tubes into a common chamber. Instead of attacking at once, as do new control groups, these test groups first mingle in a single circular column in which dark *burchelli* workers and lighter *hamatum* workers follow one another in a regular manner indicating strong individual responses to a common tactuo-chemical field of stimulation. After several minutes, however, when variations in circling have introduced sufficient interruptions in the running, reactions to odor differences appear to summate, and general combat sets in.

The Bivouac and Colony Unity

Another aspect of the army-ant pattern, the temporary nest or bivouac, as indicated in Figure 33 also presents a striking difference in the two phases of the functional cycle. This unique structure, constructed of the clustered bodies of the workers, hanging from a natural ceiling such as the underside of a log, affords the colony both a temporary shelter and a center of operations for its predatory raids, as well as serving as an efficient incubator for the great broods always present in operative colonies. Figure 33 represents the striking fact that in the nomadic phase of the cycle these nesting clusters are formed largely in the open, whereas in the statary phase they are formed in enclosed places as in the hollows of logs or trees. Observational data and the results of tests suggest that the principal factor underlying these striking differences is that the Eciton worker population, when in a high state of tension as at the end of the nomadic phase, is strongly reactive to air currents and thus can form its clusters selectively in places where air currents are much reduced. Evidence for this hypothesis has been obtained with worker groups representing colonies at different stages in the cycle, tested in the laboratory in their resistance in clusters to controlled air-current stimulation. Those from colonies in the late nomadic stage, which in the forest would then be entering enclosed bivouac sites, are the first to break and to recluster where the air is quiet. The level of individual excitation, which normally varies significantly in any colony through the functional cycle, represents an important factor in the army-ant pattern.

One important specific factor contributing to the army-ant clustering reaction is a structural characteristic, the strong recurved double hooks on the last tarsal segment of each leg. Clustering, a vital component in the army-ant adaptive system, is not to be considered simple. Among other factors indicated as significant by tests we find a susceptibility to become quiescent when the general stimulative level is low, under conditions of gentle contact, under the prevalence of colony odor, and when stretching (as through the hooking-on of other workers) induces a reaction of tonic immobility. The workers thus serve as the basic fabric of their own colony nests, may form bridges or smooth the road in raiding, or may cluster about their queen when she is halted in the nocturnal emigration.

Colony odor, a chief factor contributing to army-ant clustering, involves another important set of relationships. When various local clusters are forming in the nocturnal emigration, as is typical, the one with the best chance of becoming the colony bivouac is that entered by the queen. Army-ant workers cluster in the presence of queen-odor alone, as is shown by the formation of persistent clusters in laboratory arenas in places where the colony queen has rested only for a few minutes. Under natural conditions, a colony deprived of its queen exhibits a clearly decreasing capacity for establishing a concentrated bivouac cluster, but instead on successive nights forms increasingly diffuse gatherings which finally become carpetlike masses spread out on the ground.

Species-Typical Development a Mosaic Process

The army-ant functional pattern is thereby seen as a mosaic, to which numerous factors from numerous sources contribute. As indicated, one factor contributed by the queen is her distinctive odor, strongly unifying to the colony. The queen-odor, in fact, represents the most critical component of the general colony odor. This hypothesis is well supported by evidence that although workers of colonies with queens, belonging to the same species, normally never mix when their raids meet in the forest, a marked exception occurs when one of two colliding colonies lacks a queen. If this colony has been without its queen for as little as 12 to 20 hours, the workers intermingle readily with those of a colony of the same species when its columns are encountered, instead of becoming disturbed and remaining apart as normally occurs. The usual outcome is that the entire population of the queenless colony becomes absorbed in that of the queenright colony. To account for such results, we may postulate three factors: (1) a normally effective habituation of workers to the colony queen-odor that becomes sufficiently weakened in the queenless colony to permit most of the workers to meet the different queen-odor of another colony without disturbance, although (2) through the continuous presence of the colony queen this specific odor-habituation is normally maintained in all workers of a colony, and that (3) workers in a queenless colony lose (by virtue of volitalization) their individual coats of queen-odor within a few hours, sufficiently to permit their being received by the workers of a queen-right colony and adopted in this colony without much disturbance. It is also of interest to note that after the queenless population has entered a queenright colony with its brood, this brood is cannibalized in the course of time, whereas the brood of the queenright colony survives. Normally, therefore, the odor of the colony queen diffusing through the bivouac to the brood seems to be an important factor in the treatment of that brood by the workers, who lick, carry it about and tend it, rather than consuming it along with the prey.

The army-ant functional pattern, as Figure 34 indicates, is the product of many factors coexisting in the functional situation, introduced into that situation by conditions in the natural environment, the worker population, the broods and the queen. The interaction of these various factors is emphasized strikingly by evidence that each further operation of brood-production by the queen is initiated and completed through the effect of extrinsic conditions in the colony situation governing the amount of food and of worker-induced stimulation received by the queen. Thus, near the end of each nomadic phase, the nearly mature larval brood, by virtue of conditions in its current metamorphosis, excites the workers increasingly although at the same time it consumes less and less food. The result is an aroused colony with surplus food in which the workers now greatly increase their stimulative attentions to the queen and feed her abundantly. The queen's abdomen then increases rapidly in size as she accelerates in maturing a great brood of eggs which is laid some days later, midway in the statary phase. This is only one link, although a very critical one, in the complex army-ant functional cycle.

The recurrence of each change in the cycle thus is the product of reciprocal relationships between brood, worker and queen functions, and not of a special timing mechanism or "biological clock" endogenous to the queen (13). The cyclic pattern of army ants therefore is based upon numerous structural, physiological, behavioral and environmental factors capable of interacting under the conditions normal to the forest environment. The organization of this pattern is not determined through the heredity of any one type of individual—queen, workers or brood—nor is it additive from factors of organic maturation alone. "The organic factors basic to the species pattern have evolved in close relationship to the general environment, which therefore supplies key factors essential for their contemporary integration into a functional system" (Schneirla, 12, p. 401).

ANALYSIS OF SOCIALIZATION IN A MAMMAL

Theoretical Considerations

From birth, in neonate mammals, behavior is typified by reciprocal stimulative relationships between parent and young. The neonate attracts the female stimulatively; the female presents to the newborn a variety of tactual, thermal and other stimuli, typically of low intensity and therefore primarily approach-provoking (Schneirla, 14). On this basis the process of socialization begins. Behavioral development, because it centers on and depends upon reciprocal stimulative processes between female and young, is essentially social from the start.

Mammalian behavioral development is best conceived as a unitary system of processes changing progressively under the influence of an intimate interrelationship of factors of maturation and of experience—with *maturation* defined as the developmental contributions of tissue growth and differentiation and their secondary processes, *experience* as the effects of stimulation and its organic traces on behavior (12). There is no implication here that these two factoral complexes are sharply distinguishable in their contributions to behavioral development; our position, rather, is that such a distinction, although a theoretical convenience, constitutes a gratuitous assumption not well supported by evidence. This view of the matter is supported by the results of investigations discussed here on the behavioral development of one mammal, the domestic cat, considered in particular from the standpoint of its social behavior.[1]

Social behavior is a broad term, and one of highly variable meaning in dependence upon the age and previous developmental experience of the

---

[1] The research on mammalian behavioral development discussed in the following section of this paper was supported by grants from the National Science Foundation and from the Rockefeller Foundation. The results are to be reported in papers now in manuscript or in preparation, cited with the references.

animal. There have been very different approaches to studying the phenomena of socialization in animals, and the results frequently have been canalized by the experimenter's point of view as dictating hypotheses and method. One recent didactic appraisal of mammalian socialization is that of Scott (15), who borrowed the term "critical period" from embryology to express his idea that there is a period in the ontogeny of puppies, coming at about 18 days, which is crucial for social development by virtue of maturative processes then occurring. Apparent support for this view was derived from the finding of Fuller et al. (3) that a conditioned leg withdrawal to a buzzer paired with leg-shock cannot be established in puppies until about the 18th neonatal day. Scott took these results to mean that the indicated time marks for the puppy ". . . the beginning of the period of socialization, in which its primary social relationships are formed." The main assumption here seems to be that certain processes of maturation taken alone are crucial for the described behavioral advances and hence for a turning point in social behavior, or actually for the basis of social behavior. This conclusion we are unable to accept.

It is clear that comprehensive analytical investigations of behavioral development are needed for the solution of major problems such as that of turning points, qualitative progress from one stage to the next, and the like. An investigation of this type, to be reported in the remainder of this paper, was derived by us from the theoretical standpoint that (1) processes of mammalian socialization begin at parturition or even before, and (2) that mammalian social ontogeny involves a complex progressive organization depending upon intervening variables of maturation and of experience in the individual, in the perceptual development of the female, and in reciprocal stimulative relationships between female and young (10, 11).

Method

The general method in the studies to be discussed here involved both qualitative and quantitative procedures for observing and recording the course of events in the developmental phenomena investigated in replication, and special procedures designed for an intensive analysis of these phenomena under conditions modified in ways found significant in pilot work. To obtain quantitative records of these occurrences at all stages, behavioral items identified as significant in pilot studies were represented on the respective keys of the Aronson keyboard (Clark et al., 1), represented in Figure 35, which controlled the corresponding pens of an Esterline-Angus process recorder. Tracings representing the frequency, duration and concurrences of these items were thus obtained for analysis.

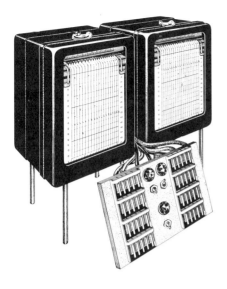

FIGURE 35
Two Aronson keyboards (below), the microswitches of which control movements of corresponding pens on one of the Esterline-Angus process recorders (above) for quantitative records of behavioral items.

Social Processes Beginning at Parturition

Studies in our laboratory by Tobach et al. (16) tested hypotheses derived from a mosaic-developmental theory of instinctive behavior in their bearing on parturition in the cat. The results, summarized below, indicated in detail that the behavioral bond between female and offspring, and therefore socialization of the young, begins with the initial stages of delivery.

We are led to characterize the event, for cats, as an interplay or even competition between the stimulative effects of endogenous events (e.g., uterine contractions; emergence of fetus) and the external results of such events (e.g., fluids, neonate). These stimulative by-products of organic processes tend to intrude themselves upon the female's attention in a somewhat variable order, timing and duration. Each one, as it arises, demands a specific perceptual and behavioral adjustment on her part. The parturitive phenomenon here is not a regular, patterned flow of events, but a series of rather sporadic organic and behavioral episodes, together with variable activities not specifically parturitive in themselves. Thus the female exhibits, in a not very predictable order, the predictable items of self-licking, licking newborn or floor, eating after-birth, general movement and sitting or lying. Intervals of intense activity indicating a high level of excitement, *a condition facilitating delivery operations,* are interspersed with intervals of exhaustion and rest, *facilitating initiation* of nursing and other stimulative relations of mother and newborn.

In these mammals, parturitive behavior is indicated as a loose assemblage of functions centering on the stimulative consequences of organic events. A sequence of hormonally-induced endogenous changes sets a loose temporal order for behavioral adjustment, dependent in sequence and timing upon the female's variable attention to competing organic and environmental stimuli. Persistently in evidence is an orientation to the posterior body and particularly to the vaginal area, a perceptual set which enormously aids normal parturitive operations. This factor, presumably based upon self-stimulative experience in youth, is very possibly indispensable for an adaptive outcome and survival of the young. (Schneirla, 12, p. 421.)

In other words, we conclude that the events of parturition, in which the neonate kitten participates rather passively and incidentally at first, provide a broad foundation for a social bond between female and young which persists and develops thereafter. The female-neonate bond, grounded particularly in processes such as licking, involves the elaboration of numerous stimulus-response processes which in time become increasingly bilateral and reciprocal. We believe that the extent and adequacy to which the conditions of pregnancy and parturition (including the female's preparturitive organic and behavioral preparation) admit a functional basis for reciprocal relationships, with the properties of the developmental situation prevalent during the litter period, govern the general trend of maternal-young relations and of socialization. This conclusion is supported by the results of further research with cats, recently completed in our laboratory, involving both detailed analytical investigations of the processes of group behavior and special research on aspects of individual development.

Ontogenesis of Orientation

Studies on the development of individual orientation, by Rosenblatt, Turkewitz and Schneirla (4, 5), show clearly that the origin point of social behavior is the home site, the home corner in our experimental cage, usually established and saturated chemically by the female in parturition or earlier in pregnancy. We find that the neonate's first adjustment to this locus occurs promptly after parturition and leads into a progressive process of orientation farther afield. In the first stage, from birth to about ten days, this process develops on a tactuo-chemical, nonvisual basis. From early hours, presence of the female quiets the neonates, as does also the presence of odor-cues on the saturated substratum of this site. If the regular floor unit is replaced by a fresh one, the tested kitten is strongly disturbed, as quantitative records of its movements and vocalization show clearly; also, in periodic orientation tests, kittens do not then re-enter the home corner readily, as they do under normal conditions.

By such testing procedures we have traced out an advancing process of orientation based on tactual and olfactory cues. Through these developments, which doubtless involve learning as a necessary factor, the kitten at 8–10 days of age, for example, can make test returns to the home corner from the corner diagonally opposite, moving with reference to the wall although only occasionally touching the wall, and passing through the intervening adjacent corner. By 12–15 days, some days after the kitten's eyes have opened, a transitional process is evident whereby the kitten now begins to make its way diagonally across the cage in the open and by the 20th day (Figure 36), a direct diagonal path can be taken. These progressive adjustments in spatial orientation advance concurrently with what we find are closely related changes in the kitten's adjustment to the female.

Development of Specialization in Feeding

In their feeding adjustments to the female, as our findings (Rosenblatt, Wodinsky, et al., 6) show, the neonates progress from the first trials. At first the newborn kittens reach the female only through a slow, variable process, always with much circuitous nuzzling and fumbling in attaining the female's mammary surface and attaching to a nipple. The quantitative results show, however, that the adjustments of individual kittens to the mammary surface begin to take on an increasingly characteristic specificity, even within the first two hours after birth. The typical result is that in the first one or two neonatal days most of the kittens in the litter are already able to take individually specific nipple positions with appreciable consistency. That is, with further approaches to the female and further attachments, certain neonates in a litter acquire an early specificity to a particular nipple or mammary region (posterior, anterior or intermediate), others suckle alternately from either of a pair of nipples, and still others are variable, suckling from any available nipple. Our conclusions, therefore, based on results from studies of 25 litters ranging in size from one to six kittens,[2] differ from Ewer's report (2) of a prevalent suckling-specificity from observations of 4 litters.

Our results on early feeding show, as do those on cage orientation, that these events undergo a steady change promoting increasing efficiency from shortly after birth, suggesting that discriminative and perceptual-motor processes basic to them progress steadily in organization and scope. The learning process postulated is an elementary pattern of conditioning, involving proximal stimuli effective through tactual, olfactory and thermal experience with the female and nest situation, with approach and suckling

---

[2] J. Wodinsky, J. S. Rosenblatt, G. Turkewitz, and T. C. Schneirla, "The Development of Individual Nursing Position Habits in Newborn Kittens." Paper presented at 1955 annual meeting, Eastern Psychol. Assn., New York City.

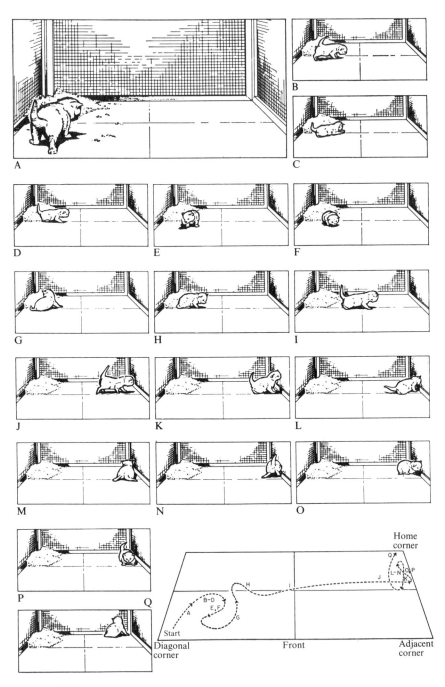

FIGURE 36

A 20-day-old kitten, set down in the diagonal corner in an orientation test, takes a course through the open field in reaching the home corner. Drawings show successive positions at 5-second intervals; diagram gives a tracing of the path.

as basic responses. Feeding processes have an obvious central significance in social development; hence our research has centered on feeding.

Normal Progress in Kitten-Female Relationships

Suckling often appears in the first-born before parturition is completed; thereafter, in the litter period, it recurs as a response that changes significantly in its organization and social relationships. At length normally, as weaning begins in the fifth week, suckling declines and is gradually replaced by self-feeding, which generally is specific by the eighth week. In the remainder of this paper, results of investigations by Rosenblatt, Wodinsky et al. (6) are reported, analyzing the development of feeding adjustments in some detail both for kittens developing in the regular litter situation and for others subjected to a technique of isolation.

Our results for the development of feeding in the normal litter situation reveal not just one suckling pattern, but variable suckling adjustments which after the described neonatal beginnings progress steadily in ways reflecting progress in perceptual, motor and motivational organization. We find that from birth there is a sequence of interrelated changes in the suckling and orientative behavior of the neonates and in the nursing and related behavior of the female. These changes are the product of complex reciprocal stimulative processes that lead, on the one hand, to weaning and independent functioning of the young and, on the other, to the gradual decline of the female's maternal behavior associated with this litter.

By means of procedures yielding both qualitative and quantitative evidence, we have traced the development of what may be called the normal suckling and nursing pattern of several litters from birth to the end of the eighth week. The general results, graphed in Figure 37 for a representative litter, may be summarized in the following terms.

In stage 1, from birth to about the twentieth day, essentially all of the feedings are initiated by the female. She approaches the kittens where they are huddled (in the home corner, as a rule), lies down with her mammary surface against them, and arches her body around them in what we call the *functional-U*. The kittens, responding to tactual and other stimuli from the female, and variously influenced by her licking operations, soon stir about and begin variable movements that, in the course of time, lead into nipple localization and to nipple-attachment and suckling. As this first stage progresses, although the female continues to initiate the procedure, the kittens become increasingly involved in the organization of feeding situations. This fact is emphasized by their rapid progress in localizing nipples, to the extent that by the fourth neonatal day most of them have established individually distinctive types of adjustment to the female.

In stage 2, which may be described as typical from about the 20th to

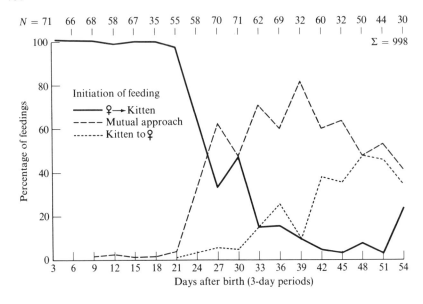

FIGURE 37

Three principal stages in the initiation of suckling in normally-raised litters in the domestic cat (data from three litters). Points on graphs show stages of responses of each type summarized for the daily observations of each three-day interval. (*N* = number of feedings observed in each interval.)

shortly after the 30th day, the initiation of feeding involves active approaches on the part of both female and kittens. Initiation of feeding approaches by kittens to the female first becomes evident under particular conditions, as for example when she is resting somewhere outside the home area, or when she is crouched over the food dish. Although either the female or the kittens may be the more active according to circumstances, the initiation of feeding remains a distinctively bilateral process throughout this period. To the approaches of the kittens, increasingly vigorous and versatile, the female nearly always responds appropriately. According to conditions, she soon assumes her nursing posture or, if already lying down, she facilitates the nipple-localization adjustments of the kittens by stretching out or at least by remaining in place. For the kittens, perceptual developments underlying improved efficiency in feeding are indicated by the results of tests demonstrating an increased facility and scope of orientation in the cage, as well as an increasing resourcefulness in transferring their activity from a specific cage locality to the female as the focus of action.

We interpret these changes as marking a steady improvement in the perceptual-motor abilities of the kittens, a developmental process for which an increasingly comprehensive motivational basis for responding to the female and other kittens is indicated. Relevant to this interpretation is the increase in the frequency and variety of casual joint activities ("play") among the kittens and of nonfeeding responses to the female such as toying with her tail. These results support the view that feeding provides a functional center for the socialization of the kittens, as feeding itself, considered at any stage, is a reciprocal activity and is inherently social.

In stage 3, which generally begins shortly after the 30th day, the initiation of suckling depends more and more and finally almost altogether upon the kittens. They now follow the female about the cage with greater frequency and increasing persistence, remaining at the place of her disappearance when she leaps to the wall shelf. When she happens to be accessible to them, they persist with vigor in attempts to nuzzle which at times result in attachment and suckling, but with increasing frequency, as though prompt counteraction by the female, may end in little more than a brief social exchange. In various ways, consequently, the kittens forcibly influence the female's behavior more and more. Her changing attitude toward the kittens is indicated clearly by the increasing frequency and duration of her stays on the shelf, at least until the kittens themselves can reach the shelf. From the time the kittens can get to the shelf, at about the 45th day, the female avoids it increasingly. In the third stage, therefore, the intimacy of the social bond between female and young has decreased with their changing behavioral relationships—i.e., as their social distance has increased.

This evidence, indicating a predictable series of changes in the formation and later in the waning and disappearance of the described reciprocal feeding relationships, is interpreted by us as centering on progressive changes in the organization and qualitative nature of these relationships and in social processes relating to them. In many ways these changes show that the development of socialization centers on feeding relationships and is essentially one of reciprocal stimulation throughout. In the processes of individual development involved, no sharp distinction can be drawn between nutritive and social adjustments, as both of these aspects are indicated in progressively diversified and indirect ways in the bilateral relationships characteristic of the litter situation.

Isolation Experiments

A principal part of this program involved research on the suckling behavior and maternal adjustments of kittens reared normally in the litter situation, in comparison with the responses of kittens returned to female and litter after isolation periods introduced experimentally at different times in the first two months of life. The aim was to analyze the normal socialization processes by determining the effects of social deprivation introduced at different times on the feeding behavior and other behavioral adjustments of kittens.

1. *General treatment and behavior of isolated kittens.* The experimental kittens were isolated in a special incubator, a cubical enclosure in which a brooder or "artificial mother" (Figure 38) was placed on the floor near one wall.[3] This brooder, constructed in a functional-U form and covered with soft toweling, was designed to constitute a model that would be attractive to the kitten by virtue of its thermal, tactual and spatial properties, and that would also present a nipple from which the isolate kitten could draw through its own efforts in suckling a synthetic formula available at a controlled temperature. The brooder was made in the functional-U form to duplicate the effect of sensory canalization normally contributed by the female lying on one side with her body arched and legs extended at right angles to her abdomen. The brooder therefore served as a crude, partial substitute for the lactating female, to the extent that it obviated the need for forced feeding by hand and other special attentions that might have been equivalent in a more comprehensive sense to the normal properties of the female. One other procedure carried out in this situation as a limited substitute for the female's normal activities was a brief daily manipulation of the isolate kitten during the first two neonatal weeks, to effect the routine stimulative operations essential to facilitate onset of defecation and urination.

By routine, each isolate kitten was first introduced manually to the nipple in the brooder, so that the process of independent feeding might be started equivalently in different subjects without any undue delays. The neonates were all able to acquire within their first three days the ability to crawl up into the brooder, locate the nipple and attach independently. From that time, self-initiated suckling occurred at regular intervals in all of the isolated subjects. In the course of time, a gradual change appeared in how each isolate approached the nipple from in front of the brooder. The earliest trend was to follow a more or less canalized path along one or the other arm of the brooder, in close contact with the soft surface. Then, after a few days, a variable approach was made through the open central area of the brooder, between the arms; also, the amount of preliminary nuzzling near the nipple decreased steadily. Finally, kittens held in isolation to the fourth week became versatile in their manner of approaching the nipple, and could reach it directly across the arms or through the central area, attaching efficiently with a minimum of nuzzling.

---

[3] This piece of equipment was developed in a prototype form in 1949 in connection with studies on parturition in the cat, was modified by Dr. Alan Frank, Fellow of the National Institute of Mental Health in our laboratory during 1950–1951, and was further improved in pilot work for the present investigation.

FIGURE 38
Week-old isolate kitten in position and suckling at
the nipple in the brooder or "artificial mother."
Rear-guard panel and milk supply are indicated.

After their isolation periods in the incubator, kittens detained there for scheduled intervals were returned individually to their respective females and litters for observations of individual reactions in the following days, with emphasis on suckling responses, on general cage orientation and on social reactions to female and littermates.

2. *Appearance of suckling after isolation.* Effective suckling responses appeared, although in different ways and in different timing, on the test returns to the female and litter situation of *all* of the kittens isolated from birth to the 7th day, from the 6th to the 23d day, and from the 18th to the 33d day. The results for the cage-return tests of these kittens are reported in Table 1.

On the other hand, suckling from the female was not accomplished in corresponding tests by any except one of the kittens isolated from the 23d to the 44th day, or by any of the kittens isolated from the 2d to the 44th day. These last kittens failed to suckle although, like the others, they remained continuously with their females from the time their tests began.

Insufficient hunger was not responsible for the failure of certain of the isolate kittens to suckle on return to the female. A strong, mounting hunger was indicated by their increasingly restless activities on return to the

TABLE 1

Records for suckling responses in isolate kittens on test returns to female and litter from the incubator.

Age and duration of isolation (days)	N	Average days isolated	% Suckling on return to female
A. Kittens suckled from brooder during isolation			
0–7	3	7	100
6–23	5	18	100
18–33	2	16	100
23–44	4	22	25
2–44	4	43	00
B. Kittens in isolation that did not suckle from the brooder			
34–49	4	16	100
47–54	3	7	100

litter situation, and independent tests showed that they would have fed readily had they been returned to the brooder. The difficulty was in feeding from the female. In a special test, two of the brooder-kittens that had not suckled were placed with their females and left for two days without food. The female was fed on schedule outside the cage, and each time she returned two mother-reared kittens also present suckled promptly. As for the isolates, no signs of suckling appeared even after they had been without food for two days. Other isolates, however, returned to the female and cage at the 49th or 54th day, after periods in the brooder in which they had fed from dishes with no opportunity to suckle, all suckled from the female (Table 1, B). The failure of certain of the experimental subjects to suckle cannot therefore be attributed either to the absence of hunger or to any "natural decline" in suckling, although the latter might seem possible from the fact that suckling normally has declined by the 44th day in litter-reared kittens.

Our findings show that suckling may arise in isolated kittens returned to the litter situation, whether or not these subjects had developed a suckling reaction to the female prior to their period in the brooder. Of three kittens isolated from birth, all suckled in the course of time after having been placed in the litter situation for testing, but of eight kittens whose isolation began after an appreciable amount of suckling experience, only one accomplished this response on its return to the litter situation. Of these eight kittens, four had suckled during 23 days in the litter situation prior to isolation, yet three of them did not suckle after their return to female and litter at 34 days after an intervening isolation period.

Failure of the feeding adjustment to the female in certain cases could not have been due to any inability to execute the action of suckling, as efficient suckling was observed in the brooder in all of the test isolates not long before they were removed for the cage tests. Furthermore, when in control tests several of the kittens that had not suckled during three days in the litter-situation tests were returned to the incubator, all of them promptly suckled from the brooder nipple. It is clear that the interference with the suckling adjustment in the litter situation was centered specifically on the female, on the litter situation itself, or on both of these.

3. *Latency in female-contact and in suckling.* The appraisal of our results for cage-return tests with respect to the relative delay of suckling, when that response appeared, provided one valuable clue as to the effects of isolation. Table 2 gives the latencies for suckling in each of the five

TABLE 2

Contact latencies and suckling latencies in kittens returned to female and litter after different periods of isolation.

Age and duration of isolation (days)	N	Individual contact latencies	Group av. contact latencies	Individual suckling latencies	Group av. suckling latencies
0–7	3	4 min 10 min 2 hr, 18 min	51 min	1 hr, 25 min 5 hr, 35 min 4 hr, 33 min	3 hr, 11 min
6–23	5	22 min 35 min 48 min 1 hr, 04 min 2 hr, 23 min	1 hr, 2 min	0 hr, 45 min 5 hr, 17 min 25 hr, 14 min 29 hr, 15 min 38 hr, 00 min	19 hr, 42 min
18–33	2	45 min 47 min	46 min	7 hr, 5 min 23 hr, 15 min	15 hr, 10 min
23–44	4	19 hr, 7 min 29 hr, 00 min 71 hr, 28 min 72 hr, 00 min	47 hr, 56 min	72 hr, 25 min No suckling in the three others	
2–44	4	1 hr, 00 min 24 hr, 40 min 44 hr, 47 min 70 hr, 00 min	35 hr, 7 min	No suckling	
34–49	4	16 min 48 min 1 hr, 49 min 93 hr, 35 min	24 hr, 7 min	24 hr, 40 min 26 hr, 5 min 50 hr, 35 min 93 hr, 35 min	29 hr, 24 min
47–54	3	1 min 6 min 31 min	13 min	0 hr, 1 min 0 hr, 33 min 5 hr, 56 min	2 hr, 10 min

groups of isolates in which this response appeared in the tests. It is seen that latencies were relatively short in both the kittens isolated from birth to 7 days and in those isolated from the 47th to the 54th day. Values for suckling latency were higher in kittens isolated from the 6th to the 23d day, and in those isolated from the 18th to the 33d day, as for these groups the average latencies were 15–20 hours and the longest delays as high as 38 hours. The maximal latencies were obtained in the group isolated from the 34th to the 49th day, for which the average was 48 hours and the longest delay 93 hours.

Analysis of the behavioral facts shows that the delay in suckling on return to the litter situation is dependent upon two different adjustments to the female by the isolate. The first of these is an initial general adjustment, called "contact latency" and recorded by us as ending when the kitten's first sustained contact with the female was achieved; the second was the subsequent interval, called by us the "suckling delay," elapsing before suckling began. In Table 2 these two measures, given for each group of isolates, are seen to be very different. The reasons for these differences become clear when the characteristic responses of litter-reared kittens to the female are compared with those of isolate kittens.

4. *Reactions to the female of litter-reared and of isolate kittens.* A study of the data in the five isolate groups in which suckling appeared indicates that in nearly all of the cases the main difficulty lay in either the initiation of the suckling act or in the performance of this act, rather than in achieving a preliminary adaptation to the female. Table 2 shows that in most cases, as in kittens isolated from the 6th to the 23d day and in others isolated from the 34th to the 49th day, the first sustained contact with the female was arrived at relatively soon, after which the accomplishment of suckling required a rather long interval. In the two groups of isolates that did not suckle (days 2–44; days 23–44) the behavior protocols indicated the existence of an additional and special difficulty in effecting a sustained contact with the female, marked by an evident tension and a heightened excitement in her vicinity, so intense and lasting that any attainment of suckling seemed out of the question.

Signs of intense disturbance, including in most cases piloerection of fur on tail and body, ear-retraction, back-arching and overt withdrawal, were observed in three of the four 23d–44th day isolates and in all of the 2nd–44th day isolates. It is also of interest that the 34th–49th day isolates, the one other group in which such disturbance signs appeared (hissing and other disturbance signs in 40%; overt withdrawal in 60%), were the group with the longest suckling delays of those subjects accomplishing the suckling adjustment to the female. The facts suggest that although in the last group the tendency for disturbance in the presence of the female had decreased sufficiently within two hours to admit a suckling adjustment to her, these reactions differed only in degree from those in the two nonsuckling groups. Had the kittens of these three isolate groups been free to run from the cage, all would doubtless have done so, thereby eliminating any chance that a suckling relationship might develop.

5. *Reactions to the female of litter-reared and of isolate kittens.* Clearly, suckling marks the accomplishment of a complex adaptive relationship between female and young for which many of the isolate kittens were not prepared under the conditions of their tests. From our results, the kitten's attainment of a sustained contact with the female, although difficult, is only a preliminary and a partial adjustment, and delays in effecting a suckling response are attributable to behavioral interferences beyond those involved in this limited relationship of female and young. We have noted the fact that in certain of the isolate groups not only the initial phase of the suckling act but also the further progress of this act was affected. To understand the difficulty in these cases, we must examine the circumstances of the isolate's adjustment both to the litter situation and to the female.

In tests of cage-orientation carried out regularly with isolates after their return, kittens in the group isolated from birth to seven days were found seriously deficient, as compared with litter-raised kittens, in their ability to orient spatially and return to the home corner even when started close by. Subject to serious shortcomings in their orientative adjustments, these isolates could not regain the home corner, and all of them spent considerable intervals of time alone away from this locale. As a result, their first contacts with the female had to occur largely by chance. When one of these isolates chanced to brush the female, the first contact was followed by a reaction of turning toward her and pushing against her body, then nuzzling into her fur. In such responses these isolates were somewhat more efficient than were neonate kittens, a fact attributable not only to greater strength, motility and other gains of maturation, but also to a certain amount of stimulus equivalence between the brooder and female in their tactual and thermal properties, as well as in spatial properties such as the functional-U. But on the other hand the returned isolates, both in their cruder orientative responses to the female and in their less efficient nipple-localizing actions as compared with normal subjects, revealed the handicap of having been deprived of certain benefits of experience with the female.

The disadvantages of isolation may be illustrated in a comparison of isolates returned at one week with litter-raised controls of the same age with respect to the important action of nuzzling. Most of the time, female-reared kittens at this age are in or near the home corner where they can soon reach the female when she is nearby. As a rule they generally locate an area of the female's abdomen soon after reaching her, and thereafter they are likely to nuzzle about only briefly before finding and attaching to a nipple, with the nuzzling usually restricted to the immediate vicinity of the nipple. In such behavior, littermates are never nuzzled, although they may be touched frequently in the orientative processes. The seven-day isolates, in contrast, after having been set down in the test, got to the female only by reaching the home corner accidentally in wandering about, or perhaps through being retrieved by the female. Their local responses differed strikingly from those of normal kittens, once the female was reached. When, for example, an isolate strayed close to the female while she was lying down, nursing the litter, she would generally respond by licking it. Typically, this action influenced the kitten's orientation, causing the kitten to turn toward the female and push, as described, against whatever part of her body happened to be touched. In such cases, isolates would commonly nuzzle over the female's entire furry surface, including paws, neck and back, although somewhat more frequently around her genital region than elsewhere. The isolate's proximal orientation to the female thus was at first very generalized and not significantly more efficient than that of a neonate. The female and the brooder evidently were equivalent to the extent that both furnished attractive low-intensity stimulation and optimal thermal stimulation, but localizing a nipple clearly was a different problem in the two situations.

These isolate kittens nevertheless operate on a different behavioral basis than do neonates, as they have had one week of physical maturation and of experience in the brooder. These differences somehow account for a handicap in adjusting to the litter situation, as we find the week-old isolates requiring definitely more time to achieve their first suckling adjustments to the female than neonates require. Analysis of the protocols shows that the difference is based on both the female's behavior and on certain aspects of the isolate's behavior. The female's nursing behavior, as we have noted, undergoes progressive changes in the first week, in relation to changes in the suckling pattern and the general behavior of the kittens that have been with her since parturition. Because these kittens as a group are now particularly attractive to the female, drawing her visually to the home corner, and because they begin suckling promptly when she arches her body around them there, they often hold her to this spot for some time. These prevalent circumstances reduce the chances that female and isolate will come together as the isolate wanders afield in the cage. The week-old isolates therefore, through their superior motility and their greater freedom as solitary individuals, are handicapped as compared with both neonates and week-old litter-reared kittens with respect to current factors in female behavior promoting the suckling relationship.

From our results, kittens isolated from the 6th to the 23d day also were clearly inferior to normally raised littermates in the initiation and early performance of suckling. Although these isolates were able to achieve their first contacts with the female early in their test periods, as for example through being attracted visually to her, their first suckling reactions had a much greater latency than those of the first-week isolates. At the same time the littermate controls were suckling once or twice each hour, each of the 6th–23d day isolates in its test continued for nearly 20 hours in an orientation to the female's face and anterior body rather than to her mammary region. Like the first-week isolates, these kittens all were generalized in their nuzzling, spending long intervals going over the bodies of other kittens and the furry nonmammary surfaces of the female, before localization of a nipple and attachment occurred. These isolates did not seem to gain any particular advantage from having been visually attracted to the female. Neither, in localizing a nipple, were they helped reliably by their early suckling experience in the litter situation prior to isolation. We conclude that their difficulties in suckling centered on the fact that the period in the brooder deprived them of specific litter experiences essential for dealing with the female at the stage of their return.

Difficulties were also great but were somewhat different in the test adjustments of kittens isolated from the 18th to the 33d day. Although these subjects, like the 6th–23d day isolates, were slow in localizing the female's mammary region, they had less difficulty in localizing nipples. Their difficulties, rather than involving this specific act, concerned adjusting to the female as an object from which to suckle.

An even longer time was required by kittens isolated later in the litter period, from the 34th to the 49th day, to make their first suckling adjustments to the female in the test returns. There is evidence that the difficulties were somewhat different in these groups of isolates; as indicated, in all of them the principal handicap seemed to be in achieving an appropriate general suckling orientation to the female rather than in the specific operations of localizing a nipple and suckling.

In the results for suckling latency, a sharp difference appeared between kittens in the groups isolated for periods starting at different times between the 6th and the 34th day, and the group isolated from the 47th to the 54th day. Although these last kittens were held in the brooder for one week from the time weaning normally begins in the litter situation, they all accomplished suckling adjustments in the return tests. Furthermore, their suckling delays were the shortest of those in all isolation groups, despite the fact that they had to accomplish their nipple localizations and attachments while the female was moving about the cage. One of these kittens had begun to suckle within one minute after the test began, and a second required less than an hour, in contrast to delays of many hours common for kittens isolated at times after the first week and before weaning time.

TABLE 3

Suckling reactions of representative subjects tested with the female after earlier periods with female and in the incubator, and of others in subsequent tests with brooder or with female.

					Next suckling test with brooder and female			
Initial period with female (days)	Following period in incubator (days)	Test with female		Subsequent period with female (days)	Brooder		Female	
		Day	Suckling latency		Day	Suckling latency	Day	Suckling latency
1–6	7–24	25th	12 hr, 15 min	25–47	48th	12 min		—
1–6	7–25	26th	19 hr, 40 min	26–47	48th	25 min		—
1–17	18–32	33rd	23 hr, 15 min	33–46	47th	10 min		—
1–24	25–40	—	—	—	—		41st	72 hr, 25 min
1–24	25–38	—	—	—	—		39th	No suckling
1–24	25–41	—	—	—	—		42nd	No suckling

6. *Suckling readjustments to the female and to the brooder.* In what ways may the acts of suckling at the female and at the brooder facilitate each other or interfere with each other? In order to compare the recall or reinstatement of these two acts, readjustment to the brooder was tested in kittens that had suckled from the female for several weeks, and readjustment to the female was tested in kittens returned to the litter after a period of isolation and feeding at the brooder nipple. All of these kittens had suckled neonatally in the litter situation, but isolation in the brooder began for two of them at the 6th day, for one at the 18th day, and for the last three at 24 days, and retesting with female or with brooder came at correspondingly later times.

As the results in Table 3 show, readjustment to the female was very difficult for the three kittens tested after having been isolated in the incubator following long initial periods in the litter situation. In their terminal tests with the female, one of these kittens had a suckling latency of more than three days and the other two did not suckle at all. On the other hand, all of the three kittens retested with the brooder made efficient suckling adjustments after relatively short latencies. These last three kittens, however, on their subsequent test returns to the litter situation from the brooder between the 25th and 35th days, at times earlier than other comparable subjects, reinstated the suckling adjustment only after latencies of from 12 to 24 hours.

Let us review the results for test returns with respect to the effects of differences in the duration of the intervening period, as concerns the nature of the suckling adjustment operative in that period. When returned to the female after intervals in the incubator ranging from 8 to 17 days, 11 kittens averaged 31 hours in their suckling latencies. In test returns to the brooder, however, after intervals with the female ranging from 10 to 36 days, 8 kittens scored a minimal suckling latency of only 12 minutes. In female tests following brooder isolation the shortest suckling latency was 33 minutes (after an isolation period of 8 days), the longest was 93 hours, and one kitten did not suckle at all in the female test after 16 days in the brooder. In brooder tests after intervening periods with the female, the shortest latency was 3 minutes after 17 days with the female, the longest was just 25 minutes after 24 days with the female, but one kitten suckled promptly in the brooder test after having been away from the brooder for 36 days. It is definite that the brooder-suckling pattern was far more readily reinstated than was the female-suckling pattern.

SUMMARY AND DISCUSSION

Our evidence from analytical research on behavioral development in army ants and in domestic cats favors for each of these a distinctive theory of the mosaic or developmental-integration type rather than a common theory using postulations of innate organization. There is no demonstrated single formula for instinctive behavior throughout the animal series. Also, there are strong arguments against strictly nativistic hypotheses of genically determined, intraneurally controlled behavior patterns in any species (Schneirla, 10). Each type of species-standard behavioral system requires investigation as a distinctive problem in development, with all hypotheses as to its nature and derivation subject to experimental test.

The army-ant species-typical pattern constitutes a functional system formed through the working together of very different processes contributed by very different types of individuals and sources in the characteristic developmental situation. Figure 33, representing the species mosaic, emphasizes the fact that the essential pattern is not inherited by any type of individual. The queen's ovulation rhythm, for example, is not innate to her as a timing process controlling the cycle, but is governed by a set of convergent biological factors which, in the colony situation with its conditions such as those related to brood-development rate, produce a species-typical reproductive schedule. The cyclic patterns of army-ant species and their chief turning points actually arise through the influence of many different contributive factors in the colony situation.

The insect and mammalian patterns we have studied represent very different functional integrative levels. There is a certain similarity between these levels in the nature of the organic factors involved—stimulative secretory processes, reproductive processes, processes of stage-conditioned sensitivity, and others. The general similarity extends further in that, in the typical functional situation, these factors contribute to the organization of a species-characteristic system or mosaic. In this system, in the case of the ants, larval cuticular secretions function in a way roughly similar to the parturitive fluids in cats, facilitating the formation of a social bond, although in the two cases the physiological details are very different. Behaviorally, such factors enter into social processes of reciprocal stimulation in both cases, essential to the formation of social bonds.

The manner in which the social bonds develop is strikingly different, however, in the insects and mammals. On the insect level, a *biosocial* organization is achieved, directly dominated throughout in its behavioral manifestations by sensory, secretory and other organic processes, and changing specifically under their impress. The recurrent cyclic shifts so characteristic of the army-ant pattern illustrate this point strikingly. On the mammalian level, although organic factors such as uterine contractions, birth fluids and others are basic to the forming of a social bond, their effects constitute intervening variables leading indirectly to a *psychosocial* system in the development of which the intimate cooperation of factors of maturation, experience and learning is paramount at all stages.

Our results substantiate the principle (10, 12) that processes of reciprocal stimulation are basic to all levels of social integration, however different their developmental history and behavioral expressions may be. Even in the army-ant system, experience plays a part, although its role here seems limited to a simple process of habituation, directly tied to organic factors as in approach-fixation to colony odors. But in the kittens, as our longitudinal studies of orientation show, factors of experience and learning play a complex and progressive role. A striking example is the expanding significance of tactual and odor cues in the kitten's early nonvisual stage of orientation; in the same neonatal period, progress in related perceptual developments involving cues from the female is indicated in our results for individual specialization in suckling. In both types of adjustment, a shift to visually dominated perceptual patterns, arising from and modifying the nonvisual system, occurs within a few days after eye-opening. The psychosocial aspect of these developmental changes in altricial mammalian young lacks a real counterpart on the insect level.

Our research has been based on the theory (Schneirla, 8, 14) that, since low-intensity stimulative effects such as contact and odor are basically approach-evocative in animal development, relationships of reciprocal-stimulation involving such stimuli play an appreciable role in socialization. We also recognize that relationships of feeding normally play a major role in social development, furnishing a center of organization for all of the reciprocal-stimulative processes involved in maintaining social bonds. Because our investigations of behavioral ontogeny in cats have been aimed at understanding species-standard patterns, our experimental situations all combine opportunities for both low-intensity stimulation and feeding.

We hold that experimental studies, as by the method of isolation, cannot be validly interpreted *except* in close reference to searching longitudinal investigation of the normal or species-standard developmental pattern. For normal behavioral development, in which the formation of a perceptual bond with and adjustment to the female as feeding object progresses without a break from the time of birth, we have described three successive, overlapping stages, of (1) female-initiation, (2) mutual initiation, and (3) kitten-initiation of the feeding adjustment and related social processes. Because feeding processes clearly reveal the nature of the social bond, and are found central to socialization, we have explored feeding adjustments comparatively as they develop in the normal litter situation and in kittens variously isolated and deprived of intervals of social experience.

Although our brooder presents attractive low-intensity stimulation and opportunities to acquire a routine feeding adjustment, it lacks motility, behavioral reactivity and individual capacities for modifying behavior, and thus constitutes a very limited substitute for the lactating female available to normally raised young. The approach-fixation that develops in isolated kittens is a perceptually limited one, very stereotyped in comparison with that developing normally. Kittens isolated from birth, along with others isolated later in the nonvisual stage, exhibit their ineptitude for normal maternal adjustments particularly in the nature of their nuzzling. In these early isolates, nuzzling is generalized to kittens and is an over-all response to the female, in distinct contrast to the versatile orientative abilities and local discriminations of normal subjects at the corresponding ages. The brooder experience is a minimal one, routine and relatively static in perceptual cues and motor processes of approach and feeding; hence the feeding reaction to it can be readily reinstated at a later time. The adjustment to the female, in contrast, is found after different isolation intervals to be out of keeping with the situation and inadequate in significant respects. Our results show that although isolation from the brooder did not significantly impair a subsequent reinstatement of the feeding response there, isolation from the situation of female and litter interfered very substantially with subsequent adjustment under those conditions.

These differences are understandable in terms of a review of results from our studies of normal events in the litter situation. A contrast of the pattern of relationships prevalent between female and young at the time the kitten was removed for isolation and that prevalent at the time of return and test discloses that the female-young relationship is always a complex and changing one in which the roles of the participants vary progressively. Because the relationships of the partners in the feeding act normally progress through three very different stages of perceptual-motor adjustments, each returned isolate is confronted by a psychological situation materially different from that prevalent at the time of removal. The differences center notably on the condition of the female, her behavior and her responses to (or attitude toward) the young.

The returned isolate must meet new conditions, and perhaps radically new conditions at certain times, without having participated in the genesis of the changed conditions. In general this presents an increasingly difficult task to kittens returned at later stages, as with time the necessary social and nutritive adjustments become more complex and more divergent from the individual's pre-isolation responses to the litter situation. In contrast, return to the brooder presents the kitten with a situation that has changed very little in its functional relevance, in ways dependent on the kitten itself. Results show that adjustment to the brooder involves a relatively simple pattern, evidently of the approach-conditioning type, substantially unimpaired by intervening litter-situation experiences and therefore reinstated readily on the kitten's return to the brooder.

Our findings consequently emphasize the necessity of a continued behavioral and functional interchange with female and littermates if the kitten is to develop an adequate suckling adjustment typical of its age group. Psychological processes concerning perceptual and behavioral organization are required in which organic factors underlying reciprocal stimulation play a basic, inextricable role. The contrast with the specific, dominant role of analogous organic processes in insects is striking, as to the resultant adaptive organization. Although in mammalian development the feeding pattern is central to the standard socialization process, it is not a simple routine mode of feeding by suckling, as in the brooder, but a perceptual adjustment adapted to the current pattern of the female and the prevalent social situation.

These considerations favor a very different view of the concept of "critical periods" from the one now held by many writers. In the social development of the cat, we are led to the idea that striking changes in the essential progression are grounded not only in the growth-dependent processes of maturation but also, at the same time, in opportunities for experience and learning arising in the standard female-litter situation. This conception of social ontogeny encourages stressing not just one or a few chronologically marked changes in the behavior pattern, but rather indicates that normally each age-period is crucial for the development of particular aspects in a complex progressive pattern of adjustment. Furthermore, the principles of development may be somewhat different for the diagnosis of different periods according to their duration, their character or their time of occurrence, and research is essential to clarify what factors at any one stage may become critical for specific or restricted as against inclusive and widely organized adjustments of the same or of later stages.

Because factors depending on experience in the normal developmental situation are crucial for progress in social adjustment, the result is that isolation at any time from the normal situation so deprives a kitten of advantages typically available in that period that on its return after isolation the subject shows characteristic defects in social adjustment. We conclude therefore that critical periods in social development are not matters of maturation per se. Rather, time-conditioned factors depending on experience in the normal situation, in close conjunction with growth-dependent factors, are necessary for both the turning points and the intervening progress in social adjustment.

Diagnosing shortcomings in social adjustment thus depends on our knowledge about disadvantageous combinations of conditions affecting factors of experience and maturation together, rather than on either of these alone. How the subject can readjust to the normal social situation after an absence in isolation is found so conditioned by a complex of factors concerning age, the duration and conditions of isolation, and the type of social situation re-encountered, that specific research seems essential to clarify what factors may be critical for any one developmental period as compared with others. The effects of atypical conditions such as those of isolation must be studied in close comparison with those holding under species-standard developmental conditions, for an adequate judgment of ontogeny in either case. Mammalian social development is thus seen as advancing from birth in ways that, for the species-characteristic outcome, continuously require not only the standard conditions of organic maturation but also the presence of the standard developmental setting with its progressively changing behavioral properties.

REFERENCES

1. Clark, E., L. R. Aronson, and M. Gordon. 1954. Mating Behavior Patterns in two sympatric species of xiphophorin fishes: Their inheritance and significance in sexual isolation. *Bull. Am. Mus. Nat. Hist.* 103: 139–335.
2. Ewer, R. F. 1954. Suckling behaviour in Kittens. *Behaviour* 15: 146–162.
3. Fuller, J. L., C. A. Easler, and E. M. Banks. 1950. Formation of conditioned avoidance responses in young puppies. *Am. J. Physiol.* 3: 462.
4. Rosenblatt, J. S., G. Turkewitz, and T. C. Schneirla. Analytical studies on maternal behavior in relation to litter adjustment and socialization in the domestic cat. III. Development of orientation. (In ms.)
5. Rosenblatt, J. S., G. Turkewitz, and T. C. Schneirla. The development of suckling and related behavior in neonate kittens—A résumé. In E. Bliss, ed., *The roots of behavior,* New York. (In ms.)

6. Rosenblatt, J. S., J. Wodinsky, G. Turkewitz, and T. C. Schneirla. Analytical studies on maternal behavior in relation to litter adjustment and socialization in the domestic cat. II. Maternal-young relations from birth to weaning. (In prep.)

7. Schneirla, T. C. 1938. A theory of army-ant behavior based upon the analysis of activities in a representative species. *J. Comp. Psychol.* 25: 51–90.

8. Schneirla, T. C. 1939. A theoretical consideration of the basis for approach withdrawal adjustments in behavior. *Psychol. Bull.* 37: 501–502.

9. Schneirla, T. C. 1941. Social organization in insects, as related to individual function. *Psychol. Rev.* 48: 465–486.

10. Schneirla, T. C. 1946. Problems in the biopsychology of social organization. *J. Abnorm. Soc. Psychol.* 41: 385–402.

11. Schneirla, T. C. 1951. A consideration of some problems in the ontogeny of family life and social adjustments in various infrahuman animals. In M. J. E. Senn, ed., *Problems of infancy and childhood: Transactions of the fourth (1950) conference.* New York: Josiah Macy, Jr. Foundation. Pp. 81–124.

12. Schneirla, T. C. 1956. Interrelationships of the "innate" and the "acquired" in instinctive behavior. In P.-P. Grassé, ed., *L'Instinct dans le comportement des animaux et de l'homme.* Paris: Masson. Pp. 387–452.

13. Schneirla, T. C. 1957. Theoretical consideration of cyclic processes in doryline ants. *Proc. Am. Philos. Soc.* 101: 106–133.

14. Schneirla, T. C. 1959. An evolutionary and developmental theory of biphasic processes underlying approach and withdrawal. In M. R. Jones, ed., *Nebraska symposium on motivation.* Lincoln: Univ. Nebraska Press. Pp. 1–42.

15. Scott, J. P. 1958. Critical periods in the development of social behavior in puppies. *Psychosom. Med.* 20: 42–54.

16. Tobach, E., M. L. Failla, R. Cohn, and T. C. Schneirla. Analytical studies on maternal behavior in relation to litter adjustment and socialization in the domestic cat. I. Parturition. (In ms.)

17. Wheeler, W. M. 1928. *The social insects.* New York: Harcourt, Brace.

ETHEL TOBACH

T. C. SCHNEIRLA

The Biopsychology of Social
Behavior of Animals

Bibliography No. 119

FUNDAMENTAL CONCEPTS IN
THE COMPARATIVE STUDY OF SOCIAL BEHAVIOR

Until forms intermediate between organic and inorganic matter are better known, the fact that all cells issue directly from other cells may be taken to indicate that no existing form of life is truly solitary and no organism is completely independent of others at all times in its history. This dependence of every individual on others is the prerequisite to social behavior. The relationships among living organisms postulated by Darwin in his theory of the evolution of forms of life suggest a basis for ordering and comparing the behavioral interactions of all species of animals.

The concept of *levels of integration* (1) postulates a hierarchical arrangement of energy (organization of matter) beginning with the simplest organized entities and increasing in the degree and elaborateness of organization from inanimate to animate forms. General categories of human knowledge which reflect such an ordering of natural phenomena are cosmology, physics, biology, and sociology. Each of these levels of organization requires distinctive instrumentation, experimental operations, and laws. For the wide range of existing animals, levels of integration are conceived as a series of progressive advances from the acellular (or "single-celled") animals through the multicellular. Each of these levels refers to animal groups which have in common a set of distinctive capacities for behavior. Any one level of integration in behavior, although certain to be similar in some respects to levels judged "lower" in the scale to which it is related through evolution, differs from them sufficiently to warrant its separate categorization. For example, the analysis of the physiologic and behavioral interactions that prevail among bees in a hive gives no adequate

From *Biologic Basis of Pediatric Practice,* edited by R. E. Cooke and S. Levin. New York: McGraw-Hill, 1968. Reprinted with permission.

preparation for studying human societies. Human social organization is not only more complex than that of the honeybee but presents *new* aspects of development, of stereotypy, and of plasticity in behavior, requiring special experimental techniques and the formulation of principles not applicable to bees. These are qualitatively different levels.

Derived from the principle of levels of integration, in a logical rather than a historical sense, is *Morgan's canon,* which states that, for scientific rigor, one must not assume higher psychologic properties when lower ones adequately account for the facts. The application of this principle, in view of existing evidence, would preclude an anthropomorphic interpretation of the social organization of the beehive and, conversely, would guard against a zoomorphic representation of human social behavior.

Any interactions of two or more organisms reflect, first of all, the behavioral abilities of each of the participating individuals. The behavioral abilities of each individual, in turn, are a reflection of its history, that is, the evolution of the species and the individual's *stage of development* (2). From the evolution of the species are derived the biochemical characteristics of the earliest stage of development, as well as factors determining the milieu in which the earliest development takes place. At each stage of development, the fusion of the past history of the individual and its interaction with present stimulation govern its properties and functions. An understanding of the history of individuals engaged in social behavior is fundamental to the adequate analysis of the phenomena of group organization.

The theory of evolution and the concepts of levels of integration, of psychologic parsimony, and of development involve principles which direct investigators toward the scientific analysis of social behavior in terms of its underlying processes.

PROCESSES BASIC TO THE ORGANIZATION
OF SOCIAL BEHAVIOR

The primary process involved in the formation of a social bond is the *approach of one organism to another.* Schneirla has proposed, in his theory postulating *biphasic processes based upon stimulus intensity* underlying behavior, that (3):

> Intensity of stimulation basically determines the direction of reaction with respect to the source, and thereby exerts a selective effect on what conditions affect the organism. This statement is derived from the generalization that, for all organisms in early ontogenetic stages, low intensities of stimulation tend to evoke approach reactions, high intensities withdrawal reactions with reference to the source.

Two basic types of response, approach and withdrawal, are proposed as giving the best operational criteria by which to describe the behavior of organisms in a given stimulus situation. These same criteria applied at all stages of development chart the behavioral changes which reflect the fusion of maturation and experience. The two response types are discerned as traceable to characteristic biphasic modes in the function of cells, tissues, organs, and systems in the afferent, conductile, and efferent spheres, which, despite general similarities, through evolution have taken on new forms and properties at different integrative levels.

The effects of the physical intensity of a stimulus are viewed as primary in that they dominate response in the early development of any organism —and throughout life in the lower integrative levels. The level attained by each species in the integration of maturation and experience in ontogeny determines the extent to which this early dominance of stimulus intensity is likely to be modified in later stages of development. In the case of acellular organisms, the initial patterns prevail; in the higher mammals, one sees the earliest modifications of initial intensity-dominated biphasic response patterns and the most complex elaboration of these biphasic modes into the greatest variety both of individualized and socialized patterns (3a).

Processes of bond formation on all social levels involve relationships of approach and consequent mutual stimulation. In the range of group patterns, however, there exist many types in which the approach aspect of the behavioral relationship is unilateral, as in relationships of parasite to host and of predator to prey. Such patterns, although not social, are often parts of a social situation, and in any case their properties make them of interest to the student of social phenomena. The analysis of these situations by the parsimonious criterion of approach and withdrawal responses is also to be desired.

In organisms such as social insects, in which the approach-response pattern is commonly elaborated during development to include the feeding of immature stages (e.g., larvae), the resultant exchange of food suggested to Wheeler a basis for the formation of social bonds. In his theoretical treatment of insect societies, Wheeler (4) offered the term *trophallaxis,* meaning the mutual exchange of food between adults and their larval young, which he considered basic for insect social life. The concept of trophallaxis has been modified and extended by Schneirla (5) to designate a wide range of processes of *reciprocal stimulation* (i.e., tactile, chemical, visual) found essential to the formation and maintenance of group organization in animals. The effect of interindividual stimulation is commonly attractive, normally accounting for group cohesion, but under exceptional conditions it can become repellent, resulting in the dispersion of group members. The processes of approach and withdrawal are both essential to the development of social behavior, particularly on higher levels, as will be demonstrated below, in such social phenomena as territoriality, aggression, weaning, and subgroup formation. The term *reciprocal stimulation* refers to processes which go far beyond the one described by the word *trophallaxis,* which denotes only exchange of food within groups.

The nature of the stimuli reciprocally exchanged between two or more animals in a social group is dependent upon the stage of development of each of the participating group members, as well as upon the group situation and factors affecting the stability of its organization.

At each stage of development, processes of *growth* (increase in number or size of cellular units), *maturation* (change in function as a result of growth and experience), and *experience* (total effect of all prior internal and external stimulation) merge and are intimately related in different configurations. These configurations are the basis for the level of integration attained by particular species and the foundation for the development of intraspecies patterns of social behavior. The *processes of reproduction,* particularly those relating to the *behavior of parents and offspring,* are central in the development of bond formation. As Allee has pointed out (6), ". . . the more closely knit societies arose from a sort of simple aggregation, frequently, but not necessarily solely of the sexual familial pattern." Essential processes have arisen in evolution through natural selection, permitting one or both parents to remain with their young for an appreciable time and admitting the development of reciprocal stimulative relations favoring interdependent behavior among individuals. Wheeler (7) thus contrasted the subsocial pattern of earwigs, in which both the female's ability to stay with her young and factors promoting group interactions were far weaker and more limited than in the ants, in which colonies or permanent social organizations exist in all species.

The analysis of the processes of biphasic modes of response, of growth, maturation, and experience and their relationships in phylogeny and ontogeny, of reciprocal stimulations, and of reproduction promoting species-characteristic patterns of parent-offspring relationship permits the ordering of group organizations and of the behavioral phenomena characteristic of them.

LEVELS OF SOCIAL ORGANIZATION

Characteristics of Association, Biosocial, and Psychosocial Behavior

Discerning similarities and differences among phyletic groups in relation to levels of integration constitutes one of the basic applications of the comparative method in the study of behavior. One principle derived from this method is that an animal's degree of stereotypy in behavior and its capacities for plasticity in modifying interactions with the environment are reflections of the level of specialization and the resources of its irritable, conductile, and reactive tissues as realized in development.

The wide range of such specialization in the animal world is reflected in the variety of types of association. An *association* may be defined as a spatially and temporally limited collection of two or more individuals. One type of association, the *aggregation,* is formed actively or passively under the influence of an external agent. A passive aggregation results when wind deposits insects on a particular bush or when a tidal wave washes marine animals into a cluster between two rocks in a tidal pool. Active aggregations are formed when animals assume a spatial relationship to one another as a result of the responses of individual organisms to stimulation from an external source.

Such responses are known as *taxis,* which is generally defined as directed orientation reactions involving the movement of the organism (Fraenkel and Gunn, 8). The focus of the definition of such reactions is on the nature of the animal's response, rather than on the source of stimulative energy. The source of stimulation is important, however, to the study of social behavior. In most instances, the energy is furnished by inanimate objects and phenomena. In the normal behavior of every animal, however, responses of the taxis type are very frequently given to stimuli produced by other animals. To be sure, in all animals part of the time and in the simplest animals perhaps most of the time the difference is not important. For the study of associative behavior, however, there is much to be gained by a differentiation between cases of an organism's orienting responses toward or away from stimuli derived from inanimate sources and responses to the stimulation afforded by other animals. We make this differentiation by terming the first instance *taxis* to distinguish it from the second example, which we term *biotaxis.* An active aggregation of barnacles on the hull of a boat is the outcome of the common response of each animal to an environmental stimulus, the tactile character of the substrate. The formation of such an aggregation does not depend upon the presence of other animals; hence, it is a taxic association of the active aggregation type.

One of the most prevalent forms of biotaxic stimuli is that of the chemical products secreted or excreted by animals. For example, the protozoan *Paramecium,* through its metabolic functions, produces a weak acid which is likely to accumulate where one or more are relatively quiescent, so that a gradient of intensities comes about. Then, as other individuals give their biotaxic reactions of approach toward the accumulation of the weak acid, an active aggregation forms. On a higher phyletic level, the production of pheromones (9) (exocrine secretions which attract or repel) by insects or other animals may comparably lead to aggregations or may lead to active dissipation of aggregations. A queen honeybee secrets a substance from her mandibular gland which attracts worker bees to her; the amniotic fluids issuing with and on the body of a newborn kitten provide a stimulus of approach value for the parturient cat; and so on, through a great variety of types.

Many other forms of stimulation provided by animals have a comparable quality of eliciting approach responses from others. The stridulation of the grasshopper is a vibratory stimulus eliciting approaches; the visual stimulus provided by the activity of individual fish in many species at particular stages of development constitutes an important factor in schooling behavior; and the tactile stimuli provided by the fur of the opossum mother elicit from the offspring the responses of approach and clasping.

Aggregations based upon biotaxic responses may provide the setting for the reciprocal stimulation of the collected animals. The forms, complexities, and permanency of group behavior resulting from reciprocal stimulation such as pheromone production dominate the interactions of the group members, and aspects of their neural equipment hold behavioral modification within distinct limits, so that patterns of action typically are determined rather directly by structural and physiologic factors. Such factors limit the storage of the trace effects of experience and restrict the use of such trace effects in new situations. The type of group bond formed in such animals is of a situationally determined character, limited in scope, and is termed *biosocial* (5).

The biosocial level of organization is exemplified by the social and migratory behavior of the army ant (Figure 39), intensively studied by Schneirla. In certain of these ants, each colony shifts alternately from a nomadic phase of vigorous daytime raids and nightly emigrations (e.g., lasting 16 to 18 days in *Eciton hamatum*) to a statary phase of weak raiding and no emigration (usually 20 days in *E. hamatum*), and the reverse. Prior to this research, the existence of a cyclic pattern was unsuspected and the idea held that these ants emigrated variably in dependence upon the local supply of their insect booty.

The cyclic pattern of these ants was found to depend essentially upon the fact that at certain times (e.g., in the enclosed pupal stage) the brood offers only a low stimulative effect to the adult population but at other times, as when it is passing through the larval stage, the brood becomes intensely excitatory to the colony. Throughout the larval stage, there is much licking, grooming, and handling of larvae by the workers; food is then dumped upon larvae. Massive stimulation from the squirming, redolent larva holds colony excitation at the behavioral level of immense daily raids and nightly emigrations as the brood develops. But when the many

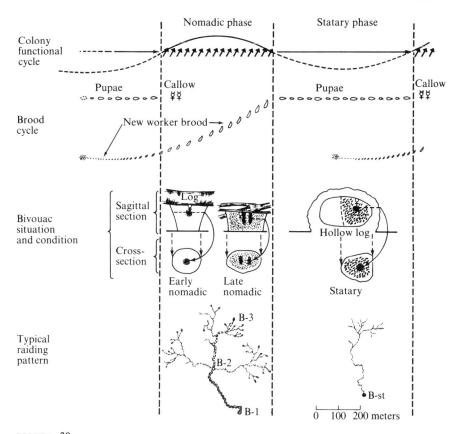

FIGURE 39

Schema of the functional cycle of the army ant, *Eciton hamatum*. From the top:
(1) The two phases of the cycle, indicated by a sine curve (arrows indicate large
daily raids and nightly emigrations in the nomadic phase); (2) typical correspondence between phases in the colony cycle and developmental stages of successive broods; (3) types of temporary nest (bivouac) in each of the two activity
phases, with an indication of the brood's position in each; (4) daily raiding
system typical in each of the principal activity phases. B-1, 2, 3, successive bivouac
sites; B-st., statary bivouac site. (From Schneirla, reference 11.)

larvae of the mature brood are well advanced in their spinning and many
have already straightened within their cocoons, on the threshold of the
pupal stage, the excitatory brood-adult processes of reciprocal stimulation
fall to a minimum, and the colony lapses into a statary phase. Just before
this happens, however, as the larvae near maturity, the metamorphosis of
their salivary glands into spin gland tissues causes them to cease feeding,
although they continue to excite the workers at high intensity as they spin
their cocoons. It is then that the queen, previously at an ebb in reproductive capacity (i.e., with contracted abdomen), begins to be the recipient

of a crescendo of social stimulation (licking, grooming) and of large-scale feeding by the workers. This change in her environment, really an outcome of the current relationship of brood and workers, constitutes a stimulative and nutritive surge from the colony to which the queen responds promptly. First she rapidly develops fatty tissues, then she matures a great brood of eggs within only about 1 week, laying these eggs about midway in the next ensuing statary phase. It is this new brood, in its larval stage, that serves to energize and maintain the next nomadic phase to its end (10, 11).

The impressive cyclic behavior pattern of the army ants thus has its basis in successive rises and falls in the level of colony excitation because of changes in reciprocal stimulative relations between the brood and the colony population. The complex and highly efficient social patterns of the army ants is derived from the interactions of individuals of limited behavioral resources. But the resources are those of varied and potent biotaxic responses which in the natural environment of the species can promote strikingly complex adaptive group patterns.

Biotaxic responses and biosocial behavior based on them are common to vertebrate social groups, as well as to invertebrate groups. The levels of organization achieved in higher mammals are a function of the extent and the speed with which the initial processes of biotaxis become elaborated and fused into higher processes as individual development proceeds, so that processes of *psychotaxis* occur (5). Psychotaxic processes arise through reactions to taxic and biotaxic stimuli which become modified through the integration of maturation and experience by virtue of such processes as conditioning, learning, and concept formation (among others), introducing a plasticity of behavior. *Psychosocial* types of bond formation then arise, in which the meanings rather than the immediate physiologic effects of stimuli are functional.

In many lower vertebrates and mammals, early approach responses of biotaxic nature facilitate the later development of psychotaxic social behavior. As an example, our studies of parturition in the domestic cat (12) show that the female, in delivering her young, responds predictably to attractive chemical stimuli presented by the amniotic fluid. Hence, although she licks in a variable manner different objects bearing this fluid, this behavior is likely to bring her soon to the neonate. Her own body and the substratum are licked energetically in a largely chance relation to the neonate, yet because the neonate presents the most fluid in a concentrated area, the female's licking soon becomes focused on the newborn as the object licked the longest and most persistently of all. After parturition, the functional-U presented by the female cat lying on her side with legs extended presents a physical pattern that in effect guides the neonate to her despite the variability of its biotaxic actions. The female's licking of the neonates from this position, localized as it is, also exerts a guiding effect on their approaches. Hence, in these animals, biosocial factors effective in the situation of the neonate play basic roles in the formation of social bonds, in this instance of establishment of a relationship betwen the nursing female and the suckling young kittens. The social organization evidenced by the domestic cat is restricted mainly to the act of mating and to the litter period. But we find that sexual behavior of the adult male cat seems to be critically dependent upon the social bond established during the litter period, indicating a psychosocial level of organization, although one of a low order.

In primates, biosocial factors operative during the early socialization of the young are elaborated into psychosocial patterns at an early age, and the complexity of group organization exemplifies psychosocial behavior of a high order. The critical, initial biotaxic stimuli may not be of a chemical nature, however. Yerkes and Tomilin (13) emphasized the importance of clasping as a factor underlying mutual approaches and other mother-young relations in chimpanzees. The significance of tactile stimulation in such matters is indicated by McCulloch's finding (14) that claspable objects could be used for young chimpanzees as incentives in delayed-response and discrimination learning tests. Normally, in primates, clinging and feeding relationships keep mother and young intimately together in the days after parturition, providing a basis for prompt returns to the mother by the infant once it acquires an independent mobility.

Yerkes (15) found chimpanzees superior to all monkeys in their perception and memory, and more varied in their creative imagination and emotional expressions. Their conspicuous superiority in response to training, adaptation to changes, and cooperation with other chimpanzees or with man favors the expectation that their group organization under natural conditions would be correspondingly more versatile and advanced than those of other known subprimates.

Recent studies by Kortlandt (16) of a chimpanzee group of about fifty individuals studied in the Congo indicate that this is the case. Although the males, after cautious reconnoitering, emerged from the forest with much stepping, shrieking, and chasing of one another, quickly occupying their usual feeding and resting ground with evident enthusiasm, the females, particularly the mothers, were usually silent, wary, and protective of their young. The mothers were highly attendant to the young, who were seldom out of sight. Chimpanzees have a longer period of offspring dependency and care than other lower primates, extending to 4 or 5 years, its greater length under natural conditions possibly retarding behavioral development as compared with that of laboratory chimpanzees. The mother-young affiliations evidently generalize readily to group associations, for offspring a few years of age were often observed feeding with other groups and riding the backs of some of the males. The young seemed very responsive to maternal signals, however, possibly because of experience with natural hazards such as leopards, in strong contrast to chimpanzee infants in zoos. In this community, two groups could be distinguished, more often apart than together: (1) a wider-ranging sexual group containing mainly adult males and females without young, often with a few mothers and offspring, and (2) smaller nursery groups of mothers with young ranging from infancy to the age of puberty, with perhaps also an adult male or two. It is interesting to note that this chimpanzee community was organized into groups distinguished by relationship to the young rather than by sex differences as in other subhuman primates. These findings suggest a pattern of considerable resiliency, with a strong internal organization based particularly upon the effective generalization of maternal-young bonds to group associations.

A description of the main types of associative behavior in the animal world has been presented according to the level of the integrative processes basic to bond formation in the various cases. Passive and active aggregations formed in response to stimuli produced by inanimate sources (i.e., taxis) have been contrasted with active aggregations formed under the influence of stimuli emanating from other animals (i.e., biotaxis). In the highest forms of social organization, the psychosocial, it is significant that processes in the early socialization of individuals are recognizably of the biosocial type, centered on taxis responses.

Contrasting Approaches to the Study of Social Behavior

Our analysis in the foregoing discussion has been concerned with the manner in which individual social behavior develops on each level. It is our position that individual development and socialization are attributable to the *fusion* of maturation and experience, hence that the functional interaction of influences from structure, physiology, and experience is a far more intimate one than that conceived in conventional views which represent the "innate" and "acquired" as readily separable in behavior (17). Both the inseparable nature of the chief developmental factors (maturation and experience) themselves and the significant differences that exist in their patterns of relationships at different stages of individual development and at different integrative levels should be recognized by any theory for the study of social behavior.

A somewhat comparable approach is that stated by Kuo (18), who proposes the following formula for the analysis of any behavior pattern:

$$(DH + ST) + PE Set. + SS) + BCF = Pred. Beh.$$
$$\quad\quad (1) \quad\quad\quad\quad (2) \quad\quad\quad\quad (3)$$

where

$$DH = \text{developmental history}$$
$$ST = \text{special training}$$

PE Set. = present environmental setting
    SS = special stimulus
    BCF = biochemical factors
Pred. Beh. = predictable behavior
    (1) = animal's past
    (2) = animal's present
    (3) = physiologic mechanisms of animal

These two theories are similar in that both are nontelic and of the interaction type. Such theories do not postulate inherited patterns of behavior but emphasize that the roles of the individual's genetic background and of its ontogenetic history must always be considered as a developmental problem. Interaction-type theories encourage phyletic comparisons, leading to the contrast of the many ways in which associative behavior arises on different integrative levels and stressing both similarities and dissimilarities.

A different type of theory directed at the study of social behavior in animals is that described by Thomas et al. (18a) as "projective" in that the emphasis is on a separation of factors underlying behavior into two general categories of instinct and the innate or hereditary as against learned or environmental.

The present writers believe that the projective type of theory relies too much on analogies and assumptions of innate behavioral patterns, evidences a lack of psychological parsimony, and strays too often toward teleologic explanatory concepts to offer the best foundation for the scientific study of social phenomena.

Allee (19) recognizes four types of groups which may be called social: (1) groups in which animals show their social habit merely through tolerating the close proximity of other individuals, (2) groups which react as units, (3) groups which show physiologic division of labor, and (4) groups which show morphologically distinct castes and a division of labor. Basic to the evolution of the more closely knit societies is the existence of ". . . an underlying pervasive element of unconscious cooperation, or automatic tendency toward mutual aid among animals." Later (20) he defined cooperation as having three levels of function: physiologic facilitation, biosocial facilitation, and psychosocial facilitation.

Tinbergen (21) views the study of social behavior as the study of the cooperation between, or among, individuals. Social cooperation, for him, depends on the innate tendency of one individual to give a signal and on the innate tendencies of the other individual to respond. In some animals, the signals and responses may become confined to specific individuals through learning; in any case, the potentialities for social behavior are presumed to be always ready in advance. Changes in the innate social behavioral patterns of given species may occur either as a result of variation in the intensity of underlying drives or as a result of learning.

Scott (22) analyzes simple or complex vertebrate social behavior into sets of relationships: (1) of *simple aggregation* based on contactual behavior; (2) of *dominance-subordination* brought about by agonistic or combative and conflictful behavior; (3) of *leadership-followership* resulting from "allelomimetic" activity occurring in pairs with some degree of mutual stimulation and of coordination; (4) of *mutual care* and *care-dependency* developed from "epimeletic" activities (i.e., giving of care or attention); (5) of *care-soliciting* or "et-epimeletic" behavior; (6) of sexual behavior; and (7) of trophallaxis, in which the participating group members engage in ingestive activities.

PHENOMENA OF SOCIAL BEHAVIOR

Sexual and Reproductive Behavior

The recent publication *Sex and Internal Secretions* (23), which shows this to be one of the best-investigated areas of vertebrate social behavior, may be consulted for detailed information. Beach (24) has stated that as one ascends the phyletic scale, the neural factors in reproductive functions dominate the hormonal factors. Aronson, in discussing this generalization, says (25):

> Although there are differences among species in the relations of gonadal hormones to sexual behavior, particularly noticeable when rodents and primates are compared, distinct phylogenetic trends are not discernible. . . . The evolution of the endocrine mechanisms controlling reproductive behavior can be approached more effectively by the analysis of individual components of the pattern than by the consideration of sexual behavior as a single, well-circumscribed entity.

Our proposal that reproductive behavior, with other social phenomena, may be characterized as biotaxic or psychotaxic subsumes these two positions. Evidence from studies of psychosocial behavior, we believe, indicates that as abstract psychotaxic stimuli become predominant in any phase of reproductive behavior, the extent to which plasticity is shown in other aspects of behavior also increases, e.g., individual mating preferences in chimpanzees (26). It should be noted that the participation of endocrine function becomes especially relevant within this framework.

PARENT-YOUNG RELATIONS

The foundation for relatively permanent social behavior has evolved many times, in somewhat parallel ways, in animals from cephalopods to primates. Essential processes have arisen in these cases, through natural selection, permitting one or both parents to stay with the young for an appreciable time and admitting the development of reciprocal stimulative relations favoring interdependent behavior among individuals.

Processes of reciprocal stimulative relations on a superior level and susceptible to an appreciable ontogenetic modification have been described by Lehrman (27) from his research on ringdoves. The parent, on its side, reflects in behavior a fusion of successive hormonal changes and of concurrent stimulative effects both from its mate and from its nest and young (and, in group situations, also from other ringdoves mating or nesting nearby). The occurrence of a species-characteristic sequence of hormonal changes, contributing to, and dependent upon, a program of reproductive actions developed in each bird under the standard conditions of individual constitutional and social history, leads to a typical pattern of reciprocal stimulative relations with species mates from hatching to mating and incubation.

Studies of animals as different as goats (Hersher et al., 28) and cats (11) have shown that in mammals also, processes of reciprocal stimulation different from those seen in lower phyla play the major role in initiating social bonds. Even before the young appear, it is probable that changes in salt metabolism associated with advanced pregnancy have contributed to an intensified responsiveness on the part of the female to the amniotic fluids during parturition. Thus Steinberg and Bindra (29) report that ". . . pregnancy increases genital licking and . . . salt availability (and consumption) decreases genital licking in the female rats. . . . In general, the pregnant females drank more salt solution, as well as water, than did the non-pregnant females."

Parturitive experience evidently is not essential for all aspects of maternal behavior in all mammals. Leblond (30) and others have reported cuddling and licking of young by estrogen-treated male and virgin female rodents, and Labriola (31) obtained the post-operative nursing of young by female rats after cesarean deliveries. Similarly, results obtained by Igel and Colvin (32) suggest that normal parturition is not essential for female dogs to establish their litter groups.

Species differences in the role of parturition in socializing the young are emphasized by Hediger's (33) contrast of one class of ungulates, typified by the goat, in which the female actively licks the young and eats placenta, amniotic sac, and umbilical cord, and a second class, typified by the camel, in which the female is relatively passive during the delivery. In the latter, the neonate emerges from the sac by its own efforts, without being licked or manipulated by the female. Yet a group organization develops thereafter in both these ungulates, with the basis of the social bond in the latter an unsolved problem.

FIGURE 40
Seven-day-old kitten, living in isolation in an incubator, stationed in the flannel-covered brooder suckling at the nipple of a temperature-controlled food supply. The food source is shown behind the partition which separates the reservoir from the chamber of the brooder. (From Schneirla and Rosenblatt, reference 34.)

Among the monkeys and apes, the experiential history of the parturient female assumes an ascendant role over hormonal and biochemical factors. The characteristic primate involvement in self-stimulative activity, which appears not to be related to tissue-need reduction, is seen very soon after parturition, illustrating what appears to be a new level of parent-young relationship. As Yerkes and Tomilin (13) reported, playful behavior between mother and infant chimpanzee, which appears early and is common, includes a variety of joint activities leading up to tumbling, rolling, and chasing. Such mothers stimulate and encourage their infants; other neglect this function or are negative and repressive. The latter may be common among those primiparous females which, as those authors note, have acted as if frightened, bewildered, or uncertain during delivery and which might later reject or refuse to handle or nurse their infants.

Results with cats in our laboratory (34) indicate that the conditions of early feeding may constitute an important factor in feline socialization (Figures 40 and 41). In fact, reciprocal behavioral relationships between mother and young evidently center on feeding operations to an important extent, as results indicate that for multikitten litters a typical series of stages takes place in which feedings are initiated first through maternal approaches, then through mutual approaches, and finally through kitten approaches.

Meanwhile, the pattern of social interchanges involved in feeding and other operations changes greatly, as is emphasized by isolation tests. Kittens detained through given intervals in an incubator containing a brooder covered with soft flannel and equipped with a nipple attached to a milk source always had significant difficulties in adapting to the changed social conditions encountered on their return to the litter situation. The greatest

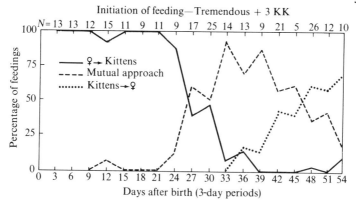

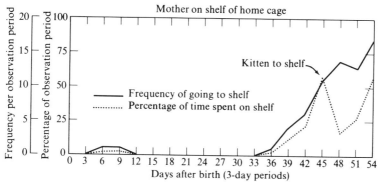

FIGURE 41

Top: Record of a representative litter of the domestic cat, showing three principal stages in the initiation of nursing-suckling episodes involving a mother and three kittens. The graphs represent the percentage of responses of each 3-day interval. Bottom: Record of the avoidance responses of the same female to her litter, as indicated by the amount of time she spends on the shelf, at first accessible only to her. Note the change after day 45, when the kittens become able to reach the shelf. (From Schneirla and Rosenblatt, reference 34.)

difficulties were seen in three kittens isolated from the twenty-fifth to the fortieth day: all became highly excited in the presence of the female, with hissing and back arching common, and one of them required 3 days for its first sucking adjustment, the other two failing completely in this respect. For these kittens isolated from the third to the fifth weeks the mother, in the meantime, had become virtually a different individual. Significantly, isolates disturbed initially by other kittens and the female in the tests, although slow to achieve social rapport, made the grade through first participating in sleeping groups. In these situations, the biotaxic attractive effects of cutaneous, thermal, and olfactory stimuli from other kittens admitted a basis for the more difficult behavioral adjustments later on.

In contrast to the feline patterns described, the role of the rhesus mother as a trophallactic stimulus is apparently modified considerably by the nature of the biotaxic clinging response. Harlow (35) has found that isolate monkeys raised from birth on "surrogate mothers" constructed of wire mesh or on wire-mesh figures covered with terry cloth preferred the latter models to the wire-mesh figures, whether these monkeys had fed from the wire mesh or terry cloth "mother." He has interpreted these results in terms of "contact comfort" as the key factor underlying normal socialization in monkeys. The role of food satisfaction is held insignificant for such matters. As inspection of the data, however, suggests that during the first 5 days more time was spent on the figures equipped with milk sources than on their foodless counterparts, hence that trophic factors may have played a role in early socialization. In the species-specific environment of the developing monkey, the progression from biotaxis to psychotaxis probably takes place by processes similar to those which may have been operating in the transition from taxic to psychotaxic responses in the monkey infants reared by Harlow on surrogate mothers.

Isolation from species mates (e.g., parent, littermates) for any considerable time in the early development of the cat and monkey as discussed above may interfere crucially with socialization. In our studies, two male kittens raised on an artificial brooder from birth to sexual maturity in isolation from other cats (except for occasional sounds and odors) proved incapable of typical mating responses, although tested regularly for more than a year. In the Wisconsin studies, monkeys raised on the surrogate mothers failed similarly in their later social and sexual adjustments. Fertilization apparently took place only incidentally in some of the females. The offspring consequently born to these females were not nursed or responded to in a species-characteristic manner.

These studies show that in two different mammals the lack of normal experiences with species mates can be more or less detrimental to social adjustment, depending on the time and duration of the detention. Later deficiencies or failures in social adjustments may be a function in part of strong withdrawal responses to the strangeness of the social situation (perhaps also with conflict between its attractive aspects on the one hand and its disturbing mobile aspects on the other hand), in part of behavioral shortcomings in the isolate in dealing with these properties, and in part of how far the isolate may have established bonds with objects only partially equivalent to the new ones.

We suggest that in these mammals, as well as in others, the social bond which is basic and prior to later species-mate responses is initiated through the female's biotaxic responses intensified by excitatory effects from the gestational and parturitive processes themselves, in a complex sequence of reciprocal stimulative events. At first the stimulative effects are biotaxic, as the female is attracted either to the fluids or to the neonate on visual, tactile, or chemostimulative bases, and the neonates are attracted to the female through biotaxic effects such as temperature, visual, auditory, and gentle contactual stimuli. These biotaxic stimuli operate reciprocally after parturition, so that within the first hours after delivery the formation of a psychosocial bond between parent and offspring is well begun. Tension relief through nursing the young must intensify the female's perceptual reactivity to them, so that as she licks and nurses them, they take on significance as objects and potential social "signs." For the young, tension relief through feeding and bladder and bowel evacuation in the instance of relatively altricially born mammals similarly organizes the percept of the parental animal. On both sides, it is probable that the reciprocal stimulative process is intensified from shortly after parturition through processes of conditioning, at first very rudimentary in nature for the neonates.

EARLY BEHAVIOR OF YOUNG
(IMPRINTING: APPROACH FIXATION)

Artificial approach fixations were first observed by Heinroth, who found that incubator-raised goslings, whose earliest approach experiences were with him, would later trail after him rather than join goslings or geese. The process by which prior experience with certain stimuli at early stages of development affects the later responses of certain birds and mammals was first descriptively named *imprägung* (imprinting) by Lorenz (36). This phenomenon has since been studied by numerous investgators (Moltz, 37) in many species of birds, particularly. Visual stimuli of the most diverse characters (e.g., disks, flickering lights) are approached and then persistently followed by the neonate duckling, chick, or other bird, provided that the given object is present early, that it is the first one shown after a post-hatching, dark-isolation period, and that it has attractive taxic properties. The stimulus to elicit imprinting must not be too large or too bright or move too rapidly; i.e., it must present a low-intensity stimulus effect if approach fixation rather than withdrawal fixation is to occur (Schneirla, 3). Auditory stimuli are also effective, if not too intense (Gottlieb and Klopfer, 38).

This type of response is probably common among sheep, goats, and other mammals with precocial young in which fixation approaches to species mates and persistent following normally occurs promptly after birth but in which young raised apart from species mates do not flock or mate with them later. In such cases, the reactions of the other animals may play an important part. For example, experiments with goats and sheep have shown that removing a kid or lamb from its mother at birth leads in most cases to the mother's rejecting the offspring on its return, but if the neonate is left with the parturient female for an hour or more, it is accepted after a period of removal (39). Once the social bond is established, the young animal enters a stage of increasing social discrimination based upon the learning of the appearance and behavioral of species mates, in which normal social experiences seem to reinforce strongly the increasing specificity of social affiliations (Collias, 40).

In animals with altricial young, these processes occur much more slowly and seem to be different psychologically. Although female rats commonly accept strange young, if the age is close to that of their own litter, they distinguish their own young from others fairly well in retrieving tests. This is accomplished on the basis of olfactory cues, as the distinction fails after removal of the olfactory bulbs (Beach and Jaynes, 41). The investigators point out that one of the difficulties of the analysis of the results is the fact that the female rats may have been responding to the next odor present on the young.

It is clear from the evidence that imprinting (or approach fixation) probably occurs in many birds and mammals under conditions strongly favoring such attachments to species mates (e.g., a parent) which are likely to be near. The adaptive value plainly consists in the apparent promptness of the fixation, particularly in precocial young. The processes responsible for the development of this biotaxic response into a psychotaxis and to further generalization leading to reproductive behavior and other social behavior are not yet well known (Hinde, 42). One factor which has been cited as having an empirical basis and theoretical relevance is the limited stage of development during which an approach fixation may take place. This has been discussed by Scott (43) and others as "the critical period" and has been extended as a concept relevant to socialization in many species. Despite Scott's statement that socialization does not take place until the organism is capable of conditioning, which he demonstrates to be 3 weeks for the dog, we contend that socialization begins at birth or even before, as discussed above (Schneirla and Rosenblatt, 44).

Territoriality

The resulting stimulus configuration and the experiential history of environmental manipulation which is termed *territorialization* appears to be predominant in adult parent-young bond formation on several phyletic levels. Among insects many patterns of altering and reorganizing the environment are seen to be essential in the formation of groups and in fostering an adult-young relation crucial for the development and later socialization of the young (45). Many species of fish, urodeles, and reptiles (turtles) similarly show complex behavioral repertories in which the delineation of areas is important to both the fertilization and parental aspects of reproduction. In ringdoves, behavioral operations concerning territories and nests seem to bear a crucial relationship to hormonal functions in the incubating parent or parents (Lehrman, 27). Among mammals too there are many species which evidence a similar dependence on these types of activities.

Riess, for example (46), reported that female rats prevented from manipulating solid objects during their youth did not nurse their young. Results from a similar study by Eibl-Eibesfeldt (47) suggest that, at least in part, the weakening of parental responses to young under such conditions may be due to inferior opportunities for establishing a territory and a nest. In research by Tobach et al. (48, 49) with mice and rats, evidence was found that experimental rearrangements of the physical aspects of the nest environs or of the social group (e.g., litter membership) accounted for serious disruptions of behavior in both mother and young, and for an abnormally high mortality rate in the young. Rowell (50) found that hamsters commonly rebuild their nests several times during the litter period. His observations that such actions stop only at about the time nursing of young has begun to decline emphasize the role of hormonal factors. The potency of the nest as a basis for bond formation in this mammal is shown by the fact that the female in many cases does not nurse young that have been born outside the nest.

It has also been shown that kittens react to local odor traces on the substratum in such a way as to remain in the "home area" in laboratory cages. Tests in which neonates were set down at varying distances from their home area toward the end of their first day showed, first, that they were disturbed when away from it and, second, that this place elicited approach responses. In successive tests, each kitten became able to reach the home area more efficiently, expanding the mastered zone first by using olfactory and tactile cues but eventually by a shift to visual cues a few days after eye opening at one week. Results indicate that in their early days these kittens reacted as though mother, littermates, and home area were equivalent to an appreciable extent in their stimulative values, but these were later differentiated increasingly (51).

The environment naturally presented to neonates has physical properties and behavioral effects typical for the species which not only favor the occurrence of the species-characteristic processes of bond formation but canalize the directions of their elaboration in development. The nest, or home, site is frequently the focus of such properties and effects. The adaptive values of the nest clearly lie in its providing a center for feeding operations as well as an appreciable protection from disturbance and marauders and a place where the young may pass their early stages of development.

Aggression

Lorenz (52) has proposed that a species which is not aggressive cannot form a social bond. The extent to which aggressiveness is present together with social-bond formation, or the reverse, constitutes an unsolved problem for research. Through the range of group behavior, aggressive actions bear so variable a relationship to social patterns as to require intensive study of particular situations before meaningful generalizations become possible. Aronson (53) has noted that many activities evident in aggressive behavior are also seen in reproduction and territorial behavior. Further, he has found that "Aggressive actions sometimes interrupt sexual activities, but under different conditions, the same actions may serve to stimulate and coordinate courtship and spawning."

Despite the similarities in the behavioral patterns of aggression and socialization, there is little difficulty in distinguishing the two types of behavior. From the projective, nativistic standpoint Tinbergen (21) defines aggressive behavior as he does socialization; that is, attacks and fighting have an important adaptive value insured by their being available innately to be touched off by innately appropriate stimuli (releasers) from the attacking animal. It is a secondary matter in his viewpoint that these instinctive responses may or may not have been modified through learning.

However, Kuo (54) studied mouse killing in kittens, often interpreted as an instinctive pattern of aggression. His results favored, instead, the view that the cat, in its typical environment and with the structural equipment of its species, normally kills rodents through an almost inevitable series of experiences, e.g., attention to a moving object, pursuit as the movement continues, biting on contact, tasting blood. According to how their early experiences with rodents varied experimentally, kittens killed rodents, were indifferent to them, or "loved" and played with the type that had been an early companion. From other extensive research, Kuo (18) found that through a wide range of animals observed (cricket, Siamese fighting fish, Japanese gray quails, chickens, rabbits, rats, guinea pigs, cats, and dogs) factors arising from the developmental history of the animal, the present environmental setting, and the individual's specific experience with the initiation of attack, defense, and defeat in relation to members of other species and to its own species all contribute to the rise of a pattern of aggression or to the lack of aggression.

As noted above, one can find in the behavioral descriptions and theories of both Tinbergen and Kuo, representing the projection and interaction types of theory, respectively, an essential agreement that the fighting pattern is somehow different from any other act. We may now consider the hypothesis, stemming from our biphasic theory of behavioral development, that in any organism those responses described as "attacking" or "fighting" constitute forms of intense, persistent approach behavior elicited at the extremes of stimulative intensity. In the ontogenetic history of individual fighting, the earliest effective stimulus is characterized both by an intensity that mounts from low to high and by a capacity to *engage,* focalize, or *hold* the animal to a train of mounting responsiveness in the situation. A persistent, focalized stimulus can thus elicit pecking in young fowl and, depending upon properties of input magnitude and the response of the stimulating individual, can lead to fighting. The chick first pecks at the partner's eye or toe, then may "fight" the *entire* object if *it* fights— that is, if *it* pecks—back. Here a mounting input from the associated organism as a focus of excitatory stimulation promotes a crescendo of processes in visceral and overt action systems sufficient to ensure an exceedingly strong approach response which by its intensity and force is likely to elicit a sudden withdrawal response from the associated organism, with a subsequent decrease in the intensity of its stimulative effect. At other times the crescendo effect on the responsiveness of the engaged individuals assumes a characteristic positive-feedback appearance similar in many respects to that seen in the copulatory act.

At higher levels, once an individual becomes conditioned on this basis to fight particular objects, the special, qualitative aspects of the object itself can elicit fighting directly. Mock fighting thus begins to be characteristic in kittens after about two weeks, when either a sudden movement or the mere appearance of a littermate can elicit the excited, quick response of strong approach, rearing, and pawing. In time, through experience, both the effective stimulus and the response pattern may specialize and elaborate far beyond the initial level of biotaxic approach or withdrawal. Then in fighting situations, the visceromotor responses of one excited mammal (e.g., arched back, hissing, in the cat), although at first briefly given at low intensities, may serve as perceptual cues for the other to react (e.g., fight back or retreat). At many levels, an animal already partially disturbed, as on entering another's territory, may withdraw promptly when the other presents disturbance signs such as a darkening of skin (as in fish) or loud, repetitive vocalization (as in blue jays or squirrels). Such responses, according to the situation and the level of animals involved, or both of these, may exert their effect either as biotaxic excitants forcing withdrawal or as recognized, perceptual cues to avoidance, that is, as psychotaxic (threat) stimuli.

By an analysis based on the concepts of biphasic behavioral development, levels of integration and parsimony, we distinguish the above classes of biotaxic and psychotaxic patterns from accessory processes which may be invoked as in the defenses and attacks of aggressive behavior. These secondary processes include nondirected hyperkinesis of a taxic nature, both extreme immobilization (death feigning) and predominantly visceral responses, such as ejection of nematocysts from hydras, the expulsion of an ink cloud from a squid, the feather ruffling in birds, or the activation of the scent gland in skunks. Although these latter responses may at times seem to be directed at the offending object, in fact they are entirely non-directional in many instances, and in other cases it is the localization of the stimulus that accounts for a positioning of the response. Such taxic and biotaxic responses, although adaptive, should not be confused with the comparably adaptive perceptual placement of blows by a fighting organism.

Hierarchical Group Organization

Basic to most social groups are relationships of reciprocal stimulation and response which are essentially cooperative in the sense that they are mutually beneficial to survival and are carried out with a degre of interdependence among individuals. Relationships of dominance-subordination were first called to attention by Schjelderjup-Ebbe (55) in his description of social hierarchies or peck orders. In flocks of domestic fowl, for example, social rank may be rated particularly by the frequency with which an individual pecks others or is pecked by them. In small groups, linear orders are frequent in which A pecks B, B pecks C and others but never A, and so on to Z, who is pecked by all but pecks none. In large flocks, complex and variable patterns are the rule.

Social hierarchies have been identified also in other domestic animals such as cattle and sheep, in arthropods, in fish, and in the wild among animals as different as lions and monkeys. Under natural conditions, however, group organization varies according to conditions. In wild rabbits, for example, Southern (56) found the organization of a colony in the reproductive period to be centered on territorial relations among the females and of dominance among certain of the males. In many ungulates, such as the red deer studied by Darling (57), outside the rutting season the stags form all-male herds in which dominance relations are more or less prominent; the females and young form separate herds which are better integrated than those of the males, with a well-defined range and usually with one adult female as leader. These matriarchal groups carry out well-coordinated group actions as in feeding and in moving about the range, including at times relationships of mutual aid, much as in comparable groups formed by elephants.

Criteria used for dominance relations in social groups are measures such as striking or accepting blows, ascendancy or retreat at food, and mounting or submission among males. Such relations are often unstable, however, and various investigators have found dominance standings to vary with individual differences in age, health, sex, sensitivity and reaction time, intelligence, and body weight, and with aspects of the situation such as availability of food. All these matters vary greatly among animal species, as well, and the dominance concept is far from universally applicable in the same way. Yerkes and Child (58) reported that for chimpanzees, size and weight (as used as criteria by Warren and Maroney, (59) in their study of wild rhesus monkeys) were unreliable factors. In the chimpanzee, for example, ascendancy at food shifts from male to female when the latter is in heat. To illustrate other complexities, Miller and Banks (60) in their study of mature rhesus monkeys found that the rankings in different measures of dominance agreed poorly. Mason (61) substantiated this finding by observing no correlation between the scores of laboratory-reared macaques in two situations testing dominance, but he also found that wild macaques maintained essentially the same standings in the two tests.

Comparative studies of social behavior emphasize differences and contrasts in the patterns characterizing different animals, as well as differences in the intragroup patterns of any one species according to its history, composition, and conditions of operation. Our conclusion is that no intragroup organization can be represented simply in terms such as those of cooperation or of dominance alone.

Play

One class of transitional behavior in mammalian ontogeny which has received insufficient scientific attention is play. In reviewing this topic, Beach (62) points out that few of the assumptions of earlier writers such as Groos have been the subjects of experimental study. Traditionally, play has been described as pleasurable, nonutilitarian, and the result of a surplus energy and general exuberance. It has been accounted for teleologically as a preparation for adult life and as a type of self-expression essential to socialization, engaged in for the sake of trial and exploration.

In such activities in Felidae, Canidae, Cetacea, and Primates, the vivid stimulative effects of sudden approaches or withdrawals by littermates, quickly increasing motor processes (often from a state of relative inactivity), almost certainly play a significant role in the maintenance and readjustment of essential social-bond processes in this stage of growing maternal independence. These changes would appear to aid the young in shifting from a perceptual and physical dependence upon the mother to nest mates as a source of cues, serving both to maintain group unity when the mother is absent and to contribute possibly to an efficient litter adjustment to predator-prey relationships. It is probably desirable to consider *play* a term for immature undifferentiated behavioral actions in the process of organization and to study this subject in close relation to other early behavior.

Weaning

This is another transitional social phenomenon focused on the shift away from female-centered activity, requiring more experimental investigation. The study by Martins (63) with dogs emphasized the fact that hormonally based changes in the nursing bitch, prior to the cessation of sucking by the litter, typically results in the bitch's regurgitation of partially digested solid food which the puppies feed upon. Current studies by Wortis (64) in Lehrman's laboratory indicate an interdependence of growth changes in the squab and hormonal changes in the parent ring-doves which bring about the rejection of begging behavior in the squab and the increase in pecking behavior.

In these studies, as well as in that by Schneirla and Rosenblatt (34) of the domestic cat, the interplay of approach and withdrawal responses in the mature and immature individuals is apparent. During the second stage of the development of feeding behavior in cats, when mutual approaches of female and young introductory to feeding increase in frequency, the kittens direct more and more of their actions at female and littermates until the behavior takes on the form of intense, hyperactive approach responses (play) in which the other animal is licked, clawed, pawed at, mouthed, and climbed upon. As one significant outcome, because much of this activity is directed at the female's mouth and face, the kittens get a taste of adult food. Not only the kittens' frequently rough behavior, but also the specific effects of growth changes in the young such as increasing strength and activity and the use of emerging teeth, all disturb the female and cause her to avoid the young increasingly. Once conditioned to the mother's food, the kittens next respond to adult food encountered during wanderings about the cage and begin to feed independently.

Communication

Wide differences exist among animals in species patterns of communication. There are many instances of visual and auditory signals, usually given as a product of an animal's excitement, which characteristically elicit definite social reactions such as approach, feeding, or flight. Odors from cutaneous glands are commonly important in the life of mammals; for example, deer and other ungulates, by rubbing their heads against projections on trees, leave thereon the secretion of the preorbital gland which serves as a biotaxic stimulus to conspecifics (Hediger, 33).

Although these stimuli are normally effective in the lives of a great variety of animals, it remains to be established that they are symbolic, intentional, and codified, and thus constitute language. This term has been used, nevertheless, for complex communication patterns such as that reported for honeybees by von Frisch (65). A bee returning from a new source of nectar not only excites other bees by dancing in a particular fashion but thus influences the direction and the distance of their flights so that they are likely to find the new food source. It is still not clear, however, how flying at a particular angle to the sun's rays and to the plane of light polarization can influence the bee to run in a particular direction on the comb in the dark. Such processes seem to be essentially biotaxic and physiologic, as variations that appear in the dance according to whether the finder encounters a headwind or tailwind on the outgoing flight are seemingly a proprioceptive effect dependent upon energy expenditure. The work of Dethier (66) with the blowfly suggests that the dance itself may be a fortuitous metabolic by-product of feeding and flight. Complex as the bee's dancing is and efficient as it is in social behavior, the predominance of transient biochemical effects, stereotypy, and low degree of plasticity in insect behavior stamp this dance and the response of the bees in the hive as a biosocial pattern involving biotaxic stimuli. In this class, however, the bee dances seem to mark the height of specialization. Descriptively, the bee seems to tell others where to go, but psychologically the process does not satisfy the scientific criteria defining language.

The mimicking of sound patterns which has been noted in birds and porpoises similarly does not constitute language; neither are the gurgles and cries of the human infant in its first year a language, although they are communicative as they are responded to appropriately by the mother according to the situation. Usually after twelve months, however, the infant has mastered (1) sound symbols, or *words,* which (2) are used in *anticipation* of their social effects; (3) these become modified and conventionalized according to social experience, and (4) usually after two years they are capable of being rearranged in codified, socially meaningful ways. No lower animal exhibits these characteristics in its vocal or other communication, although in many instances the patterns are complex, as in many birds and as in howler monkeys, which have more than twenty describable sounds uttered and responded to in roughly corresponding situations (Carpenter, 67).

Cooperation

On the biosocial level, cooperation, that is, coordinated effort on the part of a group, occurs through biotaxic effects; on the psychosocial level it can become directionalized and intentional within the limitations imposed by neural potential. Although social insects offer many striking instances of producing a common result in acting together, as with a group of ants that pulls food toward and into the nest, analysis of the act shows that these successes are the results of individuals incidentally acting similarly in the same situation rather than intentionally (Schneirla, 45). At the highest infrahuman level, primate cooperation is frequent but somewhat deficient, simple, and limited, and as Riopelle (68) has shown, rhesus monkeys usually learn more from an inefficient companion's error than from the successful actions of one who has mastered the problem. Crawford's experiments with chimpanzees (69) showed that these lower primates are capable of gestural behavior which is used in solving a problem cooperatively. Gestures by a trained chimpanzee, however, failed to elicit effective weight-lifting responses from an untrained animal. Only in those situations in which both animals had previously incorporated the necessary action into their behavioral repertoire were the gestures useful.

It is well established that in monkeys and other primates in the wild the mothers frequently offer guidance to their young, but this is often unilateral as in the case of the rhesus mother described by Altmann (70), which frequently retrieves its offspring by the tail forcibly. Altmann also reports that howler monkey mothers, which on the whole do very little to interfere with the social actions of their infants, may nevertheless frequently facilitate these actions as by holding a branch when the youngster is about to cross a gap in group travel.

The chimpanzee's most characteristic type of cooperation is limited in time, with one partner helping less than it is helped in return, which is a unilateral type of cooperation (as indeed man's often also is). Chimpanzee friendships are common in the laboratory, and such pairs cooperate better than either member does with others. Hebb and Thompson (26) describe experiments in which chimpanzees show attitudes of mutual defense in threatening situations, as do porpoises (which are presumably intermediate psychologically between dog and chimpanzee). Such behavior in the different species requires more complete experimental investigation before the taxic nature of these patterns can be defined. Human cooperation at its best is bilateral and can extend to a complex and elaborately organized plan perhaps operating over a considerable time even with the participants separated.

Tradition and Culture

A final question of importance for the comparison of animal social patterns is that of tradition. Although lower animals such as birds and insects have their territories which have been used for long series of generations, female primates pass on patterns of social interaction to their infants (71), and so on, these show scant resemblance to the essence of human folklore, history, and conventionalized tradition as given systematically to the young. The chimpanzee, which resembles man recognizably in its emotional attributes (Hebb, 72), approaches the human level only very remotely in its capacity for social heritage. Man has the advantage of the longest ontogenetic preparatory period, with opportunities for initial social training in every family.

SUMMARY STATEMENT

Biotaxic factors are basic to all social groups, invertebrate and vertebrate. The great difference is in the extent and the speed with which their initial influence becomes elaborated as psychotaxic patterns and merged in group behavioral processes as development proceeds. In mammals, depending upon species cortical equipment, potentialities are introduced for social perception, learning, and communicative versatility that are realized in relation to individual experience. Significantly the altricial condition of longer infancy, increasing in primates toward man, offers greater opportunities for a broader and deeper socialization of young related particularly to increasing potentialities for language, first nonverbal and finally, in man, verbal. Theoretically, man is in an infinitely better position than any lower animal, including primates, to encourage the development of infants from their early stages of generalized biotaxic responses to acquire patterns of social behavior representing the best attainments of the group culture and social heritage.

REFERENCES

1. Schneirla, T. C. 1953. The concept of levels in the study of social phenomena. In M. Sherif and C. Sherif, eds., *Groups in harmony and tension.* New York: Harper & Row.
2. Schneirla, T. C. 1957. The concept of development in comparative psychology. In D. Harris, ed., *The concept of development.* Minneapolis: Univ. Minnesota Press.
3. Schneirla. T. C. 1959. An evolutionary and developmental theory of biphasic processes underlying approach and withdrawal. In M. R. Jones, ed., *Nebraska symposium on motivation,* Lincoln: Univ. Nebraska Press.
3a. Schneirla, T. C. Aspects of stimulation and organization in approach withdrawal processes underlying vertebrate behavioral development. In D. S. Lehrman, R. Hinde, and E. Shaw, eds., *Advances in the study of behavior,* vol. 1. New York: Academic Press.

4. Wheeler, W. M. 1923. *Social life among the insects*, New York: Harcourt, Brace.
5. Schneirla, T. C. 1946. Problems in the biopsychology of social organization. *J. Abnorm. Soc. Psychol.* 41: 385.
6. Allee, W. C. 1938. *The social life of animals.* New York: Norton.
7. Wheeler, W. M. 1928. *The social insects.* New York: Harcourt, Brace.
8. Fraenkel, G. S., and D. L. Gunn. 1961. *The orientation of animals.* New York: Dover.
9. Karlson, P., and M. Lüscher, 1959. "Pheromes": new term for a class of biologically active substances. *Nature* 183: 55.
10. Schneirla, T. C. 1938. A theory of army-ant behavior based upon the analysis of activities in a representative species. *J. Comp. Psychol.* 25: 51.
11. Schneirla, T. C. 1957. Theoretical consideration of cyclic processes in doryline ants. *Proc. Am. Phil. Soc.* 101: 106.
12. Schneirla, T. C., J. S. Rosenblatt, and E. Tobach. 1963. Maternal behavior in the cat. In H. L. Rheingold, ed., *Maternal behavior in mammals.* New York: Wiley.
13. Yerkes, R. M., and M. I. Tomilin. 1935. Mother-infant relations in chimpanzee. *J. Comp. Psychol.* 20: 321.
14. McCulloch, T. L. 1939. The role of clasping activity in adaptive behavior of the infant chimpanzee. I. Delayed response. II. Visual discrimination. *J. Psychol.* 7: 283.
15. Yerkes, R. M. 1943. *Chimpanzees.* New Haven: Yale Univ. Press.
16. Kortlandt, A. 1962. Chimpanzees in the wild. *Sci. Am.* 206: 128.
17. Schneirla, T. C. 1956. Interrelationships of the "innate" and the "acquired" in instinctive behavior. In P.-P. Grasse, ed., *L'Instinct dans le comportement des animaux et de l'homme.* Paris: Masson.
18. Kuo, Z. Y. 1960. Studies on the basic factors in animal fighting. *J. Genet. Psychol.* I., II., III., and IV., 96: 201; V., VI., and VII., 97: 181.
18a. Thomas, A., H. G. Birch, S. Chess, and M. E. Hertzig. 1962. The developmental dynamics of primary reaction characteristics in children. *Proc. Third World Cong. Psychiatry,* pp. 722–726.
19. Allee, W. C. 1931. *Animal aggregations.* Chicago: Univ. Chicago Press.
20. Allee, W. C. 1952. Dominance and hierarchy in societies of vertebrates. In P.-P. Grasse, ed., *Structure et physiologie des sociétés animales.* Coll. Int. Cent. Nat. Rech. Scient., Paris, 1952, 34, p. 157.
21. Tinbergen, N. 1953. *Social behaviour in animals.* London: Methuen.
22. Scott, J. P. 1956. The analysis of social organization in animals. *Ecology* 37: 213.
23. Young, W. C., ed. 1961. *Sex and internal secretions,* vols. 1 and 2. Baltimore: Williams and Wilkins.
24. Beach, F. A. 1948. *Hormones and behavior.* New York: Hoeber.
25. Aronson, L. R. 1959. Hormones and reproductive behavior: Some phylogenetic considerations. In A. Gorbman, ed., *Comparative endocrinology.* New York: Wiley.
26. Hebb, D. O., and W. R. Thompson. 1954. The social significance of ani-

mal studies. In G. Lindzey ed., *Handbook of social psychology*. Reading, Mass.: Addison-Wesley.

27. Lehrman, D. S. 1961. Gonadal hormones and parental behavior in birds and infrahuman mammals. In W. C. Young, ed., *Sex and internal secretions*. Baltimore: Williams and Wilkins.

28. Hersher, L., A. U. Moore, and J. B. Richmond. 1958. Effect of postpartum separation of mother and kid on maternal care in the domestic goat. *Science* 128: 1342.

29. Steinberg, J., and D. Bindra. 1962. Effects of pregnancy and salt intake on genital licking. *J. Comp. Physiol. Psychol.* 55: 103.

30. Leblond, C. P. 1940. Nervous and hormonal factors in the maternal behavior of the mouse. *J. Genet. Psychol.* 57: 327.

31. Labriola, J. 1953. Effects of caesarean delivery upon maternal behavior in rats. *Proc. Soc. Exp. Biol. Med.* 83: 556.

32. Igel, G. J., and A. D. Calvin. 1960. The development of affectional responses in infant dogs. *J. Comp. Physiol. Psychol.* 53: 302.

33. Hediger, H. 1952. Beiträge zur Saugetier-Soziologie. In P.-P. Grasse, ed., *Structure et physiologie des sociétés animales*. Int. Cent. Nat. Rech. Scient., Paris, 1952, 34, p. 297.

34. Schneirla, T. C., and J. S. Rosenblatt. 1961. Behavioral organization and genesis of the social bond in insects and mammals. *Am. J. Orthopsychiat.* 31: 223.

35. Harlow, H. F., and M. K. Harlow. 1962. Social deprivation in monkeys. *Sci. Am.* 206: 2.

36. Lorenz, K. 1935. Der Kumpan in der Unwelt des Vogels. *J. Ornithol.* 83: 137; 289.

37. Moltz, H. 1963. Imprinting: An epigenetic approach. *Psychol. Rev.* 70: 123.

38. Gottlieb, G., and P. H. Klopfer. 1962. The relation of developmental age to auditory and visual imprinting. *J. Comp. Physiol. Psychol.* 55:821.

39. Blauvelt, H. 1955. Dynamics of the mother-newborn relationship in goats. In B. Schaffner, ed., *Group processes*. New York: Josiah Macy, Jr. Foundation.

40. Collias, N. E. 1952. The development of social behavior in birds. *Auk* 69: 127.

41. Beach, F. A., and J. Jaynes. 1956. Studies of maternal retrieving in rats. I. Recognition of young. *J. Mammal.* 37: 177.

42. Hinde, R. A. 1962. Some aspects of the imprinting problem. In *Imprinting and early learning, Zool. Soc. Lond. Symp. no. 8,* London, 1962, p. 129.

43. Scott, J. P. 1962. Critical periods in behavioral development. *Science* 138: 949.

44. Schneirla, T. C., and J. S. Rosenblatt. 1963. "Critical periods" in the development of behavior. *Science* 139: 1110.

45. Schneirla, T. C. 1952. Collective activities and social patterns among insects. In K. Roeder, ed., *Insect physiology*. New York: Wiley.

46. Riess, B. F. 1954. The effect of altered environment and of age on mother-young relationships among animals. *Ann. N.Y. Acad. Sci.* 57: 606.

47. Eibl-Eibesfeldt. I. 1955. Innate and learned behavior in the nest building of the Norway rat. *Naturwiss.* 42: 633.
48. Tobach, E., and T. C. Schneirla. 1962. Eliminative responses in mice and rats and the problem of "emotionality." In E. L. Bliss, ed., *Roots of behavior.* New York: Harper & Row.
49. Tobach, E., T. C. Schneirla, L. Vroman, and G. Turkewitz. The development of stress-tension adjustment in the rat. (Ms. in preparation.)
50. Rowell, T. E. 1961. The family group in golden hamsters: Its formation and break-up. *Behaviour* 17: 81.
51. Rosenblatt, J. S. 1962. The behaviour of cats. In E. S. E. Hafez, ed., *The behaviour of domestic animals.* London: Baillière, Tindall & Cox Ltd.
52. Lorenz, K. Z. 1957. The role of aggression in group formation. In B. Schaffner, ed., *Group processes.* New York: Josiah Macy, Jr. Foundation.
53. Aronson, L. R. 1957. Reproductive and parental behavior. In M. E. Brown, ed., *The physiology of fishes.* New York: Academic Press.
54. Kuo, Z. Y. 1931. The genesis of the cat's response to the rat. *J. Comp. Psychol.* 11: 1.
55. Schjelderup-Ebbe, T. 1924. Zur Sozialpsychologie der Vögel. *Z. Psychol.* 95: 35.
56. Southern, H. N. 1948. Sexual and aggressive behaviour in the wild rabbit. *Behaviour* 1: 173.
57. Darling, F. F. 1937. *A herd of red deer.* London: Oxford Univ. Press.
58. Yerkes, R. M., and M. S. Child. 1927. Anthropoid behavior. *Quart. Rev. Biol.* 2: 37.
59. Warren, J. M., and R. J. Maroney. 1958. Competitive social interaction between monkeys. *J. Soc. Psychol.* 48: 223.
60. Miller, R. E., and J. H. Banks, Jr. 1962. The determination of social dominance in monkeys by a competitive avoidance method. *J. Comp. Physiol. Psychol.* 55: 137.
61. Mason, W. A. 1961. The effects of social restriction on the behavior of rhesus monkeys. IV. Dominance tests. *J. Comp. Physiol. Psychol.* 54: 694.
62. Beach, F. A. 1945. Current concepts of play in animals. *Am. Nat.* 79: 523.
63. Martins, T. 1949. Disgorging of food to the puppies by the lactating dog. *Physiol. Zool.* 22: 169.
64. Wortis, R. P. The development of food-getting behavior in the young ringdove, unpublished doctoral thesis, Rutgers University, New Brunswick, N.J.
65. von Frisch, K., H. Heran, and M. Lindauer. 1953. Gibt es in der "Sprache" der Bienen eine Weisung nach oben oder unten? *Z. Vergleich. Physiol.* 35: 219.
66. Dethier, V. G. 1957. Communication by insects: Physiology of dancing. *Science* 125: 331.
67. Carpenter, C. R. 1952. Social behavior of non-human primates. In P.-P. Grasse, ed., *Structure et physiologie des sociétés animales.* Coll. Int. Cent. Nat. Rech. Scient., Paris, 1952, 34, p. 227.

68. Riopelle, A. J. 1960. Observational learning of a position habit by monkeys. *J. Comp. Physiol. Psychol.* 53: 426.
69. Crawford, M. P. 1937. The cooperative solving of problems by young chimpanzees. *Comp. Psychol. Monog.* 14: 1.
70. Altmann, S. L. 1962. Social behavior of anthropoid primates: Analysis of recent concepts. In E. L. Bliss, ed., *Roots of behavior.* New York: Harper & Row.
71. Imanishi, K. 1957. Social behavior in Japanese monkeys. *Psychologia* 1: 47.
72. Hebb, D. O. 1946. Emotion in man and animal: An analysis of the intuitive processes of recognition. *Psychol. Rev.* 53: 88.

VI

ON ORIENTATION
AND LEARNING

The many subjects introduced in the papers in this section center on
(1) general problems of conditioning phenomena (*Mechanisms in Conditioning* No. **27**),* (2) the nature of learning in insects, (3) orientation
in insects, (4) comparisons of learning and orientation in insects and
mammals. Dr. Schneirla's doctoral dissertation, *Learning and Orientation
in Ants* (No. 3) is omitted from this collection because of its length and
detail, but the major conclusions of this study are found in the article,
Ant Learning as a Problem in Comparative Psychology (No. **36**). This
article, as well as *Modifiability in Insect Behavior* (No. **63**), introduces
the comparisons with mammals (especially rats), and this problem is

---

* This and subsequent numbers in this introduction refer to the items in the complete
bibliography of Schneirla's works, p. 1017. Bold face numbers denote articles that are included in this volume.

treated in depth in the article, *Psychological Comparison of Insect and Mammal* (No. **97**).

Schneirla used the maze almost exclusively in these experiments (see Nos. 4, 7, 8, 21, 28, 117) because he believed that it was a particularly valuable instrument for understanding subtle differences in the nature of learning processes. He held to this position even in later years when instrumental conditioning became so popular, because he was convinced that instrumental techniques, by their very nature, tended to mask species differences in the mechanisms and quality of learning. He noted that many insects have the capacities for habituation learning, conditioned responses, temporal memory, discrimination, and complex learning. This highest learning ability of insects has been investigated for the most part by the maze technique. Schneirla recognized three steps in maze-learning: (1) an initial stage of generalized adjustment or habituation to the maze, (2) an intermediate stage of localized learning of specific segments of the maze, and (3) a final stage of intersegmental adjustment in which the part-patterns flow together. Rats learning similar mazes do so much more efficiently than insects, dropping out blind alleys during the first few trials, and without identifiable signs of distinctive stages. Moreover, insects show a considerable degree of stereotypy in learning which is not evident in mammals. When ants were required to run a mastered maze in reverse, they profited little from their earlier experiences and behaved as if the reversed maze was a new problem. Rats, on the other hand, show considerable saving through transfer.

Schneirla's confident use of the maze also stemmed from his interest in orientation and his recognition that typical maze situations have a significant resemblance to foraging in natural situations. Several of his reviews of orientation in insects are presented in this section: *Insect Behavior in Relation to Its Setting* (No. **62**), *Modifiability in Insect Behavior* (No. **63**), and *Problems and Results in the Study of Ant Orientation* (No. **71**). In these reviews, Schneirla noted that way-finding in many insects is controlled by simple taxes and kineses in which one sensory system predominates. However, in ants of the genus *Formica,* the taxes and kineses are based on the integration of several sensory systems. In addition, these insects follow pathways learned in their foraging (or maze) experiences and through such plastic learning capacities they "widen greatly the limits of the stereotyped processes of kinesis and taxis basic in their orientation." In running through a maze that is lighted from one side, the ant must move at one time or another towards or away from the light, or the light is on one or the other side. Nevertheless, when the maze is learned, "the light serves as a dominant orienting cue."

Dr. Schneirla and his colleagues were also interested in orientation in mammals. In the last paper in this section, *Development of Home Orientation in Newly Born Kittens* (No. **121**), they show that although the young kittens initially orient to the home site primarily on the basis of olfactory gradients, in a short time, associations are developed (i.e., conditioned learning) with other sources of stimulation, such as tactile and thermal stimuli, during huddling of the kittens, nursing, and associated activities of the mother and litter. Later, when the eyes open, visual associations to the home site develop, providing a basis for orientation. In contrast to the situation in insects, it is clear that learning factors enter into the orientation reactions of kittens more extensively and at a very early age.

Lester R. Aronson
Ethel Tobach

NORMAN R. F. MAIER

T. C. SCHNEIRLA

Mechanisms in Conditioning

Bibliography No. 27

CONDITIONING VS. TRIAL-AND-ERROR LEARNING

In recent years there has developed a tendency to break down the theoretical distinction between the classical notion of conditioning and that of selective or "trial-and-error" learning. This tendency has led investigators to carry out experiments closely resembling "problem-box" tests, treating the results so firmly under the dominance of conditioning concepts that possible relationships to the findings of problem-box studies proper may be overlooked. To be sure, Skinner (24) and Hilgard and Marquis (13) have differentiated conditioning and problem-box procedures, but they do not carry this distinction through to the basic mechanisms. We believe that closer analysis will disclose some fundamental differences of great importance.

For some time it has been recognized that contiguity in experience is the essential factor in the process of conditioning. On the other hand, in trial-and-error learning the selection process stands out clearly, and to deal adequately with this instance of learning it has been necessary to recognize not only the factor of contiguity but also the factor of motivation. Hence "reward" and "punishment" have figured prominently in discussions of trial-and-error learning.

It is an observed fact that when responses are accompanied by punishment they are in time less likely to come to expression, whereas those accompanied by reward are more likely to come to expression. The mechanisms responsible for these effects on behavior are, however, not agreed upon. Thorndike's earlier notion that punishment "stamps out" the learning and that reward "stamps in" the learning was an attempt to explain the facts in terms of associative bonds formed only in rewarded instances. Perhaps the problem can be dealt with more adequately if it is assumed that associations are formed in both cases, a position Thorndike (25) now accepts. The view is that in the one case the animal learns

From *Psychological Review* 49(2): 117–134. Copyright © 1942 by the American Psychological Association. Reproduced with permission.

what not to do and in the other it learns what to do, i.e., reward determines which responses will come to expression and punishment determines which will be inhibited. This point of view introduces a selection process in addition to an association process, and performance rather than the formation of associations is affected by the kind of incentive involved.

These considerations are sufficient to illustrate the fact that the particular roles of reward and punishment have for some years constituted a most troublesome theoretical problem for investigators working with maze, problem-box, and discrimination learning.

Recent experiments (1, 2, 3, 9, 18, 26) have shown that motivation may be a factor of importance in conditioning. In order to account for the facts, Culler (6) believes it is necessary to assume that the unconditioned stimulus has a dual function: that of giving rise to a response and that of serving as an incentive. Perhaps the recognition of the role of motivation in what are regarded as conditioning experiments is largely responsible for the current tendency to believe that the gap between the two forms of learning is being narrowed.

Before accepting a theoretical fusion of what may well be two distinctive forms of learning, it seems desirable to examine the evidence carefully to see whether certain of the differences between these processes may not be of basic importance. This precaution is suggested by known cases in which behavior mechanisms of qualitatively different nature present external similarities of relatively secondary importance. For instance, learning and maturation both exhibit a trend from initially generalized response to more specific behavior, yet much ground would be lost if basic differences in mechanism were to be subordinated to this feature of similarity. Only a careful examination will show whether similarities or differences more adequately represent essential behavior mechanisms. Thus emphasis upon certain similarities may well have led investigators to overlook or to minimize some differences of primary importance between the processes of conditioning and of trial-and-error learning.

In a general treatment (21) we have analyzed the learning process in terms of concepts primarily bearing upon what occurs in the animal rather than in terms of the situation. This analysis led us to distinguish between association formation which depends upon contiguity, and selection which depends upon reward or punishment. It seems desirable to apply that distinction here, beginning with a rudimentary diagram showing how the association and selection processes operate in conditioning and problem-box situations.

In Figure 42 the typical problem-box setting is diagrammatically represented as a situation (Sit.) which elicits a series of responses (R_1, R_2, . . . R_x, R_y). The order in which these reactions appear may depend

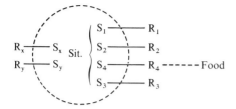

FIGURE 42
Diagrammatic representation
of selective learning.

upon the excitatory threshold of each manner of responding, or it is possible that the responses are an expression of a tendency to vary behavior (15, 19, 20). In any case the responses arise as parts of the repertoire that the animal brings to the experiment. Now because of the experimental set-up only one of these reactions to some aspect of Sit. can occur in contiguity with food and so become associated with it. It is this response which gains in preference and finally dominates over other activity. When it dominates we say that the animal has mastered the problem. The animal, however, has not learned a *new* response—rather a response with a low excitatory threshold has been made dominant, or we may say it has become selected or preferred.

In conditioning the situation is quite different. Here it is the unconditioned stimulus which determines the nature of the response. Since this stimulus initiates the response it cannot be a reward or a punishment for the response. The conditioned stimulus occurs repeatedly in contiguity with the unconditioned stimulus and soon it alone elicits the response. Initially the conditioned stimulus showed no signs of producing the response in question. We cannot therefore say there has been a shift in dominance. Rather, we may say that a previously ineffective stimulus has been transformed into an effective one, and that contiguity of the ineffective (conditioned) and the effective (unconditioned) stimuli has been the necessary condition.

Once the conditioned stimulus adequately elicits the response, however, the experimental conditions may become changed. If one then presents the unconditioned stimulus after the response occurs (the method of reinforcement often employed to prevent experimental extinction), the important aspect of the problem-box procedure is duplicated. Likewise, if the conditioned stimulus calls out the critical response promptly enough, the unconditioned stimulus (e.g., food; shock) will *follow* rather than precede the response. Here also the unconditioned stimulus can function as incentive even though no change in the external procedure has been introduced. In further trials the excitatory value of the conditioned response, or part of it, can thus be increased by selective learning. Since reinforcement occurs only when certain elements are present, the response may become progressively more specific, depending upon the nature of the unconditioned stimulus (e.g., food or shock used as unconditioned stimuli can serve as incentives more readily than light). Thus an animal conditioned to give foot-flexion in response to a bell, through the contribution of selective learning may gradually decrease the amplitude of the flexion to the minimum necessary to clear the grill. The animal's behavior now appears to be anticipatory in nature as is the case in all selective learning. From the above we can also see why conditioned responses frequently differ from the original unconditioned response.

That the *initial* phase of the conditioning procedure is an important one becomes apparent if we try to use the method of reinforcement (or reward) from the outset. Suppose we wish to train a dog to salivate to a bell. We place the dog in the bell situation and wait until he salivates before food is given. Under such conditions it would be extremely difficult, if at all possible, to train the animal. Since salivation to a bell is not a part of the dog's regular repertoire of behavior, one could not reward the act. Once, however, the bell has developed some excitatory value for salivation (by conditioning) the method of reinforcement can proceed.

Thus we may distinguish two phases in the conditioning *procedure,* a first phase in which a neutral stimulus is given excitatory value and a second in which a selective process operates. In Pavlovian experiments attention has been concentrated upon the characteristics of the first phase although the second phase may sometimes have been present. In the first phase contiguity alone determines the nature of events. It is in the second phase that the conditioning procedure can become comparable with trial-and-error learning.

Our analysis thus leads to agreement with Culler (6) in that the unconditioned stimulus may potentially have two functions, one for determining the response, the other for motivating it. Culler points out that these different functions of the unconditioned stimulus account for two stages in the development of the conditioned response, but he does not show why the stages appear as they do. The foregoing analysis emphasizes the fact that the successive stages grow directly out of the procedure, and makes it clear that it is the procedure rather than any intrinsic property of the unconditioned stimulus which leads to a shift in its function as training progresses.

The postulation of these two different phases in the procedure of conditioning permits us readily to integrate certain experimental findings which have seemed inconsistent with previous results, some of them among the reasons Culler has advanced for attributing a dual function to the unconditioned stimulus.

1. Culler and Mettler (7), also Girden, Mettler, Finch and Culler (12), have found that conditioned responses can be established in de-

corticate animals virtually as readily as in normal animals. Shurrager and Culler (23) obtained conditioning with similar ease in dogs when only a small part of the spinal cord remained in function. However, the conditioned responses formed in neurally-reduced dogs of these types are very generalized, and never reach the stage of a specific response. This seems to mean that association by contiguity is more primitive than selective learning, since it can proceed in the absence of cerebral cortex although selective learning is then excluded. The assumption that learning may take place on different neural levels is supported by experiments on conditioning under curare (10, 11). The postulation of two qualitatively different learning mechanisms makes understandable the fact that the first stage in conditioning can occur unimpaired although the second is excluded in spinal and decorticate animals.

2. Brogden (1) has found that after a conditioned response has been established a reward (food) may be substituted for the unconditioned stimulus (escape from shock) without leading to extinction of the response. If the unconditioned stimulus may acquire the role of incentive during the second phase of the conditioning procedure, it is to be expected that other incentives will function equivalently. That one incentive may be safely replaced by another in selective learning is a well-known fact.

3. Finch and Culler (9) and Brogden (2) found that they were able easily to develop a fifth order of conditioning although Pavlov had set the third order as the limit.

In order to accomplish this Finch and Culler first conditioned leg flexion to a tone. Since the flexion was produced by a shock grill on which the foot was placed, the animal soon escaped shock by a conditioned flexion. When this stage was reached, the selective phase could enter into the learning and prevent extinction. To establish the second order, a light-flash was presented with the tone. When the animal failed to flex the leg, shock to the thorax was administered and soon the light alone produced leg flexion. Since the tone produced leg flexion, a secondary conditioned response to light could be established and selection could then proceed as in the first order. By the time the third order of conditioning was reached it is reasonable to suppose that the leg flexion as a response to the general experimental situation was well within the animal's behavior repertoire. Under these conditions any new stimulus might call out leg flexion; hence the response was readily subject to selection and the first (or associative) stage of the conditioning procedure was probably not required. In establishing the third order, a stream of water was given with the light. Did the light in this case function as did the original unconditioned stimulus? We believe the light could have been omitted without changing the outcome. The point is that the stream of water followed by thoracic shock soon would have brought leg flexion to expression, since this response had been selected as a means for avoiding shock. If this was the case then it follows that trial-and-error learning rather than higher-order conditioning occurred in the above experiments.

The fourth and fifth orders of conditioning were then obtained with such ease that the experimenters believed they could have advanced readily to an indefinite number of higher orders. Since "higher-order conditioning" should introduce added difficulties with each further step, the absence of such difficulties here offers further reason for believing that our analysis is a plausible one.

The same analysis would apply to Brogden's experiment (2) in which a food reward replaced the "escape from thoracic shock" in the selective function.

There are no indications that the postulated second (selective) stage was involved in the Pavlovian experiments. This may be attributed to the use of a nonvoluntary response (salivation) and to the fact that Pavlov did not present reinforcement in a selective manner. We have thus implied that the exclusion of the selective stage would account for Pavlov's inability to carry conditioning beyond the third order. (Furthermore, the Russian experimenters had to contend with experimental extinction, since their critical response was not maintained by a selective learning.)

4. Brogden, Lipman and Culler (3) conditioned guinea pigs to run in a rotator in response to a 1000-cycle tone. Shock was used as the unconditioned stimulus. In one group the running shut off the shock and so afforded relief, in another group the response was not thus rewarded.

During the first 75 to 100 trials the two groups showed essentially identical progress, the running in response to the buzzer being part of the pattern in about twenty per cent of the trials. After 100 trials, however, the two groups progressed quite differently. The group that was rewarded for running responded by running one hundred per cent of the time, after an average of 206 trials; the group not rewarded in this manner showed questionable increase in the tendency to respond by running. Instead, the animals of the latter group held their breath and tensed their body musculature. The experimenters believed that the group which responded to the tone by running duplicated the unconditioned response, whereas the other group showed anticipatory behavior.

It seems reasonable, however, to regard holding the breath, tensing the muscles, and leaping forward all as parts of the unconditioned response to shock. Since tone was coupled with shock, it could call out any part or all of this pattern. The experimenters measured only the running and this aspect was equally shown by both groups during what we regard as the associative stage.

The one group, however, was rewarded for running and, as a consequence, it is to be expected that this aspect of the response would become more and more selected. The other group may have minimized the shock effects by tensing the musculature (the experimenters considered this to be the case), and if this is true this aspect of the pattern should become selected. If the tensing did not relieve the shock effects then we should expect the response to tone to remain generalized. (The data are not sufficiently detailed to determine which of these alternatives occurred.)

In any case the final response was distinctly different in the two groups and we believe the second or selective stage to be responsible for the difference. The experimenters believe the form of the incentive resulted in two contrary forms of conditioning. Since selective learning is an established fact, it seems unnecessary to postulate two forms of conditioning to account for the findings.

5. Kellogg (14) emphasizes the presence of individual differences in the form of the conditioned leg flexion. From the types of this response which occur in different dogs he believes the notions of "stimulus substitution" and "anticipatory responses" in conditioning can both be shown. From our analysis Kellogg's results are to be expected. Individual differences in selective learning are the rule, since each animal selectively learns from its own repertoire. Because Kellogg's dogs were able to avoid shock by flexing the leg we believe the marked individual differences observed were due to the *selective learning* occurring after the first stage.

6. Loucks (18) found that the dog could not be conditioned to a buzzer when shock to the motor area of the cortex was used as the unconditioned stimulus for leg flexion. This indicates that the unconditioned stimulus must have effective sensory relations as well as a purely motor function, since only the sensory aspect of the unconditioned stimulus was lacking in this experiment. However, a change in procedure entirely altered the outcome of the experiment. When the animal was given a food reward each time leg flexion occurred, positive results were obtained.

Loucks contends that motivation made possible the establishment of a conditioned response otherwise unobtainable. According to our analysis conditioning did not occur in this experiment. Rather, cortical shock in the buzzer situation elicited a response, and reward was able to function selectively. Under these conditions foreleg flexion became associated with reward just as string-pulling becomes associated with reward in the problem-box situation. The first stage, i.e., the association between a neutral stimulus and the experience of the unconditioned stimulus, was thus omitted. Since selective learning is facilitated when an animal is "put through" a given act, it is not surprising that Loucks was able to obtain selective learning under conditions in which cortical shock offered a very effective way of manipulating the desired response.

That this distinction is real and not merely verbal in nature can be demonstrated through the fact that the two interpretations lead to opposite conclusions in certain critical instances.

Crisler (5) and Light and Gantt (17) have shown that conditioning can occur without the animal making the critical response during training. It is merely necessary to present the conditioned and unconditioned stimuli in contiguity. Thus, Light and Gantt prevented the unconditioned stimulus from producing a response by crushing the motor roots of the essential spinal nerves. On regeneration of the destroyed motor pathways it was found that the buzzer, which had been paired with the shock to leg (unconditioned stimulus), now produced leg flexion. This result could not have occurred had not the training somehow established an association between the buzzer and shock experiences. It thus follows that making the critical response is not essential for the development of true conditioning.

In trial-and-error learning, however, actively making the response is very important, since the critical action must come to expression if it is to be selected. Thus, if our contention that Loucks's experiment involved trial-and-error learning is correct, it follows that negative results would be obtained if the Loucks's experiment were repeated with the motor nerves crushed but using buzzer and cortical shock as he did. If, however, it is claimed that ordinary conditioning occurred, this modification should not affect the findings, since making the response is not essential to conditioning.

SENSORY-SENSORY VS. SENSORY-MOTOR CONNECTIONS

It appears to us that much of the confusion in the interpretation of conditioning data arises from a failure to analyze what has happened to the animal. As a rule, interpretations are based on what the animal *does*. Behind the animal's behavior are the mechanisms responsible for the behavior, and an improved understanding of the mechanisms should throw needed light on the overt occurrences. The point can be nicely demonstrated in connection with an extension of our preceding discussion.

In conditioning, we are told, the conditioned stimulus becomes a *substitute* for the unconditioned stimulus, which apparently means that both occupy similar functional positions once training is effective. This generally accepted view is graphically presented in Figure 43-A. The dotted line indicates the functional connection which is assumed to arise through training.

An obvious alternative suggested by the traditional doctrine of the association of ideas is indicated in Figure 43-B. Here the dotted line

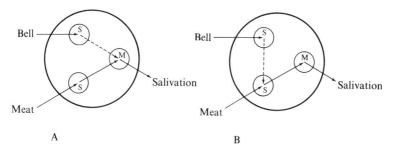

FIGURE 43
Diagrammatic representation of two interpretations of the conditioning process. The large circles indicate the field of cortical function; the small circles indicate sensory and motor regions. A. Conditioning viewed as a *substitution* process. B. Conditioning viewed as an *extension* process.

suggests a very different functional connection. The first diagram indicates that a *sensory-motor* connection is established, whereas the second offers a *sensory-sensory* connection as the essential dynamic change. It is the latter which Maier and Schneirla (21, Chap. XV) have regarded as most probable.[1]

In the first case the term "substitution" is a pertinent description of the postulated change, but in the second this term is misleading. Rather the term *extension* is more appropriate, as indicating the enlargement of a sensory pattern controlling the critical response. Although the second alternative is seldom considered it seems to best fit the facts. Let us consider some experimental findings which bear significantly on this question.

Loucks (18) found that cortical shock to the motor area could function as a conditioned stimulus, but *not* as an unconditioned stimulus. If conditioning depends upon an association between two sensory cortical patterns, then it is clear why cortical shock is thus limited in its functions. In Figure 44-A the dotted line represents our conception of the new dynamic relationship which is established when cortical shock is the conditioned stimulus. Shock to the leg furnishes the sensory component arousing motor cortex, which in turn elicits the unconditioned defense reaction. When cortical shock is introduced as unconditioned stimulus, however, the activated cortex directly gives rise to leg flexion and its function is then purely motor. Figure 44-B shows that a sensory component is absent in this experiment, and since negative results were obtained when a buzzer

---

[1] The implications of this question extend far beyond the field of mammalian conditioning. Thus we have based our theoretical comparison of psychological capacities among the lower vertebrate classes and in fact among the higher invertebrate groups as well—(21, Chaps. V–X) upon *sensory integration* as the process critical for the qualitative nature of behavior.

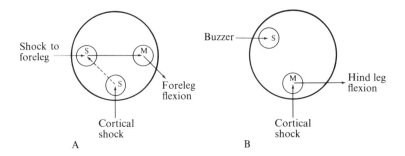

FIGURE 44
Diagram showing the role of cortical shock in conditioning. The large circles indicate the field of cortical function; the small circles indicate sensory and motor regions. A. Field of cortical function when cortical shock serves as the *conditioned* stimulus. B. Field of cortical function when cortical shock serves as the *unconditioned* stimulus.

was used as the conditioned stimulus, we are led to regard the sensory aspect of the *unconditioned* stimulus as essential for positive results. If conditioned responses depend upon a sensory-motor connection, it is difficult to account for these negative findings. (We have already shown how the addition of reward can transform the negative to positive results.)

The outcome of an experiment by Shipley (22) also favors the sensory-sensory interpretation. He first conditioned a wink response to a light flash by presenting the light with a strike below the eye (US). Next he conditioned finger withdrawal to the same strike below the eye by presenting the strike (CS) with shock to finger (US). The crucial test was now to reintroduce the light flash. In nine of his fifteen human subjects finger-withdrawal was obtained with the flash, which had never been paired with shock to finger. If we postulate a sensory-motor connection as the essential relationship, the system is like that sketched in Figure 45-A. But the acquired connections involved here, x and y, provide no direct route between the cortical components of flash and finger-withdrawal, and it is necessary to postulate highly questionable backward-running associations or kinesthetic components to account for the findings. If, however, we assume that conditioning develops sensory-sensory functional relations, the system is like that diagrammed in Figure 45-B. Here the acquired associative relationships x and y furnish a direct functional connection between the cortical pattern set up by the flash and that controlling the finger-withdrawal. Apparently Shipley did not consider this alternative.

In an experiment by Cason (4) on the conditioned wink response, a sound was paired with a shock below the eye. After this training the subjects reported that the shock when presented alone seemed weaker

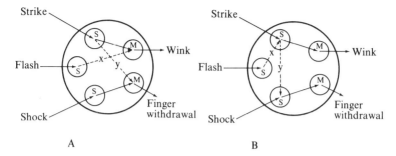

Strike — Wink · Flash — Shock — Finger withdrawal

A   B

FIGURE 45

Comparison of *sensory-motor* and *sensory-sensory* views as applied to Shipley's experiment. The large circles indicate the field of cortical function; the small circles indicate sensory and motor regions. In A, the acquired connections, x and y, do not account for the association of "flash" and "finger-withdrawal" functions. In B, the acquired connections, x and y, effectively account for the association of these cortical functions.

("and lacking in something") than when it was accompanied by the buzzer. At first this difference had not been present. In order to account for this summation effect, it appears necessary to postulate the development of a sensory-sensory connection.

Other human findings are significant on this point. Recently Leuba (16) reported the conditioning of imagery processes. For example, a hypnotized subject was presented with the snapping of a cricket and the odor of creosote in combination. When awakened and presented with the snapping of the cricket, the subject was caused to sniff and report a peculiar odor. In this case also, the assumption of a controlling cortical pattern centering around a sensory-sensory connection serves to account most adequately for the results.[2]

SUMMARY AND CONCLUSIONS

For some time the problem of the relation between conditioning and selective (trial-and-error) learning has been a source of controversy in

[2] It may be asked why it was necessary to use hypnotized subjects to produce this effect. The answer seems to be that since implicitly aroused images are readily distinguished by the waking subject from direct perceptions, the imagery process is readily suppressed and not reported. Hence the *response* aspect of conditioning affords much better evidence of training and accordingly is commonly emphasized in the literature. However, the significant fact that normal subjects may anticipate the unconditioned stimulus supports our view that the counterpart of Leuba's sensory pattern also exists in the conditioning of waking individuals.

the study of learning. Because the conditioning phenomenon can be studied conveniently and described in relatively simple terms the possibility of reducing all learning to conditioning has been an attractive one. Recent evidence on the apparent function of motivation in conditioning has tended to broaden the conditioning concept so that the differences between selective learning and conditioning seem to have been broken down or at least substantially reduced. In this paper we have offered some cogent reasons for retaining the distinction.

Our analysis has served to point out that in the *first stage* of the conditioning *procedure* a neutral stimulus develops excitatory value for a response it previously did not control. The essential condition for this change in the animal is contiguity between the experience of the neutral stimulus and the experience of the unconditioned stimulus. Then a *second stage* may develop. Once the neutral stimulus has become a conditioned stimulus, the response it elicits may be rewarded or punished. Unconditioned stimuli such as food and shock can function in this stage in the same way that "reward" and "punishment" function in problem-box learning. Thus during this stage a selective learning is involved; as a result the conditioning procedure ceases to be unique and assumes the psychological characteristics of trial-and-error learning. Then, as in all selective learning, the critical response becomes more and more specific the more effectively it leads to reward or to escape from punishment.

Before a response can become selected, it must be in the animal's repertoire. It is characteristic of Pavlovian conditioning procedure to utilize a response which is not likely to be available in a given situation unless its unconditioned stimulus is present. However, in problem-box and other trial-and-error situations, the critical response is available in the situation and a specific unconditioned stimulus is not required to bring it to expression.

Thus selective learning depends upon reward and punishment as well as on contiguity, whereas associative learning requires only contiguity in experience. Failure to distinguish these as qualitatively different forms of learning leads to inconsistencies, since it results in overlooking the possibility that different learning situations may involve the two mechanisms in different ways. We have pointed out that the conditioning procedure first introduces purely associative learning, but then may admit selective learning depending upon certain special conditions. The principal conditions determining this change concern a possible function of the unconditioned stimulus as incentive and probably also the degree to which the critical response is voluntary and thus subject to selection. If these conditions are fulfilled, the conditioning procedure frequently used may result in a pattern which has the characteristics of both associative and selective learning.

Since the first stage of the conditioning procedure is unique in requiring an unconditioned stimulus, we believe that the term "conditioning" should be restricted to the changes occurring during this stage. It is the resulting limited routine type of response which Pavlov originally designated as "conditioned." Performing tests which are in reality problem-box experiments and terming the process "conditioning" does not reduce problem-solving to conditioning, but merely confuses the issue.

Restricting the term "conditioning" in the above sense serves to focus attention upon the nature of the associative process. We have offered evidence and considerations favoring the view that the essential change, as studied in conditioning, involves a new dynamic relationship between the sensory cortical pattern of the conditioned stimulus and that of the unconditioned stimulus. Thus we maintain that the key process is a modified sensory integration. The commonly accepted view of conditioning as depending upon a new sensory-motor connection seems inconsistent with experimental findings. Rather than speak of conditioning as "stimulus substitution" it is more advisable to regard it as the extension or qualitative enlargement of the pattern of stimulation which will elicit the critical response.[3]

---

[3] Comment by Dr. Maier on Dr. Stephens' paper, "Expectancy vs. effect—Substitution As a General Principle of Reinforcement," appearing in *Psychological Review* 49(2).

The latter portion of Dr. Stephens' paper shows that he has been confronted with the same problem with which we have been primarily concerned. His solution also shows some similarities to ours. The basic difference in my estimation is that Stephens' paper represents an attempt to reduce (or elevate) conditioning to trial-and-error learning, whereas our paper attempts to reduce only the latter portion of conditioning (the stage at which reinforcement occurs) to trial-and-error learning. Since he does not break the conditioning procedure into two phases, his interests may turn to a quantitative aspect of the problem. We emphasize a qualitative stage and cannot deal with quantitative aspects until the qualitative stages have been distinctly separated. The stages being qualitatively different demand quite different units of measurement.

That our first stage (association by contiguity) is a real one is supported by Stephens' attempt to explain the conditioned leg flexion in which the leg flexion does not achieve avoidance of shock. According to his analysis such conditioning procedure would lead to a tendency other than leg flexion.

The very fact that this procedure produces responses *simulating* the unconditioned response lead to the development of the notion of conditioning. Only recently has the emphasis been placed upon certain differences between the conditioned and the unconditioned responses. The differences have been explained by regarding the conditioned responses to be anticipatory in nature. Stephens goes a step further in differentiating the two responses and in so doing fails to account for the similarities.

Stephens' criticism of expectancy when used as an explanatory principle is very convincing. It seems that our sensory-sensory integration accounts for instances in which anticipatory behavior is apparent and at the same time does not require the concept of expectancy to explain it.

It also seems that Stephens' analysis of selection would be more convincing if he clearly distinguished between conditioning and problem-box situations. To regard food as an unconditioned stimulus in a problem-box situation in which a string must be pulled so broadens the meaning of the term that its basic connotation is lost.

REFERENCES

1. Brogden, W. J. 1939. Unconditioned stimulus-substitution in the conditioning process. *Am. J. Psychol.* 52: 46–55.
2. Brogden, W. J. 1939. Higher order conditioning. *Am. J. Psychol.* 52: 579–591.
3. Brogden, W. J., E. A. Lipman, and E. Culler. 1938. The role of incentive in conditioning and extinction. *Am. J. Psychol.* 51: 109–117.
4. Cason, H. 1923. The conditioned eyelid reaction. *J. Exper. Psychol.* 5: 153–196.
5. Crisler, G. 1930. Salivation is unnecessary for the establishment of the salivary conditioned reflex induced by morphine. *Am. J. Psychol.* 94: 553–556.
6. Culler, E. A. 1938. Recent advances in some concepts of conditioning. *Psychol. Rev.* 45: 134–153.
7. Culler, E. A., and E. A. Mettler. 1934. Conditioned behavior in a decorticate dog. *J. Comp. Psychol.* 18: 291–303.
8. Culler, E. A., J. D. Coakley, and P. S. Shurrager. 1939. Differential effects of curare upon higher and lower levels of the central nervous system. *Am. J. Psychol.* 52: 266–273.
9. Finch, G., and E. Culler. 1934. Higher-order conditioning with constant motivation. *Am. J. Psychol.* 46: 596–602.
10. Girden, E. 1940. Cerebral mechanisms in conditioning under curare. *Am. J. Psychol.* 53: 397–406.
11. Girden, E., and E. Culler. 1937. Conditioned responses in curarized striate muscle in dogs. *J. Comp. Psychol.* 23: 261–274.
12. Girden, E., F. A. Mettler, G. Finch, and E. Culler. 1936. Conditioned responses in a decorticate dog to acoustic, thermal, and tactile stimulation. *J. Comp. Psychol.* 21: 367–385.
13. Hilgard, E. R., and D. G. Marquis. 1940. *Conditioning and learning.* New York: D. Appleton-Century Co.
14. Kellogg, W. N. 1938. Evidence for both stimulus-substitution and original anticipatory responses in the conditioning of dogs. *J. Exper. Psychol.* 22: 186–192.
15. Krechevsky, I. 1937. Brain mechanisms and variability: I. Variability within a means-end-readiness. *J. Comp. Psychol.* 23: 121–138.
16. Leuba, C. 1941. The use of hypnosis for controlling variables in psychological experiments. *J. Abn. Soc. Psychol.* 36: 271–274.
17. Light, J. S., and W. H. Gantt. 1936. Essential part of reflex arc for establishment of conditioned reflex. Formation of conditioned reflex after exclusion of motor peripheral end. *J. Comp. Psychol.* 21: 19–36.
18. Loucks, R. B. 1935. The experimental delimitation of neural structures essential for learning: The attempt to condition striped muscle responses with faradization of the sigmoid gyri. *J. Psychol.* 1: 5–44.
19. Maier, N. R. F. 1929. Reasoning in white rats. *Comp. Psychol. Monogr.* 6: 93.

20. Maier, N. R. F. 1939. The specific processes constituting the learning function. *Psychol. Rev.* 46: 241–252.
21. Maier, N. R. F., and T. C. Schneirla. 1935. *Principles of animal psychology.* New York: McGraw-Hill.
22. Shipley, W. C. 1933. An apparent transfer of conditioning. *J. Gen. Psychol.* 8: 382–391.
23. Shurrager, P. S., and E. Culler. 1940. Conditioning in the spinal dog. *J. Exper. Psychol.* 26: 133–159.
24. Skinner, B. F. 1938. *The behavior of organisms.* New York: D. Appleton-Century Co.
25. Thorndike, E. L. 1931. *Human learning.* New York: Century.
26. Zener, K., and H. G. McCurdy. 1939. Analysis of motivational factors in conditioned behavior: I. The differential effects of changes in hunger upon conditioned, unconditioned, and spontaneous salivary secretion. *J. Psychol.* 8: 321–351.

T. C. SCHNEIRLA

Ant Learning as a Problem in
Comparative Psychology

Bibliography No. 36

Solomon's well-known counsel to the sluggard stands as a testimonial to the antiquity of man's interest in the activities of ants. Like the weather, these insects are always around, forcing themselves upon our attention in various ways both theoretical and practical. Among the theoretical problems of long standing, wondering how ants reach food and find their way home unquestionably stands near the head of the list. Actually, the question of ant orientation or way-finding was one of the first to stimulate serious investigation as a problem in animal behavior. Let us see how this led to the notion that learning has a place in the picture.

The first investigation of ant way-finding was Bonnet's simple finger-test (1779): by rubbing a finger across the route of an ant procession he set up a disturbance which suggested that the travelers were following an actual trail on the ground. Such tests provided the basis for the chemical-trail conception, which held sway in the early literature and now remains as a popular notion that ants in general make their way by following a chemical track.

If all ant orientation were that simple there would be little point in introducing the subject into a serious psychological treatise. However, the phenomenon usually is much more complex and has a variety of forms, as was made increasingly clear through the 19th century by a series of enthusiastic investigators from Huber (1810) to Forel (1874) and many others.

Although we are mainly interested here in the ant's ability to "straighten her path," as Lubbock (1881) spoke of this insect's learning ability in first calling it to attention, until comparatively recently the main interest of investigators centered on "the senses that guide the ant." If this preoccupation with "sensory control" occasions surprise, let it be remembered that for a considerable time maze investigations of rat learning were focused largely upon the same problem. Perhaps it is a matter of more than inci-

From *Twentieth Century Psychology*, edited by P. L. Harriman. New York: Philosophical Library, 1946. Reprinted with permission.

dental interest to psychologists that the word "learning" itself has been traced to an early root meaning "to follow a track" (Smith, 1912).

Ant orientation proves to be a highly involved phenomenon varying greatly in form among different species. Lubbock was one of the first to demonstrate its great complexity, through work with the garden ant *Lasius niger* showing that this insect establishes its route in dependence upon the direction of light as well as upon the character of chemical traces upon the pathway. On the other hand, Forel's (1908) tests led him to conclude that many species run according to a succession of images, furnished through vision as well as through the "topochemical sense,"—the latter permitting the reception of chemical and tactual stimuli in complex combinations from objects along the path. Later on Cornetz (1910) patiently followed Algerian ants through their wanderings in the open, completed many tracings of routes to and from food-places and performed tests which convinced him that beyond sensory effects the ant must possess an "unknown direction sense." To him it seemed inconceivable that visual and other sensory cues alone could account for results such as the ability of *Myrmecocystus* and *Tapinoma* individuals to make their way fairly directly toward the nest after having been transferred from their route to a "strange" locality. However, Santschi (1911) and others objected that Cornetz's tests were not critical, since his controls and in particular his precautions to exclude visual guidance were not adequate. Around this general question there developed in the first quarter of the present century a lively controversy involving a number of European investigators, producing a variety of conclusions which were seemingly at cross purposes and generally very confusing. Beneath the apparent chaos, however, a solution to the problem was being worked out. This was finally shown when Rudolf Brun (1914), a Swiss psychiatrist interested in the problem mainly through the influence of Forel, was led to carry out comprehensive field and laboratory tests on the way-finding of a number of species.

Brun's work, based upon the studies of his predecessors which he extended and integrated, brought out the fact that ant orientation is first of all a matter of a patterned sensory control. The sensory pattern, he demonstrated, is different in different species, and may vary in the same species according to conditions. He differentiated between ants such as *Formica* species in which individual foraging is typical and visual effects from large objects cooperate with tactual and other sensory effects, and ants such as *Tapinoma* species in which collective foraging is typical and effects such as light-direction are superadded to a basis of chemical-trail orientation. To account for the formation of these sensory patterns, Brun adopted the "memory-theory" of Semon, concluding that in passing through new terrain the ant "ecphorizes" (i.e., imprints neurally) successive sensory effects which as "engrams" (i.e., memory traces) may be rearoused on further expeditions, guiding the traveler along her route.

Thus contributions to the solution of the orientation problem inevitably had to find some basis in learning-theory. However, Brun's application of Semon's memory-doctrine, like Forel's "succession of images" idea, did not meet the central problem of learning. We find in both of these notions a characteristic evasion of the primary question, to explain how the ant's route changes in the course of successive journeys from a highly involved and circuitous path to a fairly direct one with few detours. How the ant "straightens her path," to use Lubbock's expression, actually embodies the difficult problem of selective learning, which requires us to account not only for the disappearance of certain of the initial activities but also for the gradual development of a new arrangement of activities. The Semon theory does not meet the problem of *selection* in learning, since in effect it merely tells us that through experience changes occur in neural function which may influence subsequent behavior when rearoused. The question to be answered concerns why certain changes are more persistent than others, and why certain ones effectuate in adaptively significant behavioral organizations and others do not.

The fact is that the development of investigations upon ant orientation has given us an impressive amount of information concerning the sensory cues involed, but has not dealt with the genesis of the individual insect's ability to utilize given patterns of sensory cues in way-finding. Most of the European investigators have really taken this learning process for granted, by carrying out their tests with insects able to make their way successfully when first observed. New techniques are necessary if we are to discover how the route is established in the first place.

The maze method has served this purpose, since in the maze we have a representation of the foraging situation under controlled laboratory conditions in which the subject's behavior may be studied in detail from beginning to end. It is an interesting historical fact that the first maze studies on ants were conducted by Fielde (1902) only a few years after the first rats were run in a maze of Hampton Court pattern by Small. Primarily to test the ant's "sense of smell," Fielde used a maze of her own design in which the ants (*Aphaenogaster piceum*) were forced to travel both ways along an open diagonal path from which concentrically arranged detours led off to each side. By marking some of the ants distinctively with water colors, Fielde was able to follow their individual travels. Far more valuable than her findings here on "smell," she discovered that individual ants tended to establish their own routes independently of others, and that in going and coming (carrying their own pupae back to the next through the maze) the subjects gained speed by cutting down the number of excessive movements. She also reported that the ants "appeared to follow the line of least resistance, or to be influenced by inconvenience"; moreover, that there appeared to be no essential relationships between the outgoing and returning routes of given individuals.—Much confusion might have been avoided if investigators of ant orientation had noticed the significance of this last finding, at a stage when many of them were following the Piéron (1904) dictum that on her return trip the ant simply reverses her outgoing movements.

There followed the studies of Turner (1907) with *Formica subsericea* and other species, from which he reported the first learning (time) curves for ants, as evidence that "the show and exploring gait with which most species make the first few trips of the initial experiment of any series, when contrasted with the rapidity of the later movements, indicates that the ants learn the way home."

As evidence that the "comparative" point of view was influential in studies of animal learning at this stage, despite a general preoccupation with the rat, there are Shepard's (1911; 1914) reports in which results for ant and rat learning tests are discussed together. Using two *Formica* species in a special maze, with precautions to control the effect of chemical traces (by fitting pasteboard lining-units in the alleys) and vision (direction of illumination), Shepard not only studied the importance of sensory cues but also attacked the problem of error-elimination. With the ants free to pass through the maze between their nest and a food-place, studies of successive trips made by particular subjects (marked temporarily, or distinguished through anatomical peculiarities) showed that the ants were capable of learning to avoid blind alleys and also demonstrated that the basis of this change lay in the discrimination of chemical, visual, and other sensory differences at the respective junctions of true path and blind alley. If a lamp remained on one side throughout original learning, shifting it later to the opposite side of the maze produced a substantial disturbance in behavior, indicating the importance of light-direction cues for specific adjustments in the route. Or after all pathway linings had remained in place through a series of runs, exchanging the lining units of the true-pathway and blind-alley alternatives at a given junction accounted for serious difficulties in the vicinity, with a noticeable tendency to turn into the blind alley. The subjects were also disturbed by changes in the pattern of the maze (such as blocking off a previous true-pathway unit and introducing a new one), although they were able to readjust in the course of further runs. The ant's maze-learning thus seemed to be a matter of considerable complexity, which Shepard was able to describe as a trial-and-error process resembling that of the rat although of a much simpler order.

Such work does more than merely to demonstrate that another animal is capable of learning mazes; beyond improving our conceptions of insect psychology it has relevance to general problems of broad psychological interest. Specifically, insect maze work affords us a valuable way of studying

FIGURE 46
Maze pattern designed for rats; also mastered by ants.
(S, start; F, food-box.)

the learning process under organic and psychological conditions which appear to be significantly different from those in mammalian behavior.

Our main object in this chapter is to explore the possibilities of studying insect problem-solving as a distinctive attack upon the learning phenomenon. What important similarities and what differences will be found in the ant, which completely lacks cereb cortex, and a representative lower mammal which possesses cortex? At first sight the similarities appear to be more important than the differences. That is an impression usually given initially by the fact that not only are some ants capable of mastering mazes which prove to be fairly difficult for naive rats (Figure 46), but also that similar

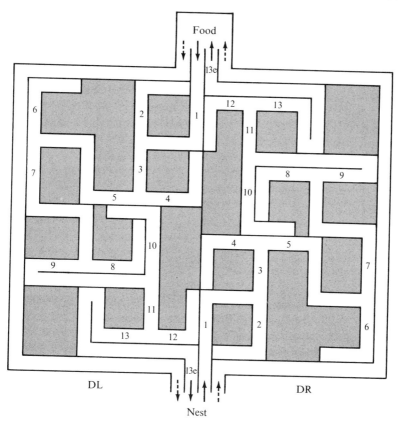

FIGURE 47
Maze pattern D, used as a problem opposing passage from nest to food-place (situation DR) or from food-place to nest (situation DL). By using the simple pathway around the maze, either of these situations may be presented as a single problem.

learning curves of the "negatively accelerated" type are obtained (Figure 48). It is only on closer examination that some prevalent differences in performance become apparent which lead us to view the ant's maze-learning process as a qualitatively distinctive instance of complex learning. In view of this fact it is apparent that this instance of learning must be dealt with first of all in its own terms before comparisons with other animal performances can have much validity.

As we have pointed out, a chief advantage of the maze situation rests in the fact that it permits us to present under controlled conditions certain obstructions which are essentially equivalent to difficulties encountered in the natural foraging situation. To improve experimental control, in the

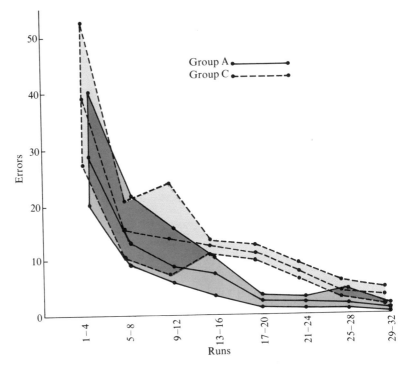

FIGURE 48
The general-average error curves for group A (normal) and group C (experimental) in situation DL. The differently shaded zones represent the intervals between the maximal and minimal performances in the respective groups (4 ants each group).

writer's recent experiments (1941; 1943) the maze has been presented as an obstacle to the ant's passage from nest to food-place, or from food-place to nest, but the subject ordinarily is prevented from returning through the pathway used in reaching the food-place. In the double maze shown in Figure 47, maze pattern D may be used under either or both of two general conditions in the foraging run (i.e., R, nest to food-place: L, food-place to nest), with simple paths around the maze for phases of the run in which the maze is not used. As a regular problem, however presented, the maze must be run through from alley 1 to alley 13e.

In the experiments we shall discuss, steps were taken to confine effective sensory cues in learning to the intra-maze situation itself. The main reason was that when extra-maze cues such as directionalized light are available, the problem is simplified for the subject in a way that greatly increases the experimenter's problem of understanding the learning process from the performance records. For this reason, diffuse illumination was used, the light nondirectionalized and effectively equal in intensity for all sections of the maze. With other precautions such as a hood screening off the observer (who watched events through any one of four small apertures symmetrically arranged around the sides of the hood), this served to confine effective sensory cues to the maze alleys themselves. All alleys of the maze were lined with bristol-board pathway units covering floor and walls, and the maze was covered with glass, as in Shepard's situation, to permit a control of chemical and related cues within the maze.

With these arrangements in the main experiment, the maze was presented under very different conditions to two principal groups of subjects. One group, A, the normal subjects, was permitted to learn the maze with the pathway linings undisturbed throughout; the other group, C, was subjected to an unstable intra-maze situation by virtue of numerous exchanges in the position of pathway linings throughout the course of learning. (Or, in other cases in group C, a different set of pathway linings was inserted after every trial.) The object of this method was to set up a critical difference in the availability of intra-maze cues which might cast light upon the essential process of learning.

In all of this work the species used was *Formica incerta,* an individual-foraging ant of the subfamily *Camponotinae* which adapts very well to laboratory conditions and appears to represent the maximum performance level of ants in this type of problem. Only one ant was admitted to the maze in a given session, and others were excluded by means of a system of entrance and exit doors which also permitted controlling the movements of the given subject.[1] The selected subject was admitted for as many runs as she would make in a given series, i.e., learning by the "massed repetitions" method, which seems to be typical of foraging in the natural situation. The ants were distinguished from one another by means of readily identified symbols on enamelled tissue attached to the dorsal surface of the gaster with rubber cement. Shorthand records were kept of the subject's movements, in particular the nature and locality of maze activities classed as "errors" (i.e., retracing; entrances into blind alleys); the records also included feeding time, maze time, and time in nest between runs.

For reasons to be considered later, these ants perform at their best when

---

[1] The colony is prepared for work at a given time of day by feeding it every day at this time through the preceding two weeks. The learned ability to forage at a special time, known as "temporal memory" (Grabensberger, 1933), insures that the subject will be available for work at that time. Unfortunately, other members of the colony, similarly trained, are also especially active and impede operation of the apparatus by gathering near the maze doors. The difficulty recurs each time the return of the record ant rearouses ants in the nest. However, if the others are not admitted to the maze, their appearance from the nest is inhibited in time through learning, so that after an hour or two the maze subject may be the only individual seen outside the nest.

running through the maze from food-place to nest (Schneirla, 1933), carrying small bits of raw beef. Groups A (stable maze situation) and C (unstable intra-maze cues) were both tested under that condition, hence any differences in their results may be attributed to the single difference between them, affecting conditions within the maze. Although negatively accelerated error curves are typical in both groups, as Figure 48 suggests, subjects in the experimental group C required more runs to master the maze than normal subjects (A) and exhibited special difficulties beyond those of normals. A comparison of the results for these groups proves to be a most useful way of disclosing how this problem situation is learned by ants.

Through such a comparison we find that three principal stages may be identified in the course of the ant's maze-learning: in succession, (1) an initial stage of general maze adjustment (Schneirla, 1941), (2) an intermediate stage of specific localized learning (Schneirla, 1943), and (3) a terminal stage of intersegmental organization. Let us briefly survey the evidence for this description of the habit.

In their early runs the ants of both groups behave similarly and accomplish similar improvements, dropping errors such as running on alley ceilings, returning repeatedly to the starting point, circling on walls and in corners, and turning back frequently from points in open alleyway. Such changes are responsible for the initial abrupt drop which characterizes the individual error curves (Figure 49), a change which typically runs its course within the first 8 or 10 runs. This series of trials brings generalized improvements in behavior not bound to any particular locality in the maze, representing a broad adjustment to the situation which may be roughly characterized as "maze-habituation." In these early runs the ant becomes able to run smoothly through maze alleys, without turning back unless an obstruction (i.e., a corner or end-wall) is encountered. Can we say that a "route" (i.e., a particular path to the end-point of the maze) has been learned?

A study of the errors which drop out during these early runs shows that they are not particular or localized activities but rather are random, variable movements which produce retracing or incidentally arise through retracing anywhere in the maze. This learned change is apparent even on the first run, when after much variable activity and back-tracking in the first parts of the situation the subject runs more smoothly and passes through the latter part of the maze with definitely fewer errors, although these alleys are distinctive in pattern and she has not passed through them previously. The benefits of initial-habituation learning thus may be elicited in any part of the situation regardless of its pattern, for these changes do not depend upon the specific local patterning of the maze. The critical fact is that through this initial stage there is no identifiable shortening of en-

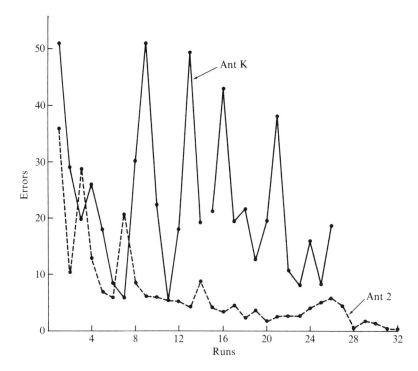

FIGURE 49

Error curves for two *Formica incerta* subjects learning situation DL. The record of the superior subject (No. 2) was made in a consecutive series of runs, that of the inferior subject (K) on two different days, with an interval of three days following the 14th run.

trances into blind alleys anywhere in the maze, nor is there any change in the proportion of blind-alley turns to true-pathway turns at the choice-points which would indicate a developing ability to avoid blind alleys. Blind-alley entrances are reduced in frequency, but simply as an outcome of a reduction of retracting generally. It appears that under our conditions the subjects do not learn a particular route during the initial stage, but are essentially restricted to a habituation-learning.

A comparison of groups A and C is enlightening as to the distinction between the first two stages of learning. In their early runs subjects in group C seem to be much more disturbed than A subjects and make more errors, yet these are the same kinds of errors and they are dropped similarly in the two groups. The C subjects spend more time in the maze and have more difficulty than A subjects, yet toward the end of the first ten runs we find that the two groups have reached a comparable level of improved performance (see Figure 48). This suggests that the learning which has been accomplished is generalized in nature, and not dependent upon particular local cues, since it occurs in group C despite an inconstancy of local stimulation. What is acquired seems to be a nonspecific "alley-running set," a generalized way of behaving in the situation rather than specialized adjustments to stimulus cues as fixed patterns or local landmarks. However, as later events show, these early developments open the way for a specific mastery of the problem, and are really essential if such specialized learning is to occur.

To further progress in learning the maze the initial stage contributes a smooth-running behavior in the situation, insuring in particular a routine manner of approaching choice-points and entering blind alleys. This may be described as a yielding of the habituated subject to movement-mechanics effects dependent upon the pattern of local alley-sequences, a rudimentary type of "set" which we have termed "centrifugal swing" (Schneirla, 1929). The stereotypy in locomotion thereby accomplished materially influences the further course of learning, determining especially the relative difficulty experienced by the subject in eliminating different blind alleys. At this point, when stereotypy is critically essential for the accomplishment of new learning, whatever introduces undue variability in behavior may seriously retard or even block further progress. The fact we have mentioned, that maze D was more difficult when presented in the run to foodbox than in the run to the nest (Schneirla, 1933), may be attributed to a large extent to the greater variability of behavior which characterized the ant's run from the nest. Further events in group C to be described show that even in the optimal situation, when running with food to the nest, reducing stereotypy at this juncture impairs the new stage of learning.

The intermediate stage, which typically begins in situation DL (see Figure 47) at about the 8th to 10th runs, is identifiable in normal subjects in terms of the representative phases of blind-elimination, which are: (1) the dropping of the second arm of the blind essentially as a unit; (2) full-length entrances to first arms gradually are displaced by very short entrances; and finally (3) the short first-arm entrances fall off in favor of direct true-path entrances. Although this process advances at different rates according to the difficulty of the respective blinds (i.e., how strongly centrifugal swing forces turning into the given blind), when studied comparatively for all sections of the maze the regular order of its successive phases in normal subjects reveals a similar process of specific learning at all difficult choice-points.

These processes have been called *specific* because the manner in which they begin and run their course shows that they occur independently in the respective choice-point localities. At basis this localized learning may be understood as a matter of discrete conditioned-response processes, with the initiating factor in each case the blocking of progress at the dead-end of the given blind (Schneirla, 1943). We may regard this last experience as the unconditioned stimulus for the inhibition of forward progress, for which stimulus patterns experienced earlier in the given blind become equivalent successively in the order of their temporal and spatial relations. These originally effective experiences may be considered the "new" or "conditioned" stimulus patterns which successively are added to the stimulus-complex adequate to elicit avoidance of the given blind-alley situation. From the manner in which blind-avoidance characteristically improves, we may say that first the subject turns around only when actually blocked, next in response to stimulation close to the dead-end itself, then still earlier in the blind in response to the pattern effective at the elbow, and finally the stimulus-pattern encountered at the choice-point becomes adequate to call out avoidance of the blind as a whole. Basically, then, we view the process of blind-dropping which follows the initial stage as a set of conditioned-response adjustments originating independently in each section of the maze where detour-blocking occurs.

The local adjustment described develops as a unitary process which under normal conditions (i.e., the situation of group A) expands regularly to become controlled by prominent stimulus-patterns successively more remote from the nuclear unconditioned effect. However, as the results for group C (Figure 48) show, when irregularity and variation impair the sequence of events in the blind-situation from trip to trip, the elimination process develops abnormally and as a rule incompletely. This we have suggested above, in stressing the importance of behavior-stereotypy as a prerequisite for intermediate-stage learning.

This theoretical description of the local adjustments is not completed by the postulation of nuclear conditioning processes alone. Our findings necessitate the further postulation that as each segmental-learning process advances it becomes qualitatively modified into a selective-learning process, based upon the differential effectiveness of alternative responses near the choice-point. To express the idea briefly, we may view the situation at a fairly advanced stage, when upon barely turning into the blind (generally less than one inch around the choice-point corner) the ant sometimes quickly turns to the side of the true pathway, but at other times hesitates tensely for a brief interval and then proceeds deeper into the blind. This act of pausing on the threshold, as it were, suggests that a focal stimulus-effect encountered there has aroused a more or less complete inhibition of further progress into the blind. That the inhibitory agent is an active process of "braking" forward locomotion is indicated not only by the tenseness of posture during the pause, but also by the forward spring (onward into the blind) or rapid volte face (into true pathway) which follows it, as though released from restraint. The signs of postural tension are even more evident when the subject happens to reach the elbow ending the first arm, frequently taking the form of successive short advances beyond the corner before the ant can leave the blind. We may say that at this juncture the aroused tension-response is resolved into free movement most promptly after a short entrance into the first arm, much less promptly and effectively at the first elbow—and that this difference gives these adjustments a correspondingly different facilitation in the selective process. Gradually, at different rates in the different blind localities, this selection process advances so that the initial centrifugal-swing-enforced blindward turn is dominated more and more effectively by the stimulus pattern of the true-pathway turn. This last response, when the blind-avoidance process has advanced sufficiently, is very effectively facilitated by the unrestrained movement which follows a briefly aroused tension-effect at the choice-point.

To summarize, we may say that each blind is eliminated by an expansion of the crude blind-end reaction through successive phases involving the addition of more remote stimulus-foci to the system, leading into a selective competition of the respective differently facilitated adjustments. Through this process there develops an "anticipation" of the blind-end in the form of a *set* away from its side; then finally when this tension-response can be touched off in the immediate vicinity of the choice-point, it may function as a factor added to the facilitation of the direct true-path turn.

These processes of segmental learning constitute the major events of the intermediate stage, accounting for a gradual fall in the error curve when they are effectuated, or for a plateau in the curve when they are retarded (e.g., as a group C, Figure 48) or more fully arrested (e.g., as in the case of ant K, Figure 49). Understanding the nature of this process is greatly assisted by an examination of plateau phenomena like those evidenced in group C, laboring under inconstant intra-maze conditions. After having accomplished the initial-stage habituation, the subjects of this group began to eliminate entrances into blinds, but virtually from the start this occurred much more slowly and variably than in group A subjects. The only phase of blind-elimination that was effectively completed was the first, the dropping of second-arm entrances; later stages leading to complete elimination progressed erratically, and seldom ran their entire course in any choice-point locality. Not only was the blind-shortening process considerably *retarded* in group C, but there was a marked *delay* in reaching the point at which there began a regular increase in direct true-path turns at choice-points. In group A the frequency of direct true-path turns rose from 49% at trip 8 to 96% at trip 32; however, in group C this value remained near 50% until trip 20, and reached its maximum of 85% only at trip 40. The upshot was that although the complete mastery of all six choice-points was accomplished by normal subjects within 32 runs, at the 45th run not one group-C subject had mastered all of the blinds. The curves in Figure 49 express clearly the difference which existed in the performances of these two groups throughout the intermediate stage.

The handicap of group C may be attributed to the marked variability which appeared in their behavior following the general maze adjustment of the initial stage. We may say that the disturbance of the tentatively established movement-stereotypy at this critical point disordered the manner in which the focal stimulus-patterns were encountered just before blocking occurred in the given blind, thereby interfering with expansion of the nuclear blind-conditioning process in the segment. This disarrangement of the temporal sequence of events from trip to trip greatly complicated the selective-learning process; the typical behavior difficulties of these subjects indicating clearly that too many interfering adjustments developed in each locality to permit a consistent, regular advance in blind-shortening. Furthermore, the marked delay in the mastery of choice-point adjustments by group C shows that under normal conditions such learning depends upon reaching a fairly advanced stage in the blind-shortening process. Even under conditions of a constant maze environment, subjects like ant K (Figure 49), which are inferior in stereotyping their initial maze adjustment, cannot progress far in the segmental learning process.

This dependence upon a regularity of stimulus events in the problem situation, and the necessity of stereotyping early behavior if specialized learning is to occur effectively suggests a constitutional limitation of the terrestrial insect for trial-and-error learning. An inconstant maze situation of the type presented to group C apparently demands wider resources for selective learning than the ant possesses. To be sure, this insect can master limited alterations in a learned situation (such as a change in the principal direction of illumination,—Schneirla, 1929) provided that such changes may be encountered successively in the same form. Judging from comparable experiments with the rat in which environmental changes have been introduced more complexly (e.g., Honzik, 1936), lower mammals have wider resources than social insects for learned adjustment to a shifting environment.

We have traced the ant's maze adjustment to the point at which local difficulties have been overcome through independent learning processes. Ordinarily, after the initial stage, there is no particular improvement in the running of true-pathway until the segmental learning has reached an advanced stage. Then, in what may be called the *terminal stage,* a unitary maze adjustment is established on a new basis. In effect, when the local choice-point adjustments have extended spatially so that they influence behavior at increasing distances from the critical junctions, they begin to interfere with one another in adjoining sections of the maze, forcing new adjustments in the running of true pathway where they overlap. In normal subjects, the development of a new way of leaving the given choice-point

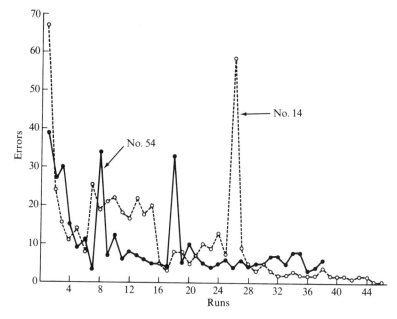

FIGURE 50

Two *Formica incerta* learning curves from situation DL, illustrating special difficulties in the intermediate period which may (as in No. 14) or may not (as in No. 54) lead directly to a general improvement of the maze response. (See text.)

presents the possibility of an interference with the established mode of approaching the next choice-point. Proceedings are further complicated by the fact that approach to a given choice-point typically changes as an extension of the local learning process, building up literally backward from the junction. As a consequence, new difficulties usually develop in the running of true pathway once the blinds are fairly well mastered. Then, frequently after passing an alley or two beyond a choice-point, the subject will hesitate or stop abruptly, perhaps retracing one or more times in the vicinity, unable to adjust to the situation after entering it somewhat differently than before.

Although such reciprocal interferences between learned segments are a typical source of new errors in the terminal stage, through behavior difficulties thereby arising new true-pathway adjustments may become established which link the segmental adjustments into a truly unitary maze response. In Figure 50 the two error curves, one (case No. 14) representing the eventual completion of this terminal-stage process, the other (No. 54) an inability to readjust to the new difficulties, with intersegmental errors persisting to the end. The case of subject No. 14 is somewhat extreme, in that difficulties mounted simultaneously in two areas of the maze, between choice-points 4, 5 and 6, 7 and between 6, 7 and 8, 9. The disorientation in the two true-pathway sequences rose to a high peak on trip 26, however, in both zones new readjustments were promptly accomplished, so that after trip 30 the maze run was completed consistently at a level of efficiency previously unobserved. Although the completion of the terminal stage usually occurs more gradually than with this subject, the case typifies the manner in which an interaction of intermediate-stage adjustments may lead to an improved organization of the maze response.

To sum up, this interpretation of the ant's maze learning holds that a generalized maze habituation first occurs, providing a basis in stereotyped behavior for the subsequent learning of segmental adjustments, and that finally a unitary organized maze behavior may arise through the interaction of these "islands" of learning once they have reached a fairly advanced stage of development.

This process appears to have its closest parallel in the stereotyped procedure of typical rote learning in which a problem is mastered in terms of the literal order of its component segments, describable as a rudimentary type of performance in mammalian subjects. The rote-like manner in which ants characteristically master these maze problems resembles rather closely the stereotyped progress of rats in learning mazes after serious cortical loss.

From this view, we should expect to find outstanding qualitative differences when the ant's characteristic maze adjustment is compared with that of normal mammalian subjects. As far as comparisons can be made at the present time, they tend to confirm that expectation. When normal rats are tested in maze-pattern D under conditions broadly equivalent to those holding for ants in group A, they master the problem within relatively few runs (all of 10 subjects within 12 runs), in a facile manner quite different from the rather labored and stereotyped process of distinctive stages found in ants. From the rat's first run there are indications of intersegmental relationships in the situation, together with rapid and complex true-pathway readjustments and the elimination of some of the blinds virtually as wholes. With ants, pattern D is useful as a means of studying the learning process; however, rats master this problem with such facility that only very general statements can be made concerning the process of their learning. A comparison of the general error curves in Figure 51 will serve to emphasize the marked difference between the performance of ants and rats.

The effect of reversing the maze following original learning clearly reveals the inferiority of the ant's adjustment. When ants are introduced into the last alley after having learned the maze D, so that now they must run through it from alley 13e to alley 1, they seem very disoriented and learn

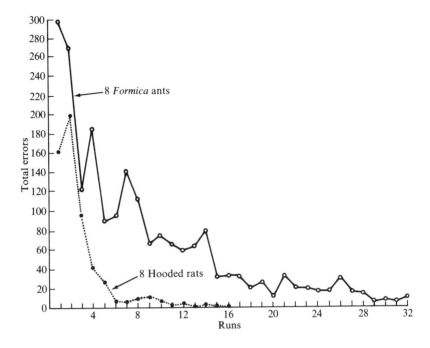

FIGURE 51
Cumulative error curves for groups of ants and rats learning pattern D.

this problem (if at all) only in the course of a long series of runs. On the other hand, after having learned pattern D rats master the reversed problem quite readily, obviously profiting by transfer effects from the original learning. It is apparent that these animals must have learned the original problem in very different ways, since only the rat can utilize its learning effectively under the changed conditions.

The ant's limitations are discernible in original learning, in the fact that the segments of the problem primarily are learned strictly in terms of local adjustments. This restriction of the terms of learning extends even to the fact that forward-going blind-alley elimination, a distinct and readily recognizable process as we have seen, is not assisted or influenced in any identifiable way by the experience of running into the blinds when retracing. During the development of blind-elimination, the shortening of entrances becomes increasingly apparent in forward approaches to the choice-points, yet at the same time there is no dependable sign of blind-shortening when blinds are entered during back-tracking. Such entrances into blinds decrease in strict dependence upon the reduction of retracing, and finally disappear only when retracing itself drops out, clearly in a very different manner than we have described for forward-going entrances. In this maze pattern the choice-points were all T's in the forward direction and L's in back-tracking (Figure 47), affording a marked dissimilarity in the approaches to blinds from the two directions. For the ant, this evidently excluded any common effects in learning, i.e., from the two directions of approach any given blind apparently was psychologically a very different situation. With this handicap the ants learned nothing specific about the maze when retracing which could assist them later in running the reversed maze; furthermore, any effective transfer from the original forward-going accomplishments was excluded on the same basis. In decided contrast to this state of affairs, rats in the original learning of pattern D were able to shorten blind-alley entrances both in forward-going and in retracing, and also exhibited a definite "saving" when introduced to the reversed pattern. Improving greatly on the performance of ants, the rats in their original learning were able to establish a somewhat common basis of response to any difficult segment of the problem however approached.

Numerous experimenters (e.g., Spence, 1932; Spragg, 1934) have reported evidence for intra-maze transfer in the rat, indicating the existence of integrative learning even during early trials. A notable fact is that the most rapid progress in avoiding blinds appears at the last choice-point and at other distinctive choice-points, demonstrably influencing adjustments at other critical junctions on the basis of pattern similarities such as the direction of turn. Specific transfer effects comparable to these do not appear in the ant's learning, in which the local segments of the problem evidently are mastered independently. For example, when a special group of ants was introduced to situation DL with just one blind (at choice-point 8, 9), they eliminated this blind alley much as did subjects that had the full number of six blinds. In other words, the fact that in the complete pattern two other blinds (No. 4, and the terminal blind, No. 12) turned *left* as did the comparison blind (No. 8) did not influence the subject's mastery of the latter situation. This finding indicates that in learning a given segment of the problem the ant is held to the specific terms of the local stimulus situation, disclosing as do the above results a distinctly inferior capacity for problem-organization as compared with the rat.

The ant's proneness for highly stereotyped and situation-fixed learning has been illustrated by her inability to show any effective transfer of learning when a mastered maze pattern is reversed. This characteristic shows itself even more strikingly in the learning of maze segments which (to the experimenter) are identical in pattern, when these are presented simultaneously in different situations. For example, one group of *Formica incerta* subjects was presented with maze D twice on each trip, running through facsimile patterns in reaching the food-place and in returning to the nest (Figure 47). After this difficult round trip had been learned (Schneirla, 1934), the entrance problem was modified by blocking alley 9a and opening its previously "blind" alternative alley 8 as a true pathway. The exit problem (DL) was not changed, i.e., in this run alley 8 remained a blind, alley 9 true pathway. Following the change, in their *entrance* runs the ants were at first greatly disturbed at choice-point 8–9, persistently repeating the learned entrance into the now-blocked alley 9, and back-tracking after very short entrances into alley 8, as characteristic errors. In the course of less than twelve runs, however, all three of the tested subjects eliminated the tendency to enter alley 9 and consistently turned directly into alley 8. The interesting fact was that throughout the series of readjustive DR runs, on the *return* trip through the facsimile D pattern (in DL) there were no signs of disturbance and no false moves in passing choice-point 8–9. In that situation, shortly after having had great difficulty in passing through the corresponding part of situation DR, on every return run through DL, the subjects continued to make the direct turn into alley 9. In this way the ants demonstrated in their behavior that for them "pattern D" was a distinctly and rather completely different problem on the two phases of each round trip.

With the normal rat as subject, we should expect to find evidences of a largely common process of learning when a given maze pattern is encountered successively in different situations, resulting in disturbances in all situations when post-learning changes are made locally in one situation alone. In other words, in the original learning process of the rat each run through the pattern in any one of the situations would influence the common habitual adjustment. In this type of test the characteristic stereotypy of the ant's procedure in learning constitutes an advantage so far as restricting the disturbing effects of local change is concerned, yet in the last analysis this is a doubtful advantage since it depends upon a constitutional inferiority in the insect mode of learning.

These results serve to cast doubt upon the validity of the Piéron (1904) hypothesis, widely accepted by writers upon insect orientation. This hypothesis holds that in normal foraging "the return is a function of the outgoing trip" in the sense that the ant is able to repeat its outgoing journey in reverse when returning to the nest. Piéron's judgment, the basis of this ability must lie in a "muscular memory." In opposition to this notion that a close functional relationship exists between the two phases of the foraging trip, our findings show that the outward and return runs are distinctively different experiences to which the insect learns separate and independent adjustments. The Piéron hypothesis calls for important transfer effects in mastering the two phases of the run, yet in our investigations no evidences of such relationships have appeared. The two phases of the run seem to be mastered as essentially independent problems, whether or not the ant returns through the "same" maze alleys (Schneirla, 1929) or through a facsimile pattern (i.e., through the alleys in the literal order of entrance). Psychologically, the ant's habit seems to be bound by the specific conditions of the given situation in which it is learned, a feature which reminds us of the characteristic limitations of recall in human rote learning.

This interpretation of our subject's limitations is significant beyond the maze-learning of the ant, judging by the findings of other experimenters (Hannes, 1930; Opfinger, 1931) with other insects in very different situations. Opfinger presented the honeybee with a distinctive visual environment during each principal phase of the foraging trip, exposing a *blue* patch at the food-place during the *arrival* flight, a *white* patch beneath the food-place during *feeding,* and a *yellow* patch during the *departure* flight. Then, in post-training tests, all of these stimulus-patches were laid out at random on the feeding table, together with various new stimuli. Characteristically, as long as the *blue* patch was present the bees alighted upon it in greatest numbers upon their *arrival* from the hive, but when this patch was removed the bees responded on an unlearned basis, behaving as though the "feeding stimulus" (the white) and the "departure stimulus" were quite as new as the others. These results disclose the interesting fact that for the specific act of arrival there was only one adequate stimulus in the test—the (blue) one experienced during *arrival* in the training period. Although the other two stimuli present in the preparatory period may have been effective in connection with their respective situations, they lack any demonstrable influence upon the arrival flight. This is evidence for a psychological independence among the three phases of the foraging act, each more or less isolated in terms of a specific control by its distinctive stimulus setting. These results from another insect as subject and a different problem situation corroborate our maze findings in suggesting that stereotypy and situation-specific recall are prevalent characteristics of insect learning.

It is evident from this description that the process of problem-solving in insects differs qualitatively in rather fundamental ways from that of the rat. There are similarities, of course, in the general trend of the error curves and in the fact that the *Formica* ant can learn mazes which prove to be fairly difficult for naive rats. However, closer examination reveals differences which suggest a fundamental disparity in the learning processes of insect and mammal. What initially is called the "same" problem is learned very differently by the two animals. Thus we learn that the contour of a learning curve alone is a feature of questionable significance until the underlying organization of the performance is known. The point is vividly illustrated by the fact that some of our error curves (e.g., Figure 50) exhibit sudden drops in their latter stages which strikingly resemble mammalian curve patterns often taken to indicate the presence of "insight learning."[2] The basis of the sudden change is a reorganization of the habit, it is true; however, this reorganization in the ant proves to be a process scarcely answering the criteria of human "insight." Far from insight, the ant accomplishes its readjustment in the problem through a relatively crude interaction of serial reactions which have developed independently in adjoining sectors of the problem. In the study of insect behavior, surprising things may be observed which superficially suggest a high level of psychological process,[2] but which on closer analysis prove to be much simpler.

More than once in the literature it has been suggested that a common qualitative process is involved in all maze learning, if not in all learning. A notable example is the unique treatise of Bierens de Haan (1937), in which a survey of the entire field of animal maze-learning centers around the following proposition (p. 212).

> Detour and maze are only different in degree; running the maze can be regarded as the making of a complicated detour. Both are based on the grasping, directly present or gradually developed, of spatial relations with regard to the goal . . . in both cases the animal strives to reach a goal, tries to do this by the shortest detour, now that the straight way is closed, makes use of different sensations, forms ideas about the way to the goal, etc. In learning the way in a maze the animal acquires a knowledge of the maze and the spatial relations of its parts, in principle not different from that of a man who learns to find the way home in a foreign town.

Evidence on maze-learning in inframammalian animals is reported in early sections of the monograph, and from this Bierens de Haan seems to conclude circumstantially that these cases fall within his goal-orientation interpretation later offered for the rat. Yet as we have pointed out in a specific comparison, a strong case can be made for the thesis that basic and essential qualitative differences exist between the characteristic learning processes of insect and mammal.

It is not our problem here to discuss the validity of goal-orientation concepts as generalized attempts to explain mammalian learning. It is in order, however, to say that the adequacy of such a conceptualization of learning has not been established by any means, notwithstanding conclusions such

---

[2] From this point of view a long series of impressive performances by insects is described very entertainingly by Hingston in his book, *Instinct and Intelligence*, the deductive interpretive procedure of which is suggested by the title. Concerning such procedures, Remy de Gourmont said: "The question of instinct is perhaps the most enervating of all. The simple-minded think it is resolved when they oppose against it the other word: intelligence. That is the elementary statement of the problem, and nothing more. Not only does it not explain anything, but it is opposed to every explanation" (1932, p. 157).

as White's (1943, p. 185) that the "principles of perceptual learning and path-goal behavior . . . ought to be the explicit and universally accepted foundation of all learning theory." In this connection it is the application of this doctrine to insect learning to which we must take exception. Unfortunately, it is not an easy matter to discuss "goal" concepts of animal learning, since their implications typically are as vague and elusive as they are numerous. To justify the introduction of "path-goal" concepts, however, it is reasonable to ask for a demonstration that the subject's learning process is influenced in identifiable ways by anticipation of a goal (i.e., by response in advance to a spatially remote incentive). We have not found such evidence for the ant.

A deductive application of Gestalt conceptions to the maze situation has led Snygg (1936) to describe the rat's maze learning as a process of "perception," in which blind-alley adjustments are individuated as special patterns from a generalized goal-awareness established during the first few runs. While the relevance of this doctrine for the rat is still a moot question, it is scarcely supported by the ant's maze performance (Schneirla, 1943, pp. 171 ff.). To be sure, at first sight the occurrence of an initial stage of generalized learning followed by a stage of specialized local adjustments might appear consistent with such a view. However, in the initial stage a general habituation to the maze situation is learned, rather than a general start-finish orientation. This habituation permits the subject to run smoothly in maze alleys, until physically obstructed; thus her behavior may be described as a yielding to the effect of pattern-sequences upon movement mechanics, without any qualitative relationship to the location of the end-point. There is no identifiable set toward a "goal"—on the other hand, the initial stage contributes a movement-stereotypy which in the ant is essential if specific adjustments are to develop in the problem.

Although much human learning is influenced by the anticipation of goals, insect learning seems to be restricted within the bounds of a much simpler motivation. For the insect a more adequate concept is "drive," denoting an organic energizing factor which activates the subject but does not carry with it a "goal set"—an organic "push" rather than a "pull" (or striving) toward an incentive. When this drive is sufficiently aroused (e.g., through "trophallactic" stimulation in the nest; through picking up or imbibing food at the food-place), the subject is impelled to continue moving until a situation is reached which instigates a new organic phase (e.g., picking up or imbibing food releasing or regurgitating food, respectively). However, the drive serves to keep the subject moving in the problem situation, and thereby makes possible learning in rote-like fashion a specific route to a food-place (or to the nest). At first the route is established piecemeal in terms of particular segmental adjustments, lacking interrelationships with other segments or with the end-point. Finally the independent expansion of these local patterns leads to their interaction, a process through which a unitary response to the problem may develop. Psychologically, the ant learns its route very differently than does a man (i.e., a goal-learning man) who learns the way home in a foreign town. To illustrate anthropomorphically, the procedure of the *Formica* subject in mastering her maze path reminds us somewhat of the cheerful but stupid fairy-tale character who had to be off but didn't know where he was going because he hadn't learned the way.

Although we have pointed out some fundamental limitations of the ant's learning capacity, the phenomenon is nevertheless impressive in its own setting and has great adaptive significance. The ability of some members of a colony to master foraging routes obviously is a highly important feature of colony organization, and plays a crucial role in the behavior pattern of the species. It must be kept in mind however that this performance, at first sight very similar to trial-and-error learning in higher animals, stands at a definitely lower psychological level than the performance of the mammal at its characteristic best. The fact seems to be that "trial-and-error learning" can be a very different kind of process, according to the nature of the organism in which it occurs. As a broad comparison, we may offer for consideration the obvious fact that while in human trial-and-error learning a "purpose"—i.e., the involvement of goal anticipation—is sometimes a dominant directive factor, this is unfortunately not always the case. Perhaps, by improving our understanding of how some animals learn in the constitutional absence of this great advantage, another step may be taken toward better insight into its proper place in human learning.

REFERENCES

Bierens de Haan, J. A. 1937. *Labyrinth and Umweg.* Leiden.
Bonnet, C. 1779. *Oeuvrez d'histoire naturelle et de philosophie.* T.1re (Observation sur de petites Fourmis, etc.) Neuchâtel.
Brun, R. 1914. *Die Raumorientierung der Ameisen,* Jena.
Cornetz, V. 1910. Trajets de Fourmis et retours au nid. *Inst. Gen. Psychol.,* Mém. No. 2, pp. 167.
Fielde, A. 1901. Further study of an ant. *Proc. Acad. Nat. Sci. Phila.,* 53: 425–449.
Forel, A. 1874. Les Fourmis de la Suisse. *Nouv. Mém. Soc. Helv. Sci.* Zurich, 26: 447.
Forel, A. 1908. *The senses of insects.* London.
Brabensberger, W. 1933. Untersuchungen über das Zeitgedachtnis der Ameisen und Termiten. *Z. Vergl. Physiol.* 20: 1–54.
Hannes, F. 1930. Über die verschiedenen Arten des "Lernens" der Honigbiene und der Insekten überhaupt. *Zool. Jb., Zool. Physiol.* 47: 89–150.

Honzik, C. H. 1936. The sensory basis of maze-learning in rats. *Comp. Psychol. Monog.* 13(4): 113.

Huber, P. 1810. *Recherches sur les mocurs des fourmis indigènes.* Paris. Genève.

Lubbock, J. (Avebury) 1881. *Ants, bees, and wasps.* London.

Maier, N. R. F., and T. C. Schneirla. 1935. *Principles of animal psychology.* New York: McGraw-Hill.

Opfinger, E. 1931. Über die Orientierung der Biene an der Futterquelle. (Die Bedeutung von Anflug und Orientierungsflug für den Lernvorgang bei Farb-, Form-, und Ortsdressuren.) *Z. Vergl. Physiol.* 15: 431–487.

Piéron, M. H. 1904. Du rôle du sens musculaire dans l'orientation de quelques éspeces de fourmis. *Bull. Inst. gen. Psychol.*, 4re Ann., No. 2, 168–186.

Santschi, F. 1911. Observations et remarques critiques sur le mécanisme de l'orientation chez les Fourmis. *Rev. Suisse Zool.* 19: 303–338.

Schneirla, T. C. 1929. Learning and orientation in ants. *Comp. Psychol. Monog.* 6 (4): 1–143.

Schneirla, T. C. 1933. Motivation and efficiency in ant learning. *J. Comp. Psychol.* 15: 243–266.

Schneirla, T. C. 1934. The process and mechanism of ant learning. *J. Comp. Psychol.* 17: 303–328.

Schneirla, T. C. 1941. Studies on the nature of ant learning. I. The characteristics of a distinctive initial period of generalized learning. *J. Comp. Psychol.* 32: 41–82.

Schneirla, T. C. 1943. The nature of ant learning. II. The intermediate stage of segmental maze adjustment. *J. Comp. Psychol.* 35: 149–176.

Smith, L. P. 1912. *The English language.* London.

Shepard, J. F. 1911. Some results in comparative psychology. *Psychol. Bull.* 8: 41–42.

Shepard, J. F. 1914. Types of learning in animals and man. *Psychol. Bull.* 11: 58.

Snygg, D. 1936. Maze learning as perception. *J. Genet. Psychol.* 49: 231–239.

Spence, K. W. 1932. The order of eliminating blinds in maze learning by the rat. *J. Comp. Psychol.* 14: 9–27.

Spragg, S. D. S. 1934. Anticipating responses in the maze. *J. Comp. Psychol.* 18: 51–74.

Turner, C. H. 1907. The homing of ants. *J. Comp. Neur. Psychol.* 17: 370–378, 399–401.

White, R. K. 1943. The case for the Tolman-Lewin interpretation of learning. *Psychol. Rev.* 50: 157–186.

T. C. SCHNEIRLA

Insect Behavior in Relation to Its Setting

Bibliography No. 62

The life of individual insects involves an intimate relationship with an environment characteristic of the species (Allee et al., 1949). This fact is not the subject of ecology alone but also concerns the physiologist and student of behavior. Thus, the effective environment (the habitat) of an insect depends not simply upon where the active life of this insect may begin, but also upon the nature and variations of organic properties such as sensitivity and upon the behavior repertoire. Inevitably, this is a reciprocal matter. Hence the present chapter is aimed at an understanding of insect behavior in terms of the different conditions under which insects live.

BEHAVIOR PATTERN AND EFFECTIVE ENVIRONMENT MUTUALLY DETERMINATIVE

Species Habitat and Behavior

Characteristically, the newly emerged insect finds itself in a situation favorable to its continued life, a "niche" (Elton, 1927) or local environment characteristic of its species. Often this initial situation can be attributed to parental behavior, which serves to narrow down or to specialize the prospective environment of the progeny. Thus, each young bee emerges into a comb-hive situation that bears certain inevitable physiological and behavioral consequences influencing its life course (Von Frisch, 1948; Grout, 1949); young worker ants emerge into a nest situation with ecological properties characteristic of the species (Talbot, 1934; Gregg, 1947) as well as potential influences upon behavior (see [*Collective Activities and Social Patterns among Insects,* in Part VII of this book]).

The extent to which the effective early environment depends upon parental behavior, especially in solitary insects, may be suggested by two

From *Insect Physiology,* edited by K. Roeder. New York: John Wiley and Sons, 1953. Chap. 26. Reprinted with permission.

examples. The chalcid wasp *Trichogramma evanescens* normally oviposits upon the eggs of a moth, but occasionally places its eggs upon objects such as sand particles or small seeds (Salt, 1935). Dragonflies typically lay their eggs upon water, but occasionally they oviposit upon surfaces such as glass or tar (Ziegler, 1910). In each instance, very different but equivalent conditions appear to have been in some way adequate to elicit the female's response. Such cases emphasize the way that parental behavior is often an important factor in determining the initial environment of the developing individual. Usually, but not always, this is a favorable, adaptive environment.

The effective postemergence environment of the individual—or, more properly, the various situations which it frequents in activities such as feeding, coming to rest, or nesting—depends to a great extent upon the organic equipment characteristic of its species. For example, in solitary insects such as butterflies, responses to outer conditions bearing upon the places that may be frequented are known to be influenced by: sensory equipment (Dethier, 1947a; Hovanitz, 1948), organic condition and its temporary variations (Rabaud, 1922), factors of neural function (see [Roeder, 1953,] Chaps. 17 and 19), and effector equipment (Clausen, 1940). To illustrate in terms of sensory factors, many butterflies and other insects are attracted to plants inconspicuous to the human eye by virtue of a visual sensitivity to ultraviolet light absent in man (Lutz, 1924; Bertholf, 1932). It is very probable that the time of maximal activity and the characteristic resting places of diurnal insects (e.g., most butterflies) and of nocturnal insects (e.g., most moths) are influenced fundamentally by visual properties such as intensity thresholds and capacity for light adaptation.

In social insects, however, the environmental situations in which individuals live are determined less directly. The nesting place of a colony depends in most ant species, for example, upon the initial environmental responses of its founding queen after the mating flight and upon her capacities for survival under adverse conditions; furthermore, it depends upon whether colonies of the species can shift their nesting sites under nonoptimal conditions (Kennedy, 1927; Wheeler, 1928, 1933; Chapman, 1931; Emerson, 1938). Factors of physiological toleration are likely to influence habitat-maintaining behavior or in extreme cases to determine the survival or extinction of entire colonies.

"Preferred Temperature" and Maintenance of Optimal Environment

Reactivity to temperature typically plays an important part in the process of reaching and maintaining an optimal situation. Krogh (1914) suggested that the influence of temperature as a habitat factor is two-

582

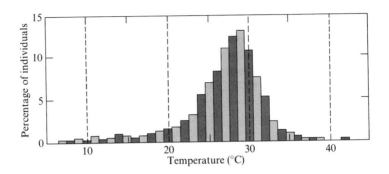

FIGURE 52
Reactions of stable flies (*Stomoxys calcitrans*) to temperature gradients in the Herter apparatus, in percentage of reactions at each temperature; 75% of the records fall between 23° and 31.5°C. (After Nieschulz, 1934.)

fold: a relatively prompt effect mediated by the central nervous system, and a slower effect through the alteration of general metabolism ([Roeder, 1953,] Chap. 5). Both types of effects must be considered in understanding the characteristic "preferred temperature" of a species, i.e., that part of the ecological range in which the insect in usually found, and within which optimal conditions presumably lie.

Various methods have been used to test reactivity to temperature conditions in a variable field (Fraenkel and Gunn, 1940). For example, the Herter (1924) "temperature organ," despite its shortcomings (Gunn, 1934), has proved useful. This apparatus is essentially a long box, within which temperature varies from a high at one end to a low at the other end, and the part within which the insect comes to rest, or spends the greatest time, is taken to indicate its "preferred temperature." Chauvin (1949b) has described an "actograph," an apparatus in which the insect responds to a gradient in which both the atmospheric and the substratal temperatures are under control.

All insect species have characteristic norms of "temperature preference" about which they vary more or less according to conditions. For example, in gradient tests conducted by Nieschulz (1934) the "preference zone" of the stable fly *Stomoxys calcitrans* was 22–32° C, with its peak at 29° C (Figure 52), and that of the lesser housefly *Fannia canicularis* was 10–28° C, with a less distinct peak at 21.5° C. Under free conditions, *Fannia* tends to appear earlier in the year and to frequent environmental situations of lower temperature than *Stomoxys*. The nests of various species of ants are distributed through a given region in relation to prevalent local temperatures (Talbot, 1934; Gregg, 1947), with characteristic differences even among closely related species (Gösswald, 1942).

Attaining the "optimum," a matter usually crucial for characteristic life processes, may be illustrated in tests with individual arthropods. Totze (1933) tested the thermal reactions of the tick, an arachnid, in a circular area heated in the center and cooled at the margin. Individual ticks reached a "preferred temperature" (between 16–18° C) by virtue of variable turning and avoiding reactions when areas of higher or lower temperature were entered. With a Herter temperature organ as well as localized "artificial fingers" to test *Pediculus,* the human body louse, Homp (1938) found that the insect reached its optimal range (26.4–29.7° C) through restless movements and avoiding reactions in other parts of the gradient field. Thus, the louse wanders about over the body of the host until an area optimal in temperature is reached, whereupon it settles down and begins feeding (Fraenkel, 1930). The adaptive significance of such facts is suggested by Herter's (1934) finding that the optimal temperature of fleas and bedbugs (ca. 35° C) approximates the average skin temperature of their mammalian hosts.

Environmental Conditions and Activity Pattern

The daily routines of most insects vary in close relation to temperature conditions (Kennedy, 1927; Talbot, 1943; Allee et al., 1949). For example, the activities of most diurnal insects typically undergo a reduction or a cessation during the hottest part of the day. According to Fraenkel (1929, 1930), the desert locust is inactive below 17° C, but begins to stir and move about as the air temperature rises above this value. Through random wandering, the hoppers reach warm, sunny spots, where aggregations gradually form. The insects typically remain in their "basking posture," at right angles to the sun's rays, until the air temperature has risen to about 28° C, whereupon they begin to move. Conditions of temperature and light are critically effective in the migratory behavior of locusts (Kennedy, 1945; Peilou, 1948).

Thermal conditions in the local environment usually influence general responsiveness in basic ways. An illustration is found in Chapman's (1923) study of the bulrush leaf-mining beetle, *Taphrocerus gracilis.* At high temperatures the adult beetles are positive to light and promptly fly off when stimulated mechanically; at low temperatures they are photonegative and mechanical stimulation produces contraction of the appendages and falling. The experimenter discerned an adaptive function in this differentiation of response according to temperature, since further feeding is possible after an escape in light, whereas contraction in dim

584

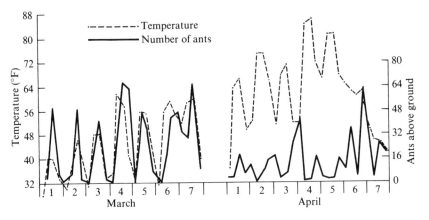

FIGURE 53
Amount of extranest activity of a colony of the ant *Prenolepis imparis* during the
first week of March and the first week of April, 1942. (In April the temperatures
ranged above the species optimum.) Broken line: temperatures recorded daily at
four spaced intervals from 7:30 A.M. to 10:00 P.M.; solid line: the total numbers
of ants seen at the corresponding times. (After Talbot, 1943.)

light typically rolls the beetle passively into a resting position in the
crevices between leaf bases and stalk.

Temperature is basic to seasonal variations in behavior (Allee et al.,
1949). An example is given in Figure 53. Hibernation and dormancy
(Sanderson, 1908; Baumberger, 1917; Roubaud, 1922; Chapman, 1931),
common among temperate-zone insects that survive the winter, represent
a suspension of active behavior under physiologically dominant temperature conditions. Many tropical insects are diurnal in the rainy season,
but shift at least partially to nocturnal activity during the dry season
(Schneirla, 1949). In such matters the influence of variations in humidity and light also is complexly involved as a rule (Chapman, 1931;
Wigglesworth, 1939). The activities of the harvester ant *Pogonomyrmex
californicus* at all times of year are related to the surface temperature of
the ground (Michener, 1942), and ants of this species living in the Mojave
desert seldom are active above ground except in early morning and late
evening or night.

The "preferred temperature" typically varies according to the condition of the insect at the time. Agrell (1947b) found that exposing the
carabid beetle *Harpatus pubescens* to specific temperatures during a fast-
ing period led first to the "selection" of higher temperatures than in control specimens. Preadaptation to a higher or lower temperature may shift
the "preference" upward or downward according to the species (Herter,
1924).

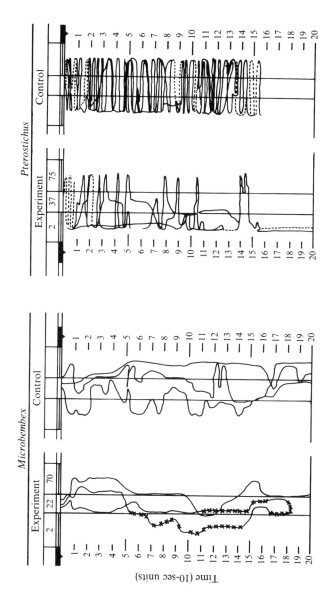

FIGURE 54

Reactions of a diurnal dune insect (a digger wasp, *Microbembex* sp.) and a nocturnal beech forest insect (a carabid beetle, *Pterostichus* sp.) in a humidity gradient (columns headed *Experiment*) and in standing air (columns headed *Control*). Crosses in the tracings for *Microbembex* indicate digging. Horizontal distance indicates movements lengthwise of the cage; vertical distance, time in 10-second intervals. Numbers at heads of the *Experiment* columns indicate the evaporation in hundredths of cubic centimeters in each third of the cage during the 20-minute experimental periods. (After Shelford, 1914.)

More lasting alterations in thermal reactivity occur in dependence upon growth stages. For example, Thomsen and Thomsen (1937) tested larvae of the housefly *Musca domestica* in a temperature gradient ranging from 9° to 50° C. For young larvae in the feeding stage, 30–37° C was the preference zone, whereas that of mature larvae close to pupation fell below 15° C. Correspondingly, the movements of fly larvae in the dungheap environment vary according to developmental stage, in close relation to the prevalent condition of temperature sensitivity. Metabolic reactions to temperature changes are discussed in [Roeder, 1953,] Chap. 5.

Although thermal factors are frequently critical, as a rule no environmental factor affects behavior independently of others. Moisture typically is effective in close conjunction with temperature (Wigglesworth, 1939); however, its role varies, for Shelford (1914) found that insects such as wood-boring beetles normally exposed to evaporation gradients react more precisely to moisture differences in laboratory tests than others (Figure 54).

Light is often critical, sometimes as the main factor restricting some insects to a subterranean habitat and others to a nocturnal activity schedule. Williams (1936) found in light-trapping tests that noctuid moths, ordinarily most active around midnight, were captured in greatest numbers on dark nights, less on nights with a partly clouded full moon, and least on nights with bright moonlight. Illustrations of environmental determination are plentiful in the methods used for control of pest insects by utilizing their characteristic reactions to external stimuli (Hewitt, 1917; Dethier, 1947a). For example, tea infested with beetles of the species *Oryzaephilus surinam* was passed along a conveyor belt, the vibration of which activated the pests so that heat from below readily forced them to the surface, where a strong directed light drove them to one side and off the belt into an oil bath (Robertson, 1944).

Biological-Behavioral Relationships Prescribing the Habitat

The dependence of the characteristic species behavior pattern upon the species habitat for its occurrence is illustrated impressively by cases such as Riley's (1892) classic study of the close biological and behavioral relationship of the moth genus *Pronuba* to the yucca plant (Figure 55). In the southwestern United States and in Central America most species of yucca are cross fertilized by particular species of moths, and the respective moths have their sole place of development and larval feeding in the yucca. The emergence of the moth from its chrysalis in the spring corresponds closely with the time of opening of the yucca flowers, which frequently remain open for one night only. After dusk, the fertilized female flies about and reaches a yucca flower (through olfaction; Rau, 1945)

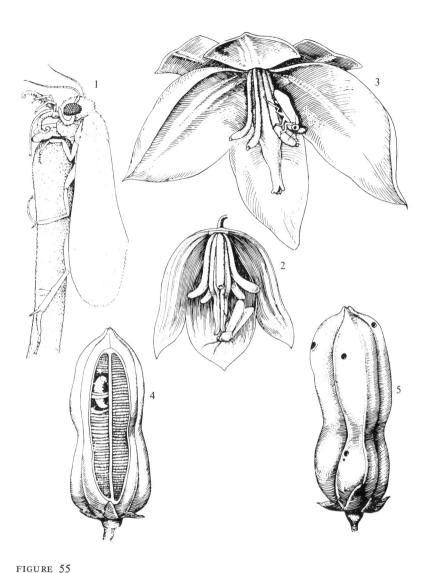

FIGURE 55

Yucca moth and yucca plant. (1) Female of *Pronuba yucasella* gathering
pollen from the anthers of a yucca plant. (2) Female *Pronuba* stuffing pollen
into the stigmatic funnel of a flower of *Yucca whipplei* (front petals removed). (3) Female *Pronuba* on yucca flower (near petals removed), shown
in the normal position of ovipositing. (4) *Pronuba* larva shown within a mature pod of *Yucca angustifolia* (with near lobe removed). (5) A pod of
yucca showing constrictions resulting from *Pronuba* puncture, and exit holes
of the larva. (After Riley, 1892.)

from the anthers of which she collects a load of pollen. Then she flies to another flower where, in a head-downward position, she thrusts her specialized ovipositor into the pistil (young fruit), where an egg is laid. Then the moth runs or flies to the top of the stigma where she stuffs her pollen mass into the funnel with her tongue. When the larva hatches, it feeds first on the juices of the ovules and then on the seeds, and matures as the remaining seeds ripen. Then it descends to the ground by a silken thread which it spins, and pupates in the soil below the plant.

The biological adaptations of the yucca to the moth are numerous, as are the organic and behavioral adaptations of the moth to the plant. A critical factor in the synchronization is the emergence of the moth when its species of yucca is in bloom. Riley observed that, in some southern areas where yucca flowering tends to be irregular or late, fertilization fails, and the plant is scarce.

The characteristic species "niche" involves an especially close relationship of food-taking and sheltering behavior in the many insects whose lives center around particular plants (Brues, 1946). Very often the plant is the sole source of food, shelter, and special protection, as in the species of *Pseudomyrma* and the many other ants found intimately associated with plants (Wheeler, 1910b, 1921; Bequaert, 1922; Weber, 1943). When the Cecropia tree of the American tropics dies, there dies also the colony of the vicious, stinging myrmecine ant (*Azteca* sp.) which has lived within it, feeding from its extrafloral nectaries and driving off other insects (Eidmann, 1944). The ant colony perishes not because of any locomotor incapacity but because of its strong fixation for the plant within which it has lived and obtained food. Among predatory and parasitic insects, instances are common in which a single prey or host species represents an indispensable feature of the environment. Many of the species of coccinellid ("ladybird") beetles common in English woods prey exclusively on one or another species of aphids. When the local supply of their aphid prey is exhausted, the beetles are unable to get other food, and they die of starvation (Elton, 1927).

MAJOR BEHAVIOR MODES IN
RELATION TO ENVIRONMENT

Feeding Behavior and Characteristic Environmental Foci

Many factors are involved in determining the environment of an insect species. The insect's own properties of sensitivity and behavior frequently determine the nature of effective environmental foci in species feeding processes. The patterns of food getting in most insects fall reasonably well into one of the following four types or combinations of them (Brues, 1936, 1946): (1) vegetarians, feeding on plants, e.g., lepidopterous species in which the larvae feed on plants characteristic of the species; (2) predators, living on captured animal tissue, e.g., the doryline ants; (3) scavengers, feeding on dead tissue or derivative materials of plants or animals, e.g., dung beetles and sarcophagid flies; and (4) parasites, feeding more or less fixedly upon the tissue of a "host" organism.

Examples of both simple and complex, extensive and limited environments are found in all of these groups and their transitional forms. Many insects take a variety of food types or are omnivorous in that they feed on animal and plant substances and perhaps refuse as well. Although the larvae of certain Lepidoptera (e.g., *Lymantria monacha;* Hundertmark, 1937) are influenced by visual factors, as are the adults, the role of chemical stimuli is widely predominant in their attraction to food plants. The focal stimuli here are particular "essential oils" characteristic of the plants. The specific attraction of cabbage butterflies (*Pieris brassicae*) to their plant depends upon mustard oils, for Verschaffelt (1910) found that the larvae took all leaves smeared with such substances. Dethier (1937) similarly demonstrated the specific effect of milkweed latex upon the milkweed butterfly, *Danais plexippus*. Scavengers, attracted to odors such as decomposing flesh, are less specific in their feeding. Correspondingly, their oviposition responses as adults are more generalized than those of adults in the vegetarian species (Brues, 1946; Dethier, 1947a).

Perhaps the greatest variety exists in the spatial range and characteristic focal stimuli of the predatory insects. The raids of the North American ant *Formica sanguinea* are carried out extensively to points at considerable distances from the home nest (Talbot and Kennedy, 1940), with the "enslavement" of the unconsumed brood of the "host" ant species once it develops; whereas coccinellid beetles capture and devour their insect prey close at hand. The "worm lion," larva of the dipteran *Vermileo comstocki,* captures prey by reflexly reacting to tactual stimuli received at the bottom of its self-made sand pit (Wheeler, 1930) much as "ant lions," the larvae of species of *Myrmeleon* in the neuropteran family Myrmeleontidae. Among the scavengers, the larvae of the manure worms are space-limited and simple in behavior, whereas many ants that feed largely upon dead insects forage at considerable distances from their nest sites. Parasitic insects such as body lice may lead a fairly mobile life until the host is found, whereupon a contracted existence begins.

An interesting contrast is seen between the free-ranging adults of many insects and their relatively sessile larvae, not only in scope of activity but also in the type of food taken. In many herbivorous insects the mature female lays her eggs upon a plant characteristic of the species, upon which the larva feeds, although as in many lepidopterans the adults feed upon the nectar of flowering plants (Brues, 1946). Although the adult females of many solitary wasps feed upon nectar, they sting and oviposit upon other insects which provide nourishment for their developing larvae (Clausen, 1940).

Among hymenopterous insects that as adults attack other insects upon which their young subsequently feed, the prey tends to be characteristic of the species. For example, among solitary wasps of vespoid families, the psammocharids predominantly attack spiders, the scholids attack scarabaeid beetles, and the dryinids attack various species of Homoptera. Comparable specializations are found in the sphecoid groups. In these wasps, the pouncing attack and stinging that precedes oviposition evidently depends upon a stimulus characteristic of the given prey. The involvement of olfaction is suggested by the fact that the victim typically is of the species upon which the wasp fed while a larva.

Among other Hymenoptera such as chalcids and ichneumonids in which the attack of the adult female is generally followed at once by oviposition directly upon the prey, the act evidently depends upon an olfactory effect influenced by the larval feeding situation (Thorpe and Jones, 1937; Dethier, 1947a). In the ichneumon *Megarhyssa lunator,* which attacks wood-boring larvae, the female evidently responds to a more or less specific olfactory stimulus. Thus oviposition occurs most frequently in infested trees; furthermore, the ovipositor frequently reaches the tunnel of the host (e.g., the larva of *Tremex*) by drilling through bark and intervening wood if these are not too hard. The actual finding of the host, however, depends upon the movements of the ichneumon larva once it has hatched (Riley, 1888). Females of the ichneumon *Pimpla instigator,* when presented with a small paper cylinder bearing a drop of fresh blood from the host (a *Pieris* chrysalid), become highly excited and repeatedly drill the ovipositor through the paper (Picard, 1921). Salt (1937b) demonstrated that olfactory stimuli govern the oviposition response of the chalcid *Trichogramma* to moth eggs, the characteristic host, and furthermore that the reaction is inhibited if the egg bears the chemical traces of a previous visit by another *Trichogramma* female.

Since evidence is rather sparse regarding what basic factors influence the attacking of a characteristic prey or the "selection" of particular kinds of food by different solitary insects, the consideration of species variability is in its preliminary stages. There seem to be all degrees of species variation in such reactions, from relative fixity to great plasticity. Frequently, the degree of variation may depend to a considerable extent upon what is at hand in the insect's habitat. It is well known that many insects, in laboratory tests, will take foods or attack prey not available in their natural environments (Wladimirov and Smirnov, 1934). Consequently, the "normal" species responses and their variability are difficult to appraise.

Although many shifts in diet may be explained as results of environmental change alone, others must be set down to changes in the insects themselves (Brues, 1936, 1946; Dethier, 1947a), as when new strains or "races" appear with altered modes of reaction. Pictet (1911) and MacBride (1934) claimed that such alterations result from the hereditary consolidation of acquired (learned) changes. MacBride, for example, forced stick insects (*Carausius morosus*) to feed on ivy instead of their typical food, privet leaves, and found that further generations fed more readily on ivy than on privet when presented with both. It is likely, however, that such experiments have not excluded a selection of particular strains from the original stock.

Learning may play some part in determining species diet. According to Thorpe and Jones (1937) and Thorpe (1938, 1939), larvae of the ichneumon species *Nemeritis canescens* reared on *Meliphora,* the waxmoth, in their oviposition responses as adults favored *Meliphora* as host rather than their normal victim, *Ephestia,* the flour moth. Such results favor regarding the altered behavior as a "habituation" to a substitute stimulus, a generalized type of learning. Under natural conditions such a change might constitute an "isolation" effect of possible importance for genetic selection (Thorpe, 1946).

Insect Behavior Altering the Effective Environment

Most insects are not passive creatures dominated by their surroundings, since the nature of their typical species setting, the habitat as well as the temporary extrinsic situation, depends upon their own processes. Both morphological and physiological factors are frequently combined with behavior in such relationships, as is illustrated by many of the "protective" patterns described by Cott (1940). For example, the stick insect *Carausius* typically becomes pale on a light ground and dark on a black one, through hormonally excited exoskeletal pigmentary changes elicited visually (Giersberg, 1928). Coupled with this feature is the "akinesis" response through which the stick insect is ordinarily immobilized on some bush in the daytime, and the unique external morphology which undoubtedly reduces its visibility to common predators. Conditions such as akinesis are reflex responses (Rabaud, 1919; Chap. 18) to environmental stimuli such as light and mechanical stimulation, which are inoperative at night when the stick insect moves about and feeds. In the Orthoptera, morphological characters such as a camouflaging green or brown color and appropriate body form are frequently combined with behavioral characters such as immobility or very slow movement under some conditions and rapid locomotion under others. In the grasshopper, slow movement or quiescence may shift quickly into a leap when the insect is disturbed in feeding; in the mantis, a slow approach to prey may break into a quick pounce (Roeder, 1937). Akinetic resting positions are common among both larvae and adults of the Lepidoptera, in which by virtue of posture and appearance the insect is merged into its background (Cott, 1940; Stephenson and Stewart, 1946). Through such processes, the insect becomes less prominent in the environment of its enemies or its prey.

Often a change in organic condition leads to behavior that alters the living situation, as in lepidopterous larvae which at first live on or within their food plants but at larval maturity shift to a very different place (e.g., the soil), in which pupation occurs. Similarly the developing stages of many forms, such as the larval caddis worm (Trichoptera) with its mobile shelter and moth pupae with their fixed ones, effectively modify the immediate environment. Through active behavioral processes, the newly fertilized queens of many ants frequently determine the specific situation in which the eventual colony has its nest (Wheeler, 1910b; Gregg, 1947). Behavior of the royal pair is similarly effective in many termites. However, Emerson (1938) reports that colonies of the tropical American termite *Constrictotermes cavifrons* reach their typical nest situations (on living trees, smooth-barked and with slanting trunks) through emigrations of established colonies rather than through the behavior of the founding pair.

Insects compete variously with other insects and other animals within the range of conditions to which species may become adapted. Insects are found adequately adjusted to environments at very low and at very high temperature extremes, at widely different altitudes, in both fresh and salt water and in the air, in an amazing variety of habitats (Chapman, 1931; Gregg, 1947; Alee et al., 1949). Not only are their morphological and physiological adaptations highly varied and their resistance to adverse conditions specialized (Kennedy, 1927; Wigglesworth, 1939), but also their behavioral adjustments to the environment are greatly diversified.

Workers of social-insect colonies commonly construct shelters which specialize the brood and colony environment in ways characteristic of the species. Ground-dwelling ants excavate galleries and chambers in a species-typical pattern (Wheeler, 1910b; Forel, 1921–1923, 1929; Gösswald, 1942; Talbot, 1948); workers of the tropical ant *Oecophylla smaragdyna* fasten together leaves into nests by employing their silk-spinning larvae as shuttles (Doflein, 1905; Karawajew, 1926). Although such nests insulate the population both ecologically and against enemies, the effective environment of social insects is enlarged beyond the physical bounds of the nest through foraging activities in particular. In contrast, solitary insect burrowers, with the exception of flying forms such as solitary wasps, are commonly insulated and at the same time are contracted in the scope of their activities (and effective environment) by virtue of their shelters.

The nests of insects, considered as agencies that specialize and modify the effective environment, are typically extended in their insulation function through physiological adjustments and also through modes of behavior that serve to meet ecological hazards. Some social insects, through a withdrawal into their nests, where they cluster, and by virtue of physiological changes such as those of dormancy and hibernation, are able to meet the conditions of the temperate-zone winter (Eidmann, 1942). Similarly, on different levels of adjustment, the arduous conditions of a tropical dry season are met both behaviorally and physiologically by indigenous insects.

The evolution of active temperature-control functions in the honey bee may have led to the elimination of hibernation through natural selection. Not only is a sheltered colony environment obtained through responses of daughter colonies, as to hollow trees, in swarming (Sendler, 1940), but also there is a heat potential in the food and a capacity to store this in the hive. There are also certain group reactions to temperature that operate to control environmental conditions (Grout, 1949). In winter, when hive temperature falls below 14° C, the bees form a compact cluster within which their body heat raises the temperature; in summer, when hive temperature rises above 34° C, a fanning of wings begins, which serves to maintain an even temperature on the combs (Armbruster, 1922a; Dunham, 1931). Comparable adjustments to overheated nests have been reported for social wasps by Steiner (1930) and Schwarz (1931).

The range and complexity of the species environment differs greatly among insects, from the relatively homogeneous and contracted setting typical of wood-boring beetles to the extensive and variable situation of adult dragonflies. In solitary insects, as we have seen, such matters frequently vary in dependence upon life stage, or upon temporary organic condition. In contrast to the sedentary larval stage of the tiger beetle, *Cicindela campestris,* posted in the upper part of its burrow, capturing by means of tactually elicited responses any insect that passes sufficiently near, the adult is a highly mobile insect, taking insect prey by swift, visually elicited movements (Imms, 1947).

Among social insects there are wide species differences in the range of normal colony operations around the nest site. For example, in the temperate zone, colonies of ponerine ants are small and mainly restricted to a subterranean life, their diminutive and nearly blind workers operating at short distances, capturing prey through chemotactic sensitivity. However, in the tropics, the colonies of ponerine species are commonly larger and mainly terrestrial, with their large, visually sensitive workers foraging

594

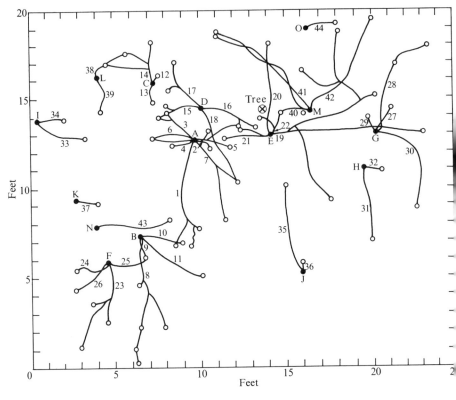

FIGURE 56
The nesting sites (A–O) of fifteen colonies of the ant *Prenolepis imparis* in the vicinity of a pear tree in a yard at Tiffin, Ohio. The odor trails (solid lines) established from July 19 to August 31, 1941, are numbered in sequence of their establishment. Black circles represent nests; light circles represent pieces of fruit or other food. (After Talbot, 1943.)

over considerable areas around the nest site (Haskins, 1939). A colony of the Algerian harvester ant, *Messor barbarus,* studied by Pickles (1944) foraged within an estimated area of 2348 sq. yd around the nest, and at a maximum distance of 50 yd. Among the species studied by Pickles (1936, 1937) in England, *Formica fusca* averaged a foraging area of 236 sq. yd, and *Myrmica ruginodis* 36.7 sq. yd, but *Acanthomyops flavus* operated scarcely beyond the aphid ground at the nest. In contrast, honey bees and other bees often forage at distances greater than 2 mi from the hive (Rau, 1929; Rayment, 1935).

Insects function effectively in various ways as parts of one another's environments (Wheeler, 1928; Forel, 1929; Maidl, 1934). Among the social insects, relations range from a mutual facilitation or tolerance to various degrees of competitiveness, the competition often being greatest, as in ants, between species of similar ecology and behavior (Morley, 1944, 1946a). Overlapping areas are the rule among adjacent colonies, with competition seldom taking the form of outright combat. The *Messor barbarus* colony studied in Algeria by Pickles (1944) was at first only 18 ft from a colony of the closely related *M. aegyptiacus,* and occasional battles occurred until the *aegyptiacus* colony removed its nest to a distance of 27 ft. Then fights were rare, although the *aegyptiacus* foraging area still lay within that of the *barbarus* colony. Headley (1943) found fifty-eight nests of five different ponerine and myrmecine species within only 500 sq. ft of ground in a mixed upland wood. In an orchard lot of 1860 sq. yd surveyed by Talbot (1943), there were eighty-eight nests of *Prenolepis imparis* with an extensive overlapping of foraging grounds, and no terrain was used exclusively by one colony alone (Figure 56). Interrelationships among colonies of social insects are discussed further in [*Collective Activities and Social Patterns among Social Insects* in Part VII of this book].

ORIENTATION OF INSECTS IN THEIR LIFE ZONES

It is evident that the dimensions of an insect's environment depend upon its mobility in space and time as well as upon the nature of its reactions and physiological adjustments. Therefore at this point we should consider the capacities of insects for orientation, that is, for maintaining a position or a course of movement with respect to extrinsic stimulus foci and prevalent fields of stimulation.

Orientation in Relation to Quantitative and Spatial Aspects of Stimulation

The study of insect orientation has centered first of all about the relationship of the animal's movements to direct and generalized properties of stimulation such as intensity, direction, and spatial aspects. A theory of such relationships was outlined by Loeb (1918) through an extension of the *tropism* concept first developed by botanists to account for bending of plants under stimulation. Loeb's theory, based upon the prevalence of bilateral symmetry in the pattern of sensory, nervous, and effector tissues, postulated that an equality or inequality in the strength of stimulation of receptors on the two sides of the body would set up a corresponding equality or inequality in nervous impulses to the action system on the two sides, resulting in an equality of tonus and straightforward movement, or an inequality of tonus and a "forced movement" toward one side. A forced response to light thus was called *heliotropism,* to contact, *thigmotropism,* to chemical stimulation, *chemotropism,* and so on. If an inequality of stimulation should produce a forced movement, according to Loeb, the unequal tonus and the forced movement would continue until a position of equal stimulation had been attained.

The shortcomings of this theory concerning insect orientation have been pointed out by numerous writers, especially by Mast (1911), Holmes (1905), and Kühn (1919). These and other writers criticized the forced-movement theory for its postulates concerning tonus; also they found it too simple to cover facts such as orientation through varied movements and the varied complex forms of animal orientation. In [Roeder, 1953,] Chap. 18 some objections based upon a consideration of nervous function are discussed. Numerous later theorists (e.g., Rose, 1929; Blum, 1935; and Viaud, 1948) have taken their departure from the Loeb concept of bilaterally symmetrical relationships in orientation. Kühn (1919) undertook a major revision of the basic orientation problem, in which Loeb's emphasis upon the existence of bilateral symmetry in animal structure and function, as well as his stress upon reflex processes, was utilized. At the same time, consideration was given to the variety of apparent types and the complexity of animal orientation.

Discussions of the basic problem of orientation have centered around reactions to light, both because of the prevalence and adaptive scope of such reactions and because of their variety and range of elaboration. A convenient classification of orientation types is offered by Fraenkel and Gunn (1940), derived from the system of Kühn, which will be followed here in a simplified form.

Under *kinesis* are included reactions that do not involve a specific orientation of the body axis in relation to a stimulus source. Thus a relatively photonegative animal such as the cockroach (Szymanski, 1914) reflexly stirred to activity by light, may reach an optimal situation by continuing its variable movements while in the light but slowing down or stopping when it enters a dark area. In a comparable manner, insects disturbed by dryness of the air may reach a humid zone (Gunn, 1937), in a response process involving a rough proportion between the intensity of general stimulation and the rate of response at any given time (*orthokinesis;* Fraenkel and Gunn, 1940).

Orientation may combine both generalized and more specific types, as when an animal enters the border of an environmental gradient such as that of gases emanating from a central source. At first the stimulative effect is diffuse in such a case, and arouses random movements. Thus parasitic insects may be excited at a distance by the odor of their host (Dethier, 1947a). However, as the gradient increases closer to the source, movement takes on a more specific directional character which leads finally to a direct approach to the source. In this way, a kinesis-type of orientation

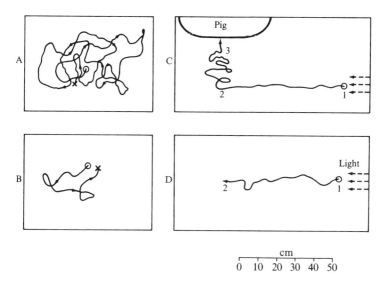

FIGURE 57

Orientation in the hog louse *Haematopinus suis* L. A. Olfactory kinesis: movements of a louse set down at O on a floor of blotting paper over blood. After moving variably for 14 minutes, the louse came to rest at ×. B. Control: a louse on blotting paper over water stops after 3½ minutes of movement. C. Taxis movements (light and olfaction): in directed light (indicated by arrows), a louse moves away from the source (1–2) until at 2 deviations appear because of an olfactory gradient based on the presence of a host. At 3 the parasite begins to move directly toward the source (8–9 cm away). D. Control, phototaxis alone: in a field of light directed as in 3, a louse moves (1–2) almost directly away from the source. (After Weber, 1929.)

may introduce a taxis type (Figure 57). Examples of such situations are found later in this chapter, in the discussion of orientation to nonvisual conditions.

The *taxis* type of orientation involves more or less "directed" reactions to spatially differentiated stimulation (Mast, 1911; Rose, 1929). In *klinotaxis* (Kühn, 1919; Fraenkel and Gunn, 1940), the animal becomes oriented through a succession of different movements, each somewhat "directed" in character through a differential stimulus effect. Klinotactic responses presumably are typical in housefly maggots (and others with a generalized light-sensitivity over anterior segments), which become photonegative when they have finished their period of feeding. In laboratory tests (Mast, 1911; Herms, 1911; Loeb, 1918), when a light is placed directly ahead, the maggot becomes reoriented (i.e., headed away from the source) through the prompt interruption of head-end oscillations toward the light, and the facilitation of movements away from the light.

In *tropotaxis* (Kühn, 1919; Fraenkel and Gunn, 1940), orientation is accomplished through a direct turn toward the more stimulated side (i.e., in a photopositive animal), without variable movements being essentially involved. Thus, when headed toward two equally intense lights in laboratory tests, an insect exhibits a tropotactic reaction when it takes a course on the line between the lights, turning toward one or the other of them when close to the source (Figure 58). When set down in a uniformly lighted field with one eye covered, an insect capable of phototropotaxis, if effectively photopositive, performs circus movements toward the open eye (e.g., the water scorpion, *Ranatra,* tested by Holmes and McGraw, 1913). Such results indicate that the normal tropotactic orientation of a photopositive insect (e.g., when moving directly toward light) involves the arousal of bilaterally equivalent effector processes through the equivalent innervation of symmetrically placed photoreceptors, or (when turning toward a light on one side) of bilaterally different effector processes through unequal innervation of symmetrically placed photoreceptors (Fraenkel and Gunn, 1940). The nervous aspects of this question are discussed in [Roeder, 1953,] Chap. 18.

It is important to note that the same organism may be capable of more than one type of orientation even in the same situation and the same behavior sequence. Also, insects capable of the complex types may behave in terms of the simpler. Thus ants of a species such as *Formica fusca* may respond on a kinetic basis when a bright, diffuse light suddenly reaches a place where they huddle with their larvae, or if strong directed light suddenly strikes them they may move directly away from it (i.e., klinotactically). Under other conditions, as we shall see, such insects are capable of much more complex patterns of orientation. In general, the more complex the receptor-nervous-effector equipment of the insect, the less readily orienting behavior can be diagnosed in terms of the simpler patterns.

The Problem of "Sign" in Orientation

Before proceeding to more complex types of insect orientation, it is desirable to consider a fundamental problem which is often minimized or neglected (Maier and Schneirla, 1935; Viaud, 1948). This is the question of "sign," or the typical trend (in klinokinesis) or direction (in tropotaxis) of response in a field of stimulation. Insects are frequently spoken of as *photopositive* (e.g., butterflies) or *photonegative* (e.g., the cockroach), although a consideration of the facts show that most insects may be positive or negative to light according to conditions (Maier and Schneirla, 1935, Chap. 4 and 6). "Sign" is thus a relative term for representative species tendencies. The typical phototactic "sign" of any species

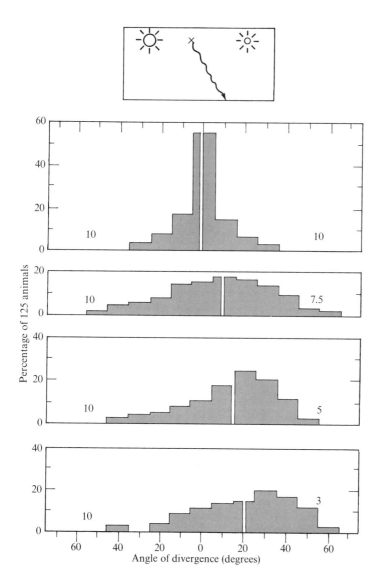

FIGURE 58

Behavior of photonegative larvae of the meal moth, *Ephestia kuehniella,* started between two beams of light, the left constant in intensity (= 10), the right reduced successively in intensity in four tests (10, 7.5, 5, and 3, respectively) as indicated. As the relative intensity of the left light increases, the angle of divergence from it becomes greater. (After Brandt, 1934.)

depends upon species metabolism and may vary temporarily both according to external conditions such as the intensity of stimulation and to organic conditions.

In other words, species have different "thresholds" of differential response to stimulation, and rather than speak of a "photonegative" species one should speak of a "typically photonegative species" to indicate that the trend is to remain out of light or to turn away from directed light. For instance, when tested under the same conditions, the "wild" strain of *Drosophila ampelophila* was highly photopositive when active, whereas three wing mutants "curled," "strap," and "vestigial" were decreasingly less photopositive in that order (McEwan, 1918).

The basic dependence of sign of response to light upon the characteristic metabolism of a species, and its variations upon temporary changes in organic condition is indicated by a variety of results (Jackson, 1910; Mast, 1911; Wodsedalek, 1911; Loeb, 1918; Dolley and Golden, 1947). Allee and Stein (1918) found that nymphs of the mayfly species *Epeorus humeralis* from running water were normally photopositive to daylight, whereas nymphs of *Leptophlebia* sp. from quiet water were normally photonegative. *Epeorus* had the higher rate of metabolism; however, when alcohol and other agents were used, which depressed metabolism, *Epeorus* specimens became photonegative. Conversely, raising the metabolic rate of *Leptophlebia* specimens made them photopositive for a time. Phipps (1915) obtained similar results with amphipod crustaceans from different stream environments. Phototactic sign changes in dependence upon life stage, or upon physiological condition, in various insects. Thus, lepidopteran caterpillars typically become photonegative after feeding; queen ants photonegative after mating. Newly hatched blowfly larvae are at first positive to weak light, but soon become negative to all but very low intensities (Herms, 1911). In light of a given intensity, young individuals of the dronefly *Eristalis tenax* reverse their phototactic reactions at somewhat higher temperatures than older flies (Dolley and Golden, 1947) (Figure 59). The view that the characteristic "phototactic signs" of species depend upon organic properties such as thresholds of sensitivity (Ewald, 1913) is supported by studies upon other arthropods (Viaud, 1948) as well as other invertebrates (Hess, 1924). Other suggestive results are considered below.

Significant Variations in Phototaxis

Many insects when placed in a diffuse field of light with one eye covered will circle until they are away from the light, and continue the circus movements when again headed toward the source (Garrey, 1918). However, Garrey's results of this type with the robber fly *Proctacanthus* were

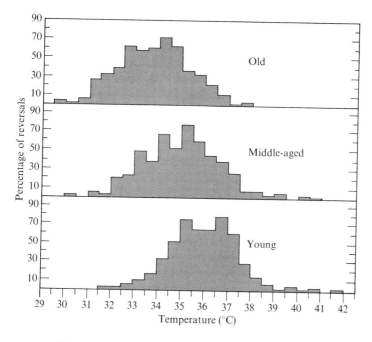

FIGURE 59

Temperatures at which specimens of *Eristalis tenax* consistently moved from light into a darkened compartment, thereby reversing their typical positive phototropism. (With increasing age the reversal occurred at successively lower temperatures.) (Adapted from Dolley and Golden, 1947.)

not obtained by Holmes (1905) with the water scorpion *Ranatra* and by Dolley (1916) with *Vanessa antiopa* (= *aglais*). The last two insects, when repeatedly headed toward a light as one-eyed specimens, were able to stop circling after a time and go in a fairly straight course toward the source. Because of the gradual straightening of the course, Holmes thought that "learning" was involved. However, Clark (1928), in experiments with the water boatman *Notonecta,* was able to show that the eventual straight course toward light depended upon a gradual increase of the light-sensitivity threshold in the unblackened eye, through visual adaptation in that eye. Specimens with one eye exposed to light for 30 min went straight toward the light on their first trial, just as specimens that had made repeated runs and straightened out their course in light meanwhile; but specimens kept in the dark for an equivalent time showed no sign of such a change. Investigators have demonstrated many types of temporary change in orientation tendency due to change in the effect of stimuli such as light, temperature, and humidity, based upon starvation, satiation, and various transitory organic conditions other than sensory adaptation.

However, there are insects that are able to make transverse courses toward a light, or to pass directly toward one of two lights, under conditions not attributable to visual adaptation or other transitory organic conditions. Mast (1923) found that a strongly photopositive dronefly *Eristalis tenax* with one eye blinded, when placed at a distance from a single light, progressed directly toward the source from the outset. With stimulation of the antero-median ommatidia of either eye (with the other eye blacked over) *Eristalis* would turn to the opposite side or walk around a curve toward the source, whereas with stimulation of the lateral and posterior ommatidia it would turn to the side of the unblacked eye. Clark (1928) found similar results with *Notonecta*. This illustrates the photic response called *telotaxis* by Kühn (1919), a direct course toward a light that stimulates only a part of one eye. The ability of many insects to move toward a light that acts upon only one eye evidently involves an arousal of anterior ommatidia in that eye adequate to set up forward progress reflexly, whereas responses to the stimulation of the functionally different lateral and rear ommatidia are nervously inhibited (Fraenkel and Gunn, 1940). Thus, the dung beetle *Geotrupes sylvaticus,* advancing toward one of two lights, may continue its progress even if the second light has been made stronger during the trial (Honjo, 1937). A possible basis for a functional difference in these sets of ommatidia is suggested by the finding of Dolley and Wierda (1929) that in the eye of *Eristalis* the ommatidia 23° to the rear are fifty-five times as sensitive as the anterior ommatidia. Thus a light intensity that affects the (less sensitive) anterior ommatidia at an effective low intensity and elicits a forward-going response arouses a different effector system, producing avoidance [withdrawal], when it acts upon more sensitive latero-posterior ommatidia, and is thus effective as a strong stimulus (Figure 60). "Turning-toward" or "forward-going" are typical reactions to "weak" stimulation, and "turning-away" to strong stimulation, in the invertebrates (Maier and Schneirla, 1935).

Thus telotaxis, as a specialized type of insect orientation, evidently depends upon different thresholds in ommatidia over the compound eye, such that adequate stimulation of different ommatidia may call into play neural and action mechanisms with correspondingly different arousal thresholds [see Roeder, 1953, chap. 18]. In a detailed analytical experiment with *Notonecta* in which various parts of the two eyes were covered in different combinations, with tests in diffuse light, Lüdtke (1938) obtained results confirming this theory. He found that the direction of the turning response called out by stimulation of particular ommatidia depends on the effective intensity of light, i.e., a stimulus just exceeding the intensity threshold of these ommatidia elicits a response *opposite* to that

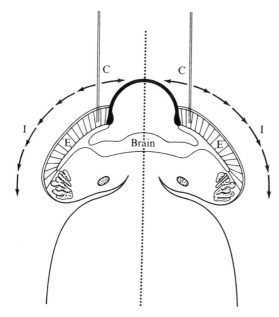

FIGURE 60
Sketch representing a horizontal section of the head
of the dronefly *Eristalis tenax*. Arrows show the
predominant turning tendency when ommatidia
under the respective points are stimulated by light
beams. E, eye; C, contralateral turning, from
stimulation of antero-lateral ommatidia; I, ipsilateral
turning, from stimulation of antero-lateral, lateral,
and posterior ommatidia. (After Mast, 1923.)

called out by a considerably stronger light. Complex phototactic orientation patterns, therefore, would seem to depend not only upon different
sensitivity thresholds of ommatidia over the compound eye but also upon
specialized sets of neural and effector mechanisms capable of responding
to respectively different receptor-arousal processes.

Other Types of Visually Controlled Orientation

Among the more generalized visual reactions important for environmental adjustment is the hovering reaction observed by Wheeler (1899)
in syrphid and other small flies that collect in swarms, a reaction termed
anemotropism by him. Midges, for example, can orient themselves against
a slight breeze and maintain almost a constant position headed into the
wind. The reaction, currently not well understood, may be visually determined. J. S. Kennedy (1939) found that mosquitoes, tested in a wind

with a moving background, first responded to the movement of the visual background by turning and flying into the wind, then became stationary or moved slowly relative to the ground. The response was particularly prompt when the background was moved from front to rear.

A somewhat different problem is raised by a type of reaction that Alverdes (1930) has called *skototaxis* on the assumption that it involves an approach to darkness as such. An illustration is found in an experiment by Hundertmark (1936), in which prefeeding caterpillars of the black arch butterfly, *Lymantria monacha,* were tested under visual conditions such as are normally involved in their approach toward food plants from a distance. When caterpillars at this stage were started from the center of a circular area, they tended to head directly for one of four upright black patches placed at intervals around the circumference, and to mount the structure upon reaching it. Among rectangles of equal width, a block 19 cm high was approached by 80% of the specimens, whereas 5% approached a block 5 cm high (Hundertmark, 1937). Degree of contrast also was important. With very broad strips, the caterpillars approached the edges but not the center, a fact unfavorable to the "black reaction" concept. Although Fraenkel and Gunn (1940) consider this is a reaction to "shape," the circumstances suggest that it may be related to *telotaxis*. An apparently similar response appears in first-stage *Dixippus morosus* nymphs (Kalmus, 1937a), which move in alignment with the black-white edges when placed on a surface floored with parallel black strips.

The various types of orienting responses described thus far appear to be grounded in basic organic properties of the organism, and to be elicited according to extrinsic conditions such as intensity and direction of light. They are subject to variations according to other factors such as temperature and humidity which affect the organic condition and sensitivity of the animal. Among the forms of orientation that are perhaps more specialized in nature, the *light-compass reaction* (Santschi, 1911; von Buddenbrock, 1917) may involve a simple (habituated) and temporarily maintained "set" or adjustment tendency toward light. As an example, the larva of the tortoise-shell butterfly, *Vanessa uricae,* wanders randomly in the dark, but, when a single light is introduced, the caterpillar may move in a curved path for a period of minutes with the light on its left side, then may shift to a different light adjustment (von Buddenbrock and Schulz, 1933). A comparable response was observed by Ludwig (1934) in the caterpillar of the gypsy moth, *Lymantria* (= *Porthetria*) *dispar,* which was able to crawl in a regular spiral with reference to a single light source, seldom approaching the light directly. Fraenkel and Gunn (1940) place such behavior in the same class with the movements of foraging Hymenoptera such as ants and bees moving in a learned relation to the sun (Santschi, 1911; Wolf, 1927, 1930). Although the two cases appear to be somewhat alike in their apparent sensory-motor mechanism, the type of adjustment exemplified by the foraging ant or bee involves important differences (in particular a plastic relationship to environmental conditions and the insect's condition) that require placing it in a superior category of orientation (Maier and Schneirla, 1935), considered later in this chapter.

Broadly speaking, spatial range is greater in insects with a repertoire of visual reactions than in those less developed visually and more dependent upon the other fields of sensitivity. Not only does a visual basis in orientation give the insect greater behavior scope but also a wider variety of responses to surrounding conditions, and often a considerable degree of precision in reaction as well. Furthermore, an interesting variety of special relationships can arise between processes of visually determined responses in the behavior repertoire and particular environmental conditions attained through such responses. The typical fixity of such relationships suggests that the underlying organic mechanisms have evolved under the influence of the specific kinds of environmental conditions concerned.

Orientation to Nonvisual Conditions in the Environment

Specific orientations to tactual stimuli are often critically important in insect behavior. Mealworm larvae, for example, creep along in contact with a surface, and when a break is reached turn reflexly according to the previous contact (Crozier, 1924). "Turning-to" reactions elicited by weak contact are of significance in the "communication" of social insects (Wheeler, 1928; Schneirla, 1941). What Fraenkel and Gunn (1940) term *low thigmotaxis,* that is, maintenance of a position or a line of movement through gentle pressure against a touched surface, is common among more sessile insects. Many insects (e.g., roaches, beetles) at certain times of day are to be found only in holes or crevices. In these typically photonegative insects, which generally reach their shelters through more or less random photokinetic reactions, the tactuomotor effect comes into play when the resting place is reached. An earwig, for example, hits upon a crevice through random movements, then maintains its position by pressing its body firmly between the surfaces (Weyrauch, 1929). Thus a position gained essentially through light-sensitivity can be kept through tactually elicited responses. Weyrauch found that earwigs remained in niches between glass plates, where light reached them in full intensity.

Numerous insects find their food almost exclusively through olfaction, for example, the dung beetles *Scarabeus* (Heymons and Lengerken, 1929) and *Geotrupes* (Warnke, 1931). When still at a distance from their food, the beetles turn variably and circle, more or less, with an increasing frequency of direct movement as they near the source until finally (typically within 50 cm) they move straight toward the source. Similar results were obtained by Otto (1949) for *Drosophila, Vespa,* and *Geotrupes.* The ichneumon *Habrobracon* is excited at a distance by olfactory stimuli received from its host, and, when nearby, moves directly upon it (Murr, 1930). Although the larvae (wireworms) of the click beetle, *Agriotes obscurus,* studied by Thorpe, Crombie, Hill, and Darrah (1947), cannot respond to airborne odors from their food plants in the open, they orient readily when below ground through some substance emanating from the plant and dissolved in the soil. The experimenters believe that the processes involved are mainly chemotactic. Barrows (1907) stated that the fruitfly *Drosophila melanogaster* oriented toward fermenting fruit on an olfactory basis; Flügge (1934) reported that the flies turned accurately at about 40 cm into a column of air containing mashed-pear or jam "odor" and then moved upwind. When the antennae were shellacked over, the flies responded only when very close to the source. The blue-bottle fly, *Calliphora erythrocephala,* orients similarly toward meat (Hartung, 1935), either when flying or running, and proceeds directly toward a source from distances of 6.4–12 cm.

Behavioral effects of various chemical attractants and repellents upon insects have been surveyed by Dethier (1947a). Although distance responses to odors are commonly involved in mating reactions and food-getting, they are seldom precisely made at any considerable distance from the source, but appear to involve an initial excitatory (kinesis) function involving variable movements. Often, olfaction increases the precision of a response initiated by other stimuli. Götz (1936) found that *Vanessa* (= *Aglais*) caterpillars, which typically reach their food plant, the nettle, by moving toward the dark patch of leaves (or when nearby, the stalk), are more likely to mount the stalk if leaves lie near its base.

Olfaction is also involved in the differentiation of environmental effects. Schaller (1926) found that the water beetle *Dytiscus* initially took musk most readily among various chemicals presented to it, but could be food-conditioned to prefer coumarin. Von Frisch (1920, 1950b) found honey bees able to distinguish a whole series of odors. He trained bees to visit a foodbox scented with one (e.g., Messina orange) and to avoid boxes scented with a number of others. Thus, blossoms of various flowers may be discriminated by a bee hovering nearby. Olfaction assists bee foraging in still other ways; for example, through scent-gland secretion deposited reflexly by an excited forager bee on the flower where she has found nectar, other bees are attracted to that flower. Also, a learned discrimination of flower odors borne upon the bodies of finder bees entering the hive aids the specific responses of foragers. Bees that have been collecting nectar from buckwheat blossoms become conditioned to the odor, and, when this odor is effective during the "dance" of a returned finder, leave the hive and fly to their foraging area. Von Frisch (1943, 1950b) has found that if fresh blossoms are placed at food places near the hive, the bees become conditioned to this odor and are more likely to forage among the same blossoms (e.g., red clover) in more distant fields.

As we shall see, chemoreceptive processes also extend the scope and complexity of orientation in insects such as the trail-making ants, many of which would be exceedingly limited in coping with surrounding conditions in the absence of such capacities. It is apparent that the adjustments of insects to conditions around them differ considerably in complexity and extent from one species (e.g., sessile) to another (e.g., motile).

PROVISIONAL ORIENTATION

Flying Insects

The taxis patterns of insect orientation are highly stereotyped, reflex-like adjustments to environmental stimuli. In contrast to these, many insects, and particularly those which leave a home point on successive foraging trips, display types of way-finding which are relatively plastic and almost always require a learned development in the individual. Way finding typically involves a sequence of changes in orientation, improving efficiency according to special circumstances in individual experience. This pattern, qualitatively superior to the *taxis* type, may be termed *provisional orientation*. To include such adjustments under *compass orientation,* as Fraenkel and Gunn (1940) do, involves a distinct underestimation of their differences from the stereotyped and species-standardized taxis patterns.

This type of orientation was studied in a simple form by Brown and Hatch (1929), who found that a temporary habituation to general visual properties of a situation permitted whirligig beetles to maintain a fixed position in a tank through active movements of swimming against the current. Similarly, under natural conditions, the beetles remain beneath an overhanging branch near a stream edge. The orientation was found to have a visual basis, for the beetles scattered in the dark. They also scattered in a quick "fright" reaction when a large white (or black) spot was introduced into a previously uniform black (or white) field. As a more complex instance, Ferton (1905) demonstrated that the solitary bee *Osmia* can return successfully to its nest in a snail shell even though the shell is shifted at intervals through a series of positions. This is a learned reaction to visual cues, exemplified by Bouvier's (1901) classic test in which *Bembex* flew at once to a flat stone that had been left near its nest entrance for 2 days and subsequently transferred to a position 20 cm from the entrance.

Tinbergen (1932) extended this test with the bee-wolf, *Philanthus triangulum*. Once habituated to a ring of pegs around the nest entrance, this wasp on its return would fly promptly to the ring even when it had been moved to a position 30 cm from the nest. Van Beusekom (1948) found that the habituated stimuli in such cases may be changed within limits without losing their effectiveness. After the wasp had been habituated to a pine-cone ring, for example, a half-ring of cones would attract it, although somewhat less effectively than the full ring. Because such visually controlled reactions elicit a specialized response (return to the nest) rather than a generalized one, they represent a higher development in learning than was evidenced in the whirligig beetle tests (Maier and Schneirla, 1935).

Processes of provisional orientation are basic to the foraging and homing activities of social insects. When Rau (1929, 1931) transported mining bees from their nest and released them, mature bees were able to return with a high degree of success over distances even greater than 1 mile, whereas younger bees returned less frequently and the effective distances were shorter. That the "bee line" of the honey bee forager is established through an initial learning is suggested by the manner in which young bees at first circle in short flights near the hive and gradually increase the distance of the journey on successive departures. Once the bee becomes involved in foraging, its nectar-gathering visits generally tend to be restricted to blossoms in a certain small area, or even to specific plants (von Frisch, 1914, 1948, 1950b; Minderhoud, 1931), shifting only when the supply of nectar is exhausted (Butler, Jefree, and Kalmus, 1943). In an operating hive, some of the foragers visit particular food places in one direction, some in another direction, so that altogether a foraging area of several square miles may be covered. The orientation of the bee during her two-way flight is essentially a matter of visual control (Wolf, 1927, 1930). The established visual guidance may depend not only upon outstanding landmarks such as houses, roads, and trees (von Frisch, 1948) but also foraging over uniform terrain may depend upon the direction of the sun's rays (Wolf, 1927) and polarized light from the sky (von Frisch, 1950b). Orientation in the hive is mainly dependent upon olfactory and tactual cues (Kalmus, 1937b).

Terrestrial Insects

Some of the most involved cases of provisional orientation in the foraging of insects are found among the ants. The diversity of obstacles they encounter as crawling and running organisms is inevitably greater than that in the flying insects. There is an extensive literature (summarized by Brun, 1914, and by Schneirla, 1929) based on investigations of the sensory factors controlling ant orientation. Very striking differences are found, at times even among closely related species, in the typical pattern of orientation.

In the ants, workers forage in the area around their nest in a variety of situations and to greatly different spatial extents in different species. Typically, each individual expands her foraging range in the course of time. In most of the species wandering "explorations" (Cornetz, 1914) occur in the initial stages of individual or colony foraging, as, for example, in the first spring activities. In further stages the paths to food places are straightened or systematized in a manner dependent mainly upon the species capacities for sensory control and learning. In some species spiraling predominates in the initial wandering, in others radial excursions (complicated by local circlings), which increase in extent, in still others a looped path with angular changes (Weyrauch, 1935). As Weyrauch pointed out, these are all definitely more adaptive in a ground-covering sense than is the "primitive" random wandering of arthropods such as the mite (an arachnid). Another characteristic feature of obvious adaptive importance is the sinuous, meandering progress of terrestrial insects in general.

A broad and necessarily crude distinction may be made between species that typically forage on collective trails, and species in which foraging occurs more or less through individual specialization. In the *collective foragers,* olfactory cues typically control general progress, e.g., chemical traces are followed more or less persistently, as is shown by the interruptions caused when a finger is rubbed across the track. In trail-dependent species such as the army ants (*Eciton* spp.), the chemical traces are laid down in a stereotyped fashion and are followed directly by newcomers on a predominantly "slavish" olfactory basis (Schneirla, 1938). In other ants such as *Lasius* (*Acanthomyops*) *fuliginosus* the direct route is established gradually as a resultant of a tangle of winding scent trails (Carthy, 1950).[1] Brun (1914) concluded, from tests involving the interchange of trail sections—that the chemical nature of the trail, the degree of its chemical polarity, or both might differ in dependence upon conditions such as the substance carried. The simple polarization theory of Bethe (1898) has been criticized on various grounds by numerous writers (e.g., Wasmann, 1901; Forel, 1903; Chauvin, 1944), and important species differences have been demonstrated (Carthy, 1950). There are differences not only in the manner in which olfaction may function in the trailing of

---

[1] Carthy (*op. cit.*) has succeeded in bringing out the chemical traces of this species by dusting lycopodium powder on glass across which the ants run.

different species (Brun, 1914; MacGregor, 1948), but also in the role of other sensory factors. Forel (1908), in his concept of *topochemical* sense, postulated a differential use of odor cues according to their spatial distribution among objects and over contours on the path.

One important factor that is differently combined with olfaction in some species, according to conditions, is a virtual orientation to the principal direction of illumination (Lubbock, 1887; Santschi, 1911). In Brun's (1914) "confinement experiment," a *Lasius niger* individual en route toward the nest would be shut under a small box for 2 (or 4) hr. When released, after some wandering, the ant usually set off on her former line with respect to the direction of sunlight, although this, of course, diverged by a specific angle from the path she was following when confined (Figure 61). In Santschi's (1911) "mirror experiment," direct sunlight was shut off from a *Tapinoma* or *Messor* trail by means of a screen, and a mirror was used to reflect the light on the ants from the opposite side. Laden ants typically reversed their direction of progress, but returned to the first direction when original conditions were restored.

In the *individual foragers,* orientation follows a pattern that differs qualitatively from the one described above. Huber (1810) discovered that trail-breaking tests did not disrupt the orientation of *Polyergus rufescens,* and Forel (1874) reported similar results for *Formica rufa,* suggesting that vision might be involved. However, Cornetz (1914) thought that an "unknown direction sense" must be implicated in cases where a transported ant proceeded directly toward the nest after wandering briefly—with vision excluded only on circumstantial grounds. Comparable results led Piéron (1904) to postulate a "muscular memory" as a general guide in orientation, and Szymanski (1911) a "sense of angles." Santschi (1911, 1923) and Brun (1914) proved many camponotine species capable of orienting with respect to the direction of illumination (i.e., after Santschi's light-compass pattern),[2] to prominent objects or to light-and-shadow patterns, and only occasionally to olfactory cues, as along an alley through grass or when close to the nest. Such ants do not follow trails as a rule, but pass individually in variable ways along ant "thoroughfares" or broad "areas of passage."

It is apparent that in different species of ants the potentialities for foraging and other activities outside the nest vary in relation to sensory physiology and underlying patterns of orientation (Brun, 1914; Rabaud, 1928; Icard, 1928; Schneirla, 1929). The chemical-trail pattern in olfaction-dominated species typically entails collective foraging, sometimes at con-

---

[2] Schifferer (unpub.; see von Frisch, 1950*b*) has found for *Lasius niger,* and Vowles (1950) for *Myrmica laevinodis* and *M. ruginodis,* that foragers can orient themselves according to the plane of polarization of light from the sky.

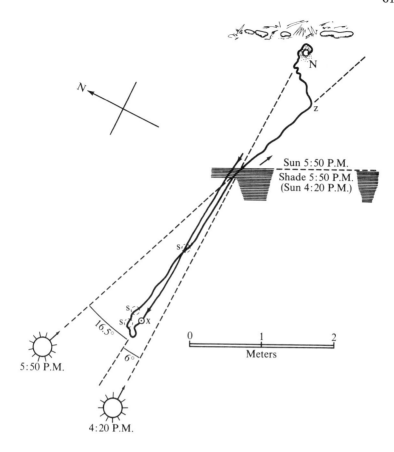

FIGURE 61

Brun's confinement test. At 4:20 P.M. a worker of *Lasius niger* that had been passing from the nest (N) on a course deviating about 6° to the north of the sun-line, was confined at X by a small box which shut out the light. At 5:50 P.M., when the box was removed, long shadows covered the area except for sun flecks at spots marked S and for the sunlit zone indicated near the nest. When released, the ant (after circling) moved variably on a line directly away from the light, except for brief indications (at the S spots) of orientation on a preconfinement basis. The latter tendency clearly appeared when the ant entered full sunlight near the nest, until her course was altered at Z (evidently by chemical tracks). (After Brun, 1914.)

siderable distances from the nest. The army ants, although held slavishly to chemical trails, through their nomadism are capable of a regular environmental expansion greater than that in any other social insect (Schneirla, 1938, 1949). On the other extreme we find camponotine species in which individual foraging is common, and in which each ant largely learns her own route (Schneirla, 1929, 1943). In such cases, the pattern of orientation is truly provisional in that it depends upon a learned relationship between organism and environment capable of further change as environmental conditions change. Although social insects such as ants and bees under simplified conditions are capable of rigid and primitively stereotyped orientation patterns of the kinesis or taxis type (Minnich, 1919; Hecht and Wolf, 1929), provisional orientation accounts for their characteristically enlarged and socially exploited environments.

ACTIVE INTERZONAL MOVEMENTS IN INSECTS

Varieties of Territorial Change

The effective environment of insects often varies greatly in space and time by virtue of interzonal movements. Characteristic shifts in environmental situation occur in many insects more or less through their own activities (Williams, 1930; Fraenkel, 1932c). Beyond excursions involved in the homing of hymenopterous insects, wanderings such as those of caterpillars in columns, which finally return to the nest, and the individual wanderings of others (e.g., some beetles), insect changes of abode through active movements are not uncommon. Sometimes this is accomplished individually, as by the mature caterpillar of the processionary moth, which in spring descends to the ground where chrysalis formation occurs beneath the surface (Bouvier, 1922); sometimes it is done en masse, as in the shifting of an established nest site by a colony of social insects (Arnold, 1914; Broekhuysen, 1948). In some ants (e.g., *Formica* spp.) a fixed nest site is usually changed only under great environmental pressure such as drought; in others (e.g., most doryline species) the colonies shift their locations readily and regularly.

Instances of exodus movements, in which some home site or a previous living area is vacated, have been reported in all the major groups, such as various flies, beetles, Lepidoptera, Odonata, and Hymenoptera (Fraenkel, 1932c). Often the relocations depend upon an initiating impulse introduced through individual growth, as in the habitat shifts of mature lepidopteran larvae, the flight of sexual forms in colonies of social insects (Wheeler, 1910b, 1928), and the springtime mass flights of freshly hatched dragonfly imagos (Fraenkel, 1932c). The swarming exodus-flight that leads to the foundation of new honey bee colonies is an outcome of characteristic biological changes within the parent hive, associated with congestion in the brood area (Demuth, 1921; Grout, 1947) and population conditions leading to the production of virgin queens (Rösch, 1925; Sendler, 1940; Kuwabara, 1948). Or the initiating condition may be essentially external, as it presumably is in wild colonies in Africa of *Apis dorsata* (Imms, 1931) and *A. mellifera,* which often move considerable distances evidently in response to seasonal desiccation and related nutritive conditions in the colonies (Vossler, 1905).

Many Odonata and Lepidoptera stage seasonal mass movements in given directions and over considerable distances (Fraenkel, 1932c; Williams, 1930, 1945). Many of these are conditioned by particular events in species biology, and depend largely upon the activities of the insects themselves. The springtime movements of imaginal *Libellula* and *Aeschna* dragonflies, for example, occur when a succession of warm days brings a mass maturation and emergence after a certain delay in development (Hill, 1911; Fraenkel, 1932c). In the eastern United States, butterflies typically move along the coastline, first westward from New England and then southward (Shannon, 1916), and comparable flights have been reported both for tropical and temperate zone species. The fact that, of eighteen recorded cases of such mass flights, fifteen have been against the wind, indicates that they involve a directionalized and active movement (Williams, Cockbill, and Gibbs, 1942).

The mass interzonal movements of locusts, which occur in every major nonpolar area of the world, present the additional complication of a bidirectional displacement occurring at different times of year. Typically there is a permanent breeding zone in which relatively sedentary *solitaria*-type individuals of the species are found continuously, and in which the *gregaria* form is produced when conditions of season (e.g., dryness, heat) and food are present. An important breeding ground in Africa is in reedy areas in the French Sudan. As Uvarov's phase theory explains (Faure, 1932; Imms, 1938; Key, 1950), a mass increase in the permanent zone is characterized by the appearance of *gregaria*-type individuals in large numbers. This type is migratory. In the African desert the *gregaria*-type nymphs begin to wander about 8 days after emergence.

As Fraenkel (1929, 1932c) describes their behavior, the locusts first wander in different directions, then become oriented in a common direction through mass pressure in particular. They assemble in sunny places, or move along and feed, mainly in dependence upon prevailing temperature. With many variations, a general direction of progress typically prevails, which Fraenkel (1932c) attributes to relatively constant external factors. For instance, the larvae of *Schistocerca gregaria* in the Trans-Jordan mountains are observed to move mainly eastward. Hoppers of the imago stage continue the movement in swarms, progressing more rapidly by flight. Although the directionalized movement itself is probably an outgrowth of pressure conditions existing in congested areas (Fraenkel, 1932c), reactions to the direction of sunlight are involved (K. Chapman, 1944), as well as optically controlled responses of other types, tactually controlled reactions to fellow hoppers in the band (J. S. Kennedy, 1954), and the directionalizing effects of topography and temperature (Pielou, 1948). Pressure of numbers from behind is evident, and separate bands often move variably. Waloff (1946) reports that, in the locust bands of eastern Africa, with some important exceptions, the major trends of migration are down the prevailing winds; however, old mature swarms tend to fly against the wind. In this way, grasshoppers native to the Sahara Desert move by stages in the spring and finally invade the plain of Algeria to the Mediterranean littoral. After the hoppers pass through various solitary generations in this general area, a southward movement ensues through which the permanent breeding areas in the Sahara are regained. Different generations appear to be involved in the northward journey of more than 1000 miles as well as in the southward journey, which occurs at intervals of a few years. It is probable that physiological changes associated with the metabolic constitution of the *gregaria* type and with sexual maturation are basically involved in the general susceptibility to environmental stimulation and the persistent movements of the *gregaria* phase (Faure, 1932; Imms, 1938; Chauvin, 1941; Key, 1950).

Many butterflies and diurnal moths are known to carry out long mass movements that are bidirectional, often under different seasonal conditions (Williams, 1930, 1945). Perhaps the best known case is that of the Monarch butterfly, *Danais plexippus,* which ranges (with color and pattern differences) through the length of the Americas (Williams, Cockbill, and Gibbs, 1942). This species has a northerly migratory race in North America, a southerly migratory race in South America, and a nonmigratory race in Central America. In the autumn this butterfly begins to mass in trees and shrubs, then broad collective movements start southward (in the northern hemisphere), along "flyways" which are not well known at present. Although the fall-migrant males contain mature sperm, the female is then reproductively immature. However, the spring migration, which is northward in the northern hemisphere, begins soon after eggs have begun to ripen in the ovaries of the female. Typically the butterflies move by day and rest in the vegetation at night. How a general direction is maintained during the several weeks of the autumnal southward flight and the springtime northward flight (i.e., in the northern hemisphere) is not specifically known. Visual effects (light direction, retinal stimulation by distant objects) and wind pressure are possible orienting factors (Williams, 1930). Although the role of visual factors during nighttime movements remains in doubt, a directed flight is possible as long as there is some extrinsic influence such as wind. It is interesting to note that the moths, which are largely nocturnal, do not carry out flights comparable to those of the diurnal Lepidoptera.

Among fifteen species of Lepidoptera known to migrate, there is good evidence for a return (i.e., oppositely directed) flight in ten of them. For instance, in India there are large flights of various lepidopteran species to the south in the late autumns and to the north in the early springs of many years, comparable to those carried out by the Monarch, Red Admiral, and others in North America. Others may have been overlooked through the fact that the northward flight typically involves fewer numbers more scattered in flight and less conspicuous, as in the Monarch and in many European species (Williams et al., 1942). The successive oppositely directed flights may be made mainly by individuals of different generations. It is interesting to note that, whereas the American species appear to increase their numbers in the north during the summer and decrease them in the south during the winter, the reverse is true in the European species.

However, cases of unidirectional mass movements by insects are not uncommon. Beebe (1949) has described seasonal flights of insects of every order and especially Lepidoptera moving in recurrent waves through Portachuelo Pass in Venezuela. The flights are southward only, away from feeding grounds and toward barren savannahs, with no evidence of any returns by the participants or their descendants. A common basis may be crowding through overpopulation in the areas of origin.

The Question of "Migration" in Insects

Although the adaptive significance of individual movements based upon growth changes is fairly evident, that of many of the mass displacements is not too clear. Before their biological significance can be understood, it will be necessary to gain a better comprehension of their character. Many of the mass departures (e.g., in dragonflies, locusts, and butterflies) evidently extend the species range, increase the complexity of the effective environment, and relieve local population pressures in various cases. Yet the specific relationship of the departing individuals to the permanent population in the regular species territory seldom is very clear.

Until the various forms of insect mass movements have been investigated adequately, inclusive theoretical conclusions as to the status of such movements must be regarded as tentative. Heape (1931) classified most collective insect movements as "emigrations" rather than migrations because he found them based upon "alimentary" factors rather than gametic (i.e., reproductive) processes, and because no "return at a later season" was believed to be involved. Thus, except for certain locusts and the Monarch butterfly, the term "migration" was restricted to the specific characteristics of the vertebrate pattern as represented in birds and fishes. However, insect movements must be understood in their own terms before their degree of resemblance to movements of other animals can be evaluated. Notwithstanding Heape's emphasis upon "alimentary factors," as Williams (1942) has pointed out, the mass movements of most butter-flies do not occur until an advanced adult stage when their feeding is near its end.

The movement of the doryline ants, which have long been regarded as nomadic (Wheeler, 1910b), is classified as "emigration" by both Heape (1931) and Fraenkel (1932c), mainly on the basis of Vosseler's (1905) premature conclusions that the nomadic movements of *Dorylus nigricans* colonies are initiated by food-exhaustion in a particular temporary nesting area. Yet, as a matter of fact, in the American dorylines and perhaps in the subfamily generally, the initiation of a series of nomadic movements in a colony actually depends upon ("trophallactic") stimulative effects from a large larval brood, the cessation of the series upon the enclosure of this brood in cocoons. This pattern of events, continuing throughout the year in dependence upon recurrent rhythmic changes in colony *reproductive processes*, involves corresponding *alternate changes* between two distinctively different ecological situations, the nesting sites of the "nomadic" and the "statary" activity phases (Schneirla, 1938, 1949). Thus it meets the commonly accepted criteria of "migration."

Whether or not the distinctive collective movements of insects conform more or less to the vertebrate pattern, most of them are regular and important features of behavior in their species and serve in some significant way to extend its environmental range of operations.

SUMMARY

Although parental or group behavior operates to specialize the habitat of progeny, properties of individual sensitivity and behavior influence the characteristic habitat. Temperature reactions are crucial for habitat in many insects. Both daily and seasonal changes in behavior routine and living situation frequently are closely related to extrinsic variations. Correspondence of environmental adjustments with metabolic condition and growth changes illustrates the role of organic processes underlying action in space and time.

Insects are not passive, situation-dominated creatures, but through their own properties and activities often modify their environments significantly. Factors of sensitivity and action influencing mode of food-taking often define individual or group environment sharply. Responses of parasitic or predatory insects depend upon numerous conditions, including habituation learning, that may serve to focalize response to host. In social insects, activities both outside and inside the nest may specialize the environment appreciably, as may group relationships ranging from toleration and mutual facilitation to competition.

Since capacities for mobility in space and time condition the life zone, orientation pattern is critical for physiology, ecology, and behavior study. Kühn's modification of Loeb's theory applies to phenomena of orientation ranging from generalized kinesis types to specialized taxis types. "Sign" is a useful concept for representing directionality of orientation. Specialized taxis patterns depend upon factors in receptor field and sensitivity, conduction, and response in the species. The predominance of visual as against nonvisual sensory capacities seems basic to many characteristic habitat differences. Many insects extend their life zones through processes such as chemical-trail formation, others through capacities for learning an orientation pattern according to prevalent conditions. Many insects carry out local or interzonal habitat changes as mass movements. Some of these occur irregularly, according to conditions such as food supply or population pressure; others more regularly, grounded in intraorganic processes resembling those considered prerequisite to vertebrate migration.

REFERENCES

Agrell, I. 1947b. Some experiments concerning thermal adjustment and respiratory metabolism in insects. *Arkiv. Zool.* 39: 1–48.

Allee, W. C., and E R. Stein. 1918. Light reactions and metabolism in may-fly nymphs. *J. Exp. Zool.* 26: 423–458.

Allee, W. C., A. E. Emerson, O. Park, T. Park, and K. P. Schmidt. 1949. *Principles of animal ecology.* Philadelphia: W. B. Saunders Co.

Alverdes, F. 1930. Tierpsychologische Analyse der intracentralen Vorgänge, welche bei decapoden Krebsen die locomotorischen Reaktionen auf Helligkeit und Dunkelheit bestimmen. *Z. Wiss. Zool.* 137: 403–475.

Armbruster, L. 1922a. Über den Wärmehaushalt im Bienenvolk. *Arch. Bienenkunde.* 4: 268–270.

Arnold, G. 1914. Nest-changing migrations of two species of ants. *Trans. Proc. Rhod. Sci. Assoc.* 13: 25–32.

Barrows, W. M. 1907. The reactions of the pomace fly, *Drosophila ampelophila* Loew, to odorous substances. *J. Exp. Zool.* 4: 515–537.

Baumberger, J. 1917. Hibernation: a periodical phenomenon. *Ann. Entomol. Soc. Am.* 10: 179–186.

Beebe, W. 1949. Insect migration at Rancho Grande in North-central Venezuela, general account. *Zoologica* 34: 107–110.

Bequaert, J. 1922. Ants in their diverse relations to the plant world. *Bull. Am. Mus. Nat. Hist.* 45: 333–583.

Bertholf, L. M. 1932. The extent of the spectrum for Drosophila and the distribution of stimulative efficiency in it. *Z. Vergleich. Physiol.* 18: 32–64.

Bethe, A. 1898. Dürfen wir den Ameisen und Bienen psychische Qualitäten zuschreiben? *Pflügers Arch. Ges. Physiol.* 70: 15–100.

Beusekom, G. van. 1948. Some experiments on the optical orientation in *Philanthus triangulum* fabr. *Behaviour* 1: 195–225.

Blum, H. F. 1935. An analysis of oriented movements of animals in light fields. *Cold. Spr. Harb. Symp. Quant. Biol.* 3: 210–223.

Bouvier. E. L. 1901. Les habitudes des bembex. *Année Psychol.* 7: 1–68.

Bouvier, E. L. 1922. *The psychic life of insects.* New York: Century.

Brandt, H. 1934. Eine Gewohnheitsbildung in der Bewegungsrichtung der Mehlmottenraupe *Ephestia kuehniella* Zeller. *Z. Vergleich. Physiol.* 21: 545–551.

Broekhuysen, G. J. 1948. The brown house ant. (*Pheidole megacephala,* Fabr.) *Union S. Africa Bull.* 266, Dept. Agr. Entomol. Ser. 7: 1–40.

Brown, C. R., and M. Hatch. 1929. Orientation and "fright" reactions of whirligig beetles (*Gyrinidae*) *J. Comp. Psychol.* 9: 159–189.

Brues, C. T. 1936. Aberrant feeding behavior among insects and its bearing on the development of specialized food habits. *Quart. Rev. Biol.* 11: 305–319.

Brues, C. T. 1946. *Insect diary.* Cambridge, Massachusetts: Harvard Univ. Press.

Brun, R. 1914. *Die Raumorientierung der Ameisen und das Orientierungsproblem in Allgemeinen.* Jena: Fischer.

Buddenbrock, W. von, 1917. Die Lichtompassoewegungen bei den Insekten, insbesondere den Schmetterlingsraupen. *Sitzber. Heidel. Akod. Wiss. Math.-Naturwiss. Klasse* 8B: 1–26.

Buddenbrock, W. von, and E. Shulz. 1933. Beiträge zur Kenntnis der Lichtom pass bewegung und der Adaptation des Insektenauges. *Zool. Jahrb. Zool. Physiol.* 52: 513–536.

Butler, C. G., E. Jeffree, and H. Kalmus. 1943. The behaviour of a population of honeybees on an artificial and on a natural crop. *J. Exp. Biol.* 20: 65–73.

Carthy, J. D. 1950. Odour trails of *Acanthomyops fuliginous. Nature* 166: 154–156.

Chapman, K. 1944. The role of light-compass orientation in migrating locusts. *J. Entomol. Soc. S. Africa* 7: 17–19.

Chapman, R. N. 1923. Observations on the life history of *Taphrocerus gracilis* (Say). (Beetle, family *Buprestidae*). *Cornell Univ. Agr. Exp. Sta. Mem.* 67: 3–13.

Chapman, R. N. 1931. *Animal ecology, with especial reference to insects.* New York: McGraw-Hill.

Chauvin, R. 1941. Contribution a l'étude physiologique du criquet pèrlerin et du déterminisme des phénomènes grégaires. *Ann. Soc. Entomol. France* 110: 133–272.

Chauvin, R. 1944–1945. Sur l' expérience de Bethe. *Anneé Psychol.*, pp. 148–155.

Chauvin, R. 1949b. Sur le préférendum thermique des insectes. I. Les techniques d'étude du thermopréférendum. *Physiol. Comp. et Oceol.* 1: 76–88.

Clausen, C. P. 1940. *Entomophagous insects.* New York: McGraw-Hill.

Cornetz, V. 1914. *Les explorations et les voyages des fourmis.* Paris: Flammarion.

Cott, H. B. 1940. *Adaptive coloration in animals.* London: Methuen.

Crozier, W. J. 1924. On stereotropism in *tenebrio* larvae. *J. Gen. Physiol.* 6: 531–540.

Demuth, G. S. 1921. Swarm control. *U.S. Dept. Agr. Farmers' Bull.* 1198.

Dethier, V. G. 1937. Gustation and olfaction in lepidopterous larvae. *Biol. Bull.* 72: 7–23.

Dethier, V. G. 1947a. *Chemical insect attractants and repellants.* Philadelphia: Blakiston.

Doflein, F. 1905. Beobachtungen an der Weberameisen (*Oecophylla smaragdina*) *Biol. Zentralbl.* 25: 497–507.

Dolley, W. L. 1916. Reactions to light in *vanessa antiopa*, with special reference to circus movements. *J. Exp. Zool.* 20: 357–420.

Dolley, W. L., and L. H. Golden. 1947. The effect of sex and age in the temperature at which reversal in reaction to light in *Eristalsis tenax* occurs. *Biol. Bull.* 92: 178–186.

Dolley, W. L., and J. L. Wierda. 1929. Relative sensitivity to light of different parts of the compound eye in *Eristalsis tenax. J. Exp. Zool.* 53: 129–140.

Dunham, W. 1931. Hive temperatures for each hour of the day. *Ohio J. Sci.* 31: 181–188.

Eidmann, H. 1942. Die Überwinterung der Ameisen. *Z. Morphol. U. Ökol. Tiere* 39: 217–275.

Eidmann, H. 1944. Zur Kenntnis der Ökologie von *Azteca muelleri* em. (Hym. Foricidae), ein beitrag zum Problem der Myrmecophyten. *Zool. Jahrb. System. Ökol. Geog.* 77: 1–48.

Elton, C. 1927. *Animal ecology.* London: Sidgwick and Jackson.

Emerson, A. E. 1938. Termite Nests—A study of the phylogeny of behavior. *Ecol. Monogr.* 8: 247–284.

Ewald, W. F. 1913. On artificial modification of light reactions and the influence of electrolytes on phototaxis. *J. Exp. Zool.* 13: 591–612.

Faure, J. C. 1932. The phases of Locusts in South Africa. *Bull. Entomol. Res.* 23: 293–405.

Ferton, C. 1905. Sur l'instinct des hyménoptéres melliferes et rauisseurs. *Ann. Soc. Entomol. France* 74: 56–104.

Flügge, C. 1934. Geruchliche Raumorientierung von *Drosophila melanogaster. Z. Vergleich. Physiol.* 20: 463–500.

Forel, A. 1874. Les fourmis de la Suisse. *Zurich, Nuv. Mem. Soc. Helvetica Sci. Nat.* 26: 1–452.

Forel, A. 1903. Nochmals Herr Dr. Bethe und die Insektenpsychologie. *Biol. Zentralbl.* 23: 1–3.

Forel, A. 1908. *The senses of insects.* (Translation) London. Methuen.

Forel, A. 1921–1923. *Le monde social des fourmis.* Genèva: Kundig.

Forel, A. 1929. *The Social World of Ants.* (2 vols., translated by C. K. Ogden) New York: Boni.

Fraenkel, G. 1929. Untersuchungen über Lebensgewohnheiten, Sinnesphysiologie und Sozialpsychologie der wandernden Larven der Afrikansichen Wanderheuschrecke *Schistocerca gregaria* (Forsk.). *Biol. Zentralbl.* 49: 657–680.

Fraenkel, G. 1930. Die Orientierung von *Schistocerca gragaria* zu strahlender Wärme. *Z. Vergleich. Physiol.* 13: 300–313.

Fraenkel, G. 1932c. Die Wanderungen der Insekten. *Ergeb. Biol.* 9: 1–238.

Fraenkel, G., and D. L. Gunn. 1940. *The orientation of animals.* Oxford: Clarendon Press.

Frisch, K. von. 1914. Der Farbensinn und Formensinn der Bienen. *Zool. Jaharb. Zool. Physiol.* 35: 1–182.

Frisch, K. von. 1920. Über die "Sprache" der Bienen. *Münch. Med. Wochenschr.* 67: 566–569.

Frisch, K. von. 1921. Über die "Sprache" der Bienen. *Munch. Med. Wochenschr.* 68: 509–511.

Frisch, K. von. 1922. Über die "Sprache" der Bienen. *Munch. Med. Wochenschr.* 69: 781–782.

Frisch, K. von. 1943. Versuche über die Lenkung des Bienenfluges durch Duftstoffe. *Naturwissenschaften* 31, 39: 445–460.

Frisch, K. von. 1948. *Aus dem Leben der Bienen,* 4th Ed. Wien: Springer-Verlag.

Frisch, K. von. 1950b. *Bees—Their vision, chemical senses and language.* Ithaca, New York: Cornell Univ. Press.

Garrey, W. E. 1918. Light and muscle tonus of insects, the Heliotropic mechanisms. *J. Gen. Physiol.* 1: 101–125.

Giersberg, H. 1928. Über den Morphologischen und Physiologischen Farbwechsel der Stabheuschrecke *Dixippus* (*Carausius*) *morosus. Z. Vergleich. Physiol.* 7: 657–695.

Gösswald, K. 1942. Rassenstudien an der roten Waldameise *Formica rufa* L. auf Systematischer Ökologischer, Physiologischer und Biologischer Grundlage. *Z. Angew. Entomol.* 28: 62–124.

Göetz, B. 1936. Beiträge zur Analyse des Verhaltens von Schmetterlingsraupen beim Aufsuchen des Futters und des Verpuppungsplatzes. *Z. Vergleich. Physiol.* 23: 429–503.

Gregg, R. E. 1947. Altitudinal indicators among the formicidae. *Univ. Colorado Studies, Ser. D,* 2: 385–403.

Grout, R. A. 1949. *The hive and the honey-bee.* Hamilton, Illinois: Dadant and Sons.

Gunn, D. L. 1934. The temperature and humidity relations of the cockroach (*Blatta orientalis*) *Z. Vergleich. Physiol.* 20: 617–625.

Gunn, D. L. 1937. The humidity reactions of the wood louse, *Porcellio scaber* (Latreille). *J. Exp. Biol.* 14: 178–186.

Hartung, E. 1935. Untersuchungen über die Geruchsorientierung bei *Calliphora erythrocephala. Z. Vergleich. Physiol.* 22: 119–144.

Haskins, C. P. 1939. *Of ants and men.* New York: Prentice-Hall.

Headley, A. E. 1943. Population studies of two species of ants, *Leptothorax longispinosus* Roger and *Leptothorax curvispinosus* Mayr. *Ann. Entomol. Soc. Am.* 36: 743–755.

Heape, W. 1931. *Migration and nomadism.* Cambridge: Heffer.

Hecht, S., and E. Wolf. 1929. The visual acuity of the honey bee. *J. Gen. Physiol.* 12: 727–760.

Herms, W. B. 1911. The photic reactions of sarcophagid flies, especially *Lucilia caesar* linn and *Calliphora vomitoria* linn. *J. Exp. Zool.* 10: 167–226.

Herter, K. 1924. Temperaturoptimum und relative Luftfeuchtigkeit bei *Formica rufa* L. *Z. Vergleich. Physiol.* 2: 226–232.

Herter, K. 1934. Ein verbesserte Temperaturogel und ihre Anwendung auf Insekten und Säugetiere. *Biol. Zentralbl.* 54: 487–507.

Hess, W. 1924. Reactions to light in the earthworm, *Lumbricus terrestris* L. *J. Morphol. Physiol.* 39: 515–542.

Hewitt, C. G. 1917. Insect behaviour as a factor in applied entomology. *J. Econ. Entomol.* 10: 81–84.

Heymons, R., and H. von Lengerken. 1929. Biologische Untersuchungen an Copruphagen Lamellicorniern. *Z. Morphol. u. Ökol. Tiere* 14: 531–613.

Hill, M. D. 1911. Migrations of dragon flies (Odonata) and of ants (Hymen). *Entom. News.* 22: 419–421.

Hingston, R. W. G. 1929. *Instinct and intelligence.* New York: Macmillan.

Holmes, S. J. 1905. The selection of random movements as a factor of phototaxis. *J. Comp. Neurol.* 15: 98–112.

Holmes, S. J., and K. W. McGraw. 1913. Some experiments on the method of orientation to light. *J. Anim. Behav.* 3: 367–373.

Homp, R. 1938. Wärmeorientierung von *Pediculus vestimenti*. *Z. Vergleich. Physiol.* 26: 1–34.

Honjo, I. 1937. Beiträge zur Lichtkom passbewegung der Insekten, insbesondere in bezug auf zweig Lichtquellen. *Zool. Jahrb. Zool. Physiol.* 57: 375–416.

Honvanitz, W. 1948. Differences in the field activity of two female color phases of *Colias* butterflies at various times of the day. *Contr. Lab. Vert. Biol. Univ. Michigan* 41: 1–37.

Huber, P. 1810. *Recherches sur les moeurs des fourmis indigenes.* Paris: Paschoud.

Hundertmark, A. 1936. Helligkeits und Farbenunterscheidungsvermögen der Eiraupen der Nonne (*Lymantria monacha* L.) *Z. Vergleich. Physiol.* 24: 42–57.

Hundertmark, A. 1937. Das Formenunterscheidungsvermögen der Eiraupen der Nonne (*Lymantria monarcha* L.) *Z. Vergleich. Physiol.* 24: 563–582.

Icard, S. 1928. Comment une Fourmi partant en exploratice ou allant seule son orientation vers le nid? *Comp. Rend. Soc. Biol.* 99: 1802–1804.

Icard, S. 1928. C'est la lumière solaire qui permet a la Fourmi isolée de retrouver son orientation vers le nid. *Comp. Rend. Soc. Biol.* 99: 2011–2014.

Imms, A. D. 1931. *Social behavior in insects.* New York: Dial Press.

Imms, A. D. 1938. *Recent advances in entomology.* Philadelphia: Blakiston.

Imms, A. D. 1947. *Insect natural history.* London: William Collins Sons.

Jackson, H. H. 1910. The control of phototactic reactions in *Hyalella* by chemicals. *J. Comp. Neurol.* 20: 259–263.

Kalmus, H. 1937a. Photohorotaxis, ein neue Reaktionsart gefunden an der Eilarven von Dixippus. *Z. Vergleich. Physiol.* 24: 644–655.

Kalmus, H. 1937b. Voreversuche über die Orientierung der Biene im Stock. *Z. Vergleich. Physiol.* 24: 166–187.

Karawajew, W. 1926. Über den Nestbau von *Polyrhachis* (Subg. *Myrmhopla*) *tubifes* sp. N. (Fam. *Formicidae*). *Biol. Zentralbl.* 46: 143–145.

Kennedy, C. N. 1927. Some non-nervous factors that condition the sensitivity of insects to moisture, temperature, light and odors. *Ann. Entomol. Soc. Am.* 20: 87–106.

Kennedy, J. S. 1939. The visual responses of flying mosquitoes. *Proc. Zool. Soc. London, Ser. A,* 109: 221–242.

Kennedy, J. S. 1945. Observations on the mass migration of desert locust hoppers. *Trans. Roy. Entomol. Soc. London* 95: 247–262.

Key, H. L. 1950. A critique on the phase theory of locusts. *Quart. Rev. Biol.* 25: 363–407.

Krogh, A. 1914. The Quantitative relation between temperature and standard metabolism in animals. *Internat. Z. Physik. Chem. Biol.* 1: 491–508.

Kühn, A. 1919. *Die Orientierung der Tiere im Raum.* Jena: Fischer.

Kuwabara, M. 1948. Über die Regulation im Weisellosen Volke der Honigbiene (*Apis mellifica*) besonders die Bestimmung des neuen Weisels. *J. Faculty Sci. Hokkaido Univ.,* Ser. VI, 9: 359–381.

Loeb, J. 1918. *Forced movements, tropism, and animal conduct.* Philadelphia: J. B. Lippincott Company.

Lüdtke, H. 1938. Die Bedeutung Waagerecht 1 iegender Augenteile fur die Photomenotaktische Orientierung des Rückenschwimmers. *Z. Vergleich. Physiol.* 26: 162–199.

Lutz, F. E. 1924. Apparently non-selective characters and combination of characters including a study of ultraviolet in relation to the flower visiting habits of insects. *Ann. N.Y. Acad. Sci.* 29: 181–183.

MacBride, E. W. 1934. The inheritance of acquired habits. *Nature* 133: 598–599.

MacGregor, E. G. 1948. Odour as a basis for orientated movement in ants. *Behaviour* 1: 267–296.

Maidl, F. 1934. *Die Lebensgewohnheiten und Instinkte der Staatenbildenden Insekten.* Wien: F. Wagner.

Maier, N. R. F., and T. C. Schneirla. 1935. *Principles of animal psychology.* New York: McGraw-Hill.

Mast, S. O. 1911. *Light and the behavior of organisms.* New York: Wiley.

Mast, S. O. 1923. Photic orientation in insects with special reference to the drone-fly, *Eristalis tenax,* and the robber-fly, *Erax rufibarbis. J. Exp. Zool.* 38: 109–205.

McDougall, W. 1923. *Outline of psychology.* New York: Charles Scribner's Sons.

McEwen, R. S. 1918. The reactions to light and to gravity in Drosophila and its mutants. *J. Exp. Zool.* 25: 49–106.

Michener, C. D. 1942. The history and behavior of a colony of harvester ants. *Sci. Monthly* 55: 248–258.

Minderhoud, A. 1931. Untersuchungen über das Betragen der Honigbiene als Blutenbestauberin. *Gartenbauwissenschaft* 48: 342–462.

Minnich, D. E. 1919. Photic reactions of the honey-bee, *Apis mellifera* L. *J. Exp. Zool.* 29: 343–425.

Morley, B. D. W. 1944. A study of the ant fauna of a garden, 1934–42. *J. Anim. Ecol.* 13: 123–127.

Morley, B. D. W. 1946. The interspecific relations of ants. *J. Anim. Ecol.* 15: 150–154.

Murr, L. 1930. Über den Geruchsinn der Mehlmottenschlupfwespe *Habrobracon Juglandis Ashmead.* Zugleich ein Beitrag zum Orientierungs-Problem. *Z. Vergleich. Physiol.* 11: 210–270.

Nieschulz, O. 1934. Über die Vorzugstemperatur von *Stomoxys calcitrans.* *Z. Angew. Entomol.* 21: 224–238.

Otto, E. 1949. Untersuchungen zur Frage der geruchlichen Orientierung bei Insekten. *Zool. Jahrb. Zool. Physiol.* 62: 65–92.

Phipps, C. 1915. An experimental study of the behavior of amphipods with respect to light intensity, direction of rays and metabolism. *Biol. Bull.* 28: 210–223.

Picard, F. 1921. Le determinisme de la ponte chez un hyménoptère térébrant, le *Pimpla insigator* L. *Comp. Rend. Acad. Sci. Paris* 172: 1617–1619.

Pickles, W. 1936. Populations and territories of the ants, *Formica fusca, Acanthomyops elavus,* and *Myrmica rugenodis,* at Thornhill (Yorks). *J. Anim. Ecol.* 5: 262–270.

Pickles, W. 1937. Populations, territories and biomasses of ants at Thornhill, Yorkshire, in 1936. *J. Anim. Ecol.* 6: 54–61.

Pickles, W. 1944. Territories and interrelations of the two ants of the genus *Messor* in Algeria. *J. Anim. Ecol.* 13: 128–129.

Pictet, A. 1911. Un nouvel exemple de l'hérédité des caractères acquis. *Arch. Sci. Phys. et Nat.* 31: 561–564.

Pielou, D. P. 1948. Observations on the behaviour of gregarious hoppers of the red locust, *Nomadacris septemfasciata* Serville. *Proc. Roy. Entomol. Soc. London* 23: 19–27.

Piéron, H. 1904. Du rôle du sens musculaire dans l'orientation de quelques espèces de fourmis. *Bull. Inst. Gén. Psychol.* 4: 168–186.

Rabaud, É. 1919. L'immobilisation réflexe et l'activité normales des arthropods. *Bull. Biol.* 53: 1–149.

Rabaud, É. 1922. L'instinct. *Ann. Soc. Roy. Zool. Belg.* 53: 94–126.

Rabaud, É. 1928. *How animals find their way about.* New York: Harcourt, Brace.

Rau, P. 1929. Experimental studies in the homing of carpenter and mining bees. *J. Comp. Psychol.* 9: 35–70.

Rau, P. 1931. Additional experiments on the homing of carpenter- and mining-bees. *J. Comp. Psychol.* 12: 257–261.

Rau, P. 1945. The yucca plant, *yucca filamentosa* and the yucca moth, *Tegeticula (Pronura) yuccasella* Riley—an ecologico—behavior study. *Ann. Missouri Botan. Garden* 32: 373–394.

Rayment, T. 1935. *A cluster of bees.* Sydney: Endeavour Press.

Riley, C. V. 1888. The larger digger-wasp. *Inst. Life, U.S. Div. Entomol.* 4: 248–252.

Riley, C. V. 1892. The yucca moth and yucca pollination. *Third Ann. Rept.,* *Missouri Botan. Garden* 99–158.

Robertson, F. W. 1944. The removal of insect pests from stored products by means of behaviour stimuli. *Bull. Entomol. Res.* 35: 215–217.

Roeder, K. D. 1937. The control of tonus and locomotor activity in the praying mantis (*Mantis religiosa* L.) *J. Exp. Zool.* 76: 353–374.

Roeder, K. D., ed. 1953. Insect physiology. New York: Wiley.

Rösch, G. A. 1925. Untersuchungen über die Arbeitsteilung im Bienenstaat. *Z. Vergleich. Physiol.* 2: 571–631.

Rose, M. 1929. *La question des tropismes.* Paris: Les Presses Université de France.

Roubaud, E. 1922. Etudes sur le sommeil d'hiver pré-imaginal des muscides. Les cycles d'asthénie et l'athermobiose réactivante spécifique. *Bull. Sci. France et Belgique* 56: 455–544.

Salt, G. 1935. Experimental studies in insect parasitism. *Proc. Roy. Soc. London, Ser. B,* 117: 413–435.

Salt, G. 1937b. Sense in host selection, *Trichogramma* (Hymenoptera). *Proc. Roy. Soc. London, Ser. B,* 122: 57–75.

Sanderson, E. D. 1908. The relation of temperature to the hibernation of insects. *J. Econ. Entomol.* 1: 56–65.

Santschi, F. 1911. Observations et remarques critiques sur le mécanisme de l'orientation chez les fourmis. *Rev. Suisse. Zool.* 19: 303–338.

Santschi, F. 1923. Les différentes orientations chez leo fourmis. *Rev. Zool. Africa* 11: 10–144.

Schaller, A. 1926. Sinnesphysiologische und Psychologische Untersuchungen an Wasserkäfern und Fischen. *Z. Vergleich. Physiol.* 4: 370–464.

Schneirla, T. C. 1929. Learning and orientation in ants. *Comp. Psychol. Monogr.* 6: 1–143.

Schneirla, T. C. 1938. A theory of army ant behavior based upon the analysis of activities in a representative species. *J. Comp. Psychol.* 25: 51–90.

Schneirla, T. C. 1941. Social organization in insects as related to individual function. *Psychol. Rev.* 48: 465–486.

Schneirla, T. C. 1943. The nature of ant learning. II. The intermediate stage of segmental maze adjustment. *J. Comp. Psychol.* 35: 149–176.

Schneirla, T. C. 1949. Army-ant life and behavior under dry-season conditions. 3. The course of reproduction and colony behavior. *Bull. Am. Mus. Nat. Hist.* 94: 1–81.

Schwarz, F. F. 1931. The next habits of the diplopterous wasp *Polybia occipentalis* variety *scutellaris* (white) as observed at Barro Colorado, Canal Zone. *Am. Mus. Novitates* 471: 1–27.

Sendler, O. 1940. Vorgänge zus Bienenleben vom Standpunte der Entwicklungsphysiologie. *Z. Wiss. Zool.* 153: 39–82.

Shannon, H. J. 1916. Insect migrations as related to those of birds. *Sci. Monthly* 3: 227–240.

Shelford, V. E. 1914. Modification of the behavior of land animals by contact with air of high evaporating power. *J. Anim. Behav.* 4: 31–49.

Steiner, A. 1930. Die Temperaturregulierung im Nest der Feldwespe (*Polistes Gallica biglumis* L.) *Z. Vergleich. Physiol.* 11: 461–502.

Stephenson, E. M., and C. Stewart. 1946. *Animal camouflage.* New York: Penguin Books.

Szymanski, J. S. 1911. Ein Versuch, das Verhältens zwischen modal Verschiedenen Reizen in Zahlen auszudrücken. *Pflügers Arch. Ges. Physiol.* 138: 457–486.

Szymanski, J. S. 1914. Eine Methode zur Untersuchung der Ruheund Aktivitätsperioden bei Tieren. *Pflügers Arch. Ges. Physiol.* 158: 343–385.

Talbot, M. 1934. Distribution of ant species in the Chicago region with reference to ecological factors and physiological toleration. *Ecology* 15: 416–439.

Talbot, M. 1943. Population studies of the ant, *Prenolepis imparis* Say. *Ecology* 24: 31–44.

Talbot, M. 1943. Response of the ant *Prenolepis imparis* Say to temperature and humidity changes. *Ecology* 24: 345–352.

Talbot, M. 1948. A comparison of two ants of the genus *Formica. Ecology* 29: 316–325.

Talbot, M., and C. H. Kennedy. 1940. The slave-making ant, *Formica sanguinea subintegra* Emery, its raids, nuptual fights and nest structure. *Entomol. Soc. Am.* 33: 560–577.

Thomsen, E., and M. Thomsen. 1937. Über das Thermopräferendum der Larven einiger Fliegenarten. *Z. Vergleich. Physiol.* 24: 343–380.

Thorpe, W. H. 1939. Further experiments on olfactory conditioning in a parasitic insect. The nature of the conditioning process. *Proc. Roy. Soc. London, Ser. B,* 126: 390–397.

Thorpe, W. H. 1939. Further studies on pre-imaginal olfactory conditioning. *Proc. Roy. Soc. London, Ser. B,* 127: 424–433.

Thorpe, W. H. 1946. Animal learning and evolution. *Nature* 156: 46.

Thorpe, W. H., A. C. Crombie, R. Hill, and J. H. Darrah. 1947. The behavior of wireworms in response to chemical stimulation. *J. Exp. Biol.* 23: 234–266.

Thorpe, W. H., and F. G. Jones. 1937. Olfactory conditioning in a parasitic insect and its relation to the problem of host selection. *Proc. Roy. Soc. London, Ser. B,* 124: 56–81.

Tinbergen, N. 1932. Über die Orientierung des Bienenwolfes (*Philanthus triangulum* Fabr.) *Z. Vergleich. Physiol.* 16: 305–334.

Totze, R. 1933. Beiträgezur Sinnesphysiologie der Zecken. *Z. Vergleich. Physiol.* 19: 110–161.

Verschaffelt, E. 1910. The cause determining the selection of food in some herbivorous insects. *Proc. Acad. Sci. Amsterdam* 13: 536–542.

Viaud, G. 1948. *Le phototropisme animal.* Paris: Librarie Vrin.

Vosseler, J. 1905. Die Ostafrikanische Treiberameise. *Pflanzer* 1: 289–302.

Waloff, Z. 1946. Seasonal breeding and migrations of the desert locusts (*Schistocerca gregaria forskål*) in Eastern Africa. *Anti-Locust Mem.* London, no. 1, pp. 1–74.

Warnke, G. 1931. Experimentelle Untersuchungen über den Geruchssinn von

Geotrupes silvaticus panz. und *Geotrupes vernalis* Lin. Zugleich ein Beitrag zum Problem der Orientierung der Tiere im Raum. *Z. Vergleich. Physiol.* 14: 121–199.

Wasmann, F. 1901. Zum Orientierungsvermögen der Ameisen. *Allgem. Z. Entomol.* 6: 19–21.

Wasmann, E. 1901. Zum Orientierungsvermögen der Ameisen. *Allgem. Z. Entomol.* 6: 41–43.

Weber, H. 1929. Biologische Untersuchungen an der Schweinelaus (*Haematopinus suis* L.) unter besonderer Berücksichtigung der Sinnesphysiologie. *Z. Vergleich. Physiol.* 9: 564–612.

Weber, N. A. 1943. Notes and comments parabiosis in neotropical "ant gardens." *Ecology* 24: 400–404.

Weyrauch, W. K. 1929. Sinnesphysiologische Studie an der Imago von *Forficula auricularia* L. auf Ökologischer Grundlage. *Z. Vergleich. Physiol.* 10: 665–687.

Weyrauch, W. K. 1935. Untersuchungen und Gedanken zur Orientierung der Arthropoden die Üblichsten Wege, auf denen die Tiere ihre. Umgebung durchsuchen. 8. Teil. *Zool. Jahrb. Zool. Physiol.* 66: 401–424.

Wheeler, W. M. 1899. Anemotropism and other tropisms in insects. *Arch. Entwicklungsmech. Organ.* 8: 373–381.

Wheeler, W. M. 1910b. *Ants, their structure, development, and behavior.* New York: Columbia Univ. Press.

Wheeler, W. M. 1921. A new case of parabiosis and the "ant gardens" of British Guiana. *Ecology* 2: 89–103.

Wheeler, W. M. 1928. *The social insects.* New York: Harcourt, Brace.

Wheeler, W. M. 1930. *Demons of the dust.* New York: W. W. Norton.

Wigglesworth, V. B. 1939. *The principles of insect physiology.* New York: E. P. Dutton.

Williams, C. B. 1930. *The migration of butterflies.* London: Oliver and Boyd.

Williams, C. B. 1936. The influence of moonlight on the activity of certain nocturnal insects, particularly of the family *Noctuidae*, as indicated by a light trap. *Trans. Roy. Soc. London, Ser. B,* 226: 357–389.

Williams, C. B. 1942. The migration of butterflies. *Proc. Linn. Soc. London,* 154th Sess., pp. 86–87.

Williams, C. B. 1945. Evidence for the migration of Lepidoptera in South America. *Rev. Entomol.* 16: 113–131.

Williams, C. B., G. F. Cockbill, and M. E. Gibbs. 1942. Studies in the migration of Lepidoptera. *Trans. Roy. Entomol. Soc. London* 92: 1–283.

Wladimirow, M., and E. Smirnov. 1934. Über das Verhalten der Schlupfwespe *Mormoniella vitripennis* wlk. zu Verschiedenen Fliegenarten. *Zool. Anz.* 107: 85–89.

Wodsedalek, J. E. 1911. Phototactic reactions and their reversal in the may-fly nymphs *Heptagenia interpunctata* (Say). *Biol. Bull.* 21: 265–271.

Wolf, E. 1927. Über das Heimkehrvermogen der Bienen (Zweite mitteilung) *Z. Vergleich Physiol.* 6: 221–254.

Wolf, E. 1930. The homing behavior of bees. *J. Soc. Psychol.* 1: 300–310.

Zeigler, H. E. 1910. *Der Begriff des Instinktes Einst und Jertzt.* Jena: Fischer.

T. C. SCHNEIRLA

Modifiability in Insect Behavior

Bibliography No. 63

Notwithstanding its characteristic stereotypy, insect behavior is frequently subject to change. In the two preceding chapters some of the basic processes in changing behavior have been considered, including those related to organic changes of a relatively fluctuant nature (e.g., to sensory adaptation), of a more lasting nature (e.g., changes attributable to sexual maturity), or those induced primarily through changes in surrounding conditions (e.g., diurnal and seasonal changes). A type of plasticity observed in the control of locomotion under changed organic conditions, and essentially based upon the properties of the central nervous system, is discussed in [Roeder, 1953] Chap. 18. When an environmental change impairs the effectiveness of a behavior process, some species of insects are able to adjust to the change within the scope of their available organic capacities, others must adjust on a long-term evolutionary basis through natural selection, and still others can meet the new conditions through a learned modification of behavior (Uvarov, 1932). Insects differ considerably in the characteristic way in which learning figures in their lives.

PATTERNS OF INSECT LEARNING

Habituation Learning

Learning typically involves a more or less persistent change in the individual behavior pattern through the effects of experience upon the organism, retained in the central nervous system particularly. Since a theoretical consideration of the question is not feasible here, we shall discuss learning mainly in terms of the outstanding patterns found among insects.

Most generalized in its form is what may be termed *habituation learning,* or a conformity to a new situation through generalized adjustments often involving the inhibition of initial avoidance or "shock" responses.

From *Insect Physiology,* edited by K. Roeder. New York: John Wiley and Sons, 1953. Chap. 27. Reprinted with permission.

Examples are the "taming" of ants (Fielde, 1901; Turner, 1907), wasps (Shafer, 1948), and cockroaches (Turner, 1913) so that they remain undisturbed under new conditions, and, incidentally may be handled without becoming agitated. In the maze learning of ants, an initial stage is discernible in which the subject learns to be active in the situation without eccentric and disturbed responses, a simple and nonspecific behavior change (Schneirla, 1941).

Such cases of learning, although not precise in stimulus control or in the nature of the response, seem understandable as simple conditioning processes. They involve the inhibition of initial shock responses upon encountering a situation, and the acquisition of an ability to remain without disturbance and to be active under general stimulation from the situation. Habituation, as learned behavior, must be distinguished from instances in which peripheral changes alone are accountable for changes in activity, such as an adaptation to light underlying a modified orientation in *Ranatra* (Holmes, 1905).

Conditioned Responses

Adaptation of insects to a new situation often involves sensory-motor adjustments qualitatively similar to the conditioned-response learning first described by Pavlov for mammals. In essence, a previously ineffective stimulus comes to elicit a particular response through having appeared repeatedly together with an initially effective stimulus. As Uvarov (1932) suggested, it is probable that many forms of insect behavior formerly regarded as unlearned actually are conditioned, at least in part. Here the nature and relationships of stimuli and responses are more specific than in cases of general habituation. At times such learning may be rather generalized and in that respect similar to habituation learning. In social insects, for example, conditioning may be an important factor in the assimilation of young individuals. The suggestion is that, in early socialization, a young individual becomes conditioned to approach and make contact with any worker bearing the composite chemical always present during early feeding experiences. The original (unconditioned) stimulus here would be tactual effects adequate to elicit initial feeding reflexes (cf. Heyde, 1924). Experiments with artificially mixed colonies containing ants of different species (Fielde, 1903, 1904; Morley, 1942) suggest that such a condition may be effective to an appreciable extent for a composite odor first encountered by individuals in the callow stage. Results on larval conditioning indicate a distinct possibility that this process in social insects normally begins in the stage of larval feeding. A generalized type of conditioning also is apparently involved in cases such as the "preimaginal learning" reported by Thorpe and Jones (1937). In these experiments, the adult oviposition responses of a parasitic insect were conditioned to an abnormal host through feeding larvae upon this host rather than the normal one. Such instances seem to be transitional between habituation learning and conditioning proper, in that a generalized response (excitement) rather than a specific one has become conditioned to a given stimulus; that is, in such cases the response given to the conditioned stimulus is not specific to training, but is that most available in the insect aroused by the conditioned stimulus. In cases such as Wodsedalek's (1912) training mayfly nymphs to appear in response to a mechanical stimulus which had accompanied feeding, the response is alike in training and performance; hence the learning approximates conditioning more closely.

Varied instances have been reported in which insect learning resembles conditioned-response training in one or more important respects. In the honey bee, Frings (1944) conditioned the simple reaction of proboscis extension by combining the odor of coumarin with feeding on sugar water, von Frisch (1943) conditioned the complex response of foraging to the specific odor of blossoms placed near the sugar-water dish, and Hertz (1933) conditioned bees to take water by going to moist air. Feeding responses to chemical stimuli were conditioned in caterpillars of the milkweed butterfly, *Danais plexippus,* by Mayer and Soule (1906), the shock response of butterflies to handling was conditioned to a sound by Turner (1914), and a conditioned acceptance of meat containing quinine was established in the water beetle *Dytiscus* by Schaller (1926). Borrell du Vernay (1942) found that individuals in either larval or adult stages of the flourbeetle, *Tenebrio molitor,* could be conditioned (typically within 40–60 trials) to avoid a rough or smooth surface, whichever was paired with an electric shock.

Both the stability and the duration of a conditioned response in insects may depend upon what basic (essentially unlearned) reaction tendency this response may oppose. Thus Zerrahn (1933) found that bees could be trained to alight upon figures presented together with food only when the positive figure was greater in articulation or in contour length than the negative figure; otherwise a spontaneous responsiveness to greater visual change proved dominant. The avoidance of light by cockroaches cannot be broken down in a very lasting way through conditioning, as Szymanski (1912) and Eldering (1919) found. In Szymanski's experiment, the roach received a shock each time it ran into the darkened part of a long box, and after a series of trials (from 16 to 118 in different cases) would stop excitedly on the light-dark border and turn back into the light. In one animal this response lasted 1 hr; however, in all instances the conditioned response either failed or was very unstable on subsequent days until further retraining was given.

The stimulative feature to which an insect is conditioned in a given situation may depend upon the relative prominence of the various environmental characteristics. Verlaine (1924) found that, although wasps (*Vespa vulgaris*) ordinarily locate their nests through specific visual cues, olfactory stimuli may be used when these are outstanding in the situation. After von Frisch (1920) had trained honey bees to get sugar water from a blue box scented with tuberose, in test trials a tuberose-scented gray box was entered 146 times against 81 responses to an unscented blue box, indicating that the olfactory stimulus had been dominant in the training. However, in a retest 5 days later, the blue box was entered far more frequently than the scented gray box, suggesting that the initial predominance had somehow changed.

"Temporal Memory"

An interesting type of learned variation in behavior resembling conditioned responses, called temporal memory by the investigators, has been demonstrated in various social insects. When honey bees are always given sugar water at the same time of day, they continue to visit the feeding place and under propitious conditions may continue their visits for 6 days or longer even after food is no longer present (Beling, 1929). Typical results are shown in Figure 62. By presenting food appropriately at two different feeding places, it is possible to train the same bees to visit each in a different daily rhythm (Wahl, 1932; Lutz, 1934; Stein-Beling, 1935), and as many as five different rhythms may be established at a time. Comparable foraging rhythms have been demonstrated in experiments with ants, bees, and termites (Grabensberger, 1933, 1934). Somehow the learning depends upon the 24-hr daily interval, since attempts to train 48-hr rhythms in honey bees have been ineffective.

The temporal memory of bees appears to be based upon internal stimulative processes, from the fact that the results are apparent under darkroom conditions. For instance, learned foraging rhythms were exhibited by bees in tests at the bottom of a deep mine shaft (Wahl, 1932). The role of organic stimuli is suggested by the fact that low temperatures (2–7° C) act to delay the feeding visits, although etherizing the trained honey bees for several hours prior to the critical response time had no appreciable effect (Kalmus, 1934). A dependence of the habit upon visceral stimulation is more directly indicated by experiments upon ants and termites in which the feeding visits were delayed beyond the critical training time by drugs such as euchinine, which lower metabolic rate (Figure 63), whereas the visits were earlier than the training time with drugs such as salicylic acid, which speed up metabolism (Grabensberger, 1933, 1934).

Evidence favors the view that stimulative effects from organic rhythms

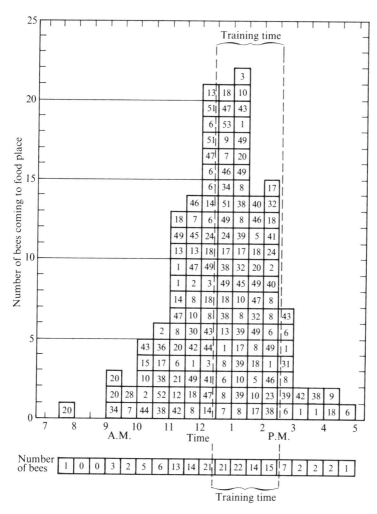

FIGURE 62

Results in normal "temporal memory" experiments with honey bees trained to visit a food place during the period 12:30–2:30 P.M., then tested. Numbers represent different marked bees trained and tested. (Of 40 bees marked during the training period, 32 appeared in the test represented here.) (After Beling, 1929.)

may be conditioned to specific time intervals used in training. From the fact that many flowers (e.g., chicory, buckwheat) exhibit diurnal rhythms in their pollen production and nectar secretion, the biological significance of such learning by insects is evident. Lutz (1934) succeeded in training the same bees to visit a different color at each of two different times,

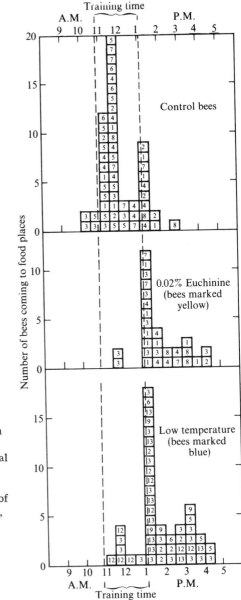

FIGURE 63
Variations in "temporal memory" in the honey bee in dependence upon physiological condition. Top. Normal results with untreated bees. Below. Results in further experiments with the same bees under two conditions of retarded metabolism. (After Kalmus, 1934.)

respectively, and suggested that in a comparable manner their visits become differentially conditioned to buckwheat and other plants that secrete nectar at different times of day. By keeping a record of the daily visits of honey bees to the different flowers of a given area, Kleber (1935) found that a fairly exact concurrence exists between secretion and frequency of visits. Not only does the greatest number of visits come when the *quantity* of secretion is at its height, but also the time of maximal *quality* of secretion is even more effective.

Discrimination Habits in Insects

It will be recalled ([see Roeder, 1953] Chap. 19, 21, and 25) that insects are capable of many types of sensory differentiation on a reflex basis. For example, the nymph of the dragonfly *Aeschna cyanea* in response to moving objects that are approximately fly-size, normally fixates at 10 cm and snaps at 10 mm, but one-eyed specimens snap at a greater distance (Baldus, 1926). The compelling effectiveness of visible movement for eliciting the snapping reactions of *Odonata* (Sälzle, 1932; Gaffron, 1934) and other unlearned reactions of insects (Plateau, 1888; Autrum, 1949) is well known. Less known is the role of learning in the modification of such reactions and the setting up of new differential reactions to stimulative differences.

Studies of color vision in insects offer enlightening examples of the way that differential training to stimulus differences may be used to explore the properties of an insect's sensitivity. Von Hess (1920), mainly from tests with the "method of preference" in which free responses to a stimulus series were recorded, concluded that the honey bee must be color blind. His principal argument was that the relative stimulative effectiveness of various spectral regions for the bee resembles that of color-blind human individuals. By means of training methods, however, von Frisch (1914) demonstrated a differential wavelength sensitivity in the honey bee, very useful in foraging. In a series of colored squares containing various hues and grays of different brightnesses, one particular "hue" would be accompanied by sugar water in the training period, or the training color with food might be placed among other hues and various grays in a checkerboard arrangement. To exclude discrimination on the basis of a specific place response, the patches would be interchanged in position at regular intervals. Olfactory cues from the stimulus patches were controlled by covering all of them with a clean plate of glass. In the test, fresh patches were placed on the table, with every stimulus patch carrying food, or all of them empty. In various training series, bees were found able to distinguish at least two hue qualities in the spectrum, and to differentiate each from various intensities of gray. The most easily established discrimination was that of yellow from blue. On the one hand, orange, yellow, and green patches were confused; on the other hand, blue, violet, and purple were confused one with another. Reds could have no specific hue quality, since they were confused with dark grays. In tests with spectral light, Kühn (1927) found that honey bees could discriminate four principal regions of the spectrum: yellow, blue-green, blue, and ultraviolet. Lutz (1924) and Lotmar (1933) found that bees can distinguish flowers visually on the basis of differences in their ultraviolet reflections alone.

Another visually effective aspect of flowers important in this connection is their "form." The problem of form discrimination was raised by Turner (1911) in experiments in which honey bees were trained to differentiate artifacts of various colors and shapes (e.g., horizontal against vertical lines of different color). Von Frisch (1914) found honey bees able to discriminate between members of pairs or members of a series of patterns, one of which was presented with sugar water in the training. In a typical procedure, four boxes were used, with each figure duplicated on the front of two of them, and with the entrance hole to each box placed exactly in the center of its figure. In training, food was present only in the box with the positive figure, but was absent from all of them (or present in all) in the test. Although the bees easily discriminated between complex figures such as one with many radii and a four-sectored one, they could not learn with any readiness to discriminate among simpler ones such as triangles, ellipses, and rectangles. This investigation was later extended by Hertz (1929, 1933) in tests involving a greater variety of figures. Although bees could learn to discriminate figures in a group of discs, squares, and triangles from those of a second group including crosses, Y-figures, and parallel lines, they were unable to learn any discriminations within either of these groups. Brokenness of outline or compactness of a figure seemed critical as a basis for learned differentiation by the bee. Untrained bees as a rule fly to figures with more broken outlines and greater internal articulation. Zerrahn (1933) accordingly found that paddle-wheel figures with many sectors were attractive in direct relation to the number of radii present. Hertz and others found for the honey bee, as Ilse found (1932b) for butterflies, that even a prolonged training does not overcome all preference for multiradial against simple figures. Complex figures are the ones that afford the greatest visual change. Examination of the sensory physiology of the bee's eye in relation to these facts led Hecht and Wolf (1929) to the conclusion that the effect of the figure (e.g., a flower) upon the eye of the bee moving over it must be equivalent to that of a flickering light (see [Roeder, 1953] Chap. 19). When five circular areas of flickering light (all at equal intensities) were presented side by side in laboratory tests, bees settled in greatest numbers on the one with the greatest flicker frequency. The conclusion is that the bee learns a visual discrimination of flowers not on the basis of their pattern or configurational properties (in the human sense) but rather in terms of their properties as intermittent lights stimulating the compound eye (Wolf, 1933b; Autrum, 1949).

As we have suggested, responses of insects to chemical stimuli are many and varied, from direct reflex adjustments to learned sensory discriminations. Evidence concerning the stimulus physiology of these matters has been considered in [Roeder, 1953] Chap. 19. Thorpe's (1938) interesting results with the ichneumon fly have been mentioned as representing what is probably a simple habituation to a prevalent extrinsic stimulus. An apparently more complex case is represented by one of Thorpe's (1939) further experiments, in which the characteristic avoidance responses of *Drosophila melanogaster* to peppermint odor could be altered either by suffusing the larval food with the peppermint or by exposing the flies (shortly after their emergence) to an airstream carrying the peppermint vapor. Adult flies so prepared were not repelled but were actually attracted to the peppermint. Thorpe (1943) has postulated two effects of the peppermint in this case: a menthol effect, which normally is repellent but which is inhibited through a habituation learning in this experiment, and an ester which is attractive and is free to exert its effect once the menthol is inhibited. If, however, the effect of the ester is not spontaneous but is learned, this learning must be more complex than simple habituation.

We have seen that numerous flying insects respond on an olfactory basis to their food or prey when close to it. In his investigation of the role of olfaction in the foraging of the honey bee, von Frisch (1920) conducted training experiments which showed this insect capable of distinguishing a large number of odors. On a table near the hive a series of boxes was presented, containing different volatilizing chemicals (e.g., perfumes, distillates). In the box with the "positive" olfactory stimulus the bees found sugar water during the training period, which was usually a few hours in duration; the remaining boxes were empty except for their respective chemicals. By interchanging the boxes in position after every trial, the experimenter assured that the habit, if acquired, would depend upon a sensory discrimination rather than upon spatial position. In certain tests, a trained acacia odor was discriminated from lavender; in others the training stimulus, oil of orange peel, was discriminated from 43 other odors and confused only with certain ones (e.g., bergamot) close to it chemically. In other tests, the training odor (e.g., rose) was distinguished from twenty-three others, some of them flower perfumes, and in special tests the training odor was discriminated even when mixed with non-training odors. Such results show that flying insects are able to respond differentially to flowers, when close to them, on the basis of learned olfactory discriminations. As we have mentioned, the discrimination may be made even more highly selective through appropriate training methods (von Frisch, 1943). A comparable complex discrimination may be involved in the maze learning of *Formica* workers, which respond to cues from their own chemical traces in the pathway but not to those of other ants, and clearly show in control tests that olfactory discriminations are involved in these critical localities in the maze (Schneirla, 1943).

COMPLEX LEARNING IN INSECTS

The foraging of insects probably involves the most complicated instances of their learning. The manner in which these habits are established and used is difficult to analyze in the field, although field studies on insect way-finding have clarified the nature of the sensory cues involved. The best opportunity for analysis and understanding of the habit is in laboratory investigations, especially with the maze method.

Typically the maze is an obstacle which intervenes between a starting point and the attainment of a terminal situation, frequently the nest. This was the situation employed in Fielde's (1901) pioneer study in which workers of the ant *Stenamma fulvum piceum* carrying brood to the nest were made to run a maze involving a series of bilateral detours from a straight diagonal path. The investigator noted that many of the ants straightened their path after rambling courses in the early runs, and furthermore that individually distinctive courses through the situation were established by many of the marked individuals. Turner (1907) later tested way-finding in the laboratory with ant species such as *Formica subsericea*, with a simpler situation. His subjects ran circuitously and variably at first, but on further trials reached the nest with brood in less time and "with greater assurance," indicating that "the ants learned the way home."

The insects most frequently used in maze investigations are cockroaches and ants. Because roaches are rather "primitive" insects in their phyletic relationships, and ants relatively highly developed, a general comparison of some typical results will be of interest. Turner (1913) tested the roach *Periplaneta orientalis* in an elevated pathway maze with three blind alleys and one long, involved alley leading to the nest. Curves of error elimination were obtained, but no subject ever reached the point where consecutive errorless trials (i.e., without retracing and blind entrances) were made. Contact with the sides of the wall-less runways was predominant. Eldering (1919) used a simple apparatus with alternative turns to a lighted open alley and a darkened alley with shock. After some of the roaches had learned the turn to the lighted alley reasonably well, the habit persisted despite varnishing of the eyes but was disrupted when one antenna was removed, because of a tendency to turn toward the remaining antenna. Chauvin (1947) found that amputation of the antennae renders the learning of a somewhat more complex maze impossible for *Blatella germanica,* although varnishing the eyes does not impair performance seriously, and Hullo (1948) obtained a great interference with the learning of simple mazes when the antennae were fastened back lightly with glue. In Eldering's experiment, when the light and dark alleys were reversed after learning, the roaches continued to go to the same side, although this now led them into the dark where a shock was received each time. Brecher (1929) obtained comparable results with *P. orientalis* in a similar apparatus. Even in the best cases, more than 110 trials were required for a consistent performance, and a stereotyped running into the "wrong" turn occurred after the alternatives had been reversed.

In the roach, therefore, we find a variable and unstable learning of simple maze situation in which tactual and olfactory control predominates, with a pronounced stereotypy of the habit once learned, and a resistance to change when the situation is altered. The shortcomings of the initial learning process are suggested by the results of Gates and Allee (1933), who found that a cockroach mastered a simple maze in a slower and more variable manner when other roaches were in the situation at the same time, presumably because collisions and irregular stimulative distractions interfered with a learned stereotyping of movement sequences.

A superior capacity for mastering mazes prevails in many ants. A complex and surprisingly plastic process of sensory control has been found in the learning of a route by workers of many species. Although Turner (1907) did not use a maze, his laboratory results on way-finding in *Formica subsericea* and other species are confirmed by other investigators, as concerns the nature of sensory control in learning. In carrying pupae from a raised stage (to which they had been transferred) to the nest, *F. subsericea* workers at first moved slowly, "as though feeling their way." However, a slow and exploring initial gait, in contrast to a consistent rapidity of later movements, indicated that the ants "learn the way home." *F. subsericea* appeared to master the route in dependence upon tactual and olfactory stimuli, with direction of illumination very important.

Turner's results were confirmed and extended by Shepard (1911) in experiments with *Formica subsericea* in a maze that involved regular blind alleys, with cardboard alley linings to control olfactory cues, and controlled illumination. From tests involving interchanges of pathway linings in position both during the learning trials and after the maze had been mastered, Shepard came to the conclusion that in the orienting process "olfaction plays a definite part, but not a controlling part." Direction of illumination was most important, since after the maze had been learned with a single lamp on one side, moving this lamp to the opposite side

638

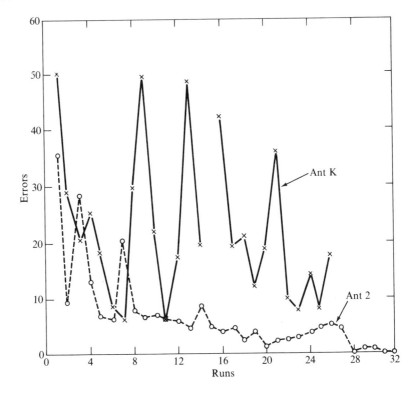

FIGURE 64
Error curves for two workers of the ant *Formica incerta* learning a six-blind maze (see Fig. 65). The record of the superior subject was made in a single series of runs, that of the inferior subject in two series, 3 days apart. (After Schneirla, 1946.)

during a maze run caused the subject to hesitate and wander, then reverse her direction of progress. Schneirla (1929) found *F. subsericea* capable of relearning a maze after changes either in the pathway linings present during initial learning or in the direction of illumination. One ant that had required more than 40 runs to learn the route to the nest through a four-blind maze, under unilateral illumination, was able to relearn it in 8 runs after the light had been shifted 180°. Then, in further tests involving 90° and 180° shifts, or light directed from two, three, or all four sides of the maze, this subject made successive facile readjustments to the problem. In later experiments with *F. incerta* (Schneirla, 1943) individual ants were able to learn a six-blind maze under diffuse illumination, i.e., in dependence upon intramaze sensory cues (Figures 64, 65). With pathway linings (i.e., chemical cues) undisturbed during original learning, this

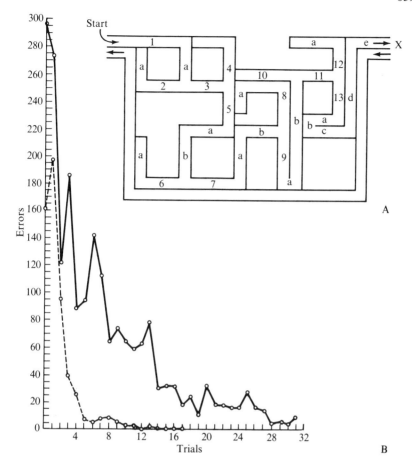

FIGURE 65

(1) Standard maze pattern D with six-blind alleys. (2) Error curves for 8 hooded rats (dotted line) and 8 ants (*Formica incerta*) (solid line) which learned this pattern, running in the direction 1 to 13e, the rats to a food-place at ✕, the ants to their nest at ✕. (After Schneirla, 1946.)

maze was mastered by the most efficient subjects in 28 to 36 runs, whereas with an intramaze situation made unstable by extensive pathway-lining changes, learning was greatly retarded and more than 40 runs were re-quired to achieve an incomplete learning. The increased role of tactual cues under these difficult conditions was indicated by a frequent touching of walls, especially in difficult choice-point localities of the maze. Wall contacts then were considerably more common than when directed light was used and chemical cues were stable.

Just as these *Formica* species readjust to changes in a learned maze situation, they modify their orientation under changing natural conditions. When visual cues are unstable or are unavailable, other sensory cues (chemical, tactual) are relied upon to a greater extent. Ordinarily sensory cues of different types are utilized concurrently (Turner, 1907; Shepard, 1911; Schneirla, 1929). Comparably, in the discrimination learned by flying insects in their arrival at food place or nest in foraging, an individual may become dependent upon specific details or upon the situation more widely, and may change its dependence upon landmarks according to prevalent conditions (Warden, Jenkins, and Warner, 1940).

In the maze learning of *Formica* workers, a sequence of three stages is discernible. In an initial *generalized stage* (Schneirla, 1941), progress occurs through a general decrease in excited and erratic behavior as an ability develops to continue running until an obstacle is encountered. Failure to learn specific adjustments is indicated at the end of this stage by entrances into blind alleys as frequently and in much the same manner as in the beginning. An unlearned postural-bias factor, termed "centrifugal swing" by Schneirla (1929, 1943), has much to do with initial tendencies to enter blind alleys. After about 8 to 12 runs in the maze shown in Figure 65, a stage of *specific segmental learning* appears, marked by shortening entrances into blind alleys and turning directly into true path alternates at choice points. After considerable progress has been made in the second stage (Schneirla, 1943), a stage of *intersegmental organization* is entered. It is apparent that the second stage depends upon accomplishment of the first, and that the third cannot occur without considerable progress in the segmental learning processes of the second stage.

PROPERTIES AND LIMITATIONS OF INSECT LEARNING

Individual and Group Differences

Comparisons of maze learning throw light upon the manner in which the habits are accomplished. Cockroaches are limited to the learning of simple mazes and seldom attain a stage of very consistent performance. In contrast, this stage is readily attained by the best performers among ants in more complex situations than a roach can be expected to learn. In mastering the "bee line," honey bees may accomplish a learning that compares favorably with that demonstrated for *Formica* ants in the maze situation. However, the conditions of learning in the bee's flight and in the terrestrial journey of the ant are very different. Although tests of honey bees in a relatively simple maze (Kalmus, 1937b) suggest how orientation within the hive is learned, important sensory and motor differences between bees and ants raise difficulties for any direct comparison of their learning.

Species differences in maze learning by ants have been reported by Schneirla (1933b), who found that *Formica exsectoides* workers required more runs and were typically more variable than *F. subsericea* workers in learning a particular maze pattern. Workers of a third species, *F. incerta,* exhibited still greater facility in mastering the same mazes.

Individual differences in learning within a species have been described for numerous insects. Eldering (1919) found that individual cockroaches differed considerably in learning a simple T-maze. Those individuals which made little progress were most disrupted when the alternatives were reversed. Wodsedalek (1911) found that some mayfly nymphs, and one individual in particular, were superior to others in learning to rise in the water when their dish was jarred. When *F. rufa* ants were tested in their ability to reach the ground from an elevated position, van der Heyde (1920) found that some individuals ceased their initial circuitous wanderings at an early point, others less quickly, and one not at all. Fielde (1901) observed that various workers of *Stenamma fulvum picea* learned individual courses in the maze, a point confirmed by Shepard (1911) and Schneirla (1929) for workers of *Formica* species. This condition arises in species in which foragers establish their routes more or less independently, although it is not apparent in species that operate collectively on a chemotactic basis—an important difference overlooked by MacGregor (1948) in his criticism of Fielde. In a complex maze, some *Formica* ants make little or no headway (Figure 64) and complete only a few runs; others are able to learn (Schneirla, 1929, 1933b). Such individual differences must depend to some extent at least upon differences in neural capacities.

Conditions Influencing Learning and Retention

Evidence concerning the retention of learned behavior by insects is still unclear. Contradictions may be due in part to differences in the conditions of investigation, to individual or species differences, or to differences in the retention value of different types of habit. According to Turner (1912) and Szymanski (1912) cockroaches conditioned to avoid the dark are more or less unstable in the habit, but can be reconditioned with a few additional shocks. In contrast, Eldering (1919) reported that cockroaches retained a position habit for periods of 1 month or more without further training. The interval between series of trials is a factor in the learning of a simple maze by roaches (Chauvin, 1947). A simple conditioned response persists for 2 or 3 days without reinforcement in the water beetle *Dytiscus* (Schaller, 1926); a learned feeding rhythm survives for as long as 6 days in the honey bee without reinforcement (Wahl, 1932). Shepard (1911) found that *Formica* workers show little loss in a moderately complex maze habit after a period as long as 3 weeks; Schneirla (1929) reported good performance in a more complex maze, and rapid recovery of full efficiency after a few trials. It is possible that, when a habit is well learned, the tendency for stereotypy evidenced in most insect learning is in itself a safeguard against types of loss to which mammals might be subject through interference from related habits.

The effect of variations in physiological condition upon learning and retention in insects is still unclear, although numerous investigators have attacked the problem. Certain observers have reported, for instance, that chemical agents such as tobacco fumes and ether somehow block "memory" in honey bees so that they are unable to return to their hive when transported (Buttel-Reepen, 1907; Phillips, 1916). Although Tirala (1923) apparently demonstrated that ether has an inhibitory effect upon performance of a learned habit, Plath (1924) and others have reported negative results. Plath suggests that the anesthetic interferes not by destroying retention but by enfeebling or even killing the bees. One of the best experiments has been performed by Rösch-Berger (1933), who tested the return of bees released in places from which they had learned their way to the hive. If these bees were liberated at the former feeding place after exposure to ether or to low temperature they returned to the hive as quickly as the control bees. Neither of these agents impaired the performance of a learned discrimination of yellow (as feeding color) from other hues. As Rösch-Berger notes, Tirala obtained his most significant results from young bees, which lacked orientation experience.

In Hunter's (1932) test of *Blatella germanica* in the Szymanski conditioning apparatus, pre-exposure to a low temperature of 3–6° C retarded formation of the dark-avoidance response and decreased retention in respectively different groups. The results favor no one explanation. With *Periplaneta americana* under the same conditions Minami and Dallenbach (1946) obtained poorer relearning scores in roaches subject to enforced activity than in quiescent or inactive subjects. Interpolated activity was thought to introduce an irritability effect that impaired relearning. Activity interpolated 10 min after original learning was more detrimental to the habit than activity interpolated after 60 min, and inferior relearning scores were obtained after interpolated rest in a light cage as compared with quiescence in a dark box. From these results the experimenters concluded that a "retroactive inhibition" had arisen through direct effects upon neural traces of the habit. However, in these last results, the possible roles of peripheral processes such as sensory adaptation on the one hand, and of a central (synaptic) neural effect on the other, are difficult to evaluate.

In an experiment by Hoagland (1931) in which *Camponotus penn-sylvannicus* (carpenter ant) workers learned to escape from a chamber through which air containing peppermint vapor passed, learning scores were about 100% better at temperatures of 27–29.4° C than at 15–25° C. Neither learning nor retention was affected appreciably by pre-exposure for 18 hr to temperatures between 15–25° C; however, a long pre-exposure to temperatures of 28.3° or 29.4° C retarded learning greatly, and also, when introduced after normal learning, increased the relearning period to more than the initial number of trials. Injurious and toxic effects were apparent under the latter condition. Thus far, in such experiments with insects, the influence of peripheral metabolic effects produced by environmental conditions such as activity and high temperature cannot be clearly distinguished from possible direct effects upon neural processes underlying learning and retention.

Stereotypy as a Limiting Factor in Insect Learning

A striking fact in the behavior of solitary wasps and other flying insects is the persistence with which they center their activities around the specific area in which they first emerge as adults. The basis would seem to be an initially established locality learning. Thorpe (1944) has summed up the evidence furnished by Rau and Rau (1918), Rabaud (1924, 1926) and others on this point. We have mentioned evidence obtained by investigators such as Ferton (1905) and Tinbergen (1934), which indicates that flying hymenopterous insects readily learn to base their orientation upon the cues available in a given situation. The facility of such learning in insects may indicate how greatly their characteristic neural processes permit a present stimulative field to dominate behavior. Hannes (1930) has characterized this as a "stamping in," which may undergo interference when olfactory stimuli are presented with the visual cues or when changes are made in visual features during the initial learning of a problem.

It is probable that the characteristic stereotypy of insect learning is closely related to this feature of *situation fixity*. Thus complex serial habits are first learned through relatively isolated local adjustments (Schneirla, 1943). A clear illustration of situation-fixed learning is furnished in some results obtained by Opfinger (1931). In these experiments, honey bees were presented with a yellow square during their arrival at the food place, a white square during the feeding interval, and a blue square on the departure flight. In subsequent tests, when these patches were set out together, in arriving the bee flew to the yellow but not to the others. In one test series, the visits were: yellow = 58, white = 0, blue = 1. The learned *arrival* response evidently is restricted to the stimulus situation effective during previous *arrival* flights in training. Recently, Opfinger (1949) has obtained comparable results with odor. That such facts disclose a prevalent feature of insect learning is suggested by results obtained in a very different setting. After a *Formica* worker has mastered a complex maze pattern presented on her run to the nest with food, this "same" pattern when presented as an obstacle between nest and food place must be learned virtually as a new problem (Schneirla, 1946).

That the fixity in insect learning depends upon more than a predominant extrinsic stimulative effect is shown by the fact that a maze pattern is learned differently when presented as an obstacle between nest and food place, and food place and nest. This is true whether it is learned by respectively different groups of ants, or by the same ants in a series of runs from nest to food place and return. The subjects eliminate blind alleys in a distinctively different manner, behave differently, and master the problem in a more regular and efficient manner in the "to nest" phase than in the "to food place" phase. Control tests under diffuse illumination show that the specificity is due in part to distinctively different patterns of stimulation (e.g., chemoreceptive) in the two situations; other considerations suggest that differences in organic condition also prevail. We have cited evidence that an insect's organic condition may dominate and canalize its responsiveness and its learning in particular external situations.

Insect and Mammalian Learning Compared

Insects ordinarily are assumed to be very different from mammals in the "character" of their behavior, yet the delineation of clear-cut qualitative differences between these animal groups is not an easy task. This is because comparative studies are deficient, not because qualitative differences are presumably absent. When 8 *Formica* ants and 8 white rats were tested in the "same" maze pattern with six blind alleys (Schneirla, 1946) all of the rats mastered the problem within 12 runs and with a minimal number of errors (an average of only about 1 per animal on each run) after the fifth run, whereas the ants required 30 or more runs to master the situation (Figure 65). The rats learned the pattern in a facile manner with choice-point adjustments beginning from the first run, with a minimal repetition of errors, and without any identifiable signs of distinctive stages. In contrast, the progress of the ants was labored, with a definite tendency to repeat certain errors; also with distinct stages of generalized and of segmental learning, in that order, prerequisite to eventual mastery of the situation.

Emphasis upon stereotypy in insect learning must not be indiscriminate, for experiments show that various insects and especially Hymenoptera are capable of relearning a changed situation (Turner, 1907; Shepard, 1911;

Schneirla, 1929). However, the characteristic inferiority of insects as compared with mammals is revealed in such processes as well as in original learning. Although the rat, with appropriate opportunities, may perform a complex serial act in terms of an anticipated end result (i.e., a goal), such processes have not been demonstrated validly in insects. The "anticipations" of an ant in the maze are strictly limited temporally and spatially; built up gradually, with no dependent trace of "acting in terms of" a remote event (e.g., the last choice point) as the rat acts in his maze learning. Confronted with the problem of running a mastered maze in reverse (i.e., starting at the previous end-point), rats show a considerable saving through transfer; ants meet the change as a new problem (Schneirla, 1946; Chauvin, 1947). By considering all maze learning as *Umweg* processes, Bierens de Haan (1937) overlooks these and other important differences.

Specifically, insects appear to have a method of problem orientation different from and inferior to that of mammals. In contrast to the rat's demonstrated capacity for transferring complex learning (Maier and Schneirla, 1935), the insect seems unable to apply a complex habit to a different situation with any adequacy, although it can transfer simple habits of the habituation type. However, although the characteristic insect pattern of learning appears subject to qualitative limitations, learning is not a negligible asset to insects. To different extents and in different ways learning contributes to food and shelter-getting, to way-finding and homing functions, and to other adjustments. Its role, although secondary, is frequently essential to the prevalent behavior pattern of a given species.

Scope of Capacities for Modifiable Behavior

We have seen that insects can modify their behavior in a variety of ways. Learning contributes to many of their environmental adjustments, both of the approach or toleration and the avoidance types. In addition to habituations and conditioned responses, sensory discriminations of many types are learned. Many insects learn serial motor patterns, as in homing, which, simple or complex, seem to have become essential to species survival. Often, variations in a familiar situation may be met through a re-learning based upon partial modification of sensory and motor processes involved in the original habit. Evolution of such capacities in a species aids it greatly in meeting environmental fluctuations.

Claims are frequently made that insects are capable of accomplishing intelligent adjustments of a high psychological order. Not unusually such contentions depend upon limited qualitative evidence of an anecdotal sort (e.g., Hingston, 1929; Cheesman, 1933; Lafleur, 1940). However interesting as narratives, such reports are usually derived without elementary scientific precautions for reliability of data and validity of interpretation; commonly they are rich in descriptive color but scanty in dependable particulars.

Perhaps the greatest source of confusion in interpreting insect behavior arises from a traditionally popular anthropomorphic disposition to regard the fact of adaptive success in an act as equivalent to a demonstration of higher-level psychological processes. Caution is necessary here, for similar end results may be attained through very different behavioral capacities and processes. For example, the mass raids of army ants are impressive in action and in booty gained, yet experimental analysis shows that they are the resultant of individual contributions deriving from elementary behavioral capacities (Schneirla, 1940, 1941). Highly "judicious" and "astute" group maneuvers are observed here, and complex mass developments, in a situation of low individual intelligence as concerns a demonstrable learning capacity. A comparable case is presented by the tropical weaver ants in the genera *Polyrhachis* (Jacobson, 1905) and *Oecophylla* (Bugnion, 1909). These construct their tree nests of leaves joined together by silk extruded from larvae manipulated by the workers as shuttles. This pattern, although complex and very adaptive, has every appearance of a thoroughgoing stereotypy. Its direct reference to hereditary processes is indicated by the fact that, although the larvae make no cocoons, their spinning glands are greatly hypertrophied (Doflein, 1905).

It is often difficult to resist accepting evidence at its face value when it appears to demonstrate a mammalian-type capacity in insects. For example, Warden, Jenkins, and Warner (1940), from a review of the evidence, reached the conclusion that the ability of solitary wasps to recognize their nests, as distinguished from the nest sites, represents a fairly high order of "abstraction." Verlaine (1924, 1932b, 1934) has reported that bees and wasps can recognize both food sources and their own nests not only through responding to a general category of geometrical forms but also in positions independent of other figures, and that bees were able to give a generalized feeding reaction to 34 different kinds of triangles. However, the abstraction-generalization concept cannot be evaluated for insects without considering to what characteristics of the situation the insects may be responding, and whether their role is really attributable to an "abstraction" process. Very erroneous conclusions may be reached if it is assumed that insects perceive and react in terms of mammalian "patterns," since experimental evidence on bees (Wolf, 1933b; Autrum, 1949) indicates that a discrimination of flicker characteristics is actually involved. If such is the case, then the equivalence of a new situation to a previously habituated one may not involve the "generalization of an abstraction," but a simpler reaction to an equivalent sensory effect without a crucial involvement of differences.

Serious claims for the exercise of higher capacities in insects have been made on the ground of a variety of observations, summarized by Thorpe (1943, 1944) in relation to the problem of "insight," by which is meant recombination of learned processes from previously isolated experiences to meet a new problem situation (Maier and Schneirla, 1935; Chap. 20). As one example, some writers (e.g., Hingston, 1929; McDougall and Mc-Dougall, 1931) have contended that insight permits eumenid wasps to repair artificial damage to their storage structures. Thus, the McDougalls used as evidence their observation that an unidentified mason wasp repaired holes made experimentally in her cell by daubing on mud pellets, although they believed that in the initial building act the mud is always spread smoothly. Unfortunately for the example, the last assumption does not appear to be correct, as the findings of Hartman (1913) indicate. One of his cases, showing that mud is applied in pellets during the original building act, is represented in Figure 66. As Thorpe (1943) maintains, no observation can be accepted as evidence for "insight" until its actual relation to the insect's normal behavior is known.

Adaptive variations in behavior may appear directly on the basis of the stereotyped species pattern and its potentialities for changes forced by different environmental conditions (Schneirla, 1949). A case in point is the famous one of the sphegid wasp *Ammophila urnaria,* observed by the Peckhams (1905) to use a small stone in tamping down the earth of its completed and stocked burrow. This act was reported by the Peckhams as a case of tool-using. Similar instances have been observed in related species (Hartman, 1905; Rau and Rau, 1918). Such behavior is known to be fairly common in some of them, and in *A. heydeni* it occurs most of the time (Berland, 1935; Molitor, 1937). Berland has pointed out that digger wasps frequently take up pebbles as an integral act in burrow closure, and accordingly the act of pebble tamping must be closely related to the normal pattern of burrow closing. The "tool" concept does not seem relevant here.

Variations in the environmental conditions under which insects perform their stereotyped activities, by their very nature, may induce behavior changes which are adaptive and thereby readily mistaken for insightful or "purposive" adjustments. An interesting case is reported in Fabre's (1922, vol. 6) study of the burying beetle *Necrophorus.* When a dead mouse is encountered on the ground, these insects dig in the soil beneath it and soon have sunk and buried the carcass. In the classical anecdote of the "frog's gibbet," burying beetles were reported to have uprooted a stake from which a dead frog had been hung, then to have buried the carcass. The evident suggestion of the anecdote is that the beetles wished to bury the body, and intelligently devised a new means to that end. However, in various tests Fabre demonstrated that the beetles never uprooted the stake

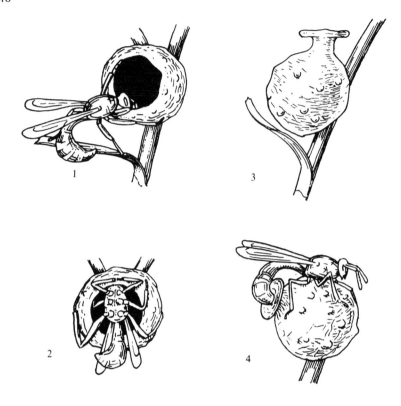

FIGURE 66

Nest construction in the mason wasp, *Eumenes belfragei*. (1) Each
load of mud is plastered on the rim, then smoothed out between mandibles and forelegs. (2) In this act, the feet are outside and the head inside
the nest. (3) View of the finished nest, on which a flanged neck has
been constructed. The tubercles or "sculpturings" on the outside result
from the fact that *less than half the loads are smoothed off in normal
nest building*. (4) Ovipositing in the finished nest, before it has been
provisioned with caterpillars. (After Hartman, 1915.)

when it slanted so that a suspended dead mouse touched the ground a few
inches from the base of the stake. They simply dug where the body
touched the ground (Figure 67). However, when the stake was perpen-
dicular and the body hung by its hind legs from raffia bonds so that it
touched the stick but did not quite reach the ground, the beetles finally released the mouse. This was not done in any special, direct manner, but
only after hours of poking and stirring around the dead animal. When, in
gnawing at the legs of the mouse, the beetles encountered the raffia bonds,
these were soon cut through just as grass roots are sheared through when

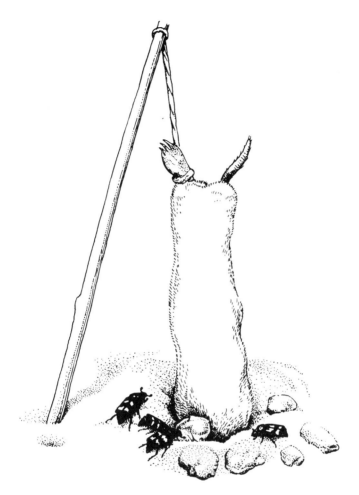

FIGURE 67
The "gibbet" test of Fabre, in which burying beetles (*Necro-phorus* sp.) were presented with a dead, suspended mole. (After Fabre, 1922, vol. 6.)

encountered ordinarily in digging. Fabre's painstaking observations and tests show clearly that the "solution" occurred not through reasoning but through enforced changes in the insect's normal pattern of behavior. Unless we consider adequately what insects are like in their normal, everyday behavioral adjustments, we are likely to misinterpret their seemingly exceptional feats.

SUMMARY

In addition to behavioral changes associated with growth or metabolic variations, most insects can modify their behavior to some extent through learning. A capacity for habituation to prevalent stimulative conditions commonly permits adjustment to new situations. Conditioned-response learning, demonstrated in various insects, frequently permits crucial environmental adjustments. Striking examples are "temporal memory" as in honey bees, and feeding responses to specific cues. Learned sensory discriminations are frequent in flying insects, and complex serial motor patterns are acquired by terrestrial foraging insects. In maze experiments, both the learned use of numerous sensory cues and the learned elimination of inefficient responses are outstanding. Ants of various species are superior to cockroaches in these respects. Both individual differences within a species and species differences in mastering problems are found.

Insect learning has distinctive characteristics. Responses to specific visual stimuli are learned with ease; more complex patterned adjustments tend to be situation-fixed and stereotyped. Specificity to the situation of learning underlies typical difficulties in transferring learned adjustments to new situations but also permits good retention after considerable periods of time. Insect learning contrasts qualitatively with that of mammals. In comparable maze problems, ants learn more slowly and less efficiently than rats, and are very inferior to rats in post-learning transfer studies. Thus, although learning contributes in many ways to environmental adjustments in insects, and may often be complex, it is not on the psychological level of mammalian learning. Claims that insects are capable of intelligent adjustments of a high psychological order seem to depend upon limited evidence which leads to exaggerated superficial similarities to mammals at their best.

REFERENCES

Autrum, H. 1949. Neue Versuche zum Optischen an Flosungsvermögen Fliegender Insekten. *Experientia* 5: 271–277.
Baldus, K. 1926. Experimentelle Untersuchungen über die Entfernungslokalisation der Libellen (*Aeschna cyanea*). *Z. Vergleich. Physiol.* 3: 475–505.
Beling, I. 1929. Über das Zeitgedächtnis der Bienen. *Z. Vergleich. Physiol.* 9: 259–338.
Berland, L. 1935. Quelques traits du comportement des Hymenopteres Sphegiens. *Ann. Sci. Nat.,* 10 series, 18: 53–66.
Bierens de Hann, J. A. 1937. *Labyrinth und Umweg.* Leiden: Brill.

Borrell du Vernay, W. von. 1942. Assoziations-Bildung und Sensibilisierung bei *Tenebrio. Z. Vergleich. Physiol.* 30: 84–116.

Brecher, L. 1929. Die anorganischen Bestandteile des Schmetterlingspuppen-blutes (*Sphynx pinastri, Pieris brassicae*). Veranderungen im Gehalt an Anorganischen Bestandteilen bei der Verpuppung. (*Pieris brassicae*). *Biochem. Zeitschr.* 221: 40–64.

Bugnion, E. 1909. Fourmi fileuse de Ceylan (*Oecophylla smaragdina*). *Arch. Sci. Phys. et Nat.* 28: 511–513.

Buttel-Reepen, H. von. 1907. Zur Psychobiologie der Hummelm. I. *Biol. Zentralbl.* 27: 576–487, 604–613.

Chauvin, R. 1947. Études sur le comportement de *Blattella germanica* dans divers types de labyrinthes. *Bull. Biol. France, Belgique* 81: 92–128.

Cheesman, E. 1933. *Insect behavior.* New York: Ballou.

Doflein, F. 1905. Beobachtungen an der Weber Ameisen (*Oecophylla smarag-dina*). *Biol. Zentralbl.* 25: 497–507.

Eldering, F. J. 1919. Acquisition d'habitudes chez les insectes. *Arch. Néerland. Physiol.,* Series 3C, 3: 469–490.

Ferton, C. 1905. Sur l'instinct des Hyménoptéres melliferes et Rauisseurs. *Ann. Soc. Entomol. France* 74: 56–104.

Fielde, A. 1901. A study of an ant. *Proc. Acad. Nat. Philadelphia* 53: 425–449.

Fielde, A. 1903. Artificial mixed nests of ants. *Biol. Bull.* 5: 320–325.

Fielde, A. 1904. On the artificial creation of mixed nests of ants. *Biol. Bull.* 6: 326.

Frings, H. 1944. The loci of olfactory end-organs in the honey bee, *Apis mellifera* Linn. *J. Exp. Zool.* 97: 123–134.

Frisch, K. von. 1914. Der Farbensinn und Formensinn der Biene. *Zool. Jahrb. Zool. Physiol.* 35: 1–182.

Frisch, K. von. 1920. Über die "Sprache" der Bienen. *Münch. Med. Wo-chenschr.* 67: 566–569.

Frisch, K. von. 1921. Über die "Sprache" der Bienen. *Münch. Med. Wo-chenschr.* 68: 509–511.

Frisch, K. von. 1922. Über die "Sprache" der Bienen. *Münch. Med. Wo-chenschr.* 69: 781–782.

Frisch, K. von. 1943. Versuche über die Lenkung des Bienenfluges durch Duftstoffe. *Naturewissenschaften* 31, 39: 445–460.

Gaffron, M. 1934. Untersuchungen über das Bewegungssehen bei Libellen-larven, Fliegen und Fischen. *Z. Vergleich. Physiol.* 20: 299–337.

Grabensberger, W. 1933. Untersuchungen über das Zeitgedächtnis der Ameisen und Termiten. *Z. Vergleich. Physiol.* 20: 1–54.

Grabensberger, W. 1944. Experimentelle untersuchungen über das Zeitge-dächtnis von Bienen und Wespen nach Verfütterung von Euchinin und Jodthyreoglobulin. *Z. Vergleich. Physiol.* 20: 338–342.

Grabensberger, W. 1944. Der Einfluss von Salicylsäure, gelbem Phosphore und weissen Arsenik auf das Zeitgedächtnis der Ameisen. *Z. Vergleich. Physiol.* 20: 501–510.

Hannes, F. 1930. Über die Verschiedenen Arten des "Lernens" der Honigbiene und der Insekten überhaupt. *Zool. Jahrb. Zool. Physiol.* 47: 89–150.

Hartman, C. 1905. Observations on the habits of some solitary wasps of Texas. *Bull. Univ. Texas Sci. Ser.* 1: 1–73.

Hartman, C. 1913. The habits of *Eumenes belfragei, Cress. J. Anim. Behav.* 3: 353–360.

Hecht, S., and E. Wolf. 1929. The visual acuity of the honey bee. *J. Gen. Physiol.* 12: 727–760.

Hertz, M. 1929. Die Organisation des Optischen Feldes bei der Biene. II. *Z. Vergleich. Physiol.* 11: 107–145.

Hertz, M. 1933. Uber die Orientierung des Bienenwolfes (*Philanthus triangulum* fabr.). II. Die Bienenjagd. *Z. Vergleich. Physiol.* 21: 463–467.

Hess, C. von. 1920. Neues zur Frage nach einem Farben Sinne bei Bienen. *Naturwissenschaften* 8: 927–929.

Heyde, H. C. van der. 1920. Quelques observations sur la psychologie des fourmis. *Arch. Néerland. Physiol.* 4: 259–282.

Heyde, K. 1924. Die Entwicklung der Psychischen Fahigkeiten bei Ameisen und ihr Verhalten bei abgeänderten biologischen Bedingungen. *Biol. Zentralbl.* 44: 623–654.

Hoagland, H. 1931. A study of the physiology of learning in ants. *J. Gen. Psychol.* 5: 21–41.

Holmes, S. J. 1905. The selection of random movements as a factor of phototaxis. *J. Comp. Neurol.* 15: 98–112.

Hullo, A. 1948. Rôle des tendances motrices et des données sensorielles dans l'apprentissage du labyrinthe par les Blattes (*Blattella germanica*). *Behaviour* 1: 297–310.

Hunter, W. S. 1932. The effect of inactivity produced by cold upon learning and retention in the cockroach. *J. Genet. Psychol.* 41: 253–266.

Ilse, D. 1932b. Zur "Formwahanehmung" der Tagfalter. I. Spontane Bevorzugung von Formmerkmalen Durch Vanessen. *Z. Vergleich. Physiol.* 17: 537–556.

Jacobson, E. 1905. Beobachtungen über *Polyrhachis dives* auf Java, die ihre Larven zum Spinnen der Nester Benutzt. *Polyrachis. Notes. Leiden Mus.* 25: 133–140.

Kalmus, H. 1934. Über die Natur des Zeitgedächtnisses der Bienen. *Z. Vergleich. Physiol.* 20: 405–419.

Kalmus, H. 1937b. Vorversuche über die Orientierung der Biene im Stock. *Z. Vergleich. Physiol.* 24: 166–187.

Kleber, E. 1935. Hat das Zeitgedächtnis der Bienen biologische Bedeutung? *Z. Vergleich. Physiol.* 22: 221–262.

Kühn, A. 1927. Über den Farbensinn der Bienen. *Z. Vergleich. Physiol.* 5: 762–800.

Lafleur, L. J. 1940. Helpfulness in ants. *J. Comp. Psychol.* 30: 23–29.

Lotmar, R. 1933. Neue Untersuchungen über den Farbensinn der Bienen, mit Besonderer Berücksichtigung des Ultravioletts. *Z. Vergleich. Physiol.* 19: 673–723.

Lutz, F. E. 1924. Apparently non-selective characters and combinations of characters including a study of ultraviolet in relation to the flower visiting habits of insects. *Ann. N.Y. Acad. Sci.* 29: 181–283.

Lutz, F. E. 1934. The "Buckwheat problem" and the behaviour of the honey-bee. *Am. Mus. Novitates* 688: 1–10.

McDougall, K. D., and W. McDougall. 1931. Insight and foresight in various animals—monkey, racoon, rat and wasp. *J. Comp. Psychol.* 11: 237–273.

MacGregor, E. G. 1948. Odour as a basis for orientated movement in ants. *Behaviour* 1: 267–296.

Maier, N. R. F., and T. C. Schneirla. 1935. *Principles of animal psychology.* New York: McGraw-Hill.

Mayer, A. G., and C. G. Soule. 1906. Some reactions of caterpillars and moths. *J. Exp. Zool.* 3: 415–433.

Minami, H., and K. M. Dallenbach. 1949. The effect of activity upon learning and retention in the cockroach, *Periplaneta americana. Am. J. Psychol.* 59: 1–58.

Molitor, A. 1937. Zur vergleichenden Psychobiologie der Akuleaten Hymenopteren auf experimenteller Grundlage. *Biol. Gen.* 13: 294–333.

Morley, B. D. W. 1942. Observations on the nest odours of ants. *Proc. Linn. Soc. London,* 154th Sess., pp. 109–114.

Opfinger, E. 1931. Über die Orientierung der Biene an der Futterquelle. (Die Bedeutung von Anflug und Orientierungsflug fur den Lernvorgang bei Farb-, Form- und Ortsdressuren.) *Z. Vergleich. Physiol.* 15: 431–487.

Opfinger, E. 1949. Zur Psychologie der Duftdressuren bei Bienen. *Z. Vergleich. Physiol.* 31: 441–453.

Peckham, G. W., and E. G. Peckham. 1905. *Wasps, Social and Solitary.* New York: Houghton Mifflin.

Phillipps, E. F. 1916. *Beekeeping.* New York: Macmillan.

Plateau, F. 1888. Recherches expérimentales sur la vision chez les arthropodes (Cinquième Partie).—a. Perception des mouvements chez les insectes. b. Addition aux recherches sur le vol des insectes aveuglés. c. Résumé général. *Bull. Acad. Roy. Belg.,* Ser. 3, 16: 395–458.

Plath, O. 1924. Do anesthetized bees lose their memory? *Am. Nat.* 58: 162–166.

Rabaud, É. 1924. Le retour au nid de *Vespa sylvestris. Feuill, Nat.* 1: 7–11.

Rabaud, É. 1926. Acquisition des habitudes et repères sensoriels chez les Guêpes. *Bull. Sci. France et Belgique* 60: 313–333.

Rau, P., and N. Rau. 1918. *Wasp studies afield.* Princeton, New Jersey: Princeton Univ. Press.

Roeder, K. D. 1953. *Insect physiology.* New York: Wiley.

Rösch-Berger, K. 1933. Das Gedächtnis der Biene nach der Narkose. *Z. Vergleich. Physiol.* 18: 474–480.

Sälzle, K. 1932. Untersuchungen an Libellenlarven über das Sehen bewegter Objekte. *Z. Vergleich. Physiol.* 18: 347–368.

Schaller, A. 1926. Sinnes Physiologische und Psychologische Untersuchungen an Wasserkäfern und Fishen. *Z. Vergleich. Physiol.* 4: 370–464.

Schneirla, T. C. 1929. Learning and orientation in ants. *Comp. Psychol. Monogr.* 6: 1–143.

Schneirla, T. C. 1933b. Some important features of ant learning. *Z. Vergleich. Physiol.* 19: 439–452.

Schneirla, T. C. 1940. Further studies on the army-ant behavior pattern. *J. Comp. Psychol.* 29: 401–460.

Schneirla, T. C. 1941. Social organization in insects as related to individual function. *Psychol. Rev.* 48: 465–486.

Schneirla, T. C. 1943. The nature of ant learning. II. The intermediate stage of segmental maze adjustment. *J. Comp. Psychol.* 35: 149–176.

Schneirla, T. C. 1946. Ant learning as a problem in comparative psychology. In P. Harriman, ed., *Twentieth century psychology.* New York: Philos. Lib. Pp. 306–316.

Schneirla, T. C. 1949. Army-ant life under dry-season conditions. 3. The course of reproduction and colony behavior. *Bull. Am. Mus. Nat. Hist.* 94: 1–81.

Shafer, G. D. 1948. *The ways of a mud dauber.* Stanford, California: Stanford Univ. Press.

Shepard, J. F. 1911. Some results in comparative psychology. *Psychol. Bull.* 8: 41–42.

Stein-Beling, I. von. 1935. Über das Zeitgedächtnis bei Tieren. *Biol. Rev.* 10: 18–41.

Szymanski, J. S. 1912. Modification of the innate behavior of cockroaches. *J. Anim. Behav.* 2: 81–90.

Thorpe, W. H. 1939. Further experiments on olfactory conditioning in a parasitic insect. The nature of the conditioning process. *Proc. Roy. Soc. London, Ser. B,* 126: 390–397.

Thorpe, W. H. 1939. Further studies on pre-imaginal olfactory conditioning. *Proc. Roy. Soc. London, Ser. B,* 127: 424–433.

Thorpe, W. H. 1943. Types of learning in insects and other arthropods. Parts I and II. *British J. Psychol.* Part I. 33: 220–234; Part II. 34: 20–31.

Thorpe, W. H. 1944. Types of learning in insects and other arthropods. Part III. *British J. Psychol.* 34: 66–76.

Thorpe, W. H., and F. G. Jones. 1937. Olfactory conditioning in a parasitic insect and its relations to the problem of host selection. *Proc. Roy. Soc. London, Ser. B,* 124: 56–81.

Tinbergen, N. 1934. Über die Orientierung des Bienenwolfes (*Philanthus triangulum* Fabr.) II. Die Bienenjagd. *Z. Vergleich. Physiol.* 21: 699–716.

Tirala, L. G. 1923. Über den Einfluss der Äthernarkose auf die Heimkehr Fähigkeit der Bienen. *Arch. Exp. Pathol. u. Pharmacol.* 97: 433–440.

Turner, C. H. 1907. The homing of ants: an experimental study of ant behavior. *J. Comp. Neurol. Psychol.* 17: 367–434.

Turner, C. H. 1911. Experiments on pattern—vision of the honey bee. *Biol. Bull.* 21: 249–264.

Turner, C. H. 1912. An experimental investigation of an apparent reversal of the responses to light of the roach (*Periplaneta orientalis* L.). *Biol. Bull.* 23: 371–386.

Turner, C. H. 1913. Behavior of the common roach (*Periplaneta orientalis* L.) on an open maze. *Biol. Bull.* 25: 348–361.

Turner, C. H. 1914. An experimental study of the auditory powers of the giant silkworm moths (*Saturniidae*). *Biol. Bull.* 27: 325–332.

Uvarov, B. P. 1932. Conditioned reflexes in insect behaviour. *Proc. V. Internat. Entomol. Congr. Paris* 1: 353–360.

Verlaine, L. 1924. L'Instinct et l'intelligence chez les Hyménoptères. I. Le problème du retour aú nid et de la reconnaissance du nid. *Mém. Acad. Roy. Belg. Cl. Sci.* 8: 1–72.

Verlaine, L. 1932b. L'Instinct et l'intelligence chez les Hymenoptèras. XX. Les sociétés des insectes ont-elles, des traditions? *J. Psychol.* 29: 784–816.

Verlaine, L. 1934. L'Instinct et l'intelligence chez les Hymenoptèras. Le relatif et l'absolu dans l'appréciation des distance chez les Guêpes. *J. Psychol.* 31: 396–407.

Wahl, O. 1932. Neue Untersuchungen über das Zeitgedächtnis der Bienen. *Z. Vergleich. Physiol.* 16: 529–589.

Warden, C. J., T. N. Jenkins, and L. Warner. 1940. *Introduction to Comparative Psychology.* Vol. II *Comparative psychology.*

Wodsedalek, J. E. 1911. Phototactic reactions and their reversal in the May-fly nymphs *Heptagenia interpunctata* (Say). *Biol. Bull.* 21: 265–271.

Wodsedalek, J. E. 1912. Natural history and general behavior of the Ephemeridae nymphs *Heptagenia interpunctata* (Say). *Ann. Entomol. Soc. Am.* 5: 31–40.

Wolf, E. 1933b. Critical frequency of flicker as a function of intensity of illumination for the eye of the bee. *J. Gen. Physiol.* 17: 7–19.

Zerrahn, G. 1933. Form Dressur und Formunterscheidung bei der Honigbiene. *Z. Vergleich. Physiol.* 20: 117–150.

T. C. SCHNEIRLA

Problems and Results in the
Study of Ant Orientation

Bibliography No. 71

I am not going to wade through this outline [see p. 665] I have given you; instead, I will talk about certain parts which seem to represent high-lights. I hope that you will find time to look into some of the other parts concerning other topics in the orientation of ants which are also important. When desirable, I shall refer to sections in the outline.

Now I think the value of ants, as experimental material, is the range and variety of patterns they give in adaptations to very different types of en-vironment in subterranean, terrestrial, and arboreal spheres. In addition to orientation processes in the normal foraging operations of workers, we have the alate males and females, with their very different reactions in-cluding those involved in the typical mating flight in the atmospheric en-vironment.

We have not only the striking characteristics in special adaptive pat-terns, as listed in Section I of my outline, but also within many species there is a range of adjustments in orientation from what we may term a low level, involving specific kinesis and taxis reactions, to a higher level of organization involving learned adjustments.

I want to contrast these two types of orientation, each one important in its way, by describing a case in which I had to clear parasitic beetles out of an ant nest in the laboratory. Here is a flat, glass-covered artificial nest, in which a colony of *Formica incerta* has established itself in earth. For some time the colony has been established in this shallow layer of earth, and many of the worker ants have learned their way from the nest via a tube to a food-place—a small, glass-covered box. These workers now travel back and forth readily during the regular feeding interval each day.

Presently we find that in this well-fed nest, the beetles are thriving and that there are 300–400 of them living with the ants and preying on the ant brood. To get rid of the beetles, I operated as follows. A lamp was placed close to the nest on one side, throwing intense light and considerable heat.

From *Proceedings of a Conference on Orientation in Animals.* Washington, D.C.: Office of Naval Research, 1954. Pp. 30–52.

In their first excitement, the ants tended to react in terms describable as kinesis and taxis—their simpler and more basic orientation patterns, we may say. Their responses of the kinesis type are indicated by variable, circuitous movements. Such reactions appear dominant among the beetles, which in the course of time drift to the side opposite the light source. In addition to taxis responses to directionalized light and to a temperature gradient, the beetles also evidently react to a humidity gradient of increasing steepness. As the earth dries out progressively from the side of the light source, increasing numbers of beetles collect in the opposite corner, which is still moist. Finally this too becomes very dry, and the beetles all perish in this little trap.

But it is different with the ants. Some of these have continued to behave in terms of kinesis and taxis reactions, shifting to the opposite side where they huddle. But before conditions reach the lethal point, they are saved through the different reactions of nest-mates. In the course of time, many of the ants that have previously learned the food-place route out of the nest have been in action. First they run out by themselves to the box, reaching the nest exit by running at right angles to the light and cutting straight across the temperature gradient. Then many of them begin to return to the nest, from which they carry out their colony mates from the huddles in which they would certainly have perished. Many make successive runs of this sort until all of the ants are out, and only the beetles remain. The ants survive, because only they have the higher type orientation reactions that will meet an emergency in which kinesis and taxis reactions lead to death.

Ants, like other social insects, exhibit the simpler and basic types of orienting adjustment which Dr. Fraenkel has discussed. The literature has been summarized by Brun (1914) and by Schneirla (1929). Reactions of the kinesis and taxis types appear, as in the above example, when ants in a resting condition are suddenly disturbed (see Outline, Sect. I-B-1). Orientation patterns of a higher type, influenced by learning, are common in the life activities of the camponotine species in particular (Outline, Sect. III and IV). The role of learning, which modifies the individual orientation pattern according to the location of food, for example, is particularly striking in species such as those in *Formica* and *Camponotus*. Orientation patterns of this plastic type have been termed "provisional orientation" by Maier and Schneirla (1935), since in them an orientation process is learned in which variations in "sign" character, in sensory control, and in locomotion along a route appear in complex dependence upon prevalent environmental circumstances.

As is indicated in Section II of the outline, there is a relatively extensive literature concerning the formation of trails by ants and the orientation of ants on trails. Only a few of the points can be mentioned here.

Many species, particularly in the ponerine, doryline, and dolichoderine subfamilies, operate on trails more or less exclusively. In the so-called "finger test" of Bonnet (1779), when ants are traveling a regular path in a column a finger is run across the route. If the ants are following a chemical trail, traffic is disrupted, and some time elapses before the column can move across the affected place. The inference is that chemical substances followed by the ants have been removed or disturbed in the test. Piéron, a French psychologist, properly objected to this test, on the ground that the ants might be disturbed by foreign substances from the finger, and not necessarily by the breaking of a chemical trail. In the crude finger-test this may often be the case, at least in part, especially with more complexly oriented species such as the frequently discussed *Lasius niger,* in which visual factors (e.g., light-direction, light-polarization) are superadded and often dominant (Outline, II-B). However, in tests with controlled cardboard pathways, Brun (1914) was able to demonstrate that, under appropriate conditions, *Lasius niger* may orient predominantly to chemical traces along its route.

In this movie * are two examples of tropical ants, both slavish chemical-trail-following species, in which the demonstration can be clear-cut. The first is a termite raider, a *Termitopone* species, which we see following a narrow line in a strict single file. If we remove a leaf from the path, even a tiny leaf, the ants stop abruptly at the spot. Traffic piles up at the break; the disturbed ants palp the ground, meander back on the trail, and it is only in the course of a few minutes that they can re-form a column across the zone of the removed leaf. Appropriate tests show that this is done through the laying down of further chemical products of their own bodies.

Here is a similar example, in a film taken of army ants on a chemical trail which they have set up during their raiding of the day. The ants with white objects are carrying prey to their temporary nest or "bivouac." Clearly they are keeping to a specific route, less than 2 cm wide. In this case also, if a leaf bridge is lifted away, traffic is disrupted and time is required to restore the trail.

I should like to say one more thing about the chemical-trail phenomenon, as illustrated in the army ants. We are emphasizing here the use of olfaction, as the predominant sense controlling orientation. But even this case is more complex. When the continuous chemical trail is interrupted, use of contact is pronounced in the restoration. In these ants, vision is virtually excluded as far as orientation is concerned. They are chemical-trail followers, which do not *learn* a route but "push" the path outward in relay

---

* Editor's note: The *Proceedings* of the Orientation Conference were published without illustrations. It was not possible to collate the same slides and films used by Dr. Schneirla in his presentation.

fashion, and any newcomer from the colony can then follow it. Covering the eyes (simple lateral ocelli) does not disturb trail orientation at all, but removing the antennae causes the worker to wander. But even in the army ants, orientation is not merely a matter of following a chemical track, as we shall see presently.

A more advanced form of chemical-trace orientation is brought out in studies such as that performed by MacGregor (Outline, II-A-3). For a *Myrmica* species, MacGregor described orientation by what he called "chemical spots." From their laboratory nest, some of the workers wandered out into an area where food had been placed in one corner. Individual workers were followed after they found the food, returned to the nest, and in a number of runs established a consistent although somewhat variable route between food-place and nest. The deviations from a specific line were least at certain places, where the lines of successive runs were superimposed. MacGregor thought that in these bottle-neck places the ants were somehow using local "chemical spots," although otherwise he did not think they were dependent upon chemical traces. Only locally, therefore, was the orientation process viewed as influenced by chemical stimuli from the substratum. How these "spots" might guide the ants was not shown in this study, nor was there an adequate control of visual and other types of sensory factor.

A hypothesis to account for such cases may be advanced on the basis of my maze studies with *Formica incerta*. In these studies (Schneirla, 1929), I found that throughout most of her run a subject could use a learned dependence upon directionalized light in particular, with a specific reliance upon olfactory differences in certain critical places. The maze was lined with closely fitted pieces of bristol board in all alleys. This permitted the control of whatever chemical products might be deposited in the repeated runs of an individual forager through the maze. Once the maze was learned and all blind-alley turns avoided, the test was made of exchanging the adjacent, oppositely-directed true-pathway and blind-alley linings at one of the junctions. The subject then was distinctly disturbed upon reaching the locality, and was likely to turn into the blind alley which she had been avoiding. In contrast, exchanging adjacent sections of lining in true pathway brought only a minor disturbance if any, and no disorientation. It is evident that at each true path-blind alley junction the ant has learned a chemical-discrimination habit, in which chemical differences between the alternative turns furnish directive cues. It is probable that a discrimination learning comparable to this is involved in the "chemical spot" orientation described by MacGregor. It is a distinctly more advanced type of orientation than the following of a continuous chemical trail as in the army ants.

The manner in which chemical trails of the various types are first set up is a problem very incompletely studied. There are very different ways of doing this (Outline, II-A-3, 4). One is the simple relay method, clearly involved in the army ants. In this sketch, army ants are advancing on a previously laid-down section of chemical trail. A small group, of about a dozen ants let us say, is directed forward on the line by tactual pressure from the base. When any ant comes to new ground, unsaturated with Eciton chemical, she advances just a short distance very excitedly, and glandular or other products are deposited as she presses her abdomen against the ground. This track can be followed by other ants as they come up, and they in turn add a little to the strip, so that the trail is lengthened gradually through collective action. In many other ants, formation of a trail is more complex. The finder ant, first to reach the food and return to the nest, in her excitement leaves a ramifying track of chemical products (e.g., anal-gland secretions). Other ants are excited on her return, and follow these traces to the food, but in the course of further runs the line is shortened considerably. Loops and wide detours in the initial complex path drop out as the ants keep more and more consistently to the best defined traces, following the chemical resultant. In many species this process is complicated by visual and other sensory factors (Outline, II-B), and in some species, as mentioned above, olfaction is involved in terms of locally discriminated chemical cues.

The next slide represents a situation in the orientation of swarm-raiding army ants. This case will help to indicate what probably happens in the formation of chemical trails by many other ants, when a collective trail emerges from circuitous individual tracks. In swarming out in one direction from their temporary nest, these army ants have formed a chemically saturated zone of increasing width. The swarm, moving in advance, leaves a saturated zone several yards wide, but only part of this area is followed by the network of columns behind the swarm, and connecting that area with the nest there is only a single column following a narrow trail. By suitable tests we can demonstrate that the ants in this basal column are following the most saturated part of a broad chemical gradient first set up in the swarm's passage. Ants transported from the column to points at the side will spiral and wander about. Those set down only a few inches from the central trail turn predominantly toward the trail, and reach it sooner and more directly than those set down farther out. Finally, with ants set down near the border of the original swarm path, wandering is nearly as random as when places clearly outside the swarm path are used. Evidently the chemical gradient is steepest near the central line followed by the column.

This type of orientation process in social insects, evidently based upon responses to a gradient of stimulation, should be studied in situations other than foraging—for example, in building operations. An interesting case has been reported by Grassé with termites which have had parts of their nest in the central queen-chamber area destroyed, so that the rebuilding process can be studied. The worker termites start building on a circumference at a certain distance from the exposed queen, first working locally in little separate groups, constructing small mounds which soon become higher pillars with their tops lengthened more and more at both ends in the circumferential direction. Finally these are joined at the top, and a wall exists around the queen, with apertures at the bottom separated by partitions. Grassé thinks that the termites have a kind of odor-form orientation, as suggested by Forel for ants (Outline, II-A-2). However, a clearer and more testable hypothesis is that the termites conduct their building operations on the basis of responses to stimulative gradients, presumably depending first upon olfactory stimuli from the queen and then upon the odorous (and possibly vibratory) stimulative effects emanating radially from each of the adjacent local groups of workers.

Turning to visual functions in ant orientation (Outline, II-B) and to cases in which vision is dominant, it is plain that we are very incompletely equipped with evidence on the neurophysiological basis of these matters. The next slide will serve as a reminder that the neurophysiological aspects of these orientation problems have interesting possibilities. For example, following the optic connections in this sketch of an ant brain, between the compound eyes and the central body we find two decussations. In the figures of some authors a bundle of uncrossed fibers is indicated for some ants, joining the outer optic ganglion with the central body. What is the significance of this equipment? And are the *mushroom bodies* the principal correlation center, as is generally thought, or is the central body? Unexplained anatomical facts such as these suggest important problems in neurophysiology lying behind the organization of orientation processes in the social insects.

The next slide will help to emphasize both the type of ant orientation in which vision is dominant and the problem of organization. The sketch is from the monograph of Rudolph Brun, now a neuropsychiatrist. An important part of Brun's investigation involved *Lasius niger*. This is a visually oriented ant on the whole, as Lubbock demonstrated (Outline, II-B), but is also influenced by chemical and tactual cues to an important extent. Here is shown the "fixation test," as Brun called it (Outline, II-B-3). In this test, an ant is traced in a direct course from a food-place toward her nest, then about midway to the nest is shut under a light-tight vessel for two hours. Meanwhile the sun's position had shifted about 23°. Then the cover is removed, releasing the ant. Usually, after some variable movements the ant sets off on a changed course which deviates from the direct course to the nest by roughly the angle through which the direction of sunlight has moved in the meantime. The outcome indicated to Brun that before she was shut up the foraging Lasius worker was returning to the nest in dependence upon the direction at which light entered specific ommatidia in her compound eyes. Such virtual orientation to the direction of illumination was called by Santschi "light-compass-orientation." Many of the camponotine ants, as well as myrmecines and others, normally seem very dependent upon the direction of illumination in their orientation. This can be demonstrated readily in laboratory tests, as Brun did with *Lasius* and *Formica* species. I have studied it in detail with *Formica incerta* in maze studies, in which a subject must make her run from nest to food-place with light directed from one side of the apparatus. Although many changes in direction must be made by the ant in passing through the maze alleys, so that she heads toward or away from the light source or has it on one side or the other in different sections of the run, once the maze has been learned the light serves as a dominant orienting cue throughout the trip. Much confusion results when the direction of illumination is changed.

Brun and Santschi did not know that many ants such as *Lasius niger* and *Myrmica* species can be oriented with reference to the plane of polarization of light from the sky. This has been demonstrated in experiments by Vowles, Carthy, and others (Outline, II-B-3). This accounts satisfactorily for Santschi's observation that a Myrmecocystus worker could maintain her direction of progress even when a tall paper cylinder held vertically over her shut out direct sunlight and left only the light from a patch of sky directly overhead. It is now clear that the many cases reported in detail by the Algerian librarian, Cornetz, which he held could not be explained in terms of known sensory functions but must depend upon an "unknown direction sense," must involve visual functions such as these.

The next slide represents the fact that in a great many if not all instances in which visual factors dominate, other fields are also involved (Outline, II-C). Under experimental conditions, when direction of illumination is changed, there are indications that olfaction and contact rise temporarily in importance. In a maze of the type shown in the next slide, proprioceptive cues (Outline, II-C-3) are at a premium as the "U" approach to each choice-point affects the mechanics of locomotion so that blind alleys are easily entered from the start and difficult to eliminate through learning. Local olfactory and tactual factors are important here, along with vision if directionalized light or other visual cues are involved. This is a reminder of how complex the orientation processes may be in the foraging of many ant species.

Another factor of importance for *Formica* and many other ants, but apparently not for most of the trail-followers, is what we may call light-distribution effects (Outline, II-B-4). This type of factor seems more complex than Santschi's light-compass orientation. In this case we evidently have to consider the pattern of light distributed over the visually-sensitive area or areas, e.g., over the three rostral ocelli. In this slide we have the so-called "constrained course" test of Brun with a *Polyergus* worker (a well-visioned species) returning in a straight path directly toward her nest, behind which there is a large pine tree. With his finger the experimenter forces the ant to run off her course, for an appreciable distance first in one direction, then successively on a line in a second direction and a third, and finally the ant is released at a point well off the line on which she was running at the start. When this test works well, the ant is able to return directly toward her nest despite the successive displacements, in what Brun calls the "closing of a polygon." He concludes that the pattern of light over the eyes, dependent upon large objects, is the visual factor responsible for the orientation in such cases. It is as though the ant moved toward, or laterally with reference to, a large dark bulk in her visual field. In one case Brun covered a rose bush beside a *Formica* worker's route, and found the ant disoriented until the bush was uncovered. The experiment was found most effective with "higher ants" such as *Formica* species, especially when the ants were operating over varied, heterogeneous terrain. With these species such tests are negative on flat uniform terrain, when the specific light-directionalization factor dominates orientation. The tests are also negative for species such as *Lasius niger,* which commonly orients with respect to direction of sunlight but which lacks ocelli, and they are negative for the collective-trail foragers.

To illustrate a complexity of factors in a relatively stereotyped case of orientation, we may take the case of the army ant circular column shown in the next slide. Columns of this kind start readily in the laboratory as the ants first follow the edge of a circular dish in close contact, or around the border of a mass of nest-mates clustered on the floor. As the temperature rises from the point at which all were clustered, more and more of the ants join in the action until all are involved. At first locomotion is slow and variable, and is specifically canalized by contact with the edge of some central island. Soon the ants are circling in a wide ring, free of the initial contact with the border. When traveling in this ring or mill, each ant is clearly influenced by a pattern of contact with other ants which run ahead, at the sides, and behind. A chemical trail is also involved, since removal of the jar around which the ants started to travel does not break up the column, but wiping over or changing the substratum does interfere. It is not simply a matter of following a chemical track, since the entire circle of ants can shift to a new place when one intense light or high temperature is introduced unilaterally. The results of simple tests together with significant features of the circling give further data for an analysis. In her persistent turning to one side with the circling column, each ant evidently reacts to a steady combination of gentle contact and olfactory change. Her "turning-to" reaction depends to an important extent upon such stimulation furnished as ants move away (i.e., provide a "drainage" effect) on the inside. This is complex, since each ant also is canalized by an inward pressure from ants on her other side, and by an onward pressure from the rear.

The organization of the circular column is more involved than this simple enumeration would suggest (Schneirla, 1944). In it, numerous tactual and olfactory factors can be identified; these function together in an interrelated system or pattern. The complexity is evident, although this case of orientation is stereotyped and must be given a lower-level status in a psychological sense. Time unfortunately does not permit going into this matter.

To illustrate what may be considered a higher-level phenomenon in ant orientation, in comparison with the army-ant case; we may return to some aspects of Formica orientation in the maze. The slide shows a maze of six blind alleys interposed as a barrier between the nest and a food-place, and a similar one as barrier between food-place and nest. In this situation, light can be directed on the maze from any one or more of the four sides. Now after a *Formica* worker has learned the maze with light always from the right side, let us say, looking from the nest, if the light is shifted to the opposite side she will be radically disturbed. But the ant can relearn the situation in considerably fewer runs and with a fraction of the effort required for original learning. This indicates not only a plasticity but also a considerable degree of integrative function of sensory factors in the orientation.

A respectable degree of integration in this orientation habit is shown in the ant's first reaction to the changed visual situation, and while she is relearning the maze, by a pronounced dependence upon tactual and olfactory cues. Not only does her behavior indicate that these factors are being relied upon more heavily in the readjustment than before, but tests can be made. If at this time, the true path and blind-alley linings are exchanged at one or more of the junctions, the ant is considerably more disturbed by such alterations than she is normally (i.e., with unchanged illumination). If regular pathway-lining changes are also made in this period of readjustment to changed lighting, the time required for adaptation to the visual change is increased very appreciably. It seems apparent that, when illumination alone is changed, a readjustment comes about through a greater reliance upon the unchanged conditions of other sensory fields. In the normal orientation of such ants there is involved what Brun calls a "global complex" of sensory factors, and these maze results show that the processes are not only interdependent and highly organized but may also change plastically to an appreciable extent as the stimulative field is modified. Through such plastic learning capacities, the most highly specialized foragers among social insects can widen greatly the limits of the stereotyped processes of kinesis and taxis basic in their orientation.

In one way or another, most foraging ants pass back and forth between their nest and a food-place through a considerable part of the day. Those mainly or entirely canalized by chemical trails in their orientation are little disturbed by diurnal changes such as the shifting angle of sunlight. On the other hand, the more visual species such as *Formica* spp. are forced to adjust on some basis to the shifting of sensory factors on which they depend. How this may happen is suggested by maze experiments in which successive learned readjustments on the part of the subject. And as we have mentioned above, such enforced readjustments are accomplished through only a partial relearning of the situation, in dependence upon stable parts of the sensory complex. In my experiments, *Formica* workers were able to meet successive 90° and 180° changes in the direction of illumination, and combinations of greater complexity, quite readily through further learning. We should bear in mind that under natural conditions, illumination normally changes only gradually, with small changes in direction from trip to trip of the forager. Presumably the problem of learning a readjustment to such environmental changes is not as difficult then as in the described maze tests. At the same time, it is probably true under natural conditions, as it is in the maze situation, that some or many of the foragers will stay in the nest after an abrupt and marked change (e.g., suddenly overcast sky) in environmental conditions.

In closing, I should like to emphasize the desirability of further experimental and theoretical studies of the very different patterns of orientation found in the various subfamilies of ants, from the stereotyped to the more plastic types.

OUTLINE

I. Principal characteristics and contrasts in the orientation of ants.
   A. As terrestrial insects, ants typically are adapted to heterogeneous environmental conditions in their various subterranean, surface, and arboreal life situations.
      1. Under appropriate conditions (e.g., when resting, suddenly exposed to light) all ants are capable of the simpler grades of orienting responses.
      2. In their typical life activities, ants exhibit orientation processes characterized by:
         a. A wide diversity of types among the principal groups.
         b. The frequent appearance of an elaborate set of orientation processes within a particular species.
   B. Principal problems recognizable in ant orientation.
      1. Simpler and more direct types of orienting adjustments:

      a. Kinesis and taxis patterns.

      b. Postural and locomotory control.

  2. Characteristic adjustments to focal aspects of the environment, such as responses to "food" objects, nesting materials, brood, queen, nestmates, "strange" insects.

  3. Individual and group way-finding processes in foraging.

  4. Orientation in group activities of nonforaging types; such as spatially coordinated activities in nest-making, intercolony territorial adjustments, mating flights, nest-changing emigrations.

II. Sensory control in foraging activities has persistently received the predominant emphasis in scientific study of ant orientation.

  A. Chemoreceptive and especially olfactory functions, first to be discovered, often have been misrepresented or overemphasized.

    1. Fundamental role of olfaction suggested by anatomical facts: receptor cells located on terminal segmented parts (funiculi) of the freely moving antennae.

    2. "Chemical-trail" concept dates almost from the classic finger-test of Bonnet (1779):

      a. Rubbing across path of ant column produces a definite interruption of traffic for an appreciable time—typically effective on the collective trails of species with poorly developed eyes, e.g., *Iridomyrmex* spp.

      b. Evidence and argument concerning polarization of chemical trails.

        (1) Bethe (1898): ant trails are directionally polarized and followed in a reflex manner, e.g., acquiring food sets off "homegoing reflex" as response to corresponding chemical traces. Evidence: reported that rotation of zinc trail-section reversed returning *Lasius niger* foragers, exchanging trail sections did not.

          (a) Forel (1903): too simple; favored the (rather vague) topochemical

          (b) or "odor-form" concept.

          (c) Wasmann (1899): too simple and reflex; favored his "odor-foot-track" concept (which was complex, obscure).

          (d) Brun's (1914) analysis contributed to clarity: In species such as *Lasius niger* used by Bethe, light-direction responses often interfere. But under appropriate conditions, greater disturbance on exchange of terminal trail-segments indicates polarization.

          Under certain conditions (e.g., larva-carrying)

the trail may be negligibly polarized, under others (e.g., return from honey-place), polarization is factor.

(2) Contemporary objections:

    (a) Chauvin (1945): rejected polarization, attributing Bethe's results to tactual breaks in trail (however, C's few field tests seem inadequate to meet Brun's cases).

    (b) MacGregor (1948): from observations on a *Myrmica* sp., concluded that chemical actually is discontinuous (but tests with other species indicate continuous chemical traces, polarized under appropriate conditions).

3. Special orienting functions involving chemical traces.

  a. Evidence for Forel's topochemical sense is shaky (e.g., Brun's perfume-test results attributable to discriminating quantitative differences on path.

    (1) However, the possibility of habituated local chemical cues [1] indicated by Turner's test with *Formica* sp.: foragers disturbed by removal of a xylol band from lab. trail.

  b. Cornetz's (1910): "odor network" around the nest entrance, assumed to guide approaches into nest, has some validity even for more visual species (e.g., *Formica rufa*).

  c. Evidence for chemoreceptive discrimination functions at critical points:

    (1) MacGregor (1948) argues against chemical trail, favors chemical "spot" guidance: he found *Myrmica* workers directionalized by specific local traces for direct progress in intervening stretches.

    (2) This seems to hold even more clearly for *Formica* spp. as maze experiments (Schneirla, 1929) show—*but* not for many other species.

    (3) Army ants are *continuous* trail-followers, yet laden ants clearly discriminate nestward turns at branches, on olfactory basis.

4. Origin and survival of chemical trails.

  a. Problem of formation of chemical trails:

    (1) In "community trailers," [2] loops and irregularities

---

[1] A "cue" may be defined as any stimulus with a directive function in a learned orientation.

[2] A species in which the traces left by one ant can be followed at once by nestmates.

gradually drop as trail is shortened (probably by following the resultant, or best-saturated line).

    (2) Two rather different types of trail origin illustrated by army-ant relay process and the "progressive straightening" pattern revealed by Eidmann's (1927) test.

  b. Continuous-trail following is never a simple phenomenon:

    (1) *Iridomyrmex* sp. swerving from lateral hot-spot.

    (2) Shifting of Eciton circular mill under unilateral disturbance.

  c. Ontogeny of chemical-trail following:

    (1) Hypothesis: Basis established in habituation to colony chemical in early feeding activities.

    (2) Evidence for gradual extension in callow army-ant workers.

  d. Time-value of survival not clearly established for any species:

    (1) Typically subject to renewal through further use, in common trailing operations nearest the nest.

    (2) In some (e.g., the leaf-cutter *Atta* sp.), tangible tactual canalization may arise—e.g., indentation of route, killing of grass by trail-chemical.

    (3) Use after interval of 3 weeks by army ants (dry season).

5. Nature of chemical traces.

  a. Santschi's observation of droplets of presumed anal-gland secretion on glass floor in wake of excited food-carrying *Tapinoma* sp. worker.

  b. Carthy's (1950) technique of dusting lycopodium powder over trail reveals (for *Lasius niger*) dashes of fluid about 4 mm long:

    (1) Believed to be an anal-gland secretion, deposited at intervals by excited worker after finding food (Kutter, 1952).

    (2) Cf. opening of scent-gland orifice by finder bee on food discovery (von Frisch and Rösch, 1926).

  c. Other sources: volatilization from general body surface, food carried (evidence from choice-point discriminations by Formica workers in maze (Schneirla, 1933).

6. Role of olfaction in other organized activities.

  a. Concerted digging in ants and wall-building by termites, cf. Grassé (1948)—hypothesis of gradient responses preferable to Forel's topochemical sense.

b. Complex individual interactions in swarm-raid organization of certain army ants (cf. orientation in circular mill).

B. Visual orienting functions outstanding in many (e.g., camponotines).

1. Species differ from zero to maximum in development of compound eyes, ocelli, and their brain connections (e.g., visual tracts).

   a. Neural functions have received little attention.

   b. Suggestive connections of mushroom bodies, central body in brain.

2. Negative or limited finger-test disturbances, or modified and variable results, typical for species with well-developed eyes.

   a. Sweeping or covering area of passage ("ant thoroughfare"), usually ineffective or limited in effect with *Polyergus* spp., *Formica* spp., *Camponotus* spp.—Huber, 1810; Forel, 1864; Fabre, 1879; Brun, 1914; etc.

   b. *Lasius niger* workers on trail over rotatable concentric table segments were disturbed when light source turned with trail segment 180°; reversed direction, but not with trail-rotation alone (Lubbock, 1883; Brun, 1914).

   c. Outcome of tests for visual factors varies greatly with species, may depend greatly upon prevalent conditions.

3. Light-direction factors.

   a. Light-compass orientation: a direct course is maintained in dependence upon continued stimulation of local sections of compound eye.

      (1) The "mirror test" (Santschi, 1911): cutting off direct sunlight with screen, reversing light direction with mirror, usually caused reversal of direction in laden returning foragers of *Camponotus* sp., *Myrmecocystus* sp., *Messor* sp., and *Tapinoma* sp.

      (2) The "fixation test" (Brun, 1914): a laden forager of *Lasius niger* returning to nest on direct course, shut under box for interval of 2–4 hr, on release typically sets off on course diverging roughly by the angle of the sun's intervening movement (e.g., by 23° after 2 hr detention).

      (3) Generally negative for many camponotine species (e.g., *Formica* spp.) except on very uniform terrain or in controlled laboratory tests (Brun, 1914) corroborated by Turner (1913) and in maze experiments by Shepard (1913) and Schneirla (1929).

        b. Polarization-plane effects.

            (1) Vowles (1950) demonstrates with *Myrmica* sp. a direct orientation to polarized light from sky, even overcast . . . similar results with other species by Miss Schifferer (von Frisch, 1950).

            (2) May account for Santschi's (1923) cases of twilight and nocturnal foraging desert ants; Cornetz's (1910 etc.) argument for "unknown direction sense based on presumed exclusion of direct light in field."

        c. Ultraviolet orientation dependent on reflection from vegetation (should be investigated).

    4. Light-distribution effects: light patches (objects), light-shaded zones, light-dark borders, other possible functions.

        a. In the mirror test, Santschi (1911) reported a *Camponotus* sp. worker first reversed her direction, then corrected when she mounted a small rise which presumably exposed for visual-cue use a nearby date tree; a *Messor* sp. worker corrected upon coming into view of a pile of sheaves.

        b. *Formica* sp. workers, after artificially enforced passages in two or three successively different directions, often set out directly for the nest upon release.

            (1) Brun (1914, 1917) denied that this "closing of a polygon" could be due to the determination of a resultant through a "kinesthetic sense of angles" as Szymanski (1911) suggested.

            (2) Rather, Brun attributed the capacity to use of large objects as visual cues.

        c. Such visual functions probably account for the frequent failure of the Santschi mirror test and similar tests with *Formica* and *Camponotus* foragers on varied terrain.

    5. Other possibilities.

        a. Interesting object-fixing capacity *suggested* in foragers of the neo-tropical "giant" ponerine, *Paraponera clavata*.

        b. "Parallax" function dependent on ocelli.

  C. Other types of sensory function *not well known.*

    1. Tactual functions may be both specific (local cues) and generalized.

        a. As possible "generalized" tactual functions, orientation to prevailing wind, stable convection currents, and the like is very possible in many species, but still undemonstrated by exact tests.

        b. General and local use of tactual cues highly probable in most species, to varying extents and in different ways.

(1) Following linear edges, touching objects, is common in the foraging of many camponotine and myrmecine species.

(2) Brun's (1914) "middleground" test: *Lasius* sp. workers, transferred to a larva heap midway on a habituated paper bridge, moved away on chance basis unless a 5 mm railing remained on one side; other evidence for tactual cues.

(3) Use of tactual cues in supporting role common in the maze-learning of *Formica* sp. workers.

c. Continuous reliance on contact (with olfaction) indicated in poorly investigated subterranean species, many nocturnal foraging species.

2. Vibratory functions (substratal, perhaps also atmospheric).

a. Many myrmecine and ponerine species have stridulatory organs producing high-frequency vibratory effects; chordotonal receptors in many, also almost all species have more or less body-surface pilosity, some have specialized integumentary spines.

(1) Substratal vibrations very probably involved in normal intra-nest orientation of many species; Haskins (1938) also demonstrated *air-vibration sensitivity* in ponerine species.

(2) Wheeler (1910) suggested that stridulation from workers in nest may assist nest return from nearby points.

3. Proprioceptive functions.

a. Kinesthesis as such undemonstrated in ants; generalized integument-buckling effects indicated by Pringle's work.

(1) Doubtful or disproved: Szymanski's "kinesthetic sense of angles" explicable on visual basis, after Santschi and Brun; Piéron's (1911) suggestion of a reversal of outgoing turns on the return to nest, through kinesthesis, is unsupported and doubtful.

(2) Orientation to slope of substratum—to position of walking surface in space.

(a) Tarsal-contact sensitivity may account for affinity to upright walking position in roofed runways (tests with anesthetized tarsal receptors desirable).

(b) Other things equal, "negative geotaxis" (i.e., upward progress on slope) characterizes most species.

(c) Brun (1914): Ants habituated to sloping laboratory paths were subjected to 180° reversal of
slope direction: with bipolar lighting, disturbance appeared at 20°, but with unipolar lighting
a greater slope was required for disturbance.

(3) Centripetal and centrifugal effects.

(a) Circular columns of nonvisually oriented army
ants, moving concentrically on a turntable, increase running speed, width and centrifugal expansion of column with speed of rotation; but at
higher speeds break, form oppositely rotating
subcircles, etc.

(b) In the army-ant mill, there is evidence for postural factors attributable to running "set."

(c) Sturdza (1942, etc.)—*Formica rufa* in rotated
dish, with slow rotation: runs in same direction
but overcompensates; with faster rotation: reversals, halts, and variations become more frequent; with visual complexity the ant may behave
almost independently of the rotation.

This suggests [the desirability of conducting
tests] on postural adjustments and locomotion
in widely different ants under various conditions of speed and interruption of substratal
rotation [as well as investigating] the reactions
of different species in crossing a rotated portion of a *learned* route.

(d) "Centrifugal swing" (as analyzed in maze-learning) a basic factor in establishing a route:
differential readiness for unilateral turning in dependence upon the preceding succession of turns.

III. Complex sensory control and integrated function the rule in ant orientation.

A. Typically, all available sensory modalities of given species are
involved.

1. Characteristic species patterns of orientation thus depend
upon:

a. Relative specialization of different sensory fields in the
species.

b. Neural and motor equipment, especially the former, as
determining capacity for change in primary responses to
given situation.

c. Stimulus characteristics of given situation.

2. In general, the orientation pattern appearing in a particular situation depends upon:
   a. Condition of the individual: resting; engaged in nest functions; engaged in successive foraging trips.
      (1) For example, resting individuals respond photokinetically or phototactically to suddenly presented lights according to their intensity, relative light-adaptation of the ant, etc.
      (2) Foragers of a visual species respond according to conditions of route, previous learning, etc.
   b. Prevalent extrinsic conditions, available sensory cues (e.g., on ant thoroughfares over varied terrain, *Formica* workers are minimally responsive to chemical features, maximally to visual).
B. Integrated functioning of sensory modalities indicated in all species sufficiently investigated.
   1. Brun's term, "global sensory function," seems appropriate for stimulus control in foraging orientation.
      a. Generalization: all available sensory cues of different modalities in a given situation function integratively to relatively different extents in a single unified process.
      b. Therefore, according to organic limitations of the species, extrinsic changes affecting one modality are likely to affect the roles of the others.
   2. Simple and complex examples are available:
      a. According to Brun, Lubbock's candle test disorients *Lasius niger* workers more in a homogeneous chemical situation (larva-carrying trail) than in a heterogeneous situation (trail from honey-place to nest).
      b. Running a partially learned maze, a *Formica* worker is more disturbed by pathway-lining (i.e., chemical) changes if unilateral illumination is also changed.
   3. Neural basis only inferred from anatomy.
C. In all investigated ant species, orientation may have an appreciable measure of plasticity.
   1. Properties for change are qualitatively very limited in *Eciton* species:
      a. Operating on canalized chemical trails, with a nondirective visual function.
      b. Chemical and tactual readjustments to changing conditions occur in a relatively gradual and cumulative manner, actually through a collective, group modification of the *stimulus cues themselves.*

2. Plasticity in orientation is relatively great in *Formica* species, in comparison with other investigated ants.

   a. After learning a maze pattern, the individual worker can master successive changes in light direction, each more promptly than the last.

   b. Here the principal change evidently is intraorganic, in the subject's learned adaptation to external sensory cues.

3. Neural basis unexplored.

IV. Ontogeny of orientation and the role of learning deserve systematic study in terms of the organic properties and limitations of each species.

A. Species genetics and ontogeny.

1. In each species we may postulate a set of characteristic, basic properties for kinesis and taxis in orientation, dictated primarily by species heredity.

2. Fundamental characteristics of ant locomotion significant for orientation:

   a. A meandering in locomotion, especially in less visual species, becomes prominent on new terrain, under changed conditions, and disturbances.

   b. An outward spiralling course modified by looping, characterizes ant progress on new terrain (Turner, 1910; Weyrauch, 1938).

3. These emerge through development as fundamental to the normal species orientation pattern, but are subject to further specialization beyond the specific dictates of tissue maturation.

   a. Postulation: individual habituation to the colony chemical, starting with feeding as a larva, provides the main basis for extra-nest orientation.

   b. In army ants, trail-following is first crude, but improves to adult status in about four days after callow workers begin activities outside the nest.

4. According to species, first, orientation within the nest, and later, outside the nest, begin in limited ways and enlarge progressively in scope.

   a. *Formica* foragers ultimately master relatively complex habits as *solitary foraging individuals*.

   b. Individual army ants probably learn little beyond the basic odor habituation to colony chemical, with possible exception of generalized qualitative discriminations at trail junctions.

B. Development of particular orientation processes thus differs greatly according to species.

1. *Rise of a collective orientation situation in species predominantly dependent on olfaction.*
    a. The army ants are a simplified, clear case: the foremost ants meander only a short distance into unsaturated terrain, incidentally laying a new stretch of chemical in their excitement; this new stretch is then followed and extended by successive new pioneers, in relay fashion.
    b. A more complex type is represented by Eidmann's (1925) case: a *Tapinoma* worker wanders around an area in a complex looping path; finally hitting on food, returns excitedly to the nest by a variable but less complex path.
        (1) The finder *evidently releases chemical secretions* in her excitement, since ants aroused from the nest can reach the same food-place better than by chance, unless a new cardboard floor is substituted.
        (2) If the food-source remains, the trail to it from the nest is straightened by degrees through further use, eventually becoming more or less direct.
2. *In still more complex cases of collective foraging, no chemical trail as such arises,* but local chemical cues (e.g., MacGregor's chemical "spots" in *Myrmica* are built up).
    a. In such cases, local chemical remnants are only partially directive, and evidently require supplementation.
    b. It is probable that additional cues are added through learning (e.g., of adjustment to directed light in the intervening stretches).
3. *In species with better developed visual properties* (e.g., *Formica*) the role of collective chemical cues is occasional and subordinate, and the *entire route is essentially a result of individual learning.*
    a. Individual learning of foraging routes can be demonstrated in laboratory maze investigations.
    b. Under natural conditions, ants of such species are capable of foraging in specific individual places at considerable distances.
4. Renewal of foraging processes after hibernation an unexplored problem.
C. Relation of the outgoing and return journeys.
    1. Generalization: the more dependent the species upon *chemical traces* in orientation, the more chances for similarity between the two phases of the foraging run.
        a. Since chemical traces *fundamentally* are generalized and capable of orientation use in either direction of progress.

b. Piéron's hypothesis is doubtful, that the ant has a "muscular memory" which on the return journey permits a repetition of the outgoing turns in reverse.

c. In the simpler cases, collective foragers leave the food-place by simply turning into the trail; in more complex cases, prompter 180° turns are possible through conditioning to directed light.

2. Generalization: the more dependent the species upon *nonolfactory cues* and particularly visual cues, the more essential are *individualized learning processes* and the more likely are the outgoing and return runs to be distinct in their routes and critical stimulus-response processes.

a. Maze experiments with *Formica* species indicate that the runs in the two directions arise as two independent sets of habits, independently learned and operative, even when true pathway sequences are the same for the two.

b. In this type, it appears that the route is mastered by each forager largely through her own individual learning processes in her own activities.

c. In the individual-foraging type, the turn-about after acquiring food may be assisted by chemical traces at well-frequented food sources, but must be considered a part of a learned route, established according to the properties of each specific orienting situation.

V. Special problems concerning group orientation in army ants.

A. Properties of orientation in mass activities.

1. Analysis of group coordination in the circular column.

a. Stimuli intrinsic to the specific group situation control the movement pattern and its variations.

b. Each individual ant moves in stereotyped fashion with reference to a locally effective chemotactual situation and the proprioceptive aspects of her locomotion.

2. Directionalization and internal organization in the raiding swarm of *Eciton burchelli* (Schneirla, 1940).

a. These properties are controlled through the collective activities of the ants themselves, although individuals within the swarm itself have not definite direction.

b. Demonstrable factors control shape and direction of progress of the swarm.

c. The entire body is both organized and directed through the highly diversified activities of its members.

B. Colony nomadism in army ants, and the *migration question* (Schneirla, 1945).

1. A colony, when in the nomadic phase, carries out a predictable succession of nightly emigrations, each over a base raiding trail of the respective day.
2. Each nocturnal shift in the specific nomadic phase may be termed an "emigration;" the series of approximately 16 shifts may be termed a "migration."

REFERENCES

Brun, R. 1914. *Die Ranmorientierung der Ameisen und das Orientierungsproblem im allgemeinan.* Jena: Fischer.

Brun, R. 1916. Weitere Untersuchungen über die Fernorientierung der Ameisen. *Biol. Zent.* 36: 261–303.

Carthy, J. D. 1951. The orientation of two allied species of British ant. *Behaviour* 3: 275–318.

Cornetz, Victor. 1910. Trajets de fourmis et retours au nid. *Inst. Gen. Psychologique, Mem.* no. 2, 1–167.

Cornetz, V. 1914. *Les explorations et les voyages des Fourmis.* Paris: Flammarion.

MacGregor, E. G. 1948. Odour as a basis for oriented movement in ants. *Behaviour* 1: 267–296.

Santschi, F. 1911. Observations et remarques critiques sur le mécanisme de l'orientation chez les fourmis. *Rev. Suisse Zool.* 19: 303–338.

Santschi, F. 1923. Les différentes orientations chez les fourmis. *Rev. Zool. Afr.* 11: 10–144.

Santschi, F. 1930. Nouvelles expériences sur l'orientation des Tapinoma par sécrétions dromographiques. *Arch. Psychol.* 22: 348–351.

Schneirla, T. C. 1929. Learning and orientation in ants. *Comp. Psychol. Monogr.* 6 (4): 143.

Schneirla, T. C. 1944. A unique case of circular milling in ants, considered in relation to trail following and the general problem of orientation. *Am. Mus. Nov.* (1253): 1–26.

Stumper, R. 1921. Etudes sur les fourmis—Recherches critiques sur l'odorat. *Bull. Soc. Ent. Belg.* 3: 24–30.

Sturdza, S. A. 1942. Verhalten der Roten Waldameisen auf horizontal gedrehten lotrechten Flächen. *Bull. Sec. Sci. Acad. Roumaine* 24: 605–609.

Vowles, D. M. 1950. Sensitivity of ants to polarized light. *Nature* 165: 184.

T. C. SCHNEIRLA

Psychological Comparison of Insect and Mammal

Bibliography No. 97

The psychological nature of an animal concerns especially the range of its abilities and resources for organizing and adaptively modifying its behavior. What is critical for comparisons is not the specific abilities so much as how they can be used in patterns and can be modified for new adaptations. Although honeybees and many ants have resources for color vision and for olfactory sensitivity superior to those of mammals, the insect may be inferior in its capacities for modifying behavior. Shepard (1914) concluded from his exploratory maze studies that ants operate on an inferior level to rats in their learning; Fabre in his classical "frog's gibbet" test found the burying beetle unable to achieve a simple novel detour solution of a type easy for most cats or dogs (granted the essential general experience).

A comparison of how insects and mammals master conditioned responses could not be expected to help much on this point, unless the method tested relative abilities for the successive conditioning and extinction, combination and recombination of opposed response tendencies. Nor would much be expected from a comparison based on operant conditioning, without more attention to the internal conditions of organization in the operant than is usual in such work.

Our present discussion is based upon studies of how the *Formica* ant (close to the peak of insect learning) compares with the rat (roughly intermediate in the mammals in learning ability) in dealing with problems of mastering and reversing spatial-discriminative associations. In the absence of data for a detailed comparison of how these animals solve the one-junction T-maze, it is sufficient to say that this is a very simple problem for the rat although I have found it more difficult for ants of *Formica* spp. Striking differences appear when the first reversals of alternatives are made. Buytendijk (1930) found that rats master the first reversal readily and with further reversals of the alternatives adapt to each change cor-

From *Psychologische Beitrage* 6: 509–520 (1962). Reprinted with permission.

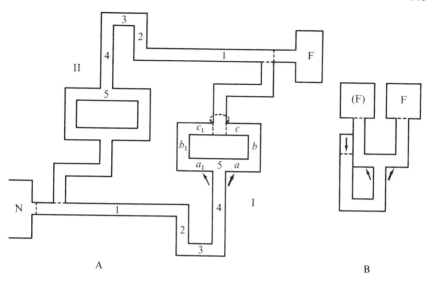

FIGURE 68

A. T-maze with U-alley approach to choice-point, in the pattern used for testing *Formica* ants. I. The problem is presented in the direction N (Nest) to F (Foodbox). The subject's passage through approach alleys 2–4 generates a strong turning bias toward side a-b-c and against side a_1-b_1-c_1. By blocking alley c or alley c_1 at its end, alley a_1 or alley a respectively is made the true-path turn at the choice-point. II. Control situation with open alternatives at 5, through which the ant returns to N. B. T-maze with U-alley approach to choice-point as adapted by Witkin (1942) for rats. From the starting compartment (arrow) shown at left, the subject passes through a U-series of alleys which gives a strong turning bias toward the right turn (heavy arrow) at the choice-point. By placing food alternately in F and in (F) as each is learned, the experimenter forces the animal to shift its adjustment to the choice-point. (From Schneirla, 1960.)

rectly with only one or two exploratory errors. *Formica* ants, however, even after a dozen reversals of alternatives in the simple T-maze, enter the newly incorrect alternative repeatedly before each successive reversal is mastered.

When the T-maze is complicated by replacing the straight approach-alley with a U-shaped succession of alleys (Figure 68-A) in free tests without food, both *Formica* ant and rat show a turning bias at the junction so strong that the "outside" turn is made more than four times as often as the inside turn (Schneirla, 1933; Witkin and Schneirla, 1937). But when food is introduced on the side of the difficult turn, rats can eliminate the easy turn and reach the food directly within less than 60 runs as a rule (Witkin, 1942); in contrast, *Formica* ants require more than 100 runs to master this problem. There are other differences: the ant progresses very

680

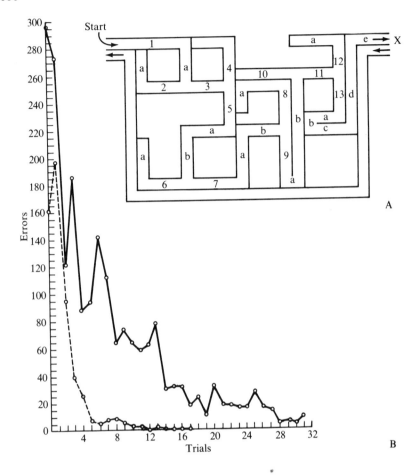

FIGURE 69
A. Maze D, with its six choice-points (2–3, 4–5, 6–7, 8–9, 10–11 and 12–13)
used as a learning test for *Formica* ants and as a comparison test for
hooded rats. In the initial learning test, each subject (the ants from the nest,
the rats from a starting-box) ran from alley 1 through the maze to the food-
box (X), —the ants returned from X to the nest via the outer pathway. B.
Curves for the initial learning of maze D by eight *Formica* ants (solid line)
and eight hooded rats (broken line). Ordinate: total errors per trial; abscissa:
trials. (From Roeder, K., ed., *Insect Physiology*. New York: Wiley, 1953.)

slowly, shortening its entrances to the blind alley by degrees, the rat more
rapidly with stages of sudden improvement.

From such results, our conclusion is that the mammal has a superior
ability for acquiring and organizing, whereby it inhibits a facile action
and substitutes a difficult one much more readily than can the ant. The rat

seems also to acquire its habit in a different way, as is shown not only by the manner in which the two animals first solve the U-maze but also, as we shall see, by their adaptations to successive reversals of the alternatives. The differences may be thrown into relief by comparing the behavior of ant and rat in learning and in adapting to modifications in a multiple-T maze.

The problem was a maze with six true path-blind alley junctions (Figure 69-A), used in appropriate scale for rat and for *Formica* ant. Striking differences appeared, first of all, in the initial learning of this problem by the two animals (Figure 69-B). Rats not only mastered the situation in fewer trials than the ants, but progressed in a strikingly different way. The ants all improved their performances much more slowly than the rats, reducing their error totals by small degrees rather than by jumps as with the rats. Under diffuse light, they needed about 32 runs to learn this maze—more than twice that for the rats.

Even more significant was the fact that the progress of each ant was describable in terms of three rather distinct stages. (1) The first stage involves a generalized learning (Schneirla, 1941), interpreted as a habituation to the situation in which erratic behavior and variable running decreases throughout the maze, but without any clear signs of improvement in avoiding blind-alley turns at the junctions or of shortening entrances into blind alleys. (2) Next, beginning at about the eighth run and plainly based upon stage 1, on intermediate stage (Schneirla, 1943) follows in which the ant gradually shortens her entrances into blind alleys and increases her true turns at junctions. I have interpreted the local processes of this second stage in the ant as involving discrete sets of conditioned-response adjustments centered in the different maze localities where forward progress is blocked. Entrances into the blind alleys are shortened gradually and from their termini, as in the T-maze, until at length the blind sequences are occasionally avoided at their entrances. In this six-blind maze, at about the eighth run, the ants show a 50 percent frequency of direct entrances—the "naive" response condition—improving this performance linearly thereafter until a 100 percent record is attained around the 32nd run. Analyses of records indicate that the ability to avoid the blind alleys at their entrances, as it improves, depends upon the slowly advancing processes of blind-shortening in each maze locality. Based upon the local conditioned-response learning, a process of selective learning is postulated for each junction in which the tendency to turn directly into the true-path alternative gradually increases in its dominance over the blind-turning response.

This selective-learning process is viewed as involving an active competition between the sensory-neuromuscular organizations of competitive responses to each junction. When this competition evidently reaches its peak—usually when blind-alley entrances have been reduced to partial, quickly reversed runs into the first arm—the existence of extreme difficulty in organizing behavior is often indicated by tense, erratic actions in subjects at the choice-points. Such behavior typically becomes marked near the end of the second stage, when the subjects have become able to avoid the long blind alleys as wholes. Then, at the moment each critical junction is reached, behavior is generally excitable and tense, and erratic new actions such as quick circling often appear. (These symptoms and their further meaning will be discussed later.)

As the local T-junction responses become regular true-path turns, this type of "nervous" behavior disappears, and the ant's regular behavior indicates that an improved organization has been attained in the maze situation. Virtual mastery of the local blind-alley difficulties, marking the end of stage 2, is essential for progress in stage 3, in which adaptation to the maze becomes a unitary, smooth-running process. By the end of stage 2, to an appreciable extent the T-junction responses represent local, insular adjustments. These local processes are still not well integrated into a system, as is indicated by the manner in which improvements at one junction then often force changes in running the intervening true-path alleys which interfere with the learned response to the next junction, giving rise to new errors there. In a sense the learned segmental adjustments go through a process of interaction, with each intruding some disorientation and incoordination in that next in the series. Typically after stage 2 a plateau appears in the learning curve, or even a rise in the error totals which may persist if stage 2 has been incompletely mastered. Usually the processes of intersegmental organization in stage 3 are accomplished gradually; at times, however, the new local difficulties may disappear in clusters after some time, thereby clarifying the situation so that an efficient organization of the inclusive maze habit seems to have been effected rather suddenly.

Not only do the rats make fewer errors and require fewer runs than the ants to master this maze problem, but their learning process in it differs markedly in several respects from that of the ants. The three stages so clearly marked in the ants cannot be distinguished reliably in the rats. The rats, in fact, progress from the very first run in shortening and eliminating their entrances into the blind alleys, moreover they drop out some of the blinds quickly and almost as units and others "by jumps" although less rapidly. The ant's pattern of eliminating blind-alley entrances gradually and by small degrees is very unlike the rat's response to this problem.

For the *Formica* ants, maze D is a complex problem, learned in a plodding, stereotyped manner in which beginning a further stage effectively depends upon having accomplished the preceding one; for the rats it is a relatively simple problem so readily mastered as not to be a useful means of studying their learning process. Spragg (1933) demonstrated that even in their early runs through a serial maze, rats commit errors indicating that they anticipate later choicepoints in the series. Such early progress in organizing the serial response as a system may well have happened with the rats in maze D, but there was nothing in the results to indicate that it happened at any stage in the ants.

Further differences of significance are found in the abilities of ant and rat to modify their maze habits once these have been learned. After *Formica* ants have mastered maze D, running through it from foodbox-to-nest in the direction from alley 1 to alley 13e and returning by a simple pathway, when each subject is started instead at alley 13e, having to run the maze in the reverse of its learned arrangement, the ants do very poorly in comparison with rats. In this reversed situation, with the exception of signs that maze habituation (gained in stage 1) is transferable, the ant gives no reliable indication of transferred learning and behaves much as do new subjects in responding to blind-alleys and choice-points. Much the same result is obtained when an ant that has learned maze D in the direction nest-to-foodbox must proceed through this maze in the direction foodbox-to-nest, now with the alleys in the same sequence (i.e., 1 to 13e) but with the maze in a different behavioral situation (Schneirla, 1934). But the rat masters such reversal problems easily and adapts readily to learned maze patterns in new post-learning situations (Shepard, 1959). It is clear that the ant's maze habit is bound to the specific conditions, including the organic conditions, of the situation in which it has been learned.

These results I have interpreted (Schneirla, 1946) to mean that an important qualitative difference exists between the ant and the rat in the nature of their learning. In its psychological organization the maze habit of an ant as a whole may be thought of as rigid, the rat's habit relatively plastic. It is not just that the ant's learning is "much less complex," as Vowles (1958) has stated, but that the inner organization of the insect's learned pattern and its susceptibility to change under new conditions is greatly inferior to the rat's as concerns what may be called "adaptive plasticity." Vowles's statement that the insect's neural properties "render necessary a functional organization of behavior far simpler than is often supposed" (op. cit., p. 29) is supported in general by the evidence discussed in this article, provided that "simpler" in this connection means a qualitatively different and inferior organizing ability, i.e., a very different kind of integrative function from that of the rat and on a distinctly lower level of plasticity.

The term "complex" is confusing here. We have seen that the *Formica* ant, organizing its behavior in learning maze D, stages a much more complex overt performance than the rat in the sense that it involves many more behavioral units. The rat, in contrast, behaves as though this problem were simpler for him, and on his superior level of organization that is substantially the fact.

The characteristic of situational-specificity in the *Formica* ant's learning, rather different from that of plasticity characterizing the rat's learning of equivalent problems, has other consequences for behavioral organization beyond those mentioned. These further differences are indicated when insect and mammal are compared with reference to their modes of interrelating alternative adjustment processes in a given adaptive situation. The maze problem used (Figure 68-A) was that, mentioned earlier, in which a single T-junction is preceded by a U-shaped path so that for both ant and rat the right turn at the junction is very easy to make, the left turn very difficult. Once the difficult left turn has been mastered in reaching food, a reversal technique is followed thereafter in which the right and left paths are introduced alternatively as the way to the food, each after the other has been mastered anew. In tests with five ants, involving from three to six double-reversals, the number of runs needed to inhibit the facile right turn fell from 80–110 to around 20, the number to eliminate the difficult left turn fell from around 20 to around 10. Significantly, the successive reversals did not produce any marked behavioral disturbances either at the T-junction or in alleys near it. Minor eccentricities appeared, resembling the tense ("nervous") behavior described for the later part of the second stage in the serial maze; these, however, were of a minor character and did not seem to interfere with progress in learning the change.

On the other hand, an eccentric pattern of behavior that appeared in both the foodbox and nest, clearly attributable to the reversal procedure, did interfere with efficiency in the main task of foraging. Initially, loading up with sugar water on reaching the foodbox had been a regular process for all of the subjects, the act usually beginning promptly after the ant darted into the compartment and continuing smoothly to its end, the "breaks" minor and coming right at the start. Under our test conditions, with regulation of concentration, temperature and drop-size of the sugar water from trial to trial, an average loading time of 115 seconds (S.D., 23 seconds) was typical of behavior in preliminary runs through a simple alley, and did not change reliably in the initial learning of the U-maze. But after a few reversals of the alternatives at the junction, the feeding act began to suffer many interruptions through eccentric actions, and also became much more variable. A subject now might at times remain in the foodbox for twenty minutes or more, or on occasion leave without having fed at all. Such behavior presumably derives from exceptional interferences in behavioral organization based upon strong competition between incompatible responses, and evidently involves an interference with visceral processes basic to the foraging run (Schneirla, 1960).

This problem, with the technique of reversal, was adapted by Witkin (1942) to the rat, with food given after each correct turn as with the ants (Figure 68-B). The rats, as expected, required far less runs than the ants to master the first reversals. Another difference soon appeared, in that although some of the subjects progressed well from change to change, others began to deteriorate. These last subjects exhibited an increasingly excitable, erratic behavior in the approach alleys and especially in the alley leading to the choice-point, often with a succession of uneven spurts and sudden stops, or with abrupt stops separating stretches of galloping. In a further study (Witkin and Klapper, unpubl.), with the alternatives distinguished visually (black vs white) at the choice-point, the degree of disturbance increased greatly among the subjects. As the reversal procedure continued under these conditions, the disturbance took the form of extreme reactions such as repeated jumping at the ceiling—often continued despite severe hemorrhage from nose injury—and violent spells of running interspersed with "freezing" in an erect, rigid posture in the alley approaching the choice-point. For most of these subjects the normal and initial reaction of passing through this situation to food was at length rendered impossible. The difficulties were plainly attributable to the animal's having to alternate a very difficult and a facile adjustment to the choice-point, with the trouble centered on approaching this locality.

In contrast, Fritz (1931), who carried out with rats many consecutive reversals of visually differentiated alternatives in a simple T-maze, found only a regular improvement comparable to that reported by Buytendijk (1930) with visually homogenous alternatives in that situation, without any signs of disturbance at the choice-point. In the U-situation, however, with visually differentiated alternatives, the reversal technique led to radical behavioral disorganization in most of the rats. The trouble centered on the choice-point to such an extent that eventually these subjects seemed unable to pass that point in the situation, as though an invisible wall existed there. Such behavior, resulting from the experimental technique, has all the marks of a neurotic condition, that is, a condition of radically disordered behavior developing in a problem situation in which the animal must adapt to alternative but contradictory conditions.

The responses of *Formica* ants to the reversal procedure in the U-situation, on the contrary, involves no such disorganization in behavioral adjustments to the problem. Instead, in the ants, a general condition of tension arises that evidently also inhibits the vegetative processes of imbibing and delivering food, essential to the foraging act. The ants show no signs of neurosis, but only a heightened excitement and a tense, nervous condition affecting behavior at the visceral level. In fact, the cephalic nervous centers of the ant, limited as they are in comparison with those of the rat, seem to be left fully unhampered with the insect free to use their resources as it may in solving the problem at hand.

It is of interest to note that a behavioral condition which may be comparable to this one of the ant has been reported by Lopatina (1956) with honeybees. In subjects that had been conditioned to visit a sugar-water source close to the hive, a post-conditioning technique of varying the interval between the conditioned stimulus and the presentation of food led to disturbed behavior with interruptions both in taking food and in dispensing it in the hive, these last actions as well as round-dancing in the hive disappearing after ten such trials. Lopatina and Chesnokova (1959) have reported related results with a simple maze problem in which visual stimuli were changed after bees had learned a discrimination between an alley marked by a blue-green filter, leading to food, and its visually unmarked alternative without food. Because the behavioral disturbance in the bee and its preconditions appear to be related to the situation and resultant nervousness we have described for the ant, an equivalent interpretation may be in order. But the hypothesis offered by the Russian investigators, that the observed behavioral disruption in the bee is the expression of a lowered level of excitation in the subject's nervous system, does not seem to follow from the results. Better support seems available for the view that the insect's difficulties in these circumstances center on a condition of increased but irregular discharge at subcephalic neural levels particularly, with a resultant heightening of organic tension that disrupts essential vegetative actions. This type of difficulty may prove to be characteristic of insects victimized by the changing of learned situations.

The *Formica* worker, as described, seems not appreciably affected by problem reversals that cause serious neurotic symptoms in the rat. Apparently, the ant cannot fall victim to problem-conflict because she is incapable of dealing with two contradictory adjustments simultaneously. The rat's difficulties, on the other hand, center on interferences in resolving the unequal alternatives, precisely because this animal is capable of responding simultaneously to contradictory action possibilities. The frequent result for the mammal, however, is one of disorganization in the appropriate performance of the alternative actions. The insect, for its part, suffers only a condition of increased tension which may cause it to desert the problem situation but is a lesser ill from which no lasting behavioral deterioration is indicated.

In their behavioral organization, insects seem to approximate the terms of the classical "bundle-hypothesis," to the extent that in their learning a fairly complex total of elements accumulates gradually to form a pattern. This pattern, however, is qualitatively inferior to that of which mam-

mals are capable. The *Formica* ant masters an involved habit in a stereotyped manner, through a gradual summative process, with the gains of one
predictable stage essential almost in toto for the next stage to begin; the
rat, in contrast, learns an equivalent situation in a qualitatively different
and superior manner, in part mastering local and inclusive situational
properties together. The rat can attain a degree of problem unity almost
from the beginning whereas the ant acquires an inferior integration only
by degrees.

The mammal's psychological superiority is shown perhaps most strikingly by the negative aspect of its susceptibility to conflict disturbances
under conditions in which the ant, on a lower organizational level, exhibits
only an increased organic tension not hazardous to the essential learned
pattern. These evidently are qualitative differences, differences in kind
rather than just in degree, which set off insect and mammal from each
other in their respective psychological natures.

SUMMARY

Insects and mammals differ strikingly in their psychological makeup.
Worker *Formica* ants learn a labyrinth of six culs-de-sac in a stereotyped
progression through well-marked stages; rats make a much simpler problem of the same labyrinth, learning without well-marked stages. Once the
problem is learned, the ants are very limited in reversing it or in relearning
under new conditions; rats show a much greater plasticity in these respects. Comparable differences are found between these animals in the initial learning and in the relearning of a problem with a single choice-point
at which competing difficult and facile alternatives are encountered. Confronted with the necessity of alternately readjusting to these alternatives as
the correct turn, the ants acquire only a "nervousness" that interferes with
their foraging, but the rats exhibit striking neurotic symptoms through
being susceptible to a major conflict in the problem. Insects and mammals seem to differ markedly in their solutions of such problems testing
their ability to organize and to reorganize behavior.

REFERENCES

Buytendijk, F. J. J. 1930. Über das Umlernen. *Arch. Néerl. Physiol.* 15: 283–
310.
Fritz, M. F. 1931. Long-time training of white rats on antagonistic visual habits. *J. Comp. Psychol.* 11: 171–184.

Lopatina, N. G. 1956. O tantse pchel. (About the dance of bees). *Pchelovodstvo* 33: 19–24.

Lopatina, N. G., and E. G. Chesnokova. 1959. Uslovnie reflexy u pchel na slozhnie razdrazhiteli. (Conditioned reflexes of bees on complex stimuli.) *Pchelovodstvo* 36: 35–38.

Schneirla, T. C. 1933. Some comparative psychology. *J. Comp. Psychol.* 16: 307–315.

Schneirla, T. C. 1934. The process and mechanism of ant learning. *J. Comp. Psychol.* 17: 303–328.

Schneirla, T. C. 1941. Studies on the nature of ant learning. I. The characteristics of a distinctive initial period of generalized learning. *J. Comp. Psychol.* 32: 41–82.

Schneirla, T. C. 1943. The nature of ant learning. II. The intermediate stage of segmental maze adjustment. *J. Comp. Psychol.* 35: 149–176.

Schneirla, T. C. 1946. Ant learning as a problem in comparative psychology. In P. L. Harriman, ed., *20th century psychology*. New York: Philosophical Library. Pp. 276–304.

Schneirla, T. C. 1960. L'apprentissage et la question du conflit chez la fourmi —Comparaison avec le rat. *J. Psychol.* 57(1): 11–44.

Shepard, J. F. 1914. Types of learning in animals and man. *Psychol. Bull.* 11: 58.

Shepard, J. F. 1959. *An unexpected cue in maze learning.* Ann Arbor: Univ. of Michigan. P. 35.

Spragg, S. D. S. 1933. Anticipation as a factor in maze errors. *J. Comp. Psychol.* 15: 313–329.

Vowles, D. M. 1961. Neural mechanisms in insect behaviour. In W. H. Thorpe and O. L. Zangwill, eds., *Current problems in animal behaviour*. Cambridge Univ. Press, Chap. 1, pp. 5–29.

Witkin, H. A. 1942. Restriction as a factor in adjustment to conflict situations. *J. Comp. Psychol.* 33: 41–74.

Witkin, H. A., and Z. Klapper. Evidence of extreme behavioral disorganization in rats running a centrifugal swing T-maze with light-dark differentiation of the choice-point alternatives. (Unpubl.)

Witkin, H. A., and T. C. Schneirla. 1937. Initial maze behavior as a function of maze design. *J. Comp. Psychol.* 23: 275–304.

JAY S. ROSENBLATT

GERALD TURKEWITZ

T. C. SCHNEIRLA

Development of Home Orientation in Newly Born Kittens

Bibliography No. 121

Among kittens the first 3 weeks of life are spent within the limited confines of the home. The mother establishes a delivery site during parturition; soon after the birth of the kittens, this site becomes the home region where all of the interactions between the mother and young, and among the young, occur. The kittens remain in the home until the beginning of the fourth week, which is long after their eyes have opened (i.e., seventh to ninth day), and they can crawl or walk the distance required to leave the home and wander around the cage. Undoubtedly, huddling of the litter and maternal nursing in the home contribute to the kitten's attachment to this region. There is an additional reason for the kitten's remaining in the home: We have found that the home becomes an orientation center for the kittens of the litter. The following is a study of the development of the home as an orientation center for kittens during the first 3 weeks of life.

When an animal adopts a posture or maintains locomotion which is related to the amount or source of stimulation in the environment, this is referred to as orientation (i.e., kinesis or taxis). Among lower invertebrates and vertebrates, orientation is based largely upon innate responses to stimulation of sensory receptors by directionalized stimuli (i.e., beam of light, chemical gradient, thermal gradient) under the appropriate organic conditions. Among newly born mammals, orientation responses are also based upon innate (i.e., present at birth) approach and withdrawal processes which enable the newborn to approach sources of weak stimulation and withdraw from sources of strong stimulation (2, 3).

Newly born mammals are characterized, however, by the rapid develop-

From *Transactions* of The New York Academy of Sciences, vol. 31, no. 3 (March 1969). Copyright © 1969 The New York Academy of Sciences. Reprinted with permission.

ment of learned orientation to new sources of stimulation based upon early experience with the mother, siblings, and home or nest environment. The development of orientation to the mother and siblings is clearly recognized as social behavior and as such is included under the term "socialization," but orientation to the home environment is also a social response since the characteristics of the home which give it behavioral significance are derived from its use as a social habitat. The study of home orientation in kittens is, therefore, a study of early social behavior and warrants inclusion in any concept of early socialization.

In the first section of this paper we shall describe the development of orientation to the home region in kittens, from birth onward, using the results of tests in three corners of the home cage and one corner of a field (i.e., unfamiliar freshly washed floor surface) situation. The following sections will deal with studies analyzing the role of home cage experience and of various sensory stimuli (i.e., olfactory and visual) in the development of home orientation. The final section will attempt to analyze the phases of development and their interrelationship in home orientation and the mechanisms of learning which are involved in the various phases.

METHODS AND PROCEDURES

Kittens

Thirteen litters of kittens, living with their mothers in a home cage, were used. Seventeen kittens were tested daily, from the first to the 16th day, on the average; and eight kittens were tested daily from the 17th to the 22nd day. Four kittens were raised in an isolation chamber from birth until the end of the first (n = 3) or second week (n = 1). They were returned to their litters and tested for their orientation to the home. Additional kittens were used to study both the effects of testing and the sensory stimuli used in orientation.

Home Cage and Field Situation

The floors of the home cage measured 36 inches square and were constructed of four 18-inch square removable floor sections, the surfaces of which were made of asbestos board, a hard but slightly porous composition board. The field duplicated in size and construction the lower half of a home cage, but it was not used as a living cage and was washed after each testing session. The home cage housed the mother and her litter between testing sessions and was not washed during the study; sawdust was removed and replaced each day in the home cage.

Test Procedure

Kittens were tested in three corners of the home cage and one corner of the field between 10 A.M. and 2 P.M. each day. The *home corner* and its quadrant, the *home quadrant,* was determined by observing the mother and litter. The neighboring corner having a wall in common with the home corner was designated the *adjacent corner* (its quadrant was the *adjacent quadrant*). The corner diagonally opposite the home corner was designated the *diagonal corner* and its quadrant the *diagonal quadrant.* The fourth corner of the home cage contained sawdust and was referred to as the *neutral corner* and its *neutral quadrant.* One corner in the field was called the home corner for each litter and its location in the field corresponded to the location of the home corner in the home cage, with respect to the cage door and the source of daylight in the testing room.

Kittens were always tested first in one corner of the field; then they were tested in each of the three corners of the home cage (except the neutral corner), in random order, each day. The kitten was placed on the cage floor with its head facing away from the test corner, towards the center of the cage, and released: The distance between the kitten's head and the border of the home quadrant in tests of the adjacent corner was about 14 inches; in tests of the diagonal corner it was about 12 inches diagonally; but it was 28 inches from the diagonal corner to the adjacent corner and then to the home quadrant, the path initially taken by kittens to reach the home.

The mother and litter were removed from the home cage before testing was begun; food dishes were removed and the sawdust was brushed into the neutral corner. Each kitten was then taken individually to be tested. Before each test of a corner, the kitten was placed on a table top where it began to vocalize (*pretest procedure*); then it was gently placed in the test corner and released. Field corner tests lasted for 2 minutes because they were disturbing to the kittens, and home cage tests lasted for 3 minutes.

The kitten's movements during a test were traced on a facsimile of the cage and field floors, and its vocalization was graded at the start of the test ("Start") and for each 15-second interval. Vocalization was graded according to the following scale: $0 = $ none, $1 = $ low, $2 = $ medium, $3 = $ loud, $4 = $ peak intensity. The duration of vocalization was the number of 15-second intervals during which any vocalization occurred.

RESULTS

Development of Home Orientation

HOME ORIENTATION

Orientation to the home, measured by terminations in the home quadrant at the end of the 3-minute tests, developed at different rates in the different corners of the home cage (Table 1). It developed earliest in the home corner tests (second to fourth-day period), several days later in adjacent corner tests (fifth to seventh-day period) when terminations in the home quadrant reached 73%, and more than 2 weeks after birth in diagonal corner tests (14th to 16th-day period). Although terminations in the home quadrant in tests started in the diagonal corner reached 42%, when this is combined with terminations in the adjacent quadrant (not shown), the reasons for which will be given later, the total was 63%.

The average age at which kittens tested in the adjacent corner completed the first of two successful trips to the home quadrant was 4.0 ± 1.9 days (n = 19) which was considerably earlier than the average age of

TABLE 1

Terminations and departures of kittens in home orientation tests from the second to the twenty-second day.

Age period (days)	Terminations (%) in home quadrant when started in:			Departures (%)				
				From home when started in:			From adjacent when started in:	
	Home	Adj.	Diag.	Home	Adj.	Diag.	Adj.	Diag.
2–4	88	34	8	12	20	33	46	33
5–7	89	73	22	12	9	14	63	50
8–10	92	73	21	13	7	0	72	33
11–13	90	72	24	12	2	0	74	76
14–16	83	78	42	19	6	14	72	61
17–19	73	76	42	45	8	23	79	50
20–22	40	84	53	73	12	18	89	71
No. of Tests	296	307	282					
Total entries and placements				296	222	87	307	101

13.8 ± 1.9 days (n = 13) at which the first of two successful trips from the diagonal corner to the home quadrant was completed.

PATHS TAKEN TO THE HOME

Paths taken to the home quadrant were not always direct; often the kitten entered other quadrants either en route to the home or in lieu of the home and had to find its way to the home from this new location. The kitten could also leave the home once it had entered this quadrant. Departures from quadrants other than the home quadrant, therefore, provide a measure of orientation to the home and of the paths taken to reach the home (Table 1).

There were few departures from the home quadrant from the earliest age: Kittens placed in the home corner or entering the home quadrant from other localities remained in the home. On the other hand, kittens placed in the adjacent corner or entering the adjacent quadrant from the diagonal corner subsequently left this quadrant. The percentage of departures from the adjacent quadrant increased from the fifth day onward from both the adjacent and diagonal corner starting localities.

The increase with age in terminations in the home quadrant and of departures from all quadrants but the home quadrant describe the two unique features of the kitten's behavior in relation to the home which enable us to characterize the home as an orientation center: Kittens approach and enter this area from various regions of the home cage and once having entered it they remain there for the duration of the test period.

Experience and Home Orientation

TEST EXPERIENCE

Kittens that were tested daily in the home cage and the field gained experience that was not normally available to untested kittens, who remained in the home region and rarely wandered or were carried out of it. To evaluate the effects of this experience on the development of home orientation, a selected number of kittens from litters that were being tested were not given their first orientation tests until either the fifth or seventh day (n = 10) or the 13th to 16th day (n = 13), the ages at which adjacent corner-to-home orientation and diagonal corner-to-home orientation normally develops.

The percentages of the kittens that remained in the home when placed there, and terminated in the home when started in the adjacent corner, at the earlier and later ages, were the same as those of the kittens that were tested daily in these localities. Among the older kittens, terminations in the home quadrant in tests started in the diagonal corner were nearly the same

(39% as against 42%). Field performances at both ages were similar in the delayed tested kittens and the daily tested kittens.

The delayed tested kittens were somewhat more aroused by the test procedure than the daily tested kittens who had by then become adapted to the handling and other manipulations required. Therefore, the delayed tested kittens vocalized for longer periods and at higher intensities and, in many tests in the home and adjacent corner, they wandered considerably more, although they finally found their way to the home and ended the test at that region.

Experience during testing, therefore, adapts kittens to the test procedures, reducing the disturbance associated with testing. Moreover, it enables kittens to adopt paths to the home from the adjacent corner and to remain in the home with less wandering. However, capacities required for the development of orientation to the home from the adjacent and diagonal corners and for distinguishing between the home cage and the field are developed within the confines of the home region itself during the normal course of a kitten's experience with the mother, littermates, and the home region.

EXPERIENCE IN THE HOME CAGE

Orientation to the home is based upon the use of sensory cues from the cage for distinguishing among the various regions of the home cage and crawling from the adjacent and diagonal regions to the home region. The question arises as to what extent kittens must have experience with the specific sensory cues of a home cage in order to develop orientative responses. Kittens normally gain this experience by living in the cage with the mother and littermates. To answer the above question, four kittens were removed at birth from the mother, littermates, and home cage, and reared individually in isolation chambers where they were fed from brooders with nipples. Three of the kittens were returned to their home cages at 6 or 7 days of age and one at 14 days of age where they were tested for their ability to orient to the home. While they were in isolation, these kittens were tested for orientation to the brooder by being placed a short distance away from it; all were able to crawl to the brooder and remain in contact with it.

The isolate kittens were unable to distinguish among the various regions of the home cage, and they showed no evidence of orienting to the home region. Their behavior in the home cage in many ways resembled that of the normally reared kittens in the field except that many of the isolates were also more active in the field than the normally reared kittens. Their vocalization in the home cage was of longer duration and greater intensity than the vocalization of normally reared kittens. There was, however, some indication, in their vocalization, that the field was more disturbing to them than the home cage; in this respect, therefore, they were able to distinguish grossly between these two regions.

The isolates were given daily orientation tests on subsequent days after their return to the home cage and litter and, gradually over the next 3 or 4 days, they developed orientation to the home region.

Analysis of Sensory Stimuli Involved in Home Orientation

FIELD TESTS

The field, unlike the home cage, did not provide the basis either for distinguishing among the different corner regions or for developing orientative responses to any particular region (i.e., home region). Although the floor and wall arrangement in the field and the relationship of the field to the room light source were similar to the home cage, out of a total of 162 tests divided about equally among the four corners of the field, there was no evidence, from the first to the 22nd day, of the development of regional differentiation or orientation. In 90 to 96% of the tests in each corner, kittens remained in the corner at which they had been placed at the start of the test and vocalized loudly throughout the test.

Activity was inhibited in the field: Kittens typically crawled forward a short distance, then turned and crawled back to the starting place, repeating this several times, at an early age. Later, the kittens remained in place or backed into the corner, vocalizing and moving their heads continually in a side-to-side motion. There was no evidence of adaptation to the field; the kittens continued to be disturbed by placement in the field and, in fact, there was some evidence that their disturbance increased as they were able to distinguish more clearly between the field and the home cages.

OLFACTORY STIMULI IN THE HOME REGION

An attempt was made to identify the nature of the stimuli which were used by kittens to orient to the home region and to determine how these stimuli were utilized by the kittens. Since orientation to the home from the adjacent corner develops before the eyes open, it is unlikely that visual stimuli are involved in this orientation. Moreover, tactual stimuli from the cage walls between the adjacent corner and both the home corner and the diagonal corner are the same, yet almost invariably kittens only crawled along the wall between the adjacent and home corners when wall-hugging played a role in home orientation. In addition, the walls of the field corners were similar to the walls in the home cage, yet wall-hugging was not prominent in the field and movement from one corner to another did not occur. Tactual stimuli are, therefore, not very likely to function as important distinguishing stimuli for orientation. In view of these considerations, our study was aimed at investigating the role of olfactory stimuli arising from the deposit of substances, by the mother and kittens, on the floor of the home cage. These substances, we believed, were deposited mainly in the home region and spread from this region outward to other cage regions. One problem, therefore, was whether, in orientating to the home region by means of olfactory stimuli, the kittens depended upon the home region as the source of these olfactory stimuli or whether there were deposited in each quadrant (i.e., adjacent quadrant) sufficient amounts of these olfactory substances to enable the kittens to find their way to the home.

Starting on the fourth day and continuing through the 18th day, a litter of four kittens was tested daily in the home and the adjacent corners using a freshly washed home quadrant in place of the one that had previously been in the cage with the mother and kittens. This quadrant then remained in the home cage overnight. On the following day, the kittens were tested with the same home quadrant, which now had a 24-hour accumulation of olfactory substances deposited by the mother and littermates; following this test, a new, freshly washed quadrant was inserted in the cage in place of the previous one and the kittens were tested again. This procedure was repeated each day throughout the testing period.

The performances of the four kittens in the tests with the 24-hour home quadrant and a fresh home quadrant can be compared with those of kittens ($n = 8$) over the same age period with a permanent home quadrant in place. In adjacent corner tests, the percentage of terminations in the home quadrant was reduced from 63% with a permanent home quadrant to 57% with a 24-hour home quadrant and to only 28% with a fresh home quadrant. When they were started in the home corner, only 48% of the kittens remained in the freshly washed home quadrant while 80% remained if a home quadrant with a 24-hour deposit of olfactory substances was in place and 93% remained if a permanent home quadrant was in place.

It was observed that kittens started in the adjacent corner crawled towards the home quadrant and began to cross the border into this quadrant. When a fresh home quadrant was in place, the kittens immediately halted when they sniffed the quadrant floor, then they backed away from the border, and came to rest in the adjacent quadrant at a site close to the border of the home quadrant. The percentage of terminations in the adjacent quadrant at this site increased from 36% with a permanent home quadrant to 43% with a 24-hour home quadrant and 70% with a fresh home quadrant. Similarly, terminations in the adjacent quadrant, usually at this site, also increased when kittens were started in the home quadrant with a 24-hour quadrant or a fresh-home quadrant in place. They increased from 6% with a permanent home quadrant to 20% with a 24-hour home quadrant and 48% with a fresh home quadrant.

Olfactory stimuli from the home region, arising from substances deposited in the home by the mother and kittens, provide the cues to which the kittens respond in orienting to the home. Removal of these stimuli from the home quadrant disrupts orientation in tests of the home corner, and it causes kittens to avoid entering the home quadrant after they have reached its border and sniffed the cage floor. However, *it does not prevent kittens from crawling towards the home region* in tests started in the adjacent corner: When they reach the border of the home quadrant, after they avoid entering this quadrant, they come to rest at a site nearest to what was formerly the home region.

After the kitten's eyes have opened on the seventh to ninth day, vision may begin to play a role in orientation, initially as a supplement to olfaction but later as the dominant sensory modality of orientation. The use of vision and olfaction in orientation to the home was studied in a litter of three kittens that were tested daily from the 13th to the 21st day under three cage conditions: (1) cage unaltered, (2) olfactory cues on the cage floor reduced by removing the four floor sections and replacing them, temporarily, with freshly washed quadrants, and (3) visual cues from the cage and its surroundings reduced by placing grey wall panels over the inside walls of the home cage. Kittens were tested in the unaltered cage first; then tests with either visual or olfactory cues reduced were made in random order on successive days.

In adjacent corner tests, the effect of reducing either visual or olfactory cues in the home cage was to cause reduction in returns to the home from 92% returns with the cage unaltered to 50–59%; the reduction of visual cues was as effective as the reduction of olfactory cues. A significant proportion of the kittens could make use of either visual or olfactory cues to find their way to the home. Returns to the home from the diagonal corner, accomplished in 83% of the tests with unaltered cages, was affected more by the reduction of olfactory cues (only 25% returns to home) than the reduction of visual cues (50% returns to the home). However, olfactory cues in themselves could not guide kittens to the home as well as the combination of olfactory and visual cues. We must conclude, therefore, that visual cues are employed by kittens in returns to the home from the diagonal corner, but their use is dependent in some way upon the presence of olfactory cues. In home corner tests, in which kittens do not have to approach the home from a distance, visual cues were of less importance than olfactory cues; nevertheless, using visual cues alone, kittens remained in the home quadrant in 67% of the tests. In the unaltered cage, kittens remained in the home in all of the tests while with visual cues blocked from view and olfactory cues present, the kittens were able to remain in the home quadrant in 92% of the tests.

We have found that orientation to the home region is based upon olfactory stimulation arising from the deposit of substances on the floor of the home cage, presumably by the mother and littermates. The olfactory stimuli used by the kitten in orientating from the adjacent corner to the home quadrant are present on the floor of the adjacent quadrant in a pattern that forms either a gradient or pattern that imposes directionality upon the kitten's movement between the adjacent corner and the home quadrant. Since, as we shall show, there is an orientation from the diagonal corner to the adjacent quadrant which develops in the same manner as orientation from the adjacent corner to the home, but at a slightly later age, the gradient of olfactory stimulation on the floor is distributed cagewide, as a result of the spread of olfactory substances from the mother and kittens from the home to cage regions at a distance from the home, with a decrement.

A freshly washed home quadrant, devoid of the familiar odor of the home cage, induces an interruption of crawling followed by head withdrawal, pivoting, turning, and crawling away. The kitten's withdrawal reaction is much stronger in an entire cage area devoid of the familiar home cage odor, as in the field. Orientation to a home area is precluded by the absence of a region that can serve as an orientation center and, instead, the kitten becomes restricted in its movement, draws its limbs up against its body, moves its head slowly in side-to-side motion, and vocalizes continuously and at a high intensity. There is no adaptation to the field during the three weeks of testing.

After the eyes open, vision begins to play a role in the kitten's orientation to the home, but it does not supplant the use of olfaction during this period and it is still less effective in orientating to the home than olfaction. In some orientative situations in the cage, vision only supplements olfaction as a guide to the home.

Regional Differentiation and the Development of Home Orientation

REGIONAL DIFFERENTIATION: VOCALIZATION IN THE HOME CAGE AND FIELD

The duration and intensity of vocalization during home tests in which kittens were placed in the home, adjacent, and diagonal corners provided a measure of the kitten's ability to recognize its location in the home cage. Further, since kittens vocalize only when they are disturbed (i.e., they are hungry, cool, or interrupted during suckling and out of contact with mother) and become quiet again when the disturbance is removed (i.e., they are fed, warm, or regain contact with mother and resume suckling), vocalization in orientation tests is a measure of the disturbance produced by the cage locality. Since kittens were set to vocalizing by the pretest procedure, the reduction of vocalization by the placement in a cage corner indicates that the corner reduces the kitten's disturbance.

By the fourth day, kittens recognized the home cage as different from the field, and within the home cage they differentiated between the home quadrant and the adjacent and diagonal quadrants, according to average measures of the duration of vocalization. They vocalized for the entire duration of the 2-minute field tests. In the 3-minute tests of the home quadrant, vocalization averaged 1 minute 15 seconds compared to around 2-minute durations of vocalization in the adjacent and diagonal quadrants. At the end of the seventh day, the three home cage regions had already been clearly distinguished from one another, and in each quadrant vocalization was of shorter duration than during the earlier period.

The intensity of vocalization during the course of the tests showed even more clearly that kittens recognized the home cage and the field, and each of the three cage localities in the home cage, early in testing. At the start of tests during the first 4 days (Figure 70), vocalization intensity was initially at a medium level as a result of the pretest procedure. In the field, it rose almost immediately and remained at a high level throughout the tests while in the corners of the home cage it gradually declined. The decline was more rapid and the final level reached was lower in the home and adjacent corner tests than in the diagonal corner tests. Some difference between the home and adjacent corners was also apparent in the intensity at which vocalization leveled off during the last 2 minutes of the tests.

According to the two measures of vocalization, each measuring a different aspect of vocalization and giving only slightly different results, the kittens showed the ability to differentiate between the home cage and the field, and among the three corners of the home cage as early as the fourth day. Not only were the cage localities recognized, but the home locality reduced the pretest disturbance of the kittens to a greater extent, and more rapidly, than the adjacent quadrant, which in turn was more effective than the diagonal quadrant. The emergence of the home region as an orientation center was in fact based on its ability to reduce the disturbance produced in kittens by removal from the home and on the ease with which kittens recognized this region.

The home emerged as an orientation center and the adjacent and diagonal quadrants were recognized by kittens and exerted an initial quieting effect upon them, even before the development of orientation to the home from the adjacent corner. This orientation developed during the period from the fifth to seventh day. There were also further developments in vocalization during this period (Figure 71). Vocalization in the field rose even more rapidly and to a higher level of intensity than earlier. In the

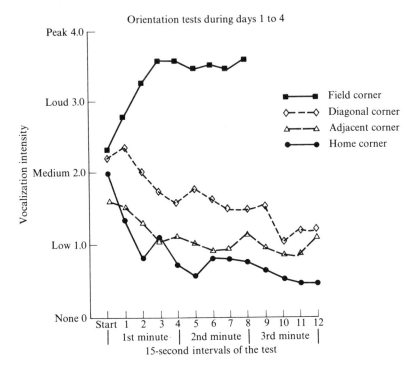

FIGURE 70
Orientation tests of a group of 8 kittens for age period 1–4 days. Average intensity of vocalization is presented for successive 3-minute tests in the home, adjacent, and diagonal corners of the home cage and during 2-minute tests in a corner of the field. Vocalization is recorded at the start of and during successive 15-second intervals.

home cage there was an initial rapid decline in vocalization intensity during the first 30 seconds in all of the corners (home corner not shown); the kittens immediately recognized that they were in the home cage. After the initial decline, vocalization continued to decline in the home corner and remained low throughout the tests (not shown). In the adjacent and diagonal corners, vocalization increased in intensity, rising higher in intensity in the diagonal corner than in the adjacent corner and remaining higher in that corner. The kittens were therefore making two discriminations: They recognized the home cage and, further, they recognized their location within the home cage. They became slightly disturbed in the adjacent region and more disturbed in the diagonal quadrant, but their disturbance in the adjacent corner was relieved towards the end of the test after many of the kittens had entered the home quadrant.

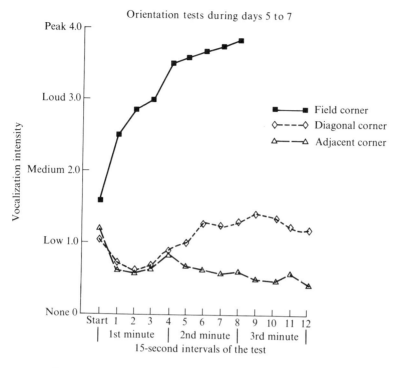

FIGURE 71

Orientation tests of a group of 8 kittens for age period 5–7 days. Average intensity of vocalization is presented for successive 3-minute tests in the adjacent and diagonal corners of the home cage and during 2-minute tests in a corner of the field. Vocalization is recorded at the start of and during successive 15-second intervals.

Development with regard to vocalization, already evident in the earlier periods, continued during the eighth to 10th day of testing (Figure 72). During this period, adjacent corner-to-home orientation was well established in most of the kittens, but home orientation from the diagonal corner had not yet begun. The diagonal corner continued to exert a disturbing effect upon the kittens after their initial reaction to being placed in the home cage. Before the end of the first minute of the diagonal corner test, the kittens recognized where they were located and began to vocalize louder as evidence of their disturbance. In the adjacent corner, there was a steady decline in vocalization in the first minute during which most of the kittens crawled to the home but those that remained in the adjacent quadrant vocalized louder. In the home corner, vocalization was at a minimum almost from the start of the test. Because all corners of the home cage were

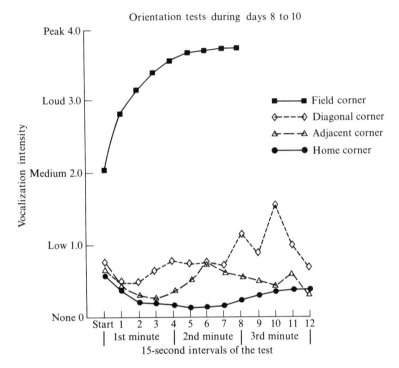

Orientation tests during days 8 to 10

FIGURE 72
Orientation tests of a group of 8 kittens for age period 8–10 days. Average intensity of vocalization is presented for successive 3-minute tests in the home, adjacent, and diagonal corners of the home cage and during 2-minute tests in a corner of the field. Vocalization is recorded at the start of and during successive 15-second intervals.

increasingly effective in quieting the kitten, the contrast between vocalization in the field, which rose immediately and remained high, and the home cage was greater during this period than during earlier periods.

REGIONAL DIFFERENTIATION AND THE
DEVELOPMENT OF HOME ORIENTATION

The early movements of the kittens when placed in each of the three home cage localities and in the field corners were quite similar, as shown in Figure 73 (all "A's"). The kitten usually crawled a short distance forward, pivoted, resumed crawling in a new direction, then pivoted again and resumed crawling in still another direction. The short movements forward, pivoting, and turning traced a circuitous path that did not carry the kitten a great distance from the starting point nor show any general orientation in one direction or another. The only indication that kittens were

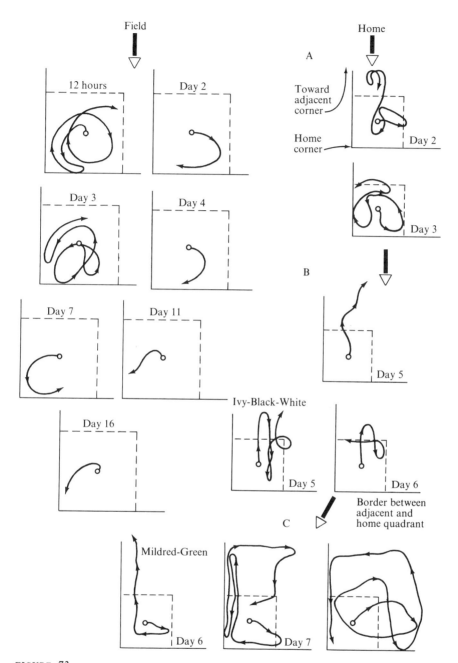

FIGURE 73

Paths taken by kittens in tests of home corner and one corner of the field from the first to the 22nd day. Paths, traced from the original records, show by arrows the distance and the direction crawled for successive 15-second phases. Developmental phases in the home corner are labeled A, B, C.

capable of recognizing the various cage localities and the field was found in the duration and intensity of vocalization, which differed, as we have seen, among the various corners and between the corners and the field.

Beginning on the second to the fifth day, there was a gradual change in the kitten's crawling in the adjacent corner which was the first indication of an orientation to the home quadrant (Figure 74, Adjacent B). Although kittens did not reach the home quadrant, crawling movements in the direction of the home quadrant were continued without interruption for longer periods while crawling movements in other directions (e.g., into the corner), particularly those movements that were headed towards the diagonal quadrant, were shortened; the kitten paused, then pivoted and crawled back towards the starting point. Significantly, the initial direction of crawling was towards the home quadrant, but this was often interrupted before the kitten reached the boundary of this quadrant (Figure 74, Adjacent B).

After the fifth day, in many kittens, the initial movement in the direction of the home quadrant was continued without being interrupted by pivoting until after the kitten had crossed the boundary and entered the home quadrant (Figure 74, Adjacent C). When it reached the home quadrant, the kitten crawled forward a short distance, then pivoted and resumed crawling further into the home quadrant. Forward movements into the home continued while those which headed the kitten back in the direction of the adjacent quadrant were interrupted by pivoting and the kitten turned back into the home quadrant. At this time wall-hugging became prominent: As kittens neared the home quadrant, they came into contact with the wall between the adjacent and home quadrants and crawled for a time in contact with the wall until they reached the home corner.

A different course of development occurred in the home quadrant when the kitten was started in the home corner (Figure 73, Home A). After the initial phase during which there was frequent pivoting and short periods of crawling, the kitten's movements in the direction of the adjacent quadrant were gradually lengthened while crawling in other directions, particularly the neutral corner, was shortened (Figure 73, Home B). In the next phase, when the kittens that were started in the adjacent corner began to reach the home quadrant and enter it, the kittens started in the home corner crawled directly towards the adjacent quadrant but, when they reached the border between the two quadrants, they turned and crawled along the border, soon turning back into the home quadrant. Although this border was crossed without hesitation by kittens entering the home quadrant from the adjacent quadrant, nevertheless, it was hardly ever crossed by kittens that approached it from the home quadrant.

The development of home orientation in diagonal corner tests was quite different from what was described above with regard to the adjacent cor-

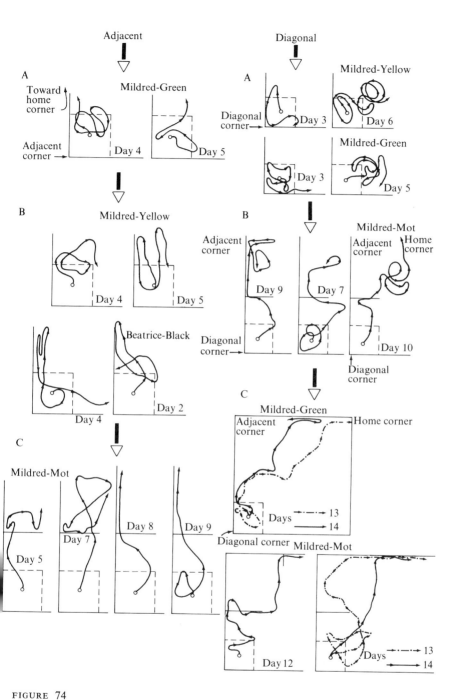

FIGURE 74

Paths taken by kittens in tests of adjacent and diagonal corners of the home cage from the first to the 22nd day. Paths, traced from the original records, show by arrows the distance and the direction crawled for successive 15-second phases. Developmental phases in each corner are labeled A, B, C.

ner. Orientation to the home quadrant directly was a late development which was preceded by orientation to the adjacent quadrant as the first leg of the trip to the home (Figure 74, Diagonal B, C). This too appeared at a later age than the corresponding orientation from the adjacent corner to the home. Initially, kittens that reached the home crawled first to the adjacent corner and then turned and crawled to the home. Shortly after this, the kittens continued as before to crawl towards the adjacent quadrant but, instead of crawling into the adjacent corner, they now turned towards the home when they reached the border of the adjacent quadrant and crawled directly to the home quadrant (Figure 74, Diagonal B, C). In subsequent tests (days 14–16), the path to the home through the center of the cage was straightened; kittens crawled or walked, at this age, diagonally across the cage to the home. It is likely, as we have seen, that visual cues supplemented olfactory cues in this latter development.

The above description of phases in the development of home orientation in diagonal corner tests suggests that a gradient of the olfactory stimulus, sufficiently well defined to enable kittens to discriminate zones of greater olfactory stimulation from zones of less olfactory stimulation, developed slowly in the diagonal quadrant and that, when it formed, it appeared first in the region between the diagonal corner and the adjacent quadrant. Kittens followed this gradient initially and were led far into the adjacent quadrant where they could then pick up the trail to the home which they used when they were placed in the adjacent corner at the start of tests. Soon after this, presumably, deposits spread in a fanlike shape directly from the home into the diagonal quadrant. Kittens moving towards the adjacent quadrant now encountered this part of the cagewide gradient before entering the adjacent region and turned towards the home, crawling now with reference to the gradient that led them directly into the home region.

Turning now to the field tests, after the initial phase of crawling in a circuitous path near the starting point (Figure 73, Field), a phase which was somewhat shorter in duration in the field than in the home cage corners, the kittens' behavior was quite different and in contrast to their behavior in the home cage. Between the second and fourth day, movement became increasingly restricted as kittens performed only a single pivoting or backing action which carried them into the corner where they remained with the limbs drawn up against the body tightly, the head moving slowly in a side-to-side motion, and loud vocalization repeated continually throughout the test period. Disturbance and restricted movement in the field continued for nearly the entire 3 weeks of testing with no evidence of any reduction until the 19th day. As the kitten recognized its location in the home cage more rapidly and was, therefore, quieted more quickly, the disturbance produced by the field test mounted more rapidly as the kitten also recognized more rapidly that it had been placed in the field. Any adaptation that might have developed in the field itself was, therefore, obscured by developments in the home cage.

DISCUSSION

Our study shows that the home region of the living cage develops as an orientation center for the kittens during the first 3 weeks after birth. Not only do the kittens remain in the home region when they are placed there, but they also gradually develop the ability to find their way back to it when they are removed and placed at a distance in the adjacent and diagonally opposite corners of the home cage. Kittens orient and find their way to the home by responding to odorous substances that have been deposited on the floor of the home region and then spread to other regions of the home cage. These olfactory substances are derived, presumably, from the fur and bodies of the mother and kittens (i.e., litter odors) and, as such, are familiar to the kittens.

The study of the development of home orientation is, therefore, a study of how newly born kittens adapt to the socially conditioned environment of their early life. Learning plays an important role in this early adaptation. The odors deposited on the floor of the home region are first encountered during the kitten's activity with the mother and littermates. Kittens raised apart from the mother and litter, in isolation, and then returned to the home cage fail to orient to the home and show only a gross differentiation of the home cage from the field, a region lacking the litter odors. Although an initial direct response to litter odors may be involved in the kitten's orientation behavior, it is more likely that the litter odors acquire their behavioral significance for the kittens by association (i.e., conditioned learning) with other sources of stimulation in the litter, for example, the tactile and thermal stimuli encountered during huddling, nursing, and other activities with the mother and littermates.

Approach responses appearing initially to these stimuli (2, 3) provide the basis, through conditioning, for the kittens' responses to the litter odors that are also found on the mother and littermates. It is also likely that early recognition of the mother and nipple position preferences, as well as nipple localization are based upon olfactory discrimination by kittens (1). The transfer of these odors to the cage floor enables equivalence reactions to develop, leading the kittens to approach or remain in the vicinity of the litter odor and to withdraw or become disturbed in the absence of the odor. Moreover, in a gradient of the litter odors, the kittens crawl towards the stronger and away from the weaker olfactory stimulus. Further development of home orientation is then, in large part, dependent upon the distribution of these odors in a graded pattern on the floor of the home cage.

Home orientation develops in phases which are dependent upon the developing capacities of the kittens to perceive differences in the intensity of olfactory stimulation at different regions of the home cage and to crawl from one region of stimulation to another. Trail-following is somewhat more complex than simple approach, however, since it involves continual alternation of approach and withdrawal (i.e., interruption of approach and turning away from forward path) responses in relation to the varying intensities of olfactory stimulation encountered during crawling. An important consideration in each phase of orientation development, therefore, is the spatial distribution of the odorous deposits on the floor of the home cage.

When vision begins to function, some time after the ninth day, the kittens gradually develop visual orientation to the home region, after a transition period during which olfactory and visual stimuli jointly guide the kittens in their orientation. Soon after the beginning of visual functioning, the kittens' center of orientation shifts to the mother and littermates and, as a consequence, home orientation recedes.

Many features of the development of orientation to the home region can be understood by assuming that kittens, crawling between the adjacent corner and home region, are continuously oriented with reference to a gradient of familiar olfactory stimulation. The kittens maintain the forward direction of their crawling when they receive an increasing intensity of olfactory stimulation, but turn away when the intensity of olfactory stimulation is unchanged or decreases. This assumption is certainly supported by many of our observations.

Deposits of odorous substances by the mother and litter were constantly accumulating on the floor of the home region and were spread, chiefly by the mother, to other regions of the home cage. These substances reached the far corners of the home cage in sufficient amounts for kittens placed in any of these regions at the start of tests to temporarily become quiet when they recognized their location. Thus a gradient of olfactory stimulation was gradually formed on the cage floor with its source (i.e., high intensity of the olfactory stimulus) at the home region and with concentric and graded zones of decreasing olfactory stimulation radiating outward.

The olfactory gradient was *not* symmetrically distributed in a fan shape which spread from an axis in the home region nor did it develop at the same rate in all directions. It was skewed towards the sawdust corner as a result of the interference by other odors or prevention of the spread of litter odors into this corner by the sawdust. In addition, the gradient was established more rapidly along the wall leading into the adjacent corner because the wooden ledge bordering the cage floor absorbed the odorous substance on the floor more easily than the floor.

The gradient of olfactory stimulation was built up gradually during the

3-week period of testing. Not until it was sufficiently steep over a small enough area of the cage floor for kittens to detect an increment in the intensity of olfactory stimulation during scanning of the floor ahead of them with side-to-side head movements while crawling was it effective in orienting kittens to the home. This, however, was in part a function of the developing olfactory acuity and discrimination of the kitten.

Regional differentiation among the corners of the home cage, based upon differences in the olfactory stimulation in each cage locality, developed earlier in the kittens (i.e., first to fourth day) than orientation to the home from the adjacent and diagonal corners. This leads us to believe these three widely separated cage localities could differ significantly in the amount of olfactory material deposited or spread in each, while the cage regions located between these localities were not as yet sufficiently graded in olfactory stimulation, within areas scanned by kittens during their crawling, to provide a basis for orienting to the home.

The earlier development of home orientation from the adjacent corner was based upon an early appearance of a gradient of olfactory stimulation on the intervening floor area. In the early stages of the development of adjacent corner-to-home orientation, circuitous movement, prominent during the first few days, receded, and continuous forward crawling developed with less frequent interruption and pivoting. A kitten in the adjacent quadrant crawling in the direction of home, along a gradient of increasing olfactory stimulation, continued to crawl forward for an extended period. It soon paused, however, then pivoted, turned, and resumed crawling in a new direction. If the new direction of crawling carried it laterally or back towards the adjacent corner, crawling was interrupted shortly after it had started, and the kitten pivoted or turned and resumed crawling once again. Although kittens did not reach the home quadrant from the adjacent corner during this early stage, their general direction of movement was oriented towards the home, and they approached closer to the home quadrant during each successive test. Significantly, the initial direction of crawling taken by kittens when released on the floor at the start of tests in the adjacent corner was in the direction of the home.

Entries into the home quadrant from the adjacent corner were initiated and became more frequent in the next phrase of orientating: Kittens adopted an initial direction of crawling towards the home and maintained it with few pauses and little pivoting until they had entered the home quadrant and reached the home region.

Improvements in this and the next phase of orientation in the adjacent corner were based upon advances in the kitten's ability to follow the gradient of olfactory stimulation leading to the home. The basis of these advances lies in maturational changes in crawling enabling the kittens to maintain continuous forward crawling without pausing and pivoting and in changes in olfactory sensitivity and discrimination enabling the kittens both to perceive small differences in the intensity of olfactory stimulation along the stimulus gradient and to turn more rapidly in the direction of the stronger olfactory stimulus. Further, there is evidence of selective learning in the more rapid forward crawling of kittens in response to increasing olfactory stimulation and their slower crawling, followed by pausing and turning, in response to decreasing olfactory stimulation. Guidance by tactual stimulation from the cage wall also aided the kitten in maintaining continuous forward crawling during the latter phases of orientation.

The extended period of circuitous movement in diagonal corner tests, continuous vocalization at a high intensity, and evidence that departures from this quadrant were oriented equally in the direction of the neutral and adjacent quadrants, early in testing, indicate that the cagewide olfactory gradient reached this quadrant only after the eighth day. The olfactory gradient first appeared in the region between the diagonal and adjacent quadrants, and kittens followed it, much as they did the earlier olfactory gradient between the adjacent and home quadrants, in orienting to the adjacent quadrant. After reaching the adjacent corner, the kittens continued on to the home. Two later developments, however, led to improved orientation to the home, directly across the center of the cage. The first of these was the spread of the olfactory gradient directly from the home to the diagonal quadrant, leading kittens then to crawl diagonally across the cage to the home without first entering the adjacent corner. The second was the gradual introduction of vision to guide orientation to the home. Direct approach to the home using visual cues was then possible but, as we have seen, vision was introduced slowly and at first was used jointly with, and largely in dependence upon, olfactory stimulation.

In home corner tests, kittens were quickly calmed and, during early tests, they came to rest near the starting place soon after the beginning of the test. Later, however, they began to crawl in the direction of the adjacent quadrant. Whether they followed an olfactory gradient, moving from a region of stronger to one of weaker stimulation, or whether there was no clearly defined olfactory gradient in the home quadrant itself cannot be determined. Nevertheless, upon reaching the boundary between the home and adjacent quadrants, the kittens turned and crawled back towards the center of the home quadrant after crawling along the border for a distance. Visual orientation appeared earlier in the home corner tests than in tests started in other regions of the home cage. It is significant that as vision became increasingly important in the orientation of kittens and olfactory stimuli in the home receded in importance, kittens began to leave the home quadrant earlier than they stopped returning to it from the adjacent and diagonal quadrants. The absence of disturbance in the home, compared to the continued low level disturbance that was still aroused in kittens that were placed outside the home, enabled home corner-tested kittens to move more freely and they left the home at an earlier age.

The kitten's behavior in the field tests can best be understood with reference to (1) the high level of disturbance aroused in them, which induced virtual withdrawal and restriction of movement, and (2) the absence of a gradient of familiar olfactory stimuli, which provided no stimuli to guide their movement out of the corner in which they were placed. Not until vision became an important avenue of stimulation did the kittens crawl or walk out of the test corner and wander in the field, continuing, however, their intense and prolonged vocalization.

REFERENCES

1. Kovach, J. K., and A. Kling. 1967. Mechanisms of neonate sucking behavior in the kitten. *Anim. Behav.* 15: 91–101.
2. Schneirla, T. C. 1959. An evolutionary and developmental theory of biphasic processes underlying approach and withdrawal. In M. R. Jones, ed., *Nebraska symposium on motivation.* Lincoln: Univ. Nebraska Press. Pp. 1–42.
3. Schneirla, T. C. 1965. Aspects of stimulation and organization in approach/withdrawal processes underlying vertebrate behavioral development. In D. S. Lehrman, R. A. Hinde, and E. Shaw, eds., *Advances in the study of behavior,* vol. 1. New York: Academic Press. Pp. 1–74.

VII

ON THE BEHAVIOR AND SOCIAL ORGANIZATION OF INSECTS

Dr. Schneirla's interest in ant behavior (an interest that developed during his college years) expanded greatly when he made his first trip to Barro Colorado Island, Canal Zone, Panama, to study the behavior of the doryline army ants. His interests were two-fold. First, he was dissatisfied with the then current limiting explanation of the unique migratory and raiding behavior of army ants that characterized such behavior as inborn or instinctive. He felt that the various behavior patterns could be profitably subjected to causal analysis and explanation in terms of biological processes. Second, he was deeply concerned about the then prevalent anthropomorphic descriptions of army ant behavior, particularly of the mass raiding patterns. After two months work in Panama, he had solved the basic problem and could state confidently that the migratory (nomadic) and nonmigratory (statary) phases of army ant behavior were related to the condition of the brood. Thus, an active larval brood stimulates the workers to the extent that the daily raids lead to daily migrations to a new bivouac site. When the larvae pupate and are hence quiescent, the workers are less active, the daily raids are smaller and do not end in migration. In this first study, Schneirla also provided detailed descriptions of the raiding patterns of the two common species of Panamanian army ants with numerous preliminary explanations of the controlling biological and environmental factors. He published his first results in 1933 in a paper entitled *Studies of Army Ants in Panama* (No. 5).* This article is not reproduced here, because it has primarily historic interest. Following two more trips to Barro Colorado Island, he wrote a comprehensive report, *A Theory of Army-Ant Behavior based upon the Analysis of Activities in a Representative Species* (No. **16**), which is the first paper in this section. This was followed by a long series of studies, extending over many years, in which Schneirla analyzed many features of army ant behavior, such as the role of the queen, production of sexual broods, behavior of the male, the adaptive nature of the bivouac, colony division, regulation of the queen's reproductive cycle by the conditions in the colony, etc. These studies culminated in an analytical and integrative paper, *Theoretical Considerations of Cyclic Processes in Doryline Ants* (No. **81**), in which Schneirla interrelated major behavioral activities, biological processes, and environmental influences in a complex and all inclusive feedback system. He summarized this in his well-known model or diagram (Fig. 99 of this paper), which he reused many times in later articles and lectures. It is of great interest that he conceived of this complex system and presented it with logic and precision without recourse to such concepts as endogenous rhythms or innate patterns of behavior—concepts which he always believed provided pseudoexplanations that tended to direct the investigator away from the real problems and the real solutions in behavioral science.

In later years, Schneirla extended his studies of doryline ants to the old world genus *Aenictus* in the Philippine Islands and to the nearctic genus *Neivamyrmex* in southeastern Arizona. The comparisons of the behavior of these species with the *Ection* species of Panama are considered in several articles, *Theoretical Consideration of Cyclic Processes in Doryline Ants* (No. **81**) in this section and articles 83, 92, 102, 113, and 120 (see complete bibliography, p. 1017). All of Schneirla's research findings on ants are synthesized in his book *Army Ants: A Study in Social Organization* (No. **122**), which was almost complete at the time of his death and which was published by W. H. Freeman and Company in 1971.

Although Schneirla concentrated his efforts on the army ants, his interests in the evolution of social behavior led him to write an important

---

* This and subsequent numbers in this introduction refer to the items in the complete bibliography of Schneirla's works, p. 1017. Bold face numbers denote articles that are included in this volume.

chapter (reprinted in this section), *Collective Activities and Social Patterns among Insects* (No. **64**) for the monumental volume *Insect Physiology* edited by K. D. Roeder.

Because many readers may wish to acquire an overall picture of Schneirla's analysis of army ant behavior without delving into the intricacies and details of his scientific articles, we are reprinting here two popular articles, *The Army Ant* (No. **44**), which was written with Gerard Piel and published in *Scientific American,* and *Dorylines: Raiding and in Bivouac* (No. **110**) from *Natural History* magazine.

Lester R. Aronson
Ethel Tobach

T. C. SCHNEIRLA

A Theory of Army-Ant Behavior based upon the Analysis of Activities in a Representative Species

Bibliography No. 16

Within the past decade the word "instinct" has been given a new meaning in psychology. Theorists have had cause to become aware that the available evidence scarcely encourages mysticism in the treatment of basic activities, and that a more thoroughgoing explanation is required by our rapidly growing fund of knowledge on the problem. In many ways child psychology has developed and strengthened the mechanistic or naturalistic explanation of original behavior in man, and animal psychology has similarly progressed in the special study of numerous vertebrate groups.

Insect behavior has long served as a rich source of examples for the convenient use of antinaturalistic or seminaturalistic writers about "instinct." A treatment such as that offered in Hingston's *Instinct and Intelligence* (1929) would give the impression that a teleological or nonmechanistic treatment of insect activities is well justified even at the present time. Such is far from being the case. Animistic thinking about insects is discouraged by the force of Wheeler's (1923) strong presentation of the "trophallaxis" theory of social organization, a theory which is well supported by studies such as Heyde's (1924) on the appearance of individual adjustments in the colony, by the work of von Frisch (1923, etc.), of Rösch (1930, etc.) and of many others. Preoccupation with a metaphysical treatment is not a valid excuse for ignoring the implications of abundant experimental evidence. To apply a name to a given behavior phenomenon, to say that the animal performs the activity for a certain purpose, or to imply that the process of the adjustment is of the same nature as it is assumed to be in man, does not contribute effectively toward

From *Journal of Comparative Psychology* 25:51–90. Courtesy of the American Psychological Association.

explaining the phenomenon. A satisfactory account of the behavior is given only when the observations are accurately reported, when factors of causal significance are disclosed and identified, and when the way in which these factors bring about the phenomenon is demonstrated. That this approach to the problem of the origin and organization of behavior modes in insects offers the only real solution is shown by treatments such as those of Ziegler (1910), of Imms (1931), and of Maier and Schneirla (1935).

No insect behavior appears more subject to a teleological interpretation than do the activities of army ants, of species in the tribus Ecitini (Forel). Their behavior, exemplified by that of the type species *Eciton hamatum* Fabricius (Schneirla, 1933), has irresistibly tempted many writers to offer an anthropomorphic description. The name "army ant" suggests the manner in which these ants pillage wide areas in mobile columns headed by groups of individuals (e.g., *E. hamatum*) or by swarms (e.g., *E. burchelli*). Wroughton (1892) in describing the forays of an Indian ant in a closely related genus, averred that

> The notion irresistibly forced on anyone, watching these manoeuvres, is that they are either the result of preconcerted arrangement, or are carried out by word of command.

Highly mystifying is the additional fact that a colony does not develop a permanent nest, but engages in periodic migrations, forming at each temporary nesting site a larger cluster (the "bivouac") composed of the hooked-together bodies of the many thousands of colony members. It is not surprising that many scientific writers by indulgence, and many popular writers through naiveté, have endowed these ants with capacities (e.g., ". . . a skilfully planned flanking attack . . . ," ". . . preconcerted arrangement . . . ," ". . . recognizing the necessity of a forced march . . . ,") which appear to lie beyond investigation. Such implications contribute in no way to a solution of any problem in behavior.

Only in consequence of detailed observational and experimental study may we hope to work out the causal factors which underlie the characteristic behavior of a given animal; a self-evident rule which is frequently ignored by impatient theorists. The present writer selected army-ant behavior as a good example of "insect instinct," and has endeavored to observe this fundamental rule while working toward a solution of the problem. The investigation was conducted mainly along the lines of field observation. Habitually, the validity of observational data was checked by repeating the given observation many times, and by means of appropriate supplementary tests under field or laboratory conditions.

The scene of operations was one ideally suited to the needs of this or practically any behavior investigation, the 7 square miles of lower tropical zone rain-forest terrain which comprises the Barro Colorado Island reservation in the Panama Canal Zone.[1] The only possible complaint is that it is not always easy to keep one's particular problem in the foreground, because of strong distractions furnished by the rich variety of animal and plant life present on the Island.

THE GENERAL PROBLEM

Three periods of work during as many rainy seasons have been devoted to the investigation of raiding and related activities, or better, the entire representative behavior pattern, in *Eciton hamatum* and other *Eciton* species. The first two periods fell during the early months of the rainy season (June and July). The results of that work have been reported, in part (Schneirla, 1933, 1934).[2] The third period (August and September, 1936) was given over mainly to a detailed study of a single colony of *E. hamatum*. This colony was regarded as a test case, and every attempt was made during this investigation to check the accuracy of predictions based upon previous work with numerous colonies over shorter periods of time. The activities of this test colony, which will be designated 36A, will be reported as representative of *E. hamatum* during the rainy season months June to September. Since this species is not only the taxonomic type of the subgenus *Eciton Latr.* but the behavior type as well, the theoretical analysis to be offered may properly be regarded as an account of the characteristic Eciton behavior pattern.

RESULTS: A REPRESENTATIVE CASE REPORT

CONDITION OF THE TEST COLONY WHEN FIRST OBSERVED

Colony 36A was first encountered on August 5, 1936, and a record of its condition and activities was maintained during the following six weeks. On September 16, my departure from the Island forced the termination of this record.

When discovered, colony 36A was clustered in a cylindrical "bivouac" which depended from the lower surface of a fallen tree trunk and reached to the broad surface of a broken limb about 14 inches below. The worker population was estimated to include approximately 40,000 individuals.

[1] The writer welcomes this opportunity to acknowledge the many ways in which Mr. James Zetek, the Custodian of Barro Colorado Island, has helped along this work.
[2] The first studies were assisted by Grants-in-Aid from the National Research Council.

In addition, there was an advanced brood of pupae enclosed in cocoons and about to hatch (ca. 30,000 individuals), a second brood of very young larvae, the inevitable ecitophiles, and a queen. (The queen was observed four days later during a migration of the colony.)

Various dependable signs indicated that on August 5 this colony was about to terminate one condition of activity, the *statary condition,* in which for a period of days there occurs no migration, and was on the point of entering a different condition of activity, the *nomadic condition,* in which there occurs a daily change in bivouac site. The best evidence for this was that the workers were beginning to open the cocoons of the advanced brood of pupae. Almost without exception one finds that an *Eciton hamatum* colony does not change its bivouac site from the time the larvae spin their cocoons until the time they are hatched as developed workers (i.e., as "callows"). Further, physical clues indicated that the colony had been clustered in this place for a number of days. When the ants had vacated the spot, a circular whitish area was to be seen on the bark against which the lower end of the cylindrical mass had rested, extending over the exact area which had been covered by the colony. The bleached appearance of this area, which was in contrast with the dark surrounding bark, may be explained by the action of Eciton-produced chemicals upon the bark itself. From other observations we may say that this distinct change could have been produced only during a period of days. Further, the condition of raiding supported the belief that the colony was then in the statary phase of activity. From the bivouac, a single raiding column led away, terminating in numerous well-branched auxiliary columns about 300 meters distant. To have but a single well-developed raiding system is very characteristic of a colony that is *statary.* We may conclude from these facts, which are thoroughly supported by other evidence on such cases, that the colony 36A had been clustered at this site for about 16 days previous to August 5.

It was very fortunate that the study could begin with a colony which was just emerging from one activity phase and about to enter a different phase. At the end of the following day (August 6), practically all of the cocoons had been opened, and the colony was in process of migrating to a new bivouac site. This marked the beginning of a period of nomadic activity.

THE BEHAVIOR OF COLONY 36A
FROM AUGUST 5 TO SEPTEMBER 16

Table 1 presents a concise report of the activities of this test colony during the 42-day period in which the study was conducted. The table is

TABLE 1 (Continued)
General activities of colony 36A, August 5 to September 16, 1936.

Date	Bivouac site (see Fig. 75)	Condition of the brood	Condition of raiding activity	Behavior toward end of the day
Aug. 5	Site A, beneath log	Two broods:: (1) tiny larvae, (2) advanced pupae	A single raiding system, with very long trail	No migration. General return to bivouac after 4:00, completed during evening
Aug. 6	Still at site A	Pupal brood now completely hatched	More active; single system on the 8/5 route	Raiding merged into migration after 3:00. New bivouac started approximately at 5:00
Aug. 7	Site 1, beneath log	Newly hatched callows; also tiny larvae	Three systems, vigorous raiding	Migrated over raiding trail toward East; starting at 2:30
Aug. 8	Site 2, beneath vine	Same: callows; young larvae	Three systems, vigorous raiding	Migrated over raiding trail to NE; started 5:30, delayed by rain
Aug. 9	Site 3, beneath log	Same (queen nonphysogastric)	Three systems, vigorous raiding	Migrated over raiding trail to E, started after 6:30 (heavy rain)
Aug. 10	Site 4, under vines	Same; callows active in raids	Four systems, one poorly developed	Migration developed slowly after 4:30, over raiding trail to NE
Aug. 11	Site 5, beneath root	Same	Three systems, one branched close to bivouac	Migration over raiding trail to SW; rapidly developed after 3:30
Aug. 12	Site 6, under palm leaf	Larvae active, probably feeding	Three principal raiding systems	Migration over raiding trail to SW x S; 4:00. Delayed by "struggle"
Aug. 13	Site 7, under log	Larvae distributed in bivouac	Three principal systems; active	Migration toward SW over raiding trail; started slowly after 3:00
Aug. 14	Site 8, under vines	Larvae feeding actively	Three principal systems; active	Migration toward SW over raiding trail; started 2:30; delayed by rain
Aug. 15	Site 9, under vines	Larvae medium-sized; active	Three systems, vigorous raiding	Migration toward NW x N over raiding trail; began slowly after 4:30
Aug. 16	Site 10, under log	Same	Four systems, one weakly developed	Migration began 2:30, over raiding trail to W, N; specific after 5:15
Aug. 17	Site 11, vines, log	Same	Three systems, vigorous raiding	Migration began 2:45, over raiding trail to NW x N; unusually prompt

(continued)

TABLE 1—Continued

Date	Bivouac site (see Fig. 75)	Condition of the brood	Condition of raiding activity	Behavior toward end of the day
Aug. 18	Site 12, mass of vines	Same	Four systems, one soon abandoned	Migration began 3:30, over raiding trail to NE; not specific until 7:00
Aug. 19	Site 13, under wide palm leaf	Larvae very active	Three vigorously developed systems	Migration over trail to NW x N, after 2:15. New bivouac started 6:10
Aug. 20	Site 14, under large log	Larvae large, well advanced	Four systems, one abandoned in A.M.	Migration over raiding trail to NW, delayed by rain (started 2:30)
Aug. 21	Site 15, between buttressed roots	Same	Four systems, one not well developed	Migration over W raiding trail; delayed by "struggle" near bivouac
Aug. 22	Site 16, under log	Same	Three systems, well developed	Migration over raiding trail to NW, after 2:30. Delayed by raiding
Aug. 23	Site 17, well under palm log	Larval cocoon-spinning began in afternoon	Four raiding systems, one inconsequential	Migration began slowly after 3:15, over raiding trail to NW
Aug. 24	Site B, under crossed logs	Cocoon-spinning completed on 8/24	Three systems, two very weak	No migration. Weak outward movement in afternoon; general return to bivouac after 4:00
Aug. 25	Site B, exposed to rain	Larval brood completely enclosed	Two systems, one poorly developed	No migration. General return to bivouac after 2:30
Aug. 26	Site B, rain disturbing	Same	One raiding system, mildly active	General return to bivouac after 2:30, completed in early evening
Aug. 27	Site B	Same	Single raiding system toward SW	New trail to NW started 2:00; general return; weak evening raiding
Aug. 28	Site B. Rain forced formation of small secondary cluster nearby, well under same log		Fairly vigorous raiding toward E	General return after 3:00; probably no night raiding
Aug. 29	Site B. Partial return from secondary to the principal cluster		Fairly vigorous raiding toward W	After 1:30, new raiding system to SW; general return delayed by rain
Aug. 30	Site B. Secondary cluster grows larger, due to rain		Fairly vigorous raiding toward E	General return after 2:30. No night raiding
Aug. 31	Site B. Ants have mainly returned to the principal		Two weak systems, to S, and	General return after 3:00, completed by 6:45

		larvae		
			W	...return after 3:00, completed in early evening
Sept. 2	Site B. Same status	Same	One system, weakly developed to S	General return after 2:30; no night raiding
Sept. 3	Site B. Nearby cluster now larger	Same	One weak system, developed to NW	General return after 3:30, completed in early evening
Sept. 4	Site B. Rain forced ants, carrying cocoons, into secondary cluster	Same	One, the extension of 9/3 route	General return after 3:00, no night raiding
Sept. 5	Site B. Shift completed to site 1 meter from the first	Same	One fairly active system toward SW	Practically all ants returning after 4:00; no night raiding
Sept. 6	Site B, far beneath log	Enclosed brood now in pupal form; eggs present	Route of 9/3 weakly used; new system toward NW	Return fairly complete at 6:30, probably no night raiding
Sept. 7	Site B	Enclosed pupae; large batch eggs	Vigorous system toward SE	New system to N developed after 2:00; steady return after 4:00
Sept. 8	Site B	Same	Two: vigorous one to W, weak one to E	Afternoon raiding not very active; all returning after 4:00
Sept. 9	Site B	Same	Two: fairly vigorous W; weak N	Traffic mainly inward after 3:00, probably no night raiding
Sept. 10	Site B. further under log (rain)	Same	One: vigorous raiding to NW	Raiders predominantly returning after 4:00
Sept. 11	Site B. cluster appears larger	Same. Cocoon-opening began in afternoon	Two vigorous systems: one to NW, one to S	Migration over SE raiding trail after 3:15; moved only 20 meters
Sept. 12	Site 1b	Pupal brood now hatched; 2d brood tiny larvae	Four systems, two very actively used	Migration over raiding trail to E, SE; direction not specific until after 7:00, because of "struggle"
Sept. 13	Site 2b, between rocks	Callows; very small larvae	Three systems, one rather weak	Migration started slowly after 4:30, over raiding route to S
Sept. 14	Site 3b, beneath log	Same	Three systems, all well developed	Migration well under way at 2:30, over raiding trail to SW
Sept. 15	Site 4, in vine mass	Same. Captured colony; queen nonphysogastric	Three very active systems	Migration started 2:00, over NW raiding trail; colony captured at 5:30: brood, queen, removed

best studied in connection with Figure 75, a contour map on which are sketched the various bivouac sites occupied during the period. In this figure the successive routes of migration may be followed to the respective new bivouac sites, and from each site the general direction of the main raiding systems may be traced.

It is to be noted that, after leaving the statary site A on August 6, the colony established itself at a different bivouac site and raided over new territory on each of the following 17 days. During this *nomadic period* the successively visited localities were most energetically pillaged. In morning hours, the ants would rapidly extend the trails which had begun to form during the previous night even before the new bivouac cluster had been established. The directions in which the principal raiding systems were developed from a given bivouac site are shown in the figure. Usually three well-used systems appeared by noon, indicated at the bivouac site by as many principal trails extending in different directions. By this time, within 120 meters or more from the bivouac, all branch trails usually had dropped away, but far out, each trunk line would first present numerous branches, terminating finally in a complex system of auxiliary trails. Toward late afternoon all but one of the principal raiding systems would be vacated gradually as the ants began their exodus to the new bivouac site. The new bivouac was always established in the evening or early night far out somewhere on the remaining raiding trail. Frequently, as a result of rain, the bivouac-change movement was prolonged into the early hours of the following day.

It will be recalled that several thousand callow workers were hatched shortly before the colony left site A. Within four or five days after that time these new workers (distinguished from adults by their light golden-yellow coloration), began to appear on the raiding trails. At first, such individuals were to be seen only within a short distance of the bivouac, but in time that distance increased as the callows apparently became fully functioning members of the colony. Near the end of their first week, but not before, callows might be seen anywhere on the raiding trails, carrying booty or apparently participating in the raids.

In the course of this nomadic period a further brood of many thousands

FIGURE 75
Terrain in the northeastern section of Barro Colorado Island over which the army ant colony 36A worked between August 5 and September 16, 1936. A, statary site occupied by the colony when discovered; 1–17, sites occupied during successive days of the nomadic period (August 7–23); B, statary site occupied from August 24–September 11; 1b–4x, sites occupied in the first days of a further nomadic period. Solid lines show the beginnings and the general directions of the principal raiding trails from each bivouac. Dotted lines show the successive migration routes. Scales: length of N–S arrow, 100 meters; contour interval, 6.1 meters.

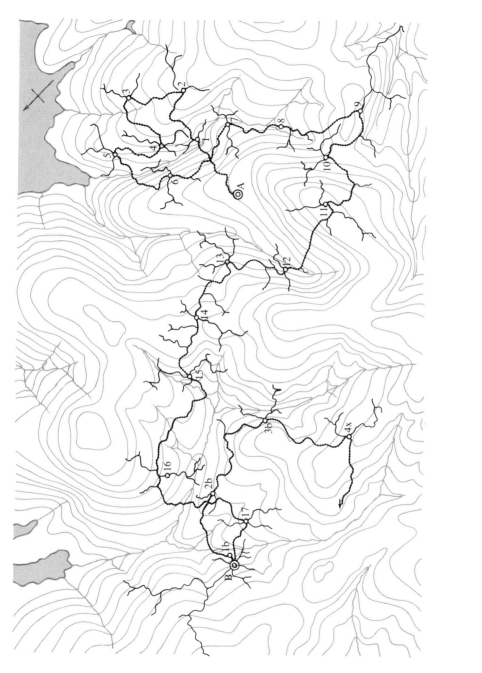

was passing through the larval stage of development. On the 17th nomad day individuals of this brood were fully grown larvae. These larvae began to spin on August 23, and the cocoon-spinning evidently was completed on the following day, when the colony was clustered at site B.

The colony remained in its bivouac on site B until September 11, a *statary period* of 19 days. Certain minor changes in the position of the cluster, forced by heavy rains, served to make the colony progressively less accessible to observation during this period. From the beginning of the statary phase, raiding was greatly reduced in vigor and in number of participants, as compared with the preceding nomadic phase. On a typical day of statary-phase raiding these values were approximately one-third as great as during a nomad day, this comparison extending to the number of raiders as well as to the development of raiding trails and the amount of captured booty.

From one day to the next during this period the principal raiding trails suggested in Figure 75 were successively developed in different directions. Usually only one trail was used actively on a given day, perhaps on one or two following days as well, or its use resumed after an interval of a few days. Frequently a trail was extended to more than 400 meters from the bivouac before being abandoned. Thus a territory of more than 300 meters radius around the bivouac was rather thoroughly pillaged during the colony's stay at site B.

Commonly the ants were observed to resume the use of an old trail or to begin a new trail during the late afternoon.[3] However, there seldom was much activity on the trails after 6:00 P.M., by which time most of the raiders had returned to the bivouac. (Table 1 will assist the study of such matters.) Night raiding apparently occurred infrequently during the statary period.

The hatching of the brood of pupae began on the afternoon of September 11, after 18 statary days. On that day there occurred a marked spurt in raiding activity. By evening a few hundred callows had been hatched, and the colony moved to a new bivouac site, which was, however, only 25 meters distant from the preceding site. Furthermore, in comparison with the typically vigorous migration of the nomadic colony, this bivouac-change was delayed and was sluggishly effected. Nevertheless, it defi-

---

[3] In the second instance of use the ants generally followed the identical original route, with occasional minor deviations, for more than 100 meters from the bivouac, making their first advance hesitantly and in the typical "relay" fashion. When one considers the heavy daily rains and the opportunity for volatilization during the intervening days, this ability to utilize the original "chemically saturated" trail suggests not only the possession of delicately sensitive chemoreceptors by these ants, but also the strength of the qualities which permitted the chemical traces to persist.

FIGURE 76
A flash-sheet photograph of the September 15
bivouac of colony 36A, *Eciton hamatum,* taken
from above at one side. The colony was clustered
into an irregular cylinder approximately 14 inches
in diameter and 7 inches in height. The removal
of vines and rubble for a proper exposure of the
bivouac so disrupted traffic on the three principal
raiding trails that ants cannot be seen on them.
Shortly after this photo was taken, the colony
was etherized and captured.

nitely marked the end of a statary period and the beginning of a nomadic
period of colony activity.

During the following days the colony raided very actively, in representative nomad fashion, from successively occupied bivouac sites. On the
evening of the fourth nomadic day, September 15, a new bivouac-change
movement was progressing vigorously when the bulk of the colony was
captured after etherization. The queen (her gaster minimal in size), a new
brood of many thousand very young larvae, the ecitophiles (see Wheeler,
1925), and representative workers were removed. The remnants of the
colony were dumped late at night on site 4 (x, Figure 75), from which
the ants had been taken. On September 18 no traces of the ants were to
be seen on that site or in its vicinity. Unquestionably the ants which re-

vived had completed the migratory movement along the fresh trail, and the casualties had been cleaned up by small forest scavengers.

A GENERAL THEORY OF ECITON ACTIVITIES

Even a casual survey of the foregoing report discloses a direct correspondence between the activity of colony 36A and the condition of its brood. It will be convenient to examine this parallel in a summary of the facts (Table 2). The observations reported in the preceding section and summarized in Table 2 are thoroughly supported by data from shorter studies of more than sixty other *Eciton hamatum* colonies. Furthermore, the investigation of numerous colonies in other *Eciton* species (e.g., *E.*

TABLE 2
A summary of the Table 1 observations on colony 36A. This shows the typical correspondence existing between colony activity and the condition of the brood.

Time	Nature of colony activity	Condition of the developing young
(Probably from about July 16 to August 5–6)	Statary: Located on constant bivouac site. Raiding activity confined to a single trail system each day.	Advanced pupal brood enclosed in cocoons; hatched August 5–6. New brood of very young larvae present on August 6.
From August 6 to August 23	Nomadic: Colony now raids vigorously each day, over three well-developed systems. A migration occurs each evening.	A brood of newly hatched and voracious workers present on August 6. Also a second brood of developing larvae which are increasingly active. These spin their cocoons on August 23–24.
From August 24 to September 11	Statary: Located on constant bivouac site. Raiding typically weak; usually single system each day.	Brood of larvae metamorphosing into pupae within cocoons. Clutch of eggs laid during this period; present as tiny larvae on September 11. Advanced pupal brood hatched from cocoons on Sept. 11.
After September 12	Nomadic: Vigorous raiding; nightly migration.	Thousands of newly hatched, active and voracious workers. Brood of developing larvae present.
Study terminated September 16		

burchelli, E. praedator, E. vagans) has shown that a similar correspondence between brood condition and the general state of colony activity prevails in their case, although apparently with somewhat different time relations. On the basis of this evidence we may now work out a theoretical account of the Eciton behavior pattern. This theory will be stated in terms of *E. hamatum* behavior.

The basis of the nomadic phase, its rise and persistence

We will be able to show that the activity of the newly-hatched worker brood accounts for the beginning of the nomadic phase of colony activity. We will also show that the activity of a further brood, when it passes through the larval stage, maintains the colony in the nomadic condition during that time. These two factors basically account for the phenomena of nomadic behavior.

ACTIVITY OF NEWLY HATCHED CALLOWS
FIRST SETS THE COLONY INTO NOMADIC BEHAVIOR

When the enclosed brood of the statary period has developed from the larval stage into the advanced pupal stage, the movements of the full-term pupae within their cocoons exert a stimulative effect upon the adult workers which hold the cocoons or are stationed nearby in the cluster. The excited workers, as a consequence, are observed to move about carrying the cocoons of "stirring" pupae. Soon other workers are drawn into the excitement, catching hold of the cocoon, and, in the ensuing counter-twisting and pulling movements, the cases are torn open by the sharp mandibles of adult workers (Schneirla, 1934, p. 320 f.). It is the antennal and leg reflexes, and to a minor extent the trunk reflexes of the full-term pupae, which first cause the workers to respond to the cocoons. That the movements of the enclosed pupae *do* excite the adults to activity which incidentally results in the hatching of the brood is shown by the outcome of laboratory tests.

One group of 60 *E. hamatum* workers from a nomadic colony was given a batch of 40 cocoons containing advanced pupae all of which had begun to "stir." Within four hours most of the pupae had been shucked from their cases. The group was next presented with 40 cocoons containing pupae at the same advanced stage of development but dead as a result of cephalic puncture by a needle. Although these cocoons were huddled, carried about, and licked by the workers, only two of them were torn open, and these only partially. A test with another group of workers which was first presented with motionless enclosed pupae, then with active enclosed pupae, turned out similarly.

It is evident that this phenomenon represents a crude type of so-called "communication," which depends upon the general (not specific: see Eidmann, 1927; Maier and Schneirla, 1935, pp. 168–170) arousal of movement through incidental contact and probably also chemical stimulation furnished by the movements of the callows. The disturbance of the workers, occasioned by the brood activity, is transmitted throughout a colony by means of incidental antennal and bodily contacts among the agitated workers as they run about the bivouac. Sufficiently aroused individuals are thereby occasioned to leave the bivouac cluster and depart on a raiding trail.[4] It will be suggested below that this terminal reaction of the sufficiently excited adult worker may be regarded as a "general, learned response." As a consequence of all this, general external observation alone shows that the colony now is maintaining a higher degree of excitement than on previous days, during the statary phase. The facts also show that the greatly augmented excitement of the brood-hatching episode brings the colony from relative quiescence into that pitch of raiding activity which in vigor and in number of participants leads inevitably to a migration at the end of each day of raiding. Just why this outcome is inevitable under these conditions we shall see presently.

The persistence of the nomadic phase during the ensuing days is dependent at first upon the newly hatched workers. During four days (or approximately that length of time) these individuals do not appear on the raiding trails to any extent, but continue to serve as a source of stimulation within the bivouac cluster. They consume large quantities of food. However, it would be a mistake to conclude that the marked increase in food consumption is the essential and direct cause of the fact that the workers continue to raid vigorously, although W. Müller (1886) in another connection was led to that conclusion. Although there lies in his suggestion a hint of the true state of affairs, it is actually a teleological interpretation and as such is very misleading. It is the restless movements of the callows, and not the incidental fact that they feed "ravenously," which excite the adults tactually and perhaps chemically and thus raise the level of their activity. To these stimuli the excited adult workers respond by presenting food (in all probability, a learned response), licking the bodies of the callows with their tongues, intermittently dashing about stimulating one another with oscillating antennae or bodily contacts, or by hurriedly leav-

---

[4] That this result is attributable to the appearance of an increased *general* excitement in the worker, and not to a *specific* change in the worker's behavior, is suggested by facts such as the following. It is frequently possible to start *new* raiding forays and even to determine their general direction, by breaking open on one side or another the bivouac cluster of a statary army-ant colony. This test works best in the late afternoon, when the one established raiding trail is thronged with returning workers; obviously, because workers which are excited to leave the bivouac are then forced to take another direction.

ing the bivouac. In observing these events, one is led to conclude that the final effect, the departure from the bivouac, occurs as a result of the summation of stimuli and not as a consequence of special (i.e., distinctive) stimulation. The presence of the callows maintains this state of affairs for a few days after the cocoons have been opened, but then the strength of the effect becomes materially reduced.

This conclusion is suggested by an important change in the behavior of the callows themselves. Since they appear on the raiding trails with increasing frequency as time goes on, we are led to the conclusion that a process takes place whereby the new individual is caused to respond by leaving the bivouac when adequately aroused (by internally arising stimuli, or otherwise), rather than by bustling about within the bivouac stimulating other ants as she does at first. The function of the callows in originating or propagating excitement through their disturbed and irregular movements within the bivouac must disappear as a consequence of this change.

It is reasonable to believe that the important change described above comes about in a manner which is fundamentally the same as that suggested by Heyde's (1924) results. Heyde found that the young campono-tine worker shortly after hatching merely remains in place and exhibits excited anterior-end movements when lacking food or when stimulated by another individual. However, she soon comes to move about the nest restlessly under these conditions, and within 2 to 4 days she leaves the nest and forages when exciting stimuli are presented. In Heyde's treatment the mechanism of the change is obscure, since the early response is termed a "reflex," the later response an "instinct."

In view of other evidence on the appearance of foraging activities in newly hatched insects (e.g., Steiner, 1932), it is reasonable to hypothetically attribute the above behavior change mainly to the influence of *learning* (Maier and Schneirla, 1935, pp. 170–173).

THE NOMADIC PHASE IS MAINTAINED AS A
RESULT OF THE ACTIVITY OF DEVELOPING LARVAE

When the passing of the excitatory agency which initiates this period would otherwise permit the colony to lapse into the relatively sessile statary condition, a new and more lasting excitatory factor comes into effect. The newly nomad colony possesses a brood which is then in the early larval stage, the eggs having been laid by the queen during the statary period. The movements of these larvae, particularly the active twisting movements of their anterior ends, shortly become an important source of stimulation to adult workers. For this it is important that the larvae as they grow larger and become more active are not massed together in the very center of the bivouac as before, but are held by individual workers or are piled in small numbers in the spaces between ant-strands throughout the interior of the bivouac.

Consequently, "trophallaxis" (Wheeler, 1923, expressed here as the interstimulative relationship of larvae and adult workers, reaches a high value which it maintains until the larvae have spun their cocoons. However, as regards the essential nature of the brood's contribution to this process, it is not the fact that the larvae feed ravenously or "require" large quantities of food, as Müller (1886) suggested. In speaking of the marked change in activity displayed by a previously rather inactive colony of *E. burchelli* which he had been observing, Müller remarked (1886, p. 87) that

> Der Punkt, wo der Wechsel eintritt, fällt ungefähr zusammen mit dem, wo sich die letzten Larven einspinnen, und dieses zusammentreffen ist jedenfalls kein zufälliges. Larven brauchen ja im allgemeinen, besonders kurze Zeit vor der Verpuppung, bedeutend mehr Nahrung als die fertigen Insekten, und so scheint nichts natürlicher, als dasz das Nahrungsbedürfnis der Gesellschaft ein geringeres wird und die Tiere entsprechend weniger auf Beute ausgehen, nachdem alle Larven eingesponnen.

"Nahrungsbedürfnis" suggests the point, yet misses it. We are warranted in assuming only that the afferent consequences of the larval growth processes result in random activity which *incidentally* exerts a powerful excitatory effect upon the workers. This relationship is, none the less, a highly adaptive one. Through its influence, at advanced stages in their development, the larvae exert a more pronounced stimulative effect than before. This indirectly forces the procuration of the larger quantities of food which the brood then is able to consume, since the adults raid more actively when more excited.

As the larvae advance in their development the colony is increasingly active in daytime raiding, and nocturnal raiding is engaged in by greater numbers of workers than before. The raiding systems now extend much further from the bivouac site into surrounding territory, also the distance between one bivouac site and the next shows a noticeable increase as the larvae near their full development. The colony retains the nomadic condition of behavior throughout the larval development, since the very active raiding of each day inevitably results in an evening migration. An analysis of the bivouac-change movement in its close relation to raiding will demonstrate this fact.

THE COLONY MIGRATION VIEWED AS THE
DIRECT OUTCOME OF MAXIMALLY VIGOROUS RAIDING

In the preceding section of this paper it is implied that augmented raiding activity which is aroused by the hatching of a pupal brood and maintained throughout the development of a further larval brood accounts for the nightly migratory movement, which is the essential characteristic of the nomad activity phase. Despite heavy rains or other interferences the colony, once it has entered the nomadic condition, changes its clustering site at the end of each day. We may proceed to show why this behavior persists during the larval development, but disappears once the larvae have spun their cocoons.

In summarizing and interpreting the facts we need include only those items which suggest how the very active "three-system" raiding of a given (nomad) day passes smoothly into a bivouac-change movement. Typically, when the vigorous raiding of morning subsides during the midday hours, three principal trails lead from the bivouac to as many broadly extended raiding fronts where the trails branch extensively in tree-like manner. (As Table 1 shows, this contrasts sharply with the single principal trail which is typically developed in a comparable length of time by a statary colony.) There occurs a spurt in raiding activity during the early afternoon, without much doubt because of atmospheric changes which regularly come at that time (e.g., temperature, humidity changes). Ants throng from the bivouac in greater numbers, and respond to the principal trails in dependence upon (a) the extent to which the different trails have become saturated with "booty chemical" by captures dragged into the bivouac during morning raiding, and (b) the physical accessibility of the respective trail entrances.[5] The first of these two factors usually prevails in the end, and governs the identity of the route taken in the migration, but the second factor sometimes causes ants to take another route in considerable numbers and thereby greatly delays the completion of the bivouac-change. Hence, in most cases, the migration occurs over the trail system from which the greatest supply of booty has been returned to the bivouac in the morning. Although it is not feasible to elaborate the matter in this connection, in all probability the response to the principal trails (as well as to outlying trail-junctions) mainly depends upon a chemoreceptively controlled discrimination which is gradually learned by the ant during her early days on the raiding trails. At 11:30 A.M., after having studied the raiding systems, one may consequently predict with considerable accuracy which of the three main routes will be the line of the evening migratory movement.

As the afternoon lengthens, more and more ants stream from the biv-

---

[5] These statements regarding the effect of "booty chemical" and the accessibility of trail entrances are based upon the results of various trail-alteration tests and upon observations of complete days of raiding in which regular estimates or sample measurements were made of booty-return and other important events at strategically located places in the raiding systems. The writer decided against unduly lengthening this paper by introducing such quantitative records in any form.

ouac. The majority of the new recruits run onto the trail over which a predominantly outward movement first started by virtue of the factors we have mentioned. The outward movement along this route in time becomes more pronounced and continuous at the expense of the other routes, and for two reasons in particular. First, ants are both forced into and "sucked" into this trail. Individuals which have been aroused by the general turmoil at the base of the bivouac meet with frequent collision when they turn back toward the bivouac, and the resultant effect of the repeated tactual stimulation thereby received causes them to turn in the direction of greater freedom of movement. The "sucking" action is provided by the recurrent and rapid evacuation of the chemically well-saturated area at the source of this trail. In their responses to the "booty chemical," newcomers move very readily into this zone; and then they are forced to "keep going" by the press of numbers behind them. Second, the excited ants are not only less likely to turn onto the other routes because of ineffective chemical stimulation at the sources, but even when started in motion on these trails soon hesitate and turn back as a result of repeated collision with returning raiders.

Thus during the late afternoon one of the principal trails is thronged with unladen ants leaving the bivouac, and with booty-laden ants from other raiding systems. Their number increases steadily, since the departing workers incidentally arouse others in a geometrically progressive continuum. Ants which return to the bivouac on the other principal trails, many of them laden with booty, also join this column by virtue of sheer physical coercion if nothing else.

This outward movement is obstructed and at first dissipated by counter forces which are encountered at a distance from the bivouac. The migratory movement is disrupted in various ways at places from which trails lead into distant zones where raiding is actively progressing. At such trail bifurcations the migrating ants may at first turn into the alternative paths in equal numbers, and the return of previously raiding ants also causes confusion there. However, such deterrences undergo a gradual reduction in their effect, because of the fact that ants which start their return with booty on this crowded trail system have many collisions with the hurrying outward-bound ants. The repeated interference with forward motion causes these laden ants to hesitate and then to reverse their direction of progress, or to deposit their burdens at trail junctions.

As a factor which contributes to the development of the general migratory movement we must not underestimate the importance of continued raiding in the outermost and widely spread portions of the trail system in question. This activity removes ants in considerable numbers from the trails which lie further back toward the bivouac, and may in itself account for the occurrence of a general outward movement on certain advanced branch trails even before the migratory movement assumes form at the bivouac site.

The route which is eventually taken by the migratory column through the complex and newer part of the trail system depends in particular upon the manner in which raiding has progressed along the alternative routes which lead from the respective junction points. This of course means that after a given period of raiding the alternatives at a given junction will differ chemically (i.e., one of them more booty-saturated than the other) and in the traffic on them, not to mention differences in natural obstruction to passage. These, it will be recognized, are among the principal factors which govern the manner in which the migration settles upon one of the available routes leading from the bivouac. To this extent the problems are almost identical. The forces which govern the behavior of ants at a given trail bifurcation are frequently so equalized for the two alternative trails that the migratory movement is interrupted there for some time. As we have suggested above, in such cases there occurs a "struggle" with predominant traffic diverted first to one of the trails, then to the other, and interchangeably (Schneirla, 1933, pp. 277–280). This phenomenon may also be observed at the bivouac when two of the principal alternative routes there are about equally "favored." Table 1 suggests that in many instances the migration of colony 36A was delayed in this manner.

From Table 1 it is to be seen that the migratory movement typically becomes recognizable as such after about 2:30 P.M. In the movement of the newly nomad colony, the callow workers do not appear in numbers within the first hour or two, but then begin to appear and soon throng the column. Later on during the movement one sees adult workers carrying small packets of tiny larvae, the new brood. In the following days of the nomad period, however, ants carrying single larvae appear on the trail early during the migration, due to the fact that now the brood is not packed near the center of the bivouac cluster as was formerly the case, but is distributed throughout the interior of the cluster.[6] The minim workers appear in numbers only toward the latter hours of the migration, since these individuals typically reside well within the bivouac and do not leave it as readily as do the larger workers.

It is not for many hours, until the bivouac has become reduced to a sparse apple-sized cluster of ants, that the queen appears. She is preceded for a meter or more, and followed, by a greatly thickened column of

---

[6] This change is attributable to the fact that as the larvae grow, and move more vigorously, their stimulative effect upon the workers increases, and hence they are more likely to be picked up and carried about the cluster, or held in place by individual workers hooked into the ant-strands.

highly excited workers. I have never seen the queen leave the bivouac earlier in the movement, but on three occasions have waited out the movement and observed her at the very end of the migration.[7] Her gaster is minimal in size during nomad days, and she runs easily and fairly rapidly when on the trail. She is not dragged along by the workers, but moves under her own power. In fact, the workers obstruct the queen's progress by swarming around her and by hanging to her legs and abdomen. Nevertheless she succeeds in moving her body and the workers that cling to it over the winding route of 200 meters or more. After she passes the column soon ends, as a rule.

The new bivouac cluster is established somewhere in the advanced raiding zone. We have described the manner in which confusion arises at trail junctions as raiders laden with booty collide with members of the migratory column. At length it becomes impossible for ants laden with brood, outward-bound from the bivouac, to pass beyond one or another of the far-advanced trail junctions, since their further progress is effectively impeded by hurrying raiders. These disoriented travelers join equally disturbed booty-carriers in clustering nearby along the route. Callow workers, in particular, cluster with great readiness because they are easily disoriented. Usually several clusters are formed at various places along the route, but most of them disappear soon after the weakening of interruptive conditions permits the migratory movement to proceed. Occasionally the eventual bivouac site is not established until well toward the end of the evacuation from the previous site. The formation of the new bivouac cluster depends first upon sufficient obstruction at a given place in the advanced raiding zone to impede the migration in a protracted manner, and second, upon the fact that Eciton individuals cluster readily in the dark and at a temperature below ca. 23° C.

The new bivouac cluster typically is established at or near the bifurcation of a raiding trail, because confusion and disorientation are particularly localized at such places. The path along which the ants moved from the previous bivouac site is seldom used at all during the raiding of the following day, for the same reason that any raiding trail ceases to hold ants after booty has become sparse in the area entered by its branches. However, during and after the formation of the new bivouac, raiding continues along the trails which lead onward divergently from the site. Daylight arouses the ants to greater activity, and with increased numbers of participating workers, the raiding systems which were started during the previous night are rapidly extended into new territory.

---

[7] Apparently F. Nevermann observed his *E. lucanoides* queen near the termination of a migration, although this is difficult to ascertain from Reichensperger's (1934) account [of the capture].

The described pattern of behavior is very typical of *Eciton hamatum* and *E. burchelli,* and apparently in its essential outlines also holds for the other *Eciton* species. A colony of *E. hamatum* practically never occupies the same bivouac site on two successive days during the period which follows the release of a pupal brood from cocoons and which covers the larval development of a further brood. To summarize, the foregoing theory is built upon the fact that a brood of larvae which contains many thousands of individuals all at the same stage in development, incidentally stimulates the adults through its activity and thereby greatly increases the general level of colony excitement. This accounts for the marked vigor of each day's raiding, and for the development of raiding systems by great numbers of workers to an extent which makes a colony migration inevitable at the end of the day. When the maintaining cause ceases to function, colony excitement is markedly reduced and the value of raiding activity falls considerably below the threshold necessary for a general migration. Consequently the colony then enters a very different activity phase in which true migration does not occur.

Basis of the statary phase, its rise and persistence

We will be able to show that the effective removal of the immense larval brood as a source of stimulation ends the nomadic phase of activity, and the absence of this or other special agencies of arousal leaves the colony in a relatively sessile condition for a period of days.

As soon as the larval brood of our test colony 36A had become enclosed, on August 24, following the cocoon-spinning which required almost two days for its completion, the state of colony activity changed markedly. The cocoon-spinning got under way on the afternoon of August 23, and in the meantime very active raiding was in progress on three extensively developed trail systems. At the end of this day the colony migrated over one of the principal raiding trails to a new bivouac site. With this we may sharply contrast events of the following day. Raiding activity then was greatly reduced, with but one fairly well-developed trail system appearing. No migratory movement occurred at the end of the day.

Somewhat before 3:00 P.M. the raiders began to return toward the bivouac along their one developed principal trail. Few individuals were to be seen leaving the colony site, although ants in small groups were observed surging about near the base of the bivouac. By early evening practically all of the raiders had vacated the trails, and at 9:00 P.M. all of the stragglers had come in. This sketches colony behavior approximately for each of the 19 days during which the colony remained in its bivouac at site B. Raiding activity was at a relatively low ebb throughout the period.

There was no possibility of a migratory movement occurring on any occasion, although now and then the raiders did not all return to the bivouac in the evening but continued to raid in small numbers through the early night hours.

It will be worth while to inquire why, during the statary phase, the typical afternoon resurgence of raiding does not eventuate in migration to a new bivouac site. An explanation may be offered which is consistent with the evidence of *E. hamatum* and other species as well, and which completes the circle in its agreement with the foregoing theoretical analysis of the nomadic condition.

Briefly, we may say that the marked and persistent reduction in raiding activity during the statary phase renders ineffective those conditions which are essential for the occurrence of the migratory movement. It will be recalled that during the statary phase, raiding is only about one-third as vigorous and extensive as it is during the nomadic phase. The citation of some significant observational results will show why, at this low value, raiding is subthreshold with respect to the production of a colony migration.

Commonly, toward noon of a statary day, there is a noticeable decrease in the number of workers passing from the bivouac toward the zone of raiding. This means that booty-laden ants in their return toward the bivouac encounter little interference, and that consequently traffic on the one principal trail is predominantly inward during the midday hours.

As a result, colony members caused to leave the cluster in the regular activity spurt of the early afternoon are not able to make effective headway over the principal trail.[8] The numbers are very insufficient to force predominant outward travel on this one booty-saturated route; and even when the balance is artificially swung in their favor by virtue of a 15-minute experimental interruption of inward traffic (far out on the trail), the change is temporary and the outcome finally is no different. Consequently, most of the newly aroused "would-be" raiders mill about at the base of the bivouac, and the result of their activity is at best the limited redevelopment of a chemical trail used on some previous day, or the partial development of a new trail. The newly utilized (or renewed) raiding route cannot be pushed out very far at the time, since relatively few ants come into the work and since raiding activity dies away in early evening, probably because darkness and lowered temperature act as deterrents to activity.

Thus we find that the conditions which were described as prerequisite

---

[8] As we have suggested, it is highly probable that the characteristic afternoon increase in colony activity depends upon atmospheric changes in temperature and in humidity which regularly come at that time of day (Schneirla, 1933, pp. 296–297).

to the occurrence of a migratory movement are all absent in the statary colony. In the lack of an active brood the colony becomes sluggish in its general behavior, since the adult ants are not as active as are larvae or newly hatched ants when deprived of food. The summation of interindividual stimulation is consequently less effective in sufficiently exciting many ants to the extent that they are caused to leave the bivouac and give their learned response to the raiding trails. Normally, the statary period cannot end until the developed pupae are hatched, since it is their restless movements which set off the process described in our analysis of nomadic behavior.

CERTAIN ALTERNATIVE EXPLANATIONS FOR THE STATARY CONDITION

Among the alternative explanations of this phenomenon offered by earlier students of the problem, three deserve some consideration here.

The first of these we mention on the strength of the probability that certain portions at least of the old-world genus *Dorylus* behave similarly to the American *Eciton* species. Vosseler (1905) advanced the hypothesis that the African doryline *Anomma molesta* must occupy the same nesting site until the colony has exhausted the available supply of booty in the surrounding region. In the case of Central American army ants there is no evidence that this factor is of any importance for rainy-season activities, although it is possible that during the dry season the mounting restlessness of starved adult workers may increase raiding activity to the point at which colony migration occurs. As seen from Table 1, in the statary period a single raiding system generally is sufficient to take up all ants which are caused to leave the bivouac at a given time. On successive days a single raiding system may be pushed to a much greater distance from the colony site than is characteristic of the nomad colony, but then this trail system will be virtually abandoned for a few days or perhaps permanently abandoned as a system is pushed out in some other direction. The available supply of booty certainly is a principal controller of the manner in which a given trail is formed and of the time during which it remains in active use, but there is no reason to believe that migration of the colony can occur before the enclosed brood reaches the stage at which hatching throws other factors into play.

Müller (1886), impressed by the fact that an *E. burchelli* colony apparently could not be driven from his brother's garden for days, conjectured that the ants must possess a queen heavy and bulky with eggs and consequently difficult to transport. At first sight this hypothesis might seem reasonable, since the facts suggest that the queen regularly becomes physogastric during the statary period, and that during the nomadic period her gaster remains minimal in size.

The queen apparently deposits her thousands of eggs at some time during the latter half of the statary period, since in examining scores of colonies which had become nomadic only within the immediately preceding days I have found a large brood of very young larvae in practically all cases. Unfortunately, the successive minor shifts in position which are forced by rains usually serve to make the bivouac cluster of the statary colony practically unassailable, and consequently physogastric *E. hamatum* and *E. burchelli* queens have not been captured, to my knowledge.

On the other hand, I have taken 5 *E. hamatum* queens and one *E. burchelli* queen from as many definitely nomadic colonies, and in every case the queen's gaster was minimal in size. Circumstances indicate that non-physogastric *E. hamatum* queens captured by Wheeler (1925) and by F. E. Lutz, as well as an *E. lucanoides* queen taken by F. Nevermann (Reichensperger, 1934), were all removed from nomadic colonies. Although the apparent facts as to the queen's condition appear to favor Müller's hypothesis, it is safe to predict that a statary colony deprived of its queen would nevertheless fail to migrate until its pupal brood had hatched. Furthermore, it is difficult to see how the physogastric condition of the queen could prevent a migratory movement which was otherwise aroused, since we have evidence that in the nomadic colony the queen takes to the trail only at the very end of the movement. (As calliope she cannot direct the parade.) The possible mechanism of Müller's hypothesis is obscure, moreover. The assumption that a queen swollen with eggs may be chemotropically so attractive to the workers that they must remain close to the bivouac is vitiated by the evident fact that the queen lays her eggs at least a few days before the statary period ends. It is not easy to see how the queen's weakness because of fatigue from the arduous act of oviposition could "somehow" hold the colony in place still longer. Finally, the "queen-transport" hypothesis may be abandoned on the strength of the relationship we have traced between the hatching of a new worker brood and the ending of a statary period.

A third assumption, that the ants of the statary colony are unable to carry the bulky cocoons and hence are forced to remain in place, is scarcely tenable. Army ants commonly are able to carry very bulky prey such as large wasp pupae, and *E. burchelli* raiders move large grasshopper legs and other over-size booty objects. The ants readily transport their own cocoons when a heavy rain or an artificial disturbance forces the statary colony to shift its position. In the laboratory a procession of Ecitons which includes cocoon-carriers will circle the base of a glass jar for hours. Finally, the fact may be mentioned that during the last days of the nomadic period the ants carry their nearly full-grown larvae readily, and cover longer distances in their migrations than at previous times when the larvae were smaller.

No one of these three hypotheses contributes much to our understanding of the problem. In our general theory we have summed up the evidence to show which factors are actually responsible for the occurrence of a nomadic and a statary condition of activity in the same Eciton colony at different times. We have shown in general how these factors function in bringing about the activity changes. Briefly, the state of colony behavior depends upon the condition of the brood, since stimulation which may be received from the active brood determines the presence of that degree of excitement which is necessary for vigorous raiding, and hence accounts for the migratory movement which can develop only as a result of a day of very active raiding.

A somewhat different approach should further clarify the nature and causes of the Eciton behavior pattern.

The essentially rhythmic character of Eciton activities

Two important rhythms are evident in the activity of an army-ant colony: first, the day-night oscillation in raiding activity, and second, the periodic alternation of the nomadic and statary activity conditions over intervals of approximately eighteen days.

THE DAY-NIGHT RHYTHM, BASED MAINLY UPON PHOTOKINESIS

With respect to the *day-night rhythm,* even a cursory survey of the record for our test colony 36A shows the presence of this feature during both the nomadic and the statary periods. We may briefly summarize the facts in the following manner.

	Daytime condition	*Nocturnal condition*
Nomadic period	Vigorous raiding throughout the day, with morning and afternoon activity "peaks." Migratory movement begins regularly in mid-afternoon.	Raiding usually is continued during the night, but is far less vigorous than during the day.
Statary period	Daytime raiding is only about one-third as vigorous as in the nomadic period. True migratory movement is absent.	Nocturnal raising usually is absent or is very weak, with practically all of the raiders returning to the colony site in late afternoon or evening.

The appearance of the characteristic day-night rhythm in both the statary and nomadic activity phases is basically attributable to the stimulative effect which light exerts upon the ants, i.e., to photokinesis.

The histological evidence reported by Werringloer (1932) favors the view that visual sensitivity is available to most if not all *Eciton* species despite their relatively undeveloped primary (lateral) ocelli.

Although numerous tests have shown that in the formation or the following of raiding trails, orientation is not materially dependent upon vision, sensitivity to light appears very important for such matters as the diurnal prominence of raiding in most *Eciton* species. Further, we may predict that special study will show that species differences in the visual receptor are mainly responsible for the surface life of some species (e.g., *E. hamatum*), the semihypogaeic life of others (e.g., *E. praedator*), and the more exclusively subterranean life of other species (e.g., *E. coecum*). This photokinetic effect is apparent in the behavior of captured colonies which are placed in laboratory nests, particularly in that such a colony ordinarily clusters in the shade or with its cylinder inclined away from the lighted side. This feature is attributable to the fact that when light strikes the colony from one side the hanging mass soon breaks up on that side as the ants become active and disengage themselves. In the dark of night or when covered in the daytime, captive army ants usually are fairly inactive and hang quietly in their cluster, but in the light they appear in numbers and eddy about in circuitous columns.

The existence of a day-night rhythm mainly controlled by light is of fundamental importance for the activity pattern which we have theoretically analyzed. Under natural conditions, with the arrival of daybreak the light arouses the ants and causes raiding to begin or to increase greatly in vigor. The photokinetic effect apparently makes the ants susceptible to social stimulation in both the statary and the nomadic phases of colony life. When in the latter condition the colony is much more readily aroused than at other times, and interindividual stimulation is subject to a much higher degree of summation because the existence of an active brood multiplies the general exciting effect of *any* stimulative agency. Under these conditions, when daylight bestirs individuals on the outer edge of the cluster, those free to move exert a contact-chemical effect upon workers within the cluster. The prompt arousal of the brood causes this effect to spread much more rapidly and to attain a higher maximum than is possible in the statary phase.

The effective arousal of raiding at dawn, which insures that the raiding systems will be developed during the day, is thus indirectly responsible for the fact that the migratory movement of the nomadic colony begins toward the day's ending. (Only under extraordinary conditions does it begin at other times.) As we know, the bivouac-change phenomenon is preconditioned by the existence of well-developed raiding systems and by the presence on these systems of great numbers of raiding ants, and these are conditions which can prevail only toward the end of a day of raiding.

The timing of events in the day-night activity cycle therefore depends mainly upon the photokinetic factor.

Temperature changes also are of some importance, although laboratory tests suggest that temperature is subordinate to light in determining this rhythm. In a manner which deserves special study, the regular diurnal temperature variations are mainly responsible for the existence of two "peaks" in raiding activity, one in the later part of the morning, and one in mid-afternoon. The significance of this fact for the general behavior pattern is grasped upon recall of the strategic relationship that the regular afternoon spurt in raiding bears to the development of the colony migration. Similarly, the nightly reduction in colony activity doubtless is partially dependent upon the fall in temperature which regularly begins in early evening and reaches its lowest point during the early morning hours.

Worthy of mention is the further possibility that in the adult worker regular visceral changes are in part responsible for the day-night oscillation in general activity. Although there is no direct evidence for this factor in the case of army ants, it is predictable as an influence which may arise in the individual through the conditional learning of a response originally dependent upon external conditions. It is reasonable to suggest this possibility, since visceral rhythms have been shown to exist in arthropods (Patterson, 1933), and since experiments have been conducted which show that in insects such rhythms apparently may function independently of external factors (Lutz, 1931, 1932; Wahl, 1932).

Certainly the day-night rhythm in the activities of these ants is a matter of great importance for the general pattern of their behavior. There is a need for special ecological and psychological research into the problem which will clarify our understanding of the rise of this effect in the individual and its function in colony life.

THE NOMAD STATARY RHYTHM

The second principal rhythm displayed in Eciton behavior is the alternation of the nomadic and the statary activity phases. We have described and analyzed this rhythm for *E. hamatum,* but there is good reason to believe that the phenomenon appears in many (if not in all) of the Central American species during at least the first half of the rainy season. Within that period *E. hamatum* colonies regularly alternate between the two major conditions of activity, at approximately 18-day intervals. Whether this rhythm also characterizes colony behavior at other times of the year remains to be discovered. In all probability it extends through the rainy season months (ca. May through November), but is modified or considerably restrained during the dry season. It is apparent that an investigation of Eciton behavior during the dry season should disclose evidence of great significance for many biological and psychological problems.

THE QUEEN'S OVULATION CYCLE AS PACEMAKER FOR
THE NOMAD-STATARY RHYTHM IN COLONY BEHAVIOR

In view of our evidence, the ultimate determining cause of the periodicity in general colony activity is not obscure. We know that nomadic behavior appears only when the colony possesses an active brood, and that statary behavior is characteristic of the colony which possesses an enclosed brood. The discovered rhythmic occurrence of these conditions during the rainy season consequently must depend upon a cyclic ovulation process in the queen, since this process governs the time at which successive lots of eggs are laid and hence mainly controls the frequency with which new broods appear.

Although we have little direct knowledge of the queen's ovulation cycle, a variety of evidence encourages the inference that during the rainy season she lays enormous clutches of eggs at *regular* intervals of approximately 36 days. Since the clutch of eggs which accounts for an entire brood apparently is laid within a period of a few days (perhaps within little more than [seven] days), the members of a brood pass through given stages of their development in pace with one another and all reach maturity practically at the same time.[9] Consequently the stimulative effect which an active Eciton brood exerts upon the adult workers must begin and must cease rather abruptly. This fact is of the greatest importance for the Eciton behavior pattern; in fact the regularity of the queen's ovulation cycle is the basic and most essential feature in this pattern.

But it must be emphasized that only in an indirect manner does the queen's ovulation cycle set the pace for changes in colony activity. This cycle governs the regular appearance of a brood, and as we know, colony behavior varies in relation to the appearance and the withdrawal of an active brood as a source of incidental stimulation. Thus the egg-production cycle of the queen controls colony behavior in a devious manner, although

---

[9] In field examinations of the broods of many Eciton colonies, 1 have found only broods which contained individuals of very nearly the same age. The cocoon-spinning of the larvae, or the hatching of a pupal brood, are events which always occur within [4 to 5] days. This statement is strongly borne out by a population study of three captured Eciton colonies together with their broods. Further, in this study the number of individuals in the broods and the relative frequency of the polymorphic types was found to be much the same in the brood population as it was in the adult worker population. This suggests great constancy in the conditions under which the eggs mature, and in the conditions under which the brood develops. While a representative adult worker population includes 40,000 or more individuals by actual count, the three broods gave the following population totals: a brood of advanced *E. hamatum* pupae, 32,479 individuals; a brood of advanced *E. burchelli* larvae, 36,888 individuals; a brood of advanced *E. burchelli* pupae, 31,298 individuals. The results of this population study are to be reported in a future paper. The actual work was performed in a very capable manner by Mr. Frank Trainor, whose services were made available by the Gibson Committee and by the C.W.A.

the two series of events parallel each other closely. This inevitable though indirect relationship is a fact of great significance for adaptation.

In the fact that a process which depends upon the queen indirectly functions as the pacemaker for regular changes in colony behavior, we find a relationship which has remarkable survival value. Various facts already cited show that the queen becomes physogastric because of the maturation of thousands of eggs during the statary period, and deposits these eggs at some time before the colony begins to migrate; but that her gaster is minimal in size while the ants are nightly on the march during the nomadic period. Thus the queen is not excited to move on long journeys along very rough trails at times when the intersegmental membranes of her gaster are so greatly stretched as to risk her death through their rupture. This is one more highly significant fact which is attributable to the dominance which a biological process (the queen's ovulation cycle) indirectly exerts over a psychological process (social stimulation as governor of the colony activity pattern).

In the foregoing theory we have attempted to show how various physiological and behavior characteristics of the army ant queen, the developing brood, and the adult worker population fit nicely together to produce a total behavior pattern which is a remarkably efficient adaptive instrument. Given an army ant colony which possesses a queen capable of producing great quantities of eggs in single batches at regular intervals, in a tropical environment which is very conducive to regularity and to stability in such activities, and a complex cyclic series of behavior changes inevitably follows. The relationship of the events in this series has been outlined no further than is necessary to show how each part of the series depends upon certain antecedent events. Further progress is made in this analysis when one considers the psychology of the worker individual: her distinctive behavior as a product of special organic equipment, and her susceptibility to social stimulation in the performance of usual activities, the latter a consequence of limited and stereotyped learning in the course of a gradual initial process of socialization and during later experience.

SUMMARY AND CONCLUSIONS

The behavior pattern of Central American army ants offers a representative problem in "instinct." In the present paper, evidence on this problem is summarized in terms of behavior conditions in the type species, *Eciton hamatum,* and is subjected to a theoretical analysis. Numerous colonies of different *Eciton* species have been studied, but the evidence is represented here in a report of activities displayed by a colony of *E. hamatum* which was kept under effective observation during a 42-day period in the rainy season of 1936. This colony was subjected to detailed study as a test case.

The findings strikingly confirmed conclusions which had been drawn from previous work. When first observed, the colony had almost completed a period of *statary* behavior, during which raiding activity was minimal and no migration occurred. Then, after hatching a new brood of workers, the colony entered a period of *nomadic* behavior during which raiding activity was maximal and a migration occurred at the end of each day. This period lasted for 17 days, during which time a new brood developed through the larval stage. After these larvae had spun their cocoons the colony entered a new *statary* period, which lasted for 19 days. During this period, while the cocoon-enclosed brood passed into and through the pupal stage of development, the colony remained in place and did not migrate. When this brood hatched from its cocoons the colony again became *nomadic,* and at that time was found to possess a new brood of very young larvae. Thus, during the period of this investigation, the test colony passed alternately through statary and nomad periods, with a direct correspondence appearing in all instances between colony activity and the condition of the brood. With respect to all of the features which are essentially representative of Eciton behavior, predictions based upon earlier work were verified in the special study of this colony.

Derived from the findings of the entire investigation, a theory to account for the representative Eciton behavior pattern is presented. For convenience, this theory is expressed in terms of conditions in *E. hamatum.* In the rainy season (at least) the queen's ovulation cycle serves as pacemaker for the alternation of the major conditions of colony activity (i.e., the nomadic and the statary conditions), but does so in an indirect manner. The queen (very apparently) produces an immense clutch of more than 30,000 eggs at intervals of approximately 36 days. The activity of this brood when in the larval stage maintains the colony in the *nomadic* condition until the brood becomes enclosed. This effect is based upon an incidental form of "communication," in which actively moving larvae incidentally excite the workers and this excitement increases progressively throughout the colony because of interindividual stimulation among the workers. Consequently the colony is aroused to a pitch of excitement at which raiding is carried on very energetically by large numbers of individuals. This response, raiding, may be regarded as a crude learned reaction which is elicited from the socialized worker by a summation of tactual and chemical stimuli within the bivouac. Any stimulation which increases general excitement will augment raiding (i.e., the result can be produced artificially). It is shown that the high degree of activity which produces three or more extensively developed raiding systems during each day of this period *inevitably* leads to a colony migration which practically always begins in the afternoon. The manner in which colony migration develops from raiding under these conditions is analyzed in some detail. One important observation which shows the close relationship of these two phenomena is the fact that the migratory movement of a colony always takes place over one of the raiding trails developed during the given day. The basis of this theory is thus the indirectly established fact that the queen's ovulation cycle is responsible for the presence, at intervals, of a special source of exciting stimuli, and thus accounts indirectly for the periodic recurrence of the nomadic behavior phase.

This interpretation of nomadic behavior checks fully with a parallel analysis of statary behavior. Once the brood has become enclosed within cocoons, the colony becomes *statary* and remains in this condition for many days. The workers forage much less actively and in definitely smaller numbers than before; only a single raiding system is developed on a given day as a rule, and consequently the colony remains on the same site during this period. Thus, when an active developing brood (or a brood of newly hatched workers) is not present, colony excitement drops markedly, and raiding activity is subthreshold with respect to the development of a migration. Consequently a colony in the statary condition does not migrate until its enclosed brood hatches into callow workers. The hatching of the pupae from cocoons depends primarily upon the fact that workers respond to the activities of full-term pupae as these "stir" within their cases.

The statary-nomad cycle in general colony behavior, with each of its two periods lasting about 18 days, roughly, is thus governed incidentally by the condition of the developing brood. It is apparent that this cycle, furnishing the basic features of the Eciton behavior pattern, finally depends upon the physiological properties of the fertile queen. This relationship has important consequences for adaptation.

For the specific characteristics of the nomadic or statary phases of behavior, the typical day-night fluctuation in the vigor of foraging is of regulatory importance. The day-night variation in raiding activity mainly depends upon the excitatory effect of light (i.e., upon photokinesis), which makes the ants very susceptible to social stimulation and other stimulation and thus arouses or greatly increases raiding activity each morning. A day-night temperature variation is of secondary importance. Regular diurnal temperature variations appear to be mainly responsible for the afternoon resurgence of activity on raiding trails during which the migration develops. Because of these effects, the raiding activity of a nomadic colony gets a fresh start each morning, and the migration consequently can occur only in the late afternoon or evening when the raiding systems have been widely developed.

It is thus shown that factors arising within the colony are basic in determining the army-ant behavior pattern, and that factors external to the colony impart to this phenomenon the temporal and other special characteristics which are so representative of Eciton activities.

The outcome of this investigation suggests the advisability of studying an "instinct," or any inclusive behavior mode, by working toward a disclosure of the essential causal factors, directly or indirectly studying their relationships, and finally by organizing the entire fund of evidence into a logically integrated account of the phenomenon. The use of "ends achieved," or of "adaptive significance" and similar teleological devices to explain a given behavioral phenomenon, as substitutes for knowledge of causal-effect relationships, is a logically unsound practice which has no essential function in scientific thinking.

REFERENCES

Eidmann, H. 1927. Die Sprache der Ameisen. *Rev. Zool. Russe* 7: 39–47.
Frisch, K. v. 1923. Über die "Sprache" der Bienen. *Zool. Jahrb., Zool. Physiol.* 40: 1–186.
Heyde, K. 1924. Die Entwicklung der psychischen Fähigkeiten bei Ameisen und ihr Verhalten bei abgeänderten biologischen Bedingungen. *Biol. Zent.* 44:624–654.
Hingston, R. W. G. 1929. *Problems of instinct and intelligence*. New York: Macmillan.
Imms, A. 1931. *Social behavior in insects*. New York: Dial Press.
Lutz, F. E. 1931. Light as a factor in controlling the start of daily activity of a wren and stingless bees. *Am. Mus. Nov.*, no. 468, pp. 1–9.
Lutz, F. E. 1932. Experiments with Orthoptera concerning diurnal rhythm. *Ibid.*, no. 550, pp. 1–24.
Maier, N. R. F., and T. C. Schneirla. 1935. *Principles of animal psychology*. New York: McGraw-Hill.
Mann, W. M. 1916. The ants of Brazil. *Bull. Mus. Comp. Zool.* 60: 399–490.
Mergelsberg, O. 1934. Über den Begriff der Physogastrie. *Zool. Anz.* 106: 97–105.
Müller, W. 1886. Beobachtungen an Wanderameisen (Eciton hamatum Fabr.). *Kosmos*, 10 Jahrg., 18: 81–93.[10]
Patterson, T. 1933. Comparative physiology of the gastric hunger mechanism. *Ann. N.Y. Acad. Sci.* 34: 55–272.
Reichensperger, A. 1934. Beitrag zur Kenntnis von Eciton lucanoides Em. *Zool. Anz.* 106: 240–245.
Rösch, G. A. 1930. Untersuchungen über die Arbeitsteilung im Bienenstaat.

---

[10] Müller's ant was not *E. hamatum*, but was actually *Eciton burchelli* Westw., as Wheeler ascertained by examining specimens preserved from the colony.

II. Die Tätigkeiten der Arbeitsbienen unter experimentell veränderten Bedingungen. *Z. Vergl. Physiol.* 12: 1–71.

Schneirla, T. C. 1933. Studies on army ants in Panama. *J. Comp. Psychol.* 15: 267–299.

Schneirla, T. C. 1934. Raiding and other outstanding phenomena in the behavior of army ants. *Proc. Nat. Acad. Sci.* 20: 316–321.

Steiner, A. 1932. Die Arbeitsteilung der Feldwespe *Polistes dubia. Z. Vergl. Physiol.* 17: 101–152.

Vosseler, J. 1905. Die Ostafrikanische Treiberameise (Siafu). *Der Pflanzer,* 1 Jahrg. 19: 289–302.

Wahl, O. 1932. Neue Untersuchungen über das Zeitgedächtnis der Bienen. *Z. Vergl. Physiol.* 16: 529–589.

Werringloer, A. 1932. Die Schorgane und Sehzentren der Dorylinen nebst Untersuchungen über die Facettenaugen der Formiciden. *Z. Wiss. Zool.* 141:432–524.

Wheeler, W. M. 1923. *Social life among the insects.* New York: Harcourt, Brace.

Wheeler, W. M. 1925. The finding of the queen of the army ant Eciton hamatum Fabricius. *Biol. Bull.* 49: 139–149.

Wroughton, R. 1892. Our ants. (Part II, 177–178.) *J. Bomb. Nat. Hist. Soc.,* 1892.

Ziegler, H. E. 1910. *Der Begriff des Instinktes einst und jetzt.* Jena: Fischer.

T. C. SCHNEIRLA

GERARD PIEL

The Army Ants

Bibliography No. 44

Wherever they pass, all the rest of the animal world is thrown into a state of alarm. They stream along the ground and climb to the summit of all the lower trees searching every leaf to its apex. Where booty is plentiful, they concentrate all their forces upon it, the dense phalanx of shining and quickly moving bodies, as it spreads over the surface, looking like a flood of dark-red liquid. All soft-bodied and inactive insects fall an easy prey to them, and they tear their victims in pieces for facility in carriage. Then, gathering together again in marching order, onward they move, the margins of the phalanx spread out at times like a cloud of skirmishers from the flanks of an army.

That is how Henry Walter Bates, a Victorian naturalist, described the characteristic field maneuvers of a tribe of army ants. His language is charged with martial metaphor, but it presents with restraint a spectacle which other eyewitnesses have compared to the predatory expeditions of Genghis Khan and Attila the Hun.

Army ants abound in the tropical rain forests of Hispanic America, Africa and Asia. They are classified taxonomically into more than 200 species and distinguished as a group chiefly by their peculiar mode of operation. Organized in colonies 100,000 to 150,000 strong, they live off their environment by systematic plunder and pillage. They are true nomads, having no fixed abode. Their nest is a seething cylindrical cluster of themselves, ant hooked to ant, with queen and brood sequestered in a labyrinth of corridors and chambers within the ant mass. From these bivouacs they stream forth at dawn in tightly organized columns and swarms to raid the surrounding terrain. Their columns often advance as much as 35 meters an hour and may finally reach out 300 meters or more in an unbroken stream. For days at a time, they may keep their bivouacs fixed in a hollow tree or some other equally protected shelter. Then, for a restless period, they move on with every dusk. They swarm forth in a solemn, plodding procession, each ant holding to its place in line, its forward-directed antennae beating a hypnotic rhythm. At the rear come throngs of larvae-carriers and, at the very last, the big, wingless queen, buried under a melee of frenzied workers. Late at night they hang their new bivouac under a low-hanging branch or vine.

The army ant, observers are agreed, presents the most complex instance of organized mass behavior occurring regularly outside the home-site in any insect or, for that matter, in any subhuman animal. As such, it offers the student of animal psychology a subject rich in interest for itself. But it also provides an opportunity for original attack on some basic problems of psychology in general. The study here reported, covering the behavior of two of the *Eciton* species of army ants, was conducted by Schneirla over a 16-year period with extended field trips to the Biological Reservation on Barro Colorado Island in the Panama Canal Zone and to other ant haunts in Central America. In undertaking it, he had certain questions in mind. The central question, of course, was how such an essentially primitive creature as the ant manages such a highly organized and complex social existence. This bears on the more general consideration of organized group behavior as an adaptive device in natural selection. There was, finally, the neglected question of the nature of social organization. This is primarily a psychological problem because it concerns the contribution of individual behavior and relationships between individuals to the pattern of the group as a whole. It was expected that reliable data on these questions in the instance of the army ant might throw light on similar questions about human societies.

The ant commends itself to study by man. Measured by the dispassionate standard of survival, it stands as one of the most successful of nature's inventions. It is the most numerous of all land animals both in number of individuals and number of species (more than 3,500 at present count). It has occupied the whole surface of the globe between the margins of eternal frost. Its teeming cities are to be found even on isolated atolls in mid-Pacific. The oldest of living orders, the ant dates back 60 million years to the early Jurassic period. More significant, the societies of ants probably evolved to their present state of perfection no less than 50 million years ago. Man, by contrast, is a dubious experiment in evolution that has barely got under way.

In the esteem of political philosophers, from Solomon to Winston Churchill, ants have shared honors with the two other classes of social insects, the bee and the termite. Of the three, the ant is by far the most various and interesting. Bees live in hives; termites burrow almost exclusively in wood. Ants are not so easily pigeonholed. Lord Avebury, a British formicologist, marveled at "the habits of ants, their large communities and elaborate habitations, their roadways, possession of domestic

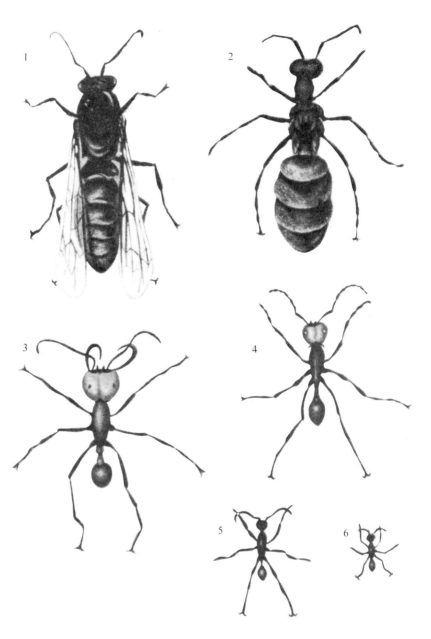

FIGURE 77

Table of organization of an army ant colony is fixed by specialization in structure and function of its individual members, here shown 2.5 times life-size. (1) Winged male (its appearance suggests the evolutionary link of ants to wasps) lives only long enough to mate a queen. Organization and behavior of the colony are polarized around queen (2) and her reproductive function. Workers, graded in size from major (3) down to minim (6) tend to specialize according to their size in defense, food-gathering or in nursing of offspring.

FIGURE 78
Worker major is equipped with a wasp-like sting in its tail as well as with big mandibles. Its aggressive response to extra-colony stimuli makes it the "soldier" of army ants.

animals and, even, in some cases, of slaves!" He might have added that ants also cultivate agricultural crops and carry parasols. It is the social institutions of ants, however, that engender the greatest enthusiasm. The late Henry Christopher McCook, in his *Ant Communities and How They are Governed, A Study in Natural Civics,* credited the ant with achieving the ultimate in democratic social order. The sight of an army ant bivouac put the British naturalist Thomas Belt in mind of Sir Thomas More's *Utopia.* The Swiss naturalist Auguste Forel urged the League of Nations to adopt the ant polity as the model for the world community.

The marvels of ant life have led some thinkers into giddy speculation on the nature of ant intelligence. Few have put themselves so quaintly on record as Lord Avebury, who declared: "The mental powers of ants differ from those of men not so much in kind as in degree." He ranked them ahead of the anthropoid apes. Maurice Maeterlinck, author of *The Life of the Ant,* hedged: "After all, we have not been present at the deliberations of the workers and we know hardly anything of what happens in the depths of the formicary." Others have categorically explained ant behavior as if the creatures could reason, exchange information, take purposeful action and feel tender emotion. Describing a tribe of army ants on the march in his book *Insect Behavior,* the American naturalist Paul Griswold Howes has "lieutenants keeping order or searching out the ground to be hunted or traveled next" and the privates in the line "obeying commands" and evincing "a wonderful sense of duty." Belt noted, as a matter of course, that "light-colored officers" keep the "common dark-colored workers" in line. R. C. Wroughton concluded from the precision of ant armies' maneuvers that "they are either the result of preconceived arrangement or are carried out by word of command."

Obviously anthropomorphism can explain little about ants, and it has largely disappeared from the current serious literature about ant behavior. Its place has been taken, however, by errors of a more sophisticated sort. One such is the concept of the "superorganism." This derives from a notion entertained by Plato and Aquinas that a social organization exhibits the attributes of a superior type of individual. Extended by certain modern biologists, the concept assumes that the biological organism, a society of cells, is the model for social organizations, whether ant or human. Plausible analogies are drawn between organisms and societies: division of function, internal communication, rhythmic periodicity of life processes and the common cycle of birth, growth, senescence and death. Pursuit of these analogies, according to the protagonists of the superorganism, will disclose that the same forces of natural selection have shaped the evolution of both organism and superorganism, and that the same fundamental laws govern their present existence.

This is of course a thoroughly attractive idea. It is representative, in the field of psychology, of current efforts in other fields of science to unify all observed facts by a single theory. But it possesses a weakness common to all Platonistic thinking. It erects a vague concept, "organism" or "organization," as an ultimate reality which defies explanation. The danger inherent in this arbitrary procedure is the bias which it imposes upon the investigator's approach to his problem. It reduces the gathering of evidence to the selection of appropriate illustrations and examples. This is a pitfall of which the investigator must be especially wary in the study of social behavior. Too often in this field theories and conclusions are composed of nine parts of rationalization to one part of evidence. The investigator in social science must be ruthless in discarding his preconceived notions, taking care to retain only the bare conceptual framework that is inductively supported by the already established evidence on his subject. In the gathering of new evidence he must impose on his work the same rules of repetition and control which prevail in the experimental sciences. Wherever possible he should subject his observations to experimental tests in the field and laboratory. In the area we are discussing this kind of work may at times seem more like a study of ants than an investigation of problems. But it yields more dependable data.

One of the most helpful sources of evidence concerning the ant is the study of the ant in its "more than royal tomb" of amber. This is the paleontologist's ant, trapped eons ago in the sticky gum of a conifer and thereby preserved intact for examination by scientists today. They find that the fossil ant is in all major respects identical with its twentieth-century descendants. From this evidence biologists reason that since the social behavior of the ant is primarily a function of its biological make-up, ant societies must be as ancient as the ant. This conclusion is supported by studies of ant behavior. The contemporary ant, as will be shown, exhibits a comparatively limited capacity for learning. On the other hand, there is little that it needs to learn when it crawls out of the cocoon. By far the greater part of its behavior pattern is already written in its genes and represents the "learning" of its race, acquired many generations ago in the hard school of natural selection.

The individual ant, as a matter of fact, is ill-equipped for advanced learning. By comparison with the sensitive perceptions of a human being, it is deaf and blind. Its hearing consists primarily in the perception of vibrations physically transmitted to it through the ground. In most species, its vision is limited to the discrimination of light and shadow. These deficiencies are partially compensated by the chemotactual perceptions of the ant, centered in its flitting antennae. Chiefly by means of its antennae, the ant tells friend from foe, locates its booty, and, thanks to its habit of signing its trail with droplets from its anal gland, finds its way home to the nest.

In an investigation of ant learning, Schneirla found that individual ants are capable of significant feats of progress in a given situation, but that on the whole ant learning is by rote. His subject in this study was the common garden Formica ant, which is known to forage freely within a radius up to 75 meters around its nest. The learning situation was presented by a maze, interposed between the laboratory nest and feeding box, with maze passages open on the return route to the nest. Each individual ant was identified and followed by means of a number pasted on its gaster (abdomen). The ants betrayed no evidence of purposive behavior. Compared to the rat, which in the same maze pattern may acquire a pronounced "goal set" and make straight for the other end of the maze after relatively few runs, the ants were at first quite haphazard in their behavior. It required almost a dozen runs before they ceased crawling aimlessly on the floors and walls of the first alley in the maze. Their learning curves then ascended steeply to a flat plateau; thereafter, they made as many wrong turns at the last choice points in the maze as they did at the first.

Control of clues provided in the maze by ant chemicals and variations in lighting revealed that the Formica ant possesses considerable learning capacity in its kinesthetic or "muscle" sense. Nevertheless, this study shows that the ant acquires merely a generalized maze habit, not an understanding of mazes. This conclusion is reinforced by another comparison with the rat. Confronted with abrupt changes in the maze layout, the rat will often exhibit plain evidence of emotional conflict, represented by an over-all deterioration of its learning progress. Ants, in the same situation, merely blunder ahead.

How the essentially uncomplicated repertory of the individual ant contrives, when ants act in concert, to yield the exceedingly complex behavior of the tribe is one of the most intricate paradoxes in nature. This riddle has been fruitfully explored during the past generation under the guidance of the concept of "trophallaxis," originated by the late William Morton Wheeler of Harvard University, who ranks as the greatest of U.S. formicologists. Trophallaxis (from the Greek *trophe,* meaning food, and *allaxis,* exchange) is based upon the familiar observation that ants live in biological thrall to their nestmates. Their powerful mutual attraction can be seen in the constant turning of one ant toward another, the endless antennal caresses, the licking and nuzzling. In these exchanges they can be seen trading intimate substances—regurgitated food and glandular secretions. Most ants are dependent for their lives upon this biosocial intercourse with their fellows. There is strong evidence that, as between larvae, workers and queen in a given tribe, there is an interchange of coenzymes necessary to the existence of all. Army ant queens unfailingly sicken and die after a few days when isolated in captivity.

Trophallaxis, or "the spirit of the formicary," as Maeterlinck was pleased to call it, is therefore essentially chemical in nature. As can be seen by the mutual attractions and repulsions of ants for one another, their social chemicals are not only specific to species but also specific to colonies. Schneirla's most acute memory of his 16-year association with army ants is the characteristic Eciton odor which emanates from their columns, an odor reminiscent of potato blossoms. It is obscured near their bivouacs by the fetid smells which emanate from the decaying fragments of booty clinging to individual ants. The army ant queen, less exposed to offal, is distinguished by a delicate, indefinable odor. All this suggests that biochemists may here find a field for studies which should yield more effective ant repellents and poisons, as well as shed new light on animal behavior.

The well-established concept of trophallaxis naturally suggests that clues to the complex behavior of the ant armies should be sought in the relationships among individuals within the tribe. Most investigators have looked elsewhere, with invariably mistaken results. In attempting to explain, for example, why an ant army alternates between periods of fixed bivouac and nomadic wandering, a half-dozen reputable scientists have jumped to the simplest and most disarmingly logical conclusion: food supply. The ants,

FIGURE 79
Reproductive cycle motivates behavior of army ant colony. Events are synchronized by visceral punctuality of the queen. Precisely spaced broods develop from eggs, go through the larval and pupal stages and emerge from cocoons in orderly succession. The coincident behavior cycle provides statary bivouac at egg-laying crisis. Behavior cycle consists of alternate periods of stay in fixed bivouac and of daily bivouac shift. Emergence of the callow workers from cocoons energizes the colony to resume nomadic wandering. Nomadism is further sustained by maturing of the larvae. When larvae spin cocoons, colony goes back into fixed bivouac, in hollow tree or similarly secluded recess.

Reproductive cycle

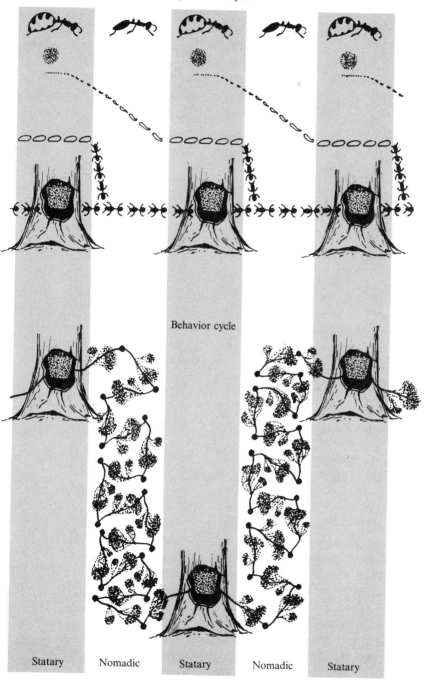

Behavior cycle

Statary   Nomadic   Statary   Nomadic   Statary

FIGURE 80
Bivouac is a more or less cylindrical hollow cluster of the members of a colony. It builds from above downward as strings and filaments of ants, hooked together leg to leg, descend from log or vine. This is a typical nomadic period bivouac, hanging exposed in the open.

they declared, stay in one place until they exhaust the local larder and then move on to new hunting grounds. Schneirla has shown, however, that the true explanation is quite different.

The migratory habits of the ant armies follow a rhythmically punctual cycle. The *Eciton hamatum* species, for example, wanders nomadically for a period of 17 days, then spends 19 or 20 days in fixed bivouac. This cycle

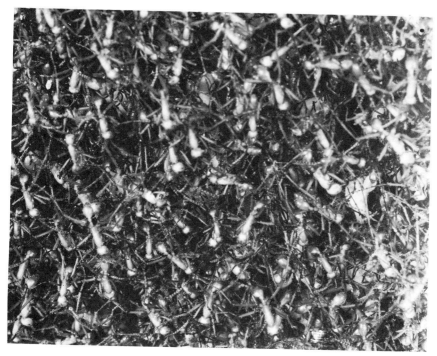

FIGURE 81

Close-up of bivouac suggests "fur of some terrible animal." Outer "tissue" of structure, as shown here, is made of workers major and intermediates. Minims concentrate around queen within. When pouchlike bivouac is poked with stick, larvae and cocoons pour out.

coincides precisely with the reproductive cycle of the tribe. The army goes into bivouac when the larvae, hatched from the last clutch of eggs, have gone into the pupal state in their cocoons. At the end of the first week, the queen, with her gaster swollen to more than five times its normal volume, goes into a stupendous five- to seven-day labor in which she delivers 20,-000 to 30,000 eggs. The daily foraging raids, which meanwhile have dwindled to a minimum, pick up again as the eggs hatch into a great mass of larvae. Then, on about the 20th day, the cocoons yield a new generation of callow workers, and the army sets off once more on its evening marches.

In determining this pattern of external social events Schneirla logged a dozen ant armies through one or more complete cycles, and upwards of 100 through partial cycles. Observations were set down in shorthand in the field. The coinciding pattern of internal biological events was documented by brood samples taken from many different colonies at various stages in the reproductive cycle. In the course of the last field trip, from November

1947 to March 1948, broods of more than 80 colonies were sampled, most of them repeatedly at intervals of a few days. In addition, detailed examinations were made of 62 queens in various phases of their physiological history and many of these were preserved for further study.

A sentimentalist considering this new picture of the army ant's domestic habits may find an explanation for its behavior more affecting than the food theory: the ants stay in fixed bivouac to protect the queen and her helpless young through the time when they are most vulnerable. Doubtless this is the adaptive significance of the process. But the motivation which carries 100,000 to 150,000 individual ants through this precisely timed cycle of group behavior is not familial love and duty but the trophallactic relationship among the members of the tribe. A cocooned and slumberous pupa, for example, exerts a quieting influence upon the worker that clutches it in its mandible—somewhat as a thumb in the mouth pacifies an infant. But as it approaches maturity and quickens within its cocoon, the pupa produces precisely the reverse effect. Its stirring and twitching excite the workers to pick up the cocoon and snatch it from one another. As an incidental result, this manhandling effects the delivery of the cocoon's occupant. (Cocoons in which the pupae were killed by needle excited no such interest among the workers and remained unopened.)

The stimulus of the emerging brood is evident in a rising crescendo of excitement that seizes the whole community. Raiding operations increase in tempo as the hyperactive, newly delivered workers swarm out into the marching columns. After a day or two, the colony stages an exceptionally vigorous raid which ends in a night march. The bivouac site is left littered with empty cocoons. Later in the nomadic period, as the stimulus of the callow workers wanes, the larvae of the next generation become the source of colony "drive." Fat and squirming, as big as an average worker, they establish an active trophallactic relationship with the rest of the tribe. Workers constantly stroke them with their antennae, lick them with their mouth parts and carry them bodily from place to place. Since the larvae at this stage are usually well distributed throughout the corridors and the chambers of the overnight bivouac, their stimulus reaches directly a large number of the workers. This is reflected in the sustained vigor of the daily raids, which continue until the larvae spin their cocoons.

These observations are supported by a variety of experimental findings in the field and laboratory. The role of the callow workers in initiating the movement to break bivouac was confirmed by depriving a number of colonies of their callow broods. Invariably, the raiding operations of the colony failed to recover from the lethargic state characteristic of the statary periods. Some tribes even extended their stay in fixed bivouac until the larvae grew large and active enough to excite the necessary pitch of activity. To test the role of the larval brood, captured tribes were divided into part-

FIGURE 82

Queen in labor has already delivered several thousand eggs, still has upwards of 20,000 to go. Exoskeletal plates of her enormously swollen gaster are widely separated, exposing the distended membrane. Workers attend labor excitedly, snatch up eggs when they emerge.

colonies of comparable size. The group with larvae showed much greater activity than those that had no larvae or that had cocoons in the early pupal state.

The interrelationships among members of the colony thus provide a complete explanation for the behavior cycle of the army ant. It should be observed, in conclusion, that the whole complex process is carried out by individuals which do not themselves originate the basic motivations of their behavior.

Long before the intricacies of its domestic existence were suspected, the army ant's reputation as a social animal was firmly established by its martial conduct in external affairs. It does not require an overactive imagination to perceive the classic doctrines of offensive warfare spelled out by the action of an ant army in the field. It carries through the maneuvers of wheeling, flanking and envelopment with a rutless percision. But to find its motivations and explain its mechanics, one must consult the ant, not von Clausewitz.

Army ant raids fall into one of two major patterns. They are organized either in dense swarms which form at the head of the column or in a deli-

FIGURE 83
Column of army ants on a bivouac-shift march
is an inch wide, may stretch upwards of 300
meters in length. In this picture, the queen appears just above center, buried under excited
workers. Attraction of queen is indicated also
by a reversal in travel of workers ahead.

cate tracery of capillary columns branching out at the forward end of the
main raiding column. Both types of raiding are found in subgenera of each
of the common species of Central American army ant. The *Eciton eciton*
species was selected for this study because it leads its life entirely on the
surface of the jungle floor and is thus accessible to continuous observation.
Whether the army ants raid in swarm or column, however, the essential
mechanics of their behavior are substantially the same.

The bivouac awakes in the early dawn. The stir of activity begins when
the light (as measured by photometer) reaches .05 foot candles, and it
mounts steadily as the light increases. In strands and clusters, the workers

tumble out of the bivouac into a churning throng on the ground. A crowd-ing pressure builds up within this throng until, channeled by the path of least resistance, a raiding column suddenly bursts forth. The ants in the column are oriented rigidly along the line of travel blazed by the chemical trail of the leaders. The minims and medium-sized workers move in tight files in the center. The "workers major," displaced by the unstable footing afforded by the backs of their smaller fellows, travel along each side. This arrangement no doubt lends suggestive support to the major's legendary role of command. It has an adaptive significance in that it places the big-gest and most formidable of the workers on the flanks. Unless disturbed, however, the majors hug the column as slavishly as the rest. The critical role of the tribal chemical in creating this drill sergeant's picture of order may be demonstrated by a simple field experiment. Removal of the chemi-cally saturated litter from the trail brings the column to an abrupt halt. A traffic jam of ants piles up on the bivouac side of the break and is not re-lieved until enough ants have been pushed forward to re-establish the chemical trail.

Appearances are less ordered at the front of the column, where the "scouts" and "skirmishers" are most frequently observed. The timid in-dividual behavior of the forward ants scarcely justifies such titles. Com-pared with the Formica, the Eciton is a far less enterprising forager. It never ventures more than a few inches into the chemically-free area ahead. Even this modest venturing is stimulated principally by physical impact from the rear. At the end of its brief pioneering sally, the Eciton rebounds quickly into the column. It is here that the critical difference between column and swarm raiding arises. The column-raiding ants are somewhat freer in their pioneering behavior and so open new pathways more readily. In the swarm raiders the comparatively reluctant progress of the forward elements creates a counterpressure against the progress of the column. This forces the head of the column into a broad elliptical swarm which arrays itself at right angles to the line of march. With ants pouring in from behind, the swarm grows steadily in size as it moves for-ward, often achieving a width of more than 15 meters.

The path of an ant army, whether in swarms or columns, shows no evidence of leadership. On the contrary, each individual makes sub-stantially the same contribution to the group behavior pattern. The army's course is directed by such wholly chance factors as the stimulus of booty and the character of the terrain. On close inspection, therefore, it appears that the field operations of ant armies approximate the principles of hydraulics even more closely than those of military tactics. This im-pression is confirmed by analysis of the flanking maneuver as executed by the swarm raiders. A shimmering pattern of whirls, eddies and momen-tarily milling vortices of ants, the swarm advances with a peculiar rocking motion. First one and then the other end of the elliptical swarm surges forward. This action results in the outflanking of quarry, which is swiftly engulfed in the overriding horde of ants. It arises primarily, however, from an interplay of forces within the swarm. One of these forces is generated by the inrush of ants from the rear. Opposed by the hesitant progress of the swarm, the new arrivals are deflected laterally to the wing which offers least resistance. This wing moves forward in a wheeling motion until pressure from the slow advance of its frontal margins counterbalances the pressure from the rear. Pressure on the opposite wing has meanwhile been relieved by drainage of the ants into the flanking action. The cycle is therewith reversed, and a new flanking action gets under way from the other end. External factors, too, play a role in this cycle. The stimulus of booty will accelerate the advance of a flank. The capture of booty will halt it and bring ants stampeding in for a large-scale mopping-up party. But raiding activity as such is only incidental to the process. Its essential character is determined by the stereotyped behavior of the individual ant with its limited repertory of responses to external stimuli.

The profoundly simple nature of the beast is betrayed by an ironic catastrophe which occasionally overtakes a troop of army ants. It can happen only under certain very special conditions. But, when these are present, army ants are literally fated to organize themselves in a circular column and march themselves to death. Post-mortem evidence of this phenomenon has been found in nature; it may be arranged at will in the laboratory. Schneirla has had the good fortune to observe one such spectacle in nature almost from its inception to the bitter end.

The ants, numbering about 1,000, were discovered at 7:30 A.M. on a broad concrete sidewalk on the grounds of the Barro Colorado laboratories. They had apparently been caught by a cloudburst which washed away all traces of their colony trail. When first observed, most of the ants were gathered in a central cluster, with only a company or two plodding, counterclockwise, in a circle around the periphery. By noon all of the ants had joined the mill, which had now attained the diameter of a phonograph record and was rotating somewhat eccentrically at fair speed. At 10:00 P.M. the mill was found divided into two smaller counterclockwise spinning discs. At dawn the next day the scene of action was strewn with dead and dying Ecitons. A scant three dozen survivors were still trekking in a ragged circle. By 7:30, 24 hours after the mill was first observed, the various small myremicine and dolichoderine ants of the neighborhood were busy carting away the corpses.

This peculiarly Eciton calamity may be described as tragic in the classic meaning of the Greek drama. It arises, like Nemesis, out of the very aspects of the ant's nature which most plainly characterize its otherwise successful behavior. The general mechanics of the mill are fairly obvious.

FIGURE 84
In laboratory, circular-column milling by army ants is spontaneous and common event. Mill may be started by a few ants circling a dish or short-cutting square corners of nest.

The circular track represents the vector of the individual ant's centrifugal impulse to resume the march and the centripetal force of trophallaxis which binds it to its group. Where no obstructions disturb the geometry of these forces, as in the artificial environment of the laboratory nest or of a sidewalk, the organization of a suicide mill is almost inevitable. Fortunately for the army ant, it is rare in the heterogeneous environment of nature. In the diversity of its natural habitat, the stereotyped army ant is presented with innumerable possibilities for variation in its activity. The jungle terrain, with its random layout of roots and vines, leaves and stones, liberates the ant from its propensity to destroy itself and diverts it into highly adaptive patterns of behavior.

The army ant suicide mill provides an excellent occasion for considering the comparative nature of social behavior and organization at the various levels from ants to men. Other animals occasionally give themselves over to analogous types of mass action. Circular mills are common among schools of herring. Stampeding cattle, sheep jumping fences blindly in column and other instances of pell-mell surging by a horde of animals are familiar phenomena. Experience tells us that men, too, can act as a mob. These analogies are the stock-in-trade of the "herd instinct" schools of sociology and politics. They are cited by those who hold that emotionalized, individually degraded, regimented patterns are the rule in group behavior of mankind.

We are required, however, to look beyond the analogy and study the relationship of the pattern to other factors of individual and group behavior in the same species. In the case of the army ant, of course, the circular column really typifies the animal. Among mammals, such simplified mass behavior occupies a clearly subordinate role. Their group activity patterns are chiefly characterized by great plasticity and capacity to adjust to new situations. This observation applies with special force to the social potentialities of man. When human societies begin to march in circular columns, the cause is to be found in the strait-jacket influence

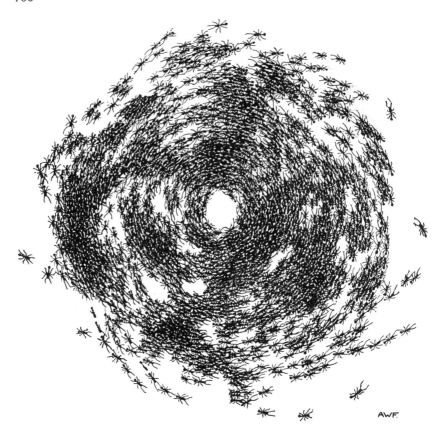

FIGURE 85

Circular column described in text is shown here in drawing traced from photograph. Tendency to form such columns betrays essential mechanics of army ant behavior. This mill developed from cluster of ants that had been isolated accidentally on a sidewalk. Stereotyped ants slavishly followed chemical trail laid by first few individuals that ventured out of cluster. As heat of day speeded travel of ants, the resulting centrifugal force increased the size of the mill to an outside diameter of about seven inches.

of the man-made social institutions which foster such behavior. The phenomenon of milling, it turns out, has entirely different causes and functions at different levels of social organization. The differences, furthermore, so far outweigh the similarities that they strip the "herd instinct" of meaning.

The same reservations apply to the analogies cited to support the superorganism theory. Consider, for example, the analogy of "communication." Among ants it is limited to the stimulus of physical contact. One excited ant can stir a swarm into equal excitement. But this behavior resembles the action of a row of dominoes more than it does the communication of information from man to man. The difference in the two kinds of "communication" requires two entirely different conceptual schemes and preferably two different words.

As for "specialization of functions," that is determined in insect societies by specialization in the biological make-up of individuals. Mankind, in contrast, is biologically uniform and homogeneous. Class and caste distinctions among men are drawn on a psychological basis. They break down constantly before the energies and talents of particular individuals.

Finally, the concept of "organization" itself, as it is used by the superorganism theorists, obscures a critical distinction between the societies of ants and men. The social organizations of insects are fixed and transmitted by heredity. But members of each generation of men may, by exercise of the cerebral cortex, increase, change and even displace given aspects of their social heritage. This is a distinction which has high ethical value for men when they are moved to examine the conditions of their existence.

T. C. SCHNEIRLA

Collective Activities and Social Patterns among Insects

Bibliography No. 64

Because fossils of insects closely similar to many present-day social ants, bees, wasps, and termites have been found in the Baltic amber deposits, Wheeler (1923) concluded that the social pattern had evolved in these insects substantially in its present form by the beginning of the Tertiary Period, about 60,000,000 years ago. For with the traces of social insects are found fossilized remnants of beetles and other insects like those now found as parasites and "guests" in their nests, and other clues to highly developed social functions. It would appear that social patterns, long established as they have been in many insects, must be thoroughly grounded in stable, genetically controlled factors. Nevertheless, their nature does not lend itself to an immediate understanding of the way in which they actually are propagated through species heredity.

FACTORS CONTRIBUTING TO COLLECTIVE BEHAVIOR

Association, Subsocial, and Social Groups

About 6000 of the more than 500,000 known species of insects are definitely social (Imms, 1931), in that they form relatively persistent, self-maintained, and integrated assemblages, in which group unity is based upon an interdependence of the individuals. According to Wheeler (1928), the social pattern has arisen independently in at least twenty-four different groups of insects, from the *Isoptera* to the *Hymenoptera*.

More or less clearly distinguishable from the social form is the more temporary and fluctuant aggregation termed an "association" by Alverdes (1927). Here the existence of the group derives from independent individual random or *taxis* orientations to extrinsic conditions (e.g., light, chemicals, humidity) and not from interindividual relationships. How-

---

From *Insect Physiology*, edited by K. Roeder. New York: John Wiley and Sons, 1953. Chap. 28. Reprinted with permission.

ever, as Allee (1938) has suggested, the principles underlying such animal groups must have been implicated in various ways in the evolution of true social organizations.

Group patterns in insects range from temporary aggregations formed through similar but independent individual responses to attractive environmental conditions, through subsocial forms in which individual biology affects the group habitat, to representative social forms dependent upon the biological and behavioral interrelationships of individuals (Wheeler, 1923, 1928).

The association type of insect aggregation is typified by temporary groups of ladybird beetles (Coccinellidae), which form in the autumn before hibernation time. As an example of a subsocial or rudimentary social group, we may take the case of the earwig *Forficula,* in which the female remains with her eggs where they were deposited in a chamber in decaying wood or in the soil, and the small group of mother and young stays together for a few days after emergence. Lhoste (1944) has reported that earwigs become relatively inactive when grouped, on the basis of a definite interattraction, but that injurious physiological effects may ensue if the usually short duration of the aggregation is prolonged. All species of ants and termites, and many bees and wasps, form colonies or true social aggregations. There are, of course, many transitional forms between the asocial and social types of aggregation.

Biological Preconditions of Social Patterns

Careful studies by Wheeler (1923, 1928) and many others have led to the postulation of certain major biological prerequisites for the evolution of insect social patterns. These essential factors may be discerned in a review of the stages whereby the complex social pattern of existing ants, for example, presumably originated among a group of wasp-like ancestors. The first important prerequisite concerns the ability of the female to lay her eggs under special environmental conditions (Nielsen, 1932). This may have undergone a sequence of changes through conditions that may be represented by a review of existing wasps. First, instead of scattering her eggs in the general living area, the female lays them on some object that eventually serves as food for the developing young. In some wasps such as mutillids the usual host is another insect. In a more advanced stage (most sphecoid wasps, for instance) the female prepares a shelter such as a burrow, stocks it with prey paralyzed by stinging ("mass provisioning"; Roubaud, 1910), lays an egg upon the prey, and then leaves the scene, never to return. A further stage ("progressive provisioning") is attained in the Bembecidae, in which the female remains in the cell with the egg, bringing in further prey from time to time as the larva develops.

In the vespoid wasp *Polistes* and others of the more socially advanced types, the female not only remains with the first young but also bridges further generations after a colony has been established. Thus the evolution of biological factors that permit the female to remain for some time with her young led to the formation of a rudimentary family, which, as C. H. Kennedy (1940) maintains, is antecedent to more complex insect social forms.

Further social evolution is preconditioned by organic specializations in the female, which prolong her life, increase her fecundity, and extend it in time and in regularity, and augment her attractiveness to the offspring (Wheeler, 1928). Specialization in the males and the degree of selectivity among them also become important for productivity (Snell, 1932). Very important is the evolution of the worker caste as one of neuter females, a "hunger form" (Wheeler, 1923) arising essentially as a special adaptation to conditions of food scarcity. These features permit an overlapping of generations, which is essential for a more highly integrated society.

Biological factors basic to the survival and greater internal consistency of an insect population are numerous (Bodenheimer, 1937; Emerson, 1939). Specializations promoting more adequate shelters, together with physiological mechanisms extending "environmental control," lengthen the life of social groups by warding off environmental hazards. Thus hibernation and dormancy permit colonies of ants and others to survive the temperate-zone winter. Other specializations such as polymorphism increase the brood-tending processes of the colony and contribute to greater efficiency in foraging. Foraging efficiency is essential for a sustained colony life under external hardships and increasing internal needs. In fact, Descy (1925) properly allots a primary role in insect social evolution to the development of a capacity in the workers to forage and return to the nest. This capacity generally depends not only upon sensory-motor adaptations increasing the range and efficiency of operations but may also depend upon neurophysiological properties underlying the ability to learn a route. Most essential for social integration are sensory, neural, and motor factors contributing to effective interindividual responsiveness. Mechanisms underlying colony integration and unity are considered later in this chapter.

The Formation of New Colonies

The principal mechanisms of colony production in the social insects are (1) *swarming* and (2) *independent activity* of the parental forms. Although swarming is almost exclusively present in honey bees, and independent activity of the parental forms exclusive in termites and predominant among the ants, in many instances both types are present in the same group. Thus in temperate-zone wasps of the genus *Polistes,* fertilized females produced near the end of the season survive the winter, and in the following spring may found new colonies individually; however, under the continuously equable atmospheric and food conditions of the tropics, the colonies of other species survive from year to year and some of them produce new colonies by periodically giving off swarms (Imms, 1931).

In swarming, or colony fission, daughter colonies are formed by the emigration from the parental colony of reproductive individuals (usually the female alone) accompanied by workers in a group which varies in size according to the species. In honey bees, swarming may result from overpopulation and crowding, which introduce trophic conditions adequate to produce young queens (Sendler, 1940; Grout, 1949). In colonies with old queens whose egg-laying powers are reduced, swarming occurs more readily than in younger colonies (Demuth, 1921). The old queen leaves the hive accompanied by some of the workers, and one of the daughter queens replaces her in the parental colony. In populous colonies, further swarms may subsequently emerge, based upon daughter queens. In certain species of tropical American doryline ants, colony division occurs annually in the dry season through a pattern akin to "swarming," its complex behavioral processes dependent upon the production of a sexual brood containing many alate males and a few wingless young queens (Schneirla and Brown, 1950).

In independent colony formation the male and female pair (as in termites) or the fertilized queen alone (as in most ants and some wasps) is able to establish a colony without initial worker assistance. Among the ants, the fertilized queen typically descends to the ground after the marriage flight and (now photonegative as a physiological consequence of insemination) loses her wings and digs a small cavity or enters a small sheltered niche (Eidmann, 1928, 1931). Here she brings up her first brood of workers (Figure 86), nourishing the larvae on a salivary secretion containing the products of her degenerated wing musculature, abdominal fat body, and some of her eggs. This form of colony founding, which Wheeler (1933) terms the "claustral" type, particularly requires the queen's capacity to feed the first brood on her own organic reserves. The first workers open and extend the nest, feed the brood, and begin external foraging, whereupon the queen settles into an exclusive reproductive specialization. In some of the Australian ponerines and particularly in *Myrmecia* species (e.g., *regularis*), Wheeler (1933) has shown that the absence of wing-muscle tissue and other reserves is correlated with a type of "progressive provisioning" of the incipient colony in which the founding queen leaves her cell at intervals and secures insect food

772

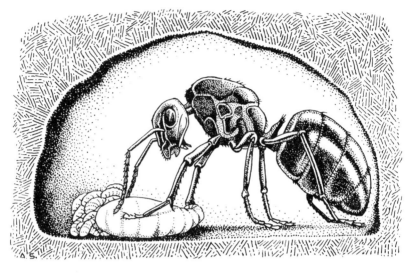

FIGURE 86
A colony-founding dealate queen of *Camponotus ligniperdus,* represented
in her self-made subterranean cell with the larvae of her first brood.
(After Eidmann, 1928.)

which is given to her larval brood. This resembles the primitive vespine
pattern, in contrast to the *claustral* pattern, which centers around the
possession of nitrogenous and lipoid reserves by the queen.

The dependent form of colony foundation is characterized by the fact
that the queen (usually smaller than queens of the independent-founding
species) lacks metabolic reserves of her own, and can found a new colony
only through a special reliance upon her own colony or one of another
species. In the ant genus *Carebara,* which contains thief ants living in the
nests of tropical termites, the huge queen carries with her on her nuptial
flight, hanging to the tufted hairs of her legs, several minute workers from
her parental nest. After the queen has established her cell in some termitarium, these workers rear her brood and make their minute galleries
through which they enter the termite quarters (Wheeler, 1928). The
queen of the African *Bothriomyrmex* gets into the nest of *Tapinoma ni-
gerrimum* through being pulled in by *Tapinoma* workers, stations herself
on the brood or on the *Tapinoma* queen, and thus acquires the basic odor
of the invaded colony. The typical sequel is that the interloper succeeds in
killing the *Tapinoma* queen by sawing off the latter's head with her mandibles, whereupon a *Bothriomyrmex* brood is soon produced which gradually takes over the nest. Wheeler (1928) states that in no less than
fourteen genera and seventeen species of ants new colonies are established

by the queen somehow displacing the queen in nests of other species. The list is increasing (Stumper and Kutter, 1950).

Other Insects and Other Organisms as Social Factors

Nearly every species of social insect has interrelationships of some kind with other insects or arthropods that fit to some extent into the processes of its social life. Such relationships are most pronounced and have been studied most intensively in the ants.

The interrelationships of ants with other ants (or with termites) have many varied patterns and degrees of intimacy. Numerous types of relationships exist between colonies of different genera or even sub-families, which have separate nests, queens, and broods but which live to some degree in a relationship of biological and behavioral significance. These include the "compound nests" of Wasmann (1891) and Wheeler (1923, 1928). A relatively distant relationship is represented by the interterritorial competition of colonies, a more intimate one by the depredations of one ant (usually a small and aggressive species) upon the food of another. Thus the thief ant *Solenopsis molesta* typically has its nest on the margin of a *Formica* nest, with its diminutive workers gaining access to the nest of the larger ant through tiny galleries. This situation usually involves a unilateral food dependence. A nonpredatory relationship (termed "plesiobiosis" by Wheeler, 1928) sometimes exists between separate colonies of two or more species living in juxtaposed but not intercommunicating nests, with the workers more or less hostile when they meet, but with the weaker species feeding on the refuse of the stronger and with a degree of incidental mutual protection against intruders.

A closer approach to mutualism is represented by what Forel (1898) has called "parabiosis." This condition is illustrated by the association in a single spherical "ant garden" of the small species *Crematogaster parabiotica,* which lives marginally in the bolus and rushes forth on slight disturbances, and the larger *Camponotus femoratus,* which lives centrally and rushes out when drastic disturbances occur (Wheeler, 1921). Beyond this protective association and a mutual tolerance represented by freely intercommunicating galleries, the two species have common foraging routes, but keep their broods and queens apart. Finally, there is the condition in which a colony of one species intermingles in the same nest with one of a different species as its true "guest." Thus *Leptothorax emersoni* lives intimately with *Myrmica canadensis,* the small workers of *Leptothorax* feeding on the surface secretion of the host and also being fed by *Myrmica* with regurgitated food (Wheeler, 1903). In the nests of the Central American fungus-growing ant *Sericomyrmex amabilis,* Wheeler (1928) frequently encountered guest colonies of the ant *Cepobroticus symmetochus,* which is in a genus not known to tend fungi. Workers of the two species live intimately and amicably together, occasionally licking one another and both feeding themselves and their broods on the fungus that is tended by the *Sericomyrmex* alone.

When colonies representing closely related species are joined socially, the combination typically is effected only at the cost of a considerable biological or behavioral modification in one or both of them. Thus, in the many genera and species of ants that are chronic social parasites, biological specializations have evolved in the queen that fit her both behaviorally and chemotactically for intrusion into and adoption in the host colony (Emery, 1909; Wheeler, 1928). In the relationship known as "slavery" or *dulosis,* the "dependent" queen of the slave-making species *Formica sanguinea* frequently initiates her colony by entering a nest of its regular host *F. fusca* (Wheeler, 1906; Burrill, 1910; Emery, 1915; Talbot and Kennedy, 1940). Once established, the *sanguinea* colony conducts forays against *fusca* in the vicinity. The unconsumed part of the captured *fusca* worker brood usually develops and becomes part of the host colony, functioning in the regular nest duties as what Wheeler (1928) terms "auxiliaries" rather than slaves. The species of *Polyergus,* the "amazons," also install their young queens in *fusca* nests (Emery, 1909), from which the workers of the eventual *Polyergus* society gain slave increments for their populations by raiding *fusca* colonies periodically (Burrill, 1908; Emery, 1911; Wheeler, 1916b). Dependent colony foundation is essential in both these dulotic species; however, established *sanguinea* colonies can and often do function normally without any *fusca* members, whereas *fusca* are necessary for the survival of *Polyergus* colonies. Ant colonies of different species have all degrees of interrelationship in their social life from one extreme of a combative pattern to the other, in which patterns of mutualistic colony life are found.

An important part of the feeding pattern and hence the social medium of many ants concerns other insects such as aphids, scale insects, tree hoppers, and coccids localized mainly outside the ant nests (Bequaert, 1922). Jones (1929) found more than 50 species of the genus *Aphis* variously attended by 253 species of ants. The ants typically obtain a honeydew secretion from the plant-feeding insects by stroking them with their antennae. The North American *Lasius* species of the subgenus *Acanthomyops* obtain most of their sustenance from such sources. They regularly tend and protect the aphids, construct "tents" of detritus over them where they feed, often carry them into their nests during inclement weather, hold their eggs in the nests in winter, and place the emerged aphids upon growing plants in the spring. Through simpler behavioral relationships than these, the excretions of Homoptera are also regularly obtained by honey bees as well as by certain bumblebees and stingless bees.

In termites, a close dependence of the entire social structure and its peculiarities upon the nature of food consumed has been pointed out by Wheeler (1928). The predominant diet of cellulose or humus in termites has provided a selective basis for their most striking characteristics: their tunneling in wood; their degenerate eyes and marked photonegativity in strong light (Richard, 1951); their soft integument together with special defenses such as the nasute glands of the soldiers in some species; and impregnable nests (in some) constructed of their own hardened fecal material. As another character, interindividual feeding relations are basic to colony unity and responsible for spreading the indispensable symbiotic protozoa, which are physiologically as well as morphologically distinct in many species (Dropkin, 1941). Without their symbiotic protozoa, most termites soon die (Cleveland, 1923). However, in highly evolved species of termites that have developed modes of cultivating and feeding on fungi, symbiotic protozoa are absent (Wheeler, 1928; Emerson, 1939; Grassé and Noirot, 1945).

Trophic roles of various kinds are also played by an assortment of insects, arachnids, land isopods, and myriapods, living in the nests of social insects in various relations with the occupants. At least 2000 arthropod species are known to live with ants of various species, 700 species with termites, and other specialized forms with social wasps and social bees (Wheeler, 1923, 1928). These relationships have evolved with greatest frequency and elaborateness in ants. That the presence of the ant "myrmecophiles" centers about food was demonstrated in Janet's (1897) pioneer study.

The classification offered for ants by Wasmann (1910) represents various degrees of intimacy in the relationship of the "guest" to the host. First, there are *parasites* proper (e.g., mites), which live either within or on the bodies of the hosts. The *synecthrans,* or hostile species, (such as swiftly moving staphylinid beetles) are disturbing to their hosts but elude their attacks through diminutive size or agile movement, and generally are predatory on the ants or their brood. For example, the staphylinid beetle *Megastilicus humeralis,* common within the nests of *Formica rufa,* effectively defends itself from seizure by raising the tip of its flexible abdomen and emitting a pungent vapor, which invariably drives off the attacking ant (Donisthorpe, 1927). *Synoeketes* are commensals and scavengers, which are either passed over entirely by their hosts or are "indifferently tolerated" through being neutral and undisturbing in chemotactic effect (Wheeler, 1928). This group includes beetles, fly larvae, and isopods, many of which are somewhat predatory or parasitic, others somewhat symbiotic in their relations with the ants. The *true guests* or *symphiles,* those most intimately incorporated into the life of the colony, are mainly beetles, which exhibit a considerable variety of remarkable behavioral and struc-

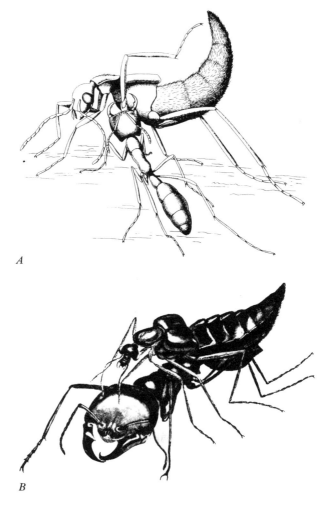

A

B

FIGURE 87
A. Small intermediate worker of the driver ant, *Dorylus nigricans,* licking a leg articulation of a staphylinid beetle (*Smectonia gridellia*) present in the nest as a "guest." B. A "guest beetle" (*Smectonia gridellia*) stroking a major worker of *Dorylus nigricans* with antennae. (Reproduced from Patrizi, 1948, by permission.)

tural adaptations to their hosts. The symphiles are licked, fed, and even reared by virtue of their attraction to the ants based upon the secretion of glandular exudates. Themselves capable of licking the host ants, or stroking them with modified antennae (Figure 87), the guests in turn are fed upon regurgitated food, or prey freely upon the ant brood. The influence of the symphiles, rather than neutral or benign, may be deleterious and in extreme cases may upset the trophic balance of the colony by causing the ants to neglect their brood as well as their foraging, with abnormal or defective individuals appearing in the brood as a result (Wasmann, 1915).

Wheeler (1928) noticed the significant fact that the myrmecophiles are most numerous and varied in the nests of the most highly socialized ants and termites. Contrary to the view of Wasmann (1910, 1915) who believed that special "symphilic instincts" on the part of the ants were responsible for the relationship, both Wheeler and Schimmer (1910) have maintained that the specific evolutionary adaptations occur mainly on the side of the myrmecophiles. Wheeler (1928) maintained that the behavior of the ants in this relationship is really that involved in ordinary interindividual responses in the colony, with limited modifications now and then based on "slight ontogenetic changes."

CONDITIONS UNDERLYING ORGANIZATION IN THE INSECT COLONY

Interindividual Stimulative Relations and the "Trophallaxis" Concept

Stimulative relations among individuals in the ant colony are complex and varied, as Wheeler's (1923, 1928) reviews of the question have shown. Outstanding relations of this type normally present in ants are the following: in founding the colony, the queen licks and handles the eggs, and later feeds the first larvae and callow workers with a regurgitated substance; workers soon begin to feed the queen and continue to do so throughout the life of the colony; workers lick and handle the eggs, also lick fatty exudates from the body surface of the larvae; workers are strongly attracted to the queen on a chemotactic basis, and are constantly licking and touching her body; workers regurgitate liquid food to larvae, to the queen, and to one another; workers frequently are in contact with one another, huddling together, licking and cleaning one another's bodies, touching antennae, and so on.

Considering such relationships basic to colony unity and organization, Wheeler (1928) conceptualized them under the term "trophallaxis." This term signifies relationships of food exchange, or of stimuli related to food in their sensory and behavioral effect, among adult individuals, between adults and developing young, and between adults and myrmecophiles in a colony (Schneirla, 1946). Trophallactic relations between adults and larvae were first observed by Janet (1903), who reported that in *Vespa* a salivary secretion produced by a stimulated larva was promptly lapped up by the nurses. The significance of such a reciprocal feeding for colony organization was elucidated by Roubaud (1916), also from observations on wasps. A growing mass of evidence (Wheeler, 1918, 1923, 1928) leaves no doubt that an exchange of stimulative effects goes on constantly and complexly in feeding and other nest activities in all social insects (Figure 87). Rather than being a set of auxiliary events, these occurrences are expressions of integrative processes basic to and accountable for colony unity.

Unmistakable variations are found in colony cohesion and interindividual responsiveness in dependence upon the scope of trophallactic relations within the colony, particularly as between the workers and brood. Thus, among ants, colony organization is clearly much looser in some of the primitive ponerine species, in which brood-adult relations are at the minimum, than in camponotine species in which brood-adult relations are complex and extensive (Haskins, 1939). The ontogeny of these processes is of particular interest.

Appearance of Socialized Behavior in the Individual Insect

Beyond observations on ordinary colony functions, studies of early individual behavior have been enlightening as to the nature and significance of interindividual stimulative relationships. The larvae of ants (Wheeler, 1918), bees (Lineburg, 1924), and wasps are known to undergo stimulative exchanges with adults during feeding. The responses of larvae in such exchanges may be a function not only of specific organic processes such as mouthpart reflexes and salivary secretions but also may change through use. As one possibility, larvae may acquire a generalized conditioned responsiveness to a characteristic chemotactic stimulation presented by workers and to a background of nest chemical present during the act of feeding.

The adult behavior pattern of the species does not appear fixedly in a newly emerged social insect, but changes significantly in time, as is shown by the studies of Rösch (1925) with bees, Steiner (1932) with wasps, and Heyde (1924) with ants. When Heyde removed mature ant pupae of *Formica* and other species from cocoons, she found that their fighting, brood care, digging, and feeding responses appeared more slowly than those of callows that emerged into groups of adults. Any one type of behavior was first observed in the form of simple, local responses, then in an extended form. Feeding is a significant example. When food is presented to the early callow worker of many ants, her mandibles open wide and the liquid is ingested. Throughout the entire act the callow's antennae oscillate, and usually her front legs also beat rapidly. The act does not occur spontaneously after the callow appears from her cocoon, but at first persistent stimulation by an adult worker is required. The unfed, newly emerged callow moves about restlessly, and, when an adult worker is encountered, antennal stimulation and initial regurgitation from the adult elicits the callow's feeding responses. According to Heyde, after a number of such feedings, the rapid antennal and front-leg oscillations of early feeding take place only at the outset, and are quickly displaced by a slow oscillatory motion of the antennae. However, the rapid movements of the anterior members remain as a regular feature of responses to nest mates, appearing with a special prominence under conditions of marked excitement as after intervals of food deprivation. These results suggest that, within a few days after emergence, callows of ant species such as *Formica* or *Camponotus* become more specifically responsive to adult workers, and also that the initially crude reflex feeding activities undergo certain (possibly conditioned) modifications. Furthermore, the initial responses to regurgitation, modified as a part of the individual's repertoire of reactions to others contacted in the nest, may play a role in colony "communication." In the doryline ants, in which no feeding of adults or young occurs by regurgitation, only brief and perfunctory antennal contacts are observed in the encounters of adult workers.

At this point we may suggest that a basic factor in early callow responses to adult workers may be a *turning toward* weak stimulation, possibly conditioned to characteristic colony stimuli in the callow worker if not also earlier in the larva. Results such as those from "mixed colony" tests to be considered below suggest that the turning-and-approach response of the early callow becomes specifically conditioned to the prevalent nest chemical. Also, the erogenous effects of weak local stimulation (to antennae and mouthparts in particular) may exert a reflex "arresting" effect and thereby may acquire a reinforcing role in the above process. Thus a simple form of learning may play a role in the colony adjustments of some social insects.

The presence of food interchange by regurgitation may be assured in many social insects, granted adequate developmental conditions, through the presence of specific organic mechanisms. The significant fact that regurgitation occurs in those ants that have a crop or distensible anterior stomach divided by a narrow muscular valve from the posterior stomach was first called to attention by Forel (1874, 1921–1923). Forel termed the crop the "social stomach," because liquid food can be held within it by a strong muscular valve, pumped back to mouthparts, and there consumed by other individuals, and only the part that gets through the valve into the posterior chamber or "individual stomach" cannot be regurgitated.

Normally, a worker leaves the colony center when the crop is empty, forages about and returns when it is filled; and in the nest readily regurgitates its contents in successive encounters with nest mates. So coercive is the adequate stimulation of reiterated antennal contact and so prompt the usual delivery of regurgitated food as to suggest the existence of a virtually automatic mechanism underlying the act. The anatomical basis may be a neural connection such as the *recurrens nerve* described by Janet (1904) for *Myrmica rubra*. From his morphological findings, we learn that this nerve passes from the frontal ganglion to the hypocerebral ganglion, from which a pair of fine connectives reaches the abdomen. These nerves pass to the prestomachal ganglion, from which the crop and gizzard are innervated. Through a neural connection of this kind the adequate stimulation of head receptors might readily induce a stereotyped regurgitation of crop contents. The potential importance of such a process merits careful investigation.

The research of Rösch (1925) discloses important functional changes in the worker bee in a definite sequence depending upon growth. Normally, feeding of the smallest larvae is carried out by the young worker from her sixth to fifteenth days and is related to the condition of the pharyngeal glands, since it ends with their atrophy; comb-building is similarly correlated with the condition of the wax glands, and the worker begins consistent foraging when these glands atrophy shortly after the twentieth day. These times may vary considerably in dependence upon changed hive conditions (Rösch, 1925, 1930) and especially upon trophic conditions in the colony (Kuwabara, 1948).

The foraging honey bee ordinarily makes many successive food-gathering trips and delivers her load each time to bees in the hive. Similar conditions prevail among ants. It is a reasonable hypothesis that the motivational or "drive" basis of food-delivery processes in the forager is derived through interindividual feeding activities during early stages of the worker's colony life. Results should repay study.

"Nest-Mate Recognition" among Social Insects

That the reactions of mutual acceptance or rejection in social insects depend upon olfactory processes to a great extent is indicated by a variety of evidence. Wheeler (1923, 1928) has pointed out that the lipoid coating of ants' cuticle and the hairy investment of bees offers an excellent base for capturing and retaining gases and solutions, and that the ordinary oral interchanges and close associations of the members of an insect colony present abundant opportunities for effecting a synthesis of the prevalent chemicals. Social insects in general have an exceedingly acute chemical sensitivity (Dethier, 1947a), and are capable of learning olfactory discrimination habits. Yet the nature of the chemical patterns involved and the basis of their role have been difficult to establish (Melander and Brues, 1906; Stumper, 1922).

Hive acceptance of the bee queen on an olfactory basis is suggested by the means ordinarily used to introduce a new queen to a queenless hive. The usual practice is to place the queen in a small screen cage in the hive between brood combs, restrained by a candy stopper through which the workers must eat their way. This insures that the queen will become impregnated with hive odor before the workers are in actual contact with her (Grout, 1949). By creating the proper behavior situation and insuring an equivalence of odor pattern, Mathis (1948) was able to introduce and have accepted two or more young queens into a single queenless hive of honey bees. In all probability queens of the social-parasitic species of ants introduce themselves into the host colonies on a comparable chemotactic basis (Wheeler, 1928; Morley, 1942).

Significant results have been obtained in experiments on artificially mixed colonies of ants. Bethe (1898) washed workers of one species successively in water and alcohol, then bathed them in a broth of body fluids of a species by which they were normally attacked. When placed with the foreign species these treated workers were at first accepted, but were attacked after a time when the superimposed chemical evidently had volatilized away. Ants of ordinarily inimical species were successfully combined into the same mixed group by Fielde (1903) as mature pupae artificially removed from their cocoons. But after a few months the group became somewhat unstable, and occasional attacks were observed. Two different colonies of *Nasutitermes banksi,* initially inimical on an olfactory basis, were joined together successfully by Emerson (1928) through mixing termites and nest material together in a jar. Morley (1942) obtained a mixed colony containing ants of *Formica, Myrmica,* and other species by including *Acanthomyops* species. The intense odor of *Acanthomyops* was generally tolerated and evidently masked disturbing odorous differences long enough for a conditioned mutual acceptance to occur. He believes that each species has a characteristic basic odor, which is a composite of different organic chemicals (e.g., from poison glands or anal glands) merged through trophallactic interchanges with those of the group (e.g., larval and queen secretions) and the environment (e.g., nest soil, characteristic food), thereby forming a common chemical that individuals of the colony are conditioned to accept. Morley reports for ants that mixed-colony tests are more successful with closely related species than with species which are biologically more distant from one another. Somewhat different results were obtained by Nogueira (1950) with stingless bees (Meliponinae), in which certain species considered by taxonomists to be closely related were definitely less compatible when placed in common colonies than other species, considered more closely related.

The role of a sensory discrimination process in normal reactions to nest mates and to strangers is suggested by the fact that bees of different hives may be combined without attacks when under the influence of smoke fumes, and that ants of normally inimical species, placed together when emerging from the effects of ether, behave as nest mates for a time. Brun's (1910, 1912) argument against olfactory differentiation and in favor of "psychological plasticity" in the nest-mate "recognition" of ants neglects the relevance both of prevalent level of arousal and of sensory acuity in relation to possible olfactory masking effects. There need be no conflict between the concepts of sensory discrimination and of learning (i.e., conditioning) in this connection. The role of stimuli such as contact and stridulation in such behavior deserves study.

"Communication" in Social Insects

Insect "communication" has been investigated most extensively in the honey bee. Bonnier's (1906) observation that the number of bees arriving at a food place varied in direct relation to the number of flowers available has been clarified by the extensive studies of von Frisch (1920, 1950b). The finder's behavior is complex. A bee returning with food to the hive performs characteristic movements on the comb, described by von Frisch (1923) as the "round dance" and the "waggle dance" (Figure 88). In the round dance the finder circles first to one side, then to the other; in the waggle dance she moves in half circles alternating in direction, with a straight run intervening in which her body, and especially her abdomen, oscillates. Significant facts have been discovered concerning this behavior (von Frisch, 1946, 1947, 1950b). The finder performs a round dance when food has been brought from sources within 50 to 100 m from the hive, a waggle dance when the source is more distant. With increasing distance the number of waggle runs falls, rapidly at first, then more slowly. With sources at 200 m, it is about 30/min; at 2000 m, it is about 13/min; and at 4000 m it is about 9/min. Also, a relationship has been found between the direction of the finder's straight median run and the location of the food place with respect to the sun (von Frisch, 1946, 1949, 1950b). With finders dancing on a vertical comb, when the food source lies toward the sun the waggle run is upward, when the food source lies away from the sun it is downward, and when the source deviates from the sun's position by a given angle the run deviates correspondingly to right or to left from the vertical. On the comb in the dark, the direction of the arrival flight to the hive somehow becomes transposed to a gravity control of movement; or it may be controlled directly by light, even by polarized rays if light reaches the comb.

That the finder's dance arouses other bees is indicated by the departure of many secondary bees from the hive when dancing is vigorous and frequent (as when food is plentiful), of few when dancing is weak or absent

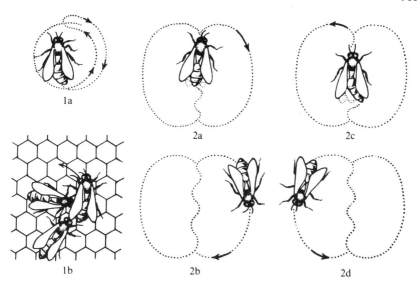

FIGURE 88

At left (1a) the "round dance" of a finder honey bee upon returning from a food place 100 m from the hive; below (1b) the responses of aroused secondary bees. At right (2a, b, c, d) successive stages in the "waggle dance," indicating (2a, c) the oscillations performed during the median run. (Modified from von Frisch, *Aus dem Leben der Bienen,* Springer-Verlag, 1948, by permission.)

(as when food is scanty). There is evidence that the dancing somehow influences the secondary bees in specific ways. For instance, after a colony had been trained to visit two different feeding places, one at 10 m and the other at 300 m from the hive, two tests were performed. When ample food was placed at 10 m but none at 300 m, the returning finders performed round dances on the comb, and virtually all of the secondary bees went to the 10 m place. But with the food reversed, the returning finders performed waggle dances and the great proportion of secondary bees went to the 300 m place. Depending upon the distance of the food place, the dances differed, and on the whole different groups of bees were aroused.

We have mentioned differences in the waggle dance corresponding to the direction of the food place. That such differences influence secondary bees was demonstrated in the following experiment: After a few bees had fed on a lavender-scented card on a stand 250 m south of the hive, seven stands bearing cards with the same scent but without food were set up on the south side at 15° intervals, all at 200 m but in different directions from the hive. During the next hour, visits were paid as follows to the stands: *east side—*45° divergent from original food line, 8 bees; 30° divergent, 13 bees; 15° divergent, 58 bees; *food-line stand—*132 bees; *west side—*

15° divergent, 37 bees; 30° divergent, 7 bees; and 45° divergent, 3 bees. Thus the dancing also somehow affords cues as to the distance and direction of the food source from which the finder has come. The nature of the actual transmissive process is not known. Von Frisch (1947, 1950b) has found that the effect persists after shellac has been applied to the abdomens of the finder bees so that the product of the scent gland cannot be released.

A fact of great importance for species adaptation is discernible in the dependence of dancing upon the organic excitatory condition of the finder. Thus vigorous dancing occurs in finders returning to a starved hive even from sparse food sources, or to a normal hive from rich food sources, and dancing decreases sharply when food of lower concentration is substituted (von Frisch, 1948). Similarly, dancing is aroused more easily in the fall when the honey flow is sparse than in the spring when it is greater (Lindauer, 1948).

The finder bee transmits not only tactual stimuli but also olfactory cues to other bees on the comb (von Frisch, 1923). In addition to an excitatory and attractive effect exerted by the scent-gland secretion (Sladen, 1902), other olfactory effects influence the behavior of the secondary bees in specific ways. A finder bee experimentally dusted with rose pollen while sipping nectar, in her dance on the comb, specifically excites rose-pollen foragers no matter what flower she has visited (von Frisch and Rösch, 1926). Although scents carried on the body surface become weak through volatilization in long flights, a perfume unweakened by distance is released when honey is regurgitated from the finder's stomach (von Frisch, 1943, 1946). When a finder delivered sugar water scented with phlox, aroused bees came to phlox—although nectar is not attainable from the phlox flower with the bees's short proboscis—and neglected nearby cyclamen containing accessible nectar.

According to Emerson (1929) disturbances are transmitted through a termite colony tactually and mechanically, and possibly also through olfactory effects such as by special secretions (e.g., the nasute glands of soldiers), according to the species. Knocking of heads against the substratum by excited individuals in a *Leucotermes tenuis* colony occurs at a rate of 10/sec, a snapping of mandibles is characteristic in many species, and stridulatory vibrations produced by *Reticulitermes flavipes* were picked up and amplified with suitable apparatus (Emerson and Simpson, 1929). Both Emerson and Grassé (1937) regard these stimulus effects as essentially excitatory and only incidentally determinative of the response.

Although Wasmann (1899) and other writers have endowed ants with a code of antennal symbols, much simpler interindividual relationships seem to prevail. Eidmann (1927) reported that a *Myrmica laevinodis*

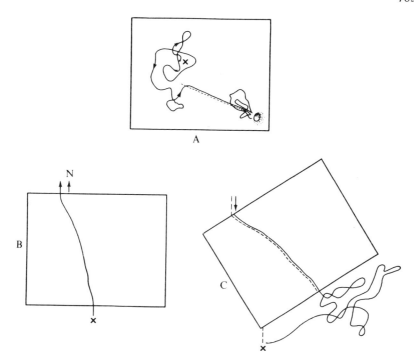

FIGURE 89

Tests on "communication" and trail-following behavior in ants. A. Trailing in the Chilean ant *Solenopsis gayi*. The experimenter rubbed the gaster of a *gayi* worker across the paper floor of the area, along the route indicated by stippling. A worker set down at × wandered until the artificial trail was crossed, then followed it to the nest entrance. B. A *Pheidole* (sp.) worker returned excitedly from a food place at × to the nest N, crossing the paper-floored area along the line indicated. C. The paper was immediately shifted in position. Aroused secondary *Pheidole* workers from the nest followed the trail to the edge of the paper, then wandered. (After Goetsch, 1937b.)

worker on finding a piece of food would run excitedly to the nest center where antennal contacts were made with other workers; these issued excitedly, circled around, and presently found the food. When both the finder ant and the paper floor of the food area were removed after arousal of the nest, the newcomers did not discover the food except by chance (Figure 89). Similar results have been obtained by Santschi (1930) and by Goetsch (1934), with evidence in numerous species that anal-gland secretions incidentally deposited on the substratum by excited finder ants could be followed to the food. Goetsch (1934) found that *Pheidole pallidula* and other species could follow artificial trails made by rubbing the abdomen tip of a worker of the species against the substratum along a given course. A comparable and highly stereotyped incidental trail-making by ants reaching new ground is effective in the forays of army ants (Schneirla, 1933a).

In well-visioned ant species, such as *Formica fusca,* the secondarily aroused workers ordinarily do not go specifically to the food source unless they have previously learned the route themselves. Under some conditions, such as discovering food after a period of starvation, the finder becomes very agitated, the movement of her antennae and the oscillations of her front legs being more vigorous than at other times. The greater the agitation of the finder the more widespread is her general excitatory effect on other members of the colony, but her actions influence only incidentally the nature, direction, and scope of response in the other ants. Hence the observed result of the return of a very agitated forager to the nest is the appearance of larger numbers of more widely ranging foragers than would have been seen after the return of a less agitated ant.

In many ants, eccentric and often violent activities appear under conditions of extreme agitation, as when an "enemy" has been met. Typical activities are opening wide or snapping the mandibles, thumping the gaster against the substratum, advancing the body in a succession of quick, jerky movements, and the like. From his careful studies of such behavior in 20 species of ants, Goetsch (1934) concluded that its effect upon nest mates is due not to the significance of particular movements but to their intensity and amplitude, and to accompanying secondary stimuli as from formic acid or anal-gland secretions. No adequate evidence exists to show that in such exchanges a "language" or "code" effect is involved in the sense that the finder "deliberately" offers a descriptive or indicative (i.e., symbolic) representation of what she has encountered and where it may be found.

INDIVIDUAL PARTICIPATION AND COLLECTIVE FUNCTION

Sex Dimorphism, Polymorphism, and the Social Structure

The presence of diversified types of individuals in a colony population characterizes most of the social insects, with the exception of the social parasites. In addition to the male-female dichotomy, the existence of various developmental and adult types within the sexes (Wheeler, 1928; Emerson, 1939) is significant for the successful adaptation and internal organization of the colony. The development and persistence of insect populations, as well as the extent to which functional specialization can appear, depend particularly upon the egg-laying properties of the queen and upon factors that influence differentiation of progeny.

The Dzierzon rule, which applies generally to the social insects, states that male individuals appear from unfertilized eggs, female types from fertilized eggs (Light, 1934; Flanders, 1946a, b). The restriction of the principal or exclusive egg production of the colony to a single "queen" (as in honey bees and most ants) or a small number of egg-laying females is significant for the appearance and growth of an insect colony (Forel, 1929; Bodenheimer, 1937).

The colonies of most species of social insects contain, in addition to one or a few fertile females, a relatively infertile or completely unfertile female type known as the "worker." It is generally held that the eggs from which queen and worker types develop are equivalent in their genetic makeup (Grout, 1949—bees; Wheeler, 1928—ants; Light, 1934—termites) so that under appropriate conditions any female type may be produced from any fertilized egg.

The worker or neuter-type female apparently is differentiated from the queen type by nutritional factors, which may differ somewhat in various social insects. It is well known that if newly hatched honey bee larvae are transferred from worker cells to queen cells before the third day of larval life, they develop into queens (Park—see Grout, 1949). Wheeler (1923) considered the worker ant a "hunger form," inadequately nourished because of larval numbers and conditions of food scarcity. The worker as a larva is held (through underfeeding) to an incomplete development of the body (especially the ovaries), and as an adult performs strenuous labors on slender rations so that a condition of more or less sterility (i.e., alimentary castration) is typically enforced. Flanders (1946a, b) has suggested that for honey bees the trophic (nutritive) differentiation may begin in early stages of oögenesis, with the queen-producing fertilized eggs possessing a metabolic superiority from initial stages because they undergo less absorption of nutrient in passing along the tubes than do worker-producing fertilized eggs.

Despite the weight of the traditional view that honey bee queens are differentiated from workers through receiving "royal jelly" (a nitrogenous, glandular product) after the third day, Haydak (1943) has pointed to the significant fact that the queen larvae are fed continuously throughout their development, whereas after the third day worker larvae are fed only at intervals (Lineburg, 1924). Kuwabara (1948) has advanced evidence favoring the view that queens are differentiated developmentally from workers on a quantitative rather than a qualitative trophic basis. It is important to note that the production of the annual sexual brood containing queens occurs when food is most plentiful in ants (Wheeler, 1928), bumble bees (Cumber, 1949), and other social insects. In termites there is evidence (Castle, 1934b) that an exudate or other secretion by the queen, received by workers through normal trophallactic interchanges (Emerson,

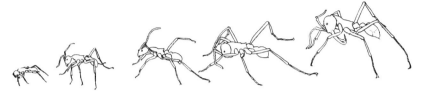

FIGURE 90
Representative types in the continuous polymorphic worker series of the army ant *Eciton hamatum*. The worker minor (left) is 4.0 mm in body length, the worker major (right) 10.5 mm; the intervening types (intermediate workers) represent equidistant intervals along the population base line. (Drawn from a photograph by Schneirla.)

1939) constitutes a chemical coordinating agent serving to inhibit the production of additional queens. When the termite queen is removed, secondary queens are produced, but this may be delayed if alcohol extracts from the primary queen are fed to the workers.

The production of differentiated (polymorphic) types of workers is generally attributed to differences in trophic conditions affecting developmental stages. In wasps, honey bees, and many ants, essentially monomorphic workers are produced with only a limited difference in size. Some ants (e.g., *Pheidole* spp.) produce more or less broken worker distributions generally with two types (dimorphic) strikingly different in size and perhaps also qualitatively in structure; others produce continuous series in which there are marked differences in size and often also in structure (Figure 90). The most common polymorphic types or "castes" are the workers minor, the intermediate workers, and the workers major (frequently called "soldiers"). Such differences may depend not only upon the amount of food received in the larval stage (Wheeler, 1928; Wesson, 1940) but also as in termites upon the differential effectiveness of "social hormones" which are known to control (at least in part) the proportions of workers and soldiers (Castle, 1934b; Light, 1934). The exudates of soldier termites tend to inhibit the development of soldier types, so that the production of the soldier caste is effectively reduced when that type is superabundant in the colony.

Stable Functional Differences Associated with Polymorphism

The queens of certain social insects and especially ants are photopositive until fertilization and loss of the wings has occurred, then become photonegative and claustral and are worker-like in their behavior in founding the nest and producing the first brood. Once a small worker population is present, however, the colony-founding queen becomes essentially an egg-producing unit in the colony (Wheeler, 1903, 1906, 1928; Eidmann, 1928). A worker-like behavior may reappear in fertile queens deprived of their worker populations. This change, which emphasizes the basic biological affinity of the queen and worker types, is a functional differentiation of key importance in colony foundation. In some wasps, the egg-laying queen continues in a worker-like function (Verlaine, 1932a), in others (Gaul, 1948), the queen becomes specialized reproductively.

The manner in which the colony function of worker insects may be related to morphological differentiation is illustrated by the succession of functions through which honey bee workers typically pass in dependence upon growth stage (Rösch, 1925), a situation also found in *Polistes* wasps (Steiner, 1932). Various observers (Forel, 1874; Buckingham, 1910; Heyde, 1924) have noted that worker ants at first are typically engaged in brood-tending, building, and other activities within the nest, and do not leave the nest in foraging until some days after their emergence.

A stable functional differentiation, or "division of labor" as it is usually termed, is outstanding between the major and minor castes of termite workers. The soldiers of many termite species are quite incapable of gnawing or perforating wood in a worker-like manner, but must be fed by the workers through a regurgitation of liquid food, and soon perish in the absence of workers (Grassé, 1937). They do not engage in foraging or building like smaller workers, but remain relatively quiescent in the termitarium or move along slowly in the roofed galleries. However, when any considerable mechanical disturbance occurs, the soldiers move to the source, where their defensive properties become evident, whereas the smaller workers usually retreat. The nasute soldier of *Nasutitermes cavifrons,* studied by Emerson (1926), for a time has a defensive role in the colony and on disturbance ejects a caustic secretion through its frontal tube, but later undergoes a molt and transforms into an individual with a characteristic worker structure and worker behavior.

The large-headed soldiers of the leaf-cutter ant *Atta cephalotes* appear to have a comparable narrow specialization as nest defenders. A similar condition exists in the largest workers of many *Camponotus* species (Buckingham, 1910; Kiil, 1934; Lee, 1939). Certain tropical American *Eciton* (army ant) species have a continuous polymorphic series ranging from large-headed soldiers with great hook-shaped mandibles through intermediates to very small minim workers. The soldiers cannot engage in the ordinary activities of the mass raid, but demonstrate their protective function by rushing to the scene of any intensive disturbance with open mandibles. Most of the raiding is carried out by workers in the intermediate castes. The largest workers of *Colobopsis,* a subgenus of *Camponotus* (carpenter ants) insert their truncated heads individually into the small circular opening of their nests in hollow stalks or twigs, effectively serving as stoppers (Wheeler, 1910b; Forel, 1921). The Asiatic weaver ant *Oecophylla smaragdina* is sharply dimorphic with a small and a larger worker type (Cole and Jones, 1948). Doflein (1905) and others report that in construction of the characteristic *Oecophylla* carton tree nests the leaves are held together by the larger workers, whereas the larvae are held and oscillated as shuttles by the smaller workers.

In the ants, the polymorphic workers of *Eciton* and *Atta* species, mentioned above, present extremes very different from each other in morphology and in behavior (Figure 90). The most specific function of the worker major in both these genera is colony defense; the most specific function of the minim workers is tending the eggs and smallest larvae. The intermediate workers, however, perform varied and over-lapping functions. Goetsch (1937b) has shown that there is a close correspondence between structural peculiarities (over-all size, size of mandibles, length of legs) and behavioral function. Similar functions are performed differently by the castes, as Lutz (1929) found in the carrying of leaf segments by workers of *Atta cephalotes*. The weight of the individual burden proved to be roughly 5 mg more than twice that of the carrier, a relationship due not to a "choice" of appropriate burdens by the ants but to matters such as difficulty in balancing over-sized pieces. In polymorphic ants, structural characteristics thus appear to operate in delimiting function both directly and indirectly. In *Atta,* a direct limitation upon function is illustrated by the inability of the largest and smallest workers to manipulate leaves, an indirect influence by the intermediate workers hitting upon leaf segments of "appropriate" size.

Numerous studies have been made of functional differentiation in species of *Camponotus* which have polymorphic worker series without well-defined structural differences except in body size. Investigators are agreed that in such species all the workers participate in most activities, but that the different "types" take part to relatively different extents in the different activities. These differences can be summarized as follows:

1. The largest individuals participate most readily in fighting, especially in major disturbances (Buckingham, 1910; Kiil, 1934; Lee, 1939) but are not so active in other colony activities such as foraging. During food exchange they are more often receivers than donors (Buckingham, 1910; Lee, 1939).
2. The intermediate workers do most of the foraging, and much regurgitating of liquid food (Kiil, 1934; Buckingham, 1910; Lee, 1939).
3. The small intermediate workers are active in tending aphids, regurgitating food, and digging and caring for the brood (Pricer, 1903; Lee, 1939; Chen, 1937; Kiil, 1934).

4. The minors are most active in tending the brood, transporting other workers, and regurgitating and digging (Buckingham, 1910; Kiil, 1934; Lee, 1939).

The above results are typical for an ant which has a continuous worker series, such as *Camponotus pictus*. But in the dimorphic *Pheidole pilfera* (Buckingham, 1910) the differences in activity between the major and minor workers are greater and more distinct.

Individual Differences in Function in Monomorphic Worker Populations

In social insects with relatively homogeneous worker populations, functional specialization exists on less apparent bases. We have seen that the principal sequence of functional changes in honey bee workers corresponds to organic changes that appear with age (Rösch, 1925). In queenless hives the feeding of small larvae appears earlier in young bees than in normal hives, and is related to a precocious development of the pharyngeal glands during the first 10 hr after emergence (Kuwabara, 1948). In as many as six genera of ants (e.g., the "honey ants," *Myrmecocystus* spp.), nectar is stored in the crops of workers that have permanently distended abdomens (Leonard, 1911). Wheeler (1910b) confirmed McCook's (1882) surmise that there are no initial structural differences between these "repletes" and other workers, but that any worker may become a food-reservoir if the process is begun during the callow stage when the integument is soft and distensible. Workers thus functionally specialized have been termed "physiological castes" by Wheeler (1928).

Even in homogeneous populations of social insects, individual differences in function probably exist on a more or less permanent basis. In various species of ants (e.g., *Lasius* and *Formica*), Lubbock (1882) and Fielde (1901) observed that some individuals are much more active than others in foraging. Schneirla (1929, 1933b) found striking individual differences among *Formica* workers in their ability to learn a maze. A minority of the foragers in a honey bee colony serve as "finders" (von Frisch, 1948; Oettingen-Spielberg, 1949). According to Pardi (1946, 1948) "dominance" is exhibited by some of the workers in *Polistes* colonies, in that they regurgitate more frequently than they receive food, and are more active within the nest than "subordinate" members. Pardi reports a tendency for better developed ovaries among "dominant" members of a colony; however, Deleurance (1948) finds that ovariectomy affects neither these behavioral differences nor nest-founding behavior in general. Combes (1935, 1937) reported that most of the various labors in the normal ant colony are performed by a minority of hyperactive workers. Chen (1937) demonstrated that in every caste of *Camponotus herculeanus* workers there are individual differences in digging activity, with the "leaders" starting more readily and doing more work than others. There is a gradient of effectiveness ranging from a short latency and high working rate to a great latency and low rate. Such individual differences evidently depend upon differences in metabolic rate, since the "leaders" were considerably more susceptible than the "followers" to the action of ether, drying, and starvation.

Thus, in worker populations with reduced polymorphism, each worker becomes able to participate to some extent in all worker functions, and individual differences become relative rather than absolute (Buckingham, 1910; Wheeler, 1928). The only lasting functional specialization in wasp workers is egg laying (Verlaine, 1932a), a function assumed by the most active workers (Pardi, 1948). Some workers are slow to shift from one type of activity to another, others characteristically shift more readily as conditions change. As Verlaine (1932a) observed for wasps, persistence in a given kind of activity may be a matter of a specific (stereotyped) learning, which opposes variation. In vespine colonies, according to Gaul (1948), the distribution of brood nursing, water collecting, foraging, and other functions differs from day to day, although the labor division remains fairly constant in any given day. The same individuals may remain at the same task for an entire day and often longer. Adlerz (see Kiil, 1934), and Fielde (1901) observed that ants of certain species used individually characteristic routes over considerable times, and in Schneirla's (1929, 1933c) maze experiments individual *Formica* workers completed as many as 100 closely consecutive runs through a complex situation. Combes (1935, 1937) found that workers of camponotine species may be individually engaged in particular types of nest function over periods ranging from one to several days. However, within the nest the same ant may be observed from time to time engaged in different functions (Buckingham, 1910; Chen, 1937).

A relative specialization of individual function is notable in foraging. Individual honey bees usually confine their flights to a relatively small foraging zone and one type of flower for a considerable period (von Frisch, 1948). This is also observable in the foraging of ants (Brun, 1914; Kiil, 1934); for example, in *Lasius niger,* the same individual worker may be found in regular attendance upon a given aphid colony for days at a time (Eidmann, 1927, Kiil, 1934). Such specializations are, of course, subject to change, and depend upon temporary physiological state, external circumstances, food supply, and nest condition. Habituation and learning may play important parts here. It is probable that in all social insects there are individual differences in the readiness and the frequency with which workers in the populations shift their function, and in the relative effectiveness of their contributions to colony life.

INDIVIDUAL AND GROUP IN INSECT SOCIETY

General Effects of Group Situation

The group setting is an essential environment for all social insects, for two reasons especially (Wheeler, 1928; Bodenheimer, 1937; Allee, 1938; Grassé, 1946). One basic group effect is due to the creation of a modified physicochemical medium by a collective population. The nest situation itself, together with the presence of nest mates, may be essential for the individual's primary physical welfare. Ants re-excavate a new nest in the disturbed soil of the old one more readily than in new soil. In many species of termites the workers die promptly when they lack the intestinal Protozoa obtainable in the collective situation. Isolated honey bees soon die, and large groups survive longer than very small groups, as with many ants and termites (Grassé and Chauvin, 1942). Such effects depend partially upon the physiological consequences of trophallactic interchange (e.g., "social hormones"). However, in *Stigmatomma* spp. and certain other ponerine ants in which colony unity is low and trophallactic relationships are minimal, isolated workers survive very successfully over long intervals if adequately fed (Haskins, 1939).

Problem of Specific Relationships

With the habituated nest environment as a basis for colony unity, stimulative interchanges in the colony are effective in facilitating and coordinating group functions. Such processes have been considered in connection with the subjects of communication and trophallaxis. Inter-individual stimulative relationships exist which may be generalized or specific according to circumstances. Francfort (1945) observed that small isolated groups of three or four *Lasius emarginatus* workers were relatively sluggish in digging and brood tending, but when their compartment was set next to a similar box containing a normally functioning colony of their species, with only a gauze partition between, the workers in the small group behaved more like workers in a normal colony. Since this result was not obtained if the partition was glass, the effect seems attributable to odor. In Chen's (1937) investigation with *Camponotus* workers, reaction time in starting to dig was shorter and more soil was dug by ants in a group than by isolated individuals. Slower workers were more influenced by the presence of other workers than were "leaders." The results show that *two* associates somehow had a greater effect upon an individual's digging than *more than two*. Such studies merit continuation on an analytical level, with attention to the kind of function performed.

The nature of the individual's contribution to group coordination, and the way the individual is drawn into group function, are not well known. The temptation to lapse into anthropomorphism is always strong (e.g., "helpfulness"; Lafleur, 1940). Hingston (1929) adopts the view of Herbert Spencer that ants summon help from nest mates and cooperate deliberately, although simpler explanations for effective cooperation are available (Wheeler, 1910b; Eidmann, 1927; Goetsch, 1934). When numerous ants jointly pull a large piece of food toward the nest, the act is not purposefully cooperative but results from their independent responses to sensory cues established for the homegoing journey (Cornetz, 1912). Although workers may arouse others in the colony in various ways, the results of careful studies do not suggest that the arousal is codified as an appeal for help (Rabaud, 1934; Goetsch, 1934; Grassé, 1939). Social insects are ordinarily responsive to tactual, chemical, and other stimulative effects presented by nest mates, but the effect (although frequently complex) apparently accounts for joint action not through an intentional communication of "knowledge" but through an *arousal* accompanied by *incidental orienting effects*. Use of the term "leaders" (e.g., Chen, 1937) for those individuals with the greatest influence upon particular group functions misrepresents the nature of the individual's role in group cooperative activity. The leading worker often functions as an "excitement center" (Morley, 1946a) through which other ants are aroused and presented with incidentally directive stimuli (Schneirla, 1941). Although individual effects upon insect groups are varied and often complex, there is no valid reason to believe that they include a planful or symbolic direction of cooperative effort in the human sense.

SOME COLLECTIVE FUNCTIONS IN INSECTS

Nest Building as a Group Function

The social insects make their nests in the earth, on the surface, and in trees, achieving with many types of materials an impressive variety of patterns (Maidl, 1934). The nests of bees are usually made in cavities; those of wasps are commonly fabricated from a paper of chewed wood pulp; termites excavate in soil or wood, and many are capable of agglutinating together (with fecal fluid, saliva, or both) particles of soil or detritus into special structures; ants present a wide range in burrowing or in constructing special structures. Whether the nest is accommodated to a cavity or is completely assembled by the insects, the nest typically represents the labors of a large part of the community.

As a rule the pattern of nest constructed is characteristic of the species. In species of the wasp subfamily Polistinae, the colonies typically construct of "paper" a single naked comb suspended from a pedicel; whereas colonies of vespine species typically make of similar material a series of vertically superimposed combs enclosed within a paper envelope, with a flight hole at the bottom (Janet, 1903; Maidl, 1934). In termites, which make their nests of agglutinated materials, striking differences are found, represented by a contrast between the earth carton nests constructed by the species of *Nasutitermes* and the large, mushroom-shaped termitaria constructed of agglutinated soil by species of *Cubitermes* (Emerson, 1938). Among ants, characteristic differences between even closely related species (Gösswald, 1942; Talbot, 1948) in the ecological situation, material, and general shape, as well as in the internal organization of nests, suggest the predominant influences of genetic factors upon collective behavior in nest building.

Emerson (1938) holds that, since the nest of an insect colony results from the collective activity of a large number of workers, it may be considered a morphological expression of the population behavior pattern, in a sense expressing the genetics of the species. Typical worker responses to environmental conditions such as light direction, temperature, rainfall, and humidity may be expressed both in the general location of the nest and its shape (Freisling, 1939; Gregg, 1947), as in the north-south orientation of the spire-shaped nests of many tropical termites (Escherich, 1909; Emerson, 1938) and the shape and tilt of the mound constructed by many ants (Andrews, 1927; Maidl, 1934). More evidence is needed concerning what environmental conditions are influential in nest location and nest making, and their effect upon individual and group behavior at various stages of construction.

The complexity of the architectural results achieved by social insects has led some writers (e.g., Escherich, 1911) to entertain the notion that a common idea or plan must dominate the workers, and others (e.g., Wasmann, 1899) to invoke a system of language symbols. Such presumptive anthropomorphic concepts generally are not indulged in by careful students of the phenomena (Emerson, 1938; Grassé, 1939). However, impressive results are achieved collectively, and the specific nature of collusion among individuals is not at all easy to grasp. For example, Chen's (1937) results disclose interindividual stimulative effects, but in quantitative and not specific qualitative terms. From his studies on nest construction in wasps, Rabaud (1937) was led to minimize direct and specific collective effects of worker upon worker, and to conclude that the nest is an indirect result of the interattraction that groups independently working individuals. Freisling (1939) also emphasized independence in function. This view seems largely adequate to characterize the initial stage of nest-building labors in which workers function more or less separately (e.g., with each ant digging in a separate place). However, it falls short of accounting for the further stages in which qualitatively differentiated results emerge through more concentrated activity in certain places, and for the eventual emergence of an architecturally distinctive result (Grassé, 1939).

In observing the nest-excavation activities of ants, one is impressed by the manner in which an initial conglomeration of disparate individual activities gradually becomes narrowed down into obviously interrelated individual functions. Although individual differences generally exist, in that some workers are more persistently active in particular localities and in particular ways, these differences are relative, and in general each worker performs various types of tasks successively, in different places. It would appear that the individual worker at any time is "in touch with" only a limited part of the general situation to which she responds according to both its *physical* and its *social-stimulative* properties. These types of stimulative effect seem to fuse into a common pattern as the work proceeds, promoting more and more adequately organized interindividual relationships. In his study of nest reconstruction by termites, Grassé (1939) observed that, although there is no direct contact between neighboring groups of workers, building the apical T-branches of adjacent pillars around the royal cell somehow is accomplished. A limited (nonvisual) distance sensitivity with spatial properties is indicated. Such effects may be influential through mechanical and chemical gradient patterns rather than through the spatially and behaviorally more complex topochemical process of Forel (1908, 1929) postulated by Grassé as involved in this situation. Here a complex result is achieved through responses of workers to progressively different chemotactic situations as the structure develops.

Other Organized Activities in Insects

An important type of collective behavior in the insect colony involves temperature and humidity adjustment through the active responses of workers (Steiner, 1930). Honey bees cluster on the combs at temperatures below 15° C, and as we have seen any appreciable rise of hive temperature above 34° C is opposed by a wing-fanning reaction of workers. Thus conditions in the brood area remain fairly stable despite wide diurnal fluctuations in external temperature (Armbruster, 1922a; Dunham, 1931). In certain species of *Polistes* (Steiner, 1930; Rau, 1931; Weyrauch, 1936) and *Polybia* wasps (Schwarz, 1931), fanning occurs in the brood area when the nest becomes overheated, and in addition the workers apply water to the nest envelope. These responses may prove to be essentially direct and relatively independent reactions of individual workers to atmospheric conditions, simple in organization although high in adaptive value.

The most complex collective behavior occurring regularly in insects outside the nests takes place in the raids of certain camponotine ants and in the predatory forays of doryline species (Schneirla, 1940). So impressively complex and effective are the maneuvers in these mass forays that Wroughton (1892) was led to say that they occurred "as if by word of command," and Belt (1874) termed the white-headed major workers of *Eciton* "officers" with the implication that they must exert some important control over operations.

However, a systematic investigation of the development and operation of the great daily swarm raids of the Central American species *Eciton burchelli* has shown that, although complexly organized, these collective functions occur on a relatively low psychological level (Schneirla, 1940, 1941). Each individual behaves according to local circumstances affecting her at the time. Thus any ant may participate briefly in the broad basal "pressure" effect which mainly directionalizes the mass away from the temporary nest; she may next be drawn into one of the commissural columns that (through group chemotactic stimulative effects) serve to interrelate local operations in the swarm; next function as a "pioneer," making a short advance into new terrain; next become a raider pouncing upon some moving insect; and so on.

In the colonies of terrestrial *Eciton* species, which construct new temporary nests nightly through clustering their own bodies into patterned masses (Schneirla, 1933a), the role of organic, physical, and group-behavioral factors affecting individual reactions clearly differs according to the stage of operations. Each individual worker, upon arriving at the new nest site, meets one aspect of a distinctive physical and behavioral situation. She responds differently according to the prevalent circumstances, in a manner qualified by her organic makeup (i.e., caste) and condition of activity (e.g., whether larva- or booty-laden, or unladen). The eventual nest pattern consequently depends both upon the characteristics of the environmental situation and upon organic factors underlying species behavior.

These social patterns, appearing in insects very limited in their individual stimulus-response repertoires (Schneirla, 1944a), clearly illustrate how complex operations of high adaptive value may appear in psychologically simplified organisms in a collective behavior situation. As Emerson (1938) has said, social insects are capable of collective performances which often closely resemble the "intelligent" adjustments of the higher mammals. However, the resemblance seems to be a superficial one between functions which, in insects and in mammals, are basically very different although they may often be similar in their general outcome.

SUMMARY

Social insects maintain persistent groups based upon interdependence among individuals, in contrast to "associations" which lack interindividual organization. Insect societies evolved through selection of factors permitting a fertile female to remain with her brood, advancing with her fecundity and attractiveness to offspring. Male specialization and unisexual polymorphism contributed further. Efficiency of insect populations increased with physiological and behavioral capacities promoting environmental control, as in shelter making and foraging. Independent colony-foundation processes illustrate the efficacy and ontogenetic specialization of these factors.

Wheeler's trophallaxis concept characterizes processes arising through interindividual stimulative exchanges and attractions as in feeding and grooming, considered basic to colony unity. Species differ in colony cohesion according to capacities for trophallactic processes. Ontogeny centers around an individual socialization grounded particularly in species-characteristic organic processes promoting social regurgitation and food taking. Trophic variations introduced through colony behavior, with genetic and induced physiological factors, account for many specializations. A learned habituation to colony chemical underlies feeding adjustments and nest mate "recognition." Colony unity depends upon this factor as well as upon effective trophallactic relationships.

Insect communication develops through trophallactic processes, expanded into foraging. It involves a generalized arousal of nest mates as by a returning food-finder, typically through contact-chemical stimulation, often with qualitative directive effects as well. Degree of agitation of the finder determines extent of colony arousal and extent of response in foraging nest mates. Specific stimulative effects (e.g., olfactory) incidentally presented by the finder often influence nest mates qualitatively. Distance and orientation of aroused honey bees are somehow influenced by the finder's behavior in a specialized manner, still unexplained. Group cooperative phenomena such as nest building develop through initial responses given independently, followed by progressively more complex interindividual relationships based upon stimulative-gradient effects in situation and group. Insect group activities are frequently complex in nature and highly adaptive, but occur on a psychological level below that of mammalian social perception.

REFERENCES

Allee, W. C. 1938. *The social life of animals.* New York: W. W. Norton.
Alverdes, F. 1927. *Social life in the animal world.* New York: Harcourt, Brace.
Andrews, E. A. 1927. Ant mounds as to temperature and sunshine. *J. Morphol. Physiol.* 44: 1–20.
Armbruster, L. 1922a. Über den Wärmehaushalt im Bienenvolk. *Arch. Bienenkunde.* 4: 268–270.
Belt, T. 1874. *The naturalist in Nicaragua.* London: Murray.
Bequaert, J. 1922. Ants in their diverse relations to the plant world. *Bull. Am. Mus. Nat. Hist.* 45: 333–583.
Bethe, A. 1898. Dürfen wir den Ameisen und Bienen psychische Qualitäten zusschreiben? *Pflügers Arch. Ges. Physiol.* 70: 15–100.
Bodenheimer, F. S. 1937. Population problems of social insects. *Biol. Rev.* 12: 393–430.
Bonnier, G. 1906. Les abeilles n'exécutent—elles que des mouvements réflexes? *Année. Psychol.* 12: 25–33.
Brun, R. 1910. Zur Biologie und Psychologie von *Formica rufa* und anderen Ameisen. *Biol. Zentralbl.* 30: 524–528; 529–545.
Brun, R. 1912. Zur Psychologie due Künstlichen Allianzkolonien bei den Ameisen. *Biol. Zentralbl.* 32: 308–322.
Brun, R. 1914. *Die Raumorientierung der Ameisen und das Orientierungsproblem im Allgemeinen.* Jena: Fischer.
Buckingham, E. 1910. Division of labor among ants. *Proc. Am. Acad. Arts and Sci.* 46: 425–507.
Burrill, A. C. 1908. A slave-making foray of the shining Amazon (*Polyergus lucious* Mayr) *J.N.Y. Entomol. Soc.* 16: 144–151.
Burrill, A. C. 1910. How sanguinary ants change at will the direction of column in their forays (*F. sanguinea* Var.) *Bull. Wisconsin Nat. Hist. Soc.* 8: 123–131.
Castle, G. B. 1934b. Caste differentiation, *Zootermopis* (Isoptera). In C. A. Kefoid, ed., *Termites and termite control.* Berkeley, California: Univ. California Press. Chap. 24 (II). Pp. 292–310.
Chen, S. 1937. Social modification of the activity of ants in nest-building. *Physiol. Zool.* 10: 420–455.
Cleveland, L. R. 1923. Symbiosis between termites and their intestinal protozoa. *Proc. Nat. Acad. Sci. U.S.* 9: 424–428.
Cole, A. C. and J. W. Jones. 1948. A study of the weaver ant *Oecophylla smaragdina* (Fab). *Am. Midl. Nat.* 39: 641–651.
Combes, M. 1935. Observations d'après les quelles l'activité des fourmis serait le fair d'une minorité de travailleuses dans tous les groupements étudies. *Ann. Sci. Nat.* 18: 97–102.

Combes, M. 1937. Existence probable d'une elite non differenciée d'aspect, constituant les veritables auvrieres chez les Formica. *Comp. Rend. Acad. Sci. Paris* 204: 1674–1675.

Cornetz, V. 1912. "L'illusion de l'entraide chez la fourmi." *Rev. Idées* 15: 1–12.

Cumber, R. 1949. The biology of bumble-bees, with special reference to the production of the worker caste. *Trans. Roy. Entomol. Soc. London* 100: 1–45.

Deleurance, E. 1948. L'indépendence de l'état ovarien et de la fondation du nid chez *Polistes* (Hyménoptères-Vespides) *Comp. Rend. Acad. Sci. Paris* 226: 514–516.

Deleurance, E. 1948. Le comportement reproducteur est indépendant de la presence des ovaries chez *Polistes* (Hyménoptères Vespides). *Comp. Rend. Acad. Sci. Paris* 227: 866–867.

Demuth, G. S. 1921. Swarm control. *U.S. Dept. Agr. Farmers' Bull.* No. 1198.

Descy, A. 1925. La vie sociale chez les insectes. *Ann. Sci. Nat. Zool.* 7: 87–105.

Dethier, V. G. 1947a. *Chemical insect attractants and repellants.* Philadelphia: Blakiston.

Donisthorpe, H. S. 1927. *The guests of British ants.* London: Routledge.

Dropkin, V. H. 1941. Host specificity relations of termite protozoa. *Ecology* 22: 200–202.

Dunham, W. 1931. Hive temperatures for each hour of a day. *Ohio J. Sci.* 31: 181–188.

Eidmann, H. 1927. Die Sprache der Ameisen. *Rev. Zool. Russe* 7: 39–48.

Eidmann, H. 1928. Weitere Beobachtungen über die Koloniegründung Einheimischer Ameisen. *Z. Vergleich. Physiol.* 7: 39–55.

Eidmann, H. 1931. Die Koloniegrundung von *Lasius flavus* F. nebst Weiteren Untersuchungen über die Koloniegründung der Ameisen. *Biol. Zentralbl.* 51: 657–677.

Emerson, A. E. 1926. Development of a soldier of *Nasutitermes* (*constrictotermes*) *cavifrons* (Holmgren) and its phylogenetic significance. *Zoologica* 7: 69–100.

Emerson, A. E. 1929. Communication among termites. *Fourth Internat. Congr. Entomol.* Ithaca, New York. II. Trans. 722–727.

Emerson, A. E. 1938. Termite nests—a study of the phylogeny of behavior. *Ecol. Monogr.* 8: 247–284.

Emerson, A. E. 1939. Populations of social insects. *Ecol. Monogr.* 9: 287–300.

Emerson, A. E., and R. C. Simpson. 1929. Apparatus for the detection of substratum communication among termites. *Science* 69: 648–649.

Emery, C. 1909. Über den Ursprung der dulotischen, parasitischen und Myrmekophilen Ameisen. *Biol. Zentralbl.* 29: 352–362.

Emery, C. 1911. Beobachtungen und Versuche an *Polyergus rufescens*. *Biol. Zentralbl.* 31: 625–642.

Emery, C. 1915. Histoire d'une société expérimentale de *Polyergus rufescens*. *Rev. Suisse. Zool.* 23: 385–400.

Escherich, K. 1909. *Die Termiten Oder Weissen Ameisen.* Leipzig: Klinkhart.

Escherich, K. 1911. *Termitenleben auf Ceylon.* Jena: Fischer.

Fielde, A. 1901. A study of an ant. *Proc. Acad. Nat. Sci. Philadelphia* 53: 425–449.

Fielde, A. 1903. Artificial mixed nests of ants. *Biol. Bull.* 5: 320–325.

Flanders, S. E. 1946a. The mechanism of sex control in the honey bee. *J. Econ. Entomol.* 39: 379–380.

Flanders, S. E. 1946b. Control of sex and sex-limited polymorphism in the hymenoptera. *Quart. Rev. Biol.* 21: 135–143.

Forel, A. 1874. Les fourmis de la Suisse. *Zürich, Nuv. Mem. Soc. Helvetica Sci. Nat.* 26: 1–452.

Forel, A. 1898. La parabiose chez les fourmis. *Bull. Soc. Vaud. Sci. Nat. 4ᵉ S.* 34: 380–384.

Forel, A. 1908. *The senses of insects* (translation). London: Methuen.

Forel, A. 1921–1923. *Le monde social des fourmis.* Genève: Kundig.

Forel, A. 1929. *The social world of ants* (2 vols., translated by C. K. Ogden). New York: Boni.

Francfort, R. 1945. Quelques phénomènes illustrant l'influence de la four-milière sur les fourmis isolées. *Bull. Soc. Entomol. France* 50: 95–96.

Freisling, J. 1939. Die Bauinstinkte der Wespen (*Vespidae*). *Z. Tierpsychol.* 2: 81–98.

Frisch, K. von. 1920. Über die "Sprache" der Bienen. *Münch Med. Wochenschr.* 67: 556–569.

Frisch, K. von. 1921. Über die "Sprache" der Bienen. *Münch Med. Wochenschr.* 68: 509–511.

Frisch, K. von. 1922. Über die "Sprache" der Bienen. *Münch Med. Wochenschr.* 69: 781–782.

Frisch, K. von. 1923. *Über die "Sprache" der Bienen.* Jena: Fischer.

Frisch, K. von. 1946. Die Tänze der Bienen. *Öst. Zool. Z.* 1: 1–48.

Frisch, K. von. 1947. The dances of the honey bee. *Bull. Anim. Behav.* 5: 1–32.

Frisch, K. von. 1948. *Aus dem Leben der Bienen,* 4th ed. Wien: Springer-Verlag.

Frisch, K. von. 1949. Die Polarisation des Himmelslichtes als Orientierender Faktor bei den Tänzen der Bienen. *Experientia* 5: 142–148.

Frisch, K. von. 1950a. Die Sonne als Kompass in Leben der Bienen. *Experientia* 6: 210–221.

Frisch, K. von. 1950b. *Bees—their vision, chemical senses, and language.* Ithaca, New York: Cornell Univ. Press.

Frisch, K. von, and G. A. Rösch. 1926. Neue Versuche über die Bedeutung von Duftorgan und Pollenduft für die Verständigung im Bienenvolk. *Z. Vergleich. Physiol.* 4: 1–21.

Gaul, A. T. 1948. Additions to vespine biology. V. The distribution of labor in the colonies of hornets and yellow-jackets. *Bull. Brooklyn Entomol. Soc.* 43: 73–79.

Goetsch, W. 1934. Untersuchungen über die Zusammenarbeit in Ameisenstaat. *Z. Morphol. u. Ökol. Tiere* 28: 319–401.

Goetsch, W. 1937b. *Die Staaten der Ameisen.* Berlin: Springer.

Gösswald, K. 1942. Rassenstudien an der roten Waloameise *Formica rufa* L. auf Systematischer Ökologischer, Physiologischer und Biologischer Grundlage. *Z. Angew. Entomol.* 28: 62–124.

Grassé, P.-P. 1937. Reciterches sur la Systematique et La Biologie des Termites de l'Afrique Occidentale Française. *Ann. Soc. Entomol. France* 106: 1–100.

Grassé, P.-P. 1939. La reconstruction du nid et le travail collectif chez les termites supérieurs. *J. Psychol. Norm. Pathol.* 27: 370–396.

Grassé, P.-P. 1946. Societés animales et effet de groupe. *Experentia* 2: 77–82.

Grassé, P.-P., and R. Chauvin. 1946. L'effet de groupe et la survie des neutres dans les sociétés animales. *Rev. Sci. 82ᵉ Ann.* 7: 461–464.

Grassé, P.-P., and C. Noirot. 1945. La transmission des flagellés symbiotiques et les aliments des termites. *Bull. Biol. France et Belgique* 79: 273–292.

Gregg, R. E. 1947. Altitudinal indicators among the Formicidae. *Univ. Colorado Studies, Ser. D,* 2: 385–403.

Grout, R. A. 1949. *The hive and the honey-bee.* Hamilton, Illinois: Dadant and Sons.

Haskins, C. P. 1939. *Of ants and men.* New York: Prentice-Hall.

Haydek, M. H. 1943. Larvae food and development of castes in the honey bees. *J. Econ. Entomol.* 36: 778–792.

Hingston, R. W. G. 1929. *Instinct and intelligence.* New York: Macmillan.

Imms, A. D. 1931. *Social behavior in insects.* New York: Dial Press.

Janet, C. 1897. *Rapports des animaux myrmécophiles avec les fourmis.* (Note 14). Limoges: Ducortieux.

Janet, C. 1903. *Observations sur les Guêpes.* Paris: Carré et Naud.

Janet, C. 1904. Anatomie du Gaster de la *Myrmica rubra.* Paris: Carré et Naud.

Jones, C. R. 1929. Ants and their relations to aphids. *Colorado Exp. Sta. Bull.* 341: 1–96.

Kennedy, C. H. 1935. Definitions of the animal family and the animal society. *Sixth Congr. Internat. Entomol.* 1,2: 33–44.

Kiil, V. 1934. Untersuchungen über Arbeitsteilung bei Ameisen (*Formica rufa* L., *Camponotus herculeanus* L. and *C. ligniperda* Latr.) *Biol. Zentralbl.* 54: 114–146.

Kuwabara, M. 1948. Ueber die Regulation im Weisellosen Volke der Honigbiene (*Apis mellifica*), besonders die Bestimmung des neuen Weiisels. *J. Faculty Sci. Hokkaido Univ.,* Ser. VI, 9: 359–381.

Lafleur, L. J. Helpfulness in ants. *J. Comp. Psychol.* 30: 23–29.

Lee, J. 1939. Division of labor among the workers of the Asiatic carpenter ants. (*Camponotus japonicus* var. *Aterrimus*). *Peking Nat. Hist. Bull.* 13: 137–145.

Leonard, P. 1911. The honey ants of Point Loma. *Trans. San. Diego Soc. Nat. Hist.* 1: 85–113.

Lhoste, J. 1944. L'«Effet de Groupe» chez *Forficula auricularia* L. *Bull. Soc. Zool. France* 69: 97–105.

Light, S. F. 1934. The constitution and development of the termite colony. In

C. A. Kofoid, ed., *Termites and Termite Control.* Berkeley, California: Univ. California Press. Chap. 3.

Lindauer, M. 1948. Über die Einwirkung von Duft- und Geschmacksstoffen sowie anderer auf die Tänze der Bienen. *Z. Vergleich. Physiol.* 31: 348–412.

Lineburg, B. 1924. Growth and feeding of honey bee larvae. *U.S. Dept. Agr. Bull.* 1222: 25–37.

Lubbock, J. 1882. *Ants, bees, and wasps.* (Rev. Ed., 1932) New York: Appleton.

Lutz, F. E. 1929. Observations on leaf-cutting ants. *Am. Mus. Novitates* 388: 1–21.

Maidl, F. 1934. *Die Lebensgewohnheiten und Instinkte der Staatenbildenden Insekten.* Wien: F. Wagner.

Mathis, M. 1948. Colonies d'abeilles *Apis mellifica* var. *punica,* entretenant et Nourrissant plusieurs dizaines de reines, vierges et fecondées. *Comp. Rend. Acad. Sci. Paris* 226: 1925–1927.

McCook, H. C. 1882. *The honey ants of the Garden of the Gods, and the occident ants of the American plains.* Philadelphia: J. B. Lippincott.

Melander, A. L., and C. T. Brues. 1906. The chemical nature of some insect secretions. *Bull. Wisconsin Nat. Hist. Soc.* N.S. 4: 22–36.

Morley, B. D. W. 1942. Observations on the nest odours of ants. *Proc. Linn. Soc. London,* 154th Sess., pp. 109–114.

Neilsen, E. T. 1932. Sur les habitudes des Hyménoptères aculeates solitaires. *Entomol. Meddel.,* Copenhagen, 18: 1–57, 87–174.

Neilsen, E. T. 1933. Sur les habitudes des Hyménoptères aculeates solitaires. *Entomol. Meddel,* Copenhagen, 18: 259–336.

Nogueira-Neto, P. 1950. Bionomic notes on Meliponins. *Rev. Entomol.* 8: 305–367.

Oettingen-Spielberg, T. zu. 1949. Über das Wesen der Suchbienen. *Z. Vergleich. Physiol.* 31: 454–489.

Pardi, L. 1946. La "Dominazione" E Il Ciclo Ovarico Annuale iu *Polistes gallicus* (L.) *Boll. Instit. Entomol. Univ. Bologna* 15: 25–84.

Pardi, L. 1948. Dominance order in *Polistes* wasps. *Physiol. Zool.* 21: 1–13.

Patrizi, S. 1948. Contribuzioni alla Conoscenza Delle Formiche e dei Mirmecofili Dell' Africa Orientale. *Boll. Instit. Entomol Univ. Bologna* 17: 158–167.

Rabaud, É. 1934. Les Fourmis s'entr'aident-elles? *Bull. Soc. Entomol. France* 39: 153–155.

Rabaud, É. 1937. *Phénomène social et sociétés animales.* Paris: Alcan.

Rabaud, É. 1941. A Propos de L'hémaphrorrhée des Lépidoptères. *Bull. Soc. Entomol. France* 46: 72.

Rau, P. 1931. Additional experiments on the homing of carpenter and mining bees. *J. Comp. Psychol.* 12: 257–261.

Richard, G. 1951. *Le phototropisme du termite á Cou Jaune (Calotermes flavicollis* Fabr.) *et ses bases sensorielles.* Paris: Masson. Ser. A. 2359.

Rösch, G. A. 1925. Untersuchungen über die Arbeitsteilung im Bienenstaat. *Z. Vergleich. Physiol.* 2: 571–631.

Rösch, G. A. 1930. Untersuchungen über die Arbeitsteilung im Bienenstaat. 2. Die Tätigkeiten der Arbeitsbienen unter Experimentell Veränderten Bedingungen. *Z. Vergleich. Physiol.* 18: 474–480.

Roubaud, E. 1910. Sur la biologie des Synagris (Hymen) évolution de l'instinct chez les Guêpes solitaires. *Ann. Soc. Entomol. France* 79: 1–21.

Roubaud, E. 1916. Recherches Biologiques sur les Guêpes Solitaires et Sociales D'Afrique. *Ann. Sci. Nat. Zool.* 10: 1–160.

Santischi, F. 1930. Nouvelles expériences sur l'orientation des Tapinoma par sécrétions dromographiques. *Arch. Physiol.* 22: 348–351.

Schimmer, F. 1910. I. Wissenschaftliche Mitteilungen. 1. Über die Wasmannsche Hypothese des "Duldungsinstinktes" der Ameisen gegenüber Synöken Myrmekophilen. *Zool. Anz.* 36: 81–95.

Schneirla, T. C. 1929. Learning and orientation in ants. *Comp. Psychol. Monogr.* 6: 1–143.

Schneirla, T. C. 1933a. Studies on army ants in Panama. *J. Comp. Psychol.* 15: 267–299.

Schneirla, T. C. 1933b. Some important features of ant learning. *Z. Vergleich. Psychol.* 19: 439–452.

Schneirla, T. C. 1933c. Motivation and efficiency in ant learning. *J. Comp. Psychol.* 15: 243–266.

Schneirla, T. C. 1940. Further studies on the army-ant behavior pattern. *J. Comp. Psychol.* 29: 401–460.

Schneirla, T. C. 1941. Social organization in insects as related to individual function. *Psychol. Rev.* 48: 465–586.

Schneirla, T. C. 1944a. A unique case of circular milling in ants, considered in relation to trail following and the general problem of orientation. *Am. Mus. Novitates* 1253: 1–26.

Schneirla, T. C. 1946. Ant learning as a problem in comparative psychology. In P. L. Harriman, ed., *Twentieth Century Psychology.* New York: Philos. Library. Pp. 306–316.

Schwarz, F. F. 1931. The nest habits of the Diplopterous wasp *Polybia occidentalis* variety *Scutellaris* (white) as observed at Barro Colorado, Canal Zone. *Am. Mus. Novitates* 471: 1–27.

Sendler, O. 1940. Vorgänge aus Bienenleben vom Standpunte der Entwicklungsphysiologie. *Z. Wiss. Zool.* 153: 39–82.

Sladen, F. W. L. 1902. A scent-producing organ in the abdomen of the worker of *Apis mellifica. Entomol. Monthly Mag.* 38: 208–211.

Snell, G. D. 1932. The role of male parthenogenesis in the evolution of the social Hymenoptera. *Am. Nat.* 66: 381–384.

Steiner, A. 1930. Die Temperaturregulierung im Nest der Feldwespe (*Polistes gallica* var. *Biglumis* L.). *Z. Verlgeich. Physiol.* 11: 461–502.

Steiner, A. 1932. Die Temperaturregulierung im Nest der Feldwespe, *Polistes gallica* var. *Biglumis* L. *Z. Vergleich. Physiol.* 17: 101–152.

Stumper, R. 1922. Quantitative Ameisenbiologie. *Biol. Zentralbl.* 42: 435.

Stumper, R., and H. Kutter. 1950. Sur le stade ultime du parasitisme social chez les Fourmis, atteint par *Teleutomyrmex schneideri. Comp. Rend. Acad. Sci. Paris* 231: 876–879.

Talbot, M. 1948. A comparison of two ants of the genus *Formica*. *Ecology* 29: 316–325.

Talbot, M., and C. H. Kennedy. 1940. The slave-making ant *Formica Sanguinea subintegra* Emery, its raids, nuptual flights and nest structure. *Entomol. Soc. Am.* 33: 560–577.

Verlaine, L. 1932a. L'Instinct et l'intelligence chez les Hyménoptères. XVIII. La spécialisation et le divison du travail chez les Guêpes. *Bull. Soc. Roy. Sci. Liége,* pp. 186–191.

Wasmann, E. 1891. Die Zusammengesetzten Nesten und Gemischten Kolonen der Ameisen. Münster: Aschen Buchdruck.

Wasmann, E. 1899. Die Psychischen Fahigkeiten der Ameisen. *Zoologica* 11(26): 133.

Wasmann, E. 1910. Über das Wesen und den Ursprung der Symphilie. *Biol. Zentralbl.* 30: 97–102, 129–138, 161–181.

Wasmann, E. 1915. Neue Beiträge zur Biologie von *Lomechusa* und *Atemeles,* mit kritischen Bemerkungen über das echte Gastverhäitnis. *Z. Wiss. Zool.* 114: 233–402.

Wesson, L. 1940. An experimental study of caste determination in ants. *Psyche* 45: 105–111.

Weyrauch, W. K. 1936. Das Verhalten sozialer Wespen bei Nestüberhitzung. *Z. Vergleich. Physiol.* 23: 51–63.

Wheeler, W. M. 1903. Ethological observations on an American ant (*Leptothorax emersonian* Wheeler). *J. Psychol. Neurol.* 2: 1–31.

Wheeler, W. M. 1906. The queen ant as a psychological study. *Popular Sci. Monthly* 48: 291–299.

Wheeler, W. M. 1910b. *Ants, their structure, development and behavior.* New York: Columbia Univ. Press.

Wheeler, W. M. 1918. A study of some ant larvae with a consideration of the origin and meaning of the social habit among insects. *Proc. Am. Phil. Soc.* 57: 293–343.

Wheeler, W. M. 1921. A new case of parabiosis and the "Ant Gardens" of British Guiana. *Ecology* 2: 89–103.

Wheeler, W. M. 1923. *Social life among the insects.* New York: Harcourt, Brace.

Wheeler, W. M. 1928. *The social insects.* New York: Harcourt, Brace.

Wheeler, W. M. 1933. *Colony-founding among ants.* Cambridge: Harvard Univ. Press.

Wroughton, R. C. 1892. Our ants. *J. Bombay Nat. Hist. Soc.* Part II. 1–29.

T. C. SCHNEIRLA

Theoretical Consideration of
Cyclic Processes in Doryline Ants[1]

Bibliography No. 81

Predatory expeditions and colony movements are traditionally well known for the ant subfamily Dorylinae.[2] But until recently, changes of nest site in the colonies of these ants were described as sporadic and irregular, somehow enforced on a nutritive basis. Both Heape (1931) and Fraenkel (1932), reviewing the earlier evidence, classified the driver and army ants as irregular emigrants rather than migrants, as the colonies were presumed to undertake changes of nesting site only when booty had been cleared from an occupied area. This conception proves to be wrong (Schneirla, 1946).

Recent investigations (Schneirla, 1933, 1938, 1949; Raignier and Van Boven, 1955) show that emigrations in these ants occur in periodicities

From *Proceedings* of the American Philosophical Society, 101(1): 106–133 (February 1957). Reprinted with permission.

[1] It is a pleasure to acknowledge the following sources of support for the research from which this paper derives. Early stages were made possible by grants-in-aid from the National Research Council, the American Philosophical Society, and the National Academy of Sciences. At later stages, laboratory studies of preserved material have been assisted under grants from the National Science Foundation and from the Committee for Research in Problems of Sex, National Research Council. Field and laboratory research was principally supported in the period 1948 to 1954 by contracts between the Biological Sciences Division, Office of Naval Research, U.S. Navy, and the American Museum of Natural History, and by grants from the Council Research Fund of this Museum.

Evidence of great value to this investigation has been made available by Dr. Harold Hagan, Professor Emeritus of Biology, City College of New York, and by Dr. Roy Whelden, Haskins Laboratory, Union College, from histological and cytological studies carried out by them on preserved Eciton queens and other material collected by us in the field.

It is also a pleasure to acknowledge the efficient assistance of Drs. Eleanor Lappano, now Research Assistant at the Rockefeller Institute, New York, and Dr. John Tafuri, now Assistant Professor of Biology at Xavier College, Cincinnati, Ohio, particularly in the study of larval development in *Eciton*.

[2] In the cosmopolitan ant subfamily Dorylinae (see Forel, 1891; Emery, 1885, 1910; Wheeler, 1910, 1922) are included two tribes of particular interest to this paper, tr. *Dorylini* Forel of the Old World and tr. *Ecitonini* Forel of the New World. In a recent taxonomic survey of the *Ecitonini,* Borgmeier (1955) has raised groups formerly designated as subgenera to generic rank as follows: genus *Eciton* (= subgenus *Eciton s.str.*), genus *Nomamyrmex* (*g.nov.*), genus *Labidus* (= subgenus *(E.) Labidus*) and genus *Neivamyrmex* (= subgenus *(E.) Acamatus*).

characteristic of species, through other than nutritive causes. My own investigations have centered around two species in the tropical American genus *Eciton,* known as "army ants." The functional pattern of these species, in all probability the most specialized in the subfamily, will be considered first, and a theory formulated which may throw light on conditions in other dorylines.

CYCLIC FUNCTION IN THE EPIGAEIC ECITONS

The Nomad-Statary Pattern

CONTRASTING ACTIVITY PHASES

The species *Eciton hamatum* and *E. burchelli* are among the few in the subfamily which may be termed *epigaeic,* in that they have evolved a dominantly terrestrial way of life. Their nesting, raiding, and emigrating occur mainly on or above the surface, in contrast to the more subterranean patterns otherwise predominant in the subfamily. In the tropics and subtropics of the world are hundreds of other species all more or less strongly hypogaeic, or subterranean, especially in their nesting activities, some largely or entirely subterranean in their predatory operations as well.

Eciton hamatum and *burchelli* present a striking regularity in all of their principal colony operations, clearly related in its evolutionary background to the physical conditions of surface life. Their functional pattern as a whole is cyclic, its predictable periodicity based upon rhythmic processes to be considered. Colony functions in these species center around two well-marked repetitive activity phases, as schematized in Figure 91. There is first a highly active phase, the *nomadic,* in which successive large daily raids occur, each ending in an emigration at the day's end. Each successive temporary nest or bivouac established in this phase is on or above the surface of the forest floor and largely exposed except for a natural ceiling such as the undersurface of a log from which it hangs to the ground (Schneirla et al., 1954).

There follows an interval of greatly reduced activity and relatively sessile existence in the colony, the *statary* phase, in which raids are much smaller, and on some days absent. The colony now remains at the same nesting site, usually in a well-sheltered place as inside a hollow tree or log, without emigrating. In these species, the behavioral and functional properties of this phase are clearly distinguished from those of the nomadic phase.

In *Eciton* colonies these two phases recur in regular alternation throughout the year. This fact has been established both through long-continued studies of single colonies at various times of year and through the com-

808

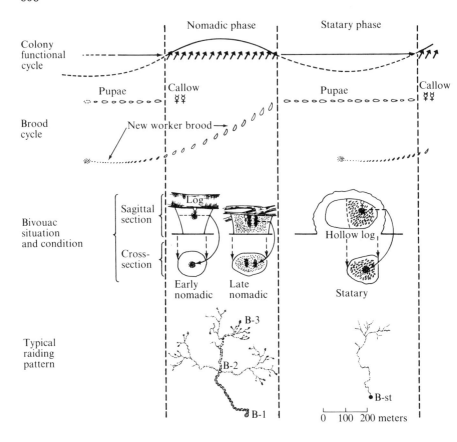

FIGURE 91

Schema representing concurrent events in the nomadic and statary phases of the Eciton functional cycle, based on *Eciton hamatum*.

Colony functional cycle. Crest of sine wave, nomadic phase: arrows represent large daily raids, ending in nightly emigrations. Trough of sine wave, statary phase: line represents reduced raiding, absence of emigration.

Brood cycle. One complete brood series is represented, from left—eggs, larvae, and enclosed pre-pupal and pupal stages, to newly emerged callow workers at right.

Bivouac. At left, exposed bivouac cluster of the nomadic phase, suggesting principal changes in brood distribution; at right, sheltered bivouac of the statary phase, suggesting new brood as egg mass centered below queen, advanced brood as enclosed pupae.

Raiding pattern. Left, three-system column raid of the nomadic phase, developed from the bivouac at B-2; previous night's emigration line, B-1 to B-2; emigration line after current raid ends, B-2 to B-3. Right, single-system column raid of the statary phase, from the fixed bivouac site B-st.

TABLE 1
Duration of phases (all-worker broods only) in the functional cycles of two Eciton species observed at different times of year (1932–1952).

	E. hamatum								E. burchelli							
	Rainy season				Dry season				Rainy season				Dry season			
	Nomadic		Statary		Nomadic		Statary		Nomadic		Statary		Nomadic		Statary	
	Cases	Days	Cases	Days	Cases	Days	Cases	Days	Cases	Days	Cases	Days	Cases	Days	Cases	Days
	5	16	1	18	4	16	1	18	1	11	1	19	1	13	2	19
	6	17	3	19	7	17	2	19	1	12	1	21	1	15	6	20
	4	18	9	20	2	18	11	20	1	13	2	22	2	16	7	21
							11	21	1	15			2	17	2	22
							1	22								
Average	16.9		19.6		16.8		20.3		12.8		21		15.7		20.5	
Range	16–18		19–20		16–18		18–22		11–15		19–22		13–17		19–22	

parative study of numerous colonies over shorter periods of time (Schneirla, 1949). As Table 1 shows, the phase durations are highly predictable according to species. The average duration of the nomadic phase is seventeen days for *hamatum,* with a year-around range of just three days, but for *burchelli* this phase is shorter and more variable. No seasonal difference is indicated for *hamatum,* but for *burchelli* this phase tends to be longer in the dry season. The two species are more alike in the duration of the statary phase, which is uniformly longer in both than is the nomadic phase.

COLONY BEHAVIOR AND BROOD CONDITION

Predictability of phase durations in these species indicates a basis in regular events affecting the colonies. Investigation shows that in all colonies each of these phases begins and ends in close correspondence with certain major changes in the condition of the great broods always present in the colonies (op. cit.). For most of the year, only all-worker broods are present; however, the relationship holds also for the exceptional sexual brood (Schneirla, 1948; Schneirla and Brown, 1950). Evidence on colony behavior and brood development demonstrates (Schneirla, 1938, 1949) that not only the regular colony functional cycle but survival of the colony itself in these ants is based upon the concurrence of these conditions.

Eciton all-worker broods occur in distinctive successive generations, each with 50,000 individuals or more in *E. hamatum,* 120,000 or more in *burchelli.* As Figure 91 shows, at the start of each nomadic phase a brood of mature pupae emerges from cocoons as young adults, and during this phase a further brood passes through its larval stage, reaching larval maturity at the end of the phase. As this current brood undergoes its prepupal and pupal development (enclosed within cocoons) in the following statary phase, a new brood appears as eggs laid midway in the phase. New broods are produced at intervals of 35–37 days in *hamatum,* 32–37 days in *burchelli,* the durations of the cycle in the two species, respectively. These events continue, year around, through the life of the colony without any break in the repetition of the cyclic changes.

Colony function reaches its highest level of intensity in the nomadic phase when active brood stages are present, its lowest in the statary phase when the brood is relatively quiescent. This difference in activity level is most prominently expressed in terms of a difference in the daily mass forays or raids. Raiding, carried out on chemical trails developed each day, differs radically in strength in the two phases. In *E. hamatum,* the typical nomadic-phase pattern of three large treelike systems of raiding trails (with terminal groups of pillaging workers) contrasts sharply with the single trail system usual in the statary phase (Figure 91). Systematic

TABLE 2

Concurrent daily traffic counts of raids in three colonies of Eciton hamatum
(records taken near bivouac between 10:30 A.M. *and noon*).

Colony and phase	Number of days	Outgoing traffic (Ants/min)		Incoming traffic (Ants/min)		Incoming, laden (Ants/min)	
		Range	Average	Range	Average	Range	Average
'52 H-C [a]							
Nomadic	12	65–242	130	27–171	106	27–166	80
Statary [b]	11	0–143	58	0–147	43	0– 86	27
'52 H-O							
Nomadic	11	26–122	60	14– 80	50	2– 60	27
Statary [b]	6	0– 58	15	0– 28	12	0– 26	8
'49 H-35							
Nomadic	8	24–109	61	19–146	67	15–126	55
Statary [b]	17	0– 92	28	0– 74	26	0– 54	20

[a] Colony '52 H-C was much larger than either of the other two colonies.
[b] Occasional statary days without raiding. (See Table 4.)

traffic counts for three colonies of this species, taken daily, gave the results in Table 2. Within the ninety minutes before noon, when raiding traffic as a rule reaches its peak in the statary phase, both outgoing and incoming traffic are more than twice as great during the nomadic phase as in the statary phase. The estimated ratio of three to one seems closer to actuality, as nomadic-phase raids reach their peak output before midmorning as a rule; also, days without raids are not uncommon in the statary phase, especially in the dry season.

As mentioned, both Heape (1931) and Fraenkel (1932) relegated the doryline ants to the class of sporadic emigrants rather than migrants, on the assumption of Vosseler (1905) that colony movements somehow occur in response to exhaustion of food in the nesting locality. This assumption is contradicted by the evidence for Eciton raiding in relation to the occurrence of emigration (Schneirla, 1938, 1944b, 1945).[3] Raignier and

---

[3] There are good reasons for considering their pattern of cyclic series of displacements, alternating with resting phases, as a case of migration (Schneirla, 1945). One important reason is that the colony movements have their basis in reproductive processes, an important condition of migration in general (Marshall, 1936). The separate nightly bivouac-change movements may be termed *emigrations* and regarded as contributing to *a migration:* the total displacement involved in the series of movements of one nomadic phase. Through these successive emigrations the colony regularly changes its ecological situation from that characteristic of the nomadic phase to that of the statary phase (Schneirla *et al.,* 1954), a reversal somewhat comparable to the vertical migrations whereby certain tropical birds in mountainous areas reverse their ecological situation with seasonal regularity.

Van Boven (1955) reached a similar conclusion from their study of African dorylines. Whatever role local food supply may have played in the evolution of nomadism in these ants, the determination of emigrations in the existing behavioral system has a different basis.

RECIPROCAL STIMULATIVE PROCESSES IN SOCIAL FUNCTION

The fact is that in these *Eciton* species an emigration can occur only as an outcome of a large raid, and that statary-phase raids are insufficiently developed to produce this result (Schneirla, 1938, 1944b). The differential is provided by stimulation from active brood. First, callow workers are very attractive and excitatory to adults. From the moment these new workers emerge from their cocoons they are feverishly licked and groomed, and their almost incessant movements are powerfully stimulative to the older workers of the colony. Second, the more advanced larvae are very attractive and excitatory to workers, who lick, stroke, and handle them incessantly. Adult workers evidently derive a variety of tactual and chemotactic stimuli as well as secretory products from active brood at both of these stages, which always occur in the nomadic phase of colony function. In contrast, in the statary phase the brood, cocoon-enclosed and passing through the quiescent prepupal and pupal stages, lacks potency in this respect. The cocoons, held in place or heaped in the bivouac interior, often seem to have a quieting effect upon the workers. Laboratory tests show that workers from a nomadic colony are more excitable and reactive than are those from a statary colony.

Excitatory effects based on individual associations with brood usually do not stop with the stimulated worker herself but are transmitted widely through the colony, permutated and increased through a variety of worker interactions. Through interindividual stimulative relations normal to colony communication, colony excitation is maintained at a high level, as long as an active brood is present. Active brood (callows, larvae, or both) is the necessary energizing source of high excitation in a nomadic colony, and brood excitation may be broadly represented as a massive energizing effect essential to nomadic colony functions such as raiding and emigration. In this sense the stimulative effects (tactual and chemotactic) are expressible as a summated quantitative value differing according to brood condition at each point in the functional period. The results of our investigations bearing upon these considerations are expressed as an empirical curve in Figure 92, in which each of the postulated intracolony energizing factors is represented quantitatively in its estimated contribution at different stages of the functional cycle, in relation to the theoretical level of arousal essential for emigration, or the "emigration threshold."

This view of the stimulative process is based upon observational and

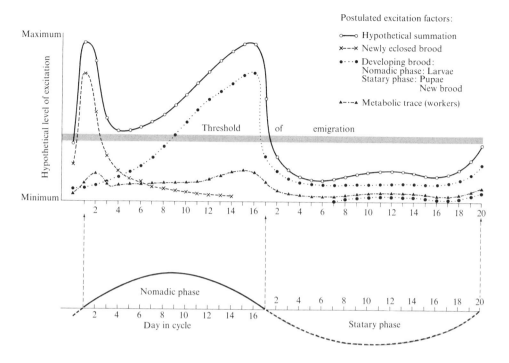

FIGURE 92

Schema of the principal social-excitation factors (top) underlying the Eciton functional cycle (sine curve bottom). Excitation-factor curve in upper figure represents empirically based judgments of the total stimulative effects of the respective factors at successive stages in the cycle (see text). The level of colony excitation as represented is based upon both observed and quantified variations in the raiding output.

laboratory studies with adults in relation to brood at various stages during the two phases of the cycle. Even casual observation shows that the stimulative processes are not always unilateral, but are often reciprocal as between active brood and workers, and at certain times even as between enclosed brood and workers. In this general respect the Ecitons resemble other ants, for which Wheeler (1928) characterized the reciprocal relationship as "trophallaxis," or the exchange of food. Processes characterized by this term were held by Wheeler, on general consideration, as basic to colony organization and unity in the social insects.

The army ants offer in detail a striking support of the *trophallaxis* theory of colony function and unity, *if* the theory is extended beyond the specific implications of Wheeler's concept (Schneirla, 1952; LeMasne, 1953). True, the transfer of nutrient substances and other organic products is common in the Ecitons (Wheeler and Bailey, 1920; Wheeler, 1928): excited workers dump booty on larvae or larvae on booty, workers obtain cuticular secretions and the like through licking larvae or callows, and so on. These biochemical gains are no doubt contributive to and essential to brood development as well as to colony health and normal function. However, adult-brood relationships go beyond nutritive gains as such to include a variety of stimulative effects in the olfactory, gustatory, and tactual modalities. Workers become excited when passing close to larvae (even when separated by a gauze screen), and larvae also when workers are close, indicating olfactory arousal. A comparable arousal on a tactual basis is evidenced by the manner in which artificial stimulation of larvae to their characteristic anterior writhing motions stirs nearby adults to begin or to increase action. The incidental touching of larvae by passing workers has equivalent effects.

The definition of "trophallaxis" consequently must be extended from the effects of exchange of nutrient as such to the many and varied ways in which specific stimulation independent of nutrient gains arouses or increases action or serves to facilitate physiological processes in the colony. The dissemination of stimulative effects is indispensable for the normal function, organization, and unity of the colony. In these processes, nutrient gains although important constitute only a part of the functional pattern, a sustaining by-product in a sense, as concerns arousal and maintenance at high intensity of large-scale worker functions.

Our findings indicate that for the extrabivouac functions of raiding and emigration, the aggregate of stimulative effects from brood may be considered the major factor determining the level of colony behavior at any point in the cycle. The brood-energizing factor is therefore held to be the *necessary* factor for nomadic behavior and for propagation of the cyclic pattern itself (Schneirla, 1938, 1952). In these terms, normal behavior and function in the terrestrial *Eciton* colony may now be examined in further detail.

Analysis of the Eciton Nomad-Statary Cycle

BROOD-STIMULATIVE FACTORS IN NOMADISM

The callow-excitation factor initiating nomadism. The shift from nomadic to statary function is a striking one in both *Eciton hamatum* and *burchelli.* In a relatively lethargic condition one day, the colony next day stages a large raid and emigrates after dusk. This is the day on which as a rule removal from cocoons of all of the mature pupal brood is accomplished in *E. hamatum,* usually the major part but not all of the brood in *E. burchelli.* The bivouac then becomes the scene of intense and growing excitement. The newly emerged callow workers are persistently active, rushing about in an erratic and "nervous" manner, feeding voraciously in the hours following eclosion. The workers are very responsive to these young adults, often running up and dropping morsels of booty among them (Wheeler and Bailey, 1920), stroking and licking their body surfaces. The level of general excitement in the population rises greatly over that of the preceding days, as is indicated for example by a noticeably increased responsiveness of the workers at dawn. This external stimulus, reaching a community already well aroused, excites the workers into a vigorous and rapidly growing exodus (Schneirla, 1938, 1940). The resulting raid, well above the statary level in excitement, numbers of participants, and in scope and complexity, exceeds the threshold essential for an emigration to occur as sequel.

The eclosion of a mature pupal brood, by releasing into the colony a relatively sudden, massive social stimulation, initiates a new nomadic phase in previously statary colonies of both *E. hamatum* (Schneirla, 1938) and *E. burchelli* (Schneirla, 1944b). The one difference is a secondary one already mentioned, namely, that in *E. hamatum* the pupal eclosion is nearly always completed throughout the brood on the first nomadic day, whereas in *burchelli* nomadism commonly begins with as much as one-third of the pupal brood (always the smallest members) still enclosed in cocoons. This difference suggests that the threshold of colony arousal essential to nomadic function may be expressed in terms of a critical ratio between the population of active brood and the population of adult workers.[4]

Although the nomadic phase invariably begins in an explosive manner in these species, as Figure 92 indicates, the excitatory callow-adult relationship responsible for the change persists at high intensity only for a few days. But in these epigaeic army ants, the nomadic phase persists well beyond this time to a predictable end. For its continuation, new causal agents seem necessary.

As may be seen in Table 1, the nomadic phase normally continues to a duration of 16–18 days in *E. hamatum* and 12–16 days in *E. burchelli*. But persistence of the nomadic condition through these species-typical intervals in the epigaeic Ecitons cannot be due to the effect of the callow-

---

[4] Both brood and adult population are much larger in [*Eciton*] *burchelli* colonies than in *hamatum*. The difference may depend upon a disproportionately greater communicative extension of the brood-excitation effect in a larger colony population than in a smaller one. This assumption is supported by the fact that in the rare cases of *E. hamatum* becoming nomadic prior to complete eclosion of the mature pupal brood, colonies of maximal size for the species are involved. Significantly, in the African driver ants, Raignier and Van Boven (1955) find that statary intervals are broken by emigration before more than a minor part of the great nymphal brood of the colony (always the largest individuals) is sufficiently mature for independent locomotion.

stimulative factor which initiates the phase. For in about 5 days after the phase begins, the callows have subsided markedly in the degree of excitement and variability of their behavior and in voraciousness; they now behave more and more like adult workers. As their integument darkens during this interval, the callows become more difficult to distinguish from adult workers, both in appearance and in behavior. Laboratory tests show that their stimulative effect upon adults tends to decrease sharply after the second post-eclosion day, and has reached a minimum after the fifth day (cf. Figure 92).

Excitatory factors in the transitional stage. But the colony does not therefore lapse to the low statary level of general excitation, either in extrabivouac or in intrabivouac activities. Worker populations maintain a condition of increased excitement even in the absence of further brood-excitation factors. Colonies in the field continue their initial nomadic excitement, although decreasingly, after brood other than callow types has been largely removed. Workers from nomadic colonies at this stage, held in laboratory nests without brood, remain more active for some days than groups of the same size taken from statary colonies.

On such grounds, a "metabolic trace" factor may be postulated in the worker population (Figure 92), persisting from the stage of intense callow excitation.[5] This condition, presumably a survival from the initial burst of brood-stimulative and associated nutritive gains, serves to prevent the worker population from lapsing to a state of low responsiveness and activity as external stimulation from callows falls sharply. It may be postulated as essential to the continuation of nomadism in terrestrial *Eciton* colonies, although not as the main factor.

Larval-excitation factor continuing nomadism. In contrast to the more hypogaeic dorylines, in the epigaeic Ecitons the larval brood now begins to function as a major source of stimulation promoting nomadism. In *E. hamatum* and *burchelli*, a new brood is produced roughly at five-week intervals, from eggs laid midway in the statary phase of the preceding cycle (see Figure 91). Figure 92 suggests how this brood enters as an essential factor in colony function. When nomadism begins, these larvae are diminutive, and as an aggregate (as compared with the callow brood) can have only a relatively minor trophallactic effect. At this stage the

---

[5] Such a factor seems frequently involved in insect behavior. As an example, Long (1955) found that mass feeding episodes in the caterpillars of *Pieris brassicae* and the extra stimulation furnished through summations of interindividual contacts in caterpillars of *Plusia gamma* induced a higher level of activity which could persist in solitary specimens. Comparably, through physiological trace effects of summated stimulative and trophic experiences in the colony situation, Eciton workers from a nomadic colony, when stimulus-tested individually or collectively in standard ways, prove more reactive than workers from a statary colony.

young brood is concentrated in a single mass near the center of the bivouac (Figure 91). Composed of eggs and microlarvae, this brood evidently then exerts a low stimulative effect on the colony, not communicated widely through the bivouac by the minim workers largely engaged in handling it.

At the fourth or fifth nomadic day as Figure 92 indicates, the stimulative effect of the larval brood has begun to accelerate. Its central position in the bivouac is now more extended, with larger larvae more marginal and attended by intermediate workers as well as minors. It is observed that larvae down into the intermediate sizes have begun to feed, a result paralleled by the histological finding (Lappano, 1955; Tafuri, 1956) that in brood samples at the fifth nomadic day, these larvae as well as the larger castes have functional salivary glands, still lacking in the smaller larvae (see Table 3). Test groups of workers in the laboratory given larvae from a colony in its *fifth* nomadic day become much more active than groups of equal size given equivalent numbers of larvae from a colony in its *second* nomadic day. But at this stage, when the larval brood has just begun to accelerate in growth rate, the cumulative excitatory effect of this brood upon workers is still relatively low.

In the interval between the second and sixth nomadic days, there are indications of a fall in the vigor of colony functions as in raiding. Nomadism then is most sensitively affected by artificial brood reductions or natural causes inhibiting colony functions (Schneirla and Brown, 1950). In the dry season, when environmental depressive effects are maximal, 69 days recorded in the continuous nomadic sequences of 9 colonies of *E. burchelli* involved subnormal raiding and failure to emigrate on 9 days, of which 7 were in the first 6 days of the nomadic phase, and 4 on the third day. A comparable susceptibility is seen in *E. hamatum* only when broods are reduced, as occurs naturally at colony division when callow and larval broods are divided between two daughter colonies (Schneirla, 1956). In the two daughter colonies of '48 H-27, the first 9 days of a nomadic phase were recorded before the study had to terminate. There were 4 days with subnormal raids and no emigration, all between days 2 and 5 of the phase, and each colony failed to raid or move on the third day; thereafter, in each daughter colony, function increased steadily in vigor to the normal level.

The interpretation is that normally, between the second and sixth nomadic days, the worker population falls from its initial high level of excitement to the lowest condition of the phase because the excitatory effect of the callow brood has fallen sharply and that of the larval brood has only begun to rise. For this interval, the summated effect of three indicated brood-excitatory factors is postulated for the maintenance of nomadic function in the colony. Although each of the three factors then seems to be

TABLE 3
Summary of Lappano's (1955) results on developmental characteristics of labial glands and time of appearance in the all-worker larval brood of Eciton burchelli.

Larval size category	Proliferation of posterior, basophilic portion [a]	Cells of posterior glandular portion increase in size, degree of vacuolization [a]	Lumen blocked posteriorly, absent anteriorly (2nd abdominal segment) [a]	Dense cytoplasm in posterior cuboidal cells; vacuolization irregular [b]	Disintegration in midsection proceeds posteriorly; products fill lumen [b]	Accumulation of acidophilic materials in lumen progresses anteriorly [b]
Largest (potential major workers)	Last statary, 1st nomadic day	3d nomadic day	5th nomadic day	8th nomadic day	10th nomadic day	10th nomadic day
Middle sizes (potential intermediate workers)	3d nomadic day	5th nomadic day	7th nomadic day	··········	11th nomadic day	11th nomadic day
Smallest (potential workers)	Mainly by 6th nomadic day	7th nomadic day	8th nomadic day	10th nomadic day	13th (last) nomadic day	13th (last) nomadic day

[a] Changes believed to indicate onset of capacity for salivary secretion in gland. These time values correspond closely to those established behaviorally for the onset of feeding in larvae: first in the largest, last in the smallest individuals of the series.
[b] Changes believed to indicate onset of spin-substance secretion in gland. Only after disintegration occurs in the blocked midregion of the gland can the acidophilic material (probable spinning fluid) pass anteriorly so that spinning may begin. Chronology of histological change here also corresponds in general to times at which spinning is observed to begin in the different larvae.

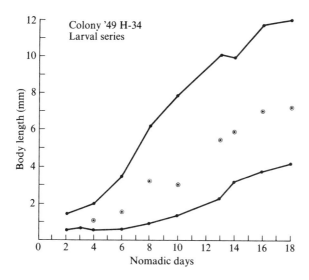

FIGURE 93
Increase in body length in the larval brood of a colony
of *Eciton hamatum* sampled (N = 50–100) at intervals
through a nomadic phase. Upper curve, body length
in mm of largest larvae (potential workers major) in the
successive samples; lower curve, body length in mm of
smallest larvae (potential workers minima) in the successive samples; intermediate points, average for each
sample.

at a low point in its strength, as Figure 92 suggests, their joint effect is
normally sufficient to raise colony excitation above the threshold essential
for nomadic function.

But after the first few nomadic days the larval brood exerts a clearly
increasing stimulative effect upon the adult population, evidently com-
mensurate with its acceleration in growth (Figure 93). This brood occupies an expanding central zone in the bivouac (Figure 91), its larger
members farther out toward the margin, its smaller members inward, in
proportion to size (Schneirla et al., 1954). As the phase wears on past its
midpoint, more and more of the intermediate and larger workers become
directly involved with the brood: licking, stroking or holding the larvae
individually in the bivouac, feeding them, or carrying them in the emigration. As this brood progresses toward maturity, the intensity of nomadic function, as indicated by increases in the vigor of raiding and extent
of emigration, mounts steadily to a climax.

Review: stimulative factors supporting nomadism. To take stock,
Figure 92 represents the estimated gross effects of the three principal so-

cial-stimulative factors postulated as essential for nomadic function in the epigaeic army ants. Factor 1, the *callow-brood effect,* is held to initiate the phase. Factor 2, the *metabolic traces* in the workers from excitatory and nutritive effects of active brood, is given a secondary role, yet evidently a critical one when other stimulative influences are at their lowest in the phase. In the epigaeic Ecitons, factor 3, the *larval stimulative factor,* is at first a minor agent but increases in its excitatory effect roughly in relation to developmental status of the brood. It is this factor, replacing the callow-brood effect as major stimulative agent, that is held responsible for sustaining colony function at a high level through a nomadic phase of predictable duration.

This phase and its termination as a sustained interval of nomadism seem unique to the Ecitons. In the last few days of the phase, larvae feed decreasingly as maturity approaches and spinning begins, first in the largest individuals and last in the smallest. Paralleling this behavior change, Lappano's histological studies summarized in Table 3 reveal in *Eciton* larvae a progressive atrophy of the basophilic salivary gland tissue associated with feeding, along with an increase in acidophilic secretory substance associated with spinning. These changes are readily identified at this time, the former beginning anteriorly in the tubular labial-gland complex, the latter beginning posteriorly and progressing anteriorly until it has displaced the atrophied salivary tissue. These changes, also, are identified first in the largest larvae or potential workers major, last in the smallest or potential workers minima. But, as mentioned, *although feeding drops off from the largest to the smallest members of the brood as spinning begins, the total excitatory effect of this brood on workers mounts steadily to the time when spinning predominates in the brood.*

Then, rather precisely when most of the larvae have become enclosed in their first filmy envelopes, there is an abrupt reduction in worker activities outside the nest, marked by smaller raids (Table 2) and no emigration. The nomadic phase then is ended through an abrupt fall in the level of brood-stimulative effects. On one day the colony is nomadic; next day, with the brood enclosed and much less excitatory to workers, the colony has become statary.

THE STATARY PHASE AS A SPECIFIC BEHAVIORAL CONDITION

The statary phase may be viewed as a condition in which the worker population has only a minimal stimulation from the brood. As long as the advanced brood is enclosed, with little more than the behavioral processes of the worker population alone to stimulate large-scale activities outside the bivouac, the threshold of raiding development essential for emigration is then never reached (Figure 92). Consequently, the statary phase nor-

TABLE 4

Frequency of raiding on the corresponding days of consecutive statary phase series in two Eciton *colonies of different species (Schneirla, 1949).*

E. hamatum, colony '46 H-B				E. burchelli, colony '46 B-I			
Sum for three successive statary phases				Sum for four successive statary phases			
Statary days	Days observed	Raids [a] observed	% days of raiding	Statary days	Days observed	Raids [b] observed	% days of raiding
1– 2	6	6	100	1– 3	11	11	100
3– 4	6	3	50				
5– 6	5	1	20	4– 6	12	8	66
7– 8	3	0	0				
9–10	4	2	50	7– 9	8	2	25
11–12	4	1	25				
13–14	4	1	25	10–12	9	4	44
15–16	5	4	80				
17–18	4	3	75	13–15	6	2	33
				16–18	8	5	62
19–20	5	5	100	19–21	12	12	100

[a] Raids weak: days 5, 10, 16 (one each). Raid late in starting: days 10, 16 (one each). Raid started *artificially* after 2 P.M.: days 16, 17 (one each).
[b] Exceptionally weak: day 10 (2 raids). Raid morning only: days 10, 12 (one each). Raid afternoon only: days 6, 7, 15, 18 (one each).

mally persists until the enclosed brood has reached pupal maturity and eclosion, when a callow excitation effect of high intensity is introduced, adequate to initiate a new nomadic phase.

Eciton colonies are restricted to a low level of activity in their statary phases; however, behavior is by no means constant throughout. An appreciable variability is suggested by Table 4, in which are given the frequencies of raiding through consecutive statary phases in two *Eciton* colonies of different species. In both colonies, raids occurred daily in the first few and the last few days of the phase, but in the intervening days were reduced in frequency. Furthermore, parallel differences are found in the *vigor* of raiding, with the strongest statary forays almost always those of the first few and the last few days of the phase.

The greater frequency and strength of raids in the initial statary days may be attributed to the fact that the mature larval brood continues its cocoon-spinning activities for a few days after the statary phase has begun. Then, as laboratory tests show, the movements of the larvae within their cases excite the adult workers to greater activity, both in responding to the larvae and in general colony function. Significantly, spinning always lasts a day or two longer in *E. burchelli* than in *E. hamatum,* and, as Table 4 indicates, a corresponding difference is found in the raiding.

A comparable effect of the brood on colony activity occurs in the last few days of the statary phase, when the pupal brood is nearly mature. Then, starting with the largest members, pigmentation begins and reflex activities of increasing intensity are noted, first in antennal funiculi and leg tarsae, then in the trunk as well. Tests show that not only tactual stimulation, but chemotactic effects also, are available to workers through these changes. In fact, the actual behavioral processes through which mature pupae are finally removed from their cocoons by workers arise through such stimuli, which cause the adults to pick up the cocoons, carry them about and tug at them with some excitement, thereby starting the openings which pupal struggles aid in enlarging (Schneirla, 1934).

The described variations in colony function in the course of a statary phase, attributable to relatively slight variations in the stimulative effect of an enclosed brood upon an adult population, further emphasize the need to reinterpret "trophallaxis" as *reciprocal stimulative processes.* It may be concluded that the major brood-stimulative factors we have found critical for setting off a nomadic phase (the callow-excitation effect) and for maintaining this phase to its conclusion (the larval-excitation effect) owe their energizing force not to what exchanges of nutrient substances may be involved but to the efficacy of stimulative processes affecting the level of colony behavior. Nutrient exchange may be considered a by-product, facilitative when present but not necessary to the brood-aroused communicative processes permutated into higher intensities in colony behavior.

ROLE OF THE QUEEN IN THE ECITON CYCLE

Regularity of reproductive processes.   Behind these events of the Eciton functional cycle stands the queen as the source of the massive broods appearing at regular intervals. As she is solely responsible for the egg series of each new brood, and as she produces these egg series at regular intervals, she is in this sense the pacemaker of the cycle (Schneirla, 1944a). This performance is formidable, involving as it does the delivery of a great series of eggs within a limited period of days about midway in each statary phase. In *E. hamatum* the queen lays more than 50,000 eggs at intervals of about 36–37 days, in *E. burchelli* she lays more than 120,000 eggs at intervals of 32–37 days. What timing mechanism controls this rhythm?

The hypothesis of a control strictly endogenous to the queen can be examined at present only by indirection. There is one striking indication that periodic ovulation in the Eciton queen is not a response to an internal "time clock." When a colony has its infrequent, usually annual sexual brood of males and fertile females, the interval between broods is shortened by nearly one week in both of the investigated species. This difference may be attributed to a more accelerated larval development of the sexual forms than with all-worker broods (Schneirla, 1948; Schneirla and Brown, 1952). But the queen's next egg brood is then delivered as usual, midway in the following statary phase, in time with the colony cycle although much earlier than a strictly endogenous control might have dictated. This suggests that the stimuli essential for oviposition are extrinsic to the queen, and come either from the physical environment or from within the colony situation.

Among conceivable extrinsic controls, none of the more obvious physical periodicities seems likely. First of all, neither of the two established *Eciton* species rhythms falls into step with the periods of any regular physical event such as lunar phases as Weber (1943) suggested. Also opposing a linkage controlled by such events is the fact that among a number of colonies operating in the same general area at any one time, no significant correlation of phases is found (Schneirla, 1949; Schneirla and Brown, 1950). The answer must lie somewhere within the functions of the *Eciton* colony itself.

Figure 94 shows an Eciton queen in the fully contracted condition, which prevails through most of the nomadic phase, and one in the physogastric condition with maximally enlarged gaster, normally invariable for these queens during the period midway in each statary phase. These conditions alternate regularly (Schneirla, 1944a), making it clear that a contracted queen is not necessarily a virgin or a young female, as was previously assumed (e.g., Wheeler, 1925; Borgmeier, 1933; Bruch, 1934). The time relations of the transition from one to the other of these conditions in the two species are indicated in Figures 95 and 96, in terms of the gaster length of queens measured at different stages in the functional cycle. It is clear that the condition of the functional queen in any epigaeic Eciton colony is *reversible* with respect to physogastry, and always predictable from colony behavior or from the condition of the developing broods present (cf. Figures 91 and 95, 96).

Conditions initiating physogastry. The histological studies of Hagan (1954) with queens of *Eciton hamatum* and *burchelli,* and others of the genus collected by me in Panama and in Mexico, show that the increase in gaster length toward the end of the nomadic phase as indicated in Figures 95 and 96 parallels the only progress of the cycle into a condition of egg delivery (Figure 97). There is then a recrudescence of the fatty tissues of the abdomen, with an accelerated maturation of oöcytes to completion in the ovarioles. This condition advances to full physogastry and egg-laying, midway in each statary phase, a process which (from field observations) lasts about seven days in the queen of *E. hamatum* and about ten days in the queen of *E. burchelli.* But why does this change in the queen (marked

824

FIGURE 94

Functional queens of *Eciton burchelli,* photographed in the laboratory after removal from their colonies. Top: a queen ('46 B–IV) captured on the tenth statary day of her colony, when she was *physogastric* and at the height of egg-laying. Bottom: a young colony queen ('52 B–I$_8$) with *contracted gaster* (gaster length, 10.4 mm), taken from her colony near the end of the statary phase in which her first egg-laying had occurred. Her gaster, although still somewhat distended, is approaching the minimal size characteristic of the nomadic phase (cf. Figure 96).

by an increase in volume of the gaster) begin late in each nomadic phase, and not at some other time in the cycle?

The available facts indicate that the Eciton queen's periodic resurgence into physogastry is due to a change in her relationship to the colony, based upon conditions which can arise, normally, only once in each cycle. This is the time mentioned, when a larval brood nearing maturity excites the workers increasingly, but feeds decreasingly. Then, as raids increase in size, a food surplus arises and persists in the colony. The highly aroused workers busy themselves not only with the larval brood, but also increasingly with the queen. She receives mounting social stimulation through antennal stroking, licking, mouth contacts, and other grooming from workers, which must excite her to feed more and more voraciously on the food heaped around her in the bivouac. It is very probably the high pitch and persistence of stimulation from workers that primarily induces the voracious feeding, and not simply the abundance of food. Food surpluses may arise at other times in the nomadic phase, without bringing the queen to physogastry.

It appears, then, that approach to maturity in the larval brood brings with it behavioral and trophic conditions adequate to change the queen from a contracted condition into full reproductive function. The egg-laying condition evidently is set off by *extrinsic* factors, and no timing mechanism intrinsic to the queen need be postulated. When the necessary turn of events is reached in the functional cycle, the normal Eciton queen responds to her full reproductive capacity.

Therefore, the Eciton cycle may be considered a self-rearousing system, in which the reproductive unit is linked periodically into a critical participation. Actually, the function of the queen herself sets off processes which at a later stage, in a feed-back manner depending upon brood development, serve to arouse the specific timing mechanism for her next contribution to the repetitive cyclic pattern.

Exogenous and endogenous control of ovulation. At other times in the cycle, the queen's reproductive processes are held to a low level, evidently conditioned upon limited stimulative and trophic advantages. Points in the functional cycle at which significant rises occur in these conditions coincide with times at which Hagan finds appreciable advances in the development of overlapping generations of oöcytes within the queen. In the schema representing his results in Figure 97, two significant changes are indicated for the time near the end of the statary phase at which a propitious trophic situation exists by virtue of conditions incident to pupal maturity. Here a maximal larval excitation of the colony promotes increased raiding, although meanwhile the brood consumes decreasing amounts of food. Significantly, Hagan's histological studies of the queen show that at

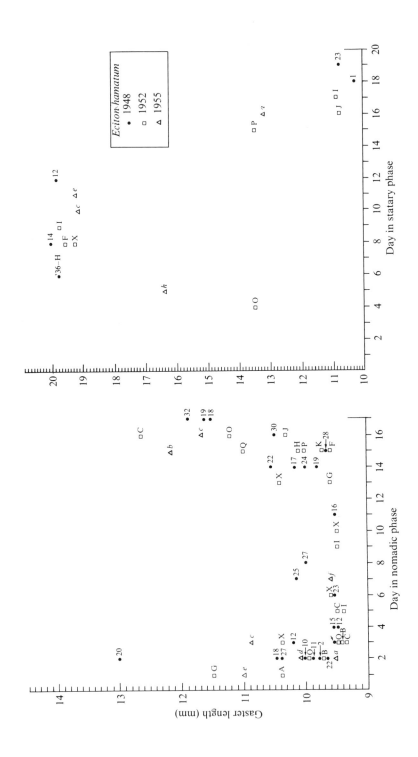

this time (1) a new oöcyte generation makes its appearance, and (2) the previous oöcyte generation exhibits a limited developmental spurt.

But rigid limitations seem to hold for such advances in the ovulative processes of the queen. Thus when nomadism begins and the callow brood feeds voraciously, the queen promptly loses the condition of partial physogastry characteristic of this stage in the cycle. Figures 95 and 96 show that her gaster length then falls to a minimum indicating full contraction before the third nomadic day. In Figure 97 it may be seen that a leveling off then occurs in the development of the two current oöcyte generations from the limited accelerations just preceding.

The persistence of limited oöcyte development and a fully contracted gaster from this time nearly to the end of the nomadic phase would seem attributable to the presence of active brood. Voracious broods first of new callows, then of growing larvae, suggest a competitive situation maintaining low stimulative and trophic conditions for the queen, holding her at a low level of reduced metabolism with reproductive processes distinctly subdued. (In this condition, the role of inhibitory secretory factors may be suspected.) Hagan finds that the queen exhibits only a very slow and limited advance in ovulative processes through the nomadic phase nearly to its end, when the next acceleration occurs as the larval brood nears maturity.

The case is different with the young queen of a new daughter colony, just after a colony division has taken place (Schneirla and Brown, 1950; Schneirla, 1956). Once established in the new colony, the primiparous queen is maintained in partial physogastry by means of a continuous overfeeding throughout the *entire* first nomadic phase following her eclosion. Oöcyte maturation evidently is brought thereby to a much more rapid completion than in adult functional queens. The young queen thereby reaches full physogastry and delivers a mass of eggs approaching normal brood size in the first statary phase after division—only about three weeks after her fertilization and less than thirty days after she emerged from her own cocoon.

FIGURE 95

Gaster length in mm of queens of *Eciton hamatum* measured at specific different times in the functional cycle. Symbols designate the queens of different colonies for convenience in comparing those measured more than once (e.g., queen '52-X, 3d and 10th nomadic days, 8th statary day). Queens '48 H-20 (2nd nomadic day) and H-25 (7th nomadic day) had somewhat flabby gasters and were judged to be elderly; queen '48 H-27 (8th nomadic day) was a callow queen recently established in a daughter colony after a colony division, and hence subject to overfeeding (see text). Gaster lengths of 9.4, 10.0 and 10.2 mm correspond to gaster widths of 5.0, 5.5, and 5.6 mm, and to body weights of 0.122 g, 0.132 g, and 0.135 g, respectively. [The letters and numbers following the symbols designate individual queens.]

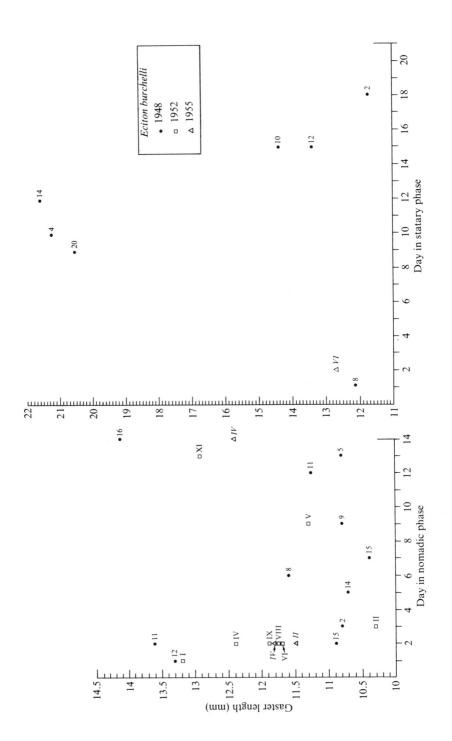

Accordingly, we see that the Eciton queen's reproductive functions synchronize with the colony cycle from the beginning, although for the first broods somewhat differently from later. The Eciton pattern seems to involve a close control of the reproductive unit at all times, mainly through the effect of external processes in the colony functional situation. Whatever endogenous factors in the queen operate to curb the interim rate of ovulation [6] would seem to be maintained by minimal social stimulation and low feeding until the time when a sharp rise in these conditions operates to remove the block and admit the completion of an ovulation.

The initiation and termination of the alternating phases in the Eciton functional cycle seem to hinge upon major stimulative changes brought into play when a brood completes a principal stage in its development. That is, the duration of the nomadic phase depends upon a regular time relationship holding between eclosion of a mature pupal brood and attainment of larval maturity by the next brood. Similarly, the duration of a statary phase is precisely dependent upon the time required for an enclosed brood to attain pupal maturity. In these two *Eciton* species, as we have seen, durations of the two alternating functional phases are highly predictable. It is evident that conditions affecting the rate of development in the massive discrete Eciton broods must be very regular and must have a high degree of stability characteristic of stages in the cycle.

ENVIRONMENTAL ADJUSTMENTS CRITICAL
FOR THE ECITON CYCLE

The bivouac and related processes. With respect to the problem of the developmental milieu in these nomadic insects, too involved for a systematic treatment here, three main points may be considered. First is the fact that the temporary nest or bivouac of a colony also functions as the *incubator* of its broods. The successive bivouacs of a nomadic phase afford the developing larval brood a series of microclimatic situations all very similarly stable in their properties as concerns internal temperature conditions, and therefore humidity also (Schneirla et al., 1954). Not only are the

FIGURE 96
Gaster length in mm of queens of *Eciton burchelli* measured at specific different times in the functional cycle. Queen '48–8 (6th nomadic day) was suspected to be a callow recently established in a daughter colony after colony division, and hence subject to overfeeding. Gaster lengths of 10.2 and 10.5 mm correspond to gaster widths of 5.2 and 5.5 mm, and to body weights of 0.143 and 0.152 g, respectively. [The letters and numbers following the symbols designate individual queens.]

---

[6] As, for example, secretory factors; also, physical sequelae of the previous egg-laying, as Hagan's results suggest.

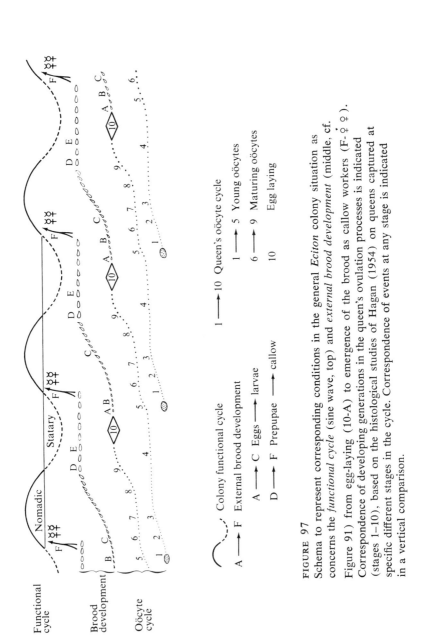

FIGURE 97

Schema to represent corresponding conditions in the general *Eciton* colony situation as concerns the *functional cycle* (sine wave, top) and *external brood development* (middle, cf. Figure 91) from egg-laying (10-A) to emergence of the brood as callow workers (F-♀♀). Correspondence of developing generations in the queen's ovulation processes is indicated (stages 1–10), based on the histological studies of Hagan (1954) on queens captured at specific different stages in the cycle. Correspondence of events at any stage is indicated in a vertical comparison.

Functional cycle

Brood development

Oöcyte cycle

~ ~ ~ ~ ,   Colony functional cycle

A ──► F   External brood development

A ──► C   Eggs ──► larvae

D ──► F   Prepupae ──► callow

1 ──► 10   Queen's oöcyte cycle

1 ──► 5   Young oöcytes

6 ──► 9   Maturing oöcytes

10   Egg laying

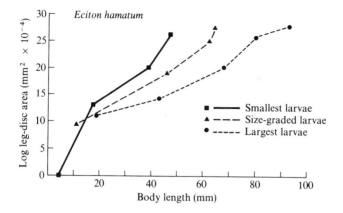

FIGURE 98
Ratio of a local anatomical character (*log* leg-disc area, *ordinate*) to a measure of over-all size (body length, *abscissa*) in larvae from successive samples of an *Eciton hamatum* brood through the nomadic phase (from Lappano, 1955). From the origin, successive points on each curve represent average for larvae in samples collected on the 2nd, 6th, 10th, and 14th nomadic days, respectively. (N = 5 in each measured lot of smallest and of largest larvae; N = 20 in each lot of size-graded or intermediate larvae.)

characteristic atmospheric variations of the tropical day leveled off so that a high regularity prevails in larval development, but conditions in the controlled microclimate facilitate a differential development through the brood population. One important outcome may be mentioned.

In an *E. hamatum* brood there is a time difference of about one week between the laying of the first and the last eggs of the series. At larval maturity this time difference, as measured by the onset of spinning in the largest and the smallest members of the brood, has narrowed to about three days. Quantitative studies of preserved broods (Lappano, 1955; Tafuri, 1956) have shown that the intermediate and minor members of a worker-brood series both in this species and in *E. burchelli* develop at correspondingly more rapid rates than do the potential workers major, maturing from the earliest-laid eggs (Figure 98). Significantly, our studies on the ecological properties of the bivouac (Schneirla et al., 1954) show that the highest temperatures exist at bivouac center where the smallest brood members are located, lower temperatures at the margin where the largest are located—in fact, that the bivouac regularly presents an ecological gradient to the brood (Jackson, 1956). The regularity in diurnal bivouac conditions on which these facts depend is traceable particularly to behavioral reactions of the worker population normal to their daily functional routine and to the daily march of atmospherically induced responses (Schneirla et al., 1954). Factors contributing to the regulation of bivouac properties must be considered vital for the adaptation of these Ecitons to a surface life.

Adaptations concerning food supply. Another principal environmental factor to which the Eciton cycle is adjusted is booty or food. Army-ant emigrations do not depend upon local food-scarcity as was formerly thought, as convincing evidence can be brought for a very different theory (Schneirla, 1938, 1944b, 1945). Even so, the fact is that mechanisms of the Eciton functional cycle normally furnish an adequate solution of the colony food problem. When active broods (callows, growing larvae) are present and the food-consuming capacity of the colony is highest, nomadism is maintained through the intense brood-stimulative processes outlined above. The colony thereby, ipso facto, is assured a fresh hunting area on each further day, different from that of the preceding day. Although worker reactions characteristic of the stage operate against entering previously worked areas, and favor new ground, the nightly emigration has causes only indirectly related to food-need or food-supply. With a comparable indirectness, when the food-consumption capacity of the colony is lowest in the statary phase, emigration does not occur; instead the colony carries out successive daily raids from the same base but over radial trails established successively in different directions (Schneirla, 1945).

Through the Eciton cycle, a broad correspondence exists between magnitude of the colony food-consuming capacity on the one hand, and on the other the ability of the colony to gather food (through the size of daily raids) and the chances of finding more food (through emigration to new ground). This adaptive relationship is attributable to fluctuations in the level of brood-excitation effects, incidentally and indirectly controlling food supply. *The effect is independent of whether or not the brood, source of determinative stimulation, can feed at the time.* This fact is indicated by a higher level of daily raiding both in the initial and in the final days of a statary phase (Table 4), owing specifically to a greater stimulative effect from *enclosed* brood than in the intermediate part of the phase. Besides, a new nomadic phase occasionally begins before more than a small part of the mature callow brood has emerged from cocoons and is feeding. This is seldom seen except with very large colonies, in which the communicative permutation of brood-excitatory effects evidently is greatest. Although Eciton workers are psychologically simple creatures incapable of a process of perceptual expectancy for an impending increase in colony food needs, the outcome of the described situation is highly adaptive—as effective as a housewife's buying more groceries for expected visitors.

Adaptations to the day-night rhythm. A third environmental condition to which the epigaeic Ecitons are sensitively adapted is that of atmospheric factors such as light, temperature, and humidity. The characteristic Eciton daily routine of raiding followed (under appropriate conditions) by emigration is attuned directly to the day-night rhythm (Schneirla, 1938, 1940, 1944b). Werringloer's (1932) histological study of the eyes and their central connections in several species of American dorylines showed *E. burchelli,* the most epigaeic, to have the largest lateral ocelli and best developed neural connections; *Labidus coccus,* one of the most hypogaeic, tiny ocelli and minimal nerve connections. Adaptation to a surface life evidently has entailed a specialization of the visual system. This is only one factor, as a comparative consideration of hypogaeic dorylines shows.

Because the terrestrial Ecitons are photokinetically responsive to light in a highly sensitive manner, their activity routine involves the daily development of a raid, followed by an emigration or by none according to internal conditions in the colony. Consequently their activity phases are divided, as it were, into more or less equivalent units (e.g., in *E. hamatum,* 17 successive nomadic days), clocked by environmental conditions. The Eciton daily routine is mainly light-conditioned, with other physical factors involved secondarily. Increasing temperature facilitates the development of a raid each morning, high temperature with intense radiation inhibits raiding activities at midday—preparing the colony for a resurgence of activity with return of more equable outer conditions in early afternoon— falling temperature at dusk depresses activity as does failing light, stopping the raid and paving the way for a continued exodus or for return to the bivouac (Schneirla, 1938, 1940, 1945; Schneirla et al., 1954).

The changing excitation level of an epigaeic Eciton colony during the functional cycle is clearly indicated by typical variations in responsiveness to environmental changes. In the nomadic phase, the workers are sensitively reactive to the first morning light, and raiding starts promptly at dawn. Although the midday depression involves a marked reduction of traffic on trails from the bivouac, traffic always continues, and the columns are promptly crowded again in early afternoon. Conditions are very different in the statary phase, and particularly in its intermediate days (cf. Tables 2 and 4). Now the colony response is greatly reduced at dawn and exhibits a noticeable inertia; raiding builds up much more slowly or may fail altogether. The midday depression reduces raiding to a minimum, and in the dry season, when this effect is greatest, traffic often stops for some time for a considerable distance from the bivouac. Nomadic colonies in contrast are able to continue their raiding at such times.

In all three respects—the bivouac, adjustments concerning food supply, and reactions to light and other physical conditions on the surface—the epigaeic Ecitons exhibit adaptations essential to a regular life on and above the forest floor. These mechanisms and related types of behavior all contribute essentially to the maintenance of the highly specialized cyclic functional pattern characteristic of these species. It will be interesting to compare them in these respects with the more or less hypogaeic doryline species.

COMPARISON OF EPIGAEIC AND HYPOGAEIC DORYLINES

Colony Function in the African Anomma and the Epigaeic Ecitons

Recently, Raignier and Van Boven (1955) have reported that in the African driver ant subgenus, *Dorylus* (*Anomma*), the immense colonies interrupt long sedentary intervals with continuous emigrations each lasting 2–3 days. The colony movements, although somewhat variable in time of occurrence, come most frequently at intervals of about 20–25 days in the best studied species, *D.* (*Anomma*) *wilverthi*. Significantly, these emigrations occur at times when a major part of the all-worker brood is in a mature pupal condition with individuals of the largest castes already ambulant as partially-pigmented callows. The colony then settles in a new subterranean nest from which it conducts successive raids through an interval of 20 to 25 days before a further emigration may occur. These authors also discern in *D.* (*A.*) *wilverthi* a less frequent inter-emigration interval of 11 days as well as one approximating 2 months when a developing male brood is present. In a less studied species, *D.* (*A.*) *nigricans,* an inter-emigration interval of more than 100 days is reported, but in that case also the infrequent emigration is characterized by the presence of a majority of mature pupae in the brood (Cohic, 1948).

The situation reported for these African driver ants obviously bears some resemblance to the cyclic pattern in the epigaeic Ecitons of the New World. However, in *Anomma* the nomadic interval is very short and seems to involve just one bivouac-change movement of the colony, and also the interval spent in fixed nests is considerably more irregular in duration than in Eciton.

Raignier and Van Boven (1955, p. 241), as did Cohic (1948), find this state of affairs in the driver ants consistent in general with the terms of my theory for cyclic nomadic function in the Ecitons, in which nomadic function is attributed to causes dependent upon brood condition. Since, when emigration occurs in *Dorylus* colonies, mature nymphal forms always preponderate in the brood, it is stated that ". . . leur réserve énergétique et leur grande activité excitent la colonie au point qu'un déménagement s'ensuit." We may conclude that the principal if not the sole excitatory agency underlying emigrations in colonies of the investigated *Anomma* species is equivalent to that which I have described as the *callow-excitatory factor* (Schneirla, 1938) postulated as initiating a nomadic phase in colonies of epigaeic *Eciton* species. It is therefore not clear on what grounds the authors (op. cit., p. 55) conclude that the causes setting an *Anomma* colony into movement are very different from those I have identified in *Eciton.* The main difference actually lies in what *follows* the emigration. Although the authors (op. cit., p. 241) recognize that the basis of emigration in *Anomma* lies in reproductive processes, they offer only a very general suggestion as to how they think the adult population is aroused. As a more specific hypothesis, consistent with the modified trophallaxis concept I have found applicable to the Ecitons, the arousal may be attributed to the *summative effect of tactual and chemotactic stimuli from the brood.*

One striking difference between *Anomma* and *Eciton* is that, although nomadism in the former is confined to a single long colony movement, in the latter it involves a continuous phase at an increased level of activity with successive nightly emigrations. In both cases, we may say that the callow-excitation factor holds the colony in a highly aroused condition for about three days, then subsides as a major excitatory agent (cf. Figure 92). Raignier and Van Boven seem disinclined to adopt the concept of a functional cycle for the African dorylines studied. But even a single colony displacement lasting three days may be considered a *nomadic phase,* when based upon a brood-stimulated excitatory condition in the colony, and when it recurs at more or less regular intervals. Furthermore, the distinctive intervening periods in which the colony operates from a fixed site, with successive raids in different directions, clearly resemble *statary* intervals as I have described them for the epigaeic Ecitons (Schneirla, 1933, 1938, 1945). This latter condition holds until the maturation of a further nymphal brood occurs and the colony again emigrates. Contrary, then, to the conclusion of Raignier and Van Boven (1955, p. 241), the concept of a functional cycle involving alternating nomadic and statary phases seems applicable to *Anomma,* although in certain details the picture differs from that in the epigaeic Ecitons.

The major difference is that in *Anomma* the capacity for emigration disappears after one colony movement, whereas in the Ecitons it continues through a much longer phase. Theoretically, we may attribute the initiation of nomadism in both cases to the callow excitatory factor. But Raignier and Van Boven (op. cit., p. 241), without a specific citation, state for me that "Cet auteur trouve que chez les Doryles americains, le passage de la période sédentaire à la période nomade est occasionné par un appel croissant des larves à la nourriture." *On the contrary,* I have consistently held, that *newly eclosed callow brood* furnishes the stimulative effect initiating a nomadic phase (e.g., 1938, p. 64; 1952). To the stimulative effect of the *larval* brood I have attributed the *continuation* of nomadism in the epigaeic Ecitons, a factor viewed as thereby overlapping that of the callow brood in its arousal function. But also, diametrically opposing the sense of the above statement, I have postulated the larval factor also as one of *stimulative arousal*, and *not* "un appel à la nourriture." The latter expression would suggest the "Nahrungsbedürfnis" concept of Müller (1886), which I questioned as follows [Schneirla, 1938, p. 69]:

> Nahrungsbedürfnis suggests the point yet misses it. We are warranted in assuming only that the afferent consequences of larval growth processes result in random activities which incidentally exert a powerful excitatory effect upon the workers. . . . This indirectly forces the procuration of the larger quantities of food which the brood is then able to consume, since the adults raid more actively when more excited.

In any case, no larval-excitatory factor seems indicated in *Dorylus* as far as influencing the arousal of an emigration is concerned. Raignier and Van Boven always found larvae in the minority in the broods of emigrating colonies. But it seems possible that stimulative effects from developing larvae may account for a crescendo of raiding prior to emigration, and, somewhat as in *Eciton,* also (indirectly) promote ovulation in the queen.

It seems likely from Raignier and Van Boven's brood-samples that the Anomma queen may lay more or less continuously, but that a limited physogastry with a more intensive laying within 5–6 days may occur at intervals of about 3 weeks (op. cit., p. 254), most frequently after arriving at a new nest.[7] But they find that in about one-third of the cases, the phase of intensive egg-laying begins a few days *before* the exodus. It is concluded that in one period of about 21 days, between emigrations, a quantity of eggs from some hundreds of thousands to as many as a million may be laid.

Egg-laying in Anomma queens is found (op. cit.) much more variable and more extended in time than I have found it in Eciton queens, in which it is restricted to an interval of about 7 days in *E. hamatum* and 10–12 days in *E. burchelli,* with a 2- to 3-day peak of delivery coming after the midpoint in each. Yet in Anomma queens there *is* a periodicity in the occurrence of high points in egg production, which Raignier and Van Boven attribute to an endogenous rhythm depending upon processes intrinsic to the queen. This conclusion may be premature. Further evidence concerning the effect on the Anomma queen of social stimulative processes and trophic conditions within the colony may indicate her egg-laying rhythmicity to be conditioned essentially by these, somewhat as I have found in *Eciton.*

---

[7] This condition prevailed in a colony of *Dorylus* (*A.*) *nigricans arcens* in Ibadan, Nigeria, from which Dr. L. R. Aronson captured a physogastric queen, large quantities of eggs, and a great brood of mature pupae. The colony had just finished an emigration.

The hypothesis of a brood-stimulative basis for such occurrences remains to be tested for *Anomma.* The statary phase indicated for *D.* (*A.*) *nigricans* (which is usually also the interbrood period in this species) is much longer than that typical for *D.* (*A.*) *wilverthi.* This wide difference would seem more likely to be based upon conditions holding for brood development than upon very different endogenously controlled ovulative rhythms in the queens of the two species. In view of the emphasis due the role of temperature in brood development (Schneirla et al., 1954), it is significant that Raignier and Van Boven (1955, pp. 192, 194) report a higher and more regular temperature ("physiologique") in the compact brood area of the subterranean nests of *wilverthi* than in the diffuse brood areas in the nests of *nigricans* colonies. Longer statary intervals and longer inter-brood periods may be due simply to a much slower rate of development in the brood of the latter.

A Perspective on Some Hypogaeic New World Dorylines

The hypogaeic nesting tendency, with or without surface foraging, evidently predominates in the remaining doryline genera of the world. Unfortunately, evidence concerning behavior and biological functions in these groups is at best sparse, and deficient on critical points. Something may be gained, however, by summarizing the fragmentary evidence for best-known species in genera other than *Eciton* in the tribe *Ecitonini.*

The epigaeic tendency, most predominant in the genus *Eciton* in species such as *burchelli* and *hamatum,* is somewhat reduced in other species of the same genus such as *rogeri.* These, although at times found in surface bivouacs under humid conditions in deep forest, at times carrying out full column raids on the surface, are persistently subterranean in nesting and often make extensive use of underground avenues in their raids and emigrations. This capacity for intermittent surface operations, coupled with predominant subterranean nesting, also typifies species such as *E. vagans* and *E. dulcius.* Scattered evidence suggests that these species may approximate to differing degrees the functional and brood cycle of the epigaeic Ecitons. In humid forests with good cover, somewhat exposed bivouacs are found containing large larval worker broods, with the colonies raiding extensively, then emigrating; whereas other colonies are found in sheltered sites with enclosed pupal broods, settled and inactive, often then with signs that eggs have been laid (Schneirla, 1947).

Nomamyrmex crassicornis (= *E.* (*Lab.*) *crassicorne*) is persistently hypogaeic in its nesting, indicated by the fact that although its branching columns are frequently seen above ground in humid tropical American forests, the nest and queen are unreported. In humid forest, surface raiding operations occur often, exposed at times over areas up to 50 meters, but may disappear quickly underground. The emigrations, which may continue day and night for 30 hours or more, usually expose their columns on the surface for limited distances only, as in crossing streams. Each of three different emigrations of this species I was able to watch continuously for 12 hours or more contained many tens of thousands of callow workers. *Nom. hartigi* is reported as even more hypogaeic than *crassicornis* (Borgmeier, 1955).

Labidus praedator (= *E.* (*Lab.*) *praedator*) stages extensive swarm raids on the surface, more vigorously by day but also frequently at night. The species is strongly hypogaeic in its nesting, and colonies seem to occupy particular subterranean sites for long periods of time, often for months (Sumichrast, 1868; v. Ihering, 1912). Forel (1906) reported Fiebig's observation in Paraguay of an emigration column with workers carrying nymphs. On four occasions I have watched at length emigration columns of this species in which ran tens of thousands of callow workers, with great numbers of unopened small cocoons being carried along. The concurrence of emigration with the maturation of worker pupae in great numbers appears to be common in this species. Prior to such emigrations, the bivouac becomes partially exposed at the surface, e.g., permeating a log. Observations suggest that the queen may lay great quantities of eggs at these times. Luederwaldt (1918) observed a bivouac of *praedator,* in part exposed at the surface, in which he found numerous worker pupae and empty cocoons, and also eggs and microlarvae, with the queen physogastric. In a bivouac which I examined in detail in Eastern Chiapis in Mexico (Schneirla, 1947) countless chambers in a mouldy log were packed with a great enclosed brood of mature pupae, and in extensive chambers in the ground below were large quantities of eggs and microlarvae.[8] This pattern was substantially duplicated in two other observations, one of which was followed within 48 hours by an emigration. Statary nests occupied for intervals of six months or even longer have been reported for this species (Luederwaldt, 1918; Borgmeier, 1955).

Labidus coecus (= *E.* (*Lab.*) *coecum*), strongly hypogaeic, seldom is surface-exposed save for short stretches of column, even then usually largely beneath cover or roofed over with detritus particles. Raiding, elusive and mainly subterranean, seems to occur both night and day. To the statement of Wheeler and Long (1901) that *Lab. coecus* is "entirely subterranean," Creighton (1950) adds that, like many other army ants of strong hypogaeic tendency, this species will forage above ground "when the circumstances are suitable." This species evidently has *Dauernester;*

---

[8] This large colony was not raiding at the time, but was found quite by accident, after I had traced back the single foraging column of a colony of *Eciton vagans* to the same log, in which the two colonies were found in closely adjacent statary bivouacs.

e.g., v. Ihering (1912) observed one colony continuously for more than four months, when it occupied an abandoned termite nest and chambers in the soil below. Weber (1941) found a colony occupying a rotted stump and the soil beneath, with "eggs and very young larvae," as well as whitish "cocoons of workers" containing pupae. The queen was distended with eggs. There is no evidence thus far to synchronize these events with emigration.

The genus *Neivamyrmex* (= *Acamatus*), which ranges from Iowa to Patagonia, has 113 currently described species (Borgmeier, 1955), in contrast to 12 in *Eciton*, 8 in *Labidus*, and 2 in *Nomamyrmex*. All are mainly hypogaeic. Although, of the described species, workers are known for 48 and all adults for 12, colony function and brood cycle are virtually unknown.

Neivamyrmex nigrescens (= *E. (Acam.) schmitti*).   In Texas, Wheeler (1900, 1910), in Argentina, Bruch (1934), and in northern Mexico, Creighton (1950) found colonies beneath stones at the surface, with partially physogastric, egg-laying queens present (cf. Holliday, 1906; Smith, 1942). Creighton (1950) suggests that a chambered nest of *Neiv. nigrescens* discovered by Wheeler and Long (1901) beneath a stone actually involved "a statary phase . . ." and that "the 'nest' was actually a permanent bivouac made during the period when the brood was about to pupate." Behavioral and biological conditions in Neivamyrmex colonies, and the conditions under which the nests are changed, are virtually unknown. Wheeler (1900) suggested for Texas species that the same nest is occupied during the winter and spring months, with departure to "resume their marauding expeditions . . . after the brood is raised in late spring." It is probable that brood production continues during the warm months.

Two suggestive cases concerning brood have come to my attention. In Georgia, Dr. E. S. Ross [9] found a colony nesting within and just below a log in the deep woods, with some thousands of mature pupae present, the largest castes pigmented; and Mr. Carl Rettenmeyer [9] found a colony near Lawrence, Kansas, from which a "small sample of mature larvae and a large sample of pupae nearing eclosion" were taken. A few days later, the colony was gone. The possibility exists that emigrations of Neivamyrmex colonies may occur in connection with the maturation of pupal broods.

DISCUSSION

The doryline ants throughout the tropics and subtropics of the world have retained primitive carnivorous dietary properties based on predatory foraging activities, and have developed reproductive capacities supporting

---

[9] Personal communication.

large colonies, through an evolution evidently centered around nomadic patterns in colony function. This seems to hold throughout all doryline genera of the world, notwithstanding the probability that the Old and New World representatives have been isolated from the time of their theoretical common predoryline ancestor.

The outcome of evolution to date in this large formicine subfamily supports Wheeler's (1928) generalization that a predominantly carnivorous way of life cannot be maintained in a social insect with large colonies having permanent nesting sites. Dorylines universally seem able not only to shift their nesting sites and zones of foraging, but to do so in a more or less cyclical way. What all sections of the subfamily evidently have retained, and modified or specialized convergently, are mechanisms underlying predatory, nomadic species patterns closely related to large-scale reproductive processes through which such patterns are dynamized and sustained. An early stage in the evolution may have involved changes in colony nesting site enforced through depletion of food in the occupied zone. This is no longer true for any well-known doryline. Rather, the nomadic changes now seem due to stimulative colony arousal mechanisms based upon reproductive processes. But the prodigious reproductive capacities characteristic of the unique dichthadiigynes, or highly specialized queens functioning singly in doryline colonies, may have evolved in intimate relationship with selection processes effective through the trophic situation of their colonies. In the epigaeic Ecitons we find that this relationship still exists, although now in a specialized, self-rearousing pattern in which the critical reproductive factor is keyed off by stimuli released within the colony functional system itself. This formula may hold to some extent for all existing dorylines.

We are currently in a position to compare the functional pattern of certain doryline species in the Old and New Worlds, at least in a general way. It is unlikely that any doryline species departs from the pattern of a nomadic, predatory life based upon reproductive processes, established for *Eciton* and now indicated for *Anomma* as well. It seems likely that all doryline species will be found to possess a cyclicity in these functions, sustained through a recurrent system of excitatory relationships between colony behavioral processes and brood properties. This type of system, with massive brood-stimulative effects critical for major phases in colony behavior and their changes, prevails in the epigaeic Ecitons and is also indicated in the African driver ants.

The epigaeic *Eciton* species, best known at present, seem most highly specialized of all in their colony functional pattern. They are evidently more divergent in their specializations from the other, essentially hypogaeic dorylines of the Old and New Worlds than either of these is from the other. The inference seems justified that, whereas the Ecitons of the American tropics had a continuous environment of deep forest with heavy cover prevalent in which to pass the critical part of their evolution, the others including the African *Anomma* must have evolved under conditions of intermittent forest cover, of savannah conditions and the like. For the Ecitons, therefore, a selection process prevailed favoring the persistence and integration of factors consolidating colony adaptation to conditions on and above the forest floor. In contrast the other dorylines, evolving under conditions of broken or variable forest cover, were forced to subterranean adaptations in their nesting, all of them partly and some of them mainly if not entirely in their foraging as well.

The principal factors through which the specialized functional pattern of the epigaeic Ecitons has arisen are schematized in Figure 99, with their chief interrelationships indicated. One factorial complex involves physical properties of the terrestrial environment such as the diurnal rhythms in light, temperature and humidity, or as the seasonal cycle. The characteristic Eciton routine of daytime raiding and nighttime emigration is clearly conditioned upon day-night physical variations, and first of all upon light. *Eciton* species such as *E. burchelli,* as Werringloer (1932) found, have much better developed lateral (pseudo) ocelli with much better nervous connections than have members of the hypogaeic American doryline genera. Thus light has a distinctive photokinetic effect: the surface-dwelling colonies are aroused to build up their foraging systems in the daytime but are capable only of emigration and other more lethargic activities at night. Their visual equipment admits for them an effective light adaptation, and also, in their case, a heavier exoskeletal pigmentation opposes disruptive effects through intense light and surface radiation, permitting a scope of daytime surface operations far beyond that possible for species in other doryline genera.

The epigaeic specialization of the Ecitons clearly rests upon properties of the workers first of all. Sensitivity to light and to other physical radiation, as suggested, would seem critical for the consistently superior Eciton tolerance of surface conditions, and for relative differences among species in other genera in this respect. Werringloer's findings indicate a gradation in the photosensory factor among American dorylines from the most epigaeic species, *E. burchelli,* with best developed and best pigmented lateral ocelli, to *Labidus mars,* evidently most completely hypogaeic and the one American doryline species known to be *eyeless.* Comparative tests of mine on workers with experimentally covered eyes, as with *E. burchelli* and the very hypogaeic *Labidus coecus,* indicate that susceptibility to infracuticular radiative disturbance may be *least* in the epigaeic species and *greatest* in the most hypogaeic species. Other ecologically effective properties of the workers, as those affecting species temperature optima and relative desiccation tolerance, must also be ranked high in this respect.

Eciton rogeri workers, although much more light-shy than *E. hamatum,* not uncommonly expose sections of their column raids on the surface; however, the rarity of even partially surface-exposed bivouacs in *rogeri* suggests a higher humidity optimum than in *hamatum.*

There is no reliable indication that worker properties affecting behavior in the raid (e.g., factors of sensitivity and of secretion underlying formation and use of trails; efficacy of mandibular bite and of sting, overall strength) are decisive for epigaeic or hypogaeic tendency. *Nomamyrmex crassicornis* resembles *E. hamatum* in the size range of its workers and in the branching-column aspect of its raids (often extended over considerable surface areas), yet the nests of the former are strictly hypogaeic and its emigrations are seldom seen. These species both take soft-bodied prey (e.g., insect brood) and are therefore competitive to an appreciable extent. *Neivamyrmex pilosus,* although in another genus and with much smaller workers, develops branched-column raids very similar to those of the above two species, but on a smaller scale, and captures soft-bodied booty, also relatively smaller. This species seems to be almost as fixedly hypogaeic in nesting and in basal raiding operations as *Nom. crassicornis.* As another comparison, *Eciton burchelli,* very epigaeic, and *Labidus praedator* (a hypogaeic nester as is *Neiv. pilosus*) have a similar swarm-raiding pattern (Schneirla, 1940) and capture a wide range of comparable booty, although in *Lab. praedator* both swarms and booty are smaller, roughly in relation to the smaller size of the workers.

Type of prey and type of raiding system appear not to distinguish the epigaeic species sharply from the hypogaeic, therefore, nor do virulence and persistence of attack. In both of these latter respects *Lab. praedator* and numerous other hypogaeic dorylines must be ranked before the epigaeic *E. hamatum.* Although the Ecitons tend to be larger in body size than the hypogaeic doryline species, there are exceptions (e.g., *Nom. crassicornis*), and the absence of a strict relationship suggests that the importance of this factor is secondary.

The extent of polymorphic differentiation among workers seems not closely related to relative epigaeic tendency, as in general the more markedly polymorphic *Labidus* species tend little more toward surface life than do the relatively more monomorphic species of the genus *Neivamyrmex.* However, from the fact that *Eciton* species all exhibit a wide polymorphic range extending to large workers major, the possibility cannot be excluded that some relationship may have existed between selective processes bearing on diversity in worker development and those contributing to an epigaeic way of life. Life on the surface involves not only ecological hazards, but also the danger of attacks against brood by a variety of predators including large mammals. Lacking the workers major, with their high arousal thresholds adapting them as defense units under conditions of extreme disturbance, and with their large, needle-sharp, tong-shaped mandibles as deterrents to the largest molesters, the epigaeic Ecitons probably could not have arisen in tropical forests containing mammals such as anteaters and coatis.

The formation of open, hanging bivouac clusters above ground is an exclusive property of the Ecitons, when colonies are in the condition of increased excitement peculiar to the nomadic phase. Colonies of hypogaeic species in other genera (as in *Anomma*) also apparently have periodic times of increased excitement when in some species their nests are formed nearer to if not at the surface. Even then, however, the colony almost always remains partially rooted in the soil, and does not extend its nest above the surface except with the ecological protection of shelters such as the enclosing walls of hollow stump, log or debris. This resembles, without duplicating, the statary bivouac situation of *Eciton* colonies.

The open bivouac cluster is an inseparable characteristic of the Ecitons, in which they are exposed to surface conditions, and particularly to the light-dark rhythm upon which their daily routine of raiding and emigration depends. For this surface-adaptive accomplishment, characteristics of workers, brood, and queen all are essential (Figure 99). In all, exposure-tolerance properties are essential beyond those in the corresponding individual types of hypogaeic species. In the workers, better-developed tarsal hooks and effective clustering reactions are essential for the linking of bodies in large hanging masses. Here the larger workers, morphologically specialized, are indispensable, as is indicated by the larger cylindrical clusters and more frequent hanging bulb-clusters formed by the larger, stronger workers of *E. burchelli* than by those of *E. hamatum* (Schneirla et al., 1954).

Nomadism in the dorylines seems dependent upon an interrelationship between characteristic worker properties and those of a specialized brood, accounting for relatively abrupt changes in trophallactic excitation conditioning critical variations in colony function. The massive arousal effect based upon maturation of a pupal brood seems to function similarly in all sufficiently known dorylines. This factor initiates nomadic phases in the Ecitons, and in the hypogaeic *Anomma* energizes single emigrations occurring at well-separated intervals. Scattered evidence for the hypogaeic American dorylines indicates that a pattern like that of *Anomma* may be approximated in their case. When better known, this may come to be regarded as the basic or "primitive" doryline pattern.

Thus far, the continuous nomadic phase of successive emigrations has been found only in the Ecitons, and may be a specific outcome of epigaeic specialization. In the Ecitons, a regular overlapping of synchronized broods involves the invariable presence of a larval brood in its early stages, when nomadism begins. A new factor enters thereby which can function as

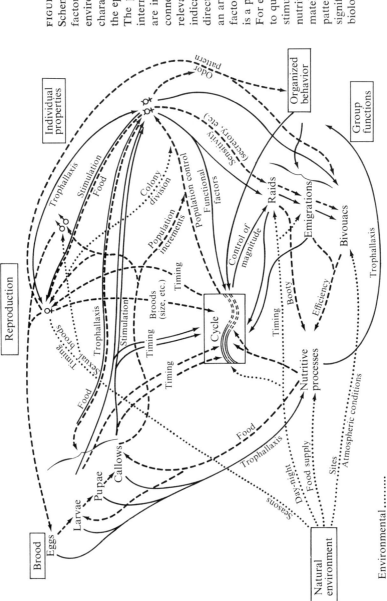

FIGURE 99

Schema to represent the principal factors contributed by the natural environment and by major individual characteristics in the population to the epigaeic Eciton behavior pattern. The principal empirically established interrelationships of these factors are indicated by the respective connecting lines, the general adaptive relevance of each relationship is indicated by a label, and the main direction of the adaptive effect by an arrow direction. Differentiation of factors as "biological" or "behavioral" is a procedure of approximation. For example, food given by workers to queen and to brood has *both* a stimulative (behavioral) and a nutritive (biological) function, intimately related; the species odor-pattern has a variety of behavioral significance closely bound up with its biological properties, and so on.

Environmental ....
Biological ----------
Behavioral ————

major colony energizer after the callow-stimulative effect has waned. Such a precise synchronization of broods would require, as control, either (1) a highly regular endogenous cyclic timing mechanism in the queen, (2) a precise external physical rhythm, or (3) a regular pattern of interrelationships among the functions of the main participants (worker population, broods, and the queen) in the colony routine. The last alternative is favored by available evidence.

The fact of regularity in brood development cannot be overestimated in its importance for the species-predictable Eciton cycle. The bivouac is an incubator for the brood, and an efficient one the properties of which seem due to a number of factors (Schneirla et al., 1954). First of all, worker reactions to the odor field of the queen (posted in the upper center) seem essential to weld the cluster together, for a colony from which the queen has been taken soon forms less compact, increasingly diffuse bivouacs. This worker-queen relationship must contribute to centering of the brood in the cluster, a condition clearly essential to the thermo-regulation of brood development. The efficiency of the bivouac as brood incubator also may be related critically to a series of worker reactions to changing environmental conditions through the day, whereby for example the interior is ventilated in the heat of the day, and insulated from the outer atmosphere in a heat-conserving manner at night.

A routine of worker responses to the daily march of changes in the physical environment may be held vital for the emigration, which in these epigaeic species normally can occur only as a sequel to raiding (Schneirla, 1938). Dawn initiates the raid in a nomadic colony, midday environmental events contribute to further essential changes, and dusk makes the exodus dominant by closing off foraging activities. In outline, this is a threshold phenomenon. Through this regular process, new foraging ground inevitably becomes available on each further day in this phase, indirectly assured by active brood stimulatively energizing the adult population. The automatic nature of this brood-adult relationship, for which food transfer is incidental, is shown through the study of points in the cycle at which the excitatory process occurs at maximum although the brood then feeds only minimally if at all. Without these brood-adult relationships characteristic of the daily routine, the Eciton brood-development schedule would be greatly disordered or at least more variable, disturbing the regularity of the nomad-statary cycle and as a consequence endangering colony existence.

The light-determined schedule of the daily Eciton routine, a worker-environment relationship, has the additional effect of assuring through a regular nightly emigration: (1) minimal interruption of raiding activities by bivouac-change traffic and (2) minimal exposure of the brood to environmental hazards. Vital to success in the regular epigaeic nomadism in colonies of Eciton magnitude is the fact that colony translocation in the early nighttime hours involves an exposure of broods (callows, larvae) *only* at the time of day when atmospheric conditions are fairly uniform on the forest floor and nearest the brood optimum.

Within the surface bivouac of the nomadic Eciton colony, conditions obtain which are vital in still other ways for the normal cyclic function of the colony. These adaptive results are gained through (1) trophic and environmental relationships of the colony which not only facilitate regularity in brood developmental processes but also (2) admit and control a species-predictable range of polymorphic differences in the brood. The first condition regulates the time required by the unitary brood to complete the larval and the pupal stages, thereby setting time limits for the nomadic and statary phases. More specifically, the properties of the bivouac as a specialized environment greatly increase the precision with which brood-stimulative factors initiate or terminate changes in the colony functional cycle. In Eciton bivouacs once settled after the emigration, the smallest members of the brood (developing from eggs laid last in the series) are always held in the center, the larger types more peripherally in relation to size. Thus the smallest members, virtually always in the zone of highest temperature (Schneirla et al., 1954), can complete their development in a shorter time than respectively larger individuals (Figure 98). Consequently, the time-differential holding for the egg series is greatly reduced at later stages—e.g., in *E. hamatum,* from *ca.* 7 days at laying to *ca.* 3 days at larval maturity. The brood-stimulative effect thereby exerts a much more concentrated and a more intense impact upon the colony than if time relations at egg-laying held throughout. To this state of affairs we may attribute the fact that in the Ecitons the larval brood becomes a major factor influencing colony function, accounting for a striking time-limited change in colony behavior at its maturity.

In contrast, in the hypogaeic dorylines (as in *Anomma*), no larval-stimulative influence is as yet indicated in colony function, certainly none with the critical phase-timing role found in *Eciton.* It is likely that, for one thing, the time disparity in developmental rate in the brood series is too great to permit more than secondary influences on colony function until pupal maturity is attained. Numerous factors concerning queen, brood properties and colony ecological situation may be responsible for the difference. As concerns the brood factor, in the subterranean bivouacs of the driver ants, Raignier and Van Boven find that in the more concentrated clusters of *A. wilverthi* a "physiological temperature" prevails, evidently responsible for shorter brood-developmental intervals and shorter inter-emigration intervals than in *nigricans,* which lacks this ecological advantage.

The second condition mentioned above facilitates a greater polymorphic specialization in the graduated brood series than would otherwise be possible, so that worker types arise as different in their functional properties as the minima (essential in the centralizing and care of eggs and small larvae), the intermediates (essential for the brood gradient in bivouac; outstanding in raiding and in bivouac formation), and the workers major. The latter, as we have mentioned, are a unique defensive type critical for doryline adaptation to an epigaeic habitat.

Specialization of the doryline dichthadiigyne as a single colony reproductive capable of large-scale ovulative function presumably occurred intimately in relation to the evolution of brood-stimulative mechanisms underlying nomadism. In the Ecitons the queen must have undergone still further specialization with secondary advances of the social group to an effective epigaeic adaptation. One important specialization is the capacity for disjunctive broods separated by resting intervals. This property contributes to surface-adaptive advantages gained through more precise and more diversified brood-stimulative factors than are indicated in the case of hypogaeic dorylines. The Anomma queen, for example, seems to lay eggs over longer intervals or perhaps continuously, with periods of intensive production intervening. This condition, as compared with that of *Eciton,* may be considered basic to a lesser scope (i.e., reduction to a crucial pupal-arousal effect only) and greater time variability of brood stimulative effects as factors in the colony functional cycle. From Hagan's findings the Eciton queen is shown capable of initiating a new brood generation before the previous one has completed ovulation, a capacity fundamental to the adaptive asset of *over-lapping broods* which makes possible a continuous nomadic phase. Through this property of the queen, the waning stimulative effect of a new callow brood is replaced smoothly in *Eciton* by the growing stimulative effect of a young larval brood, so that no break occurs in nomadic function until its completion at larval maturity.

On grounds already considered, I believe it is impossible to account for the reproductive periodicity of the Eciton queen either on the hypothesis of a strictly autonomous endogenous rhythm or as a response to an *extra-colony* physical rhythm. Rather, from evidence summarized in this paper, both the initiation of ovulation and certain well-marked intervening stages in the process, as well as the completed maturation and delivery of each specific brood generation as eggs, may be considered physiological responses of the queen to certain stimulative and trophic conditions in the colony adequate to instigate such changes. These we have described as feed-back relationship of the queen with the colony functional situation, through which she is *indirectly* responsible for the regular appearance of brood-excitatory factors critical for the colony functional cycle as well as for timing her own reproductive functions. All in all, however, the efficient operation of this complex timing mechanism depends upon a number of specialized functional interrelationships dependent upon the properties of workers, brood, and queen (Figure 99).

Raignier and Van Boven imply that the Anomma queen delivers her broods on the basis of an endogenous rhythm. Their evidence, however, seems inconclusive. In fact, their results as concern delivery of eggs and maturation of broods actually encourage a hypothesis of situation-stimulated queen function consistent with the theory offered above for *Eciton*. If we assume that new reproductive episodes in the queen are aroused through the effect upon her of trophic and stimulative changes in the colony, reported variations in the timing of egg-laying in queens of *A. wilverthi* become more understandable, as does the much longer interbrood interval suggested for the queen of *D. (A.) nigricans*.

Finally, one of the most striking aspects of Eciton epigaeic adaptation is a process of population control through which a complete colony emigration can be accomplished within a single night. Obviously, specializations in the queen are involved, since the Eciton queen lays considerably smaller broods than does the Anomma queen, for example. In contrast, hypogaeic tropical dorylines, characteristically with larger colonies than in *Eciton,* present a pattern of single emigrations with intervening stops over much longer intervals, relatively independent of the diurnal rhythm. In this process, brood-exposure in the daytime is reduced through worker behavioral mechanisms (as clustering and forming arcades of detritus) not observed in the Ecitons. Evidence considered earlier in this paper indicates that adaptive mechanisms influencing population control and the degree of hypogaeic life in general must involve not only the queen but all types of individual in the colony. If such mechanisms are to be considered ancestral or primitive on the grounds that hypogaeic patterns must be so classified, then it would seem that they have been lost or occluded in the course of epigaeic specialization.

CONCLUSIONS

1. In the ant subfamily Dorylinae, a predatory, carnivorous way of life has been widely combined selectively with large colonies, by virtue of a periodic nomadism in a cyclical pattern stabilized through a control by reproductive processes.

2. A nomad-statary pattern seems to hold in some form in all of this subfamily, with the essential energizing effect exerted by active stages of developing broods.

3. The Ecitons of tropical America, evolved under conditions of continuous deep forest and good cover, evidently have the most complex functional pattern of the group. Their essentially epigaeic adaptation is keyed

to the diel light rhythm and the march of atmospheric changes as well as to other surface conditions. This pattern is centered around interrelationships among a complex set of factors arising through epigaeic adaptations in workers, queen, and brood.

4. The characteristic Eciton nomad-statary pattern is energized by two principal brood-stimulative factors: (1) a callow-excitatory factor initiating the nomadic phase, and (2) a synchronized larval-excitatory factor maintaining and at length closing this phase at a species-characteristic duration.

5. A general similarity is discernible between the functional pattern of the Ecitons and that of the African *Anomma* in the colony-energizing effect exerted by a brood at nymphal maturity, initiating nomadism.

6. Limitation of *Anomma* to a single continuous emigration of the colony in what may be regarded as a short nomadic phase is attributable to the absence of a larval-stimulative factor of sufficient strength to maintain the phase as in *Eciton*.

7. Adaptation in terms of a nomad-statary functional cycle may have evolved homologously in epigaeic and hypogaeic doryline species of both Old and New Worlds, with secondary differences as noted above.

8. With the Eciton queen perhaps the most specialized of all, the dichthadiigynes in the dorylines generally may approximate a periodic pattern in reproductive function. Queens of epigaeic and hypogaeic species may differ mainly in the precision with which successive ovulative episodes are delimited, and in the capacity for overlapping successive generations.

9. Cyclical variations in the reproductive functions of all doryline queens may depend, as in *Eciton,* not on an autonomous endogenous rhythm but on excitatory effects arising periodically through the trophic and social-stimulative situation of the colony.

REFERENCES

Borgmeier, T. 1933. A rainha de *Eciton rogeri* Dalla Torre. (Hym. Formicidae). *Rev. Entom.* 3: 92–96.

Borgmeier, T. 1955. Die Wanderameisen der Neotropischen Region (Hym. Formicidae). *Studia Entomologia,* Nr. 3, Ed. Vozes Limitada, Petropolis, R. J. Brasil.

Bruch, C. 1934. Las formas femeninas de Eciton. *Anal. Soc. Cien. Argent.* 118: 113–135.

Cohic, F. 1948. Observations morphologiques et ecologiques sur *Dorylus* (*Anomma*) *nigricans.* Ill. (Hym. Dorylidae). *Rev. Fr. Ent.* 14: 229–276.

Creighton, W. S. 1950. The ants of North America. *Bull. Mus. Comp. Zool.* 104: 1–585.

Emery, C. 1895. Le problème des Dorylus. *Bull. Soc. Ent. Fr.*, lxxi–lxxiv.

Emery, C. 1910. Sous-famille Dorylinae (Hym., Form.). In Wytsman's *Genera Insectorum*, Fasc. 102: 1–34.

Forel, A. 1891. Ueber die Ameisensubfamilie der Doryliden. *Verh. Ges. deutsch. Naturf. Aerzte* 63: 162–164.

Forel, A. 1906. Fourmis neotropiques nouvelles ou peu connues. *Ann. Soc. Ent. Belg.* 60: 225–249.

Fraenkel, G. 1932. Die Wanderungen der Insekten. *Ergeb. Biol.* 9: 1–238.

Gallardo, A. 1920. Las hormigas de la República Argentina—Subfamilia dorilinas. *An. Mus. Nac. Hist. Nat Buenos Aires* 30: 281–410.

Hagan, H. 1954. The reproductive system of the army-ant queen, *Eciton* (*Eciton*). Part 1. General Anatomy. *Am. Mus. Nov.*, no. 1663: 1–12; Part 2. Histology. *Ibid.*, no. 1664: 1–17; Part 3. The oöcyte cycle. *Ibid.*, no. 1665: 1–20.

Heape, W. 1931. *Emigration, migration and nomadism.* Cambridge: Heffer.

Holliday, M. 1904. A study of some ergatogynic ants. *Zool. Jb., Syst.* 19: 292–328.

Ihering, H. von. 1912. Biologie und Verbreitung der brasilianischen Arten von *Eciton. Entom. Mitteilungen* 1: 226–235.

Jackson, W. B. 1957. Microclimatic patterns in the army ant bivouac. *Ecology.* In press.

Lappano, E. 1955. A morphological study of polymorphism in the larva of the army ant, *Eciton burchelli*, and comparisons with that of *Eciton hamatum.* (Ph.D. thesis on file in the library of Fordham University, New York City.)

LeMasne, G. 1953. Observations sur les relations entre le couvain et les adultes chez les fourmis. *Ann. Sci. Nat. Zool.* 15: 1–56.

Long, D. 1955. Observations on sub-social behavior in two species of lepidopterous larvae, *Pieris brassicae* L. and *Plusia gamma* L. *Trans. Roy. Ent. Soc. Lond.* 106: 421–437.

Luederwaldt, H. 1918. Notas myrmecologicas. *Rev. Mus. Paulista* 10: 31–64.

Marshall, F. 1936. Sexual periodicity and the causes which determine it. *Phil. Trans. Roy. Soc. Lond.*, Ser. B, 226: 423–456.

Müller, W. 1886. Beobachtungen an Wanderameisen (*Eciton hamatum* Fabr.). *Kosmos*, 10 Jahrg., 18: 81–93.

Raignier, A., and J. Van Boven. 1955. Étude taxonomique, biologique et biométrique des Dorylus du sous-genre Anomma (Hymenoptera Formicidae). *Ann. Mus. Roy. Congo Belge, Tervuren*, N.S., Sci. Zool., 2: 359.

Reichensperger, A. 1934. Beitrag zur Kenntnis von *Eciton lucanoides* Em. *Zool. Anz.* 106: 240–245.

Schneirla, T. C. 1933. Studies on army ants in Panama. *J. Comp. Psychol.* 15: 267–299.

Schneirla, T. C. 1934. Raiding and other outstanding phenomena in the behavior of army ants. *Proc. Nat. Acad. Sci.* 20: 316–321.

Schneirla, T. C. 1938. A theory of army-ant behavior based upon the analysis of activities in a representative species. *J. Comp. Psychol.* 25: 51–90.

Schneirla, T. C. 1940. Further studies on the army-ant behavior pattern.—

Mass organization in the swarm-raiders. *J. Comp. Psychol.* 29: 401–460.

Schneirla, T. C. 1944a. The reproductive functions of the army-ant queen as pace-makers of the group behavior pattern. *J. N.Y. Entom. Soc.* 52: 153–192.

Schneirla, T. C. 1944b. Studies on the army-ant behavior pattern.—Nomadism in the swarm-raider *Eciton burchelli. Proc. Am. Philos. Soc.* 87: 438–457.

Schneirla, T. C. 1945. The army-ant behavior pattern: Nomadstatary relations in the swarmers and the problem of migration. *Biol. Bull.* 88: 166–193.

Schneirla, T. C. 1947. A study of army-ant life and behavior under dry-season conditions with special reference to reproductive functions. 1. Southern Mexico. *Am. Mus. Nov.,* no. 1336: 1–20.

Schneirla, T. C. 1948. Army-ant life and behavior under dry-season conditions with special reference to reproductive functions. II. The appearance and fate of the males. *Zoologica* 33: 89–112.

Schneirla, T. C. 1949. Army-ant life and behavior under dry-season conditions. III. The course of reproduction and colony behavior. *Bull. Am. Mus. Nat. Hist.* 94: 5–81.

Schneirla, T. C. 1952. Basic correlations and coordinations in insect societies with special reference to ants. *Coll. Int., Cent. Nat. Rech. Sci.* XXXIV, 1950: 247–269.

Schneirla, T. C. 1956. A preliminary survey of colony division and related processes in two species of terrestrial army ants. *Insectes Sociaux* 3: 49–69.

Schneirla, T. C., and R. Z. Brown. 1950. Army-ant life and behavior under dry-season conditions. 4. Further investigation of cyclic processes in behavioral and reproductive functions. *Bull. Am. Mus. Nat. Hist.* 95:267–353.

Schneirla, T. C., and R. Z. Brown. 1952. Sexual broods and the production of young queens in two species of army ants. *Zoologica* 37: 5–32.

Schneirla, T. C., R. Z. Brown, and Frances Brown. 1954. The bivouac or temporary nest as an adaptive factor in certain terrestrial species of army ants. *Ecol. Monogr.* 24: 269–296.

Smith, M. R. 1927. A contribution to the biology and distribution of one of the legionary ants, *Eciton schmitti* Emery. *Ann. Ent. Soc. Am.* 20: 401–404.

Smith, M. R. 1942. The legionary ants of the United States belonging to *Eciton* subgenus *Neivamyrmex* Borgmeier. *Am. Midl. Nat.* 27: 537–596.

Sumichrast, F. 1868. Notes on the habits of certain species of Mexican hymenoptera presented to the American Entomological Society. *Trans. Am. Ent. Soc.* 2: 39–44.

Tafuri, J. 1955. Growth and polymorphism in the larva of the army ant (*Eciton* (*E.*) *hamatum Fabricius*). *J. N.Y. Entom. Soc.* 63: 21–41.

Vosseler, J. 1905. Die ostafrikanische Treiberameise (Siafu). *Pflanzer, Jg.* 1, Nr. 19: 289–302.

Weber, N. A. 1941. The rediscovery of the queen of *Eciton* (*Labidus*) *coecum* Latr. *Am. Midl. Nat.* 26: 325–329.

Weber, N. 1943. The ants of the Imatong Mountains. *Bull. Mus. Comp. Zool.* 93: 265–389.

Werringloer, A. 1932. Die Sehorgane und Sehzentren der Dorylinen nebst Untersuchungen über die Facttenenaugen der Formiciden. *Z. wiss. Zool.* 141: 432–524.

Wheeler, W. M. 1900. The female of *Eciton sumichrasti* Norton, with some notes on the habits of Texas Ecitons. *Am. Nat.* 34: 563–574.

Wheeler, W. M. 1910. *Ants, their structure, development, and behavior.* New York: Columbia Univ. Press.

Wheeler, W. M. 1921. Observations on army ants in British Guiana. *Proc. Am. Acad. Arts Sci.* 56: 291–328.

Wheeler, W. M. 1922. Keys to the genera and subgenera of ants. *Bull. Am. Mus. Nat. Hist.* 45: 631–710.

Wheeler, W. M. 1925. The finding of the queen of the army ant *Eciton hamatum* Fabricius. *Biol. Bull.* 49: 139–149.

Wheeler, W. M. 1928. *The social insects.* New York: Harcourt, Brace.

Wheeler, W. M., and I. W. Bailey. 1920. The feeding habits of Pseudomyrminae and other ants. *Trans. Am. Philos. Soc.* 22: 235–279.

Wheeler, W. M., and W. H. Long. 1901. The males of some Texas Ecitons. *Am. Nat.* 35: 157–173.

T. C. SCHNEIRLA

Dorylines: Raiding and in Bivouac

Bibliography No. 110

PART I

BROOD IS KEY TO CYCLES IN LEGIONARY ANTS

The doryline, or legionary, ants of the world are all raiders, living mainly on arthropod prey, and are all nomadic, without permanent nests. As one of the eight or so subfamilies of ants, they are specialized along these lines, presumed to be an ancient off-shoot from the primitive ponerines, which arose from the wasplike ancestors of all ants. The dorylines—in contrast to their probable ancestors, the early ponerines, which themselves have continued as a large, distinct subfamily characterized by raiding behavior, a carnivorous diet, and relatively small colonies—have maintained the predatory pattern but with much larger colonies and with strong emphasis upon large group forays and nomadism as their way of life.

Doryline genera differ greatly among themselves in the degree and the nature of their specialization of the common subfamily behavior pattern. The most primitive and simplified of all may be the genus *Aenictus* of the Old World. Although *Aenictus* interested me increasingly from the time of my first research on American dorylines in Panama, it was thirty years before the circle rounded so that I actually could see and study the *Aenictus* genus in the field.

My research began with army ants of the tropical American genus *Eciton,* perhaps the most specialized of all dorylines. In this genus, *E. burchelli* and *E. hamatum* are among the few species of all *Eciton* (and hence of all dorylines) well adapted behaviorally and biologically to surface conditions.

E. burchelli and *E. hamatum* are closely similar in the external structure of their queens, males, and workers, and so are regarded by sys-

Part I is from *Natural History* 74(8): 44–51. Copyright © 1965 by The American Museum of Natural History. Reprinted with permission.

FIGURE 100
Area of *Aenictus* investigation was on Negros Island in the Philippines.
The Mindanao Sea is in the background.

tematists as closely related. The anatomical similarities in their worker series—which are polymorphic, or differentiated both in size and structural gradations from the minim to the major workers—are shown in Figures 104 and 105. Although the two species are much alike in their degree of surface adaptation, some important differences exist between them, particularly in their patterns of raiding and in their typical prey. *E. burchelli* is the well-known tropical American swarm raider, an excitable ant whose mass forays are large and complex (in Panama and Mexico I have seen their advancing swarms exceed 65 feet in width), whereas *E. hamatum* is a less excitable ant whose raids are marked by widely branched columns extended into new terrain by small groups that also begin pillaging operations. The striking difference in the typical raiding patterns of these two species is represented in Figure 109. The species also differ greatly in their booty. *E. burchelli* captures a wide variety of arthropod prey ranging from spiders and leaf-insects—torn up and carried back in pieces to the temporary nest—to ants and their brood; *E. hamatum,* in contrast, specializes on ants and their brood carried, as a rule, in whole.

Perhaps the most striking aspect of behavior common to the two species is that of the functional cycle, which presents two alternating phases. One of these phases covers an interval of species-typical length in which the colony carries out vigorous daily raids that generally end in nighttime emigrations to new nesting sites. I have called this the "nomadic phase." The other also involves an interval of species-typical length in which, however, raids are small or sometimes absent and emigrations highly exceptional. This I have called the "statary phase." The nomadic phase in *E. hamatum* usually lasts 16 to 18 days, in *E. burchelli,* 12 to 17 days; the statary phase is usually 20 or 21 days long in both species. Because the durations of these phases (hence of the successive cycles of any colony throughout the year) depend upon the interactions of complex functions based upon the properties of brood, queen, and workers, these values, predictable for each species, seem phenomenally precise.

The fundamentals of the cycle, first worked out for these *Eciton* species, may be summarized briefly. Each statary phase in *Eciton* ends when a large new brood matures and emerges as young workers, an event that so greatly arouses the colony as to shift it at once into high, so to speak, in a new nomadic phase. The basis of the excitation lies in a variety of mass-stimulative tactual and chemical effects exerted upon the colony by an emerging brood of callow workers. These workers take a few days for their postpupal maturation, during which the colony remains in its newly excited condition. The large broods of *Eciton* overlap in time so that a new brood of young larvae becomes the major energizer of the colony as the stimulative effect of the callow brood falls to the level of the regular adult workers. As the new larval brood grows, its effect on mass arousal also increases, and the colony stages more and more vigorous raids and emigrations. But as soon as these tens of thousands of larvae become mature and spin their cocoons, their excitatory effect upon the colony quickly drops to a low level. Then nomadic behavior ceases and a statary phase begins. With a relatively low degree of stimulation from the brood, the worker population now raids only weakly, and the colony does not emigrate at all. The statary condition persists for about three weeks, or until the enclosed brood matures and, in its turn, introduces a high stimulative effect sufficient to set off a new nomadic phase.

Colony behavior among these *Eciton* species maintains the described alternate phasic changes throughout each year. The nomadic and statary changes in each colony correspond closely in their duration to regular variations in the quantitative level of mass stimulation from successive great broods. I use the term "mass" for these effects because in these dorylines the members of any one of the annual series of all-worker broods begin and pass through the stages of their development at nearly the same time. In *E. burchelli* successive all-worker broods appear at intervals of about 36 days, each brood containing 200,000 or more individ-

FIGURE 101
Workers of *Aenictus* move over leaf bridge on raiding trail with insect booty. Large piece is carried by group at lower center.

uals; in *E. hamatum* the interval is about the same, each brood containing about 80,000 young. These facts prepare one to appreciate what potent effects the broods can exert upon colony behavior as their activity levels and secretory properties change radically from one developmental stage to the next—rising steadily during the larval stage; falling to a low point held until near the end of the pupal stage when a moderate rise occurs; rising abruptly with full pupal maturation and emergence as callow workers.

In another genus of American dorylines, *Neivamyrmex,* which I studied in Alabama and at the Southwestern Research Station of The American Museum of Natural History in Arizona, a comparable nomadic-statary cycle was demonstrated. Recently Mr. Howard Topoff, working in association with my project, obtained evidence that the workers of *N. nigrescens*

FIGURE 102
Bivouac of *Eciton hamatum* colony, now in its nomadic behavioral phase, forms an open cluster 20 inches high in hollow between buttressed roots.

show a sharply higher condition of physiological activity (as in oxygen consumption) during a nomadic phase than during a statary phase. As would also be expected from my theory of brood stimulation, this level normally increases through the nomadic phase to a high point reached near the end, but is abnormally low in colonies with greatly reduced larval broods.

The known species of *Eciton* and *Neivamyrmex,* although distinctive structurally and in many aspects of their behavior, resemble one another so closely in the phase durations and evident brood-stimulative causation of their functional cycles as to justify our referring to them together as the E-N group in comparing them with other of the dorylines.

However, a different state of affairs seems to exist in other dorylines, such as the Afro-Asian driver ants in the genera *Anomma* and *Dorylus.* These ants, and apparently also the tropical American genus *Labidus,* present markedly variable activity schedules in which single emigrations of the great colonies occur at irregular intervals that range from a few

FIGURE 103
In contrast to *Eciton hamatum,* an *Aenictus laeviceps* colony gathers under dry leaves in a platter type of cluster. Both species are well adapted to surface conditions.

days to around two months in length. Between emigrations, a colony remains at the same nesting site, raiding from it in different directions on some days—somewhat as colonies of the E-N group do in their statary phases. *Aenictus,* however, resembles the E-N genera in its colony behavior, and we may include it in an E-N-A group characterized by regular, clearly marked nomadic-statary cycles.

Aenictus, an Old World genus of more than 46 known species, ranging from Africa through Asia into the Philippines, New Guinea, and Australia, is distinctive in several respects. In contrast to the other four genera mentioned, the ants in all *Aenictus* species are relatively small. *Aenictus* workers, only about 3 mm long in some species to 5 mm long in others, are exceeded in size by all but the smallest workers of the genera we have discussed, and contrast strongly with body lengths of 12 to 13 mm in the major workers of *Eciton* and *Anomma.* The males of *Aenictus* are also correspondingly smaller, as are the queens. Another striking difference is that although the workers of the other genera are polymorphic (presenting differences in size and structure in a series ranging from the minim to the major workers), the workers of any *Aenictus* colony are nearly monomorphic (closely similar in size and structure). Still other differences are in colony and brood populations:

Species	Estimated worker population	Estimated worker brood
Anomma wilverthi	10–20,000,000	1,000,000
Labidus praedator	3–6,000,000	800,000
Eciton burchelli	1,000,000	200,000
Eciton hamatum	250,000	80,000
Neivamyrmex nigrescens	150,000	50,000
Aenictus laeviceps	100,000	35,000

My interest in *Aenictus* dated from the time when, shortly after my *Eciton* work began in 1932, I read a paper by the eminent Italian ant taxonomist Carlos Emery. Based on studies of preserved material, he arrived at the conclusion that *Aenictus* might be one of the most archaic dorylines and therefore one closest to the primitive trunk near the ponerines. With time I became increasingly interested in the comparative behavioral importance of the relatively small size of *Aenictus* workers and colonies and monomorphism in the workers.

Investigating the behavior of existing species is a relatively new approach to the study of evolutionary relationships. In contrast with this approach, the taxonomists' classifications derive mainly from the study and comparison of structures in extinct and in existing forms. The approach through behavior study is necessarily the more devious one, for the relationship of structure to behavior is nearly always indirect and involved,

Eciton burchelli

Eciton hamatum

FIGURE 104
Polymorphic *Eciton* workers are from 3 to 13 mm long.

Aenictus laeviceps

FIGURE 105
The monomorphic *Aenictus* workers
measure about 2.7 to 3.5 mm.

Aenictus gracilis

and the nature of structural-behavioral relationships still proves highly refractory to investigation. But the behavior of insects (and of other invertebrates) is more closely related to, and more directly influenced by, specific structural characteristics than is that of mammals. From progress already made in discerning the significance of behavioral data for evolutionary relationships in both invertebrates and vertebrates, new approaches along these lines should furnish valuable clues to research and theory. Experience with *Aenictus* has strengthened this interest in evolutionary relationships.

One who encouraged pursuing the *Aenictus* problem was Dr. J. W. Chapman, who studied these and other ants during his long period of service as missionary, biologist, and administrator at Silliman University in Negros Island, southern Philippines. Even during the war, when the Chapmans were forced by the Japanese military (who considered them dangerous) to move high into the mountains west of Dumaguete, Dr. Chapman studied colonies of *Aenictus,* whose activities he thought fitted well the pattern of the *Eciton* cycle as I had described it. Sadly enough—although it was Dr. Chapman's enthusiastic letters about the abundance of *Aenictus* colonies in the Dumaguete area that finally took me there—before either his own monograph on *Aenictus* ecology or our results on the functional cycle could be published, he was accidentally killed.

It was the palm-thatched Chapman cottage on the mountain slopes above Dumaguete that, upon his invitation, became the headquarters of our *Aenictus* project when I began it in 1961. Subsequent field investigations have been carried out by an able group of Filipinos directed by my collaborator, Professor Alfredo Reyes, who is with the Silliman University Department of Biology.

At first we worked in the upper forest in an area about 3,000 feet square marked off in coordinates for accurately tracing colony movements. By degrees, however, the investigation shifted down to a much larger area that included a plateau of mixed cover and a deep gorge of heavier cover, as new colonies for study were found there. Gradually,

FIGURE 106
Cleto, a member of the research group, marks the entrance to an underground bivouac. The ant colony's main raiding trail is shown by string on the right.

also, the daily schedule of research lengthened until it stretched—to meet the *Aenictus* schedule—around the clock.

Doryline activity schedules vary greatly, according to genus and species and to the conditions of the area and the colony. For example, the two surface-adapted *Eciton* species, *E. hamatum* and *E. burchelli,* start their nomadic-phase raids at dawn and build them up during the day. Toward dusk they shift into an emigration that is completed during the night. *Neivamyrmex nigrescens,* of our southern states, less surface-adapted than these *Eciton* species but also a surface raider, generally starts its nomadic raids at dusk and emigrates later in the nightly schedule. These dorylines clearly have quite different daily schedules in the nomadic phase, with the two *Eciton* species day-active in raiding and *N. nigrescens* night-active, although the nomadic raids of all three are long and nearly always end in colony emigrations. These daily nomadic schedules contrast with behavior in the two surface-adapted species of *Aenictus* on which we concentrated. The *Aenictus* colonies, when nomadic, proved capable of raiding or emigrating at any time of day or night, with variations relating mainly to colony condition.

FIGURE 107
Workers congregate in laboratory nest. Maturing larvae are in the lower right corner. Excitation by larval broods stimulates more energetic raiding.

Although at present we can only speculate as to the basis of this generic difference, sensitivity to light is probably the main factor. Most of the New World dorylines, including the E-N group, have small, specialized eyes (lateral ocelli) that cause arousal by light although they play no demonstrable role in orientation. *Aenictus,* whose workers have no eyes at all, reacts to light in tests. Significantly, the surface-adapted species have pale spots in places such as the sides and corners of the head. These may mark the location of subdermal light-sensitive cells. Such spots are absent, however, in other, more subterranean *Aenictus* species, which seem light-shy and in the daytime operate underground or beneath surface cover, unless they are in the dim light of heavy forest. We found that *Aenictus* raids, early in the nomadic phase, begin most frequently toward dusk. On subsequent days, they shift increasingly to morning starts. But throughout most of the phase, paralleling a clearly increasing colony excitement, they can begin at almost any time. A hypersensitivity to light, which inhibits daytime raiding aboveground, may prevail early in the no-

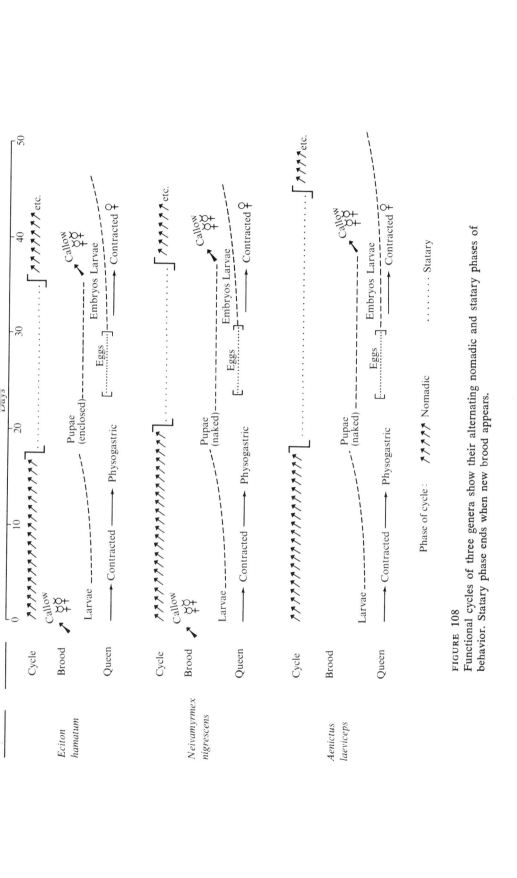

FIGURE 108

Functional cycles of three genera show their alternating nomadic and statary phases of behavior. Statary phase ends when new brood appears.

madic phase, and may be succeeded in that phase by a condition in which light becomes attractive and daytime surface activity increases as the level of colony excitement rises.

Our studies were concentrated on *Aenictus laeviceps* and *A. gracilis,* the two dominant surface-adapted species in the Dumaguete area. When colonies of these species are nomadic, they commonly raid on the surface even in full daylight. How far surface adaptation has progressed in *A. laeviceps* and *A. gracilis* is shown by the fact that their colonies, when nomadic, usually form their bivouacs on the surface itself—although generally under a light cover, such as leaves—in simple, disk-shaped clusters that enclose the broods and queen. In the last nomadic days, however, a tendency toward underground bivouacking appears, and subterranean (or deeply concealed) sites are the rule in the statary phase. A generic similarity in nesting reactions, dependent upon changing colony condition in the cycle, is indicated by the similar behavior of *E. hamatum* and *E. burchelli;* both shift from exposed surface bivouacs to sheltered sites in late nomadic days and to deep shelter (in hollow logs or trees) to start the statary phase. From our evidence, both *Eciton* and *Aenictus* readily enter more sheltered sites as they become disturbed by such conditions as air currents, higher temperatures, and dryness, typical of the open sites occupied in the nomadic phase.

However, the surface clusters formed by colonies of these *Aenictus* species in the nomadic phase may be considered primitive in comparison with the complex, highly specialized nomadic bivouacs typical of *E. burchelli* and *E. hamatum.* The *Eciton* species are also much more highly specialized than *Aenictus* in their patterns of raiding. The raiding forays of all dorylines are carried out on chemical trails, made as ants in the advance groups enter new terrain and in their excitement deposit body secretions that can be followed by others who, in pressing on, extend the trail similarly in relay fashion.

The main development of an *Aenictus* raid involves a stage of exodus from the bivouac, in which a heavy column divides and redivides while the raiders accumulate booty in caches at the trail junctions; and then (in the simplest case) a stage of reversed traffic, in which the booty is transported to the bivouac. In more complex cases, successive new outbursts from the bivouac may occur, reinforcing the raid and extending the front, before a lasting reversal of traffic toward the bivouac occurs or the entire colony emigrates over trails formed during the raid. The raiding systems of *Aenictus* are smaller and simpler than the branching systems of *E. hamatum.* Although the nomadic-phase raids of *E. hamatum* last through the entire interval of daylight and often build up to a distance of more than 800 feet, those of *Aenictus* generally last only from part of an hour to a few hours and usually do not extend more than 65 feet.

FIGURE 109
Top. Raiding patterns of *Eciton
hamatum* (A), *Eciton burchelli* (B),
and *Aenictus laeviceps* (C). The
Aenictus gracilis pattern is similar to
C. Bottom. Daily schedules compare
activities of *Eciton, Neivamyrmex,*
and *Aenictus.*

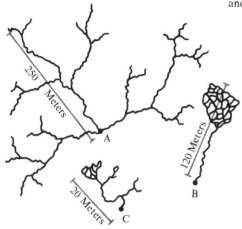

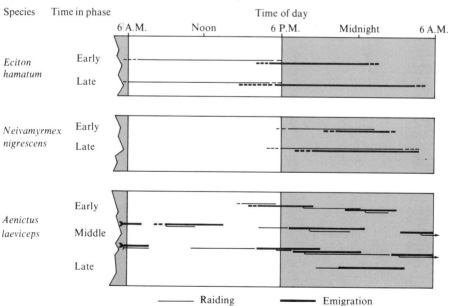

Daily Schedule of Activities
(Nomadic phase)

A simpler and more direct relationship seems to exist between raiding and emigration in *Aenictus* than in the E-N group. *Aenictus* colonies, even when nomadic, often show quiescent intervals at the bivouac during which no ants emerge. These intervals may occur at almost any time and last from part of an hour to several hours. But this does not mean that a relatively dormant condition then exists in the colony, as it does in the statary phase. Laboratory observations indicate that these pauses in external activities arise mainly through processes that hold ants within the bivouac, and particularly through worker actions with the brood, such as feeding. External conditions may also play a part, as on hot, bright days when quiescent intervals occur more frequently about midday than at other times. Even *Eciton* species, which never stop their nomadic raids throughout the day, often exhibit a slowdown in the midday period.

The start of a new *Aenictus* raid, after either an emigration or an interval of external quiescence, is marked by the sudden appearance from the bivouac of a few dozen agitated workers that rush back and forth on the trail, their numbers usually increasing rather suddenly. Often this event approaches the magnitude of an explosion of forces in a rushing column or a spreading mass. In the raids of excited nomadic *Aenictus* colonies, the stage of exodus and of dividing and redividing columns is followed by a stage of pillaging, in which networks of columns with variable terminal groups form and re-form as the ants reach a productive area, such as a group of ant nests, then surge on and repeat the process in another area. Often the raiders seem to be following the victims' own chemical trails, as when a column surges directly to the prey's nest from a yard or two away. Many times the prospective victims are aroused in advance by their own foragers that have met the *Aenictus* frontal wave, so that when the raiders arrive, the disturbed occupants are already rushing forth with their brood to scatter and huddle under leaves until all is again quiet. In this way, as well as by defense, in larger colonies the victims may salvage some of their young. It is quite possible that the *Aenictus* become attracted to the species odors of their common victims, and the victims repelled by that of their common enemy, through simple processes of conditioned-response learning.

As inspections of the booty returned to caches or to the bivouac suggest, the victims include a variety of arthropods, both social and solitary, as well as other invertebrates. *Aenictus* booty covers a wide range, even including vegetable matter, with various species of ants and their broods most frequent, but with termites, wasps and their brood, roaches, spiders, beetles, and a host of others also taken. The *Aenictus* are quick, have strong jaws and virulent stings, can usually rush numbers to the scene of a heavy fight, and are not often worsted when the raid issues from an ex-

FIGURE 110
Posed workers of *Aenictus laeviceps* attack one of *Polyrachis bihamata*. Colonies of tree-dwelling *Polyrachis* are often victims of *Aenictus* raids.

cited nomadic colony. Pulling at a victim from all sides, often in chains of interlocked bodies, *Aenictus* are capable of tearing to bits even the large earthworms they sometimes attack in their underground burrows. Frequent victims among the ants are colonies of tree-nesting *Camponotus* and *Polyrachis,* the latter often succumbing despite the heavy armor and body spines of their workers and the sutured-leaf nests that enclose their broods.

In vigorous raids, *Aenictus* columns regularly mount the lower vegetation and even get high into tall trees, where invasions into the nests of ants and of wasps, such as the large tropical *Ropalida* sp., often prove fruitful. Despite the strong, snapping jaws of the wasps, which crush many of them, the *Aenictus* tear through the paper walls into brood cells from which the young are dragged out together with the huge bodies of those adults that stayed to fight. Such raids may last for hours when vigorous nomadic-phase raids of legionaries strike large colonies of ants or wasps.

An *Aenictus* colony makes a substantial haul of booty on nomadic-phase raids simply by pushing forward its dragnet of dividing and redividing columns over a widening zone. The first raiders to emerge with pieces of booty usually reverse their direction quickly to the rear and are soon on their way to a booty cache or the bivouac. Turning correctly at trail branches is simplified because these branches, through the forward momentum of the initial dividing groups, are likely to be Y-shaped with their bases pointed toward the nest. For the booty-carriers, it is not a matter of knowing where the nest is, but merely a process of following a chemical track and bucking traffic. After a time, however, when outgoing traffic has lessened and the laden traffic has increased, the booty-carriers seem to be aided by a new olfactory cue, and can take the correct (nestward) trail by turning to the side that is saturated with booty odor. This saturation of the trail, as in E-N raids, is caused both by the direct contact of dragged heavy pieces with the ground and by volatilization from lighter, carried pieces.

Aenictus raids sometimes continue for hours, with the colony collecting thousands of pieces of arthropod booty from the area through which it is passing. This booty, whether returned to the current bivouac or left in caches until carried to the next bivouac in an emigration, is soon consumed by the colony and especially by the brood.

FIGURE 111
Colony of *Aenictus* emigrates to new bivouac.
Each worker carries a larva.

PART II

EMIGRATION PATTERNS ARE COMPLEX

Part I of this discussion of legionary ants focused on raiding operations, in which *Aenictus* reveals its doryline relationship in such primary operations as forming branched chemical trails and attacking prey. It is clear that the behavior of *Aenictus* is complex, although primitive and simple in comparison with that of *Eciton*. This point is illustrated further in the emigrations, which in *Aenictus* arise more directly from raiding than in *Eciton*.

Part II is from *Natural History* 74(9): 40–47. Copyright © 1965 by The American Museum of Natural History. Reprinted with permission.

FIGURE 112
Queen, *arrow,* covered by worker ants, passes in
an emigrating *Eciton* column.

As an *Aenictus* raid continues, two important changes are likely to follow sooner or later after much booty has been returned to the rear:
caches are formed and a new outpouring of traffic may begin. Caches are
booty dumps that usually are formed near the main trail branches where
raiders drop their loads and rush back into combat, or where others release their loads after having been blocked in traffic. The second change,
a new outpouring of workers upon the trail, results from a long caravan
of booty carriers entering the bivouac.

The prompt result may be an emigration—that is, a complete movement of the colony, with its entire worker personnel, its queen, its
transported brood, and accumulated booty—to a new site reached by fol-

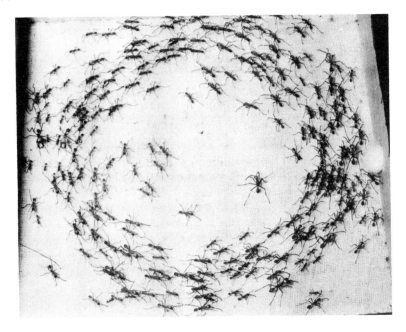

FIGURE 113
Excited workers in the nomadic phase move in circles
in a laboratory nest.

lowing the chemical trails of raiding. Early in the nomadic phase, however, with the presence of many callow workers that become agitatedly active when food is gone, the new exodus leads more often to an extension of raiding than to an emigration. When an emigration then occurs, the workers bearing packets of tiny larvae usually do not appear from the bivouac until some time after the exodus has begun. But later on in the phase, when the larvae are larger, more widely distributed through the bivouac cluster, and a potent excitant to workers, their actions—and, quite probably, their increased odorous effects when unfed—have the evident result of causing workers to grasp them and carry them forth promptly.

Brood carrying from the bivouac may begin soon after the main traffic reversal is under way, if chiefly unladen workers return from the raiding front, but is slower if the return of booty has been greater. Once brood carrying from the bivouac begins, however, it continues (barring interruptions, as by heavy rain) until the entire colony has moved. At the height of the movement the column often exceeds a half inch in width, appreciably thinning ahead of traffic blocks caused by groups of workers struggling along with oversized pieces of booty.

Another and more predictable cause of column thinning during emigra-

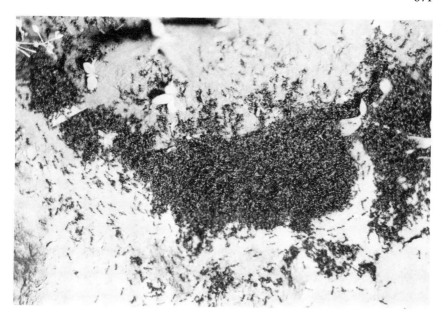

FIGURE 114
Bivouac (above) of a colony of *Aenictus laeviceps* forms beneath a rock. The emigration column enters below center.

tion is the passage of the queen. She moves along steadily under her own power, but somewhat more slowly than the general stream of workers (which runs at the rate of about one yard in twenty-two seconds); also, she is slowed by the workers that surge in masses around, over, before, and after her. One used to seeing the sizable queens of *Eciton* in their emigration runs is unprepared for seeing one of the relatively diminutive *Aenictus* queens running the route. Still, these queens, both the large *Eciton* and small *Aenictus,* are highly attractive to the workers, which form similar long entourages about them in the emigration. The entourage of the *Aenictus* queen is usually a yard or two long, in comparison with the several yards usual for *Eciton*. In both cases, the queen has a group of unladen workers before and after her in the column. These are a kind of royal guard that is regularly clustered around her in the bivouac—evidently older workers strongly odor-affiliated to the queen. In *Eciton,* older workers compose both the entourage of emigration and the queen's cluster in the bivouac. This is clear from their darker appearance, as age brings with it an increased pigmentary darkening.

The prompt transformation of raiding into an emigration seems to be a distinct *Aenictus* characteristic that we may consider primitive, in contrast to the far slower and more complex transformations typical of the

FIGURE 115
Colony of *Eciton hamatum* is agitated (right) as queen and her entourage, on log, leave during a nocturnal emigration.

Eciton-Neivamyrmex, or E-N, group. As the *Aenictus* larval brood grows and its stimulative potency increases, emigrations occur more frequently, until the daily total may be three or four. This impressive power of the brood to arouse, maintain, and increase colony nomadism offers excellent evidence for W. N. Wheeler's concept of "trophallaxis" (food exchange). However, our evidence warrants substituting the term "reciprocal stimulation," which more adequately conveys the broader meaning of a complex, bilateral process of varied tactual and chemical effects (including nutritive and neurosecretory effects) between workers and brood, with the queen also involved.

Emigrations early in the nomadic phase, in the absence of interruptions, usually run their course quickly in *Aenictus,* with the entire colony of about 100,000 workers, as well as brood and queen, moved to the new bivouac site within little more than two hours. This interval is considerably shorter than in *Eciton,* because of the smaller size of the workers and the smaller colony populations. *Eciton* emigrations at a comparable time in the phase take a minimum of five to six hours in *E. hamatum,* and much longer in *E. burchelli.* As Figures 104 and 105 show, the workers of *Aenictus* are much smaller than those of *Eciton.* In addition, their colony and brood populations are correspondingly smaller than other dorylines in the E-N-A genera and in *Anomma.* Many important differences in colony function and behavior seem related to these differences.

As the *Aenictus* nomadic phase progresses, interesting changes appear.

First the emigrations take an increasing time to run their course. The larvae are now larger and must be carried by the individual workers. They are held head-end forward and slung back under the worker's body in a characteristic ponerine manner. In late nomadic days, once the larva-carrying column is well under way, it is likely to overrun the zone of raiding into new terrain, so that treks of as much as eighty to one hundred yards may occur. Some of our records suggest that, in so doing, the colony hits upon and follows a chemical trail developed earlier by another colony of the species. Relatively great distances are thereby covered, incidentally insuring new, unworked terrain for the successive raids. In twenty-six emigrations carried out by a colony of *A. laeviceps* in one nomadic phase of eighteen days, a total ant-trail distance of more than two-thirds of a mile was covered.

Causes of the shift from raiding to emigration, although still unclear, evidently center upon stimulative relationships between workers and the larvae they feed. Laboratory observations suggest that the workers are attracted increasingly to individual larvae as their size and stimulative potency increase, and that one of two reactions may occur: workers drop food upon active larvae or pick up vigorously wriggling larvae and carry them off. Observational results suggest that the latter reaction occurs with increasing frequency as the food supply runs low. Behavioral changes seem to sweep quickly through the simple *Aenictus* bivouac cluster, however, and once the workers on one side of the mass are well started in carrying out the larvae, the procedure probably causes others to follow suit.

There are also interesting differences in the ways in which raids and emigrations begin as the nomadic phase extends in *Aenictus*. As the typical eighteen-day phase advances, emigration steadily becomes less predictable as an event following the exodus stage of raiding. Often two or more reversals of traffic may occur, each followed by an exodus that extends raiding, before an outpouring with brood marks the start of an emigration. Another new feature is that the exodus with brood may begin rather suddenly, either after an interval in which booty-laden returns to the bivouac are scanty or after an interval of (external) quiescence following the return of all raiders to the bivouac. "Quiescence" does not mean that the colony is dormant, as indications are that actions centered on brood feeding continue within the cluster. If we view an *Aenictus* emigration as the result of the mass excitation of workers to feeding relations with the brood, we can better understand that the threshold of emigration in their colonies can be reached more directly through uniform intrabivouac behavior and simpler relations with the raiding operations than can be found in the *Eciton-Neivamyrmex* group.

In *Eciton*, emigration is a complex event that has several prerequisite stages in the development of a day-long sequence of raiding operations

Species

Day in phase

Colony

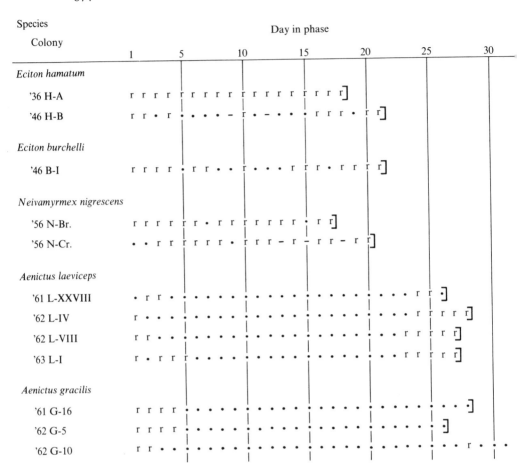

FIGURE 116
Raiding frequency in the statary phase is different for three genera. *Eciton* and *Neivamyrmex* both show decrease, while *Aenictus* ceases surface raiding.

synchronized with the march of environmental events between dawn and dusk. In *Neivamyrmex nigrescens* it is a complex process that occurs as part of routine nightly events arising from a raid begun at dusk. In the simpler activity sphere of *Aenictus,* both raiding and emigration are far less related to events in the day-night cycle, far more directly centered upon events within the colony. Thus, they often appear to occur by chance. The role assigned to chance in predicting these results, however, may be expected to decrease as mass behavioral processes and their underlying conditions within the colony become better known.

The more prompt and more direct occurrence of emigration in *Aenictus*

FIGURE 117
Monomorphic brood of mature worker larvae has just been removed from an
Aenictus laeviceps bivouac. Colony had been in early stages of the statary phase.

seems attributable not only to simpler raiding operations but also to more
direct and uniform processes of communication between worker and
brood populations in the bivouacs. Although this hypothesis rests upon
scattered evidence, the brood-stimulative theory from which it derives is
a strong one. One fact of significance for the entire process of cyclic colony behavior is that the brood and worker populations of *Aenictus* are
quasi-monomorphic, that is, they are composed of similar individuals that
react in much the same manner under the same conditions. This, together
with the relatively small colonies, means that a wave of excitation (due
to increased actions of larvae, perhaps also to secretions released by larvae
in the unfed condition) can spread far more quickly across the shallow
platter-shaped *Aenictus* bivouacs than across the more complexly organized, internally diversified bivouacs of the E-N group. In the simpler
Aenictus bivouac situation, once the reaction of suddenly grasping larvae

FIGURE **118**
Workers from a newly statary *Eciton* colony are busy with larvae.

and moving out is under way in one place, other workers respond quickly to the exit cues. The speedy transformation of *Aenictus* raiding to emigration seems explicable on the basis of relatively simple group behavioral relations.

But in the heterogeneous, large populations of E-N colonies, the complexity of raiding operations opposes quick reversals of colony behavior, and in the bivouacs, subgroups engaged in differing behavioral operations are inevitably present, most of them resisting the stimuli to radical behavioral changes (such as that of grasping larvae and moving off) until raiding is far advanced. With *Eciton,* I have been able to force premature emigrations only by means of widespread, intensive stimulations of bivouac surfaces, as by using a mirror to direct the hot, bright rays of a sun-fleck against the mass for several minutes.

In the complex daytime situation of a nomadic *Eciton* colony, extensive excitations of workers (through the return of a long procession of booty carriers) can lead to waves of exodus from the bivouac. These waves are

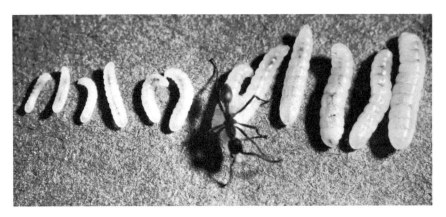

FIGURE 119
Large larvae of *Eciton hamatum* will be major workers; small will be minim.

generally absorbed in the expansion of the great raiding systems until darkness terminates the raids and promotes such uniform behavior as stereotyped trail following. In the advanced evolutionary status of *Eciton,* the more complex behavioral relationships between brood and workers basic to raiding and emigration have become synchronized with the regular day-night sequence of external events. In *Aenictus,* which has retained the primitive condition of smaller, more uniform colony populations, these patterns of mass behavior are controlled essentially within the colony, so they are simpler and operate much more freely in time. Even so, *Aenictus* belongs with the E-N groups in its cyclic functions.

In all three genera, the nomadic phase is governed by the duration of the main sweep of development in which the brood stimulates the adult population intensively—about eighteen days in *A. laeviceps* and *A. gracilis,* nineteen days in *N. nigrescens,* and sixteen to eighteen days in *E. hamatum.* In all three, the maintenance of a high level of nomadic function depends similarly upon summated stimulative events from the brood, and not a hypothetical "need for food." When the level of brood excitation falls sharply with larval maturation, as in *Eciton,* and with postlarval growth changes, as in *Neivamyrmex* and *Aenictus,* the colony lapses into the statary condition.

Because *Aenictus* has a nomadic-statary cycle equivalent to that of *Eciton* and *Neivamyrmex,* these three form an E-N-A group of genera in the dorylines in which colony functional phases change regularly and according to stimulative changes depending upon the brood. The most striking similarity between the archaic *Aenictus* and the far more specialized E-N genera is the duration of nomadic phases. Certainly the most striking difference is in the duration of the statary phase, which is about twenty-

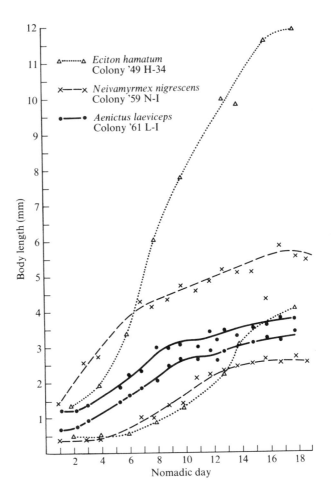

Growth rates and size ranges differ for larvae of three
doryline genera. Upper curves depict a brood's largest
members; lower curves depict smallest.

eight days in both *A. laeviceps* and *A. gracilis* in contrast to twenty or
twenty-one days in the *Eciton* species studied and eighteen or nineteen
days in *N. nigrescens*.

This statary-phase difference is surprising, for in all three genera the
principal cause of the statary phase is the onset of the pupal stage in a
maturing brood. The crucial point, however, is how this phase ends, an
event that in *Eciton* and *Neivamyrmex* depends specifically upon the
emergence of the brood as callow workers. But in *Aenictus* the statary

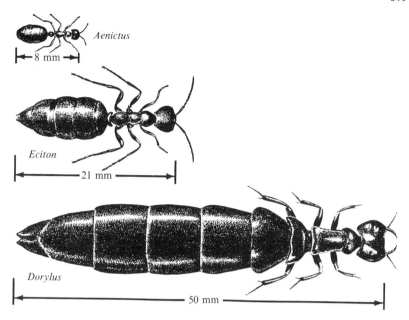

FIGURE 121

Batches of about 35,000 eggs are laid regularly by the queen of *Aenictus laeviceps*. Queen of *Eciton burchelli* lays batches of 225,000 at regular intervals. Queen of *Dorylus wilverthi* lays more than 1 million irregularly.

phase cannot end for this reason, as the pupal brood has matured in the first three weeks of the statary phase. The brood then merges into the general worker population during the days remaining before nomadism begins.

This difference requires us to compare functional events in the three genera during the statary phase. In all three, the phase begins in much the same way: first the larval brood matures; then the queen becomes gravid and delivers a new batch of eggs in a single series. In all three genera, the delivery of eggs begins at about the end of the first statary week and ends within eight to ten days (around statary-day 16). In all three, the queen seems to function similarly during this event: that is, in maturing and delivering the new batch of eggs she responds to changes in the colony situation centered on an abrupt shift in its stimulative and nutritive conditions enforced through brood changes at the end of the preceding nomadic phase. All circumstances indicate that as the larvae mature and cease feeding they continue for a time to excite the colony at a high level, accounting for a wave of grooming and feeding the queen by workers, which soon brings her into the gravid condition.

DORYLINE GENERA		TYPE OF FUNCTION

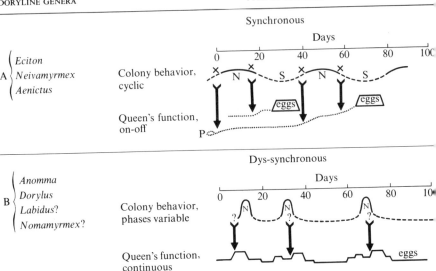

FIGURE 122

Regular cyclic functions of Group A are based on synchronous reproduction processes; varying functions of B are based on dys-synchronous reproduction.

The differences seem to center on how the new brood begins its development in each of the three genera. Let us start with the E-N broods, from which polymorphic workers develop. The causes of polymorphism, certainly complex, seem attributable in these ants to certain advantages of the first-laid eggs that result in developmental superiorities over those next in the series, these over the next ones, and so on. It is quite possible that the advantages of the first-laid eggs begin before they are laid, in their losing the least through ovisorption (absorption of nutriment) as they pass down the ovarioles of the queen as oöcytes. Accordingly, they are the first to become embryos, then the first to become microlarvae and to feed. Thus they gain advantages over the others in social stimulation and in feeding—advantages they maintain throughout the larval and pupal stages of development. The result is that individuals developing from first-laid eggs become major workers, whereas individuals produced later in the series become intermediate, minor and minim workers respectively.

Aenictus resembles *Eciton* and *Neivamyrmex* closely in the schedule of egg delivery, but it differs radically in the developmental circumstances in its colonies that finally produce monomorphic, rather than polymorphic, broods. First, the queen, although she is relatively small, delivers a relatively large batch of eggs on a schedule close to that of E-N; second, the workers pass through the statary phase not just underactive and on a re-

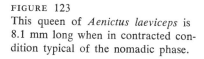

FIGURE 123
This queen of *Aenictus laeviceps* is
8.1 mm long when in contracted condition typical of the nomadic phase.

duced level physiologically (as do those of E-N colonies), but so near a
condition of dormancy that after the first four or five days of the phase
they remain in their underground bivouac without engaging in any surface
raiding at all.

These circumstances seem to result in effects on the brood and colony
that may account both for the longer statary phases of *Aenictus* and for
the way *Aenictus* colonies end this phase. Three hypotheses may be offered regarding the factors that affect the new brood in its earliest stages:
(1) the oöcytes are all reduced so radically in their nutritive contents
through extreme ovisorption in the queen that they start at much the same
low physiological level; (2) at this low ebb, the eggs offer far less attraction to the workers than in *Eciton* and *Neivamyrmex,* so there is far less
handling and licking of the eggs by workers—an activity that promotes
a differential early development in the egg series in the E-N; and (3) the
workers are unresponsive to the eggs by virtue of their own low physiological condition. (Significantly, the eggs in species of archaic ponerine
genera, such as the Australian bulldog ant *Myrmecia,* are in a dry condition after laying and are passed over by workers until they enter the
early larval stage.)

As a result, all the eggs of a new *Aenictus* brood begin and pass through
their development in nearly the same condition and at the same pace. It is
interesting to speculate as to what secretions (of queen, workers, and
brood) in E-N colonies may be deficient or even lacking in *Aenictus.*

It is clear that radical differences in function exist between *Aenictus*
and E-N. Even the maturation of the pupal brood after about three weeks
in the statary phase, an event that promptly stirs E-N colonies into no-

FIGURE 124
Early in statary phase, the queen becomes gravid and
takes on physogastric condition of egg production.

madism, seems to be only a partial excitant to *Aenictus,* which at that
period begins to raid weakly without any signs of emigrating. *Aenictus*
colonies become nomadic only when the new brood has reached the early
larval condition and is feeding. Thus, for them, the essential to set off
nomadism seems to be the ending of a preliminary pupal-maturation excitatory effect and a subsequent excitatory effect centered upon the minim
larvae.

Despite these differences, similarities in the timing and general properties of factors essential to the E-N-A types of nomadic-statary cycles suggest a common evolutionary origin. It would seem, on the other hand,
that their hypothetical common ancestors must have diverged early from
the ponerine-like stock from which arose *Anomma, Labidus,* and other
dorylines of great colony populations that exhibit isolated nomadic episodes of markedly irregular timing. The probably archaic conditions of
smaller colonies and monomorphic population seem to have succeeded
well enough in *Aenictus* to have been retained through its evolution in the
Old World.

Ancient conditions in the New World, however, presumably offered the primitive dorylines a greater variety of habitats in the forested and other terrain invaded by them than existed in the Old World. Far more extensive adaptive radiations may have arisen, advancing them much further into specializations than in the *Aenictus*-like stock remaining in the Old World, although the evolution of both continued to center on the nomadic-statary cycle. Consequently, in *Eciton* and *Neivamyrmex*, under the resulting conditions of greater selective pressures, a far greater diversity in species structure, function, and behavior arose than in *Aenictus*. We therefore find closely related species of *Eciton*, as for example *E. hamatum* and *E. burchelli*, strikingly different in these respects, whereas closely related species of *Aenictus*, as for example *A. laeviceps* and *A. gracilis*, are strikingly similar.

This preliminary comparison of existing doryline ants points to the co-existence—in this subfamily—of genera with large colonies that exhibit quasi-cyclic, irregular nomadism and other genera with smaller colonies that exhibit cyclic, regular patterns of nomadic behavior. As an exercise in insect social behavior, it also indicates a high degree of plasticity in factors basic to the evolution of the latter—the E-N-A type of cyclic behavior—from which there rose the highly specialized patterns that are characteristic of *Eciton*, as well as the primitive *Aenictus* system of predatism and nomadism.

VIII

ON ASPECTS OF
MAMMALIAN BEHAVIOR

Dr. Schneirla's research and articles on mammalian behavior reflect his views on major topics in comparative psychology. In fact, the choice of problems that he and his colleagues selected for investigation were based on the premise that they would demonstrate the heuristic value of his theoretical orientation. Therefore, to review his position on various topics in behavior, we selected a theoretical article, *A Consideration of Some Conceptual Trends in Comparative Psychology* (No. 57) * as the first paper in this section, bearing in mind that it fits just as readily in Part I.

In the article, *Psychological Problems in the Orientation of Mammals* (No. 72) (which would readily fit into Part VI), Schneirla emphasizes the importance of understanding behavior in terms of psychological levels, when he writes, ". . . there are levels of orientation capacity which are not just differences in degree, . . . but which are qualitatively distinct." Similarly in reference to perception he distinguishes between *stimulus-*

---

* This and subsequent numbers in this introduction refer to the items in the complete bibliography of Schneirla's works, p. 1017. Bold face numbers denote articles that are included in this volume.

response relationships, in which the response is forced by the sheer strength of the stimulus, and *perceptions,* in which the stimulus has learned pattern properties. He postulates, moreover, levels of perception in which there is increasing knowledge of objects and situations.

The importance of a developmental approach is emphasized in the article, written with E. Tobach, *Eliminative Responses in Mice and Rats and the Problem of "Emotionality"* (No. **100**). In this study, emotionality was defined by the rate of defecation in an open field and by related tests (avoidance conditioning and approach impedence). The authors showed that the defecatory reaction is dependent on specific features of the test situations and on the developmental histories of the individuals. From this it is argued that the defecatory reaction is not necessarily determined by innate factors and is not equivalent to a general characteristic such as "emotionality."

Dr. Schneirla's continuing criticism of nativistic explanations of behavioral phenomena would not be so convincing if he did not provide alternative methods of analysis and alternative explanations. One such example is his analysis, previously discussed, of the social and cyclical behavior of army ants (*A Theory of Army-Ant Behavior based upon the Analysis of Activities in a Representative Species,* No. **16**, in Part VII). Another example, reprinted here, is the study with J. Rosenblatt and E. Tobach on *Maternal Behavior in the Cat* (No. **104**). Here the authors demonstrated that the physiological events of parturition and the organic by-products of these events (e.g., appearance of neonate, placenta, and amniotic fluid) initiate various female activities. Uterine contractions, for example, cause the female to orient to her anogenital and abdominal regions and to lick these regions. Later, the attractive amniotic fluid, which covers the neonate, reinforces the licking of the kitten by the female. Events such as these establish a bond between mother and litter that is strengthened and modified by events during the litter period—events which eventually lead to the dissolution of the bond as the litter matures. In this way behavior during parturition and the litter period are explained in terms of internal biological events interacting with the external stimuli stemming from these internal events.

Other reports (not printed here) of related studies of feline behavior are: *Early Socialization in the Domestic Cat as Based on Feeding and other Relationships, Between Female and Young* (No. 95), *The Behavior of Cats* (No. 98), and *Development of Sucking and Related Behavior in Neonate Kittens* (No. 99).

Lester R. Aronson
Ethel Tobach

T. C. SCHNEIRLA

A Consideration of Some Conceptual Trends in Comparative Psychology[1]

Bibliography No. 57

HAVE WE A COMPARATIVE PSYCHOLOGY?

One might say that ideally comparative psychology exists when the comparative methods of science are applied to psychological problems. This must have been, in part at least, what Wundt had in mind in writing his *Vorlesungen* . . . (181). Potentially, such a program would appear to offer a good basis for bringing together and integrating too-divergent fields such as animal, child, and social psychology. Of course this type of approach has not disappeared altogether from psychology, for in recent years we have had an American edition of Werner's *Comparative Psychology of Mental Development* (171), utilizing animal, child, cultural, and social evidence in dealing with common psychological problems, and there is developmental psychology (103) which offers a somewhat limited and loose kind of alliance of child and animal study. However, the precontemporary and contemporary trends have led us from such integrative advances, for the most part, undoubtedly in some measure because of the difficult and tenuous nature of extrapolations among these disciplines. On the whole, comparative psychology is currently regarded as contained by animal psychology. But the digestion and assimilation have been uneasy and incomplete at best.

Although a sound use of the comparative method would be expected to unify and mutually strengthen all psychological fields having to do with problems of development, we have at the present time no articulate and integrated advance of the kind. One's strong impression is that no forward-

From *Psychological Bulletin* 49: 559–597. Copyright © 1952 by the American Psychological Association. Reprinted with permission.

[1] The basis of a paper delivered by invitation at the symposium on Conceptual Trends in Psychology, annual meeting of the American Psychological Association in Chicago, September 1, 1951.

looking program of the kind extends through animal psychology. Konrad Lorenz, the central figure in a vigorous contemporary group of European students of animal behavior, has commented as follows (87, pp. 239 f) upon one symptom of our situation:

> Since the days of Charles Darwin the term "comparative" has assumed a very definite meaning. It indicates a certain rather complicated method of procedure which, by studying the similarities and dissimilarities of homologous characters of allied forms, simultaneously obtains indications as to the phyletic relationships of these forms of life and as to the historical origin of the homologous characters in question. I need not enlarge on the details of this method which is a commonplace to biologists and physiologists. We all know perfectly well what we mean by "comparative" anatomy, morphology, physiology, and so on. But it is all the more misleading if psychologists, who evidently are not familiar with what we mean when we speak of the comparative method, apply the same term in a very loose sense to all behaviour studies concerned with different forms of life. I must confess that I strongly resent it, not only from the terminological viewpoint, but also in the interests of the very hard-working and honest craft of really comparative investigators, when an American journal masquerades under the title of "comparative" psychology, although, to the best of my knowledge, no really comparative paper ever has been published in it.

If this somewhat abrupt comment is even partially correct, we have cause for concern. If the *Journal of Comparative and Physiological Psychology* does not live up to the senior term in its name, there may be cause for editorial study as to how far the journal *can* be representative under its present editorial program. But since this journal undoubtedly is representative of current developments to an appreciable extent, reactions such as that quoted above must be given very serious consideration.

Let us define the feasible limited objective: a comparative psychology of animal behavior, as the study of similarities and differences in adjustive capacities and personality among the types of living organisms (128). To what extent, if at all, do we have such a subject in American psychology? There appears to be no waning of interest in carrying out studies with animal subjects. In the decades from 1888 to 1940, in the annual total of articles appearing in 14 psychological journals, the percentage of articles dealing with animals below man has risen steadily from 3.5 to 15.2 percent (20). Our deviations, whatever they may be, evidently cannot be attributed to any neglect to carry out investigations with lower animals.

The answer may lie in how and to what extent we study animals. A few years ago (127), I compared the *Journal of Animal Behavior* in its content from 1911 to 1918 with the *Journal of Comparative Psychology* in its content from 1938 to 1941, as to the kinds of animals used as subjects for the reported studies. A striking difference appeared, typified by the fact that while papers on invertebrate animals fell from 33 to 5 percent, papers on the rat rose from 19 to 66 percent. No recent change in this trend is apparent, for Beach (13) found later on that in 1946 and 1948, respectively, rats were the subject of 72 and 66 percent of the papers in the *Journal of Comparative and Physiological Psychology,* all submammalian animals just 4 and 6 percent. This trend toward concentrating on a single mammalian species as subject in the investigations of animal psychologists cannot be taken to mean that we have solved even the principal problems concerning inframammalian animals, notwithstanding the fine beginnings made earlier in this century by Yerkes, Jennings, Thorndike, and our other pioneers in the comparative field. Of course, in this space we cannot hope to offer any substantial analysis of the complex developments in biology and psychology, not to speak of the world in general, which must underlie the described symptoms. The practical consideration of paramount importance here is not how many types of animals we use in our investigations, but whether or not we use the comparative methods of science in working with them. Or perhaps the more primary question is whether we are even interested in such a goal.

Actually, we have developed no discipline of comparative psychology, either in investigation or in theory, of any substantial proportions. Just last year, a scientist in another field was prompted to write that "The life sciences and the sciences of the minds of both animals and men have been neglected too long" (174). Of course there has been a considerable amount of investigation of special problems such as sensory processes, neural mechanisms in learning, problem solving, and higher processes (48, 92, 101, 102, 128, 165). The rat psychologists must not be held lightly, for they have accomplished many useful things (27). But their work has not favored, and in many ways has opposed, a trend toward a consistent, comparative study of behavioral adjustments and psychological capacities throughout the animal series. This is true notwithstanding the fact that the studies on animal capacities carried out by psychologists such as Thorndike, Yerkes, Watson, Lashley, Hull, and Tolman, to mention some contrasts, have occupied a basic and indispensable position in the development of modern American psychology.

However, the fact is not at all obscure that American psychologists have turned from comparative method to an anthropocentric interest in exploring specific problems, from more naturalistic procedures and attitudes to a technical, instrumental emphasis in pursuing these problems. Here we may consider a bit of human behavior which seems not unrepresentative of the general situation. Just last year at a conference, one of our well-known animal psychologists, speaking under the title "Levels of Integration along the Phylogenetic Scale—Learning Aspect" (45), explained that he would limit his discussion mainly to primates, because they are closest to man and well studied. Now primates are fine animals, interesting and important, but in a comparative sense they are not a very large part of the phyletic baseline. This attitude, we must admit, is typical, a sign of the times and no reflection on zeal or intelligence. In actuality, American psychology has turned sharply away from the beginnings of a comparative methodology perceptible earlier in this century.

Presumably, the broad responsibility of psychologists *as psychologists* concerns investigating all aspects and relations of behavior, personality, and social organization in the universe. Instead, with respect to animal investigations, the following anonymous statement seems to be the consensus:

> The principal if not exclusive problem of psychologists is learning about man and his psychological properties and putting this knowledge to good use. We learn most about man by studying man; however, lower animals closest to man can be used advantageously as subjects, because more conveniently obtained and manipulated. They are then used as substitutes for human subjects, and are considered equivalent to human subjects in the situation and problem of study.

This is assuredly a pivotal point in investigative and theoretical attitude, which certainly has led to much valuable knowledge for psychology in general. Some of the underlying assumptions, however, may not be as defensible as seems to be generally assumed. On the one hand, it seems manifest from a large body of sound experimental findings that, for many basic problems in reception and other areas in physiological psychology, rats may serve very well in place of human subjects. But many psychologists, for example Tolman (161) and Hull (61), largely take for granted the rat's equivalence to man as subject for many presumptive psychological problems, and especially for learning.

This conclusion is not foregone, as Köhler (68) has reminded us recently, although first admitting that "Even the rat may reveal great secrets." However, he then says, "But essential characteristics of man are barely discernible in the modest rodent; and what is barely discernible will easily be ignored. So . . . a selection of subjects for reasons of method gradually turned into a selection of special material evidence. . . . Knowledge has been and is being gained by separate rushes which aim at quite particular goals and for the time being at not much else. . . . Take the conditioned reflex, a notion about which scientific bias actually threatened to center." Köhler believes, however, that a "strong interest in the conditions of experimental proof," which he finds dominant among American psychologists, will overcome the hazards, and also that a trend toward a widened horizon of investigative and theoretical interest is apparent. Can we hope that such is the case?

It is very probable that a strong inclination at present discernible among general psychologists in the United States, to doubt the significance and even the relevance of animal evidence for human psychological theory (e.g., 7), is in good part a reaction to the conditions referred to by Köhler in the above statements. These critics, from a strictly anthropocentric standpoint, do not seriously accept the post-Darwinian premise (165, 166) that studying the animal "mind" is an unfulfilled responsibility of scientists. Not long ago Gordon Allport (7) gave explicit utterance to such a view, particularly on the ground that the gap in psychological capacities between man and his brute relatives is too great for any real help to be expected from infrahuman studies. Far from strongly negating such narrow views, most American animal psychologists at present seem to be *really* nonevolutionary minded, in the sense that they show no special zeal to find how man differs mentally from lower animals and vice versa, but rather focus strenuously on general problems without much attention to phyletic lines.

This practice seems dangerous to the depth and breadth of scientific behavior studies, even for the limited goal of understanding man. Even to justify using animals such as the rat, in a completely anthropocentric sense, as equivalent to man in given respects, there would have to be a substantial use of comparative techniques. How else could we demonstrate that whatever animals might be convenient to use were not too dissimilar mentally from man to meet the specific needs of the problem? Really, the entire discussion here seems rather schizoid to the present writer.

Criteria such as those now prevalent, emphasizing phyletic similarities and minimizing differences, may perhaps be taken to represent a contemporary form of anthropomorphism which subtly avoids mentalistic terminology but inevitably becomes loaded with equivalent implications. The point, of course, is not any serious encroachment of the specific superficialities of traditional mentalism, for the attitude of contemporary American animal psychologists is avowedly objective and *non*mentalistic. Indeed, the specific superficialities of traditional mentalism are seldom noted. To the arguments of European phenomenalists such as Bierens de Haan (16) for a subjective and inferential description of animal "mind," we may oppose the comment of Boring (19) with respect to one contemporary objective system, that of Skinner (143): "The statements of functional dependency that result from such experimentation leave the concept of a controlling mind in the same limbo to which phlogiston has been consigned." Quite so! But, all the same, the mentalists may argue, with reason, that the operational and operant systems have made no great strides toward solving the problems of "mental organization" toward which the disowned concepts were directed. A useful hint for objective theorists may be found in Lashley's (77) remark that "the question 'What is the mental state of an animal?' means then: what is the level of organization of its activities." Statements such as this should be inspiring to those interested in the development of a comparative psychology (although they will not satisfy the minority of phenomenologists in our midst). For a discipline of serious contrasts is implied, with emphasis upon the significance of differences as well as similarities in capacities and adjustment patterns. But a scanning of the panorama of current American psychology suggests that we are not too close to this ideal. To investigate, perhaps the most efficient procedure is to undertake a brief comparative study of how some of our chief concepts are used contemporaneously.

"THE INNATE"

In a symposium on heredity and environment (157) published in the *Psychological Review* in 1947, Beach (12) says, "In agreeing to discuss any aspect of the so-called heredity-environment problem one naturally infers that the artificiality of the implied dichotomy is obvious to everyone." Unfortunately, this natural inference did not hold even in that symposium, for in summarizing Hunter was able to say: "It will come as a surprise to many psychologists that all five of the distinguished contributors to this symposium have emphasized the roll of heredity in the determination of behavior" (157, p. 348). Now does "artificiality" in the first statement mean only that the dichotomy is "man-made," or that it is "man-made, and spurious"? If the latter alternative is the truer of the two, the surprise must be all the greater. It is the opinion of the writer, in his present somewhat uneasy role of trend-spotter, that a really weak dichotomy was accepted implicitly in the symposium. For the contributors agreed in general that the "anti-instinct writers" (55, 71) of the twenties went too far; then, in general, both by implication and by explicit ideology, they swung strongly toward the opposite extreme. We may inquire how far this procedure is a function of new evidence and of valid theoretical advances.

From the general literature one may gather that the aforementioned symposium did represent certain general trends toward a positivistic and recurrent emphasis upon behavior patterns as innate. "Instinct" certainly had the leading conceptual role. One of the contributors, in discussing whether so-called hereditary behavior is "innate or acquired," made the following statement (100, p. 336):

Adult rats, fully watered and fed, will hoard five to twenty pellets per day if placed in hoarding apparatus and left there. Since the rat only eats one or two pellets a day, this is plainly hoarding. And since it comes out spontaneously without training, it is plainly instinctive. Of course, rats may have learned to hoard early in infancy because of competition for food in their home cages, but hoarding is so universal in laboratory rats, always fully watered and fed, that such learning is unlikely.

Certainly, many animal psychologists have not ceased to rely upon the criterion of universality to bolster an argument for pattern innateness, despite lessons from the past such as that conveyed by the "coenotrope" concept of Smith and Guthrie (146). For that matter, the main load of argument also frequently rests upon the criterion of early appearance, with experiential factors rejected out of hand if there are no obvious indications of them or if the experimenter has not introduced them programmatically (i.e., operationally). And in this exceedingly controversial field, teleological implications frequently lurk under the guise of supposedly functional terms. It may be suggested, for instance (63), that pulling-in or dragging-in behavior would be a proper operational substitute for the possibly improper term "hoarding," at least until we know more about what the rat's intentions are in such behavior. Retrieving behavior is also recognizable as a kind of "pulling-in" activity; and a common use of this term suggests the desirability of investigating possible relationships between these patterns.

There is no denying that much of our contemporary literature in this field is set along nativistic and preformistic lines. But also, as Anastasi and Foley (8) point out in a timely critique, psychologists often (and biologists not infrequently) "define heredity indirectly, vaguely, or inconsistently, especially when it comes to the domain of behavior phenomena." As these authors say, the definition of both heredity and environment, especially for the purpose of psychological investigation, is exceedingly difficult. They offer a provisional consideration of behavior etiology in terms of structural and functional factors instead of heredity-and-environment. How far such substitute dichotomies may be expected to reduce the fallacies in the hoary one of nature and nurture is not too clear. However, Anastasi and Foley believe the substitute should promote general understanding of statements such as Jennings's (65) that: "That which is directly inherited . . . is the set of genes, with the accompanying cytoplasm," in relation to Holt's (55) reminder that "No potential character ever is 'already contained' in anything . . . [so] that the applicability of the concept of heredity to behavior phenomena is indirect and remote." How well have the implications of statements such as these, based on sound theory in modern genetics, received consideration from animal psychologists and behavior students on either side of the Atlantic, in their investigations of so-called "innate behavior"?

The implication that "beyond the genes, which are the really inherited part of the organism, lies a problem of development," often seems elusive to behavior students. It seems unfortunate for progress along these lines that certain of our leading theorists have withdrawn somewhat from outpost positions once boldly taken. In the heredity-environment symposium, for example, Carmichael (23) discussed "The Growth of the Sensory Control of Behavior Before Birth" without reference to or use of his earlier significant theoretical contribution to this question (22), bearing on the development in utero of integrations of intrinsic and extrinsic factors influencing embryonic growth and activities. What intervening events in science have led to such changes is not clear. The significance of drug-inactivity studies with lower vertebrates (21, 164) for this question now appears somewhat equivocal. The recent study of Fromme (40) indicates that a drugged condition of inactivation has different effects upon development of aquatic locomotion in frog tadpoles, depending upon whether the drug acts prior to stage 17 or during the critical stage 17–20 interval. When these matters have been clarified, there remains the question of how far evidence from such processes on the amphibian level can be extrapolated to the level of mammalian development. Although, as Sperry (154) says, "Holt (1931) and others earlier minimized neural organization available through maturation alone," it is equally dangerous to swing to the opposite extreme for vertebrates *in general* on the basis of results suggesting the role of matured neural paths for some of the *simpler* responses in the *lower* vertebrate classes.

Currently, emphasis is surely light on the need for systematic ontogenetic behavior studies and analysis of developmental stages considered as interrelated. Analysis is usually cross sectional, and is introduced by frequently arbitrary assumptions about procedures which supposedly rule out the determinative role of extrinsic factors during early stages. For example, the method of isolation, in which a laboratory animal is raised away from others of its kind, is very often adopted as a presumably rigid control for experiential factors. However, the risk of leaning upon this crudely teleological criterion is indicated by a consideration of how the individual animal itself, as a representative of "its own kind," may be a factor through processes based upon self-stimulative events in its own private activities. Consider a hypothesis, based on this point, with reference to the controversial problem of whether chicks recognize other chicks to any important extent on an innate basis (58, 110). Since a segregated chick usually chirps when warmed, when fed, and in similar situations, a factor of learning may be introduced favoring its approach to other chicks as against ducklings, etc., in later "choice" tests. Controlling possibilities such as this represents a challenge to the theoretical vigilance and instrumental ingenuity of the investigator.

It is clear, as Leuba (82) states, that a systematic study of innate nature is needed. This should involve analytical approaches to the problem of behavior development in a variety of animals. Another need seems to be a new methodological equipment of improved controls on the experimental intervention of preconceived ideas of innate behavior patterning. It is suggested (124) that even an insect has an ontogeny which must be considered if we are to understand its full-blown behavior pattern.

As Hall (42) reminds us, the nature-nurture question is a pseudo-argument, which has not brought science closer to understanding the contributions of heredity to behavior patterns. The field of genetics in biology has concerned itself largely with morphology, whereas psychologists have studied behavior largely in pre-Mendelian terms. The growing interest in a joint discipline of "psycho-genetics," which Hall discusses, stresses the need for a *rapprochement* of these two fields in investigation. Such studies, performed on a systematic basis, should be very useful, as one source of evidence for a systematic theoretical examination of "innate nature." But investigations of hereditary-and-behavior correlations must be paralleled or extended by analytical studies of ontogenic stages in each animal type, if evidence from such research is to be properly evaluated and validly explained in theory.

There are very different attitudes toward the value for animal psychology of studies on morphological and physiological factors underlying behavior. Skinner (31) for instance maintains that a science of behavior may be developed without reference to neurology; Loucks (88) asserts on the other hand that neurology and neurophysiology cannot be excluded. Discussing the difficulties, Lashley (76, 77) points to the fact that in some organisms where the relations are simple and direct (e.g., the earthworm) it has been possible to show correlations between specific structures and behavior, but in more complex reactions in which the influence of hereditary factors appears to be heavy (e.g., nesting in birds), clear correlative analyses have been baffled. Obviously, an even weightier challenge to understanding the role of structure in behavior is encountered in the processes of behavior modifiability. The challenge, however, is to improve theory, not to retreat with agility. How well such theory is improved may determine the relevance of evidence from psychogenetics for the problems of "innate behavior" and of ontogeny alike.

Now evolutionary theory and systematics in biology have placed a fundamental emphasis upon structural relationships among animal groups, implying some more or less important significance for adaptive adjustments in the respective groups. In the recent development of this field

(65) this emphasis has been extended very actively to the consideration of behavioral factors in the adjustive repertoire of species. Animal psychologists, as Nissen (106) says, have found it difficult to see "how major psychological emergents are demonstrated to coincide with major and abrupt changes in structural characteristics differentiating larger taxonomic groups, especially the phyla." This difficulty certainly rests to a great extent in the lack of analytical comparative studies on patterns of behavior and their variations in related groups. The generalization that a direct involvement of structural factors in the functional determination of behavior patterns decreases phyletically from lower invertebrates to mammals (92) may be considered only a rather tenuous introduction to the necessary programmatic investigations.

If psychologists neglect to carry out such research systematically, others will attempt it, in their own ways. Biologists have recognized for some time that behavioral characteristics may be useful as clues to taxonomic affinities (85, 112). The heuristic value of this fact has greatly stimulated interest of biologists in animal behavior. Thus Lorenz (85, 86, 87), leader of an enthusiastic contemporary group of European zoologists devoted to studying behavior, has been led to say (87, p. 238) that:

> . . . behavior patterns are not something which animals may do or not do, or do in different ways, according to requirements of the occasion, but something which animals of a given species have got, exactly in the same manner as they "have got" claws or teeth of a definite morphological structure. . . . From the recognition of this fact it is only a very short step to the systematic comparison of the innate behavior patterns characteristic of allied species. . . . [The term comparative] indicates a rather complicated method of procedures which, by studying the similarities and dissimilarities of homologous characters of allied forms, simultaneously obtains indications as to the phyletic relationships of these forms of life and as to the historical origin of the homologous characters in question.

Such conclusions seem inevitable to those whose experience is bounded largely by specific behavior observations together with the realities of morphology. There is, however, much more to this than meets the eye, and perhaps psychologists should pay more careful attention to the validity of attempts to draw up principles of behavior in direct parallel with principles of morphology.

Not just because of its practical use to taxonomists, but more important, to observe and learn its nature, Lorenz urges behavior as an important object for biologists to study. He presents them with a rather neat, positivistic theoretical system (85, 86) whereby behavior patterns are viewed as innately determined through intracentral processes in the nervous system, with specific stimulative effects acting as "releasers" to trigger them off. Lately, Lorenz (87) has begun to speak of natively determined patterns as "endogenous behavior." The investigations are essentially observational, qualitative, and relatively simple, mainly on birds although with studies on insects, fishes, and other forms also involved. The approach is avowedly comparative. However, since the theory is essentially preformistic, with an a priori emphasis upon the "native" aspects of behavior, a really comparative methodology of animal psychology has not yet appeared and may find difficulties in growing within this context. The proneness to impose a similar rigid nativistic ideology upon behavior in different and even widely different animals may be suggested by the final statements in a recent paper by Lorenz (87, p. 266 f.):

> . . . it is high time that social and group psychology began to occupy itself with the physiological side of behavior and more especially with the innate processes of which I spoke above. It is high time that the collective human intellect got some control on the necessary outlets for certain endogenously generated drives, for instance "aggression," and some knowledge of human innate releasing mechanisms, especially those activating aggression. Hitherto it is only demagogues who seem to have a certain working knowledge of these matters and who, by devising surprisingly simple "dummies," [2] are able to elicit fighting responses in human beings with about the same predictability as Tinbergen does in sticklebacks.

The Lorenz system has been criticized as "too simple." With all due credit to its desirable emphasis upon behavior study, the present writer wonders about the validity of its basic postulates.

That the Lorenz conceptual system is not without its appeal to American psychologists is indicated by the numerous references to it in the recent handbook (155) in which, however, no critical appraisal is undertaken. There are indications, it must be said, that a preoccupation with a presumed native predetermination of behavior may lead to overlooking necessary controls or significant aspects of evidence. Thus from an investigation frequently cited as evidence for Lorenzian principles, Tinbergen and Kuehnen (160) reported that the gaping (i.e., bill-opening) reactions of young thrushes are released initially by mechanical stimuli, but after the tenth day also by visual stimuli such as a black disc within a given size range in diameter. However, some observations by Lehrman (81) raise a serious question as to the validity of the Tinbergen-Kuehnen interpretation of the visual stage as natively determined. In the days

---

[2] Models, artifacts, used in the investigation of "releasers."

immediately preceding that stage, the young nestling's eyes are likely to open during the latter part of the bill reaction (for example, while the parent bird is sitting on the side of the nest). A contiguity of stimuli is thereby effective with the critical response, which may introduce conditioning as a factor preparatory to the visual phase.

It is doubtful whether any methodology can be successfully comparative without a thoroughgoing concern for ascertaining the characteristics of ontogeny in each behavior system studied, as a step preliminary to the intellectual process of comparing behavior patterns and personality in different animals.

LEARNING

By and large, American animal psychologists have worked most intensively in the field of learning problems (52, 101, 155). Different methods have been used and differing theoretical viewpoints have arisen, represented currently by the stress of Hull's (61, 62) theory on "reinforcement processes" and by Tolman's (161, 162) on "field-cognition" processes in learning. At present, methods are more similar than previously; however, theoretical differences are still rather sharp between these two systems in particular (79, 80, 152). By and large, theoretical trends in this field are much too complex to receive any amount of treatment in the present context; hence we shall limit our discussion to some general comments which appear to be in order.

An observant bystander outside the immediate field of intensive investigation and research on learning readily gains the impression that those carrying on work in this field often are likely to grossly underestimate their own roles in the situation, as complexes of experimental variables. The crucial responsibility thus involved is indicated by Melton's (98) statement: "Stimulus response and field theorists frequently engage in the same types of investigations, with similar situations, but with such conditions imposed as to maximize the applicability of their own conceptual structure or minimize the applicability of the opponent's conceptual structure." It would seem that among the causes of contradictory results, in addition to the variations in investigative situation and poorly known conditions mentioned by Brogden (155), the experimenter himself must play a large and frequently uncontrolled role. His responsibility for narrowing down the scope of experimentation so that a limited and "unnatural" view of the phenomenon may be obtained in the end, is suggested by Brogden's (155) reminder that "The response has rarely been the independent variable," although it may be an important variable. Aiming for strict control, an experimenter laboring under the weight of a conventionalized theory may acquire a sort of "tunnel vision" which blocks from view aspects of the phenomenon which happen not to lend themselves to convenient study under his methods, or within his attitude. Though aiming to attain a *strict* experimental control, through losing the relation of trees-focused-upon to the forest he risks the loss of validity in the study of nature. Is it possible that the contemporary field of animal-learning investigation has become overspecialized along these lines?

The conditioning and the trial-and-error approaches to the study of learning both have existed in various forms for some time, often with applications to very different contexts (52, 166). The influence of Pavlov's (111) and Thorndike's (158) findings and theory tended to be somewhat different in American psychology. Thus, after Watson's (168, 169) inspired theorizing based on conditioning theory to a great extent, some investigators emphasize contiguity and reinforcement (152); after Thorndike's versatile studies of learning, with or without the influence of McDougall (97), other investigators emphasize the initiative, goal-seeking tendency, or cognition of the organism (80). Maier and Schneirla (92, 93) distinguished between contiguity and selection as conditions making for qualitatively different processes in the learning adjustment; Skinner (142, 143) and Hilgard and Marquis (53), from an operational point of view, distinguished between classical and instrumental patterns of conditioned learning. Culler and associates (29), in particular, reported results corroborating a qualitative distinction. To Kendler and Underwood (67), from the reinforcement standpoint, the results seemed insufficient for such a distinction; however, to Birch and Bitterman (18) the evidence seemed adequate, and further evidence was cited to support the position of Maier and Schneirla (93). Reinforcement-contiguity theorists (62, 152) hold their lines to a concept of monomorphic learning without essential change. Tolman (163) has recently accepted the premise that qualitatively different learning processes exist; however, his distinguished processes *all* have the characteristics of cognitive mechanisms. It seems quite probable that both reinforcement and cognition formulae may be reducing the phenomena of learning to what may represent a *valid* phase, but a *different* phase of the problem range.

Thus far, the principal emphasis in studying learning has been upon the highly specialized investigation of a few mammalian types, without too much emphasis upon differences in patterns. The relatively few comparative studies attempted have brought interesting results. Thus, although a spider monkey investigated by Lashley (77) could not master a similarity relationship in a matching problem, this was easy for a chimpanzee. "An attempt to analyze the learning process here results in the discovery of apparently different processes." Rats and *Formica* ants in suitable scale replicas of the "same" maze pattern not only learned the situation in a strikingly different manner, but adapted to postlearning changes very differently, thus evidencing different types of learned organization (126). Although available theories present no very promising resources for dealing with comparative evidence, analytical studies of learning in very different animal types should reward us with important new evidence and fresh theoretical insight.

Because of limited evidence, conclusive phyletic comparisons concerning the properties of fixation (i.e., trace formation) or of organizational capacities in learning are premature. It is difficult to see how valid comparisons can be made, outlining the scope and nature of either similarities or differences, until the learning and learning-transfer processes have been exposed in each important animal type.

With respect to the feasibility of neurophysiological postulations in the study of animal learning, very different views exist. As a rule, neither Tolman nor Hull utilizes neurophysiological concepts in his theorizing. Skinner (31, 143) maintains that a science of behavior can be built up without recourse to neural postulates. Lashley (72, 76), on the other hand, consistently has utilized neural references in his learning studies, and recently Hebb (47) has offered a "redintegrative" theory of learning and perception, grounded in concepts of neural change with experience. It is to be hoped that we may soon discover a trend toward a genuine consideration of ontogeny and personality development in learning theory.

INTELLIGENCE

A direct challenge to the soundness of this concept is presented by Lashley (77) when, after stating that the spider repairing a web appears to exhibit an appreciation of spatial relationships of the same nature as concepts of spatial relationships basic to mammals, remarks that "The mechanisms of instinctive and intelligent behavior thus seem fundamentally the same." While no doubt overgenerous to the status of arthropod capacities, and although unsupported by analytical evidence, this comment nevertheless calls attention to our lack of systematic comparative studies of adaptive behavior on different levels. As Hebb (48) concludes, "We shall almost certainly find that the conception of a general level of intelligence is useless and that we shall have to learn how to define, not a single continuum, but a number of continua, requiring qualitative as well as quantitative analysis of behavior."

A stock definition of animal intelligence, "the capacity to meet new environmental conditions successfully," does not hold up well against the questions: "What conditions? How new? And how met?" To evaluate the process dependably, we must know more about the conditions of adjustment and the ontogenetic prerequisites than is usually known. Effective adjustment to an "emergency" offers an unstable criterion for intelligent behavior, for it is conceivable that different animals meet their respective crisis situations with equal degrees of success but on the basis of very different organizational processes.

"Complexity," often used as a criterion, is hardly standardized in meaning and is a weak pillar to support evaluations. As Nissen (106) states, although "the recurring term in phyletic comparisons is increasing complexity . . . [it is] of course too broad to be useful, unless the complexity is further specified." For example, in keeping with a complex morphological makeup, the starfish is capable of complex locomotive processes, in the sense of a very involved neural and stimulus-response repertoire, in which, however, a low-grade integration is predominant (43, 145). It is doubtful that complexity may be taken as evidence for intelligence status, unless the concomitant qualitative characteristics are known. *Formica* ants can learn complex mazes, but the habits are organized in ways inferior to those of the rat, and their application of the habit to new situations is also inferior (126). In a "molecular" sense, trial-and-error solutions by higher mammals may be more *complex* than "insight" solutions.

One great difficulty is that the composite variable to be measured and compared, intelligence capacity, is necessarily influenced to variable extents by auxiliary factors such as sensory acuity, motor dexterity, and motivation. This entire "assisting caste," as Nissen (106) terms it, must be made functionally equivalent in the compared subjects, or otherwise controlled. It is of course an exceedingly difficult prospect to determine a weighting for the sensitivity factor, for instance, in animals as different as the rat and spider. For similar reasons, McBride and Hebb (96), after endeavoring to compare the intelligence of dolphins with that of higher vertebrates, reached the conclusion that at present no adequate method exists for this purpose. Not only do the auxiliary factors seem inextricably involved in the pattern, but the problem-solving process itself may be elusively different in different types of organism. These considerations suggest a need for really systematic efforts to solve the problem, not for giving up.

That results from original learning tests offer an elusive basis for comparing intelligence is indicated, for instance, by the difficulty Searle (133) experienced in trying to isolate a learning factor in analytical tests with "bright" and "dull" strains of rats. And in the "same" test situation, very different patterns of mastery may appear in initial learning (94). An extrapolation of human intelligence-test theory promises better results. A few beginnings have been made in devising batteries of tests in which, in various problem contexts, the ability to adapt a learned repertoire to new situations is measured systematically. Fischel (37, 38), in an interesting programmatic attempt to compare different animals in such terms, has tested reptiles, birds, dogs, and human subjects in a comparable situation. The subject is first permitted to master a characteristic adjustment to each of two lures of different attractiveness, then is tested in his ability to use these adjustments appropriately in a combined presentation.

Evaluating different ways of utilizing past experience is of course a most difficult assignment, as the history of the multiple-choice test has shown (150, 184). Using the discrimination-generalization test (cf. 114) in a programmatic way, Harlow (44) and his collaborators have outlined the manner in which a monkey advances by stages of experience in the situation through successive "learning sets," from simple to complex and plastic reaction modes. Harlow criticizes the S-R theorists for their failure to investigate adequately the experience variable in its contributions to new situational adjustments. In most learning experiments, insufficient attention has been paid to this variable (1, 25, 92). Preparation is of course critical (66, 109), since experimenters working on both the animal (17) and the human levels (33) have obtained trial-and-error or insight solutions, depending upon the manner in which part-processes were contrib-uted through controlled preliminary experience.

There is discernible in the literature a disposition to question the existence of an important qualitative difference between trial-and-error and insight solutions. Although this attitude is quite proper, and in accordance with Morgan's "canon," it may encourage too narrow a view in studying this crucial question. For instance, from his discrimination-generalization experiments, Harlow (44) is inclined to believe that insight is but a further stage of trial-and-error process in sequential learning, and not really qualitatively different from it. Prior to these Wisconsin experiments, however, Maier and Schneirla (92) questioned the adequacy of abstraction-generalization methods by themselves for differentiating "higher processes," on grounds which have not been controverted. These processes are undeniably related, but possible qualitative differences between them are not necessarily brought out by all types of test situation. The Wolfe and Spragg (178) investigation, designed to find whether Maier's (89) evidence for "combination of isolated experiences" could be reduced to the strict terms of contiguity-learning theory, did not succeed in this respect (90). In an answer to G. Allport's (7) challenge for clear evidence of higher processes in infrahuman animals, Seward (134) mustered strict criteria for insightful solutions which he found were met by Maier's recombination tests as well as by five other methods used to investigate such capacities in lower mammals.

Methodological and theoretical vigilance is of course essential to guard against the postulation of exaggerated solution capacities. Unfortunately, Morgan's canon is not accorded a basic place with equal seriousness by all students of animal behavior. Thus, in evaluating the remarkably man-like solutions achieved by monkeys in the Liège investigations, Lashley (74) concluded that the results were so influenced by uncontrolled varia-bles (e.g., experimenter-derived cues) as to be without value for apprais-ing the level of the solution processes involved (see also 56). As another example, a sudden fall in a learning curve may indicate a solution process of high or low qualitative status; the shape of the curve is not a critical indication in itself, but the judgment must depend upon a detailed analysis of the experimental results (92).

Often the status of an observed situational adjustment seems to depend upon a sweeping characterization rather than upon a critcial study of how the situational properties are met. Thus if maze learning is defined broadly along the lines of hormic theory as "goal response," then round-about solutions may be attributed to all animals, from the earthworm to man, which have been able to learn some kind of maze (15). On the other hand, the concept of "Umweg" may acquire value for solution compari-sons among widely different animals provided that tests and evaluation of results are guided by strict criteria (38). Yet again, the criteria of Umweg-solution are called into question by experiments such as those of Schiller (120, 121), from which roundabout solutions are reported for various inframammalian animals including cephalopods and minnows. In the same sense, the present criteria and meaning of "delayed-response" adjustments are really not adequate to appraise some reports of Thorpe (159), who describes cases in which solitary wasps maintained a route despite forced lateral deviations, and of Baerends (10), who cites the return of observed solitary wasps after intervals of time to provision appropriately each of two or three different burrows. Such developments remind us that some years ago the adequacy of the delayed-response method for calibrating higher adjustive capacities was challenged (92). One major difficulty is in controlling the extent to which critical cues are supplied by the animal or by the environmental situation. Far too little attention is being accorded to the question of evaluative criteria in discussing such problems. This condition seems not unrelated to a strong current tendency to merge superficially similar kinds of performance in very different animal types under the same phenomenal headings. Unclear comparisons with poorly devised concepts are considerably worse than no comparisons at all.

PERCEPTION

The application of this term to broadly different types of adjustment has increased to such an extent that clarification is urgently needed. On the one hand, experimental investigations have been directed at the analysis of perceptual phenomena (47, 73), and the continuity-discontinuity controversy (75, 153) is another expression of efforts to study the nature of situational meaning and organization in perceptual discriminations. On the other hand, use of the term on a vague qualitative basis in the general literature has increased rather than decreased.

There exists a widespread tendency to employ the word "perception" rather loosely to any case in which an animal senses an object or situation and reacts to it in a manner considered "adaptive" (e.g., 119, 156). Whether the response is to be considered a reaction simply and directly elicited on an uncomplicated sensory-motor basis, or an appropriate reaction to the pattern of a recognized familiar object or situation, is very often very unclear. In the absence of specific evaluative criteria or even of a disposition to be critical in the matter, if such practices continue, the scientific role of this term in any conceptual sense may be reduced to that of a minus factor. Thus it is difficult to trace the specific implications of a statement such as Hartley's (156) for certain birds, that ". . . recognition of some enemies results from innate powers." Certain stimulative and behavioral relationships are described or implied in such cases, but the unknown status of the adjustment would seem to merit a more operational and less presumptive characterization.

Scattered experimental developments suggest that it is important to be vigilant for differences in the sensory-integrative processes underlying adjustments to situations by animals. For example, Hertz (50, 51) investigated the visual adjustments of bees to a variety of artifacts, and formulated a rather complex theory to account for the bee's ability to single out from the first those with greater brokenness of outline or greater internal complexity. Particular training was not needed; in fact, such response tendencies strongly opposed any training of positive reactions to the opposite visual condition. The investigations of Wolf (176) disclosed that such visually determined reactions in the bee are attributable to differences in flicker effect, and not to a visual pattern organization in the human sense so far as was discernible.

Unfortunately, the problem of "innate" contributions to perception has not been attacked very systematically and analytically on any subhuman level. The nature of differences between "those animals whose repertoire of perceptions is more or less limited to the relatively small number determined by innate organization . . . [and] those animals whose perceptual organizations are primarily acquired . . . ," as Nissen (106) suggests the distinction, is very poorly understood. What physical characteristics such as intensity, rate of movement, size, and so on, may produce adaptive reactions in animals without benefit of specific experience, is a subject that must be approached through methods appropriate to the animal type concerned. It is encouraging to note a disposition on the part of some psychologists to meet such problems frontally. Hebb (47), for one, has endeavored to develop a theory of perceptual development on the mammalian level, in the light of both native factors and of ontogenetic processes.

At the same time, less inductive approaches to these problems are in evidence. It is with problems concerning sensory apprehension and adjustment that Lorenz and his associates (156) have been especially involved. They have observed and classified for a considerable number of animals, particularly birds but also fishes and certain other lower vertebrates, the types of stimulus-effect ("releasers") which will produce given species-characteristic reactions. These reactions, as mentioned before, are considered innate and intraneurally determined, each with its corresponding extrinsic releaser, or trigger stimulus. The execution of the releasing-stimulus activity represents the end or goal toward which appetitive behavior is directed (85, 87). The releasing stimulus (156) is typically named according to the observer's appraisal of the animal's (adaptive) behavioral relation to the situation of occurrence (e.g., an "enemy" valence). No particular differences are set up by these investigators between the postulated "innately given" qualities of objects or situations and the perceptual characteristics of learned, familiar situations in which the character of adjustment depends upon experience (47, 81). Usually the releaser or the "sign stimulus" is described rather teleologically by the observer, whether it depends upon those features "most typical for the object" or "a configuration of features" (11). Some psychologists, troubled by the characteristic employment of observer-subjective naming devices instead of critically selected operational terms, may wonder as to our safeguards for reliability in weighting "innate" and "experience" variables, and for presuming to distinguish them in theory, when investigative methods are really cross sectional rather than ontogenetic. In view of our lack of adequate criteria for controlling such factors, the assurance of the outspoken Lorenz group is amazing.

Clarification is surely needed for the problem of "innately given" sensory adjustments to objects and situations, and their relation to the contribution of learning. How far are qualitative aspects (i.e., "meaning character") of the situation presumed to differ for the animal in innately controlled cases as against instances in which learning intervenes? To what extent and how does a pigeon "perceive *her young*," when upon their removal to a short distance she returns to sit upon the nest, while they shiver in full view? In preliminary investigations, Riess (118) found that female rats, after they had passed their early postweaning life in isolation without ever having handled or carried objects of any kind (subsisting entirely upon powdered food), in the parturition situation were very inferior in all respects to normal mothers, and lost all of their young promptly. What was the deficiency of these rats in early experience, as compared with normal rats? The hypothesis that the absent factor here is a perception of objects-to-be-approached-and-dealt-with (i.e., as "incentives") seems to merit testing. It appears that without the lacking factor a "maternal behavior pattern" cannot be formed.

The importance of experience for the development of visual perceptual adjustments in chimpanzees is indicated by Riesen's (116) investigation with chimpanzees raised in darkness from birth to 16 months of age. Since, in tests then carried out, objects evidently had no more meaning for these animals than for newborn chimpanzees, questions arise concerning the normal ontogeny of perception. (The possible contribution of previous perceptual training through other sensory modalities—e.g., somesthetic—as factors in re-education through intersensory transfer (78) will bear further consideration.) Such experiments indicate the development of a renewed interest in the ontogeny of individual perception in lower animals.

Investigations of the development of external drive controls in motivation contribute to an understanding of perceptual development. An early contribution was Woodworth's (180) concept of habits becoming transformed into drives through experience; a recent development has been the concept of "externalization of drives" (9). A predominant assumption is that motivational growth in mammals involves the specialization of the drive-behavior pattern with respect to particular learned situational adjustments. The characteristics of objects and situations which are connected with the relief of needs thus become focalized in perception, in a manner which much research on discriminative learning has been directed toward clarifying. The relationship of such processes to meeting the conditions of the environment is strikingly represented in the more rapid and effective acquisition of token-reward habit by chimpanzees (177) than by the cat (147), and its more plastic use by the former animal.

In the theory projected by Hebb (47) to account for ontogenetic perceptual development, the growth of perceptual patterns is traced for a mammalian animal from the naive stage through the first stages of learning. A developing action basis of expectancy and attention, a simple and molar one in this case, is followed through in an inductive procedure. This theory, which is characterized as a "redintegrative" developmental theory, appears to furnish a sound approach and good basis for further ontogenetic theory in child and animal psychology. Perception at any stage is regarded as involving an expectancy which is selective in function, and which thereby influences situational adjustments and further learning. What is learned at any stage depends on what can then be perceived, i.e., it is a function of how far the perceptual systems have advanced.

An inductive theory of perceptual development such as this calls attention to the problem of set or expectancy in situational adjustment and learning. It contains a further potentiality: namely, that relatively limited sets or adjustive patterns may represent early stages of more dynamic and versatile systems of expectancy, according to the animal's capacities for such advances. Is a conceptual clarification developing through such considerations—in that the term "set" may be applied more specifically to a functionally earlier, more limited (in selective scope) and stereotyped adjustive pattern? It is possible that, in contrast, a concept such as Maier's (91) "direction" represents the more dynamic expectancies of a later stage, through which the organism may overcome the bonds of specific contiguities more readily than before.

A groping for the relationship between perceptual and conceptual processes is currently apparent. It seems possible that perceptual systems, under appropriate conditions, may lead to conceptual systems. One interesting experimental development may be subject to reinterpretation in this light. After the Hayeses (46) had raised an infant chimpanzee under home conditions as closely similar as possible to those normal for a human infant, they reached the conclusion that this infant was inferior in no identifiable way to a human infant in its course of development until the language stage was reached in the latter. The principal psychological deficiency of chimpanzee ontogeny thus is attributed to the absence of a verbal language. On the other hand, it seems possible that preliminary stages of perceptual development, difficult to follow in observational studies, are partially similar in man and chimpanzee but also different in subtle qualitative ways. The hypothesis that the infant chimpanzee never reaches the threshold of perceptual-meaning-organization and nonlinguistic conception which is prerequisite for verbal-symbol mastery demands testing.

What is the relationship between perception and conceptual processes in mammalian ontogeny? Some writers seek an answer along the path of a "lumping" procedure. Thus Leeper (80) insists that the principal characteristics of "inductive concept formation are also to be found in discrimination learning and conditioning, and much of trial-and-error learning." These characteristics are given as differentiation and some generality of application. Whether this is to be considered a speculative exercise, or an introduction to a serious systematic reductive operation on the part of cognitive theory, is not altogether clear. It is often forgotten that in such exercises there is also a responsibility for trying to discern the significance of qualitative differences in the compared processes and capacities. It seems worth suggesting that a greater theoretical gain may lie in regarding these processes as successive stages in the development of an individual, i.e., in viewing conditioning as a process prerequisite to the more complex organizations of trial-and-error or selective learning, perception as a prerequisite to more highly involved functions of conceptual mastery, and the like. What is needed, perhaps, is a closer application of the comparative method to the tracing of stages in the development of personality on different animal levels.

A COMPARATIVE SOCIAL PSYCHOLOGY OF ANIMALS

Animal social investigations employing the comparative method are still uncommon, although there are indications of new developments both in research and in theory (4, 125). Psychologists have been less active here than biologists (26, 132). There are, however, a few indications of convergent developments in biology, psychology, and sociology (3, 131), pointing to further systematic investigation of social phenomena in animals. Advances are needed particularly in studying what differences may be significant for differentiating various types of animal societies, while at the same time their similarities are taken into account.

It is probable that the study of animal social behavior has resources which have not been brought to the investigative level attained by the study of human group dynamics (4, 126). Although much of the animal work is still descriptive, there are some detailed and systematic studies with implications for further research (24, 30, 57, 123).

The general conceptual trend is still influenced by intergroup similarities, much less by contrasts. An example is the concept of "dominance hierarchies," which has appealed to many laboratory investigators, including psychologists (26, 95, 104, 122). The "peck-right" concept has furnished a convenient way of describing the group behavior of vertebrate animals, and dominance-submission relations certainly have proved to be an outstanding aspect of group relations, as studied both in laboratory and field. It is now apparent, however, that this concept is somewhat like that of "extroversion-introversion" in the sense that it represents not just one social parameter such as aggression relations (26, 95), but a number of variables such as ascendance (186), prestige, and the like. Its main limitations may be summed up by saying that the dominance concept represents only one aspect of group behavior, which does not necessarily reveal the factors essential to group structure or may even reveal them in a negative way (125, 129).

The "dominance-hierarchy" concept, moreover, has influenced the attention and thought of students at the expense of concepts relating to the more positive and central aspects of group structure, so that the potentialities of concepts such as "cooperation" (3, 28, 41, 125, 185) seem largely unrealized. Although it is true of course that, as Zuckerman (188) has said, a comparative social psychology cannot exclude reference to the principle of dominance, it is now clear that unless dominance behavior is viewed in its relation to other social factors, investigation and theory in this field are certain to be seriously limited and distorted (3, 125).

The usefulness of other concepts such as "cooperation" has been reduced greatly by tendencies to use them in a phyletically generalized way. Thus questions concerning the rise of gregariousness and the properties of group organization in different animal types have been approached only to a limited extent in research and theory. Investigations inspired by "innate" behavior theory (156) emphasize a descriptive type of study, concentrate on individual aspects of social behavior, and do not attack the problems of group structure in analytical ways. It should be noted that questions of group communicative behavior have been attacked on several levels (14, 39, 107, 115, 125, 187), although mainly only in preliminary ways. However, an adequately comparative program of study of such phenomena is long overdue, particularly to clarify the relationships of concepts such as "sign," "signal," and "symbol," as well as the criteria of "language" (14, 115), all of which appear to suffer from a heavy load of speculation and a minimum of systematic research. Research on questions concerning levels of phenotypic relationships through successive generations in lower animal groups, certainly basic to a needed re-evaluation of the broad problem of "culture" (4, 125, 137), should enlist the active attention of social psychologists, sociologists, and anthropologists alike.

It would seem that a sufficient number of objective studies of group behavior have been carried out (24, 28, 30, 57, 123, 132) on widely different types of animals and groups, with prospects of others in a more intensive vein, to justify a new and more concentrated attack upon theoretical problems common to all group organizations. The basic biological aspects of such phenomena have been investigated theoretically by Allee (3, 5) in particular. The central idea for a consistent theoretical statement as to the properties of "gregariousness" on different levels seems to be available in the potentialities of Wheeler's (172) concept of "trophallaxis" (i.e., food-exchange relationships). This concept has potentialities for a much broader extension in physiological psychology as a means of appraising the variant social impacts of fundamental biological processes in the growth and maintenance of different types of animal groups. A preliminary conceptualization of widely different types of group patterns, e.g., insect and higher mammalian structures, on this basis, has been offered by Schneirla (125, 129) as the "biosocial" and the "psychosocial."

A limited but promising vigorous trend toward the study of animal group behavior has been apparent, and an inevitable enlargement of interest in the questions of the relationship of familial functions to the origin and continuance of larger groups is to be expected. There are a few beginnings in research on individual socialization in different animal types.

A flourishing positivistic conceptualization of individual and group relationships in evolution, with the group characterized as "supraorganism" (5, 6, 34, 35), has been found by some biologists to have heuristic value. On the other hand, it has been criticized (108, 125) for having weaknesses common to general analogies, which in this case readily lead to serious misrepresentations of individual and group characteristics, and do not suggest or encourage comparative analysis.

ASPECTS OF METHOD AND ATTITUDE

Attitudes and practices concerning method are of course critical for the possibility of a genuine comparative basis for animal psychology. A few important points may be considered here. There appears to be a growing awareness that in the vast experimental literature on rat behavior, really very little psychological information about the pre-experimental antecedents and life of the experimental subjects is given as a rule. The subjects are usually regarded as "naive" and "inexperienced" if they have had no *specific* experience, to the experimenter's knowledge, in the *specific* kind of situation he is investigating. Of course, the literature for some time has not lacked reminders, and often strong reminders (1, 25, 48, 63, 66, 109, 117), of the fact that perceptual, emotional, motivational, and other influential aspects of the rat's personality must be considered and controlled as important experimental variables. Christie (25) calls attention to the probability that "these variations might have an appreciable effect upon the behavior of adult rats and might underlie some of the contradictory findings reported in the literature." Of this, it would seem, we can be positive.

This fact calls attention to the attitudes and predilections of the investigator himself as a most important variable in research on animal behavior. The reasons for a common lack of attention to the experience factor, and a general disposition to assume it to be homogeneous in the group and thus controlled, unfortunately cannot be considered simple and readily correctible. The symptoms center about a strong tendency to focus upon a specific problem without any adequate consideration of its broader naturalistic implications. There is in general too little interest in the ontogeny of behavior and personality development as important problems demanding investigation. Mainly for this reason, no doubt, a myopia is detectable for experiential factors which may influence behavior phenomena in somewhat obscure and indirect ways, and for their possible equivalence in function to "training" designedly introduced by the experimenter. As an example, Hudson (59) points out that:

Observation of the behavior of an animal during the course of a typical conditioning experiment will often suggest that important aspects of the learning process are not available for scrutiny by that method. Resistance of the animal to being placed in the apparatus, for example, may develop long before the appearance of a conditioned motor response. This, as a relevant aspect of the learning, is sometimes overlooked.

Hudson emphasizes the significance of rapidly learned and very important perceptual reactions for the behavior of subjects in test situations. Cage life contributes psychological factors of this sort, however difficult they may be to identify. This point deserves renewed emphasis, to counteract the implicit assumption that, if subjects are "naive" for the *specific* problem, "training" then becomes a function of the experimenter's specific operations. This limitation may defeat the efforts of the most hard-working investigator for "rigid control."

As these considerations suggest, much contemporary work in animal psychology tends toward a segmental approach to the organism, through an intense concentration upon specific problems without a full appreciation of their behavioral setting. Thus, rigid control of a small-scale situation in the study of learning may mean a poor control in regard to the broad problem of personality development. A heavy burden is placed on the experimenter, proceeding operationally. Through his own subjective impressions and selective processes in evaluating the phenomenon, he decides what independent variables he shall measure and what "dependent variables" he shall control—devising situation, apparatus, and procedure accordingly. An experimenter, an S-R experimenter in particular, thus may not realize what he excludes when he selects for the animal what the animal is to learn. Planned along the line of "rigid" thought processes dictated by a particular theoretical structure, the experimenter's preconception of the phenomenon may be so imposed upon the investigative process that it becomes not a *test* of anything so much as it is a *demonstration* of that theory. As Harlow (44) has pointed out, S-R theorists do not really control the experience variable in learning studies, notwithstanding their stress upon a "historical" approach to learning. A similar error is made at times by cognitive psychologists in postulating systematic solution tendencies and insight in the animal's approach to a situation (69, 70) without adequate attention to simpler alternative factors (175).

These are certainly not arguments against control in research on behavior problems; on the contrary, they suggest the need for basic *improvements* in control. Pre-experimental anecdotalists attributed higher mental processes to lower animals, or denied such processes, largely on the basis of stories. Their experimentally-minded successors, objectively oriented, may themselves indulge in a similar procedure more subtly derived from uncontrolled implicit processes in the experimenter as thinker and perceiver. The expression *molar approach* is often used when the approach really is segmental. Research may be concentrated upon taking kinds of data which are partial, and thus may favor a really spurious answer to the problem. In the vast and devious literate on maze-learning in rats, how often would obscure results be clearer in their implications if the investigator had reported his data in terms of "kinds of errors" instead of (or in addition to) "error totals"? The experimenter's sagacity determines *what is significant* when he plans the investigation. He may be or feel under pressure to produce results, and thus may attempt a specialized study prematurely. As Sears (31) puts the matter, in appealing for really "molar" investigations in child study: "A kymograph cannot catch what is the essence of the child's conduct, whereas a human observer can." This is not a light or obvious point, as an uninformed bystander might think.

No argument is intended against quantitative methods in animal study, when the appropriate stage has been reached. The neglect of instrumental approaches at the required points in research may be serious for the validity of theory, as is suggested by Köhler's (68) statement that ". . . enthusiasm is no safe substitute for a high reliability of differences."

The compulsive advance of some psychologists toward phenomenalism, a development for which Tolman deserves a good measure of credit (151), must be recognized at least in part as one contemporary reaction to operationism, rigid use of quantitative methods, and deductivism in studying animal behavior. There has resulted an emphasis upon a strictly individualistic qualitative study of behavior which is often a poor substitute for a frank, pre-experimental "mentalistic" study of animals.[3] Such an approach may effectively exclude a consideration of behavior in a broadly naturalistic and social context, in the way that Sherif (136, 137) and Hebb (47), for example, undertake to study behavior.

An emphasis upon *similarities* in process and capacity is predominant in current animal psychology. For example, does the loose habit of applying the term "learning" to instances of temporarily changed behavior in lower invertebrate animals imply some essential equivalence to "learning" in mammals? Such phenomena in the low invertebrates exhibit features much like those of sensory adaptation and muscular fatigue in higher animals, occurrences not ordinarily spoken of as "learning." The terms

---

[3] It is interesting to note that, for different explicit reasons, S-R theorists (61, 151) and phenomenonalist theorists (148, 149) are inclined to exclude physiological evidence more or less completely. Notwithstanding this trend, physiological psychology continues to be a flourishing field of investigation (155).

perception and learning are endowed a priori with some vague essence of equivalence wherever used, or the characteristics of "cognition" are found generalizable throughout a range of processes from conditioning to reasoning. In effect, neither S-R nor cognitive theories have as yet shown their worth to differentiate the various kinds of adjustive and organizing process through the animal series, although some attempts have been made (60, 61, 62, 161, 162).

The concept "purpose," long a center of controversy in biology (2, 32, 83) and in psychology (31, 55, 97), has been receiving some study in behavior work. To this trend not only the behavioristic criticisms of Watson (168) but the more eclectic "purposive behaviorism" of Tolman (161) has contributed. Previously offered as representing impulsions toward goal or end situations through the entire scale of organisms, this concept is now more clearly seen as a confusion of "adaptive behavior" with a vaguely conceived mental process (55, 85, 92, 129). The term "purpose" itself is held to require the satisfaction of certain operationally definable criteria which thus far have validated the postulation of "anticipation," "expectancy," "goal-gradient," and similar higher-level processes only in higher mammals.

A clearer understanding of the relationship of quantitative methods to observational and essentially qualitative methods is very desirable. It may be contended that there need be no fundamental dissimilarity between observation and formal experimentation, considered as scientific disciplines (36, 130). To be sure, an important part of every behavior student's training should be learning how to recognize, and discount, an observational report which is merely anecdotal and hence unreliable. By the same token, he should also learn the clues to unreliability in experimental reports. "Hit-and-run" studies are found in both areas. Observational study, if performed systematically with an adequate methodology, can have the advantages of experimental control held as standard in laboratory work. Furthermore, a systematic observational investigation, through progressive stages of test and control, must inevitably lead into more formally devised laboratory experiments as an indispensable part of the program.

These considerations suggest the advantages of correlative studies of animal behavior adjustments under natural and under man-devised (i.e., laboratory) conditions. A striking illustration is offered in the work of Hediger (49), who has compared with insight the adaptive behavior of the same animal types in the wild and under conditions of confinement in zoos. In general, however, animal psychology has been very deficient in attention to its naturalistic aspects. We should plan to learn how various types of animals may utilize their capacities (e.g., learning) in meeting the typical hazards and arduous trials of their habitats. By remedying this lack, we should gain a more adequate appreciation of the important types of animals as integrated, functioning organisms, and should be in a better position to select validly what is important for laboratory study.

THE DOCTRINE OF LEVELS

A concept of "levels" in capacities and organization follows inevitably from the theory of evolution. According to the levels doctrine, existing systems, both organic and inorganic, are viewed as comparable in their structural and functional characteristics (105, 108, 125, 129), and as capable of being ranked with respect to their degrees and kinds of similarities and differences in these respects. Such a concept offers the broad framework for a systematic study of phyletic similarities and differences which is urgently needed by animal psychology if it is to develop a comparative methodology.

One immediate gain from this viewpoint is vigilant attention to the validity of extrapolations from one system to another. How far, for example, may mechanical models be used in the study of organic and behavioral systems (167, 173)? The gains to be realized through a reference from mechanical calculating devices to the function of a mammalian brain may be elusive, since rough similarities may be stressed and crucial differences (e.g., the role of the human planner and operator of the machine) not really taken into account. As another example, evidence from the study of spinal-reflex systems has been extrapolated to the level of brain function, thereby imposing the pattern of a lower-level system upon a higher functional level in the organism. The investigations of animal psychologists, and of Lashley (72, 76) in particular, have gone far toward freeing psychology from theoretical error along this line.

A contemporary example of a reductionistic (144) theory is that of Lorenz (85, 87). This theory bases postulations concerning the innate control of general behavior patterns upon results such as von Holst's (156), obtained from the study of *lower*-level neurophysiological functions in *lower*-vertebrate locomotion. The extrapolation here is from one type of pattern, locomotion (which might be considered a lower-level function in the individual), to organizations concerning the *whole* individual in action. Although it is a secondary matter here, the validity of the conclusions deduced from the lower-level function itself (i.e., of an endogenous, intraneural control of *patterns*) has been called into question (84, 170). Studies on the deficiencies of conditioned-response learning patterns in decorticate mammals (139) and the deficiencies of a reeducative recovery of locomotor control in spinal mammals as compared with intact individuals (140) serve to emphasize the qualitative differences of lower and higher part-processes in the organism.

The concept of levels has frequently come into discussion in the biological literature (105, 108, 113), less frequently in psychology (135, 182). Discussion of its potentialities for behavioral comparisons have been only introductory (125, 129) and occasional. The idea certainly is not a novel one with reference to behavioral capacities, since Aristotle described vegetative, sensitive, and rational souls for plants, animals, and man respectively, and both C. Lloyd Morgan (99) and Yerkes (182) utilized the essential principle of functional levels.

Certain generalizations may be derived from a preliminary comparative consideration of behavioral capacities in the principal types of living animals (92, 129). First of all, the relevance of evidence concerning morphological equipment may be considerably different according to the type of organism studied. Simply stated, in organisms considered lowest in a psychological sense, organic structure is found to have a rather immediate or "directly determining" efficacy for behavior, relatively unlike its significance for the pattern of behavior in higher organisms, in which varying stages of development and intervening part-processes must be considered. A second generalization is that any functional part-process (e.g., a sensitivity factor) may have different functional significance on different behavioral levels, according to the nature of the whole system within which it functions. Thus, on one level, knowledge about a particular functional component may be expected to have a different bearing upon whole-individual organization from that on other levels. This generalization sharply challenges the validity of extrapolations from level to level when the comparison is made in terms of similarities alone. In other words, extrapolations from level to level concerning similar part-processes have no necessary validity. If recapitulation doctrine has its limitations for modern biology (54), it has far less intrinsic validity for the theoretical psychologist.[4]

Consequently, the principles of behavior must be worked out carefully on an inductive basis for each important type of animal, as a foundation for carrying forward a valid system of interlevel comparisons. Comparisons based on similarities alone may be worthless, however striking they may be. Also, behavioral complexity as such offers no dependable basis for interlevel extrapolations, since complexity is found both in qualitatively high and in qualitatively low functional levels. The clear inference is that unless animal psychologists accept the task of making thoroughgoing functional studies of the principal and widely different types of living organisms, their generalizations will have validity only for the levels studied.

It is evident that knowledge and theory concerning phyletic positions

---

[4] A limited heuristic value may be granted to Haeckel's law as applied to behavior, but no assured a priori place in theory.

and evolutionary background, as determined on biological grounds, must be treated as challenging and introductory by the animal psychologist, for whom the essential question concerns the degree of phyletic relationship or the lack of such relationships. For the psychologist, working contemporaneously, there remains the task of determining the significance of such evidence for the interpretation of behavioral capacities and organization in each type of living organism. Biologists consider existing animal forms as an incomplete series from which transitional forms have largely disappeared through natural selection (141). Psychologists must therefore study animal types as they find them, and rank them accordingly.

The levels viewpoint also emphasizes the dangers inherent in the teleological practice of naming behavior functions according to similar adaptive outcomes, such as food-getting, or protective behavior. Behavioral similarities alone, and similar adaptive results, offer deceptive clues to underlying processes in different animal forms. In terms of the levels concept, we become alert not only for evidence warranting the postulation of qualitative similarities, but also for qualitative differences at crucial turning points in the phyletic scale. A tendency to rely closely upon evidence concerning morphological turning points thus becomes educated through the consideration of behavioral qualifications. It is to be expected that difficulties will be experienced in relating such behavioral qualifications to structural turning points (76, 77), for at progressively higher psychological levels the relationship of specific structural equipment to behavior becomes increasingly devious.

Consequently, the meaning of the terms "part-process" (the molecular) and of more inclusive organization (the molar) must be worked out in a study of behavioral development and organization on each functional level. Then, by contrasting various levels, light may be thrown upon common problems in the field, such as learning. Premature comparisons, ruled by a preoccupation with similarities alone, cannot have much validity for a scientific, hence comparative, psychological theory.

Without doubt, a comparative study of behavioral development and capacities on different animal levels should stimulate investigations on the development of human capacities and personality, in ways perhaps otherwise unrealized. The answer to challenges of the relevance of animal-behavior evidence for human psychology is not that, in the absence of such evidence, irresponsible conclusions will be drawn and applied in any case, both in lay and in scientific circles. More significant is the greater breadth of view which can be obtained through comparative methods in studying the wide range of psychological problems.

This discussion may end with its initial statement concerning a defensible ideal in comparative psychology. One reason for encouraging such a discipline is to gain a valid grasp of man's similarities and differences with respect to lower animals, to replace the often irresponsible speculation which otherwise flourishes in general theory. A wider ideal is that the effective use of the comparative methodology of science in the basic fields of animal, child, and social study is certain to contribute to the conceptual development of all of these fields and thus benefit psychology as a whole.

REFERENCES

1. Adams, D. K. 1929. Experimental studies of adaptive behavior in cats. *Comp. Psychol. Monogr.* 6: 1–168.
2. Agar, W. E. 1943. *A contribution to the theory of the living organism.* Melbourne: Melbourne Univ. Press.
3. Allee, W. C. 1938. *The social life of animals.* New York: Norton.
4. Allee, W. C. 1948. Animal sociology. *Encycl. Britannica,* 1948 ed., vol. 1, pp. 971–972.
5. Allee, W. C. 1949. Extrapolation in comparative sociology. *Scientia* 84: 135–167.
6. Allee, W. C. et al. 1949. *Principles of animal ecology.* Philadelphia: Saunders.
7. Allport, G. W. 1947. Scientific models and human morals. *Psychol. Rev.* 54: 182–192.
8. Anastasi, A., and J. P. Foley. 1948. A proposed reorientation in the heredity-environment controversy. *Psychol. Rev.* 55: 239–249.
9. Anderson, E. E. 1941. The externalization of drive. I. Theoretical considerations. *Psychol. Rev.* 48: 205–224.
10. Baerends, G. P. 1941. Fortpflanzungsverhalten und Orientierung der Grabwespe Ammophila campestris Jus. *Tijdschr. v. Entom.* 84: 71–275.
11. Baerends, G. P. 1950. Specializations in organs and movements with a releasing function. In *Physiological mechanisms in animal behaviour.* New York: Academic Press.
12. Beach, F. A. 1947. Evolutionary changes in the physiological control of mating behavior in mammals. *Psychol. Rev.* 54: 297–315.
13. Beach, F. A. 1950. The snark was a boojum. *Am. Psychologist* 5: 115–124.
14. Bierens de Haan, J. A. 1930. Animal language in its relation to that of man. *Biol. Rev.* 4: 249–268.
15. Bierens de Haan, J. A. 1937. *Labyrinth und Umweg.* Leiden: Brill.
16. Bierens de Haan, J. A. 1947. Animal psychology and the science of animal behaviour. *Behaviour* 1: 71–80.
17. Birch, H. G. 1945. The relation of previous experience to insightful problem-solving. *J. Comp. Psychol.* 38: 367–383.
18. Birch, H. G., and M. E. Bitterman. 1949. Reinforcement and learning: The process of sensory integration. *Psychol. Rev.* 56: 292–308.

19. Boring, E. G. 1948. Review of *Current trends in psychology* (Wayne Dennis, ed.). *Psychol. Bull.* 45: 75–84.
20. Bruner, J. S., and G. W. Allport. 1940. Fifty years of change in American psychology. *Psychol. Bull.* 37: 757–776.
21. Carmichael, L. The development of behavior in vertebrates experimentally removed from the influence of external stimulation. *Psychol. Rev.*, 1926, 33: 51–58; 1927, 34: 34–47; 1928, 35: 253–260.
22. Carmichael, L. 1936. A re-evaluation of the concepts of maturation and learning as applied to the early development of behavior. *Psychol. Rev.* 43: 450–470.
23. Carmichael, L. 1947. The growth of the sensory control of behavior before birth. *Psychol. Rev.* 54: 316–324.
24. Carpenter, C. R. 1934. A field study of the behavior and social relations of howling monkeys (Allouatta palliata). *Comp. Psychol. Monogr.* 10: 1–168.
25. Christie, R. 1951. Experimental naïveté and experiential naïveté. *Psychol. Bull.* 48: 327–339.
26. Collias, N. 1944. Aggressive behavior among vertebrate animals. *Physiol. Zool.* 17: 83–123.
27. Crannell, C. W. 1947. Are rat psychologists responsible for fission? *Am. Psychologist* 2: 22–23.
28. Crawford, M. P. 1937. The cooperative solving of problems by young chimpanzees. *Comp. Psychol. Monogr.* 14: 1–88.
29. Culler, E. 1938. Recent advances in some concepts of conditioning. *Psychol. Rev.* 45: 134–153.
30. Darling, F. F. 1937. *A herd of red deer*. London: Oxford Univ. Press.
31. Dennis, W., ed. 1947. *Current trends in psychology*. Pittsburgh: Univ. Pittsburgh Press.
32. Driesch, H. 1908. *The science and philosophy of the organism*. London: Black.
33. Durkin, J. E. 1937. Trial-and-error, gradual analysis, and sudden reorganization: An experimental study of problem solving. *Arch. Psychol.* 30 (210): 1–85.
34. Emerson, A. E. 1939. Social coordination and the superorganism. *Am. Midl. Nat.* 21 : 182–209.
35. Emerson, A. E. 1942. Basic comparisons of human and insect societies. In R. Redfield, ed., *Biological Symposia* 8: 163–176.
36. Emlen, J. T. 1950. Techniques for observing bird behavior under natural conditions. *Ann. N.Y. Acad. Sci.* 51: 1103–1112.
37. Fischel, W. 1948. *Die höheren Leistungen der Wirbeltiergehirne*. Leipzig: Barth.
38. Fischel, W. 1950. *Die Seele des Hundes*. Berlin, Hamburg: Parey.
39. Frisch, K. v. 1951. *Bees—Their vision, chemical senses, and language*. Ithaca: Cornell Univ. Press.
40. Fromme, A. 1941. An experimental study of the factors of maturation and

practice in the behavioral development of the embryo of the frog, *Rana pipiens. Genet. Psychol. Monogr.* 24: 219–256.

41. Galt, W. 1940. The principle of cooperation in behavior. *Quart. Rev. Biol.* 15: 401–410.
42. Hall, C. S. 1951. The genetics of behavior. In S. S. Stevens, ed., *Handbook of experimental psychology.* New York: Wiley. Pp. 304–329.
43. Hamilton, W. F. 1921. Coordination in the starfish. I, II, III. *J. Comp. Psychol.* 1: 473–488; 2: 61–76; 3: 81–94.
44. Harlow, H. 1949. The formation of learning sets. *Psychol. Rev.* 56: 51–65.
45. Harlow, H. 1950. Levels of integration along the phylogenetic scale—learning aspect. In J. H. Rohrer and M. Sherif, eds., *Social psychology at the crossroads.* New York: Harper.
46. Hayes, K. J., and C. Hayes. 1951. The intellectual development of a home-raised chimpanzee. *Proc. Am. Philos. Soc.* 95: 105–109.
47. Hebb, D. O. 1949. *The organization of behavior.* New York: Wiley.
48. Hebb, D. O. 1950. Animal and physiological psychology. In C. P. Stone, ed., *Annual review of psychology,* vol. II. Stanford, Calif.: Annual Reviews, Inc. Pp. 173–188.
49. Hediger, H. 1950. *Wild animals in captivity.* London: Butterworths.
50. Hertz, M. 1931. Die Organisation des optischen Feldes bei der Biene. *Z. Vergl. Physiol.* 14: 629–674.
51. Hertz, M. 1933. Ueber figurale Intensitäten und Qualitäten in der optischen Wahrnehmung der Biene. *Biol. Zbl.* 53: 10–40.
52. Hilgard, E. R. 1948. *Theories of learning.* New York: Appleton-Century-Crofts.
53. Hilgard, E. R., and D. G. Marquis. 1940. *Conditioning and learning.* New York: Appleton-Century.
54. Holmes, S. J. 1948. *Organic form and related biological problems.* Berkeley: Univ. California Press.
55. Holt, E. B. 1931. *Animal drive and the learning process.* New York: Holt.
56. Honigmann, H. 1942. The number conception in animal psychology. *Biol. Rev.* 17: 315–337.
57. Howard, W. E., and J. T. Emlen. 1942. Intercovey social relationships in the valley quail. *Wilson Bull.* 54: 162–170.
58. Howells, T. H., and D. O. Vine. 1940. The innate differential in social learning. *J. Abnorm. Soc. Psychol.* 35: 537–548.
59. Hudson, B. B. 1950. One-trial learning in the domestic rat. *Genet. Psychol. Monogr.* 41: 99–145.
60. Hull, C. L. 1937. Mind, mechanism, and adaptive behavior. *Psychol. Rev.* 44: 1–32.
61. Hull, C. L. 1943. *Principles of behavior.* New York: Appleton-Century-Crofts.
62. Hull, C. L. 1945. The place of innate individual and species differences in a natural-science theory of behavior. *Psychol. Rev.* 52: 55–60.

63. Hunt, J. McV. 1941. The effect of infant feeding frustration upon adult hoarding in the albino rat. *J. Ab-Norm. Soc. Psychol.* 36: 338–360.
64. Jennings, H. S. 1930. *The biological basis of human nature.* New York: Norton.
65. Jepsen, G. L., E. Mayr, and G. G. Simpson. 1949. *Genetics, paleontology, and evolution.* Princeton: Princeton Univ. Press.
66. Karn, H. W., and J. M. Porter, Jr. 1946. The effects of certain pretraining procedures upon maze performance and their significance for the concept of latent learning. *J. Exp. Psychol.* 36: 461–469.
67. Kendler, H. H., and B. J. Underwood. 1948. The role of reward in conditioning theory. *Psychol. Rev.* 55: 209–215.
68. Köhler, W. 1943. A perspective on American psychology. *Psychol. Rev.* 50: 77–79.
69. Krechevsky, I. 1932. "Hypotheses" in rats. *Psychol. Rev.* 39: 516–532.
70. Krechevsky, I. 1933. Hereditary nature of "hypotheses." *J. Comp. Psychol.* 16: 99–116.
71. Kuo, Z. Y. 1924. A psychology without heredity. *Psychol. Rev.* 31: 427–448.
72. Lashley, K. S. 1929. *Brain mechanisms and intelligence.* Chicago: Univ. Chicago Press.
73. Lashley, K. S. 1938. The mechanism of vision: XV. Preliminary studies of the rat's capacity for detail vision. *J. Gen. Psychol.* 18: 123–193.
74. Lashley, K. S. 1940. Studies of Simian intelligence from the University of Liège. *Psychol. Bull.* 37: 237–248.
75. Lashley, K. S. 1942. An examination of the "continuity theory" as applied to discriminative learning. *J. Gen. Psychol.* 26: 241–265.
76. Lashley, K. S. 1947. Structural variation in the nervous system in relation to behavior. *Psychol. Rev.* 54: 325–334.
77. Lashley, K. S. 1949. Persistent problems in the evolution of mind. *Quart. Rev. Biol.* 24: 28–42.
78. Leeper, R. W. 1935. Study of a neglected portion of the field of learning —the development of sensory organization. *J. Genet. Psychol.* 48: 41–75.
79. Leeper, R. W. 1944. Dr. Hull's *Principles of behavior. J. Genet. Psychol.* 65: 3–52.
80. Leeper, R. W. 1951. Cognitive processes. In S. S. Stevens, ed., *Handbook of experimental psychology.* New York: Wiley. Pp. 730–757.
81. Lehrman, D. S. A critique of Lorenz's "objectivistic" theory of animal behavior. *Q. Rev. Biol.,* in press.
82. Leuba, C. 1940. The need for a systematic study of innate nature. *Psychol. Rev.* 47: 486–490.
83. Lillie, R. S. 1945. *General biology and philosophy of organism.* Chicago: Univ. Chicago Press.
84. Lissmann, H. W. 1950. Proprioceptors. In *Physiological mechanisms in animal behaviour.* New York: Academic Press. Pp. 34–59.
85. Lorenz, K. 1935. Der Kumpan in der Umwelt des Vogels. *J. f. Ornith.* 83: 137–213.

86. Lorenz, K. 1937. Ueber die Bildung des Instinkbegriffes. *Naturwiss.* 25: 290–330.
87. Lorenz, K. 1950. The comparative method in studying innate behaviour patterns. In *Physiological mechanisms in animal behaviour.* New York: Academic Press. Pp. 221–268.
88. Loucks, R. B. 1941. The contribution of physiological psychology. *Psychol. Rev.* 48: 105–126.
89. Maier, N. R. F. 1929. Reasoning in white rats. *Comp. Psychol. Monogr.* 6 (3): 1–93.
90. Maier, N. R. F. 1935. In defense of reasoning in rats: A reply. *J. Comp. Psychol.* 19: 197–206.
91. Maier, N. R. F. 1940. The behavior mechanisms concerned with problem solving. *Psychol. Rev.* 47: 43–58.
92. Maier, N. R. F., and T. C. Schneirla. 1935. *Principles of animal psychology.* New York: McGraw-Hill.
93. Maier, N. R. F., and T. C. Schneirla. 1942. Mechanisms in conditioning. *Psychol. Rev.* 49: 117–134.
94. Marker, Charlotte, and M. Dolgin. 1942. Simple and complex bases for the solution of various tests in the Carmichael elevated-maze situation. *J. Genet. Psychol.* 60: 259–269.
95. Maslow, A. H. 1936. Dominance-quality and social behavior in infrahuman primates. *J. Soc. Psychol.* 11: 313–324.
96. McBride, A. F., and D. O. Hebb. 1948. Behavior of the captive bottlenose dolphin. *J. Comp. Physiol. Psychol.* 41: 111–123.
97. McDougall, W. 1911. *An introduction to social psychology,* 4th ed. Boston: Luce.
98. Melton, A. W. 1950. Learning. In C. P. Stone, ed., *Annual review of psychology.* Stanford, Calif.: Annual Reviews, Inc. Pp. 9–30.
99. Morgan, C. L. 1894. *An introduction to comparative psychology.* London: Scott.
100. Morgan, C. T. 1947. The hoarding instinct. *Psychol. Rev.* 54: 335–341.
101. Moss, F. A., ed. 1945. *Comparative psychology.* New York: Prentice-Hall. (Rev. Ed., C. P. Stone, Ed., 1950.)
102. Munn, N. L. 1933. *Animal psychology.* Boston: Houghton Mifflin.
103. Munn, N. L. 1938. *Psychological development.* New York: Houghton Mifflin.
104. Murchison, C. 1935. The experimental measurement of a social hierarchy in Gallus domesticus: I. The direct identification and direct measurement of Social Reflex No. 1 and Social Reflex No. 2. *J. Gen. Psychol.* 12: 3–39.
105. Needham, J. 1929. *The skeptical biologist.* London: Chatto.
106. Nissen, H. W. 1951. Phylogenetic comparison. In S. S. Stevens, ed., *Handbook of experimental psychology.* New York: Wiley. Pp. 347–386.
107. Nissen, H. W., and M. P. Crawford. 1936. A preliminary study of food-sharing behavior in young chimpanzees. *J. Comp. Psychol.* 22: 383–419.

108. Novikoff, A. 1945. The concept of integrative levels in biology. *Science* 101: 209–215.

109. Patrick, J. R., and R. M. Laughlin. 1934. Is the wall-seeking tendency in the white rat an instinct? *J. Genet. Psychol.* 44: 378–389.

110. Pattie, F. A. 1946. Howells on the hereditary differential in learning—A criticism. *Psychol. Rev.* 53: 53–54.

111. Pavlov, I. 1927. *Conditioned reflexes.* London: Oxford Univ. Press.

112. Petrunkevitch, A. 1926. The value of instinct as a taxonomic character in spiders. *Biol. Bull.* 50: 427–432.

113. Redfield, R., ed. 1942. *Levels of integration in biological and social systems.* Lancaster, Pa.: Cattell Press.

114. Révész, G. 1925. Experimental study in abstraction in monkeys. *J. Comp. Psychol.* 5: 293–343.

115. Révész, G. 1944. The language of animals. *J. Gen. Psychol.* 30: 117–147.

116. Riesen, A. H. 1947. The development of visual perception in man and chimpanzee. *Science* 106: 107–108.

117. Riess, B. F. 1945. A possible explanation of "freezing" behavior in rats. *Science* 102: 570–571.

118. Riess, B. F. An experimental investigation of instincts in the white rat. The effect of restricted infantile environment on maternal behavior. *J. Comp. Physiol. Psychol.*, in press.

119. Russell, E. S. 1934. *The behaviour of animals.* London: Arnold.

120. Schiller, P. H. 1948. Delayed response in the minnow. *J. Comp. Physiol. Psychol.* 41: 233–238.

121. Schiller, P. H. 1949. Delayed detour response in the octopus. *J. Comp. Physiol. Psychol.* 42: 220–225.

122. Schjelderup-Ebbe, T. 1922. Beiträge zur Sozialpsychologie des Haushuhns. *Z. Psychol.* 88: 225–252.

123. Schneirla, T. C. 1940. Further studies on the army-ant behavior pattern. Mass organization in the swarm-raiders. *J. Comp. Psychol.* 29: 401–460.

124. Schneirla, T. C. 1941. Social organization in insects, as related to individual function. *Psychol. Rev.* 48: 465–486.

125. Schneirla, T. C. 1946. Problems in the biopsychology of social organization. *J. Abnorm. Soc. Psychol.* 41: 385–402.

126. Schneirla, T. C. 1946. Ant learning as a problem in comparative psychology. In P. L. Harriman et al., eds., *Twentieth century psychology.* New York: Philosophical Library. Pp. 276–305.

127. Schneirla, T. C. 1946. Contemporary American animal psychology in perspective. In P. L. Harriman et al., eds., *Twentieth century psychology.* New York: Philosophical Library. Pp. 306–316.

128. Schneirla, T. C. 1948. Psychology, comparative. *Encycl. Britannica* 18: 690–760.

129. Schneirla, T. C. 1949. Levels in the psychological capacities of animals. In R. W. Sellars et al., eds., *Philosophy for the future.* New York: Macmillan. Pp. 243–286.

130. Schneirla, T. C. 1950. The relationship between observation and experi-

mentation in the field study of behavior. *Ann. N.Y. Acad. Sci.* 51: 1022–1044.

131. Scott, J. P. 1945. Social behavior, organization, and leadership in a small flock of domestic sheep. *Comp. Psychol. Monogr.* 18: 1–29.

132. Scott, J. P., ed. 1950. Symposium: Methodology and techniques for the study of animal societies. *Ann. N.Y. Acad. Sci.* 51: 1101–1122.

133. Searle, L. V. 1949. The organization of hereditary maze-brightness and maze-dullness. *Genet. Psychol. Monogr.* 39: 279–325.

134. Seward, J. P. 1948. The sign of a symbol: A reply to Professor Allport. *Psychol. Rev.* 55: 277–296.

135. Shepard, J. F. 1914. Types of learning in animals and man. *Psychol. Bull.* 11: 58 (Abstract).

136. Sherif, M. 1947. Some methodological remarks related to experimentation in social psychology. *Int. J. Opin. Att. Res.* 1: 71–93.

137. Sherif, M. 1948. *An outline of social psychology.* New York: Harper.

138. Sherrington, C. S. 1906. *The integrative action of the nervous system.* New Haven: Yale Univ. Press.

139. Shurrager, P. S., and E. Culler. 1940. Conditioning in the spinal dog. *J. Exp. Psychol.* 26: 133–159.

140. Shurrager, P. S., and R. A. Dykman. 1951. Walking spinal carnivores. *J. Comp. Physiol. Psychol.* 44: 252–262.

141. Simpson, G. G. 1950. *The meaning of evolution.* New Haven: Yale Univ. Press.

142. Skinner, B. F. 1935. Two types of conditioned reflex and a pseudo-type. *J. Gen. Psychol.* 12: 66–77.

143. Skinner, B. F. 1938. *The behavior of organisms.* New York: Appleton-Century.

144. Sloane, E. H. 1945. Reductionism. *Psychol. Rev.* 52: 214–223.

145. Smith, J. E. 1950. Some observations on the nervous mechanisms underlying the behaviour of starfishes. In *Physiological mechanisms in animal behaviour.* New York: Academic Press. Pp. 196–220.

146. Smith, S., and E. R. Guthrie. 1921. *General psychology in terms of behavior.* New York: Appleton.

147. Smith, M. F. 1939. The establishment and extinction of the token-reward habit in the cat. *J. Gen. Psychol.* 20: 475–486.

148. Snygg, D. 1941. The need for a phenomenological system of psychology. *Psychol. Rep.* 48: 404–423.

149. Snygg, D., and A. W. Combs. 1949. *Individual behavior.* New York: Harper.

150. Spence, K. W. 1939. The solution of multiple choice problems by chimpanzees. *Comp. Psychol. Monogr.* 15: 1–54.

151. Spence, K. W. 1944. The nature of theory construction in contemporary psychology. *Psychol. Rev.* 51: 47–68.

152. Spence, K. W. 1950. Cognitive versus stimulus-response theories of learning. *Psychol. Rev.* 57: 159–172.

153. Spence, K. W. 1951. Theoretical interpretations of learning. In S. S.

Stevens, ed., *Handbook of experimental psychology*. New York: Wiley. Pp. 690–729.

154. Sperry, R. W. 1951. Mechanisms of neural maturation. In S. S. Stevens, ed., *Handbook of experimental psychology*. New York: Wiley. Pp. 236 280.

155. Stevens, S. S., ed. 1951. *Handbook of experimental psychology*. New York: Wiley.

156. Symposia of the Society for Experimental Biology, No. IV. 1950. *Physiological mechanisms in animal behaviour*. New York: Academic Press.

157. Symposium on heredity and environment. 1947. *Psychol. Rev.* 54: 297–352.

158. Thorndike, E. L. 1911. *Animal intelligence*. New York: Macmillan.

159. Thorpe, W. H. 1950. A note on detour experiments with Ammophila pubescens Curt (Hymenoptera; Sphecidae). *Behaviour* 2: 257–263.

160. Tinbergen, N., and D. J. Kuehnen. 1939. Ueber die auslösenden und richtungsgebenden Reizsituationen der Sperrbewegungen von jungen Drosseln (Turdus m. merula L. und T. e. ericetorum Turton). *Z. Tierpsychol.* 3: 37–60.

161. Tolman, E. C. 1932. *Purposive behavior in animals and men*. New York: Century.

162. Tolman, E. C. 1948. Cognitive maps in rats and men. *Psychol. Rev.* 55: 189–208.

163. Tolman, E. C. 1949. There is more than one kind of learning. *Psychol. Rev.* 56: 144–156.

164. Tracy, H. C. 1926. The development of motility and behavior reactions in the toadfish (*Opsanus tau*). *J. Comp. Neurol.* 40: 253–369.

165. Warden, C. J., L. Warner, and T. N. Jenkins. 1935. *Comparative psychology*. Vol. 1. *Principles and methods*. New York: Prentice-Hall.

166. Washburn, M. F. 1936. *The animal mind*, 4th ed. New York: Macmillan.

167. Waters, R. H. 1948. Mechanomorphism: A new term for an old mode of thought. *Psychol. Rev.* 55: 139–142.

168. Watson, J. B. 1914. *Behavior: An introduction to comparative psychology*. New York: Holt.

169. Watson, J. B. 1919. *Psychology from the standpoint of a behaviorist*. Philadelphia: Lippincott.

170. Weiss, P. 1950. Experimental analysis of co-ordination by the disarrangement of central-peripheral relations. In *Physiological mechanisms in animal behaviour*. New York: Academic Press. Pp. 92–111.

171. Werner, H. 1940. *Comparative psychology of mental development*. New York: Harper.

172. Wheeler, W. M. 1928. *The social insects*. New York: Harcourt, Brace.

173. Wiener, N. 1949. *Cybernetics*. New York: Wiley.

174. Wigner, E. P. 1950. The limits of science. *Proc. Am. Philos. Soc.* 94: 422–427.

175. Witkin, H. A. 1942. "Hypotheses" in rats: An experimental critique.

III. Summary evaluation of the hypotheses concept. *Psychol. Rev.* 49: 541–568.

176. Wolf, E. 1933. Das Verhalten der Bienen gegenüber flimmernden Feldern und bewegten Objekten. *Z. Vergl. Physiol.* 20: 151–161.

177. Wolfe, J. B. 1936. Effectiveness of token-rewards for chimpanzees. *Comp. Psychol. Monogr.* 12: 1–72.

178. Wolfe, J. B., and S. D. S. Spragg. 1934. Some experimental tests of "reasoning" in white rats. *J. Comp. Psychol.* 18: 455–469.

179. Woodger, J. H. 1929. *Biological principles—A critical study.* New York: Harcourt, Brace.

180. Woodworth, R. S. 1918. *Dynamic psychology.* New York: Columbia Univ. Press.

181. Wundt, W. 1863. *Vorlesungen über die Menschen- und Thierseele.* Leipzig: Vosz.

182. Yerkes, R. M. 1905. Animal psychology and criteria of the psychic. *J. Philos. Psychol. Sci. Math.* 2: 141–149.

183. Yerkes, R. M. 1907. *The dancing mouse.* Leipzig: Vosz; New York: Macmillan.

184. Yerkes, R. M. 1916. The mental life of monkeys and apes: A study of ideational behavior. *Behav. Monogr.* 3, Ser. No. 12, 1–145.

185. Yerkes, R. M. 1933. Genetic aspects of grooming, a socially important primate behavior pattern. *J. Soc. Psychol.* 4: 3–25.

186. Yerkes, R. M. 1939. Social dominance and sexual status in the chimpanzee. *Quart. Rev. Biol.* 14: 115–136.

187. Yerkes, R. M., and A. W. Yerkes. 1929. *The great apes.* New Haven: Yale Univ. Press.

188. Zuckerman, S. 1932. *The social life of monkeys and apes.* London: Kegan, Paul.

Psychological Problems in the Orientation of Mammals

Bibliography No. 72

I hope you have all seen this brief outline [see p. 938], and we will try to follow it so that problems I don't happen to comment on, and which may interest you, can be brought up.

You will notice that in the first section, on the ontogenetic aspects of animal orientation, we are emphasizing native factors and the experimental study of behavior development.

Now animal psychologists have by no means been backward in studying these problems. Dr. Hebb, for one, has carried out some important investigations on early orientational behavior in rats, discussed in his important book. Many significant analytical studies have been carried out; consider, for example, the frequently overlooked investigations of Kuo on the development of pecking in domestic fowl and of mouse-killing in kittens. But these have been too few—we know too little about the *development* of orientation patterns, not just in mammals, but in animals in general. Patterns on all levels must be studied carefully from the standpoint of ontogeny. This is an important need for advance in the field.

Phylogeny and ontogeny are often mixed up in a very confused manner. Our knowledge concerning ontogeny is too limited to justify the confidence of some writers about the presumed "endogenous" or innate basis of a pattern which appears universally in a species. This is an explicit attempt to state the typical basis of the psychologist's objection to "instinct" theory. It is very easy to conclude that a behavior pattern is determined in the genes or dependent upon an innate determining center in the central nervous system, as do Lorenz and Tinbergen, when no real attention has been paid to ontogeny and when the relation of both genes and nervous centers to behavior patterns is so poorly known as concerns development (Schneirla, 1952).

The fact is that a behavior pattern can appear universally in a species

From *Proceedings of a Conference on Orientation in Animals*. Washington, D.C.: Office of Naval Research, 1954. Pp. 193–209.

without being determined on a purely native *basis as a pattern*. This is not to exclude the influence of hereditary factors, of course. In the feeding pattern of ring doves which I mentioned previously, hereditary factors are certainly present, but the feeding pattern is not innate as a pattern. There has been too much jumping to conclusions on these matters, when the real nature of the process through which the pattern appears is very likely to be most subtle and elusive to investigation and when important ontogenetic conditions are easily overlooked.

The psychologist has had his fingers burned along these lines, and has learned that premature nativistic conclusions are dangerous to the truth. In this field, as in the general field of orientation, we are likely to be fascinated by the theme "I love a mystery!" and to leap as readily to hypotheses of unknown native determinants as some students of migration and homing have to "unknown direction senses." We are all very intrigued by something we can't explain, but to jump right out of the field of known evidence, and to neglect important experimental clues already in the literature (as Kuo's "instinct" investigations have been neglected) is inexcusable for scientists. That is, this is an inexcusable behavior if we are studying the problems scientifically, and trying to get at the truth.

Now that is part of the motivation of the psychologists to whom Dr. Galambos has referred. These psychologists have little confidence in nativistic and preformistic claims for behavior determination on what they consider superficial or insufficient evidence. It is necessary to examine very carefully some of the strong claims for a nativistic determination of behavior patterns, in comparison with how little interest is shown by the claimants in the ontogeny or individual history of these patterns. In particular we must be careful not to confuse a lower-order type of activity like a visceral rhythm with more wholistic patterns like food-getting or way-finding. For example, I would hesitate to extrapolate any principle directly from Dr. Brown's rhythmic processes in Crustacea to general behavior patterns even in insects, much less in higher vertebrates.

There are different *orders* of behavior in the individual, from the lowest orders of reflex to higher orders in which the anterior nervous system plays a controlling part, and the same principles do not apply to these a priori, any more than the same principles cover lower and higher *levels* of behavior in the animal series.

More must be learned about how the patterns of orientation behavior arise in the individual. I should like to refer again to the study by Mr. Lehrman on feeding relations between parent and young ring doves. His results show that the eventual behavior patterns, and specifically the orientation of the young bird to the parent in feeding, cannot possibly be understood without considering what happens to the reflex processes of the young bird when they get caught up in a succession of behavioral interactions with the parent. A behavior pattern eventuates to which genetically given factors contribute, but the *pattern* cannot arise without benefit of the parent-young behavioral relationships certain to arise in ontogeny.

The problem of perception, loosely speaking, concerns how an animal "sees its world." In his *Organization of Behavior*, Dr. Hebb has shown that the nativistic doctrines in themselves can give only a very misleading answer to this problem. That this is true for birds as well is indicated by a study made by Dr. A. Siegel with ring doves in our laboratory. Groups of experimental doves were provided with translucent head-hoods which they wore continuously from hatching to adulthood. These hoods were light-permeable, so that pathological conditions in the eye were excluded, but deprived the birds of visual definition—outlines and light-darkness differences were ruled out. The experimental subjects wore their translucent hoods to young adulthood, and then were tested in the learning of a visual pattern discrimination (triangle vs. circle) in comparison with adults raised normally. The visually deprived doves were not only very significantly inferior at the outset and retarded in learning this discrimination, their habit was inferior to that of the normals, and they had difficulties that were due neither to deficiencies in visual acuity nor to motor handicaps. They were equivalent to the controls in visual acuity and had no identifiable pathological defects in the retina or otherwise. The experimental birds were also inferior to normal subjects in transferring the discrimination habit, when required to relearn it in using the hemi-retina of the other eye which had been covered in the initial discrimination learning.

There would therefore seem to be something in the normal experience of a ring dove from hatching to early adulthood, in seeing objects and reacting to seen objects during its normal developmental history as an individual, that contributes to the perceiving of patterns such as those used in the test. This contribution of normal experience may be what is suggested by the expression "learned meaning." Such experience is normal for all ring doves not forced to wear translucent hoods from the time of hatching.

We had better consider the meaning of the term "perception" here, since this term has been used in a very sweeping way by many writers. Of course, like the term "acuity," perception means many things, and often means very different things to different people. Let me suggest here a line of attack that is desirable for the clarification of our nomenclature.

We may postulate a level of stimulus-response relationships in which the response is given in a coerced or forced manner according to the sheer physical properties of the extrinsic stimulus. The term "perception" very probably should be reserved for the level in which the character of meaning first appears—that is, in which the visually effective object has pattern properties dependent upon its learned significance. It is necessary to postulate advanced levels of perception, distinguishable in species of increasingly higher capacity for modifiable behavior, in which more and more can be learned about objects and situations. These differences in level would be suggested by the expressions "sign," "signal," and "symbol" as terms for maximal capacities—the last representing a characteristic of perceiving which has been demonstrated only in the higher mammals.

This is a most important problem for the understanding of orientation. It is the problem for which von Uexküll attempted to offer an answer through his "Umweltforschung," or investigation of the animal's surrounding world. Hediger, Director of the Basle Zoo, is a representative contemporary scientist who has thought much about this problem. Many of you are familiar with his *Wild Animals in Captivity,* in which he endeavors to analyze the significance of objects and situations for the adjustments and orientation of animals in [their] characteristic surroundings.

More studies should be made on the ontogeny of these matters. We should compare the manner in which orientation develops, first to the mother and later to an expanding environment. It would be interesting to carry out detailed comparisons of the ontogeny of such adjustments in blind-born mammals such as the dog in comparison with mammals that have vision from birth—ungulates, for example. Important changes occur in the orientation of blind-born mammals in the presight period, which we do not as yet have the techniques to investigate adequately.

Under I-B in the outline, aspects of developmental study, I should like to point out that we have a great deal of evidence on early stimulogenous and developmental-motor conditions in various mammals, such as rat, cat, and guinea pig. We have much evidence on the human level, as well, but this mass of evidence is still largely a catalog of events rather than a basis for an adequate theory of the organization of orientation or other behavior patterns.

Under I-B2, the development of drive and motivational systems, our attention is called to an important set of problems which should be studied in relation to the properties of orientation. "Approach" and "avoidance" are terms used for the direction of orientational adjustments to objects and situations. For lower invertebrates there is the much-neglected problem of "sign," to which Dr. Blum has referred. In mammals we have various perceptual levels in which approach or withdrawal adjustments are related to the meaningful perception of objects or situations. Following a theory suggested in an earlier article (Schneirla, 1939) and developed further in a recent paper (Schneirla, 1948), I have assembled from a scattered literature a variety of evidence which seems enlightening on this subject. Briefly, using the human level as example, I think it is profitable to postulate the following ontogenetic process. An initial, forced nonpurposive reaching, through experience with objects and situations, furnishes the basis for a perceptually oriented, anticipative reaching in the infant. Furthermore, I believe that the acquired pattern of perceptual reaching is the prelude to and basis for more extensive encroachments into the environment, to more widely expanded orientation capacities in crawling and then in walking toward objects and situations. We might go further into the later stage of "vicarious approach," when there is an imaginative orientation toward absent objects and situations. This is intended to suggest a transition by stages, in an expanding perceptual-motor development that gives the individual a more and more versatile command over a constantly expanding environment in which he can find his way and operate with increasing efficiency. Of course, orientation with respect to other individuals must be included in this process. At first, the other individual is not a *fact* to the infant and is not perceptible by the infant. He reaches out, but at first as a stimulatively enforced response, to the sheer physical delivery of certain energy to his receptors and nervous system. Only later does he reach toward a "face." There are important problems here which have been passed over very lightly but should be very rewarding to adequate investigation.

Under Section II-A in the outline we come to the contributions of the maze method. American psychologists have been criticized, by themselves as well as by outsiders, for having carried such work to extremes of overspecialization. This criticism no doubt is very deserved in some respects and partially in others. Yet there is much of value in the maze literature, and in it much valuable evidence concerning animal orientation is lying unused. For example, in the detailed literature on the "sensory control of maze-learning" (see Maier & Schneirla, 1935, Chap. 16), there is evidence which throws valuable light on the function of exteroceptive fields on general mammalian space orientation, in comparison with the function of proprioception and especially of kinesthesis. This evidence should be better known—it is far from valueless.

The maze work also throws valuable light on the manner in which mammals master orientation habits of a simple or a complex nature. To begin with, here are two examples of studies on the orientation of naive animals. Yoshioka studied adult rats in a T-maze, feeding the subject whether he turned to right or to left, and recording the frequency of turning for each animal. He found a significant correlation between the right-or-left turning tendency in many of the animals and the direction of curvature of the nasal bone. This study therefore identified an organic factor (no doubt one of many) which has a demonstrable effect upon the orientation of an animal in a strange situation. Biel (1935) required a lengthy article for the summary of maze work on factors determining the right or left turning of rats at choice points.

Another important set of effects in the naive orientation responses of mammals at turning points depends upon the mechanics of movement, and I have characterized this as "centrifugal swing." Witkin and I (1939) studied this matter with naive rats in this simple U-maze situation (drawing on blackboard). With a U-sequence of alleys preceding the critical junction, naive rats turned to the "outside" alternative (i.e., away from the side of the "U") 86 percent of the time in the first six runs. In a further study, Witkin used this situation with a somewhat complicated technique to study the development of "conflict" difficulties in rats. When it was necessary for the subject to adjust first to one alternative as a systematic way of getting to a food-place, and then to the other in this U-approach maze, with numerous shifts alternatively from one to the other, some of the rats developed behavior syndromes of a highly interruptive and erratic kind. Some of them finally became unable to run the maze at all.

Applying the same test to the ant, under comparable conditions, I found no such indications of "conflict" difficulties. Apparently the ant was not at all troubled by what is conflict for the rat—and does not become disoriented through too much interference as does the rat. We may say that for the rat, there may exist a tendency to make two alternative turns at the same time in this situation, but not for the ant. Such results indicate that the social insect is a much more stereotyped animal in its orientation processes than is the mammal, and develops its orientation very differently through learning. From a broad comparison with other maze studies, it seems probable that partially decorticated rats would be more like insects than like normal rats in their learned orientation under these conditions. Shock also has the effect of simplifying the white rat's behavior at choice points, and stereotyping it so that the animal becomes more or less immune to conflict-engendering situations that greatly trouble normal subjects.

With the next slide,* I want to return to the question of the sensory control of maze learning. Those of you who know something of the literature on this subject are able to recall how much attention has been given to attempts to isolate the function of kinesthesis (cf. Maier & Schneirla, 1935, Chap. 16). In the work of Shepard, such studies have been carried to an advanced point by using the "unit-alike" maze, in which there is a series of pathway combinations which are all alike except one, the unique section. In detailed investigations, it was shown that the unique unit could be readily localized by trained rats, so long as they were able to use what Shepard calls "floor cues." But if auditory and vibratory cues are eliminated by padding the floor adequately (as by running animals on cloth over sand), then the animal can locate the unique unit only by chance. He

---

* Editor's note: The *Proceedings* of the Orientation Conference were published without illustrations. It was not possible to collate the same slides used by Dr. Schneirla in his presentation.

has all of the kinesthetic or muscle-sensitivity of normal animals, as well as what we may call the skin-tension-pattern factor, but his learned orientation habit cannot operate on that alone. Qualitative guidance of orientation in the maze evidently demands a certain amount of exteroceptive control—and in the alley maze this means audition in particular. The sensory basis of the "floor cue" has not been identified very definitely as yet, but there is reason to suspect that it is body-vibration in part, and in part auditory (e.g., sound-reflection effects from running feet).

If we are working with the problem of how a mammal acquires its orientation in a general environment comparable to the maze, the floor-cue is a subtle factor that must be reckoned with. If uncontrolled it will surely account for spurious results that are likely to be mistaken as evidence for a "general orientation" to the points of the compass, for instance. The evidence on "general orientation" solutions of maze problems requires reviewing in this light.

DR. HASLER: Can you stuff the ears on the rats and have much effect?

DR. SCHNEIRLA: Deafening the rats would reduce it, but not eliminate it. It is evidently due to body-vibration cues in part. Both these cues and specific auditory cues evidently are very materially reduced by a suitable padding of the floor, which drops accuracy in locating the unique unit to zero or almost to zero. . . .

I might mention that we have had a classic instance of alleged "unknown direction sense" in ants. Cornetz thought he had eliminated all sensory factors including directionalized light, so that when homegoing ants still seemed well oriented, he began to speak of an "unknown direction sense." But later, Santschi and Brun showed that Cornetz's results could be explained to an appreciable extent at least as due to reliance upon a directionalized effect of diffuse illumination (e.g., under a canopy of Eucalyptus boughs), and more recently it has been shown that many ants can be virtually oriented to the plane of light polarization. "Unknown direction sense" should be regarded as a strictly preliminary and challenging term, for what we don't know.

Under Section II-B in the outline are numerous problems that should be considered here. If time permitted, I should like to discuss evidence on visual and other types of discrimination in orientation. Such discussions should begin with a consideration of evidence concerning stimulus- and difference-thresholds in orientation, for the sensory modalities involved. These matters should also be considered in relation to their neurophysiological relationships in function, as an introduction to the study of mammalian orientation. A careful analysis of these matters is needed, by psychologists, neurophysiologists and sensory physiologists, working collaboratively. There is an extensive, scattered literature here which needs bringing together for use in the study of space orientation.

Among the less obvious aspects of these problems, one sensory factor of possibly great importance seems to have been overlooked for the most part. This factor we may call the "skin-tension-effect," the pattern of sensory impressions afforded through the differential stretching of skin as an animal makes a succession of movements. This factor may be very important in acquisition of skill, for example, or at critical moments in an orientation series. In the skilled manipulation of objects or in the manipulation of the body as in tumbling, etc., the varying patterns of skin-stretching may furnish orienting cues of great importance. The maze techniques furnish a relatively convenient way of testing this hypothesis. For instance, controls might readily be carried out in which portions of skin on the limbs and over the body are desensitized, either during or after an orientation habit is learned. This hypothetical factor may well account for some of the directive function that has been assigned to kinesthesis by some writers. The maze evidence would lead us to place kinesthesis in a supporting but nondirective role in controlling oriented movement, rather than in a directive role comparable to that of the exteroceptors.

With the next slide we pass to the organization of spatial-temporal orienting systems (Outline, II-C). In this connection, the question of "territory" is important, and that recalls some of Dr. Davis's remarks. There is much to be considered here, in connection with problems of space orientation. A comparative consideration would be of interest, of territory in lower vertebrates, birds, and different mammals.

[An operational definition of territory would be "the space which an animal will defend."] I am not sure that we need to hold ourselves to that here, but perhaps it would be better to consider all space within which a given individual or given group operates—this is much more than "territory" as the term is regularly used in discussions of social behavior, etc., in animals.

Let us speak of the "normal range" of the individual or group, as a more convenient concept for studying the breadth of spatial adjustments. As an example, the next slide shows the effective normal space of one hippopotamus studied by Hediger. Here are the best used trails, converging on the central resting point as is typical of this animal. Here are the identified "signal" points, which are distinguishable through repeated scenting operations by the animal. How does the animal perceive this situation, in using it and in getting about from point to point in it? What Hediger calls the "flight distance" (the minimal distance of approach to a disturbing object such as man before withdrawal occurs) is different for example according to whether the hippo is near the center of the margin of this zone. This indicates a different perception of the molestor and a different orientation process, according to where the animal happens to be within its zone. Hence a different perceptual adjustment to the parts of the living space themselves.

An important set of problems is raised by this question of differing flight distance. Let me illustrate flight distance with a sketch: here is the animal, and here is the disturbing object, a man. Hediger works out the flight distance for different animals in response to man, and this data is very useful for designing livable cages to which the animal can adjust with the least difficulty. This question of flight distance takes us back to the problem of native factors in orientation. Now in fishes and amphibians the size of an object will be very important in determining whether the animal will approach or withdraw. There are factors to be considered here, closely related to the genetic make-up and the contribution of maturation in the different animals. These or comparable factors are also involved basically in the mammals in determining naive flight responses, but there is much more. After experience with the given object, its initial size effect may be overcome or even reversed in mammals, but not to anywhere near that extent in the lower vertebrates and invertebrates, where it has definite limits of change often near zero. The higher we go in the animal series, the more cortex an animal has among the mammals, the greater the mastery an individual can acquire over the nature of an object and the more versatile his capacity to deal with it. The spatial system of the mammal is not merely more extensive and complex, its perceptual significance for the animal is on a distinctly higher level.

To illustrate the superiority of the spatial-temporal system of the mammal over lower animals, I should like to discuss the different ways in which rats and ants master mazes (cf. Schneirla, 1946). Here is a maze pattern for which *Formica* ants required about 30 trips to master, when they learned it, but which rats learned in 12 runs or less. But the most striking difference is not just in the fact that the mammal required less experience to learn this particular orientation habit, it is rather in how the habit is mastered and in what is acquired. In the ant's learning of this maze we find three fairly distinctive stages, but in the records of the rats no such differentiation of stages can be made. The rat's learning of the orientation habit is much more involved, and of a distinctively higher type.

To indicate the extent of the difference, we may consider how the choice-points are learned. The pattern shown in this slide, as we see, has six different choice-points. In the first place each ant must learn for herself to discriminate the true-path and blind-alley turns at each of these junctions. Even when we leave the alley linings already scented by subject No. 1 in place in the alleys when No. 2 first enters, after No. 1 has mastered the maze, No. 2 is not helped much. The chemical on the pathways helps her to make a generalized adjustment to the maze, entering the alleys with less excitement than otherwise, but does not give her the discriminations at choice points. These she must learn for herself. She cannot get the habit by following a scent trail, as might an army ant. The choice-point discriminations are learned individually, but in a cruder and more stereotyped way than by a rat.

Another comment on the nature of discriminations at choice points. Dr. Hasler indicated that discriminations were made by the salmon at stream branches, on a chemical basis. This is a simpler type of generalized discrimination, I believe, and more comparable to that of the army ant turning toward the trail branch which bears the greater concentration of booty odor. It is a generalized discrimination, good for any bifurcation of route in a series never before encountered, and not at all specific to other characteristics of any locality. The discrimination habits of the *Formica* ant appear to be of a somewhat higher order, specific to each locality in the orientation situation and distinctively learned for each locality. The rat's choice-point discriminations are also distinctive to the localities, but have other properties which place them in a higher category than those of the *Formica* ant.

For one thing, in the ant's learning of the maze there is no evidence for a special anticipation of the last turn—the final choice-point—as in the rat. If we put a unique turn in the middle of the maze (e.g., the one right-going true path turning in a series of left turns) the rat makes errors at preceding choice-points which show that he is anticipating this unique turn. Not so with the ant.

The difference can be shown in another way, by a test reversal of the maze after it has been learned. When the ant has learned a given pattern, the maze is now turned around so that the subject enters from the previous exit end. She now is entering the learned situation once more, but seems quite unable to profit by her experience, and needs a considerable number of runs to learn it. In actuality, it is practically a new problem for her. The only advantage is a generalized odor habituation to the situation which adjusts her to run the alleys with less excitement—otherwise it is a different situation. But for the rat, matters are otherwise. He starts with some hesitation at the previous exit point, but as a rule can then scamper through with little difficulty. Now both *Formica* ant and rat had occasion to reverse their directions many times during the initial learning series. But after learning, only the rat can profit by this experience in the reversal test. With only a little readjustment, he can use his choice-point discriminations in the reverse direction. In this respect, the ant is oriented as though in a new situation. Choice-point discriminations with such limitations are a lower order of orientation habit.

I mentioned the fact that the rat usually learns this particular pattern in about 12 trials. Once, in an experimental psychology class, I had a (human) subject, a girl who was a C student and probably in the vicinity of 105 I.Q., who couldn't learn a stylus version of this pattern in 60 trials. There were indications from the verbal reports that her trouble was not actual stupidity, but rather holding fast to a very incorrect idea about how the problem could be solved. There was no indication that any of the rats had such ideational handicaps in learning the maze.

Now for the ant, rat, and this human subject, there are marked differences in the organization of this orientation problem. The ant is on a very reduced, stereotyped level. Her learning is complex, to be sure, but it is qualitatively inferior to that of the rat. The nature of the local discriminations, and the organization of the whole problem, must be considered inferior in her case. These matters are critical when we are trying to evaluate the status of spatial adjustments in the orientation of different animal types. . . .

The chemical traces do help the *Formica* ant to get through a maze, but not as critical cues except at choice-points. They are more in the nature of stimuli supporting a generalized habituation. The army ant orients by following a chemical track, but the *Formica* ant is considerably beyond that.

DR. HASLER: What happens if a new lining is introduced after the maze has been learned?

DR. SCHNEIRLA: The ant is disturbed, but relearns in less trials than would be needed at any earlier point in the learning series. Specific cues for directional turning are needed only at choice-points. Even here, the ant is far from lost if odor is changed or removed, since she has other learned cues, and visual cues particularly.

In the next slide there is shown a situation which was studied by Marker and Dolgin in our laboratory, and which was solved by rats in one of two very different ways depending on the experimental method. In this Trueblood elevated maze, rats of group I were started at A and fed on reaching A_1, rats of group II were started at A and fed at B_1, in their first series of runs. At the second choice-point, X, the group I rats had a difficult turn to make, opposed by the mechanics of movement in running around the preceding turns (or, as we put it, by "centrifugal swing"); rats of group II had an easy turn at this point, favored by centrifugal swing. There were reliable indications that the rats of these two groups learned very differently. To take group II first, they had an easier time and needed fewer runs than did group I. After the first few runs they went rapidly past both choice points, with only exceptional hesitancy at X. The rats of group II needed more runs than I; they ran more slowly on the whole, and hesitated frequently at X.

We interpret the outcome as a lower-level habit in the case of group I, which evidently paid more attention to cues at the choice-point since the rats exhibited what Muenzinger calls "vicarious-trial-and-error responses" there. They depended closely upon choice-point cues in making the run, but there was no indication that the end-point at the food-box was anticipated; rather, it seemed to be reached by stages. These rats seemed to learn in a more stereotyped fashion than those of group II, which evidently acquired the run as a unitary operation, with the food-box anticipated from the start. These rats were matched litter mates, equivalent in learning capacity. But under the conditions, the rats of group II evidently used their best capacities for modifiable behavior and acquired a higher-level orientation habit, whereas those of group I were not using their capacities at maximum and acquired a lower-level orientation habit. The difference seems to have been determined by the experimental method.

Very frequently, whether a mammal uses its best capacities for organization depends on the way we set up the situation. I believe that this little experiment illustrates the possibility that we can get a higher or a lower type of orientation adjustment from this mammal, through learning, according to the effect of the learning situation.

In the last slide we will consider another contrast in mammalian problem orientation. Tolman has utilized a concept which he terms "means-end-readiness" or "expectancy," and which he lately is applying to what he calls "cognitive maps" (i.e., meaningful spatial relationships in a problem situation). He extends this concept to almost every learned problem adjustment of which the rat is capable. But as we saw in the last example, under some conditions rats may adjust in terms of what Tolman regards as typical, the "cognitive" type of solution (as in group I of the Marker-Dolgin experiment), and under other conditions a simpler type of orientation is learned. Lower-level problem solutions do not involve a spatial organization in which anticipation of remote points is dominant.

The slide illustrates the 3-way problem of Norman Maier, which gets at the superior orientation abilities of the rat. In his basic experiment with this situation, Maier tested two groups of rats, both of which had been given a general habituation to the apparatus, running freely from table to table over the elevated pathway, without being fed anywhere. The rats of group *L* were then started at Table 1 and were fed when they reached Table 3 on several runs in succession; the rats of group *R* had no training beyond the habituation period. Then in a test, the rats of both groups were fed briefly on Table 2, after which they were placed on Table 1 to see where they would go. Rats of the *L* group went to Table 3, following the dictates of their learned habit. But in 80 percent or more of the trials, rats of the *R* group went to Table 3 and found the food.

The interpretation is that the rats of group *L* have a simple orientation habit of a lower-level type which works only in the situation of initial learning; rats of group *R* have a preparation for a generalized behavior in the situation, and Maier concludes that they accomplish the higher-level solution of combining the experience of being fed on Table 2 with getting from Table 1. Maier found that these two types of solution are affected differently by decortication: ability L drops away gradually with increasing size of lesion, as does learning a maze, whereas ability R falls away very sharply after 18 percent of the cerebral cortex is lost.

These two response types seem to represent very different levels of orientation capacity in mammals. The L type centers around a specific learned organization of the sensory cues from room and tables, controlling a definite pattern of movement on the elevated pathways. The R type involves a perceptual familiarity with the room but is not influenced by a specific learned orientation that will dominate the problem response, therefore the R rats are free to demonstrate their best capacities to reorganize their spatial adjustments, and evidence for a simple reasoning capacity appears in this case.

There are many important types of investigation and problem that could be mentioned in this connection. I have hit only some of the high spots. But what I have tried to say can be boiled down to just two things. One is that there are levels of orientation capacity which are not just differences in degree, or quantitative differences in the same capacity, but which are qualitatively distinct. And we must look more closely at various applications of the concept "perception," as it is often used in a generalized way through the animal series, to find how many important differences in qualitative level are overlooked or misconstrued in this procedure.

The second point concerns the ontogeny of these matters. I think we should drive not just for more evidence about ontogeny, to have more descriptions of developmental processes underlying adult orientation patterns, but should pay more attention to the manner in which capacities and abilities appear. The hypothesis that some capacities and behavior patterns appear through endogenous or purely native determination is just one possibility to be tested. It may be correct in some instances, but we have to find when, and how far it applies. I believe that we can get at the truth of these matters only if we pay more attention to the appearance of orientation capacities in individual development. It is the development of behavioral capacities in space and time that we must stress in our investigations, if we are ever to understand these patterns adequately.

OUTLINE

I. Ontogenetic aspect: appearance of individual perceptual adjustments.
  A. Nature and qualitative contributions of native factors.

    1. Specific experimental studies scattered: Examples: Lashley-Russell, Hebb, Riesen.

    2. Descriptive studies: e.g., Langworthy on pouch-young opossums; chimpanzee-human comparison by Jacobsens and Yoshioka.

    3. Evidence desirable on ontogeny of each orientation type; e.g., contrast of environmental and social adjustments of blind-born and birth-visioned mammals.

  B. Some aspects of developmental study.

    1. Evidence scattered, largely unexploited.

      a. Significance of stimulogenous evidence?

      b. Significance of developmental-motor evidence?

    2. Studies needed on ontogeny of space-time adjustments:

      a. "Drive" and "motivational" systems in the individual.

      b. Ontogeny of approach-withdrawal adjustments requires study.

    3. Development and variations of adjustment to social group.

    4. Bases and processes in perceptual development.

II. Experimental studies on properties of orientation in mammals.

  A. Contributions of maze method.

    1. Kinesthesis and proprioceptive factors.

    2. Contrasts in sensory control according to situation-type.

    3. Factors influencing development of learned adjustment:

      a. Basic organic and mechanics-of-movement factors.

      b. Condition of organism (neural equipment; motivation).

      c. Aspects of situation: complexity; qualitative status.

    4. Studies emphasizing very different qualitative aspects of learned orientative adjustment:

      a. S-R vs. "cognitive" functions.

      b. Different interpretations of Krechevsky's "hypotheses."

      c. Meanings of "general orientation" in maze:

        (1) Bierens de Haan's emphasis on goal orientation.

        (2) Shepard's "floor cue" and short-cut orientation.

  B. Studies on basic sensory properties of orientation.

    1. Analytical study of "naive" sensory effects needed (e.g., "artifact" studies of object "recognition").

    2. Discrimination studies:

      a. Stimulus range, difference-threshold studies.

      b. Significant difference in results according to method of testing.

    3. Problems in stimulus-cue localization.

    4. Sensory integration:

      a. Basic properties (summation; inhibition; transfer).

      b. Modifiability; new patterns.
  C. Organization of spatial-temporal systems.
    1. Evidence from serial-learning studies.
      a. "Order of mastery" in maze learning.
      b. Postulation of "goal" orientation.
        (1) Conditions governing presence or absence of "end-point" anticipation.
        (2) S-R interpretations; Tolman's "cognitive maps."
    2. Evidence on selective processes.
      a. Factors influencing scope and qualitative level:
        (1) Cortical assets; "intelligence."
        (2) Organic condition; motivation.
        (3) "Set"; "attention"; "attitude."
        (4) Nature and scope of experience.
      b. Appraisal of environmental adjustments:
        (1) Early "imagery" studies.
        (2) v. Uexküll's "Umweltforschung."
        (3) Delayed-response studies.
        (4) "Cue," "sign," "signal," "symbol."
        (5) Abstraction-generalization; anticipation.
    3. Higher-process studies:
      a. Insightful orientation: box-stacking tests, etc.
      b. Short-cut orientation solutions.
      c. Impromptu organization of experiences.
III. Varied theoretical approaches.
  A. Instinctivist and preformist theories.
  B. Phenomenistic and mentalistic theories.
  C. Inductive, naturalistic approaches.
  D. Deductivist, operationistic theories.

REFERENCES

Buel, J. 1935. Differential errors in animal mazes. *Psychol. Bull.* 32: 67–99.

Hebb, D. O. 1949. *The organization of behavior.* New York: Wiley.

Hediger, H. 1950. *Wild animals in captivity.* London: Butterworth.

Hediger, H. 1951. *Observations sur la Psychologie animale dans les Parcs nationaux du Congo Belge.*—Explor. Parcs Nat. du Congo Belge.—Fascicule 1. Bruxelles: Hayez.

Kuo, Z. Y. 1930. The genesis of the cat's responses to the rat. *J. Comp. Psychol.* 11: 1–30.

Kuo, Z. Y. 1932. Ontogeny of embryonic behavior in Aves. V. The reflex concept in the light of embryonic behavior in birds. *Psychol. Rev.* 39: 499–515.

Krechevsky, I. 1932. "Hypotheses" in rats. *Psychol. Rev.* 39: 516–532.

Maier, N. R. F. 1932. The effect of cortical destruction on reasoning and learning in rats. *J. Comp. Neurol.* 54: 45–75.

Maier, N. R. F., and T. C. Schneirla. 1935. *Principles of animal psychology.* New York: McGraw-Hill.

Marker, C., and M. Dolgin. 1942. Simple and complex bases for the solution of various tests in the Carmichael elevated-maze situation. *J. Genet. Psychol.* 60: 259–269.

Redfield, R., ed. *Levels of integration in biological and social systems.* Lancaster, Pa.: Cattell Press.

Schneirla, T. C. 1939. A theoretical consideration of the basis for approach-withdrawal adjustments in behavior. *Psychol. Bull.* 37: 501–502.

Schneirla, T. C. 1946. Ant learning as a problem in comparative psychology. In P. Harriman, ed., *20th century psychology.* New York: Philosophical Library. Pp. 266–305.

Schneirla, T. C. 1948. Psychology, comparative. *Encyclopedia Britannica,* vol. 18, pp. 690–760.

Schneirla, T. C. 1952. A consideration of some conceptual trends in comparative psychology. *Psychol. Bull.* 49: 559–597.

Siegel, A. 1953. Deprivation of visual form definition in the ring dove. *J. Comp. Physiol. Psychol.* 46: 115–119.

Tolman, E. C. 1932. *Purposive behavior in animals and men.* New York: Century.

Witkin, H. 1942. Restriction as a factor in adjustment to conflict situations. *J. Comp. Psychol.* 33: 41–74.

Witkin, H., and T. C. Schneirla. 1937. Initial maze behavior. *J. Comp. Psychol.* 23: 275–304.

Yoshioka, J. 1928. A note on right or left going position habit with rats. *J. Comp. Psychol.* 8: 429–433.

ETHEL TOBACH

T. C. SCHNEIRLA

Eliminative Responses in Mice and Rats and the Problem of "Emotionality"

Bibliography No. 100

In 1932, Yoshioka (1932) observed that food-deprived rats placed in an enclosure with food accessible often responded in early trials by defecating and urinating but not by feeding. Introduced successively to the same situation, however, most of the animals began to feed, and eliminative responses in the enclosure ceased. Hall (1934c) viewed this phenomenon not in the context of learning theory, as had Yoshioka, but in relation to individual differences in adjustment. He (1938) gave the following four facts as evidence for characterizing these responses as "emotional":

1. They occur in situations recognized to be emotionally arousing in character.
2. They are linked with other reactions set off by impulses traveling over the autonomic nervous system.
3. They disappear as the originally strange situation becomes familiar.
4. As the number of animals defecating and urinating decreases, the number of animals eating increases.

According to Hall (1938), the proof that such behavior affords a valid measure of individual differences is that the same animal that defecates in the novel situation does not feed, whereas the nondefecating animal does feed.

In later work by Hall and co-workers, and by others, Criteria 3 and 4 were modified or dropped (Anderson, 1939; Bindra and Thompson, 1953; Broadhurst, 1957a, 1957b; Hall and Whiteman, 1951; Lindzey, 1951; Martin and Hall, 1941; Stern, 1957; Willingham, 1956). The second cri-

From *Roots of Behavior,* edited by E. Bliss. New York: Harper and Brothers, 1962. Reprinted with permission.

terion has received relatively little attention. No studies have been reported in which other autonomic activities were measured in correlation with defecation and urination. Rather, in this respect, the research has been indirect, involving either operative procedures aimed at the clarification of the role of the adrenal medulla (Fuller, Chambers, and Fuller, 1956; Moyer, 1958) or pharmacological investigations of drug effects, with the defecatory reaction as the dependent variable (Broadhurst, Sinha, and Singh, 1959; Jones, 1944; Ryall, 1958; Taeschler and Cerletti, 1959).

Although Hall uses the term "emotional," he prefers the word "emotionality," considered "a convenient concept for describing a complex of factors . . . a group of organic, experiential, and expressive reactions . . . a general upset or excited condition of the animal" (1934c). He has also referred to such behavior as "timidity" or "fearfulness," a view which has found some support (Anderson, 1938; Geier, Levin, and Tolman, 1941), but which other investigators (Billingslea, 1940, 1942; Bindra and Thompson, 1953; Hunt and Otis, 1953; Willingham, 1956) have considered related to other aspects of behavioral organization.

Hall's first criterion for the phenomenon is that it must occur in "emotionally arousing situations." There have been two approaches to the problem of defining "emotionally arousing situations" which can elicit the defecatory reaction. In one, the intensity of the stimulus situation presented to the animal in the open-field test has been investigated. Hall (1938) specified that the animal in the open-field test should be stimulated by a high intensity of light. Later investigators (Broadhurst, 1957a; Evans and Hunt, 1942) found that the open-field test becomes a more reliable indicator of emotional defecation when its stimulative intensity is increased.

Another approach to studying the relation between noxious stimulation and the defecatory response has been to stimulate young mice and rats at various stages of development and later to test them in the open-field situation. Hall and Whiteman (1951), working with offspring of crosses between C57 and dba mice, found that animals subjected to a noxious auditory stimulus defecated more than did control pups. Stanley and Monkman (1956), working with dba/1 mice, did not find a comparable effect when animals were shocked during the litter period. Griffiths and Stringer (1952), with rats, used several forms of noxious stimulation during the litter period but found no differences in defecation in adulthood.

Other investigators have used "manipulation" of the animal as an early experience designed to affect the incidence of defecation or number of boluses in the open-field test. The noxious character of this treatment is less readily defined than is that of shock or auditory stimulation, but its general, over-all stimulative effect is apparent. It is not clear from the literature on "manipulation" studies (Bovard, 1958) how this treatment acts as a disturbance to the animal. Although Weininger (1956) showed that rats handled outside their home cages defecate less than nonhandled controls in their home cages, Ader (1959) and Mogenson and Ehrlich (1958) found no differences in defecation between handled and nonhandled rats in the open-field test. Levine (1959) also, who manipulated mice prior to weaning, observed no differences in amount or incidence of defecation in a runway situation designed to study "aggression." In an earlier study with rats, however, he found that handled rats defecated less than nonhandled rats (1956).

The second approach to clarifying the concept "emotion" as related to the defecatory reaction has been to "validate" the "emotionally arousing situations" which elicit the response. Parker (1939) used various forms of noxious stimulation designed to arouse the emotions of "fear" and "escape behavior" and found that the defecation scores of rats in all of these situations intercorrelated significantly and positively. Hall (1934b) presented food behind a wire-mesh barrier in an open-field test and found a significant decrease in defecation, which he took to indicate the effect of "frustration." O'Kelly (1940) also created a "frustration" situation by using a barrier to prevent rats from leaving a brightly lit area as they had been doing and found a significant increase in defecation and urination. The crucial factors may concern differences in the nature or in the degree of frustration, in the techniques used, or in all of these.

Hunt and Otis (1953) have shown that a defecatory reaction can be conditioned in an "anxiety"-producing situation. The only attempt to test the hypothesis that the defecatory reaction is related in some way to "anxiety" was a study on rats by Moyer (1957) in which he found no correlation between defecation and the "anxiety" advanced by Mowrer as a factor in conditioned-escape responses.

"Anxiety" has been defined experimentally for man by the work of Welch and Kubis (1947) on the basis of Pavlov's (1927) finding that more excitable dogs condition more quickly than phlegmatic animals. Their report that human subjects judged "anxious" in a psychiatric examination condition more rapidly than normal subjects was substantiated by Bitterman and Holzman (1952) and by Taylor (1951). Runquist and Ross (1959), using a physiological measure of emotionality in human subjects, also found a correlation between conditioning scores and emotionality. James (1953) pointed to a need for experimental investigation of the relationship between "emotionality" and conditioning and cited several examples of the possibility of such a relationship in dogs.

Levine (1959), although not studying the problem in the context outlined above, did find a correlation between the defecatory reaction and conditioning rate in Sprague-Dawley rats. The relationship was a positive one, so that animals which conditioned quickly in the avoidance situation were low in amount of defecation. If the concept of human anxiety is in any way related to that of emotionality in the defecatory reaction, the correlation should have been a negative one, i.e., animals high in amount of defecation should condition quickly.

Although Hall does not include in his list of criteria his genetic characterization of the defecatory reaction, the idea is implicit and explicit in his work and in that of others, that the behavioral pattern is "something quite fundamental to the animal" (1938), an innate factor related to the functioning of the autonomic nervous system which is more constitutionally than situationally determined. Hall (1938) bred two strains of rats selectively: "emotional" rats which defecated consistently in the test situation and "nonemotional" rats which did not defecate in the test situation. According to Hall (1938), the fact that such a breeding program could be carried out supports his psychogenetic view of the defecatory reaction. Recently, Broadhurst (1959) has stated that the "rat's defecation in the open field is determined by a polygenic system having a low degree of dominance and a moderate heritability . . ." suggesting that defecation indicates a "high degree of susceptibility to environmental effects . . . ."

Although Broadhurst's statement might imply a disagreement with Hall's (1938) position that experience is not an important variable in the defecatory response mechanism, it is clear that he considers defecation in the generalized open-field situation a genetic trait, i.e., an innate characteristic. If the level of defecatory reaction is thus held to be constitutionally characteristic of the individual, two questions are raised: (1) Are there any measures of the level of defecatory response which may differentiate individuals as to this characteristic at all stages of development? and (2) Is this activity really characteristic of an individual animal in all situations?

Although a developmental study using both cross-sectional and longitudinal methods is required to answer these questions (Schneirla, 1956), no studies are found in the literature involving developmental indicators of the defecatory reaction. Schneirla (1956) has pointed out the need for an experimental analysis in which external and internal factors are viewed as interrelated and as differently integrated at all stages of development. Despite Hall's (1951) plea for a strictly genetic approach, the existence of an interaction between phenotypic physiological characteristics and the developmental situation is tacitly accepted in his insistence upon the maintenance of a *constant* environment, and by his own work with Whiteman (Hall and Whiteman, 1951). Clearly, experimental investigations are needed of the effects of different types of experience on the type of individual response under study here.

Two aspects of the phenomenon seem to lend themselves to such experimental study. First, as rodents do not defecate and urinate spontaneously at birth, onset of defecation presents itself as an early indicator of phenotypic variation perhaps responsive to various types of experience during development. Second, the defecatory response seems to be most easily and reliably elicited in a situation not specifically experienced earlier by the animal. Consequently, it would seem that an animal experiencing novel situations frequently in early life might defecate less than otherwise in a novel test situation encountered in later life.

Other aspects of the problem of "emotionality" will be considered, in regard to the defecatory reaction in situations designed to be "emotionally arousing," and in regard to a needed validation of the "anxiety" concept of this behavioral pattern. Thus, by observing the same animals in many different situations, we may also investigate the hypothesis that defecatory reactivity is constitutional on an innate basis.

SUBJECTS

B Albino C mice were used, the colony derived from breeding pairs from the Roscoe B. Jackson laboratory.

METHODS AND PROCEDURE

The methods used in this investigation combine the longitudinal and cross-sectional types of investigation. Subjects representing all groups were studied concurrently, and the experiment involving a particular group was repeated until the prescribed number of subjects was obtained. Where possible, litters were assigned to different groups. The replication of experiments took approximately five months (July 1, 1956 to November 20, 1956).

Table 1 shows the experimental design.

Development of Defecatory Response

To study the development of the defecatory response, litters were assigned to one group which was raised in an environment unvarying as to its principal physical and social aspects. In each litter in this group, some animals (Group UPUS-A; see Table 1) were observed daily in a modified open-area situation from their day of birth until weaning. To control for the effects of the manipulation involved, some animals from each litter (Group UPUS-B) were kept meanwhile in a carrier without being exposed to the bright light of the testing situation. The fact that mice, like many other mammals, do not defecate spontaneously for an appreciable time after birth recommended the inclusion of another group (UPUS-C),

TABLE 1
Experimental design.

	I. Development aspect						II. Environmental aspect						III. Control	
GROUP	UPUS						VPUS		UPVS		VPVS		MC	
LITTER-PERIOD ENVIRONMENT														
"Physical" aspect (cage)	Unvarying (standard laboratory cage)						Varying		Unvarying		Varying		Unvarying	
"Social" aspect (dam and litter)	Unvarying						Unvarying		Varying		Varying		Unvarying	
	Pups of each litter equally assigned to the following subgroups						Pairs of litter mates assigned to the following subgroups						Pups of each litter assigned to each subgroup	
SUBGROUP	A		B		C	D	A	B	A	B	A	B	1	2
	1	2	1	2										
OBSERVATIONS Litter period	Open-area test daily (4 min)		Kept in container during testing of Subgroup A		Open-area test daily (2 hr)	Open-area test on 1 day only (4 min)	Open-area test daily (4 min)	Kept in container	Open-area test daily (4 min)	Kept in container	Open-area test daily (4 min)	Kept in container	Cage cleaned every 5 days; no other treatment	
Postweaning period	Open-area test and approach impedance (4 min)	Avoidance conditioning	Open-area test and approach impedance (4 min)	Avoidance conditioning			All animals in all groups tested after weaning in the standard open-area situation, and subjected to approach impedance						Open-area test and approach impedance (4 min)	Avoidance conditioning
	Avoidance conditioning		Avoidance conditioning										Avoidance conditioning	
NUMBER OF SUBJECTS	10	10	10	10	18	385	10	10	10	10	10	10	12	12

to find whether the four-minute duration of the open-area test was sufficient to elicit the response and also whether the animals would defecate and urinate spontaneously despite the lack of any stimulation by the dam over an extended period. This "extended period" was set at two hours, as pilot experiments revealed that mice could be removed from the litter for a period of two hours daily without seriously affecting their viability or growth rate. To control for the effects of these types of daily manipulation, the remaining litter mates (UPUS-D) were tested in the open-area situation on one day only. Litters were standardized as to size because of possible effects on the defecatory response after weaning (Seitz, 1954). In this way, a litter of seven or eight in this group would be assigned as follows:

Subgroup A: Observed daily in the open-field test—2 pups.
Subgroup B: Kept in container while litter mates A observed—2 pups.
Subgroup C: Kept for two hours daily in an open-field situation—2 pups.
Subgroup D: Tested only once in the open-field situation—1 or 2 pups.

Pups were marked individually on the day of birth by a system of ear clipping.

To supplement the regular UPUS-D pups obtained from the assignment of the experimental litters to the various subgroups, additional pups were taken from regular colony litters. All animals in the UPUS-D group were left with the female at all times, except for the one test.

To further control the effect of a high amount of manipulation during the litter period, another group (the manipulation control—MC—see Table 1) was incorporated into the design. These animals were handled once every five days in the course of cage cleaning only.

Effect of Varying the Aspects of Environment During the Litter Period

To observe the development of the defecatory reponse and the effects of a varying litter environment, four groups were set up as follows.

Group UPUS: *u*nvarying *p*hysical and *u*nvarying *s*ocial aspects of the environment.
Group VPUS: *v*arying *p*hysical and *u*nvarying *s*ocial aspects of the environment.
Group UPVS: *u*nvarying *p*hysical and *v*arying *s*ocial aspects of the environment.
Group VPVS: *v*arying *p*hysical and *v*arying *s*ocial aspects of the environment.

In each of the four groups, litter mates were assigned to Subgroups A and B as described above, with the exception that the first group (UPUS) also contained Subgroups C and D.

All scheduled environmental changes in the social or physical aspects of the environment, or in both of these, were made daily. Pups to be tested were removed from the home cage, and at the end of the test period were placed in the new situation, i.e., one in which either the physical or social aspects, or both of these, had been altered.

Postweaning Tests

At weaning, all animals were placed in individual maintenance cages with food and water. On the day after weaning, all animals in the VPUS, UPVS, and VPVS groups were presented with the open-field test described below. In Groups UPUS and MC, only half of each group was tested (see Table 1).

OPEN-FIELD TEST AND APPROACH IMPEDANCE

Upon return to the maintenance cage after observation in the open-field test on the day after weaning, subjects were deprived of water. Three hours after the observation, they were given water for one hour. This routine was continued so that in this part of the experiment each animal was deprived of water for 20 hours before each observation.

For this test, the animal was placed in the center of the enclosure. Two minutes after its entry, an interval timer rang, and a water bottle was placed at the center of the open-area enclosure. At the end of two minutes, the interval timer rang once more, and the animal was removed. One trial was given daily for 10 days. On Days 11 and 12, the water bottle placed in the enclosure was empty. On Day 11 the animal was not given any water in its home cage, so that at the time of observation on Trial 12 it had been without water for 44 hours. This procedure of presenting a dry water bottle after water deprivation proved significant for testing impedance of a bottle-approach response (Ghent, 1957; Siegel and Stuckey, 1947).

AVOIDANCE CONDITIONING

After the defecatory reaction had been studied in the open-air situation, animals from Groups UPUS-A-1 and B-1, and from MC-1 so studied, together with their litter mates (UPUS-A-2, UPUS-B-2, and MC-2) not experienced in this open-field testing, were conditioned to give an avoid-

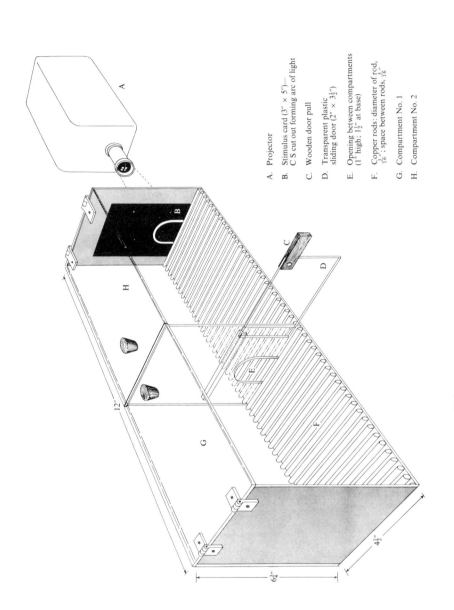

A. Projector
B. Stimulus card (3″ × 5″) —
   C S cut out forming arc of light
C. Wooden door pull
D. Transparent plastic
   sliding door (2″ × 3½″)
E. Opening between compartments
   (1″ high; 1½″ at base)
F. Copper rods: diameter of rod,
   $\frac{3}{16}$″; space between rods, $\frac{1}{16}$″
G. Compartment No. 1
H. Compartment No. 2

FIGURE 125

Avoidance conditioning apparatus (Diagram courtesy of
The American Museum of Natural History, New York).

ance response to a lighted arc with electric shock as the unconditioned stimulus (Figure 125).

For a conditioning trial, the animal was placed in Compartment 1, and the door was opened. If the subject entered Compartment 2 before the CS was given, it was shocked until it re-entered Compartment 1. If an animal entered Compartment 2 after the CS was presented, and before shock, a CR was noted as made. After Compartment 2 was entered, the animal was returned to Compartment 1, and the next trial was begun. The criterion of conditioning was reached when an animal made five successive CR's.

Intervals between "door-opening" actions ranged from 15 to 45 seconds. The first trial (each door opening, CS, and shock equal one trial) started 35 to 120 seconds after the animal was placed in Compartment 1 at the beginning of each day's session. Daily sessions lasted approximately 12 minutes.

APPARATUS

The various types of cages and nesting materials used are described in Table 2.

The open-field enclosure used for tests in the litter period was a solid

TABLE 2
Cages used for various groups and animals.

Standard laboratory cage: solid metal cage, wire-mesh cover; gravity-type water bottle; measurements: 7¼ × 9¾ × 8 inches. Groups UPUS and UPVS. Sawdust.

Glass tank: standard two-gallon aquarium, wire-mesh cover; gravity-type water bottle; measurements: 10 × 8½ × 6¾ inches. Groups VPVS and VPUS.

Glass dish: a round glass dish with convex sides; wire-mesh cover; gravity-type water bottle; measurements: 9¼ inches in diameter and 5 inches high. Groups VPVS and VPUS.

Round cage: an all-mesh metal cage with a solid metal cover; a water bottle is inserted through the mesh sides; measurements: 9 inches in diameter and 7¼ inches high. Groups VPVS and VPUS.

Large cage: a solid metal cage with wire-mesh cover; gravity-type water bottle; measurements: 16 × 11¾ × 5¼ inches. Groups VPVS and VPUS.

Individual laboratory cage: a solid metal cage with wire-mesh cover; gravity-type water bottle; measurements: 10 × 6 × 8 inches. (Post-weaning maintenance.) Sawdust.

Nesting materials: sawdust; fine gravel; nonsterile absorbent cotton; packing material (an absorbent paper cloth); strips of ½-inch white crepe paper. Groups VPVS and VPUS.

Food: loose on floor in all cages.

metal cage 10 × 6 × 5 inches high, painted a flat gray. A 100-watt bulb was suspended over the center of this cage. The open-area enclosure used for postweaning tests had a circular wall of metal 24 inches high and 30 inches in diameter standing on a metal floor 30 inches in diameter. The metal was painted a flat gray. A 300-watt bulb hung over the center of the enclosure.

The conditioning apparatus consisted of two adjoining chambers, connected by a door and floored with parallel copper rods for electrical conduction (Figure 125). The entire apparatus was enclosed and lighted from within, creating a one-way screen for viewing the animal. An Applegate constant current stimulator was used to deliver 130 microamperes of current to the floor of the apparatus at all resistances of the circuit.

GENERAL LABORATORY CONDITIONS AND TESTING PROCEDURES

The colony was maintained on a reversed lighting schedule so that the animals could be observed during their active period. Observations took place in rooms other than the colony room. With the exception of the postweaning period during the open-field testing, food and water were always present. After weaning, animals were maintained in individual cages. Weaning took place at 21 days of age.

All equipment and the enclosures and apparatus were swabbed with 95 percent alcohol between observations.

BEHAVIORAL DATA RECORDED

In the open-area observations prior to weaning, written records were made of the animal's activity, with times noted as far as possible. The occurrence of eliminative responses was recorded both during the tests and when the animal was in the carrying case before and after the tests.

For postweaning tests in the open-area situation, an Esterline-Angus reaction recorder with the Aronson (Clark and Aronson, 1951) keyboard was used to record ambulatory activity, circling, and the following important responses: washing and grooming, number of fecal boluses and occurrence of micturition, time to reach wall, all crossings of open area, all movements to center from wall or to wall from center, approaches to the water bottle, duration of drinking acts, standing up to or climbing leg of apparatus, nosing and drinking drops of water on the floor, standing up at wall, and jumping. In addition, the number of boluses and occurrence of micturition in the container before and after observations were recorded.

In all conditioning trials, data were taken on a check sheet as to jumping, number of fecal boluses, micturition, washing, grooming, complete or partial entries into Compartment 2, rigidity or freezing, and conditioned responses with times noted as far as possible.

RESULTS

No sex differences were found on any of the measures analyzed, except that in the incidence of micturition during the open-field tests after weaning, as discussed below. No significant correlations were found between defecation and micturition at any stage of the experiment. Comparisons of the behavior of animals raised under the "split-litter" conditions as well as of the litter mates assigned to different groups showed that differences among the various groups were due to treatment rather than to litter differences. Table 3 shows the results obtained in all the subdivisions of the experiment.

DEVELOPMENTAL DATA

Onset of Spontaneous Defecation and Micturition

Mice, like most mammals, for an appreciable period after birth require urogenital stimulation for elimination to occur. In this study, significant differences were found among the groups with regard to the first appearance of defecation and micturition.

Using as the "score" the day on which defecation was first seen, with techniques for analysis of matched samples, no differences were found between animals tested in the open-area situation and their litter mates kept in the carrying case (Groups VPUS and VPVS). In Groups UPUS and UPVS, the animals observed in the open-field test started defecating spontaneously at an earlier age than their litter mates kept in containers. It was also found that UPUS-A mice showed spontaneous defecation later than UPVS-A animals, and that UPVS-B animals started defecating later than UPVS-B mice.

Eliminative Responses Throughout the Litter Period

The four groups studied in litter situations of varying stability may be compared not only with one another but in particular with two control

TABLE 3
Analyses of the defecatory responses in different situations.

| | DIFFERENCES AMONG GROUPS WITH DIFFERENT EXPERIENCE | | | |
Measures	Open-field tested pups (Subgroup A) vs. container-held pups (Subgroup B) (during the litter period)	Comparisons among all groups	Between-group comparisons	Within-group comparisons
		Litter period		
Age at which defecation first seen in open-field test	UPUS-A < UPUS-B UPVS-A < UPVS-B	Significant	UPVS-A < UPUS-A UPVS-B < UPUS-B	
Number of pups giving response on each day of litter period	Not significant		Day 11: UPUS-D > UPVS Day 12: UPUS-D > UPUS-A & B Day 13: UPUS-A & B <UPVS UPUS-C, UPVS, VPUS > UPUS-D Day 14: UPUS-A & B, UPUS-C, UPVS, VPVS > UPUS-D Day 18: UPUS-A & B > UPUS-D	UPUS-D: Day 10 > Day 9 Day 12 > Day 13 Day 12 > Day 14
		Post-weaning period (mean defecation rate)		
A. Open-field test				
Trial 1, Part 1	Not significant	Significant	UPUS = UPVS < VPUS < VPVS	
Trial 1, Part 2	Not significant	Significant	VPVS > VPUS	
Trials 2–11, Part 1	Not significant	Not significant		
Trials 2–10, Part 2	UPVS-A < UPVS-B	Significant		
B. Approach-impedance trials				
Trial 11, Part 2	Not significant	Not significant		
Trial 12, Part 1	Not significant	Not significant		
Trial 12, Part 2	Not significant	Significant	VPVS = UPVS < MC-1; VPUS = UPUS > MC-1	
Trial 11, Part 2: increase over median Trials 2–10, Part 2			UPUS = VPUS = UPVS > MC-1	

C. Avoidance conditioning

"Door-only" trials	Not significant	Not significant
"Door-only and CS trials	Not significant	Not significant
Conditioning trials	Not significant	Not significant

Measures	Mean defecation rate Trials 2–10, Part 2	Approach-impedance reaction score	Conditioning rate
Onset of defecation		VPUS-A − .776[a]	
Approach-impedance reaction score	UPUS-B-1 − .717[a] UPUS-A-1 + .731[a]		
Conditioning rate			
Defecatory reaction on first trial of "door-open" and CS			MC-1 + .809[b]
Mean defecation rate on conditioning trials			MC-1 − .685[b]

No other correlations were found to be statistically significant

[a] N = 10; RHO = .564; $p = .05$; RHO = .746; $p = .01$.
[b] N = 12; RHO = .506; $p = .05$; RHO = .712; $p = .01$.

groups—the two-hour group (UPUS-C) and the cross-sectional group (UPUS-D). It is not clear from the present experiment whether the two-hour separation from the female should be characterized as disturbing or as analogous to what might happen in the nest situation. Although in this experiment no observations were made in the nest situation, observations of litters in the colony room seemed to indicate protracted periods during which the female neither licked nor nursed the pups, and when spontaneous defecation and urination may have taken place in the home cage. These intervals, when female and pups were separated in the home cage, were very short at the beginning of the litter period but lengthened gradually, the longer intervals probably coming at about the tenth day (cf. Williams and Scott, 1953). In any event, the data of the two-hour group make an interesting standard against which to compare the other groups.

In the case of the cross-sectional group, the comparison is more tenable. These animals were taken from regular colony litters and tested only once as a control on the effects of continuous testing of the same animal. Some of the animals came from litters which were handled daily (UPUS-D group), and an analysis disclosed no difference between these animals and those from colony litters.

In the following analyses, animals in the group tested in the open area were first compared with those kept in the container, but no differences were found among them as to the number of animals defecating on any one day. Accordingly, the animals were combined into six groups: the UPUS, VPUS, UPVS, VPVS, UPUS-D, and the UPUS-C groups.

Starting on Day 10, significant differences begin to appear among the groups in the number of animals defecating. Generally these differences among the groups are a reflection of the characteristics of Groups UPUS-C and UPUS-D. Group UPUS-C reached a maximum earlier than any of the other groups and maintained it throughout the litter period. Group UPUS-D showed a significant increase on Day 10 and continued significantly higher than other groups until Days 13 and 14. On these days, not only was this group significantly lower than the other groups, but the decreases from Day 12 to Day 13 and to Day 14 were statistically reliable. (A two-by-two chi-square analysis—Siegel, 1956—was significant at less than the 5 percent level of probability.) From Day 15 until weaning there were no more significantly different relationships among the groups, except on Day 18 when UPUS-D had a lower frequency of animals defecating than UPUS-A and UPUS-B.

Throughout the litter period no differences were found among the four groups with varying degress of environmental stability, except on Day 13 when UPUS-A-1, UPUS-A-2, UPUS-B-1, and UPUS-B-2 had less animals defecating than Group UPVS.

Time of Eye Opening

The eyelids of the mouse normally fuse in utero approximately five days before birth and then reopen about Day 14 (Bennett and Gresham, 1956; Takebe, 1939), with some variation as we have found. In this study, "day of eye opening" was marked as that day when both eyes were open. Although there were no differences between the subgroups (A and B) of each group, or among the four main groups (UPUS, VPUS, UPVS and VPVS), all of these groups opened their eyes earlier than the animals in UPUS-C.

Two-by-two χ^2 analyses of defecation and eye-opening frequencies on Days 13 and 14 revealed no relationship between the two phenomena. That is, an animal that had opened its eyes on a given day would not be more likely to defecate than an animal that had not yet opened its eyes.

POSTWEANING OBSERVATIONS IN THE OPEN-FIELD SITUATION

Defecatory Reaction

Each trial was divided into four intervals: Pretesting (animal in the case to the observation situation); Part 1 (animal in the enclosure without the water-bottle apparatus); Part 2 (in the enclosure after the water-bottle stand was introduced); and Postobservation (animal in the case to the home cage). Counts were made of the number of fecal boluses in the case before and after the observation and in the enclosure in each part of the observation, and each occurrence of micturition was noted. As each of these parts of the trial varied in duration, a defecation rate was calculated by dividing the number of boluses by the duration in seconds of each part of the trial.

The first trial in the open-field situation was run before any deprivation was introduced, and the data from this trial are treated apart from both the trials in which the animals were deprived and from the behavioral-impedance trials (i.e., the second part of Trial 11 and Parts 1 and 2 of Trial 12).

The incidence of defecation in the carrying case before and after the trials was random, although defecation was more frequent before trials than after. On Trial 1, however, enough animals defecated before the observation to warrant an analysis. No reliable differences were found among the groups or their subgroups. As defecation was too sporadic before the observations in the subsequent trials, these data were not

TABLE 4
Mean rate of defecation—trial 1, part 1 (Mann-Whitney "U" Tests)

Groups	Mean rates	Comment
UPUS-A-1 and UPUS-B-1	20.45	Differs from all groups except UPVS
UPVS	23.20	Differs from all groups except UPUS
VPUS	26.65	Differs from all groups
VPVS	30.55	Differs from all groups
MC-1	12.90	Differs from no other group

analyzed. The one reference to the rate of defecation before observations (Yeakel and Rhoades, 1941) reports no relationship between preobservation defecation and defecation during the observation.

Defecation after the trials was not frequent enough to admit an analysis of data for Trial 1 or for subsequent trials.

Using the Friedman two-way analysis of variance technique it was found possible to arrive at average defecation rates for each animal for the first part of Trials 2 through 11 and the second part of Trials 2 through 10, as there were no significant differences among the days or the groups.

The data for the first trial reveal significant differences among the groups for Part 1 and for Part 2 of the test. For Part 1 of Trial 1, no differences were found between animals observed in the open field prior to weaning and their controls kept in the cotainers. They were, therefore, combined and treated as one group. The differences among all the groups were significant (Kruskal-Wallis analysis of variance, $p = .02 - .01$).

A similar analysis conducted for Part 2 of Trial 1 showed no differences between the groups tested in the open-field situation during the litter period and their controls; hence these were combined. There was an over-all difference due mainly to differences between VPUS and UPVS animals. The VPUS group was lower than the UPVS group.

Micturition

Micturition took place so rarely as to exclude analysis. There was a slight (not statistically significant) tendency for females to urinate more frequently than males. In each group between seven and nine animals urinated on a mean of 1, 2, or 3 trials. When urination did take place there was also a slight but not significant tendency for it to occur in Part 2 rather than Part 1.

APPROACH-IMPEDANCE REACTION

Defecatory Reaction

In Part 2 of Trial 11, the animals were presented with an empty water bottle. Using the median defecation rate on Days 2 through 10 for all groups, each animal in a group was rated for Part 2 of Day 11, as above or below the median. Below are listed the number of animals in each group above or below the median:

	UPUS	VPUS	UPVS	VPVS	MC-1
Above median	10	13	10	7	3
Below median	6	7	8	12	9

The discrepancy in total number of animals in each group is due to cases with rates equivalent to the median in Part 2 of Day 11.

From these results, it was found that Groups UPUS and VPUS differed significantly from Group MC-1 ($p = .05 - .02$). Group UPVS when compared with Group MC-1 showed a higher frequency above the median ($p = .10 - .05$). In general, it would appear that Groups UPUS, VPUS, and UPVS were fairly similar in that there was an increase in defecation when the empty water bottle was presented, but Groups VPVS and MC-1 were more alike in showing a decrease in defecation.

The animals were then deprived of water for a period of 44 hours before Trial 12. In Part 2 of Trial 12 they were again presented with an empty water bottle. Again, no statistically significant difference was found among the groups in defecation rates on Part 1 of Trial 12. The difference among the groups on Part 2 of Trial 12 was statistically significant, however (Kruskal-Wallis test; $p < .01$).

The main source of the group differences centered on Group MC-1 which differed from all other groups. No other comparisons between pairs of groups were significant.

When the defecation rates in each group were analyzed in two-by-two comparisons, as to the number of animals showing a decrease from Trial 11 in defecation rate, Groups VPUS, VPVS, and MC-1 did not show a significant decrease in defecation rate in Part 2 of Trial 12, whereas Groups UPUS and UPVS did. The factor of lack of fecal material may be discounted (Broadhurst, 1957a; Hall, 1936).

A further analysis of the behavior of the animals in Trial 12 revealed a significant relationship between defecation and attempts at drinking from the empty water bottle. A Mann-Whitney "U" test was performed between

TABLE 5

Defecatory reaction in part 2 of trial 12
(Second approach—impedance situation)

Groups	Mean defecation response
UPVS	5.7
VPVS	7.4
MC-1	9.8 (differs from all groups)
UPUS	11.1
VPUS	12.3

the defecation rates of the following two groups (whatever their pre-weaning experience): (1) all animals that were consistent drinkers and also attempted to drink on Trials 11 and 12 were compared with (2) all animals that were consistent nondrinkers and did not attempt to drink in Trials 11 and 12. "Consistency" was determined by applying the one-sample runs test to each animal. The latter group (i.e., the nondrinkers) had a significantly higher defecation rate than the drinking animals. Furthermore, there was no statistically significant difference between random drinkers that attempted to drink on Trials 11 and 12 and random drinkers that did not.

Locomotion

Although there were no group differences in the absolute duration of locomotion in Trials 11 and 12, a statistically significant number of animals in each group increased in locomotor activity in Part 2 of Trial 11 above the mean locomotion level for Trials 2 through 10. A chi-square comparison of consistent drinkers, consistent nondrinkers and random drinkers revealed that a significant number of nondrinkers decreased in locomotor activity in Part 2 of Trial 12, whereas drinkers and random drinkers increased in locomotion in the second approach-impedance test.

In the open-area test some animals exhibited a pattern involving locomotion between the wall and the center of the enclosure, with or without reaching the center or wall. In some instances this was done shortly before the water-bottle apparatus was introduced. This activity was exhibited primarily, however, by animals that showed random drinking and random "wall going." In Part 2 of Trial 12 there was a change in the animals exhibiting this pattern.

Correlation Between Defecatory Reaction
and Reaction to Approach-Impedance

Seven behavioral indices were used to qualify an animal's reaction to the empty water bottle: a change in wall-going or in center-staying behavior, wall-to-center locomotion with or without reaching wall or center, biting the tube, climbing tube more than momentarily, standing up at wall (if not done in earlier trials), urinating in Part 1 of Trial 12 and in Part 2 of Trials 11 and 12 (if not in earlier trials) and failure to drink in Trial 12 (if animal was a consistent drinker and an attempt to drink had been made in Trial 11).

Animals in each group were ranked by these indices, and the rankings were correlated with several defecatory indices: onset of defecation prior to weaning, defecation rate in Part 1 of Trial 1, mean defecation rate in Part 1 of Trials 2 through 11, in Part 2 of Trials 2 through 10, and in Part 2 of Trial 12. Two significant rank-order (RHO) correlations were found: in Group VPUS-A animals, a negative correlation was found between onset of defecation and severity of reaction in the approach-impedance trials, i.e., animals defecating early tended to react more severely to approach-impedance. Group UPUS-B-1 showed a negative correlation between severity of reaction and defecation rate in Part 2 of Tests 2 through 10, i.e., animals which reacted severely in the approach-impedance trials tended to be low in defecation rate during the postweaning open-field testing under water deprivation conditions. (See Table 3.)

AVOIDANCE CONDITIONING

No statistically significant differences were found among any of the groups in conditioning rate, in defecatory reaction, or in other behavioral measures observed.

CORRELATIONAL ANALYSIS

None of the correlations among the defecatory reactions in any of the various test situations reached statistical significance. Significant correlations were found, however, between the conditioning rate and defecatory reaction. For Group UPUS-A-1 animals a positive correlation was found between conditioning rate and mean defecation rate in Part 2 of Trials 2 through 10. For Group MC-1 the correlation was positive between conditioning rate and defecation rate on the first day of presentation of "door-open" plus CS, and it was negative between conditioning rate and defecation rate in conditioning trials.

DISCUSSION

The Defecatory Response as a Fundamental Characteristic of the Organism

This research has been directed particularly at the properties of the defecatory reaction in rodents, widely accepted as a measure of "emotionality." We have noted especially the view of Hall, according to which this reaction is considered a constitutionally fixed process, a basic trait running through behavior, differentiating individuals in disturbing situations at different stages of development.

We do not exclude hypothetical characteristics of maturation and experience that may be sufficiently pervasive to render certain reactions of an animal more constant than seems possible for defecatory reactions as studied under our conditions. By adopting the view that the defecatory reaction is highly dominated by the animal's perception of conditions in the prevalent situation, and that this reaction may therefore vary considerably under different conditions of stress, apparent inconsistencies in our results are resolved. Thus, individuals may have different thresholds for the defecatory response in different situations or may be more comparable in terms of patterns of defecatory reactivity than in terms of the simple occurrence or nonoccurrence of defecation.

It is evident from our experimental design that introducing the mice to new situations at different ages may have confounded the developmental changes of the defecatory response with responses to a specific treatment. In further investigations, a control for this factor should be included. Nonetheless, because both developmental and cross-sectional techniques were used in this study, certain comparisons are admissible, and conclusions may be drawn from them. The differences between groups at different stages of development, the lack of significant correlations within individuals during the same period of the experiment, and the longitudinal comparisons within particular stages of development are all reliable. At first sight, the finding of certain relationships at some stages but not at others may seem contradictory. It is our belief, however, that this type of finding throws light not only on certain contradictory results in the literature but also on the complexities of open-system phenomena such as behavioral development that do not seem consistent with hypotheses of constitutionally determined constancy.

Experiential Factors in the Defecatory Response

One outcome of the view that the defecatory reaction is a basic and pervasive individual characteristic has been to limit investigations of the role of experience in the development of individual patterns and levels of this reaction. From our results, it is clear that when the physical aspects of environment vary, defecatory reactions under disturbing test conditions increase and that when both physical aspects and social aspects vary the level of defecatory reactions is higher.

The possibility must be considered that varying the physical aspects of environment has effects upon mice equivalent to those of lowering response thresholds to noxious stimulation, rather than increasing the effects of adaptivity to disturbances. This interpretation involves the unproved assumption that the defecatory response necessarily indicates disturbance and must be adaptive. Now it is known that mice to an appreciable extent organize their home-cage areas into feeding zones distinguishable from defecation zones (Warne, 1947; Williams and Scott, 1953). In females subjected to our conditions, when this propensity for living-area organization operated against the necessity (as in the physical-change group) to rebuild nests and reorganize living areas daily, the general level of disturbance may have been raised very considerably. The possibility of ramifying disturbance effects in female and young is suggested by the finding of Carrière and Isler (1959) that frequent housing changes in a group of C3H mice resulted in a lowered thyroid function, although without detectable changes in adrenal weight.

Although Anderson and Anderson (1938) found no differences between "emotional" and "nonemotional" subjects, Yeakel and Rhoades (1941) reported heavier thyroid glands in the Hall strain of "emotional" rats than in the "nonemotional" strain. On the good possibility that frequently enforced housing changes reduce thyroid function appreciably, and that in mice and rats a comparable relationship exists between thyroid weight (and possibly function) and defecatory response, it follows that our mice raised under constant environmental conditions would be expected to show a higher defecatory rate in the tests than those raised under conditions of physical instability. Under our conditions, this did not prove to be the case.

Furthermore, the lack of evidence for the prediction that a preweaning environment in which the physical aspects were frequently varied would result in a lowered defecatory response supports the suggestion of Anderson (1937–1938) and Lebo (1953) that the defecatory response can become habituated to specific situations without there being any generalized habituation to "strangeness" as such. This means, in effect, that rather than habituating mice to "novelty" our preweaning manipulation had so exposed them to disturbances differing in kind and in degree that the effects of such disturbances later waned after their initial appearance in a given test situation.

The Definition of "Emotional" Defecation

It might be objected that, in the present study with mice, the techniques used and the results obtained may indicate that we are not dealing with "emotional" defecation as defined by Hall, and that evidence of individually consistent defecatory patterns otherwise admissible was somehow excluded. Hall (1938) stated that "emotional" defecation refers only to that defecatory reaction which ceases under conditions of familiarity with the situation first stimulating the response. Under conditions such as those in our open-field tests, mice, in contrast to rats, do not cease their defecatory response. This reaction may, therefore, prove useful as an index of generic- and species-specific adjustments to disturbing conditions, as with Farris and Yeakel's (1945) finding that strains of rats can be distinguished by differences in the continuance of their defecatory responses.

Characteristics of Situations Eliciting the Defecatory Response

A stricture offered (Hall, 1938) for situations that elicit the defecatory reaction concerns their "emotion"-arousing characteristics. Three of the techniques used in our experiment that could be so interpreted are: the open-field tests during the litter period, the approach-impedance test, and the avoidance conditioning test. Although our investigation did not test the concept of "emotion" in animals, and although we are not undertaking a theoretical critique of this concept, our evidence indicates that in studying the defecatory response we are dealing with the upper and disruptive part of a continuum of excitatory stimulative intensities. Accordingly, we find significant differences among the mice in regard to some aspects of the defecatory response in two of the situations—that is, the open-field testing during the litter period and the approach-impedance situation—but do not find a statistically significant difference in the defecatory response with the introduction of electric shock.

In the results from open-field tests given in the litter period, there were no signs of individual differences in measures such as, first, incidence of defecation prior to weaning, or second, the number of days of recorded defecation up to the time of eye opening. In three different group comparisons, however, reliable differences in onset-of-defecation were found under conditions indicating that the differences were related mainly to the prevalent intensity of stimulation. Thus, the UPUS and UPVS animals presented with the open-field tests began their spontaneous defecation earlier than did litter mates held in containers during the test periods, and the UPUS animals (raised under unvarying physical and social environmental conditions) were later in their onset-of-defecation than the UPVS animals (raised under unvarying physical but varying social conditions). If onset-of-defecation is more related to the processes underlying defecatory reactivity in stressful situations than to specific aspects of growth (e.g., motor properties), it would appear that in mice subjected to disturbance during the litter period there is a hastening of the appearance of the defecatory response in ontogeny.

In analyzing the effects of the approach-impedance test on mice, we find an increase of locomotor activity. This result was observed not only in Part 2 of Trial 12 but also in Part 2 of Trial 11, and it seemed directly related to the drinking or nondrinking proclivities of the animals. Consistent drinkers and random drinkers increased in their locomotion, whereas consistent nondrinkers decreased. Furthermore, the type of locomotion was striking in its character as specifically related to this situation. Under these impedance conditions, increases were common not only in general locomotion but also in partial movements either to the center or to the wall. When this behavior was analyzed in relation to responses of licking or not licking the water bottle, it was found that animals approaching the bottle evidenced more of this vacillatory locomotion than did animals not attempting to drink.

Accordingly, in analyzing the responses of mice to the approach-impedance test, we find that alterations thereby entailed in the open-field test had the effect of inducing behavior of an evidently nondirective and unstabilized character not as frequently observed in the open-field situation itself. Thus, the animals did not keep to one locality or to one type of response, but alternated in these respects in phases of short duration. These activities and their described changes, clearly apparent and readily quantified, may be accepted as reliable indicators of disturbed behavior.

Accompanying these changes in locomotor behavior was a decrease in defecation rate in most animals. If approach-impedance tests such as ours are sufficiently disturbing to initiate a condition of frustration, our results are consistent with those of Hall (1934b) in tests with rats presented with a wire-mesh barrier around food in the open-field situation.

The last of the three situations which might be considered "emotion"-arousing was that of avoidance conditioning. In this test, we introduced electric shock, more clearly noxious than any characteristics of other testing situations used. Despite this fact, no reliable changes were found in defecatory reactivity under these conditions as against those in other tests, either in the frequency of defecation or in the number of boluses. It is of course conceivable that the shock was not sufficiently intense to have produced distinct differences in this respect; this idea, however, is opposed by the fact that in all significant behavioral respects the animals indicated strong reactions of withdrawal in this situation.

"Emotionality" or the Defecatory Response and "Anxiety"

The dominant experimental interest in this area has concerned finding a technique for investigating disturbed behavior in lower animals—and particularly one which might aid the understanding of disturbed behavior in man. In the complex literature, often the existence of a relationship between conditions such as "emotionality" and "anxiety" has been assumed without supporting evidence. Because we have found such questions abstruse, in this investigation we have employed operationally the occurrence of "defecatory reactions" as a more objective term than "emotionality," and have used the term "anxiety" as an expedient only to introduce the more exact concept of a "conditioning rate." One notable precedent for this step is Pavlov's delineation, from his work with dogs, of a relationship between conditioning rate and degree of emotional excitability.

Although, in general, no correlation was found in our study between the defecatory reaction and rate of conditioning, the three significant correlations found involved two of the three groups tested in the open-area situation prior to conditioning, (i.e., MC-1 and UPUS-A-1). Two of these correlations were positive: (1) conditioning rate as against defecatory reactivity in Part 2 of Trials 2 through 10 and (2) defecatory reactivity on the first day that *"door-open" and CS* were presented as against *conditioning rate*. The second correlation means that animals that conditioned quickly tended to rank low in defecatory reactivity on the first day of conditioning. The only value to correlate negatively with conditioning rate was defecatory reactivity during the actual pairing of the conditioned and unconditioned stimuli. If it were permissible to consider defecatory responsiveness in rodents somehow analogous to human "anxiety," the latter result would make possible equating the defecatory reaction with "anxiety."

In view of our findings, however, of such a negative correlation in only one group of six, it is questionable whether behavioral conditions of the type reported for Pavlov's dogs are analogous to those we have found in mice under conditions of high defecatory reactivity. It is also doubtful whether both conditioning-rate measures and defecatory reactivity may be accepted as criteria of "anxiety" as involved in the disturbed reactions of infrahuman animals. Further study of the two phenomena seems warranted, however, in light of their quantifiable characteristics and in respect to the few suggestive correlations we have found.

To a great extent, we think, the vagueness of terms such as "emotionality" and "anxiety" rests upon untested assumptions of an underlying unity in all individual disturbed behavior, frequently assumed to have a common innate basis. In our judgment, our failure to find inclusive and uniform trends in "defecatory reactivity" at different stages of development and in disturbing situations of different character suggests an inherent weakness in these last assumptions of a *constitutional unity* and a *common innate basis* underlying "emotionality." It seems clear, however, that hypotheses of "innateness" and of "constitutional unity" should be tested independently, with adequate controls on developmental and situational factors.

Our results suggest that the term "defecatory reactivity" is not to be used synonymously with concepts such as "emotionality" and "anxiety," but that aspects of disturbed behavior evidently not appraised adequately by the defecatory-reactivity criterion may be studied advantageously through the use of other objective concepts such as "conditioning rate," under experimentally differentiated types of background and test conditions. Objective standards such as those admitted by criteria such as "defecatory reactivity" should be used for disturbed behavior to the extent that they can be supported experimentally. These two concepts, as examples, may prove valuable as mutually complementary instruments to carry out the types of developmental research that are clearly indispensable to understanding the over-all problem of "emotionality" (or "disturbance") in behavior. It is along these lines particularly that the problems of phyletic similarities and differences in adaptation to disturbing conditions may be studied to best advantage.

CONCLUDING STATEMENT

The defecatory reaction, often considered synonymous to "emotionality" or "autonomic reactivity" as studied in rats, from results on investigations of disturbed behavior in mice is viewed as a situationally specific response rather than an individually generalized pattern resting upon a native or constitutional basis. Developmentally controlled studies show that defecatory reactivity is likely to increase or decrease according to the nature of the disturbing situation and according to the given individual's developmental history, rather than to remain always on a level typifying the individual's measurable responses. Defecatory reactivity, which is therefore not found equivalent to any presumably general characteristic such as "emotionality," is affected by the nature of individual developmental experience, differentiated in this investigation in terms of stability or instability of the physical or of the social aspects of the individual's pre-weaning environment.

REFERENCES

Ader, R. 1959. The effects of early experience on subsequent emotionality and resistance to stress. *Psychol. Monographs.* 73(2): 1–31.

Anderson, E. E. 1937–1938. The interrelationships of drives in the male albino rat. II. Intercorrelations between 47 measures of drives and of learning. *Comp. Psychol. Monographs.* 14(6): 1–119.

Anderson, E. E. 1938. The interrelationship of drives in the male albino rat. III. Intercorrelations among measures of emotional, sexual and exploratory behavior. *J. Genet. Psychol.* 53: 335–352.

Anderson, E. E. 1939. The effect of the presence of a second animal upon emotional behavior in the male albino rat. *J. Social Psychol.* 10: 265–268.

Anderson, E. E., and S. F. Anderson. 1938. The relation between the weights of the endocrine glands and measures of sexual, emotional, and exploratory behavior in the male albino rat. *J. Comp. Psychol.* 26: 459–474.

Bennett, J. H., and G. A. Gresham. 1956. A gene for eyelids open at birth in the house mouse. *Nature* 178: 272–273.

Billingslea, F. Y. 1940. The relationship between emotionality, activity, curiosity, persistence and weight in the male rat. *J. Comp. Psychol.* 29: 315–325.

Billingslea, F. Y. 1942. Intercorrelational analysis of certain behavior salients in the rat. *J. Comp. Psychol.* 34: 203–211.

Bindra, D., and W. R. Thompson. 1953. An evaluation of defecation and urination as measures of fearfulness. *J. Comp. Physiol. Psychol.* 46: 43–45.

Bitterman, M. E., and W. H. Holtzman. 1952. Conditioning and extinction of the galvanic skin response as a function of anxiety. *J. Abnorm. Social Psychol.* 47: 615–623.

Bovard, E. W. 1958. The effects of early handling on viability of the albino rat. *Psychol. Rev.* 65: 257–271.

Broadhurst, P. L. 1957a. Determinants of emotionality in the rat. *Brit. J. Psychol.* 48: 1–12.

Broadhurst, P. L. 1957b. Emotionality and the Yerkes-Dodson Law. *J. Exp. Psychol.* 54: 345–352.

Broadhurst, P. L. 1959. Application of biometrical genetics to behaviour in rats. *Nature* 184: 1517–1518.

Broadhurst, P. L., S. N. Sinha, and S. D. Singh. 1959. The effect of stimulant and depressant drugs on a measure of emotional reactivity in the rat. *J. Genet. Psychol.* 95: 217–226.

Carrière, R., and H. Isler. 1959. Effect of frequent housing changes and of muscular exercise on the thyroid gland of mice. *Endocrinology* 64: 414–418.

Clark, E., and L. R. Aronson. 1951. Sexual behavior in the guppy, *Lebistes reticulatus* (Peters). *Zoologica* 36: 49–66.

Evans, J. T., and J. McV. Hunt. 1942. The emotionality of rats. *Am. J. Psychol.* 55: 528–545.

Farris, E. J., and E. H. Yeakel. 1945. Emotional behavior of gray Norway and Wistar albino rats. *J. Comp. Psychol.* 38: 109–118.

Fuller, J. L., R. M. Chambers, and R. P. Fuller. 1956. Effects of cortisone and adrenalectomy on activity and emotional behavior of mice. *Psychosom. Med.* 18: 234–242.

Geier, F. M., M. Levin, and E. C. Tolman. 1941. Individual differences in emotionality, hypothesis formation, vicarious trial and error and visual discrimination learning in rats. *Comp. Psychol. Monographs* 17: 1–87.

Ghent, L. 1957. Some effects of deprivation on eating and drinking behavior. *J. Comp. Physiol. Psychol.* 50: 172–176.

Griffiths, W. J. Jr., and W. F. Stringer. 1952. The effects of intense stimulation experienced during infancy on adult behavior in the rat. *J. Comp. Physiol. Psychol.* 45: 301–306.

Hall, C. S. 1934a. Defecation and urination as measures of individual differences in emotionality in the rat. *Psychol. Bull.* 31: 604.

Hall, C. S. 1934b. Drive and emotionality: factors associated with adjustment in the rat. *J. Comp. Psychol.* 17: 89–108.

Hall, C. S. 1934c. Emotional behavior in the rat. I. Defecation and urination as measures of individual differences in emotionality. *J. Comp. Psychol.* 18: 385–403.

Hall, C. S. 1936. Emotional behavior in the rat. II. The relationship between need and emotionality. *J. Comp. Psychol.* 22: 61–68.

Hall, C. S. 1938. The inheritance of emotionality. *Sigma Xi Quart.* 26: 17–27.

Hall, C. S. 1951. The genetics of behavior. In S. S. Stevens, ed., *Handbook of experimental psychology.* New York: Wiley. Pp. 304–330.

Hall, C. S., and P. H. Whiteman. 1951. The effects of infantile stimulation upon later emotional stability in the mouse. *J. Comp. Physiol. Psychol.* 44: 61–66.

Hunt, F. H., and L. S. Otis. 1953. Conditioned and unconditioned emotional defecation in the rat. *J. Comp. Physiol. Psychol.* 46: 378–382.

James, W. T. 1953. Morphological and constitutional factors in conditioning. *Ann. New York Acad. Sci.* 56: 171–183.

Jones, M. R. 1944. Some observations of effects of phenobarbital on emotional responses and air-induced seizures. *J. Comp. Psychol.* 37: 159–163.

Lebo, D. 1953. A simplified method for measuring emotional defecation in the rat. *Science* 118: 352–353.

Levine, S. 1956. A further study of infantile handling and adult avoidance learning. *J. Personality* 25: 70–80.

Levine, S. 1959. Emotionality and aggressive behavior in the mouse as a function of infantile experience. *J. Genet. Psychol.* 94: 77–83.

Lindzey, G. 1951. Emotionality and audiogenic seizure susceptibility in five inbred strains of mice. *J. Comp. Physiol. Psychol.* 44: 389–394.

Martin, R. F., and C. S. Hall. 1941. Emotional behavior in the rat. V. The incidence of behavior derangements resulting from an air blast stimulation in emotional and non-emotional strains of rats. *J. Comp. Psychol.* 32: 191–204.

Mogenson, G. J., and D. J. Ehrlich. 1958. The effects of early gentling and shock on growth and behaviour in rats. *Canad. J. Psychol.* 12: 165–170.

Moyer, K. E. 1957. Relationship between emotional elimination and the persistence of an anxiety motivated response. *J. Genet. Psychol.* 90: 103–107.

Moyer, K. E. 1958. Effect of adrenalectomy on emotional elimination. *J. Genet. Psychol.* 92: 17–21.

O'Kelly, L. I. 1940. The validity of defecation as a measure of emotionality in the rat. *J. Genet. Psychol.* 23: 75–87.

Parker, M. M. 1939. The interrelationship of six different situations in the measurement of emotionality in the adult albino rat. *Psychol. Bull.* 36: 564–565.

Pavlov, I. P. 1927. *Conditioned reflexes,* trans. and ed. by G. V. Anrep. London: Oxford Univ. Press.

Runquist, W. N., and L. E. Ross. 1959. The relation between physiological measures of emotionality and performance in eyelid conditioning. *J. Exper. Psychol.* 57: 329–332.

Ryall, R. W. 1958. Effect of drugs on emotional behavior in rats. *Nature* 182: 1606–1607.

Schneirla, T. C. 1956. Interrelationships of the "Innate" and the "Acquired" in Instinctive Behavior. In P.-P. Grassé, ed., *L'Instinct dans le comportement des animaux et de l'homme.* Paris: Masson. Pp. 387–452.

Seitz, P. F. D. 1954. The effects of infantile experiences upon adult behavior in animal subjects: I. Effects of litter size during infancy upon adult behavior in the rat. *Am. J. Psychiat.* 110: 916–927.

Siegel, P. S., and H. L. Stuckey. 1947. The diurnal course of water and food intake in the normal mature rat. *J. Comp. Physiol. Psychol.* 40: 365–370.

Siegel, S. 1956. *Non-parametric statistics for the behavioral sciences.* New York: McGraw-Hill.

Stanley, W. C., and J. A. Monkman. 1956. A test for specific and general behavioral-effects of infantile stimulation with shock in the mouse. *J. Abnorm. Social Psychol.* 53: 19–22.

Stern, J. A. 1957. The effect of frontal cortical lesions on activity wheel and open-field behavior. *J. Genet. Psychol.* 90: 203–212.

Taeschler, M., and A. Cerletti. 1959. Differential analysis of the effects of phenothiazine-tranquilizers on emotional and motor behavior in experimental animals. *Nature* 184(1): 823.

Takebe, K. 1939. Experimental hypoplasy and hyperplasy of the centers of vision in the mouse. *J. Fac. Sci.* 5: 165–189.

Taylor, J. A. 1951. The relationship of anxiety to the conditioned eyelid response. *J. Exper. Psychol.* 41: 81–92.

Warne, M. C. 1947. A time analysis of certain aspects of the behavior of small groups of caged mice. *J. Comp. Physiol. Psychol.* 40: 371–387.

Weininger, O. 1956. The effects of early experience on behavior and growth characteristics. *J. Comp. Physiol. Psychol.* 49: 1–9.

Welch, L., and J. Kubis. 1947. The effect of anxiety on the conditioning rate and stability of the PGR. *J. Psychol.* 23: 83–91.

Williams, E., and J. P. Scott. 1953. The development of social behavior patterns in the mouse, in relation to natural periods. *Behaviour* 6: 35–64.

Willingham, W. W. 1956. The organization of emotional behavior in mice. *J. Comp. Physiol. Psychol.* 49: 345–348.

Yeakel, E. H., and R. P. Rhoades. 1941. A comparison of the body and endocrine gland (adrenal, thyroid, and pituitary) weights of emotional and non-emotional rats. *Endocrinology* 28: 337–340.

Yoshioka, J. G. 1932. Learning vs. skill in rats. *J. Genet Psychol.* 41: 406–416.

T. C. SCHNEIRLA

JAY S. ROSENBLATT

ETHEL TOBACH

Maternal Behavior in the Cat

Bibliography No. 104

The apparent maternal efficiency of cats suggests to many that the animals carry out the essential series of acts in a rigid order and on a fixed native basis. The prevailing concepts are derived from observations of domestic cats; much less is known about conditions among pumas, jaguars, lions, leopards, and tigers—the wild cats. Knowledge essential for comparisons is sparse, not only about different species but also about variations within any species (Lindemann, 1955; Rosenblatt and Schneirla, 1962). Even the question of how domestic cats behave maternally when they become wild, as happens often in large cities or out-of-season in resort areas, is largely a matter of conjecture. For these reasons, this article will concern itself mainly with maternal behavior in the domestic cat, *Felis catus,* which the writers of this chapter and others studied intensively in the seven years following 1949 (Rosenblatt, Turkewitz, and Schneirla, 1961; Schneirla and Rosenblatt, 1961; Tobach, Failla, Cohn, and Schneirla, in preparation).

Cats have altricial young, in which the eyes open some days after birth (about one week in the domestic cat) and action advances slowly in strength and coordination. Maternal-young relations consequently have a development quite different from that of the precocial young of other mammals such as ungulates.

Maternal behavior for the cat may be defined as characterized by exaggerated licking of self and of young, and encircling, nursing, retrieving, remaining near, and returning to the young. Maternal functions in cats have been discussed in one or another respect by Cooper (1942, 1944), Günther (1954), and Leyhausen (1956, 1960), often to limited extents by others in scientific articles, and of course still more often in popular publications.

It is well established that the conditions under which maternal behavior

From *Maternal Behavior in Mammals,* edited by H. L. Rheingold. New York: John Wiley and Sons, 1963. Reprinted with permission.

occurs are dependent on neurohormonal processes. Discussions of recent evidence of the neurohormonal basis of reproductive behavior have been offered by Beach (1948, 1958) and by Lehrman (1956, 1961). Physiological processes underlying the initiation and maintenance of lactation have been described in great detail (Hain, 1935; Hall, 1957; Harris, 1955; Leblond, 1937; Meites, 1959; Nicoll, Talwalker, and Meites, 1960; Riddle, 1935; Riddle, Lahr, and Bates, 1935, 1942; Rothchild, 1960a; 1960b). The bases of retrieving, nestbuilding, and other aspects of maternal behavior are not yet as clear. Although most of the research has been done with the rat, rabbit, and dog, it is likely that the primacy of a neurohormonal control of maternal behavior will be found applicable to the cat as well. Bard's (1936) findings indicate that the full pattern of sexual behavior in the female domestic cat may depend strictly upon hormones; Michael (1958) found that in the cat, in contrast to the rat and rabbit, both sexual receptivity and the associated postural responses depend upon ovarian hormones. Racadot (1957a, 1957b) found indications of modified thyroid function in female domestic cats during parturition which reach their peak soon thereafter and persist in nursing individuals to the end of lactation. As far as a relationship exists between this function and that of the neurosecretory axis (alterations in which follow it in time), he believes that the thyroid modifications may be primary.

Certain factors underlying maternal behavior are significant for what follows. First, because maternal behavior in its developed form constitutes a *pattern* (that is, an organized system of activities and processes), it is important always to specify whether all the activities and processes, or just certain ones, occur under given conditions. Second, it is essential to know not only the extent and intensity of the activities and processes, but also their degree of organization under the conditions of study. For example, the fact that pregnant rats, as well as hormone-injected virgin females and males, retrieve young although not lactating does not necessarily supply evidence of what lactation may contribute to the more complete pattern. Nor does the finding that full-term female rats after caesarean deliveries continue to retrieve young and build nests (Labriola, 1953) contribute any evidence of the function of absent factors such as licking membranes and neonates and ingesting placenta in the normal development of the pattern (Schneirla, 1956). Third, as maternal-like behavior is always in flux, undergoing consecutive changes of some type from the time of the first effects in pregnancy to the time of weaning, the appearance and the change of both the elements and the pattern must be viewed always as matters of development. That the whole process of maternal behavior is neurohormonally controlled, rather than only hormonally controlled (Clegg, 1959), emphasizes the value of psychological and behavioral factors as well as situational factors affecting general physiology for understanding both the pattern and its elements (for example, Nicoll et al., 1960).

For the preceding reasons we regard strictly nativistic theories as outworn (Schneirla and Rosenblatt, 1961). To understand maternal behavior, we need the evidence of biochemical and neurophysiological excitation and transmission as well as the facts of experience, learning, and socialization (Schneirla, 1951, 1956). We need to know also the factors of early experience which play an elusive but important role in the development of sexual behavior in the male domestic cat (Rosenblatt and Aronson, 1958). As Lehrman (1956) has pointed out, there is evidence that the hormonal setting of maternal behavior and of its basic processes appears susceptible to exteroceptive stimulation, that anterior pituitary (as well as other) secretions may be conditioned to specific stimuli (for example, those provided by the young), that qualitatively different responses may be conditioned to the same internal excitatory condition at different intensities, that a particular activity may be based upon an organic need and appetite (as in the case of licking for salts, Barelare and Richter, 1938) and that for all these processes the peripheral conditions of the animal (for example, local cutaneous sensitivity; heat exchange) may have important and changing relationships to pertinent intraorganic conditions and the progress of behavior.

In keeping with the mating cycle of cats in northern latitudes, litters tend to occur during two seasons, from mid-March to mid-May and from mid-July to late August (Scott and Lloyd-Jacob, 1955). Many wild species may be similar (Eckstein and Zuckerman, 1956), but the lion and tiger have no fixed breeding seasons. Domestic cats in northern Europe have heat periods twice a year, in spring and early fall; in the northern United States anestrum lasts from September to January; variations in amount of illumination, however, influence these periods (Asdell, 1946). In our laboratory, with light maintained at approximately springtime conditions and certain other conditions observed, litter production tends to be fairly uniform throughout the year. In contrast to the conventional range in term for housecats of 60 to 65 days, under our conditions the range has tended to be 63 to 68 days, and similarly Scott and Lloyd-Jacob (1955) reported a range of 64 to 68 days with an average of 66 days. Records for number of young in the litter under our conditions give a range of 1 to 7 and a mode around 4. The reported range of litter size for the lion is 2 to 6,[1] that for the tiger 1 and 6, and most other

---

[1] Cooper (1942) reported a total of 159 lion cubs born in 64 zoo parturitions (mean = 2.48); Steyn (1951) found that in four different zoos, over periods of ten or more years, the litters of lions contained 1 to 6 young with an average close to 3.

Felidae tend to have fewer than six cubs in a litter (Asdell, 1946).[2]

BEHAVIOR AND CONDITIONS OF PREGNANCY

Advance of pregnancy is marked behaviorally in the domestic cat by decreasing activity and agility, with less frequent climbing or jumping. In the last third of pregnancy, when weight is accelerating, appetite increases and licking of genital and abdominal areas is likely to be augmented. Distention of the mammae with occasional signs of active secretion, together with tumescence at the vulva, rising body weight, and evident maximum size of embryos on palpation, indicate approach to term.

In the last weeks of pregnancy, the cat is described, conventionally, as seeking a dry, dark, wind-protected, and undisturbed situation with cover and preferably with a soft substrate, in which the young are delivered and reared (Cooper, 1944; Leyhausen, 1956); the lioness, similarly, as taking a sequestered place near water and a good hunting ground (Wells, 1934). The fixation of a desirable locality seems to be usual, but the degree of seclusion essential may vary with the female and her background—wild or untamed individuals virtually going into hiding, sociable and home-adjusted housecats more often taking exposed places. Among alternatives, the one with softer substratum, if darker and thermally optimal, is likely to be adopted.

As pregnancy advances, the females of wild species are reported to become more retiring. A nesting place or den, frequented and used for sleeping, is saturated with the odors of urine, food, and body secretions. With the four corners of a large, screened cage available, our pregnant domestic cats nearly always settled on one corner at the back as the resting place in pregnancy, maintaining it as the site of parturition and of litter care. Nervous, maladjusted females tend to be more variable. Place-fixation constitutes an important although incidental contribution to the early habituation and orientative development of the young.

Increased cutaneous sensitivity of thoracic, abdominal, and pelvic areas—apparently general in cats late in pregnancy—may facilitate the characteristic place-fixation of that time as well as the later encircling of neonates. The African lioness in advanced pregnancy pulls out with the incisors hair around the nipples, as do also pseudopregnant and parturient females (Cooper, 1942). Beginning often before parturition, females of

---

[2] Problems of health and maintenance are of paramount importance. A large screen-wire cage equipped with wall shelf, adequate diet supplemented for lactating females with five drops of viosterol and a pinch of edible bone meal daily, careful handling including abdominal support for pregnant animals, and prompt attention to all disorders are features to be emphasized.

various cat species may become irritable, defensive in general, and even actually aggressive.[3] Self licking, normally a frequent item in the domestic cat's repertoire (Leyhausen, 1956), is prominent in behavior from the time of pregnancy, presumably in relation to increased endogenous excitation as well as to the increased sensitivity of ventral zones and to special secretions and fluids. Sensory and other organic conditions fundamental to such behavior changes may be reasonably attributed to the neurohormonal factors of pregnancy.

PRELIMINARIES TO PARTURITION

The imminence of delivery is indicated by the appearance of colostrum in the mammae, vulvar distension, sometimes with a pinkish mucoid discharge, and by scratching of the substratum, alternating with a squatting posture resembling the defecatory crouch of normal females and kittens. "Calling," although uncommon among our laboratory females, is described by Cooper (1944) as a frequent and "distinctly recognizable vocal pattern" in his Siamese housecats at this time.

An abbreviated protocol of typical behavior just preceding parturition in the domestic cat is presented [as Protocol I at the end of this paper].

PARTURITION

A few general descriptions of delivery in various feline species have appeared, notably those of Cooper (1944) and Leyhausen (1956) for the domestic cat, and of Cooper (1942) for the lion. Cooper (1942) noted these activities of a parturient lioness: a considerable amount of vocalizing, squatting and lying supine, kneading of the abdomen and hair pulling from abdomen and tail, rolling and pacing, and frequent licking of the genitalia. Cooper (1944) reported a detailed description of parturition in a multiparous pure-breed Siamese housecat. Although it showed marked behavioral disturbances unless her owners were nearby, in certain respects his findings are comparable with those we obtained for the births of 66 kittens in 17 parturitions.

Our study (Tobach et al., in preparation) used females of heterogeneous stock excluding selected strains. Each female was habituated during pregnancy to a standard 36 inch square and high mesh-wire cage

---

[3] The possibility that events of the late stages of pregnancy may constitute a "stressor" complex inducing neural and hormonal changes leading to general irritability and facilitating later changes such as colostrum and milk letdown is indicated by the finding of Nicoll et al. (1960) that nonspecific stressors can induce lactation in rats primed with extradiol.

and was accustomed to the presence of observers and to a routine of observations. The main course of events and the occurrence of definite activities were recorded either with routine symbols on a timescale or for quantitative data with an Aronson keyboard controlling the chart of an Esterline-Angus recorder. The observer did not intervene during parturition except to mark neonates with tape-collars on delivery, to remove the sac when loss of the neonate seemed imminent, and to palpate the female when parturition seemed near its end. In the 17 parturitions, all the young were viable except for two stillborn kittens of one female and one of another.

An abbreviated protocol of typical behavior in the domestic cat in parturition is presented [as Protocol II at the end of this paper].

The cat is a multiparous animal, that is, giving birth to more than one offspring in a litter. The succession of deliveries of kittens in a litter provides an opportunity for comparing not only the actions of any one female during the different kitten births of a given litter but also the parturitive behavior of different females. The results are presented in a form to facilitate both such comparisons; a kitten birth is distinguished from a parturition, the delivery of a litter.

The data support the following formulations:

1. Female behavior is the outcome of an interplay or competition between the stimulative effects of endogenous events (such as uterine contractions and the passage of the fetus) and of exogenous stimuli resulting from the by-products (that is, fluids, neonate, and placenta) of these organic processes. Although the female displays a fairly predictable repertoire of parturitive behavior, no pattern of behavioral acts is indicated in our evidence.

2. Parturitive behavior is exemplified by variable actions of licking which, in being shifted variably from the female's own body to the newborn or surroundings, indicate the path of the female's attention. Intrinsic or extrinsic stimuli may affect her behavior according to the rate, intensity, and distinctness of their appearance in the scene of parturition.

Organic Events Marking Kitten Birth Intervals

From our evidence, certain organic events in parturition are sufficiently distinct to be used as means of distinguishing successive intervals within any kitten birth. These events are (1) onset of abdominal contractions; (2) appearance of the fetus as it pauses in the vulva; (3) passage of the fetus from the vulva (fetus-delivery); and (4) passage of the placenta from the vulva (placenta-delivery). By these events we have reliably distinguished four successive intervals in a kitten birth as: (1) the contraction interval; (2) the emergence interval; (3) the delivery interval;

978

TABLE 1
Frequency of common sequences of organic events in delivery.

Sequences	Birth order of neonate in litter						Total
	First (K-1)	Second (K-2)	Third (K-3)	Fourth (K-4)	Fifth (K-5)	Sixth (K-6)	
C,FA,FD,PA,PD [a]	1			2	1		4
C,FA,FD,PD	3	4	7	4	3	1	22
C,FD,PD		2	3	4	2		11
C,FD,PA,PD			1				1
Total	4	6	11	10	6	1	38

[a] C, onset of contractions; FA, fetus arrested in vulva during emergence; FD, delivery of fetus; PA, placenta arrested in vulva during emergence; PD, delivery of placenta.

and (4) the placental interval. In this way, characteristics of the kitten births, such as duration and activities of the intervals, may be compared from case to case.

Empirically, the termination of a kitten birth was set as the onset of contractions for the next kitten birth; termination of a parturition, however, could not be set by delivery of the placenta of the last kitten born; hence at times after placental deliveries palpation was necessary to determine whether there were any unborn fetuses.

In 38 of 51 kitten births analyzed, contractions, fetus-delivery, and placenta-delivery occurred consistently and in that order (Table 1). These occurrences were therefore considered standard and as those regularly influencing the behavior of the parturitive cat. Fetus-pausing-in-vulva occurred twenty-six times in these otherwise typical sequences; placenta-pausing, in contrast, occurred only five times.

The data did not indicate a relationship between the durations of kitten births and their order in the sequence. For example, short kitten births did not tend to be early in a parturition and longer ones late, or the reverse. There was a wide range of variation in the durations of the intervals in kitten births (for example, contraction intervals lasting from 12 seconds to 1½ hours and delivery intervals from 32 seconds to over 50 minutes). As might be expected, intervals of long duration, because they contained a greater frequency of specific female activities than those of shorter duration, complicated statistical analyses of the data.

Among 51 kitten births observed, 13 were atypical by our criteria. In 6 of the latter, a fetus and placenta were delivered simultaneously. In two cases there was an overlapping of kitten births; in one the interval began with the delivery of one fetus and ended with contractions referable to the next, in the other it began with the delivery of one placenta and ended with the delivery of that referable to a forthcoming fetus. The other cases were scattered and variable in nature. No evidence was found for significant differences in the duration of typical and atypical kitten births.

Female Behavior During Kitten Birth Intervals

The definition of the kitten birth intervals as bounded by endogenous events aids in relating the female's activities in each phase of a kitten birth to the changes in stimulative conditions. At any one time, endogenous stimuli (such as those arising from uterine contractions and the passage of the fetus) and exogenous stimuli (that is, from by-products such as fluids, membranes, fetus, and placenta) of the organic processes produced a changing stimulus scene to which the female responded differentially. The shifts in the female's behavior in successive intervals (Table 2) reflect the predominance of the one as opposed to the other source of stimulation.

The following descriptions of parturitive behavioral items will aid in tracing the flow of events from interval to interval.

A reliable sign of the actual onset of parturition is the first clear indication of contractions of abdominal musculature, considered the accompaniment of uterine contractions. We have distinguished reliably between displacements of the abdominal wall due to uterine contractions and those from fetal movements alone; the first but not the second is accompanied by leg movements (flexing, also raising) of slight or greater amplitude.

During the contraction and emergence intervals one type of activity, gross body movements, is more in evidence than in the delivery and placental intervals (Table 2). These postural changes were attributed predominantly to excitation from endogenous sources because no specific extrinsic changes were found regularly coincident with them. Thus squatting, straining, and crouching, brought together because they could not be reliably differentiated, often resembled the normal female postures of defecation and micturition and commonly occurred at times when the progress of a fetus in the birth canal might have been acute. Scratching, which appeared in the contraction and emergence intervals but not later, markedly resembled the normal feline action of covering urine or feces. Rolling (Figure 126), rubbing, and lordosis, other gross bodily actions observed during kitten births, occur in female mating behavior. Circling, as we observed it (Figure 127), had all the earmarks of a perceptual adjustment to a disturbance localized in the posterior body; hence Cooper's (1944) term, "nesting," is misleading for this activity as it suggests a purely extrinsic orientation.

During the first two intervals (contraction and emergence), as well as

TABLE 2
Parturitive behavior in kitten birth intervals.

Items	Contraction	Emergence	Delivery	Placental
Gross body movements				
Scratching floor	3	2		
Squatting, straining, or crouching	10	9	4	1
Bracing body	2	1		3
Rolling or rubbing	6	1	1	
Lordosis	2	1		
Circling		2	2	1
Nosing				
Kitten: last born	2			1
born previously		1	4	1
Placenta	2			2
Surroundings	2	3	1	1
Licking				
Self: general	15	13	27	18
genital-abdominal	20	11	22	18
Kitten: last born	18	8	33	21
born previously	15	8	22	16
Fetal membranes		1	1	
Cord			9	2
Placenta	2		1	9
Surroundings	7	8	6	5
Chewing				
Cord	1		1	1
Placenta			1	1
Ingesting				
Fetal membranes			7	2
Cord			4	1
Placenta	1	1		23
Action with kitten				
Dangling kitten from: vulva	1	2	7	
mouth	1		1	1
Sitting or lying on kitten	3	3	1	5
Stepping on kitten	1			1
Pawing kitten	2 .			1
Curling or rolling up		1		2
Carrying, mouthing, or retrieving	3	2	1	6
Nursing	4	2	3	4
Number of intervals observed	37	29	38	29

Note: The table may be read as follows: for example, in 3 out of 37 contraction intervals, a parturient female scratched the floor. The frequencies in each column are not additive; a female may have been observed doing any number of the listed activities during an interval.

FIGURE 126
Sudsie rolling during an apparent episode of uterine contractions preceding the delivery of the fourth kitten.

FIGURE 127
Persian carrying out a rapid circling movement, dragging a partially delivered fetus still attached by its cord.

FIGURE 128
Mabel, early in parturition, responding to birth fluids by licking damp spot on floor.

in subsequent intervals of the kitten birth, actions of nosing and licking the kittens, as well as self and surroundings, were observed.

Licking (Figures 128, 129, 130), by far the most frequent response in parturition, was recorded whenever the female passed her tongue over a surface such as her body, a neonate, or the floor.

Our females in all phases of parturition often actively touched the nose to a fetus, placenta, or to fluids on the floor. This action, termed nosing to include the item sniffing, often difficult to distinguish, may not infrequently have been based on very slight olfactory cues; for example, when a female touched her nose to a place where she or a neonate had been lying.

The parturitive female's actions with her kittens varied from direct responses to a neonate as pawing (Figure 131) or licking to clearly incidental responses as dragging it about the cage while still attached by the cord. An incidental action was sitting or stepping on kittens during responses to herself or to the fetus in delivery. The female's enclosing response was a response to neonates which differed sharply from rolling or rubbing. Clearly directed at the kittens, it involved the female's approaching and standing close to one or more of them, then lying on her side as she drew the front legs ventrocaudally and the rear legs ventro-

FIGURE 129
Mabel in posture characteristic of anogenital licking.

FIGURE 130
Rita licking neonate which is still attached; the placenta remains
undelivered.

984

FIGURE 131
Sudsie makes a quick postural thrust of left rear leg, thereby
"pawing" against body of neonate just delivered.

anteriorly, thus enclosing the kittens near her abdomen. This occurred
most frequently near the kittens, whereas no identifiable extrinsic situation
accompanied rolling or rubbing.

Under our conditions, retrieving was infrequent in the parturitive situation. In different occurrences, it varied from lifting and transporting a
neonate to grasping its body briefly in the jaws and releasing it promptly
with or without lifting. These responses did not differ reliably in frequency
in the intervals of parturition.

Although enclosing occurred, nursing was infrequent in the parturitions
observed, being recorded in only 4 of 14 kitten births in 3 females.
Whether or not nursing occurred did not appear to affect other activities
in the respective intervals.

Behavioral Shifts in Relation to Stimulative Events

LICKING

To examine the hypothesis that the different organic events of parturition and their by-products set off different female activities, each of 14 kitten births, recorded in its complete form, was analyzed for the frequency

of the various groups of behavioral items which occurred in each interval. The items of each of the principal activity groups: (1) scratching floor, (2) squatting and bracing, (3) rolling, rubbing, and lordosis, and (4) licking and ingestion (Table 2) were found to be aroused in a different birth interval with frequencies approaching significance ($p = .10–.05$, Friedman two-way analysis of variance). Each birth interval may therefore be viewed as characteristically different from any of the others with respect to the relative potencies as well as the specific nature of endogenous and exogenous stimuli acting on the parturient female.

Further evidence of significant changes in the female's activities from interval to interval in a kitten birth appears in two types of analysis of the data. First, although no one type of activity initiated any one interval more often than did any other type of activity, it was found that most of the intervals began with a new overt response by the female, sharply breaking her foregoing actions. Genito-abdominal licking and licking the last kitten born are responses exemplifying this conclusion. The contraction interval was initiated more frequently by genito-abdominal licking than was the placental interval, whereas licking the latest born kitten was seen more frequently as the first response during the delivery interval than during the placental or emergence periods. These data show that, although no particular activity consistently followed any given organic event, that event influenced the probability of the occurrence of one of at least two actions in the female's repertoire immediately after the event. Thus the initiation of a contraction period by a series of intrusive endogenous stimuli had a greater likelihood of causing the female to orient to her genito-abdominal region, and thus lick herself specifically, than did stimuli associated with placental delivery. To the latter stimuli, as will be shown, the female was likely to react by promptly ingesting the placenta after its delivery. Similarly, licking the neonate followed the complete passage of the fetus from the female's body more frequently than it followed either the arrest of the fetus or the delivery of the placenta. During the emergence interval, gross body movements dominated to the exclusion of licking the neonate; also, after the delivery of the placenta, when the placenta itself offered a stimulus which for the time being was more potent than others, the newly emerged fetus was licked to a lesser extent than after its own delivery.

Second, a comparison of the frequency and duration of the various behavioral items shown by the female during the different kitten birth intervals indicated that changes in stimulus conditions strongly tended to be responsible for changes in the female's behavior. As mentioned, by-products of the organic processes (such as fluids, neonate, and placenta), variably present during the different intervals, served as potent organizers of behavior, witness the prominence of licking and ingestion. It is important to note, however, that the presence of these by-products was subject to individual differences in the sequence of the organic events themselves and in reactivity among the females (Table 1), being highly variable among the different females.

Not only were the activities of different females in any one interval of a kitten birth highly varied, but the same female might, in any given interval of different kitten births, display one, a few, or all of these actions in almost any combination. With licking the item emphasized, some 25 sequences of activities were found for each of the four intervals in kitten births, without any of the combinations proving to be characteristic of any one interval. With the focus on activities other than licking, appropriate analyses showed the same result. Cooper's (1944) conclusion that variability prevails in the cat's parturitive activities may be clarified by the statement that our data offer no evidence for patterning except for conjunctions of events arising through interactions between the parturitive female, her organic processes, and the external environment.

Because of this lack of patterning in the parturitive process, dealing with the individual behavioral items became more feasible. As can be seen in Table 2, the frequency of the intervals in which licking occurred was greater than the frequency with which any other behavioral item occurred in all intervals. Between 27 and 53% (median 30%) of the parturient female's time was spent in one or another form of licking. No other activity approached licking in the amount of time devoted to it.[4] The predominance of licking made it desirable to differentiate the stimuli to which the licking response was made. The following areas were distinguished: (1) female's body, that is, genito-abdominal area versus general self-licking; (2) kitten, that is, the latest born; (3) fetal membranes; (4) cord; (5) placenta; and (6) surroundings (Table 2). Signs of the interplay or competition of endogenous and exogenous stimuli are most clearly indicated in the changes that occur in licking in the different intervals.

Self-licking, common in all phases of kitten birth, was more frequent than neonate licking in the emergence interval and not reliably less frequent at other times. During the contraction intervals, self-licking, usually genito-abdominal in locus, was predominant and more frequent than licking of latest kitten. The general level of licking activity was heightened in the fetus delivery and the placenta delivery intervals; these were the

---

[4] A very considerable quantity of fluid, attractive to the female, appears from the vulva in connection with neonate delivery. Wislocki (1935) reported that the quantity of amniotic fluid attached to the hair of the embryo at term amounts to as much as 10 to 20 grams, and may exceed by two to four times the volume of the free fluid within the cavity.

times when both the newborn and the earlier born kittens were licked most frequently.

On the whole, the orientation of licking in the cat's parturition does not seem to be a devious question. Self-licking and neonate licking often occurred in close sequence, practically as parts of the same act, suggesting that licking occurred rather indiscriminately when fluids were present. In 31 of 39 cases of fetus-arrested-in-vulva, for example, when the fetus emerged, the female directed her licking equally at herself genito-abdominally, at the floor and at the fetus; 8 females did not lick anything. This fact, together with the equivalent latencies of fetus licking and self-licking, as discussed below, indicates that licking activities tended to occur as responses to fluids rather than to the neonate or to other objects.

Consistent with this point, genito-abdominal self-licking occupies significantly more time within delivery intervals when the focus of stimulation centers more specifically on the vulva than within contraction intervals when stimulation is predominantly intraorganic and diffuse. The excitatory effect is then intense and dominates attention just as in contraction intervals general self-licking was more frequent than either genito-abdominal self-licking or licking of the latest born kitten. But in the delivery interval, licking of the latest born kitten occupied more time than either genito-abdominal self-licking or licking of previously born kittens. Nor was it surprising to find that the longest acts of licking the latest born kitten occurred in the delivery intervals, with licking in the placental, contraction, and emergence intervals decreasing in that order.

The latency of licking last kitten born was significantly less ($p = .01$) for the delivery interval (mean = 3.3 second; median = 2 second) than for the contraction interval (mean = 25 second; median = 10 second) by the Mann-Whitney "U" test. This result we attribute to a greater variety in extrinsic stimulation (as from fluids) in the delivery interval than in the contraction interval.

Contrary to a frequent assumption, the female does not promptly lick a newborn fetus. Rather, in a total of 38 delivery intervals for which the data are subject to analysis, the neonate was licked first in only 20 cases. Moreover, the latency of licking did not differ significantly whether the female or the neonate was the first object to be licked, but general self-licking occurred significantly sooner than either genito-abdominal or neonate licking. Of 58 cases, however, 52 females licked the neonate in the delivery interval.

OTHER BEHAVIORAL SHIFTS

On empirical grounds, we distinguished licking from chewing-and-ingesting, although, in both cases, fluids were often imbibed. The differentiation of these acts was often aided more by a shift in the female's

FIGURE 132
Sudsie chewing at cord of latest delivered fetus; the fetus is now free, although the placenta is still undelivered; left rear leg elevated in a common parturitive posture.

orientation than by a change in the dominant action, as when a postural shift indicated increasing effort in mouthing and swallowing the placenta or cord.

In feline parturition highly adaptive effects often come about as incidental results. Typical is the action of severing the cord while at the same time clamping it so as to prevent hemorrhage. This is clearly an incidental outcome of other responses rather than a direct or specific action of the female with reference to the cord (Figures 132 and 133). Placenta eating involves actions that not only sever the cord more or less promptly but through an inevitable pulling and stretching have the effects both of clamping the portion that remains attached to the kitten and so weakening it as to hasten its rupture at the end of that section. Of 51 instances in which the cord remained intact after fetus and placenta had been delivered, in 35 the cord was broken incidentally as the female handled the placenta, in 1 case through pawing before placenta eating occurred, in 4 cases through her variable activities, in 9 cases by the experimenter as an emergency act.[5] One of the other two cases involved a direct response,

---

[5] It should be noted that the figures represent groupings of the data on different bases. Thus although 51 placentas were delivered intact, the female's first reaction to the placenta was observed in only 37 cases.

FIGURE 133
Duchess chewing at cord of a just delivered fetus whose body dangles from it; placenta still undelivered.

with the female taking the placenta in her jaws and pulling it from the vulva; another was questionable because she weakened the cord through vigorous licking at frequent intervals. A binominal test of the results indicates that in a high predominance of the cases severance of the cord occurred through placenta eating.

As a rule, the female responded promptly to the placenta when it appeared, often beginning to chew it and perhaps consuming it altogether before it had emerged completely from the vulva. Of 37 placental deliveries, in 20 the female's first reaction was to the after-birth, either nosing, licking, or ingesting it, and in only 4 cases was there no definite response. Of the 33 cases of definite response, the placenta was completely consumed in 29. Of 20 cases in which the female responded first to the placenta in this interval, in 19 it was eaten completely. No relationship was indicated between the sequence of births and either latency of response to the placenta or the rate or completeness of its consumption.

Cooper (1942) states that the parturient lioness, especially when primiparous, is likely to cannibalize neonate cubs by simply going on from eating the afterbirth. The case may be different in domestic cats. Under our conditions, at any rate, a total of 73 kitten births occurred without any instances of cannibalism (Tobach et al., in preparation); a very few instances were observed, however, in the postpartum resting interval and in the days immediately thereafter (Rosenblatt, Turkewitz, and Schneirla, 1962).

VARIABILITY AND LACK OF PATTERNING OF BEHAVIORAL EVENTS

To substantiate the conclusion that variability resulting from the interplay of endogenous and exogenous stimuli was an obvious feature of the parturitive behavior of the female, two aspects of the delivery process were considered for critical evaluation. The first was the question of a possible change in behavior from the birth of the first kittten to the birth of later kittens.

Both the frequency and variety of external stimulation increase necessarily with the further kitten births of a parturition; hence the character of the neonate as a stimulus object may be somewhat different when it is the fourth born (K-4) than when it is the first of the series (K-1). Furthermore, the effect of earlier kitten births might be to increase fatigue and promote satiation to new stimuli, or, on the other hand, to accelerate responses to stimuli previously experienced. It is interesting to note, however, that in an analysis of behavioral characteristics of the different intervals in succeeding kitten births, no differences of significance were found.

The second comparison was related to parity. One group of three primiparous females was contrasted with a group of three multiparous females, each cat delivering a litter of four kittens. Little difference was found between primiparous and multiparous subjects either in the repertoire or in the influence of specific activities, except that in the delivery interval the multiparous females were more likely to lick the new kitten first and to lick themselves genito-abdominally than were the primiparous females. The results indicate a somewhat greater frequency of gross bodily movements in the primiparous animals in the contraction and emergence intervals than in other intervals, perhaps indicating that inexperienced females tend to be more responsive to intraorganic sources of excitation. On the other hand, a tendency for more gross bodily movements in the multiparous than in the primiparous females during the placental interval would suggest previous experience making the placenta an attractive edible object. These results may mean that the experienced multiparous subjects tend to be relatively more relaxed and more responsive to extrinsic conditions and somewhat less disturbed by the entrance of intraorganic stimuli in the parturitive situation than the primiparous.

Résumé and Discussion of Parturition

We view the events of parturition in the domestic cat as the outcome of an interplay or at times even a competition between the stimulative effects of endogenous occurrences (such as uterine contractions and the first passage of the fetus) and of the external situation particularly as it is altered by the sequelae of such events (for example, the fluids, neonate, and afterbirth). These stimulative by-products of intraorganic processes tend to intrude upon the female's attention in an order, timing, and duration variable from case to case. Each of these occurrences, as it arises, demands a specific perceptual and behavioral adjustment.

Thus parturition in the domestic cat cannot be viewed as a regular, patterned flow of events; rather, it is a series of sporadic organic and behavioral episodes broken by activities not themselves specifically parturitive. The female thus exhibits, in a not very predictable sequence, predictable items such as self-licking, squatting, licking neonate or substratum, eating afterbirth, and sitting or lying. The organic events centering on uterine contractions set off periods of intense activity indicating a high level of excitement, a condition facilitating expulsion of the fetus and delivery operations in general. Alternating with these intervals of intense activity are times of fatigue in which action is restrained, a condition facilitating the first continuous postnatal stimulative exchange between female and neonates.

Parturitive behavior in the cat may thus be characterized as a loose assemblage of functions centering on the stimulative effects of a crude succession of organic events and of their external consequences. The temporal order of behavioral adjustments and their timing thus depend upon the manner in which these internal and external occurrences may displace one another in competing for the female's variable attention. A persistent factor is an orientation to the posterior body and especially to the vaginal area, perhaps due both to earlier self-experience and to currently increased stimulation from these zones. This orientation, together with the internal stimulative factors, seems indispensable for an adaptive outcome and survival of the young.

The relatively secondary differences between primiparous and multiparous females seem to involve some increase in the neonate's potency as an object to be licked and of the birth zones and objects (for example, fetus, afterbirth) as related, as well as a more relaxed condition of the multiparous females in which they are more responsive to extrinsic conditions and less to organic excitation than are primiparous females. A statement of Steyn's (1951, p. 51) that ". . . young lionesses are not always the best mothers" may have a similar basis.

THE POSTPARTUM RESTING INTERVAL

In the events of parturition, the neonate kitten evidently participates rather passively and incidentally at first, the female in a variable and somewhat diffuse fashion depending upon outer and inner environmental circumstances. These events nevertheless intensify stimulative interactions between female and young and thus provide a broad basis for a social bond which persists and develops thereafter. The tie between mother and young, grounded particularly in actions such as licking and their gratifications, involves an elaboration of these other numerous stimulus-response processes which in time become increasingly bilateral and reciprocal. Parturition thus initiates in the female a long interval in which she deals continuously with her young as attractive entities and so becomes capable of the more complex activities constituting their care.

Directly after parturition in our cats there came an interval of several hours in which rest with the kittens superseded general activity. After the last kitten birth, decrease in the level of activity may have been somewhat slower to appear in primiparous than in multiparous subjects. In all cases there ensued an interval of about 12 hours in which the female lay nearly continuously with the kittens, encircling them.

The manner in which this resting group was formed after parturition and the manner and time at which general suckling by kittens began tended to be highly variable. Cooper (1944) noted that in one case the first actual suckling responses occurred 35 minutes after birth. Ewer (1961) reported suckling as appearing often during the first hour and in nearly all cases by the end of the second hour. In just 4 of our 17 cases, nursing of neonates began during parturition; in the others, it developed only slowly during the postpartum resting interval.

The home site, or home corner in our experimental cage situation, was established as a behavioral refuge and customary resting place and saturated chemically by the female very early in parturition and often during pregnancy. Slowness to establish such a home site and variability in using it may prove to be indications of unstable behavior in the female, impairing her adequacy as a mother. The earliest direct adjustment of the female to the kittens that promotes a feeding relationship is the reaction called "presenting," which in its first appearance may be described as simply lying down around the kittens with her ventral surface arched toward them and her front and rear legs extended to enclose them. There was wide variation in the first appearance and the early frequency of this posture.

The female's response of presenting and encircling is usually given to the main body of the litter, but on occasion it occurs with individual kittens. In the early postparturitive days she returns to the litter in the home corner at frequent intervals, each time upon her arrival making motions that might cause them to awaken and feed. In the postpartum resting interval, however, when the departures are fewer than they are later on, the kittens usually do not awaken promptly on the female's return. At times, when they fail to respond, she continues in the encircling posture, at other times she leaves and returns soon to repeat encircling.

In connection with intervals of neonate encircling, the female tends to orient the neonates not only by her movements and the little bay or functional-U she forms around them, but also by attractive optimal thermal stimuli from her body and attractive (turning-to-eliciting) tactual stimuli delivered through both licking and bodily contacts. The female's behavior thus serves incidentally as well as directly through licking to guide the neonates to her and to the resting place.

After parturition, a resting group forms in a manner that varies from case to case. Suckling usually begins during female-neonate contacts within the first hour after birth (see also Ewer, 1961). Freed of its membranes, the neonate rights itself, then soon crawls slowly and ir-regularly forward through alternate paddlelike movements of the forelegs and uncoordinated pushing by the hind legs at intervals (Langworthy, 1929; Prechtl and Schleidt, 1950, 1951; Rosenblatt and Schneirla, 1961). In side-to-side movements of the head the neonate touches its nose variably to the floor so that a limited zone just ahead is effectively "scanned." Thus, through variable circumstances arising in connection with its own erratic actions, either during parturition or within the resting interval, the viable neonate comes into contact with the fur of the mother. Then, in response to tactual, thermal, gustatory (Pfaffman, 1936), and possibly olfactory stimuli, the young kitten begins to climb her body and promptly nuzzles in her fur. Nuzzling continues until one of many contacts with a protruding nipple elicits slow headfirst withdrawal and then nipple grasping and suckling. The female's licking of herself and of the kittens in this resting interval, a factor of importance for the first suckling, usually continues at about the same level as in the last kitten birth.

THE LITTER PERIOD

General Behavioral Characteristics

During the first 2 days after parturition, the mother cat rather con-sistently maintains her nursing group at the home site. As a rule, this situation is interrupted only at about 2-hour intervals when she rises, stretches, moves about, and feeds (or, under natural conditions, forages in the vicinity). After the first 2 days, these breaks tend to come more frequently. Then, on her return to the huddle, she stands over the group and arouses the usually sleeping kittens by licking them vigorously, then lies down encircling them; whereupon suckling resumes promptly.

The mother's encircling the kittens has the effect of quieting them, as does also (our tests show) the presence of odor cues in the home site for which the mother herself is mainly responsible. The first stage of the neonate's adjustment to this locality, thus intimately dependent upon the presence of and stimulation from the female, begins with parturition, continues for about 10 days, and develops on a tactuo-chemical (non-visual) basis (Rosenblatt, Turkewitz, and Schneirla, in preparation).

During the parturitive period, the female appears unresponsive to the occasional crying of neonates, even passing close to a shrieking kitten or standing on one without orienting to it. Her excited condition at this time may inhibit attention, or the cue may lack perceptual meaning or, as is more likely, both factors may operate. Shortly after parturition, however, she begins to respond to the vocalizing of the young, usually of individuals away from the home corner. It is well known (Leyhausen, 1956) that the postpartum female cat does not usually retrieve her young on sight, even when they lie close to the nest, but often does so on hearing them. Usually within a day or two the mother, in response to its shrieking, will leave the nest to retrieve a marooned kitten. She behaves thus only when the sound reaches a sufficiently high level.

When the disturbance level in the litter situation rises so that the female's state of tension is increased sufficiently, she may continue for a considerable period to shift the kittens from place to place in the cage in an agitated manner. Female tigers, when disturbed, move their young to a distance, carrying them in the jaws (Burton, 1933). Causey and Waters (1936) point out that domestic cats carry their young most frequently by the nape of the neck and less frequently by the shoulders; variation is considerable, and to an appreciable extent it is a matter of convenience which part is grasped. In our subjects this act seemed somewhat random and indirect on the few occasions when it appeared during parturition and in its more frequent occurrences in early postpartum days. The act of retrieving soon improves, reaching a peak in readiness and in technique after about one week, but thereafter declines in frequency. This change may not express a lesser readiness for retrieving so much as a sharp drop in the vocalization of kittens away from the nest after the 5th or 6th day postpartum.[6] Later, however, the mother's readiness to transport her young individually to a different nesting place increases. The tendency seemed to be strongest between the 25th and the 35th days, probably because in this period the females showed a stronger susceptibility to the disturbing effects of extrinsic local conditions.

The time spent by the female in nursing the kittens typically falls off

---

[6] At this time, although retrieving is much less frequent from places close to the home site, it occurs about as often as before to kittens marooned at greater distances (for example, 12 to 18 inches). Nearby, the kittens vocalize less than before and are themselves able to return; farther away their orientation is still inefficient; hence they are prone to vocalize intensely and for longer periods.

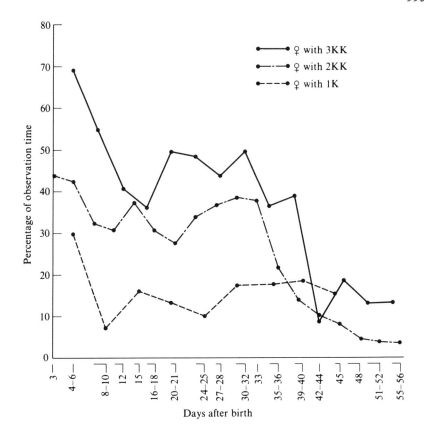

FIGURE 134
Time spent by three cats in nursing their kittens; data based on daily 2-hour observation periods.

during the first 2 weeks from an initial high point related to the number of kittens in the litter (Figure 134). In a litter of three kittens the mother at 4 days spent 70% of her time nursing the young, but a mother with two kittens spent little more than 40% of her time in this activity. Typically, after the second week, a plateau was approximated at a definitely lower level. For mothers with two or three kittens this new level approximated 30 to 50%, but for a mother with one kitten it was 15% or lower. One kitten appears to motivate the female's readiness to nurse disproportionately less than do two or more kittens (Rosenblatt, Wodinsky, Turkewitz, and Schneirla, in preparation, a).

The female contributes incidentally to the development of orientation in her young to the home site and to surrounding areas. Odor cues based on the female's earlier occupancy of this area are increasingly useful to the kittens in the nonvisual returns to the nest site. Frequently also, when the female leaves the nest, she drags some of the kittens, still attached and suckling, and after dropping off nearby they gain a further opportunity to improve their local orientation through learning. In our experimental living cages, kittens of 3 to 4 days already showed an increasing ability to return to the home corner from the adjacent corner. Frequently, a subject would stop and vocalize, whereupon the mother might intervene as described. About 12 to 15 days the kittens had begun to increase their ability to make their way to the nest across the open on the diagonal, and by the 20th day they were all proficient in this act. In the meantime, they had begun to move directly toward the female when she was seen.

The common belief that the female cat teaches her kittens to hunt seems to have some basis. Wells (1934, p. 87), experienced with lions, states that ". . . the wild lioness puts her youngsters through an intensive course of training in hunting and killing before casting them adrift. . . ." Tiger cubs begin to hunt for themselves at about 17 months, but are with the female until about 2 years of age (Burton, 1933). Because the kittens gain experience in catching and eating prey through following the female, they are on hand when she kills and thus are conditioned to become excited in the presence of such objects (Wilson and Weston, 1947). Although the maternal influence has not been shown to be specific tuition, as is often implied, it is unquestionably important for the initiation and organization of predatory behavior in the young. Kuo (1930, 1938) demonstrated that kittens reared with females that killed rodents periodically in the presence of their young later killed rodents significantly earlier and more frequently than kittens raised alone or with a small rodent. In fact, only half the kittens raised alone ever killed rodents and the others did so less frequently than did kittens raised in maternal rodent-attack situations. Notwithstanding the need for further research on this problem, in our judgment Kuo's main findings stand despite Leyhausen's (1960) criticisms.

Typical Development of Maternal-young Feeding Relationships

Through procedures yielding both qualitative and quantitative evidence we have traced the development of the normal nursing and suckling patterns of several litters of domestic cats from birth to the end of the 8th week. The general results are graphed in Figure 135 and summarized in Table 3 in terms of how the *feeding approaches,* or behavior specifically initiating feeding, occur at different times in the course of development of a representative litter. The evidence may be summarized in the following terms.

1. Stage 1 (*female approaches*). In stage 1, from birth to around the

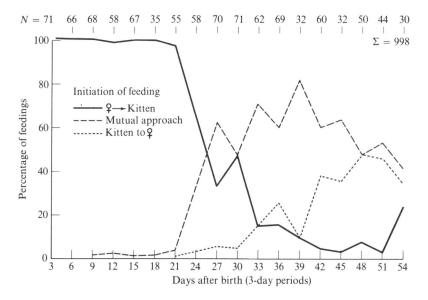

FIGURE 135
Initiation of feedings in three litters of cats, based on daily 2-hour periods of observation. N is number of feedings observed in each 3-day period. (From Schneirla and Rosenblatt, 1961.)

20th day, nearly all the feedings are initiated by the female. As she nears the grouped kittens, the mother lies down, arching her body around the kittens and presenting her mammary surface to them, relaxes and evidently "lets down" the milk as they begin to draw on the nipples. Her licking, and other varied stimuli presented by her, orient the kittens and facilitate their attachment and suckling. This is the basic feeding situation in which the female regularly stimulates and aids suckling by licking accessible kittens at intervals as well as by occasionally stretching and effecting slight changes in her posture. When she returns to the sleeping group after foraging, as described, she arouses them by licking, then "presents" and initiates another feeding episode.

In the first stage, the female's behavior changes in subtle ways in relation to developments in the behavior of the kittens. From the first postpartum hours, the kittens make gradual progress in their feeding adjustments to the mother (Wodinsky, Rosenblatt, Turkewitz, and Schneirla, 1955). At first the neonates reach the female through a slow, variable process, always with much nuzzling and fumbling in attaining her mammary surface and attaching to nipples. Adjustments of individual kittens take on an increasingly specific, individually characteristic form almost from the beginning (Rosenblatt et al., in preparation, a). Usually,

TABLE 3
Initiation of feedings.

STAGE I—FEMALE TO KITTENS

1. Female approaches kitten (KK), encircles (licks); KK nuzzle, attach.
2. Female approaches KK, sits among KK (licks); KK nuzzle, attach.
3. Female encircling KK after nursing, arouses KK; KK nuzzle, attach.
4. Female encircling KK in nest; KK awake, nuzzle, attach.
5. Female sitting among KK in nest; KK crawl to female, nuzzle, attach.
6. Female lying near KK in home area, no contact; KK crawl to female, nuzzle, attach.
7. Female sitting near KK in home area, no contact; KK crawl to female, nuzzle, attach.

STAGE II—MUTUAL APPROACH

8. Female lying away from home area; KK crawl to her, nuzzle, attach.
9. Female sitting outside home area; KK crawl to female, nuzzle, attach.
10. Female stands or sits at food dish; KK nuzzle; female leaves food, lies or sits; KK nuzzle, attach.
11. Female stands or sits at food dish; KK nuzzle, attach; female leaves, lies or sits; KK follow, nuzzle, attach.
12. Female stands or sits at food dish; KK nuzzle, attach; female remains at food.
13. Female at food dish; KK nuzzle, attach; female leaves, makes self available for nursing.
14. KK wander in vicinity of female; female lies down; KK approach, nuzzle, attach.
15. KK wander in vicinity of female; female sits; KK approach, nuzzle, attach.
16. Female lying or sitting, nursing KK; K wanders, turns towards her; nuzzles, attaches.

STAGE III—KITTENS TO FEMALE

17. Female wanders around cage; KK follow, approach female, nuzzle; female sits or lies; KK nuzzle, attach.
18. Female wanders around cage; KK follow, approach female, nuzzle, attach; female remains standing, then sits or lies; KK nuzzle, reattach.
19. Female wanders around cage; KK follow, approach, nuzzle, attach; female remains standing.
20. Female comes down from shelf; KK immediately approach, nuzzle, attach.
21. Female on floor; K on shelf, comes down, approaches female, attaches.
22. Female and KK on shelf; nursing.
23. KK vocalize towards female on shelf; female comes down; KK immediately approach and attach.
24. KK climb to female on shelf; immediately nuzzle and attach.

within the first two neonatal days, the majority of the kittens in any litter are already able to take individually specific nipple positions with appreciable regularity. With further experience, certain neonates in a litter thus come to suckle in a particular place or at a particular nipple pair in the front, the center, or the back. Some suckle alternately at either of two positions, whereas others seem to suckle at any available place. The results indicate differences in suckling specificity in more than twenty-five litters ranging from one to seven kittens. It is understandable that Ewer (1959), having worked with four litters, would be likely to emphasize the specificity of early nipple localization at the expense of individual and group variability.

The increasing involvement of the kittens in the organization of feeding situations as the first stage progresses is emphasized by the rapidity with which they advance in locating nipples so that by the fourth neonatal day most of them have become proficient in reaching the female and in attaching themselves. As Figure 135 indicates, however, the mother holds the role of the initiator of feeding situations until near the end of the third week.

2. Stage 2 (*mutual approaches*). In the second stage, which typically runs from about the 20th to shortly after the 30th day, the initiation of feeding involves active approaches by mother and kittens. The kittens, now increasingly ambulant outside the home site, begin to make feeding approaches to the female in different situations, for example, when she is resting outside the nest or crouching over the food dish and feeding. Although the nature of these situations varies increasingly, with either the female or the kittens the more active according to conditions, the initiation of feeding remains a distinctively bilateral process throughout this stage. When the kittens start the approach, the female nearly always responds appropriately, either by lying at once or, if already lying, by facilitating nipple localizations by kittens through stretching out or at least remaining in place. The kittens, on their part, respond promptly and efficiently to the mother when she presents and display an increasing adaptivity in transferring their reactions from the home site as a specific locality to the female as a focus of action.

The mother and kittens are constantly interacting, the interchanges involving subtle visual, tactual, auditory, and even olfactory cues. Although most of the auditory cues arise from movements, general reactions to vocalizing may occur. Moelk (1944) questions whether many of the vocal exchanges are direct; in her opinion one of the very few specific ones occurs after about 9 weeks when the kitten "greets" the mother upon meeting her or responds to her "murmur of greeting." "When a kitten irritates the mother by chewing and clawing her feet and tail, the irritation may find vent in growl and anger-wail" (p. 203), which, however, are doubtful as controls of kitten behavior. So far as the mother directly controls the kittens she does so behaviorally, by cuffing them, dragging them off, or turning away from one that disturbs her.

To an appreciable extent the mother thus far has accommodated her behavior to developments in the young through which they have acquired an increasingly comprehensive perceptual and motivational basis for responding to her and to littermates. She thus submits to or even joins the constantly more varied casual joint activities ("play") of the kittens including nonfeeding responses of the kittens to herself such as romping around and pouncing over her, pawing her, toying with her tail, and the like. But, near the end of the 4th week, the amount of such attentions she will tolerate at any one time seems to be on the decrease. From our results her acceptance of continued kitten encroachments would show an increasing rate of extinction between the 25th and the 35th days.

The mother, therefore, as the active center of the feeding group, through the first stage and well through the second, has provided a functional basis for the socialization of the kittens; feeding is essentially a reciprocal and social activity.

3. Stage 3 (*kitten approaches*). In the third stage, which generally is under way shortly after the 30th day, the initiation of suckling depends increasingly and finally almost altogether on the kittens. They now follow the mother around the cage with increasing frequency and persistency, often even pursuing her and remaining where she disappears when she evades them by leaping to the wall shelf. When the female is accessible, the kittens persist vigorously in their attempts to nuzzle. This at times results in attachment and suckling but more and more, through counteractions by the mother, may be limited to only a brief social exchange.

In many different ways therefore the kittens actively concentrate their ambulant responses upon the female and forcibly influence her behavior more and more strongly in the direction of avoidance.

Two successive types of behavioral relationship between mother and young in stage 3 are represented by the series of items 17 to 19 and 20 to 24 in Table 3. The changing attitude of the mother toward the kittens is shown by the increase in frequency and duration of her stays on the shelf (Figure 136). But from about the 45th day, when the kittens begin to reach the shelf through their own efforts, the female avoids this place more and more as it ceases to be a refuge.

The results point therefore to a predictable series of changes in the formation and waning of mother-young relationships; these are essential to the social bond which centers on reciprocity in the organization of the litter's social behavior (Schneirla and Rosenblatt, 1961). In stage 1 the kittens' suckling operations are gratifying to the female as are the stimulative patterns characteristic of her other meetings with them; in stage 2

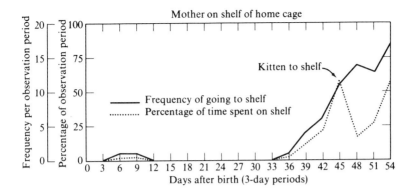

FIGURE 136
Shelf-going behavior of a female with litter of three kittens, based on daily 2-hour observation periods. Arrow indicates day when kittens first reached the shelf.

these effects still predominate although the pattern of relationships is becoming complicated by occasional maternal withdrawal from the kittens; in stage 3 the withdrawal responses specialize into avoidance as the kittens' vigorous pursuits of the mother and other encroachments upon her mount. In other words, in the third stage, the strength of the social bond between female and young decreases as behavioral relationships shift from a reciprocal to a unilateral status.

It is apparent that in cats, as the litter stage advances, a basis for weaning is laid in the changing behavioral relationships of mother and kittens. At this time in domestic cats in the open, and at the corresponding time in wild cats (Wilson and Weston, 1947), the female, who now spends increasing amounts of time away from the litter, upon return usually brings slain prey to her kittens. In view of the possibility that such changing relationships occur not only in other cats but in mammals more widely, Adamson's (1960) statement that the lioness regurgitates food to her cubs (that is, probably as nursing wanes) before they join her in hunting is suggestive. It is also significant for this point that Martins (1949) reported regurgitation by female dogs to their pups in the weaning period under conditions suggesting a basis in changing behavior relationships between mother and young (Schneirla, 1956).

Further evidence of the increasing disturbance that the kittens' relationships with the mother acquire in the third stage comes from a comparison of shelf-going behavior in females with single kittens and in females with two or three kittens. In the one-kitten situation, the female began a regular procedure of shelf climbing shortly after parturition and continued it through the litter association, with no perceptible change other than a slight rise between the 30th and 40th days. Females with two or more kittens, in contrast, exhibited a slight tendency for shelf climbing at the 3rd to 5th days, but soon lost this tendency, and such behavior did not reappear in their case until the 25th to 30th days when it became pronounced. The continuation of shelf climbing in the one-kitten females we attribute to a persistently low attraction value of the single kitten; its prompt disappearance in females with more than one kitten, to a stronger bond with the young. In Figure 134 we see that after the first few days the one-kitten female spent a minimal part of her time in nursing, whereas two-kitten and three-kitten females spent an important part of their time thus and probably more than would be expected from the larger feeding numbers alone.

It is interesting, however, that one-kitten females, with what may be characterized as low maternal motivation, showed no indications of avoiding the one kitten at the time when mothers with litters were showing the sharp decrease in amount of nursing and increase in kitten avoidance. The distinction of three stages in the litter period is therefore less applicable to the one-kitten mother who might continue her low-level bond with the young for months. In fact, associations of a mother cat with a single kitten involving the maintenance of a stereotyped suckling pattern have been reported as lasting until sexual maturity in the young. The single-kitten mother seems to lack the behavioral disturbance, effective with litters of two or more kittens, that appears to contribute to decreased nursing and increased evasion of the young, and thereby to weaning.

The mother evidently contributes to weaning not only by incidentally emphasizing sources of solid food behaviorally, but in particular by making the infantile mode of feeding more and more difficult at a time when the young are more and more capable of getting their food independently.

RESPONSES TO STRANGE YOUNG

Preliminary studies were made in which the kittens were removed at parturition; then at 7, 12, and 15 days the female's maternal responses were tested to *one* as against three kittens. To the introduction of one kitten the female reacted with encirclement, also by approaching the kitten at intervals and accepting its approaches as in normal litter situations. Introducing three kittens had a very different effect at 15 days postpartum. The female was very disturbed, attacked the kittens, retreated as far as possible from them, avoided contacts, and showed high excitement when they neared her. The suggestion is that a maternal motivation that is low but sufficient for the acceptance of one kitten is not equal to the task of accepting three.

FIGURE 137
Week-old isolate kitten in suckling position at the brooder. The milk supply is indicated behind the rear guard panel. (From Schneirla and Rosenblatt, 1961.)

Because kittens shortly after birth are able to distinguish their own mother from other littering females, and with increasing effectiveness in the course of time, a distinct initial hesitancy to suckle from the strange female may be expected. The kittens, however, soon adapt to the female, who reacts in kind. A littering female usually accepts strange kittens not too much older than her own unless an eccentricity in their behavior (as through isolation) causes a series of disturbing encounters. Then in all cases but one the female reacted by withdrawing from the situation of disturbance. Thus the difficulties had to be initiated by the kitten, with the female having to summate to the point of intolerance.

EXPERIMENTAL ANALYSIS THROUGH ISOLATION STUDIES

As another approach to studying the normal development of female-young adjustments, kittens were isolated at different times in an incubator containing a brooder or "artificial mother." Empirically, the minimal normal contributions of the female to the neonate were appraised as: (1) attractive weak tactual and optimal thermal stimulation, (2) orientative guidance in feeding (through the "functional-U"), and (3) a stable food supply. The brooder as first used in 1951 is shown in Figure 137.

This situation supplied female-factor one through its optimal temperature and cover of soft toweling, factor two through its U shape with either arm furnishing tactual guidance to the base, and factor three through the nipple at the base with its temperature-controlled synthetic food supply. To complete the initial situation, as a female substitute, regular manual guidance in feedings was given all neonates during the first 3 days, also brief daily manipulative stimulation during the first two neonatal weeks to facilitate the onset of defecation and urination.

The variety of stimulation normally supplied by the female to the neonates, although initially incidental to her role, has cumulative psychological effects far beyond those of the active guidance and stimulation supplied by the experimenter with the brooder. The "artificial female" was thus no mother substitute as was found when the isolates were tested by being returned to the litter situation after different intervals.

First, a striking difference appeared in the results for kittens segregated in pairs in the brooder as against single isolates (Rosenblatt, Wodinsky, Turkewitz, and Schneirla, in preparation, b). The brooder adjustments themselves were very different in these cases. Although two nipples were available to each pair of kittens segregated in the brooder, virtually always when one kitten held one nipple, the other kitten, instead of taking the second nipple, left this food source unused while it nuzzled its mate then in the act of suckling. The mate is attractive not just because it presents a soft, warm surface but because this object emphasizes these stimulative properties by being motile and reactive. As further results of the isolation experiments show, these characteristics are basic to the female's normal attraction for the young and to her potent effect upon their feeding and other normal activities.

Following their isolation periods in the incubator, the kittens held there as single occupants for scheduled intervals were returned to the female and litter to test their individual reactions to the female, littermates, and situation. Although suckling appeared in all the kittens isolated from birth to the 7th day, from the 6th to the 23rd day, and from the 18th to the 33rd day, it did not appear immediately on any of the returns. Instead, suckling required up to 3 hours in the birth-to-7-day group, 20 hours in the 6 to 23rd day group, and 15 hours in the 18 to 33rd group. Analysis of the results shows that the delay in female suckling centers on two different adjustments to the female: an initial general adjustment, "contact latency," scored when the kitten made its first sustained contact with the female; and a more specific adjustment through which suckling appeared after a "suckling delay."

Attainment of a sustained contact with the female, although only a preliminary and partial adjustment in itself, depended upon adaptations both to the living situation and to the female. In the cage orientation tests, isolates returned from the brooder at 7 days were significantly inferior to the litter-raised kittens in their ability to orient spatially to the home corner and return to it even from close by. Hence these kittens soon became marooned away from the home corner and, consequently, the initial contact with the female had to occur by chance and was greatly delayed. When one of them happened to brush the female, the initial contact was followed by the kitten's turning towards her and then by a pushing against her body and nuzzling persistently into her fur. In their cruder orientative reactions, and especially in the low efficiency of their nipple-locating actions as compared with normal subjects, the isolate kittens revealed the handicap of having lost the first week of experience with the female.

The nuzzling reactions of these kittens differed significantly from those of normals. One-week-old female-reared kittens locate an abdominal area very soon after having reached the female, and thereupon nuzzle very little before achieving an attachment, with this nuzzling confined to the immediate nipple area. Any littermate touched in the preliminary orientative process is never nuzzled, although this response is common in 3-day-old neonates with litter experience. The 7-day isolates, in contrast, reached the female through much wandering, which brought them to the home corner accidentally, if at all, or perhaps through a retrieval elicited by their squealing. If an isolate happened to wander close to the female while she was lying down, she would lick it; this licking then would cause the isolate to turn toward her and push, as described, against whatever part of her body was touched. This was a crude reaction; the isolate would nuzzle over the female's entire body including even paws, neck, and back, although somewhat more frequently around her genital area. Thus the isolate's proximal orientation to the female was initially quite generalized and not more efficient than that of a neonate kitten. Female and incubator were equivalent to the extent that each furnished attractive tactual and thermal stimulation, but localizing a nipple was clearly a very different problem in the two cases, requiring specific experience with the main object involved.

In their adjustments to the female, the birth-to-7-day isolates clearly behaved differently from the neonates. They took longer for the first suckling engagement than did neonates. Analysis of the protocols discloses that they had a special difficulty, absent in the relatively simple and invariable situation of the initial postpartum resting group. The female's nursing pattern had changed progressively in the first week in relation to the behavioral development of the kittens that had been with her since parturition. These kittens, now specifically attractive to her as a group, began their suckling promptly when she encircled them in the home corner, and often held her there for some time. This condition greatly lowered the chances that the female would respond to the isolate's crying and retrieve it from a distance. Consequently, the first week isolates were at a distinct disadvantage in comparison with neonates as to factors in female behavior facilitating the first suckling.

The female, as an active agent with complex potentialities for reciprocal stimulative relationships with young, was thus hardly equivalent to the brooder to which the isolates had adjusted. But it is interesting that kittens isolated from the 6th to the 23rd day also were clearly inferior to normal littermates in the return tests, notwithstanding their early experience with the female. Although they also soon achieved their first contacts with the female, being attracted to her visually, the latency of their first suckling reactions was much greater than that for the first week isolates. Although littermate controls suckled twice in each hour, each of the 6 to 23rd day isolates continued for more than 20 hours in a persistent orientation to the female's face and anterior body. These kittens also, as with the first week isolates, were generalized in their nuzzling, spending long intervals nuzzling over the bodies of other kittens and the furry nonmammary surfaces of the female before nipple localization occurred. Visual attraction to the female did not seem to help them much in their main task nor did early suckling experience in the litter situation noticeably help them in localizing a nipple on return. We conclude that the deficiencies were due to their having been deprived of the opportunity to advance their feeding and social adjustments to cope with modifications that had occurred in the female's behavior during their absence.

The deprivation differed for kittens isolated from the 18th to 33rd day. Although they were also slow in localizing the female's mammary region, they had less difficulty in localizing nipples than the others. Their main drawback lay rather in adapting to the female as an object from which to suckle. A similar difficulty occurred in the kittens isolated from the 34th to 44th day; they needed even more time for their first suckling adjustments. The deprivation seems to have handicapped them in effecting an appropriate suckling orientation to the female rather than in the specific operations of localizing a nipple and suckling.

In the five isolate groups in which suckling finally appeared, the principal difficulty lay not in the preliminary adjustments to the female, although these were deficient, but in the more intimate adaptation required by suckling. In the two isolate groups that failed to suckle in the tests, the data indicated a special difficulty in making any sustained contact with the female, with a considerable degree of tension and excitement when near her, so intense and lasting as to exclude any suckling adjustment. Responses in the female's presence involved hissing and other indications of marked disturbance up to overt withdrawal in three of four 23rd to 44th day isolates and in all of the 2nd to 44th day isolates. Also, the 34th to 49th day isolates, the one other group in which disturbance signs appeared, showed the longest latency of all accomplishing the suckling adjustment. Although their disturbance with the female decreased sufficiently within 2 hours to admit a suckling relationship, their responses to the female still showed withdrawal tendencies and signs of "fright" differing only in degree from those in the two nonsuckling groups. It is quite likely that the members of all three of these groups would have left the litter situation altogether had this been possible.

To examine the deficiencies of the brooder as a substitute for the female, readjustment to the brooder was tested in kittens that had suckled at the female for several weeks, and readjustment to the female was tested in kittens that had just completed lengthy periods at the brooder. Three kittens that had initial periods with the female in which all had suckled were placed in the brooder at the 25th day. When, after 2 weeks they were retested in the litter situation, they had great difficulty in readjusting to the female. One had a suckling latency of more than 3 days and the other two did not suckle at all. By way of contrast, the two kittens that spent an early period (day 6 to 24) at the brooder, equivalent to that spent with the female by the others, but then had been placed with the female on the 24th day to remain with her in a suckling relationship while the others were at the brooder, reinstated brooder suckling almost at once on their terminal tests at 49 days. The sixth kitten, similarly prepared and transferred from the female to the brooder for a test on the 47th day, needed only 10 minutes to reinstate suckling at the brooder. But the last three kittens, taken from the brooder at times preceding the 25th and 35th day respectively, when tested with the female, needed periods of from 12 to 23 hours to reinstate female-suckling—much longer suckling latencies than those obtained either in female-return tests at later ages or in brooder-return tests at any age.

The length of the intervening period has a very different effect on suckling adjustments according to whether the tested kitten has been with the brooder or with the female. After intervals in the brooder of from 8 to 17 days, 11 kittens averaged 31 hours in their suckling latency when tested with the female. But in tests with the brooder after intervals with the female ranging from 10 to 36 days, 9 kittens scored a minimal suckling latency of only 12 minutes. In female tests after brooder isolation the shortest latency was 33 minutes and followed an isolation of 8 days; the longest was 93 hours, with 1 kitten not suckling at all after 66 hours in the brooder. The shortest latency in brooder tests after an intervening period with the female was 3 minutes after 17 days with the female, the longest was 25 minutes after 24 days with the female, but one kitten suckled at once after having been away from the brooder for 36 days spent partly with the mother and partly alone and feeding from a dish.

These results show clearly that the brooder suckling pattern was reinstated far more readily than was the pattern of female suckling in kittens that had fed from one or the other during equivalent periods in early development. The kitten's capacity to recall an earlier suckling adjustment therefore depends on the conditions under which it developed in relation to conditions prevalent in the test. The difficulties or the failures of subjects to reinstate the female suckling pattern under certain conditions must have been due to specific differences in the circumstances prevalent in the litter situation at the time of the test as against those prevalent there before the subject's absence. As the investigations of normal litter conditions have shown, during the time of these absences from the litter situation important changes were occurring in the female's behavior with respect to the kittens which affected the entire relationship of mother and kittens. In contrast, the brooder situation, which had not changed in the meantime independently of the kitten, presented no such difficulties in the tests.

SUMMARY

In the domestic cat, the specific processes antecedent to maternal behavior begin during pregnancy, with a reconditioning and reorientation by the female to her own changing organism marked by intensified self licking and by fixation of a resting place. The entire pattern involves a complex progressive organization depending on the intervening variables of physiological change in the female and the young, the developmental changes in the perception of both, and upon complex and changing reciprocal relationships between female and young.

Basic factors in the female introduced essentially by neurohormonal changes are: secretory process (for example, prolactin) specific to stages; raised metabolic level; local tumescence; direct reproductive changes (for example, contractions, expulsion of fetus); sequelae of reproductive changes such as release of fluids; and in both female and young, stage-conditioned factors of sensitivity and action. These factors provide the basis for the rise of a specialized pattern of mutual adjustment in which the female is, of course, the primary active agent.

The female's changing organic status and physiological condition facilitate her habituation to a resting situation prior to parturition; the events of parturition such as uterine contractions hold her to this situation; licking fluids and eating placenta fix first the situation and then the young as attractive and initiate a behavioral bond with the neonates. There is no unitary, template basis for the patterning of behavior. Behavioral processes of different types become dominant and change in the parturitive situation according to the interplay or competition of stimuli arising from internal organic function with external stimuli from fluids, neonate, and afterbirth, sequelae of the birth-processes.

From the time parturition begins, the consequences of events such as licking fluids, fused with associated gratifications such as those from cutaneous stimulation and from eating afterbirth, dominate the female's behavior. These occurrences, in a continuous and changing succession, focus the female first on her own body and then on the young when they appear. These sources of satisfaction are an excellent basis for a perceptual attachment to the young which intensifies in time and which is essential for the normal status of caring for the young.

The strength of the social bond as a function of the extent to which an adequate pattern of reciprocal stimulation can develop between mother and young is clearly indicated by the differences found in the motivation of one-kitten and of multi-kitten mothers. Cues from the female are essential for the socialization of the young, for in the early postpartum situation the female's licking is an important guide in the first suckling adjustments of the neonate, and later in the litter stage her behavior influences the young in getting solid food. Thus relationships of feeding normally are basic to the female's role in the socialization of the young, furnishing a center of organization for the reciprocal stimulative processes maintaining the social bond.

Maternal motivation and the neurohormonal conditions maintaining it remain high in the feline mother through both the stage in which she makes the approaches and the stage in which overt approaches are mutually initiated, but weaken and change in the further stage in which increasingly vigorous approaches of the young often verge on harrying or pursuit. It is possible that her increasing avoidance of the young represents a behavioral condition appropriate for changes in hormonal secretions necessary for the waning of maternal behavior and favoring sexual receptivity. Maternal behavior is often long continued in the one-kitten litter in which the sequelae of disturbed relations do not arise as they do between mother and more than one offspring. But normally in the domestic cat the changes of the third stage promote weaning and the dissolution of the bond between mother and young. A waning attachment to the litter and the rise of physiological and behavioral changes favoring mating are evidenced by the frequency with which fertilization occurs in female cats before the actual end of the litter period.

PROTOCOL I

Abbreviated protocol of typical behavior just preceding parturition in the domestic cat.

Case Mabel, 31 July 1953, 10:25:00 A.M. *To 7:08:35* P.M. Reddish discharge at vulva. Feeds, lies, licks self generally; pronounced fetal movements; cries and pants; digs at sawdust; scratches floor; digs, lies, cries repeatedly; digs, sits down slowly elsewhere; crouches. 1:30 P.M.: drinks milk, lies on side panting; salivates heavily; digs in sawdust; digs on bare floor; licks meat but does not feed. 4:50 P.M.: mounts to shelf for first time today, cries and pants. 4:54 P.M.: down and to food dish without feeding, lies, digs in sawdust, twice; vulvar discharge thinner and increasing in quantity; digs; lies and half-rolls into genital-licking position but without any licking; palpation of nipples shows that female is lactating; licks self generally, also genitally; drinks milk; feeds briefly; digs, four times; general self-licking. 5:31 P.M.: onto shelf; vocalizes; general self-licking. 5:32 P.M.: down from shelf; urinates and covers; vaginal discharge; digs on bare floor and in sawdust with increasing speed and intensity; defecates and covers. 5:37 P.M.: lies. 6:25 P.M.: female assumes genital-licking position but does not lick. 7:08:35 P.M.: first contraction.

PROTOCOL II

Abbreviated protocol of typical behavior in the domestic cat in parturition.

Case Della, 3 May 1951. This case, in which four kittens were born, has been selected as the most representative with respect to parturitive behavior and related events, although labor was overlong for the second kitten.

FIRST KITTEN (K-1). *Contraction interval* (4:26:34 to 4:37:10): Contractions; female lifts hind leg; contractions; rolls; scratches bare floor; crouches; contractions; lifts rear leg; rolls; contractions. *Emergence interval* (4:37:10 to 4:56:10): Female shifts onto hip; licks food; lifts rear leg; contractions; lifts rear leg; licks self generally; lifts rear leg; shifts position; contractions; shifts position; contractions; shifts position; stands; contractions; licks fetus. *Delivery and placental intervals combined* (4:56:10 to 5:04:28): Neonate and afterbirth delivered together; female eats afterbirth to completion; chews cord; licks neonate; noses neonate; licks floor; noses floor; licks neonate; neonate gets covered with sawdust, female sits on it; female licks self generally.

SECOND KITTEN (K-2). *Contraction interval* (5:04:28 to 5:31:26): Contractions; female licks K-1; braces rear legs; lordosis; retrieves K-1 and licks it; retrieves K-1, licks it; grips K-1 in jaws; licks K-1; grips K-1 in mouth; paws K-1; licks K-1; lies down on K-1; stands; pants; braces; licks K-1; lies, curled around K-1; licks K-1; contractions; lies on side, K-1 at head; contractions; K-1 nuzzles female's foreleg and vocalizes; female shifts position; lifts rear leg; contractions; lifts rear leg; lies on K-1; stands; braces; stands; circles; licks K-1; gets up; sits and licks K-1; licks self generally; licks K-1. *Emergence interval* (5:31:26 to 6:26:18): Fetus visible in vulva; female circles; licks K-1; licks self generally; K-1 vocalizing steadily; female stands; shifts position; noses floor; vocalizes; circles; braces; sits down; licks K-1; shifts position; nuzzles K-1; licks self generally; licks K-1; licks self generally; licks own abdomen; contraction; licks K-1; braces; K-1 inspected by *E* [observer]; female mouths K-1 as *E* holds it; contraction; female noses floor; *E* weighs and tags K-1; female stands and vocalizes; contraction; female lies on side; braces; circles; retrieves K-1; licks K-1 while sitting on K-2 (fetus); contractions; scratches floor; lies on K-1; licks K-1; licks self generally; licks fluids on floor; licks K-1; licks floor. *Delivery interval* (6:26:18 to 6:27:20): As female licks floor and circles, K-2 emerges; free of sac, vocalizing promptly and continually; female continues licking fluids on floor, circling, and then licks K-2 while K-2 clings to her tail; female continues to lick both fluids on floor and K-2 (the floor was licked for 40 seconds in four bursts of licking, and K-2 was licked in three bursts lasting 40 seconds). Female licks floor; circles; licks K-1. *Placental interval* (6:27:20 to 6:46:22): Afterbirth delivered; female licks K-2; licks afterbirth; chews cord; eats placenta; licks K-2; licks self generally; retrieves K-2; licks K-2; licks K-1; licks K-2 at length; licks K-1 briefly; licks self abdominally and generally for extensive period during which she retrieves K-2 three times; licks K-1 and K-2 briefly; alternately licks K-2 and self generally; licks K-1 and K-2 briefly; licks floor; female mouths K-1; circles; lies down in presenting position; *E* tags K-2.

THIRD KITTEN (K-3). *Contraction interval* (6:46:22 to 6:56:46): Contractions; female licks self generally; licks K-1; licks self abdominally; squats; licks K-1; licks self genitally; licks self generally; licks K-1; licks K-2; contractions; squats; licks self generally; licks self abdominally; contractions. *Emergence interval* (6:56:46 to 6:58:04): Fetus visible; female stands; strains; defecatory crouch; licks self genitally; contractions. *Delivery interval* (6:58:04 to 7:02:40): K-3 born; female licks self abdominally; licks K-3; paws K-3; eats sac; licks self generally; licks K-3 and K-2; stands up dangling K-3; female drags K-3 as she moves about. *Placental arrest interval* (7:02:40 to 7:10:18): Placenta of K-3 visible in vulva; female licks self generally; licks K-3; licks self genitally; licks cord; licks K-1 and K-2; circles several times dragging K-3. *Placental interval* (7:10:18 to 7:14:40): Afterbirth delivered as female stands; female eats placenta; retrieves K-2 and sits on K-3; licks K-2 briefly.

FOURTH KITTEN (K-4). *Contraction interval* (7:14:40 to 7:28:44): Contraction; licks K-3; licks K-1; licks self generally; licks self abdominally; licks K-3; drags K-3 by cord; mouths K-3; retrieves K-3; steps on K-2; licks K-2; licks floor; shifts; stands; lies down; contraction. *Emergence interval* (7:28:44 to 7:29:14): Fetus visible; contraction; female lies on side; licks floor. *Delivery interval* (7:29:14 to 7:40:18): K-4 delivered; female licks K-4 and cord; stands with fetus dangling from vulva; licks self generally; licks abdominal area and cord; licks self generally;

licks K-4; circles, dragging K-4; lies down; rises. *Placental interval* (7:40:18 to 8:00:00): Afterbirth falls out; female eats afterbirth; licks K-4; licks K-2; licks floor; retrieves K-3; licks K-4; retrieves K-3, dragging K-1; licks K-4; licks self generally; retrieves K-1; licks K-1 and K-2; *E* palpates female, weighs kittens; female licks K-1, K-2, K-3, K-4 and self generally; licks K-3; protocol ends.

REFERENCES

Adamson, Joy. 1960. *Born free.* New York: Pantheon.

Asdell, S. A. 1946. *Patterns of mammalian reproduction.* Ithaca, N.Y.: Comstock.

Bard, P. 1936. Oestrual behavior in surviving decorticate cats. *Am. J. Physiol.* 116: 4–5.

Barelare, B. Jr., and C. P. Richter. 1938. Increased sodium chloride appetite in pregnant rats. *Am. J. Physiol.* 121: 185–188.

Beach. F. A. 1948. *Hormones and behavior.* New York: Hoeber.

Beach, F. A. 1958. Neural and chemical regulation of behavior. In H. F. Harlow and C. N. Woolsey, eds., *Biological and biochemical bases of behavior.* Madison: University of Wisconsin Press. Pp. 263–284.

Burton, R. G. 1933. *The book of the tiger.* London: Hutchinson.

Causey, D., and R. H. Waters. 1936. Parental care in mammals with especial reference to the carrying of young by the albino rat. *J. Comp. Psychol.* 22: 241–254.

Clegg, M. T. 1959. Factors affecting gestation length and parturition. In H. H. Cole and P. T. Cupps, eds., *Reproduction in domestic animals.* New York: Academic Press. Pp. 509–538.

Cooper, J. B. 1942. An exploratory study on African lions. *Comp. Psychol. Monogr.* 17(91): 1–48.

Cooper, J. B. 1944. A description of parturition in the domestic cat. *J. Comp. Psychol.* 37: 71–79.

Eckstein, P., and S. Zuckerman. 1956. The oestrous cycle in the mammalia. In A. S. Parkes, ed., *Marshall's physiology of reproduction,* vol. 1, part I., 3rd ed. London: Longmans, Green and Co. Pp. 226–396.

Ewer, R. F. 1959. Suckling behaviour in kittens. *Behaviour* 15: 146–162.

Ewer, R. F. 1961. Further observations on suckling behaviour in kittens, together with some general consideration of the interrelations of innate and acquired responses. *Behaviour* 17: 247–260.

Günther, S. 1954. Klinische Beobachtungen über die Geburtsfunktion bei der Katze. *Arch. Exp. Vet.-Med.* 8: 739–743.

Hain, A. M. 1935. The effect (a) of litter-size on growth and (b) of oestrone administrated during lactation (rat). *Quart. J. Exper. Physiol.* 25: 303–313.

Hall, K. 1957. The effect of relaxin extracts, progesterone and oestradiol on maintenance of pregnancy, parturition and rearing of young after ovariectomy in mice. *J. Endocrin.* 15: 108–117.

Harris, G. W. 1955. *Neural control of the pituitary gland.* London: E. Arnold.

Kuo, Z. Y. 1930. The genesis of the cats' responses to the rat. *J. Comp. Psychol.* 11: 1–35.

Kuo, Z. Y. 1938. Further study on the behavior of the cat toward the rat. *J. Comp. Psychol.* 25: 1–8.

Labriola, J. 1953. Effects of caesarean delivery upon maternal behavior in rats. *Proc. Soc. Exper. Biol. Med.* 83: 556–557.

Langworthy, O. R. 1929. A correlated study of the development of reflex activity in fetal and young kittens and the myelinization of tracts in the nervous system. *Contr. Embryol., Carneg. Instn.* 20(114): 127–171.

Leblond, C. P. 1937. L'Instinct maternel. Nature et relations avec la glande mammaire, l'hypophyse et le système nerveux. *Rev. Franc. Endocr.* 15: 457–475.

Lehrman, D. S. 1956. On the organization of maternal behavior and the problem of instinct. In P.-P. Grassé, ed., *L'Instinct dans le comportement des animaux et de l'homme.* Paris: Masson. Pp. 475–520.

Lehrman, D. S. 1961. Hormonal regulation of parental behavior in birds and infrahuman mammals. In W. C. Young, ed., *Sex and internal secretions.* Baltimore: Williams and Wilkins. Pp. 1268–1382.

Leyhausen, P. 1956. Das Verhalten der Katzen (Felidae). *Hand. Zool., Berl.* 10(21): 1–34.

Leyhausen, P. 1960. Verhaltensstudien an Katzen. *Z. Tierpsychol.,* Beihelf 2.

Lindemann, W. 1955. Über die Jugendentwicklung beim Luchs (*Lynx L. Lynx Kerr*) und bei der Wildkatze (*Felis S. Silvestris Schreb*). *Behaviour* 8: 1–45.

Martins, T. 1949. Disgorging of food to the puppies by the lactating dog. *Physiol. Zoöl.* 22: 169–172.

Meites, J. 1959. Mammary growth and lactation. In H. H. Cole and P. T. Cupps, eds., *Reproduction in domestic animals,* vol. 1. New York: Academic Press. Pp. 539–593.

Michael, R. P. 1958. Sexual behaviour and the vaginal cycle in the cat. *Nature,* London 181: 567–568.

Moelk, M. 1944. Vocalizing in the house-cat; a phonetic and functional study. *Am. J. Psychol.* 57: 184–205.

Nicoll, C. S., P. K. Talwalker, and J. Meites. 1960. Initiation of lactation in rats by nonspecific stresses. *Am. J. Physiol.* 198: 1103–1106.

Pfaffmann, C. 1936. Differential responses of the new-born cat to gustatory stimuli. *Ped. Sem. and J. Genet. Psychol.* 49: 61–67.

Prechtl, H., and W. M. Schleidt. 1950. Auslösende und steuernde Mechanismen des Saugaktes. I. Mitteilung. *Z. Vergl. Physiol.* 32: 257–262.

Prechtl, H., and W. M. Schleidt. 1951. Auslösende und steuernde Mechanismen des Saugaktes. II. Mitteilung. *Z. Vergl. Physiol.* 33: 53–62.

Racadot, J. 1957a. La thyroïde de la chatte durant la gestation et la lactation. *C. R. Soc. Biol.* 151(5): 1005–1007.

Racadot, J. 1957b. Neurosécrétion et activité thyroïdienne chez la chatte au cours de la gestation et de l'allaitement. *Ann. Endocr.,* Paris 18: 628–634.

Riddle, O. 1935. Aspects and implications of the hormonal control of the maternal instinct. *Proc. Am. Phil. Soc.* 75: 521–525.

Riddle, O., E. L. Lahr, and R. W. Bates. 1935. Maternal behavior induced in virgin rats by prolactin. *Proc. Soc. Exp. Biol. Med.* 32: 730–734.

Riddle, O., E. L. Lahr, and R. W. Bates. 1942. The rôle of hormones in the initiation of maternal behavior in rats, *Am. J. Physiol.* 137: 299–317.

Rosenblatt, J. S., and L. R. Aronson. 1958. The influence of experience on the behavioural effects of androgen in prepuberally castrated male cats. *Anim. Behav.* 6: 171–182.

Rosenblatt, J. S., and T. C. Schneirla. 1962. Behaviour of the cat. In E. S. E. Hafez, ed., *The behaviour of domestic animals.* London: Baillière, Tindall and Cox. Pp. 453–488.

Rosenblatt, J. S., G. Turkewitz, and T. C. Schneirla. 1961. Early socialization in the domestic cat as based on feeding and other relationships between female and young. In B. M. Foss, ed., *Determinants of infant behaviour.* London: Methuen. Pp. 51–74.

Rosenblatt, J. S., G. Turkewitz, and T. C. Schneirla. 1962. Development of suckling and related behavior in neonate kittens. In E. L. Bliss, ed., *Roots of behavior.* New York: Hoeber. Pp. 198–210.

Rosenblatt, J. S., G. Turkewitz, and T. C. Schneirla (in preparation). Analytical studies on maternal behavior in relation to litter adjustment and socialization in the domestic cat. II. Development of orientation.

Rosenblatt, J. S., J. Wodinsky, G. Turkewitz, and T. C. Schneirla (in preparation, a). Analytical studies on maternal behavior in relation to litter adjustment and socialization in the domestic cat. III. Maternal-young relations from birth to weaning.

Rosenblatt, J. S., J. Wodinsky, G. Turkewitz, and T. C. Schneirla (in preparation, b). A study of individual isolates and segregated pairs of kittens in relation to normal adjustments in the litter situation.

Rothchild, I. 1960a. The corpus luteum-pituitary relationship: the association between the cause of luteotrophin secretion and the cause of follicular quiescence during lactation; the basis for a tentative theory of the corpus luteum-pituitary relationship in the rat. *Endocrinology* 67: 9–41.

Rothchild, I. 1960b. The corpus luteum-pituitary relationship: the lack of an inhibiting effect of progesterone on the secretion of pituitary luteotrophin *Endocrinology* 67: 54–61.

Schneirla, T. C. 1951. A consideration of some problems in the ontogeny of family life and social adjustments in various infrahuman animals. In M. J. E. Senn, ed., *Problems of infancy and childhood* (Trans. 4th Conference, 1950). New York: Josiah Macy, Jr. Foundation. Pp. 81–124.

Schneirla, T. C. 1956. Interrelationships of the "Innate" and the "Acquired" in instinctive behavior. In P.-P. Grassé, ed., *L'Instinct dans le comportement des animaux et de l'homme.* Paris: Masson. Pp. 387–452.

Schneirla, T. C., and J. S. Rosenblatt. 1961. Behavioral organization and genesis of the social bond in insects and mammals. *Am. J. Orthopsychiat.* 31: 223–253.

Scott, P. P., and M. A. Lloyd-Jacob. 1955. Some interesting features in the reproductive cycle of the cat. *Studies on Fertility* 7: 123–129.

Steyn, T. J. 1951. The breeding of lions in captivity. *Fauna and Flora, Transvaal,* 2: 37–55.

Tobach, E., M. L. Failla, R. Cohn, and T. C. Schneirla (in preparation). Analytical studies on maternal behavior in relation to litter adjustment and socialization in the domestic cat. I. Parturition.

Wells, E. F. V. 1934. *Lions Wild and Friendly.* New York: Viking Press.

Wilson, C., and E. Weston. 1947. *The Cats of Wildcat Hill.* New York: Duell, Sloan and Pearce.

Wislocki, G. B. 1935. On the volume of the foetal fluids in sow and cat. *Anat. Rec.* 63: 183–191.

Wodinsky, J., J. S. Rosenblatt, G. Turkewitz, and T. C. Schneirla. 1955. The development of individual nursing position habits in newborn kittens. Paper read at Eastern Psychol. Assoc., New York.

Bibliography

1. 1928 Schneirla, T. C. Review of Georges Dwelshauvers, *Les Méca-nismes Subconscients* (Paris: Félix Alcan, 1925). *Am. J. Psychol.* 40: 146–147.

2. 1928 Schneirla, T. C. Review of W. S. Walsh, *The Mastery of Fear* (New York: E. P. Dutton & Co., 1925). *Am. J. Psychol.* 40: 154–155.

3. 1929 Schneirla, T. C. Learning and orientation in ants. *Comp. Psychol. Monogr.* 6: 1–143.

4. 1933 Schneirla, T. C. Motivation and efficiency in ant learning. *J. Comp. Psychol.* 15: 243–266.

5. 1933 Schneirla, T. C. Studies on army ants in Panama. *J. Comp. Psychol.* 15: 267–299.

6. 1933 Schneirla, T. C. Some comparative psychology. *J. Comp. Psychol.* 16: 307–315.

7. 1933 Schneirla, T. C. Some important features of ant learning. *Z. vergl. Physiol.* 19: 439–452.

8. 1934 Schneirla, T. C. The process and mechanism of ant learning. *J. Comp. Psychol.* 17: 303–328.

9. 1934 Schneirla, T. C. Raiding and other outstanding phenomena in the behavior of army ants. *Proc. Nat. Acad. Sci.* 20: 316–321.

10. 1934 Schneirla, T. C. The process and mechanism of ant learning. *Psych. Bull.* 31: 614–615.

11. 1934 Schneirla, T. C. The relationship between the two principal "instinctive" activities of army ants. *Psychol. Bull.* 31: 745–746.

12. 1935 Maier, N. R. F., and T. C. Schneirla. *Principles of animal psychology.* New York: McGraw-Hill, 529 pp. (Reprinted with supplementary articles. New York: Dover Pub., 1964, 683 pp.)

13. 1937 Witkin, H. A., and T. C. Schneirla. Initial maze behavior as a function of maze design. *J. Comp. Psychol.* 23: 275–304.

14. 1937 Schneirla, T. C. Analysis of the army-ant behavior pattern: the nature of an "instinct." *Psychol. Bull.* 34: 710–711.

15. 1938 Crafts, L. W., T. C. Schneirla, E. E. Robinson, and R. W. Gilbert.

Recent experiments in psychology. New York: McGraw-Hill, 417 pp.

16. 1938 Schneirla, T. C. A theory of army-ant behavior based upon the analysis of activities in a representative species. *J. Comp. Psychol.* 25: 51–90.

17. 1938 Schneirla, T. C. The problem of organization in ant learning. *Psychol. Bull.* 35: 639.

18. 1939 Schneirla, T. C. A theoretical consideration of the basis for approach-withdrawal adjustments in behavior. *Psychol. Bull.* 37: 501–502.

19. 1940 Schneirla, T. C. Further studies on the army-ant behavior pattern. *J. Comp. Psychol.* 29: 401–460.

20. 1940 Schneirla, T. C., and N. R. F. Maier. Concerning the status of the starfish. *J. Comp. Psychol.* 30: 103–110.

21. 1941 Schneirla, T. C. Studies on the nature of ant learning. I. The characteristics of a distinctive initial period of generalized learning. *J. Comp. Psychol.* 32: 41–82.

22. 1941 Schneirla, T. C. Social organization in insects as related to individual function. *Psychol. Rev.* 48: 465–486.

23. 1941 Schneirla, T. C. Review of C. S. Warden, T. N. Jenkins, and L. H. Warner, *Comparative psychology: A comprehensive treatise.* Vol. II: *Plants and invertebrates* (New York: Ronald Press, 1940). *Psychol. Bull.* 38: 105–108.

24. 1941 Sampson, B. H., and T. C. Schneirla. The appearance of nail-biting in a rat; a fixation in a frustrating problem situation. *J. Comp. Psychol.* 32: 437–442.

25. 1942 Schneirla, T. C. German psychological warfare. *Psychol. League J.* 5: 9–18.

26. 1942 Schneirla, T. C. "Cruel" Ants—and Occam's razor. *J. Comp. Psychol.* 34: 79–83.

27. 1942 Maier, N. R. F., and T. C. Schneirla. Mechanisms in conditioning. *Psychol. Rev.* 49: 117–134.

28. 1943 Schneirla, T. C. The nature of ant learning. II. The intermediate stage of segmental maze adjustment. *J. Comp. Psychol.* 35: 149–176.

29. 1943 Schneirla, T. C. Postscript to "Cruel" Ants. *J. Comp. Psychol.* 35: 233–235.

30. 1944 Schneirla, T. C. Studies on the army-ant behavior pattern.—Nomadism in the swarm-raider *Eciton burchelli. Proc. Am. Phil. Soc.* 87: 438–457.

31. 1944 Schneirla, T. C. A unique case of circular milling in ants, considered in relation to trail following and the general problem of orientation. *Am. Mus. Novitates,* no. 1253, pp. 1–26.

32. 1944 Schneirla, T. C. The reproductive functions of the army-ant queen as pace-makers of the group behavior pattern. *J. New York Entom. Soc.* 52: 153–192.

33. 1944 Schneirla, T. C. Behavior and ecological notes on some ants from South-Central Florida. *Am. Mus. Novitates,* no. 1261, pp. 1–5.

34. 1944 Schneirla, T. C. Nomadism in the swarm-raiding army ants as an instance of animal migration. *Anat. Rec.* 89: 552.

35. 1945 Schneirla, T. C. The army-ant behavior pattern; nomad-statary relations in the swarmers and the problem of migration. *Biol. Bull.* 88: 166–193.

36. 1946 Schneirla, T. C. Ant learning as a problem in comparative psychology. In P. L. Harriman, ed., *Twentieth century psychology.* New York: Philos. Library. Pp. 276–305.

37. 1946 Schneirla, T. C. Contemporary American animal psychology in perspective. In P. L. Harriman, ed., *Twentieth century psychology.* New York: Philos. Library. Pp. 306–316.

38. 1946 Schneirla, T. C. Problems in the biopsychology of social organizations. *J. abnorm. Soc. Psychol.* 41: 385–402.

39. 1946 Schneirla, T. C. Studies on the relation between learning and social activities in ants. *Year Book Am. Philos. Soc. 1945,* pp. 168–170.

40. 1947 Schneirla, T. C. A study of army-ant life and behavior under dry-season conditions with special reference to reproductive functions. I. Southern Mexico. *Am. Mus. Novitates,* no. 1336, pp. 1–20.

41. 1947 Schneirla, T. C. Herbert Spencer Jennings: 1868–1947. *Am. J. Psychol.* 60: 447–450.

42. 1948 Schneirla, T. C. Psychology, Comparative. *Encyclopaedia Britannica* 18: 690–708. Revised in 1959, vol. 18: pp. 690–708 and in 1962, vol. 18: pp. 690Q–703.

43. 1948 Schneirla, T. C. Army-ant life and behavior under dry-season conditions with special reference to reproductive functions. II. The appearance and fate of the males. *Zoologica* 33: 89–112.

44. 1948 Schneirla, T. C., and G. Piel. The army ant. *Sci. Am.* 178: 16–23. Available as a separate offprint No. 413, San Francisco: W. H. Freeman and Co.; Condensed in *Scientific American Reader,* Sci. Am. Board of Editors (eds.), New York: Simon and Schuster, 1953, pp. 411–422; *The college omnibus,* L. F. Dean (ed.), 8th ed., New York: Harcourt, Brace, 1955, pp. 56–63; and *Twentieth century bestiary,* Sci. Am. Board of Editors (eds.), New York: Simon and Schuster, 1955, pp. 54–67.

45. 1948 Schneirla, T. C. Biological and behavioral aspects of sexual brood production in army ants. *Anat. Rec.* 101: 693.

46. 1949 Schneirla, T. C. Levels in the psychological capacities of animals. In R. W. Sellars, V. J. McGill, and M. Farber, eds., *Philosophy for the future.* New York: Macmillan. Pp. 243–286.

47. 1949 Schneirla, T. C. Army-ant life and behavior under dry-season conditions: 3. The course of reproduction and colony behavior. *Bull. Am. Mus. Nat. Hist.* 94: 1–81.

48. 1949 Schneirla, T. C. Problems in the environmental adaptation of some new-world species of doryline ants. *Anales Inst. Biol. Mex.* 20: 371–384.

49. 1949 Schneirla, T. C. Studies on army-ant behavior and its biological basis. *Year Book Am. Philo. Soc. 1948*, pp. 160–163.

50. 1950 Schneirla, T. C. The relationship between observation and experimentation in the field study of behavior. *Ann. N.Y. Acad. Sci.* 51: 1022–1044.

51. 1950 Schneirla, T. C., and R. Z. Brown. Army-ant life and behavior under dry-season conditions: 4. Further investigation of cyclic processes in behavioral and reproductive functions. *Bull. Am. Mus. Nat. Hist.* 95: 263–353.

52. 1951 Schneirla, T. C. The "levels" concept in the study of social organization in animals. In M. Sherif and J. N. Rohrer, eds., *Social psychology at the crossroads*. New York: Harper. Pp. 83–120.

53. 1951 Schneirla, T. C. A consideration of some problems in the ontogeny of family life and social adjustments in various infrahuman animals. In *Problems of infancy and childhood*, Trans. 4th Conference, M. Sehn (ed.). New York: Josiah Macy, Jr. Foundation. Pp. 81–124.

54. 1951 Schneirla, T. C. Carpenter Ants. *Nat. Hist.* 60: 227–238.

55. 1951 Schneirla, T. C. Review of K. v. Frisch, *Bees, their vision, chemical senses and language* (Ithaca: Cornell University Press, 1950). *Ecology* 32: 562–565.

56. 1951 Schneirla, T. C. The Dances of the Bee. Lecture accompanying 16 mm. film by K. v. Frisch. Distribs. Mauthner-Pikelny, % Pikelny, Brooklyn, N.Y., and Psychol. Cinema Reg., University Park, Pa.

57. 1952 Schneirla, T. C. A consideration of some conceptual trends in comparative psychology. *Psych. Bull.* 49: 559–597.

58. 1952 Schneirla, T. C. Basic correlations and coordinations in insect societies with special reference to ants. *Colloques Internationaux du Centre National de la Récherche Scientifique. Structure et Physiologie des Sociétés Animales* 34: 247–269.

59. 1952 Schneirla, T. C. Problems in the ontogeny of family life and social adjustments in various infrahuman animals. Part I. *Child-Family Digest* 6: 22–23; Part II. *Child-Family Digest* 6: 76–99.

60. 1952 Schneirla, T. C., and R. Z. Brown. Sexual broods and the production of young queens in two species of army ants. *Zoologica* 37: 5–32.

61. 1953 Schneirla, T. C. Basic problems in the nature of insect behavior. In K. Roeder, ed., *Insect physiology*. New York: John Wiley. Pp. 656–684.

62. 1953 Schneirla, T. C. Insect behavior in relation to its setting. In K. Roeder, ed., *Insect physiology*. New York: John Wiley. Pp. 685–722.

63. 1953 Schneirla, T. C. Modifiability in insect behavior. In K. Roeder, ed., *Insect physiology*. New York: John Wiley. Pp. 723–747.

64. 1953 Schneirla, T. C. Collective activities and social patterns among

insects. In K. Roeder, ed., *Insect physiology.* New York: John Wiley. Pp. 748–779.

65. 1953 Schneirla, T. C. The concept of levels in the study of social phenomena. In M. Sherif and C. Sherif, *Groups in harmony and tension.* New York: Harper. Pp. 54–75.

66. 1953 Schneirla, T. C. Algunas diferencias estacionales en las funciones biologicas de ciertas especies de hormigas guerreras (Secuela de las investigaciones iniciadas en al sureste de Mexico). *Mem. del Cong. Cient. Mex.* VII, Cient. Biol.: 375–384.

67. 1953 Schneirla, T. C. The army ant queen: Keystone in a social system. *Bull. l'Union Int. Etude Insectes Sociaux* 1: 29–41.

68. 1953 Schneirla, T. C. Military ants. *O.N.R. Research Rev.* Feb.: ii, 1–8.

69. 1954 Schneirla, T. C., R. Z. Brown, and F. C. Brown. The bivouac or temporary nest as an adaptive factor in certain terrestrial species of army ants. *Ecol. Mongr.* 24: 269–296.

70. 1954 Schneirla, T. C. Introductory statement. In T. C. Schneirla, ed., *Proceedings of a conference on orientation in animals.* Washington, D.C.: Office of Naval Research. Pp. ix–x.

71. 1954 Schneirla, T. C. Problems and results in the study of ant orientation. In T. C. Schneirla, ed., *Proceedings of a conference on orientation in animals.* Washington, D. C.: Office of Naval Research. Pp. 30–52.

72. 1954 Schneirla, T. C. Psychological problems in the orientation of mammals. In T. C. Schneirla, ed., *Proceedings of a conference on orientation in animals.* Washington, D.C.: Office of Naval Research. Pp. 193–209.

73. 1954 Schneirla, T. C. Correspondence. *Insectes Sociaux* 1: 293–294.

74. 1955 Schneirla, T. C. Driver Ants. *Encyclopedia Americana* 9: 337–338.

75. 1955 Schneirla, T. C. Biological and behavioral aspects of sexual brood production in army ants. *Anat. Rec.* 101: 43.

76. 1955 Tobach, E., M. L. Failla, R. Cohn, and T. C. Schneirla. Analytical studies of maternal behavior and litter relations in the domestic cat. I. Parturition. *Anat. Rec.* 122: 423–424.

77. 1956 Schneirla, T. C. Interrelationships of the "innate" and the "acquired" in instinctive behavior. In *L'Instinct dans le comportement des animaux et de l'homme.* Paris: Masson. Pp. 387–452.

78. 1956 Schneirla, T. C. A preliminary survey of colony division and related processes in two species of terrestrial army ants. *Insectes Sociaux* 3: 49–69.

79. 1956 Schneirla, T. C. The army ants. *Smithsonian Inst. Ann. Report, 1955.* Publ. 4244: 379–406. (Revised 1960 in W. P. True, ed., *Smithsonian treasury of science.* New York: Simon and Schuster. Pp. 663–696.)

80. 1957 Schneirla, T. C. The concept of development in comparative psychology. In D. B. Harris, ed., *The concept of development.* Minneapolis: Univ. Minn. Press. Pp. 78–108.

81. 1957   Schneirla, T. C. Theoretical consideration of cyclic processes in doryline ants. *Proc. Am. Philo. Soc.* 101: 106–133.

82. 1957   Schneirla, T. C. A comparison of species and genera in the ant sub-family Dorylinae with respect to functional pattern. *Insectes Sociaux* 4: 259–298.

83. 1958   Schneirla, T. C. A field investigation of the behavior and biology of representative species of army ants in the southeastern United States. *Year Book Am. Phil. Soc. 1957*, pp. 283–284.

84. 1958   Schneirla, T. C. The behavior and biology of certain nearctic army ants. Last part of the functional season, southeastern Arizona. *Insectes Sociaux* 5: 215–255.

85. 1958   Tobach, E., T. C. Schneirla, B. Sang, P. Gold, K. Steele, and R. Wortis. Hopping behavior in mice of pre-weaning age. *Anat. Rec.* 131: 604.

86. 1958/   Schneirla, T. C. The study of animal behavior: Its history and rela-
     1959   tion to the museum. I. *Curator* 1: 17–35 (1958); II. *Curator* 2: 27–48 (1959).

87. 1959   Schneirla, T. C. An evolutionary and developmental theory of bi-phasic processes underlying approach and withdrawal. In M.R. Jones, ed., *Nebraska symposium on motivation* 7: 1–42. Lincoln: Univ. Nebraska Press.

88. 1960   Schneirla, T. C. L'Apprentissage et la question du conflit chez la fourmi—comparaison avec le rat. *J. Psychol. Norm. et Path.* 57: 11–44.

89. 1960   Schneirla, T. C. Instinctive behavior, maturation—experience and development. In B. Kaplan and S. Wapner, eds., *Perspectives in psychological theory*. New York: Intern. Univ. Press. Pp. 303–334.

90. 1960   Schneirla, T. C. Instinctive behavior. In *Encyclopedia of science and technology*. New York: McGraw-Hill. Pp. 146–147. (Revised, 1967, in press.)

91. 1960   Tobach, E., L. Vroman, G. Turkewitz, and T. C. Schneirla. Physiological effect of pre-weaning manipulation in two strains of rats. *Anat. Rec.* 138: 387.

92. 1960   Tobach, E., L. Vroman, G. Turkewitz, and T. C. Schneirla. Infantile experience with specific visual stimuli as related to later differential approach responses in rats. *Anat. Rec.* 138: 385.

93. 1961   Schneirla, T. C. The behavior and biology of certain nearctic doryline ants. Sexual broods and colony division in *Neivamyrmex nigrescens*. *Z. Tierpsychol.* 18: 1–32.

94. 1961   Schneirla, T. C., and J. S. Rosenblatt. Behavioral organization and genesis of the social bond in insects and mammals. *Am. J. Orthopsychiat.* 31: 223–253.

95. 1961   Rosenblatt, J. S., G. Turkewitz, and T. C. Schneirla. Early socialization in the domestic cat as based on feeding and other relationships, between female and young. In B. M. Foss, ed., *Determinants of infant behavior*. London: Methuen. Pp. 51–74.

96. 1961 Schneirla, T. C., E. Tobach, R. Laupheimer, and K. Grossman. The use of a computer in a study of behavior in rats during the litter period. *Am. Zool.* 1: 393–394.

97. 1962 Schneirla, T. C. Psychological comparison of insect and mammal. *Psychol. Beitr.* 6: 509–520.

98. 1962 Rosenblatt, J. S., and T. C. Schneirla. The behaviour of cats. In E. S. E. Hafez, ed., *The behaviour of domestic animals.* London: Ballière, Tindall & Cox. Pp. 453–488.

99. 1962 Rosenblatt, J. S., G. Turkewitz, and T. C. Schneirla. Development of sucking and related behavior in neonate kittens. In E. Bliss, ed., *Roots of behavior.* New York: Harper. Pp. 198–210.

100. 1962 Tobach, E., and T. C. Schneirla. Eliminative responses in mice and rats and the problem of "emotionality." In E. Bliss, ed., *Roots of behavior.* New York: Harper. Pp. 211–231.

101. 1962 Schneirla, T. C. Preface to American edition of L. V. Krushinskii's *Animal Behavior, Its Normal and Abnormal Development.* New York: Consultants Bur. Pp. ix–xii.

102. 1962 Tobach, E., T. C. Schneirla, L. R. Aronson, and R. Laupheimer. The "ATSL": An observer-to-computer system for a multivariate approach to behavioural study. *Nature* 194: 257–258.

103. 1963 Schneirla, T. C. The behaviour and biology of certain nearctic army ants: Springtime resurgence of cyclic function—southeastern Arizona. *Anim. Behav.* 11: 583–595.

104. 1963 Schneirla, T. C., J. S. Rosenblatt, and E. Tobach. Maternal behavior in the cat. In H. L. Rheingold, ed., *Maternal behavior in mammals.* New York: John Wiley. Pp. 122–168.

105. 1963 Schneirla, T. C., and J. S. Rosenblatt. "Critical Periods" in the development of behavior. *Science* 139: 1110–1115.

106. 1963 Tobach, E., and T. C. Schneirla. A note on seasonal variation in nest-building behaviour in the domestic rabbit (*Oryctolagus cuniculus*). *Anim. Behav.* 11: 491–493.

107. 1964 Schneirla, T. C. Studies on foraging and learning in ants. In E. O. Wilson, ed., *Research problems in biology: Investigations for students.* Series 4. Biol. Sci. Curric. Study. New York: Anchor Books–Doubleday. Pp. 152–159.

108. 1965 Schneirla, T. C. Aspects of stimulation and organization in approach/withdrawal processes underlying vertebrate behavioral development. In D. S. Lehrman, R. Hinde, and E. Shaw, eds., *Advances in the study of behavior,* vol. 1. New York: Academic Press. Pp. 1–71.

109. 1965 Schneirla, T. C. Cyclic functions in genera of legionary ants (subfamily Dorylinae). *Proc. 12th Int. Congr. Ent. London,* pp. 336–338.

110. 1965 Schneirla, T. C. Dorylines: raiding and in bivouac. Part 1. *Nat. Hist.* 74 (8): 44–51; Part 2. *Nat. Hist.* 74 (9): 40–47.

111. 1965 Lappano-Colletta, E. R., U. Geduldig, and T. C. Schneirla. An improved histological technique for refractory insect brood ma-

terial in research on doryline ant behavior. *Nature* 207: 959–960.

112. 1966   Schneirla, T. C. Behavioral development and comparative psychology. *Quart. Rev. Biol.* 41: 283–302.

113. 1966   Schneirla, T. C. Development and comparative psychology. *Wissenschaft. Zeitschr. der Karl-Marx Universität Leipzig* 15: 455–465.

114. 1966   Schneirla, T. C., and A. Y. Reyes. Raiding and related behaviour in two surface-adapted species of the old world doryline ant, *Aenictus. Anim. Behav.* 14: 132–148.

115. 1966   Schneirla, T. C. *Instinct and aggression.* Reviews of Konrad Lorenz, *Evolution and Modification of Behavior* (Chicago: The University of Chicago Press, 1965) and *On Aggression* (New York: Harcourt, Brace & World, 1966). *Nat. Hist.* 75: 16.

116. 1967   Tobach, E., Y. Rouger, and T. C. Schneirla. The development of olfactory function in the rat. *Am. Zool.* 7: 792–793.

117. 1967   Weiss, B. A., and T. C. Schneirla. Inter-situational transfer in the ant *Formica schaufussi* as tested in a two-phase single choice-point maze. *Behaviour* 28: 269–279.

118. 1968   Schneirla, T. C., R. R. Gianutsos, and B. S. Pasternack. Comparative allometry in the larval broods of three army-ant genera, and differential growth as related to colony behavior. *Am. Nat.* 102: 533–554.

119. 1968   Tobach, E. and T. C. Schneirla. The biopsychology of social behavior of animals. In R. E. Cooke, and S. Levin, eds., *Biologic Basis of Pediatric Practice.* New York: McGraw-Hill. Pp. 68–82.

120. 1969   Schneirla, T. C. and A. Y. Reyes. Emigrations and related behaviour in two surface-adapted species of the old-world doryline ant, *Aenictus. Anim. Behav.* 17: 87–103.

121. 1969   Rosenblatt, J. S., G. Turkewitz, and T. C. Schneirla. Development of home orientation in newly born kittens. *Trans. N.Y. Acad. Sci.* 31: 231–250.

122. 1971   Schneirla, T. C. *Army ants: A study in social organization.* Edited by H. R. Topoff. San Francisco: W. H. Freeman and Co.

Index